Using
Word Version 6 for
Windows™, Special Edition

Ron Person

Karen Rose

with

Robert Voss, PhD

Mathew Harris

Lorry Laby

Ralph Soucie

Colin Bay

que

Using Word Version 6 for Windows™, Special Edition

Library of Congress Catalog No.: 93-86247

ISBN: 1-56529-469-6

95 94 93   6 5 4 3 2 1

Interpretation of the printing code: the rightmost double-digit number is the year of the book's printing; the rightmost single-digit number, the number of the book's printing. For example, a printing code of 93-1 shows that the first printing of the book occurred in 1993.

Screen reproductions in this book were created with Collage Plus from Inner Media, Inc., Hollis, NH.

Publisher: David P. Ewing

Director of Publishing: Mike Miller

Managing Editor: Corinne Walls

Marketing Manager: Ray Robinson

Credits

Publishing Manager
Chuck Stewart

Acquisitions Editor
Sarah Browning

Product Development Specialists
Elden Nelson
Steve Schafer
Joyce Nielsen
Robin Drake
Bryan Gambrel
Jim Minatel

Production Editor
Michael Cunningham

Editors
Ginny Noble
Lori Cates
Heather Northrup
Pamela Wampler
Cindy Morrow
Chris Nelson
Mary Morgan
Brad Sullivan
Elsa Bell
Chuck Hutchinson
Mary Anne Sharbaugh
Chris Haidri
Tom Hayes
Patrick Kanouse
Linda Seifert
Phil Kitchel

Technical Editor
Jeff Adams
Randall Bryant
Tish Nye
Anne Poirson

Book Designer
Amy Peppler-Adams

Cover Designer
Jay Corpus

Production Team
Jeff Baker
Angela Bannan
Danielle Bird
Paula Carroll
Charlotte Clapp
Brook Farling
Michelle Greenwalt
Carla Hall
Heather Kaufman
Caroline Roop
Amy Steed
Tina Trettin

Proofreading/Indexing Coordinator
Joelynn Gifford

Production Analyst
Mary Beth Wakefield

Graphic Image Specialists
Dennis Sheehan
Sue VandeWalle
Tim Montgomery
Teresa Forrester

Indexers
Michael Hughes
Joy Dean Lee
Craig Small

Composed in *Goudy* and *MCPdigital* by Que Corportion

About the Authors

Ron Person has written more than 14 books for Que Corporation, including *Using Excel for Windows,* Special Edition; *Excel for Windows Hot Tips*; *Using Windows 3.1,* Special Edition; and *Windows 2.1 QuickStart*. Ron is one of Microsoft's original twelve Consulting Partners. He has an M.S. in physics from The Ohio State University and an M.B.A. from Hardin-Simmons University.

Karen Rose has written four books for Que, including *Using Microsoft Windows 3.1,* Special Edition; *Windows 3.1 QuickStart*; and *Using WordPerfect 5.1*. Karen teaches Word for Windows and desktop publishing and has taught for the Sonoma State University. She is the publisher and owner of Little Red Book Press, a publisher of hand bound books.

Ron Person & Co., based in San Francisco, has attained Microsoft's highest rating for Microsoft Excel and Word for Windows consultants: Microsoft Consulting Partner. The firm is a recognized leader in training developers and support personnel in Visual Basic for Applications and the application languages used by Microsoft Excel, Word for Windows, and Microsoft Access. The firm's developer courses have enabled many corporations to develop their own financial, marketing, and business-analysis systems. If your company plans to develop applications using Microsoft's Visual Basic for Applications, Word Basic, or Microsoft Access Basic you should contact Ron Person & Co. regarding on-site courses for support personnel, advanced users, and developers. For information on course content, on-site corporate classes, or consulting, contact Ron Person & Co. at the following address:

Ron Person & Co.
P.O. Box 5647
Santa Rosa, CA 95409

(415) 989-7508   Voice
(707) 539-1525   Voice
(707) 538-1485   FAX

Acknowledgments

Using Word Version 6 for Windows, Special Edition, was created through the work and contributions from many professionals. We want to thank the people who contributed to this effort.

Thanks to everyone at Microsoft. Their energy and vision have opened new frontiers in software. The accessibility of Word for Windows to all levels of users shows the benefits of Microsoft's usability labs and testing. Word's success in the marketplace is tribute to a great product.

Thanks to the software consultants and trainers who helped us write and technically edit *Using Word Version 6 for Windows*, Special Edition. Technical editing was done by a group of very capable consultants and MIS support personnel; however, the responsibility for errors that may have slipped through their knowledgeable gaze lies solely with us. There were many 16 hour days and missed weekends required to finish this book and we appreciate the work of the following people:

Robert Voss, PhD, deserves special thanks for his help in bringing this book together. In addition to applying his writing and training skills to the original writing, Bob also dove into the final edits. Bob has made a significant contribution to many of Que's best-selling books. Bob is a senior trainer in Microsoft Excel and Word for Windows for Ron Person & Co.

Mathew Harris, is a computer consultant in Oakland, California, who has been doing training, support, and technical writing since 1980 for corporations and non-profit organizations. He is the author of *The Disk Compression Book* and has made significant contributions to four other Que books. He can be reached on CompuServe at 74017,766.

Anne Poirson is a *Microsoft Consulting Channel Partner in Excel*. Anne was the main technical editor for the book. Anne owns the consulting firm, Computer Synergy, located in Cleveland, Ohio. She has over twenty years experience developing custom software applications for firms such as General Electric, Newport News Shipbuilding, and BP America. In addition to her computer science degree, Anne is a graduate of General Electric's Financial Management Program.

Lorry Laby, is a trainer and technical writer in Santa Rosa, California, who supports companies and municipal governments that use Word for Windows and WordPerfect. Lorry has written numerous computer guides and text books.

Ralph Soucie, long-time contributing editor to *PC World* and the author of a popular book on Microsoft Excel, is also a Microsoft Excel consultant and lives in Jonesport, Maine. His Excel consulting and training practice includes Boston and the eastern seaboard.

Colin Bay, is a software technical writer in Portland, Oregon, who has considerable experience using Word to create finished documentation. His writing helped us meet a last minute schedule change.

Tish Nye technically edited portions of the book. She has nine years as a computer trainer and is the Human Resources Information Systems Coordinator for the City of Indianapolis.

Jeff Adams did technical edits. He is the managing editor for *TVRO* magazine in Fortuna, California.

Randall Bryant supports over 600 people as the network administrator at Hurco. He also did technical edits.

Que Corporation is the largest publisher of trade computer books in the world. Their quality is recognized by their leadership in sales and by their holding tightly to the largest number of books on the best-seller's lists. That can only be possible due to the insight, creativity, and hard work of the many people at Que who help produce these books. We want to thank the many people who put this book together:

Charles Stewart is the title manager who gave this book the vision and guidance it took to get this book completed.

Mike Miller made the book more accessible with his suggestions on organization and the slant toward task orientation.

Michael Cunningham is the senior editor who worked weekends and many long nights. As I worked past midnight I would marvel that I was getting phone calls, downloads, and FAXes from Michael who was in a time zone two hours later.

Ginny Noble is the production editor who worked with Michael to ensure that this book would meet its nearly impossible deadline. Her objectivity helped clear the way when the written words became overwhelming.

Trademark Acknowledgments

Contents at a Glance

Introduction 1

Part I Everyday Word Processing

1 What's New in Word for Windows 6 15
2 Getting Started in Word for Windows 29
3 Creating and Saving Documents 63
4 Managing Documents and Files 93
5 Editing a Document 115
6 Using Templates as Master Documents 165
7 Using Editing and Proofing Tools 185
8 Previewing and Printing a Document 215

Part II Formatting Documents

9 Formatting Characters and Changing Fonts 243
10 Formatting Lines and Paragraphs 285
11 Formatting with Styles 337
12 Working with Columns 383
13 Setting the Page Layout 401

Part III Creating Special Documents

14 Managing Mail Merge Data 447
15 Mastering Envelopes, Mail Merge, and Form Letters 465

Part IV Mastering Special Features

16 Creating and Editing Tables 507
17 Creating Bulleted or Numbered Lists 549
18 Building Forms and Fill-In Dialog Boxes 573
19 Organizing Content with an Outline 613
20 Calculating Math with Formulas 629
21 Displaying Formulas and Equations 641

Part V Publishing with Graphics

22 Inserting Pictures in Your Document 659
23 Framing and Moving Text and Graphics 687
24 Drawing with Word's Drawing Tools 717
25 Creating Banners and Special Effects with WordArt 773
26 Graphing Data 799
27 Desktop Publishing 827

Part VI Handling Large Documents

28 Inserting Footnotes and Endnotes 877
29 Creating Indexes and Tables of Contents 893
30 Tracking Revisions and Annotations 933
31 Adding Cross-References and Captions 949
32 Assembling Large Documents 969

Everyday Word Processing

Formatting Documents

Creating Special Documents

Mastering Special Features

Publishing with Graphics

Handling Large Documents

Part VII Word & Other Applications

Word & Other Applications

33 Using Word with Other Windows
    Applications   993

34 Converting Files with Word for
    Windows   1021

Part VIII Customizing Word

Customizing Word

35 Customizing and Optimizing Word
    Features   1037

36 Customizing the Toolbar, Menus,
    and Shortcut Keys   1051

Part IX Automating Your Work

Automating Your Work

37 Automating with Field Codes   1071

38 Recording and Editing Macros   1123

39 Building More Advanced Macros   1139

Part X Reference

Appendixes

Appendix A Support Services   1157

Appendix B Installing Word for
            Windows   1159

Appendix C Character Sets   1167

Index   1173

Table of Contents

Introduction   **1**

Why You Should Use This Book 1
Why You Should Use Word for Windows 2
    Word for Windows Has Accessible Power 2
    Word for Windows Works in the Windows Environment ..3
    Word for Windows Shows You Results 3
    Word for Windows Reduces Support 4
    Word for Windows Helps WordPerfect Users 5
Working with Word for Windows 5
    Word Processing in Daily Business 6
    Word Processing for Legal and Medical Documents...........6
    Word Processing for Scientific and Technical Documents ..7
    Word Processing for Financial Documents 7
    Word Processing for Graphic Artists and Advertising..........8
    Word Processing for Specific Industries 8
How This Book Is Organized 9
Conventions Used in This Book 11

I   Everyday Word Processing   **13**

1   What's New in Word for Windows 6   **15**

Better Access to Features 15
    Tip of the Day 15
    Shortcut Menus...16
    Tabbed Dialog Boxes...16
    Wizards to Guide You 17
    Full Screen View...17
    Automatic Corrections 18
    Copy and Paste Formatting 18
    AutoFormat 18
    Style Gallery 19
    Easier Column Formatting 19
    More and Movable Toolbars 20
More Power 20
    Working with Other Windows Applications 20
    Inserting or Linking to External Databases 21
    Manage Data with the Data Form 22
    Customizable Toolbars 22

Better File Management 22
Forms That Include Pull-Down Lists, Edit Boxes,
    or Check Boxes 23
Improved Mail Merge 24
Improved Envelope and Label Printing 24
Improved Indexing and Tables of Contents
    or Authorities 24
Cross-References 24
Drawing Directly on the Document 25
Drop Caps 26
Callouts Attached to Objects 27
Organizer for Managing Macros, Styles, AutoText,
    and Shortcut Keys 27
Improved Compatibility 28

2 Getting Started in Word for Windows   29

Starting and Quitting Word for Windows 29
Understanding the Word for Windows Screen 31
Using the Mouse 35
Understanding Windows and Word for Windows Terms ...37
    Mouse Actions 37
    Keyboard Actions 38
Choosing Commands 40
    Saving Time with Shortcut Menus 40
    Choosing Commands with the Keyboard 41
    Using Drag-and-Drop Commands 42
    Troubleshooting 42
Using the Toolbars 42
    Getting Help on Tools 44
    Displaying or Hiding Toolbars 44
    Moving, Resizing, and Reshaping Toolbars 45
Working in Dialog Boxes 47
    Selecting a Tab in a Dialog Box 48
    Selecting Option Buttons and Check Boxes 48
    Editing Text Boxes 49
    Selecting from List Boxes 51
    Command Buttons and Closing Dialog Boxes ...52
Getting Help 52
    Searching for a Topic in Help 53
    Jumping Between Help Topics 54
    Getting Help in Dialog Boxes 54
    Closing the Help Window 55
    Troubleshooting 55
    Getting the Tip of the Day 56
Manipulating Windows 57
    Switching Between Applications 57
    Switching Between Document Windows 57
    Minimizing, Maximizing, and Restoring Windows ...58

Moving a Window 59
Sizing a Window 59
Closing a Document Window 60
From Here... 61

3   Creating and Saving Documents   63

What You Need to Know About Creating and
Saving Documents 63
Understanding File Names 64
Understanding Directories.. 64
Setting the Default Directory 66
Creating a New Document 67
What You Need to Know About Creating a
New Document 68
Creating a New Blank Document 69
Creating a New Document from a Template 70
Creating a New Document with a Template Wizard 70
Troubleshooting Creating a New Document 71
Opening an Existing Document 72
What You Need to Know About Opening a Document..... 72
Opening a Document 72
Opening a Recently Used File 74
Opening Non-Word for Windows Files 74
Opening a Document While Starting
Word for Windows 75
Troubleshooting Opening a Document 76
Working in a Document 76
What You Need to Know About Working in
a Document 76
Troubleshooting Working in a Document 78
Working with Multiple Documents 78
What You Need to Know About Working with Multiple
Documents 78
Saving a Document 80
What You Need to Know About Saving a Document 80
Saving Your Document.. 81
Saving Files with a New Name 82
Saving with Summary Information to Make Documents
Easier to Find 83
Saving Without Renaming 84
Saving Many Documents at Once 85
Automatically Saving Documents 85
Creating Automatic Backups 86
Saving with Fast Save 87
Saving for Other Word Processors or Applications 88
Saving a Document as a Protected File 88
Troubleshooting Saving Files 90
Closing a Document 90
From Here... 91

4 Managing Documents and Files   93

What You Need to Know About Managing Documents
  and Files 94
Finding Files 95
  What You Need to Know About Finding Files 95
  Searching Different Drives or Directories 96
  Searching for Specific Files or Different File Types 97
  Searching by Summary Information or Text in
    the File 98
  Searching by Date Saved or Created 101
  Saving Search Criteria 102
  Troubleshooting Finding Files 103
Viewing Documents and File Information 103
  What You Need to Know About Viewing
    Documents and File Information 103
  Sorting File Lists 104
  Previewing Documents 105
  Viewing File Information 107
  Viewing Summary Information 107
  Editing and Adding Summary Information 108
Managing Files 109
  What You Need to Know About Managing Files 110
  Opening Found Files 110
  Printing Found Files 111
  Copying Found Files 111
  Deleting Found Files 112
From Here... 113

5 Editing a Document   115

Controlling Your Document's Appearance On-Screen 115
  Selecting the Correct View for Your Work 116
  Editing in Normal View 120
  Editing in Full Screen View 120
  Editing in Page Layout View 121
  Zooming In or Out 121
  Editing in Outline View 124
  Modifying the Screen Display 124
Moving in the Document 127
  Moving and Scrolling with the Mouse 127
  Moving and Scrolling with the Keyboard 129
  Going to a Specific Page 129
  Going to a Bookmark 130
  Moving the Insertion Point a Relative Distance 131
  Moving to Previous Locations 133
Selecting Text 133
  Selecting Text with the Mouse 133
  Selecting Text with the Keyboard 135

Deleting Text..138
   Troubleshooting 138
Typing over Text 139
Hyphenating Words 139
   Inserting Regular and Nonbreaking Hyphens 140
   Inserting Optional Hyphens Throughout
      a Document 140
Undoing Edits 142
Inserting Frequently Used Material 142
   Creating an AutoText Entry 143
   Inserting AutoText 144
   Deleting AutoText 145
   Using the Spike 145
   Printing AutoText Entries 146
Correcting Spelling Errors as You Type 146
   Creating AutoCorrect Entries 146
   Using AutoCorrect 148
   Deleting an AutoCorrect Entry 148
Marking Locations with Bookmarks 149
   Creating Bookmarks 149
   Editing, Copying, and Moving Bookmarked Text 150
   Moving to or Selecting a Bookmark 151
   Deleting Bookmarks 151
Moving, Copying, and Linking Text or Graphics 152
   Understanding the Clipboard..152
   Moving Text or Graphics 153
   Copying Text or Graphics 154
   Using the Mouse to Move and Copy Items 155
   Linking Text 157
   Troubleshooting 158
Working with Multiple Windows 159
   Viewing Different Parts of the Same Document 159
   Cutting and Pasting Between Documents........................160
Working with Pages 161
   Repaginating a Document 161
   Inserting Manual Page Breaks 161
From Here… 163

6   Using Templates as Master Documents   165

What You Need to Know About Templates 167
Using Templates as a Pattern for Documents...........................168
   Opening a New Document 169
   Using Word's Predefined Templates...................................169
   Opening Templates Troubleshooting...................................172
Adding Additional Features with Add-Ins 173
   Loading Add-Ins 173
   Removing Add-Ins 174

Using Wizards to Guide You in Creating Documents 174
    Creating Documents with Wizards 174
    Wizards that Come with Word 174
Changing a Template 175
    What You Need to Know About Changing a Template ... 176
    Changing a Template 176
    Setting Default Formats in the Normal Template 177
    Making Template Features Available to All Documents .. 177
    Changing Template Features from Within
        a Document 178
Creating a New Template 179
    Creating a New Template Based on an
        Existing Template 179
    Creating a Template Based on an Existing Document 180
Using Information from Another Template 180
Transferring Template Contents Using the Organizer 182
From Here... 183

7   Using Editing and Proofing Tools   185

Using Find and Replace 187
    Finding Text 187
    Replacing Text 190
    Finding and Replacing Formatting 193
    Finding and Replacing Special Characters 198
Checking Your Spelling 200
    Checking Your Document's Spelling 201
    Setting Spelling Options 204
    Creating a Custom Dictionary 205
    Troubleshooting Tool Menu Commands 207
Checking Your Grammar 207
    Selecting Grammar Rules 209
    Testing the Readability of a Document 211
Using the Thesaurus 212
Proofing in Other Languages 213
Counting Words 214
From Here... 214

8   Previewing and Printing a Document   215

Selecting a Printer 215
Setting Up Your Printer 217
    Installing a Printer in Windows 217
    Using Special Print Setups 219
    Setting Up Printer Memory and Font Cartridges 221
Previewing Pages Before Printing 222
    Using Page Layout View 222
    Using Print Preview 223
Printing the Current Document 227
    Printing Multiple Copies 227
    Printing Part of a Document 228
    Printing Different Types of Document Information 230

Controlling Printing Options 232
    Printing a Draft 232
    Printing Pages in Reverse Order 233
    Updating Fields 233
    Updating Links 233
    Background Printing 234
    Printing Form Input Data Only 234
    Selecting the Paper Source 234
    Printing Multiple Unopened Documents 235
Sending Documents Electronically..236
    Printing to a File 236
    Printing to a Fax Machine 237
    Sending Documents to Others in Your Workgroup........238
From Here… 239

II Formatting Documents   241

9 Formatting Characters and Changing Fonts   243

What Is Character Formatting? 243
Viewing Formatted Characters 244
    Understanding Screen Fonts and Printer Fonts 245
    Troubleshooting the Screen View of Characters 245
Selecting Characters to Format 246
Formatting Characters 246
    Formatting with Menu Commands 247
    Formatting with Keyboard Shortcuts 250
    Formatting with the Formatting Toolbar 251
    Troubleshooting Character Formatting..........................254
Changing Fonts..254
    Changing Font Type 256
    Changing Font Size 257
Changing the Default Character Formatting 259
Copying Formatting 259
Applying Special Character Formatting Options 260
    Hiding Text 261
    Changing Character Colors 264
    Making Superscript and Subscript Text 264
    Underlining Text 265
    Adjusting Character Spacing 267
    Switching Uppercase and Lowercase 268
Starting Paragraphs with a Drop Cap 269
Inserting Special Characters and Symbols 272
    Using the Symbol Dialog Box 273
    Customizing the Symbol Dialog Box 274
    Inserting Special Characters from the Keyboard 275
Using Fonts Correctly 276
    Understanding Types of Fonts..276
    Understanding Your Printer's Capabilities 278

Understanding How Windows Works with Fonts 279
Using TrueType 279
Enabling TrueType Fonts 280
Installing and Deleting Soft Fonts 282
From Here... 284

10 Formatting Lines and Paragraphs   285

Understanding Paragraph Formats 285
Displaying Paragraph Marks 286
Using Paragraph Formatting Techniques 289
Formatting Paragraphs with Menu Commands 291
Formatting Paragraphs with Shortcut Keys 291
Formatting Paragraphs with the Formatting
Toolbar 292
Formatting Paragraphs with the Ruler 293
Duplicating Formats 294
Troubleshooting 295
Aligning Paragraphs 295
Aligning with Menu Commands 296
Aligning with the Formatting Toolbar 297
Aligning with Keyboard Shortcuts 297
Troubleshooting 298
Setting Tabs 298
Using the Tabs Dialog Box 300
Using the Ruler to Set Tabs 302
Setting Default Tabs 304
Troubleshooting 305
Setting Indents 306
Using the Paragraph Command to Set Indents 307
Creating a Hanging Indent 308
Using the Ruler or Formatting Toolbar to Set Indents 309
Using Keyboard Shortcuts to Set Indents 313
Setting Default Indents 313
Numbering Lines 315
Adding Line Numbers 315
Removing or Suppressing Line Numbers 317
Adjusting Line and Paragraph Spacing 318
Adjusting Paragraph Spacing 318
Adjusting Line Spacing 320
Inserting a Line Break 323
Shading and Bordering Paragraphs 324
Enclosing Paragraphs in Boxes and Lines 325
Shading Paragraphs 332
From Here... 335

11 Formatting with Styles   337

Using Styles versus Direct Formatting 337
Choosing a Formatting Method 339
Formatting a Document Automatically 341

Applying Styles with AutoFormat 343
Reviewing Format Changes 345
Setting AutoFormat Options 347
Getting the Most from AutoFormat 348
Using the Style Gallery 349
Using Word for Windows Standard Styles 351
What You Need to Know About Standard Styles 351
Redefining Standard Styles 354
Applying, Copying, and Removing Styles 355
Resolving Conflicts Between Paragraph and
    Character Style 355
Applying Paragraph Styles 356
Applying Character Styles 356
Copying Styles 358
Removing Character Styles 359
Creating Styles 359
Naming the New Style 359
Creating a Style by Example 360
Creating a Style with a Menu Command 362
Creating a Style Based on an Existing Style 364
Changing Styles 365
Deleting a Style 366
Giving a Style a New Name or Alias 366
Redefining a Style 367
Changing the Normal Style 369
Updating Styles 370
Changing the Base of a Style 371
Creating Style Shortcut Keys 373
Following One Style with the Next Style 375
Sharing Styles Among Documents 375
Displaying Styles with the Style Area 378
Checking Formats 379
Overriding Styles with Manual Formatting 379
From Here… 381

12 Working with Columns 383

Creating Columns 383
What You Need to Know About Columns 384
Calculating the Number and Length of Columns 384
Understanding Sections 385
Creating Columns of Equal Width 387
Creating Columns of Unequal Width 389
Typing and Editing Text in Columns 391
Adding a Line Between Columns 391
Viewing Columns 392
Changing Columns 393
Changing the Number of Columns 394
Changing the Width of Columns and the Spacing
    Between Columns 395

Removing Columns 397
Starting a New Column 397
Balancing Column Lengths 398
Troubleshooting Columns 399
From Here... 399

13   Setting the Page Layout   401

Setting Margins 402
Setting Margins with a Precise Measurement 403
Setting Margins Visually 408
Determining Paper Size and Orientation 411
Changing Page Setup Defaults 413
Creating Headers and Footers 414
Adding Headers and Footers 414
Including Different Headers and Footers in
Different Parts of Your Document 417
Determining a Header's or Footer's Distance
from the Edge 421
Formatting and Positioning Headers and Footers 422
Editing Headers and Footers 422
Deleting Headers and Footers 423
Hiding the Text Layer While Creating or
Editing Headers and Footers 424
Inserting Page Numbers 424
Inserting Page Numbers 424
Removing Page Numbers 425
Formatting Page Numbers 426
Numbering Different Sections in a Document 427
Inserting a Date and Time 428
Inserting Line Numbers 429
Changing Layouts Within a Document 432
Dividing a Document into Sections 432
Removing Section Breaks 434
Copying Section Formatting 435
Changing the Section Break Type 435
Finding Section Breaks 435
Aligning Text Vertically 436
Controlling Where Paragraphs and Pages Break 437
Controlling Paragraph Breaks 437
Inserting Page Breaks 439
Repaginating in the Background 440
Selecting the Paper Source 441
From Here... 443

III   Creating Special Documents   445

14   Managing Mail Merge Data   447

What You Need to Know About Managing Data 448
What You Need to Know About the Database Toolbar............449

Inserting a Database from a File 450
Inserting a Database 451
Creating a Data Source for Mail Merge 453
Creating a New Data Source 454
Working with an Existing Data Source 458
Using Data from Another Application 459
Managing Information in the Data Source 460
Finding or Editing Records with the Data Form 460
Sorting a Data Source 462
Renaming, Inserting, or Removing Fields from
a Data Source 462
Inserting or Removing Records from a Data Source 463
Scrolling Through the Data Form 464
From Here... 464

15 Mastering Envelopes, Mail Merge, and Form Letters   465

Printing an Envelope 466
Printing an Envelope with Bar Codes or FIM Codes 469
Customizing Envelopes with Text and Graphics 470
Merging Mailing Lists and Documents 470
What You Need to Know About Mail Merge 471
Specifying a Main Document 473
Specifying a Data Source 474
Creating a New Data Source 476
Editing the Main Document 478
Creating a Data Source Document 483
Quickly Merging to Printer or Document 483
Controlling the Merge Process 485
Selecting Specific Records to Merge 486
Using Letterhead While Merging 490
Merging Envelopes 491
Creating Mailing Labels 494
Making Mail Merge More Efficient 498
From Here... 503

IV Mastering Special Features   505

16 Creating and Editing Tables   507

What You Need to Know About Tables 507
Creating Tables 509
What You Need to Know About Creating Tables 509
Creating a Table with the Table Wizard 509
Using the Table Insert Table Command 512
Using the Insert Table Button 513
Displaying or Hiding Gridlines and End Marks 514
Typing and Moving in a Table 515
Using Indents and Tabs in a Cell 517
Attaching Captions to Tables 517

Editing Tables 519
   What You Need to Know About Editing Tables 519
   Selecting and Editing Cells 519
   Moving and Copying Cells 521
   Changing Column Width 525
   Changing Row Height and Position 528
   Adding or Deleting Cells, Rows, or Columns 531
   Troubleshooting Editing a Table 534
Merging and Splitting Cells and Creating Table Headings 535
   Merging Cells 535
   Creating Table Headings 535
   Splitting Cells 536
Formatting a Table 536
   What You Need to Know About Formatting a Table 536
   Formatting a Table with Table AutoFormat 537
   Selecting Border Formats 538
   Selecting Shading and Colors 540
Numbering Rows and Columns 542
   Adding Numbers with the Numbering Button 542
   Adding Numbering with the Menu 543
Splitting a Table 543
Sorting Tables 544
Converting a Table to Text 545
Converting Text to a Table 545
Calculating Math Results in a Table 547
   What You Need to Know About Calculating
   Math in a Table 547
From Here… 548

17 Creating Bulleted or Numbered Lists   549

Creating Bulleted Lists 550
   Creating Bulleted Lists with Menu Commands 551
   Creating Bulleted Lists with the Toolbar 552
   Ending the Bulleted List 553
   Adding Subordinate Paragraphs to a Bulleted List 553
   Customizing Bulleted Lists 554
Creating Numbered Lists 557
   Creating Numbered Lists with Menu Commands 557
   Creating Numbered Lists with the Toolbar 559
   Ending the Numbered List 559
   Adding Subordinate Paragraphs to a Numbered List 560
   Customizing Numbered Lists 561
Creating Multilevel Lists 563
   Customizing Multilevel Lists 565
Splitting a Numbered or Bulleted List 567
Removing Bullets or Numbering 567
Creating Numbered Headings 567
   Customizing Numbered Headings 569
   Removing Heading Numbers 571
From Here… 571

18 Building Forms and Fill-In Dialog Boxes   573

Form Basics 574
Building Forms 577
    Creating and Saving the Form Structure 577
    Adding Form Fields 578
    Protecting and Saving the Form 581
Using an On-Screen Form 583
    Filling in an On-Screen Form 584
    Saving an On-Screen Form 586
    Troubleshooting Forms 586
Customizing Form Fields 586
    Customizing Text Form Fields 588
    Customizing Check Box Form Fields 591
    Customizing Drop-Down Form Fields 592
    Formatting Form Fields 594
    Disabling Form Fields 594
    Naming and Finding Fields in a Form 594
    Adding Help to a Form 595
    Adding Macros to a Form 597
    Protecting and Unprotecting a Form with a Password 598
    Protecting Part of a Form 599
Converting Existing Forms 600
Printing a Form 601
    Printing the Filled-In Form 601
    Printing Form Data Only 602
    Printing a Blank Form 602
    Troubleshooting Printing a Form 602
    Saving Data Only 603
Building Forms with Fill-In Dialog Boxes 604
    Using {fillin} Fields 605
    Reusing Field Results 606
    Saving and Naming the Template 608
    Updating Fields in a Form 609
    Creating a Macro to Update Fields Automatically 609
From Here… 611

19 Organizing Content with an Outline   613

Viewing an Outline 613
Creating an Outline 617
Formatting Your Outline 618
Promoting and Demoting Headings 618
    Using the Mouse to Promote or Demote Headings 619
    Using Keyboard Shortcuts to Promote or
        Demote Headings 620
Collapsing and Expanding an Outline 620
    Using the Mouse to Collapse or Expand Headings 621
    Using Keyboard Shortcuts to Collapse or
        Expand Headings 622

Fitting More of the Outline into the Window 622
    Using the Mouse to See More of the Outline 623
    Using Keyboard Shortcuts to See More of the Outline 624
Reorganizing an Outline 624
Numbering an Outline 625
Using Outline Headings for a Table of Contents 625
Replacing Outline Headings 626
    Using Custom Styles to Create an Outline 626
    Globally Replacing Outline Headings 628
    Removing Text from Within an Outline.......................... 628
Printing an Outline 628
From Here... 628

20   Calculating Math with Formulas   629

Using Word's Math Functions or a Spreadsheet? 629
Performing Calculations 630
Using Bookmarks to Perform Calculations in Text 631
Performing Calculations in a Table 633
    Specifying Table Cells in a Formula 634
    Entering a Formula in a Table 635
    Using Table Values in a Formula outside the Table 637
Recalculating Formulas 637
    Troubleshooting Calculations 638
From Here... 639

21   Displaying Formulas and Equations   641

What You Need to Know about Displaying Formulas
    and Equations 641
Building an Equation 643
    Inserting an Equation 644
    Typing in the Equation Editor 645
    Selecting Items in an Equation 645
    Entering Nested Equation Templates 645
    Entering Symbols 647
    Adding Embellishments 648
Formatting an Equation 649
    Controlling Spacing 649
    Positioning and Aligning Equations 650
    Selecting Fonts 651
    Selecting Font Sizes 652
Working with Matrices 653
Viewing Equations 654
Editing an Equation 654
Printing Equations 655
From Here... 655

V   Publishing with Graphics   657

22   Inserting Pictures in Your Document   659

Reviewing Compatible Formats 660
Installing the Import Filters 661
Inserting and Copying Pictures into Your Document 661
    Inserting Pictures into Your Document 662
    Copying Pictures into Your Document 665
    Inserting Picture Objects in Your Document 666
    Inserting Pictures in Frames and Text Boxes 669
Working with Pictures 671
    Selecting Pictures 671
    Resizing and Cropping Pictures 672
    Adding Lines and Borders 676
    Moving or Copying a Picture 680
    Displaying and Hiding Pictures 681
Editing and Converting Pictures 683
    Converting Picture Objects 683
From Here... 685

23   Framing and Moving Text and Graphics   687

Framing Text, Pictures, and Other Objects 688
    Framing Text 689
    Formatting Text Within a Frame 690
    Framing Pictures and Other Graphic Objects 691
    Framing Tables 692
    Inserting a Blank Frame 693
    Inserting Text or Graphics in a Blank Frame 694
    Framing Objects Together 694
    Including a Caption in a Frame 695
    Working in Different Views 695
    Troubleshooting Frames 696
Selecting and Removing Frames 697
    Selecting a Framed Object 697
    Removing a Frame 699
Moving and Positioning Frames 699
    Moving a Frame with a Mouse 700
    Moving and Copying Frames 701
    Positioning a Frame Horizontally 702
    Positioning a Frame Vertically 705
    Positioning a Frame in a Margin 706
    Anchoring a Frame 707
Wrapping Text Around a Frame 708
Sizing Frames 710
    Sizing Frames with a Mouse 711
    Sizing Frames with the Keyboard 712
Bordering and Shading Frames 713
From Here... 715

24 Drawing with Word's Drawing Tools   **717**

What You Need to Know About Drawing 717
Displaying and Understanding the Drawing Toolbar 719
     Displaying the Drawing Toolbar 719
     Understanding the Drawing Tools 719
Choosing the Line and Color for Drawing 722
Using a Menu Command to Change Drawing Color or
     Line Pattern 723
     Setting Colors and Line Patterns Using the
         Drawing Toolbar 727
Drawing and Coloring Shapes and Lines 727
     Understanding the Drawing Screen 727
     Scrolling the Page 728
     Basic Procedure for Drawing 729
     Selecting Shapes, Lines, and Whole Drawings 730
     Troubleshooting the Selection Process 732
     Drawing and Coloring Lines 732
     Drawing and Coloring Arrows 734
     Drawing and Coloring Rectangles or Squares,
         and Ellipses or Circles 735
     Drawing and Coloring Arcs and Wedges 738
     Drawing and Coloring Freeform Shapes and Polygons ... 739
     Creating Shadowed Lines and Shapes 742
     Using the Drawing Grid 743
     Troubleshooting Your Drawings 744
Changing Lines and Shapes 745
     What You Need to Know About Changing Objects 745
     Basic Procedure for Changing Drawing Objects 746
     Changing or Removing a Shape's Fill or Pattern 747
     Changing Line Style and Color 748
     Removing the Line Around a Shape 749
     Changing Arrows or Removing Arrowheads 750
     Resizing a Line or Shape 750
     Changing the Shape of a Freeform Shape 751
     Rotating Shapes and Lines 752
     Flipping Shapes and Lines 753
     Troubleshooting When You Change an Object 753
Moving, Copying, Deleting, and Positioning Lines
     and Shapes 753
     Moving Lines and Shapes 754
     Copying Lines and Shapes 755
     Deleting Shapes and Lines 755
     Aligning Lines and Shapes to Each Other or to
         the Page 755
     Positioning Lines and Shapes 757
Including Text or Another Picture in a Drawing 759
     Inserting Text Boxes 759
     Inserting Picture Containers 761
     Troubleshooting Text Boxes and Picture Containers 763

Adding and Changing Callouts 763
    Inserting a Callout 764
    Changing a Callout 764
Rearranging a Drawing's Layers 766
    What You Need to Know About Rearranging Layers 767
    Moving Objects in Front of or Behind Each Other 767
    Layering Objects Below or Above the Text 769
    Framing Objects to Move Them into the Text 769
Gouping and Ungrouping Lines and Shapes 770
    Grouping Objects 771
    Ungrouping Groups 771
    Troubleshooting Grouping 772
From Here… 772

25 Creating Banners and Special Effects with WordArt   **773**

What You Need to Know about WordArt 773
Creating a WordArt Object 775
    Starting WordArt 775
    Entering and Editing the Text 777
    Understanding WordArt's Commands, Lists,
        and Buttons 778
    Exiting WordArt 780
    Getting Help in WordArt 780
    Troubleshooting WordArt 780
Adding Special Effects 780
    What You Need To Know about WordArt Effects 781
    Shaping the Text 782
    Changing the Font or Font Size and Inserting
        Symbols 782
    Applying Bold, Italics, or Even Caps 784
    Flipping and Stretching Letters 785
    Rotating, Slanting, and Arcing Text 787
    Aligning the Text 788
    Adjusting Spacing Between Characters 789
    Adding Borders 790
    Adding Color, Shading, or a Pattern 792
    Adding Shadows 794
Editing a WordArt Object 795
From Here… 798

26 Graphing Data   **799**

Creating a Chart 799
    Understanding the Data Sheet Layout 801
    Typing Data for a New Chart 803
    Creating Charts from a Table 803
    Copying Data from Word for Windows or
        Other Applications 804

Importing Worksheet or Text Data 805
Importing a Microsoft Excel Chart 806
Editing Existing Charts 807
Entering Data for Overlay Charts 808
Editing the Data Sheet 808
Selecting Data 808
Replacing or Editing Existing Data 809
Inserting or Deleting Rows and Columns 810
Copying or Moving Data 810
Including and Excluding Data from a Chart 810
Changing Data by Moving a Graph Marker 811
Changing the Chart Type 811
Selecting the Original Chart Type 811
Customizing an Existing Chart Type 814
Formatting the Data Sheet 816
Adjusting Column Widths in the Data Sheet 816
Formatting Numbers and Dates 817
Custom Formatting of Numbers and Dates 819
Adding Items to a Chart 819
Adding Titles and Data Values 820
Adding Floating Text 821
Adding Legends, Arrows, and Gridlines 821
Formatting the Chart and Chart Items 822
Sizing Your Chart 822
Changing Patterns and Colors 823
Formatting Fonts and Text 823
Formatting Axes 824
Rotating 3-D Charts 825
Exiting or Updating Graphs 826
From Here… 826

27   Desktop Publishing   827

Designing Your Publication 829
Planning Your Publication 829
Using the Building Blocks of Design 830
Understanding the Elements of Effective Design 834
Using Word for Windows Desktop Publishing
Capabilities 837
Tools to Help You Work 838
Working in Different Views 838
Changing the Viewing Options 838
Using the Toolbars 839
Using Templates 839
Using Wizards 839
Using Styles 839
Spelling and Grammar Checkers 839
Laying Out the Page 840
Paper Size 840
Paper Orientation 840
Margins 841

Facing Pages for Newsletters, Catalogs, Magazines,
and Books 841
Binding Gutters for Extra Margin Width 841
Changing the Page Layout Within a Document 842
Including Headers and Footers 842
Positioning Text and Graphics in the Margins 842
Designing with Text 843
Selecting the Font 843
Selecting the Font Size 844
Choosing Text Styles and Color 844
Using Typesetting Characters 845
Controlling the Letter Spacing 845
Using Titles, Headings, and Subheadings 846
Determining Alignment and Justification 846
Adjusting Line and Paragraph Spacing........................... 847
Keeping Text Together 848
Maintaining Consistent Formatting 848
Indenting Paragraphs 849
Creating Lists 849
Using Text as Graphics 849
Working with Columns 850
Creating Snaking, Newspaper-Style Columns 851
Controlling Column Length 852
Varying the Number of Columns in a Publication 852
Creating Side-by-Side Columns 853
Creating Sideheads 853
Incorporating Illustrations 854
Including Photographs 854
Creating Illustrations in Other Programs 855
Adding Captions 855
Sizing and Cropping Illustrations.................................... 855
Knowing Where to Position Illustrations 856
Drawing in Word for Windows 856
Repeating Graphics on Every Page 857
Creating Transparent Graphics 857
Creating Logos with WordArt 857
Using Ready-Made Computer Art...................................... 858
Leaving a Blank Space for Pictures 858
Wrapping Text Around Graphics
(and Other Text) 858
Framing and Moving Text and Objects 859
Framing and Grouping Items Together 859
Using Lines, Boxes, and Shading 860
Putting Information in a Box 861
Creating an Empty Box for Illustrations Added
After Printing 861
Lines Above and Below Paragraphs 862
Including Lines Between Columns 862
Shading and Coloring Paragraphs 863

Printing Your Publication 863
    Understanding Your Own Printer's Capabilities 864
    Printing an Original for Outside Duplication 864
    Getting Your Printing Job Typeset 864
Desktop Publishing Examples 865
    Creating a Page Full of Business Cards 865
    Creating a Folded Brochure 866
    Creating an Ad 868
    Creating a Simple Newsletter 869
    Creating Letterhead and an Envelope 870
    Creating a Four-Column Newsletter 871
From Here... 873

VI Handling Large Documents   875

28 Inserting Footnotes and Endnotes   877

What You Need to Know About Inserting Footnotes and
    Endnotes 877
Inserting Footnotes and Endnotes 878
    Changing the Appearance of Reference Marks 881
Editing and Viewing Footnotes and Endnotes 882
    Viewing Footnotes and Endnotes 882
    Formatting and Editing Footnotes and Endnotes 883
Finding Footnotes 883
Deleting, Copying, and Moving a Footnote or Endnote 884
Converting Footnotes and Endnotes 885
Customizing Note Settings 886
    Customizing Note Separators 887
    Placing Footnotes 888
    Customizing Numbering 890
From Here... 891

29 Creating Indexes and Tables of Contents   893

Creating Indexes 893
    Creating Index Entries 894
    Including a Range of Pages 897
    Customizing Index Entries 898
    Assembling a Simple Index 899
    Formatting an Index 901
    Updating or Replacing an Index 903
    Deleting an Index 903
    Fixing an Index as Text 904
    Creating Multiple-Level Index Entries 904
    Creating Cross-Reference Index Entries 906
    Automatically Creating Index Entries 907
Creating Tables of Contents 909
    Creating a Table of Contents Using Outline
        Headings 909

Creating a Table of Contents Using Any Style 912
Creating a Table of Contents Using Any Text 914
Troubleshooting Tables of Contents 916
Creating a Table of Figures or Other Tables 917
Creating Tables of Figures and Other Tables
Using Styles 917
Creating Tables of Figures and Other Tables
Using Any Text..920
Creating a Table of Authorities 923
Creating Citation Entries 923
Editing Citation Entries 925
Assembling a Table of Authorities 925
Customizing Citation Categories 926
Updating, Replacing, or Deleting Tables of Contents
and Other Tables 927
Updating a Table of Contents or Other Table 927
Replacing a Table of Contents or Other Table 928
Deleting a Table of Contents or Other Table 928
Limiting Tables of Contents and Other Tables 929
Formatting Tables of Contents and Other Tables 929
Formatting with Styles 930
Formatting with Field Code Switches 930
From Here... 931

30 Tracking Revisions and Annotations   933

What You Need to Know About Revisions and
Annotations 933
Using the Revision Marks Feature 934
Marking Revisions 935
Showing Revisions 936
Accepting or Rejecting All Revisions 936
Accepting or Rejecting Individual Revisions 937
Customizing Revision Marks 938
Protecting Documents for Revisions 939
Merging Revisions and Annotations 940
Troubleshooting Revisions 941
Comparing Documents 941
Using Annotations 942
Inserting Annotations..943
Finding and Viewing Annotations 944
Including or Deleting Annotations 945
Protecting Documents for Annotations Only 945
Printing Annotations 946
Troubleshooting Annotations 946
From Here... 947

31 Adding Cross-References and Captions   949

What You Need to Know about Cross-References
and Captions 949
Creating Cross-References 951

Adding Cross-References 952
Cross-Referencing Another Document 954
Updating Cross-References 954
Formatting Cross-References 955
Creating Captions 955
Inserting Captions Manually 956
Inserting Captions Automatically 957
Creating New Caption Labels 959
Changing Caption Labels 960
Deleting a Caption Label 961
Changing Caption Numbering...961
Including Chapter Numbers in a Caption 962
Formatting Captions 963
Editing Captions 963
Updating Captions 964
Framing a Caption with Its Object 964
Editing and Deleting Cross-References and Captions 964
From Here… 967

32 Assembling Large Documents   969

What You Need to Know About Assembling a
    Large Document 971
Creating a Master Document...971
Creating a New Master Document 972
Creating a Master Document from an Existing
    Document 975
Creating a Master Document by Combining
    Documents 976
Troubleshooting 976
Working with the Master Document 976
Formatting the Master Document 977
Printing a Master Document 978
Sharing a Master Document 978
Troubleshooting 979
Working with Subdocuments within the
    Master Document..979
Opening Subdocuments from Within a
    Master Document..980
Rearranging Subdocuments in a Master Document.........980
Splitting, Merging, and Deleting Subdocuments 980
Inserting Tables of Contents, Indexes, and
    Cross-References 982
Troubleshooting 982
Working with Individual Files...982
Setting Starting Numbers...983
Creating Chapter Numbers...984

Printing Individual Files 985
Creating a Table of Contents..985
Inserting Chapter Numbers 986
From Here... 989

VII Word & Other Applications   991

33 Using Word with Other Windows Applications   993

Starting Applications from the Microsoft Toolbar 994
Choosing to Paste, Link, or Embed Data 995
What You Need to Know about Data Formats 998
Exchanging Data Through Files 999
Transferring Data with Copy and Paste 999
Embedding Data 1000
Creating an Embedded Object..1001
Editing Embedded Objects 1006
Converting Embedded Objects 1007
Troubleshooting Embedded Objects 1008
Linking Documents and Files 1008
Linking Documents to Entire Files 1009
Linking Documents to Part of a File 1011
Troubleshooting Linked Files 1013
Managing Links 1014
From Here... 1019

34 Converting Files with Word for Windows   1021

Converting Files from Word Processors, Spreadsheets,
or Databases 1021
Examining the File Types that Word for Windows
Converts 1021
Installing Converters 1023
Converting a File into Word for Windows Format 1024
Troubleshooting Converting a File into Word
for Windows 1025
Saving Word for Windows Documents to Another
Format 1026
Seeing Which Converters You Have Installed......................1027
Modifying Conversion Options...1028
Improving Conversion Compatibility 1029
Controlling Font Conversion in Documents 1030
Font Conversions for Documents Converted to
Word for Windows 1030
Font Conversions for Documents Converted from
Word for Windows to Another Format 1032
From Here... 1033

VIII   Customizing Word   1035

35   Customizing and Optimizing Word Features   1037

Customizing Commonly Used Features 1037
Improving the Performance of Word for Windows 1038
    Modifying Word for Windows Settings 1039
    Managing System Memory 1041
Starting Word or Documents on Startup 1043
    Loading or Running Word When Windows Starts 1043
    Loading Documents When Windows Starts 1044
    Loading a Document When Word Starts from
      an Icon 1044
    Starting Word with Special Settings 1045
Making Menus, Toolbars, and Shortcut Keys Globally
    Available 1046
Customizing the Workspace and Display 1046
Customizing Mouse Settings 1047
Customizing Word for the Hearing or Movement
    Impaired 1048
From Here... 1049

36   Customizing the Toolbar, Menus,
and Shortcut Keys   1051

Understanding Where and When Customizing Occurs 1051
Customizing and Creating Toolbars 1052
    Adding Tools 1052
    Reorganizing Tools 1054
    Creating Your Own Toolbar 1056
    Putting a Command or Macro on a Toolbar 1058
    Choosing Custom Tool Faces 1059
    Drawing Your Own Tool Faces 1060
    Transferring Toolbars with the Organizer 1061
Customizing the Menu 1062
    Adding Commands to Menus 1062
    Removing or Resetting Commands 1064
    Adding or Removing Menus 1065
Assigning Commands and Macros to Shortcut Keys 1066
From Here... 1068

IX   Automating Your Work   1069

37   Automating with Field Codes   1071

Understanding the Basics of Fields 1073
    Examining the Types of Fields 1073
    Understanding the Parts of Fields 1074
    Field Code Shortcut Keys 1075

Viewing and Printing Field Codes 1076
    Displaying Field Codes 1077
    Displaying Field Results as Shaded 1078
    Printing Field Codes 1078
Inserting Field Codes 1079
    Inserting Field Codes 1080
    Inserting Field Code Switches or Bookmarks 1080
    Inserting Field Codes Manually 1082
Moving Between Fields 1083
Editing Fields 1084
    Creating Complex Fields by Nesting 1085
    Deleting Fields 1085
Formatting Field Results 1085
    Formatting Numbers, Dates, and Text Case 1087
    Preserving Manual Formats 1087
    Formatting with Custom Numeric Formats 1090
    Formatting Date-Time Results 1094
Updating, Unlinking, or Locking Fields 1096
    Updating Fields 1096
    Undoing or Stopping Updates 1097
    Locking Fields to Prevent Updates 1098
    Unlinking Fields 1098
Getting Help on Field Codes 1098
A Reference List of Field Codes 1099
From Here… 1122

38 Recording and Editing Macros   1123

Recording Macros 1124
    Deciding How Your Macro Will Work 1125
    Specifying Where Macros Are Stored 1125
    Preparing to Record a Macro 1126
    What Gets Recorded 1127
    Recording a Macro 1128
    Recording a Sample Macro 1129
    Troubleshooting Recording a Macro 1131
Running a Macro 1132
    Troubleshooting Macros 1134
Editing a Macro 1134
Saving a Macro 1136
Using Word for Windows Sample Macros 1136
From Here… 1137

39 Building More Advanced Macros   1139

Understanding and Modifying Recordings 1139
Modifying the MyWorkspace Macro 1141
Using Input Boxes to Enter Data 1143
Creating Automatic Macros 1146

Managing Macros 1148
Getting Help on Macros 1150
Debugging Macros 1152
From Here… 1154

X   Reference   1155

Appendix A Support Services   1157

Resources, Consulting, and Support 1157
    Microsoft Corporation 1157
    CompuServe 1157
    Que Corporation 1158
    Ron Person & Co. 1158

Appendix B Installing Word for Windows   1159

Hardware Requirements 1159
Installing Word for Windows 1160
    Starting the Installation Process 1160
    Choosing the Features to Install 1162
    Finishing the Installation 1165

Appendix C Character Sets   1167

Index   1173

Introduction

Word for Windows is the best-selling word processor available for Windows. In competitive reviews, Word for Windows has received the highest rating from every major reviewer and magazine. Its features range from those of an easy-to-use word processor to those that make it the most powerful and customizable word processor.

Why You Should Use This Book

Previous editions of *Using Word for Windows* have sold more copies than any other book on word processing in Windows. It is not just a rehash of the manual by writers who aren't familiar with Word for Windows. This book has in it the knowledge that comes from time spent on the front-lines of business—helping individuals, departments, and corporations learn how to work effectively using Windows software. Our work has included helping business people who are just getting started with word processing to teaching corporate developers how to program in the Word and Excel application languages. We have seen the confusion caused by some areas in the manuals and have expanded and clarified these areas. We've tried to include tips and tricks that have been learned over time—many of which are either not in the manuals or difficult to find.

Throughout the book, Tips and Notes highlight combinations of features or tricks that make you more productive. These Tips and Notes are set off from the text so that you can get at them quickly without having to wade through a swamp of black ink.

Word for Windows 6 is an extensive upgrade from Word for Windows 2 and a significant improvement over Word for Windows 1. Throughout the book, new features specific to Word for Windows 6 are marked by a Version 6 icon (shown at the right of this paragraph). If you used Word for Windows before, watch for these icons so that you can quickly learn about new features. If you used a previous version of Word for Windows, you should read Chapter 1, "What's New in Word for Windows." It will give you a visual catalog of the major new features in Word for Windows 6.

Using Word Version 6 for Windows, Special Edition, includes extensive sections on how to get the most out of WordArt, Microsoft Graph, Equation Editor, and Microsoft Query—applications you can use to create publishing titles, create charts and graphs, insert equations, or retrieve data from external databases. You will also learn how to integrate Word for Windows 6 with other Windows applications. You can paste, link, or embed data from another Windows application into your Word document. This book will help you understand the differences, advantages, and disadvantages among these three methods of exchanging data.

Why You Should Use Word for Windows

Many reasons exist for choosing Word for Windows as your word processor, including its wide array of features, its accessibility, its power, and its ability to exchange data and graphics with other Windows applications. For those of you standardizing on a word processor, the choice of Word for Windows is an easy one. For those of you already using one or more word processors, Word for Windows can increase productivity and decrease support costs. Because of its capability to coexist with other word processors, you can begin a gradual transition toward Word for Windows.

Word for Windows Has Accessible Power

Word for Windows is the most powerful word processor, but it has features that make it the easiest to use and easiest to get help.

Most people do not need or use advanced word processing features regularly. On most days, you want a convenient word processor that doesn't get in the way. Word for Windows toolbars, shortcut menus, and excellent on-line help make it one of the easiest word processors to learn. You can also customize the screen display and menus to make the program even more straightforward and easy to use. Although Word's advanced features don't get in the way, they are there to handle any type of specialized work you need, such as drawing on a document, outlining, importing, or linking to mainframe database, desktop publishing, and the list goes on.

Word makes these advanced features, that you may only use occasionally, easy to learn. The toolbars shown in fig. I.1, for example, enable you to click a button to do the most frequently used commands, such as opening or saving files, inserting bulleted lists, making tables or columns, or formatting for bold with centered alignment. You can even customize the toolbar to fit your needs by adding or removing buttons for specialized commands.

Fig. I.1
Select text and click buttons on toolbars to execute many commands.

Word for Windows Works in the Windows Environment

If you know any other Windows application, you already know how to use Word for Windows menus and commands, choose from dialog boxes, use the Help window, and operate document windows. Another advantage of Windows is that you can easily transfer data between applications, embed graphics or text in a Word for Windows document, or link graphics or text between applications. Fig. I.2 shows a Word for Windows document linked to Microsoft Excel charts and tables. You can easily switch between the two applications.

Word for Windows gives you access to Object Linking and Embedding (OLE). With OLE, you can embed text, graphics, and charts into a Word for Windows document and not have to worry about misplacing the file that the text, graphics, or charts came from. The data is embedded along with the result. Double-click an embedded object, like the chart in fig. I.2, and the appropriate application immediately loads the object so that you can edit it. Word works with both OLE 1 and OLE 2 so that you can embed or link with older or the most up-to-date Windows applications.

Word for Windows Shows You Results

Word for Windows enables you to zoom from a 25% to 200% view of your document—exactly as it will appear when printed. You can edit and format text or move framed objects while you are in any zoomed view. If you are using TrueType fonts, you are guaranteed to see what will print. Word has the features necessary to do most desktop publishing. Fig. I.3 shows a page zoomed out to show almost an entire page.

Fig. I.2
You can paste,
link, or embed
data from other
Windows applica-
tions so that your
word processor
really gives you
the ability to
integrate data from
many different
sources.

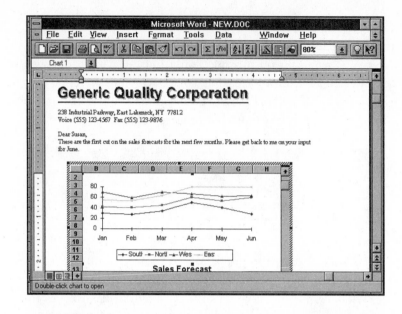

Fig. I.3
Word has the
commands and
buttons to do
desktop publishing
that satisfies most
business and
personal needs.

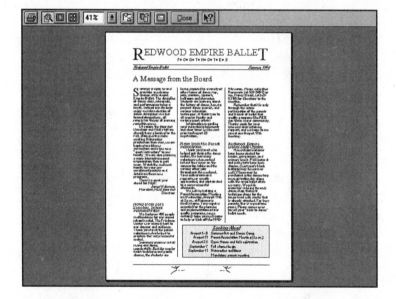

Word for Windows Reduces Support

Word for Windows contains extensive help files you can use to get an
overview of a procedure. To get help, just press the F1 key. When the Help
window appears, you can click topics about which you want additional
information. Press Alt+F4 to put the Help window away. In fact, anytime a
dialog box or alert box appears and you want more information, just press F1.

If you are working in a macro, you can even move the insertion point inside a macro statement (code) and press F1 to see detailed help about that specific statement. When you need more extensive help or tips and tricks, refer to this book.

Word for Windows Helps WordPerfect Users

Word for Windows not only does a good job of translating WordPerfect documents and graphics, it can help you learn Word for Windows. When you install Word for Windows, or at any later time, you can turn on the capability to use WordPerfect menus and navigation keys. While the WordPerfect help system is on, you can press a WordPerfect key such as Ctrl+F8 for fonts and the WordPerfect Help dialog box, shown in fig. I.4, will appear with the appropriate WordPerfect menu. (Fig. I.4 shows the highest level WordPerfect menu.) Use the same keystrokes you would use in WordPerfect. When you finish making menu choices, Word for Windows displays a *stick-em* note describing what to do, or actually makes the Word for Windows menu and dialog choices for you. As you watch it make the correct choices, you learn how to use Word for Windows.

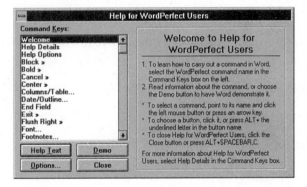

Fig. I.4
WordPerfect users can retrieve their WordPerfect documents and get help with commands.

If you are a professional typist who likes a clean, clear screen to work on, you can choose the View Full Screen command to remove the menu bar, status bar, scroll bars, ruler, ribbon, and toolbar so that the Word for Windows screen is clear. Pressing Esc or clicking the Restore button returns the screen to its original view.

Working with Word for Windows

Word for Windows has features that fit many working environments. Even beginning and intermediate operators can customize Word for Windows to fit specific job needs. This section includes several examples of the many types of documents you can produce with Word for Windows.

Word Processing in Daily Business

Word for Windows makes repetitive work very easy. As a professional typist doing daily business work, you can use some of the following Word for Windows features:

- Automatically format standard types of documents with the AutoFormat command.

- Use template Wizards to guide you through building brochures, newsletters, letters, and so on.

- Create forms that contain pull-down lists and check boxes to replace your office's printed forms.

- Use print preview or page layout views to see results before you print.

- Use the mail-merge capabilities that guide you through mailings and labels.

- Automatically generate envelopes.

- Use templates to hold repetitive documents, formatting styles, macros, text you want entered automatically, and shortcut keys.

- Choose the symbol you need from a table.

- Insert tables that look like spreadsheets by clicking a toolbar button.

- Format numbered and bulleted lists by clicking a toolbar button.

- Add toolbar buttons for the commands you use frequently.

- Portrait (vertical) and landscape (horizontal) pages in the same document.

Word Processing for Legal and Medical Documents

Legal and medical documents present unique word processing requirements that Word for Windows is built to handle:

- AutoText to eliminate typing long words and repetitive phrases

- One of the best outliners available

- Tables of authorities and automatic cross-referencing

- Annotations, hidden text, and revision marks

- Numbered lines with adjustable spacing

- Inserting graphics or pictures

- Drawing directly on the document with drawing tools

Word Processing for Scientific and Technical Documents

When you write scientific or technical papers, you need to include references, charts, tables, graphs, equations, table references, footnotes, and endnotes. Word for Windows will help your technical documents with the following:

- An equation editor that builds equations when you click equation pieces and symbols

- Drawing and graphing tools built into Word for Windows

- The capability to insert many different types of graphics files as well as AutoCAD files

- Spreadsheet-like tables for data

- Mathematics in tables

- Embedding or linking with Excel, the leading Windows worksheet

Word Processing for Financial Documents

The reader's initial impression of a financial report comes when the cover page is turned. Word for Windows gives you on-screen tables, similar to spreadsheets, and links to Microsoft Excel and Lotus 1-2-3 for Windows worksheets and charts. You will find the following productive features:

- Commands and structure very similar to Microsoft Excel

- Ability to operate Microsoft Excel or Lotus 1-2-3 and Word for Windows simultaneously and switch between them

- Embedding of Microsoft Excel worksheets so that they can be updated within the Word document

- Linking of Microsoft Excel or Lotus worksheets so that changes in the original worksheet appear in the Word document

- Row-and-column numeric tables that can include math

- Ability to use Microsoft Query to download and link to mainframe or server data

- Borders, shading, and underlining to enhance columnar reporting

- Tables and charts linked to other Windows applications

Word Processing for Graphic Artists and Advertising

Until now, testing page layouts and advertising design required two applications: a word processor and a desktop publishing program. Word for Windows combines both. Although Word for Windows doesn't have all the "free form" capabilities of a publishing application like Aldus PageMaker, Word for Windows still gives you many features, such as the following:

- Wide range of graphic file import filters

- Text wrap-around graphics

- Movable text or graphics

- Borders and shading

- Parallel or snaking columns that include graphics

- Print preview or an editable page layout view that zooms 25% to 200%

- Compatibility with PostScript typesetting equipment

- Linking of body copy and graphic files into a single, larger master document

- Drawing directly on the document

- Automatic captions and callouts that are tied to the graphic or position

Word Processing for Specific Industries

Word for Windows is a fully customizable word processor. Therefore, industry associations, custom software houses, and application developers can tailor Word for Windows features to fit the needs of specific vertical industries or to integrate with their own custom applications. For example, they can create custom menus, toolbars, and shortcut keys that operate existing commands or run programs written in Word's extensive WordBASIC programming language. To aid developers, Word for Windows includes the following:

- WordBASIC, an extensive macro programming language with more than 400 commands

- A macro recorder and editing tools

- Customizable toolbars, menus, and shortcut keys

- AutoText for industry-specific terms

- Customized templates to package documents with customized features

- Personal and foreign language dictionaries

- Integration and data exchange with other Windows applications

How This Book Is Organized

Word for Windows is a program with immense capability and a wealth of features. It can be straightforward and easy to learn if approached correctly. This book is organized to help you learn Word for Windows quickly and efficiently.

If you are familiar with Word for Windows 2, then you should scan the table of contents for new features and look through the book for pages marked with the Version 6 icon that marks new features. Many of the Word 2 commands have been moved so that they are more accessible to the average user and so that Microsoft Excel and Word have a similar menu structure.

Using Word Version 6 for Windows, Special Edition, is organized into the following parts:

- Part I: Everyday Word Processing

- Part II: Formatting Documents

- Part III: Creating Special Documents

- Part IV: Mastering Special Features

- Part V: Publishing with Graphics

- Part VI: Handling Large Documents

- Part VII: Word & Other Applications

- Part VIII: Customizing Word

- Part IX: Automating Your Work

Part I helps you learn the fundamentals of Word for Windows that you will need for basic letters, and gives an overview of the new features in Word 6. If you are familiar with Word 2, you should start with Chapter 1 and learn the new features in Word 6. Chapters 2 through 6 describe the basics you will need to know for opening, creating, editing, and saving documents. Chapter 7 describes proofing tools such as Word's spelling checker, thesaurus, and grammar checker. Chapter 8 closes Part I by showing you how to preview your document and print.

Part II teaches features that help you format the document. You will begin by learning how to format characters in Chapter 9. Chapter 10 then describes how to format paragraphs with such features as alignment, indentation, and borders. One of the most useful chapters in Part II is Chapter 11. Chapter 11 covers styles, which are useful to anyone who uses a format repetitively for headings, titles, and so on. Chapter 12 describes how to use multiple columns if you need to create newsletters, brochures, or scripts. Finally, Chapter 13 describes how to set overall page layout with such things as margins, page orientation, and type of paper.

In Part III you learn how to automate mailing lists and bring data into Word from outside databases. You will learn how to use Word's built-in database or link Word to data files stored on disk, in a network server, or on the mainframe. Chapter 15 describes how to use that data to create form letters, envelopes, and labels.

Part IV describes the many special features that make Word the most powerful word processor. You will learn how to number lists and insert special symbols. If you like to put a structure to your document before starting, you'll definitely want to learn about Word's outliner. And virtually everyone should learn how to use tables in Word. Tables are spreadsheet-like grids that help you organize text, lists, numbers, and even graphics.

If you want to use a word processor to do work similar to desktop publishing, then Word is the one you should use. Part V describes how to use Word's built-in drawing tools and how to import graphics drawn in drawing programs. Chapter 23 shows you how to frame text or graphics so that you can make anything moveable on-screen. You can drag items anywhere on the page and the text wraps around it. Part V also describes the *applet* programs, WordArt and Graph, included with Word for Windows. These programs enable you to create fancy titles and banners, or build charts like those created by a program such as Excel.

If you write contracts, build large manuals, print a book with many chapters, or work with thesis or formal term papers, then you should turn to Part VI. You will learn how to create footnotes and endnotes, indexes, tables of contents or authorities, and print documents that are larger than will fit in Word's memory.

Part VII shows you the advantage Word has when working with other applications in the Windows environment. You can copy and paste, link, or embed data between Windows applications. This section also describes how to convert documents and data from non-Word programs.

Even if you don't know how to program, you can customize Word to the work and look that you want. Part VIII describes how to customize Word's features using the Tools Options menu. In addition, it shows you how easy it is to reorganize Word's menus, add new commands to toolbars, and add shortcut keys to cut down on your work.

The final section, Part IX, describes how to automate Word and add new features through the use of the macro recorder. Word has a powerful built-in programming language that you can use even as a beginner. These two chapters describe how to record a process that you do frequently and then modify that recording. You can then run your recorded procedures from menu commands, buttons on toolbars, or shortcut keys.

The appendixes contain information about installing Word for Windows, important telephone numbers, and a table of the Windows character set.

Conventions Used in This Book

Conventions used in this book have been established to help you learn to use the program quickly and easily. As much as possible, the conventions correspond with those used in the Word for Windows documentation.

Letters pressed to activate menus, choose commands in menus, and select options in dialog boxes are printed in boldface type: File **O**pen. Names of dialog boxes are written with initial capital letters, as the name appears on-screen. Messages that appear on-screen are printed in a special font: Document 1. New terms are introduced in *italic* type.

Two different types of key combinations are used with this program. For combinations joined with a comma (Alt, F), you press and release the first key and then press and release the second key. If a combination is joined with a plus sign (Alt+F), you press and hold the first key while you press the second key.

An icon is used throughout this book to mark features new to Version 6 of Word for Windows.

The code continuation character ➥ is used to indicate that a breaking code line should be typed as one line. Here's an example:

```
    ToolsOptionsSave .CreateBackup = 0, .FastSaves = 1,
➥ .SummaryPrompt = 0, .GlobalDotPrompt = 0, .NativePictureFormat = 0,
➥ .EmbedFonts = 0, .FormsData = 0, .AutoSave = 0, .SaveInterval = "",
➥ .Password = "", .WritePassword = "",
➥ .RecommendReadOnly = 0
```

Even though the preceding example runs across five lines, the code continuation character tells you that the code fragment should be typed as one line. The code continuation character is your cue to continue typing a code fragment as one, long line.

Part I

Everyday Word Processing

1 What's New in Word for Windows 6

2 Getting Started in Word for Windows

3 Creating and Saving Documents

4 Managing Documents and Files

5 Editing a Document

6 Using Templates as Master Documents

7 Using Editing and Proofing Tools

8 Previewing and Printing a Document

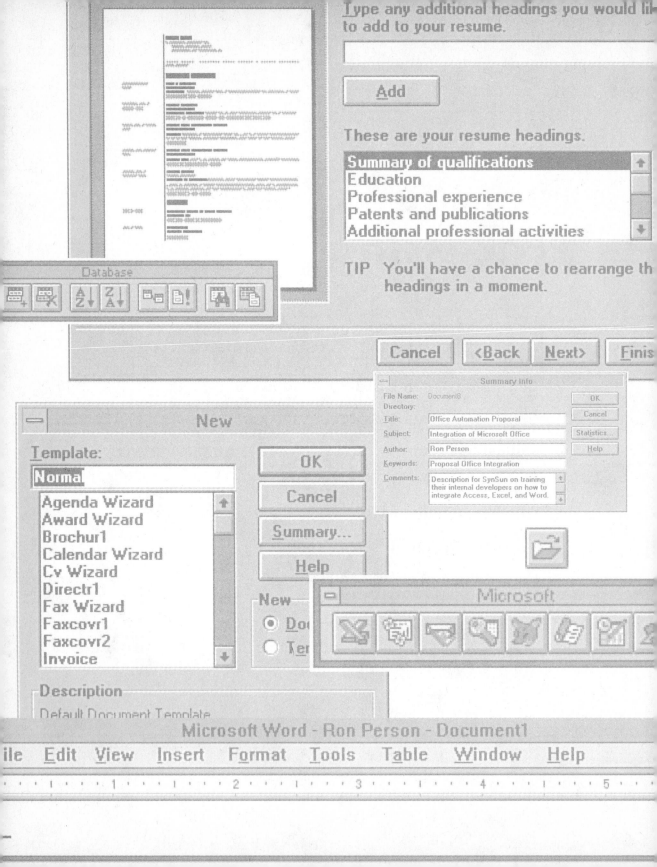

Type any additional headings you would lik
to add to your resume.

Add

These are your resume headings.

Summary of qualifications
Education
Professional experience
Patents and publications
Additional professional activities

TIP   You'll have a chance to rearrange th
      headings in a moment.

Database

Cancel   <Back   Next>   Finis

Summary Info

File Name: Document8   OK
Directory:
Title: Office Automation Proposal   Cancel
Subject: Integration of Microsoft Office   Statistics...
Author: Ron Person   Help
Keywords: Proposal Office Integration
Comments: Description for SynSun on training
             their internal developers on how to
             integrate Access, Excel, and Word.

New

Template:

Normal

Agenda Wizard   OK
Award Wizard
Brochur1   Cancel
Calendar Wizard
Cv Wizard   Summary...
Directr1
Fax Wizard   Help
Faxcovr1
Faxcovr2   New
Invoice   ● Doc
                   ○ Ter

Microsoft

Description

Default Document Template

Microsoft Word - Ron Person - Document1

ile   Edit   View   Insert   Format   Tools   Table   Window   Help

. . . 1 . . . . 1 . . . . 2 . . . . 1 . . . . 3 . . . . 1 . . . . 4 . . . . 1 . . . . 5 . . .

Chapter 1

What's New in Word for Windows 6

Word for Windows 6 is much easier to use than Word for Windows 2, and yet it has more powerful features. Microsoft has tested Word for Windows in its usability laboratory to find ways to make Word's features more accessible to you.

This chapter is a catalog of a few of the most important changes and new features in Word for Windows 6. If you are an experienced Word for Windows user, browse through this chapter to find what's new and what powerful features have been added.

Changes in Word for Windows are of two types: features that have been made easier and more accessible and features that have been made more powerful. Of course, the improvements to Word don't easily fall into one category or another because all the new features combine power with accessibility.

Better Access to Features

Microsoft understands that powerful features aren't important unless you can use them. In Word for Windows 6, the features you use most often are more accessible and much easier to use.

Tip of the Day

Applications such as Word for Windows are becoming easier to use with pull-down menus and tabbed dialog boxes, but when you become very proficient in certain tasks, you probably find yourself wishing for faster, more productive ways to work. Although you could use the Search button in Help to learn

For Related Information
■ "Getting a Tip of the Day," p. 56

about Word's many shortcuts, a more fun way to learn these shortcuts is to activate the Tip of the Day feature (see fig. 1.1). This feature displays a different shortcut each time you start Word. When you've learned everything there is to know about Word, you can turn off the Tip of the Day feature.

Fig. 1.1
Learn helpful tips about Word each time you start the program.

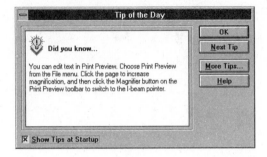

Shortcut Menus

For Related Information
■ "Saving Time with Shortcut Menus," p. 40

With pull-down menus that lead into tabbed dialog boxes, you can quickly get at hundreds of options. You use some of these options and features more frequently than others, however. For this reason, Microsoft has added *shortcut menus* (see fig. 1.2). Shortcut menus appear when you click the right mouse button on text, an object, or a screen element such as a toolbar. The shortcut menu appears (right under the pointer) depending upon which item you clicked. It takes a little while to remember that you don't always have to go to the main menu, but shortcut menus become addictive quickly.

Fig. 1.2
Shortcut menus appear when you click the right mouse button on text, objects, or screen elements such as toolbars.

Tabbed Dialog Boxes

For Related Information
■ "Working in Dialog Boxes," p. 47

Word has so many different features and options that there is no way they can all be available from the menu. Instead, Microsoft has kept the menus short and has made hundreds of options available in dialog boxes. Because there are so many options available, they are now grouped together into tabbed "cards" within the dialog box (see fig. 1.3). You can switch between different groups of options by clicking the tab or pressing Alt and the appropriate letter to choose a different tab.

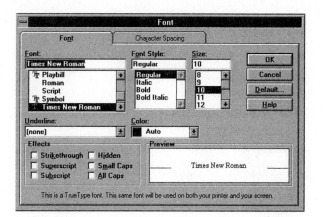

Fig. 1.3
With Word's new tabbed dialog boxes, you have quick access to many options.

Wizards to Guide You

Wizards guide you through the process of creating special or complex documents (see fig. 1.4). To open a Wizard, choose the File New command and select the Wizard. Word comes with Wizards that help you create documents such as a fax cover sheet, brochures, calendars, legal pleadings, business or personal letters, resumes, and complex tables that include fancy formatting.

For Related Information
■ "Using Wizards to Guide You in Creating Documents," p. 174

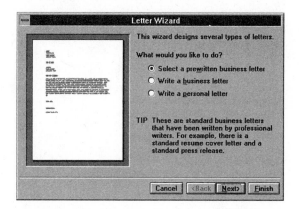

Fig. 1.4
Wizards guide you through producing complex documents.

Full Screen View

Some typists are distracted by menus, toolbars, and scroll bars. If you are such a typist, work in Word's new Full Screen view. To display the full screen, just choose the View Full Screen command (see fig. 1.5). Return to the previous view by pressing Esc or by clicking the Full Screen button.

For Related Information
■ "Controlling Your Document's Appearance On- Screen," p. 115

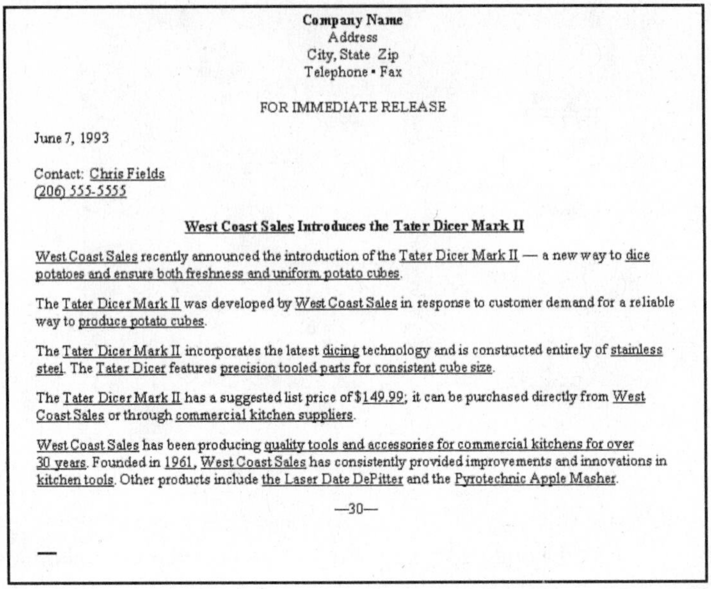

Fig. 1.5
The new Full
Screen view makes
your document
appear as though
you are typing on
a white page that
fills the entire
screen. Extraneous
screen elements
are hidden.

Company Name
Address
City, State Zip
Telephone • Fax

FOR IMMEDIATE RELEASE

June 7, 1993

Contact: Chris Fields
(206) 555-5555

West Coast Sales Introduces the Tater Dicer Mark II

West Coast Sales recently announced the introduction of the Tater Dicer Mark II — a new way to dice
potatoes and ensure both freshness and uniform potato cubes.

The Tater Dicer Mark II was developed by West Coast Sales in response to customer demand for a reliable
way to produce potato cubes.

The Tater Dicer Mark II incorporates the latest dicing technology and is constructed entirely of stainless
steel. The Tater Dicer features precision tooled parts for consistent cube size.

The Tater Dicer Mark II has a suggested list price of $149.99; it can be purchased directly from West
Coast Sales or through commercial kitchen suppliers.

West Coast Sales has been producing quality tools and accessories for commercial kitchens for over
30 years. Founded in 1961, West Coast Sales has consistently provided improvements and innovations in
kitchen tools. Other products include the Laser Date DePitter and the Pyrotechnic Apple Masher.

—30—

Automatic Corrections

With Word's new AutoCorrect feature, you can type a word or abbreviation
and Word will automatically replace it with the text or graphic you have
previously specified. This can make legal and medical typing more productive—type an abbreviation, and it automatically converts to the correct word
or phrase. You also can set AutoCorrect to automatically correct mistakes you
frequently make such as changing "hte" to "the" or capitalizing the first letter
in a sentence.

Copy and Paste Formatting

When you need to reapply multiple formats, reach for the tool that looks like
a paintbrush. The Format Painter button on the Standard toolbar enables you
to select text that has formatting applied, and then click and drag the text
you want reformatted. When you release the mouse button, the copied format is applied.

**For Related
Information**
■ "Copying
Formatting,"
p. 259

■ "Formatting a
Document
Automatically,"
p. 341

AutoFormat

The AutoFormat feature enables you to type a document and then apply a
standardized set of formats to the document with a single command. Using a
set of rules about what defines a heading, title, body copy, figures, tables, and
so on, Word examines your document and applies styles to each element.
You then can manually redefine each style or use the Style Gallery to change
the overall appearance of the document.

Style Gallery

If you want to create a standardized appearance in your documents with less work, you can use the Style Gallery (see fig. 1.6). The Style Gallery is a collection of formatting styles that are applied as a group to an entire document. You can actually see a sample of what the active document will look like as you select each different style in the gallery.

For Related Information
■ "Using the Style Gallery," p. 349

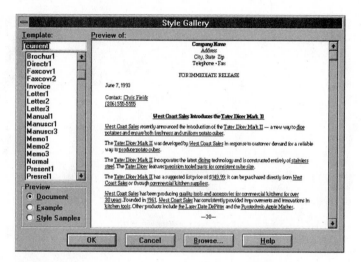

Fig. 1.6
The Style Gallery enables you to change the appearance of your entire document by changing entire collections of formatting styles.

Easier Column Formatting

Newspaper or snaking columns make text more readable. They give the eye a shorter distance to travel to see part of a sentence. With the Word 6 Format Columns command, creating columns is much easier to do than in Word 2 (see fig. 1.7). In Word 6, you can even create unevenly spaced columns.

For Related Information
■ "Creating Columns," p. 383

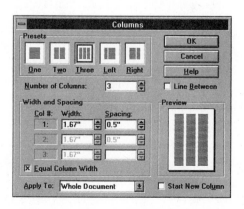

Fig. 1.7
The Columns feature makes columns very easy to apply. In Word 6, you can even create unevenly spaced columns.

More and Movable Toolbars

For Related Information
■ "Using the Toolbars," p. 42

Toolbars give you quick access to commands. Word 6 has more toolbars, which you can move and reshape on-screen (see fig. 1.8). Using either the View Toolbars command or a right mouse click on a toolbar, you can display or hide a toolbar. Dragging in a toolbar's gray area moves it while dragging an edge reshapes it.

Fig. 1.8

Word's large number of movable toolbars gives you quick access to your most frequently used commands when you use a mouse.

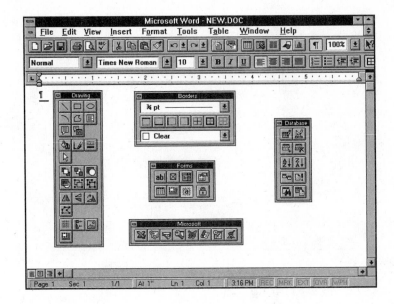

More Power

Word is one of the most powerful word processors. With it, you have such varied capabilities as being able to link to mainframe databases and all the desktop publishing features of a publishing program.

Working with Other Windows Applications

For Related Information
■ "Embedding Data," p. 1000

Word has gained even more flexibility and power when working with other Windows applications. In addition to its previous ability to copy and paste or link to data in other Windows applications, Word now includes OLE automation. This means that you can edit or modify embedded objects from applications such as Microsoft Excel 5 from within your Word document. Notice that in fig. 1.9 the Word menu and toolbar reflect the Excel chart object that is selected in the document.

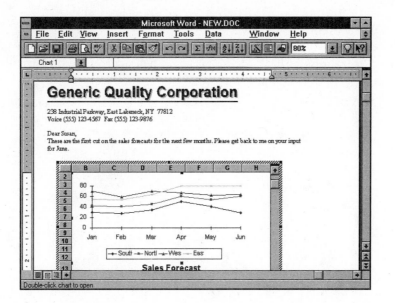

Fig. 1.9
Word works even
better with other
Windows applica-
tions. You can edit
data from OLE 2
applications such
as Excel 5 while
staying in your
Word document.

Inserting or Linking to External Databases

Whether you are in a major corporation or a small business, you probably
have information in a database that you could use with Word for Windows.
For example, you may need that information to print mailing labels, send
form letters to customers, or create a new price sheet or catalog. Word now
has the ability to get information from most databases found in PC, SQL
Server, or mainframes (see fig. 1.10). Word also works with Microsoft Query,
the application that lets you search and retrieve information from within
relational databases.

**For Related
Information**
■ "Creating a
Data Source for
Mail Merge,"
p. 453

Fig. 1.10
You can insert or
link to selected
data on PC, SQL
Server, or main-
frame databases.

For Related Information
■ "Creating a Data Source for Mail Merge," p. 453

Manage Data with the Data Form

Mailing lists and product information are much easier to maintain with Word's Data Form (see fig. 1.11). You can use the Data Form to find records and edit them in Word.

Fig. 1.11
Use Word's built-in Data Form to find, edit, or delete information in one of Word's data sources.

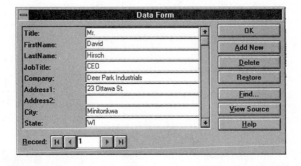

Customizable Toolbars

For Related Information
■ "Customizing and Creating Toolbars," p. 1052

If you frequently use a command or feature and need quick access to it, you can assign it to a custom tool on your own created toolbar or an existing toolbar (see fig. 1.12). You can even draw your own tool faces and assign macros to tools.

Fig. 1.12
You can customize existing toolbars or create your own toolbars.

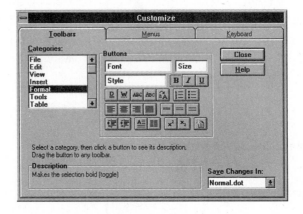

Better File Management

For Related Information
■ "Finding Files," p. 95

It doesn't take very long before you have hundreds of documents on your disk and finding a specific document becomes tedious and frustrating. Word's new Find File command lets you find files by different characteristics so you don't have to decipher an inscrutable eight-letter file name (see fig. 1.13). You can even preview a file's contents.

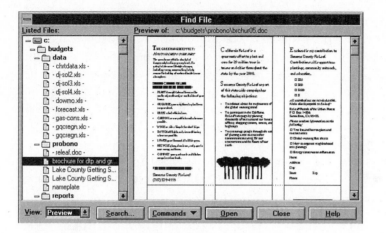

Fig. 1.13
Finding and previewing files is significantly easier with the new Find File feature.

Forms That Include Pull-Down Lists, Edit Boxes, or Check Boxes

Word processors seem to lend themselves to doing forms, yet they can't manage to fill in the blanks on forms. Consequently, many businesses continue to inventory hundreds of pounds of pre-printed forms. Word helps you reduce the cost of storing and printing forms with its new forms feature, shown in fig. 1.14. In a normal word processing document, you can now insert edit boxes, check boxes, and pull-down lists. You don't have to have to know how to program, all you have to do is make selections in a dialog box.

For Related Information
■ "Building Forms," p. 577

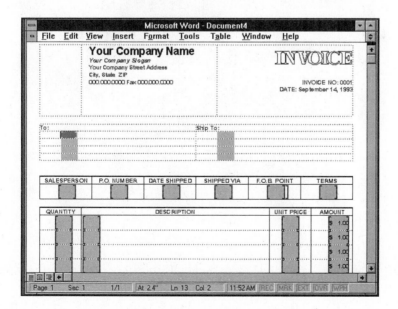

Fig. 1.14
Word's new forms feature enables you to easily put edit boxes, check boxes, and pull-down lists within a normal document.

**For Related
Information**
■ "Mastering
   Envelopes, Mail
   Merge, and
   Form Letters,"
   p. 465

■ "Creating
   Indexes and
   Tables of
   Content,"
   p. 893

Improved Mail Merge

Mail merge is often looked at as a difficult task in word processing, yet it's something that many small and medium sized businesses do frequently. Word now uses the Mail Merge Helper, a series of dialog boxes, to guide you through merging data into form letters, envelopes, and labels. You can even choose the layout for the types of envelopes and labels.

Improved Envelope and Label Printing

Envelopes and labels are not only preaddressed for you, all the formatting is laid out as well (see fig. 1.15). Select standard-sized envelopes and labels or create custom settings (see fig. 1.16).

Improved Indexing and Tables of Contents or Authorities

If you work with major reports, proposals, or legal documents, you will find Word's indexing, table of contents, and table of authorities features much improved (see fig. 1.17). You have more formatting options and these features are easier to use.

Fig. 1.15
The labels tabs contain lists of layout definitions for most standard business labels.

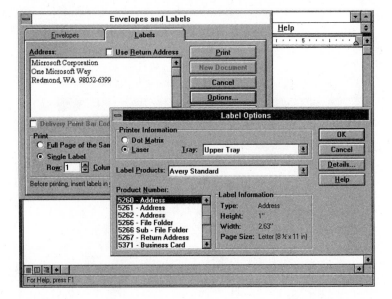

**For Related
Information**
■ "Creating
   Cross-
   References,"
   p. 951

Cross-References

One of the time consuming jobs in proposals and authoritative documents is cross-referencing tables, figures, and comments. With a little guidance, Word takes care of the job for you. You don't even have to move back and forth in a document to see what you want to cross-reference. Word keeps track of different types of content and topics and presents it to you so you can select the topic you want to cross-reference.

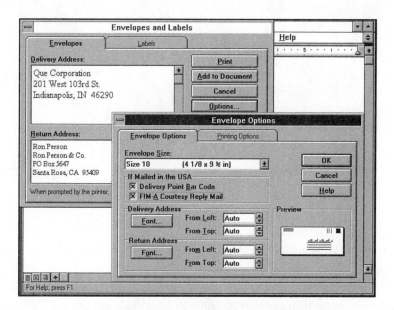

Fig. 1.16
The envelope options enable you to position addresses on different-sized envelopes as well as automatically print postal delivery bar codes.

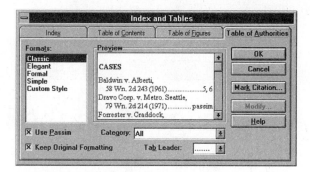

Fig. 1.17
The formatting and features in Word's indexing and table generation capabilities are improved.

Drawing Directly on the Document

Word 2 had Microsoft Draw, an add-in drawing program. Word 6 has incorporated all of Draw's drawing tools directly into Word (see fig. 1.18). Also, there are now three graphics layers into which you can put your drawing or imported graphic. You can put drawings under the text to get a watermark-like effect, in with the text so the text wraps around the graphic, or over the text as an overlay.

For Related Information
■ "Drawing with Word's Drawing Tools," p. 717

Fig. 1.18

All of Microsoft Draw has been incorporated directly into Word. You even have a choice of putting your graphics behind, with, or in front of text.

Drop Caps

For Related Information
■ "Starting Paragraphs with a Drop Cap," p. 269

Drop caps are large letters that designers use to make you aware of a new chapter or section (see fig. 1.19). They look fancy and attractive, but in Word 2, they took a few formatting tricks to accomplish and then you couldn't be extremely precise with their positioning. In Word 6, drop caps are available as a formatting option.

Fig. 1.19

Publishers use drop caps to make new chapters and sections obvious. They are now a choice on the Format menu.

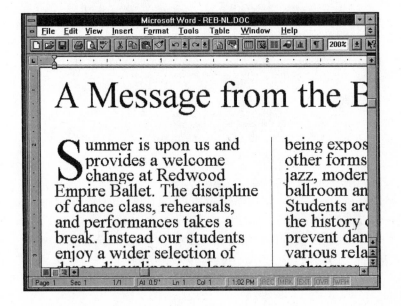

Callouts Attached to Objects

Anyone doing technical documentation or training materials in a word processor has wished for the ability to do callouts. *Callouts* are text boxes that explain elements of a picture or drawing, as you see in fig. 1.20. Well, those documentation and training writers can now put away their desktop publishing programs and stay in Word. Callouts in Word are easy to insert and can be formatted and attached to locations on-screen so they stay with the object they describe.

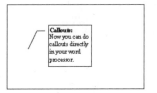

For Related Information

■ "Adding and Changing Callouts," p. 763

Fig. 1.20
A feature like a callout once required a desktop publishing program. Now trainers and technical writers can do all their work in Word.

Organizer for Managing Macros, Styles, AutoText, and Shortcut Keys

In Word 2, you could attach a document to another template when you wanted to use a style, macro, or shortcut key from that template, but to transfer features between documents or templates was a difficult or impossible task. Now you only need to display the Organizer to move macros, styles, AutoText entries, or shortcut keys between documents (see fig. 1.21). If you have a feature in one document that you want in another document, call in the Organizer.

For Related Information

■ "Transferring Template Contents Using the Organizer," p. 182

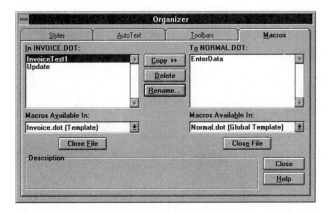

Fig. 1.21
If you like a feature in one document, use the Organizer to move it to any document you want.

Improved Compatibility

For Related Information

■ "Converting Files from Word Processors, Spreadsheets, or Databases," p. 1021

Word has many filters and converters to import word processing documents, worksheets, database records, and graphic files. Word 6 adds compatibility options that take into account the different ways that non-Word programs handle special features. Because you are probably not familiar with the nuances between programs, Word recommends settings when you import a file from another application.

Chapter 2

Getting Started in Word for Windows

The basics of using Word for Windows are the same as the basics for using any other Windows program. If you are familiar with another Windows application, such as Microsoft Excel, you may not need to read this "basics" chapter (or perhaps a quick scan is all you need). If you are a new Windows user, however, you will find this chapter important for two reasons: you will become comfortable navigating Word for Windows; and you will have a head start on the next Windows program you learn.

In this chapter, you learn how to control not only Word for Windows menus and dialog boxes but also the windows that contain Word for Windows and its documents. By the time you finish this chapter, you will be able to use the mouse and the keyboard to choose commands from menus, select options from dialog boxes, access the extensive help system, and manipulate windows on-screen. Beyond these basic tasks, you should be able to organize windows so that you can access and use multiple documents at once or "clear away your desktop" so that you can concentrate on a single job.

Some of the important things you will learn in this chapter are:

- Starting and quitting Word for Windows

- Choosing commands and selecting from dialog boxes

- Operating Word for Windows from keyboard or mouse

- Manipulating windows

Starting and Quitting Word for Windows

To activate Word for Windows:

1. Start Windows by typing **WIN** and pressing Enter.

2. Activate the Word for Windows 6 group window by clicking on the window or double-clicking the window's icon. If you are using the keyboard, press Ctrl+Tab until the the Word group window is activated; the title bar will darken when the window is active. If the Word group is an icon, press Ctrl+Tab until the icon is highlighted, and press Enter.

Fig. 2.1 shows the Word for Windows 6 group window with the Word for Windows icon selected.

Fig. 2.1
The Word for Windows icon selected in the Word for Windows program group window.

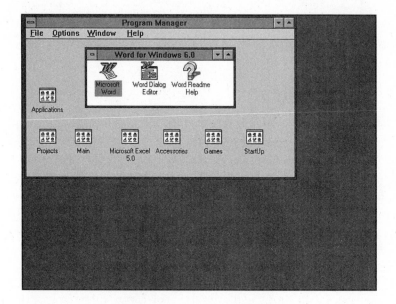

To start Word for Windows:

1. Double-click the Word icon, or press the arrow keys until the title of the Word icon is highlighted and press Enter.

You also can start Word for Windows by choosing a document file from the File Manager. To start Word for Windows and load the document, double-click the file name for a Word for Windows document (DOC), or select the file name and press Enter.

Close—or "quit"—Word for Windows when you are finished working for the day or when you need to free memory for other applications. To quit Word for Windows:

1. If you are using the keyboard, press the shortcut key combination Alt+F4 or choose the File Exit command by pressing Alt, F, X. If you are using a mouse, click the File menu, then click the Exit command.

> **Note**
>
> If this procedure does not work, check to see whether the PATH command in the AUTOEXEC.BAT file gives the directory where the WINWORD.EXE file is located. If this procedure still does not work, you may need to *associate* Word for Windows files with Word for Windows. To learn how to associate files with an application, see the Windows manual or *Using Windows 3.1*, Special Edition, from Que.

To learn how to use the mouse and keyboard for carrying out commands and other procedures, see "Understanding Windows and Word for Windows Terms" later in the chapter.

2. If you made changes to any document, Word displays an Alert box asking whether you want to save your current work. Choose the Yes button or press Enter to save your work, or choose the No button to quit without saving.

Understanding the Word for Windows Screen

One advantage of Windows applications is the ability to run several applications and display them on-screen simultaneously. Chapters 33, "Using Word with Other Windows Applications," and 34, "Converting Files with Word for Windows," describe how to run Word for Windows and other Windows or DOS applications together and transfer information among them. This capability can save you time when you transfer data into or out of Word for Windows, create automatically updated links from Word for Windows and other Windows applications, or embed Word for Windows data into other Window application documents.

Each Windows application, like Word for Windows, runs in its own application window. Because some application windows can contain multiple document windows, you can work simultaneously with more than one document. Fig. 2.2 shows the Word for Windows application window with two document windows inside.

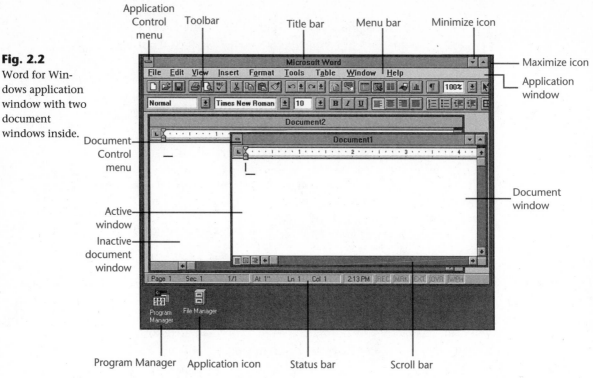

Fig. 2.2
Word for Windows application window with two document windows inside.

Table 2.1 lists and describes the parts of a Word for Windows screen shown in fig. 2.2.

Table 2.1 Parts of Word for Windows and Windows Screens	
Part	**Description**
Application window	The window within which Word for Windows runs.
Application icon	The icon of a running application.
Document window	The window within which documents are displayed.
Application Control menu	The menu that enables you to manipulate the application window.
Document Control menu	The menu that enables you to manipulate the active (top) document window.
Active window	The window that accepts entries and commands; this window is shown with a solid title bar and is normally the top window.
Mouse pointer	The on-screen arrow, I-beam, or drawing tool that indicates the current location affected by your mouse actions.

Part	Description
Insertion point	The point where text appears when you type.
End of document marker	The point beyond which no text is entered.
Title bar	The bar at the top of an application or document window.
Menu bar	A list of menu names displayed below the title bar of an application.
Toolbar	A bar containing tools (buttons) that, when chosen with the mouse pointer, produce a function or action.
Minimize icon	A down arrowhead at the right of a title bar that stores an application as an application icon at the bottom of the screen; equivalent to the application Control Minimize command.
Maximize icon	An up arrowhead at the right of a title bar that fills available space with the document or application; equivalent to the Control Maximize command.
Restore icon	A double arrowhead at the right of a title bar that restores an application or document into a sizable window; equivalent to the Control Restore command. (Not shown in fig. 2.2.)
Scroll bar	A gray horizontal and vertical bar that enables the mouse to scroll the screen; a scroll box in the bar shows the current display's position relative to the entire document.
Status bar	A bar at the bottom of the screen that shows what Word for Windows is prepared to do next; watch the Status bar for prompts, explanations of the current command, buttons under the mouse pointer, or guidance.
Indicators	These display modes of operation, such as NUM when the numeric pad is on, SCRL when the Scroll Lock has been pressed, or EXT when the Extend mode is on.

Fig. 2.3 shows the elements within Word in more detail. The document window, Document 1, has a solid title bar, indicating that it is the active document window. You can have multiple document windows open at the same time. Most entries and commands affect only the active document window. Inactive windows are normally behind the active window and have a lighter colored or cross-hatched title bar.

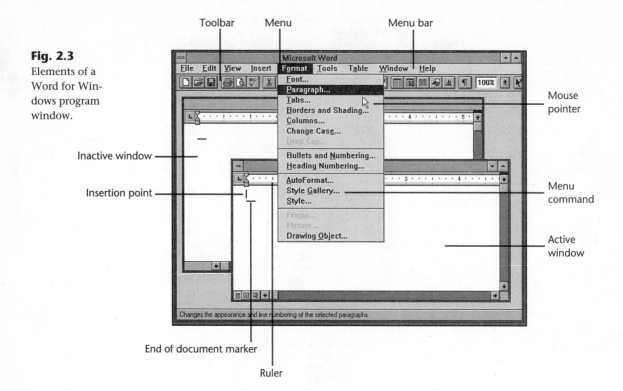

Fig. 2.3
Elements of a
Word for Win-
dows program
window.

The components in a Word screen are described in table 2.2.

Table 2.2 Parts of the Word Screen	
Part	**Description**
Active window	The document window that accepts entries and commands; this window has a solid title bar and is normally the top window.
Inactive window	Inactive windows contain documents that are loaded, but are not affected by commands; these windows have a lighter colored title bar and are normally behind the active window.
Menu bar	A list of menu names displayed below the title bar of an application.
Menu	A pull-down list of commands.
Command	A function or action chosen from a pull-down menu.

Part	Description
Toolbar	A bar containing buttons that gives quick access to commands and tools, such as the spell checker, bold, italic, edit cut and edit paste, styles, and fonts. A toolbar can be moved to different locations and reshaped to a different orientation.
Ruler	A bar containing a scale that indicates tabs, paragraph indents, and margins in the paragraph where the insertion point (cursor) is located. The ruler can be used with the mouse to format paragraphs quickly.
Mouse pointer	The on-screen pointer that shows the mouse location.
Insertion point	The point where text appears when you type.
End of document marker	The point beyond which no text is entered.
Split window icons	Dark bars at the top of the vertical scroll bar that you can drag down to split a window into two views of the same document.

Using the Mouse

The mouse is an optional piece of hardware that attaches to your personal computer and enables you to move the on-screen pointer as you move the mouse with your hand. In Word, you can control the program with mouse movements or with keystrokes, but, most users will find that Word is easier to learn and to use with the mouse. Some Word actions, such as drawing graphical objects, require the use of a mouse; other actions, such as moving text, are significantly easier when you use a mouse. All menu commands and many other procedures features are all accessible through the use of the keyboard. You will find that combining mouse actions, touch-typing, and short-cut keys is the most productive way to work.

You can run the Mouse program and switch the left and right mouse button controls. This is useful if you are left-handed. To find the Mouse program, start the Control Panel from the Main group window of the Program Manager. See your Windows documentation or *Using Windows 3.1,* Special Edition, from Que for more information about using the Control Panel functions.

The mouse pointer changes appearance depending on its location. You usually see the mouse pointer as an arrow when it is in the menus or as a vertical I-beam shape when it is over a text area of your document. When you use the mouse pointer for drawing graphical objects or for embedding objects on a document, its shape changes to a crosshair (a thin cross). Each shape signals to you what action you can perform at that location.

Table 2.3 shows and explains the different shapes of the pointer.

Table 2.3 Mouse Pointer Shapes		
Pointer Appearance	**Screen Location**	**Function**
⬚	Menu	Select commands
	Scroll bars	Scroll through document
	Objects or selected text	Move, size, or select objects
⬚	Left edge of text	Select lines or paragraphs
⬚	Selected text with mouse button depressed	Mouse moves selected text
I	Text	Type, select, or edit text
⬚	Window corner	Resize two sides of window
⬚	Window edge	Resize single side of window
↕	Corner or side handle of selected frame or object	Resize selected picture, frame, or object picture
✛	Window center object edge	Move window or object
↓	Top of table	Select column
⬌	Left or right edge of any cell in a table	Widen or narrow column
⬚	Split bar	Split window into two panes
⬚	Anywhere	Get help specific to next item selected

Pointer Appearance	Screen Location	Function
☝	Help window	Select help items
⌛	Anywhere	Wait while processing

Everyday Word Processing

Understanding Windows and Word for Windows Terms

For Related Information

■ "Selecting Text with the Mouse," p. 133

All Windows applications, including Word for Windows, require the same keyboard and mouse actions to select what is changed on-screen or to give commands. By learning the actions named in table 2.4, you will learn how to operate menus and to select items within any Windows application.

Table 2.4 Windows and Word Actions	
Action	**Description**
Select	Highlight or mark a section of text, menu name, command, dialog box option, or graphical object with the keyboard or with mouse actions.
Choose	Execute and complete a command. You may execute some commands when you select the menu command. Other commands execute when you select OK from a dialog box.
Acitvate	Bring an application or document window to the foreground. When you are working with more than one application or more than one document within word, the active window is the window you are working in.

Mouse Actions

Mouse techniques are simple to learn and to remember. These techniques make using Word for Windows much easier. In fact, for such work as moving and copying text, scrolling through a document, and drawing and embedding objects, the mouse is nearly indispensable. Table 2.5 describes the mouse actions that you use in carrying out Word operations.

Some mouse actions have a different effect when you hold down the Shift or Ctrl key as you click, double-click, or drag with the mouse. As a general rule, holding down the Shift key as you click selects text between where your in-sertion point was, and the location where you Shift+Click. Holding down the Ctrl and clicking or double-clicking also has different effects, depending on what is selected when you carry out this action. You will learn about using the mouse in combination with the keyboard in the appropriate sections throughout the book.

Table 2.5 Mouse Actions

Action	Description
Click	Place the tip of the mouse pointer or the lower portion of the I-beam pointer at the desired location and then quickly press and release the left mouse button *once.* This action selects a menu, command, moves the insertion point, or selects a graphical object so that you can work with it; this action also places the insertion point in text boxes.
Right-click	Position the tip of the mouse pointer in the desired location on a document or toolbar and then click the right mouse button. This action displays a menu appropriate to the item on which you clicked.
Double-click	Position the tip of the mouse pointer or the lower portion of the I-beam pointer at the desired location and then quickly press the left mouse button *twice.* This action is often a shortcut for carrying out a command or opening a dialog box from the Word screen. In Word, you can select a word by double-clicking anywhere in the word.
Drag	Position the tip of the mouse pointer, center of the cross-hair, or the lower portion of the I-beam on an item; then hold down the left mouse button as you move the mouse pointer. This action selects multiple items, cells (in a worksheet), or text characters, or moves graphical objects.

Keyboard Actions

The keyboard is most useful for typing text and numbers, performing fast operations with shortcut keys, and operating with portable or laptop comput-ers that don't have a mouse. Don't forget, however, that the best way of oper-ating Word for Windows and other Windows applications is through the combined use of mouse and keyboard. Table 2.6 lists and describes the key-board actions that you will use in Word for Windows.

Table 2.6 Keyboard Actions

Action	Description
Type	Type, but do not press the Enter key.
Enter	Press the Enter key.
Alt	Press the Alt key.
Alt, letter	Press the Alt key, release it, and then press the underlined letter or number shown. The active letters that appear underlined on-screen appear in bold print in this book.
Letter	Press only the underlined letter shown in the menu, command, or option.
Alt+letter	Hold down the Alt key as you press the underlined letter.
Alt, hyphen	Press the Alt key, release it, and then press the hyphen key.
Alt, space bar	Press the Alt key, release it, and then press the space bar.
Tab	Press the Tab key.
Esc	Press the Esc key.

Throughout this book, you see combinations of keys indicated with a plus sign (+), such as Alt+F. This combination means that you must hold down the Alt key while you press F. After pressing F, release both keys. (This book shows capital letters, as with the F, but you don't need to hold down the Shift key unless indicated.)

Keystrokes that appear separated by commas should be pressed in sequence. Alt, space bar, for example, is accomplished by pressing and releasing Alt and then pressing the space bar.

If you have a mouse, try using both mouse actions and keystrokes to perform commands and tasks. You soon will find that the keyboard works well for some commands and features and that the mouse works well for others. A combination of mouse and keyboard usually is the most efficient. The Quick Reference card bound inside the back cover of this book shows both keyboard and mouse shortcut methods.

The keyboard also is useful for many shortcut keys. These shortcut keys are listed in the appropriate areas throughout this book.

The 12 function keys give you a shortcut method of choosing commands that you normally choose from a menu. Some function keys use other keys in combination. When two or more keys are listed with a plus sign, hold down the first key(s) as you press the second key.

Notice that key combinations are listed on the right side of some pull-down menus. These key combinations execute the command immediately, without going through the menu and menu item. Instead of choosing the **Edit Clear** command, for example, you can press the Delete key.

If you are working in Word for Windows and forget a function key or shortcut key combination, choose the **Help Contents** command, choose Reference Information, and then choose the Keyboard Guide topic for keyboard listings and shortcuts.

For Related Information

■ "Quick Reference Card," inserted in back of this book.

Choosing Commands

Word for Windows uses the same menu-selection methods used by all Windows applications. You can control commands with the mouse, keystrokes, directional keys, or shortcut keys. You often can mix your methods of menu selection by starting with one method and finishing with another.

You cannot use a shortcut key while a menu is pulled down or a dialog box is displayed.

Notice that some commands in a menu may be gray. These commands are unavailable at that current point in Word operation.

Commands in the menu that are followed by an ellipsis (...) need more information from you before they execute. These commands display dialog boxes that ask you for more information.

In Word for Windows, you can back out of any pull-down menu or dialog box by pressing Esc. If you are using a mouse, you can back out of a menu by clicking on the menu name a second time or by clicking on the Cancel button in a dialog box.

Saving Time with Shortcut Menus

You can save yourself time by using shortcut menus. Shortcut menus display the most frequently used commands that relate to the selected item or object.

To display a shortcut menu, click with the right mouse button on the item or object for which you need a shortcut menu. If you are using a keyboard, select the item and then press Shift+F10. For example, to open a shortcut menu that applies to text, select the text you want to work with, and click with the right mouse button on the text.

Shortcut menus appear under the mouse pointer or at the top left of the document window, if activated by keyboard. Select a command by clicking it or by pressing the up- or down-arrow key and then pressing Enter. To remove a shortcut menu, click outside the menu or press the Esc key.

The following figures show a few shortcut menus, and the captions indicate the items with which the menus appear.

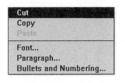

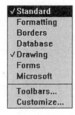

Fig. 2.4
A right-click on selected text displays a shortcut menu for text.

Fig. 2.5
A right mouse click on an object displays a shortcut menu to quickly manipulate the object.

Fig. 2.6
A right mouse click on a toolbar displays a shortcut menu for other toolbars.

Choosing Commands with the Keyboard

When you are familiar with the Word for Windows menus, you can perform the following steps to touch-type commands:

1. Press Alt to select the menu bar.

2. Press the underlined letter in the menu name; for example, press F for File. The menu pulls down.

3. Press the underlined letter in the command name; for example, press O for Open.

You do not need to wait for the menu to appear when you touch-type commands.

Hold down the Shift key as you click the File menu and you will see a helpful command, Close All. Choose Close All to close all open documents. You will be prompted to save documents that have changed.

Using Drag-and-Drop Commands

You can save a great deal of time in Word for Windows when moving or copying text if you learn how to use *drag and drop*. Drag-and-drop commands are executed using the mouse and enable you to do with a simple mouse action what might require many keystroke steps. For example, to move selected text you only need to select the text, then move the pointer into the selected text and *drag* the selection. You will see a gray insertion point indicating where the text will be inserted. Position the insertion point and let go of the mouse button to *drop* the text. If you want to make sure you can use drag-and-drop commands, choose the Tools Options command and select the Edit tab. Within the Edit tab select the **Drag-and-Drop Text Editing** check box.

Troubleshooting

When I try to choose a command from a menu, it is grayed out.

When a menu command is grayed out, it means the command is not available at that time for some reason. For example, until you have used the Edit Copy or Edit Cut command to move text to the clipboard, the Edit Paste command will be grayed out and unavailable. You must carry out some other action before you can use a grayed out menu command.

Using the Toolbars

The toolbars in Word for Windows give you quick access to frequently used commands and procedures. Tools on toolbars can only be used with a mouse (or similar pointing device). To use a tool on a toolbar, click the tool that represents the command or procedure you need. You decide which toolbars are displayed and where they appear on-screen. Toolbars are always accessible because they float above document windows.

In Word for Windows, you can display and work with more than one toolbar at a time. Word for Windows has eight predefined toolbars, described in the following list.

Everyday Word Processing

- *Standard toolbar*. The Standard toolbar contains the tools most frequently used during document creation, file handling, and printing.

- *Formatting toolbar*. The Formatting toolbar contains tools used for formatting fonts, setting alignment, applying numbering or bullets, applying format styles, and formatting borders.

- *Forms toolbar*. The Forms toolbar contains tools to help you insert edit boxes, check boxes, lists, and tables. You can also change the properties of a form field and lock the form when you are finished.

- *Database toolbar*. The Database toolbar contains tools to help you sort lists, edit a database, add or delete columns from a database, start mail merge, and insert data from a database outside of Word for Windows.

- *Drawing toolbar*. The Drawing toolbar contains tools for drawing, filling, reshaping, and grouping objects in the document.

- *Borders toolbar*. The Borders toolbar enables you to quickly apply borders and change their thicknesses.

- *Microsoft Toolbar*. The Microsoft toolbar contains tools so you can quickly start and activate other Microsoft Windows applications.

■ *Word for Windows 2.0 toolbar.* The Word for Windows 2.0 toolbar is the toolbar used in the previous version of Word for Windows.

Word for Windows comes with many tools that are not on the predefined toolbars. To customize predefined toolbars, you can drag off the tools that you do not need and drag on the tools that you do need. This is described in Chapter 36, "Customizing the Toolbar, Menus, and Shortcut Keys."

If someone has used Word for Windows before you, the predefined toolbars may be modified. Additional custom toolbars may be available to you that previous users have created or that have been created to assist you with specific tasks.

Getting Help on Tools

To see what a tool does, move the mouse pointer over the tool and read the description in the status bar at the bottom of the Word for Windows window.

When you need help using a tool, click the Question Mark (?) tool, if available, and then click the tool you want help with. If the ? tool is not visible, press Shift+F1 and click a tool. A Help window appears to show you how to use the tool. Press Alt+F4 or choose the File Exit command to close the Help window.

Displaying or Hiding Toolbars

You can use the View Toolbars command or the toolbar shortcut menu to display and hide toolbars on-screen.

To display a toolbar:

1. Choose the View Toolbars command to display the Toolbars dialog box shown in fig. 2.7.

2. Select the toolbar that you want to display. Toolbars with selected check boxes will be displayed.

3. Choose OK. Word for Windows displays the toolbar you selected. The toolbar is displayed in the last position in which it was used.

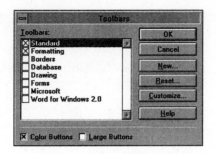

Fig. 2.7
The Toolbars
dialog box.

Everyday Word Processing

To display a toolbar if you are using a mouse and a toolbar is currently displayed:

1. Click with the right mouse button in the toolbar to display a shortcut menu.

2. Click the name of the toolbar you want to display.

You can hide a toolbar in three ways:

■ You can click the toolbar with the right mouse button to display the toolbar shortcut menu. In the shortcut menu, displayed toolbars appear with a check mark. Click the name of the displayed toolbar that you want hidden.

■ If a toolbar is in a floating window, you can close it by clicking once on the window's Control menu icon (a small box) to the left of the toolbar's title bar.

■ Finally, you can close a toolbar by choosing the View Toolbars command. When the Toolbars dialog box appears, deselect toolbar check boxes you do not want displayed, then choose the OK button.

Word for Windows records the toolbars and their locations. When you restart Word for Windows, the toolbars you last used will be available to you.

Moving, Resizing, and Reshaping Toolbars

You can move and reshape toolbars to fit the way you want to work. Toolbars can be *docked* in a position along an edge of the window or they can *float* free in their own window. Docked toolbars are one tool wide or high. You can reshape toolbars that float in a window and drag them wherever they are most convenient to use. Fig. 2.8 shows floating and docked toolbars.

Fig. 2.8
Floating and
docked toolbars.

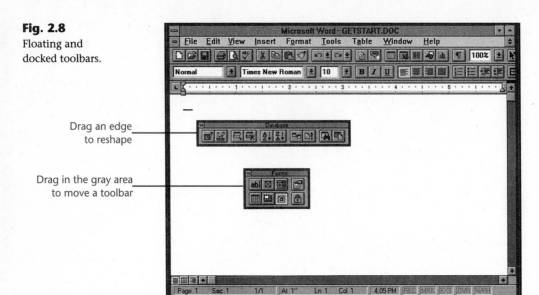

Drag an edge
to reshape

Drag in the gray area
to move a toolbar

To move a toolbar, click in the gray area around the edge of the toolbar and drag. If you drag the toolbar to an edge of the window, the toolbar docks against the edge. A toolbar is ready to dock when its gray outline becomes thinner.

Toolbars docked against a left or right edge may be too narrow for tools with a pull-down list, such as the Style tool, to display. While docked against a left or right edge, these toolbars replace wide tools with tool buttons. Clicking on a button displays the appropriate dialog box.

Toolbars also can float free in a window. To move a floating toolbar, click in the gray area along one of the wide edges and drag. You can resize a floating toolbar window by dragging on a border. To return the toolbar to a dock, drag the floating toolbar's title bar to an edge of the screen and then release.

If you use a monitor with higher than VGA resolution, the normal size of buttons may be too small for you to easily see. You can manually switch between normal tools and larger tools by choosing the View Toolbars command, selecting the Large Buttons option, then choosing OK.

Toolbars that have colored buttons will display in color if you have the Color Buttons check box selected in the Toolbars dialog box. When it is deselected, color buttons appear in shades of gray.

Working in Dialog Boxes

In the pull-down menus, commands that require additional information are followed by an ellipsis (...). Choosing one of these commands displays a dialog box in which you enter needed information. The Format Font command, for example, results in the dialog box shown in fig. 2.9. This dialog box contains tabbed sections, the tabs showing across the top of the dialog box. Each tabbed section contains a different type of formatting.

For Related Information
■ "Customizing and Creating Toolbars," p. 1052

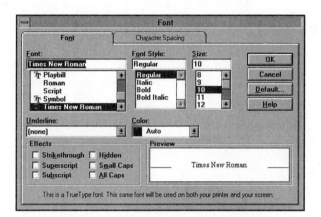

Fig. 2.9
A dialog box containing tabbed sections with boxes, check boxes, and lists.

Dialog boxes contain different types of items. These items are described in more detail in the sections immediately following. To familiarize yourself with Word for Windows dialog box items, read the following list:

■ *Tab.* Multiple sections of a dialog box. Only one group at a time is displayed and each group contains related options.

■ *Text box.* A box in which you can type and edit text, dates, or numbers.

■ *Option button.* A button that gives you one choice from a group of options. These are sometimes called "radio buttons."

■ *Check box.* A square box that can be turned on or off.

■ *List box.* A list or pull-down list that scrolls to display available alternatives.

■ *Command button.* A button that completes or cancels the command; some buttons give you access to additional options.

Selecting a Tab in a Dialog Box

A dialog box like the one shown in fig. 2.9 may contain more than one tab. The tabs appear within the dialog box as though they are cards within a card file—all related options are on the same card. For example, all options relating to formatting fonts are in the Font tab of the Format Font dialog box. The titles of each section appear across the top of the dialog box as though they were tabs on filing cards.

To select a tab by keyboard:

Press Alt+*letter*, where *letter* is the underlined letter in the tab's name.

or

Hold down the Ctrl key and press the Tab key until the tab title you want displayed is selected.

To select a tab with the mouse:

Click the tab title.

Selecting Option Buttons and Check Boxes

Fig. 2.9 shows check boxes, which appear as squares. Fig. 2.10 shows groups of option buttons, which appear as circles. You can select only one option button from within a group, but you can select one or more check boxes.

Fig. 2.10
A dialog box with groups of option buttons.

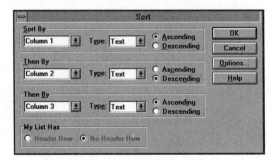

Check boxes are square boxes that you can turn on or off and use in combination with other check boxes. A check box is on when an X appears in the box.

To select or deselect a check box, click the check box that you want to change. From the keyboard, press Alt+*letter* where *letter* is the underlined letter in the name of the check box.

To select an option button with the mouse, click the button. To clear an option button, you must click another in the same group. A dot within the option indicates that the option is on. Remember that you can select only one button in a group.

To select an option button from the keyboard, hold down the Alt key and then press the underlined letter of the option group you want. Alternatively, press Tab until an option in the group is enclosed by dashed lines. After you select the group, press the arrow keys to select the option button that you want from within the group.

When you are using a keyboard and making a succession of changes in a dialog box, pressing the Tab key is probably the easiest way to move between items in the box. (Shift+Tab moves in the reverse direction.) The active item is enclosed in a dashed line or contains the flashing insertion point for text editing. To change a check box that is enclosed by the dashed line, press the space bar. To change an option button in a group enclosed by the dashed line, press the arrow keys.

Editing Text Boxes

You use text boxes to type information, such as file names and numbers, into a dialog box. You can edit the text within a text box the same way you edit text elsewhere in Word for Windows.

To select characters with a mouse, click in the text where you want the insertion point, or drag across text to select characters or words. Double-click a word to select the entire word.

Select	Mouse Action
Multiple letters	Drag across letters
Word	Double-click word
Words or formula terms	Double-click word; then drag

To select text with the keyboard, press the Alt+*letter* combination for the text box. Press the left- or right-arrow key to move the flashing insertion point and then type the text you want to insert.

Delete characters to the right of the flashing insertion point by pressing the Del key. Delete characters to the left of the insertion point by pressing the Backspace key.

Keep in mind that the insertion point and the I-beam are not the same. The insertion point is where typing or deletions will take place. The I-beam is the mouse pointer—it moves when you move the mouse. The insertion point moves to where the I-beam is only when you click the mouse button.

To select multiple characters using the keyboard so that you can delete or replace them by typing, perform these actions:

Table 2.7 Text-Editing Actions

Mouse Action	Result
Click I-beam in text	Moves the insertion point (flashing cursor) to the I-beam location.
Shift+click in text	Selects all text between the current insertion point and the I-beam.
Drag	Selects all text over which the I-beam moves while the mouse button is held down.

Keyboard Action	Result
Left/right-arrow key	Moves the insertion point left/right one character.
Shift+arrow key	Selects text as the insertion point moves left or right.
Ctrl+left/right-arrow key	Moves the insertion point to the beginning of the preceding/next word.
Shift+Ctrl+left/right-arrow key	Selects from the insertion point to the beginning of the preceding/next word.
Home	Moves the insertion point to the beginning of the line.
Shift+Home	Selects from the insertion point to the beginning of the line.
End	Moves the insertion point to the end of the line.
Shift+End	Selects from the insertion point to the end of the line.

To insert text in a text box using the mouse, click the I-beam at the location where you want the text, and then type the text. If you use a keyboard, press the Alt+*letter* combination or the Tab key to activate the text box, and then press one of the cursor-movement keys shown in table 2.7 to position the insertion point. Then type.

Text you type replaces the selected text only when the Typing Replaces Selection check box is selected from the Edit tab of the Tools Option command.

You can copy and paste in edit boxes within dialog boxes. This can be useful with commands such as Find or Replace. To do this, select text using the techniques described here, then press Ctrl+X to cut, Ctrl+C to copy, or Ctrl+V to paste. You can even copy and paste between dialog boxes or from a document into a dialog box.

Selecting from List Boxes

In some cases, Word for Windows will give you many alternatives from which to select. The Font tab of the Format Font dialog box, for example, shows you lists of fonts (refer to fig. 2.9).

Some list boxes show only the current selection in what appears to be a text box. To see the entire list of alternatives, you must pull down the list. Fig. 2.9, for example, shows the Underline pull-down list in the up position. Fig. 2.11 shows the list pulled down to make the selection easier.

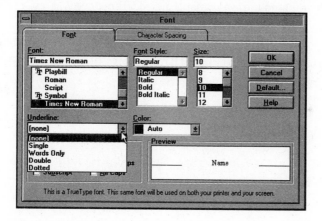

Fig. 2.11
The Underline pull-down list.

To select an item from a list box:

1. If the list is not displayed, click the down arrow to the side of the list or activate the list box by pressing Alt+*underlined letter*.

2. When the list is displayed, click the arrowheads in the scroll bar to scroll to the name you want. Then click the name you want to select it.

   or

Alternatively, select the name you want by pressing the up-arrow key, down-arrow key, Home key, or End key.

3. Choose OK.

In most dialog boxes, you can double-click a name in a list box to select the name and choose OK in one operation. You cannot double-click a name in a pull-down list box.

Before you select a command button such as OK, make sure that the name you want to select from the list box is selected (highlighted), not just surrounded by a dashed line.

Command Buttons and Closing Dialog Boxes

Command buttons usually appear at the upper-right corner or down the right side of dialog boxes. You usually use these buttons to execute or cancel a command. With a mouse, you can click a command button to choose it.

From the keyboard, you can choose a command button in three different ways. If the command button contains an underlined letter, press Alt+*underlined letter*. If a button is bordered in bold, press Enter to choose the button. In most cases, pressing Enter will choose OK. Choose Cancel by pressing Esc. You can select any command button by pressing Tab until the button is bordered in bold and then pressing the Enter.

Getting Help

Windows and Word for Windows have Help information to guide you through new commands and procedures. Word's Help files are extensive and explain topics that range from parts of the screen to commands, dialog boxes, and business procedures.

Tip
You can print the contents of any Help screen using the File Print Topic command in the Help window menu.

To get help in Word or a Windows application, choose a command from the Help menu or press F1, or click the question mark (?) button, then click the item of interest. The Help Contents command or F1 will display the window shown in fig. 2.12. From this window, you can learn how to use Help or you can see the contents of all Help topics. Notice that you can access or control Help information in different ways. You can use the menus at the top of the Help window, or you can use the buttons under the menus to Search for a topic or to see a History of all the previous topics you have viewed.

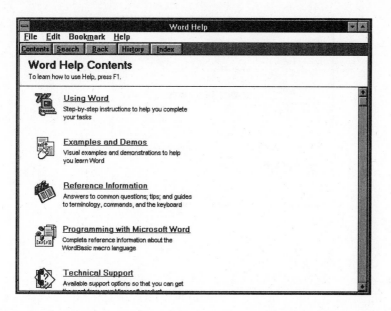

Fig. 2.12
The Help Contents
window lists the
topics you can get
help on.

Command buttons are located under the menu and help you move through
the Help topics. Choose a button by clicking on it or by pressing Alt+*letter*.
The following command buttons help you move through information:

Button	Action
Contents	Shows the index or contents of Help at the highest level.
Back	Returns to the preceding Help topic. With this button, you can retrace the topics you have viewed back to the initial Help Index.
History	Shows a list of the previously selected topics. Double-click a topic to return to it or press the up- or down-arrow keys to select the topic, and then press Enter.
Search	Displays a list of key words. Choosing a key word displays a list of Help topics related to that key word. Choosing from the topics displays the Help screen for that topic.

Searching for a Topic in Help
The Search dialog box enables you to find topics related to the subject you
need help with. To use Search, choose the **Help Search** command. If the Help
window is already displayed, choose the **Search** button. The dialog box
shown in fig 2.13 appears.

Fig. 2.13

The Search dialog box.

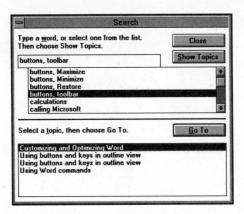

If you are using a mouse, click the Search button to display the Search dialog box. Type a word in the top box or select a topic from the top list and then choose the Show Topic button. The bottom list will display topics related to the word. Select a topic from the bottom list and choose the Go To button.

If you are using the keyboard, press Alt+S to activate the Search mode, and then press Alt+W to choose the top list. Type a topic in the text box. As you type, the list scrolls to topics that start with the letters you type. To scroll through the list, press Tab so that a topic in the list is enclosed with dashes, and then press the up- or down-arrow key. Press Enter to choose the Show Topic button, and the Go To list will fill with related topics. Press the up- or down-arrow key to select a topic, and then press Enter to choose the Go To button.

Jumping Between Help Topics

Hot words or phrases appear within the actual Help text. These words or phrases have a solid or dashed underline and are displayed in green, meaning that the word or phrase is linked to additional information. Words or phrases with definitions appear with a dashed underline.

To jump to the topic related to a solid underlined word, click the word, or press Tab until the word is selected and press Enter.

To display the definition of a word that appears with a dashed underline, click the word or tab to the word and press Enter. Click again or press Enter to remove the definition.

Getting Help in Dialog Boxes

You can get help for any dialog box or error message that appears in Word for Windows. When any dialog box from a command or from an error message appears, press F1 to get help. Fig 2.14 shows the Help message that appears when you press F1 or click the **Help** button when the **Font** tab in the Font dialog box is active.

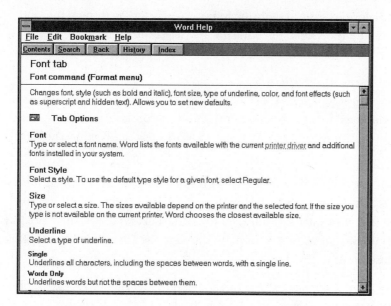

Fig. 2.14
The Help message that appears after pressing F1 or clicking the Help button when the Font tab in the Font dialog box is active.

To learn what action a command performs or how a portion of the screen works, press Shift+F1 and then click that command or portion of the screen. You can also click the ? button in the Standard toolbar. Notice that the mouse pointer changes to a question mark that overlays the pointer. You can press Shift+F1 to ask a question about the item you click.

Closing the Help Window

Because Help is an actual application, you need to close its window when you are done. To remove the Help window, double-click the Control menu icon to the left of the Help title bar; or press Alt, space bar, and then C for Close, or press Alt+F4.

Troubleshooting

A dialog box displays an error message that you don't understand.

Press F1. A help window appears with an explanation of the error. Read the help window and follow the recommendations to resolve the problem.

When I press Shift+F1 to display the question mark cursor so I can get context-senstive help, a Help for WordPerfect Users dialog box appears.

The Help for WordPerfect Users option is turned on, which is why you get this dialog box instead of the question mark cursor. To turn off this option, choose the Tools Options command and select the General tab. Clear the check box for the Help for WordPerfect Users option and choose OK.

Getting the Tip of the Day

Often we get so involved with daily tasks we forget to look for ways to improve our work or to improve our skills. Word comes with a feature called the Tip of the Day that is a painless way to learn a few of the many shortcuts in Word.

Figure 2.15 shows the Tip of the Day dialog box that appears when you start Word. The Did You Know box in its center reveals one of Word's shortcuts each time Word starts. If you want to see the next tip in the Tip of the Day, just choose the Next Tip button. To switch to the Tip index in Word's Help, choose the More Tips button.

If you have memorized all the tips and don't want Tip of the Day to appear, just deselect the **S**how Tips at Startup check box that is at the bottom left of the dialog box. You can display the Tip of the Day dialog box at any time by choosing the **H**elp Tip of the Day command from Word's menu.

Fig 2.15
Tip of the Day appears when you start Word so that you can learn Word's many shortcuts.

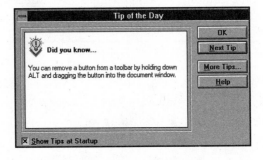

Manipulating Windows

When you use Word for Windows, you can display and run more than one application in Windows or use multiple documents while you are in Word for Windows. Seeing that much information on your screen can be confusing unless you keep your windows organized. Just as you organize folders and papers on your desk, you can organize your Windows applications and Word for Windows documents.

You will see two types of windows on-screen. An application window contains an application, such as the File Manager, Microsoft Word for Windows, or Excel. A document window contains a Word for Windows document. You can open multiple document windows within the Word for Windows window.

Switching Between Applications

You can work in an application or document only when its window is active. The active window has a solid title bar. In most cases, the active window is also the top window. In a few instances, however, such as during the process of linking documents together, the active window may not be on top.

If you are running Word for Windows with other Windows or non-Windows applications, you can switch between application windows by activating the application whose window you want. Press Ctrl+Esc to display the Task List. To choose an application from the Task List, double-click its name or press the up- or down-arrow key to select the application, and then press Enter.

You also can cycle between applications by holding down the Alt key and pressing Tab. A dialog box or a title bar shows which application will be activated. Release all keys when you see the title of the application that you want to activate.

Switching Between Document Windows

Because Word for Windows makes working with several documents easy, you frequently may have more than one window on-screen. Each *document window* may contain a different document. You can affect only the active document window, however. From within the Word for Windows window, if you can see the window, you can make it active by clicking on it with the mouse pointer. If you cannot see the document window, move the other document windows so that you can see it.

To switch to another window from the keyboard, choose the **Window** menu and then press or click the number of the document window that you want to activate. The name of each document appears in the menu. You can cycle between document windows by pressing Ctrl+F6.

Minimizing, Maximizing, and Restoring Windows

You soon will find that your computer desktop can become as cluttered as your real desktop. To gain more space, you can store applications or document windows by minimizing them so that they become small symbols (icons) at the bottom of the screen.

When you need one of the applications or documents that has been minimized, you can restore the icon to its former window at the original location and size. When you want a window to fill the entire available area, you can maximize it.

To maximize an application or document window with the mouse, click the maximize icon for the active window, or double-click in the title bar of the window. To maximize an application or document window from the keyboard, press Alt, hyphen to display the document Control menu, or press Alt, space bar to display the application Control menu. Press X for the Maximize command.

You can minimize application or document windows so that they are stored temporarily at the bottom of the screen. To use the mouse to minimize a window, click the minimize icon. From the keyboard, press Alt, hyphen to display the document Control menu or press Alt, space bar to display the application Control menu. Press N to choose Minimize.

You can restore Word for Windows and document windows from their maximized or minimized sizes into their previous window size. If Word for Windows or a document is an icon at the bottom of the screen, double-click it. If Word for Windows is maximized, click the double-headed icon to the right of the Word for Windows title bar to restore it to a window. If a document is maximized, click the double-headed arrow to the right of the menu bar. With the keyboard, press Alt, space bar to select the Word Control menu or press Alt, hyphen to select the document Control menu, and then choose Restore.

Moving a Window

With multiple applications or multiple Word for Windows documents on-screen, you will want to move windows for the same reason that you shuffle papers on your desk. You can move a window with the mouse or the keyboard by following these steps:

- If you are using a mouse, activate the window that you want to move. Drag the title bar until the shadow border is where you want the window to be located. Release the mouse button to fix the window in its new location.

- From the keyboard, select the application or document Control menu by pressing Alt, space bar for the application Control menu or Alt, hyphen for the document Control menu. Press M to select Move. A four-headed arrow appears in the title bar. Press an arrow key to move the shadowed outline of the window. Press Enter to fix the window in its new location, or press Esc to retain the original location.

Sizing a Window

You often want to see only part of an application or document window. The following steps show you how to change the size of the window by using the mouse or the keyboard.

To resize a window with the mouse:

> Drag the window edge or corner to the location you want, then release the mouse button.

To resize a window from the keyboard:

1. Activate the window.

2. Press Alt, space bar for the application Control menu or Alt, hyphen for the document Control menu.

3. Press S for Size.

4. Press the arrow key that points to the edge you want to reposition.

5. Press the arrow keys to move that edge.

6. Press Enter to fix the edge in its new location or press Esc to cancel.

Closing a Document Window

When you finish with a document, you should close the window to remove it from the screen and to free memory. If you made a change since the last time you saved the document, Word displays an Alert dialog box, as shown in fig 2.16, asking whether you want to save your work before closing. Choose Yes if you want to save your most recent changes before closing a document.

Fig. 2.16

An Alert dialog box.

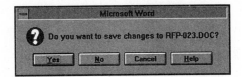

There is an important difference between closing a document window and closing the document. If more than one window is open on a document, you can close a window without closing the file. However, if there is only one document window or if you choose File Close, you close the file and all document windows that show that file.

To close the active document window with a mouse when more than one window is open on a document:

Double-click the document Control menu icon on the left side of the document's title bar (when the document is in its own window).

To close the active document window by keyboard when more than one window is open on a document:

Press Alt, hyphen to choose the document Control menu and press C for Close.

To close the file so that all windows using a document close:

1. Choose the File Close command. The window closes if no changes have been made to the document since the last save.

2. If you made changes to the document after the last save, a dialog box appears, asking you to confirm whether you want to save your changes.

   In the dialog box, choose the No command button if you don't want to save the changed version of the file or choose the Yes command button to save your changes.

3. If you chose Yes, and the file has not been saved before, a Save As dialog box appears. Enter a new file name and choose OK.

To close all visible documents, hold down the Shift key as you choose the File menu. The Close All command will be available in place of Close. Choose Close All to close all visible documents.

From Here...

For information relating directly to controlling Word for Windows and working with document windows, you may want to review the following chapters:

- Chapter 3, "Creating and Saving Documents," teaches you to create and save a new document, open existing documents, and close a document.

- Chapter 4, "Managing Documents and Files," teaches you to use Word's powerful file management features, including how to search for files, and how to preview, open, print, copy, and delete files that you find using the Find File command.

For Related Information
- "Saving a Document," p. 80
- "Closing a Document," p. 90
- "Working with Multiple Documents," p. 78

Everyday Word Processing

Chapter 3

Creating and Saving Documents

Word processing basics begin with creating a new document, typing the text, and saving the document. You need to know how to accomplish these basic tasks before you move on to learning the more advanced tools that Word for Windows offers for working with your documents. In this chapter, you learn how to create a new document, open an existing document, and how to save your documents. You also learn how to work with more than one document at the same time.

What You Need to Know About Creating and Saving Documents

When you are working on a document in Word for Windows, the document is stored in the memory of your computer. This memory is often referred to as *RAM*, or *random-access memory*, and it is a temporary location for the programs and documents you use when you are working with your computer. When you exit a program or turn off your computer, whatever was stored in memory is removed. For this reason, you need a permanent storage location for your programs and files. Floppy disks and hard disks are used for this purpose. They are magnetic media, much like the cassette tapes that are used to record music, on which information from your computer can be stored for as long as you want.

When you first open Word for Windows, you are presented with a blank document. You can begin typing text into this document right away. Until you save the file, the work you do is only temporarily stored in the

In this chapter, you learn to do the following:

- Create a new document

- Save your document

- Open an existing document

- Work with more than one document at a time

computer's memory. Eventually, you need to save this document onto a disk, either the hard disk in your computer or a floppy disk, using the File Save command. When you first save the document, you need to give it a name, which you do in the Save As dialog box. From then on, you have the choice of saving the file with the same name, or saving it with a new name, which you can do using the File Save As command.

Understanding File Names

The first time you save a new document, you must give it a name and assign it to a disk drive and directory. Word for Windows files use standard MS-DOS file names. Remember these simple rules when naming files:

- A DOS file name can have an extension up to three characters long.

- A DOS file name can be from one to eight characters long (excluding the three-letter extension).

- You can use letters A through Z (uppercase or lowercase), numbers 0 through 9, hyphens (-), underscores (_), and exclamation points (!).

- You cannot use periods (.) or blank spaces. A period separates a file's first name and extension. Substitute legal characters (such as underscores) for blanks.

- You cannot use spaces or the following characters in file names: asterisks (*), plus signs (+), equal signs (=), commas (,), colons (:), semicolons (;), question marks (?), brackets ([and]), slashes (/ or \), bars (|), greater than (>), or less than (<). You can use a period (.) only to separate the file name from the extension. Legal characters include !, @, #, $, %, ^, &, (,), _, -, {, and }. Use the exclamation point or another legal character as the first character in a name when you want the name to be first in the alphabetical listing of names.

- Word for Windows provides its own extension, DOC. You can override this default when you name your file by including a period and an extension. Using the Word for Windows default extension is better, however, because the extension helps you to identify each file's type and eases the task of opening files. (By default, Word for Windows lists only files with the DOC extension in the Open dialog box.)

Understanding Directories

When you save a file on the hard disk in your computer, it ends up in a directory on your hard disk. Directories are analogous to the file drawers and file folders you use in your office to help you organize and locate your paper files. You can locate files more easily if you store related files together in a directory. For example, you could store all the business letters you create in Word in a directory named \LETTERS and all your proposals in a directory named \PROPOSAL. Don't store the files you create in the directories where your program files are stored. If you ever have to reinstall or upgrade Word, you could lose any files you stored in the program directories. Also, because many files are already in the program directories, you will not have as much room to store your own files if you use these directories. Create your own directories and subdirectories, which are directories that branch off of another directory, for storing your files.

The first time you use the File Open or File Save As command, Word for Windows assumes that you want to open or save a document in the Word for Windows directory. Instead, you usually want to open or save a file in one of your own directories or subdirectories. For example, you may have a directory named C:\WINWORD6\LETTERS. You must tell Word for Windows where the file you want to open is located or where you want to save a file— whether that location is a different directory or subdirectory, a different drive on your hard disk, or a floppy disk in drive A or B. To switch directories or drives, use the appropriate list boxes in the Open and Save As dialog boxes, as discussed in the following paragraphs.

The selected directory and drive for the files listed in the File Name box is listed in the path statement above the Directories list box (see fig. 3.1). If you see the path C:\WINWORD6\LETTERS, for example, you know you are looking at a list of files on drive C, in the directory WINWORD6, and in the subdirectory LETTERS. A backslash separates drives and directories.

The Directories list box includes all directories and subdirectories on the selected drive. An icon that resembles a file folder represents each directory. Open file folders indicate open directories; closed file folders indicate closed directories. If you want to open a file in a subdirectory contained within a directory, you first must open the directory.

To change disk drives or directories in the Open dialog boxes, follow these steps:

1. Scroll the Drives list to display the drive where the file you want to open is stored.

2. Select the drive where the file you want to open is stored, if it is not already selected.

3. Scroll the Directories list to display the directory where the file you want to open is stored.

4. If necessary, open a directory to display the subdirectory where the file you want to open is stored.

5. Select the directory or subdirectory where the file you want to open is stored.

6. Select the File Name text box and select or type the file name.

7. Choose OK.

You can use the same procedures as just described in the Save As dialog box to change drives and directories when you are saving a file.

Fig. 3.1

You can change drives and directories in the Save As dialog box or the Open dialog box.

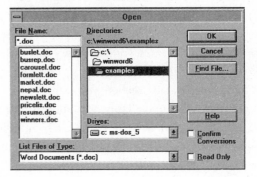

Setting the Default Directory

When you first choose the File Open command or File Save As command, you see a listing of files in the \WINWORD directory. Because you should reserve this directory for the Word program files and store the files you create in Word in other directories, you will need to switch to some other directory to find the file you want. After you have switched directories in the Open dialog box (or the Save As dialog box), that directory becomes the current directory until you close Word, and whenever you choose the File Open command or File Save As command, the files in that directory are listed.

You can change the default directory, which is the directory that appears when you first choose the File Open command or File Save As command. Making the directory where you store the files that you use most often your default directory can save you some time when you open and save files.

To change the default directory, follow these steps:

1. Choose the Tools Options command.

2. Select the File Locations tab. The File Locations folder is displayed (see fig. 3.2)

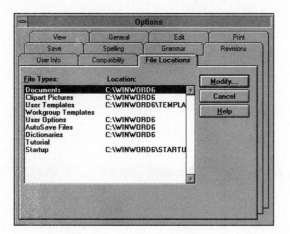

Fig. 3.2
You can change the default directory for Word for Windows documents.

3. Select Documents in the File Types list.

4. Choose the Modify button.

5. Select the directory you want to use as the default from the Directories list or type the full path name for the directory in the Location of Documents text box.

6. Choose OK and then choose Close.

Creating a New Document

When you first start Word for Windows (see Chapter 2, "Getting Started in Word for Windows"), you see a blank document, ready for typing (see fig. 3.3). This new document is named Document1 to indicate that the document is the first one you have created since starting the program.

If your new document isn't the first one you have seen since starting Word for Windows, however, the document is numbered accordingly: the second new document is called Document2, the third is Document3, and so on. Even if you save and close Document1, the next new document in the current working session is numbered Document2.

Fig. 3.3
A blank document, ready for you to begin entering text.

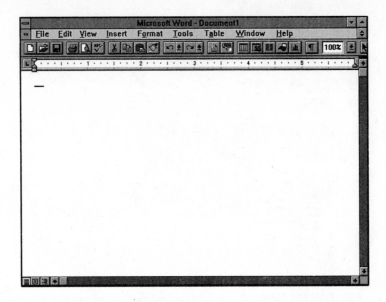

You can create a new document in Word in three ways. New documents can be based on three different types of *templates*. These templates contain frequently used text, formatting styles, macros, and custom settings. The three different templates that documents can be based on are the following:

■ NORMAL.DOT, which contains the default settings for standard documents.

■ Custom templates that come with Word (such as Faxcovr1) or that you create that contain predefined text, formatting styles, macros, and custom features necessary for a specific type of document.

■ Template Wizards, which are templates combined with intelligent dialog boxes that guide you through the process of completing the document. Wizards come with Word (Calendar Wizard, for example) or they can be built by individuals familiar with Word BASIC.

The following sections describe how to open documents based on these three different types of templates.

What You Need to Know About Creating a New Document

When you create a new document, Word bases the new document on a template. Unless you specify otherwise, Word uses the Normal template, NORMAL.DOT, as the basis for your new document.

A template is a predefined set of formatting characteristics, such as type style, margin width, tab settings, and so on, and can also contain boilerplate text, such as a letterhead. Word comes with templates for creating standard business letters, memos, fax cover sheets, and many other types of documents. These templates save you the trouble of having to type standard text, such as the To, From, and Subject fields in a memo, and they help you produce documents that are formatted consistently from one to the next.

You also can create your own templates. For example, you may want to base your document on a special template you have created called Letters that includes formatting to match your company's letterhead. Unless you choose otherwise, however, Word for Windows bases new documents on the Normal template. You can think of NORMAL.DOT as the global template, which contains the settings that are used by default for new documents.

Creating a New Blank Document

When you want to start writing in a blank document, you will often use the NORMAL.DOT template as a basis for the new document. Opening a document based on NORMAL.DOT is very easy.

To start a new document, follow these steps:

1. Choose the File New command or press Ctrl+N. The New dialog box appears (see fig. 3.4).

Fig. 3.4
Start a new document from the New dialog box.

2. Choose OK.

You also can start a new document by clicking the New Document button (the first button on the left of the Standard toolbar). A new document based on the Normal template is opened.

Creating a New Document from a Template

When you use the File New command to open a new document, the New dialog box appears on-screen (refer to fig. 3.4). In the New dialog box, you see a list of Templates in the Template list. By default, the Normal template is selected. This is the template that a new document opened with the New Document button is based on. You will probably use the Normal template for most of your documents. However, you can choose one of the other pre-defined templates if you want, or you can choose a custom template that you have created.

To open a new document based on a template, follow these steps:

1. Choose the File New command or press Ctrl+N. The New dialog box appears (refer to fig. 3.4).

2. Select the template you want to base your document on from the Template list.

3. Choose OK.

Creating a New Document with a Template Wizard

When you choose the File New command, you will see a list of Wizards in the Template list. Wizards provide on-screen guidance as you create a new document. For example, if you choose the Fax Wizard, you are guided through the entire process of creating a fax cover sheet, step-by-step. All you need to do is follow the instructions in the dialog boxes as they appear on-screen. A series of VCR-like buttons along the bottom of the Wizard dialog boxes enable you to move from one dialog box to the next.

To create a new document using a Wizard, follow these steps:

1. Choose the File New command or press the Ctrl+N key.

2. Select the Wizard you want to use from the Template list.

3. Choose OK. A Wizard dialog box is displayed, as shown in fig. 3.5.

4. Follow the steps presented to you in the Wizard dialog box, using the buttons at the bottom of the dialog box to move from box to box.

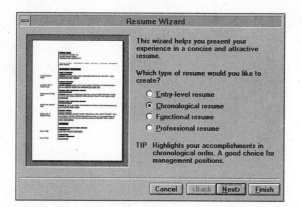

Fig. 3.5
Wizards guide
you through the
process of creating
a new document.

Note

Most of your documents will probably be based on the Normal template. If you
don't like the predefined settings in the Normal template, you can modify them so
that all new documents based on the Normal template use your preferred settings
and you don't have to change them for each new document. For example, if you
want to use different margin settings or a different font, you can change these settings in the Normal template. For more information on how to modify a template,
see Chapter 6, "Using Templates as Master Documents."

Troubleshooting Creating a New Document

*I opened a new document using one of the templates that comes with Word and
typed in some text that I always want to appear in documents using this template.
I saved the document, but when I open a new document using this template, the text
I typed doesn't appear in the document.*

To edit a template, you must work directly with the template. Choose the
File Open command, switch to the \WINWORD6\TEMPLATE directory, and
select Document Template in the List Files of Type box. Select the template
you want to modify in the File Name list box and choose OK. Edit the template to your liking and then save it. Now, whenever you open a new document template based on this template, the changes you made will apply to
the new document. See Chapter 6, "Using Templates as Master Documents,"
for more information on templates.

**For Related
Information**
- "Changing a
  Template,"
  p. 175

- "Recording
  and Editing
  Macros,"
  p. 1123

Opening an Existing Document

The great advantage to word processors is that you can use the same files repeatedly. You can return to the same document as many times as you want to print it, edit it, or add new material to it. Or you can open an existing document and use parts of it in a new document.

You are not restricted to opening files created by Word for Windows. When you install Word, you are given the option of installing one or more conversion files that allow you to open files created by other programs, for example, WordPerfect. Word's conversion capability allows you to view and edit a document created by another user using a different program or to convert documents you created on another word processor as you make the transition to Word for Windows.

You can speed up the process of opening a file by automatically opening Word and a document at the same time from the File Manager.

What You Need to Know About Opening a Document

Opening a file involves locating the file in a drive and directory and knowing what type the file is. Word for Windows, by default, lists only files that end in the extension DOC in the Open dialog box. The program also can open other files: template files, which end in the extension DOT, and files created by other programs, which have various extensions. To open a file with an extension other than DOC, you must specify the extension you want to list by choosing the file type in the List Files of Type box in the Open dialog box or by typing the extension preceded by the *. characters in the File Name box and then pressing Enter.

Tip
You can move quickly to a file in the File Name list by typing the first few letters of the file name in the File Name text box.

You can use wild cards to help you locate the type of file you want—an asterisk (*) means any character or characters, and a question mark (?) means any single character. If you want to locate all files that end in the extension EXT, for example, type *.EXT in the File Name box. If you want to list files with any name that ends in any extension, type *.* in the File Name box.

Opening a Document

You use the File Open command to open an existing document. First, you must switch to the drive and directory where the file is stored, and then select the file from the list of files in the Open dialog box.

To open an existing document, follow these steps:

1. Choose the File **O**pen command or press Ctrl+O or click the Open button on the Standard toolbar (the second button from the left). The Open dialog box appears (see fig. 3.6).

Fig. 3.6
Select the file you want to open in the Open dialog box.

2. If necessary, select a different disk drive in the Drives list (see "Under-standing Directories," an earlier section in this chapter).

3. If necessary, select a different directory in the **D**irectories list (see "Understanding Directories," an earlier section in this chapter).

4. If necessary, select a different file type in the List Files of **T**ype box.

5. Select the Read Only option if you want to prevent changes to the original document.

   The Read Only option prevents the use of the File **S**ave command, which replaces the original version with the changed document. Documents opened with Read Only must be saved with the File Save **A**s command and a new file name.

6. In the File Name text box, type the name of the file you want to open, or select the file you want to open from the File **N**ame list.

7. Choose OK.

> **Note**
>
> Through the Open dialog box, you can access the Find File command. You can use this command to find files using summary information, file information, or any string of characters that appears in the file. After you find a file, you can open, print, view, copy, or delete it. For details about the Find File command, see Chapter 4, "Managing Documents and Files."
>
> After you open a file, you can quickly return to the place in the document where you left off when you last closed the file. Press Shift+F5 and the insertion point moves to where it was when the file was last saved.

Opening a Recently Used File

Word remembers the last several documents you have used and lists them at the bottom of the File menu. You can quickly open any of these documents by selecting it from the list.

To reopen a recently closed file, follow these steps:

1. Choose the File menu.

2. Select the file name from the bottom of the menu by clicking the file you want to reopen or typing the number of the file you want to reopen.

> **Note**
>
> You can specify how many files appear in the list at the bottom of the File menu by choosing the **Tools Options** command and selecting the General tab. Select or type the number of entries you want to appear in the list in the Recently Used File List option and choose OK. You can specify up to nine files.

Opening Non-Word for Windows Files

Word for Windows can open files created by other programs such as the Windows Notepad (or any other application that creates a text file), WordPerfect, Word for DOS, WordStar, WindowWorks, and others. You use the normal File Open command, but then you must identify the file type so that Word for Windows can convert the file into its own format. (Word for Windows proposes the file type it thinks the file should be, which is usually correct.)

To open non-Word for Windows files, follow these steps:

1. Choose the File Open command, or click the File Open button on the Standard toolbar.

2. Select the drive and directory containing the file you want to open.

3. In the File Name box, specify the extension of the file you want to open. (For example, to list all files ending in the extension WP5, type ***.WP5**.)

4. From the list of files in the File Name box, select the file you want to open.

5. To display the Convert File dialog box, which will confirm the format from which the file is being converted, select the Confirm Conversions option.

   If you do not select this option, Word immediately converts the file without indicating the original format of the converted file.

6. Choose OK.

If there is no converter for the file, the Convert File dialog box appears. Select a substitute converter from the list and choose OK. The other option is to return to the Program Manager and run the Word for Windows setup program. You will have the chance to install additional converters found on Word for Windows installation disks. For more information on converting and using files from other applications, read Chapter 34, "Converting Files with Word for Windows."

Opening a Document While Starting Word for Windows

From the File Manager, you can start Word for Windows and open a file at the same time. This is handy if you use the File Manager to help you find a file and you want to immediately open the file without switching back to Program Manager and opening Word first.

To open a file from File Manager, follow these steps:

1. In the File Manager, display the window containing the Word for Windows document you want to open.

2. Double-click the file with the mouse. If you are using the keyboard, press Tab to move into the file window, then press the arrow keys to select the file and press Enter to start the file. Word for Windows starts and displays the document you selected.

Troubleshooting Opening a Document

When I choose the File Open command and switch to the directory where my file should be stored, I don't see the file listed in the File Name list.

If you saved the file with an extension other than DOC, you will not see the file listed. To list the file, you must change the extension in the File Name text box to match the extension on the file you are looking for. Or you can type ***.*** in the File Name text box to list all files. To avoid this problem, don't add an extension to your Word documents when you save them. Word automatically adds the DOC extension and these files will be listed by default in the File Name list.

Whenever I try to open a particular document in Word, I get a dialog box asking me for a password. How can I access this document?

Someone must have saved the document as a protected file. This means you must know the password that was assigned to the document in order to open it. Find out from others who have worked on the document what the password is.

For Related Information

- "Finding Files," p. 95
- "Opening Found Files," p. 110
- "Converting Files from Word Processors, Spreadsheets, or Databases," p. 1021
- "Seeing Which Converters You Have Installed," p. 1027

Working in a Document

When you have opened a new or existing document, you need to know how to work with that document. This section introduces some of the basic concepts and procedures you need to know to work in a document. Many of the concepts and procedures discussed in the following section will be familiar to you if you have worked with other word processors. If you have never used a word processor, you need to become familiar with these basics before you start working with a document in Word for Windows.

What You Need to Know About Working in a Document

When you create a new document in Word for Windows, you see a blank typing screen (except for the helpful tools at the top, bottom, and right). A vertical bar—the insertion point—flashes at the top left. Below the insertion point is a horizontal line called the *document end mark*. When you begin typing, your characters appear on-screen to the left of the insertion point, which moves to the right as you type.

If you have never typed in a word processor before, you immediately become aware of one difference from typing on a typewriter: you don't have to press the Enter key at the end of every line. You continue typing past the end of the right margin, and Word for Windows wraps sentences around to fit within the margins.

Press the Enter key only to mark the end of a paragraph or to insert a blank line. Pressing Enter inserts a paragraph mark. (Normally you don't see paragraph marks on-screen; if you want to see them, see Chapter 10, "Formatting Lines and Paragraphs.")

There are two important reasons for pressing Enter only when you want to end a paragraph. First, if you add or delete text from the paragraph, the word-wrap feature ensures that the paragraph stays intact. If you press Enter at the end of each line and then add or delete text, each line ends where you pressed Enter, whether it's at the beginning or middle of the line. Second, as you learn in Chapter 10, "Formatting Lines and Paragraphs," a paragraph is a special set of text with its own useful formatting commands, such as alignment, indents, line spacing, and tabs.

When you type text on-screen, you can use all the characters on your keyboard. Besides the normal characters you see on your keyboard, however, Word for Windows offers many special characters you can type, including bullets, typesetting quotes, wide dashes, and many others. For details about entering these characters, see Chapter 9, "Formatting Characters and Changing Fonts."

When you type in Word for Windows insert mode, you add text to an existing document between the existing words. In some cases, you may prefer to type in the overtype mode so that new text types over existing text.

If you want to switch from the insert mode to the overtype mode, press the Insert (or Ins) key on your keyboard. OVR becomes dark in the status bar at the bottom of the screen. Press the Insert key a second time to return to insert mode. If your status bar isn't displayed, you don't see a screen message reminding you that you're in the overtype mode. (To display the status bar, choose the Tools Options command and select the View tab. In the Window group, select Status Bar so that an X appears in the check box.)

If you prefer to use the overtype mode all the time, you can customize Word for Windows to use the overtype mode as the default (see Chapter 35, "Customizing and Optimizing Word Features").

> ### Caution
>
> Be careful when you use the overtype mode. It is very easy to forget to return to the insert mode and then type over text that you didn't want to replace.

You can move to a location where you were previously working in your document by pressing Shift+F5. Word remembers the previous three locations of the insertion point, so you can return to any of these locations by pressing Shift+F5 until you get to the location you want. When you first open an existing document, pressing Shift+F5 returns you to where the insertion point was located when you last closed the document.

Troubleshooting Working in a Document

Whenever I try to enter new text, the new text I enter overwrites the text that was already in my document. How can I prevent this?

This happens when you are in the overtype mode. Press the Insert key to return to the insert mode. When you type in the insert mode, the new text is inserted after the insertion point and any existing text is moved to make room for the new text.

For Related Information

■ "Selecting the Correct View for Your Work," p. 116

■ "Moving in the Document," p. 127

■ "Selecting Text," p. 133

Working with Multiple Documents

In Word for Windows, you can work with several documents simultaneously. Each new document you create or each existing document you open resides in its own document window on your screen. (For details on the difference between the program window and document windows and on moving and sizing windows, see Chapter 2, "Getting Started in Word for Windows.")

One great benefit to working with multiple documents simultaneously is that you can easily copy or move text between them. This feature eases the task of creating two different versions of one basic document or borrowing from an existing document as you build a new one.

What You Need to Know About Working with Multiple Documents

To work with multiple documents, you simply open additional new or existing documents as discussed in the previous sections. You can work with up to nine documents at a time. As you open successive documents, they appear in document windows that hide the previously opened documents. To work with these documents, you can switch between them in this full-screen mode, or you can arrange the windows so that you can see at least a portion of each of them. Only one window can be active at a time. The window on top, with the different-colored title bar, is the active window. It displays the document in which you are working.

To arrange multiple document windows, choose the **Window Arrange All** command. Word for Windows reduces the size of each window so that you can see them all on-screen. You can resize or move these windows using normal Windows techniques.

To switch between full-screen document windows, follow these steps:

1. Choose the **Window** menu, which lists all currently open files.

2. Select the name of the file to which you want to switch.

As an alternative to using the **Window** menu to switch between open documents, you can click the window you want to select, or use Ctrl+F6. Press Ctrl+F6 repeatedly to cycle through all open documents. This method is the quickest when you have only two files open. To restore any window to its full-screen size, click the maximize arrow at the top right of the window, or choose the Control Maximize command (Ctrl+F10).

To open a second copy of the current file, the one in the active window, follow these steps:

1. Choose the Window menu, which lists all currently open files.

2. Choose the New Window command.

When you open multiple copies of the same file, the first file name in the title bar ends with :1, the second with :2, and so on. You can switch between these windows in the same way you switch between any document windows, but any edits you make to one are made to all, and you can save the document from any of the windows displaying that document. If you close the document using the File Close command, all copies of the document are closed. To close just one of the windows for the document, select the control menu for that window (click the control menu bar or press the Alt+Hyphen keys) and choose the Close command.

**For Related
Information**
■ "Editing a
Document,"
p. 115

> **Note**
>
> You can open a second window and then change the way you view that document in the new window. In this way, you can have two different views on the same document. For example, you can view the document as an outline in one window and view the document normally in the second window. See Chapter 5, "Editing a Document," for information on selecting different views of your document.

Saving a Document

By now, you probably have heard the lecture advising you to save your document frequently. Saving your work stores the work as a file on disk. Until you save, your work exists only in your computer's memory. Thus, if the electricity goes off, even for a very short time, everything in your computer's memory is lost—including your work.

Saving frequently also reduces the time required for Word for Windows to store your work on disk. In effect, you save time by saving often.

Once you have saved a file, you can save it again with the same name or save a new copy of the file with a different file name and storage location. You can attach summary information to the file when you save it, which makes it easier to find the file when you want to work on it again.

You can tell Word to automatically save your document at specified time intervals and to make a backup copy of your file each time you save a document. In this way, if you have forgotten to save a file and your power fails or some other problem occurs, you will at least be able to recover some of your lost work.

You can save a document created in Word for Windows in other formats so that you can transfer the document to other computers that do not have Word installed. For example, you can save a document as a WordPerfect file to give to someone who uses WordPerfect. You can also save a document as a protected file to limit access to the document and prevent anyone from altering the document unless you give them access to it.

What You Need to Know About Saving a Document

The first time you save a document, you need to give it a file name and decide on what disk and in which directory you want to store it. After you have saved a file for the first time, you can save it again with the same file name or you can save a new file, with a different file name. This is what you would do if you wanted to save successive drafts of a document as you worked on it.

Saving Your Document

The first time you save a document, you must name it and decide where you want to store it.

To save and name a file, follow these steps:

1. Choose the File Save As command or press F12 or choose the Save button on the Standard toolbar (the third button from the left). The Save As dialog box appears (see fig. 3.7).

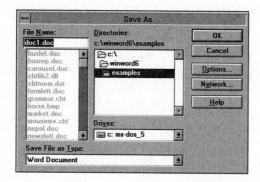

Fig. 3.7
Use the Save As dialog box to name a file and assign where you want it stored.

2. Type a file name in the File Name box.

3. In the Drives list, select the drive where you want to save your file. Use this option to save your file to a floppy disk in drive A or B, for example, or to save the file to a different drive on your hard disk. (See "Understanding Directories," an earlier section in this chapter).

4. In the Directories list box, select the directory where you want to save your file. (See "Understanding Directories," an earlier section in this chapter).

5. Choose OK.

6. If you have selected the option to display the Summary Info dialog box when you first save a file, fill in the dialog box when it appears and choose OK (see "Saving with Summary Information to Make Documents Easier to Find," later in this chapter). You can bypass the dialog box by choosing OK without entering any information.

You can change the default directory that is listed when you first choose the File Save command or File Save As command. See "Setting the Default Directory," an earlier section in this chapter.

Note

If you are familiar with directory path names, you can save a file into another directory by typing the path name and file name in the File Name box of the Save As dialog box. To save a file named REPORTS into the CLIENTS directory on drive C, for example, type the following path name and then choose OK or press Enter:

C:\CLIENTS\REPORTS

Saving Files with a New Name

You can use the File Save As command to save a named file with a new name, which creates a backup of your file. If you have a file called LETTERA.DOC, for example, you can save your file a second time, giving it the name LETTERB.DOC. You then have two versions of the same file, each with a different name. You can save the new version of your file in the same directory as the original, or in any other directory or drive.

Revising your file before saving it with a new name is a common practice. You then have the original file and the second, revised file, each with a unique name. Using this method, you can store successive drafts of a document on disk. You can always return to an earlier draft if you need to.

To save a named file with a new name, choose the File Save As command, change the file name in the File Name box, change the drive or directory if you want, and then choose OK.

Note

You can use the File Save As command to make sequential backups of important documents. The first time you save a file, name the file with a number, such as FILE01. Then each time you save the file again, rename the document with the next higher number: FILE02, FILE03, and so on. The file with the highest number is always the most recent version. When you finish the project, you can delete the files with low numbers.

Be sure to name the files FILE01 and FILE02—including the zero—so that the files stay in order in dialog box lists. If you don't, FILE11 is listed before FILE3 because files are listed alphabetically and numerically. This rule is especially important in the Open dialog box, where you want to be sure you open the most recent version of your file.

Saving with Summary Information to Make Documents Easier to Find

Summary information includes descriptive notes that can ease the task of organizing and finding files later, after you have created many files. You can attach summary information to your document when you first create the file, while you work on the file, or when you save the file.

To add summary information when you create a new document, follow these steps:

1. Choose Summary in the New dialog box. The Summary Info dialog box appears (see fig. 3.8).

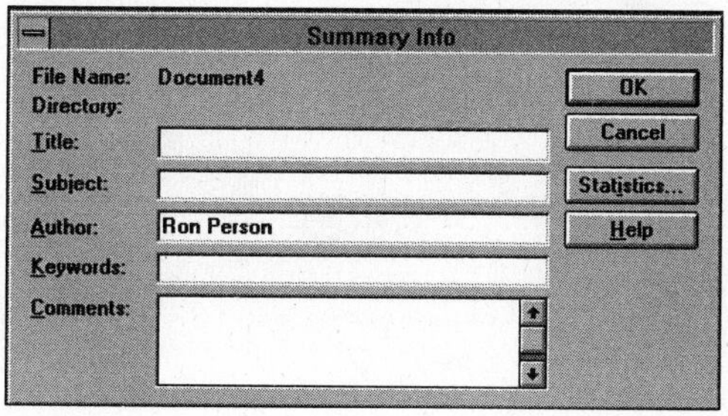

Fig. 3.8
Use the Summary Info dialog box to attach useful information to your documents.

2. Fill in any of the fields with descriptive text. Include as much (up to 255 characters) or as little information as you like.

3. Choose OK.

You can add or edit the summary information at any time by choosing the File Summary Info command to display the Summary Info dialog box. The Statistics option in this dialog box tells when you created the document, when the document was most recently saved, and how many pages, words, and characters the document contains.

To view the statistics for a document, follow these steps:

1. Select Statistics in the Summary Info dialog box. The Document Statistics dialog box appears (see fig. 3.9).

2. Take note of the statistics that interest you.

3. Choose OK.

If you want to be prompted to enter summary information when you save a file, you can select an option to display the Summary Info dialog box whenever you choose the File Save As command. Choose the Tools Options command and select the Save tab. Select the Prompt for Summary Info option and choose OK. Now, whenever you first save a file, the Summary Info dialog box appears. If you don't want to enter summary information for that file, choose OK to bypass the dialog box.

Fig. 3.9
The Document Statistics dialog box provides detailed information on your document.

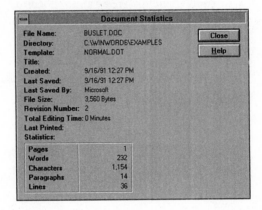

Whichever method you choose, including summary information is a wonderful time-saver. In Chapter 4, "Managing Documents and Files," you learn how to use this information to locate misplaced files or files whose names you don't quite remember. The Summary Info dialog box also helps you cope with the limited file naming rules of DOS. Although you must still limit the names of your files to eight letters, you can attach a title to any of your documents and then list the files in any subdirectory along with their titles, using the Find File command. You can include any text up to 255 characters in any of the Summary Info fields. No naming or character restrictions exist.

Filling in the Summary Info box may seem like a nuisance, but try the box before giving it up. When you learn how to use the powerful Find File command, you see that summary information helps you find files much more easily than by using the cryptic eight-letter DOS file name.

Saving Without Renaming

Every time you save a document with a unique name, you create a new file on disk—a good way to keep backups of your document. Not all files are so important, however, that you need multiple backups. In that case, you can save the document to its existing file name, replacing the current version of the file.

Remember that when you save without renaming, you erase and replace the existing file with the new file.

To save without renaming, choose the File Save command or press Shift+F12 or click the Save button on the toolbar (the third button from the left).

Saving Many Documents at Once

If you have several documents open at once, you can save them all simultaneously by showing the File Save All command. The Save As dialog box appears for any documents that have not been saved before.

Files you normally don't see, including glossary and macro files, also are saved when you use this command.

Automatically Saving Documents

You can tell Word for Windows to automatically save your documents at specified intervals. AutoSave files are saved with a name different from your file name, but always with the ASD extension. AutoSave files are saved in the TEMP directory specified in your AUTOEXEC.BAT file. Normally, this is the \WINDOWS\TEMP directory. You can change the directory in which AutoSave files are saved by following these steps:

1. Choose the Tools Options command and select the File Locations tab.

2. Select AutoSave Files from the File Types list and choose Modify. The Modify Location dialog box appears.

3. Specify the drive and directory where you want AutoSave files to be stored and choose OK. You also have the option of creating a new directory for your AutoSave files in the Modify Location dialog box.

To turn on automatic saving, follow these steps:

1. Choose the File Save As command or press F12 and select Options.

    or

    Choose the Tools Options command and select the Save tab.

    The Save tab is displayed (see fig. 3.10).

2. Select the Automatic Save Every option.

3. Select or type the time interval, in minutes, between automatic saves in the Minutes text box.

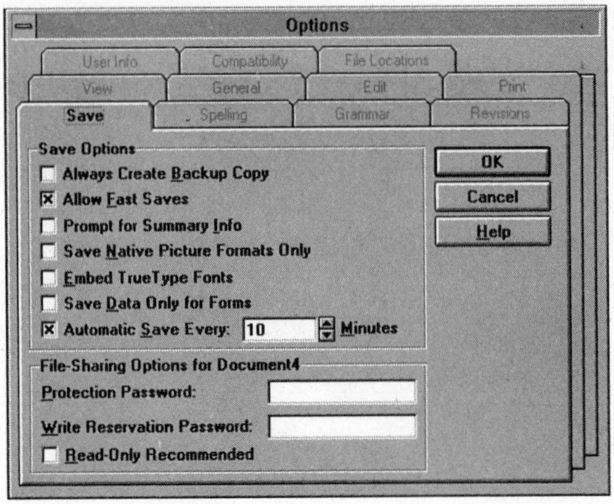

Fig. 3.10

You can specify several save options in the Save tab.

4. Choose OK.

As you are working in your document, Word periodically saves your document. A message in the status bar indicates that your file is being saved.

If a power failure or other problem causes Word to shut down while you are working on a document, and you have selected the automatic save option, you can recover everything that was entered up until the last automatic save. The next time you start Word for Windows, any files that were open when Word shut down will automatically be reopened. Any recovered file will be displayed in a window with " (Recovered) " next to the document name in the title bar.

Creating Automatic Backups

You can tell Word to create a backup copy of your document every time you save it. When you choose this option, Word saves the previous version of the document as a backup file and gives it the same file name as the original, but with the extension BAK.

To create backup copies of your documents, follow these steps:

1. Choose the File Save As command or press F12 and select Options.

   or

   Choose the Tools Options command and select the Save tab.

   The Save folder is displayed (refer to fig. 3.10).

2. Select the Always Create **B**ackup Copy option.

3. Choose OK.

If you lose work because Word shuts down due to a power failure or some other problem, you can open the backup copy. You must save a file more than once before a backup copy is created. The backup copy is stored in the same directory as the original document.

Saving with Fast Save

You can speed up the process of saving a file by selecting the Allow **F**ast Saves option. With this option selected, Word for Windows saves faster because the program saves only the changes, not the entire document. Fast saves occur only with the **S**ave command, not the Save As command. If you have selected the Always Create **B**ackup Copy option (see previous section), you cannot use the fast save feature because backups can be made only with full saves.

To turn on the fast saves feature, follow these steps:

1. Choose the File Save **A**s command or press F12 and select **O**ptions.

or

Choose the Tools **O**ptions command and select the Save tab.

The Save folder is displayed (refer to fig. 3.10).

2. Select the Allow **F**ast Saves option.

3. Choose OK.

Note

When you select the Allow **F**ast Saves option to save time when saving files, the files you save take up more disk space than those created using a full save, because Word must keep the original file plus the changes. To free up disk space, choose the **File** Save **A**s command, choose the **O**ptions button, clear the Allow **F**ast Saves check box, and choose OK twice when you make your final save for the document. Doing this will create a smaller file.

Everyday Word Processing

Saving for Other Word Processors or Applications

When you save a file in Word for Windows, the document is saved in Word for Windows format. Word for Windows, however, enables you to save your file in many formats. You may need to save a file into another format, such as WordPerfect format. At other times, you may need to save the file in Text (ASCII) format so that you can import the file into a different type of program.

To save your file in a non-Word for Windows format, follow these steps:

1. Choose the File Save As command or press F12. The Save As dialog box appears (refer to fig. 3.7).

2. In the File Name box, type the file name without an extension.

3. Select the file format from the Save File as Type list box.

4. Choose OK to save your file.

Word for Windows assigns an appropriate extension to the file name. To learn more about saving a file to a different file format, refer to Chapter 34, "Converting Files with Word for Windows."

Word for Windows displays only the types of files for which converters have been installed in the Save File as Type list box. If the word processor you need doesn't appear, reinstall Word for Windows using the custom installation option. You will be given the chance to install converter files without reinstalling all of Word for Windows.

Saving a Document as a Protected File

If you share files or your PC with other users, you may want to prevent people from opening some files or from modifying others. To prevent users from opening a file, you can assign a Protection Password. The next time you open the file, you must type the password. Another option is to assign a Write Reservation password, which allows anyone who knows the password to open the document and make and save changes to it. A user who does not know the password can open the file as a read-only document. They can read the document but cannot make and save changes to that document.

You can also assign the Read-Only Recommended option to a document. When a document with this option assigned is opened, a dialog box appears advising the user to open the document as a read-only document to which changes cannot be saved. However, the user does have the option of opening the document normally and saving changes to the document. For maximum protection, therefore, assign a password to the document.

You can also limit changes to a document to annotations, which are comments in a document that are viewed in a separate annotation pane, and marked revisions, which can be incorporated into the document only by a user who knows the password. See Chapter 30, "Tracking Revisions and Annotations," for details on protecting a document for annotations and revisions.

If you have created a form in a Word for Windows document, you can protect the document against all changes except entries into the form fields. See Chapter 18, "Building Forms and Fill-In Dialog Boxes," for details on how to protect a form.

To assign a password to a document, follow these steps:

1. Choose the File Save **As** command or press F12 and select **O**ptions.

   or

   Choose the Tools Options command and select the Save tab.

   The Options dialog box appears with the Save tab selected (refer to fig. 3.10).

2. To assign your file a password, select either the **P**rotection Password or **W**rite Reservation text box and type a password.

   As you type, you see only asterisks—no written record of your password exists anywhere. Your password can consist of up to 15 characters, including letters, numbers, symbols, and spaces.

3. Choose OK. Reenter the password in the Confirm Password dialog box and choose OK.

4. Choose OK at the Save As dialog box to save the file.

Caution

When a file is password-protected, no one can open that file without the password—including you. Don't forget your password.

To change or delete a password, follow the same procedure, but delete the existing password (which still appears only as a string of asterisks) and type the new password (or not, if you want to remove the password).

To assign the Read-Only Recommended option to a document, follow these steps:

1. Choose the File Save As command or press F12 and select Options.

   or

   Choose the Tools Options command and select the Save tab.

2. Select the Read-Only Recommended option.

3. Choose OK.

For Related Information
■ "Protecting and Saving the Form," p. 581

■ "Protecting Documents for Annotations Only," p. 945

■ "Saving Word for Windows Documents to Another Format," p. 1026

Troubleshooting Saving Files

Periodically, Word saves the document I am working on. I find this annoying, because it distracts me when I am entering text into the document.

You need to turn off the AutoSave feature in Word. Choose the Tools Options command, select the Save tab, clear the Automatic Save Every option, and choose OK.

I made some changes to a document and wanted to save the document with a new name. When I clicked the Save button on the toolbar, the document was saved with the same name and I lost my original document.

To save a document with a new name, you must use the File Save As command to open the Save As dialog box, where you can enter a new name for the document. The Save button on the Standard toolbar opens the Save As dialog box only the first time you save a document. After that, it saves the document with the same file name you gave it when you first saved it.

Closing a Document

After you finish working on a document and save the file, you may want to close the document, especially if you have several documents open.

To close a document, choose the File Close command. If the document is in a window, you can close it by double-clicking the dash icon at the top left corner of the document window. When a document is maximized to full screen, the dash icon appears in the menu bar to the left of File. Be careful not to double-click the bar icon in the top left corner of the Word for Windows window, or you will close Word.

If you have made changes since you last saved, Word for Windows asks whether you want to save your changes. Respond Yes to save them. (If you haven't named the document, the Save As dialog box appears, and you must name the file.) Respond No to discard changes. Choose Cancel to cancel the close, or choose Help to access the Word for Windows help window.

From Here...

The following chapters are good ones to study after you have learned the basic skills discussed in this chapter:

- Chapter 5, "Editing a Document." Learn how to edit the documents you have created.

- Chapter 7, "Using Editing and Proofing Tools." Learn how to use the excellent tools provided by Word for editing and proofing your documents, including the Spell Checker and Find and Replace.

- Chapter 8, "Previewing and Printing a Document." Learn how to preview how your documents will look on the printed page and how to print your documents.

Chapter 4

Managing Documents and Files

Although word processors undoubtedly offer a tremendous advantage over the typewriter for producing written documents, one fact remains: you accumulate Word files as fast as you accrued paper files before the advent of the word processor. Word for Windows, however, can help you to find and manage these files with its Find File command.

The Find File command enables you to search for files by file name, location, author, and date the files were created or last saved. Alternatively, you can use the information you've entered in the Summary Info dialog box (refer to Chapter 3, "Creating and Saving Documents"). You can also search for specific text that occurs in a document. You can specify search criteria as broad or narrow as you want. The more you narrow your search, the fewer files will be found.

The files that are found using the criteria you have specified are listed in the Find File dialog box (see fig. 4.1). From there, you can browse through the directories that were included in the search, sort the files in the list, and preview any file without opening it in Word. Furthermore, you can view information about a file, specifically the file name, title, size, author, and date last saved; or you can view the summary information you have entered for a file.

You can accomplish many other file-related tasks from the Find File dialog box. You can select as many files as you want in the list, and then open, print, copy, or delete the files. The capability to work with multiple files is a powerful feature of the Find File command and a great time-saver.

In this chapter, you learn to do the following:

- Find files
- View files and file information
- Manage found files

Fig. 4.1
All the files that
meet the search
criteria you specify
are listed in the
Find File dialog
box.

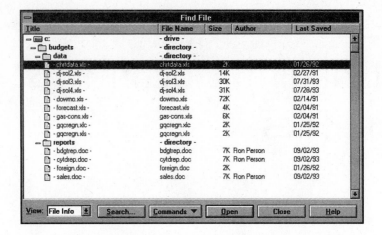

What You Need to Know About Managing Documents and Files

When you save a file, you give it a file name and then decide where you want
to store the saved file. As the number of files you create in Word increases,
you will want to come up with some sort of system for organizing your files.
The easiest way to do this is to set up directories on your hard disk that contain related files. For example, you might have a directory for business letters
and another for personal correspondence. You might also have a directory for
each of the projects on which you are working. When you save a document,
you want to be sure that you do so in the appropriate directory. In this way,
it is easier to retrieve the document if you need to work with it again. For
more information on working with file names and directories, refer to Chapter 3, "Creating and Saving Documents."

After you have decided where your files are stored, you still need to locate
them when you need to work with them again. If you haven't worked with a
document for a long time, you can easily forget its name or location when
you want to reopen it. Or you might want to look over a group of related
documents without having to open each one in Word. You can use the Find
File command to bring together a list of related files or to find a specific file.

Once you have found the files that match the criteria you specified, you can
browse through the directories included in the search until you find the file
or files you want to work with. You can preview any file to make sure it is the
one you want, and then open, print, copy, or delete the file. If you want to

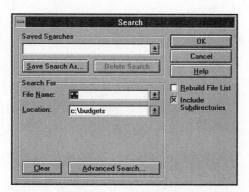

act on several files at once, you can select them first and then issue one of the commands that acts on these files. You can select a group of files, for example, and then copy them to a floppy disk to back them up, or print several files at once without opening the files in Word.

Finding Files

Before you can use the Find File command to manage your files, you need to find the files you want to work with. Your search can be very narrow; for example, you can look for a particular file with a familiar file name. Or you can search for a group of files that match whatever criteria you specify. This section shows you all the different ways you can search for files.

What You Need to Know About Finding Files

You begin your search for files by using the Find File command in the File menu. Alternatively, you can choose the Find File button in the Open dialog box. To find files, you must specify the *search criteria* that Find File uses to look for the files. The first time you use the Find File command, Word for Windows displays the Search dialog box so that you can describe the files or directory you want to search. After you have done your first search with Find File, the next time you choose the Find File command, it will display the list of files that match the criteria you last searched for.

To change the found files shown in the listing, you must specify new or additional criteria and then initiate a new search in the Search dialog box (see fig. 4.2). You can limit your search to a file with a specific file name; to all Word files that end with the extension DOC; or to all types of files, regardless of extension. If you want to limit the scope of the search to a particular disk drive or to certain directories on a disk, you can specify the location for the search.

Fig. 4.2
You specify the criteria for a simple file name or directory search in the Search dialog box.

Everyday Word Processing

Using the Advanced Search command (see fig. 4.3), you can narrow down the list of files that must be found. You do this by specifying additional criteria, such as the file creation or save date, author name, summary information, or specific text strings (such as a word or phrase).

Fig. 4.3
You can enter
additional search
criteria in the
Advanced Search
dialog box.

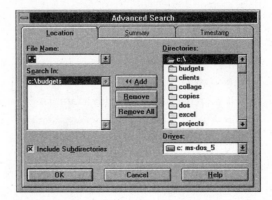

After you have specified search criteria, you initiate a new search by choosing OK in the Search dialog box. If you need to cancel a search before it is completed, choose Cancel. The files meeting the new search criteria are listed in the Find File window. For instructions on how to view file information and preview the files in the list, see the section "Viewing Documents and File Information" later in the chapter.

Searching Different Drives or Directories

If you know where the files you are looking for are located, you can specify that only certain directories be searched. This speeds up the process of finding the files because Find File does not have to search your entire hard disk. For example, you might know that the files you want to find are in one or more of the subdirectories of the WINWORD directory. In this case, you can limit the search to those subdirectories. You can also specify a different drive for a search, such as a floppy drive.

To specify the directories to be searched, follow these steps:

1. Choose the Find File command from the File menu or the Open dialog box. The Find File dialog box appears (refer to fig. 4.1), listing the files that meet the current search criteria.

2. Choose the Search button in the Find File dialog box. The Search dialog box appears (refer to fig. 4.2).

3. From the Location list, select the drive you want to search.

4. Choose the Advanced Search button and select the Location tab. The Location tab in the Advanced Search dialog box is displayed (see fig. 4.4).

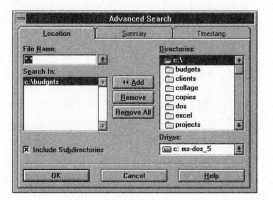

Fig. 4.4
Use the Location tab to specify where to search for files.

The directories that are currently searched are listed in the Search In list.

5. To add a directory to the Search In list, select the directory in the Directories box and choose the Add button.

6. To remove a directory from the Search In list, select the directory in the list and choose the Remove button. To remove all directories from the Search In list, choose the Remove All button.

7. To include all the subdirectories of the directories listed in the Search In list, select the Include Subdirectories check box.

8. Choose OK in the Advanced Search dialog box; then choose OK in the Search dialog box to begin the search.

The files matching the location criteria and other criteria specified are listed in the Find File dialog box.

Searching for Specific Files or Different File Types

By default, Word for Windows searches for all Word for Windows files in the specified directories (or on the entire drive if no path has been specified). However, you can also search for a specific file or different types of files. If the files are compatible with Word for Windows, you can open or print them; you can copy or delete the files you find, even if they are not compatible with Word for Windows.

To search for different file types, follow these steps:

1. Choose the Find File command from the File menu or the Open dialog box. The Find File dialog box appears (refer to fig. 4.1), listing the files that meet the current search criteria.

2. Choose the Search button. The Search dialog box appears (refer to fig. 4.2).

3. In the File Name box, type the name of the file for which you want to search, including the file extension.

4. To search for a file type instead, pull down the File Name list and select the type of file for which you want to search.

   or

   In the File Name box, type the extension of the file type for which you want to search. You can use wild-card characters. An asterisk (*) represents any string of characters; you can search for files ending with the extension TXT by typing ***.TXT**. A question mark (?) represents any one character; you can search for LETR?.DOC to search for files named LETR1.DOC, LETR2.DOC, LETRB.DOC, and so on.

   By default, Word replaces the existing file list with a new list of files matching the current search criteria. To add the files that match the new criteria to the existing list, choose the Advanced Search button and select the Summary tab. Next select Add Matches to List from the Options list and choose OK.

5. Choose OK.

Searching by Summary Information or Text in the File

One of the best advantages to including summary information in all your Word files is that you can search for files by text contained in any of the summary information's fields. For example, you can add a title to a document and then use it to search through files. In this way, Word for Windows enables you to override the DOS limitation of an eight-character file name. You can also search for a file based on any of the text contained in it. To learn how to add summary information to your Word files, refer to Chapter 3, "Creating and Saving Documents."

To search by summary information or any text in the file, follow these steps:

1. Choose the Find File command from the File menu or the Open dialog box. The Find File dialog box appears (refer to fig. 4.1), listing the files that meet the current search criteria.

2. Choose the Search button and then the Advanced Search button. The Advanced Search dialog box appears (refer to fig. 4.3).

3. Select the Summary tab. The Summary tab appears. (Fig. 4.5 shows a partially complete Summary tab.)

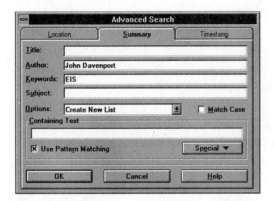

Fig. 4.5
You can use summary informa- tion to help you find files.

4. In the appropriate text boxes, type the summary information to be searched for:

Text Box	Searches for
Title	Text you enter in the Title box
Author	Text you enter in the Author box
Keywords	Text you enter in the Keywords box
Subject	Text you enter in the Subject box

5. Select Match Case to match upper- and lowercase exactly.

6. If you need to search the contents of a Word document, enter the text you want to search for in the Containing Text box. To add special sym- bols or wild cards to the text you are searching, select the Use Pattern Matching check box, and then choose the Special button to display a list of special characters. To insert a character in your search text, select that character.

7. From the Options list, select one of these options:

Option	Description
Create New List	Replaces the existing list
Add Matches to List	Adds the new list to the exiting list
Search Only in List	Searches for criteria only in the existing list (this option does not apply when you search a different drive or directory)

8. Choose OK twice.

A few rules exist for searching files by summary information or text in the file. You can type as many as 255 characters in any of the summary information fields in the Summary tab (shown in fig. 4.5). You can use partial words or any combination of upper- and lowercase letters. If you type **ba** or **Ba** in the Title field, for example, you get a list of files containing the words *bank* or *abandon*, as well as any other files that have the letters *ba* in their titles. (Select the Match Case option to match upper- and lowercase exactly.) If you want to search for a phrase, such as *bank loan*, enclose it in double quotation marks, as in **"bank loan"**. You can use wild cards in your search, and you can combine words, as the following examples show:

To Search for	Type in the Text Box
Any single character	? (question mark) *Example:* type **ba??** to find *bank* or *band*
Any string of characters	* (asterisk) *Example:* type **ba*** to find any word that begins with the letters *ba*
A phrase (such as *bank loan*)	" " (quotation marks enclosing the phrase) *Example:* type **"bank loan"**
One word or another word	, (comma) *Example:* type **bank,loan** to find files containing *bank* or *loan*
One word and another word	& (ampersand or space) *Example:* type **bank & loan** or **bank loan** to find files containing *bank* and *loan*
Files not containing	~ (tilde) *Example:* type **bank~loan** to find files containing *bank* but not *loan*

Searching by Date Saved or Created

You can search for files based on the date you created or last saved them. This feature is convenient, especially when used with other search criteria. For example, you can search for files containing the title words *bank* and *letter* that were created between June 1 and June 30 of last year.

To search for files by date created or saved, follow these steps:

1. Choose the Find File command from the File menu or the Open dialog box. The Find File dialog box appears (refer to fig. 4.1), listing the files that meet the current search criteria.

2. Choose the Search button and then the Advanced Search button.

3. Select the Timestamp tab. The Timestamp tab appears (see fig. 4.6 for a completed Timestamp tab).

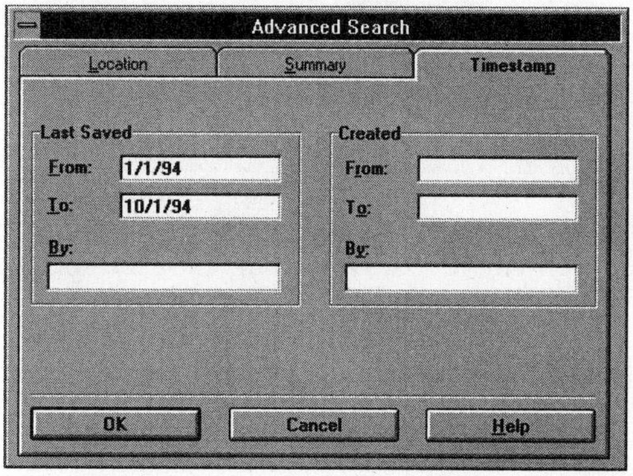

Fig. 4.6
You use the Timestamp tab to date criteria for a search.

4. To search files by date last saved, type in the From box the beginning date of the range of dates you want to search for. In the To box, type the ending date. Use the format *mm/dd/yy* (for example, 6/1/93).

   To search files by date created, type in the From box the beginning date of the range of dates for which you want to search. In the To box, type the ending date.

5. You can specify the author of the file by typing the name in either the Last Saved **By** or the Created **By** box.

6. Choose OK.

Saving Search Criteria

If you have entered a set of search criteria and you want to be able to reuse it for future searches, you can save the criteria with a name. When you want to reuse the criteria, you select the named set of criteria from the Search dialog box and then initiate a new search.

To save search criteria, follow these steps:

1. Choose the Find File command from the File menu or the Open dialog box. The Find File dialog box appears (refer to fig. 4.1), listing the files that meet the current search criteria.

2. Set up the search criteria you want, as outlined previously.

3. Choose the Save Search As button in the Search dialog box. The Save Search As dialog box appears (see fig. 4.7).

Fig. 4.7
You can name a
set of search
criteria, save it,
and reuse it.

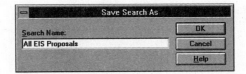

4. In the Search Name text box, type a name for the search criteria.

5. Choose OK.

6. To start a search with these criteria, choose OK.

To reuse saved search criteria, follow these steps:

1. Select the set of criteria you want to use from the Saved Searches list in the Search dialog box.

2. Choose OK to begin the search using the saved criteria.

The name of the set of search criteria used in the search appears at the top of the listed files.

Troubleshooting Finding Files

I included a network drive in my search criteria, but Find File is not searching on this drive.

You must first connect to the network drive before Find File can search that drive. To connect to a network drive, choose the Search button in the Find File dialog box and then choose the Advanced Search button in the Search dialog box. Next choose the Network button in the Advanced Search dialog box. In the Connect Network dialog box select the drive to which you want to connect. Choose OK. Now the network drive is included in the search.

When I attempt to search for a file, using a string of text that I know is in the document, Word doesn't locate the file I am looking for.

If you save files by using the Allow Fast Saves option, Find File ignores such files when it searches using text entered in the Containing Text field of the Advanced Search dialog box. You need to turn off the Allow Fast Saves option to avoid this problem. Choose the Tools Options command and select the Save tab. Clear the Allow Fast Saves option and choose OK.

Viewing Documents and File Information

After you have found the files you want to work with, you can sort the list of found files; then you can view file information or preview a file. Viewing file information and previewing files can help you manage your documents. For example, you can preview a file before you open or print it, so that you know you are working with the right document. Or you can view file information to find out which is the most recent version of a document on which you have been working.

What You Need to Know About Viewing Documents and File Information

After you have completed a search using whatever criteria you specify, all the files matching the criteria are listed in the Listed Files box in the Find File dialog box (see fig. 4.8). The matching files are listed by directory, starting with the root directory. Each directory containing files that match the criteria is represented by a folder in the Listed Files box. The name of the directory appears on the right side of the folder icon. Closed folders have a plus sign (+) next to them and can be opened to display the files in the folder. To do this,

For Related Information
- "Understanding File Names," p. 64
- "Understanding Directories," p. 64
- "Saving with Summary Information to Make Documents Easier to Find," p. 83

you simply double-click the folder or click the plus sign. Open folders are displayed with a minus sign (–) next to them. To close a folder, double-click it or click the minus sign.

Fig. 4.8

The Find File dialog box displays a list of files matching your search criteria.

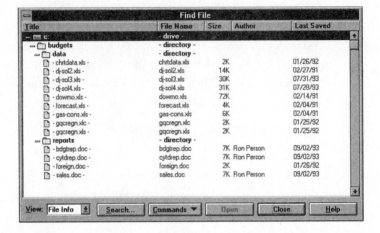

Before you can view a file or its information, you must select the file. To select the file, click the file name with the mouse, or press the Tab key until the focus (the dotted lines) is in the Listed Files box. Then use the up- and down-arrow keys to select the file.

This section describes how to sort a list of files, preview a file, and view file information.

Sorting File Lists

If the list of files in a directory is long, you might want to sort the listed files. You can sort by file name, author, size, creation date, or date last saved. You can sort also by using the name of the person who most recently saved the file. You can list the files by file name or by title entered in the Summary Info dialog box (refer to "Searching by Summary Information or Text in the File" in an earlier section of this chapter).

To sort a list of files, follow these steps:

1. Choose the Find File command from the File menu or the Open dialog box.

2. Choose the Commands button in the Find File dialog box. Then choose Sorting. The Options dialog box is displayed (see fig. 4.9).

3. In the Sort Files By list, select one of the following sorting options:

Fig. 4.9
In the Options
dialog box, you
can select how you
want to sort and
list files.

Everyday Word Processing

Option	How Files Are Listed
Author	Alphabetically by author
Creation Date	Chronologically by the file creation date (most recent date first)
Last Saved By	Alphabetically by name of person who most recently saved the files
Last Saved Date	Chronologically by the date files are saved (most recent date first)
Name	Alphabetically by name (default choice)
Size	Numerically by file size

4. Select one of the following List Files By options:

Option	How Files Are Listed
Filename	By file name
Title	By title used in the Summary Info for each file

5. Choose OK.

The files in all the directories in the Listed Files box of the Find File dialog are sorted.

Previewing Documents

One of the most useful features in the Find File dialog box is the capability to preview a document. When you are making decisions about what files you want to open, copy, print, or delete, it is helpful to be able to preview their contents quickly, without having to open them.

To preview a file, follow these steps:

1. Choose the Find File command from the File menu or the Open dialog box.

2. From the View list in the Find File dialog box, select Preview (see fig. 4.10).

Fig. 4.10
You can view files listed in the Find File dialog box with one of three methods.

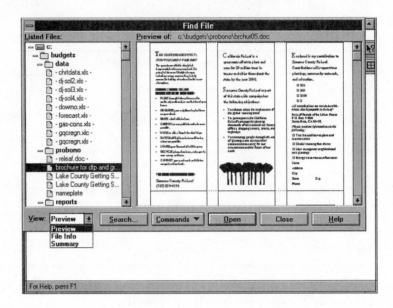

3. From the Listed Files box, select the file you want to preview.

A reduced view of the file contents is displayed in the Preview of box (see fig. 4.11). You can move through the file by using the scroll bars or the keyboard.

Fig. 4.11
You can view the contents of a file without opening it.

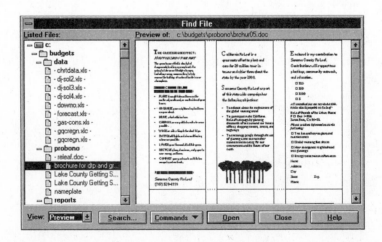

If you select a non-Word file, it is converted, provided that the necessary converter has been installed. You can run the Word Setup program to install additional converters (see Appendix B).

> **Note**
>
> Selecting Preview as the view in the Find File dialog box will slow you down if you don't have a fast computer. The reason is that the Preview area has to be redrawn each time you select a new document from the file list. Use the File Info or Summary view to speed things up.

Viewing File Information

You can view information for a file instead of viewing the file's contents. When you select the File Info view, information for each file in the file list is displayed next to the name of the file. You see different information, depending on how you have sorted the file list. For example, if you sort by name, the title, size, author, and date last saved are displayed. If you sort by creation date, the Last Saved field is replaced by the Created field.

To view file information, follow these steps:

1. Choose the Find File command from the File menu or the Open dialog box.

2. Select File Info in the View list at the bottom of the Find File dialog box (refer to fig. 4.10).

The file information for each file in the list is displayed in columns adjacent to the list (see fig. 4.12). You can change the width of any of the columns. To do this, move the mouse pointer over the right border line of the column heading for the column whose width you want to change. When the mouse pointer changes to a double-headed arrow, drag the border to a new position.

Viewing Summary Information

If you have chosen to add summary information to your Word files (refer to Chapter 3, "Creating and Saving Documents"), you can view this information in the Find File dialog box. The information can include title, author name, subject, keywords, and comments that you enter in the Summary Info dialog box. The summary information automatically includes other statistics about the file, including the creation date, date last saved, and size of the file. Therefore, even if you don't add summary information when you save the file, you will see some information when you view the summary information.

Fig. 4.12
You can use the
File Info view to
view information
about the files
listed in the Find
File dialog box.

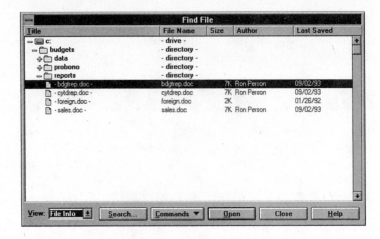

Tip
If you have already
opened a docu-
ment, you can
view and edit its
summary informa-
tion by choosing
the File Summary
Info command.

To view summary information, follow these steps:

1. Choose the Find File command from the File menu or the Open dialog box.

2. Select Summary in the View list at the bottom of the Find File dialog box (refer to fig. 4.10).

The summary information and document statistics are displayed for the file selected in the Listed Files box (see fig. 4.13).

Fig. 4.13
You can view the
summary informa-
tion for a file
in the Find File
dialog box.

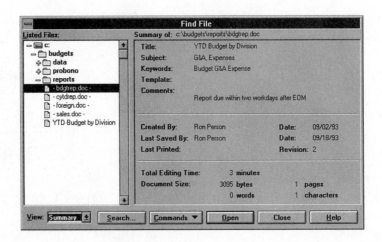

Editing and Adding Summary Information

If you didn't add summary information to a Word file when you created or saved it (refer to Chapter 3, "Creating and Saving Documents"), or if you want to edit the summary information for a file, you can do so from the Find File dialog box.

To edit or add summary information, follow these steps:

1. Choose the Find File command from the File menu or the Open dialog box. The Find File dialog box appears.

2. From the Listed Files box, select the file with which you want to work.

3. Choose the Commands button, and then choose **Summary**.

4. Fill in or edit any of the fields. Include as much information (up to 255 characters) or as little as you want.

5. Choose OK.

Note

Use the Summary Info box to attach a descriptive title to all your Word documents. Then list the files by title in the Find File dialog box. This makes it much easier to identify your files in the file list and helps you work around the eight-character limitation for DOS file names.

For Related Information
- "Opening a Document," p. 72
- "Saving with Summary Information to Make Documents Easier to Find," p. 83
- "Converting Files from Word Processors, Spreadsheets, or Databases," p. 1021

Managing Files

After you have found the files that meet the search criteria you specified, you can accomplish many tasks with these files by using the commands in the Find File dialog box. You can open, print, copy, or delete a file or group of selected files—all from this dialog box. The fact that you can select more than one file at a time from the Listed Files list is a tremendous time-saver. For example, if you want to print several files at once, you can find all of them with the Find File command. Then you can select all the files you want to print, and issue one print command. This approach is much simpler and quicker than opening each of the files, one by one, from within Word and printing them separately. You can use the same approach to copy or delete groups of files. This capability, along with being able to preview the contents of a file without having to open it, greatly facilitates the process of managing your files.

What You Need to Know About Managing Files

Before you issue various commands to manage your files, you need to select one or more of the files with which you want to work. To select a file with the mouse, click the name of the file you want; or press and hold down the Ctrl key and click multiple file names (see fig. 4.14). If you want to select several sequential files, press and hold down the Shift key and then click the first and last file you want. (Press and hold down the Ctrl key and click a second time to deselect any file you select by mistake.)

Fig. 4.14
Multiple files selected in the file list.

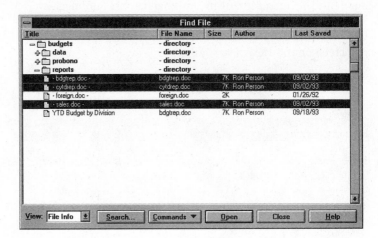

To select a file with the keyboard, press the Tab key until the focus (the dotted line) is in the Listed Files box. Then use the up- or down-arrow key to move to the file you want to select. To select multiple files that are not contiguous, press Shift+F8. Then move to each file you want to select, and press the space bar. Press Shift+F8 again to turn off the multiple-selection mode. To select multiple contiguous files, press the up- or down-arrow key to select the first file. Next press and hold down Shift and then press the up- or down-arrow key to extend the selection.

Opening Found Files

After you use the Find File command to find and select a file, you can open it from the Find File dialog box. You can also open more than one file.

To find and open documents, follow these steps:

1. Choose the Find File command from the File menu or the Open dialog box.

2. Select the file or files you want to open (refer to "What You Need to Know About Managing Files" earlier in this section).

3. Choose the Open button.

4. If you want to prevent yourself from modifying any of the files you open, choose the Commands button. Then choose the Open **Read** Only command.

When you choose the Open button, all files are opened, each in its own document window. For more information on working with multiple documents, refer to Chapter 3, "Creating and Saving Documents."

Printing Found Files

You can use the File **Print** command to print the open document. If you want to print several documents with the same printing parameters at once, however, use the Find File command to first find and then print the files.

To print documents from the Find File dialog box, follow these steps:

1. Choose the Find File command from the File menu or the Open dialog box.

2. Select one or more files you want to print (refer to "What You Need to Know About Managing Files" earlier in this section).

3. Choose the Commands button and then the **Print** command. The Print dialog box appears.

4. Select the printing options you want. Then choose OK.

If you select multiple documents to print, they all print with the parameters you identify in the Print dialog box. For more information on printing, see Chapter 8, "Previewing and Printing a Document."

Note

If you routinely need to print the same set of documents, such as those you hand out for a seminar, set up a search criteria set that finds only those files. Then save the search criteria set. Whenever you need to print these documents, select the set of criteria from the Saved Searches list. Next run the search and select all the found files. Then issue the **Print** command.

Copying Found Files

You can use Find File to copy selected files from one location to another. Similarly, you can use a combination of techniques to move files. You must first copy them to their new location and then delete them from their original location.

To find and copy files, follow these steps:

1. Choose the Find File command from the File menu or the Open dialog box.

2. Select one or more files you want to copy (see "What You Need to Know About Managing Files" earlier in this section).

3. Choose the Commands button and then the Copy command. The Copy dialog box appears (see fig. 4.15).

Fig. 4.15
You can copy files to another location by using the Copy dialog box.

4. If the destination is on another drive, select the drive from the Drives list.

5. If you want to create a new directory to copy the files to, select the directory that the new directory is to be a subdirectory of, and choose the New button. Type the name for the new directory and choose OK.

6. In the Directories box, select the directory to which you want to copy the file(s). Or type the path name in the Path text box.

7. Choose OK.

Files are copied to a new location with their original name and extension. Using Find File to copy files is a good way to make backups on a floppy disk.

Deleting Found Files

To find and delete files, follow these steps:

1. Choose the Find File command from the File menu or the Open dialog box.

2. Select the files you want to delete (see "What You Need to Know About Managing Files" earlier in this section).

3. Choose the Commands button and then the Delete command. A dialog box asks you to confirm the deletion.

4. Choose Yes to delete the files, or choose No if you don't want to erase them. (Select Help to learn more about deleting files.)

Note

You cannot delete a file that is currently open. Nor can you delete a file from which you cut or copied text during the current work session.

From Here...

For information related to finding and working in documents, review the following chapters:

- Chapter 3, "Creating and Saving Documents." This chapter shows you how to save a document with Summary information, which makes the document easier to find.

- Chapter 8, "Previewing and Printing a Document." If you need to print single documents, you may want to use the File Print command. You can preview a document before printing.

For Related Information

- "Working with Multiple Documents," p. 78

- "Saving with Summary Information to Make Documents Easier to Find," p. 83

- "Controlling Printing Options," p. 232

- "Converting Files from Word Processors, Spreadsheets, or Databases," p. 1021

Chapter 5

Editing a Document

As you begin working with Word for Windows, start by gaining a solid understanding of the basics. For example, several different options exist for viewing your document: you can work very fast in normal mode, or you can slow down and zoom in to do detailed work by choosing the page layout view and enlarging it up to 200 percent. You can move around in your document in many ways, using the mouse and keyboard techniques. You should understand one of the most important principles in working with Word for Windows: Select, then do. You can move and copy text and objects from one part of your document to another, from one document to another, or even from one application to another.

Controlling Your Document's Appearance On-Screen

In Word for Windows, you can display your document in the way that best fits what you need to do. As you work, you can use normal view to see the body text as it will print, use outline view for outline expansion or contraction, and use page layout view to see the entire page exactly as it will print, including columns, headers, footers, and page numbers. You can use master document view to ease the creation and reorganization of long documents. (For more information about master documents, see Chapter 32, "Assembling Large Documents.") Full screen view can be set to display only your document text, excluding all other screen elements. In all these views you can type, format, and edit. (A sixth view under the File menu, print preview, shows thumbnail pictures of how pages will print, but you cannot edit in this view. For more information on print preview, see Chapter 8, "Previewing and Printing a Document.") The sections that follow describe the various Word for Windows views.

In this chapter, you learn these basics (and more) of editing, and you will learn many handy shortcuts such as using the following features:

- Use the AutoText feature to save time when you are entering repetitive text

- Use the AutoCorrect feature to automatically correct misspelled words as you type

- Mark a frequently visited location in a document with a bookmark

- Copy text between documents

- Work with several documents open at once

You can also add or remove screen elements, such as scroll bars and the status bar, in these views. Screen elements are controlled by selections you make with the **Tools Options** command (see the section "Modifying the Screen Display" later in this chapter).

Fig. 5.1 shows the screen modified to provide access to the menu bar and a maximum of typing space.

Fig. 5.1

The Word for Windows screen, modified to display the menu bar and a maximum of typing space.

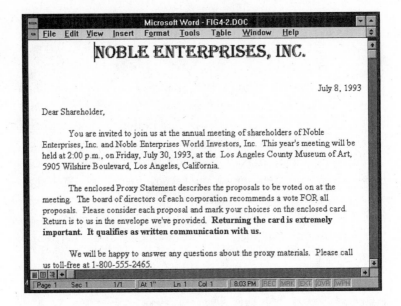

Selecting the Correct View for Your Work

The work you do will help you choose the best screen view. If you are a production typist, you may desire as much on-screen typing space as possible. If, on the other hand, you are desktop publishing and constantly using various Word for Windows tools, it might help to work in page layout view and to have certain tools easily accessible at all times. For example, you can choose the Drawing toolbar to display the Microsoft Draw tools on-screen. You can customize the view of your document as you change tasks.

The following figures show the types of views you can choose. These views include normal (fig. 5.2), full screen (fig. 5.3), page layout (fig. 5.4), outline (fig. 5.5), and master document (fig. 5.6) views.

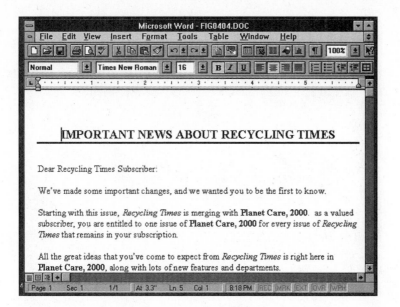

Fig. 5.2
The normal view,
which is used for
basic typing and
editing.

IMPORTANT NEWS ABOUT RECYCLING TIMES

Dear Recycling Times Subscriber:

We've made some important changes, and we wanted you to be the first to know.

Starting with this issue, *Recycling Times* is merging with **Planet Care, 2000**. as a valued subscriber, you are entitled to one issue of **Planet Care, 2000** for every issue of *Recycling Times* that remains in your subscription.

All the great ideas that you've come to expect from *Recycling Times* is right here in **Planet Care, 2000**, along with lots of new features and departments.

You don't have to do a thing, because we've taken care of all the subscription details. Sit back and enjoy reading your copy of **Planet Care, 2000**.

We're sure that you'll be delighted, because we're continuing to bring you the most up-to-date information on recycling products and techniques. You'll also find regular columns and practical tips developed by leaders in the field.

Fig. 5.3
The full screen
view, which you
use to maximize
typing space.

Fig. 5.4

The page layout
view, which shows
how your page
will appear in
print.

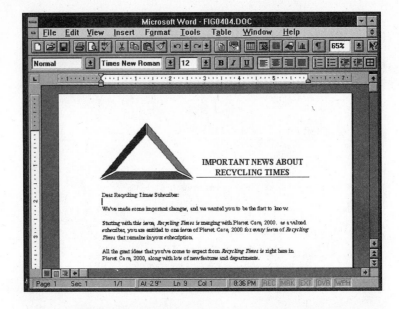

Fig. 5.5

The outline view,
which shows topic
levels of an
outline or entire
document.

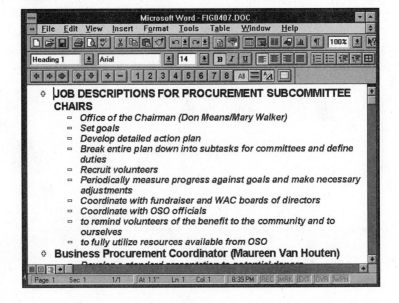

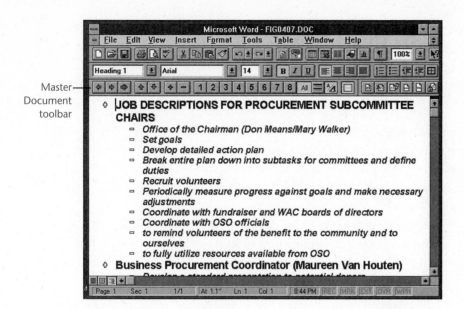

Master Document toolbar

Fig. 5.6
The master document view, which you use to assemble a long document from several shorter ones.

Everyday Word Processing

There are three ways that you can change the view. You can use menu commands, shortcut keys, or the view buttons that are at the left end of the horizontal scroll bar. If you are editing a master document and you use either the shortcut keys or the view buttons to select outline view, Word for Windows automatically places the document in master document view.

To change the view using menu commands, follow these steps:

1. Choose the View menu. Notice that the currently selected view is marked with a bullet.

2. Choose the view you want: Normal, Outline, Page Layout, or Master Document.

To change the view, you can use the following shortcut keys or view buttons:

Shortcut key	Button	View
Alt+Ctrl+N		View Normal
Alt+Ctrl+O		View Outline
Alt+Ctrl+P		View Page Layout

The Word for Windows 6 toolbar provides three Zoom buttons. The leftmost button is View Zoom Whole Page, which zooms to a view of the whole page in page layout view. The center button is View Zoom 100, which shows a full-size page in normal view (Word for Windows default view). The rightmost button is View Zoom Page Width, which zooms the page to show the full width of the text (in normal view) or the full width of the page (in page layout view).

Editing in Normal View

Use *normal view* for most of your typing and editing. In this view, which is the Word for Windows default view, you see character and paragraph formatting as they will print. Line and page breaks, tab stops, and alignments are accurate. The area outside the text body—the area containing headers, footers, footnotes, page numbers, margin spacing, and so on—does not show. You also cannot see the exact placement of such features as snaking columns, positioned paragraphs, or text wrapping around fixed paragraphs or objects.

To display normal view:

Choose the View Normal command, or press Alt+Ctrl+N.

The selected option appears with a bullet to the left of the option.

Editing in Full Screen View

 Use *full screen view* when you want to maximize the typing area. Full screen view is comparable to normal view in its display of character and paragraph formatting, line and page breaks, tab stops, and alignments. However, the title bar, the menu bar, all toolbars, the scroll bars, and the status bar are all removed from the screen in full screen view. The ruler remains. (See "Displaying or Hiding Toolbars" in Chapter 2.) A special toolbar containing only the Full button appears at the bottom of the screen to indicate that full screen view is currently displayed. Fig. 5.3 shows a document in full screen view with the Full Screen toolbar displayed.

To display the full screen view:

Choose the View Full Screen command.

To return to the previous view:

Click the Full button.

or

Press the Esc key.

When you exit full screen view, you return to the previous view. For example, suppose that you are typing in page layout view and switch to full screen view. When you click the Full button or press Esc, you will return to page layout view.

You can move the Full Screen toolbar to a new location on-screen. To move the Full Screen toolbar in full screen view, drag the title bar on the button. After you position the Full Screen toolbar where you want it, release the mouse button.

You can also resize and close the Full Screen toolbar. To resize the Full Screen toolbar, place the pointer on an edge of the toolbar until the pointer becomes a two-headed arrow. Drag the toolbar to enlarge it or make it smaller. To close the Full Screen toolbar, double-click the rectangle in its upper-left corner. To redisplay the Full Screen toolbar, press Alt+V to display the View menu, then choose the **T**oolbars command while you are in Full Screen view. Finally, select the Full Screen toolbar so that there is an X in the check box.

If you don't want the Full Screen toolbar to appear as a floating window over your document, double-click its title bar. The button will immediately move to the top of the screen and become a full-screen width toolbar.

Tip
To redisplay the Full Screen toolbar, you must first be in full screen view, then use the View Toolbars command.

Editing in Page Layout View

In *page layout view*, your document shows each page as it will appear when printed. You can scroll outside the body copy area of the page to see such items as headers, footers, footnotes, page numbers, and margin spacing. Snaking columns and text that wraps around fixed-position objects appear as they will print. Although you can see exactly how the page will print, you still can type and make formatting changes.

To change to the page layout view:

Choose the View Page Layout command, or press Alt+Ctrl+P.

Fig. 5.4 shows a document in the page layout view. Notice the vertical ruler along the left side of the screen. You can use it to change the top and bottom margins of the document. Chapter 13, "Setting the Page Layout," describes how to change margins using the ruler.

Zooming In or Out

You can use the View Zoom command to further hone your screen view.

To see more of your document, follow these steps:

1. Choose the View Zoom command.

2. When the Zoom dialog box shown in fig. 5.7 appears, select the desired magnification. The lower the magnification, the more you will see of your document on-screen.

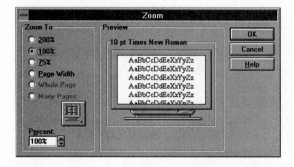

To change the screen magnification from the toolbar:

Click the Zoom button's down arrow (this is the button beside the percentage box near the right side of the toolbar). Then select the preset percentage or document size.

or

Select the Zoom button's edit box, type a new percentage between 10% and 200%, and then press Enter.

Naturally, you can zoom in for a closer look by selecting 200% magnification. This could be useful if you work with small font sizes or if you need to precisely align objects while doing desktop publishing. If none of the preset magnification options (200%, 100%, and 75%) meets your needs, you can enter your desired magnification in the Percent box. You can select within the range of 10% to 200%.

If you are working with your document in page layout view, you can use the zoom feature to see the entire page at the same time, or to view several pages at once.

To see the entire page at once, follow these steps:

1. Choose the View Page Layout command if you are not already in page layout view.

2. Choose the View Zoom command.

3. Select the **W**hole Page option.

One screen is equal to one printed page. Fig. 5.8 shows a page zoomed to Whole Page in page layout view. Whole Page view is available only in page layout view.

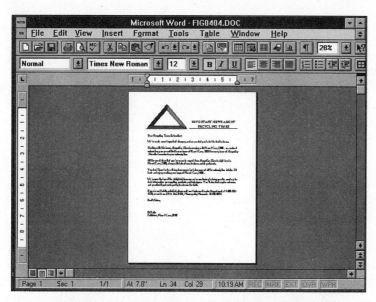

Fig. 5.8
An entire page displayed with the Whole Page zoom option.

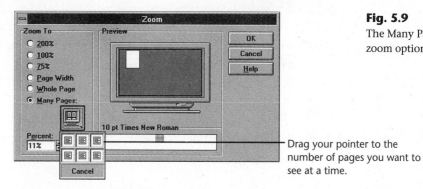

Drag your pointer to the number of pages you want to see at a time.

Fig. 5.9
The Many Pages zoom option.

Use the Many Pages option in page layout view to see and edit the layout of a group of pages.

To see more than one page at a time, follow these steps:

1. Choose the **V**iew **P**age Layout command, if you are not already in page layout view.

Tip
You can also change the number of displayed pages by increasing or decreasing the value in the Percent box in the Zoom dialog box.

2. Choose the View Zoom command.

3. Click the Many Pages icon. A grid appears (see fig. 5.9).

4. Drag across the grid to indicate how many of up to 6 pages you want displayed.

Editing in Outline View

In *outline view*, your document shows the levels of outline structure. The Outline bar appears at the top of the screen to enable you to promote and demote outline topic levels (see fig. 5.5). Outlining is described in Chapter 19, "Organizing Content with an Outline."

To change to outline view:

Choose the View Outline command or press Alt+Ctrl+O.

The horizontal scroll bar at the bottom of the screen includes three buttons for changing the view. You can choose the first to switch to normal view, the second to switch to page layout view, and the third to switch to outline view.

Modifying the Screen Display

With the Tools Options command, you can further modify the display to fit your preferences. You can, for example, request that tab and paragraph marks be displayed as special characters, that margins be displayed as dotted lines, or that horizontal and vertical scroll bars be displayed. The Options dialog box presents each option on an index tab that is pulled to the front when you click its name or index tab. The View tab contains options that change the appearance of the screen.

To change your screen's appearance, follow these steps:

1. Choose the Tools Options command. The Options dialog box appears, as shown in fig. 5.10. Select the View tab.

2. Select the appropriate options (see table 5.1).

3. Choose OK.

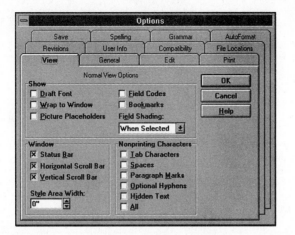

Fig. 5.10
The View tab in the Options dialog box.

Table 5.1 View Options in the Options Dialog Box

Show Group

Option	Function
Draft Font	Displays the document without formatting or graphics, to speed up editing.
Wrap to Window	Displays the document with line breaks to fit the current window width.
Picture Placeholders	Displays placeholders instead of the full pictures or graphics on-screen to speed up editing.
Field Codes	Displays field code type and switches (if any in field braces).
Field Shading	Shades fields never, always, or when selected.
Bookmarks	Displays a thick I-beam symbol in the position of each bookmark.

Window Group

Option	Function
Status Bar	Displays status bar.
Horizontal Scroll Bar	Displays horizontal scroll bar.
Vertical Scroll Bar	Displays vertical scroll bar.
Style Area Width	Controls width for the area by the left margin where the style name is displayed. (If the width is too narrow, the name is cut off.)

(continues)

Table 5.1 Continued

Nonprinting Characters Group

Option	Function
Tabs	Displays tabs as right arrows.
Spaces	Displays spaces as dots.
Paragraph Marks	Displays paragraph marks as ¶.
Optional Hyphens	Displays optional hyphens as _.
Hidden Text	Varies, depending on the particular type of hidden text.
All	Displays all marks along with text boundaries.

Figs. 5.11 and 5.12 show two screens of the same document in page layout view. Each screen uses different options in the view mode Options screen. The screen displays were modified with the Tools Options command.

Fig. 5.11
A screen displaying scroll bars but no status bars.

To quickly show all special formatting marks, click the ¶ button on the Standard toolbar or press Shift+Ctrl+* (Show All). To remove the marks, click the ¶ button again or press Shift+Ctrl+* again.

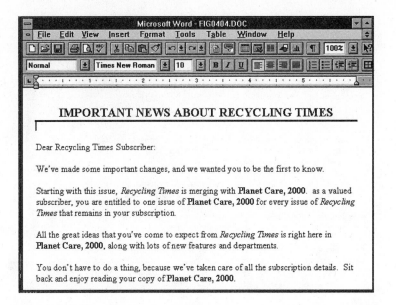

Fig. 5.12
A screen with the scroll bars and status bars hidden.

For Related Information

■ "Previewing Pages Before Printing," p. 222

■ "Setting Margins with a Precise Measurement," p. 403

■ "Creating an Outline," p. 617

■ "Creating a Master Document," p. 971

■ "Recording and Editing Macros," p. 1123

Moving in the Document

If you're familiar with word processing, you will learn to move efficiently through a Word for Windows document in no time at all. But don't stop trying to learn more, because Word for Windows provides a number of unique methods to cut your visual search time to the absolute minimum.

Moving and Scrolling with the Mouse

To relocate the insertion point by using the mouse, scroll so that you can see the location you want, and then click the I-beam pointer at the character location where you want the insertion point.

Using your mouse pointer in the horizontal and vertical scroll bars enables you to scroll the document easily so that a new area is displayed. Fig. 5.13 shows the parts of the scroll bars, which include the scroll box and page view icons. The scroll box shows the screen's location relative to the entire document's length and width. Page layout view displays page icons, which you can click to turn a page. The horizontal scroll bar includes three buttons for changing the view.

If you use a mouse, display the horizontal and vertical scroll bars so that you can scroll with the mouse. If you use the keyboard, turn off the horizontal and vertical scroll bars to have more room on the typing screen.

Fig. 5.13
The horizontal and
vertical scroll bars.

Table 5.2 lists the scrolling methods you can use with the mouse and the scroll bars.

Table 5.2 Using the Mouse and the Scroll Bars	
To move	**Click**
One line	Up or down scroll arrow
One screen up or down	Gray area above or below the scroll box in the vertical scroll bar
One page	Page icons (in page layout view)
Large vertical moves	Drag vertical scroll box to a new location
Horizontally in small increments	Right or left scroll arrow
Horizontally in relative increments	Drag horizontal scroll box to a new location in the horizontal scroll bar
Into left margin	Left scroll arrow while holding Shift (normal view); left scroll arrow (page layout view)

Don't forget to click the I-beam at the new typing location after the text you want to edit scrolls into sight. If you scroll to a new location and leave the insertion point at the old location, your typing or editing appears at the old location.

Moving and Scrolling with the Keyboard

The arrow keys ($\uparrow$, $\downarrow$, $\leftarrow$, and $\rightarrow$) and cursor-movement keys (PgUp, PgDn, Home, and End) move the insertion point as you would expect. Combine these keys with the Ctrl key, however, and they become powerful editing allies. Table 5.3 shows cursor movements you can make with the keyboard.

Table 5.3 Moving and Scrolling with the Keyboard	
To move	**Press**
One character left	Left-arrow key
One character right	Right-arrow key
One line up	Up-arrow key
One line down	Down-arrow key
One word to the left	Ctrl+left arrow
One word to the right	Ctrl+right arrow
To end of a line	End
To beginning of a line	Home
One paragraph up	Ctrl+up arrow
One paragraph down	Ctrl+down arrow
Up one window	PgUp key
Down one window	PgDn key
To bottom of window	Ctrl+PgDn
To top of window	Ctrl+PgUp
To end of document	Ctrl+End
To start of document	Ctrl+Home

Going to a Specific Page

When you need to move to a specific page number, use the Edit Go To command. The Edit Go To command works with page numbers only when the document has been paginated. (You can also use Go To to move to specific sections, lines, bookmarks, annotations, footnotes, endnotes, fields, tables, graphics, equations, or objects. Creating bookmarks is covered later in this chapter. You can read about going to other locations in your document in the section called "Moving the Insertion Point a Relative Distance.")

To move to a specific page, follow these steps:

1. Choose the Edit Go To command or press F5. The Go To dialog box, shown in fig. 5.14, appears. (Your dialog box may appear with another option selected. Click Page in the Go to What box.)

2. Type a page number in the Enter Page Number text box.

3. Choose Go To.

Fig. 5.14
The Go To dialog box.

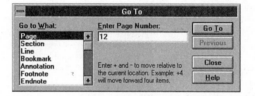

Going to a Bookmark

Bookmarks are locations in a document or sections of a document to which you assign a name. If you are familiar with Microsoft Excel or Lotus 1-2-3, bookmarks are similar to range names.

To go to a bookmark, follow these steps:

1. Choose the Edit Go To command or press F5. The dialog box shown in fig. 5.14 appears.

2. Choose Bookmark in the Go to What box. The edit box becomes Enter Bookmark Name.

3. Type the name of the bookmark or click the down arrow to the right of the Enter Bookmark Name box to see a list of bookmarks and select one of the bookmarks.

4. Choose Go To.

"Creating Bookmarks" later in this chapter describes how to create bookmarks.

Moving the Insertion Point a Relative Distance

You can move a relative distance from the insertion point's current location with the **Edit Go** To command. The move can be in increments of pages, lines, sections, footnotes, annotations, fields, tables, graphics, equations, or objects. You can even move to a location that is a certain percentage of the way through the total document. The Next and Previous options move the insertion point to the next or previous item you select.

To move a relative distance, follow these steps:

1. Choose the **Edit Go** To command or press F5 to display the Go To dialog box.

2. Choose one of the options listed in Go to **What** box.

3. Enter the number or other identifier you want to go to.

   or

   Click the **Next** or **Previous** button. (These buttons appear when appropriate.)

   or

   Enter a percentage that represents the distance you would like to move through the document.

4. Choose Go To.

5. Choose Close or press Esc.

Sections, footnotes, annotations, tables, graphics, and equations are numbered from the beginning of the document. Enter the number of the item you want to move to. You can use a plus sign (+) to indicate a relative number forward in the document or a minus sign (–) to indicate a relative number backward in the document. For example, 9 is the ninth footnote in the document, but +9 is the ninth footnote forward from the current position.

Table 5.4 shows the actions to take to move the insertion point to a particular location.

Table 5.4 Moving to a Relative Location	
To move insertion point	**Type or Select**
To page *n*	*n*
Forward *n* pages	+*n*
Backward *n* pages	-*n*
To section *n*	*n*
Forward *n* sections	+*n*
Backward *n* sections	-*n*
To line *n*	*n*
Forward *n* lines	+*n*
Backward *n* lines	-*n*
To bookmark	*name of bookmark*
To annotation	*reviewer's name, then choose next or previous*
To footnote *n*	*n*
Forward *n* footnotes	+*n*
Backward *n* footnotes	-*n*
To field	*field name*
To table *n*	*n*
Forward *n* tables	+*n*
Backward *n* tables	-*n*
To graphic *n*	*n*
Forward *n* graphics	+*n*
Backward *n* graphics	-*n*
To equation *n*	*n*
Forward *n* equations	+*n*
Backward *n* equations	-*n*
To object	*object name*
n percent through document	*n*%

n is the number of units (pages, lines, sections, footnotes, annotations, tables, graphics, equations) you want to move forward or backward from the current location.

Combine move codes and their relative numbers to move to the exact location you want. When Page is selected in the Go To **What** list, the following code, for example, moves the insertion point to the 12th line on page 15 in the 3rd section:

s3p15l12

Moving to Previous Locations

To return the insertion point to the last three locations where an action occurred, press Shift+F5. Each of the first three presses moves the insertion point to the immediately preceding place of action. Pressing a fourth time returns the insertion point to the starting location.

Pressing Shift+F5 after opening a document returns the insertion point to its location when you last saved the document.

Selecting Text

Word for Windows uses the principle common to all good Windows software: Select, then do. Whether you want to delete a word, format a phrase, or move a sentence, you must select what you want to change before choosing the command. As with other commands and features, you can use the mouse or the keyboard to select text. Many shortcuts and tips also are available for selecting text quickly.

Selecting Text with the Mouse

Selecting text with the mouse is easy and convenient. You can select any amount of text from a single character to the entire document. You also can combine mouse and keyboard selection techniques. Use whichever method or combination is effective for you.

To select a small amount of text with the mouse, follow these steps:

1. Click and hold the mouse button at the beginning of the text you want to select.

2. Drag the pointer in any direction across the text you want to select.

If the pointer touches the edge of the window as you are dragging, the window scrolls in that direction if more text exists.

To select from the current insertion point to a distant location, follow these steps:

1. Click the I-beam at the beginning of the text to relocate the insertion point.

2. Hold down the Shift key or press F8 (Extend Selection).

   While you are in Extend Selection mode, EXT appears on the status bar at the bottom of the screen.

3. Scroll the screen so that the end of text you want selected shows.

4. Click the I-beam at the end of the text.

5. Release the Shift key if you held it down in Step 2, or press Esc if you pressed F8 in Step 2.

As an alternative, position the insertion point where you want to start the selection, scroll until the end of the text is visible, and then hold down the Shift key while you click the I-beam where you want to end the selection.

To deselect text:

Click the mouse anywhere in the document window.

You can select specific units of text, such as words, sentences, lines, paragraphs, or the whole document, by using one of the techniques listed in table 5.5. Notice that clicking or dragging in the selection bar, as indicated in fig. 5.15, is a shortcut for selecting text. The selection bar is the blank vertical space on the left side of the Word for Windows document. Text never extends into this area.

If you frequently select the same block of text or need to select text under macro control, use a bookmark. Bookmarks are described later in this chapter.

Table 5.5 Selecting Blocks of Text with the Mouse	
Text to select	**Mouse action**
Word	Double-click the word
Sentence	Press Ctrl and click in sentence
Line	Click in selection bar (blank margin to left of text)

Text to select	Mouse action
Multiple lines	Click in selection bar and drag up or down
Paragraph	Double-click in selection bar
Document	Press Ctrl and click in selection bar
Rectangular block of text	Click at the top left of the rectangle you want, and then hold Alt while you drag to select a rectangular block of text

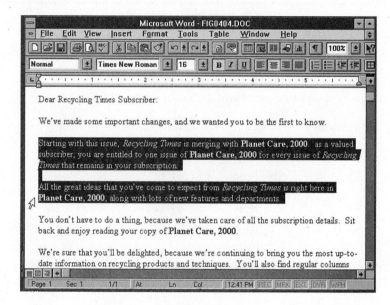

Fig. 5.15
Using the mouse to select text in the selection bar.

Selecting Text with the Keyboard

If you are a touch typist, you don't need to move your fingers from the keyboard to select text. Word for Windows enables you to select varying amounts of text quickly and conveniently.

The method most convenient for selecting text is to hold down the Shift key as you move the insertion point. Some of these key combinations are listed in table 5.6. You can select text by using Shift in combination with any move key.

Table 5.6 Selecting Text with the Shift Key	
To select	**Press**
A word	Shift+Ctrl+left- or right-arrow key

(continues)

Table 5.6 Continued	
To select	**Press**
To beginning of line	Shift+Home
To end of line	Shift+End
One line at a time	Shift+up- or down-arrow key
To beginning of document	Shift+Ctrl+Home
To end of document	Shift+Ctrl+End

You can select large amounts of text or an amount relative to your current location by combining the F8 (Extend Selection) key with the F5 (Go To) key and a move code.

To select large amounts of text with the keyboard, follow these steps:

1. Move the insertion point to the beginning of the text you want to select.

2. Press F8 (Extend Selection).

3. Press F5 (Go To).

4. Select the item you'd like to move to, and enter the number or other identifier that represents the relative location of the end of your selection, as described earlier in the section "Moving the Insertion Point a Relative Distance."

5. Choose Go To.

6. Press Esc to remove the Go To dialog box.

To select the next 20 lines in your document, for example, press F8 (Extend Selection) and F5 (Go To). Select Line and enter +20, and then choose Go To. Press Esc to exit Extend Selection mode.

Press Ctrl+5 to select the entire document. This shortcut works only with the 5 key on the numeric keypad. Num Lock can be on or off.

To select an entire table, place the insertion point inside the table and press Alt+5 on the numeric keypad. Num Lock must be off.

Another way of selecting text with the keyboard is to use the F8 (Extend Selection) key to select the text that the insertion point subsequently moves over.

To select from the insertion point to a distant location, follow these steps:

1. Move the insertion point to the beginning of the text you want to select.

2. Press F8 (Extend Selection).

3. Press one of the keys listed in table 5.7.

4. Press Esc to exit Extend Selection mode.

Table 5.7 Selecting Text in the Extend Selection Mode

To select	Press
Next or previous character	Left- or right-arrow key
A character	That character
End of line	End
Beginning of line	Home
Top of previous screen	PgUp
Bottom of next screen	PgDn
Beginning of document	Ctrl+Home
End of document	Ctrl+End

When out of Extend Selection mode, you can press any arrow key to deselect the selected text.

You also can use Extend Selection mode to select specific units of text, such as a word, sentence, or paragraph.

To select specific units of text, follow these steps:

1. Move the cursor into the text.

2. Press F8 (Extend Selection), as indicated in this chart:

To select current	Press F8
Word	2 times
Sentence	3 times
Paragraph	4 times
Section	5 times
Document	6 times

If the insertion point is in a field code when you press the F8 key, the field code and then the next larger block of text are selected. (Field codes are hidden codes used to automate Word for Windows processes. Reading Chapter 37, "Automating with Field Codes," will help you understand field codes.)

For Related Information
■ "Understanding the Basics of Fields," p. 1073

To select a unit of text smaller than the current selection:

Press Shift+F8 as many times as needed to decrease the selection.

Remember, press the Esc key, and then move the insertion point to turn off Extend Selection mode.

Deleting Text

Effective writing doesn't come easily, and good writers spend a great deal of time deleting text. Deleting is a simple operation in Word for Windows, but you should be aware of some nuances.

To delete text, first select it, using any selection technique or shortcut, and then press the Del or Backspace key. You can use one of the following key combinations to delete specific units of text:

To delete	Press
Character to right of insertion point	Del
Character to left of insertion point	Backspace
The next word	Ctrl+Del
The preceding word	Ctrl+Backspace

To make editing quick and easy with the keyboard, use the F8 or Shift key combinations to select text; then press Del or Backspace. To delete a sentence, for example, press F8 three times and then press Del. Press Esc to turn off extend mode.

Troubleshooting

Text changes its formatting when you press the Del or Backspace keys.

Word for Windows stores paragraph formatting in the paragraph mark at the end of each paragraph. If you delete the paragraph mark of a particular paragraph, it takes on the format of the following paragraph. Choose the Edit Undo command immediately to reverse the deletion and restore the paragraph formatting.

To repair the paragraph, reformat it or copy a paragraph mark from a similar paragraph and paste it at the end of the problem paragraph.

To avoid deleting a paragraph mark inadvertently, turn on paragraph marks by choosing the paragraph mark button near the right end of the Standard toolbar. Or turn on nonprinting characters by choosing the Tools Options command, View tab, and selecting the All check box in the Nonprinting Characters category.

Typing over Text

One helpful feature in Word for Windows enables you to replace selected text with your typing. Before you can replace selected text with text you type or paste from the Clipboard, you may need to select a custom setting.

To set up Word for Windows to replace selected text with new typing, follow these steps:

1. Choose the Tools Options command. The Options dialog box, shown in fig. 5.10, appears.

2. Select the Edit category by clicking its name or index tab.

3. Select the Typing Replaces Selection option.

4. Choose OK.

    Anything you type or paste replaces whatever is selected.

If you accidentally type over selected text, you can undo your mistake by immediately choosing the Edit Undo command or pressing Ctrl+Z or Alt+Backspace.

If you're in overtype mode, typing replaces the selection and text following the selection. You cannot undo overtyping, so be very careful if you're working in this mode. (You can toggle overtype mode on or off by pressing the Ins key or by selecting Overtype Mode in the Edit Settings section of the Options dialog box.)

Hyphenating Words

Hyphenation joins words used in combination or splits long words so that they can break to the next line. Splitting long words with hyphens reduces the ragged appearance of your right margin or the amount of white space between words in justified text. Word for Windows has three types of hyphens: optional, regular, and nonbreaking.

Inserting Regular and Nonbreaking Hyphens

Use regular hyphens when you want to control where a hyphen is inserted or to join two words used in combination. A regular hyphen breaks the word, when necessary, so that it can wrap at the end of a line. Use a nonbreaking (or *hard*) hyphen to join words or acronyms that you do not want broken at the end of a line. (Optional hyphens are discussed in the next section.) Table 5.8 summarizes the three types of hyphens available in Word for Windows.

Table 5.8 Types of Hyphens			
Hyphen	**Keystroke**	**Appearance**	**Function**
Regular	Hyphen	-	For words that are always hyphenated and can be split at line breaks.
Optional	Ctrl+Hyphen	⌐	To split words at the end of a line. Not displayed unless the word appears at the end of the line.
Nonbreaking	Ctrl+Shift+Hyphen	_	For words that are always hyphenated and you do not want to split at the end of the line.

Inserting Optional Hyphens Throughout a Document

The Tools Hyphenation command automatically inserts optional hyphens throughout your document. It identifies the first word in each line and, if the word can be hyphenated, Word for Windows inserts an optional hyphen. The first part of the word then is moved to the end of the preceding line of text. Optional hyphens are printed in your document only if they are needed to break a word at the end of a line.

You normally don't see optional hyphens unless they are used to break a word.

To see all optional hyphens, follow these steps:

1. Choose the Tools Options command.

2. Select the View tab.

3. Select either the All or Optional Hyphens check boxes in the Nonprinting Characters group. Optional hyphens appear as a dash with a crook.

Hyphenation should be used after you finish writing, editing, and proofreading your document.

To hyphenate a document, follow these steps:

1. Select the text you want hyphenated, or move the insertion point to the top of the document. The **Hyphenation** command hyphenates text from the insertion point to the end of the document if no text is selected.

2. Choose the Tools Hyphenation command. The Hyphenation dialog box appears (see fig. 5.16).

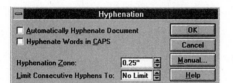

Fig. 5.16
The Hyphenation dialog box.

3. Select from among the options in the dialog box:

Option	Action
Automatically Hyphenate Document	Does not ask you to confirm each hyphenation.
Hyphenate Words in CAPS	Hyphenates words in all caps.
Hyphenation Zone	The space at the right margin within which a word can be hyphenated. To increase the number of hyphenated words and decrease right-margin raggedness, lower the number in the Hyphenation Zone box. Increase the number for less hyphenation with a more ragged right margin.
Limit Consecutive Hyphens To	Sets the maximum number of consecutive lines that can end with hyphens.
Manual	Displays each word before hyphenating in the Hyphenate At box. Use the arrow keys to move the insertion point or click where you want the hyphen to appear. Choose Yes to add a hyphen, or No to skip the word. The next word displays for hyphenation.

4. Choose OK.

5. When a dialog box appears telling you hyphenation is complete, choose OK.

Everyday Word Processing

To remove optional hyphens, choose the Edit Replace command. Type ^- in the Find What text box. Delete any contents in the Replace With text box. Choose the Find Next button to confirm each replacement or choose the Replace All button to remove all optional hyphens.

Undoing Edits

The Undo command reverses the most recent action (assuming that action can be reversed). You can undo most editing actions, such as deletions. Other actions that you can undo are Insert commands (except Insert Page Numbers), Format commands (Style), and Tools commands (except Options).

You must choose the Edit Undo command immediately after you make the mistake. If you continue working, you cannot undo your error with the Edit Undo command.

To undo the last action:

> Choose the Edit Undo command.
>
> or
>
> Press the Undo keys, Ctrl+Z or Alt+Backspace.

You can also undo any of the last several actions from the Standard toolbar. The Undo and Redo buttons keep track of the editing functions you perform. You can choose to undo or redo actions only in a series. For example, if you've just checked spelling, deleted a word, and pasted a sentence, choosing the Undo button can undo all three of those actions, the last two, or just the last one.

To undo or redo multiple actions from the toolbar, follow these steps:

1. Choose the Undo or Redo button.

2. Drag across to the number of previous actions you want to undo or redo.

3. Release the mouse button.

Inserting Frequently Used Material

Word for Windows AutoText feature is like word processing shorthand. It saves you time by storing selected text and graphics (and their formatting) that are used repeatedly. If you have a long company name that you frequently must type in documents, for example, you can abbreviate it as AutoText and insert it quickly into your document. AutoText also ensures that repetitive material is typed correctly and consistently. If you create templates for standardized documents, you should consider including AutoText entries in the templates for frequently used words, phrases, formats, or pictures. (A *template* provides a guide or pattern for creating specific types of documents. To learn more about templates, see Chapter 6, "Using Templates as Master Documents.")

AutoText is not limited to text. It can contain pictures and graphics of digitized signatures, graphic letterheads, logos, or symbols. If you frequently use a table with special formatting, you can make it an AutoText entry.

Creating an AutoText Entry

You can use the AutoText command to add text or graphics to an AutoText entry with either the Edit Autotext command or the AutoText button, available on the Standard toolbar.

To add text or graphics to an AutoText entry, follow these steps:

1. Select from your document the text, graphic, table, or combination of items that you want to add to the AutoText entry.

2. Choose the Edit AutoText command or click the AutoText button on the Standard toolbar. The AutoText dialog box appears (see fig. 5.17). Notice that the selected text is shown in the Selection box.

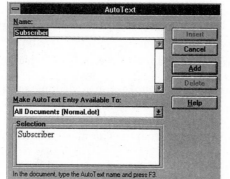

Fig. 5.17
Using the AutoText dialog box to create an AutoText entry.

3. Type an abbreviated name for the text in the Name box. Use an abbreviation you can easily remember. To change an existing AutoText entry, select the name of the entry from the list and edit it.

4. Choose the Add button.

AutoText entries belong to your current document and to a template. You can choose a template from the Make AutoText Entry Available To box. The AutoText entry will be attached to the template you select. If you choose the default, All Documents (NORMAL.DOT), your AutoText entry will be available to all future documents you create using the NORMAL.DOT template. If you choose another template, the entry will be available to future documents you create using that particular template only. When you exit Word for Windows after a session in which you created AutoText entries attached to the NORMAL.DOT template, a dialog box appears. It asks if you want to save changes that affect the global template, NORMAL.DOT. Choose Yes to keep your AutoText entries or No to discard them. You can store up to 150 entries per document with the AutoText feature.

Inserting AutoText

Once you've created an AutoText entry, it is simple to use it in your document.

To insert an AutoText entry into your text, follow these steps:

1. Position the insertion point where you want the AutoText entry to appear.

2. Type the abbreviation you gave the AutoText entry.

3. Press F3, the AutoText key, or click the AutoText button in the Standard toolbar.

When you press F3, Word for Windows replaces the AutoText abbreviation with the AutoText. (The AutoText abbreviation you type in your document must be at the beginning of a line or preceded by a space.)

If you cannot remember the AutoText abbreviation, you can access a list of AutoText entries.

To insert an AutoText entry from the Edit menu, follow these steps:

1. Position the insertion point where you want the AutoText entry to appear.

2. Choose the Edit AutoText command.

3. In the AutoText name box, type the AutoText name, or select it from the list.

4. Choose the Insert button.

Deleting AutoText

You may want to delete an AutoText entry if you no longer use it.

To delete an AutoText entry, follow these steps:

1. Choose the Edit AutoText command.

2. Type the name of the AutoText entry you want to delete in the Name box, or select the name from the list.

3. Choose the Delete button.

Using the Spike

The *spike* is a special type of AutoText entry that enables you to remove selected items from different places in your document, collect them, and insert them into your document as a group. The term *spike* comes from the old office spikes that impaled bills and invoices until they could all be dealt with at once. Contents stored in the spike are inserted just as you would insert a regular AutoText entry. You also can empty the contents of the spike and make it available to store another collection of text and graphics.

To add text or graphics to the spike, follow these steps:

1. Select the text or graphics you want to add to the spike.

2. Press Ctrl+F3, the Spike key combination. Word for Windows cuts the selected text or graphic and adds it to the spike glossary entry.

3. Select additional items in the order you want them added to the spike and repeat Step 2.

After you create a spike entry, you will see it listed as Spike in the AutoText dialog box list when you choose the Edit Autotext command.

Note that spiked selections are cut from your document, not copied.

To insert the spike's contents into your document, follow these steps:

1. Position the insertion point where you want the spike's contents to appear.

2. Press Shift+Ctrl+F3 (the Unspike key combination) to paste in the spike and remove its contents from memory.

or

Type **spike**, and then press F3 (AutoText) to paste in the spike and retain its contents so that you can paste them again.

or

Choose the Edit AutoText command. Select Spike from the list and choose Insert.

Printing AutoText Entries

For Related Information
■ "Using Templates as a Pattern for Document," p. 168

If you do not use certain AutoText entries regularly, you soon will forget what the abbreviation in the AutoText list does. To see a more complete view of each AutoText entry, including its format, print a list of AutoText entries.

To print a list of AutoText entries, follow these steps:

1. Open a document based on the template containing the AutoText entries.

2. Choose the File Print command and select AutoText Entries in the Print What list.

3. Choose OK.

Correcting Spelling Errors as You Type

Almost every typist has at least one or two typing mistakes that they make frequently. The Word for Windows AutoCorrect feature recognizes common typing mistakes and automatically substitutes the correct spelling for you. You can also use AutoCorrect to automatically type long words from an abbreviation. You could use AutoCorrect to automatically type the phrase *not applicable*, for example, everytime you type the abbreviation *na*.

The AutoCorrect feature can also change straight quotation marks into curly quotation marks, automatically capitalize the first word of every sentence, and automatically capitalize the names of days of the week.

Creating AutoCorrect Entries

You can create AutoCorrect entries in two ways. You can manually add entries using menu commands, or you can add an AutoCorrect entry while you perform a spelling check.

Adding AutoCorrect Entries with Menu Commands. To add an AutoCorrect entry through the menu commands, follow these steps:

1. Choose the Tools AutoCorrect command. Word for Windows displays the AutoCorrect dialog box (see fig. 5.18).

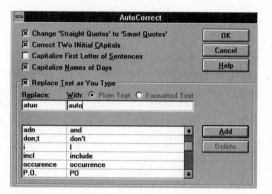

AutoCorrect
☒ Change 'Straight Quotes' to 'Smart Quotes'
☒ Correct TWo INitial CApitals
☐ Capitalize First Letter of Sentences
☒ Capitalize Names of Days
☒ Replace Text as You Type
Replace: With: ⊙ Plain Text ○ Formatted Text
atuo   auto

adn	and
don;t	don't
i	I
incl	include
occurence	occurrence
P.O.	PO

OK, Cancel, Help, Add, Delete

Fig. 5.18
Use the AutoCorrect dialog box to create new AutoCorrect entries and to set the AutoCorrect options.

2. In the Replace text box, type the misspelling that you want to have corrected automatically.

3. In the With text box, type the correct spelling of the word or phrase.

4. Choose Add to add the new entry to the list of AutoCorrect entries.

5. Choose OK.

To have AutoCorrect automatically replace the misspelling or abbreviation with the correct spelling or complete phrase, make sure that the Replace Text as You Type check box has an X in it.

Adding AutoCorrect Entries during a Spelling Check. You can also add AutoCorrect entries as you perform spelling checks on your document. To add an AutoCorrect entry during a spelling check, follow these steps:

1. Choose the Tools Spelling command to start the spelling check, if you have not already done so.

2. Choose the AutoCorrect button to add the misspelled word in the Not in Dictionary text box and the correct spelling in the Change To text box to the list of AutoCorrect entries.

3. Continue the spelling check.

See Chapter 7, "Using Editing and Proofing Tools," for more information on checking the spelling in your documents.

Using AutoCorrect

The AutoCorrect feature works automatically as you type, without any special actions on your part. AutoCorrect offers several options that you can change to suit your working style and preferences.

To change the AutoCorrect options, follow these steps:

1. Choose the Tools AutoCorrect command. The AutoCorrect dialog box appears (refer to fig. 5.18).

2. Choose among the available options in any combination. Each option is described in the following table:

Option	Result
Change 'Straight Quotes' to 'Smart Quotes'	Changes quotation marks to matched "curly" to quotes from straight quotation marks.
Correct TWo INitial CApitals	Changes the second of two capital letters at the beginning of a word to lowercase.
Capitalize First Letter of Sentences	Changes the first letter of a word beginning a sentence to uppercase.
Capitalize Names of Days	Capitalizes the first letter of names of days of the week.
Replace Text as You Type	Replaces misspelled words with correct spellings, based on the list of entries maintained by AutoCorrect.

Deleting an AutoCorrect Entry

Occasionally, you may want to remove an AutoCorrect entry because you no longer use an abbreviation, or because the AutoCorrect entry conflicts with a legitimately spelled word (it doesn't always make sense to have AutoCorrect replace misspellings such as *tow* for *two*, because *tow* is actually a correctly spelled word).

To delete an AutoCorrect entry, follow these steps:

1. Choose the Tools AutoCorrect command to display the AutoCorrect dialog box.

2. Select the entry you want to delete in the list at the bottom of the dialog box.

3. Choose the Delete button.

4. Choose OK.

Marking Locations with Bookmarks

A *bookmark* in Word for Windows is a specific named item. The item can be a portion of the document, including text, graphics, or both; or it can simply be a specific location. Spreadsheet users will readily recognize the concept—bookmarks are similar to named ranges in a worksheet.

Use bookmarks to move quickly to a given point in a document, or to mark text or graphics for efficient moving, copying, indexing, or cross-referencing. Bookmarks also are vital when you create a macro that performs an operation on a specific portion of a document.

Bookmarks can be used in calculations, much as you use a range name in a spreadsheet. The bookmark represents the location of a number, rather than the number itself. The number can change, and the calculation will reflect the new result. For example, to total an invoice, create a bookmark for each of the subtotals (job1, job2, job3, and so on). Position the insertion point where you want the total due to print. Choose Insert Field, and in the Field Codes box type an expression using the bookmark names: **=job1+job2+job3**. Choose OK. If the individual amounts change, position the cursor in the total due, press F9 to update the formula field, and the results will be updated.

Creating Bookmarks

When you create a bookmark, you assign a unique name to a location or item in the document.

To create a bookmark, follow these steps:

1. Position the insertion point at the location you want to name, or select the text or graphic you want named.

2. Choose the Edit Bookmark command or press Ctrl+Shift+F5. The Bookmark dialog box is displayed so that you can name a new bookmark, redefine an existing one, delete an existing one, or go to an existing bookmark (see fig. 5.19).

3. Type a new name for the bookmark in the Bookmark Name text box, or select from the list an existing name that you want to redefine.

4. Choose Add.

Fig. 5.19
The Bookmark
dialog box.

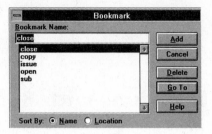

Bookmark names can be up to 40 characters long. A name must begin with a letter but can include numbers, letters, and underlines. Do not use spaces, punctuation marks, or other characters.

One way in which bookmarks can save you time is in selecting text or graphics that you frequently copy, move, or reformat. By naming the text or graphic with a bookmark, you can select the text or graphic no matter where you are in the document. Bookmarks are important when you construct macros in which a portion of text must always be found, then acted on.

You can make bookmarks visible on-screen with the Tools Options command. Choose the View category by clicking on View or its index tab. Choose Bookmarks. Open and closed brackets indicate the position of each bookmark that includes text. A thick I-beam marks the position of each bookmark that is a location only.

Editing, Copying, and Moving Bookmarked Text

The text you select and mark with a bookmark can be edited, copied, or moved. If you add text to any part of a bookmarked item, the following will result:

Add Text	Result
Between any two characters	Text is added to bookmarked text within bookmark brackets
Immediately before opening bookmark bracket	Text is added to bookmarked text
Immediately past closing bookmark bracket text	Text is not added to bookmarked
To the end of a marked table, add row	Row is included with same bookmark

You can copy a bookmarked item with the following results:

Copy Text	Result
That includes a bookmark to another document	Bookmark is inserted into the other document as well
Entire item or a portion to same document	Bookmark stays with the first item

You can delete bookmarked text with the following results:

Delete Text	Result
Part of a bookmarked item	The remainder stays with the bookmark
Entire text and bookmark and paste elsewhere	Text and bookmark moved to new location

Moving to or Selecting a Bookmark

If you want to quickly go to and select items or a location named by a bookmark, choose the Edit Bookmark command. Then select the bookmark name to which you want to move, and choose Go To. Bookmark names are listed alphabetically. To list bookmark names in the order they occur in the document, choose Sort By Location in the Bookmark dialog box.

You can also choose the Edit Go To command or press the F5 key, select the bookmark name from the Enter Bookmark Name box, and choose OK. (The Go To command is described in more detail in "Moving in the Document," an earlier section in this chapter.)

Deleting Bookmarks

You can remove bookmarks from a document. You might want to remove a bookmark if you no longer use it.

To delete a bookmark, follow these steps:

1. Choose the Edit Bookmark command.

2. Select the name of the bookmark you want to delete.

3. Choose the Delete button.

4. Choose the Close button. The bookmark is deleted and the previously marked text remains a part of the document.

For Related Information

■ "Creating Tables of Contents, Tables of Figures, and Tables of Authorities," p. 909, 917, 923

■ "Creating Cross-References," p. 951

■ "Using Bookmarks to Perform Calculations in Text," p. 631

You can undo a bookmark deletion with the Edit Undo command. You can remove a bookmark and its marked text by selecting all the text and pressing Backspace or Del. If you delete only a portion of the marked text, the rest of the text, along with the bookmark, will remain.

Moving, Copying, and Linking Text or Graphics

With Word for Windows move and copy commands, you can reorganize your thoughts to make your writing flow smoothly and logically.

Word for Windows also has the powerful capability to link text or graphics within a document or to other documents. This feature enables you to link text or graphics in one location to another location in the same document. When you change the original, the linked copy changes simultaneously.

Word for Windows incorporates *OLE*, Object Linking and Embedding. This enables you to link documents and data, such as an Excel chart, into a Word for Windows document. When you want to update the Excel chart, you can double-click the chart to bring up Excel so that the chart can be edited. The OLE features of Word for Windows are described in detail in Chapter 33, "Using Word with other Windows Applications."

Understanding the Clipboard

A section of text or a graphic being moved or copied is kept in a temporary area of memory known as the *Clipboard*. The Clipboard holds an item while it is being moved to a new location in the same or a different document. In fact, you can even move or copy text from Word for Windows to other Windows or DOS applications.

To see the contents of the Clipboard, follow these steps:

1. Press Alt+Tab until the Program Manager title appears.

2. Choose the Main group window.

3. Select the Clipboard option and double-click it or press Enter.

The Clipboard displays in its own window, as shown in fig. 5.20. The window heading shows the type of contents in the Clipboard. The Clipboard may be empty if you have not cut or copied something to it. Some commands clear the Clipboard after executing.

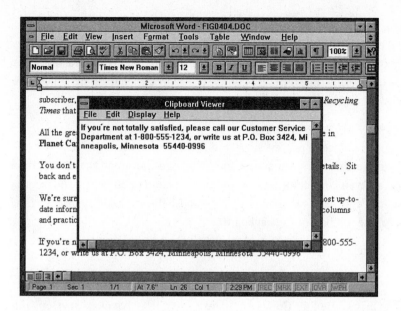

Fig. 5.20
The Clipboard
window.

To close the Clipboard:

Press Alt+F4.

Moving Text or Graphics

You probably are familiar with the concept of moving text or graphics.
A portion of text or a graphic is "cut" from the original location and then
"pasted" into a new location. The existing text at the new location moves to
accommodate the new arrival. You can perform move operations from the
menu command, from the keyboard, or from the Standard toolbar.

To move text or graphics, follow these steps:

1. Select the text or graphic you want to move.

2. Choose the Edit Cut command, press Ctrl+X, or click the Cut button on
   the Standard toolbar.

   The selection is removed from the document and stored in the Clipboard.

3. Reposition the insertion point where you want the item to reappear.

4. Choose the Edit Paste command, press Ctrl+V, or click the Paste button
   on the Standard toolbar. The selection is pasted into its new location.

If you need to accumulate and move multiple pieces of text to the same location, you will want to use the spike. The spike enables you to cut several pieces of text, move all of them to a new location, and paste them in the order they were cut. "Using the Spike," an earlier section in this chapter, describes how to use Word for Windows AutoText feature to spike your selections.

Copying Text or Graphics

Copying text uses a process similar to moving text. The difference is that copying retains the original text and inserts a duplicate in the new location. You can even copy information from one document and paste the information into another document. You can choose the copy command from the menu, the toolbar, or the keyboard.

To copy text or graphics to a new location, follow these steps:

1. Select the text or graphic you want copied.

 2. Choose the Edit Copy command, press Ctrl+C, or click the Copy button on the Standard toolbar.

   The selection is stored in the Clipboard.

3. If you want to paste into another document, open that document now. If it is already open, make it active by choosing it from the Window menu or by clicking any portion of that document if you can see it.

4. Reposition the insertion point where you want the copy to appear.

 5. Choose the Edit Paste command, press Ctrl+V, or click the Paste button on the Standard toolbar.

You can make repeated pastes of the same item until you cut or copy a new item to the Clipboard.

Shortcut keys for moving and copying text or graphics can save you time. Table 5.9 lists available shortcuts for moving and copying text or graphics quickly.

Table 5.9 Using Shortcut Keys to Move and Copy	
Keys	**Function**
Ctrl+X or Shift+Del	Cuts the selected text or graphic to the Clipboard. This shortcut works the same as the Edit Cut command.
Ctrl+C or Ctrl+Ins	Copies the selected text or graphic to the Clipboard. This shortcut works the same as the Edit Copy command. You can paste the copied material multiple times.

Keys	Function
Ctrl+V or Shift+Ins	Pastes the Clipboard's contents at the cursor's location. This shortcut works the same as **Edit Paste**.
Shift+F2	Copies the selected text or graphic one time without using the Clipboard. To use this shortcut, select what you want to copy and then press Shift+F2. The prompt Copy to where? appears at the bottom of the screen. Move the insertion point to the new location and press Enter.
Alt+Shift+up arrow	Cuts the selected paragraph and pastes it above the preceding one.
Alt+Shift+down arrow	Cuts the selected paragraph and pastes it below the following one.

Using the Mouse to Move and Copy Items

With Word for Windows, you can move, copy, and link items within a document by using only the mouse. This feature enables you to quickly move paragraphs or sentences, copy phrases, or drag pictures to new locations.

Word for Windows enables you to *frame* graphic objects or any amount of text, and then pick up the frame and place it somewhere else in the document. You can, for example, drag pictures to the center of a page and the text will wrap around them, or you can drag a paragraph to the side, enclose it in borders, and use it as a "pull-quote." To learn how to use these desktop publishing features in Word for Windows, refer to Chapter 23, "Framing and Moving Text and Graphics," and Chapter 27, "Desktop Publishing."

To move text or a graphic to a new location using the mouse, follow these steps:

1. Select the text or graphic you want to move. (If you are dragging a picture to a new location, change to page layout view before dragging.)

2. Move the mouse pointer over the selected text or graphic. The mouse pointer changes from an I-beam into a pointer over selected text or into a four-headed move pointer over graphics.

3. Hold down the left mouse button and drag to where you want the text or graphic located.

   The text pointer becomes an arrow pointer combined with a small gray box. The text insertion point appears as a grayed vertical bar. The graphic will appear as a grayed outline as it is dragged to a new location.

4. Release the left mouse button to insert the selected text or graphic.

To move text or graphics quickly, select the text or graphic you want to move. Then scroll to the screen area where you want to move the text or graphic. Hold down the Ctrl key as you click the right mouse button at the target location.

You can also use the right mouse button to cut, copy, and paste. When you click the right mouse button, a context-sensitive menu appears at the position of the insertion point (see fig. 5.21).

Fig. 5.21

A quick cut, copy, and paste menu, displayed by clicking the right mouse button.

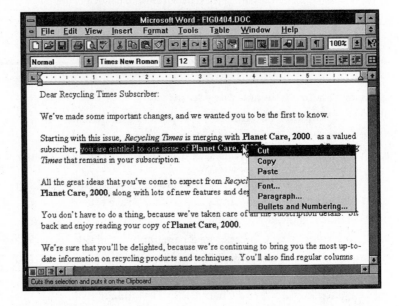

To move or copy text to a new location using the right mouse button, follow these steps:

1. Select the text or graphic you want to move or copy.

2. Place the pointer directly over the selected text and click the right mouse button to display the shortcut menu.

3. Choose Cut or Copy.

After a selection has been copied to the Clipboard (using any method), you can use the right mouse button menu to paste it in other locations.

To paste text using the right mouse button, follow these steps:

1. Position the insertion point.

2. Click the right mouse button.

3. Choose Paste.

Linking Text

A special technique exists for forging a link between the source and the destination when you copy text or an object between or within documents. The *source* is the original text or graphic that you select and copy; the *destination* is the location to which you copy the text or graphic. By linking the object as you copy it, you can automatically update the destination each time you make a change to the source. For example, a CPA might maintain a library of boilerplate paragraphs to borrow from when writing individual letters to clients advising them about tax matters. If tax laws change, the CPA can change the source (boilerplate) document and, by simply selecting a command or pressing a key, update the destination document to reflect the changes.

To copy and link text or an object, follow these steps:

1. Select and copy the text or object in the source document.

2. Position the insertion point where you want to link the text or object in the destination document.

3. Choose the Edit Paste Special command. The Paste Special dialog box appears (see fig. 5.22).

4. Choose the Paste Link option.

5. Select the type of object you want from the list in the As box.

6. Choose OK. Word for Windows inserts the linked object. This link is a field code that specifies the contents of the linked selection from the source document.

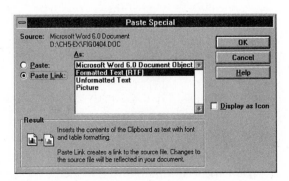

Fig. 5.22
The Paste Special dialog box.

The advantage of linking text is the ease of transferring changes between the original and the linked text. Linked text actually is created by inserting a hidden field code that links the original text to the location you indicate. An example of such a field code linking within the same document is as follows:

```
{ EMBED Word.Document.6 \s }
```

Chapter 33, "Using Word with Other Windows Applications," describes in detail links created to other documents or applications. To learn more about field codes, refer to Chapter 37, "Automating with Field Codes."

You can edit and format linked text just as you would normal text. When the linked text is updated, however, it changes to reflect the current status of the original text.

To update linked text to match any changes made to the original text, select across the entire linked text, making sure to exceed at least one end of the linked text. Press the F9 key to update all field codes within the selection. You will see the linked text update to match the changes in the original.

You can unlink linked text from its original by selecting all of the linked text and pressing Shift+Ctrl+F9. This changes the link into normal text.

To update the linked text or object (to reflect the changes made in the original), select the object to update and choose the Edit Links command. In the Links dialog box, choose Update Now. To cancel the link, choose Cancel Link.

When you update a link, Word for Windows looks for the source document in the same location where it was when you created the link. If it's not there, the link cannot be updated unless you tell Word for Windows where to find the source document. To do that, change the source document's path in the field code that is entered when you link text or an object (to see and edit the path, choose the View Field Codes command).

For Related Information

- "Moving and Positioning Frames," p. 699

- "Linking Documents and Files," p.1008

- "Understanding the Basics of Fields," p. 1073

Troubleshooting

A message appears, informs you that you don't have enough memory for a large Clipboard, and asks whether you want to discard the Clipboard.

After you cut or copy information, it is stored on the Clipboard. Discarding the Clipboard clears its contents. In most cases, the Clipboard contains the information you last cut or copied. If you no longer need this material, discard the Clipboard. If you need the information, reduce memory use and recut or re-copy the information (see the section "Improving Word for Windows Performance" in Chapter 35, "Customizing and Optimizing Word Features").

Working with Multiple Windows

You can have up to nine documents open at one time in Word for Windows. Each document occupies its own window. You can arrange these windows within Word for Windows just as you would place pieces of paper on a desk. With the Window Arrange All command, you can arrange all open windows so that each has a portion of the screen. You can even open more than one window onto the same document when you need to work on widely separated parts of the same document. And as mentioned previously, you can even cut or copy from one document and paste into another.

Viewing Different Parts of the Same Document

If you are working with a long document, you may want to see more than one part of it at the same time. This can be useful when you need to compare or edit widely separated parts of the same document.

You can expand your view in two ways. The first method is to open a new window by choosing the **Window New Window** command. This technique creates a second window containing the same document. If you are displaying a single document with the document window maximized, the title bar will appear as Microsoft Word - PAKINSTR.DOC. If you display the same document in more than one window, each document's window will show the document name followed by the window number. For example, PAKINSTR.DOC:1 and PAKINSTR.DOC:2. Fig. 5.23 shows two windows displaying the same document.

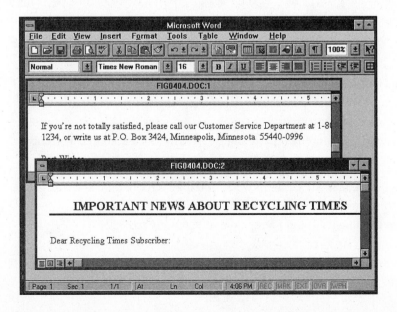

Fig. 5.23
Two windows displaying the same document, which you use to view two portions of a long document at the same time.

To close a new window, choose the document control menu by pressing Alt+ - (hyphen) and select Close. Or just press Ctrl+F4.

You also can split a window so that you can see two different areas of a document in the same window. This approach is helpful when you type lists. You can split the document's window so that the upper part shows column headings and the lower part shows the list you are typing. As you scroll the list, the headings stay in place.

To split a window with the keyboard, choose the **W**indow **S**plit command. Then press the up- or down-arrow key to position the horizontal gray line where you want the split, and press Enter. To remove the split, choose the **W**indow Remove **S**plit command.

To split the window with the mouse, look for the black bar above the up arrow in the vertical scroll bar. Drag this black bar down and release the mouse button to position the split. To remove the split, drag the black bar all the way up or down, and then release the button.

Double-click the split bar to split the screen in half. Drag the split bar to reposition the split. Double-click the split bar when the window is split, and you remove the split. (You must double-click the bar in the vertical scroll bar, not the line separating the window panes.)

Cutting and Pasting Between Documents

When you have several documents on-screen, you can move from one document window to the next in the stack by pressing Ctrl+F6 or by choosing the **W**indow command and selecting the document you want active. Press Ctrl+Shift+F6 to move to the preceding document window. You can also use the mouse to move to a specific document window—just point and click.

Displaying two or more documents on-screen at one time can be useful. If you have two similar contracts to prepare, for example, you can use **E**dit Copy to copy paragraphs from one contract, press Ctrl+F6 to switch to the other contract, and then paste the paragraphs in the second contract by choosing **E**dit **P**aste.

If you have many documents open, you may want to directly activate one. To do this, choose the **W**indow menu. At the bottom of the menu is a list of all open documents. Select the document you want active.

Working with Pages

Before you print your document, be sure that it's paginated correctly. You don't want a page to break right below a title, for example, and you may not want certain paragraphs separated onto two pages. You can let Word for Windows manage page breaks for you, or you can control them yourself.

Repaginating a Document

By default, Word for Windows repaginates whenever you make a change in your document. Word for Windows calculates how much text fits into a page and inserts a soft page break, which appears as a dotted line in normal view, or as the end of a page in page layout view. This feature is called *background repagination*. You can have Word for Windows repaginate for you, or you can repaginate manually with a command.

To change background repagination, follow these steps:

1. Choose the **T**ools **O**ptions command.

2. Select the General tab.

3. Select the **B**ackground Repagination check box to repaginate as you work and keep the page numbers in the status bar current.

4. Choose OK.

Word for Windows operates faster with background repagination turned off. To update page breaks if you have background repagination turned off, change to page layout view or print preview; Word for Windows repaginates the document.

Word for Windows repaginates automatically whenever you print, when you choose the **V**iew **P**age Layout or **F**ile Print Preview commands, or when you compile or update an index or table of contents.

Inserting Manual Page Breaks

As you work on a document, Word for Windows breaks pages every time you fill a page with text or graphics. These are automatic or *soft page breaks*. If background repagination is on, Word for Windows recalculates the amount of text on the page and adjusts soft page breaks as you work.

You can insert page breaks manually whenever you want to force a page break at a particular spot—at the beginning of a new section, for example.

Page breaks you insert are called *hard page breaks*. A hard page break appears as a heavy dotted line with the words *Page Break* centered in the line. When you insert a hard page break, Word for Windows adjusts the soft page breaks that follow. Word for Windows cannot move hard page breaks; you must adjust them yourself.

To insert a hard page break from the menu command, follow these steps:

1. Place the insertion point where you want the page break to occur.

2. Choose the Insert Break command.

3. Select the Page Break option.

4. Choose OK.

To insert a hard page break from the keyboard:

Press Ctrl+Enter.

To delete a hard page break, follow these steps:

1. Move the insertion point onto the dotted line created by the page break.

2. Press the Del key.

or

1. Place the insertion point just past the dotted line.

2. Press Backspace.

If you find a page break difficult to delete, check the Format Paragraph command for the paragraphs after the page break. If any of the Text Flow options in the Pagination group are selected (Page Break Before, Keep With Next, or Keep Lines Together), they may be causing a page break before the paragraph. Try deselecting these options.

From Here...

This chapter contains many editing shortcuts and options. Don't expect to learn them all at once. Learn what you need now, and check back occasionally to find more ways of streamlining your work. For information relating directly to editing, you may want to review the following major sections of this book:

- Chapter 7, "Using Editing and Proofing Tools," covers search and replace, checking spelling and grammar, and other proofing tools.

- Chapter 16, "Creating and Editing Tables," describes how to create and use tables.

Chapter 6

Using Templates as Master Documents

Templates can save you work and increase the consistency of any documents you create frequently. A template acts as a guide or pattern for documents of a specific type, such as form letters, letters of engagement, invoices, contracts, or proposals.

A template is a file that contains the parts of a document and features used for a specific type of document. Word for Windows templates can contain text, pictures, graphs, formatting, styles, AutoText, field codes, custom menu commands, buttons on the toolbar, shortcut keys, and macros. You can put text, formatting, and settings you use repeatedly for a specific task into a template.

When you open a new document, all the contents and features of the template are transferred to the new untitled document. The original template remains unaltered on disk.

Figs. 6.1, 6.2, and 6.3 show some examples of templates in use.

You can use templates to simplify the creation of any frequently used document. Some of the types of documents for which you will find templates useful are

- Invoices, employee records, or any standardized form

- Proposals and reports

- Memos and FAX sheets

In this chapter, you learn how to use templates to quickly produce standardized versions of formal documents or any document that you produce frequently. In this chapter, you learn about the following (and more):

- How to use and change the predefined templates provided with Word for Windows

- How to create, use, and change new templates

- How to use Wizards

Fig. 6.1
Everyday blank
documents are
based on the
NORMAL.DOT
template.

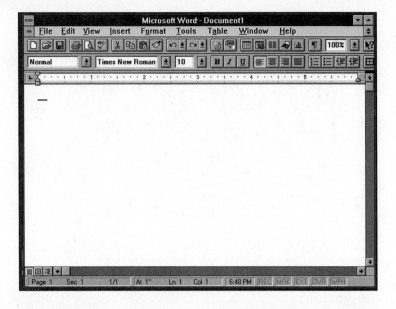

Fig. 6.2
You can base
frequently used
documents, such
as memos and
invoices, on a
custom template.

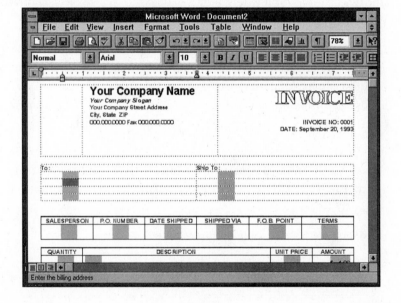

Using templates in place of preprinted forms can significantly reduce your
company's printing costs. Templates in reports ensure that all reports have
the same format and layout. You can build into the template special commands or macros needed to produce a report, such as integrating Excel charts,
so that they are readily available. When certain phrases and names are stored
in AutoText, it makes it easier to keep the spelling and formatting the same

across documents. All table and figure formatting, tables of contents, and indexes look the same from report to report because they are created and formatted with macros and styles attached to the template.

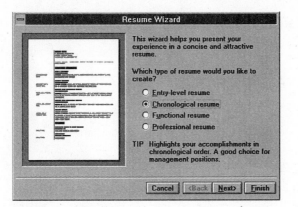

Fig. 6.3
Template Wizards guide you through document creation for documents such as meeting agendas, résumés, brochures, and newsletters. Template Wizards help you also with features such as tables.

Many companies use templates to prepare interoffice memos and FAX cover letters. The headings and document formatting are predefined and, therefore, are standardized. ASK or FILLIN fields prompt the operator for entries. The DATE and AUTHOR fields can be used to enter automatically the current date and name of the operator.

Word for Windows comes with several predesigned templates that you can use as a basis for your own business documents, including press releases, FAX cover sheets, and reports. You can modify the Word for Windows templates to meet your needs, or you can create your own templates from scratch.

What You Need to Know About Templates

Templates are normally saved by Word as files with the DOT file extension in the TEMPLATE subdirectory under the directory that contains Word. DOT files in this subdirectory appear in the Use Template list of the New dialog box. This makes templates readily accessible regardless of which directory you are working in.

All documents in Word for Windows are based on a template. Even the default new document is based on a template, NORMAL.DOT. The NORMAL.DOT file contains the formatting and default settings for the new document you open when you choose File New.

Styles, AutoText, macros, and other items stored in the NORMAL.DOT template are available to all documents at all times. Because the information stored in NORMAL.DOT is available to all documents all the time, they are said to be available *globally*.

Templates can contain the following:

- Body text, headers, footers, footnotes, and graphics with formatting
- Page and paper layouts
- Styles
- AutoText entries
- Predefined or custom macros
- Custom menus and commands
- Tools
- Shortcut keys

When you create a document based on a template, the document opens to show the body text, graphics, and formatting contained in the template. All the styles, macros, tools, and so on that are in the template are available for use with the document.

After you create a document, you can attach the document to a different template so that you can use the features (but not the text or page formatting) found in that template. Later sections of this chapter show you how you can transfer features between templates so that a style or macro you create in one template can be transferred into another template.

Using Templates as a Pattern for Documents

Most people use only a few templates. The templates they use may include the NORMAL.DOT template for everyday work or one of a few custom templates for use in memos or reports. Many people use the NORMAL.DOT template to create the blank document with which they normally work. You should examine the predefined templates that come with Word, because you might find one appropriate to your particular task.

Opening a New Document

Opening a new document is easy. To open a new document, follow these steps:

1. Choose the File New command. Notice that the NORMAL.DOT template (shown in the list as *Normal*) is already selected in the Template list (see fig. 6.4).

Fig. 6.4
Most documents are based on the NORMAL template.

2. Select a template name from the Template list. The Description box shows the type of document for which the template is designed.

3. Choose OK.

To open a new document based on NORMAL.DOT using a tool, click the New Document button in the Standard toolbar, or press Ctrl+N.

Using Word's Predefined Templates

Word for Windows comes with predefined templates you can use to create many typical business documents. Many of the templates contain custom features such as special tools, formatting styles, custom menus, AutoText, and macros for frequently used procedures. The predefined templates that come from Microsoft are described in table 6.1.

Table 6.1 Predefined Word Templates

Template	Description
Normal	Default document template
Brochur1	Classic brochure

(continues)

Everyday Word Processing

Table 6.1 Continued	
Template	**Description**
Dirctr1	Classic directory
Faxcovr1	Classic FAX cover sheet
Faxcovr2	Contemporary FAX cover sheet
Invoice	Standard invoice
Letter1	Classic letter
Letter2	Contemporary letter
Letter3	Typewriter letter
Manual1	Classic instruction/operator's manual
Manuscr1	Classic manuscript
Manuscr3	Typewriter manuscript
Memo1	Classic memo
Memo2	Contemporary memo
Memo3	Typewriter memo
Present1	Classic presentation
Presrel1	Classic press release
Presrel2	Contemporary press release
Presrel3	Typewriter press release
Purchord	Standard purchase order
Report1	Classic report
Report2	Contemporary report
Report3	Typewriter report
Resume1	Classic résumé
Resume2	Contemporary résumé
Resume4	Elegant résumé
Thesis1	Classic thesis
Weektime	Weekly time sheets

Storing Summary Information About a Document. Each Word document can have summary information attached. This summary information can remind you about the source or contents of a document. You can use Word's File Find File command also to search for key words in the summary. This can be very helpful if you forget a file's name or need a list of all files that have similar key words in the summary.

If you want to attach summary information to the document file, choose File New, then choose the Summary button from the New dialog box and complete the Summary Info dialog box (see fig. 6.5). When you save the document you have opened, the summary information is saved with the file. You can edit the summary information for the active document by choosing the File Summary Info command.

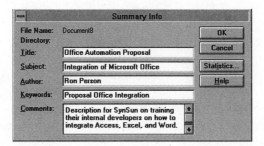

Fig. 6.5
Saving summary information with a file makes the file easier to find later.

> **Note**
>
> If you frequently use the same templates, you can save yourself time by creating a tool or menu command that opens a new document from each of these templates. Use the macro recorder to record a macro when you open a template. Assign this macro to a button on a toolbar or to a menu command.

Opening a Template on Startup. You can make Word open a specific template when it starts. To do this, open the NORMAL.DOT template. With the NORMAL.DOT template active, you will need to record a macro. Give the macro the name AutoExec. While the macro recorder is on, open a document based on the template you want. Save the NORMAL.DOT template. The next time you start Word, it automatically opens the document based on the template you specified.

If you want to load multiple templates on startup, so that the macros and styles in those templates are available, copy the DOT file for each template into the STARTUP subdirectory located under Word's directory. The STARTUP directory is the default directory used for startup files. If you do not have a STARTUP directory, choose the Tools Options command and select the File Locations tab. Select the Startup directory in the File Types list, and then choose Modify to set a new directory as the startup directory.

Opening Word for Windows 2 Templates. Templates created for Word for Windows 2 can be opened and used in Word for Windows 6. When you close a document based on the old template, Word for Windows automatically saves the document in Word 6 format. If you edit the old template, you are asked if you want to save the template in the new Word for Windows 6 format when you save the template file.

Word normally looks to the TEMPLATE directory found underneath the WINWORD directory when it searches for the templates used in the New dialog box. If you need to organize your disk so that Word looks to a different directory for its templates, choose the Tools Options command and select the File Locations tab. Select the Template directory in the File Types list, and then choose Modify to set a new directory as the template directory.

Opening Templates Troubleshooting

The template on which this document was originally based is no longer available.

It may have been erased, renamed, or moved to a different directory. You cannot use the macros, AutoText, or toolbars that were assigned to that template. You do, however, still have the styles that were in that template.

You can attach another template to the document to gain the use of the other template's features by opening the document and choosing the File Templates command. Follow the description in the section titled "Using Information from Another Template" later in this chapter.

Word's predefined templates do not appear in the Template list of the New dialog box.

If Word's predefined templates do not appear in the list, the templates may not have been installed when you installed Word for Windows. You can rerun the installation procedure and choose to install only the templates.

A custom template does not appear in the Use Template list of the New dialog box.

Templates use a DOT extension and are stored in the template directory normally found under the directory containing the Word for Windows program, WINWORD.EXE. The directory to which Word normally looks for template files is C:\WINWORD6\TEMPLATE.

Adding Additional Features with Add-Ins

Add-ins are a way of extending the capabilities of Word for Windows 6. An add-in program is not part of Word, but behaves as if it is a part of Word for Windows. An add-in program may add new menu choices to Word for Windows, or add new toolbars to Word. Like a template, the add-in program remains available until you exit Word. Add-in programs for various tasks are available from a variety of third-party vendors. For specific information about using a particular add-in, consult the documentation provided with the add-in program.

Add-in programs end with the file extension WLL. Follow the installation instructions provided with the add-in program for help in installing an add-in.

Loading Add-Ins

To load an add-in program, follow these steps:

1. Choose the File Templates command. The Templates and Add-ins dialog box appears.

2. Choose the Add button in the Global Templates and Add-ins section of the Templates and Add-ins dialog box. The Add Template dialog box appears.

3. Choose Word Add-ins in the List Files of Type list box.

4. Select the add-in you want from the File Name list. If the add-in you want is not listed, use the Directories and Drives lists to view other directories and disk drives. (If you don't know the name of the add-in, consult the documentation provided with your add-in program.)

5. Choose OK.

Word for Windows loads the add-in program.

Loading Add-Ins Automatically. You can also load add-ins automatically, every time Word for Windows starts. To load an add-in program on startup, simply copy the add-in WLL file into the STARTUP subdirectory located under Word's directory. The STARTUP directory is the default directory used for startup files. If you do not have a STARTUP directory, choose the Tools

Options command and select the File Locations tab. Select the Startup directory in the File Types list, and then choose the Modify button to set a new directory as the startup directory.

Removing Add-Ins

After an add-in is loaded, it remains available until you quit Word or explicitly remove the add-in. You might want to remove an add-in in order to make more system memory available.

To remove an add-in, follow these steps:

1. Choose the File Templates command. The Templates and Add-ins dialog box appears.

2. Select the add-in you want to remove in the Global Templates and Add-ins list.

3. Choose the Remove button. The add-in is unloaded.

4. Choose OK.

Using Wizards to Guide You in Creating Documents

Word comes with some templates that guide you through the creation of a document. These special templates are called *Wizards*.

When a Wizard template opens, it displays dialog boxes, messages, and graphics that tell you how to fill in a template or complete forms. Word comes with several Wizards that are very helpful.

Creating Documents with Wizards

Starting a Wizard is like opening any other new document. You choose File New and select a Wizard template from the Template list. Templates that contain Wizards show the word *Wizard* in their names.

Wizards that Come with Word

Wizards have you fill in information inside dialog boxes. They use your responses to fill in forms or prepare formatting. Some Wizards are simple and prepare simple documents such as FAX cover letters. Other Wizards are more complex and create newsletters, brochures, or calendars. Table 6.2 lists the Wizards supplied with Word for Windows.

Table 6.2 Predefined Word Wizards	
Wizard	**Description**
Agenda Wizard	Helps you create meeting agendas
Award Wizard	Helps you create customized award certificates
Calendar Wizard	Helps you create calendars for week, month, or year
Cv Wizard	Helps you create a résumé (curriculum vitae)
Fax Wizard	Helps you create customized FAX cover sheets
Legal Wizard	Helps you create legal pleading papers
Letter Wizard	Helps you create prewritten or customized letters
Memo Wizard	Helps you create customized memos
Newsltr Wizard	Helps you design and lay out a newsletter
Resume Wizard	Helps you create a customized résumé
Table Wizard	Helps you create and format tables

Changing a Template

You may need to change a template as your work changes. As you work with a template, you may discover styles or macros that would be useful if added to the template. Or as your business changes, the text content of the template may need to change.

You can modify templates to incorporate the specific text, graphics, styles, formatting, AutoText, and macros you need for your documents. This means you can modify templates to fit your needs, even if the template came with Word or was given to you by another Word user.

The templates that come with Word for Windows are designed to handle many daily business transactions; however, you might need to modify the template to fit your business formats more closely or to add AutoText and styles specific to your needs. For example, you might want to use the Memo1 template for creating interoffice memos, but the template might not include AutoText entries for words or phrases used in your department. You can modify Memo1 to include your own AutoText entries, change the format to fit your needs, and edit the boilerplate text.

What You Need to Know About Changing a Template

After you make changes to a template, all new documents using that template include the modifications or edits you've made to the template. Documents created from the template before it was modified, however, have access to only some of the changes to the template. For example, styles, text, graphics, page formatting, or print formatting added to the template do not transfer to existing documents. Changes in a template that are available to documents that were created from the earlier template are

- AutoText entries

- Macros

- Menus

- Shortcut keys

- Toolbar buttons

Changing a Template

If you have many changes to make to a template, it might be easier to use one of the methods described later in this chapter to create a new template from scratch or to use an existing document as the basis for the new template. When you have to make just a few modifications to a template, however, it is easier to modify the template with one of the following methods.

To change an existing template, perform the following steps:

1. Choose the File **O**pen command, click the Open button, or press Ctrl+F12. The Open dialog box appears (see fig. 6.6).

2. Select the TEMPLATE directory or the directory containing your template from the Directories list.

3. Select Document Templates (*.dot) from the List Files of Type list.

4. Choose OK.

5. Change the template by modifying text or graphics; changing formats; redefining styles or AutoText entries; or adding or changing shortcut keys, buttons, or macros.

6. Choose the File **S**ave command to save the template back to the same directory with the same name.

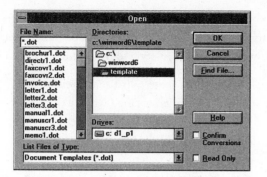

Fig. 6.6
Select the template
file you want to
modify from the
Open dialog box.

Everyday Word Processing

Setting Default Formats in the Normal Template

Word for Windows bases its default settings for a new document on a template stored in the file NORMAL.DOT. All documents you create by choosing File New and pressing Enter are based on the Normal template. Settings, such as the style, font type and size, margins, and other formats, are stored in this file.

You can change default settings for new documents in two ways. In the most powerful method, you can set new defaults for styles, AutoText, page formatting, and so on by changing the setting in the NORMAL.DOT template. If you need to change only the default for a font, style, or page layout, you can change them while editing a document using the method described in a later section, "Changing Template Features from Within a Document."

If you want to change any of the default formatting or features controlled by a template, open the NORMAL.DOT template and change the appropriate format or settings. If you want to change the appearance of the normal body text, change the Normal style. Save the NORMAL.DOT template back to the same directory with the same name.

Making Template Features Available to All Documents

If you have macros, buttons, styles, or AutoText that you want to be available to all documents, put them in the NORMAL.DOT template. A conflict might occur if the active document is based on a template that has styles, macros, or AutoText that has the same names as those in the NORMAL.DOT template.

Whenever there is a conflict between styles, macros, or AutoText with the same name, the template that created the document takes priority over the NORMAL.DOT template. For example, if your report is based on the

REPORT.DOT template that contains a style named Bulleted List, and the NORMAL.DOT template also contains a style named Bulleted List, your document will use the Bulleted List style found in REPORT.DOT.

Changing Template Features from Within a Document

Default settings are format settings specified when a document opens—settings such as which font and font size are used when you first begin to type. You can change default settings in two ways: You can open and modify the template that creates a type of document, or you can change some formats within a document and transfer the changes back to the template so that the changes become new defaults.

The types of changes that can be transferred from a document back to its template are found in the Format Font, Format Style, and Format Page Setup commands.

To transfer a format change from the document back to the template, follow these steps:

1. Open a new or existing document based on the template you want to change.

2. Choose the Format Font, Format Style, or Format Page Setup command, depending on the type of default change you want made.

3. If you choose Format Style, choose the Modify button.

4. Select the tab for the type of formatting you want changed, then select the formatting options you want to define as default settings on the template.

5. If you change the font or page setup, choose the Default button. A dialog box appears asking you to confirm the update to the template.

   or

   If you change or add a style, select the Add to Template check box.

6. Choose Yes or press Enter to update the document's template file with the selected default settings.

You may be able to save yourself some work when modifying a template by copying existing styles, AutoText, buttons, or macros from another template. Use the Organizer to copy template items. The Organizer is described in each chapter that deals with a feature that can be transferred. It is covered lightly in the "Using Information from Another Template" section later in this chapter.

Creating a New Template

Although Word for Windows comes with many predesigned templates, you probably have many documents or forms that do not fit any of the templates. You can create a completely new template, or you can create a template based on an existing document or template.

Creating a New Template Based on an Existing Template

You can create a template in much the same way you create any document. If you have a template that already has most of the features that you want, you can save time by creating the new template based on the existing one.

To create a new template based on an existing template, follow these steps:

1. Choose the File New command.

2. Select the New Template option.

3. Select from the Template list the template on which you want to base the new template. Select the Normal template if you want to start with a blank template and the default settings.

4. Choose OK or press Enter. Note that the title bar now displays *Template* rather than *Document*.

5. Lay out and format the template as you would a document. Include text that will not change between documents. The template can contain text and graphics you want to appear on all documents, formatting and styles, AutoText entries, macros, new commands, shortcut keys, and new toolbar buttons.

6. Choose the File Save command.

7. Enter a name for the template in the File Name box. The extension DOT is assigned to templates. All document template files are stored in the directory specified for Word templates.

8. Choose OK or press Enter.

Creating a Template Based on an Existing Document

You already might have a document that contains most of the text, formatting, and settings you want to use in a template. Rather than re-create the document on a template, Word for Windows enables you to create a template based on the existing document.

To create a template based on an existing document, follow these steps:

1. Choose the File Open command and open the document that you want to use as the basis for a template.

2. Modify this document by editing text and adding graphics, styles, AutoText, buttons, or macros that you want to be in the template.

3. Choose the File Save As command.

4. Select Document Template from the Save File as Type pull-down list.

5. Type the template's file name in the File Name box. You do not have to type the DOT extension. The template file automatically is saved to the directory that contains templates.

6. Choose OK.

> **Note**
>
> Templates are a key to creating forms that you use repeatedly. Word has the ability to create forms that include edit fields, drop-down lists, and check boxes. Because forms are used over and over, you will want to save forms as templates. Users can easily open the form template using the **File New** command. You don't have to worry about the form being accidentally changed, because the original template stays on disk and the user works with a copy of the form.

Using Information from Another Template

If you are working on a document and decide you want to have access to all the features in another template, you can attach that template to the document. Attaching a new template does not change the existing document text, but it does change specified settings, such as AutoText, macros, menu commands, margins, shortcut key assignments, and buttons.

To attach another template to a document, follow these steps:

1. Open the document to which you want to attach a template.

2. Choose the File Templates command. The Templates and Add-ins dialog box is displayed. Notice that the Document Template edit box displays the name of the template currently attached to the document (see fig. 6.7).

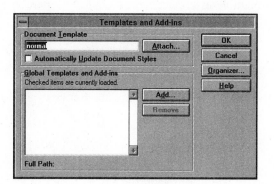

Fig. 6.7

Use features from other templates by attaching a different template containing those features to a document.

3. Choose the Attach button to display the Attach Template dialog box (see fig. 6.8).

4. Select the template in the File Name box.

5. Choose OK. The Attach Template dialog box closes.

6. Choose OK.

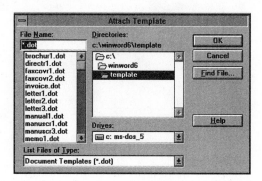

Fig. 6.8

Choose from the Attach Template dialog box the template to which you want to attach the document.

Transferring Template Contents Using the Organizer

As you work, you may find that you need a style, macro, toolbar, or AutoText that is stored in another template. Or you may develop a style, macro, toolbar, or AutoText in one document and want to use it with other documents. After you learn how to use the Organizer, you'll be able to transfer features between templates so that they are available wherever you need them.

To transfer a style, macro, toolbar, or AutoText from one template to another, follow these steps:

1. Open a document based on the template that you want to receive the feature.

2. Open the document based on the template that you want to send the feature from. If you want to transfer a style, open a document containing the style. If you want to transfer a macro, toolbar, or AutoText, open a document based on a template that contains the macro, toolbar, or AutoText.

3. Choose the File Templates command, then choose the Organizer button. The Organizer, shown in fig. 6.9, is displayed.

Fig. 6.9

Use the Organizer to transfer styles, AutoText, toolbars, or macros between templates and documents.

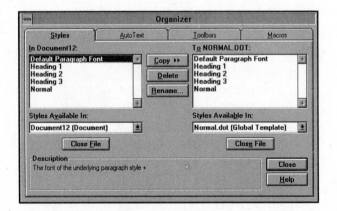

4. Select the tab for the type of feature you want to transfer.

5. Select from the lists on the left the document or template that contains the feature, then select the feature from the top left list.

6. Select from the lists on the right the document or template that will receive the feature.

7. Choose the Copy button.

8. Repeat Steps 4 through 7 to transfer additional features or choose Close to close the Organizer.

Transferring styles, macros, toolbars, or AutoText is described in more detail in the specific chapters that discuss those features.

From Here...

For information relating directly to how templates can help you and the important features that you can customize specific to a template, please review the following chapters:

- Chapter 11, "Formatting with Styles," for information on using styles and how to name frequently used styles for consistency and ease of use.

- Chapter 13, "Setting the Page Layout," for information on page and paper formatting.

- Chapter 36, "Customizing the Toolbar, Menus, and Shortcut Keys," for information on customizing Word for Windows menus and toolbars to make it easier to select editing or viewing options that you use frequently.

- Chapter 37, "Automating with Field Codes," for information on using field codes in a template to make it easier to produce documents that you create frequently and to automatically insert data in your documents.

- Chapter 38, "Recording and Editing Macros," to learn how to use macros in templates to automate the production and formatting of your documents.

Chapter 7

Using Editing and Proofing Tools

By now you're probably familiar with most of the basics of Word for Windows—how to create, edit, and save your documents. You can also use many tools to ease text entry, ensure accuracy, and make sure your document reads well.

With Word for Windows, you can use the Find and Replace feature to change text, formatting, special characters, and styles.

Before you print your document, check its spelling. Your eyes are trained to correct obvious spelling errors when you read them. However, you can still overlook a mistake when you proof a document. Use the spelling checker to catch mistakes you missed and to correct spelling when you make an error. Use Word for Windows grammar checker to correct faulty sentence construction and style. You can use the thesaurus to find just the right word, or define a term about which you're unsure.

If you need to know how many words your document contains, use the Word Count feature to gather information about the number of words, lines, paragraphs, and more.

The following two figures show a document before (fig. 7.1) and after (fig. 7.2) it was checked for spelling and grammar. The thesaurus was also used to improve some of the language.

In this Chapter, you learn to do the following:

- Search and replace for text items

- Identify special formating characters

- Check your grammar and spelling

Fig. 7.1

This rough draft of a document has not been revised using Word for Windows editing and proofing tools.

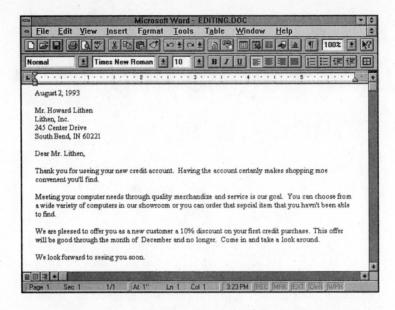

Fig. 7.2

You can polish your writing with the editing and proofing tools.

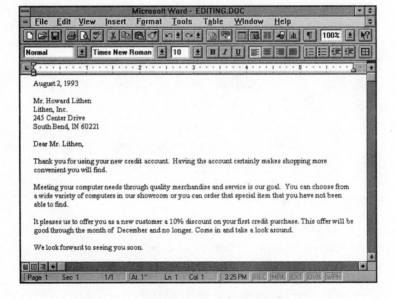

All the editing and proofing tools combine to help you hone the language of your documents. Use them for the following:

■ Catch typos and spelling errors.

■ Make sure that your grammatical usage fits the type of document.

■ Use the thesaurus to find the right replacement word. Then, use the Replace feature to exchange the new word for the original word throughout your document.

Using Find and Replace

Being able to find and replace text, formatting, styles, and special characters is an important time-saver. (This feature helps ensure that you catch every occurrence of whatever you need to find or replace.) The Edit Find command finds and selects the text, formatting, style, or special character you specify, enabling you to easily locate a certain phrase or a particular type of formatting. The Edit Replace command enables you to find and replace text, formatting, and characters. You can replace items selectively or globally (changing your entire document all at once).

Finding Text

With Word for Windows Find feature, you can quickly locate a specific word or phrase or a special formatting character in a document that is many pages long. The text can be as brief as a single letter or as long as a sentence containing up to 256 characters. You also can search for special characters, such as tabs, page breaks, line numbers, footnotes, or revision marks within your document. Alternatively, you might want to search for a particular format or style.

To find text (containing as many as 256 characters), empty space, or special characters, follow these steps:

1. Choose the Edit Find command or press Ctrl+F. The Find dialog box appears (see fig. 7.3).

Fig. 7.3
Use the Find dialog box to search through your document quickly.

2. In the Find What text box, type the text or special characters for which you want to search. (Refer to table 7.2 in the section "Finding and Replacing Special Characters" for a list of special characters.)

The text scrolls to the right if you enter more text than will fit in the box. You can enter as many as 256 characters.

3. Select one or more of the options in the Find dialog box:

Option	Effect
Search	Determines the direction of the search. Down searches from the insertion point to the end of the document or selection. Up searches from the insertion point to the beginning of the document or selection. All searches the entire document or selection.
Match Case	Matches the text exactly as you have typed it— including capital letters. Capitalization with Small Caps or All Caps is not considered: Word examines the case of the letters as they were originally typed. Do not select this option if you want to find all occurrences of the text regardless of case.
Find Whole Words Only	Finds whole words only, not parts of words. Do not select this option if you want to find all occurrences of the text.
Use Pattern Matching	Uses special search operators and expressions with which to search. See the section "Finding and Replacing Special Characters" later in this chapter.
Sounds Like	Matches words that sound alike, but that are spelled differently, such as *seize* and *sees*.
Format	Displays the Format options, including Font, Paragraph, Language, and Style. Depending on your selection, the dialog box displays the tab that contains the various types of formatting for each formatting option. (For more information on these options, refer to the section "Finding and Replacing Formats" later in this chapter.)
Special	Displays the Special options to enable you to include special codes, such as Paragraph Mark, Tab Character, and others in the search text (see fig. 7.4). You can also type these codes. (See "Finding and Replacing Special Characters" later in this chapter.)
No Formatting	Removes any formatting codes displayed beneath the text box from a previous find operation (unless you want these codes to affect the current search).

4. Choose Find Next button to begin the search.

or

Choose the **R**eplace button to display the Replace dialog box.

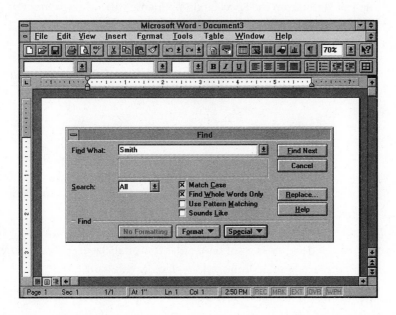

Fig. 7.4

You can include special codes with search text.

Word for Windows finds the first occurrence of the text or special character, and then moves to and selects it. The dialog box remains open so that you can immediately continue to search for other occurrences of the text or special character by choosing Find Next again.

When you're finished with your search, close the Find dialog box by choosing Cancel or pressing Esc. For example, close the Find dialog box if you want to edit the found text.

After you've closed the Find dialog box, you can repeat the search by pressing **Shift+F4**. Alternatively, you can choose the Edit Find command again. Then, choose Find Next.

If Word for Windows cannot find the text, the program displays a dialog box which indicates that Word has finished searching the document. Choose OK and try again.

Tip
You can also
display the Find
dialog box by
pressing Ctrl+F.

If you're unsure of spelling, try using *special characters* in place of letters you're not sure about. If you want to find *Smith*, for example, but aren't sure whether it's spelled with an *i* or a *y*, search for *Sm^?th*. You can insert the question mark by typing ^? (the caret character and the question mark) or by choosing Any Letter from the Special pop-up menu. Alternatively, you can search for part of a word, such as *Smi*. (Make sure that the Match Whole Word Only check box in the Find dialog box is turned off.)

If you want to search for or replace text in only a portion of your document, select that portion. Then follow the general instructions for finding or replacing.

Replacing Text

Besides searching for text, formatting, or special characters, you also can replace them automatically. If you finish your document and realize that *Mr. Smith* really should have been *Ms. Smythe*, you can use a simple menu command to search for every occurrence of the incorrect spelling and replace it with the correct version. Or if your typist underlined every title in a long list of books and you decide you want book titles to be italicized, you can search for every occurrence of underlining and replace it with italic.

Replacing text works much the same way as finding text. The only major difference is an additional Replace With text box in which you enter the text to replace the text you find. The Replace dialog box enables you to confirm each replacement. Alternatively, you can replace all occurrences of the text with a single command.

To replace text:

1. Choose the Edit Replace command or press Ctrl+H. The Replace dialog box appears (see fig. 7.5).

2. In the Find What text box, type the text you want to replace.

3. In the Replace With box, type the new text.

4. Select one or more of the options in the Replace dialog box:

Option	Effect
Search	Determines the direction of the search. Down searches from the insertion point to the end of the document or selection. Up searches from the insertion point to the beginning of the document or selection. All searches the entire document or selection.

Option	Effect
Match Case	Matches the text exactly as you have typed it—including capital letters. Capitalization with Small Caps or All Caps is not considered: Word examines the case of the letters as they were originally typed. Do not select this option if you want to find all occurrences of the text regardless of case.
Find Whole Words Only	Finds whole words only, not parts of words. Do not select this option if you want to find all occurrences of the text.
Use Pattern Matching	Uses special search operators and expressions with which to search. See the section "Finding and Replacing Special Characters" later in the chapter.
Sounds Like	Matches words that sound alike but are spelled differently, such as *seize* and *sees*.
Format	Displays Format options, including Font, Paragraph, Language, and Style. Depending on your selection, the dialog box displays the tab that contains the various types of formatting for each formatting option. (For more information on these options, refer to the section "Finding and Replacing Formats" later in this chapter.)
Special	Displays the Special options to enable you to include special codes, such as Paragraph Mark, Tab Character, and others in the search text (refer to fig. 7.4). These codes can also be typed. See "Finding and Replacing Special Characters" later in this chapter.
No Formatting	Removes any formatting codes displayed beneath the text box from a previous find operation (unless you want these codes to affect the current search).

5. Choose the Find Next or Replace All button.

If you want to confirm each change, choose Find Next. When an occurrence of the text is found, choose the Replace button to change the text or the Find Next button again to continue the search without altering the selected occurrence. (If the dialog box is covering up the selected text, you can move this box by dragging its title bar. Alternatively, you can press **Alt**, **space bar**, **M**. Then, use any arrow key and press Enter when you're finished.)

If you want to change all occurrences of the specified text without confirmation, choose the Replace All button.

Fig. 7.5

Use the Replace dialog box to change one word or phrase to another throughout your document.

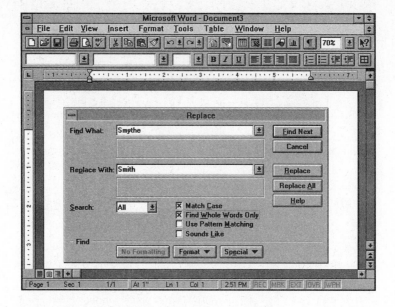

6. Choose Cancel to return to the document.

If Word for Windows cannot find the text, you see a message dialog box which indicates that Word has finished searching the document. The search item was not found.

If you want to search for or replace text in only a portion of your document, select that portion. Then follow the general instructions for finding and replacing.

To cancel a search-and-replace operation, press **Esc**.

Choosing the Replace All button saves time, but can be risky. You might want to start by confirming the first few replacements. When you are sure that you want to change all remaining occurrences of the text, choose Replace All. If you select Replace All and then realize you made a mistake, immediately choose the Edit Undo command.

Unless you specify otherwise, Word for Windows applies the original formatting to the new replacement text. If you replace the boldface word *Roger* with the plain name *Ms. Smith*, for example, the replacement is a boldface **Ms. Smith**. To override this feature, specify formatting as part of your replacement (see this chapter's section, "Finding and Replacing Formats").

You can undo a replacement by choosing the Edit Undo Replace command. If you have confirmed each replacement, the Edit Undo Replace command undoes only the last replacement (however, you can choose the Edit **Undo** Replace command repeatedly to undo replacements sequentially, starting with the last replacement). If you choose the Replace All button and make all the replacements at once, the Edit **Undo** Replace command undoes all the replacements.

You can use the Undo button on the Standard toolbar to undo all the replacements.

To undo all replacements using the Undo button:

1. Click the down arrow of the Undo button on the Standard toolbar. The box containing all the actions appears.

2. Drag to select all the Replace items listed on the Undo button pull-down.

3. Release the mouse button; all the replacements revert to the original text.

You can paste text copied to the Clipboard with the Edit Copy command into the text boxes in the Edit Find and Edit Replace dialog boxes. This feature enables you to insert large amounts of text or text using noncontiguous formats. To use the contents of the Clipboard, position the insertion point in the Find What or Replace With text box. Then press **Ctrl+V**.

Finding and Replacing Formatting

Finding and replacing formatting is similar to finding and replacing text. Suppose that you have a document with many underlined titles, and you want to italicize them instead. Or suppose that an article is sprinkled with boldface phrases, and you want to remove the boldface formatting. You can change the text, the formatting, or both the text and the formatting.

You also can find and replace paragraph formats, language, and styles. A centered paragraph, for example, can be replaced with right-alignment formatting. A paragraph written in French can be assigned to a French language dictionary rather than an English (US) language dictionary for spell checking, or a style such as Heading 1 can be replaced with another, such as Heading 2.

Finding and Replacing Formats. You can find and replace text (or special characters), formatting, or both. For example, you can find text and replace it with different text, or you can find formatted text and replace it with differently formatted text. Or, you can find only formatting, and replace it with different formatting.

To find or replace formatting:

1. Choose the Edit Find or the Edit Replace command. The Find or the Replace dialog box appears.

2. Select the Find What box. Then type the formatted text you want to locate, or leave the box blank to find only formatting.

3. To find a font or character formatting, choose the Format button and select Font from the menu that appears. The Find Font dialog box appears (see fig. 7.6). It appears the same as the Font dialog box used for formatting characters. Select the font or other options you want to find. Then choose OK or press **Enter**.

Fig. 7.6
You can include character formatting as a search or replace option in the Find Font dialog box.

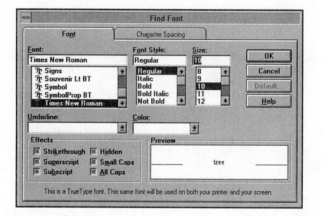

To find paragraph formatting, choose the Format button and select Paragraph from the menu that appears. The Find Paragraph dialog box appears; this dialog box resembles the Paragraph dialog box used for formatting paragraphs. Select the paragraph formatting options you want to find. Then choose OK or press **Enter**.

To find language formatting (areas of the document to which you assign a dictionary for another language), choose the Format button and select Language from the menu that appears. The Find Language dialog box displays (see fig. 7.7). Select the language assignment you want to find or replace with.

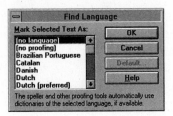

Fig. 7.7
Use the Find
Language dialog
box to search for
or replace an area
of text that has a
foreign language
dictionary assigned
to it.

To find style formatting, choose the Format button and select Style from the menu that appears. The Find Style dialog box appears (see fig. 7.8). Select the style you want to find or replace. Choose OK or press Enter.

Fig. 7.8
Choose styles you
want to find or
replace from the
Find Style dialog
box.

The font, paragraph, language, or style options you select are listed beneath the Find What or Replace With boxes.

4. To replace formatting, select the Replace With box. Then type the replacement text, or leave the box blank to replace the contents of the Find What box with formatting only.

5. To add formatting to the replacement text, choose the Format button. Select Font, Paragraph, Language, or Style. The Replace Font, Replace Paragraph, Replace Language, or Replace Style dialog box appears. Select the options you want. Choose OK or press **Enter**.

   The formatting options you select are listed under the Replace With box.

6. Choose Find Next to find the next occurrence of the specified text, formatting, or both.

   If you're replacing formatting, choose Find Next to find the next occurrence. Then choose Replace, or Replace All to find and replace all occurrences.

7. When the find or replace operation is complete, choose Cancel (or press **Esc**) to close the Find dialog box. Choose Close (or press **Esc**) to close the Replace dialog box.

Initially, check boxes are gray and text boxes are blank on the format dialog boxes. This indicates that these fields are not involved in the search or replace operation. Clicking a check box option once selects it—an x appears in the box. Clicking a second time clears the option. In this case, the option is still involved in the search or replace operation. However, you have specifically deselected that option, removing the format. Clicking a third time grays the option again so that it is no longer involved in the search or replace operation.

If you want to remove small caps from all occurrences of a certain word, for example, type it into the Find What box. Choose the Format button. Then select Font. Click the Small Caps option to select it. Choose OK to return to the Replace dialog box. Then type the same word into the Replace With box. Choose the Format button and select Font. Click the Small Caps check box twice to deselect this option. If you leave this box grayed, the formatting will not be removed.

The formatting selections you make for the Find What and the Replace With boxes remain in effect until you change them. In other words, they will be there the next time you open the Find or Replace dialog box. To remove all formatting options, select either Find What or Replace With. Then choose the No Formatting button.

You might want to always confirm the first occurrence of your search and replace operations before proceeding with a global replace.

You can use the shortcut keys for formatting characters and paragraphs in the Find and Replace dialog boxes. To specify bold formatting, for example, press **Ctrl+B**. To specify a font, press **Ctrl+Shift+F** repeatedly until the font you want is selected. See the reference card for a list of the shortcut keys.

The find and replace feature in Word for Windows is flexible, enabling you to replace text regardless of formatting, both text and formatting, or just formatting. You also can replace text with nothing (that is, delete specified text), or remove formatting. Table 7.1 outlines replacement options available when using the Find and Replace commands.

Table 7.1 Find and Replace Options

If you replace	With	You get
Text, format, or both Text	Text Format	New text, old format
Text	Format	Old text and format, plus new format
Format or text and format	Format	Old text, new format
Text	Text and format	New text, old format, plus new format
Text	Nothing	Remove Text
Format or text and format	Nothing	Remove text and format

Replacing Styles. A *style* is a combination of several formatting commands. You can have a style called Title, for example, that includes the formatting commands for Times New Roman font, 24-point size, centered, underlined, and bold. A style enables you to apply all these formats with a single command. (For more information on styles, see Chapter 11.) You can use Word for Windows Replace command to replace either a format with a style or one style with another. When you replace formatting or a style with a style, all paragraphs formatted by the replacement style take on its formatting.

For Related Information
■ "Creating Styles," p. 359

The procedure to replace a format with a style, or one style with another, is described in the section called "Finding and Replacing Formats." When you choose the Format button and select Style in the Replace dialog box, the Find Style or Replace Style dialog box displays all the defined styles (see fig. 7.8). When the style is selected in the Find What Style or Replace With Style list, the formatting commands that compose the selected style appear below the list.

Note

Each time you use the Find or Replace command, Word for Windows remembers the last words and formatting you searched for or replaced. Choose the No Formatting button in the dialog box when you need to clear formatting selections.

Finding and Replacing Special Characters

Searching for and replacing text in your document is handy and easy. Sometimes, however, you want to search for and replace other items. You can find and replace many special characters, including a wild-card character (?), a tab mark, a paragraph mark, section marks, a blank space, and many more. If you open a text (or ASCII) file with carriage returns at the end of every line, for example, you can replace each of those paragraph marks with a space. Alternatively, if you have a list that contains spaces instead of tabs, you can replace those spaces with tabs. Always be careful to confirm your changes at least once so that you don't inadvertently make an incorrect replacement.

You can find or replace special characters by using the Special button in the Find or Replace dialog box, or by using the keyboard. Table 7.2 lists the codes that you can type from the keyboard.

To insert special codes by using the Special button:

1. Choose the Edit Find or Edit Replace command.

2. Select the Find What or Replace With box.

3. Choose the Special button.

4. Select the command you want to find or replace.

To insert special codes from the keyboard:

1. Choose the Edit Find or Edit Replace command.

2. Type the appropriate code in either the Find What or the Replace With box. (Type the caret (^) character by pressing **Shift+6**.)

3. Choose the No Formatting button if you do not want the formats to influence the action of the Find or Replace command.

Table 7.2 Codes for Special Characters	
Code	**Special Character**
^p	Paragraph mark
^t	Tab character
^a	Annotation mark (Find only)

Code	Special Character
^?	Any character (Find only)
^#	Any digit (Find only)
^$	Any letter (Find only)
^^	Caret character
^n	Column break
^+	Em dash
^=	En dash
^e	Endnote mark (Find only)
^d	Field (Find only)
^f	Footnote mark (Find only)
^g	Graphic (Find only)
^l (L)	Line break
^m	Manual page break
^~	Nonbreaking hyphen
^s	Nonbreaking space
^-	Optional hyphen
^b	Section break (Find only)
^w	White space (any space—one space, multiple spaces, tab spaces—bordered by characters) (Find only)
^c	Clipboard contents (Replace only)
^&	Find What text (Replace only)
^0nnn	ANSI or ASCII characters (Replace only). *n* is the character number.

If you want to find or replace special characters, you should display nonprinting characters, such as paragraph marks and tab marks.

To display nonprinting characters from the toolbar, click the Show/Hide button on the Standard toolbar.

To display nonprinting characters from the menu:

1. Choose the Tools Options command.

2. Select the View tab.

3. Select the All check box in the Nonprinting Characters group.

4. Choose OK.

Checking Your Spelling

After you enter your text and you're fairly sure that the words are correct, check the spelling of your document. You can easily overlook spelling mistakes when you proofread your document, and you might find a word or two that you spelled wrong.

Word for Windows spelling checker quickly pinpoints words in your document that don't match those in its or the user's dictionary, or in your own custom dictionary. When you aren't sure about a word, you can ask Word for Windows to suggest alternative spellings. The program searches its dictionary for a match and offers you a list of other spellings. It can even suggest one as the most likely choice.

> **Note**
>
> Word for Windows spelling checker also searches for several other problems: double words (*the the*), oddly capitalized words (*mY*), words that should be capitalized (*california*), and words that should be all capitals (*ZIP*). You also can set additional options in the Spelling dialog box.

Spell checking begins at the beginning of your document and works forward through your document, checking its entire contents. You can check spelling in a smaller section of text by first selecting that area (it can be as little as a single word). Then, you can check the spelling as usual.

A good spelling checker gives you the confidence of knowing that your work is accurate. However, you should exercise caution. No spelling checker can tell you when you have misused words, perhaps typing *for* when you mean *four*, or *thought* when the word should be *though*. A spelling checker is an important tool, but it cannot replace thorough proofreading.

Checking Your Document's Spelling

To check spelling in your document:

1. Select the word or section of your document you want to check for spelling. If nothing is selected, Word for Windows checks the entire document from the beginning.

2. Choose the Tools Spelling command, or choose the Spelling button on the Standard toolbar. (The Spelling button resembles an ABC with a check mark.) Alternatively, press F7.

   Word for Windows scrolls through your document, matching each word against the main dictionary. The program selects words it does not recognize, and the Spelling dialog box appears. The unrecognized word is highlighted in the text and displayed in the Not In Dictionary box (see fig. 7.9). You can move the spelling dialog box if it is hiding the selected word.

3. Correct the misspelled word in the Change To text box, or select the correct word from the Suggestions list.

   If the Always Suggest option is turned on in the Spelling Options, and Word for Windows can suggest an alternative spelling, that suggestion appears in the Change To box. Other possible words will appear in the Suggestions list. If the Always Suggest option is turned off, the selected word appears in the Change To text box. (For more information on using Always Suggest, see the section "Setting Spelling Options" later in this chapter.)

   If the Always Suggest option is turned off, the Suggestions list is empty. Choose the Suggest button to display a list of possible words; then select the correct word from the list.

4. When the correct spelling appears in the Change To box, choose the Change button. The selected word changes to the spelling displayed in the Change To box. Choose Change All to change all occurrences of the misspelled word in your document.

   or

   Choose Ignore to leave the word as is. Choose Ignore All to ignore all future occurrences of the word in your document.

or

If Word for Windows finds a word it thinks is misspelled and you want to add that word to the dictionary, choose the Add button. The word is added to the selected dictionary displayed in the Add Words To box.

5. Word for Windows continues searching. Choose Cancel to discontinue the spell checking. You also can undo up to five of the previous corrections by choosing the Undo Last command.

6. A message dialog box appears when the spelling checker reaches the end of the document or the selection. If you are checking a word or a selected section, a dialog box asks whether you want to check the remainder of the document. Choose Yes or No.

Fig. 7.9

You can use the Spelling command to find misspellings and typos throughout your document.

If you started spell checking in the middle of the document, Word will return to the beginning and continue checking up to the point at which you began.

You can halt the spelling check to edit your document without closing the Spelling dialog box. Drag the Spelling dialog box away from the area that you want to edit. Then either click in the document or press Ctrl+Tab to activate the document window. After editing your document, choose the Start button in the Spelling dialog box to resume spell checking at the point at which you stopped (if you're using a keyboard rather than a mouse, press Ctrl+Tab to reactivate the Spelling dialog box).

You can use wild-card characters such as * or ? when you are searching for the spelling of a word. In the Change To text box of the Spelling dialog box, type the word, using as a wild card either * for multiple unknown characters or ? for a single unknown character. If you are not sure whether the correct spelling is *exercise* or *exercize*, for example, type **exerci?e** in the Change To text box. Then choose the Suggest button. Word for Windows displays the correct spelling of the word.

You can undo all spelling changes made during a spell check in two ways.

To undo all spelling changes from a menu command:

> Choose the Edit Undo Spelling command immediately after you complete the spell checking.

To undo all spelling changes with the Undo button:

1. Choose the Undo button on the Standard toolbar. Then, drag down through all the Spelling edits.

2. Release the mouse button.

Finding Double Words. When Word for Windows spelling checker finds double words, the Not In Dictionary box changes to the Repeated Word box, and the repeated word is displayed (see fig. 7.10).

To delete the repeated word:

1. Leave the Change To box blank.

2. Choose the Delete button. Be sure to delete unwanted spaces.

Adding Words to a Dictionary. The spell-checking process enables you to add words to a custom dictionary. When Word for Windows selects an unrecognized word that you use often, choose the dictionary to which you want to add it. The word is bypassed in future spell checks.

To add words to a custom dictionary:

1. Choose a dictionary from the Add Words To list.

2. Choose the Add button.

Tip
Another way to access Word for Windows spelling check feature is to press the shortcut key, F7.

Tip
Click on the word in the Not in Dictionary box if you want to copy it into the Change To box.

Everyday Word Processing

Caution

Be careful not to accidentally add misspelled words to the dictionary! If you want to delete a misspelled word from a dictionary, use Windows Notepad to open the dictionary and delete the word. Dictionaries are located in the Proof folder within the Msapps folder within the Windows folder.

Setting Spelling Options

One of the buttons that appears in the Spelling dialog box is the Options
button. Choosing the Options button enables you to use a non-English
dictionary or to check spelling against a custom dictionary you create. (See
the next section for information on creating a custom dictionary.) It also
enables you to select other spelling options.

Options can be set at any time.

To set options:

1. To set options before you check spelling, choose the Tools Options
   command. Then, select the Spelling tab.

   or

   To set options while checking spelling, choose the Options button in
   the Spelling dialog box.

   The Spelling tab for adjusting spelling options appears (see fig. 7.11).

2. Under Ignore, select the class of words you want Word for Windows
   to skip during every spell check. These options are presented in the
   following table:

Option	Function
Words in UPPERCASE	Ignores words in all uppercase letters
Words with Numbers	Ignores words that include numbers
Reset Ignore All	Removes all words that have been added during the current session to the Ignore All list. The next time you spell check a document during the current Word session, Word does not ignore those words.

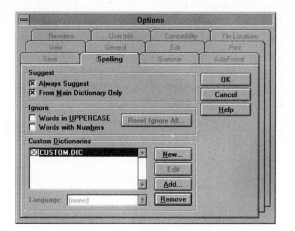

Fig. 7.11
You can customize a spelling check in the Spelling Options dialog box.

Everyday Word Processing

3. Select from the Custom Dictionaries list the dictionaries you want open. Up to ten custom dictionaries can be open during a spelling check. You might have many custom dictionaries available. However, Word for Windows checks spelling against only custom dictionaries that are open.

4. In the Suggest group, select among the following options:

Option	Function
Always Suggest	Word will always suggest corrections. Deselect this option if you don't always want suggestions (and if you want the spelling checker to work faster).
From **Main** Dictionary Only	Suggestions will come from the Main dictionary only, not from any open custom dictionaries.

5. Choose OK.

Creating a Custom Dictionary

Each time you run the spelling checker, it compares the words in your document with those in the dictionary. Word for Windows standard dictionary contains thousands of commonly used words. However, certain ones you use frequently might not be included—terms specific to your profession, for example, or your company's name, or the names of products your firm sells. You can create custom dictionaries and specify that Word for Windows consult them each time you check spelling. To learn how to open these dictionaries so that they're used when you check spelling, refer to the preceding section, "Setting Spelling Options." To learn how to add words to your custom dictionary, refer to the previous section, "Adding Words to a Dictionary."

To create a new custom dictionary:

1. Choose the Tools Options command. Then select the Spelling tab.

2. Choose the New button in the Custom Dictionaries section. A dialog box prompts you for the name of the dictionary file.

3. In the File Name box, type a name for the new dictionary ending with the extension DIC. Your dictionary is stored in the \windows\msapps \proof subdirectory. You can select another directory in which Word is to store the dictionary.

4. Choose OK.

5. To close the Options dialog box, choose OK.

You can remove a word from a custom dictionary by selecting the dictionary in the Custom Dictionaries list, then choosing the Edit button. Choose OK to close the Options dialog box. The file lists all dictionary entries alphabetically. Delete the words you no longer want. Then, save the file in Text Only format (don't change the file's name or location).

You can choose options from the Custom Dictionaries group as follows:

Choose This	To Do This
Edit	Make changes to the custom dictionary you select. You must confirm that you want to open the dictionary as a Word document.
Add	Add a custom dictionary from another directory or disk.
Remove	Remove a dictionary from the Custom Dictionary list. The dictionary must be deselected before it can be removed.
Language	Add language formatting to a custom dictionary. Only text formatted in that language will be spell checked with that custom dictionary. (See "Proofing in Other Languages" later in this chapter.) If you select (none), the dictionary will be used to spell check text formatted in any language.

Troubleshooting Tool Menu Commands

The following troubleshooting tip will help you solve one of the more frequently asked questions about choosing Tool commands.

A dialog box appears indicating that Word for Windows cannot locate a command or feature from the Tools menu.

Many Word for Windows features, such as the spelling checker, are optional during the Word for Windows installation process. If a feature or command you want to use has not been installed, you can run the Word for Windows installation procedure again. Then, you can select only the options you want to install. Run Word for Windows installation program by double-clicking the Word Setup icon in the Word for Windows group window of the Program manager. Instructions appear on-screen at the beginning of the installation process that prompt you to select the options you want to install. For example, select Proofing Tools if you need to install the spelling checker. Follow the instructions that appear to complete the installation process.

Checking Your Grammar

When you are creating a document, you might be uncertain whether your sentence structure is grammatically correct. You might use the phrase *between you and I*, for example, when the grammatically correct version is *between you and me*. Word for Windows grammar checker is used to spot grammatical errors and suggest how to correct them. The Grammar dialog box provides several choices for making changes (see fig. 7.12).

If no text is selected, Word for Windows checks the entire document beginning at the insertion point. If text is selected, only the selection is checked. A selection must contain at least one sentence.

By default, Word for Windows checks spelling and grammar. If you want to check only grammar, turn off the Check Spelling option in the Grammar tab of the Options dialog box. (To learn how to do this, see the upcoming section, "Selecting Grammar Rules.") If the Check Spelling option is selected, Word for Windows may display the Spelling dialog box before it displays the Grammar dialog box—it depends on whether it locates a spelling or a grammar error first.

To check a document's grammar:

1. Choose the Tools Grammar command.

   The Grammar dialog box appears when Word for Windows finds a sentence with a possible grammatical error or questionable style (refer to fig. 7.12). The grammatically questionable words appear in bold, and also appear in the Sentence box in the Grammar dialog box.

2. Select an option in the Grammar dialog box.

The Suggestions box offers an explanation of why a selection is ungrammatical, and if available, offers possible replacement text. You can update the sentence with a suggested correction by selecting it in the Suggestions box, and then choosing the Change button. If the Change button is grayed, the Grammar checker is unable to suggest a change. You can make a change directly in the document.

Fig. 7.12
Use the Grammar checker to flag possible errors in spelling and grammar.

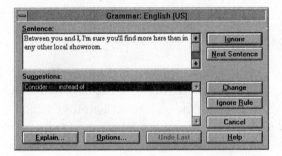

To leave the Grammar command temporarily in order to make a change in the document:

1. Choose the document window by clicking it, or by pressing **Ctrl+Tab**.

2. Edit the sentence in the document.

3. Choose the Start button that appears in the Grammar dialog box. The grammar check resumes at the insertion point after you have edited your document.

You can also choose from these Grammar options:

Choose This	To Do This
Ignore	Ignores the questioned word or phrase.

Choose This	To Do This
Ignore Rule	Skips other similar occurrences that break the same grammar or style rule.
Next Sentence	Leaves the sentence unchanged and moves to the next sentence.
Explain	Provides more information about the error. A window appears describing the relevant grammar or style rule. After you read the information, press **Esc** to clear the window and return to the Grammar dialog box.
Options	Selects different rules of grammar and style. The Grammar Options tab that appears enables you to select an option button for the rule group you want to observe for the remainder of the check. (See "Selecting Grammar Rules" later in this chapter.)

When the grammar checker reaches the end of the document, it continues checking from the beginning. If the entire document or the selected section has been checked, you see a message indicating that the grammar check is completed. Choose OK to return to your document.

If the Show Readability Statistics option is selected, a dialog box displays the information about the document. (Readability is covered later in the section "Testing the Readability of a Document.") Choose OK to return to your document.

Selecting Grammar Rules

You can choose the rules of style and grammar that are used during grammar checks. Depending on your audience, your style, and the material, you might want to follow some rules and disregard others. When you choose the Tools Options command and select the Grammar tab, you can pick from among three predefined rule groups: Strictly (all rules), For Business Writing, or For Casual Writing. You can also create up to three custom rule groups, or customize the three predefined rule groups by selecting or clearing grammar and style options.

This Rule Group	Applies These Rules
Strictly	All grammar and style rules
For Business Writing	Fewer rules; those appropriate for written business communication

(continues)

(continued)

This Rule Group	Applies These Rules
For Casual Writing	The least number of rules; those appropriate for informal written communication
Custom 1, 2, 3	Rules that you apply

To customize a rule group:

1. Choose the Tools Option command. Then select the Grammar tab. If you have already started grammar checking, choose the Options button in the Grammar dialog box. The Grammar tab appears (see fig. 7.13).

Fig. 7.13
Use the Grammar tab in the Options dialog box to choose gram-matical rules and styles you want to apply to your documents.

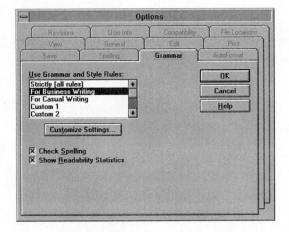

2. Select the rule group you want to change in the Use Grammar and Style Rules list.

3. Choose the Customize Settings button. The Customize Grammar Settings dialog box appears (see fig. 7.14).

4. If you base a custom rule group on an existing rule group, select the existing rule group from the Use Grammar and Style Rules list.

5. Select first Grammar, and then Style, and then select the rule check boxes for rules you want Word for Windows to observe. Clear check boxes for rules you want ignored.

6. From the pull-down lists in the Catch group, select how you want to control Split Infinitives, Consecutive Nouns, and Prepositional Phrases.

Also, indicate the maximum number of words you want in a sentence with the Sentences Containing More Words Than option.

7. Choose OK.

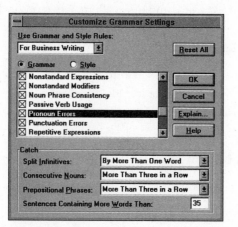

Fig. 7.14

You can customize the grammatical rules used to check your document.

Testing the Readability of a Document

Readability statistics measure how easy your writing is to read. Writing that is easier to read communicates more clearly. The *Wall Street Journal*, for example, writes at the eighth-grade level. Hemingway wrote at the sixth-grade level. Writing need not be boring when it's readable. To make his writing interesting, Hemingway used intriguing subject matter, active writing, colorful descriptions, and variable sentence lengths.

If you choose to display readability statistics, they appear at the end of grammar checking.

To display readability statistics after you use the Grammar command:

1. Choose the Tools Options command.

2. Select the Grammar tab.

3. Select the Show Readability Statistics check box.

4. Choose OK.

Word for Windows readability statistics are based on the Flesch-Kincaid index. This index assigns a reading ease score and grade level based on the average number of words per sentence and syllables per 100 words.

Using the Thesaurus

When you're not sure of the meaning of a word, or when you think you're using a certain term too often, take advantage of Word for Windows thesaurus. It defines selected words and offers alternative terms (synonyms). For example, Word for Windows synonyms for the word *information* include *intelligence*, *data*, and *facts*.

The thesaurus looks up one word at a time. If a word is selected, or the insertion point is in a word, the thesaurus looks up that word. If the insertion point is outside a word, the thesaurus looks up the word preceding the insertion point.

To display a list of synonyms and definitions for a word in your document:

1. Select the word for which you want to locate a synonym.

2. Choose the Tools Thesaurus command, or press **Shift+F7**. The Thesaurus dialog box appears (see fig. 7.15).

   The selected word is displayed in the Looked Up text box. The first meaning is displayed in the Replace With Synonym text box, followed by a list of synonyms. Its definition appears in the Meanings box.

Fig. 7.15
You can see the meaning of any word you select in the Thesaurus dialog box.

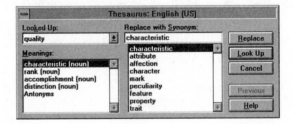

3. You have several options at this point:

Do This	For This Result
Choose a synonym in the Replace With Synonyms list.	The word moves into the Replace With Synonyms box.
Select a different meaning from the Meanings list.	A new list of synonyms appears in the Replace With Synonyms list. You can select a word from this list.
Select Related Words or Antonyms in the Meanings list.	"The Replace with list displays related words or antonyms."

Do This	For This Result
Select the word from the **Meanings** or **Synonyms** list, or type a word and choose **Look Up**.	Meanings of those new words appear.
Choose **Previous**.	The word that was previously looked up appears.

4. Choose the Replace button to replace the selected word in the document with the word in the Replace With Synonym/Antonym/Related Word box, or choose the Cancel button.

Proofing in Other Languages

If you're reading this book in English, most of your typing is probably in this language. However, your document might contain some text in Spanish, French, or another language. You can select that text, assign to it a language other than English, and all the Word for Windows proofing tools—spell checker, hyphenation, thesaurus, and grammar checker—will use the other language dictionary you specify to proof that text.

Before the language command is available, you must purchase and install the appropriate language-proofing tools for the language you will be using. If you want to check the spelling of French text, for example, you must install a French dictionary. Contact Microsoft Corporation or other vendors for information on the many language-proofing tools available.

To proof text in another language:

1. Select the text written in another language.

2. Choose the Tools Language command to display the Language dialog box.

3. Select the language from the Mark Selected Text As list. To change the language for all the text you proof, choose the Default button.

   You can choose (no proofing) from the list if you want the proofing tools to skip the selected text. This feature is useful for technical material containing terms not listed in any of the standard spelling dictionaries.

4. Choose OK.

Counting Words

The Tools Word Count command counts the number of pages, words, characters, paragraphs, and lines in a document. You can choose to include footnotes and endnotes in the count.

To count words, lines, and more of the document on the screen:

1. Choose the Tools Word Count command. The Word Count dialog box displays. Word performs the count and displays the results.

2. Select Include Footnotes and Endnotes if you want to include these items in the count. The count is redone, and the new results appear.

3. Choose the Close button.

Fig. 7.16
The Word Count command provides statistics about a document.

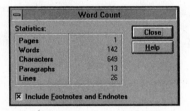

From Here...

To better understand the capabilities of the other Word for Windows tools and options, see the following chapters:

■ Chapter 15, "Mastering Envelopes, Mail Merge, and Form Letters," teaches you about creating and editing Macros.

■ Chapter 35, "Customizing and Optimizing Word Features," teaches you how to use the other options in the Tools menu.

Chapter 8

Previewing and Printing a Document

Although printing with Word for Windows can be as simple as opening a document, choosing a print command, and starting the printing operation, Word for Windows gives you many additional options. You can preview one or more pages in your document and change their margins while you're in the preview. You can print all or part of an open document. You can print a draft or a final version. You can print normal copy and graphics or print hidden text and field codes. You also can print multiple documents without opening them.

Often, your objective is not to print a document but to route it electronically to its destination. This chapter shows you how to print a document, fax a document, print it to a file, or send it via electronic mail to someone in your workgroup.

Selecting a Printer

Microsoft Windows is the common denominator that makes printing with Word for Windows easy. Any printer you install to use with Windows you also can use with Word for Windows.

Word for Windows prints on whichever installed printer currently is selected as the default printer. You can find out which printer is selected by choosing the File Print command and looking at the top of the Print dialog box (see fig. 8.1).

Fig. 8.1

The Print dialog box offers a variety of options.

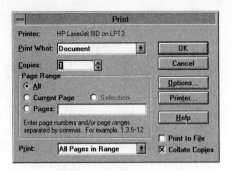

To select a printer, choose Printer in the Print dialog box. If you use only one printer, select that printer the first time you print a document with Word for Windows. After you print, your printer stays selected. If you switch between printers, you must select a printer each time you change printers.

When you select a printer, Word for Windows lists the available printers in the Print Setup dialog box (see fig. 8.2). This list includes all printers installed for use with Windows. If the printer you want to use is not on the list, you must install it in Windows. To install a printer, see the following section, "Installing a Printer in Windows."

Fig. 8.2

Click the Printer button in the Print dialog box to open the Print Setup dialog box.

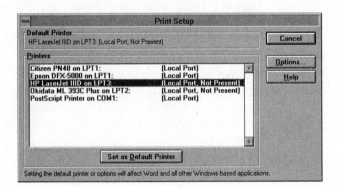

To select a printer, follow these steps:

1. Choose the File Print command. The Print dialog box appears.

2. Choose Printer in the Print dialog box.

3. Select a printer from the Printers list in the Print Setup dialog box.

4. Choose the Set as Default Printer button.

5. Choose Close to return to the Print dialog box. Choose OK to print, or Close to return to your document.

The next time you choose the File Print command, you see your selected printer listed at the top of the Print dialog box.

The Options button in the Print dialog box provides access to certain settings that affect the appearance of your printed document. You learn about these settings later in this chapter.

Setting Up Your Printer

Windows manages most details of setting up a printer. Three tasks, however, are left up to you: selecting the printer you want to use in Word for Windows, installing the printers you want to use in Windows, and changing the printer setup for special printing needs.

Installing a Printer in Windows

Selecting a printer in Word for Windows is simple—if the printer is listed in the Print Setup dialog box. If your printer is not listed, Windows does not have that printer installed. You can install a printer in Windows from within Word for Windows.

To install a printer in Windows, follow these steps:

1. In the Main window of the Windows Program Manager, start the Control Panel.

2. Choose the Printers icon from the dialog box (see fig. 8.3 for the Windows 3.1 Control Panel). The Printers dialog box appears.

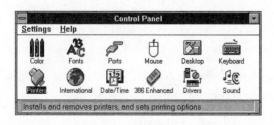

Fig. 8.3
The Control Panel provides access to Windows printer installation functions.

3. Choose the Add >> button. The Printers dialog box expands to reveal a list of available printer drivers at the bottom, as shown in fig. 8.4 (for Windows 3.1).

Fig. 8.4

Install new printer
drivers in the
Control Panel's
Printers dialog
box.

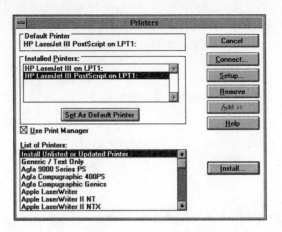

4. Select the printer you want to install from the List of Printers list and
   then choose Install.

   If your printer is not listed and you receive a printer driver—a DRV
   file—from the printer manufacturer, choose the first option on the List
   of Printers list, Install Unlisted, or Updated Printer. If your printer is not
   listed and you do not have a driver, you may be able to use the driver of
   a compatible printer model, or you can select the second driver on the
   list, Generic/Text Only. This driver does not support special fonts or
   graphics.

   A dialog box prompts you to insert one of the original Windows installation disks or the disk issued by the printer manufacturer. (If the
   printer driver is already copied onto your hard disk, you'll see no dialog
   box prompting you for a disk; in this case, skip Step 5.) Drive A is
   shown as the default, but you can enter another drive letter.

5. Insert the disk and then choose OK. You'll return to the Printers dialog
   box when the installation is complete. The new printer is listed in the
   Installed Printers list, and is selected.

   When the Install Driver dialog box appears, enter the drive and directory path that contains the new printer driver.

   If Windows does not find the driver on the disk, the dialog box reappears. Insert a different disk from the one requested and choose OK
   again. The printer driver may be on one of the other Windows installation disks.

6. Choose Connect from the Printers dialog box.

7. From the Ports list, select the port you want for that printer; then choose OK to return to the Printers dialog box.

8. Choose the Setup button. The setup dialog box appears (the setup dialog box varies from one printer to another).

9. Select the settings you use most frequently, such as printing in portrait (vertically) or landscape (sideways), the resolution, paper source, printer memory, and font cartridges. Then choose OK.

    A single printer driver program often is used for a whole family of printers. In that event, you must select your specific printer model from a list box. If your printer model is not listed, select a compatible printer driver.

10. Choose Close to complete the setup operation and close the Printers dialog box.

11. Choose the Settings Exit command, or press Alt+F4 to close the Control Panel.

Using Special Print Setups

For the most part, after you install a printer in Windows, Word for Windows completes the rest of the process of setting up the printer. Because Word for Windows makes certain assumptions about such things as paper size and orientation (portrait or landscape), you normally do not have to select these options. In Chapter 13, "Setting the Page Layout," you learn how to change the default settings. Word does enable you to choose some printing options from the Print dialog box, however.

To set options at the time you print a document, follow these steps:

1. Choose the File Print command. The Print dialog box appears.

2. Choose Printer in the Print dialog box. The Print Setup dialog box appears.

3. Select a printer from the Printers list.

4. Choose the Options button in the Print Setup dialog box. Choosing this button opens a dialog box like the one shown in fig. 8.5.

Fig. 8.5

The Print Setup
Options dialog box
for an HP LaserJet
printer.

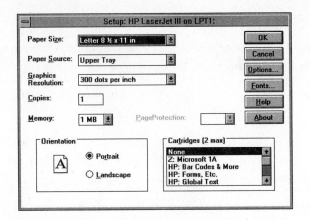

5. Select the option(s) you want. (See the section "Controlling Printing Options" later in this chapter for details on the individual options.)

6. Choose OK.

7. In the Print Setup dialog box, choose Close.

8. In the Print dialog box, choose OK.

The actual Print Setup Options dialog box that you see varies depending on the printer you select in Step 3. Fig. 8.6 shows the Options dialog box for a PostScript printer.

Fig. 8.6

The Print Setup
Options dialog box
for a PostScript
printer.

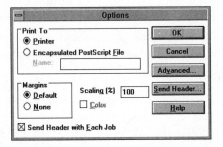

Note that the Options dialog box for the PostScript printer contains an Advanced button so that you can select advanced options. Choosing this button opens the dialog box shown in fig. 8.7. This dialog box controls options that are useful if your document contains sophisticated graphics or if you want to share the file on a network. These advanced features may be useful if you do desktop publishing with Word.

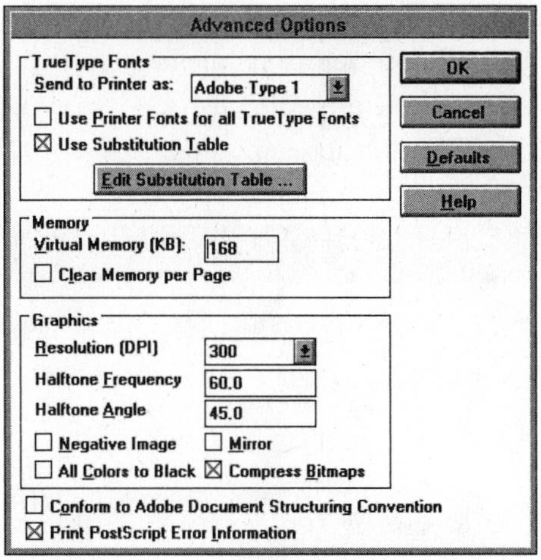

Fig. 8.7
The Advanced
Options dialog box
gives you access to
advanced printing
options.

Setting Up Printer Memory and Font Cartridges

If you use a laser printer, you may need to specify which font cartridge to use
and how much memory is in the printer. These settings affect the capabilities
of your printer, so you should not neglect to set them. You can change many
aspects of your printer setup, depending on what type of printer you have.

To set memory and select font cartridges for a laser printer, follow these steps:

1. Choose the File Print command. The Print dialog box appears.

2. Choose Printer. The Print Setup dialog box appears.

3. From the Printers list, select your printer, then choose Options. The
   Setup dialog box appears.

4. Select Memory, and select the amount of memory installed on your
   printer.

5. In the Cartridges list, select the cartridge(s) (one or two) installed in
   your printer.

6. Choose OK to return to the Print Setup dialog box.

7. Choose Close to return to the Print dialog box.

8. Choose OK to print your document, or choose Cancel to return to your
   document.

Another way to set up font cartridges or memory is from within the Windows
Control Panel. Start the Control Panel (Main group) and select the Printers

icon. When the Printers dialog box appears, select your printer from the Installed Printers list. Then choose Setup. Set memory and select cartridges as described in steps 4 and 5 in the preceding list. Choose OK to return to the Printers dialog box, then choose Close, and then close the Control Panel.

Caution

Remember to turn off your printer and then turn it back on after replacing and selecting cartridges.

Note

You can change certain print options (document size and paper source, for example) in the Page Setup dialog box. Choose the File Page Setup command. You can change other options—such as print quality and print order (along with paper source)—by choosing the Tools Options command and selecting the Print tab. The Page Setup dialog box settings override the defaults and affect only the current document. The Print tab settings change the global defaults.

Previewing Pages Before Printing

Word for Windows offers you two alternatives for viewing your document before you print. These alternatives are the page layout or print preview view.

Following are the advantages of using the page layout view to preview your printing:

In the page layout view, you can frame and then drag text or graphics to new locations. You also can drag page breaks to new locations.

The primary advantage of using the print preview view is using the preview screen's toolbar, which contains convenient buttons for zooming and displaying multiple pages.

Using Page Layout View

Different document views in Word for Windows show different perspectives on your margins. In the normal view, you don't see the margins, but you see the space between them, where your text appears. In the page layout view, you see the page as it will print, margins and all. Select this view if you want to see headers, footers, page numbers, footnotes, and anything else that appears within the margins.

At the left of the horizontal scroll bar are three buttons offering different views of documents. (If your horizontal scroll bar is not displayed, choose the Tools Options command, select the View tab, and in the Window group, select Horizontal Scroll Bar.) On the Standard toolbar is a button that displays the print preview view. Table 8.1 summarizes the effects of the document view icons.

Table 8.1 Effects of Document View Icons in the Horizontal Scroll Bar		
Button	**Name**	**Effect**
	Normal	Displays document in normal view
	Page Layout	Displays document in page layout view
	Outline	Displays document in outline view
	Print Preview	Displays document in print preview view

To view the document in page layout view, follow these steps:

1. Open the document you want to preview.

2. Choose the View Page Layout command (if the command is not selected already). Alternatively, click the Page Layout button in the horizontal scroll bar.

3. If you like, adjust the magnification by using the Zoom button or by choosing the View Zoom command.

To return to normal view, choose the View Normal command or click the Normal button at the left of the horizontal scroll bar.

Using Print Preview

The other method of seeing how your document will print is to use the print preview view.

For Related Information
■ "Editing a Document," p. 115

To see the entire document in print preview, follow these steps:

1. Open the document you want to preview.

2. Choose the File Print Preview command or use the Print Preview button on the Standard toolbar. You see a screen like the one shown in fig. 8.8.

Fig. 8.8
Display a screen representation of your printed document with the Preview screen.

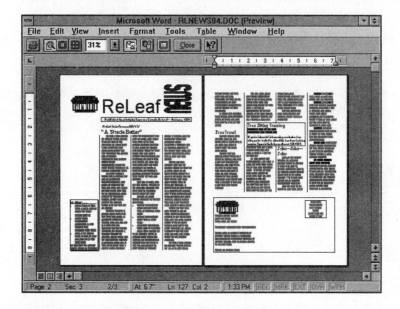

Using the Preview Icon Bar. Across the top of the Preview screen is a toolbar. You can use the buttons on the bar for the actions listed in table 8.2.

Table 8.2 Preview Screen Buttons

Button	Name	Effect
	Print	Prints the document using the printing options set in the Print dialog box
	Magnifier	Toggles the mouse pointer between a magnifying glass (for examining the document) and the normal mouse pointer (for editing the document)
	One Page	Displays document in single-page view
	Multiple pages	Displays document in multiple-page view

Button	Name	Effect
`31%` ⬇	Zoom Control	Displays a list box of zoom magnification percentages and options
	View Ruler	Toggles ruler display on and off
	Shrink to Fit	When the last page of the document contains very little text, tries to "shrink" the document to fit on one less page
	Full Screen	Toggles between full-screen display (which removes everything but the document and the toolbar) and normal display
Close	Close	Returns to your document (Cancel appears before you make changes to your document; Close appears after)
⬆?	Help	Provides context-sensitive help

In print preview, you also have access to the normal, page layout, and outline icons at the extreme left of the horizontal scroll bar (assuming the bar is displayed). Clicking any of these buttons closes the preview screen and displays the document in the view mode you selected.

You can move around in the document in the preview screen by using the PgUp and PgDn keys on your keyboard and the scroll bars. When the rulers are displayed, you adjust margins in the same manner as in page layout view. You also can edit the document.

To edit a document in print preview, follow these steps:

1. Click the Magnifier button to display the magnifying glass icon.

2. Click the part of the document you want to edit. Word displays the document at 100 percent magnification.

3. Click the Magnifier button to restore the normal Word mouse pointer.

4. Edit the document, revising text and repositioning margins on the page as described in "Using Page Layout View" earlier in this chapter.

5. After you make your changes, you can reduce the document to the previous magnification by clicking the Magnifier button again and then clicking on the document with the magnifying glass icon.

Printing from Print Preview. You can print all or part of your document from the print preview screen. You can print using the Print button or the Print dialog box.

 To print using the button, you click the Print button to print the document using the current print settings. (The Print dialog box does not appear when you click the button.)

To print using the Print dialog box, follow these steps:

1. Choose the File Print command.

2. Make the usual printing selections in the Print dialog box.

3. Choose OK.

Viewing One or Two Pages. You can view as many as 18 pages at once—although you might not find it practical to display more than six or eight.

To view multiple pages, follow these steps:

 1. Click the Multiple Pages button.

2. Move the mouse pointer over the upper-left portion of the grid that appears below the Multiple Pages button.

3. Drag the mouse pointer down and to the right until the highlighted portion of the grid reflects the number of pages you want to display. If you continue dragging, the grid expands to display additional pages to a maximum of three rows and six columns.

4. Release the mouse button. The preview screen now displays the arrangement of pages represented by the grid at the time you released the button. All other selections in the toolbar work as usual.

 To change back to single-page view again, click the One Page button.

Canceling or Closing the Print Preview Screen. To return to your editable document, select Cancel or Close from the toolbar. (The button reads Cancel if you have not made any changes to your document, Close if you have.)

Printing the Current Document

The simplest way to print is to open a document and choose the File **Print** command. By default, Word for Windows prints one copy of all pages of the currently open document on the currently selected printer without printing hidden text.

To print one copy of a document, follow these steps:

1. Open the document you want to print.

2. Choose the File **Print** command or press Ctrl+Shift+F12. The Print dialog box appears.

3. Choose OK.

To cancel printing while the Print dialog box is displayed, press Esc or choose the Cancel button. (The status bar at the bottom of the screen displays a message telling you when you can cancel the print job.) If the Print dialog box is no longer displayed and you are using the Windows Print Manager, the complete print job may already have been sent to the Print Manager. In this case, you must press Ctrl+Esc to display the Task List, activate the Print Manager, and stop your print job. If you are not using the Print Manager and the Print dialog box is no longer displayed, the print job already may have been sent to the printer.

You can bypass the Print dialog box and print your document quickly by clicking the Print button on the Standard toolbar. Word for Windows prints your document using settings previously selected in the Print dialog box.

Printing Multiple Copies

With Word for Windows' Print dialog box, you can print more than one copy of your document. In fact, you can print 32,767 copies of your document (but you may want to plan a trip to Hawaii while all those copies print). By default, Word for Windows collates the copies—a handy feature for long documents.

To print multiple copies of your document, follow these steps:

1. Open the document you want to print.

2. Choose the File **Print** command or press Ctrl+Shift+F12. The Print dialog box appears (see fig. 8.9).

Fig. 8.9
You can print
multiple copies of
your document.

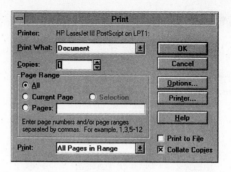

3. Select the Copies box in the Print dialog box and enter the number of copies you want to print. (Alternatively, use the increment/decrement arrows to increase or decrease the specified number of copies.)

4. Choose OK.

If print time is important, you can deselect the Collate Copies option in the bottom right corner of the dialog box. This step enables Word for Windows to run multiple documents through the printer faster. You pay for choosing this option later, however, when you have to collate all the copies by hand.

Printing Part of a Document

Word for Windows provides two ways to print part of a document. You can select the portion of your document you want to print and then choose the File Print command. You also can print the current page, selected text, or a specific range of pages.

Printing a selected area is useful when you want to print a section of a larger document but don't know on which page or pages the section is located.

To print a selected area of text, follow these steps:

1. Select the text to print.

2. Choose the File Print command or press Ctrl+Shift+F12.

3. Choose the Selection option.

4. Choose OK.

If you know exactly which pages you want to print, you can print a range of pages. Suppose that you make changes to the first three pages of a long document. In that case, you may want to print from pages 1 through 3.

To print a specific range of pages, follow these steps:

1. Choose the File Print command or press Ctrl+Shift+F12.

2. In the Pages box, enter the range of pages you want to print. (For instance, to print pages 1 through 3, enter **1-3**.)

3. Choose OK.

In the Pages box, you can specify multiple page ranges (such as **1-7,8-13,14-20**) or multiple discontinuous pages (**1,2,8,13**). You can combine ranges with individual page numbers, as shown in fig. 8.10.

You also can print pages in a certain section. To print the second section in your document, type **s2** in the Pages box. If you want to print from page 7 in the second section to page 10 in the third section, type **p7s2-p10s3** in the Pages box.

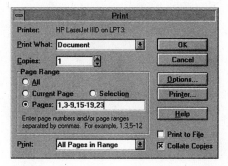

Fig. 8.10
Enter groups of page ranges and/or selected pages in the Pages box of the Print dialog box.

In a long document, it's sometimes helpful to simply print the page on which you're working.

To print the page on which you're working, follow these steps:

1. Position the insertion point on the page you want to print.

2. Choose the File Print command or press Ctrl+Shift+F12.

3. Select Current Page.

4. Choose OK.

If you're printing on both sides of the paper, you should print the odd-numbered pages in one print run and the even-numbered pages in another.

To print only the odd- or even-numbered pages, follow these steps:

1. Choose the File Print command or press Ctrl+Shift+F12.

2. In the Print box, choose the Odd Pages or Even Pages option.

3. Choose OK.

Printing Different Types of Document Information

Word for Windows documents contain associated information such as summary information, field codes, and data for forms. You can print this information with the document or separately. The first method describes how to print the ancillary hidden information with the document. The second method describes how to print the hidden information separately.

Word for Windows enables you to include the following hidden attributes as part of your printed document:

- Summary information

- Field codes

- Annotations

- Hidden text

- Drawing objects

To print hidden information with your document, follow these steps:

1. Choose the Tools Options command. The dialog box shown in fig. 8.11 opens.

Fig. 8.11
Choose the Tools Options command and display the Print Tab to specify a variety of printing options, including "nondisplaying" information to print when you print the document.

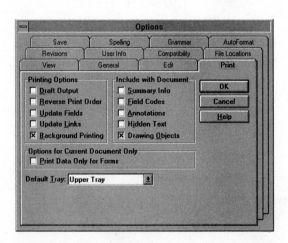

2. Select the Print tab if it is not already displayed.

3. Select the option(s) you want to print in the Include with Document group (see table 8.3). If you choose Annotations, for example, Word for Windows prints a list of the annotations associated with your document. (You can use this option to see a list of the annotations a reviewer has made to your document.)

4. Choose OK.

Table 8.3 Print List Box Options

Option	Effect
Summary Info	Prints summary of information about the document—including author, subject, print date, and number of pages, words, and characters—on separate pages at the end of the document
Field Codes	Prints field codes rather than their results
Annotations	Prints a list of annotations reviewers have attached to your document, with page number headings indicating where each annotation occurs—at the end of the document
Hidden Text	Prints any hidden text, such as table of contents entries, where text appears in document
Drawing Objects	Prints drawing objects you created in Word

Alternatively, you can print hidden information separately from the document itself, although you can select only one of the following items:

- Summary
- Annotations
- Styles
- AutoText entries
- Key Assignments

To print only a document's hidden information without printing the document, follow these steps:

1. Choose the File Print command.

2. Select Print What to open the drop-down list.

3. Select one of the options from the list.

4. Choose OK.

Controlling Printing Options

Word for Windows offers you many printing options. You can print the pages in reverse order or save time by printing a draft copy (on some printers). You can print text that usually is hidden, separately or as part of your document. You can update fields as you print, or you can print from paper in a specified bin if your printer has more than one paper source.

To set printing options, follow these steps:

1. Choose the Tools Options command and select the Print tab.

2. Select the desired options.

3. Choose OK.

The following sections describe the available printing options.

Printing a Draft

Sometimes you need a quick, plain printed copy of your document. Perhaps someone else must edit the copy, or you want to take the copy home from work to review. For a quick, unadorned print, choose a draft copy. A draft prints quickly, without formatting. Enhanced characters are underlined rather than in boldface or italic, and graphics print as empty boxes. (The exact result of a draft print depends on your printer; for example, a Hewlett-Packard LaserJet prints formatted text but no graphics in draft mode, whereas a PostScript printer does not support draft mode.)

If you select draft printing as your default, all printing will be in draft mode until you deselect that option. Alternatively, on some printers you can print in draft mode for just one time without changing the default (this option is not available for laser printers).

To select draft as your default print quality mode, follow these steps:

1. Choose the Tools Options command. Select the Print tab.

2. In the Print tab of the Options dialog box, select the **Draft Output** check box.

3. Choose OK.

To print a draft copy of a document one time using a dot-matrix printer, follow these steps:

1. Choose the File **Print** command.

2. In the Print dialog box, choose **Options**.

3. In the Printing Options group, select **Draft Output**.

4. Choose OK.

5. In the Print dialog box, choose OK.

Printing Pages in Reverse Order

Some printers have a collator that produces printed pages stacked in the correct order. Other printers stack pages with the last page on top. If your printer stacks with the last page on top, you may want to select the Reverse Print Order option to stack your pages in the correct order.

To print in reverse order, select the **Reverse Print Order** check box in the **Print** tab of the Options dialog box. Choose OK.

Updating Fields

Word for Windows files can include field codes that instruct Word for Windows to insert special information into the document. A date field, for example, inserts the current date when the document is printed. But some fields may not be updated during the printing process. To update those fields when you print, you must choose a special command. In most cases you want this option turned on.

To update fields when you print, select the **Update Fields** check box in the Print tab of the Options dialog box. Choose OK.

To learn more about fields and how they are updated, refer to Chapter 37, "Automating with Field Codes."

Updating Links

The Update Links option updates any linked information in the document before printing. To update links before you print, select the Update Links check box in the Print tab of the Options dialog box. Then choose OK.

Background Printing

The Background Printing option enables you to continue working in Word while you print a document. To print in the background while you're performing other operations in Word, select the Background Printing check box in the Print tab of the Options dialog box. Then choose OK.

Printing Form Input Data Only

For Related Information
■ "Automating with Field Codes," p. 1071

■ "Building Forms," p. 577

If you have entered data into fields on a form, printing the input data only might make it easier to compare the data in Word to the source document. To print the input data only, select the Print Data Only for Forms check box in the Print tab of the Options dialog box. Then choose OK.

To learn more about fields and how they are updated, refer to Chapter 18, "Building Forms and Fill-In Dialog Boxes."

Selecting the Paper Source

If you want to always print from a particular bin on your printer, you can change the default paper source.

To change the default paper source, follow these steps:

1. Choose the Tools Options command.

2. In the Print tab of the Options dialog box (see fig. 8.12), choose Default Tray to open the drop-down list.

Fig. 8.12
You can change the paper source with the Default Tray option in the Print tab.

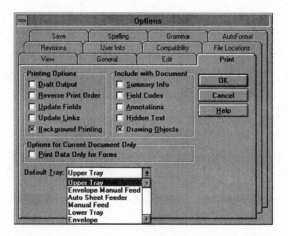

3. Select the paper source by selecting the option you want from the list box.

You also can set the paper source for your document by choosing the File Page Setup command, selecting the Paper Source tab, and selecting First Page and Other Pages options. For details, see Chapter 13, "Setting the Page Layout."

In most single-bin laser printers, you can slide your letterhead into the manual tray as far as the letterhead goes and leave your bond paper in the paper bin. After you choose OK from the Print dialog box, the letterhead is pulled in first and the bond pulled in for following sheets. As a result, on printers such as the HP LaserJet Series II, III, or IV, you do not need to go through a series of steps. Just print.

Printing Multiple Unopened Documents

Occasionally, you may want to print an unopened document or several documents simultaneously. The Find File command in the File menu enables you to open and print several documents at once or search for documents whose names have characteristics you specify.

To print one (or more) unopened documents, follow these steps:

1. Choose the File Find File command.

2. Choose Search and enter new search criteria, if you want. (Chapter 4, "Managing Documents and Files," explains your search options.) Alternatively, select a saved search from the Saved Searches box.

3. Choose OK.

4. Select the file or files to print. To select multiple contiguous files using the mouse, click the first file, hold down Shift, and click the last file. To select noncontiguous files, hold down Ctrl while you click the files. To select multiple contiguous files with the keyboard, use the arrow keys to move to the first file, hold down Shift, and use the arrow keys to move to the last file. To select noncontiguous files with the keyboard, use the arrow keys to select the first file, press Shift+F8, use the arrow keys to select the next file, and press the space bar. Use the arrow keys and space bar to select as many files as you want.

5. Click the Commands button.

6. Select Print.

7. Select any print options in the Print dialog box.

8. Choose OK.

To learn more about the Find File command, see Chapter 4, "Managing Documents and Files."

If you've assembled several Word documents into a master document, you can print the entire master document. You learn about master documents and related printing options in Chapter 32, "Assembling Large Documents."

Sending Documents Electronically

Traditionally, a printed document is the ultimate realization of something you've created in word processing, and the printed hard copy is delivered physically. Increasingly, however, documents are routed electronically. Word can print a document to a file or route it to someone else in your organization or directly to a fax machine.

Printing to a File

Someday you may need to print a document to a file and not to a printer. One way this method can be useful is to print a document setup for a PostScript printer to a file. You then can take the resulting encapsulated PostScript (EPS) file to a printer (or service bureau) to be printed on a Linotronic typesetting machine for high-quality documents.

Another use for printing to a file is to create a file that you can take to a computer that has a printer but no copy of Word for Windows. If you create the file for that printer, you can use the DOS COPY command to copy the Word for Windows file to the LPT1 printer port. The file prints even though Word for Windows is not running.

To print to a file, follow these steps:

1. Choose the File Print command.

2. Select the Print to File option; then choose OK. The Print to File dialog box appears.

3. In the Output File Name box, type the full path name of the file to contain the document; then choose OK.

You see the disk light come on as the information sent to the printer is stored in a file with the name you entered in Step 3.

When you want to resume printing to your printer, deselect the Print to File option in the Print dialog box.

> **Note**
>
> You can create a text file easily in Word for Windows. Just choose the **File Save As** command; then select the Save File as **T**ype pull-down list and select one of the text file format files that Word for Windows creates. In most cases, you should choose the Text Only (*.TXT) format.

Printing to a Fax Machine

If you have a fax board and appropriate software installed on your computer, you can print a Word document to a remote fax machine. WinFax Pro is representative of fax software packages that intercept documents that Word thinks it has sent to the printer and then route them over the phone lines to a fax machine.

To print a document to a fax machine with WinFax Pro, follow these steps:

1. Install a fax board in your computer and install and set up the WinFax Pro software.

2. Choose the **File W**in Fax command (see fig. 8.13).

Fig. 8.13
To send a document to a fax machine, select the fax software from the File menu and then fill out the Fax addressing dialog box (as shown with WinFax Pro).

3. Fill out the Fax addressing dialog box.

4. Choose the Send button.

Sending Documents to Others in Your Workgroup

You might work in a collaborative environment where several people contribute to the creation of individual documents. Perhaps you need approval from a higher-up before you send out a report or letter. If your computer is connected to a network with electronic mail capability, you can send the document by using the Send command.

The following example uses Microsoft Mail, a popular electronic mail package, for illustration.

To send a document to a colleague via electronic mail, follow these steps:

1. Choose the File Send command.

2. Enter your Mail password in the Password box in the Mail Sign In dialog box and choose OK.

3. In the window that appears, enter the recipients' names in the To and Cc boxes, or click the Address button and select the recipients from your Mail address book. Fig. 8.14 shows a completed dialog box.

Fig. 8.14
Choose the File Send command to include a Word document in an electronic note to someone in your organization. Note the icon representing the Word document.

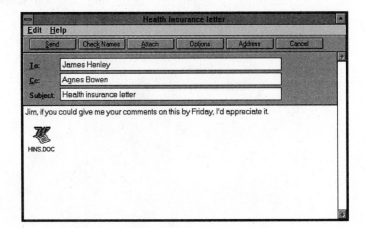

4. Add explanatory comments in the message body section.

5. Click the Send button.

For more information about sending documents with Microsoft Mail, see the documentation for Microsoft Mail or the Mail User's Guide in the documentation for Windows for Workgroups.

From Here...

For information relating directly to printing, you can review the following major sections of this book:

- Chapter 9, "Formatting Characters and Changing Fonts," describes working with different fonts.

- Chapter 13, "Setting the Page Layout," teaches you how to add headers and footers to your documents, control page breaks, and set margins.

- Chapter 15, "Mastering Envelopes, Mail Merge, and Form Letters," shows you how to print envelopes and mailing labels, access data files, and print form letters.

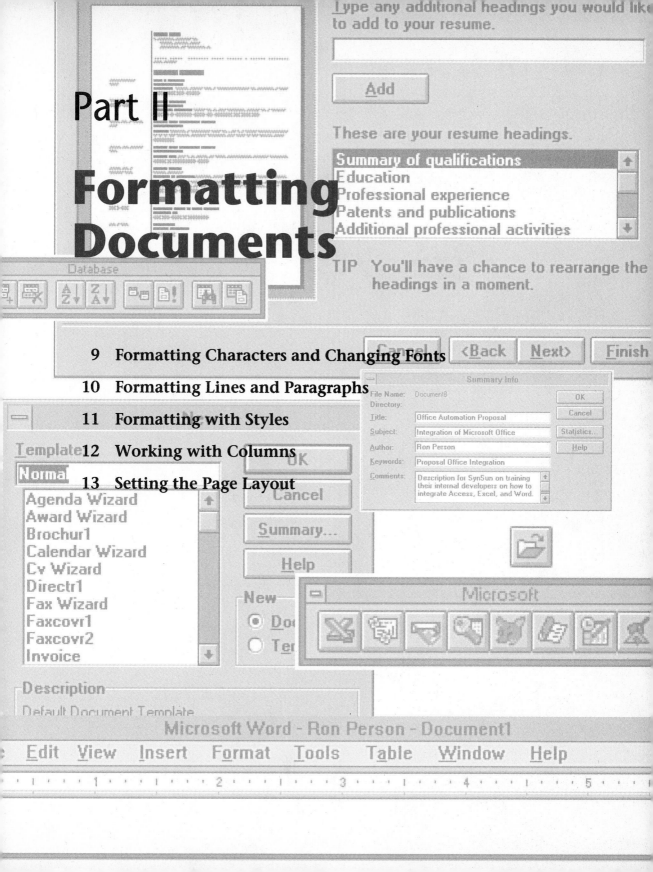

Part II

Formatting Documents

9   Formatting Characters and Changing Fonts

10   Formatting Lines and Paragraphs

11   Formatting with Styles

12   Working with Columns

13   Setting the Page Layout

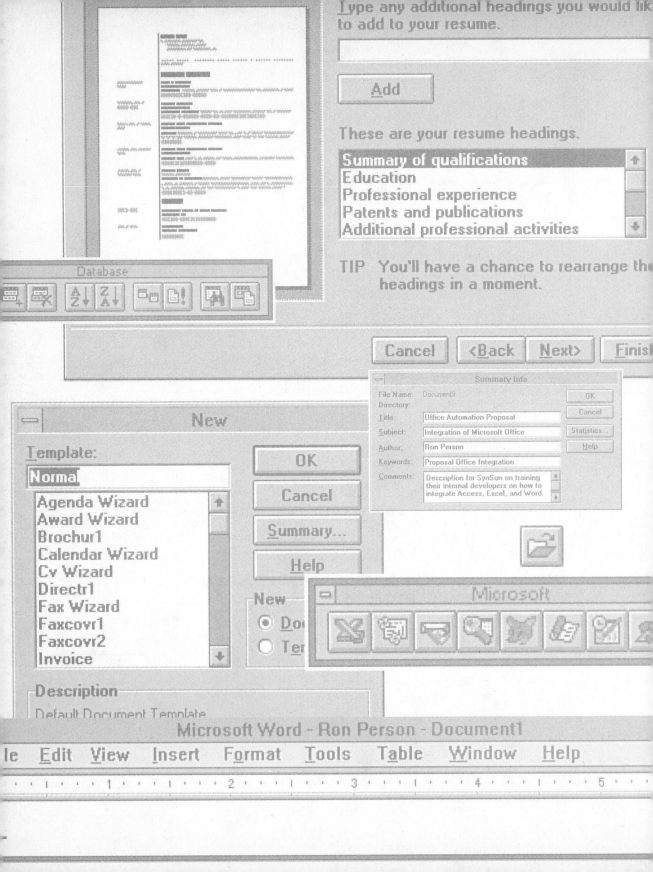

Type any additional headings you would lik
to add to your resume.

Add

These are your resume headings.

Summary of qualifications
Education
Professional experience
Patents and publications
Additional professional activities

TIP You'll have a chance to rearrange the
headings in a moment.

Database

Cancel   <Back   Next>   Finish

Summary Info

File Name: Document8
Directory:
Title: Office Automation Proposal
Subject: Integration of Microsoft Office
Author: Ron Person
Keywords: Proposal Office Integration
Comments: Description for SynSun on training
            their internal developers on how to
            integrate Access, Excel, and Word.

OK
Cancel
Statistics...
Help

New

Template:

Norma

Agenda Wizard
Award Wizard
Brochur1
Calendar Wizard
Cv Wizard
Directr1
Fax Wizard
Faxcovr1
Faxcovr2
Invoice

OK
Cancel
Summary...
Help

New
◉ Do
○ Te

Microsoft

Description
Default Document Template

Microsoft Word - Ron Person - Document1

le   Edit   View   Insert   Format   Tools   Table   Window   Help

Chapter 9

Formatting Characters and Changing Fonts

Characters—individual letters, numbers, punctuation marks, and symbols—are the smallest unit of text you can format in a Word document. You can apply formatting styles such as bold, italic, or a different font to one character or to an entire document. You can combine character formatting options; for example, you can make a word bold and italicized. You also can use as many different types of character formatting in a document as you want. Your document's title, for example, can be in a different font or larger size, subheadings can be boldfaced, and paragraphs of text can be plain text with some italic text for occasional emphasis.

What Is Character Formatting?

Character formatting options include fonts, sizes, boldface, italic, strikethrough, hidden text, colors, superscript and subscript, uppercase and lowercase, small caps, underlines, and character spacing.

Word for Windows also has many special characters to include in your document. You can create a list using bullets or decorative dingbats, for example, or you can include a copyright or trademark symbol. This chapter covers all the character formatting options.

Fig. 9.1 shows some examples of the character formatting options available in Word for Windows.

Some of the main topics covered in this chapter are

- Formatting characters

- Changing fonts

- Copying formatting

- Special character formatting

- Inserting symbols and special fonts

- Using fonts correctly

Formatting Documents

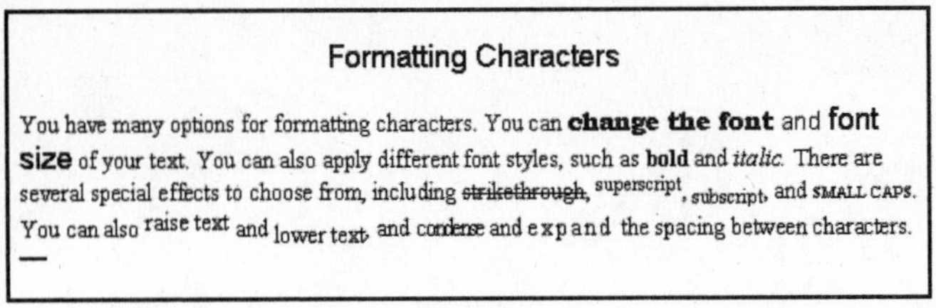

Fig. 9.1
There are many formatting options you can apply to characters in Word for Windows.

Formatting Characters

You have many options for formatting characters. You can **change the font** and font size of your text. You can also apply different font styles, such as **bold** and *italic*. There are several special effects to choose from, including ~~strikethrough~~, superscript, subscript, and SMALL CAPS. You can also raise text and lower text, and condense and e x p a n d the spacing between characters.

—

You can use character formatting to accomplish the following tasks:

- Add emphasis to text—you can boldface or enlarge important items.

- Hide notes to yourself or other readers—you can use hidden text to include notes that do not print.

- Add visual interest to text—you can change fonts to visually differentiate body text from headings.

Viewing Formatted Characters

The way characters appear on-screen depends on several factors. One factor is the selected document view. In normal view, which is the default view, you see accurate character formatting (boldface appears **bold**, for example), unless you have selected the Draft Font option using the Tools Options command. In page layout view, you see the entire page exactly as it will look in print, including character formatting. Select the view you want from the View menu.

To see character formatting in normal view, follow these steps:

1. Choose the View Normal command.

2. Choose the Tools Options command.

3. Select the View tab.

4. Deselect the **Draft Font** check box (if it is checked).

5. Choose OK.

Another factor controlling how text appears on-screen is the printer you have selected. If your printer doesn't support a font or size you use to format your text, Word for Windows may substitute the closest possible font and size.

Understanding Screen Fonts and Printer Fonts

Finally, the issue of *screen fonts* (which control the screen appearance of fonts) versus *printer fonts* (fonts the printer uses) can affect the appearance of on-screen text. If you have printer fonts for which no corresponding screen fonts are available, fonts may look blocklike on-screen (the fonts are scaled up or down from the nearest font or size) even though they print just fine.

To resolve the discrepancy between screen fonts and printer fonts, you can use TrueType fonts with Word for Windows while operating under Windows Versions 3.1 or later. TrueType is a type of built-in font-generation software that generates screen and printer fonts so that what you see on-screen is almost the same as what you print, whether you have a laser printer or a dot-matrix printer. For more details on printer and screen fonts, see "Using Fonts Correctly" later in this chapter.

If you format text with fonts your printer cannot print, you may end up with a screen that doesn't match the printed output. You can make the following change to ensure that line and page breaks appear on-screen just as they appear in print.

To be sure your document looks the same on-screen as it does in print, follow these steps:

1. Choose the **V**iew Normal command.

2. Choose Tools **O**ptions and select the View tab.

3. Deselect the **D**raft Font check box (if it is checked).

4. Choose OK.

"Using Fonts Correctly," later in this chapter, describes how to improve the correspondence between what you see on-screen and the printed result.

Troubleshooting the Screen View of Characters

The following troubleshooting tips provide the answers to some of the questions most frequently asked about the screen display.

The character formatting I've added doesn't show up on-screen.

The display options may be set to increase typing and scrolling speed rather than to display character formatting. Make sure that the normal view is set with **D**raft Font turned off in the View tab of the Tools Options command (instructions for this setting appear earlier in this section). Also make sure that the printer you have selected can print the format you have applied.

Tip
The Font list in the Formatting toolbar shows a printer icon to the left of each font available from your printer and a TT for TrueType fonts. For best results, always use one of these fonts.

Choose the File Print command, and then choose the Printer button to display the Print Setup dialog box. The printer you have selected is highlighted in the Printers list box.

I don't see the formatting codes on-screen.

Unlike some word processors, Word for Windows does not display formatting codes on-screen. Instead, you see the results of the formatting on-screen. The text appears as it will look in print. You can determine which formatting options have been applied by selecting the text and choosing the Format Font command. The dialog box indicates those options that currently are active.

Selecting Characters to Format

For Related Information
■ "Selecting Text," p. 133

You can format characters as you type or after you finish typing. To format characters as you type, choose the formatting command, type the text, and then choose the formatting command a second time to turn off the command. To format characters after you finish typing, you must remember this rule: Select, then do. Select the text to format, and then choose the formatting command. See Chapter 5, "Editing a Document," for instructions on how to select text.

Formatting Characters

Word for Windows offers no shortage of techniques for applying character formatting. If you have a mouse, you can format using tools and lists on the Standard and Formatting toolbars. If you prefer the keyboard, you can access formatting commands from the menu. You also can take advantage of many helpful mouse and keyboard shortcuts.

Whether you choose to format text before or after you type it, you must remember that most character formatting commands *toggle* on and off—you turn them on the same way that you turn them off. If you select and boldface a word and then want to remove the boldface, select the word a second time and choose the Bold command again. Toggling applies when you use buttons on the toolbars or keyboard shortcuts to apply or remove formatting. Formatting with the menu commands varies slightly.

Formatting with Menu Commands

Using a menu command is probably the most basic technique for formatting characters. Using the menu has three primary advantages: the Font dialog box displays all the character formatting commands at once; you can apply several types of character formatting simultaneously with the Font dialog box; and you can preview the results of the formatting choices you make in the Font dialog box.

To access the Font dialog box, choose the Format Font command or press Ctrl+D. The Font dialog box displays two tabs: Font and Character Spacing (see figs. 9.2 and 9.3). The options of each tab are described in tables 9.1 and 9.2. (Options marked with asterisks are detailed later in this chapter.)

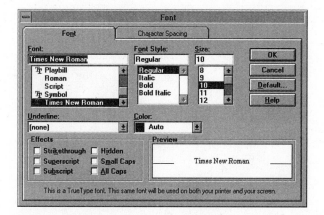

Fig. 9.2
Use the Font options to change fonts, character font styles, and effects.

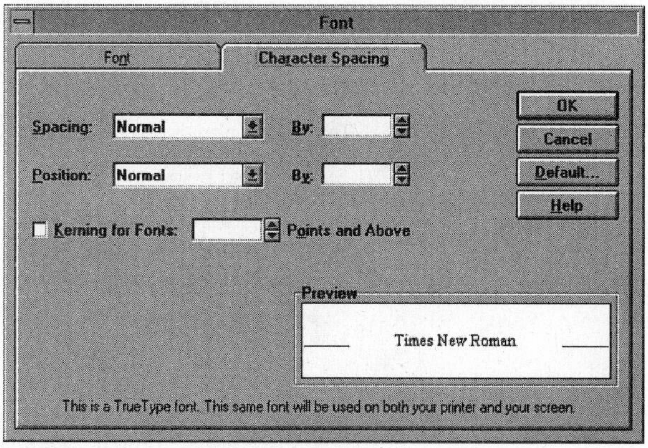

Fig. 9.3
Use the Character Spacing options to control the spacing between characters.

Formatting Documents

Table 9.1 The Font Tab Options

Group	Option	Description
Font*	Selection varies depending on printer	A typeface style. Common fonts include Times New Roman, Arial, and Courier.
Font Style	Regular	The basic font with no enhancements. Used for most typing.
	Italic	Oblique, or slanted, text: *Italic*. Often used for book or magazine names, or for emphasis. Can be combined with Bold.
	Bold	Heavy text: **Bold**. Often used for document titles or subheadings.
	Bold Italic	Bold and italic formatting combined.
Size*	8, 10, 12, etc.	Character size in points. An inch consists of 72 points (a typesetting measurement).
Underline*	None	Normal text. Used to remove underlining.
	Single	<u>Single underline</u>. The space between words is underlined.
	Words only	<u>Single underline</u>. The space between words is not underlined.
	Double	<u>Double underline</u>. The space between words is underlined.
	Dotted	Single underline. The space between the words is underlined.
Color*	Auto, Black, Red, Yellow, etc.	Changes the color of text on-screen if you have a color monitor. Prints in color if you have a color printer.
Effects	Strikethrough	Text crossed with a line: ~~Strikethrough~~. Often used when making revisions.
	Superscript*	Text raised above the baseline.
	Subscript*	Text lowered below the baseline.
	Hidden*	Text that doesn't appear or print unless you want it to. Often used for private notes or comments.
	Small Caps	Short uppercase letters: SMALL CAPS. Used for emphasis or for graphic effect.
	All Caps	All uppercase letters: ALL CAPS. Used for emphasis or for graphic effect. Harder to read than format combining uppercase and lowercase.

Group	Option	Description
Default*	n/a	Applies selected formatting to the template attached to the document as well as to the current document. All future documents based on this template will use the selections in the Font dialog box as the default font.
Preview	n/a	Shows a sample of text formatted with selected options.

Table 9.2 The Character Spacing Options

Group	Option	Description
Spacing*	Normal	Default spacing for the selected font.
	Expanded	Space between characters expanded to 3 pts.
	Condensed	Space between characters condensed to 1.75 pts.
By:*	1 pt (default), or enter your own amount	Number of points by which text is expanded or condensed. Measured in increments of tenths of a point.
Position*	Normal	Text is printed on the base line.
	Raised	Text is raised above the baseline by the increment you indicate in the **By** box.
	Lowered	Text is lowered below the baseline by the increment you indicate in the **By** box.
By:	3 pt (default), or enter your own amount	Number of points by which text is raised or lowered.
Default	n/a	Applies selected formatting to template attached to the document as well as to the current document. All future documents based on this template will use the selections in the Font dialog box as the default font.
Preview	n/a	Shows a sample of text formatted with selected options.

To format characters using a menu command, follow these steps:

1. Select the text to format, or position the insertion point where you want formatting to begin.

2. Choose the Format Font command. The Font dialog box appears (refer to figs. 9.2 and 9.3).

3. Select the Font tab or the Character tab.

4. Select the formatting option or options you want.

5. Choose OK.

The Font dialog box tabs show formatting for the currently selected characters. If the selected text is bold, for example, the Bold option is selected in the Font Style box on the Font tab. If, however, the selection includes various formatting options, no items in the list boxes will be selected and the check boxes will be shaded, indicating that the selection includes mixed formats.

Because any formatting options you select apply to all the selected text, you can use the Font dialog box to turn on or off formatting for large areas of text, even if the text includes a variety of formatting.

Formatting with Keyboard Shortcuts

You can use the keyboard to format characters in two ways. The first way is to press Alt+O, F to display the Font dialog box; you can use this dialog box to select character formatting options (as described in the preceding section). The second way to format characters with the keyboard is to use a shortcut key.

To format characters using shortcut keys, follow these steps:

1. Select the text to format, or position the insertion point where you want formatting to begin.

2. Press the appropriate key combination, described in the following table:

Format	Shortcut
Bold	Ctrl+B
Italic	Ctrl+I
Single underline	Ctrl+U
Word underline	Ctrl+Shift+W
Double underline	Ctrl+Shift+D
SMALL CAPS	Ctrl+Shift+K

Format	Shortcut
ALL CAPS	Ctrl+Shift+A
Hidden text	Ctrl+Shift+H
Superscript	Ctrl+Shift+= (equal sign)
Subscript	Ctrl+= (equal sign)
Copy formatting	Ctrl+Shift+C
Paste formatting	Ctrl+Shift+V
Remove formatting	Ctrl+space bar
Change case of letters	Shift+F3
Font	Ctrl+Shift+F. This command activates the Font box in the Formatting toolbar. Type a new font name or use the arrow keys to highlight the desired font; press Enter to select it.
Symbol font	Ctrl+Shift+Q
Point size	Ctrl+Shift+P. This command activates the Point Size box in the Formatting toolbar. Type a new size or use the arrow keys to highlight the desired point size; press Enter to select it.
Next larger point size available for selected font	Ctrl+Shift+>
Next smaller point size available for selected font	Ctrl+Shift+<
Up one point size	Ctrl+]
Down one point size	Ctrl+[

See the following sections for more information about the preceding commands.

Formatting with the Formatting Toolbar

The *Formatting toolbar* is a handy tool for quick character formatting (see fig. 9.4). You can change the style, font, or size of text, and format characters with bold, italic, or single underline. Paragraph formatting options also are included on the Formatting toolbar. For more details about paragraph formatting, refer to Chapter 10, "Formatting Lines and Paragraphs."

II

Formatting Documents

Fig. 9.4

You can select character formatting commands from the Formatting toolbar.

The following information provides general instructions for formatting with the Formatting toolbar; later in this section you will find more detailed instructions for using styles, bold, italic, and underline. Techniques for using the Formatting toolbar to format fonts and sizes are described in the sections "Changing Font Type" and "Changing Font Size" later in this chapter.

The Formatting toolbar first must be displayed before using it. To display the Formatting toolbar, follow this step:

Choose the View Toolbars command and specify the toolbars you want to display on-screen.

To format characters using the Formatting toolbar, follow these steps:

1. Display the Formatting toolbar by choosing the View Toolbars command, selecting Formatting, and choosing OK. (Do this step only if the Formatting toolbar is not currently displayed.)

2. Select the text to be formatted, or position the insertion point where you want formatting to begin.

3. Select a style from the Style list.

   or

   Select a font from the Font list.

   or

   Select a select a size from the Point Size list.

   or

   Choose the Bold, Italic, or Underline button.

You can make as many of these selections as you want. For example, you can change the font and point size for the selected text and add boldfacing.

No matter how you apply formatting to text—whether you use a menu command, a shortcut, or the Formatting toolbar—the Formatting toolbar displays the formatting for that text when it is selected.

Notice that the Formatting toolbar also includes paragraph alignment options. For details about using these options, see Chapter 10, "Formatting Lines and Paragraphs."

Selecting Styles with the Formatting Toolbar. A *style* is a set of "memorized" formatting commands. Although styles apply to entire paragraphs, they often contain character formatting. Word for Windows uses the Normal style to apply default formatting, but you can change the style easily.

To change the style with the mouse, follow these steps:

1. Position the insertion point inside the paragraph you want to format with a style.

2. Select a style from the Styles list box.

To change the style with a shortcut key, follow these steps:

1. Position the insertion point inside the paragraph you want to format with a style.

2. Press Ctrl+Shift+S to select the Styles list box.

3. Press the down-arrow key to select the style you want.

4. Press Enter.

Even if the Formatting toolbar isn't displayed, you can apply a style by pressing Ctrl+Shift+S. The Style dialog box appears. You can select a style and then choose the Apply button or press Enter. For details about creating and using styles, see Chapter 11, "Formatting with Styles."

Selecting Bold, Italic, or Underline with the Formatting Toolbar. When selected, the three-dimensional buttons on the Formatting toolbar are bright and appear pressed; when not selected, the buttons appear raised. If your selection includes mixed formatting, for example (if part of the selection is bold and the rest is not), the button will be grayed. Selecting a button—raised, pressed, or grayed—applies (or removes) formatting to all selected text.

To apply bold, italic, or underline with the Formatting toolbar, follow these steps:

1. Select the text to be formatted, or position the insertion point where you want the formatting to begin before you enter the text.

Formatting Documents

II

2. Click the Bold, Italic, or Underline button to apply the formatting you want to use.

Remember that these buttons toggle on and off. If you select a boldfaced word and click the Bold button, the bold formatting is removed from the selected word. If you select both a bold word and a normal word that *precedes* it and click the Bold button, both words are formatted as bold. If you select both a bold word and a normal word that follows it and click the Bold button, however, both words are formatted as normal.

Troubleshooting Character Formatting

Characters appear OK on screen, but they don't print as shown.

Use TrueType fonts in your documents. TrueType fonts come with Windows 3.1. In the Font list of the Font tab, TrueType fonts are preceded by a TT. TrueType fonts are designed to appear the same on-screen as they do in print. You are likely to have used a font on-screen that your printer cannot exactly reproduce. TrueType takes care of this problem. See "Using TrueType" later in this chapter for more information.

Character formatting appeared to be correct the last time the document was opened, but now the character formatting has changed. In some cases, formatting is missing.

For Related Information
■ "Aligning Paragraphs," p. 295

■ "Creating a Styles by Example," p. 360

The currently selected printer may not be the printer that was selected during the document's original formatting. If the current printer is not capable of reproducing the fonts, sizes, or styles that you originally formatted, Windows shows you the best that the current printer can do. Correct this problem by reselecting a printer that is capable of printing the formats. Choose the File Print command, choose the Printer button, and then select a new printer.

Changing Fonts

A *font* is a typeface style; all letters, punctuation, and other text characters of a given font have the same appearance. Three basic types of fonts exist: *serif*, with strokes at the ends of letters; *sans serif*, with no strokes; and *specialty*, such as symbols and script fonts.

Common fonts include Times Roman, a serif font; Helvetica, a sans serif font; and Zapf Chancery, a script font. These and other fonts are shown in fig. 9.5.

```
Times New Roman
Arial
Helvetica
Palatino
Bookman
ZapfChancery
Script
Symbol: αβχδψγλ
```

Fig. 9.5
The selection of
fonts available to
you depends on
your printer.

The printer (or printers) you installed and selected determine what fonts are available for your use. The HP LaserJet III, for example, includes CG Times, Univers, Courier, and Line printer. A PostScript printer usually includes Times Roman, Palatino, Bookman, New Century Schoolbook (serif fonts), Helvetica, Avant Garde (sans serif fonts), Zapf Chancery (a script font), and Zapf Dingbats (a symbol font). The selected printer determines which fonts you see listed in the Font list box. (The Font list also includes built-in Windows fonts such as the symbol fonts, Symbol and Fences. For more information about fonts available in Windows, see "Using Fonts Correctly" later in this chapter.)

You can add more fonts to your printer. You can buy software fonts (which tend to print slowly) and download them to a printer, or buy font cartridges to insert into your laser printer. The popular Z1A cartridge for the HP LaserJet II, for example, includes Times and Helvetica in several sizes and styles.

Because Word for Windows and other Windows programs use printer and screen fonts, you can select screen fonts in your document that your printer cannot print. If you do, what you see on-screen isn't necessarily what you get when you print. The ability to select fonts that your printer doesn't support is handy when you want to create a document that will be printed on another printer or used by a service bureau for producing a linotype. In this case, you can select fonts that you know are supported by the other printer or service bureau, and you can see on-screen how your document will look, even though you can't obtain an accurate printout on your own printer.

To make sure that your screen displays what you will actually get when you print, follow these steps:

1. Choose the Tools Options command.

2. Select the Normal View tab.

3. Deselect the Draft Font check box.

4. Choose OK.

Even with the preceding procedure, lines of text may extend into the right margin, or text in a table may appear cut off at the right border of a cell. In spite of its on-screen appearance, however, text will print accurately.

Changing Font Type

Tip
You can use the Edit Replace command (or press Ctrl+H) to search for and replace fonts (without changing the text). For details, see Chapter 7, "Using Editing and Proofing Tools."

You can change fonts with a menu command or from the Formatting toolbar. You can use either the mouse or the keyboard to make the change. This section includes instructions for all these methods.

To change the font with the mouse from the menu, follow these steps:

1. Select the text whose font you want to change, or position the insertion point where you want the new font to begin before you begin typing.

2. Choose the Format Font command, press Ctrl+D, or click the right mouse button and select Font from the shortcut menu.

3. Select the Font tab.

4. Select the font you want from the Font list or type its name.

5. Choose OK.

To change the font using the Formatting toolbar, follow these steps:

1. Select the text whose font you want to change, or position the insertion point where you want the new font to begin when you begin typing.

2. Click the down arrow to the right of the Font list box, or press Ctrl+Shift+F and press the down-arrow key to display the list of fonts.

3. Select a font from the Font list box. Press Enter if you are using the keyboard.

Changing Font Size

Font sizes are measured in *points*, the traditional typesetting measuring unit. An inch consists of 72 points; thus, an inch-high letter is 72 points, and a half-inch-high letter is 36 points. Text in a book may be 10 or 11 points.

Like fonts, your printer determines what font sizes you can use. An HP LaserJet II printer equipped with the popular Z1A cartridge includes Times and Helvetica fonts in pre-set sizes ranging from 8 to 14 points. PostScript printers and HP LaserJet III printers include scalable fonts. You can print scalable fonts from sizes as small as a barely readable 4 points to as tall as a page. (For more information about fonts and font sizes, see "Using Fonts Correctly" later in this chapter.)

Screen fonts (fonts created without TrueType) that are included in Windows rather than in the printer don't come in all sizes, even if your printer has scalable fonts. If you change text to an odd size such as 17 points, the text looks blocklike on-screen, because Word for Windows substitutes the next closest font size for the missing screen font.

You can change font sizes in three ways: with the menu command, the Formatting toolbar, or shortcuts.

To change the font size using the menu command, follow these steps:

1. Select the text you want to resize, or position the insertion point where you want the new font size to begin when you start typing.

2. Choose the Format Font command, press Ctrl+D, or click the right mouse button and select Font from the shortcut menu.

3. Select the Font tab.

4. Select the Size list.

5. Select the point size you want or type in the point size.

6. Choose OK.

The Formatting toolbar provides a quick way to change font size without using a menu command. The Formatting toolbar must be displayed before you can use it.

Tip

If the Formatting toolbar isn't displayed, you can change the font by pressing Ctrl+Shift+F to display the Font dialog box; then select a font or type in the font name and press Enter.

II

Formatting Documents

To display the Formatting toolbar, follow these steps:

Choose the **View Toolbars** command, select Formatting, and choose OK.

To change font size with the Formatting toolbar, follow these steps:

1. Select the text you want to resize, or position the insertion point where you want the new size to begin when you start typing.

2. Select a size from the Point Size list box by clicking the down arrow next to the font size, or press Shift+Ctrl+P and type in a size or use the down-arrow key to select a size, then press Enter.

Tip

Even if the Formatting Toolbar isn't displayed, you can change point size by pressing Ctrl+Shift+P to display the Font dialog box; select or type a font size and press Enter.

Another shortcut is available for increasing or decreasing point size to the next size listed in the Font Size list on the Formatting toolbar or in the Font dialog box. If sizes 9, 10, and 12 are listed, for example, you can increase 10-point text to 12 points, and you can decrease 10-point text to 9 points.

To use keyboard shortcuts to change point size, follow these steps:

1. Select the text you want to resize before you enter text, or position the insertion point where you want the new size to begin.

2. Press Ctrl+Shift+> to increase the point size.

    or

    Press Ctrl+Shift+< to decrease the point size.

Note

You can replace a font size in your document just as you can replace text. If all of your headlines in a report are 14 points and you want to change them to 12 points, for example, you can use the **Edit Replace** command to make the global change quickly (see Chapter 7, "Using Editing and Proofing Tools").

Changing the Default Character Formatting

Word for Windows uses the Normal style (contained in the Normal template) to control the default character and paragraph formatting choices for all documents. The Normal style's default type font, Times New Roman, has a default size of 10 points. If you always work with some other character formatting settings, you can apply those settings to the Normal style. Your new defaults take effect for the current document and for all future documents (but not for existing documents).

To change default character formatting, follow these steps:

1. Choose the Format Font command.

2. Select the new defaults you want to use from either the Font or Character Spacing tabs.

3. Choose the Default button.

4. Choose the Yes button to indicate that you want to change the Normal template.

Because you requested a change to the Normal template, when you exit Word for Windows, you see a message box asking whether you want to save changes to Word for Windows. Choose Yes. For more information about styles, see Chapter 11, "Formatting with Styles." For more information about templates, see Chapter 6, "Using Templates as Master Documents."

For Related Information
- "Using Styles versus Direct Formatting," p. 337

- "Changing a Template," p. 176

Copying Formatting

If you do much repetitive character formatting, you can save some time by repeating or copying formatting between characters. You can use two different methods: the Edit Repeat command and the Format Painter button.

You can use the Edit Repeat command to copy formatting immediately after you have formatted characters. The command repeats only the *one* most recent edit. If you use the Font dialog box to apply several formatting choices at once, the Repeat command repeats all those choices because you made them as a single edit. But if you use the Repeat command after making several formatting choices from the keyboard or with the Formatting toolbar, the command repeats only the one most recent choice.

To repeat character formatting with the **Edit Repeat** command immediately after formatting characters, follow these steps:

1. Select the new text to format.

2. Press F4, or choose **Edit Repeat**.

To use this technique, you must perform it immediately after performing the edit that you want to repeat.

The Standard toolbar includes a button for copying character formatting. To copy character formatting with the Format Painter button, follow these steps:

1. Select the text whose format you want to copy.

2. Click the Format Painter button on the Standard toolbar. The mouse pointer changes to a paintbrush with an I-beam.

3. Select the text you want to change and release the mouse button. The selected text automatically takes on the new formatting when you release the mouse button.

You can copy the formatting to more than one location by double-clicking the Format Painter button in Step 1, selecting the first block of text to which you want to copy the formatting, and releasing the mouse button. Then select each additional block of text to which you want to copy the formatting, and release the mouse button. When you have finished copying the formatting, click the Format Painter button again or press Esc.

If you find that the formatting you copied or added is not to your liking, you can remove all character formatting. The remaining formatting is part of the style to which the text is attached.

For Related Information

■ "Using Paragraph Formatting Techniques," p. 289

To remove all character formatting, follow these steps:

1. Select the text whose character formatting you want to remove.

2. Press Ctrl+space bar.

Applying Special Character Formatting Options

Many formatting options are simple and straightforward: a font is a specific character set design; size is measured in points; boldfaced text is heavier than normal text. Other options, however, aren't quite so obvious, and to use them, you may need to specify some criteria that further controls the option. For example, you can specify how high you want superscript text to appear in relation to the text baseline.

All the character formatting options described in this section toggle on and off. To remove superscripting, for example, you must select the Superscripted text, choose Format Font to access the Font dialog box, and choose Superscript again.

Hiding Text

At times, you may want to include in your document *hidden text*—text that disappears until you choose a command to display it. When displayed, hidden text has a dotted underline (see fig. 9.6). Hiding text doesn't affect the text formatting.

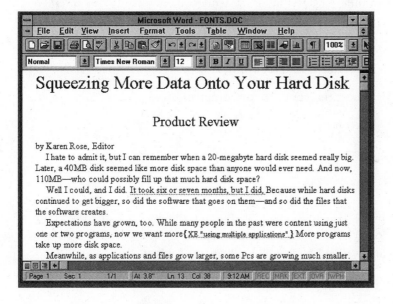

Fig. 9.6
Hidden text has a dotted underline on-screen; when printed, it has no underline.

You can format any text, such as notes to yourself, as hidden text. Word for Windows also uses hidden text to format table-of-contents entries, index entries (as shown in fig. 9.6), and annotations.

To hide text with the menu command, follow these steps:

1. Select the text you want to hide, or position the insertion point where you want hidden text to begin.

2. Choose the Format Font command.

3. Select the Font tab.

4. Select the Hidden check box.

5. Choose OK.

To hide text with the keyboard shortcut, follow these steps:

1. Select the text you want to hide, or position the insertion point where you want hidden text to begin.

2. Press Ctrl+Shift+H.

You can toggle hidden text on and off with the keyboard shortcut, as long as the text is selected. You also can display all hidden text on the screen in normal, outline, page layout, or master document views. If you intend to print hidden text, display it before you decide on final page breaks. Otherwise, page numbering and page breaks may be inaccurate.

To display hidden text, follow these steps:

1. Choose the Tools Options command.

2. Select the View tab.

3. Select the Hidden Text check box (see fig. 9.7).

4. Choose OK.

If you have not indicated that you want hidden text displayed on the Tools Options View tab, you can toggle the display of hidden text on and off with the Show/Hide ¶ button on the Standard toolbar.

To display the Standard toolbar, follow this step:

Choose the View Toolbars command, select Standard, and press Enter.

To hide and display hidden text with the Show/Hide ¶ button, follow this step:

Click the Show/Hide ¶ button on the Standard toolbar.

You also can see hidden text with the File Print Preview command if you choose to print hidden text.

To print hidden text all the time, whether or not the text is displayed, follow these steps:

1. Choose the Tools Options command.

2. Select the Print tab (see fig. 9.8).

3. Select the Hidden Text check box.

4. Choose OK.

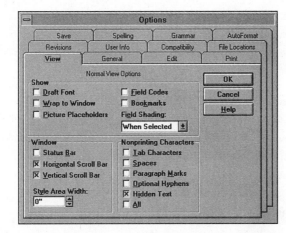

Fig. 9.7
Select the Hidden Text option to display hidden text on-screen.

Fig. 9.8
Select the Hidden Text option on the Tools Options Print tab to print hidden text.

Formatting Documents

To include hidden text only when you print the current document, follow these steps:

1. Choose the File Print command.

2. Choose the Options button. The Tools Options Print tab appears.

3. Select the Hidden Text check box.

4. Choose OK.

Note

You can format any character as hidden text, even a page break or paragraph mark, but doing so affects the page numbering in a table of contents. For an accurate page count, remove the hidden formatting by using the Edit Find command to locate the hidden character and remove the hidden formatting. For details about finding and replacing formatting, refer to Chapter 7, "Using Editing and Proofing Tools."

Changing Character Colors

If you have a color monitor, you can make good use of the 16 different colors available for text in Word for Windows. On an office task list, for example, you can format each person's duties in a different color so that they easily can see who must do which job. You also can format different levels of priority as different colors: for example, red items must be done right away; blue can wait. If you have a color printer, you can print text in color.

To color text, follow these steps:

1. Select the text to color, or position the insertion point where you want the new color to begin.

2. Choose the Format Font command.

3. Select the Font tab.

4. Select a color from the Color list.

5. Choose OK.

Auto color, also listed in the Color list, is the color you select for Window Text in the Colors section of the Control Panel. Auto color is usually black.

Making Superscript and Subscript Text

Sometimes you may need to use subscripts and superscripts. You may use these features in scientific notations (for example, H_2O) or in references such as trademark or copyright symbols (for example, Microsoft™).

In calculating where superscripts and subscripts appear in relation to normal text, Word for Windows begins with the text baseline. You use the same procedure to add and remove both superscripts and subscripts.

To add or remove superscripts and subscripts, follow these steps:

1. Select the text you want to raise or lower, or position the insertion point where you want raised or lowered text to begin.

2. Choose the Format Font command.

3. Select the Font tab.

4. In the Effects group, select Superscript to raise text, or select Subscript to lower text. An X indicates that the feature is active.

5. Choose OK.

By default, Word for Windows raises superscript 3 points above the baseline and lowers subscript 3 points below the baseline. You can change the vertical position of superscript, subscript, or any text or graphic, however, in the Font dialog box on the Character Spacing tab.

To change the vertical position of text, follow these steps:

1. Select the text you want to raise or lower.

2. Choose the Format Font command.

3. Select the Character Spacing tab.

4. Choose Raised or Lowered from the Position box.

5. In the By box, accept 3 points as the default distance to raise or lower text, click the up or down arrows to change the distance, or type in a new amount.

6. Choose OK.

Underlining Text

Word for Windows offers four types of underlines: *single*, which underlines words and the space between words; *words only*, which underlines words but not the space between words; *double*, which double-underlines words and the space between words; and *dotted*, which underlines with dots the words and the space between words.

Tip

To superscript text by 3 points, select the text and press Shift+Ctrl+= (equal sign). To subscript text by 3 points, select the text and press Ctrl+= (equal sign).

Formatting Documents

To add underlining from the menu command, follow these steps:

1. Select the text you want to underline, or position the insertion point where you want underlining to begin.

2. Choose the Format Font command.

3. Select the Font tab.

4. In the Underline list box, select Single, Words Only, Double, or Dotted.

5. Choose OK.

Tip
To place an under-line below a super-script only, select the superscript—not the surround-ing text—before issuing the Under-line command. Subscripted text is always underlined just below the subscripted characters.

To remove underlining with the menu command, follow these steps:

1. Select the underlined text.

2. Choose the Format Font command.

3. Select the Font tab.

4. Select None from the Underline list box.

5. Choose OK.

To add or remove underlining with shortcut keys, follow these steps:

1. Select the text you want to underline or the text from which you want to remove underlining. Or position the insertion point where you want underlining to begin when you start typing.

2. Press one of the following shortcut keys:

Shortcut	Result
Ctrl+U	Single underline
Ctrl+Shift+W	Single underline, words only
Ctrl+Shift+D	Double underline

 To use the Formatting toolbar to add or remove underlining, follow these steps:

1. Select the text you want to underline or the text from which you want to remove underlining. Or position the insertion point where you want underlining to begin when you start typing.

2. Click the Underline button on the Formatting toolbar.

Adjusting Character Spacing

The normal spacing between letters in a word is right for most situations. Occasionally, however, you must fit more text on a line. Condensing the line can make the text fit. Sometimes, such as in large headlines, you also must condense the space between two individual letters to improve the headline's appearance. This process is known as *kerning*. The change in spacing is determined by the font design and the particular pair of letters being kerned.

In other instances, you may want to increase the space between letters to fill out a line or to create a special effect. Expanding makes text wider. For examples of condensed and expanded text, see fig. 9.9.

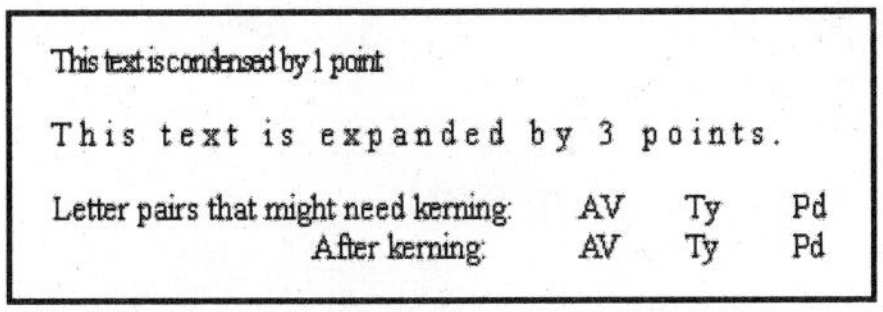

```
This text is condensed by 1 point

This  text  is  expanded  by  3  points.

Letter pairs that might need kerning:    AV    Ty    Pd
                        After kerning:    AV    Ty    Pd
```

Fig. 9.9
Use condensed and expanded text to change the spacing between characters.

By default, Word for Windows expands and condenses the spacing between characters by 3 points. You can change the distance in increments of 0.1 of a point. You need this level of precision for kerning.

In the Font dialog box's Character Spacing tab, watch the Spacing Preview box to see how your text looks after condensing or expanding.

To condense or expand the space between characters, follow these steps:

1. Select the text you want to condense or expand, or position the insertion point where you want condensed or expanded text to begin when you start typing.

2. Choose the Format Font command.

3. Select the Character Spacing tab.

4. In the Spacing box, select Expanded or Condensed.

5. In the **By** box, accept the default, click the up or down arrows to increase or decrease the amount, or type in a new amount.

6. Choose OK.

Note

If you select the **K**erning for Fonts option in the Character Spacing tab of the Font dialog box, Word will automatically adjust the kerning for TrueType or Adobe Type Manager fonts. You can specify the point size at and above which you want automatic kerning to be applied in the **P**oints and Above box.

To return expanded or condensed text to normal, follow these steps:

1. Select the text you want to return to normal, or position the insertion point where you want normal text to begin.

2. Choose the **F**ormat **F**ont command.

3. Select the Character Spacing tab.

4. In the **S**pacing box, select Normal.

5. Choose OK.

Switching Uppercase and Lowercase

You can use a Word for Windows shortcut to change letters from uppercase to lowercase, or vice versa (the result depends on the case of selected text).

To change the letter case from the menu command, follow these steps:

1. Select the text whose case you want to change, or position the insertion point in or to the left of the word whose case you want to change.

2. Choose the **F**ormat **C**hange Case command. The Change Case box appears (see fig. 9.10).

3. Select a case-change option from the following:

Option	Result
Sentence case	First character of the sentence to uppercase, all other characters to lowercase
lowercase	All lowercase

Option	Result
UPPERCASE	All uppercase
Title Case	First character of each word to uppercase, all other characters to lowercase
tOGGLE cASE	Switches uppercase to lowercase and lowercase to uppercase

4. Choose OK.

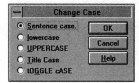

Fig. 9.10
Use the Format
Change Case
command to alter
letter case quickly.

To change the letter case from the keyboard, follow these steps:

1. Select the text whose case you want to change, or position the insertion point in or to the left of the word whose case you want to change.

2. Press Shift+F3 to change the case. You toggle among three options: all uppercase, all lowercase, first character uppercase. Continue to press Shift+F3 until the case is as you want it.

> **Note**
>
> The terms *uppercase* and *lowercase* come from the days when type was set by hand from individual letters molded from lead. The capital letters were stored in the upper case above where the typesetters assembled their text, and noncapital letters were stored in the lower case.

Starting Paragraphs with a Drop Cap

You can add visual interest to a paragraph by starting it with a *drop cap*, a large capital letter or first word that is set into a paragraph. The top of the drop cap or word aligns with the top of the first line of the paragraph. Succeeding lines are indented to allow space for the dropped text. Drop caps usually mark the beginnings of key sections or major parts of a document.

II

Formatting Documents

If you select a different font for the drop cap, choose one that blends with the rest of the paragraph. Sans serif initial letters should be used with sans serif paragraphs; serif drop caps go well with paragraphs in serif fonts. Alternatively, you may combine an elegant script or cursive drop cap with a paragraph in a serif font. Figs. 9.11 and 9.12 illustrate some uses of drop caps.

Fig. 9.11

A drop cap using the same font as the body text.

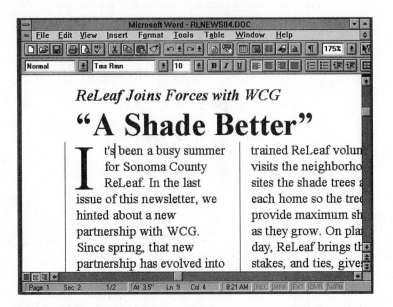

Fig. 9.12

A drop cap using a decorative font to enhance the text.

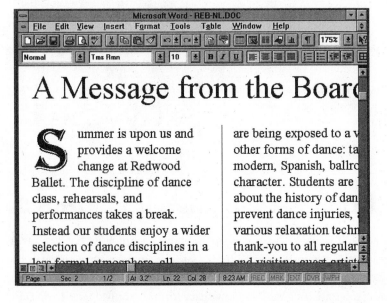

When you select a drop-cap format, Word for Windows places the selected text in a frame. The rest of the paragraph wraps beside the frame. For information about frames, see Chapter 23, "Framing and Moving Text and Graphics."

Note

To increase horizontal spacing between the drop cap and the body text, follow these steps. Select the drop cap. A frame will show around the drop cap when it is selected. Next choose the Format Frame command. In the Frame dialog box that appears, increase the Horizontal Distance from Text to approximately 0.1". You may want to experiment with this distance. Choose OK.

To create large dropped capital letters, follow these steps:

1. Select the first letter, word, or segment of the paragraph you want to format as a dropped cap.

2. Choose the Format Drop Cap command. The Drop Cap dialog box appears (see fig. 9.13).

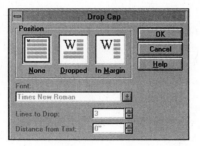

Fig. 9.13
You can design drop caps with the Format Drop Cap command.

3. Select Dropped or In Margin in the Position group to place the drop cap as follows:

Option	Result
Dropped	Dropped flush with the left margin, inside the main text area
In Margin	Dropped in the left margin

4. Select a font from the Font box.

5. In the Lines to Drop text box, type or select the number of lines you want the capital to drop into the paragraph. The default is 3 lines.

6. In the Distance from Text text box, type or select the distance you want between the drop cap and the paragraph text.

7. Choose OK.

If you are in normal view, Word for Windows asks whether you want to switch to page layout view to see the dropped cap as it will appear in print.

Choose the Yes button to switch to page layout view.

To remove dropped capital letters, follow these steps:

1. Select the first letter, word, or segment of the paragraph from which you want to remove the drop cap.

2. Choose the Format Drop Cap command.

3. Select the None option from the Position group.

4. Choose OK.

For Related Information
- "Framing Text, Pictures, and Other Objects," p. 688

- "Using Text as Graphics," p. 849

The drop cap text is inserted into a frame and can be resized and repositioned. To learn more about working with frames, see Chapter 23, "Framing and Moving Text and Graphics."

Inserting Special Characters and Symbols

You can include many special characters in your document. Symbol fonts such as Symbol and Zapf Dingbats, for example, contain *dingbats* (decorative characters such as bullets, stars, and flowers) and scientific symbols. You can use foreign language characters such as umlauts (ü) and tildes (ñ), or ANSI characters such as bullets and *em dashes* (wide hyphens used in punctuation). You also can use invisible characters such as discretionary hyphens (which appear only when needed) and nonbreaking spaces (which prevent two words from separating at the end of a line).

Two techniques give you access to special characters. You can use the Symbol dialog box, which shows a keyboard of special characters to choose from, or you can use a series of special keystrokes.

Using the Symbol Dialog Box

The Symbol dialog box, shown in fig. 9.14, gives you access to symbol fonts and ANSI characters. A symbol font, Symbol, is included with Word. Other symbol fonts may be built into your printer; for example, most PostScript printers include Zapf Dingbats. ANSI characters are the regular character set that you see on your keyboard, plus another hundred or so characters that include a copyright symbol, a registered trademark symbol, and many foreign language symbols.

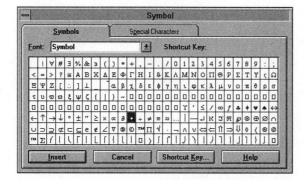

Fig. 9.14
You can insert symbols from the Symbol dialog box.

To insert symbols from the Symbol dialog box, follow these steps:

1. Position the insertion point where you want the symbol to appear.

2. Choose the Insert Symbol command. The Symbol dialog box appears.

3. From the Font list box, select the font for which you want to see symbols. (Select Normal Text to see ANSI characters.)

4. Click a symbol to select it and/or to see it enlarged, or press tab until the highlighted symbol in the box is selected (surrounded by dotted outline), and then use the cursor-movement keys to move the selection to the symbol you want.

5. Choose the Insert button.

6. Insert more characters by repeating Steps 3 through 5.

7. Choose the Close button.

Be sure to scan through all the interesting and useful symbols available in the Symbol and the Normal Text fonts.

Inserted symbols are actually field codes embedded in your document. This arrangement prevents you from accidentally selecting your symbol and changing it to a different font. Changing a symbol's font can change the symbol into a letter; for example, if you format text as Zapf Dingbats to include square bullets in your document, and then change the bullets to Times Roman, the bullets turn into *n's*.

To delete an inserted symbol, follow these steps:

1. Position the insertion point to the right of the symbol and press Backspace.

   or

1. Select the symbol you want to delete.

2. Press the Del key.

Customizing the Symbol Dialog Box

You may insert certain symbols, such as the copyright or trademark symbols, frequently in your work. You can customize the Symbol dialog box by adding shortcut keys. You then can use the shortcut keys to insert symbols directly from the keyboard.

To add shortcut keys to the Symbol dialog box, follow these steps:

1. Choose the Insert Symbol command.

2. Click the symbol for which you want to add a shortcut key.

3. Choose the Shortcut Key button. The Customize Keyboard dialog box, shown in fig. 9.15, appears. The symbol you have selected is displayed in the Symbol box.

4. Press the shortcut key combination you want to assign to the symbol. You can choose from any of the following key combinations:

Key Combination	Comments
Ctrl+ any letter or single digit	Most are previously assigned by Word
Ctrl+Shift+ any letter or single digit	Many are previously assigned by Word
Alt+ any letter or single digit	Most are not assigned
Alt+Shift+ any letter or single digit	Most are not assigned

5. Choose the Assign button.

6. Choose the Close button.

7. Repeat Steps 2 through 6 for any additional symbols you want to assign a shortcut key.

8. Choose the Close button.

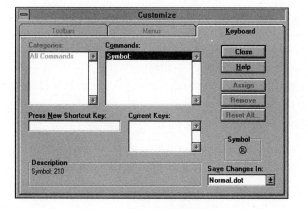

Fig. 9.15
You can add shortcut keys to symbols in the Customize Keyboard dialog box.

Inserting Special Characters from the Keyboard

You can insert special characters from the keyboard in two ways: by using shortcut keys you assign in the Symbol dialog box (see the preceding section), or by using the ANSI character numbers. You must know the ANSI character numbers for the corresponding character or symbols you want. Appendix C contains a complete list of ANSI characters.

To insert ANSI characters from the keyboard, follow these steps:

1. Position the insertion point where you want the symbol to appear.

2. Press Num Lock on the numeric keypad (so that numbers appear when you type).

3. Hold down the Alt key and, on the numeric keypad, type 0 (zero) followed by the ANSI code for the symbol you want. To type the fraction 1/4, for example, press Alt+0188 on the numeric keypad.

For Related Information
■ "Hyphenating Words," p. 139
■ "Customizing the Toolbar, Menus, and Buttons Shortcut Keys," p. 1051

If you have a symbol font such as Zapf Dingbats, or if you want to use a special character from the Symbol font, you can type and format the corresponding character with the Zapf Dingbats or Symbol font. To type a solid square (■), for example, you can type and format the letter *n* as Zapf Dingbats.

Using Fonts Correctly

With Windows and Word for Windows you can create documents that use the best capabilities of your printer. If you understand how Windows works with fonts, you can make your screen display match the printed result more closely.

A font is a set of characters with a consistent size and style. Times Roman 12 point and Helvetica 10 point, for example, are fonts. Windows is equipped with several fonts, and your printer may add more fonts. You also can purchase additional fonts for Windows and your printer.

Understanding Types of Fonts

Windows 3.0 works with two different types of fonts: fonts designed to display on-screen (screen fonts) and fonts designed to print (printer fonts). This section describes both types of fonts.

The Windows 3.1 TrueType font technology resolves many of the font problems inherent in Windows 3.0. TrueType font technology is described later in this chapter.

Understanding Printer Fonts. Depending on how the fonts are stored, Windows deals with fonts used by the printer in three ways.

Resident fonts are built into the printer. Many PostScript printers, for example, have a standard set of thirteen typefaces. (*PostScript* is a page description language.) Each *typeface* contains many fonts, such as Times Roman, Times

Roman Italic, Times Roman Bold, and so on. Laser printers also have built-in fonts. The number of built-in fonts depends on the model of the printer. Some printers contain *scalable fonts*, also known as *outline fonts*, that generate many sizes from one font outline. Many users prefer resident fonts because they print the fastest and don't take up processing power or computer memory.

> **Note**
>
> The available fonts may vary with the printer *orientation* (portrait or landscape). When you select a specific printer and change the orientation setting with the Printer Options command in the File Print dialog box, Windows determines the resident fonts for that printer and the selected orientation, and lists those fonts in the Font list.

Cartridge fonts come in hardware modules that plug into a printer. They act as resident fonts. Each cartridge contains one or more sets of fonts. Cartridges usually are used with HP LaserJet-compatible printers. During printer installation or setup, you must select, from a list, the cartridges available to the printer. This action lets Windows know which additional fonts are available. You can access the list of cartridge fonts by choosing File Print and then choosing the Printer button.

Soft fonts are generated by a software program and stored on your computer's hard disk or on the network. When you print a document that uses soft fonts, Windows sends the font information to the printer. The printer stores the font information in memory and composes a page. After the font is downloaded to memory, it stays in the printer until the printer is turned off, so that if you print another document that uses those soft fonts, they don't have to be downloaded again.

Soft fonts take up hard disk storage and slow down printing times. Most soft font generation packages have a font installer program that creates the fonts you request and stores the fonts in a directory on the hard disk. You must use the Windows Control Panel to install the soft fonts in Windows.

Understanding Screen Fonts. Windows 3.0 uses three types of fonts on-screen. *System fonts* come with Windows and are designed to match generic serif and sans serif fonts (serifs are the small marks at the end of some characters' lines). System fonts also provide special characters. Windows uses system fonts in dialog boxes, titles, and so on, and to represent printer resident or

Tip
For newer HP LaserJet printers, you can select two cartridges in the Printer Setup dialog box. To select the second cartridge, hold down Ctrl and click the second cartridge with the mouse.

Tip
If soft fonts and cartridges cannot coexist in your printer, select None in the Cartridge box in the Printer Setup dialog box, which you open by choosing the Printer button in the Print dialog box and then choosing the Options button.

Formatting Documents

II

cartridge fonts. Because a generic screen font that comes with Windows may be slightly different from a specific printer font, the screen appearance and the printed result of a font may be different.

A special form of *screen soft font* matches a printer font as closely as possible. These screen fonts are stored in software files and are available with soft fonts designed for the printer. Because these screen fonts are designed to match a specific printer's soft font, the on-screen display closely matches the printed result. Soft font generation programs usually generate a printer font and screen font of a specific typeface, size, and style at the same time, or the fonts are pregenerated on-disk. Screen fonts end with a FON extension.

Type management programs are designed to generate screen and printer fonts simultaneously. These fonts are generated on the fly rather than prebuilt like soft fonts, reducing the disk storage devoted to prebuilt soft fonts and ensuring that screen displays closely match printed results. Type management programs print pages more slowly than do some other forms of fonts. TrueType and the Adobe Type Manager are type management programs. TrueType is built into Windows 3.1. Adobe Type Manager is a program purchased separately.

Understanding Your Printer's Capabilities

Different printers have different capabilities. Some printers are not capable of advanced features such as printing small capital letters, bidirectional printing, landscape printing, or graphics. Some printers require that you change the font to change from normal to bold or italic, rather than enabling you to format the existing font with a bold or italic style. Windows is designed to use as much of your printer's capabilities as possible.

You must tell Windows which printer you have connected and which extra features are available on that printer. If you install an HP LaserJet III printer, for example, during installation you must tell Windows the amount of memory in the printer, which font cartridges are installed, and how the printer and envelope bins are handled.

If you are using a laser printer with expandable memory, be sure that you have specified correctly how much memory it has. If the printer doesn't have enough memory, or if you fail to tell Windows additional memory has been installed, Windows may not be able to print a full graphic or page of text. If a full page does not print, lower the graphic print resolution by choosing the File Print command, choosing the Printer button, and choosing Options. Then try printing again.

Understanding How Windows Works with Fonts

When you run Word for Windows in Windows 3.0, two sets of fonts are used: screen fonts and printer fonts. If you print to a printer with resident fonts or cartridge fonts, Windows uses its screen fonts to display as closely as possible how text will appear on the page. But the generic screen fonts that come with Windows 3.0 don't always represent accurately the size, shape, and spacing of the printer fonts. If you create and install custom screen fonts in Windows and print with soft fonts, Windows uses the custom screen fonts. These custom screen fonts enable Windows to represent more accurately the printed page. If the screen fonts and printer fonts don't match, however, the screen and the printed results may differ. (Custom screen fonts are created by soft font generation programs or are available on-disk with cartridges.)

The difference between screen and printer fonts can cause numerous problems:

- Words wrap differently on-screen than they do in print.

- Titles or sidebars extend further than expected.

- On-screen text extends past the margin set in the ruler.

- On-screen text in tables overfills cells in tables.

- Bold or italic formatting causes lines to appear longer than they print.

Screen fonts and printer fonts also are mismatched when you use fonts on-screen that are unavailable in the printer. (In Word for Windows, you can select a font even if the font isn't available on the current printer.) You can use this feature to create a document for printing on another printer. If you use a font not available in the printer, Word for Windows attempts to substitute a similar typeface and size when it prints. If it cannot find the requested size, it substitutes the next smallest size font in the printer.

You can avoid these problems in two ways. First, use fonts available in the printer. If a font is in the current printer, a small printer icon appears to the left of the font name in the Font list from the Formatting toolbar or the Font dialog box. Second, if you are using soft fonts or a font manager, make sure that you generate and install the screen fonts that go with the printer's soft fonts.

Using TrueType

You can use TrueType fonts with Word for Windows when the program is operating under Windows 3.1 or later. A type of built-in font-generation software, TrueType generates screen and printer fonts so that what you see on-screen is almost exactly the same as what prints, whether you have a laser or a dot-matrix printer.

When you choose the Format Font command and select the Font tab, the fonts available with your printer appear in the Font list with printer icons next to them. TrueType fonts are listed with a TT icon next to them (see fig. 9.16). After you select a new font from the Font list, read the description of the font below the Preview box. The information in this box describes the type of font you have selected and how it affects printing.

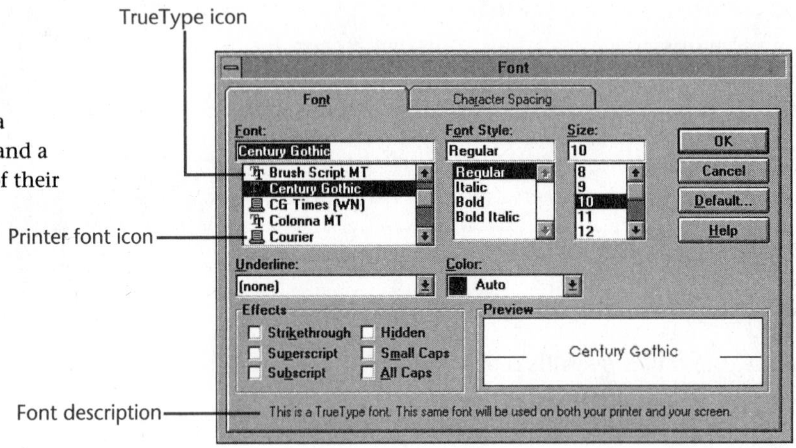

Fig. 9.16
Printer fonts appear with a printer icon and a description of their behavior.

TrueType icon

Printer font icon

Font description

You also can use screen fonts that don't match any font in your printer. Because the printer has no matching font, however, Windows selects a similar type and size of font when you print. In some cases, the printer font may be similar to the screen font; in others, it may be very different. Screen fonts that don't match a printer font appear in the Font list without an icon.

TrueType fonts give you a wide range of sizes and styles, and you can purchase additional typefaces designed for TrueType. The disadvantage of using TrueType fonts is that the generation time needed to create the screen fonts and download the characters slows system performance slightly. This slowing is only noticeable, however, on older systems.

Enabling TrueType Fonts
A basic set of TrueType fonts is installed automatically for you during the installation of Windows 3.1 or later. Some applications such as CorelDRAW!

install additional TrueType fonts. To make sure that you have these fonts available for applications such as Word for Windows, you must enable TrueType fonts. If the Font list in the Font dialog box shows TT icons with the font names Arial, Courier New, Symbol, and Times New Roman, you have TrueType fonts enabled. If the list doesn't show these fonts, you need to enable TrueType.

To enable TrueType fonts, follow these steps:

1. Open the Control Panel from the Main group window in Windows Program Manager.

2. Start the Fonts application by double-clicking the Fonts icon or by selecting the icon with the arrow keys and pressing Enter.

3. Choose the TrueType button. The TrueType dialog box appears (see fig. 9.17).

4. Select the Enable TrueType Fonts check box.

5. Select the Show Only TrueType Fonts in the Application check box if you want to see only TrueType fonts, not screen or printer fonts, in the Font list.

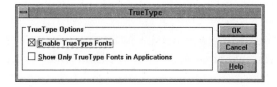

Fig. 9.17
See the installed fonts and enable TrueType with the Fonts program from the Main group.

6. Choose OK.

7. If you changed the setting for the Enable TrueType Fonts check box, another dialog box appears. Choose the Don't Restart Now button if you want to return to your Windows applications to finish work and save documents. Choose the Restart Now button if you want to restart Windows immediately. (Word for Windows asks whether you want to save any changed documents.) Keep in mind that changing the Enable TrueType Fonts check box doesn't take effect until you exit and restart Windows.

Formatting Documents

Installing and Deleting Soft Fonts

Soft fonts often generate the printer font and the screen font. The soft font software usually does three things: it generates screen and printer fonts of the size and type you want, saves files for those fonts to the hard disk, and modifies Windows WIN.INI file so that Windows knows which fonts are available and where they are located. When fonts are installed correctly, you can see the new Font listed in your font lists and print them. If font installation was incorrect or the font program didn't install the fonts in Windows, you may be able to install them yourself.

You can check whether screen fonts are installed by looking for the appropriately named FON files in the PCLFONTS directory (for HP LaserJet-compatible printers) or the directory in which fonts are installed. In most cases, the PCLFONTS directory is located off of the root directory of your hard disk. Some printers, like the newer HP Series III LaserJet printers, have appropriate screen fonts built into the printer driver. If you have such a printer, you may have screen fonts available in the driver but see no FON files on disk.

Adding or Removing Fonts. Some font manufacturers produce font generation and management programs that create files of predefined fonts for the screen and printer. These fonts are created with patterns of dots (*bit maps*) when displayed or printed. Such fonts for printers subscribing to the Hewlett-Packard PCL format store their fonts in the PCLFONTS directory.

If the font generation software doesn't automatically modify Windows WIN.INI file, you cannot see in Windows the fonts that you have installed. You can install the screen fonts and printer fonts at the same time with the Printer Font Installer that is part of many printer drivers. The following procedures describe font installation for an HP Series III LaserJet printer.

To install screen and printer fonts, follow these steps:

1. Open the Main group in Windows Program Manager and start the Control Panel.

2. Choose the Printers icon by double-clicking it or by using the arrow keys to select it and pressing Enter.

3. From the Printer dialog box, select the printer for which the fonts are designed, and then choose the Setup button. The Setup dialog box for your printer appears.

4. Choose the Fonts button. The HP Font Installer dialog box appears.

   If the Fonts button isn't displayed in the dialog box, the driver cannot install soft fonts. Check with Microsoft or the font manufacturer for instructions on installing the soft fonts.

   Fonts currently installed in the PCLFONTS directory appear in the left window of the dialog box.

5. Choose the Add Fonts button. The Add Fonts dialog box appears.

6. In the Add Fonts dialog box, type the drive and path name where the soft fonts are located (in most cases, soft fonts are located on a floppy disk containing prebuilt fonts or in a directory on the hard disk where fonts were stored by the font generation program); then choose OK.

7. Select from the right window the bit-mapped fonts you want to install into the PCLFONTS directory. You can select multiple fonts by clicking them, or by pressing the up- or down-arrow keys and then pressing the space bar to mark them. Select a font again to deselect it.

8. Choose the Add button.

   Installed fonts appear in the left side of the window.

9. Choose OK twice to return to Word for Windows.

You cannot remove font files from Windows without first uninstalling them and then deleting them. Merely deleting the files from the disk doesn't tell the WIN.INI file that the fonts are no longer available. You must uninstall the font files, and then delete them.

Installing Screen Fonts. You can install or remove screen soft fonts by using the Font program in the Control Panel. Use the Font program to add or re-move screen fonts that are separate from the printer soft fonts (if you are using font cartridges or if the font manufacturers release updated screen fonts after the printer fonts).

To install soft fonts from the disk for Windows 3.1, follow these steps:

1. Open the Main group in Windows Program Manager and start the Control Panel.

2. Choose the Fonts icon by double-clicking it or by pressing the arrow keys to select it, and then pressing Enter.

II

Formatting Documents

3. Choose the Add button. The Add Font Files dialog box appears.

4. Change to the directory containing the fonts you want to add, select the files, and then choose OK.

5. Choose OK.

Tip
Windows keeps a
list of installed
fonts in WIN.INI.
When you use the
Font program to
add or remove soft
fonts, you also are
modifying the
WIN.INI file.

You remove fonts from Windows by uninstalling them and then deleting the files, follow these steps:

1. Open the Main group in Program Manager and start the Control Panel.

2. Choose the Fonts icon by double-clicking it or by pressing the arrow keys to select it, and then pressing Enter.

3. Select from the Installed Font list the font you want to remove.

4. Choose the Remove button. When you are prompted to verify removing the font, choose Yes.

After you have uninstalled the font, you can delete the file from the hard disk.

From Here...

For information relating directly to formatting characters, you may want to review the following sections of this book:

■ Chapter 11, "Formatting with Styles." With styles, you can format your document quickly; even more importantly, you can make global formatting changes just by redefining a style. Although styles apply to paragraphs, they often contain character formatting and are useful for applying character formatting to paragraphs of text (such as body copy and headlines).

■ Chapter 22, "Inserting Pictures in Your Document." Text sometimes can function as a graphic. For example, you can create a box, type text inside, add borders, and move the box around on the page so that the rest of the text on the page wraps around the box.

■ Chapter 27, "Desktop Publishing." You can sometimes use text in a graphical way to enhance the appearance of a special document.

Chapter 10

Formatting Lines and Paragraphs

In writing, a paragraph is a series of sentences linked together to convey a single thought or idea, or to describe a single image. In Word for Windows, the definition of a paragraph is less lyrical: a *paragraph* is any amount of text—or no text at all—that ends when you press Enter. A paragraph may be the title of a story, an item in a list, a blank line between other paragraphs, or a series of sentences linked together to convey a single thought or idea.

Whatever its contents, a paragraph, once selected, is changeable. The Word for Windows paragraph formatting options cover a wide range of features that enable you to communicate your thoughts visually, as well as through your choice of words.

You might find paragraph formatting useful in many ways, including the following:

- Centering headings
- Creating hanging indents for numbered and bulleted lists
- Creating charts using the Tab command to align the columns

Understanding Paragraph Formats

In Word for Windows, a paragraph also is a formatting unit. Just as you format individual characters with character formatting options such as bold and italic, you can format paragraphs with paragraph, tab, and border formatting options, such as the following:

In this chapter, you learn how to format paragraphs and lines. Some of the most important procedures you learn are the following:

- Techniques for formatting paragraphs
- Displaying paragraph marks
- Aligning paragraphs
- Setting tabs
- Setting indents
- Numbering lines
- Adjusting line and paragraph spacing
- Adding shading and borders to paragraphs

- *Alignment.* Lining up the text of a paragraph to the left, center, right, or both margins.

- *Indents.* Indenting the left edge, right edge, or first line of a paragraph in from or out from its margin.

- *Tabs.* Creating columns of text that line up perfectly and can be adjusted easily.

- *Spacing.* Adding spaces between lines and between paragraphs.

- *Lines, borders, and shading.* Adding graphic interest to paragraphs with lines next to paragraphs, borders surrounding paragraphs, and shading to fill a border.

New paragraphs formed when you press Enter bring along the formatting from the previous paragraph. After you format a paragraph, you can continue that format into new paragraphs simply by pressing Enter. See figs. 10.1 and 10.2.

Paragraph formatting affects the entire paragraph and is stored in the paragraph mark that ends each paragraph. If you delete one of these paragraph marks, the text preceding the mark becomes part of the following paragraph. If the paragraph mark you delete contains formatting selections, that formatting also is lost. The new paragraph formed of two merged paragraphs takes on the formatting applied to the second of the two paragraphs. See figs. 10.3 and 10.4.

Displaying Paragraph Marks

When paragraph marks are hidden, you don't see them at the end of a paragraph. You can display paragraph marks, however; they look like reverse P's (see fig. 10.4). If you expect to do much text editing, you should display the paragraph marks to avoid accidentally deleting one of them and thereby losing your paragraph formatting.

To display paragraph marks from the menu, follow these steps:

1. Choose the Tools Options command.

2. Select the View tab.

3. Choose Paragraph Marks under Nonprinting Characters.

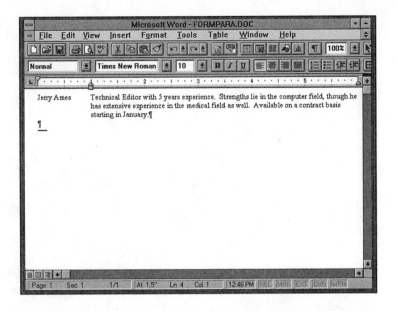

Fig. 10.1
The Formatting has been set up for the paragraph in this document.

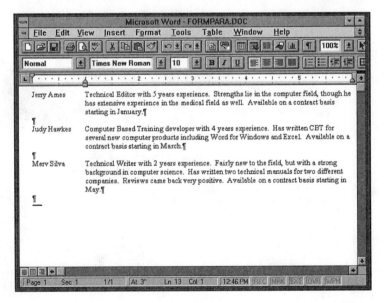

Fig. 10.2
When you press Enter, the formatting is carried forward to the new paragraph. Paragraph formatting is stored in the paragraph mark, shown in this figure.

Fig. 10.3

Display paragraph
marks to avoid
accidentally
including them
with selected text.

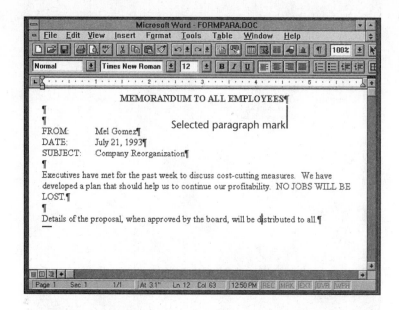

Fig. 10.4

If you delete
paragraph marks,
the text becomes
part of the next
paragraph and
takes on its
formatting. Notice
that the heading
lost its centering.

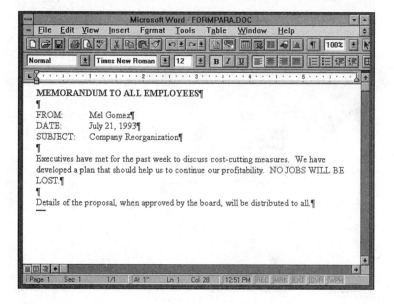

To display paragraph marks from the keyboard, press Ctrl+Shift+8.

To display paragraph marks from the Standard toolbar, click the Show/Hide ¶ button on the Standard toolbar.

> **Note**
>
> If you turn on paragraph marks by choosing **Tools O**ptions, clicking the Show/Hide ¶ button turns on and off the display of tabs and spaces only. Paragraph marks remain on.

Using Paragraph Formatting Techniques

Every new document you create based on the default Normal template is controlled by the Normal style. The Normal style formats paragraphs as left-aligned and single-spaced, with left-aligned tab stops every half inch. If you usually choose different paragraph formatting selections, change the Normal style to reflect your preferences. For details about changing styles, see Chapter 11, "Formatting with Styles."

You can format a paragraph at two times: before you begin typing or after you finish typing. To format after typing, you must select the paragraph or paragraphs you want to format. If you are formatting only one paragraph, instead of selecting the entire paragraph you can position the insertion point anywhere inside the paragraph before making your formatting selections. Paragraph formatting commands apply to the entire paragraph. For information about selecting text, see Chapter 5, "Editing a Document."

Word for Windows offers several alternative techniques for formatting paragraphs. You can use **F**ormat **P**aragraph to select many formatting options at once and to get the widest possible range of paragraph formatting options. You can use the Formatting toolbar to access paragraph formatting commands individually. You can use the ruler to set tabs and indents quickly. With keyboard shortcuts, you can format as you type. Figs. 10.5 and 10.6 show examples of selecting text and formatting it from the Formatting toolbar.

Fig. 10.5
Select the
paragraphs you
want to format.

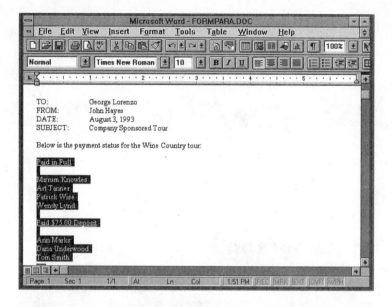

Fig. 10.6
Click the button
for the formatting
you want. The
Center button is
used in this
example.

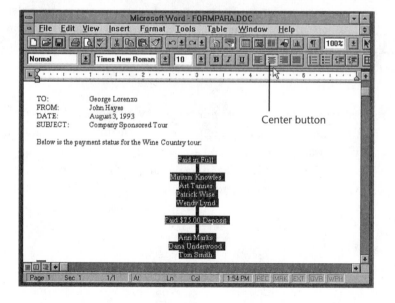

Formatting Paragraphs with Menu Commands

The Paragraph dialog box offers the greatest number of options for formatting paragraphs and shows a sample of how the formatting you choose affects your paragraph in the Preview box (see fig. 10.7). You can choose the Indents and Spacing tab to change indentation, spacing, and alignment; or you can choose the Text Flow tab to change pagination and suppress line numbers and hyphenation. Because the Paragraph dialog box provides quick access to the Tabs dialog box, you also can do quite a bit of formatting at once by choosing Format, Paragraph. See Chapter 13, "Setting the Page Layout," for more details on pagination.

Tip

You also can display the Paragraph dialog box by clicking the right mouse button and choosing Paragraph.

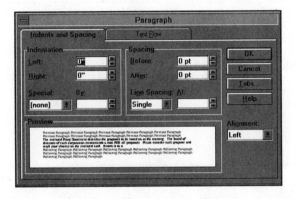

Fig. 10.7

Use the Paragraph dialog box to change the formatting of the selected text or the paragraph that contains the insertion point.

Specific instructions on using the Paragraph dialog box appear throughout this chapter.

Formatting Paragraphs with Shortcut Keys

You can choose from several shortcut keys for quick formatting changes made directly from the keyboard. To use a shortcut key for formatting, first select the paragraph or paragraphs you want to change or place the insertion point in the paragraph you want to change. Then choose one of the following commands:

To Do This	Press
Left-align text	Ctrl+L
Center text	Ctrl+E
Right-align text	Ctrl+R

(continues)

(continued)

To Do This	Press
Justify text	Ctrl+J
Indent from left margin	Ctrl+M
Create a hanging indent out one tab stop	Ctrl+T
Reduce a hanging indent by one tab stop	Ctrl+Shift+T
Single-space text	Ctrl+1
Change to 1.5-line spacing	Ctrl+5
Double-space text	Ctrl+2
Add 12 points of space before a paragraph	Ctrl+0 (zero)
Remove space before a paragraph	Ctrl+Shift+0 (zero)
Remove paragraph formatting that isn't part of the paragraph's assigned style	Ctrl+Q
Restore default formatting (from the Normal style)	Ctrl+Shift+N

Formatting Paragraphs with the Formatting Toolbar

The Word for Windows Formatting toolbar provides a quick way to choose certain paragraph formatting options, if you have a mouse (see fig. 10.8). Default paragraph formatting buttons on the Formatting toolbar include buttons for creating numbered lists and bulleted lists, for indenting and unindenting, and for controlling a paragraph's alignment. You also can access a special toolbar for creating lines and borders in your document.

To use the Formatting toolbar for alignment, follow these steps:

1. Select the paragraph or paragraphs you want to align or place the insertion point in the paragraph you want to align.

2. Choose the appropriate alignment button: Left, Centered, Right, or Justified (both margins aligned).

Toolbars are optional but useful to display if you do much formatting. If you want more typing space on-screen, however, remove the toolbar.

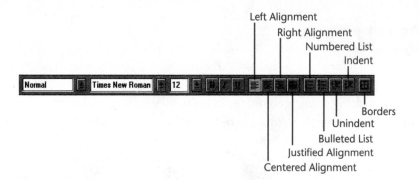

Fig. 10.8

You can change the format of selected paragraphs from the Formatting toolbar.

Note

You can add any command to the toolbar, filling in blank spaces in the toolbar or replacing existing buttons. For more details, see Chapter 38, "Recording and Editing Macros."

Several of the following sections in this chapter give specific instructions on using the Formatting toolbar.

Formatting Paragraphs with the Ruler

The *ruler* is useful for quickly setting paragraph indentations and tabs with a click of the mouse (see fig. 10.9). By default, tabs are left-aligned, but if you want a different tab style, you must select that style and then position the tab on the ruler. Displaying the ruler, like the toolbar, is also optional.

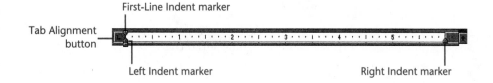

Fig. 10.9

The ruler provides quick access to some formatting options.

To display or remove the ruler, choose the **View Ruler** command. The ruler command has a check mark to its left when displayed. Choose the command again to remove the ruler.

Displaying the ruler can speed up formatting if you have a mouse; removing the ruler gives you more room on-screen. See Chapter 5, "Editing a Document," for more information about the screen display.

The sections "Setting Tabs" and "Setting Indents" in this chapter discuss using ruler options.

Formatting Documents

Duplicating Formats

The easiest way to duplicate paragraph formatting is to carry the formatting forward as you type. As you arrive at the end of the current paragraph and press Enter, the current paragraph ends and a new one begins—using the same formatting as the preceding paragraph. If, however, you use the mouse or cursor-movement keys to move out of the current paragraph, you move into a different paragraph, which may have different formatting.

Another way to duplicate formatting is to use Edit Repeat or press F4. Remember that this command duplicates only your one most recent action. The command works best when you format with the Paragraph, Tabs, or Borders dialog box, making multiple formatting choices at once.

To duplicate paragraph formatting using a mouse, follow these steps:

1. Select the text containing the formatting you want to duplicate.

 2. Click the Format Painter button in the Standard toolbar. The pointer changes to a combination insertion point and paintbrush.

3. Drag across the text you want formatted.

When you release the mouse button, the text over which you dragged changes to the copied format.

To duplicate paragraph formatting from the keyboard, follow these steps:

1. Select the paragraph whose format you want to copy.

2. Press Ctrl+Shift+C.

3. Select the paragraph(s) whose format you want to change.

4. Press Ctrl+Shift+V.

Probably the most powerful way to duplicate paragraph formatting is to use styles. A *style* is a set of formatting commands that you can apply all at once and can change globally later. Styles are easy to create—especially when you use the "styles by example" technique—and easy to use. Styles are explained in detail in Chapter 11, "Formatting with Styles."

Troubleshooting

Text changes its formatting when you press the Del or Backspace key.

Word for Windows stores paragraph formatting in the paragraph mark at the end of each paragraph. If you delete the paragraph mark of a particular paragraph, it takes on the format of the following paragraph. Choose the Edit Undo command immediately to reverse the deletion and restore the paragraph formatting.

To repair the paragraph, reformat it or copy a paragraph mark from a similar paragraph and paste it at the end of the problem paragraph.

To avoid deleting a paragraph mark inadvertently, turn on paragraph marks by clicking the paragraph mark button at the right end of the Standard toolbar. Or turn on paragraph marks by choosing the Tools Options command and selecting the Paragraph Marks option in the View tab.

I set up formatting in a paragraph and then moved to the next paragraph, but the formatting didn't carry over.

You must press the Enter key at the end of the paragraph whose formatting you want to carry over to a new paragraph. If there is already a paragraph mark following the formatted paragraph and you use the mouse or arrow keys to move into this paragraph, the new paragraph will not necessarily have the same formatting as the previous paragraph.

For Related Information

- "Using the Toolbars," p. 42

- "Controlling Your Document's Appearance On-Screen," p. 115

- "Selecting Text," p. 133

- "Creating Styles," p. 359

Aligning Paragraphs

Paragraph alignment refers to how the left and right edges of a paragraph line up (see fig. 10.10). Left-aligned paragraphs line up on the left edge but are ragged on the right (the Word for Windows default). Left-aligned text is commonly used in informal letters or in the body text in a book, such as in this book. Right-aligned paragraphs line up on the right edge but are ragged on the left. Right-aligned text can be used in headers and footers in a document, for example, for the page numbering, or when you are creating a list and want the items in the right column to line up along the right margin. Centered paragraphs are ragged on both edges, centered between the margins. Centered paragraphs are most often used for headings. Justified paragraphs are aligned on both edges and are often used in formal business letters and in text that appears in columns, as in a newsletter.

Paragraphs are aligned to the margins if no indentations are set for them. If paragraphs are indented, they align to the indentation.

Fig. 10.10

You can choose from four styles of alignment: left, centered, right, and justified.

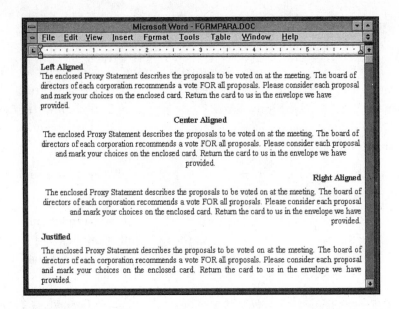

You can set paragraph alignment while you're typing or while you're editing your document. If you set alignment as you type, the alignment carries forward when you press Enter (like all paragraph formatting selections). If you set alignment later, your setting applies only to the selected paragraph or paragraphs.

Aligning with Menu Commands

You can use Format Paragraph to set alignment with a mouse or your keyboard.

Tip

To justify the last line of a paragraph, end the line with the new line command, Shift+Enter, rather than Enter.

To set alignment using the menu command, follow these steps:

1. Select the paragraph or paragraphs to align, or position the insertion point where you want the new alignment to begin.

2. Choose the Format Paragraph command. The Paragraph dialog box appears.

3. Select the Alignment option from the Indents and Spacing tab.

4. Select Left, Centered, Right, or Justified from the Alignment pull-down list, as shown in fig. 10.11.

5. Choose OK.

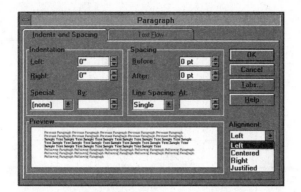

Fig. 10.11
You can choose paragraph alignment from the Alignment box in the Paragraph dialog box.

> **Note**
>
> You can choose formatting commands from the shortcut menu. Select the text you want to format, click the right mouse button, and choose Paragraph. Then the Paragraph dialog box appears.

Aligning with the Formatting Toolbar

If you have a mouse, a quicker way to set alignment is to display the Formatting toolbar and to click the appropriate alignment button. If the Formatting toolbar isn't displayed, choose the View Toolbars command and specify the toolbar(s) you want to display.

To align paragraphs with the Formatting toolbar, follow these steps:

1. Select the paragraph or paragraphs to align, or position the insertion point where you want the new alignment to begin.

2. Click the Formatting toolbar's Left, Centered, Right, or Justified Alignment button.

Aligning with Keyboard Shortcuts

One of the quickest ways to align selected paragraphs is to use Ctrl-key shortcuts from the keyboard. With this technique, you also can save screen space by not displaying the Formatting toolbar.

To align paragraphs using keyboard shortcuts, follow these steps:

1. Select the paragraph or paragraphs to align, or position the insertion point where you want the new alignment to begin.

II

Formatting Documents

2. Press the appropriate Ctrl-key combination:

Paragraph Alignment	Shortcut
Left	Ctrl+L
Centered	Ctrl+E
Right	Ctrl+R
Justified	Ctrl+J

Troubleshooting

When I inserted a page break immediately after a justified paragraph, Word justified the words in the last line of the paragraph, resulting in very wide spacing between the words.

This problem occurred because the insertion point was located at the end of the justified paragraph when you inserted the page break. Be sure to press Enter at the end of the paragraph before you insert the page break.

Setting Tabs

Working with tabs is a two-part process. First, you must set the tab stops, or you must plan to use the Word for Windows default left-aligned tab stops at every half inch. Setting the tab stops includes selecting the type of tab—left, centered, right, decimal, or bar—and specifying where the tab stops must appear. The second step in using tabs is to press the Tab key as you type your document to move the insertion point forward to the next tab stop.

A wonderful advantage to working with tabs is that after the tabs are in your document, you can move or change the tab stops, and the selected text moves or realigns with the stops.

You can set tabs in one of two ways. You can use the Tabs dialog box, which gives you precise control over where each tab is to appear and enables you to customize tabs by adding tab leaders. Alternatively, you can use the ruler to select a tab style and then to set the tab's position using the mouse.

When you work with a table or list made up of tabs, displaying the tab characters in your document is helpful. The tab characters appear as right-pointing arrows.

To display the tab characters from the Standard toolbar, click the Show/Hide ¶ button at the right end of the Standard toolbar.

To display the tab characters from the menu commands, follow these steps:

1. Choose the Tools Options command.

2. Select the View tab.

3. Select the Tabs option from the Nonprinting Characters group.

You must understand that, like all paragraph formatting options, tabs belong to paragraphs. If you set tab stops as you type text and then press Enter, the tab settings are carried forward to the next paragraph. If you add tabs later, however, they apply only to the paragraph or paragraphs selected when you set the tab stops.

Fig. 10.12 shows how each of the different tab styles affects the text to which they're applied; fig. 10.13 shows the three different tab leader styles.

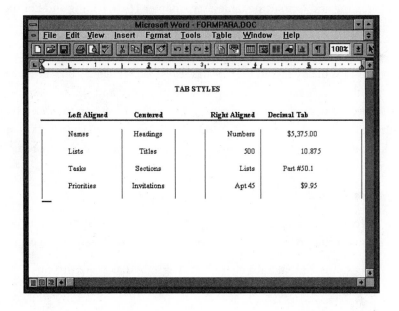

Fig. 10.12
You can select from five tab styles: left, centered, right, decimal, or bar. This example includes bar tabs set between and around the other tab styles.

Formatting Documents

Fig. 10.13
Use any of the
three leader styles
to "lead" the eye
to tabbed text.

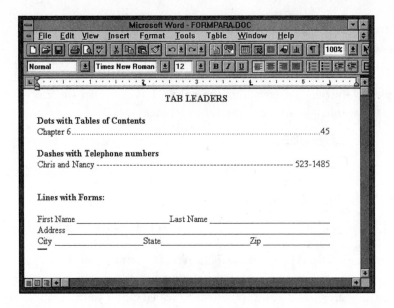

Although tabs are useful for lists, menus, tables of contents, and anything requiring tab leaders, a table sometimes works better for lists. A table contains *cells* formed by rows and columns and is the best choice when you have many columns or when the text in each cell varies in length. For details about creating and formatting tables, see Chapter 16, "Creating and Editing Tables."

Using the Tabs Dialog Box

Using the Tabs dialog box to set tabs has several advantages. You can set each tab's position precisely by typing in decimal numbers, and you can add dotted, dashed, or underlined tab leaders. (A *tab leader* "leads" up to tabbed text on the left side, as shown in fig. 10.13.) With a mouse or a keyboard, you can quickly clear existing tabs and change the default tab settings for the rest of your document. You can even reformat existing tabs.

To set tabs using the menu command, follow these steps:

1. Select the paragraph or paragraphs for which you want to set tabs, or position the insertion point where you want the tab settings to begin.

2. Choose the Format Tabs command. The Tabs dialog box appears (see fig. 10.14).

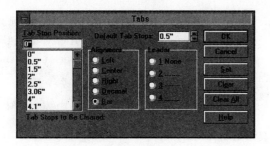

Fig. 10.14
You can set tabs at precise locations and include leaders from the Tabs dialog box.

3. Type the position of the tab stop you want to set, using decimal numbers, in the Tab Stop Position box.

4. From the Alignment group, select the tab style you want: Left, Center, Right, Decimal, or Bar.

5. In the Leader list, select the tab leader style you want (if any): **1** for no leader, **2** for a dotted leader, **3** for a dashed leader, or **4** for an underlined leader.

6. Choose the **S**et button to set the tab stop.

7. Repeat Steps 3 through 6 to set additional tab stops.

8. Choose OK.

The Tab Stop Position list box displays your tab stops after you set them.

You can reformat existing tab stops by following the same general procedure for setting tabs.

To reformat existing tab stops, follow these steps:

1. Select the tab to reformat in the Tab Stop Position list box.

2. Select the new formatting options for the selected tab stop in the Alignment and Leader boxes.

3. Choose the **S**et button.

You can access the Tabs dialog box through the Paragraph dialog box. Choose the Format Paragraph command or click the right mouse button and choose **P**aragraph; then choose the Tabs button. Alternatively, you can double-click any tab set on the ruler to display the Tabs dialog box.

Formatting Documents

Clearing Tabs. After you set tabs, you can *clear* (remove) them individually or as a group. The following technique works whether you set the tabs through the Tabs dialog box or by using the ruler (see "Using the Ruler to Set Tabs" later in this chapter).

To clear tab stops with the menu command, follow these steps:

1. Select the paragraph or paragraphs from which you want to clear tabs, or position the insertion point where you want to begin working with the new tab settings.

2. Choose the Format Tabs command.

3. Select the Clear All option to clear all the tabs.

   or

   Select the tab from the Tab Stop Position list and choose the Clear button to clear one tab. Repeat this process to clear additional tab stops.

4. Choose OK.

As you select tab stops to clear and choose the Clear button in Step 3, the tab stops that are removed are listed in the Tab Stops to Be Cleared area at the bottom of the Tabs dialog box.

Resetting the Default Tab Stops. If you do not set custom tabs, Word has preset tabs every 0.5". When you set a custom tab, all preset tabs to the left of the custom tab are cleared. You can use the Tabs dialog box to change the default tab stop interval if you routinely use the preset tabs and do not like the default tab setting. Any custom tab stops you may have set for existing paragraphs are not affected.

To change the default tab stops, follow these steps:

1. Choose the Format Tabs command.

2. In the Default Tab Stops box, type in a new default tab interval or click the up or down arrow to change the number in the box.

3. Choose OK.

Using the Ruler to Set Tabs

If you have a mouse, you can set, move, and remove left, center, right, or decimal tabs quickly, using the ruler. (Bar tabs are not available from the ruler.) The task involves two steps: selecting the tab style by clicking the Tab Alignment button on the ruler and then setting the tabs where you want them on the ruler.

The ruler displays Word for Windows' default tab stops (set every half inch, unless you change the interval) as tiny vertical lines along the bottom of the ruler. When you set your own tab stops, all default tab stops to the left are removed from the ruler.

To use this technique, you must display the ruler for access to these tools (see fig. 10.15).

Left tab   Center tab   Right tab   Decimal tab

Fig. 10.15
This ruler shows the symbols for the various kinds of tabs.

To display the ruler, choose the View **Ruler** command.

See Chapter 5, "Editing a Document," for more information about changing the screen display.

To set tabs using the ruler, follow these steps:

1. Select the paragraph or paragraphs for which you want to set tabs, or position the insertion point where you want the new tab settings to begin.

2. Click the Tab Alignment button at the far left of the ruler until the symbol for the tab style you want to use is selected: Left, Centered, Right, or Decimal.

   Fig. 10.12, shown earlier, shows examples of how each Tab Alignment style looks on screen.

3. Position the pointer just below the tick mark on the ruler where you want the tab stop to appear. Click the left mouse button to place the tab stop on the ruler.

Repeat Steps 2 and 3 to add various kinds of tab stops to the ruler, or just Step 3 to add more tab stops of the same style.

The tab stop appears as a marker in the same style as the tab style you selected from the ruler. If you don't get the tab marker in just the right place on the ruler, position the mouse pointer on the marker, hold down the left mouse button to select the marker, and drag the tab marker to the correct position.

To use the ruler to change a tab stop's alignment or to add a leader, double-click the tab stop to display the Tabs dialog box. Select the tab stop you want to change in the Tab Stop Position list and make whatever changes you want and choose OK.

Removing a Tab Stop. You can delete tab stops quickly with the mouse.

To use the mouse to remove a tab from the ruler, follow these steps:

1. Drag the tab off the ruler onto the document.

2. Release the mouse button.

Setting Default Tabs

Default tabs are set every half inch. If you find that you are changing them frequently, you can change the default tab settings in NORMAL.DOT, the template on which most documents are based. You first need to retrieve NORMAL.DOT, then change the tabs, and finally save the template.

To retrieve NORMAL.DOT, follow these steps:

1. Choose the File Open command.

2. Specify the WINWORD directory.

3. Specify the TEMPLATE subdirectory.

4. Click the down arrow of List Files of Type and choose Document Templates (*.dot).

5. Choose NORMAL.DOT.

6. Choose OK.

If you have never made any changes to the default settings in NORMAL.DOT, NORMAL.DOT will not appear in the TEMPLATE directory. If this is the case, you can create NORMAL.DOT, which can then be modified as described. To create NORMAL.DOT, open a new document, choose the Format Font command, and then choose the Default button. When asked if you want to change the default font, choose Yes. Because you didn't actually select a new font, you haven't really changed the default font. The idea is to trick Word into thinking you made a change in the default settings, so it will create a NORMAL.DOT file. Choose the File Save All command. Choose

Cancel when the Save As dialog box appears, since you don't need to save the blank document. Word will then automatically save NORMAL.DOT, and NORMAL.DOT will appear in the TEMPLATE directory, as described above.

To change the default tabs, follow these steps:

1. Choose the Format Tabs command.

2. Change the setting in the Default Tab Stops box to the interval you prefer.

3. Choose OK.

To save and exit NORMAL.DOT, follow these steps:

1. Choose the File Close command. You are asked whether you want to save the changes.

2. Choose Yes to save the changes you've made.

The next time you create a document using NORMAL.DOT, the default tab settings will match the changes you've made to the template.

Troubleshooting

When I tried to adjust the column in a table created with tabs by dragging the tab stop on the ruler, only one row in the table changed.

Tabs settings are a paragraph characteristic and are stored in the paragraph mark at the end of a paragraph. To adjust the columns in a table, you must select all of the rows (paragraphs) in the table and then drag the tab stops on the ruler.

When I select the rows in a table created with tabs, some of the tab stops are grayed on the ruler.

When you select a group of paragraphs that don't all have exactly the same tab settings, the tab stops that are not common to all of the paragraphs will appear in gray. You can drag a tab stop to a new setting, and it will then be applied to all of the paragraphs in the selection. This is a good way to synchronize the tab stops in a group of paragraphs if you accidentally change a tab setting in just one of the paragraphs.

For Related Information
- "Creating a Table," p. 509
- "Controlling Your Document's Appearance On-Screen," p. 115
- "Setting Default Formats in the Normal Template," p. 177

II

Formatting Documents

Setting Indents

A document's margins are determined by selections made in the File Page Setup dialog box. Margins apply to the entire document or to sections within the document. But individual paragraphs or groups of paragraphs can be indented from those margins and therefore appear to have their own margin settings.

Although only two side margins (left and right) are available, you can indent a paragraph in many ways (see fig. 10.16). You can indent from the left, right, or both margins. You can indent just the first line of a paragraph, a technique that often substitutes for pressing Tab at the beginning of each new paragraph. You can create a *hanging indent*, which "hangs" the first line of a paragraph to the left of the rest of the paragraph; hanging indents often are used for bulleted or numbered lists. You also can create *nested indents—* indentations within indentations.

Fig. 10.16

You can use various levels of indenting to achieve various effects.

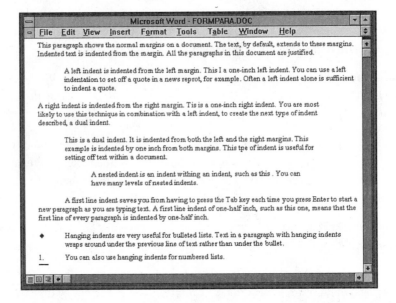

Several techniques exist for creating indents. You can use the Paragraph dialog box, typing the amount of indent for the selected paragraph or paragraphs. You can use the ruler, dragging indent icons left and right. You can use a button on the toolbar to indent or unindent paragraphs quickly or to create lists with a hanging indent. You also can use keyboard shortcuts.

Whichever technique you use, indenting belongs to the paragraph and is carried forward when you press Enter at the end of a paragraph. Alternatively, you can return to a paragraph later and format the text with an indent.

Note that numbered and bulleted lists are a special type of indented list. They are described in Chapter 17, "Creating Bulleted or Numbered Lists."

Using the Paragraph Command to Set Indents

You can use the Paragraph dialog box to set any type of indent, measured precisely. The Indentation list in the Paragraph dialog box lists three options: Left, Right, and Special (see fig. 10.17).

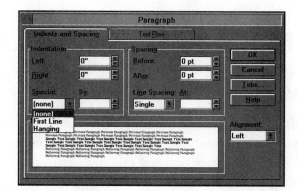

Fig. 10.17
Use the Indents and Spacing tab to change paragraph indentation.

The indentation options give the following results:

Option	Result
Left	Indents selected paragraph or paragraphs from the left margin. If the number is positive, the paragraph is indented inside the left margin; if the number is negative, the paragraph is indented outside the left margin (sometimes termed *outdenting*).
Right	Indents selected paragraph or paragraphs from the right margin. If the number is positive, the paragraph is indented inside the right margin; if the number is negative, the paragraph is indented outside the right margin.
Special	Indents the first line or lines of selected paragraph or paragraphs from left indent (or margin, if no indent is made). Click the down arrow to select either First Line or Hanging. First Line indents inside the left indent. Hanging Indent indents outside the left indent. The default indent is 0.5". Change the indent by typing a new number or by using the up or down arrow to change the number.

To set indentations using the Paragraph dialog box, follow these steps:

1. Select the paragraph or paragraphs to indent, or position the insertion point where you want the new indentation to begin.

2. Choose the Format Paragraph command. The Paragraph dialog box opens.

3. Select the Indents and Spacing tab

4. Type or select a value in the Left or Right Indentation text box.

   or

   Select First Line or Hanging from the Special list box and type or select a value in the By text box.

   You can preview the effects of the choices you make in the Preview box.

5. Choose OK.

You can create indents in measurements other than decimal inches. To create a 6-point indent, for example, type **6 pt** in either indentation box. (An inch consists of 72 points.) To create an indent of 2 centimeters, type **2 cm**; to create an indent of 1 pica, type **1 pi** (six picas per inch; 12 points per pica).

Creating a Hanging Indent

A hanging indent is used for items such as bulleted and numbered lists, glossary items, and bibliographic entries (see fig. 10.18).

To create a hanging indent, follow these steps:

1. Choose the Format Paragraph command.

2. Select the Special box by clicking its down arrow.

3. Choose Hanging.

4. Type the amount you want the first line of the paragraph to extend to the left of the rest of the paragraph.

5. Choose OK.

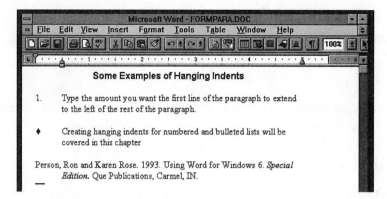

Fig. 10.18
Hanging indents can be used for creating bulleted and numbered lists and bibliographic entries.

To use a hanging indent, type a number or bullet at the left margin, press the Tab key to advance to the left indent, and then begin typing the text of the paragraph. When text reaches the end of the line, the paragraph wraps around to the left indent, not the left margin. This technique is useful for numbered and bulleted lists. (You can create hanging indents for numbered and bulleted lists automatically with the toolbar or the Bullets and Numbering dialog box. See Chapter 17, "Creating Bulleted or Numbered Lists.")

Symbol fonts such as Symbol and Zapf Dingbats are full of interesting dingbats that you can use as bullets in a list. For details about using these characters, see Chapter 9, "Formatting Characters and Changing Fonts."

Using the Ruler or Formatting Toolbar to Set Indents

With the ruler, you easily can create indents of any kind. With the Formatting toolbar, you can indent a selected paragraph to the next available tab stop.

The ruler contains triangular markers, called *indent markers*, at the left and right margins. You can drag them left and right on the ruler to set indents. The top triangle at the left margin represents the first-line indent. The bottom triangle represents the left indent. Both the top and bottom triangles move independently. You use the square below the bottom triangle to move both the first-line and left paragraph indents at once. The triangle at the right margin represents the paragraph's right indent. Fig. 10.19 shows the indent markers on the ruler.

Fig. 10.19

Use the indent markers to set left and right indentation.

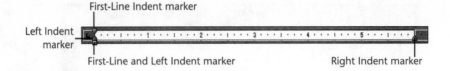

First-Line Indent marker

Left Indent marker

First-Line and Left Indent marker

Right Indent marker

Left and right indents are measured from the left and right margins, respectively. First-line indents are measured relative to the left indent. In fig. 10.20, fig. 10.21, and fig. 10.22, you can see that the position of the indent markers reflects the indentation settings for the selected paragraph.

To set indents with the ruler, you first must display the ruler. Choose the **View Ruler** command to display the ruler.

To set indentations with the ruler, follow these steps:

1. Select the paragraph or paragraphs to indent, or position the insertion point where you want the new indentation to begin.

2. To set a left indent, drag the square below the Left Indent marker to the ruler position where you want the indentation. (Notice that the top triangle moves also.)

   or

   To set a right indent, drag the Right Indent marker to the position where you want the indentation.

   or

   To set a first-line indent, drag the first-line indent marker to the position where you want the first-line indentation.

   or

   To set a hanging indent with the first line at the left margin, drag the Left Indent marker to a new position on the ruler.

Note

When you drag the left or first-line indent to the left of the left margin, the ruler automatically scrolls to the left. If you want to scroll on the ruler into the left margin without moving the indent markers, however, hold down the Shift key while you click the left scroll arrow in the horizontal scroll bar.

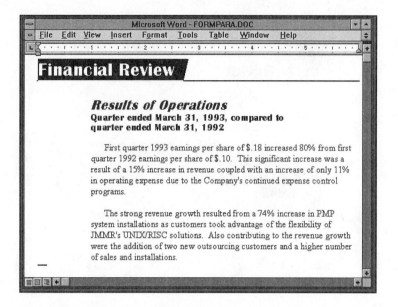

Fig. 10.20
The First-Line, Left, and Right Indent markers are set even with the left and right margins.

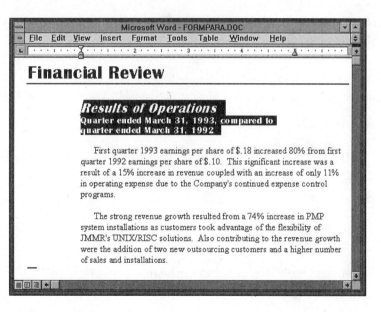

Fig. 10.21
The First-Line and Left Indent markers are set at 1.0", and the Right Indent marker has been moved to 5".

Formatting Documents

Fig. 10.22

The First-Line Indent marker is set in .25" from the Left Indent marker to create a first-line indentation.

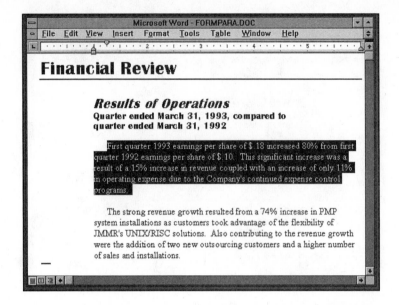

The Formatting toolbar includes two buttons for indenting a selected paragraph to the next tab stop: the Indent and Unindent buttons. You use these buttons to create left indents only—not first-line or hanging indents—and to indent to tab stops already set in the current paragraph(s). To use this technique, be sure the Formatting toolbar is displayed by choosing View Toolbars.

Unindent is used to unindent to the previous tab stop.

Indent is used to indent to the next tab stop.

To indent or unindent paragraphs using the Formatting toolbar, follow these steps:

1. Select the paragraph or paragraphs to indent, or position the insertion point where you want the new indentation to begin.

2. To indent the paragraph, click the Increase Indent button.

   or

   To unindent the paragraph, click the Decrease Indent button.

You can click the Indent button as many times as you want to continue moving the left indentation to the right. The Indent button, therefore, is an easy way to create nested paragraphs, which are like indents within indents (refer to fig. 10.16).

Using Keyboard Shortcuts to Set Indents

If you're a touch typist, you might appreciate being able to create indents by using keyboard shortcuts. Just as when you use the Formatting toolbar to create indents, keyboard shortcuts rely on existing tab settings to determine the position of indents. If you haven't changed Word for Windows default tab stops, for example, and therefore they still are set every half inch, using the shortcut keys to create a hanging indent leaves the first line of the paragraph at the margin but moves the left edge for the remaining lines of the paragraph to one-half inch.

To set indents by using keyboard shortcuts, follow these steps:

1. Select the paragraph or paragraphs to indent, or position the insertion point where you want the new indentation to begin.

2. Use one of the following keyboard shortcuts to indent your text:

Shortcut	Indentation Type
Ctrl+M	Moves the left indent to the next tab stop
Ctrl+Shift+M	Moves the left indent to the preceding tab stop (but not beyond the left margin)
Ctrl+T	Creates a hanging indent

Note

Just as you use shortcuts to format a paragraph, you can use a shortcut to remove formatting. Press Ctrl+Q to reset a paragraph to normal formatting (as defined by the Normal style). Press Ctrl+space bar to reset a paragraph to its pure style.

Setting Default Indents

One of the most commonly used letter-writing styles is modified-block style, with indented paragraphs. If you find that you frequently are changing indentations to indent paragraphs, for example, you can change the default indentation settings in NORMAL.DOT, the template on which most documents are based. You first need to retrieve NORMAL.DOT, then change the indentation, and finally save the template.

To retrieve NORMAL.DOT, follow these steps:

1. Choose the File Open command.

2. Choose the WINWORD directory.

3. Choose the TEMPLATE subdirectory.

4. Click the down arrow of List Files of Type and choose Document Templates (*.dot).

5. Choose NORMAL.DOT.

6. Choose OK.

If you have never made any changes to the default settings in NORMAL.DOT, NORMAL.DOT will not appear in the TEMPLATE directory. If this is the case, you can create NORMAL.DOT, which can then be modified as described. To create NORMAL.DOT, open a new document, choose the Format Font command, and then choose the Default button. When asked if you want to change the default font, choose Yes. Because you didn't actually select a new font, you haven't really changed the default font. The idea is to trick Word into thinking you made a change in the default settings, so that it will create a NORMAL.DOT file. Choose the File Save All command. Choose Cancel when the Save As dialog box appears, because you don't need to save the blank document. Word will then automatically save NORMAL.DOT, and NORMAL.DOT will appear in the TEMPLATE directory, as described above.

To change the indentation from the ruler, drag the First-Line Indent marker to .25".

To change the indentation using Format Paragraph, follow these steps:

1. Choose the Format Paragraph command.

2. Click the down arrow of the Special option and choose First Line.

3. Type the new first-line indentation setting in the By box.

4. Choose OK.

To save and exit NORMAL.DOT, follow these steps:

1. Choose the File Close command. You are asked whether you want to save the changes.

2. Choose Yes to save the changes you've made.

The next time you create a document using NORMAL.DOT, the indentations will match the changes you've made to the template.

Numbering Lines

Line numbers are useful in preparing manuscripts or legal documents, for reference, or if you simply need to know how many lines of text are on a page, in a poem, or in a document. You can choose the starting number for line numbering, the distance between numbers and text, the interval at which line numbers appear, and whether line numbering restarts with every new page or section or continues throughout your section. You can suppress line numbering for a specific paragraph or paragraphs.

Adding Line Numbers

You can add line numbers to sections of a document or to the entire document, if it isn't formatted into sections. For information about formatting a document in sections, see Chapter 13, "Setting the Page Layout."

To number lines, follow these steps:

1. Position the insertion point inside the section in which you want line numbers, or anywhere in the document to number a document that hasn't been split into sections. To number an entire document that has been divided into sections, select the entire document.

2. Choose the File Page Setup command. The Page Setup dialog box appears.

3. Select the Layout tab.

4. Choose the Line Numbers button. The Line Numbers dialog box appears (see fig. 10.23).

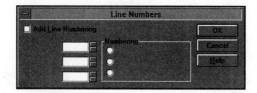

For Related Information
- "Creating Bulleted or Numbered Lists," p. 549
- "Inserting Special Characters and Symbols," p. 272
- "Setting Default Formats in the Normal Template," p. 177

Fig. 10.23
Choose line numbering options from the Line Numbers dialog box.

5. Select the Add Line Numbering option. Change the following default line numbering settings if you want.

Formatting Documents

Option	Setting	Then Type
Start At	Starting line number	Type a new starting number in the box, or click the up or down arrow to increase or decrease the starting number. (By default, line numbering begins with number 1.)
From Text	Distance between line numbers and text	Type a distance in the box or click the up or down arrow to increase or decrease the distance by tenths of an inch. (The Auto option places line numbers .25" to the left of single-column text or .13" to the left of newspaper-style columns.) If the margin or the space between columns is too small, line numbers do not print.
Count By	Interval between printed line numbers all lines are numbered, but only those numbers specified here print)	Type an interval in a box, or click the up or down arrow to increase or decrease the interval.

6. Select an option from the Numbering group to establish when line numbers restart at the first number.

Option	Restart Point
Restart Each Page	Beginning of each new page
Restart Each Section	Beginning of each new section
Continuous	None; number lines continuously throughout document

7. Choose OK.

You cannot see line numbering in Normal view. To see line numbers, choose the View Page Layout command or choose the File Print Preview command. Or you can print your document.

> **Note**
>
> You can change the formatting of line numbers by redefining the Line Number style. Refer to Chapter 11, "Formatting with Styles," for information about redefining styles.

Removing or Suppressing Line Numbers

You can remove line numbers entirely. Also, an option in the Paragraph dialog box on the Text Flow tab offers you the chance to suppress line numbers. This option clears line numbering from selected paragraphs or the paragraph containing the insertion point. (This option doesn't suppress line numbers applied in creating a numbered list, described in Chapter 17, "Creating Bulleted or Numbered Lists.")

To remove line numbers, follow these steps:

1. Position the insertion point in the section from which you want to remove line numbers, or select the entire document if it's formatted into more than one section.

2. Choose the File Page Setup command.

3. Select the Layout tab.

4. Select the Line Numbers button.

5. Choose Add Line Numbering to remove the check mark.

6. Choose OK or press Enter twice to return to the document.

To suppress line numbers, follow these steps:

1. Select the paragraphs for which you want to suppress line numbering.

2. Choose the Format Paragraph command.

3. Select the Text Flow tab.

4. Select the Suppress Line Numbers option.

5. Choose OK.

For Related Information
- "Changing Layouts Within a Document," p. 432
- "Creating Numbered Lists," p. 557

II

Formatting Documents

Adjusting Line and Paragraph Spacing

Like all word processing and typesetting programs, Word for Windows spaces lines of text far enough apart so that lines don't crash into each other. If something large is on the line, such as a graphic or an oversized character or word, Word for Windows leaves extra space.

You're not limited to using Word for Windows automatic spacing, however. You can add extra space between lines and paragraphs.

> **Note**
>
> Spacing is an excellent candidate for using *styles,* which are sets of remembered formatting commands that you easily create and apply. If your document's format includes subheadings preceded by extra space, for example, create a style for your subheadings that includes the extra space and apply the style to each subheading. For details about using styles, see Chapter 11, "Formatting with Styles."

Adjusting Paragraph Spacing

You can adjust paragraph spacing by adding extra lines before or after the selected paragraphs. After you press Enter, Word for Windows skips the specified amount of space before starting the next paragraph. This technique is useful when your document's format requires extra spacing between paragraphs, before new sections, or around graphics. Adding extra spacing before or after paragraphs is like pressing Enter a second time each time you finish typing a paragraph (see fig. 10.24).

The Preview section of the Paragraph dialog box shows the effect of your selected spacing.

> **Note**
>
> When you're printing, if you format a paragraph to include extra space before and the paragraph appears at the top of a new page, Word for Windows ignores the extra space so that the top margins of your document always remain even.

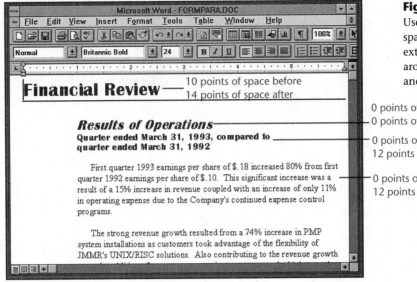

Fig. 10.24

Use paragraph spacing to add extra spacing around headings and paragraphs.

0 points of space before
0 points of space after

0 points of space before
12 points of space after

0 points of space before
12 points of space after

To adjust paragraph spacing, follow these steps:

1. Select the paragraph or paragraphs to add spacing before or after, or position the insertion point where you want the new spacing to begin.

2. Choose the Format Paragraph command.

3. Select the Indents and Spacing tab.

4. To add line spacing before the selected paragraph or paragraphs, type a number in the Spacing Before box or click the up or down arrow to increase or decrease the spacing amount in increments of half a line (see fig. 10.25).

5. To add line spacing after the selected paragraph or paragraphs, type a number in the Spacing After box or click the up or down arrow to increase or decrease the spacing amount in increments of half a line.

   You can use measurements other than decimal inches to specify spacing. To add 6-point spacing, for example, type **6 pt** in the Before or After box. To add spacing of 2 centimeters, type **2 cm**, and to add spacing of 1 pica, type **1 pi**.

6. Choose OK.

Formatting Documents

Fig. 10.25
Use the Paragraph
Indents and
Spacing tab to set
paragraph spacing
options.

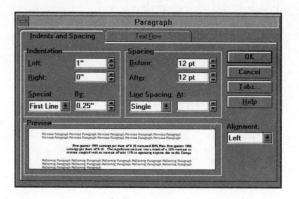

Adjusting Line Spacing

Typesetters and desktop publishers call the spacing between lines in a document *leading* (pronounced "ledding"). Typesetters have great control over precisely how much space appears between lines. They know that long lines need more spacing so that the eye doesn't lose its place in moving from the right margin back to the left. They know that font styles with small letters require less spacing between lines than fonts with big letters.

Word for Windows gives you a typesetter's control over spacing between lines in your document. The feature begins with automatic spacing and enables you to increase spacing, reduce spacing, permit extra spacing for a large character or superscript on the line, or control the spacing exactly.

Spacing is measured by lines. Normal text has single spacing of one line, but if you request spacing of .5, you get half-line spacing. Lines formatted this way are *condensed*. If you request spacing of 1.5, the paragraph has an extra half line of space between lines of text (see fig. 10.26).

You can be very specific about line spacing. If your page design requires 10-point type with 12 points of leading, for example, you type **12 pt** in the At box on the Indents and Spacing tab in the Paragraph dialog box. Word automatically changes the Line Spacing setting to Multiple and inserts a comparable number in inches.

> **Note**
>
> You can include line spacing with styles so that when you press Enter to end a paragraph, the exact spacing is inserted automatically for each style of text you type, whether it's a heading that requires 14 points of space after or body text that requires only 12 points of space after. See Chapter 11, "Formatting with Styles," for information on styles.

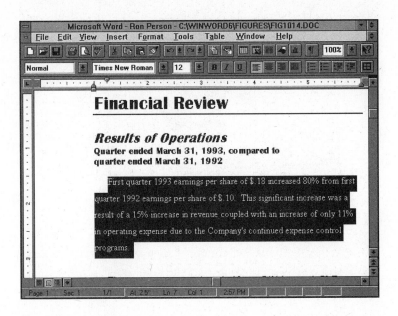

Fig. 10.26
The line spacing is set at 1.5 to put more space between the lines of the selected text.

To adjust spacing between lines using the menu commands, follow these steps:

1. Select the paragraph or paragraphs to space, or position the insertion point where you want the new spacing to begin.

2. Choose the Format Paragraph command to open the Paragraph dialog box.

3. Select the Indents and Spacing tab.

4. Choose one of the following options in the Line Spacing box:

Option	Spacing
Single	Single-line spacing (Line height automatically adjusts to accommodate the size of the font and any graphics or formulas that have been inserted into a line.)
1.5 Lines	Line-and-a-half spacing (extra half line between lines)
Double	Double-spacing (extra full line between lines)
At Least	At least the amount of spacing you specify in the At box (Word for Windows adds extra spacing, if necessary, for tall characters, big graphics, or super-/subscript.)

(continues)

(continued)

Option	Spacing
Exactly	The exact amount of spacing you specify in the At box (All lines are exactly the same height, regardless of the size of the characters in the line. Word for Windows doesn't add extra spacing for anything. Some text may be cut off if enough space isn't available. Increase the amount of spacing if characters are cut off.)
Multiple	Multiples of single-line spacing, such as triple (3), quadruple (4)

5. If you want to specify your own line spacing, type the spacing amount in the At box (with decimal numbers, such as **1.25** for an extra quarter-line of space between lines) or click the up or down arrow to increase or decrease the amount.

   You can choose a spacing amount in the At box without first choosing from the Line Spacing list. Word for Windows assumes that you want at least this spacing and provides extra spacing if needed for large characters, superscript, and so on.

6. Choose OK.

If you want to return to single-line spacing, select the paragraph or paragraphs, choose the Format Paragraph command, and then choose Single Line Spacing.

You can change line spacing to single, 1.5, or double from the keyboard. You can also add or remove 12 points of space before a paragraph.

To adjust spacing between lines from the keyboard, follow these steps:

1. Select the paragraph or paragraphs, or place the insertion point in the paragraph in which you want to change the spacing.

2. Press one of the following key combinations:

Press	To Do This
Ctrl+1	Single-spacing
Ctrl+5	1.5 line spacing
Ctrl+2	Double-spacing
Ctrl+0 (zero)	Adds 12 points of space before a paragraph
Ctrl+Shift+0 (zero)	Removes any space before a paragraph

Inserting a Line Break

When you type a paragraph formatted by a style that is automatically followed by a different style and you then press Enter, the next paragraph is formatted with the next style. Sometimes, however, you may not be ready to change to the next style. If you have a two-line subheading, for example, you may want to press Enter after the first line and still be in the subheading style, rather than switch to the next style. In this case, you want to insert a *line break*, or *soft return*, rather than a new paragraph. To end a line without inserting a paragraph mark, press Shift+Enter.

Pressing Shift+Enter breaks a line without breaking the paragraph. After you finish typing your two-line subheading, press Enter in the usual way to end the paragraph and begin the following paragraph with the next style.

If you click the Show/Hide ¶ button at the far right end of the Formatting toolbar to display paragraph marks, you see that the line end marks at the ends of lines where you pressed Shift+Enter look like left-facing arrows rather than paragraph marks (see fig. 10.27).

For Related Information
- "Changing Styles," p. 365

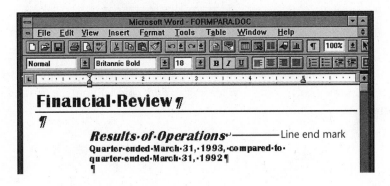

Fig. 10.27
Press Shift+Enter to create a new line without creating a new paragraph. Line end marks display as left-facing arrows rather than paragraph marks.

Formatting Documents

Shading and Bordering Paragraphs

For a finishing touch, you can add paragraph borders and shading to your document. A *border* may be a box surrounding a paragraph (or paragraphs) on all sides or a line that sets a paragraph off on one or more sides. A border can include *shading*, which fills a paragraph with a pattern. Boxes and lines can be solid black, shading can be gray, or, if you have a color monitor, they can be more colorful than a rainbow.

Borders are particularly useful in setting special paragraphs apart from the rest of your text for emphasis or wonderful graphic effects (see fig. 10.28). If you use Word for Windows for desktop publishing, you may find boxes, lines, and shading to be helpful buttons. For examples of text enhancement, see Chapter 27, "Desktop Publishing."

Fig. 10.28

Borders, lines, and shading can set paragraphs apart.

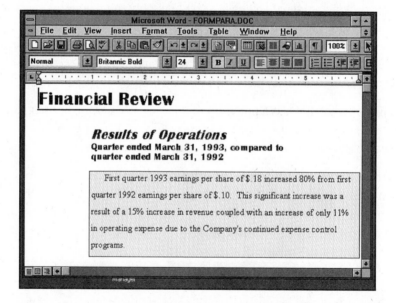

Creating colored lines, boxes, and shading is easy if you have a color monitor. If you have a color printer, you also can *print* colored lines, boxes, and shading.

Note

Service bureaus in many cities offer color printing for a per-page fee. If you want to print your document with colored lines, boxes, and shading, use your own printer to proof the pages and then take a floppy disk containing your file to the service bureau to have the final pages printed in color. Before you go to the service bureau, check to see if they have Word for Windows. You may need to reformat your document slightly for their printer.

Borders, like all forms of paragraph formatting, belong to the paragraphs to which they are applied. They are carried forward when you press Enter at the end of a paragraph. Thus, if a group of paragraphs are formatted with a box around them and you press Enter at the end of the last paragraph, your new paragraph falls within the box. To create a new paragraph outside the border, move the insertion point outside the border before you press Enter. If you're at the end of the document and have nowhere to go outside of the border, create a new paragraph and remove the border.

If you delete the paragraph mark (which stores all the paragraph formatting), the current paragraph merges with the following one, assuming its formatting. If you accidentally remove borders in this way, immediately choose the Edit Undo command to undo your mistake.

Tip
To change the color of the text inside a border, use Format Font. See Chapter 9, "Formatting Characters and Changing Fonts," for more information.

Note

Sometimes the screen display inaccurately shows text extending beyond borders or shading. This situation results from screen fonts and screen resolutions that differ from the printer's fonts and resolution. Your printed text formats within the border or shading.

Enclosing Paragraphs in Boxes and Lines

A box fully surrounds a paragraph or selected group of paragraphs. Two types of preset boxes are available: box and shadow. A line appears on one or more sides of a paragraph or selected paragraphs, or may appear between selected paragraphs. You have 11 line styles to choose from and can use any line style to create a line, a box, or a shadowed box.

You use the Paragraph Borders and Shading dialog box to create boxes, lines, and shadows. Choose the Format Borders and Shading command to access

Formatting Documents

the dialog box. In the dialog box, you can choose either the Borders tab or Shading tab. The Borders tab (see fig. 10.29) offers the following choices:

Borders Option	Effect
None	No box. Use this option to remove an existing box. (This option is used often with the Shading options to create a shaded box with no border.)
Box	A box with identical lines on all four sides.
Shadow	A box with a drop shadow on the bottom right corner.
Border	A line on one or more sides of the selected paragraph(s). Dotted lines at the corners and sides of the sample indicate where the lines appear; when they are selected, arrows point to these dotted lines. The sample displays each border as added (see fig.10.30).
From Text	The distance between the line or box and the text, measured in points. Because 72 points make up an inch, select 9 points for an eighth-inch distance or 18 points for a quarter-inch distance.
Line None	No line. Use this option to remove individual lines.
Style	A line or box in the selected line style. Options listed show exact point size and a sample display.
Color	A line or box in the selected color. Sixteen colors and gray shades are available. If you select the Auto option, the default color for text is used. This is usually black, but can be changed in the Windows Control Panel.

 You also can use the Borders toolbar to add borders and shading to selected paragraphs (see fig. 10.31). Display the Borders toolbar by choosing View Toolbars or by clicking the Borders button on the Formatting toolbar.

To create a box or line from the menu command, follow these steps:

1. Select the paragraph or paragraphs for which you want to create a box or line.

   If you create a box for more than one paragraph, the box encloses the paragraphs as a group, with no borders between them.

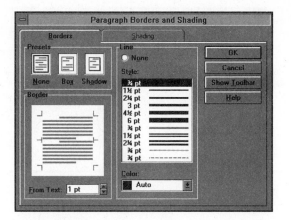

Fig. 10.29
The Borders tab from the Paragraph Borders and Shading dialog box offers options for adding lines to any and all sides of a paragraph.

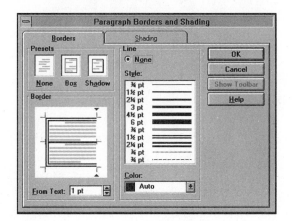

Fig. 10.30
The sample box in the Borders tab shows you which line is currently selected and gives you a preview of the lines you have inserted.

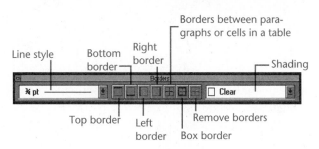

Fig. 10.31
You can add borders and shading from the Borders toolbar.

II

Formatting Documents

To Add a Box or Line to	Select
A paragraph, including paragraphs inside a table cell or frame	The paragraph
A table cell	The entire cell, including the end-of-cell marker
A frame	The frame (see Chapter 23, "Framing and Moving Text and Graphics")

2. Choose the Format Borders and Shading command. The Paragraph Borders and Shading dialog box appears.

3. Select the Borders tab.

4. To create a box, choose either Box or Shadow from the Preset group.

   To create a line, do one of the following:

   Mouse: To create a line, in the Border group click the side of the paragraph where you want the line. Triangles are used to indicate when a line is selected. If a style has already been selected from the Style group, a line with that style will be inserted. You can continue inserting using this appoach. If the None option is selected, you can select multiple lines by holding the Shift key while you click the sides you want to add lines to. Then select a line from the Style group to insert lines at all the selected locations. A line with the currently selected style will be inserted. If multiple paragraphs are selected, you can create a line between them by clicking the horizontal line between paragraphs in the Border box.

   Keyboard: Choose Border; then press any cursor-movement key to scroll through various line combinations. Triangles are used to indicate which line or lines are selected. Press the space bar to insert a line with the style that is currently selected in the Style list. If the None option is selected, select the Style box and use the arrow keys to select a style to apply to the select line or lines.

   Choosing the line style before you create borders ensures that borders take on the appearance of the selected line style. (If None is selected as the line style, borders have no line.)

5. To set the spacing between a box and the text, specify a distance in the From Text box.

6. To apply color to all your boxes and lines, choose a color from the Color list.

7. Choose OK.

To create a box or line from the Borders toolbar, follow these steps:

1. Display the Borders toolbar by clicking the Borders button on the Formatting toolbar or by choosing the View Toolbars command and specifying the Borders toolbar.

2. Select the paragraph or paragraphs for which you want to create a box or line.

   If you create a box for more than one paragraph, the box encloses the paragraphs as a group, with no borders between them.

To Add a Box or Line to	Select
A paragraph, including paragraphs inside a table cell or frame	The paragraph
A table cell	The entire cell, including the end-of-cell marker
A frame	The frame

3. Select the Line style box by clicking the down arrow and choose a line style.

4. Choose the border you want to add by clicking one of the following buttons:

Choose This Button	To Do This
	Add a border along the top
	Add a border along the bottom
	Add a border along the left edge
	Add a border along the right edge
	Add inside borders

(continues)

(continued)

Choose This Button	To Do This
	Add a box border
	Remove all borders

5. Choose shading or a pattern from the Shading box, if you want shading or a pattern added.

The width of a paragraph border (box or line) is determined by the paragraph indent. (If no indent exists, width is determined by the page margins.) If you want a paragraph's border (or line) to be narrower than the margins, indent the paragraph (see figs. 10.32 and 10.33).

Fig. 10.32
With indents set to the left and right margins, borders extend the full width of the page.

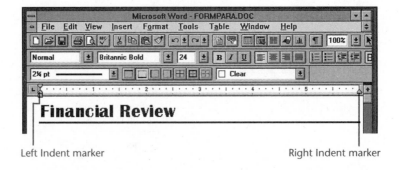

Left Indent marker   Right Indent marker

Fig. 10.33
To create a shorter border, move in the Left and Right Indent markers.

Left Indent
marker

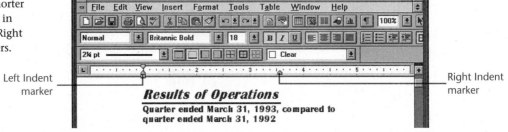

Right Indent
marker

If you select and box several paragraphs that have different indents, each paragraph appears in its own separate box (instead of all appearing together in one box). To make paragraphs with different indents appear within a single box, you must create a table and put each paragraph in a row by itself and then format a box around the table (see Chapter 16, "Creating and Editing Tables").

When paragraphs extend exactly to the margins of your page (as they always do if you don't indent the paragraphs), borders extend slightly outside the margins. If you want borders to fall within or exactly on the margins, you must indent the paragraph. To make borders fall on the margins, indent the paragraph by the width of the border: for example, if the border is the double 1-point line, which adds up to a total of 3 points in width including the space between the double lines, indent the paragraph by 3 points. Type **3 pt** in the **L**eft and **R**ight indentation boxes in the Paragraph dialog box.

Note

Remember the definition of a paragraph: any amount of text—even no text—that ends when you press Enter. If you format groups of paragraphs to have lines between them, those lines apply to blank spaces between paragraphs if you create those blank spaces by pressing Enter an extra time. To avoid extra lines between paragraphs, use the Spacing After option in the Paragraph dialog box to add blank space between paragraphs. (See "Adjusting Line and Paragraph Spacing" earlier in this chapter.)

You can remove borders all at once or line by line. Changing the line style of existing borders is essentially the same process.

To remove or change a box or line from the menu command, follow these steps:

1. Select the paragraph or paragraphs for which you want to remove or change boxes or lines.

2. Choose the **F**ormat **B**orders and Shading command.

3. Select the **B**orders tab.

4. Select the Presets **N**one option to remove all borders.

   or

   Select the Line **N**one option and then select the lines you want to remove.

5. Select the line you want to change and choose a different option from the Line Style options.

or

Select a different line color from the Line Color options.

6. Select Box or Shadow to change the Preset border style.

7. Choose OK.

To remove or change a line or box from the Borders toolbar, follow these steps:

1. Select the paragraph or paragraphs for which you want to remove or change boxes or lines.

2. Click the Borders button on the Formatting toolbar to display the Borders toolbar.

3. Click the Remove Borders button to remove all borders.

4. Choose a new line style.

5. Click the button(s) for the box(es) or border(s) you want to add.

Shading Paragraphs

Paragraphs can be shaded as well as bordered. Shading comes in various percentages of black or the selected color, and in patterns (see fig. 10.34). Percentages of black appear as grays of various intensities. For each shade or pattern, you can select a foreground or background color. *Shades* create a blended effect: a foreground of yellow and a background of blue creates the effect of green. But in *patterns*, the effect is more dramatic: in a Lt Grid pattern, for example, the yellow foreground forms a light grid pattern over a blue background. With some experimentation, you can create eye-catching results that can add visual impact to documents used for presentations or overhead transparencies. Colors are converted to shades of gray or patterns on a black-and-white printer.

You can use shading with borders so that a paragraph is surrounded by a line and filled with shading, or you can use shading alone so that no border goes around the shaded paragraph. Watch the Preview box on the Shading tab to see the effect of the patterns and colors you select. To add shading, choose the Shading tab in the Paragraph Borders and Shading dialog box. You have the following options:

Shading Option	Effect
None	No shading in selected paragraph(s).
Custom	Shading in the selected custom shading. Options shown in Shading.
Shading	Shading in the selected custom darkness or pattern. Options include increasing degrees of shading and various patterns. Clear applies the selected background color; Solid applies the selected foreground color.
Foreground	A foreground color for the selected shading pattern. Auto selects the best color, usually black. Select from 16 colors, including black and white.
Background	A background color for the selected shading pattern. Auto selects the best color, usually white. Select from 16 colors, including black and white.

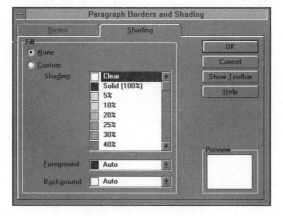

Fig. 10.34
The Shading tab from the Paragraph Borders and Shading dialog box offers options for adding varying degrees of shading and/or color to a paragraph.

Formatting Documents

To shade paragraphs with the menu command, follow these steps:

1. Select the paragraph or paragraphs you want to shade:

To Shade	Select
A paragraph, including paragraphs inside a table cell or frame	The paragraph

(continues)

(continued)

To Shade	Select
A table cell	The entire cell, including the end-of-cell marker
A frame	The frame

2. Choose the Format Borders and Shading command. (If you want borders around your selected paragraph, select the Borders tab and choose border options.)

3. Select the Shading tab (see fig. 10.34).

4. Select the Shading pattern you want. Options include Clear (uses the background color), Solid (uses the foreground color), percentages, and striped and checkered patterns such as Dk Horizontal (for dark horizontal stripes) and Lt Grid (for a grid made of light cross-hatching).

   Percentage patterns consist of foreground and background colors. The result appears in the Preview box. For best results in creating colors, however, look first for the color you want in the Foreground list.

5. Select a color from the Foreground list to color a percentage pattern or a pattern foreground.

6. Select a color from the Background list to color a percentage pattern or a pattern background.

7. Choose OK.

To shade paragraphs using the Borders toolbar, follow these steps:

1. Select the paragraph or paragraphs you want to shade:

To Shade	Select
A paragraph, including paragraphs inside a table cell or frame	The paragraph
A table cell	The entire cell, including the end-of-cell marker
A frame	The frame

2. Click the Borders button on the Formatting toolbar to display the Borders toolbar.

3. Choose the shading or pattern you want from the Shading box.

To remove shading using the menu command, follow these steps:

1. Select the paragraph or paragraphs from which you want to remove shading.

2. Choose the Format Borders and Shading command.

3. Choose the Shading button.

4. Choose None from the Fill group.

5. Choose OK.

To remove shading with the Borders toolbar, follow these steps:

1. Select the paragraph or paragraphs from which you want to remove shading.

2. Click the Borders button on the Formatting toolbar to display the Borders toolbar.

3. Choose the Clear setting from the Shading box.

From Here...

For information relating directly to formatting paragraphs, review the following chapters:

■ Chapter 11, "Formatting with Styles." Learn how to format paragraphs quickly with styles and reformat them globally.

■ Chapter 13, "Setting the Page Layout." Learn how to control where paragraphs and pages break.

■ Chapter 23, "Framing and Moving Text and Graphics." Learn how to position paragraphs exactly where you want them on a page.

■ Chapter 27, "Desktop Publishing." Learn how to use paragraphs as graphic elements in a newsletter or other publication.

For Related Information

■ "Applying Special Character Formatting," p. 260

■ "Formatting a Table," p. 536

■ "Formatting Text Within a Frame," p. 690

Formatting Documents

- Chapter 16, "Creating and Editing Tables," Chapter 24, "Drawing with Word's Drawing Tools," Chapter 25, "Creating Banners and Special Effects with WordArt," and Chapter 26, "Graphing Data." Learn how to use Word's many advanced tools to create professional-looking documents.

Chapter 11

Formatting with Styles

What gives your document style? For the most part, style is the appearance of your document: the arrangement of text on pages, the shape of the paragraphs, the characteristics of the letters, the use of lines and borders to give your document emphasis. All these elements of style are formatting choices you make while working with Word for Windows.

Style involves more than just appearance, however. Style is also readability and consistency. When your document's style is appropriate to its content and is consistent from one section to the next, the reader's job of gleaning information from your text becomes much easier.

Word for Windows offers you tools designed to make the task of developing and maintaining your document's style much easier. Appropriately, these tools are called *styles*. In Word for Windows, a style is a set of formatting instructions you save with a name in order to use them again and again. All text formatted with the same style has exactly the same formatting. If you make a formatting change to a style, all the text formatted with that style will reformat to match the new formatting.

Using Styles Versus Direct Formatting

You can create and apply two types of styles: character styles and paragraph styles. *Character styles* include any of the options available from the Font dialog box, such as bold, italic, and small caps. Character styles store only character formatting, and apply to selected text or to the word containing the insertion point. *Paragraph styles* include character and paragraph formatting, tab settings, paragraph positioning, borders and shading, and language used for spell checking. Paragraph styles can store both character and paragraph formatting, and apply to selected paragraphs or the paragraph containing the insertion point.

You can type a plain business letter and then apply a set of styles automatically with the AutoFormat command on the Format menu to give it a professional appearance. Word applies styles to common text elements, such as bulleted and numbered lists and headings. In addition, Word makes small improvements, such as changing straight quotation marks (") to curved typesetting quotation marks (" "). You can review and undo the changes Word has made and make further changes of your own.

You can also choose from among many available style groups to change the document format automatically to the style you want. The Style Gallery displays your document in other styles and lets you select from among them the one you most like.

See figs. 11.1 and 11.2 for an example of how automatic formatting can quickly change your document's appearance with styles.

Fig. 11.1
You can choose between different families of styles. This letter uses the Letter1 template.

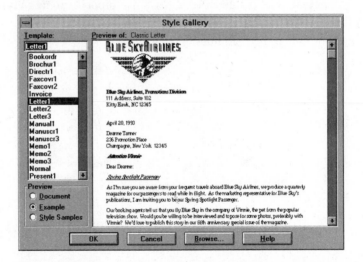

Using styles instead of directly formatting each word, phrase, paragraph, or page individually offers several benefits:

- *You save time.* You can format one word or paragraph the way you like it and copy that formatting to other words or paragraphs. The AutoFormat command applies styles automatically, quickly formatting a simple document into a professional-looking presentation.

- *You preserve consistency.* By using styles to format your document, you can be sure that each selected item or paragraph looks the same as others of its type.

- *You reduce the effort required to change your document's appearance.* By changing a style, you also change all the selected text or paragraphs associated with that style.

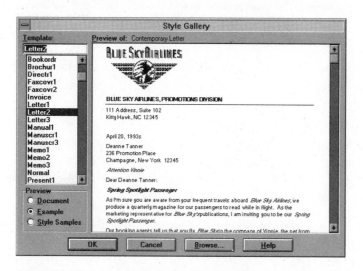

Fig. 11.2

This is the same letter using, previewed with the Letter2 template

Choosing a Formatting Method

You're always using at least one style when you work with Word for Windows. The *Normal style*, built into Word for Windows, gives your document its default formatting choices. If you have the Formatting toolbar displayed when you start a new document, you can see the Normal style in the Style box, already selected (see fig. 11.3). The Normal style's formatting selections are basic: it includes a font and font size (12-point MS Serif, 10-point Times New Roman, or a different font, depending on your printer), left alignment, and single-line spacing. Word also makes other styles available for items like page numbers, headers, and footers. You learn how to change the Normal style in the section "Redefining Standard Styles" later in this chapter.

The list of styles from which you can select depends on the *template* you select when you create a document. The default template is Normal. In addition to the Normal style, the template contains styles for indenting, table of contents, titles, headings, lists, envelopes, and many more. You can use the styles built into a template as they come, you can modify them, or you can create your own styles. (See Chapter 6, "Using Templates as Master Documents," for information about templates.)

Fig. 11.3
The Normal style is displayed in the Formatting toolbar when you start a new document.

Except for the Normal template, which is designed for general use, each template's styles have been designed to suit one particular application, such as a brochure, a fax cover sheet, or a resume. Normal style in one template may be 10 point Times New Roman, while in another template it may be 12 point Century Schoolbook. Changing the template may change the formatting of the style. Word provides a Style Gallery in which you can view the effects of changing a template and its resultant changes to the styles you use. The Style Gallery is covered later in this chapter.

You can apply and change styles in three ways. Each method has advantages and disadvantages, as described in the following paragraphs.

Method 1. The fastest formatting method is formatting automatically with the Format AutoFormat command.

> *Advantage*
>
> The formatting is done automatically without having to select styles.
>
> *Disadvantage*
>
> You have less control over the selection of styles, although you can manually override any style selections.

Method 2. The method that allows you the greatest control over the format of the text is manually formatting by creating, selecting, and/or modifying those styles available in the template upon which your document is based.

> *Advantages*
>
> You can make your document appear any way you choose by creating and selecting suitable styles.

Styles you create can be based on existing styles and/or followed by other styles. For example, you can follow a heading style with a body text style, automatically incorporating consistent spacing and other formatting.

Disadvantage

You have to create and/or select a style for each element of your document.

Method 3. The third formatting method is selecting a new template with the Format Style Gallery command.

Advantage

You can preview your document as it will appear based on each of many other templates, and then select and apply that template. For example, you can choose from three different letter styles.

Disadvantage

You have less control over the selection of styles, although you can manually override any style selections.

The following sections describe in detail each method of formatting.

Formatting a Document Automatically

Imagine that you quickly dash off an important business letter, paying no special attention to the letter's formatting. Then with a click of the mouse, the letter suddenly takes the shape of the formal business letter you had in mind. The Format AutoFormat command gives you that power.

When you choose the Format AutoFormat command, Word goes through your document paragraph by paragraph, applying appropriate styles. If you've included a list of items, each preceded with an asterisk, for example, Word reformats the list, replacing asterisks with bullets and adding the bulleted list style. Whether or not you've formatted some of the text, the AutoFormat command will complete the job. AutoFormat ensures that the formatting is consistent throughout the document and also improves the appearance. The styles Word applies come from the template that is currently attached to the document. See figures 11.4 and 11.5 for an example of a document that has been formatted with AutoFormat.

Fig. 11.4
You can type letters, documents, and memos without worrying about formatting.

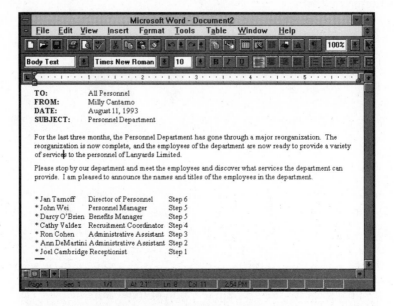

Fig. 11.5
The AutoFormat command will use its rules to apply formats, such as bullets, to your documents.

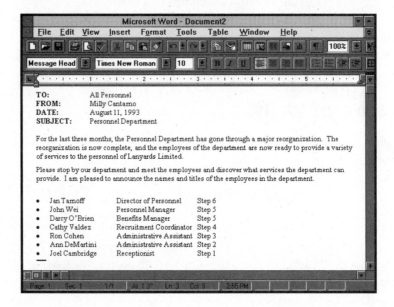

After the text has been formatted with AutoFormat, you can polish the document's appearance by manually applying styles or formatting to any elements of the document. You can also choose a new template from the Style Gallery to change the overall design of the document. Each of these topics is covered later in this chapter.

Applying Styles with AutoFormat

The AutoFormat command analyzes the document in the active window and applies a style to each paragraph that is currently formatted with either the Normal or Body Text style. The styles AutoFormat applies are designed to format common writing elements such as quotations, bulleted lists, headings, and more. AutoFormat applies styles and makes corrections as described in the following list:

- Uses its formatting rules to find and format such items as headings, body text, lists, superscript and subscript, addresses, and letter closings.

- Removes extra paragraph marks.

- Replaces straight quotation marks (") and apostrophes (') with typesetting quotation marks (" ") and apostrophes (' ').

- Replaces "(c)," "(R)," and "(TM)" with copyright ©, registered trademark ®, and trademark ™ symbols.

- Replaces asterisks, hyphens, or other characters used to list items with a bullet character (•).

- Replaces horizontal spaces inserted with the Tab key or the space bar with indents.

To format text automatically with the menu command, follow these steps:

1. Select the text you want to format. If you want to format the entire document, position the insertion point anywhere in the document.

2. Choose the Format AutoFormat command. The AutoFormat dialog box appears (see fig. 11.6).

   You can determine which changes AutoFormat makes by choosing the Options button in the AutoFormat dialog box or by changing the settings in the AutoFormat tab of the Options dialog box. See "Setting AutoFormat Options" for more information.

II

Formatting Documents

Fig. 11.6
You can automatically format a
document with
the Format
AutoFormat
command.

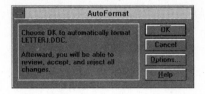

3. Choose OK to begin formatting. Word reviews the text and selects styles from the current template.

4. When AutoFormat is finished, the AutoFormat dialog box is displayed again, and you have four choices (see fig. 11.7):

Choose OK to accept all the changes.

Choose Cancel to reject all the changes.

Choose **Review** Changes to examine changes one by one, accepting or rejecting individual changes. See "Reviewing Changes" in this section for more information.

Choose **St**yle Gallery to apply styles from another template. See "Using the Style Gallery" later in this chapter for more information.

Fig. 11.7
When AutoFormat
is complete, you
can choose to
accept or reject all
changes, to review
the changes, or to
change templates
in the Style
Gallery.

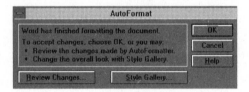

You can also run AutoFormat by clicking the AutoFormat button on the Standard toolbar (the toolbar must be displayed) or from a keyboard shortcut.

To display the Standard toolbar, follow these steps:

1. Choose the View Toolbars command.

2. Select the Standard toolbar.

3. Choose OK.

To format text automatically from the Standard toolbar, follow these steps:

1. Position the insertion point in the document you want to format or select the text you want to format.

2. Click the AutoFormat button on the Standard toolbar. Text is automatically formatted, using styles from the currently attached template and the options that are selected on the AutoFormat tab in the Options dialog box. (For more information, see the later section "Setting AutoFormat Options.") The Review option isn't available when you choose AutoFormat from the Standard toolbar.

To format text automatically with a keyboard shortcut, position the insertion point in the document you want to format or select the text you want to format and press Ctrl+K. Text is automatically formatted using styles from the currently attached template and the options that are selected in the Options dialog box. The Review option isn't available when you start AutoFormat from the keyboard shortcut.

If you don't like the result of the autoformatting, you can undo the formatting changes you've made.

To undo all changes after accepting them, click the down-arrow button next to the Undo button on the Standard toolbar and undo AutoFormat Begin.

Reviewing Format Changes

After a document has been automatically formatted, you may want to review the changes and possibly make some alterations. You can choose the Review Changes button in the AutoFormat dialog box to review the changes one by one (refer to fig. 11.7). As you review each change, you can accept or reject it. You can also scroll through the document and select specific changes for review.

Tip

You can automatically format tables with the Table AutoFormat command on the Table menu. See Chapter 16, "Creating and Editing Tables," for information.

Word indicates changes to text and formatting with temporary revision marks and color (on color monitors). With paragraph marks displayed, Word highlights the extra paragraph marks it deleted and also those to which a style was applied.

To display paragraph marks, click the Show/Hide ¶ button on the Standard toolbar.

You can also review the document with the revision marks hidden. To hide revision marks, choose the Hide Marks button in the Review AutoFormat Changes dialog box.

Table 11.1 describes Word's revision marks.

Table 11.1 AutoFormat Revision Marks	
Visual Change	**Meaning**
Blue paragraph mark (¶) (Shown lighter on a monochrome monitor.)	Applied a style to that paragraph
Red paragraph mark (¶) (Shown lighter on a monochrome monitor.)	Deleted that paragraph mark
Strikethrough character (-)	Deleted text or spaces (indicated in red)
Underline (_)	Added the underlined characters (indicated in blue)
Vertical bar in the left margin	Changed the text or formatting in that line of text

To review changes made by AutoFormat, follow these steps:

1. After Word completes the AutoFormat, choose the Review Changes button. The Review AutoFormat Changes dialog box appears (see fig. 11.8).

2. Choose from among the following options to target the change(s) you want to review:

   To see text under the dialog box, drag the box by its title bar to a new location.

   To see the entire document, use the vertical scroll bar to scroll through the document.

   To see changes one by one, use the Find buttons.

   To see the effect of another style, select the text and then select another style from the Style box on the Formatting toolbar.

3. Choose from among the following options to alter the selected change:

   To undo the displayed change, choose Reject.

   To undo the last rejected change, choose Undo Last.

   To view the document with all remaining changes and revision marks turned off, choose Hide Marks.

Undo the displayed changes and automatically move to the next change, select the Find Next after Reject check box.

4. Choose the Close button to accept all remaining changes. The AutoFormat dialog box is displayed again.

5. Choose Accept to accept all changes.

or

Choose Reject All to reject all changes.

or

Choose Style Gallery to select a different AutoFormat style.

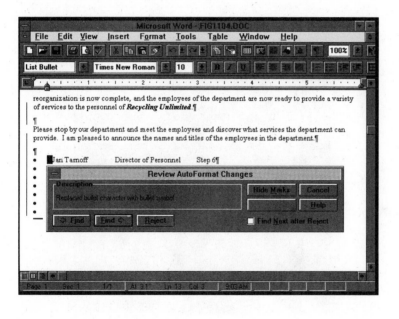

Fig. 11.8
Use options in the Review AutoFormat Changes dialog box to reject or accept the changes made by AutoFormat.

Formatting Documents

Setting AutoFormat Options

You can change the rules that Word follows each time it performs an AutoFormat. You can choose whether to apply styles to headings and lists, for example.

To change the AutoFormat formatting rules, follow these steps:

1. Choose the Tools Options command and select the AutoFormat tab (see fig. 11.9).

Tip
AutoFormat can format a document with styles you've designed if you redefine the built-in styles. See "Getting the Most from AutoFormat" and "Creating Styles" later in this chapter.

2. Select from the following groups of options you want applied (selected options are marked with an ×):

   Choose options from the Preserve group to retain styles and/or indentation you've already added to the document.

   Choose options from the Apply Styles To group to select the document parts to which you want Word to apply styles.

   Choose options from the Adjust group to standardize spacing on the items you select.

   Choose options from the Replace group to select the characters or symbols you want Word to replace.

   or

   Select those options you want turned off to remove the ×.

3. Choose OK.

Fig. 11.9
Specify the settings you want to control the changes Word makes during an AutoFormat.

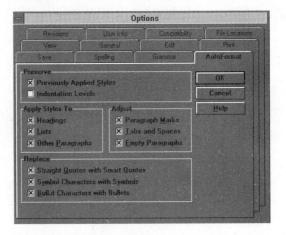

Getting the Most from AutoFormat

Any formatting you have applied using commands on the Format menu helps Word determine which styles to apply during AutoFormat. For example, styles previously applied can be preserved or changed, depending on the settings in the Options dialog box on the AutoFormat tab (see the preceding section). In addition, the following tips will help you to maximize the results you get from AutoFormat.

chapter, or by using the Format Style command, also described later in this chapter.

To learn more about using the outline view to apply heading styles, refer to Chapter 19. To learn more about creating a table of contents from heading styles, refer to Chapter 29, "Creating Indexes and Tables of Contents."

Applying, Copying, and Removing Styles

The power of styles becomes apparent when you use them to apply consistent formatting to paragraph after paragraph in your document. You can apply styles to text as you type or to selected text by choosing a style from the menu command, from the Formatting toolbar, or with a keyboard shortcut. You will mostly use the Formatting toolbar.

To display the Formatting toolbar, follow these steps:

1. Choose the View Toolbars command.

2. Select Formatting from the Toolbars list. An × appears in the check box to indicate that it is selected.

3. Choose OK.

For Related Information

■ "Creating Tables of Contents, Tables of Figures, and Tables of Authorities," p. 909, 917, 923

■ "Creating an Outline," p. 617

> **Note**
>
> The Style box in the Formatting toolbar shows the style at the position of the insertion point or of the selected text. If the text selection includes text formatted with more than one style, the Style box is blank.

Resolving Conflicts Between Paragraph and Character Style

Remember that paragraph styles can include both paragraph-level formatting commands and character-level formatting. Character styles include only character-level formatting commands. Any paragraph style you apply to text formats the entire paragraph (or the group of selected paragraphs). If a paragraph style includes character formatting, it too is applied to the entire paragraph. If you apply a character style, such as bold, to text in a paragraph, and then apply a paragraph style that includes bold, the text you boldfaced with the character style appears normal, rather than bold, because the paragraph style toggles off bold.

II

Formatting Documents

Applying Paragraph Styles

To apply a paragraph style to a single paragraph, the insertion point must first be positioned anywhere in that paragraph. You can apply a paragraph style to a group of paragraphs by first selecting those paragraphs, or at least part of each paragraph (see fig. 11.12).

Fig. 11.12

All the paragraphs will change with a new style selection because at least part of each paragraph has been selected.

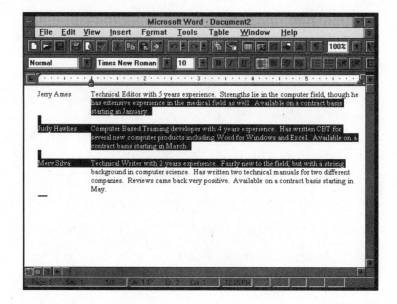

Applying Character Styles

To apply a character style, you must first select the text to which you want to apply the character style. The formatting of the new style will be added to those formats already in effect on the selected text. For example, a character style that adds bold and italic doesn't change the font or point size or other formatting applied by the paragraph style in use.

To apply a style from the menu command, follow these steps:

1. Position the insertion point inside the paragraph, or select text in the paragraph(s) you want to format with a style.

2. Choose the Format Style command. The Style dialog box appears.

3. Click the down arrow to the right of the List group and select one of the following options:

   Select the Styles in Use option to list standard styles and those you've created or modified for the current document.

Select the All Styles option to list all styles available in the document.

Select the User-Defined Styles option to list non-standard styles that you have created for the document

4. Select the style you want from the Styles group. Paragraph styles are listed in bold text; character styles are listed in normal text. The Paragraph Preview and Character Preview boxes provide a sample of how the style appears.

5. Choose Apply.

To apply a style from the Formatting toolbar, follow these steps:

1. Position the insertion point inside the paragraph, or select text in the paragraph(s) you want to format with a style.

2. Click the down arrow at the right side of the Style box in the Formatting toolbar to display a list of available styles. Paragraph styles are listed in bold text; character styles are listed in normal text.

3. Select the style you want to apply to the paragraph or selected paragraphs (scroll the list if necessary).

To apply a style from the keyboard, follow these steps:

1. Position the insertion point inside the paragraph, or select text in the paragraph(s) you want to format with a style.

2. Press any of the following key combinations:

Press This	To Apply This Style
Ctrl+Shift+N	Normal
Ctrl+Alt+1	Heading 1
Ctrl+Alt+2	Heading 2
Ctrl+Alt+3	Heading 3
Ctrl+Shift+L	List Bullet (bulleted list style)
Ctrl+Shift+S	Activates the Style box; choose the style you want from the list

Tip

The styles listed in the Style box are only a partial list of what's available. To see the entire list, hold down the Shift key while you click the down arrow next to the Style box.

Formatting Documents

When you press Ctrl+Shift+S, Word selects the currently displayed style in the Style box in the Formatting toolbar. To select another, either type a different name in the Style box, or use the arrow keys to highlight another style and then press Enter. If you type the name of a style that doesn't exist, you will create a style based on the example of the selected paragraph or paragraphs, rather than applying a style.

You can assign shortcut keys to other styles, as well. See "Creating Style Shortcut Keys" later in this chapter.

Copying Styles

You can apply the same style several times consecutively. Apply the style the first time, then select the additional text you want to format with that style, and press Ctrl+Y. Continue the procedure to apply the style in other locations. This method works for both paragraph styles and character styles.

You also can use the Format Painter button on the Standard toolbar to copy character styles to paragraphs or selected text one or several times.

To copy character styles with the Format Painter button, follow these steps:

1. Select the text or paragraph mark (¶) that has the formatting you want to copy.

2. Click the Format Painter button on the Standard toolbar.

3. Select the text you want to format with the character style. The new character style is applied to the selected text.

To copy character styles multiple times with the Format Painter button, follow these steps:

1. Select the text or position the insertion point within the text that has the formatting you want to copy.

2. Double-click the Format Painter button on the Standard toolbar.

3. Select the text to which you want to copy the formatting and release the mouse button. Continue selecting text and releasing the mouse button to copy the character style.

4. Click the Format Painter button to turn off the copy process.

Removing Character Styles

You can remove a character style and reapply the default character formatting, which will match the character formats defined for the selected paragraph style.

To remove a character style, select the text formatted with the character style you want to remove, and press Ctrl+space bar.

Creating Styles

The process of using styles of your own involves two steps. First you create the style, specifying formatting choices like paragraph indentations, line spacing, font, and font size. Then you apply that style—along with all your formatting choices—to other characters or paragraphs in your document. You can create paragraph styles in two ways: by example (using the Formatting toolbar or a keyboard shortcut) or by menu command. Creating a style by example is so easy that even a beginner can do it. Using a menu command gives you more options, including creating character styles, and isn't difficult when you understand the concept of styles. (See "Creating Styles with a Menu Command" later in this chapter.)

> **Note**
>
> Styles are saved with the document or template in which you create them. You can share styles with other documents, however. (Refer to the section "Sharing Styles Among Documents" later in this chapter.)

Naming the New Style

A new style name must be unique. If you try to create a new style with an existing name, you apply the existing style to your paragraph instead of creating a new style. If that happens, choose Edit Undo and try again. Be aware that Word for Windows includes quite a few built-in styles (like Normal and Heading 1 through Heading 9); don't create new styles using their names. For a list of built-in styles, refer to the section "Using Word for Windows Standard Styles" earlier in this chapter.

As you're naming your style, remember these rules:

■ A style name can contain up to 253 characters. Try, however, to use simple, memorable style names.

■ The name can contain spaces, commas, and aliases. An *alias* is an optional, shorter name (see "Renaming a Style" later in this chapter).

■ Style names are case-sensative—you can use uppercase and lowercase letters.

■ Illegal characters include the following: \ (backslash), { or } (braces), and ; (semicolon).

Choose a style name that makes sense to you so that you will remember it later and so that you can use it consistently in other documents. If you frequently create lists in your documents and you always format them the same way, for example, create a style called List in all the documents where you want to create identically formatted lists.

Creating a Style by Example

To create a style by example, you format a paragraph the way you want it, and then create a style based on the formatting contained in that paragraph. As you format your first paragraph (the one you will use as an example to create a style), remember that although paragraph styles are paragraph-level formatting commands, they also can contain character formatting. The character-level formatting is defined by the font, size, and other character formats of the first character of the selected text. If your example paragraph contains left and right indents and a border, those formatting choices will also be part of your style.

You can create a style by example by using the Formatting toolbar or by using a keyboard shortcut.

To create a style by example using the Formatting toolbar, follow these steps:

1. Choose the View Toolbars command and select the Formatting toolbar (if it isn't already displayed).

2. Format your example paragraph.

   You can include character or paragraph formatting, borders and shading, frames and positioning, tabs, and a language for spell checking.

3. With the insertion point still in your example paragraph, select the entire name of the existing style in the Formatting toolbar's Style box (see fig. 11.13).

4. Type the name of the style you want to create (see fig. 11.14).

5. Press Enter to create the style.

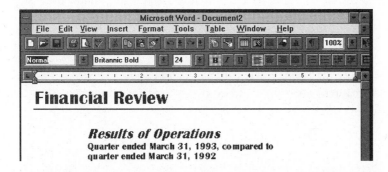

Fig. 11.13
Select the current style name in the Formatting toolbar's Style box.

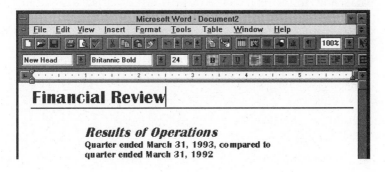

Fig. 11.14
Type the new style name to create a style by example.

After you create your style, look in the Formatting toolbar's Style box. You see your new style name displayed, indicating that its formatting choices control the appearance of your example paragraph.

To create a style by example using the keyboard, follow these steps:

1. Format your example paragraph and position the insertion point in it.

2. Press Ctrl+Shift+S. Word for Windows selects the current style name in the Style box.

3. Type the name of the style you want to create.

4. Press Enter to create the style.

Look at the Style box in the Formatting toolbar to see that your new style is now selected for your example paragraph.

You also can use a menu command to create a style by example. You might do this, for example, if you want to use a formatted paragraph as the basis for a style, but you also want to add additional formatting choices to the style.

To create a style by example using the menu command, follow these steps:

1. Format the paragraph you want to use as an example for your style, and leave the insertion point inside the paragraph.

2. Choose the Format Style command and choose the New button. (See "Creating a Style with a Menu Command" for details on using this dialog box.)

3. In the Name box, type the name of your new style.

   Notice that the Description box changes to show the selected paragraph's formatting.

4. Choose Format and make additional formatting choices.

5. Choose OK to return to the Style dialog box.

6. Choose Close.

Creating a Style with a Menu Command

If you want to create styles before you use them, rather than creating them by example, use the Format Style command. Using this command, you name a style, define its formatting characteristics, and select options such as whether to base the style on another style, whether to follow it with another style, and whether to add the style to the current template. You can also import and export styles to and from other documents and templates.

Using a menu command, you can create both types of styles: paragraph and character.

When you create a style by using the menu command, you have the option to apply the style to the currently selected paragraph or simply to add it to the list of styles you created for your document (or for your template).

All new styles you create are based on the style of the currently selected paragraph. In the next section, you learn how you can base your new style on any other style.

To create a style from the menu command, follow these steps:

1. Choose the Format Style command. The Style dialog box appears.

   Notice that the preview boxes display both the paragraph and character formatting of the currently selected paragraph. The Description box indicates the precise characteristics of the formatting.

2. Choose the New button. The New Style dialog box appears (see fig. 11.15).

3. In the Name box, type the name of your new style. Use a unique, brief, and easy-to-recall name. Refer to "Naming the New Style" for style naming rules.

   Now only the style name of the currently selected paragraph's style appears in the Description box.

4. In the Style Type box, select Character to create a character style, or Paragraph to create a paragraph style.

5. Choose Format to pull down the list of format options and select the one you want. If you want to include bold formatting as part of your style, for example, select Font to display the Font dialog box, then select the Bold option from the Font Style group.

Select This	To Select These Formatting options
Font	Font, style (bold, italic, underline), size, color, super/ subscript, and character spacing
Paragraph	Paragraph alignment, spacing, indentation, and line spacing (not available for character styles)
Tabs	Tab stop position, alignment, and leaders, or clear tabs (not available for character styles)
Border	Border location, style, color, and paragraph shading (not available for character styles)
Language	The language that the spell checker, thesaurus, and grammar checker should use for the current paragraph
Frame	Text wrapping, frame size or position, or remove frame (not available for character styles)
Numbering	Bulleted and Numbered paragraphs in various styles (not available for character styles)

Tip

If you plan to use your styles over and over in the same type of document, as in a monthly newsletter, create them in a new template. See Chapter 6, "Using Templates as Master Documents."

Tip

If you want to print a list of a document's styles (along with a description of each style), choose the File Print command, select Styles in the Print box, and then choose OK.

II

Formatting Documents

Fig. 11.15

You can create styles in the New Style dialog box.

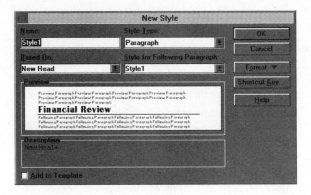

Repeat this step to include as much formatting as you want.

6. Choose OK.

To create additional styles, you can repeat steps 2 through 5 before closing the dialog box.

7. To apply your new style to the currently selected paragraph, choose Apply.

or

To exit the Style dialog box without applying the style to any paragraph, choose Close.

> **Caution**
>
> When you type the name of your new style in step 2, be sure that it is a unique name. If you type the name of an existing style and then make formatting choices, you will redefine the existing style. Any text formatted with the existing style then will take on this redefined formatting.

As part of the process of creating a style, you can assign shortcut keys to make the style easy to apply. See the later section "Creating Style Shortcut Keys."

Creating a Style Based on an Existing Style

You may need a group of styles that are similar to each other but have slight variations. For example, you may need a Table Body style for the contents of a table, and you also may need a Table Heading style and a Table Last Row style. Using the following technique, you can create a "family" of styles based on one foundation style.

To base one style on another style, follow these steps:

For Related Information
■ "Creating a New Template," p. 179

1. Choose the Format Style command.

2. Choose New.

3. Choose Name and type the name of your new style.

   When you select a style name, you see the name of the style plus any formatting attributes from the selected paragraph in the Description box. Your new style automatically is based on that existing style, unless you specify a different style.

4. Specify the name of the style on which you want to base your style in the Based On box. To display a list of styles, click the down arrow to the right of the Based On box.

5. Choose any of the Format button options to add additional formatting options to your style.

6. Choose OK to return to the Style dialog box.

7. Choose Close.

   or

   Choose Apply if you want to apply your new style to the currently selected paragraph.

Changing Styles

You can change any style, including standard styles. This capability makes it easy to adapt to the changing tasks you have to do. For example, instead of having to remember your company's new format for closing signatures, you can redefine a style you have created for closings. All you need to do is continue working like you did before; the new style definition takes care of the changes.

You can also change the design of a document by copying styles from another template. (See "Sharing Styles Among Documents," later in this chapter.) Or, you can open a template with the File Open command and modify the styles in that template in preparation for creating a document.

II

Formatting Documents

Deleting a Style

At some point, you may decide you no longer need a style. You can delete it, and all text associated with the deleted style will revert to the Normal style. You cannot delete built-in styles.

To delete a style, follow these steps:

1. Choose the Format Style command.

2. Select the style you want to delete from the Styles list.

   If you have selected a paragraph containing the style you want to delete, the style already will be selected in the Styles list box.

3. Choose the Delete button. You see a message asking whether you want to delete the style.

4. Choose Yes.

You also can delete several styles at once. Choose the Organizer button in the Style dialog box. Select the styles you want to delete and choose the Delete button. You can select a group of contiguous files by clicking the first one, and then holding down Shift while you click the last one. To select noncontiguous files, hold down Ctrl while you click each one.

Giving a Style a New Name or Alias

You can rename a style, which doesn't affect the associated text, but changes the style name throughout your document. You can choose to rename a style for two purposes: to give it a new name or to add an optional name, or *alias*. An alias is a shorter name or abbreviation that you can type quickly in the Style box in the Formatting toolbar. For example, if you're using the Heading 1 style frequently, and applying it from the keyboard, you can give the style an alias of h1. Then to apply the Heading 1 style you press Ctrl+Shift+S, type h1 (rather than the full name), and press Enter.

Standard styles cannot be renamed, but you can add an alias to them. Also, you cannot use a standard style name as an alias for another style.

To rename a style or add an alias, follow these steps:

1. Choose the Format Style command.

2. Choose the Modify button. The Modify Style dialog box appears.

3. Type the new name. To include an alias, type a comma after the new name and then type the alias.

or

To add an alias, type a comma after the current style name, and then type the alias.

4. Choose OK to return to the Style dialog box.

5. Choose Close.

Redefining a Style

When you *redefine* a style, all the text formatted with that style updates to reflect the changes you have made. Suppose that you finish a 35-page report with many subheadings formatted with a style called Subhead which includes 18-point, bold, Helvetica, centered text. Now your company's publications committee decides subheadings should be smaller and underlined. Just redefine the style Subhead to reflect the new formatting, and all the subheadings in your text will change. You can redefine styles by example or with the Format Style command.

It is as easy to modify a style by example as it is to create a style by example.

To redefine a style by example, follow these steps:

1. Choose the View Toolbars command and select the Formatting toolbar if it isn't currently displayed.

2. Reformat the paragraph you will use as an example for the redefined style. Select the paragraph (or some portion of the paragraph).

3. In the Formatting toolbar, select the current style name, or just position the insertion point to its right.

or

Press Ctrl+Shift+S and select or type the name of the style you want to redefine.

4. Press Enter. The Reapply Style dialog box appears (see fig. 11.16). You have the following options:

Choose Redefine the style using the selection as an example? to change the formatting of the current style to match the formatting of the selected text.

Choose Return the formatting of the selection to the style? to reapply the formatting of the style to the selected text.

5. Select Redefine the style using the selection as an example and choose OK to redefine the style.

Fig. 11.16
The Reapply Style dialog box appears when you redefine a style by example.

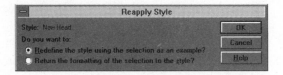

The Format Style command gives you the greatest flexibility for changing a style. You can make a change and add that change to the template on which you based the document. That way, each time you use the template in the future, the particular style will reflect the change.

To redefine a style using the menu command, follow these steps:

1. Choose the Format Style command.

2. From the Styles list, select the style you want to redefine. If the style isn't included in the list, select a different option from the List list.

3. Choose the Modify button. The Modify Style dialog box appears (see fig. 11.17).

Fig. 11.17
You can change a style's formatting in the Modify Style dialog box.

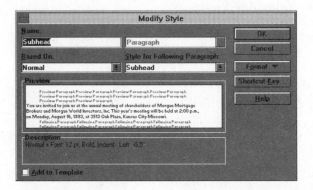

4. Select Format and select any formatting options you want to add to your style. Deselect any options you want to remove.

5. Select the Add to Template check box to make the change in the document's template, as well as in the document.

6. Choose OK to return to the Style dialog box.

   Repeat steps 2 through 6 if you want to redefine additional styles.

7. Choose Close.

> **Note**
>
> You can use the **E**dit Re**p**lace command to delete text that has been formatted with a particular style. In the Find box, choose the name of the style whose text you want to delete from the Format **S**tyle list. Leave the Replace box empty. Choose the **F**ind Next button. If the text you find is text you want to delete, choose the **R**eplace button. If you don't want to delete the text, proceed through the document with the **F**ind Next button to the next item.

Changing the Normal Style

Each time you begin a new document based on the Normal template, Word uses the Normal style to determine the font, font size, line spacing, and other formats. If you find that you are always changing the font, the point size, or some other aspect of the Normal style, you can change its default format settings.

Changing the formats defined for the Normal style in your document affects only the current document. Add the style to the template to apply the change to future documents. Existing documents are not changed unless you specifically have Word update their styles. See "Updating Styles" later in this chapter.

Remember that any change you make to the Normal style will be reflected in all styles that are based on that style, which includes most styles.

To change the default settings for the Normal style with the menu command, follow these steps:

1. Choose the File New command and select the Normal template or the template that you use for new documents.

   The Style box on the Formatting toolbar should show Normal. In a new document, the first paragraph will automatically use the Normal style.

2. Choose the Format Style command and choose **M**odify. The Normal style should be selected in the Name box. If it isn't, type **Normal**.

3. Make the changes you want to the style, using the Format options.

4. Select the Add to Template check box.

5. Choose OK to return to the Style dialog box.

6. Choose Close.

To change the default settings for the Normal style by example, follow these steps:

1. Choose the File Open command and select a document that is based on the Normal template or the template that you use for new documents.

2. Select text or position the insertion point in a paragraph that is formatted with the Normal style.

3. Select commands on the Format menu, from the Formatting toolbar, or with shortcut keys to make formatting changes you want applied to most documents. For example, you might want to choose a different font in a different point size with a first line indent of .5".

4. Click the Style box in the Formatting toolbar and press Enter. Word asks whether you want to redefine the style using the selection as an example.

5. Choose OK.

6. Choose Format Style. The Style dialog box opens with the Normal style selected in the Styles list. Select Normal if it isn't selected.

7. Choose Modify, select the Add to Template check box, and choose OK.

8. Choose Close.

Updating Styles

If you create a group of documents, each based on the same template, you'll want to make sure that any change to a style is reflected in each of the documents. For example, if you're writing a book with each chapter in a separate file, you want any changes to headers, footers, and headings to be copied to each of the document files. When you select the Automatically Update Document Styles command, Word copies the attached template's styles to the document each time you open it. The Update feature follows these rules:

■ Styles in the template that have the same name as a style in the document override the document style. The formatting from the template's style replaces the formatting from the document's style.

■ Styles not found in the document are copied from the template to the document.

■ Styles found in the document, but not in the template, are left unchanged.

Make sure that you use identically named styles in each of the documents. Otherwise, Word will not properly update the styles.

To update a document's styles each time you open it, follow these steps:

1. Place the insertion point anywhere in the file whose styles you want to update automatically.

2. Choose the File Templates command. The Templates and Add-ins dialog box appears (see fig. 11.18). The template attached to the current document is named in the Document Template box.

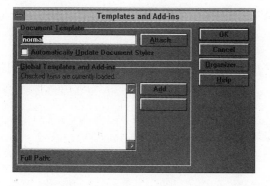

Fig. 11.18
Select Automatically Update Document Styles, and each time you open the document its styles will be updated from the attached template.

3. Select the Automatically Update Document Styles check box.

4. Choose OK.

Changing the Base of a Style

Unless you specify otherwise, a new style is based on the style of the currently selected paragraph. Often, that's the Normal style. You have the option, however, to base any style on any other style. When you do, any changes you make to the base style carry through to all styles based on that style. If you change Normal, those changes are reflected in any style based on the Normal style.

This often can be to your advantage. Suppose that you work in a legal office and you regularly type certain court documents that must always be double-spaced, in a certain font and size, and have specific margins. To help automate this task, you can create a template with the correct margins, and then modify the template's Normal style to include the correct font and size and double-spacing. You then can create additional styles based on that redefined Normal style, and they too will use the specified font and size and be double-spaced.

Keep in mind that Word for Windows standard styles are based on the Normal style, and if you alter the Normal style, your alterations will apply to all the standard styles as well.

If you don't want to alter your Normal style, you can create a base style in your document and use it as the basis for additional styles. By changing that base style, you can make extensive changes throughout a document.

To base one style on another style, follow these steps:

1. Choose the Format Style command.

2. Select from the Styles list a style whose base style you want to change.

3. Choose the Modify button. The Modify Style dialog box appears.

4. Specify the name of the style on which you want to base your style in the Based On box. To display a list of styles, click the down arrow to the right of the Based On box.

   If you want the selected style to remain unaffected by changes to any other style, select (no style) from the top of the list in the Based On box.

   When you select a style name, you see the name of the style plus any formatting attributes from the selected paragraph in the Description box. Your new style automatically is based on that existing style, unless you specify a different style.

5. Choose any of the Format button options to add additional formatting options to your style.

6. Choose OK to return to the Style dialog box.

7. Choose Close.

   or

   Choose Apply if you want to apply your new style to the currently selected paragraph.

Creating Style Shortcut Keys

A fast way to apply a style is with a shortcut key, which you can assign as part of the process of creating or redefining a style. The shortcut keys usually include pressing the Alt key plus a letter that you designate. You could assign the shortcut Alt+S, for example, to a style called Sub. You can use other key combinations if you want, but they may conflict with shortcut keys preassigned to Word for Windows built-in macros. (Word for Windows uses the built-in macro Ctrl+Shift+S, for example, to enable you to create or apply a style quickly, so you wouldn't want to assign Ctrl+Shift+S to your style Sub.) To learn more about built-in macros, refer to Chapter 38, "Recording and Editing Macros."

To create shortcut keys for styles, follow these steps:

1. Choose the Format Style command.

2. From the Styles list, select the style for which you want to create shortcut keys.

3. Choose the Modify button.

4. Choose the Shortcut Key button. The Customize dialog box opens and displays the Keyboard tab (see fig. 11.19).

5. Type a shortcut key combination in the Press New Shortcut Key box. You can use the letters A through Z, the numbers 0 through 9, Insert, and Delete, combined with Ctrl, Alt, and Shift.

   If the shortcut key combination you selected is already in use by another style or macro, Word displays the message `Currently Assigned To` and the command or macro to which the shortcut key is assigned. If the shortcut key isn't assigned, the Currently Assigned To message line displays `[unassigned]`.

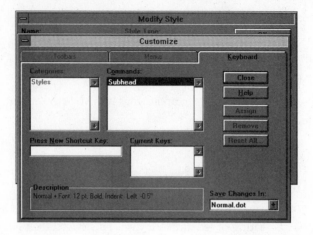

Fig. 11.19
You can assign shortcut keys to styles with the Customize Keyboard dialog box.

6. Choose the Assign button.

7. Choose the Close button to return to the Modify Style dialog box.

8. Choose OK to return to the Style dialog box.

9. Choose Close.

To remove a shortcut key, follow these steps:

1. Choose the Format Style command.

2. From the Styles list, select the style for which you want to remove the shortcut key.

3. Choose the Modify button.

4. Choose the Shortcut Key button.

5. Select the shortcut key you want to remove in the Current Keys box.

6. Choose the Remove button.

7. Choose Close to return to the Modify Style dialog box.

8. Choose OK to return to the Style dialog box.

9. Choose Close.

To apply a style with a shortcut key you have assigned, follow these steps:

1. Select the paragraph (or paragraphs) to which you want to apply the style.

2. Hold down the Ctrl, Alt, or Shift keys while you type the shortcut letter, number, function key, Ins, or Del key. (If your shortcut is Alt+C, for example, hold down Alt while you press C.)

Following One Style with the Next Style

One of the most useful style options is the ability to follow one style with another. Suppose that you're editing a complex document with many sub-headings, all formatted with styles. Text formatted with the Normal style follows each subheading. You would save time and effort if you didn't have to apply the Normal style each time you finished typing a subheading. If the style Subhead is followed by the Normal style, for example, when you finish typing a subhead and press Enter, the Normal style is applied automatically to the next paragraph. You can see this process in action by watching the Style box in the Formatting toolbar.

By default, Word for Windows follows each style with that same style so that when you press Enter, the style carries forward. In many cases, that's what you want. When you finish typing a paragraph formatted with the Normal style, you want the next paragraph also to be formatted with the Normal style. All of Word for Windows automatic styles are followed by the next style Normal.

To follow one style with another style, follow these steps:

1. Choose the Format Style command.

2. Type a new style name in the Styles box (if you're creating a new style), or select an existing style from the list.

3. Choose Modify. The Modify Style dialog box appears.

4. Select the style that you want to follow the current style from the Style for Following Paragraph list. To display a list of styles, click the down arrow to the right of the Style for Following Paragraph box.

   If you select no style, your style will be followed by itself.

5. Choose OK to return to the Style dialog box.

6. Choose Close.

Sharing Styles Among Documents

Every document you create includes styles—even if it's only the Normal style and Word for Windows other automatic styles. Each document's group of

Tip

You can add styles to a menu or toolbar. See Chapter 36, "Customizing the Toolbar, Menus, and Shortcut Keys."

Formatting Documents

styles is provided by its template, either the Normal template or a custom template you create.

In its simplest sense, using a template is the basic way you can share styles among documents. You create a template that contains certain styles you need, and then base your documents on that template. You may, for example, have a template called Letters that contains styles for formatting letters to be printed on your company's letterhead. If you regularly produce several different types of documents, you may create a template for each of them. (For details about creating templates, refer to Chapter 6, "Using Templates as Master Documents.")

At some point, however, you may want to use the styles from one document or template in a different document or template. You can do that by copying styles from one document or template to another.

A likely scenario for sharing styles is the big, multidocument publication that undergoes design revisions as the project progresses. In the beginning of the project, you create a template containing styles for formatting each document. Because all documents are based on the same template, they contain identical formatting, which preserves consistency. Later, the publications committee issues major design changes. One way to change your documents is to open each one and revise its styles. But an easier way to make the changes is to revise the styles in the template instead, and then copy the template's revised styles into each document. The template's revised styles replace the document's identically named styles, and any text associated with those styles changes to reflect the revisions.

You can copy styles to or from any document or template. If you copy an identically named style, it replaces the one in the document or template you're copying to (you will be asked to confirm the replacement); new styles are added to the document or template to which you're copying.

To copy styles from a document or template, follow these steps:

1. Choose the Format Style command.

2. Choose the **Organizer** button. The Organizer dialog box appears.

   The **In** box on the left displays a list of the styles in the currently open document or template. The **To** box on the right displays a list of the styles of the NORMAL.DOT template.

3. Select Close File (below the appropriate list) to close the current document or template style list in order to copy styles to or from a different document or template.

   Select Open File (below the appropriate list) to open a different document or template in order to copy its styles. The Open dialog box appears; select the document you want to use. If you want to select a template, use List Files of Type in the Open dialog box to choose Document Templates (*.DOT). If necessary, change directories or drives. Templates are stored in C:\WINWORD6\TEMPLATES by default.

   Select Styles Available In to select either the open document or its associated template to list styles from.

4. Select the styles you want to copy from the In or To lists. The Copy button arrows change direction to indicate the direction the styles will be copied.

   You can select a group of styles by clicking the first one you want to copy, then holding down Shift while you click the last one you want to copy. To select noncontiguous styles, hold down Ctrl while you click each one.

5. Choose Copy.

6. Choose Close.

Another way to merge a *single* style into a document is to copy into your document a paragraph formatted with a different style from another document. Be careful, though. Copying styles into your document this way doesn't override existing styles (as copying styles does). If you copy a paragraph formatted with a style called List, for example, and your existing document also contains a style called List, the new paragraph will take on the formatting of the existing List style.

Other commands for inserting text into a document, such as AutoText, Paste, and Paste Special, also can bring in new styles. You can copy in up to 50 paragraphs that contain unique style names—if you copy in more than 50, Word for Windows merges in the document's entire style sheet.

You can avoid copying the style along with the paragraph into the new document by *not* including the paragraph mark with the text you're copying.

Formatting Documents

Displaying Styles with the Style Area

If you're working with styles extensively, you can display the style area on your screen to list each paragraph's style name in the left margin (see fig. 11.20).

Fig. 11.20
Use the Style Area to display the names of the styles currently in use.

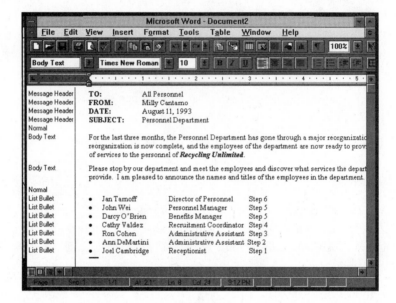

Using the style area, you can see at a glance which style is applied to each paragraph. If you have a mouse, you also can use the style area to quickly access the Styles dialog box.

To apply and redefine styles quickly, double-click the style name to display the Styles dialog box. From there, you can apply, create, or redefine a style.

The width of the style area varies. When you first display the style area, you set its width. After it's displayed, however, you can vary its width by using a mouse to drag the line separating the style area from the text to the left or right. You can close the style area entirely by dragging the arrow all the way to the left edge of the screen, or by resetting the style area width to zero.

Tip
By clicking once on the style name in the style area, you quickly can select an entire paragraph.

To display or remove the style area, follow these steps:

1. Choose the Tools Options command.

2. Select the View tab. The View dialog box lists all the view settings you can modify.

3. Type the style area width you want in decimal inches in the Style Area Width box.

   or

   Click the up or down arrows at the right end of the Style Area Width box to increase or decrease the style area width by tenths of an inch.

   or

   Type **0** (zero) to remove the style area from the screen.

4. Choose OK.

Tip

If you frequently display the style area, record a simple macro that turns on the style area. (You can even edit your macro so that it toggles the style area on and off.) Chapter 38 explains how to create macros.

Checking Formats

Formatting can be applied from a style or manually from the Format menu or other commands. You can quickly determine how formatting was applied to any text with the Help button on the Standard toolbar.

To determine how formatting was added, follow these steps:

1. Click the Help button on the Standard toolbar.

2. Click the text you want to check. A formatting box appears, showing paragraph and font formatting (see fig. 11.21). You can continue to click in other locations to see the formatting of other text.

3. Press Esc to turn off the Help feature.

Overriding Styles with Manual Formatting

Although you can do most of your formatting with styles, at times you will need to override the formatting in a style you have already applied. You may want to do something simple, like making one word in a paragraph bold, or maybe something more substantial, like italicizing a whole paragraph. You can modify the formatting in a paragraph without changing the style.

Fig. 11.21
Use the Help
button on the
Standard toolbar
to quickly check
the formatting of
any text.

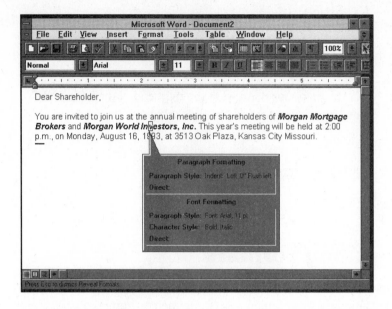

Be aware, however, of what effect your formatting will have on the paragraph if you later reapply the style. Reapplying the style may cancel some of the manual formatting changes you have made. Manual formatting works with styles as follows:

- If the reapplied style contains formatting choices in the same category as those you have applied manually, the style's choices override the manual formatting. If you have manually applied double line spacing, but the style specifies single line spacing, for example, then the double line spacing is canceled when you apply the style.

- If the reapplied style contains formatting choices unrelated to the formatting you have applied manually, the style won't affect manual formatting. If you add a border to a paragraph and then reapply a style that doesn't specify borders, for example, the border will remain.

- Some character formatting choices toggle on and off—you select bold to turn it on in the same way you select bold to turn it off. If you apply a style containing bold to a paragraph with one or two words that are bold, for example, then all of the paragraph will be bold except the one or two words that you formatted as bold manually (the style toggles them off). On the other hand, if you make a whole paragraph bold, then reapply a style that contains bold, Word for Windows leaves the paragraph bold rather than toggling off the bold.

- If you want to remove all manually applied character formatting from a paragraph formatted with a style, press Ctrl+space bar.

- If you want to remove all manually applied paragraph formatting from a paragraph formatted with a style, press Ctrl+Q.

From Here...

For information relating directly to using styles and automatic formatting you may want to review the following sections of this book:

- Chapter 6, "Using Templates as Master Documents." Templates work well with styles. You can create a special template containing styles you need for a particular type of document, and base all your documents on that template.

- Chapter 7, "Using Editing and Proofing Tools." Use the Find and Replace feature to locate and change styles automatically throughout a document. As you use styles to ensure consistency of formatting, you can use the Grammar Checker to ensure consistency of language usage.

- Chapter 38, "Recording and Editing Macros." Macros are a great way to automate some of the things you do repeatedly, such as displaying the style area.

- Chapter 19, "Organizing Content with an Outline." Word uses Heading styles to create outlines. With what you have learned in this chapter, you can redefine the appearance of these headings.

- Chapter 29, "Creating Indexes and Tables of Contents." Tables of contents and indexes also use predefined styles. By redefining them, you can easily change their appearance.

Working with Columns

12

Sometimes what you have to say isn't best said in line after line of margin-to-margin text. Often you can help keep your reader interested and make your prose look a little more inviting by dividing the text into columns. Research has shown that text of newspaper column width is much faster to read. Columns not only make information more attractive, but also more readable.

In Word for Windows, you can create two types of columns: the *snaking columns* of text you see in newspapers, magazines, and newsletters; and the *parallel columns* of text and numbers you see in lists and tables. Chapter 16, "Creating and Editing Tables," discusses tables, which consist of columns and rows of text, numbers, or dates. Tables work well for parallel columns or for data that you want to keep aligned. This chapter discusses snaking columns (sometimes called *newspaper columns*), in which the text wraps continuously from the bottom of one column to the top of the next column. Fig. 12.1 shows an example of a desktop published newsletter with snaking or newspaper columns. (To learn more about the desktop publishing capabilities of Word for Windows, refer to Chapter 27, "Desktop Publishing.")

You will learn procedures in this chapter that make it easy to create documents such as newspapers, newsletters, and brochures.

Creating Columns

In Word, you can create columns of equal or unequal width. You can include different numbers or styles of columns in different sections of your document. Newsletters, for example, often have two or more sections. The first section contains a large one-column banner and the remaining text is divided into multiple columns. You also can include a vertical line between columns.

In this chapter, you learn the following techniques:

- Calculating the number and length of columns you need

- Understanding how sections separate parts of a document with different layout

- How to create even and uneven width columns

- How to type and edit within columns

- How to insert a line between columns

- How to see the columns on screen as they will print

- How to change column layouts after they are created

II

Formatting Documents

Word for Windows gives you two methods of creating columns: the Format Columns command and the Columns button on the Word for Windows or Standard toolbar. In the normal view, you see columns in their correct width, but not side by side; only in the page layout or print preview views do you see columns side by side.

What You Need to Know About Columns

You can include as many columns in a document as you have space for on your page. You can also include different numbers or styles of columns in different parts of your document, as long as you divide your document into sections.

Fig. 12.1
Columns make many documents more attractive and easier to read.

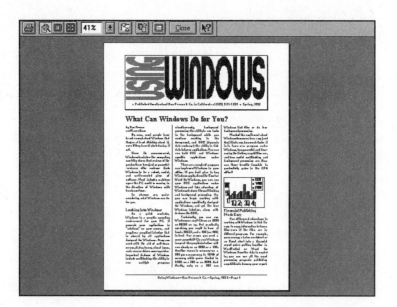

Calculating the Number and Length of Columns

Word determines how many columns you can have on a page based on three factors: the page width, the margin widths, and the size and spacing of your columns. On a wide landscape-oriented page, for example, you have more room for columns than on a narrower portrait-oriented page. Similarly, if your margins are narrow, there's more room for text on the page, and thus you can have more columns. If columns are narrow, you can fit more of them on a page than if they are wide.

In Word, columns must be at least half an inch (.5") wide. If you try to fit too many on a page, Word displays a message reading `Column widths cannot be less than .5"`. You might see this message if you change your margins, for example, making them wider so that there is less room on the page for columns. If you see the message, change either your page layout or the number, width, or spacing of your columns.

Columns are the length of the current section or of the current page if there are no sections.

Understanding Sections

A new document based on the default Normal template is a single section with a one-column format, like that shown in fig. 12.2. *Sections* are divisions within a document that can be formatted independently of one another. If you want different numbers or styles of columns in different parts of your document, you must divide it into sections. Fig. 12.3 shows a document divided into two sections. The upper section shows the title as a single column, whereas the lower section shows the body copy in three columns. Fig. 12.4 shows a document with three sections; one column for the title, two columns for the upper text, and three columns for the lower text. Sections are described in detail in the section "Changing Layouts within a Document" in Chapter 13, "Setting the Page Layout."

Fig. 12.2
This document has only a single section.

Fig. 12.3
This document
has two sections—
the title and body
copy.

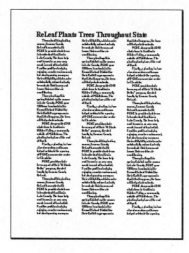

Fig. 12.4
This document
has three sections.

With columns, there are three ways you can insert section breaks. You can use the **Insert Break** command to display the Break dialog box (see fig. 12.5). Another way to insert section breaks is to use the **Format Columns** command to create columns, and specify that columns apply not to the whole document, but to "this point forward" in your document; a section break is added before the insertion point. The third way to insert section breaks is to select the text that you want to appear in different columns before you create or change the columns; a section break is added before and after the selected text (or just after the selected text if it falls at the beginning of a document).

Fig. 12.5
You can insert
section breaks
using the Insert
Break command.

Using the Break dialog box, you can specify that sections run continuously so that you can have a different number of columns on the same page, or you can specify that each section start on a new page or on the next even-numbered or odd-numbered page.

Section breaks appear in your document as a double dotted line containing the words End of Section.

When formatting your document into columns, remember the following tips:

- By default, columns apply to the whole document if your document includes no section breaks.

- Columns apply to the current section if you divide your document into sections. (Columns apply to multiple sections if multiple sections are selected.)

- You can position the insertion point where you want columns to start in your document and apply columns from that point forward. Word for Windows inserts a section break at the insertion point.

- You can select the text you want in columns and apply columns to just that selection. Word for Windows inserts a section break before and after the selected text.

Tip

All column formatting is stored in the section break mark at the end of a section. If you delete this mark, that section takes on the column formatting and section formatting of the section below it.

Creating Columns of Equal Width

There are two ways you can quickly divide your document into columns of equal width. You can use the Columns button on the Word for Windows or Standard toolbar, or you can use the Format Columns command to specify the number of columns you want.

The width of the columns depends on the number of columns you choose, your margins, and the amount of space you set between columns. For example, if you have one-inch left and right margins on a standard 8 1/2-inch paper width, and you divide your text into three columns with one-quarter inch between them, you get three two-inch-wide columns.

II

Formatting Documents

Remember that only in page layout view will you see your columns side by side.

To create equal-width columns with the Columns button, follow these steps:

1. Do one of the following to specify which part of your document you want divided into columns:

   ■ If you want to format the entire document into columns, and your document has only one section, position the insertion point anywhere in your document.

   ■ If you want to format only one section into columns and you've already divided your document into sections, position the insertion point inside the section you want formatted into columns.

   ■ If you want columns to start at a certain point in your document and you haven't divided your document into sections, position the insertion point where you want columns to start.

   ■ If you want to format selected text into columns and you haven't divided your document into sections, select the text that you want in columns.

2. If the toolbar is not displayed, choose the View Toolbars command. Select the Standard or Word for Windows toolbar and choose OK. Point to the Columns button and drag the mouse pointer down and right to display the column pull-down box. Select the number of columns you want. Fig 12.6 shows the Columns with three columns selected.

Fig. 12.6
The quickest way to format your document with columns is to use the Columns button on the Word for Windows or Standard toolbar.

3 Columns

or

Choose Format Columns. The Columns dialog box appears (see fig. 12.7).

In the Presets group, select One, Two, or Three columns. Or select Number of Columns, and type or select the number of columns you want. If you want columns to start at the insertion point, select Apply To and select This Point Forward. Choose OK or press Enter.

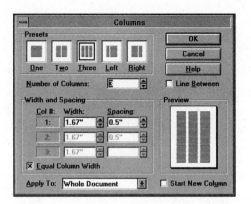

Fig. 12.7
Use presets to
quickly format
your text into
columns, or select
the number of
columns you
want.

Creating Columns of Unequal Width

Although you can easily format your document with columns by using the
Columns button, you get more options when you choose the Format Columns command instead. In the Columns dialog box, you can choose preset
columns, or you can define your own columns. Preset columns include a
wide and a narrow column; the wide column is twice as wide as the narrow
column. If you want, use preset columns as a starting point for defining your
own columns. It ensures that the columns are a consistent width.

When you create columns with the Format Columns command, you
can specify whether columns apply to the whole document, the current
section(s), the insertion point forward, or the selected text (if text is selected).
If you choose columns for the entire document, all sections are formatted
with columns. If you already divided your document into sections, Word for
Windows assumes that you want to apply columns to the currently selected
section(s). If no text is selected, you have the option to apply columns from
the insertion point forward in your document, and Word for Windows inserts a section break at the insertion point. If you select text before choosing
the command, Word for Windows inserts a section break before and after the
selected text and applies the column format only to the selected text.

Using the Format Columns command, you also can specify how wide you
want your columns and how much space you want between them.

To create columns of unequal width, follow these steps:

1. Select the text you want to format into multiple columns, or position
   the insertion point inside the section you want to format or at the
   point where you want a new number of columns to begin.

2. Choose the Format Columns command. The Columns dialog box appears (see fig. 12.8).

Fig. 12.8
To create columns
of unequal width,
use presets or
define your own
columns.

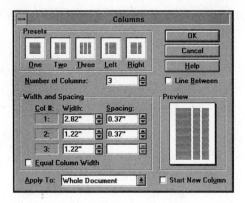

3. Optionally, from the Presets group, select Left if you want a narrow column on the left, or select Right if you want a narrow column on the right.

4. Select Number of Columns, and type or select the number of columns you want. Look at the Preview box to see how your columns will look.

5. Deselect, or clear, the Equal Column Width option if it is selected.

6. If you want to define the width or spacing for individual columns, select Col # and select the number of the column you want to change. The dialog box has space for only three column numbers; click or press the down arrow to display additional column numbers.

7. Select Width, and type or select the width you want for the selected column.

8. Select Spacing, and type or select the spacing you want to the right of the selected column (there is no space to the right of the rightmost column).

9. Select from the Apply To pull-down list the amount of text you want to format. The options shown in the Apply To list change depending on whether text is selected or whether your document contains multiple sections. Usually Word correctly guesses where you want to apply your columns, based on the location of the insertion point.

The Selected Sections option appears only when multiple sections are selected. It formats the sections you selected with columns.

The Selected Text option appears only when text is selected. This option formats the text you selected with columns. It also puts a section break before and after the selection.

The This Point Forward option appears only when no text is selected. This option formats with columns from the insertion point forward. It puts a section break at the location of the insertion point.

The This Section option appears only when the insertion point is inside one of multiple sections. This option formats with columns the section containing the insertion point.

The Whole Document option formats the entire document with columns.

10. Choose OK or press Enter.

Typing and Editing Text in Columns

Typing, editing, and formatting text in columns follows all the same rules and takes advantage of the same shortcuts for typing, selecting, and editing any other text. (Refer to Chapter 5, "Editing a Document," for details.) The following two tips will help you as you move around in and select columnar text:

- To move from one column to the top of the next column using the keyboard, press Alt+down-arrow key. To move to the top of the previous column, press Alt+up-arrow key.

- The selection bar that normally appears at the left margin of a page now appears at the left margin of each column in page layout view. When you move the mouse pointer into this area, it turns into an arrow you can use to select lines and paragraphs within a column.

If text seems narrower than the columns, it may be because the text is indented. Use the ruler or Format Paragraph command to eliminate or change the indentation settings for selected text.

Adding a Line Between Columns

Adding a vertical line between columns can add interest to your page. Lines are the length of the longest column in the section. You can see lines in the page layout view or in print preview.

To add lines between columns, follow these steps:

1. Click in the section containing columns where you want vertical lines.

2. Choose the Format Columns command.

3. In the Columns dialog box, select the Line Between option.

4. Choose OK or press Enter.

To remove lines, deselect (or clear) the Line Between option.

You can also add vertical lines on your page using the Format Borders and Shading command. If you do, and you also add lines between columns, you may see two lines between columns. For columns, the Line Between option is a better choice than using the Format Borders and Shading command because it creates lines of uniform length in the section, even if one column of text is shorter than the others.

Viewing Columns

Word for Windows has several ways to view a document. Views include normal, outline, page layout, master document, and print preview. Depending on which view you are in, columns appear differently on-screen.

Normal view is faster for text entry but does not display columns side by side as they will appear when printed. The text appears in the same width as the column, but in one continuous column. Page layout view displays columns side by side, with vertical lines between columns if you've selected that option. Section and column breaks appear only when you've displayed paragraph marks. Print preview gives an overview of the page as it will appear when printed. In all three views, you can change column width using the ruler, and you can display the Column dialog box to edit columns.

In the outline view, you see columns the full width of the page, and you can't edit them. In master document view, you see columns the full page width, but you can edit them.

When you are editing a document, you may need to view a particular section up close. At other times, you may need an overview of the entire page. The Word for Windows toolbar includes three buttons that enable you to magnify or reduce the size of the display. The Zoom Whole Page button shows you a miniature view of the whole page in page layout view. The Zoom 100% button shows you a full-size page in normal view. The Zoom Page Width button shows you the full width of the page in whichever view you're currently working. The Standard toolbar has a drop-down list with the same commands, along with several percentages at which you can view your page. You can also select magnification of 25% to 200% with the View Zoom command. For more information on zooming the view, see Chapter 5, "Editing a Document."

Changing Columns

Once you format your document with columns, you can change the columns in many ways. You can change the number of columns, or switch between equal- and unequal-width columns. You can change the width of columns or the spacing between them. You can force text to move to the top of the next column, and you can force a column to start on a new page. You can balance columns on a page so that they are as close to the same length as possible.

You can make some changes to columns using the ruler; for example, you can change their width or the spacing between them. Other changes you make using the Columns dialog box.

Before you change columns, make sure you select the text you want to change, and be sure in the Columns dialog box to apply the changes where you want them (use the Apply To list). Follow these rules for selecting text and applying the changes:

- If you want to change columns for the entire document and your document has only one section, position the insertion point anywhere in your document. In the Apply To list of the Columns dialog box, choose Whole Document.

- If you want to change columns in only one section and you've already divided your document into sections, position the insertion point inside the section you want to change. In the Apply To list of the Columns dialog box, choose This Section.

- If you want columns to start at a certain point in your document and you haven't divided your document into sections, position the insertion point where you want columns to start. In the Apply To list of the Columns dialog box, choose This Point Forward.

For Related Information

- "Controlling Your Document's Appearance On-Screen," p. 115

- "Changing Layouts Within a Document," p. 432

- "Laying Out the Page," p. 840

- "Working with Columns," p. 850

Tip

You can quickly display the Columns dialog box by double-clicking on the gray area between columns on the horizontal ruler.

II

Formatting Documents

- If you want to change columns in only part of your document and you haven't divided your document into sections, select the text that you want in columns. In the Apply To list of the Columns dialog box, choose Selected Text.

- If you want to change columns in multiple existing sections, select the sections. In the Apply To list of the Columns dialog box, choose Selected Sections.

Most of the time, Word understands where you want to apply changes by where you've positioned the insertion point, and you needn't make a selection in the Apply To list.

Because you can format text in columns in the same way you can format text that is not in columns, you may create some unexpected results. If your column is too narrow, for example, you may find yourself with a vertical strip of text that isn't very readable. Try widening the column, or lessening the space between the columns, or reducing the number of columns. Or try reducing the size of the text.

Changing the Number of Columns

You can change the number of columns using either the ruler or the Columns dialog box. You can also change between equal- and unequal-width columns. If you want to change from equal-width to unequal-width columns, you must use the Columns dialog box, but you can change from unequal-width to equal-width columns using the ruler.

To change the number of equal-width columns, or to change from unequal-width to equal-width columns, follow these steps:

1. Position the insertion point or select the text where you want changes to apply.

2. On the Word for Windows or Standard toolbar, point to the Columns button and drag the drop-down list down and to the right to select the number of columns you want.

   or

   Choose the Format Columns command to display the Columns dialog box. From the Presets group, select One, Two, or Three. Or select Number of Columns, and type or select the number of columns you want. If you are changing from unequal-width to equal-width columns, select the Equal Column Width option. Choose OK or press Enter.

To change the number of unequal-width columns, or to change from equal-width to unequal-width columns, follow these steps:

1. Position the insertion point or select the text where you want changes to apply.

2. Choose the Format Columns command to display the Columns dialog box. If you want two preset columns of unequal width, select Left or Right from the Presets group. Or, select Number of Columns, and type or select the number of columns you want.

3. If you're changing from equal-width to unequal-width columns, deselect, or clear, the Equal Column Width option.

4. Choose OK or press Enter.

Changing the Width of Columns and the Spacing Between Columns

When you first create columns, Word determines their width based on your margins and the number of columns you want. You can change the width of all or some columns.

You can also change the spacing between columns. By default, columns have half an inch (.5") of spacing between them, but you may want to decrease or increase this distance. You may want to decrease the distance if you have many columns, because the greater number of columns you have, the narrower they are, and the less space you need between them. You may want to increase the distance with fewer columns, as you might in a three-column brochure printed sideways on the page, for example.

You can change the width of columns or the space between columns in two ways: using the ruler or using the Columns dialog box. Using the ruler, you drag column margin markers to change the width and spacing at the same time.

If your columns are currently equal-width and you want to change them to unequal-width, you must use the Columns dialog box.

To change the width of columns or the space between columns using the ruler, follow these steps:

1. Make sure the ruler is displayed; if it is not, choose the View Ruler command.

2. Position the insertion point inside the section containing the columns you want to change.

3. The gray areas in the horizontal ruler indicate the spaces between columns. Move the mouse pointer over one of these gray areas until the pointer turns into a two-headed arrow as shown in fig. 12.9. Choose any gray area if your columns are all the same width; choose the gray area above the space you want to change if your columns are different widths. When columns are different widths, the gray area contains a grid-like icon as shown in fig. 12.10.

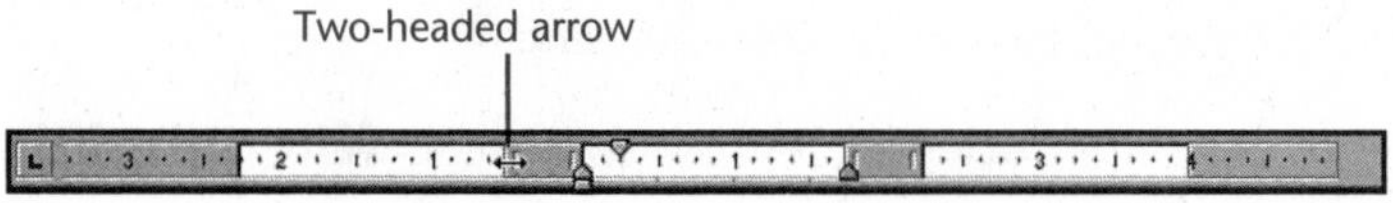

Two-headed arrow

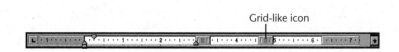

Fig. 12.9

Using the ruler, you can change the width of columns and the spacing between them. If your columns are all the same width, changing one changes them all identically.

Grid-like icon

Fig. 12.10

When columns are of unequal widths, the gray area of the ruler contains a grid-like icon.

4. Hold down the mouse button and drag the edge of the gray area away from the center to widen the space between columns, or drag it toward the center to lessen the space between columns. If columns are different widths, you can drag either side of the gray area to change the spacing in either direction.

If your columns are all the same width, changing the spacing for any one changes the spacing between them all. If they are different widths, changing the spacing for one affects only that column.

To change the width or columns or the space between columns using the Columns dialog box, or to change columns of equal width into columns of unequal width, follow these steps:

1. Position the insertion point inside the section containing the columns you want to change.

2. Choose the Format Columns command.

3. If you are changing equal-width columns to unequal-width columns, deselect, or clear, the Equal Column Width option.

4. In the Width and Spacing group, select Col # and select the column whose spacing you want to change. If your columns are all the same width, you can change only column number 1; all the rest use the same measurements.

5. In the Width and Spacing group, select Width and type or select the width you want for your column or columns.

6. In the Width and Spacing group, select Spacing and type or select the spacing you want between your columns.

7. Choose OK or press Enter.

Removing Columns

If your document is formatted into columns, you can remove them easily using either the Columns button or the Columns dialog box.

To remove columns, follow these steps:

1. Position the insertion point or select text where you want to remove columns.

2. Use the Columns button to select one column.

   or

   Choose the Format Columns command. From the Presets group, select One. Choose OK or press Enter.

Starting a New Column

When Word for Windows creates columns, it automatically breaks the columns to fit on the page. Sometimes the column may break inappropriately. On a three-column page, for example, column two may end with a heading that should be at the top of column three. By inserting a column break directly before the heading, you shift the heading to the top of the next column, keeping the heading and its following text together.

If you want a column to start on a new page, you can insert a page break.

To insert a column break, press Ctrl+Shift+Enter or follow these steps:

Formatting Documents

1. Position the insertion point at the beginning of the line where you want the new column to start.

2. Choose the Insert Break command. The Break dialog box appears (see fig. 12.11).

Fig. 12.11
Inserting a column break causes text to move to the top of the next column.

3. Select the Column Break option.

4. Choose OK or press Enter.

To insert a page break, press Ctrl+Enter or follow these steps:

1. Format your document into columns.

2. Position the insertion point where you want the break.

3. Choose the Insert Break command. The default selection is **Page Break**.

4. Choose OK or press Enter. The column continues on a new page.

Balancing Column Lengths

On pages where the text in columns continues to the next page, Word for Windows automatically balances (lines up) the last line of text at the bottom of each column. But when columnar text runs out on a page, you may be left with two full-length columns and a third column that's only partially filled. You can balance column lengths so that the bottom of all the columns are within one line of each other. Figs. 12.12 and 12.13 show unbalanced and balanced columns.

To balance the length of multiple columns, follow these steps:

1. Position the insertion point at the end of the text in the last column of the section you want to balance.

2. Choose the Insert Break command.

3. Select the Continuous Section Break option.

4. Choose OK or press Enter.

Fig. 12.12
Unbalanced
columns.

Fig. 12.13
Columns balanced
by adding a
section break at
the end of your
document.

Troubleshooting Columns

I have several columns and I want to change their width and spacing, but in the Columns dialog box I can select only column number 1.

Your columns are currently of equal width. Deselect the Equal Column Width option if you want to make them different widths.

Product lists, date schedules, and the dialog for plays all appear to use columns, but it's impossible to keep related items lined up across the columns. Adding or editing in one column changes the position of items in following columns.

Use Word's table feature to create scripts for plays, procedural steps, duty rosters, product catalogs and so on. Tables are grids of rows and columns. Information within a *cell* in a table will stay adjacent or parallel to other information in the same row, even when you add lines in the cell. Cells can contain entire paragraphs, math calculations, field codes, and even pictures. Tables are described in detail in Chapter 16, "Creating and Editing Tables."

**For Related
Information**
■ "Formatting
Lines and
Paragraphs,"
p. 285

■ "Changing
Layouts Within
a Document,"
p. 432

■ "Working with
Columns,"
p. 850

Formatting Documents

From Here...

For information relating to columns, you may want to review the following major sections of this book:

■ Chapter 16, "Creating and Editing Tables." Another way to create columns of side-by-side text is to use tables. With the grid lines turned off, tables can look like columns.

- Chapter 23, "Framing and Moving Text and Graphics." You can create "sideheads" by framing paragraphs and positioning them in the side margins of your document. You can also frame graphics, so that columnar text wraps around them.

- Chapter 27, "Desktop Publishing." Columns are frequently used in desktop publishing tasks. Even if you need only simple columns, you will find interesting tips and suggestions on how to make your work look better.

Chapter 13

Setting the Page Layout

Of the four levels of formatting—page, section, paragraph, and character—page layout is the broadest. Page layout often encompasses formatting choices that affect the entire document—for most documents, page layout choices such as margins and page size do apply to the whole document. In a change from tradition, however, Word for Windows also enables you to apply page-level formatting to portions of the document known as *sections*.

Page layout options include margins, paper size and orientation, headers and footers, page numbers, page and paragraph breaks, section breaks, vertical alignment on the page, and the paper source. By default, many page setup options, such as margins, headers and footers, and page numbers, apply to the entire document. Alternatively, you can apply these options to a designated section of text or from the position of the insertion point forward in your document.

You can include an envelope and a letter in a single document, for example, by specifying different margins, paper size, paper orientation, and paper source for the first page of the document—the envelope—than you specify for the remaining pages—the letter. Or you can create different headers and footers for different parts of a long document. Being able to divide your document into sections and specify where page layout options apply gives you great flexibility in designing your document (see fig. 13.1).

In this chapter,
you learn to do the
following:

- Set new
  margins for
  different
  documents

- Adjust the page
  orientation

- Create headers
  and footers

- Insert page
  numbers

II

Formatting Documents

Fig. 13.1
You can set margins however you want; you can choose portrait or landscape orientation and include headers and footers; and you can divide your document into sections, each of which you can format differently.

Setting Margins

Margins are the borders on all four sides of a page, within which the text of your document is confined. Margins aren't necessarily blank, however; they may contain headers, footers, page numbers, footnotes, or even text and graphics.

Word for Windows' default margins are 1 inch at the top and bottom and 1.25 inches on the left and right. You can change the margins for the entire document (if the document contains only a single section) or for parts of the document (if you divide the document into sections). If you use different margin settings regularly, you can send your settings to the Normal template so that they become the new defaults.

Different views in Word for Windows show different perspectives on your margins. In normal view, you don't see the margins, but you see the space between them, where your text appears. In page layout view, you see the page as it will print, margins and all. Select that view if you want to see headers, footers, page numbers, footnotes, and anything else that appears within the margins. To select a view, choose the View Normal or View Page Layout command.

You can change the margins in your document in two ways. First, you can make selections from the Page Setup dialog box. When you set margins this way, you control margin settings precisely. A second technique for setting margins is to use the ruler. Using this technique, you can see how margin settings affect the appearance of your page.

Setting Margins with a Precise Measurement

Using the Page Setup command to set margins gives you the greatest number of options. You can set the margins to precise measurements, establish facing pages and gutters for binding (discussed later in this chapter), set varying margins for different sections of your document, and apply your margin settings to the Normal template so that they become the new default settings.

If you want to apply margin settings to your entire document, the insertion point can be located anywhere in the document when you set your margins. If you want to apply margins to only one part of your document, however, you must do one of three things: to apply margins to a selected portion of your text, select that text before you set the margins; to apply margins to existing sections, you must insert section breaks; or to apply margins from a specific point forward in your document, position the insertion point where you want the new margins to start and then specify that the margins apply to the text "this point forward." If you apply margins to selected text, Word for Windows inserts section breaks before and after the selected text. If you apply margins from the insertion point forward, Word for Windows inserts a section break at the insertion point. Setting different margins for different parts of your document is covered in a later section in this chapter, "Changing Layouts Within a Document."

Formatting Documents

To set measured margins, follow these steps:

1. Position the insertion point inside the section for which you want to set margins. (The margins apply to the entire document unless the document has multiple sections.) Or select the text for which you want to set margins.

2. Choose the File Page Setup command. The Page Setup dialog box appears (see fig. 13.2).

Fig. 13.2
Set precisely measured margins using the Page Setup dialog box.

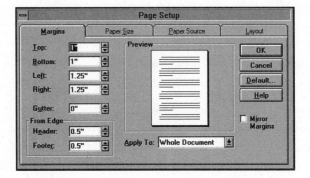

3. Select the Margins tab, if necessary. (The tab may be selected already.)

4. Choose your margin settings. For each setting, type the amount of the margin or use the increment/decrement arrows (or press the up- or down-arrow key) to increase or decrease the margin setting by tenths of an inch.

Option	Margin setting
Top	Top of page
Bottom	Bottom of page
Left	Left side of page
Right	Right side of page
Gutter	Extra space on pages for binding (see the section "Creating Facing Pages and Gutters")

5. Choose OK.

> **Note**
>
> As you select your margin settings, notice that the Preview box in the Page Setup dialog box shows you how your page or pages look.

Margins usually are measured in decimal inches, unless you change your default measurement system by using the Tools Options command (General tab). Nonetheless, you can create margins in a different measurement system by typing in amounts such as **36 pt** for 36 points (half an inch—72 points make up an inch), **3 cm** for 3 centimeters, or **9 pi** for 9 picas (one and one-half inches—6 picas make up an inch). For details, see Chapter 35, "Customizing and Optimizing Word Features." If you use the inch measurement system, the next time you open the Page Layout dialog box you see that your measurements have been converted back to inches.

Setting Different Margins for Different Parts of Your Document. For different parts of your document to contain different margin settings, your document must be divided into sections. You can create sections with different margins in several ways. You can insert section breaks manually and then format the text between the breaks or after a break with different margin settings. Alternatively, you can use the File Page Setup command to apply margins to only the selected text or from the insertion point forward in your document. When necessary, Word inserts section breaks.

The Apply To list in the Page Setup dialog box, which determines where margins are applied, changes depending on two factors: whether your document is divided into sections and whether you've selected text before choosing the File Page Setup command. Word tries to apply your margin settings logically; for example, if your document is divided into sections, and the insertion point is inside one of those sections when you set margins, then in the Apply To list Word proposes applying those margin settings to "This Section." You can select a different option in the list, however.

You can learn more about creating sections later in this chapter in the section "Changing Layouts Within a Document."

To set different margins for different parts of your document, follow these steps:

1. Position the insertion point inside the section or sections for which you want to set margins.

or

Select the text for which you want to set margins.

or

Position the insertion point where you want new margins to begin in your document.

2. Choose the File Page Setup command. The Page Setup dialog box appears. Select the Margins tab if necessary.

3. Type or select Top, Bottom, Left, and Right margins.

4. From the Apply To list, select the section to which you want to apply margins (choices on the list vary depending on the amount of text currently selected):

Option	Applies Margins to	When
This Section	Current section (No section break is inserted)	Insertion point is located within a section
Selected Sections	Multiple sections (No section breaks are inserted)	At least part of more than one section is selected
This Point Forward new	Insertion point (Inserts new-page section break at insertion point)	Insertion point is where you want margin to start
Selected Text	Selected text (Inserts new-page section breaks at beginning and end of text)	Text is selected
Whole Document	Entire document (No section breaks inserted)	Insertion point is anywhere

5. Choose OK.

Creating Facing Pages and Gutters. Facing pages in a document are the left and right pages of a double-sided document, like in a book or magazine. You can set up your document for facing pages by selecting "mirror margins" in the Page Setup dialog box (see fig. 13.3). When you do, you no longer have left and right margins; instead, you have inside and outside margins. Facing pages are ideal when you plan to print your document on both sides of the paper and want wider margins on the inside than on the outside edges.

With facing pages, you can have different headers and footers on each page and can position page numbers on opposite sides of the facing pages. In a newsletter footer, for example, you may want to position page numbers below the outside margins and the date below the inside margins.

Like margins, facing pages apply to sections. You can insert section breaks before you select facing pages, or you can create sections as part of the process. (For details, see "Setting Different Margins for Different Parts of Your Document" earlier in this chapter.)

Tip

If you include sections with different margins in your document, remember that if you delete the section break, you delete the section and thus lose its margins. If you accidentally delete a section break, choose the **E**dit **U**ndo command.

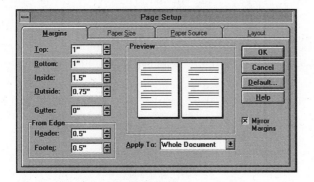

Fig. 13.3
When you choose "mirror margins," you create facing pages with inside and outside margins, rather than left and right margins.

Formatting Documents

To create facing pages, follow these steps:

1. Position the insertion point or select the text where you want facing pages.

2. Choose the File Page Setup command and select the Margins tab (if not selected already).

3. Select Mirror Margins.

4. Choose OK.

Adding Extra Margin Space in Gutters. Whether you're working with normal pages that have left and right margins or facing pages that have inside and outside (mirror) margins, you can add a gutter to leave extra space for binding. A gutter on normal pages adds space at the left edge of the page; a gutter on facing pages adds space at the inside edges of each page. To leave an extra half-inch for binding, for example, include a gutter of .5". A gutter doesn't change your document's margins, but it does reduce the printing area.

Like margins, gutters apply to sections. You can insert section breaks before you select gutters, or you can create sections as part of the process. (For details, see "Setting Different Margins for Different Parts of Your Document" earlier in this chapter.)

To set a gutter, follow these steps:

1. Position the insertion point or select the text where you want a gutter.

2. Choose the File Page Setup command and select the Margins tab (if not selected already).

3. Select Gutter and type or select the amount by which you want to increase the left margin (if you have left and right margins) or the inside margin (if you select mirror margins so that you have inside and outside margins). The Preview box shows a shaded area where the gutter appears (see fig. 13.4).

Fig. 13.4
When you select a gutter, in the Preview box you see a shaded area where the gutter appears.

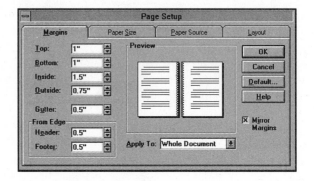

4. Choose OK.

Setting Margins Visually

A quick way to set margins for your document or for a section in your document is to click the ruler by using a mouse.

You must display a ruler to set margins with a mouse. In page layout or print preview view, Word has two rulers: a horizontal ruler, which appears at the top of your document and can be used to set left and right (or inside and outside) margins; and a vertical ruler, which appears at the left side of your document and can be used to set top and bottom margins (see fig. 13.5). Only the horizontal ruler is available in normal view.

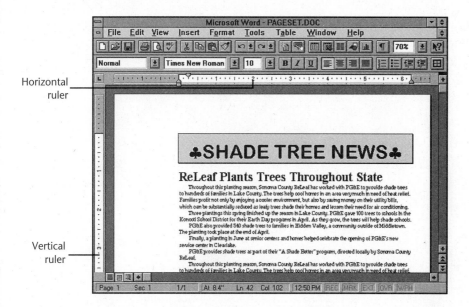

Fig. 13.5

You can set left and right (or inside and outside) margins with the horizontal ruler at the top of your document, and you can set top and bottom margins with the vertical ruler at the left edge of your document.

On each ruler is a gray or colored area and a white area. The gray or colored area indicates the margins; the white area indicates the space between the margins. The edge between the gray or colored area and the white area is the margin boundary. You can drag the margin boundaries on either ruler to change the margins for the currently selected section or sections. To make the left margin smaller, for example, you can drag the left margin boundary toward the edge of the page.

The ruler doesn't insert any section breaks into your document; it sets the margins for the entire document or for the section containing the insertion point. If you want to use the ruler to create various margins for multiple sections in your document, insert section breaks before you begin.

Use the File Page Setup command if you want to change margins in the outline or master document view.

To change margins with a ruler, follow these steps:

1. If the ruler is not displayed, choose the View Ruler command. If only the horizontal ruler appears, choose the Tools Options command, then select the View tab, and in the Window group choose the Vertical Ruler option. In the print preview view, click the Ruler button to display rulers.

2. Position the mouse arrow over the margin boundary that you want to change. When the arrow turns into a two-headed arrow, you can drag the boundary (see fig. 13.6).

Fig. 13.6

When you see a two-headed arrow, you are ready to drag the margin boundary. (If you see a one-headed arrow, you drag indents rather than margin boundaries.)

Two-headed arrow——

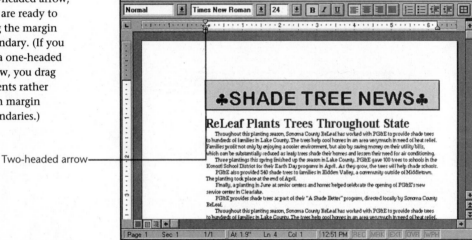

Tip

If you want to change the margins for just one or a few paragraphs, use indents instead (see Chapter 10, "Formatting Lines and Paragraphs," for details). Use the ruler to change margins only when you want to change margins for the entire document or for a large section.

3. Drag the margin boundary toward the edge of the page to make the margin smaller or toward the center of the page to make the margin wider. A dotted line on your document shows you where the new margin will appear (see fig. 13.7).

You can hold down the Alt key as you drag to see margin measurements in the ruler.

If you change your mind about dragging a margin, you can cancel your change by pressing Esc before you release the mouse button, or by choosing the Edit Undo Formatting command after you release the mouse button.

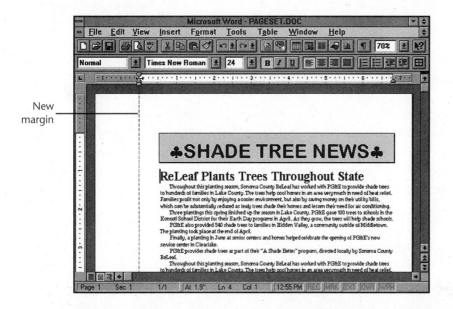

New margin

Fig. 13.7
You can drag margin boundaries to make your margins narrower or wider.

Caution

You must see the two-headed arrow so that you can drag margin boundaries on the ruler. If you see the one-headed mouse arrow, you're pointing to something other than the margin boundary—probably an indent marker. At the left margin boundary, for example, if you haven't set indents for your document, the indent markers are right on top of the margin boundary. If you move the mouse arrow so that it is between the indent markers, it turns into the two-headed margin boundary arrow.

Tip
If your document has facing pages (mirror margins), display multiple pages in the print preview view so that you can see the effect of any change you make to the inside margins. If you change the inside margin on one page, all pages in the section reflect that change.

Determining Paper Size and Orientation

You can change the paper size or orientation for your entire document or for part of your document. You may select a different paper size to create something smaller than usual, such as an invitation. You can select landscape (horizontal) orientation rather than the usual portrait (vertical) orientation to create a brochure or envelope.

Word for Windows offers several predefined paper sizes, including letter, legal, and Monarch. But if none of these sizes suits your needs, you can select a custom size instead and enter your own measurements.

For Related Information
■ "Setting Indents," p. 306

■ "Creating Columns," p. 383

■ "Changing Columns," p. 393

■ "Positioning a Frame in a Margin," p. 706

Formatting Documents

Paper size and orientation settings apply to the current section, just like margin settings. If you haven't divided your document into sections, your settings apply to the whole document, unless you choose to apply them to the currently selected text or from the insertion point forward in your document. If you apply settings to selected text, Word for Windows inserts a new-page section break before and after the selection. (The new-page section break isolates the section on a separate sheet of paper. When you're changing paper size and orientation, this format is probably what you want.) If you apply settings to the insertion point forward, Word for Windows inserts a new-page section break at the insertion point's current position.

To set paper size and orientation, follow these steps:

1. Select the text or section where you want to set paper size and orientation.

2. Choose the File Page Setup command. The Page Setup dialog box appears.

3. Select the Paper Size tab (see fig. 13.8).

Fig. 13.8
You can select a preset or custom paper size, and you can choose the paper orientation—portrait (vertical) or landscape (horizontal).

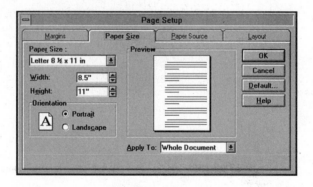

4. From the Paper Size list, select a predefined paper size.

or

In the Width and Height boxes, type or select the width and height of your custom paper size.

5. For a vertical, upright page, select Portrait from the Orientation group.

or

For a horizontal, sideways page, select Landscape from the Orientation group.

6. From the Apply To list, select the section to which you want to apply paper size and orientation settings. (For more information about the Apply To list, see "Setting Different Margins for Different Parts of Your Document" earlier in this chapter.)

7. Choose OK.

Note that if you create custom-size paper, the paper measurements you type are usually in inches, unless you change the default measurement system by choosing the Tools Options command and then selecting the General tab. You can override the default inches by typing your measurement using text that describes a different measurement system. To set a paper width of 36 picas, for example, type **36 pi**; to set a paper height of 24 centimeters, type **24 cm**.

Changing Page Setup Defaults

All new documents are based on a template, and unless you choose a different template, Word for Windows bases new documents on the Normal template, which contains default page setup choices. Because these default choices may not be exactly what you want, Word for Windows gives you the chance to change them by applying your own page setup options to the Normal template. Thus, you can use your own page setup choices as defaults. You can change the default margins, for example, if you always print on paper that requires different margin settings than those supplied by the Normal template. You can change the paper size if you normally use paper different from standard letter size.

You can change defaults for any option in the Page Setup dialog box. Then each new document you create based on the Normal template has your new defaults. (Your current document—or the text or section you've selected—also uses your new settings.)

To change the default page setup settings, follow these steps:

1. Choose the File Page Setup command.

2. On any tab in the Page Setup dialog box, make the page setup selections you want.

3. Choose the **Default** button. A dialog box asks you to confirm that all new documents based on the Normal template are affected by the change.

4. Choose OK.

Creating Headers and Footers

Headers and footers contain information repeated at the top or bottom of the pages of a document. The simplest header or footer may contain only a chapter title and page number. More elaborate headers or footers can contain a company logo (or other graphic), the author's name, the time and date the file was saved or printed, and any other information that may be needed.

You can format headers and footers like any other part of the document, but you usually position them within a page's top and bottom margins, although Word for Windows enables you to position them anywhere on the page.

Word for Windows also gives you the option of having a different header or footer on the first page of a document or section. You also can have different headers and footers on even and odd pages. This feature is useful for chapter headers in books and manuscripts. Each section of a document—a chapter, for example—can have its own headers and footers.

When you create and edit headers and footers, Word switches you to the page layout view and displays headers and footers at the top or bottom of the page, just as they appear when you print your document.

Adding Headers and Footers

When you add headers and footers, Word switches you to page layout view, activates a pane where you can create your header, displays a special Header and Footer toolbar, and dims the text of your document so that you can't edit it (see fig. 13.9).

You create your header or footer inside the pane, editing and formatting it the same way you do any text. After you finish creating the header or footer, close the Header and Footer toolbar. You can move the Header and Footer toolbar by dragging it to a different position on the page.

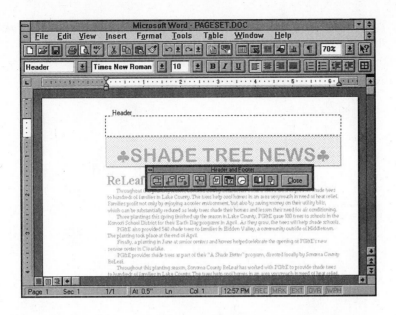

Fig. 13.9
You create headers
and footers in a
special pane.

You can include text or graphics, or both, in a header or footer. If you want, you can insert page numbers, date and time, fields, symbols, cross-references, files, frames, pictures, objects, or a database. Or you can draw a picture using buttons on the Drawing toolbar.

Buttons on the toolbar aid you in creating your header or footer (see fig. 13.10). If the status bar is visible at the bottom of your screen, you can display a message explaining each button by pausing the mouse pointer over the button.

Fig. 13.10
The Header and
Footer toolbar.

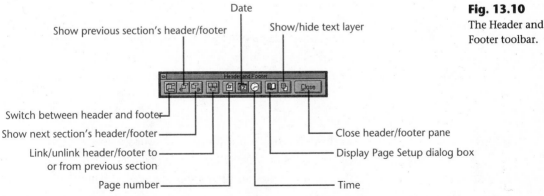

Date

Show previous section's header/footer

Show/hide text layer

Switch between header and footer

Show next section's header/footer

Link/unlink header/footer to
or from previous section

Page number

Close header/footer pane

Display Page Setup dialog box

Time

Formatting Documents

In page layout view, your document appears grayed when you're creating or editing headers or footers; headers and footers appear grayed when you're working on your document. To see both your document and its headers and footers, choose the File Print Preview command.

To add a header or footer to your document, follow these steps:

1. Choose the View Header and Footer command.

2. Type and format the text of your header. Click the following buttons to quickly add page numbers, the date, or the time:

Choose this button	To
	Insert a page number field at the insertion point
	Insert a date field at the insertion point
	Insert a time field at the insertion point

3. Click the Jump Between button to display the footer, and type and format it as you did the header (see Step 2). Alternatively, use the scroll bars or press PgUp or PgDn to scroll to the footer.

4. Choose Close or double-click your document to close the header or footer pane and return to your document.

Another way to include an automatic date or time in a header or footer is to insert a date or time field using the Insert Field command. Using this command, you can select among different formatting options for your date or time. To learn more about fields, see Chapter 37, "Automating with Field Codes."

Preventing (or Creating) Overlapping Headers or Footers and Text. If your header or footer is larger than your margin, Word adjusts the margins of your document so that there is room for the header or footer. If you don't want Word to adjust your margins, make your header or footer smaller or move it closer to the edge of the page (see "Determining a Header's or Footer's Distance from the Edge" later in this chapter). If you want text to overlap a header or footer (as you might if the header or footer is a graphic you want to appear behind text), type a minus sign in front of your margin measurement. If your header is four inches high, for example, and you want a top margin of one inch, and you want the text to overlap the header, type -1" as your top margin. You can use this technique to create a "watermark" that appears behind the text on every page of your document.

Including Different Headers and Footers in Different Parts of Your Document

Each section in a document with multiple sections can have unique headers and footers. This setup is helpful if you format each chapter in a book as a separate section. Or you can create different headers and footers on odd and even pages. You also can have a different header or footer on the first page of a document. If your document has facing pages (mirror margins), for example, you might want a right-aligned header on odd-numbered pages (which appear on the right side of a facing-page layout) and a left-aligned header on even-numbered pages (which appear on the left). In a newsletter, you might want no header on the first page.

Creating Different Headers and Footers for Different Sections. When you first create headers and footers, Word applies them to all the sections in your document. That way, all the headers and footers in your document are the same. Similarly, if you divide into sections a document with existing headers or footers, the headers and footers are the same in all sections.

If you want a different header or footer in a section, you must go to that section and unlink the existing header or footer; then you must create the new header or footer. The new header or footer applies to the current section and to all following sections. Later, if you decide you want your new header or footer to be the same as the previous header or footer, you can relink it.

If you change one header or footer without unlinking it, all the headers and footers in all the sections change.

If you want different headers and footers in different sections of your document, you first must divide your document into sections. To learn how, see "Changing Layouts Within a Document" later in this chapter. To change the header or footer in one section of your document, follow these steps:

1. Position the insertion point inside the section where you want to change the header or footer.

2. Choose the View Header and Footer command. Word selects the header for the section in which you're located. If instead you want to change the footer for that section, click the Jump Between button.

3. To unlink the header or footer, click the Link/Unlink button. The "Same as Previous" line disappears from the top right of the header or footer editing pane.

4. Create the new header or footer.

5. Choose Close or double-click your document to close the Header and Footer toolbar.

   or

   Click the Next Section button to change the header or footer in the following section.

The new header or footer applies to the current section and to all following sections.

As an alternative to Steps 1 and 2, you can choose the View Header and Footer command from within any section to activate headers and footers. Then click the Jump Between button to jump between headers and footers, or click the Next Section or Previous Section buttons to activate headers or footers in a different section.

To relink a different header or footer to the previous header or footer, follow these steps:

1. Position the insertion point inside the section containing the header or footer you want to relink.

2. Choose the View Header and Footer command. Word selects the header for the section in which you're located. If you want to change the footer for that section, click the Jump Between button.

3. To relink the header or footer, click the Link/Unlink button. Word displays a message box asking whether you want to delete the header/footer and connect to the header/footer in the previous section.

4. Choose Yes.

5. Choose Close or double-click your document to close the Header and Footer toolbar.

By relinking the header or footer to the previous header or footer, you change not only the current header or footer, but also those in all the following sections.

To make headers and footers different in all the sections, follow these steps:

1. Position the insertion point in the first section.

2. Choose the View Header and Footer command. Word selects the header for the first section. If you want to change the footer, click the Jump Between button.

3. Create the header or footer you want for the first section.

4. Click the Next Section button to move to the header or footer for the second section.

5. Click the Link/Unlink button.

6. Create the header or footer you want for the second section.

7. Continue clicking the Next Section button to move to the header or footer for the next section, clicking the Link/Unlink button to unlink that section from the previous section, and creating the new header or footer you want.

8. After you create headers and footers for all the sections, choose Close.

Creating Different First-Page Headers and Footers. Many documents have a different header or footer on the first page—or have no header or footer on the first page. In Word, first-page headers and footers apply to sections, not to the whole document. That way, you can have a different header or footer at the beginning of each section in a document that is divided into sections.

To create a different header or footer for the first page of your document, follow these steps:

1. Choose the View Header and Footer command.

2. Click the Previous Section or Next Section button to locate the section in which you want a different first-page header or footer.

3. Click the Page Setup button (or choose the File Page Setup command) to display the Page Setup dialog box.

Formatting Documents

4. Select the Layout tab.

5. In the Headers and Footers group, select Different First Page.

6. Choose OK. The header or footer editing pane for the section you're in is titled "First Page Header" or "First Page Footer."

7. If you want no header or footer, leave the header or footer editing area blank. If you want a different header or footer on the first page of the section, create it now.

8. Choose Close or double-click your document.

As a shortcut, activate a header or footer by double-clicking it in page layout view.

To remove first-page headers and footers from a section or document, follow these steps:

1. Position the insertion point anywhere inside a document containing only one section.

   or

   Position the insertion point inside the section for which you want to remove first-page headers and footers.

2. Choose the File Page Setup command.

3. Select the Layout tab.

4. Deselect (or clear) the Different First Page option in the Headers and Footers group.

5. Choose OK.

Creating Different Headers and Footers for Odd- and Even-Numbered Pages. Sometimes you want different headers and footers for the odd- and even-numbered pages in your document. In a document with facing pages (mirror margins), odd-numbered pages appear on the right side and even-numbered pages appear on the left side. You might want left-aligned headers on even-numbered pages and right-aligned headers on odd-numbered pages so that headers always appear on the outside edges of your document.

You can create different odd and even headers and footers for each section in your document.

To create different headers and footers for odd and even pages, follow these steps:

1. Choose the View Header and Footer command.

2. Click the Previous Section or Next Section button to locate the section in which you want different odd and even headers and footers.

3. Click the Page Setup button (or choose the File Page Setup command) to display the Page Setup dialog box.

4. Select the Layout tab.

5. In the Headers and Footers group, select Different Odd and Even.

6. Choose OK. The header or footer editing box for the section you're in is titled "Even Page Header" or "Odd Page Footer."

7. If you want no header or footer, leave the header or footer editing area blank. If you want a different header or footer on the first page of the section, create it now.

8. Choose Close or double-click your document.

As a shortcut, activate a header or footer by double-clicking it in page layout view.

Determining a Header's or Footer's Distance from the Edge

Headers and footers appear within the top and bottom margins of your document. You can determine how far from the edge of the page they appear. By default, they appear half an inch from the edge.

To determine a header's or footer's distance from the edge of the paper, follow these steps:

1. Choose the View Header and Footer command.

2. Click the Previous Section or Next Section button to locate the section containing the header or footer you want to affect.

3. Click the Page Setup button (or choose the File Page Setup command) to display the Page Setup dialog box.

4. Select the Margins tab.

5. In the From Edge group, select Header and type or select the distance that you want your header from the top edge of the page.

or

Select Footer and type or select the distance that you want your footer from the bottom edge of the page.

6. Choose OK to close the Page Setup dialog box.

7. Choose Close or double-click your document to return to it.

As an alternative, you can position the insertion point inside the section containing the header or footer you want to affect, then choose File, Page Setup, select the Margins tab, set the distances you want, and choose OK.

Remember that most printers have a quarter-inch nonprinting edge on all sides.

Formatting and Positioning Headers and Footers

Anything you can do to or in regular text, you can do to a header or footer. You can change the font, reduce or enlarge the size of the text, insert graphics, draw pictures, include a table, add a line or box, or add shading. You also can add tabs, change the alignment or indents, or change line or paragraph spacing.

Use any of Word's formatting techniques to make headers and footers look distinct from the text in your document. Make the characters larger or a different font. Draw a line beneath headers or above footers. Make headers and footers wider or narrower than the text with paragraph indents. Add borders or shading around headers and footers.

You can use most of the commands in the Insert, Format, Tools, and Table menus to format headers and footers. You can use the ruler to set tabs and indents.

Editing Headers and Footers

In normal view, you can't see headers or footers. In the page layout view, you can see headers and footers, but they appear dimmed. In any view, you must activate a header or footer to edit it. You can activate a header or footer using the same command you used to create it, or in the page layout view, you can double-click a header or footer to activate it. Once it is activated, you edit the header or footer using the same commands you used to create it.

If your document contains only one section, the headers and footers are the same throughout your document, and you can edit headers and footers with the insertion point anywhere within the document. If your document contains multiple sections with differing headers and footers, you must locate the header or footer you want to edit. You can do that two ways: either by activating headers and footers and then using the Previous Section and Next Section buttons on the Header and Footer toolbar to move between sections, or by first locating in your document the header or footer you want to edit and then activating it.

If you want to create different headers and footers for different parts of your document, see "Including Different Headers and Footers in Different Parts of Your Document" earlier in this chapter.

To edit headers and footers, follow these steps:

1. Choose the View Header and Footer command. Word activates the header for the section containing the insertion point. Or, in the page layout view, double-click the header or footer you want to edit.

2. To edit a footer rather than a header, click the Jump Between button or press PgDn to scroll to the bottom of the page.

3. To locate a header or footer in a different section of your document, click the Previous Section or the Next Section button.

4. After you locate the header or footer you want to edit, make the changes you want.

5. Choose Close or double-click the document.

Any time you want to edit more than one header or footer in your document, you can click buttons on the Header and Footer toolbar to move between headers and footers: the Jump Between button toggles between the header and footer in the current section; the Next Section and Previous Section buttons move you to the header or footer for the next or previous section.

Deleting Headers and Footers

You can delete a header or footer by activating it, selecting all the text or objects contained in the header or footer, pressing Delete, and then choosing Close. See the preceding section, "Editing Headers and Footers."

For Related Information
■ "Formatting Characters," p. 246

■ "Changing Fonts," p. 254

■ "Shading and Bordering Paragraphs," p. 324

■ "Changing Layouts Within a Document," p. 432

Hiding the Text Layer While Creating or Editing Headers and Footers

Normally, the text layer appears dimmed while you're working on headers and footers. If you want to hide it altogether, you can click a special button on the Headers and Footers toolbar. Text is only hidden while you're working on the header or footer.

To hide or display the text layer, follow these steps:

1. Activate headers and footers by choosing the View Header and Footer command or by double-clicking an existing header or footer in page layout view.

2. Click the Hide/Show Text Layer button. Click the button a second time to display the text layer.

3. Choose Close or double-click your document to return to it.

Inserting Page Numbers

Long documents are easier to read and reference when the pages are numbered. In Word for Windows, you can insert a page number quickly, and Word formats it as a header or footer for you. That way, you can use all the techniques for working with headers and footers to work with page numbers. See "Creating Headers and Footers" earlier in this chapter.

Inserting Page Numbers

Page numbers can appear at the top or bottom of the page and can be aligned to the center or either side of the page. When you insert a page number, Word for Windows includes a PAGE field and frames the page number. That way, you can move the number anywhere within the header or footer.

Another way to include page numbers is to insert them as part of creating a header or footer, by clicking the Page Number button on the Header and Footer toolbar. This technique is the best if you want to include text with your page number.

To insert page numbers, follow these steps:

1. Choose the Insert Page Numbers command. The Page Numbers dialog box appears (see fig. 13.11).

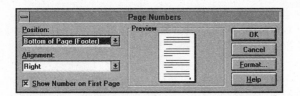

Fig. 13.11
Using the Page
Numbers dialog
box, you can
include page
numbers at the top
or bottom of the
page, in any
alignment. You
can choose
whether to show
them on the first
page of your
document.

2. In the Position list, select Bottom of Page (Footer) to position your page number at the bottom of the page as a footer or choose Top of Page (Header) to position your page number at the top of the page as a header.

3. In the Alignment list, select Left, Center, Right, Inside, or Outside to line up your page number to the center or one side of the page.

4. Select Show Number of First Page if you want a page number to appear on the first page of your document. Deselect this option to prevent the page number from appearing on the first page.

5. Choose OK.

To reposition page numbers, choose the Insert Page Numbers command and choose a different option from the Alignment list. Alternatively, in page layout view, double-click the page number to activate the Header or Footer editing pane. Select the page number and drag it to a new position (or select the frame and reposition it by choosing the Format Frame command and making selections from the Frame dialog box). Then choose Close.

Removing Page Numbers

Because page numbers appear within headers or footers, to remove them you must activate the header or footer, select the page number, and delete it.

To remove page numbers, follow these steps:

1. In page layout view, double-click the page number.

   or

   Choose the View Header and Footer command and click the Jump Between, Next Section, or Previous Section button to locate the page number.

2. Select the page number.

3. Press Delete.

4. Choose Close or double-click your document.

Formatting Page Numbers

You can format your page numbers in a variety of ways. They can appear as numbers, uppercase or lowercase letters, or uppercase or lowercase roman numerals.

You can include chapter numbers if your document's chapter numbers are formatted with Word for Windows default heading styles (Heading 1 through Heading 9) and if you've applied heading numbering by choosing the Format Heading Numbering command and making a selection from the Heading Numbering dialog box. If you include chapter numbers, you can separate them from the page numbers with a hyphen, a period, a colon, or an em dash (a wide hyphen).

You can format page numbers at the same time that you insert them, or you can format them later.

To format page numbers, follow these steps:

1. If you're creating new page numbers, choose the Insert Page Numbers command. Make selections from the Position and Alignment lists.

   or

   If you want to format existing page numbers for a single section, position the insertion point inside that section and choose the Insert Page Numbers command.

2. Choose the Format button. The Page Number Format dialog box appears (see fig. 13.12).

Fig. 13.12
You can format your page numbers as you create them or after you've already created them.

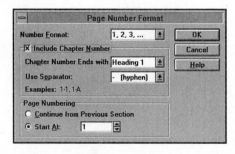

3. In the Number Format list, select the style you want your numbers to be.

4. Select Include Chapter Number if you want to include a chapter number before your page number. In the Chapter Number Ends with list, choose the style (Heading 1 through Heading 9) that you use for chapter numbers in your document.

5. If you want a separator between the chapter number and page number, make a selection from the Use Separator list.

6. Choose OK.

Numbering Different Sections in a Document

Even if your document contains more than a single section, page numbering applies by default to your entire document, and numbers are continuous throughout the document. You can start page numbering at the number you specify in any section, however. You may want page numbering to restart at "1" for each section, for example.

To create page numbering for a single section, follow these steps:

1. If necessary, divide your document into sections by inserting section breaks.

2. Position the insertion point inside the section for which you want unique page numbering.

3. Unlink the header or footer from previous headers or footers (see the section "Creating Different Headers and Footers for Different Sections" earlier in this chapter).

4. Choose the Insert Page Numbers command. Then choose Format.

5. In the Page Numbering group, select Start At and type or select the starting page number for the current section.

6. Choose OK to return to the Page Numbers dialog box; choose OK again to return to your document.

If headers and footers containing page numbers are unlinked from previous sections but you want page numbering to be continuous from section to section, choose the Insert Page Numbers command and then choose Format. Next, select Continue from Previous Section from the Page Numbering group. Finally, choose OK.

For Related Information
- "Creating Headers and Footers," p. 414
- "Changing Layouts Within a Document," p. 432
- "Creating Numbered Headings," p. 567
- "Moving and Positioning Frames," p. 699
- "Selecting and Removing Frames," p. 697
- "Understanding the Basics of Fields," p. 1073

Formatting Documents

Inserting a Date and Time

In Word for Windows, you can use several ways to insert the date and time automatically. You can use a command to insert the current date and time, as described in this section. Using this technique, you can insert the date and time as frozen—that is, the date and time do not change—or you can insert them as a field that you can update to reflect the current date and time. You can choose among many different date and time formats.

Alternatively, you can insert a date and time field. Or you can include a date and time field in a header or footer. These fields also update to reflect the current date or time.

To update a date or time field, select the field and press the F9 key. Date and time fields automatically update whenever you open or print a document.

To insert a date or time, follow these steps:

1. Position the insertion point where you want the date or time to appear. You can insert the date or time in your document or in a header or footer.

2. Choose the Insert Date and Time command. The Date and Time dialog box appears (see fig. 13.13).

Fig. 13.13
Use the Insert Date and Time command to insert a date or time.

3. Choose the date and time format you want from the Available Formats list.

4. If you want the date and time to update to reflect the current date and time, select Insert as Field.

5. Choose OK.

Inserting Line Numbers

If a document is used for reference, it is helpful to readers if the lines are numbered. You can number lines in text that a class shares or in legal briefs, for example.

You can number some or all of the lines in a document. If your document contains no section breaks, line numbers apply to the entire document. If your document contains sections, line numbers apply to the currently selected section. If you select text before you assign line numbers, Word for Windows places page section breaks before and after the selected text, isolating it on a page (or pages) by itself. If you want to apply line numbers to an entire document that contains multiple sections, select the entire document before you apply the line numbers.

Word for Windows offers many options for controlling how line numbers appear. Numbers can start at 1 or some other number, and they can appear on each line or on only some lines. They can be continuous, or they can restart at each section or page. You can measure the distance between text and the line numbers. You also can suppress line numbers for selected paragraphs.

Line numbers appear in the left margin of your page or to the left of text in columns.

To add line numbers, follow these steps:

1. Position the insertion point inside the section containing lines you want to number. (Position the insertion point anywhere inside a document that is not divided into sections.)

    or

    Select the text whose lines you want to number.

    or

    Select the entire document if it is divided into sections and you want line numbering for all the sections.

2. Choose the File Page Setup command. The Page Setup dialog box appears.

3. Select the Layout tab.

4. Choose Line Numbers. The Line Numbers dialog box appears (see fig. 13.14).

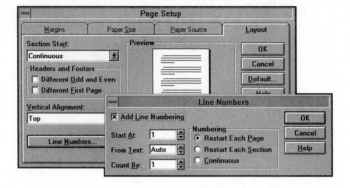

5. Select Add Line Numbering.

6. Choose OK.

7. Choose OK again to close the Page Setup dialog box and return to your document.

To format line numbers, follow these steps:

1. Position the insertion point in the section where you want to format line numbers.

2. Choose the File Page Setup command. The Page Setup dialog box appears.

3. Select the Layout tab.

4. Choose Line Numbers. The Line Numbers dialog box appears.

5. Select Add Line Numbering if you have not already done so.

6. Select Start At and type or select the starting line number.

7. Select From Text and type the distance between the line numbers and text. (Be sure your margins are wide enough to accommodate this distance.)

8. Select Count By and type or select the increment by which you want lines to be numbered. Select 3, for example, if you want every third line numbered.

9. In the Numbering group, Select Restart Each Page for numbering to start over on each page.

or

Select Restart Each Section to start over in each section.

or

Select Continuous if you want line numbers continuous throughout the document.

10. Choose OK.

11. Choose OK again to close the Page Setup dialog box.

To remove line numbers, follow these steps:

1. Position the insertion point in the section where you want to remove line numbers.

2. Choose the File Page Setup command. The Page Setup dialog box appears.

3. Select the Layout tab.

4. Select Line Numbers. The Line Numbers dialog box appears.

5. Deselect (or clear) the Add Line Numbering option.

6. Choose OK.

7. Choose OK again to close the Page Setup dialog box.

To suppress line numbers, follow these steps:

1. Select the paragraphs where you don't want line numbers to appear.

2. Choose the Format Paragraph command. The Paragraph dialog box appears.

3. Select the Text Flow tab.

4. Select Suppress Line Numbers.

5. Choose OK.

For Related Information
■ "Creating Headers and Footers," p. 414

Formatting Documents

Changing Layouts Within a Document

In early word processing programs, many formatting choices applied to your entire document. When you set the margins, they applied to the whole document. Columns, headers and footers, line numbers, page numbers, and footnotes all applied to the entire document. Word for Windows, however, offers a way to divide your document into "sections," each of which you can format differently. Each section is like a document within a document.

Sections are especially important in creating two types of documents: those with chapters and those that fall into the desktop publishing category. Sections are useful for chapters because you can force a section to start on a right-facing page (as most chapters do) and can change headers, footers, page numbers, line numbering, and so on for each chapter. Sections also are indispensable for desktop publishing, where you often need to vary the number of columns on a single page.

Dividing a Document into Sections

By default, a document contains only a single section. *Section breaks* divide your document into sections. The breaks appear as double dotted lines containing the words End of Section in normal view or in page layout view if paragraph marks are displayed (see fig. 13.15). (You can display paragraph marks by choosing the Tools Options command, selecting the View tab, and then selecting Paragraph Marks. Or you can click the Paragraph Marks button on the Standard toolbar.) The dotted lines do not print.

A section break marks the point in your document where new formatting begins. In a newsletter, for example, a section break often follows the title, so that a multiple-column format can begin. The text following the section break, along with its new formatting, can begin in your document immediately, on the next page, or on the next even-numbered or odd-numbered page. You determine where the new section formatting begins when you insert the section break.

To insert a section break, follow these steps:

1. Position the insertion point where you want the section break.

2. Choose the Insert Break command. The Break dialog box appears (see fig. 13.16).

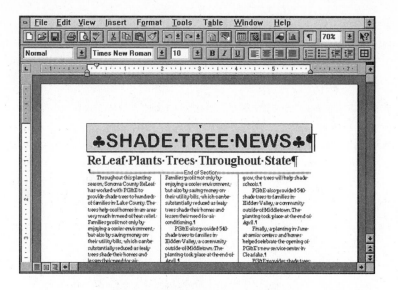

Fig. 13.15
Section breaks
appear as a
double-dotted line
in normal view
and in page layout
view when
paragraph marks
are displayed.

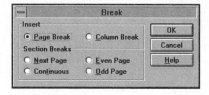

II

Formatting Documents

Fig. 13.16
In the Break dialog
box, you can insert
section breaks that
don't break the
text, or that force
the text following
the section break
to start at the next
page or at the next
even- or odd-
numbered page.

3. Select from the following Section Breaks options:

Option	Section starts
Next Page	Top of the next page in document
Continuous	Insertion point (causing no apparent break in the document)
Even Page	Next even-numbered page in the document (generally a left-facing page)
Odd Page	Next odd-numbered page in the document (generally a right-facing page)

4. Choose OK.

Use the Next Page section break when you want the new section to begin on the next page. Use the Continuous section break when you want the new section to begin at the insertion point; for example, when you create a newsletter that has different-width columns on the same page (such as a full-width title followed by a three-column story). Another use for the Continuous section break is to balance columns on a page: insert a Continuous section break at the end of a document that is divided into columns but that doesn't fill the last page.

Use the Odd Page section break for chapters when you want them to start always on a right-facing page (assuming page numbering in your document starts with page 1 on a right-facing page). Use the Even Page section break to start a section on the next even-numbered page; on facing page layouts with mirror margins, even-numbered pages usually are on the left side of the layout.

Word for Windows inserts section breaks for you on some occasions. When you format a document for columns and specify that the columns take effect from "This Point Forward," Word inserts a continuous section break at the insertion point. When you select text and format it for columns, Word inserts continuous section breaks both before and after the selected text. The same rule holds true when you make many page setup selections.

Removing Section Breaks

In the same way that paragraph marks store paragraph formatting, section break marks store section formatting. Although you can remove a section break easily, remember that when you do, you also remove all section formatting for the section preceding the section break marker that you remove. The preceding section then merges with the following section, taking on its formatting characteristics. If you accidentally delete a section break marker, immediately choose the Edit Undo command to retrieve the marker.

To remove all the section breaks in your document, choose the Edit Replace command. Select Find What, and in the Special list, choose Section Break. Then make sure that the Replace With box contains no text, and choose Replace All.

To remove a section break, follow these steps:

1. Position the insertion point on the section break.

2. Press the Del (Delete) key.

As alternatives, you can position the insertion point just after the section break marker and press Backspace; you can select the section break and press Backspace or Delete; or you can choose the section break marker and choose the Edit Cut command.

Copying Section Formatting

The section break that appears as a double dotted line stores section formatting. You can duplicate (or apply) section formatting quickly by selecting, copying, and then pasting the section break elsewhere. After you paste the section break, the preceding text takes on the formatting of the copied section break.

Another way to duplicate section formatting is to copy and store a section break as AutoText. That way, the break becomes available in all new documents and can be applied quickly and easily. To learn how to create and apply AutoText, see "Inserting Frequently Used Material" in Chapter 5, "Editing a Document."

A final way to duplicate section formatting is to include the formatting in a template—even the Normal template. Remember that by default, a new document includes only one section. That section carries certain default formatting characteristics: one column, a half-inch space between columns (if columns are selected), and no line numbers. If you always format sections differently, modify the Normal template or create a new template that includes your own custom section formatting selections. To learn about templates, see Chapter 6, "Using Templates as Master Documents."

Changing the Section Break Type

If you insert a continuous section break and want to change it to a new page section break, you must delete the existing section break and insert a new one. If you want to make this change without removing the previous section's formatting, insert the new section break after the old one and then delete the old page break.

Finding Section Breaks

If you want to find section breaks, choose the Edit Find command. Next, select Special and then select Section Break. Choose Find Next to find the next section break. You can find section breaks this way even if they are not displayed.

You can use the Edit Replace command to find a section break and replace it with something else, but you cannot replace something with a section break. Use this technique if you want to remove all the section breaks in your document: simply replace section breaks with nothing.

For Related Information

- "Creating Columns," p. 383
- "Setting Margins," p. 402
- "Creating Headers and Footers," p. 414
- "Inserting Page Numbers," p. 424
- "Aligning Text Vertically," p. 436
- "Determining Paper Size and Orientation," p. 411
- "Laying Out the Page," p. 840
- "Working with Columns," p. 383
- "Desktop Publishing Examples," p. 865

II

Formatting Documents

Aligning Text Vertically

Text is normally aligned to the top margin in your document. But you may want to align it differently—in the center of the page or justified on the page (see fig. 13.17). When you justify text, the paragraphs (not the lines within paragraphs) on the page are spread evenly between the top and bottom margins.

Fig. 13.17
You can align text in the center of the page (left side) or justified (right side). If you have a full page of text, however, centered or justified alignment does not appear different from normal top alignment.

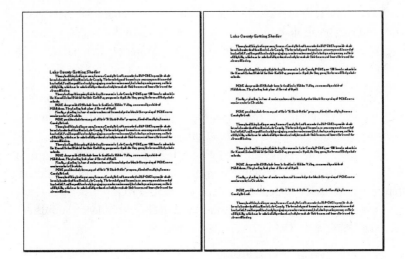

Text alignment applies to sections. If you haven't divided your document into sections, it applies to the entire document. If text fills each page, changing its vertical alignment does not make much difference; reserve this technique for pages that are not full or for sections that are less than a page in length.

To align text on the page, follow these steps:

1. Position the insertion point inside the section where you want to align text.

2. Choose the File Page Set**u**p command. The Page Setup dialog box appears.

3. Select the Layout tab.

4. In the Vertical Alignment list, select Center to center text on the page.

or

Select Justify to spread paragraphs between the top and bottom margins.

or

Select Top to align text to the top margin.

Controlling Where Paragraphs and Pages Break

As you type your document, Word automatically breaks text at the bottom margin of each page. Text continues on the next page, unless you specify otherwise. Word determines how much text appears on a page based on many factors, including margins, type size, paragraph specifications, and the size of footnotes. Displaying hidden text and field codes also can affect page breaks—hide them to see accurately how your pages will break.

You have many ways to control how text breaks on a page. You can specify that paragraphs stay together, for example, or with other paragraphs. You can specify at which line a page will break.

Controlling Paragraph Breaks

By default, paragraphs break at the bottom margin of a page and continue at the top margin of the next page. Many times you want to prevent paragraphs from breaking arbitrarily at the bottom of the page. You may want to keep a heading paragraph together with the paragraph that follows it, for example. Or you may want certain paragraphs not to break at all. You may want to avoid *widows* and *orphans*, single lines of text that appear at the top or bottom of the page.

Regardless of how you format paragraphs to control paragraph breaks, *hard* page breaks that you insert manually take precedence. If you format a paragraph to stay together on a page but insert a hard page break inside the paragraph, for example, the paragraph always breaks at the line containing the hard page break. You must remove the hard page break if you want the paragraph to stay together (see the next section).

To control paragraph breaks, follow these steps:

1. Position the insertion point inside the paragraph you want to affect.

2. Choose the Format Paragraph command. The Paragraph dialog box appears (see fig. 13.18).

3. Select the Text Flow tab.

Fig. 13.18
In the Paragraph dialog box, you can control how paragraphs break—or don't break—at the bottom of a page.

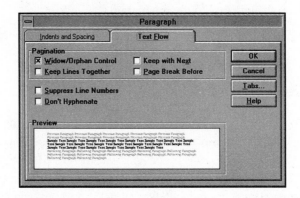

4. Select the following options you want from the Pagination group:

Select this option	To get this result
Widow/Orphan Control	Prevents single lines in selected paragraphs from appearing alone at the top or bottom of a page.
Keep Lines Together	Prevents a page break inside a selected paragraph. Moves paragraph to next page if there's not room on current page for all of it.
Keep with Next	Ensures that the selected paragraph always appears on the same page as the next paragraph. Moves the paragraph to the next page if there's not room on the current page for it and the next paragraph.
Page Break Before	Starts the selected paragraph at the top of the next page. Inserts a page break before selected paragraph.

5. Choose OK.

A nonprinting square selection handle appears in the left margin next to any paragraph for which you've selected a pagination option. If text breaks on the page in a way you don't like, look for these squares to see whether the page break is caused by a pagination option. If it is, you can remove it by following the preceding steps and deselecting (or clearing) the offending pagination option.

Inserting Page Breaks

Word inserts *soft* page breaks at the end of every page and adjusts them as necessary when you edit, add, or remove text. If you want to force a page to break at a particular place in your document, you can insert a hard page break. Word always starts text following a hard page break at the top of the following page.

In normal view, a soft page break appears as a dotted line; in page layout or print preview view, you see the page as it will print. In outline view, you don't see soft page breaks. Hard page breaks appear in the normal and outline views as a dotted line containing the words `Page Break`; they appear this way in the page layout and master document views when you display paragraph marks.

Note

Hard page breaks take priority over paragraph pagination options.

After you insert a hard page break, you can delete it, move it, copy it, or paste it.

You can insert a hard page break by using a command or a keyboard shortcut. You also can insert a page break by inserting a section break that begins on the next page, or on the next odd- or even-numbered page; see "Changing Layouts Within a Document" earlier in this chapter. To insert a hard page break, follow these steps:

1. Position the insertion point at the beginning of the text that you want to start on a new page.

2. Choose the Insert Break command. The Break dialog box appears (see fig. 13.19).

3. Select Page Break.

Fig. 13.19

In the Break dialog box, you can insert a hard page break by selecting the **P**age Break option.

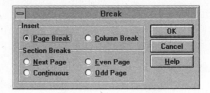

4. Choose OK.

To insert a hard page break using a shortcut, follow these steps:

1. Position the insertion point where you want the page break.

2. Press Ctrl+Enter.

Repaginating in the Background

By default, Word for Windows automatically calculates page breaks as you work on your document. In the normal, outline, or master document view, you can turn off background pagination, but in page layout or print preview views, you cannot. You may see a slight performance improvement if you turn off background repagination.

Word for Windows always repaginates when you print your document, switch to page layout or print preview view, or compile an index or table of contents.

To turn off background repagination, follow these steps:

1. Choose the View menu, and then choose the Normal, Outline, or Master Document command.

2. Choose the Tools Options command.

3. Select the General tab.

4. Deselect (or clear) the Background Repagination option.

5. Choose OK.

Selecting the Paper Source

In Word for Windows, you not only can alter margins, paper size, and paper orientation for your document or for a section of your document, but you also can specify where your printer finds the paper.

Many printers have different options for storing paper. Most laser printers, for example, have a default paper tray and a manual feed. You can specify that one section of your document be printed from the manual feed, whereas the rest of the document be printed from paper in the default paper tray. Some printers have two paper trays; you can specify that one section, such as the first page of a letter, be printed on letterhead in the first tray, whereas the remaining pages be printed on plain paper from the second tray.

As you can do with all page setup options, you can insert section breaks before you select paper source, or Word for Windows can insert section breaks for you.

To select a paper source for your document, follow these steps:

1. Position the insertion point inside the section for which you want to set the paper source. (The change applies to the entire document unless the document has multiple sections.)

   or

   Select the section for which you want to set the paper source.

   or

   Position the insertion point where you want the new paper source to begin in your document.

2. Choose the File Page Setup command. The Page Setup dialog box appears (see fig. 13.20).

3. Select the Paper Source tab.

4. From the First Page list, select the paper source for the first page of your document.

5. From the Other Pages list, select the paper source for the remaining pages of your document.

Fig. 13.20
Using the Page
Setup dialog box,
you can print
different sections
of your document
on paper from
different sources.

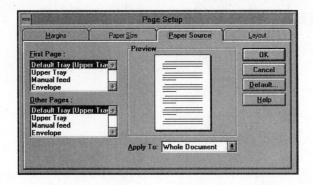

6. From the Apply To list, select the section to which you want to apply paper source settings (the list displays different options, depending on how much text is selected in the document):

Option	Applies margins to	When
This Section	Current section (No section break is inserted)	Insertion point is located within a section
Selected Sections	Multiple sections (No section breaks are inserted)	At least part of more than one section is selected
This Point Forward	Insertion point (Inserts new page section break at the insertion point)	Insertion point is where you want new margin to start
Selected Text	Selected text (Inserts new page section breaks at the beginning and end of text)	Text is selected
Whole Document	Entire document (No break is inserted); Insertion point is anywhere	

7. Choose OK.

When you print a document with various paper sizes, orientations, or sources, your printer may pause at the end of each page and wait for you to indicate that it should continue. In some cases, you may need only to access the Print Manager and "Resume" the print (see Chapter 8, "Previewing and

Printing a Document"). In other cases, you may need to press a button on the printer. Newer laser printers work well with varying paper sizes and orientations, but if you experience difficulties, check your printer manual.

If you want to apply your paper source selections to the Normal template so that they become the default settings, choose the Default button instead of pressing Enter.

From Here...

For information relating to page setup, review the following major sections of this book:

- Chapter 10, "Formatting Lines and Paragraphs," in which you can read about bordering paragraphs to see how you can add lines and shading to your page layout.

- Chapter 12, "Working with Columns," shows how you can divide your text into columns for a readable page layout.

- Chapter 22, "Inserting Pictures in Your Document," tells you how to include graphic elements in your page layout.

- Chapter 23, "Framing and Moving Text and Graphics." When you frame text or a picture, you're no longer confined to the space between the margins in your page layout. In addition, when you frame text or an object, you can wrap text around it.

- Chapter 24, "Drawing with Word's Drawing Tools." Using the buttons on the Drawing toolbar, you can create pictures that you can send to the layer behind the text.

Tip
Be sure that you have installed the correct printer driver for your printer in Windows so that Word for Windows knows which paper trays your printer has available. Refer to your Windows book or manual for details.

II

Formatting Documents

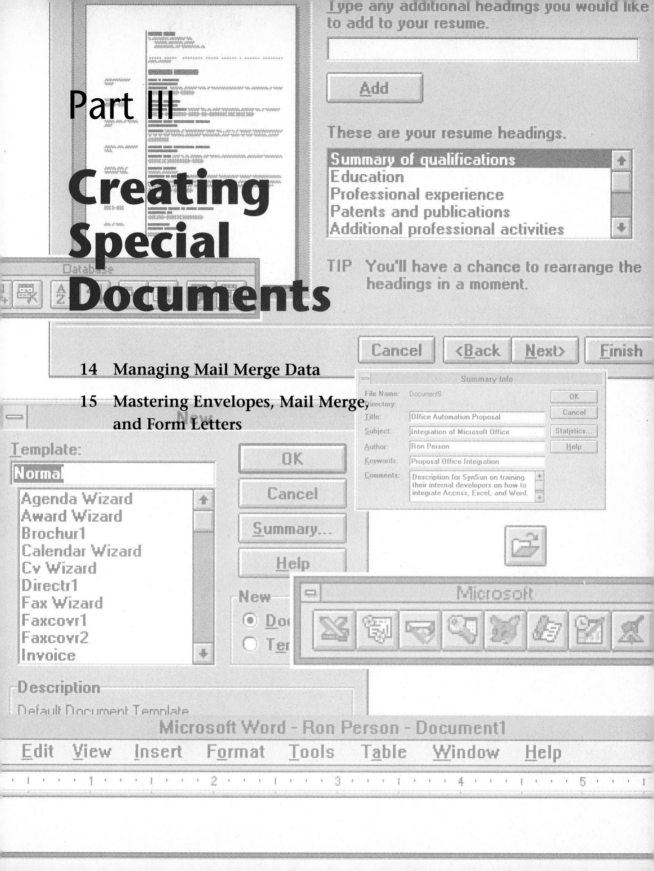

Part III

Creating Special Documents

14   Managing Mail Merge Data

15   Mastering Envelopes, Mail Merge, and Form Letters

Type any additional headings you would li
to add to your resume.

Add

These are your resume headings.

Summary of qualifications
Education
Professional experience
Patents and publications
Additional professional activities

TIP You'll have a chance to rearrange th
headings in a moment.

Cancel   <Back   Next>   Finis

Database

Summary Info

File Name:	Document8
Directory:	
Title:	Office Automation Proposal
Subject:	Integration of Microsoft Office
Author:	Ron Person
Keywords:	Proposal Office Integration
Comments:	Description for SynSun on training their internal developers on how to integrate Access, Excel, and Word.

OK
Cancel
Statistics...
Help

New

Template:

Normal

Agenda Wizard
Award Wizard
Brochur1
Calendar Wizard
Cv Wizard
Directr1
Fax Wizard
Faxcovr1
Faxcovr2
Invoice

OK
Cancel
Summary...
Help

New
◉ Doc
○ Ter

Microsoft

Description

Default Document Template

Microsoft Word - Ron Person - Document1

ile   Edit   View   Insert   Format   Tools   Table   Window   Help

. . . I . . . 1 . . . I . . . 2 . . . I . . . 3 . . . I . . . 4 . . . I . . . 5 . .

Chapter 14

Managing Mail Merge Data

Word for Windows does more than just publish text. Think of it as a report writer or publisher of database information as well. Word has the ability to retrieve, store, and manipulate rows of information such as names and addresses, billing information, invoice data, product catalog information, and so on. Some of the tasks that are commonly relegated to database report applications can be done with Word, and Word can give you a more free-form, publishing-oriented result. For example, you can use data stored or linked into Word to create:

- Form letters using name and address information. Other information can be merged into the form letters such as amounts owed, product information, or notes

- Envelopes to go with the form letters. Envelopes can be printed in sorted ZIP code order and include POSTNET and FIM bar codes to save you money

- Mailing labels that even include logos, graphics, POSTNET and FIM bar codes

- Product catalogs that include graphics and a more professionally published appearance than what is normally produced from a database report

- Sales report data in a more free-form layout. Word can publish data using features such as newspaper columns and integrated graphics that are not available in worksheets such as Excel or from database report writers.

In this chapter, you learn to do the following:

- Create a new data source document from scratch in Word

- Retrieve an existing data source file into Word or link a Word document to a data source located in an external database

- Manage data through updating, sorting, finding, editing and deleting

III

Creating Special Documents

Fig. 14.1

A data source can be as simple as a table in Word containing rows and columns of information.

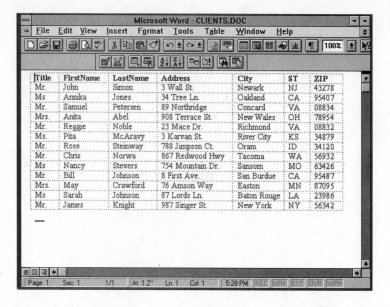

Title	FirstName	LastName	Address	City	ST	ZIP
Mr.	John	Simon	3 Wall St.	Newark	NJ	43278
Ms	Annika	Jones	34 Tree Ln.	Oakland	CA	95407
Mr.	Samuel	Petersen	89 Northridge	Concard	VA	08834
Mrs.	Anita	Abel	908 Terrace St.	New Wales	OH	78954
Mr.	Reggie	Noble	23 Mace Dr.	Richmond	VA	08832
Ms.	Pita	McAravy	3 Karvan St.	River City	KS	34879
Mr.	Rose	Steinway	788 Jimpson Ct.	Oram	ID	34120
Mr.	Chris	Norwa	867 Redwood Hwy	Tacoma	WA	56932
Ms	Nancy	Stevers	754 Mountain Dr.	Sansom	MO	63426
Mr.	Bill	Johnson	8 First Ave.	San Burdue	CA	95487
Mrs.	May	Crawford	76 Amson Way	Easton	MN	87095
Ms	Sarah	Johnson	87 Lords Ln.	Baton Rouge	LA	23986
Mr.	James	Knight	987 Singer St.	New York	NY	56342

What You Need to Know About Managing Data

Word dialog boxes and the Mail Merge Helper refer to the object containing data as the data source. The data source can be on the same computer as Word and created in a personal computer such as a Word document, an Excel worksheet, or a dBASE file. The data source can also reside in another computer to which Word is linked via a network. The other computer can contain a large database application, such as Oracle or SQL Server. Word can retrieve just the part of the database it needs from these larger databases.

Word can use as a data source information you type into a table, a data source you create with the aid of the Mail Merge Helper, a file you import from another application, or data linked into Word from a database application. The data source can be small and simple or it can be a link from Word to a corporate computer.

Information stored in the data source is normally laid out in a table format of rows and columns. Each row of information is known as a record. If the data source contains the names and addresses of clients, a record contains each individual's name, address, and specific client information. In this case, one record of information is like a card in a card file. Each row in a data source ends with a paragraph mark.

Information is arranged within records by column. These columns are known as fields. Each field, or column, contains one specific type of information. For example, the name and address data source might need one field for state and another for ZIP code. A delimiter separates each field of data. Delimiters that Word understands are commas, tabs, or separate cells in a table. If a record contains more than 31 fields, then Word cannot use a table; it uses tabs or commas instead.

Data sources need a row of titles at the top that are known as field names. The field names should describe the contents of that field in the data source. You refer to these field names when you are searching for or limiting the data used from the data source. Field names are also used to indicate where information goes when it is taken from the data source and placed into the merge document such as a form letter or label.

Field names have specific requirements. They must be no more than 40 characters long, they must start with a letter, and they cannot contain a space. Rather than use a space in a field name you may want to use an underscore character.

What You Need to Know About the Database Toolbar

Word includes a toolbar specifically designed to help you manage tables, databases, and data sources. The Database toolbar automatically displays when you open a document that has been specified as a data source for mail merge as described in Chapter 15, "Mastering Envelopes, Mail Merge, and Form Letters." You can also open the Database toolbar by selecting the View Toolbars command, selecting Database from the Toolbars list, and then choosing OK. Here's what the Database toolbar looks like:

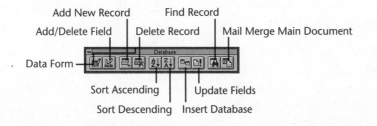

The different buttons in the Database toolbar are as follows:

Icon	Name	Description
	Data Form	Displays the Data Form, which makes adding, editing, and finding information easier in the database
	Manage Fields	Makes it easy to add, remove, or rename fields (columns) in a database
	Add New Record	Adds a new record at the current insertion point in a table or database
	Delete Record	Removes a record at the current insertion point in a table or database
	Sort Ascending	Sort the table or database in ascending order on the current field
	Sort Descending	Sort the table or database in descending order on the current field
	Insert Database	Displays the Database dialog box so that you can insert a file containing a database
	Update Fields	Updates fields and links in the document. Updates databases linked to files
	Find Records	Displays the Find in Field dialog box to help you search a database
	Mail Merge Main Document	Opens the main document attached to the current data source

Inserting a Database from a File

Small lists can be managed in a word processor; however, if you have lists or databases larger than a few hundred records, you will want to use a database application such as Microsoft Access in which to store, edit, and retrieve your data. Word makes it easy to store data in many different types of databases and then bring that data into a Word document so that it can be used as a data source for mail merge.

For Word to import or access a database file, it must have the appropriate file converters or Open Database Connectivity (ODBC) drivers installed. Installing converters and drivers can be done after Word has been initially installed. This is described in Appendix B.

Database files that Word can convert and insert include the following:

Microsoft Word

Microsoft Access

Microsoft Excel

dBASE

Paradox

Microsoft FoxPro

Word for Mac 3.x, 4.x, and 5.x

Word for MS-DOS 3.0-6.0

WordPerfect 5.x for MS-DOS or Windows

Lotus 1-2-3 2.x and 3.x

Inserting a Database

When you insert a database, you can choose to insert the data or insert a field code, which creates a link to the database file. Inserted data acts just as though it was typed in the document. Inserting a field code enables you to quickly update the database because it has a link to the file on disk. If the data in the file changes, you can easily update the list.

To insert a database that is in a file on disk, follow these steps:

1. Position the insertion point in the document where you want the database.

2. Choose the Insert Database command to display the Database dialog box, shown in fig. 14.2.

3. Choose the Get Data button to display the Open Data Source dialog box.

4. Select or type the name of the file in the File Name list. Choose OK.

   If it is possible to select part of the data source, such as a range on a spreadsheet, a dialog box like the one in fig. 14.3 appears. In this example, the Excel spreadsheet named DOWMO.XLS contains a named range, Database. Select the range or query that defines the data you want, then choose OK to return to the Insert Database dialog box.

III

Creating Special Documents

Fig. 14.2
Use the Database
dialog box to
insert all
or part of a data-
base that is in a
file from Word
or another
application.

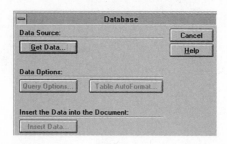

Fig. 14.3
You can insert a
portion of some
database files.

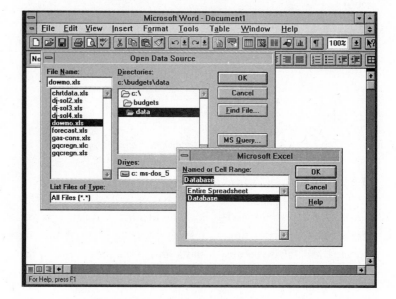

5. Select the **Query Options** button from the Database dialog box if you want the data you insert to meet certain criteria. The section titled "Selecting Specific Records to Merge" in Chapter 15 describes how to specify a Query.

6. Select the **Table AutoFormat** command if you want to be guided through custom formatting of the table.

7. Choose the **Insert Data** button to display the Insert Data dialog box, shown in fig. 14.4.

8. If you want to limit the number of records inserted, select **From** and **To** and enter the starting and ending record numbers.

9. If you want to create a link from your database to the database file on disk, select the Insert Data as Field check box.

10. Choose OK.

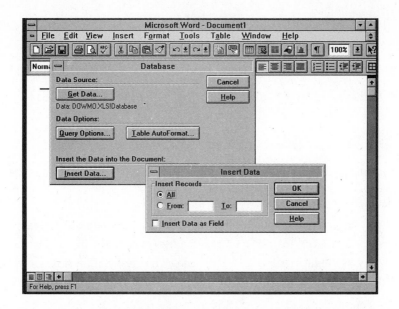

Fig. 14.4
From the Insert
Data dialog box,
you can select the
amount of data
you want and
whether the
database should be
linked to the file
on disk.

If you did not select the Insert Data as Field check, the data is inserted as if it was typed. If the check box was selected, a link is created between the document and the database file. This link is created with a field code. You can update this field code by selecting it and pressing F9. You can unlink the field code so that the database becomes fixed text by selecting the table and pressing Shift+Ctrl+F9.

Creating a Data Source for Mail Merge

The data source you use in Word for Windows can come from an existing Word document, be created new in Word, or be linked into Word from another application.

Creating a New Data Source

If the amount of data you need to store is not extensive and you do not need to share the information with other users, the easiest way for you to store and manage your data is in a Word document. You can create a data source in a Word document either manually or with the guidance of the Mail Merge Helper.

Creating a Data Source Manually. You can manually create a data source document by typing data into a document. The fields of data must be separated into the cells of a table, or separated by tabs or commas. The field names in the first row of the data source document must fit the rules for field names:

■ Names must start with a letter.

■ Names must not contain a space. Use an underscore if you need to separate words.

■ Names must not be longer than 40 characters.

■ Names must be unique. You cannot have two field names spelled the same.

You must save the document containing your data source to disk before you can use it. Try to save the document with a file name that will not change frequently. If the file name of the data source changes, you must reconnect the mail merge document in order to use the data source.

Fig. 14.1 shows an example of a table that is used as a data source for a mail merge document. Each field (column) in the table contains a type of information and each record (row) contains a group of information about a client. The information in this document could also have been separated by commas or by tabs. Fig. 14.5 shows the same information as a data source with the data separated by tabs. If you decide to use commas or tabs to separate data, use one or the other throughout the data source—do not mix them in the same document. End each record (row) with a paragraph mark if it is a comma or tab-delimited record. A record in a table is one row of the table.

Fig. 14.5

You can manually create data source documents by typing data into tables or by typing each record in a row and separating the fields with commas or tabs.

After you have created your data source document, save it and remember its name and directory. When you run a mail merge as described in Chapter 14, "Managing Mail Merge Data," the Mail Merge Helper asks you to select the file name of the data source.

If you create a comma-delimited data source and some of your data contains commas, Word may be confused as to the fields in which data belongs. To solve this problem, enclose any data that contains commas within quotes (") when you use commas to separate fields of data. The quotes around a piece of data tell Word that any comma within the quotes is part of the data.

Using the Mail Merge Helper to Create a New Data Source. If you want to be guided through the process of creating a data source document, use the Mail Merge Helper. The Mail Merge Helper is a series of dialog boxes that present options for creating some of the most commonly used field names. After you have created the field names, the Mail Merge Helper gives you a chance to enter data into the new data source. A later section of this chapter, "Finding or Editing Records with the Data Form," describes how to add more records or find and edit existing records.

The following process helps you create a data source document with the Mail Merge Helper. The Mail Merge Helper assumes you are creating a form letter and the source document at the same time. Because most people create first one or the other and then return later to merge the two together, the following steps show you how to create only the source document.

To create a new data source, follow these steps:

1. Choose the Tools Mail Merge command. The Mail Merge Helper dialog box appears.

2. Choose Create and then select Form Letters.

3. Choose the New Main Document button. This opens a blank document and returns you to the Mail Merge Helper. The Get Data button is now available.

   The blank document that opened would normally be used to create a new form letter, but you need it open only to appease the Mail Merge Helper while you create a new data source.

4. Choose the Get Data button, then select Create Data Source from the list.

Fig. 14.6

Choosing Tools Mail Merge displays the Mail Merge Helper. The Mail Merge Helper guides you through the process of creating data sources, creating main documents, and merging the data and document.

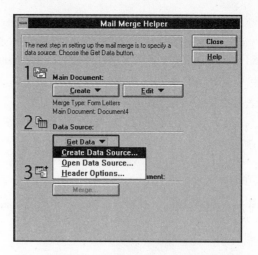

Fig. 14.7

The Create Data Source dialog box appears and gives you the opportunity to accept, add, or remove field names that will be used to name each column in the data source.

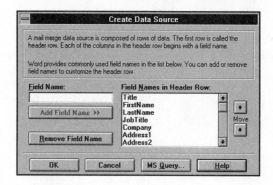

5. In the Create Data Source dialog box, add or remove field names for the columns in your data source. When the Create Data Source dialog box first appears, it shows in the Field Names in Header Row list the most frequently used field names for mail merge. Field names appear left to right across the first row of the data source in the order they are listed in the Field Names in Header Row list. Edit the field names in the list using the following steps:

■ Add a new field name to the list by typing the name in the Field Name edit box and choosing Add Field Name. The name is added to the end of the list. Field names must be 40 characters or less and start with a letter. Spaces are not allowed.

- Delete a field name from the list by selecting the name in the Field Names in Header Row list, then choose Remove Field Name.

- Move a field name up or down in the list by selecting the name and then clicking on the up or down arrows.

6. Choose OK. The Save Data Source dialog box appears.

7. Type a file name in the File Name edit box. Change to the directory in which you expect to keep the data source.

8. Choose OK to close the Save Data Source dialog box. A dialog box appears warning you that the data source you created contains no data.

9. Choose Edit Data Source to display the Data Form where you can add records to your new data source.

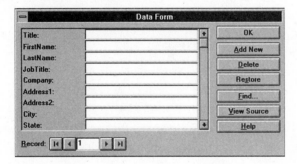

Fig. 14.8
Use the Data Form to add new data to your new data source. You can bring up the Data Form at any time to find or edit data in a data source.

10. Enter data in the Data Form. Press Tab or Enter to move to the next field of data. Choose Add New to add another record. The Data Form is described in detail in the section titled "Finding or Editing Records in the Data Form."

11. When you are finished entering data and want to save the data source, choose the View Source button. When the data source document appears, choose File Save.

If you do not save the data source document, you will be given a chance to save it when you attempt to close the blank document you opened in Step 3.

III

Creating Special Documents

Tip
View more of a
wide data source
by using the View
Zoom command to
fit more fields on
the screen.

You can see the paragraph mark that ends a row of comma-delimited data if you click Show/Hide Hidden Character button on the Standard toolbar.

Your data source document looks like a table if it has 31 or fewer field names. If it has more than 31 field names, data is separated by commas, and records end with a paragraph mark. The field names will be in the first row and data in following rows.

Working with an Existing Data Source

**For Related
Information**
■ "Creating
Tables," p. 509

■ "Creating a
Data Source
Document,"
p. 483

You can work with data sources that already exist, even if they aren't Word documents. The data may have come from a worksheet, database, or corporate mainframe.

You may want to work with an existing data source to edit its contents or to build a new main document that contains merge fields. For example, if you want to create a new form letter using a data source you already have, follow this procedure:

1. Choose the Tools Mail Merge command.

2. Choose the Main Document Create button, then select the type of main document you want to create: Form Letters, Mailing Labels, Envelopes, or Catalog. From the dialog box that appears, choose either Active Window or New Main Document to attach the data source to the existing active document or to open a new document.

3. Choose the Get Data button, and then choose Open Data Source from the pull-down list. The Open Data Source dialog box appears.

4. Change to the directory containing the data source, and then select or type the file name of the data source in the File Name box. Choose OK.

5. Choose the Edit Main Document button.

The data source is open but does not show in a window. If you want to edit the data in the data source, refer to the section later in this chapter titled "Finding or Editing Records with the Data Form."

If the appropriate file converters are installed, you can use files from other applications as a data source. For information about how to install converters, refer to Appendix B.

You can use the data source documents you used in previous versions of Word for Windows with the Mail Merge Helper in Word for Windows 6. Make sure that Word 6 has the converters installed to convert the old document into Word 6 format. After you have resaved the document, you can treat it the same as any data source.

Using Data from Another Application

Word can use the data from other applications as a data source. Your main documents in Word can link to data in other applications such as Microsoft Access or Microsoft Excel. The document can read directly from databases such as Access, Paradox, FoxPro, or dBASE through the use of Open Database Connectivity (ODBC) drivers. You also can import and convert data from any files for which you have a converter. Chapter 34, "Converting Files with Word for Windows," describes how to convert files.

Using the Mail Merge Helper with a Non-Word Data Source. To work with a non-Word data source, follow these steps:

1. Open a main document.

2. Choose Tools, Mail Merge.

3. Choose Main Document Create, and then select the type of main document you want to create: Form Letters, Mailing Labels, Envelopes, or Catalog. From the Help dialog box that appears, choose either Active Window or New Main Document to attach the data source to the existing active document or to open a new document.

4. Choose Get Data, and then select Open Data Source from the pull-down list.

5. Change to the directory containing the data source, and then select or type the file name of the data source in the File Name box. Choose OK.

   or

   If you open an Excel worksheet, you are given an opportunity to specify a range name within the worksheet that describes the data you want to bring in. If you open an Access file, you can open an Access query file and only the data that satisfies that query will be brought in.

   or

   Choose MS Query to open Microsoft Query so you can connect to and query an external data source. Microsoft Query is a separate Microsoft application that comes with Microsoft Excel 5 or Microsoft Office. When you are finished in Microsoft Query, choose File Return Data to Microsoft Word.

For Related Information

■ "Using Word with Other Windows Applications," p. 993

■ "Converting Files with Word for Windows," p. 1021

6. If the active document is not a main document that contains merge fields, Word displays a Mail Merge Helper dialog box. Choose the Edit Main Document button.

Managing Information in the Data Source

You can manage the data in your data source just as though you had a small database program built into Word. You can find or edit records using the Data Form. You can also reorganize the columns in a data source or merge together two data source files.

Finding or Editing Records with the Data Form

The information in your data source is of little value unless it is accurate. Word includes features to help you keep your data source up-to-date.

To quickly find data when the data source is in the active document, follow these steps:

1. Click within a data source.

2. Click the Find Record button on the Database toolbar to display the Find in Field dialog box shown in fig. 14.9.

Tip
When you don't know which field (column) contains the data you need to find, select the entire database search with the Edit Find command.

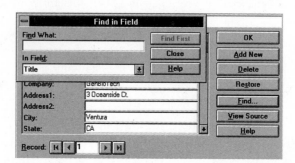

Fig. 14.9
You can find records that contain information in the field name you select.

3. Select from the In Field list the field name of the column you want to search.

4. Type in the Find What box what you are searching for under the field name.

5. Choose Find First.

6. Examine the record found or click the Find Next button to continue.

To find and edit information when a data source is in the active document, follow these steps:

1. Click within a data source.

   The database may have fields in table columns, tab-separated or comma-separated. A main document does not have to be opened or attached. It must have valid data source field names.

2. Click the Data Form button on the Database toolbar.

3. Begin at Step 3 in the next procedure to find or edit data using the Data Form.

To find data within the data source when the main document is active, follow these steps:

1. Open a main document that uses your data source.

2. Click the Data Form button in the Database toolbar or choose the Tools Mail Merge command, then choose the Edit button and select the data source. The Data Form dialog box appears.

3. Move to the first record in the data source if you want to begin the search from the first data record.

4. Choose Find.

5. Select from the In Field list the field name of the column you want to search.

6. Type in the Find What box what you are searching for under the field name.

7. Choose Find First.

When the first record satisfying your request is found, the Find What button changes to a Find Next button. Select this button to find any further occurrences of what you are searching for. A message notifies you when you have reached the last record in the database.

When you find a record you want to edit, choose Close in the Find in Field dialog box and edit the record in the Data Form.

You can delete a record by displaying it in the Data Form and then choosing **Delete**.

III

Creating Special Documents

If you delete or edit a record incorrectly, immediately choose **Restore** to return the record to its original condition. After you move to a new record when editing, you cannot restore previous edits.

Sorting a Data Source

Sorting a data source can be useful for a couple of reasons. If you are printing a large volume of mail merge envelopes or labels, you can get a discount on postage if ZIP codes are in sorted order. Another reason for sorting is if you need to create printed lists that will be searched manually.

To quickly sort a data source, follow these steps:

1. Click in the data source in the field (column) on which you want to sort.

2. Click the ascending or descending sort button on the Database toolbar.

If you have more complex sorts and your data is in a table, or can be converted to a table, use the Table Sort command described in chapter 16, "Creating and Editing Tables."

Renaming, Inserting, or Removing Fields from a Data Source

When your information needs change, you will probably have to add or remove fields (columns) from your data source. For example, you might want to add a field that includes a customer's automatic reorder date, or you might want to delete an old, unnecessary field such as a Client Priority number.

To add or remove a field in a data source, follow these steps:

1. Save your current data source under a new name. Save this file as a backup in case you make mistakes and need to return to an original copy.

2. Open the data source document and display it in the active window.

3. Click the Manage Fields button in the Database toolbar to display the Manage Fields dialog box, shown in fig. 14.10.

Fig. 14.10
Use the Manage Fields dialog box to add or remove new fields (columns) in the Data Source as your information needs change.

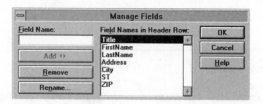

4. If you want to add, remove, or rename a field, follow these steps:

   ■ To add a field, type the new name in the Field Name edit box, then choose the Add button.

   ■ To remove a field name and its corresponding data, select the name from the Field Names in Header Row list, then choose the Remove button. Choose Yes to confirm that you want to remove the field and data.

   ■ To rename a field name, choose the Rename button, then type your name in the New Field Name edit box that appears. Choose OK.

5. When you have finished making changes to your data source, choose OK.

Inserting or Removing Records from a Data Source

It seems that the amount of information demanded only seems to grow; however, sometimes you might need to delete a record from your data source. With Word, you can easily insert or delete records.

To insert a new blank record at the bottom of the data source, you can use the Data Form as described earlier in this chapter. Alternatively, you can follow these steps:

Tip
If records to be deleted have common data, sort the field containing that data so that you can delete multiple records at one time.

1. Open and activate the data source document.

2. Click the Add New Record button on the Database toolbar.

To delete a record from the data source, follow these steps:

1. Open and activate the data source document.

2. Click in the record (row) that you want to delete. Select down through many records if you want to delete multiple records.

3. Click the Delete Record button on the Database toolbar. You are not asked to confirm that you want to delete.

If you decide you have accidentally deleted the wrong record, immediately choose the Edit Undo command. You can undo only the last record you deleted.

III

Creating Special Documents

Scrolling Through the Data Form

You can browse through records in the data source using the buttons at the bottom of the Data Form. Clicking the left or right button moves the records one at a time. Clicking the left end or right end button (VCR end controls, |< and >|) moves to the beginning or end of the data record.

If you do not have a mouse, you can move to a specific record by pressing Alt+R and typing the numeric position of the record you want to see. When you press Enter, the insertion point moves out of the Record number box and into the first field.

From Here...

For information relating directly to creating and using a data source, you may want to review the following chapters:

- Chapter 15, "Mastering Envelopes, Mail Merge, and Form Letters," shows you how to take your data and insert it into form letters, envelopes, and mailing labels.

- Chapter 16, "Creating and Editing Tables," describes how to create and edit tables. Many mailing list databases are kept in tables, so the information here is useful.

Chapter 15

Mastering Envelopes, Mail Merge, and Form Letters

Successful businesses stay in touch with their clients and customers. Staying in touch with many people is difficult, however, unless you learn how to create personalized form letters and envelopes with Word for Windows.

To make single letters easier to produce, Word for Windows has automated the process of printing an envelope. The envelope printing feature uses the address from a document to print an envelope, with or without a return address. The envelope can be printed separately or attached to the document with which it is associated. This feature is covered in the first section of this chapter.

Form letters broadcast information yet add a personal touch to your work. You may produce only a few form letters each day, but they still can automate repetitive parts of your business and give you time to improve the creative end of your work. You also can generate invoices, appointment reminders, and so on. This chapter is challenging, but working through it will pay great dividends.

You can create two types of form letters with Word for Windows: those that are filled in manually and those that are filled in from computer-generated lists. In this chapter, you learn to create an automated form letter that prompts you for information the document needs in creating an invoice. You learn also how to fill in the blanks in a form letter by merging a mailing list

In this chapter, you learn to do the following:

■ Print envelopes and include their bar code or FIM code

■ Use the Mail Merge helper to create a main document, a data source, and control the merging of data into documents

■ Do mail merge with special documents such as letter-head, envelopes, and mailing labels

■ Insert field codes that prompt you to enter a personal note in each mail merge document

with the main document. Finally, you learn Word for Windows' advanced techniques for document automation, including a form letter that combines manual fill-in with merging of information.

Printing an Envelope

Word for Windows offers an easy and quick solution to a frequent word processing problem: printing envelopes. Word for Windows can print envelopes by themselves, attached to a document, or as part of a mass mailing.

To test the envelope feature, create a short letter like the one shown in fig. 15.1.

To create an envelope, follow these steps:

1. Select the address in the letter.

   If the address is a contiguous block of three to five short lines near the beginning of the letter, you do not have to select it. Word for Windows automatically finds the address.

2. Choose the Tools Envelopes and Labels command. Word displays the Envelopes and Labels dialog box (see fig. 15.2).

3. Select the Envelopes tab if it is not already active.

4. If necessary, edit the Delivery Address information. To insert line feeds (line breaks without a carriage return), press Shift+Enter.

5. If necessary, edit the Return Address information. If you do not want to print the return address (you may be working with preprinted envelopes, for example), select the Omit check box.

6. If you need to select an envelope size, choose the Options button to display the Envelopes options dialog box (see fig. 15.3); then select from the Envelope Size list.

   The Delivery Address and Return Address options enable you to customize the fonts and positions of the addresses. You learn about the postal mailing options later in this section.

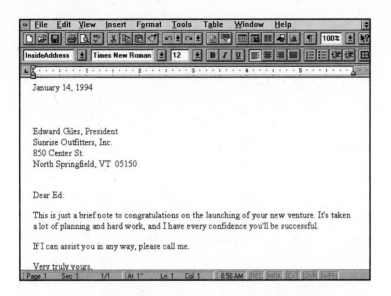

Fig. 15.1
A sample business letter.

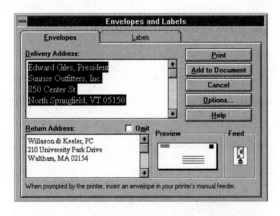

Fig. 15.2
Word will find the address in most letters and automatically display it in the Envelopes and Labels dialog box.

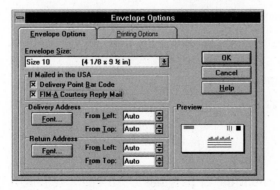

Fig. 15.3
Choose the Options button in the Envelopes and Labels dialog box to display the Envelope Options dialog box.

When you're done with your selections, choose OK.

III

Creating Special Documents

7. If necessary, load envelope(s) into your printer's feeder as indicated in the Feed box in the Envelopes and Labels dialog box.

8. Choose the Print button to print an envelope immediately.

or

Choose the Add to Document button to add the envelope as a landscape-oriented section before the first page of your document (see fig. 15.4).

Fig. 15.4
The Add to Document button inserts a landscape envelope before the first page of your document.

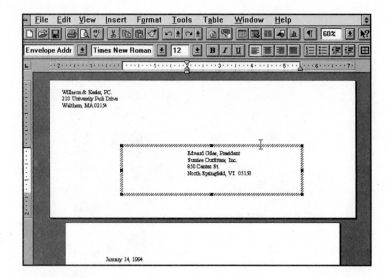

You can change the default Return Address information. Choose the Tools Options command and then select the User Info Category. In the Mailing Address text box, add or edit the return address. This becomes the default return address until you change it.

When you choose the Print button, most laser printers immediately print the envelope from the envelope bin. If you do not have an envelope feeder or envelope bin, insert the envelope, narrow side in, in the formfeed guides on top of the primary paper tray. The envelope prints first, then the document.

To reposition the Delivery Address block, change to page layout view and move the mouse pointer to the striped border until a four-headed arrow appears. When a four-headed arrow appears near the mouse pointer, drag the entire box containing the Delivery Address to a new position (see fig. 15.5).

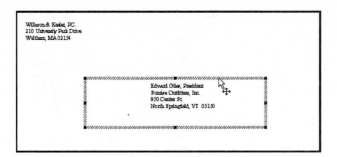

Fig. 15.5
You can drag the
address block to a
new position in
the envelope
section.

If you have trouble printing an envelope, with the envelope layout or with
envelope and paper feeding, examine the printer driver. Use the File Printer
Setup command and the Windows Control Panel. Check with your printer
manufacturer or Microsoft Corporation for a more current version of the
Windows printer driver program.

Printing an Envelope with Bar Codes or FIM Codes

Word for Windows provides a way to print machine-readable codes on envelopes so that the U.S. Postal Service can process the envelopes by machine, as
long as they are sent to addresses within the U.S., saving time and money.

You can print POSTNET codes (bar code equivalents of U.S. ZIP codes) and
Facing Identification Marks, or FIMs (vertical lines that indicate the address
side of the envelope).

To print POSTNET bar codes and Facing Identification Marks on envelope(s)
attached to the current document, follow these steps:

1. Choose the Tools Envelopes and Labels command.

2. In the Envelopes tab of the Envelopes and Labels dialog box, choose the
   Options button. Word displays the Envelope Options dialog box (see
   fig. 15.6).

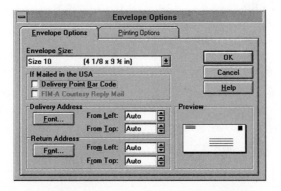

Fig. 15.6
Set envelope
printing options
in the Envelope
Options dialog
box.

III

Creating Special Documents

3. Select the Delivery Point Bar Code check box to print POSTNET bar codes.

4. Select the FIM-A Courtesy Reply Mail check box to print Facing Identification Marks.

5. Choose OK.

Customizing Envelopes with Text and Graphics

You can easily add a graphic, such as a company logo, to your envelopes, whether the graphic consists of formatted text or actual graphics.

To set up envelopes to print your logo, follow these steps:

1. Enter your logo text and/or graphics in a document.

2. Put the logo in a frame.

3. Choose the Edit Autotext command.

4. Add the logo under the name EnvelopeExtra.

5. Choose OK.

Merging Mailing Lists and Documents

One of the most powerful and timesaving features available in any word processor is mail merge. Mail merge enables you to create multiple letters or envelopes by merging together a list of names and addresses with letters, envelopes, or address labels. Mail merge can also be used for such tasks as filling in administrative forms and creating invoices from accounting files. Whenever you keep a list or get a list from other programs and you need to put information into a Word for Windows document, you should be thinking about mail merge.

The time you save by using mail merge can be tremendous. Instead of typing or modifying tens or hundreds of documents, Word can make all the documents for you. All you need to do is keep your list (names, addresses, and so on) up-to-date and create a form letter in which the data will be inserted. In fact, you can even make each document pause during mail merge so that you can enter personalized information.

What You Need to Know About Mail Merge

You need two documents to create form letters or mailing labels. One document, called the *data source*, contains a precisely laid-out set of data, such as names and addresses. The other document, the *main document*, acts as a form that receives the data. Most forms that receive data are form letters or multicolumn tables for mailing labels.

Although most people would use the term *form letter* to describe a Word main document, a main document can take the form of a mailing list, catalog, mailing labels, or letters.

Main Documents and Data Sources. The main document is like a normal document except that it contains MERGEFIELD field codes that specify where merged data will appear. In a typical form letter, for example, the main document is a form letter that needs names and addresses inserted, and the data source is a list of names and addresses.

The data source document must be organized in a very specific way, or the merge process will generate errors. The first row of the data source must be one row of names. Below the row of names are rows of data. Each row of data is a *record*, and each piece of data in the row, such as a last name, is a *field*. The row of names in the first row of the documents is the *header record*. Each name in the first row is a *field name*. Each field can be referenced by the name for that field in the heading. Chapter 14, "Managing Mail Merge Data," goes into detail on how to create and maintain a data source.

When you merge the documents, Word replaces the merge fields with the appropriate text from the data source. At merge time, you can choose to display the result as a new document on-screen or to print it directly to the current printer.

Using Word's Mail Merge Helper. Word for Windows Mail Merge Helper guides you through the three stages of creating a form letter, catalog, or other merged document:

1. Creating or identifying the main document

2. Creating or identifying the data source

3. Merging the data source and main document

III

Creating Special Documents

To start the Mail Merge Helper, follow these steps:

1. If you want to use an existing document as the main document, open that document. Otherwise, create a new document.

2. Choose the Tools Mail Merge command.

The Mail Merge Helper dialog box (see fig. 15.7) lays out the three stages in creating a merged document. Notice that the dialog box contains a lot of empty space; this space will fill up with useful information about the merge documents as you proceed.

The following parts of this section describe how to proceed through the three stages of creating mail merge documents. The Mail Merge Helper is used to centrally coordinate the mail merge documents and the final merging of main document and data source. When you choose a button in the Mail Merge Helper, you are presented with a series of windows that guide you through the stage corresponding to the button.

Understanding Word's "Decision" Dialog Boxes. The Mail Merge Helper is designed to be flexible; you can start setting up to merge at virtually any stage in the document-creation process. At appropriate points, Word requires you to make decisions or reminds you to go back and complete all necessary steps in creating a merged document.

You'll see many dialog boxes resembling the one in fig. 15.8. Although this box does not have a name, you might think of it as the "decision" dialog box.

Sometimes the decision box offers a choice between creating a new document or changing the type of the active document. Consider carefully before changing the document type; generally, you'll want to preserve the existing document in its current form.

If you fail to complete a required portion of one of the three stages in the merge process, you'll see a dialog box like the one shown in fig. 15.9. This type of dialog box essentially forces you to add detail to incomplete documents before going through with the merge. You see this dialog box only if the Mail Merge Helper detects that you have missed a step or incorrectly entered a response.

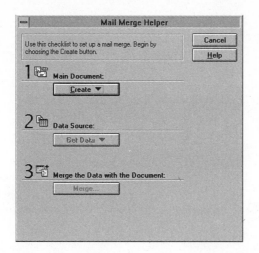

Fig. 15.7
The Mail Merge Helper dialog box is "home base" as you complete the three stages of form-letter production.

Fig. 15.8
At many different points in the merge process, Word asks whether you want to create a new, blank document or use an existing one.

Fig. 15.9
Word's Mail Merge Helper forces you to create complete documents before it will let you begin merging.

Specifying a Main Document

You can use any existing document as a main document. Simply open that document before starting the Mail Merge Helper. If you need to create the main document, however, you have the following options:

■ Use the document window that automatically opens when you start Word.

■ Choose the File New command and then follow these steps:

1. Make sure that the Document button in the New group is selected.

2. Select the template you want to use.

3. Choose OK.

It's not necessary to enter any text in the document right now; you can come back to that later.

To create a main document for a form letter, follow these steps:

1. Choose the Tools Mail Merge command.

2. Under the Main Document heading of the Mail Merge Helper dialog box, choose the Create button.

3. Choose Form Letters. Word displays a decision dialog box asking what you want to use to create the form letter.

4. Click the Active Window button to use the active document as the main document. Click the New Main Document button to open a new document, which uses the Normal document template.

Word brings you back to the Mail Merge Helper dialog box, which now displays the type of merge and the name and path of the main document under the Main Document heading.

This process illustrates the Mail Merge Helper's flexibility; if you realize in Step 4 that you don't want to use the active document, you don't have to start over again.

Specifying a Data Source

Attaching the data source to the main document does three things: it shows Word the file name and path where the data will be located, it attaches a mail-merge bar with merge tools to the top of the main document, and it enables Word for Windows to read the field names used in the data source.

If you are unfamiliar with what a data source is or you need to create a data source, read Chapter 14, "Managing Mail Merge Data." This chapter goes into detail about creating a new list or database, or using existing data from Word or other applications.

If you do not yet have a source for the data that will be merged, you should read Chapter 14 and create a data source before proceeding. An overview of creating a new data source is presented in the next section, titled "Creating a New Data Source."

To specify an existing file as a data source, follow these steps:

1. Under the Data Source heading, click the Get Data button.

2. Choose Open Data Source. Word displays the Open Data Source dialog box, shown in fig. 15.10.

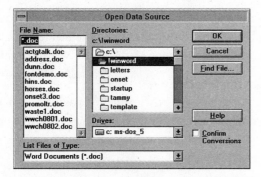

Fig. 15.10
Use the Open Data Source dialog to access a data source in Word or many other formats.

3. Select the data source from the File Name list. Word can read many different data source formats. Choose from the List Files of Type list to see other formats. Choose OK after selecting the file.

   or

   Choose the MS Query button if Microsoft Query is available on your computer. Use Microsoft Query to access specific data in a non-Word database.

Use Microsoft Query to retrieve data meeting specific criteria. The data may be on your computer, on a network, in a SQL Server, or many types of mainframe databases. Microsoft Query is available as a separate application and comes with Microsoft Excel 5.0.

Word automatically converts non-Word files for which it has converters. If you need to install a converter for a non-Word data source, such as Excel, Access, or dBASE, see Appendix B for information on installing converters.

III

Creating Special Documents

What happens next depends on whether your main document was complete when you started the merge process. If you have not yet inserted any merge fields in your main document, Word displays the dialog box shown in fig. 15.11.

Fig. 15.11
After attaching the
data source, the
Mail Merge Helper
detects that there
are no merge fields
in your main
document.

To go directly to the main document to add the merge fields, choose Edit Main Document. For instructions on inserting the merge fields in your main document, see the upcoming section, "Editing the Main Document."

Creating a New Data Source

If you did not have a data source that contained your lists of names or database of information to be merged, you will need to create one. Chapter 14 describes how to create a data source and how to manage existing data sources.

To create a new data source, follow these steps:

1. Under the Data Source heading in the Mail Merge Helper, choose the Get Data button.

   This button is available only if you attached a main document by choosing the Create button from the Main Document stage. If you want to create a data source and wait to create a main document, just attach a blank document as the main document.

2. Choose Create Data Source. Word displays the Create Data Source dialog box (see fig. 15.12).

   The Field Names in Header Row list box contains names traditionally used for fields in mailing lists. The names in the list box comprise a default list of field names.

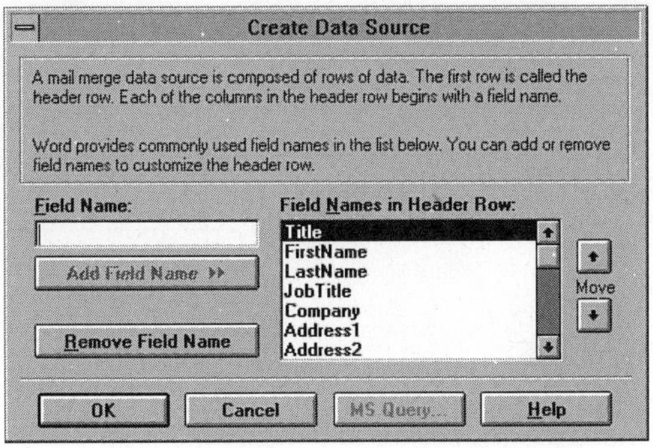

Fig. 15.12
The Create Data
Source dialog box
guides you
through creating
a data source. It
even presents the
most commonly
used headings for
mail merge data
sources.

3. Edit the list of names in the Field Names in Header Row list box, as
    described here:

    If you see any field names you won't use in your main document, select
    the name from the Field Names in Header Row, then choose the Re-
    move Field Name button. Word removes the name from the list.

    To add a field name, type it in the Field Name box and then choose
    Add Field Name.

    When you are satisfied with your list, choose OK.

    To change the sequence of names (reposition them), select a field name
    and then click the up or down arrow labeled Move. The top-to-bottom
    sequence you see in this list box determines the right-to-left sequence
    of the fields in the data source.

4. Word displays the Save Data Source dialog box. In the File Name box,
    enter a name for the data source document and choose OK.

5. Word displays a decision dialog box asking what you want to do next.
    To enter data in the data source, choose the Edit Data Source button. To
    edit the Main document so that you can insert the merge fields to cre-
    ate a main document, choose the Edit Main document button.

If you choose Edit Main document, Word displays the main document as a
normal Word document, with one exception: the Mail Merge toolbar is now
displayed below the toolbar(s) and above the ruler (see fig. 15.13). With the
main document on-screen, you can create a main document in which the
data will be inserted.

Fig. 15.13

When you choose the Edit Main Document button after using the Mail Merge Helper, Word displays the document and adds a Mail Merge toolbar.

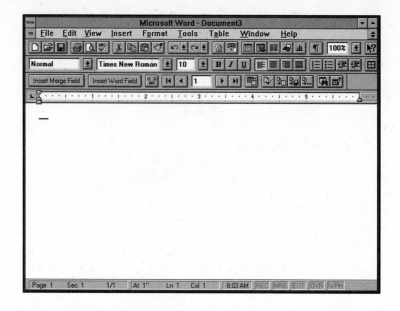

Editing the Main Document

After the data source is attached to the main document, you can edit the document by using normal typing and formatting features. Whether you start with an existing document containing body copy or a new blank document, you must enter MERGEFIELD codes to tell Word where to insert specific data from the data source. Once the data source is attached, you can use the Insert Merge Field button in the Mail Merge toolbar to insert these codes.

To insert merge fields in the main document, follow these steps:

1. Move the insertion point to where you want the first merged data to appear.

Insert Merge Field

2. Choose the Insert Merge Field button from the Mail Merge toolbar that appears under the formatting toolbar. This displays a list of the fields in your data source.

3. Select the field name from the Print Merge Fields list.

4. Choose OK or press Enter.

5. Move the insertion point to the next location where you want data inserted. Make sure to leave a space before or after the merge field just as you would leave a space before or after a word you type.

6. Continue inserting all the merge fields necessary for the form letter in this manner. Don't forget, however, to insert needed text—for example, spaces between merge fields for city, state, and ZIP code.

To add ordinary word fields, such as Date, to main documents, you can choose the Insert Field command. You can insert certain Word fields—such as Ask, Fill-in, and Next Record—by clicking the Insert Word Field button and selecting the field from the drop-down list. You learn how to do this later in the chapter.

You can delete unwanted fields from main documents in the same way you delete text in any other Word document.

You can get a sneak preview of the merged document by clicking the View Merged Data button in the Mail Merge toolbar. With View Merged Data off, your completed main document resembles the document at the top in fig. 15.14. After you click the View Merged Data button, the document appears as shown at the bottom of that figure.

By default, the main document displays the data from the first record in the data source. You can use the VCR-type control icons in the Mail Merge toolbar to browse through the entire merged document. The controls work in an intuitive manner.

Fig. 15.14 shows documents with the Field Codes option in the View tab of the Options dialog box turned off. When field codes are displayed, the document looks like that in fig. 15.15.

Checking for Errors. Browsing through the merged document is helpful in spotting problems with the merge, but when the data source contains a large number of records, you might want a higher level of assurance. You can check the entire data source for errors by clicking an error-checking button in the Mail Merge toolbar.

When you click the Check Errors button, Word for Windows reads your data source and checks for errors, such as field names that do not meet the rules for bookmarks. Word checks also to ensure that the number of field names and the number of fields in each record (row) are the same. You are also warned if the data source cannot be found or if it contains blank records.

Fig. 15.14

When the document displays the field names (top), click the View Merged Data button to display the data merged from the data source (bottom).

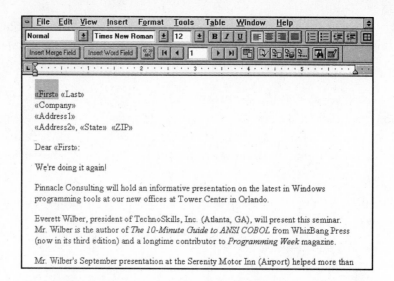

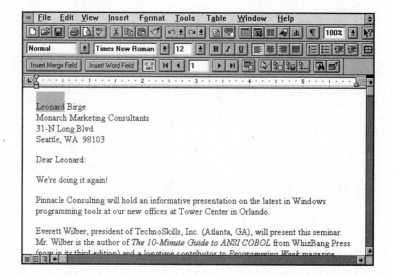

To check the main document and data source for errors, follow these steps:

1. Click the Check Errors button in the Mail Merge toolbar. The Checking and Reporting Errors dialog box appears (see fig. 15.16).

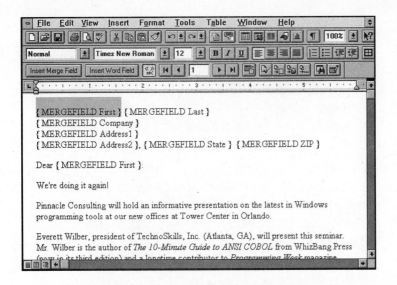

Fig. 15.15
When the Field
Codes option in
the View tab of the
Options dialog box
is turned on, the
document shows
the MERGEFIELD
field codes.

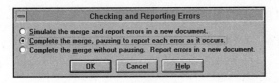

Fig. 15.16
Test your main
document and
data source with
the Check Errors
button before
starting a long
mail merge.

2. Select the error-reporting option you want. The first option simulates
the merge, and the second and third complete it; the second option
displays messages as errors occur, and the third option puts them in a
new document. If you expect some errors, consider simulating the
merge first.

3. Word next displays a dialog box. If you choose to report errors as they
occur, the first dialog box displayed might contain an error message,
like the one in fig. 15.17. Otherwise, Word displays a dialog box indicating that the operation has been completed. In any case, choose OK
to clear the dialog box (or boxes) and proceed accordingly.

III

Creating Special Documents

Fig. 15.17
This error message
appears when
Word cannot find
a field name in the
data source that
corresponds to a
merge field in the
main document.
Choose the Help
button for more
information
specific to the
problem.

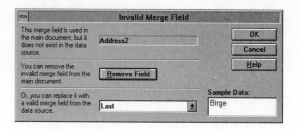

The Invalid Merge Field dialog box assists you in correcting the problem in
the merge document. Choose the Remove Field button to remove the offending field from the main document. If the field mismatch is the result of a
typographical error in the main document, you can correct it by selecting the
valid field name from the list box at the bottom of the dialog box. When you
select a field name from this list, the corresponding value from the data
source is displayed in the Sample Data box.

The following guidelines can prevent errors that commonly cause problems:

- Field names must not have spaces. Use an underscore rather than a
  space.

- Field names must not start with a number but can have a number in
  them.

- Field names must be in one row at the top of the data source.

- Field names must be unique (no duplicates).

- Each field (column) of data must have a field name.

- The number of fields in each record must match the number of field
  names.

Note

If the records in the data source are not in a table and if commas, tabs, or cells are
missing, the number of fields in a record may not match the number of fields in the
heading.

Changing the Data Source Your Main Document Is Attached to. You may have one form letter that you use with different mailing lists. In that case, you will want to attach your main document to other data sources. You use the same procedure as for attaching the original data source.

To attach a main document to a different data source, follow these steps:

1. Choose the Tools Mail Merge command.

2. Click the Get Data button.

3. If the data source is to be an existing file, choose Open Data Source. To create a new data source, choose Create Data Source.

4. Select or create the data source file, as appropriate.

Caution

Quite often, field headers in the new data source do not match the field codes in the main document. It's a good idea to check for errors immediately after you attach a main document to a new data source.

Creating a Data Source Document

The first row in the data source must contain the field names. Only one row of field names can be at the top of the data source. Field names cannot contain blanks because Word for Windows uses the names as bookmarks. Do not start a field name with a number (although a number can be in the field name). If you need to use a two-part field name, use an underscore rather than a space. Each field name must be unique.

See Chapter 14, "Managing Mail Merge Data," for more information about creating and using data sources in Word documents or in other application programs.

Quickly Merging to Printer or Document

When you are satisfied with your main document, you can merge it with the data by choosing one of three merge buttons in the Mail Merge toolbar. Table 15.1 shows how these buttons work.

III

Creating Special Documents

Table 15.1 Effects of Merge Buttons in the Mail Merge toolbar	
Button	**Effect**
	Creates the merged document and places it in a new Word document
	Creates the merged document and prints it on the currently selected printer
	Displays the Merge dialog box, which provides a wide range of options for record selection and other operations (see the next section for details)

Fig. 15.18 shows the merged document. The Form Letters1 document contains the full text of the merged document, with each of the individually addressed letters contained in a section. This document contains no field codes; you can treat it as you would any typed document. Each section break (represented by a double dashed line) starts a new page, so printing the document produces individual letters. Naturally, if you want to make changes to individual letters, you can edit them in the usual manner.

Fig. 15.18
Merging a form letter to a document can create a long document containing all the individual letters.

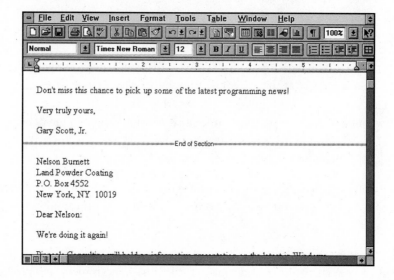

If you merge a large number of records, merge to the printer so that you do not exceed memory limits. You may want to merge a few records to a new document before printing. This enables you to see whether the merge is working correctly.

Controlling the Merge Process

Often you will not want to merge an entire data source into a letter. You may want to do 20 letters at a time, or limit the merged data to specific ZIP codes or job titles. Or you may want to merge one or two letters as a text before running a large merge job.

To control the data that's merged into your main document, follow these steps:

1. Prepare your data source and save it.

2. Open your main document. When it opens, the Mail Merge toolbar also appears.

    If Word cannot find the data source for the main document, it displays a dialog box that you can use to open the correct data source.

3. Choose the Tools Mail Merge command to display the Mail Merge Helper as shown in fig. 15.19.

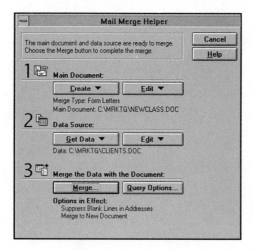

Fig. 15.19
A Mail Merge Helper that is ready to merge data shows both main document and data source types and locations.

In fig. 15.19 you can see that a Mail Merge Helper that is properly completed displays the type of main document and where it is located, as well as the data source for that main document and where the data source is located.

4. Choose the Merge button to begin the merge process. The Merge dialog box shown in fig. 15.20 displays.

Fig. 15.20

Select from the Merge dialog box how you want the merge to be performed.

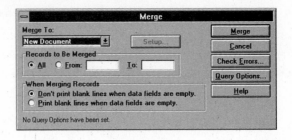

5. Select the Merge To list and select one of the following types of merges:

Merge to Printer	Produces a printed result
Merge to New Document	Produces a new document containing all resulting merged documents
Only Check for Errors	Checks the headings but does not merge

6. Select the number of records to be merged from the Records to Be Merged group:

All	Merges all records
From/To	Limits the range of data according to the record (row) numbers in the data source

7. Select from the When Merging Records group how blank lines will be handled:

    Don't print blank lines when data fields are empty.

    Print blank lines when data fields are empty.

8. Choose OK.

Selecting Specific Records to Merge

Word for Windows enables you to select which records you want to merge. You can build *rules* that limit which data is merged. The rules form English statements specifying the data you want to merge. You can use this feature if you are doing a targeted mailing to a particular area (selected by ZIP code). For example, the statement *Lastname is equal to Smith* merges only those records in which the name *Smith* appears in the Lastname field.

To select specific records for merging, follow these steps:

1. Activate the main document.

2. Choose the Merge dialog box button from the Mail Merge toolbar or choose the Tools Mail Merge command. Choose the **Merge** button to display the Merge dialog box shown in fig. 15.20.

3. From the Merge dialog box, choose the **Query Options** button to display the Query Options list shown in fig. 15.21.

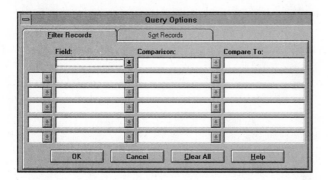

Fig. 15.21
The Query Options dialog box provides control over selection of records.

4. Select from the Field drop-down list the first field you want to limit.

5. The phrase Equal to appears in the Comparison list. If you want something other than an exact match, select the type of comparison (such as Less than or Greater than) you want to make.

6. In the Compare To text box, type the numeric value or text you want compared to the field. Fig. 15.22 shows an example that merges only those records in which the last name begins with a *P* or a letter following *P* in the alphabet.

7. After you make an entry in the Compare To box, the word And appears in the leftmost box in the next row. Select the And or Or option in this box to add another selection rule. If you want to merge only those records that meet both conditions, select And. To merge all records that meet either condition, select Or.

8. To add another rule, repeat steps 4-7.

9. To sort the resulting merged records on any of the selected fields, select the Sort Records tab (see fig. 15.23). You can sort by up to three key fields. Select (or enter) the name of the primary sort field in the Sort By drop-down list box. Enter secondary or tertiary keys, if used, in the Then By and Then **By** boxes, respectively. You can select the sort order with the option buttons to the right of the list boxes.

III

Creating Special Documents

Fig. 15.22
To select an alphabetic or numeric range of records, enter the field name, comparison phrase, and comparison value. This rule merges records with last names beginning with *P* through *Z*.

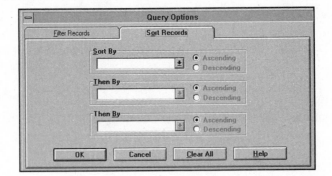

Fig. 15.23
Select the Sort Records tab to sort records in a merged document.

10. Complete the merge by choosing OK. When the merge is complete, choose Cancel from the Mail Merge Helper.

If you make a mistake, you can revise any entry or selection at any time. To start over again, click the Clear All button in the Filter Records tab of the Query Options dialog box.

When you build rules, a complete English statement is built that specifies how data from the data source is selected for merging. Fig. 15.24, for example, illustrates a rule that would be useful for mailing to a list of contributors. If the data source contains fields for amount pledged (Pledged) and amount contributed (Paid), this rule selects everyone who pledged $200 or more and paid less than $50.

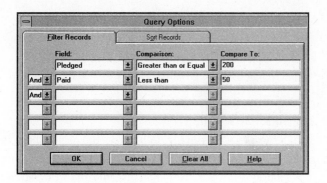

Fig. 15.24
A completed dialog box to select donors who have yet to fulfill their pledges.

Here are some tips for building rules:

- Text is compared in the same way as numbers. For example, B is less than C.

- Select ranges using And. A numeric range, for example, may be as follows:

  ZIP is Greater than 95400

  And

  ZIP is Less than 95600

  A text range may be as follows:

  State is Greater than or Equal to CA

  And

  State is Less than or Equal to NY

- Select individual names or numbers with Or. A numeric selection, for example, may be as follows:

  ZIP is Equal to 95409

  Or

  ZIP is Equal to 95412

  A text selection may be as follows:

  Title is Equal to President

  Or

  Title is Equal to Manager

III

Creating Special Documents

To personally select which records merge, create an extra field (column) with a field name such as Selection in your data document. In that column, enter a **1** in the row of each record you want to merge. Use the Record Selection dialog box to specify that you want only records with a 1 in the Selection field to merge.

Using Letterhead While Merging

The first page of a form letter is usually on letterhead paper and needs a different top margin from that of the following pages. To compensate for the difference in top margins in your normal documents and form letters, use a different header for the first page.

To create a first-page only header on the active document, follow these steps:

1. Choose the View Header/Footer command.

2. Click the Page Setup button in the Header and Footer toolbar to display the Page Setup dialog box.

3. Select the Layout tab if it is not already selected.

4. Select the Different First Page check box.

5. Choose OK.

In the header-editing box that appears at the top of the document, enter the letterhead text. This header is for the first page; the following pages will begin body copy underneath the top margin set by the document format.

If your printer has double paper bins, like the HP LaserJet Series IIID, IIISi, and 4Si, you can pull letterhead paper from the letterhead bin. If your printer has only one bin, you can stack alternating letterhead and bond in the tray, or feed letterhead into the manual feed tray. If you push the letterhead far enough into the manual feed at the appropriate time, the LaserJet pulls from the manual feed before pulling from the bin. (The HP LaserJet accepts paper from the manual feed before pulling from the bin if the printer has the default menu settings.)

Merging Envelopes

With the Mail Merge Helper, you can create mail-merge envelopes or a document that merges mail-merge envelopes and documents at the same time.

To create mail-merge envelopes, create a data source and main document, as for the mail-merge form letter described in the section "Creating a Form Letter" earlier in this chapter. Attach the data source to the main document. Be sure that the top of the main document contains a 3-to-5-line address composed of MERGEFIELD codes. If you are not mailing a main document, create a blank letter with the MERGEFIELD codes in an address block. The automatic envelope maker uses this document as a basis for its MERGEFIELD address information.

To set up for making a mass-mailing envelope based on your main document, follow these steps:

1. Activate the main document.

2. Choose the Tools Mail Merge command. (If the Mail Merge toolbar is displayed, you can click the Mail Merge Helper dialog box button.)

3. Under the Main Document heading of the Mail Merge Helper dialog box, click the Create button.

4. Select Envelopes from the drop-down list.

5. Word displays a decision dialog box. The options offered depend on the condition of the active document when you began the procedure. Click Active Window if it appears in the dialog box. Otherwise, click New Main Document.

   Word displays the Mail Merge Helper dialog box (see fig. 15.25). The information under Main Document reflects the merge type (Envelopes) and new document name.

To finish creating the mass-mailing envelope, follow these steps:

1. Under Data Source, click the Get Data button.

2. Click Open Data Source.

3. Select the data source from the File Name list, then choose OK. If necessary, browse through the directories in the usual manner. Word then displays the dialog box shown in fig. 15.26.

Fig. 15.25
The Mail Merge
Helper dialog box
changes to reflect
the fact that
you're creating a
new main
document.

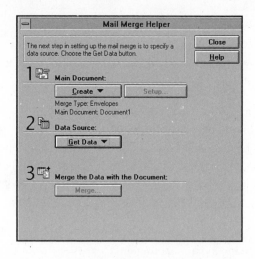

Fig. 15.26
Word displays this
dialog when it
needs to set up
your main
document.

4. Click Set Up Main Document.

5. In the Envelope Options dialog box, change any settings in the Envelope Options and Printing Options tabs and then choose OK. Word displays the Envelope Address dialog box (see fig. 15.27).

Fig. 15.27
Use the Envelope
Address dialog box
to insert the field
codes that will
insert data into
the address area of
an envelope.

6. Insert the merge fields for names and addresses, adding any necessary spaces and punctuation. You select these fields in the same way as when you created the form letter earlier in this chapter—by clicking the Insert Merge Field button and selecting the field names from the drop-down list.

   You can click the Insert Postal **Bar** Code button to print POSTNET codes on the envelopes. A dialog box prompts you for the name of the field containing the postal code.

   When you are done entering fields, choose OK. Word brings back the Mail Merge Helper dialog box.

7. In the Mail Merge Helper, click the Merge button. Your document will look something like that in fig. 15.28.

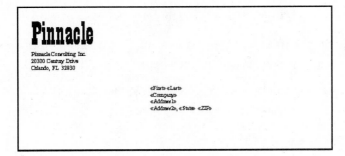

Fig. 15.28
You can create envelopes for mass mailings that use the merge fields you created for the related form-letter document. The envelopes also include graphics and logos.

The envelope is now a new document, separate and distinct from the main document. You should save the envelope main document for later use.

You might well ask why Steps 5-7 were necessary; that is, why doesn't Version 6 of Word for Windows assume that you want to attach the envelope main document to the same data source that's attached to the form letter (as did Version 2)? Actually, it's because your envelope main document will rarely change—unless you change envelope sizes. By contrast, it's quite possible that you will generate a variety of form letters, which will be saved under different document names. By forcing you to create a "stand-alone" envelope, Word 6 relieves you from having to go through the many steps just described for each envelope you create.

Word for Windows no longer provides concurrent form letter and envelope printing.

III

Creating Special Documents

Creating Mailing Labels

If you are sending many documents, mailing labels can save a great deal of time. With Word for Windows, you can easily update your mailing lists and print labels on demand.

You can design a form that prints multiple labels on a page in much the same way you create a form letter. If you've designed main documents for mailing labels in a previous version of Word for Windows, you can continue to use those documents to print mailing labels. But if you need to create a new label form, it's quite easy in Version 6 of Word.

Creating a Mailing-Label Main Document. The Labels tab of the Envelopes and Labels dialog box automates the process of creating mailing labels. For the example provided here, it is assumed that have already created a form-letter main document.

To create mailing labels for an existing form letter, follow these steps:

1. Choose the Tools Mail Merge command. (You do not need to activate the main document for the form letter.)

2. Under the Main Document heading of the Mail Merge Helper dialog box, click the Create button.

3. Choose Mailing Labels.

4. In the decision dialog box, click Active Window if it appears in the dialog box. Otherwise, click New Main Document.

5. Under the Data Source heading, click the Get Data button.

6. Choose Open Data Source. Word displays the Open Data Source dialog box.

7. Select the appropriate data source from the list, browsing through the directories as needed.

8. If Word displays a dialog box, click Set Up Main Document.

9. Word displays the Label Options dialog box. Selecting a label format is explained in the next section.

Specifying Label Size and Type. Word now displays the Label Options dialog box (see fig. 15.29). You'll probably be able to select from this dialog box the label format you want; the dialog box contains specifications for dozens of commercial preprinted label products.

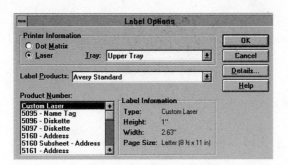

Fig. 15.29
Select a label
format from the
Label Options
dialog box.

To specify the type and size of your mailing labels, follow these steps:

1. In the Label Options dialog box, select the appropriate label group from the Label **P**roducts drop-down list:

Avery Standard	Avery U.S. products
Avery Pan European	Avery European products
Other	Products from other manufacturers

2. Select your type of label from the Product **N**umber list. If you are not using labels from any of the commercial products available in this dialog box, use the product number for the same size label. If none of the label formats produce the result you want, you will have to edit the label specifications, as explained in "Creating Custom Mailing Labels," a later part of this section.

3. If you're not sure which label type is correct, use the arrow keys to browse through the list so that you can view in the Label Information box the label and page dimensions for each type.

4. If you want to view more details about the selected label type, click the **D**etails button. Word displays a dialog box similar to the one in fig. 15.30. Choose OK to return to the Label Options dialog box. To learn how to create a custom mailing label size, see "Creating Custom Mailing Labels," a later part of this section.

5. When you are satisfied with all your selections, choose OK.

6. Word displays the Create Labels dialog box (see fig. 15.31). Insert the appropriate merge fields in the Sam**p**le Label box and choose OK. Word then displays the Mail Merge Helper.

Fig. 15.30
In this dialog box, you can preview any available label type and set custom sizes.

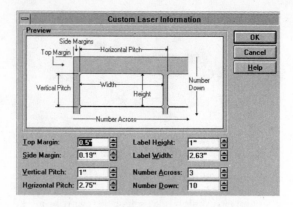

Fig. 15.31
Use the Create Labels dialog box to build a label by inserting merge field codes.

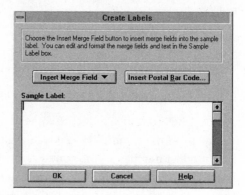

7. Click the **Merge** button to display the Merge dialog box.

8. Select the options you want and then proceed with error checking, query definition, and merging. When you are finished, click the **Merge** button.

Word creates a new document containing a table formatted for the type of labels you selected. You can merge the labels to a new document or print them in the usual manner.

Printing Labels for a Single Address. Naturally, not all your letters will be form letters. Through the Labels tab of the Envelopes and Labels dialog box, you can print a single mailing label or several labels containing the same address.

To print one or more mailing labels for a single document, follow these steps:

1. Activate the main document for the form letter.

2. Choose the Tools Envelopes and Labels command.

3. In the Envelopes and Labels dialog box, display the Labels tab.

4. Examine the fields displayed in the Address box for accuracy. Or, if you want to print return address labels, select Use Return Address.

5. If you want to print a single address label, select Single Label and specify the location of the label where you want to print. For single-wide, continuous-feed labels for dot-matrix printers, use the defaults (Row 1, Column 1). For labels on cut sheets for laser printers, you will usually have to specify the location of the next available blank label on the page, as shown in fig. 15.32.

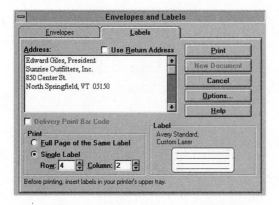

Fig. 15.32

In the Print area of the Envelopes and Labels dialog box, you can choose to print a single label. In this example, the address prints on the label in the second column of the fourth row of the label sheet.

6. If necessary, click the Options button and make changes in the Label Options dialog box. Then choose OK.

7. Make sure that the label paper is loaded in the printer; then click the Print button to print the labels.

Creating Custom Mailing Labels. You can design your own labels if you can't find the right size in the Label Options dialog box.

To change the label format to a nonstandard size when creating a mailing label document, follow these steps:

1. In the Label Options dialog box, select a label format similar to the format you want.

2. Click the Details button. Word displays the label preview dialog box.

The Preview window contains a representation of the current label format. In the bottom portion of the dialog box, enter your custom label specifications. (The annotations in the Preview window illustrate the effects of the specifications.) Enter a new value for any of the measurements (or change the amount by clicking the attached arrow buttons) and watch the Preview window reflect the change.

If you change the specifications in a way that makes it impossible to fit the specified number of labels on a page, Word displays a message.

3. When you are satisfied with all your selections, choose OK. Then click OK to confirm that you want to override the existing custom label specifications.

4. In the Label Options dialog box, Word updates the information in the Label Information box. Choose OK.

Word displays the Create Labels dialog box, where you can proceed with label creation, merging, and printing.

Caution

Do not use labels with adhesive backing designed for copiers in laser printers. Laser printers operate at high temperatures, which can melt and separate labels, creating a mess in your printer. Suppliers such as Avery have a complete line of labels of different sizes and shapes made especially for laser printers.

Making Mail Merge More Efficient

Having worked through all the basics of merging documents, you are now ready for a few of the most powerful features of Word for Windows 6. One of these features eliminates blank lines in mail-merge addresses and labels—a feature that gives you a more professional appearance. You also see how to use a main document with different data sources, without having to re-create field names. The secret is to use a header file that shows the field names. Another important topic is how to make merge documents pause and ask you for a customized entry. Finally, this section describes some of the databases you can use to manage large or complex Word for Windows mailing lists.

Quickly Inserting Word Fields in a Main Document. You can insert certain Word fields from the Mail Merge toolbar. Suppose that you want Word to insert one of two different personalized messages in your form letter, depending on whether a condition was satisfied.

To insert an IF field in a main document, follow these steps:

1. Click the Insert Word Field button to display a subset of Word fields.

2. Select If... Then... Else. Word displays the dialog box shown in fig. 15.33. Enter your comparison criteria and the two conditional texts you want in the letter; then choose OK.

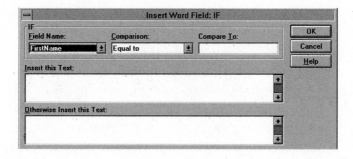

Fig. 15.33
Using the Insert Word Field button to insert an IF field displays a helpful dialog box.

If you then display field codes in the document (by choosing the Tools Options command and clicking Field Codes), the IF field will look something like the one in fig. 15.34.

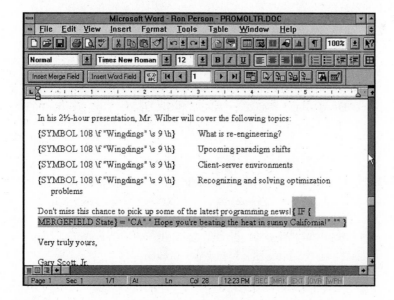

Fig. 15.34
The IF field shown in this letter will add a personal touch to recipients with a California address.

Suppressing Blank Lines in Addresses. Most business mailings include fields for information such as title, suite number, mail station, and so on. If some information is missing, however, blank lines can show up in your addresses or labels, producing an unfinished, unprofessional appearance. To ensure that blanks are skipped, after you choose the Merge button from the Mail Merge Helper the Merge dialog box appears. In this dialog box, make sure you select the Don't print blank lines when data fields are empty option. Blank lines involving a MERGEFIELD are skipped if they end with a paragraph mark (¶). Lines ending with a line feed (Shift+Enter) are not skipped.

Using One Main Document with Different Data Sources and Field Names. If you use a database program to maintain your mailing lists, you will appreciate this section. Your database program may generate data sources that do not have a *header record*, the top row that contains field names. Instead of opening what may be a huge data source and adding a top row of field names, you can attach a header file. This also enables you to use many data sources without having to change the MERGEFIELD in a main document. A *header file* contains a top row of field names, which are used with the data source. The header file can contain a single row of names or be an existing data source with the correct field names. The header file must have the same number of field names as there are fields in the data source.

To create a separate header file, follow these steps:

1. Be sure that the main document is the active document.

2. Choose the Tools Mail Merge command.

3. Click the Get Data button.

4. Select Header Options. Word displays the Header Options dialog box.

5. Choose Create. Word displays the Create Header Source dialog box (see fig. 15.35).

6. Edit the list of field names as you did earlier in the chapter when you created a data source. To remove the selected field name, click **Remove Field Name**. To add a field name, enter it in the **Field Name** box and click Add Field Name. When you are satisfied with your list, choose OK, The Save Data Source dialog box will appear.

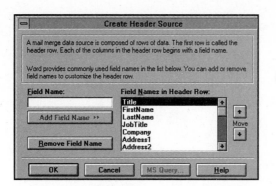

Fig. 15.35
The Create Header Source dialog box works much like the Create Data Source dialog box.

7. Enter a file name for the header source in the File Name box in the Save Data Source dialog box; then choose OK.

Word displays the Mail Merge Helper dialog box, updated for the new header source. The header source you created is attached immediately to the active main document. You still must attach a data source to the main document. The data source itself should not contain a header record because Word for Windows will merge the row of names as it would a data record.

To print with separate header and data sources, be sure that you attach the header and data sources in the Mail Merge Helper dialog box before you choose the Merge button.

Requesting User Input During a Mail Merge. Word for Windows can automate and personalize your written communication at the same time, but for truly personal form letters, you can put FILLIN fields in form letters so that you can type custom phrases into each mail-merge letter.

FILLIN is a Word field (as opposed to merge fields) that can automate document creation. You learn about fields in depth in Chapter 37, "Automating with Field Codes." The following example illustrates how Word fields can be useful in form letters.

Fig. 15.36 shows a main document with a FILLIN field in the second paragraph of the body text. During the merge operation, this field displays a dialog box that prompts the user to enter a personalized message to the recipient. The \d switch and the text that follows tell Word for Windows to display Go Blue against the Wildcats in the Silicon Bowl! as a default response.

III

Creating Special Documents

Fig. 15.36

Use the FILLIN field when you want to prompt the user to type information in merged letters.

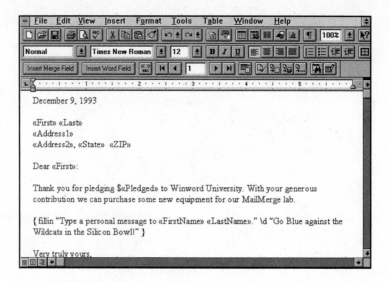

To enter the FILLIN field in your document, insert or type the following field code where you want the results to appear:

{fillin \d "Go Blue against the Wildcats in the Silicon Bowl!" }

Naturally, you can type the FILLIN field code in the document (remember to press Ctrl+F9 to create the field characters {}), or you can insert it with the Insert Field command.

To personalize the letter, you need to know to whom you are sending it. To display in the fill-in dialog box the name of the person being addressed, type a prompt in quotes; then in the quotes, use the Insert Merge Field button to insert a MERGEFIELD of the person's name. The field should look like the following:

{fillin "Type a personal message to
 {mergefield Firstname} {mergefield Lastname}" \d "Go
 Blue against the Wildcats in the Silicon Bowl!" }

Notice that the MERGEFIELD code is inside the quotes that enclose the prompt. For more information on using prompts and defaults in FILLIN fields, see Chapter 37, "Automating with Field Codes."

From Here...

For more information relating to the printing of form letters, labels, and envelopes, review the following chapters of this book:

■ Chapter 14, "Managing Mail Merge Data," describes the creation and management of data sources in greater detail.

■ Chapter 18, "Building Forms and Fill-In Dialog Boxes," shows how to create form documents.

■ Chapter 37, "Automating with Field Codes," covers entering and editing fields; and using computational fields to calculate amounts in a table to create invoices, statements, or other documents containing computed numbers.

III

Creating Special Documents

Part IV

Mastering Special Features

16   Creating and Editing Tables

17   Creating Bulleted or Numbered Lists

18   Building Forms and Fill-In Dialog Boxes

19   Organizing Content with an Outline

20   Calculating Math with Formulas

21   Displaying Formulas and Equations

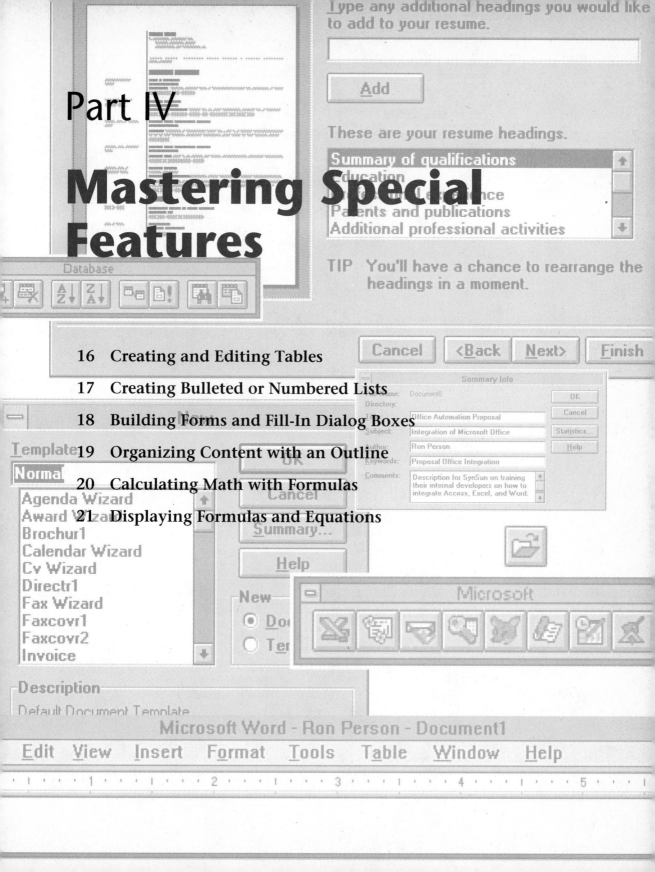

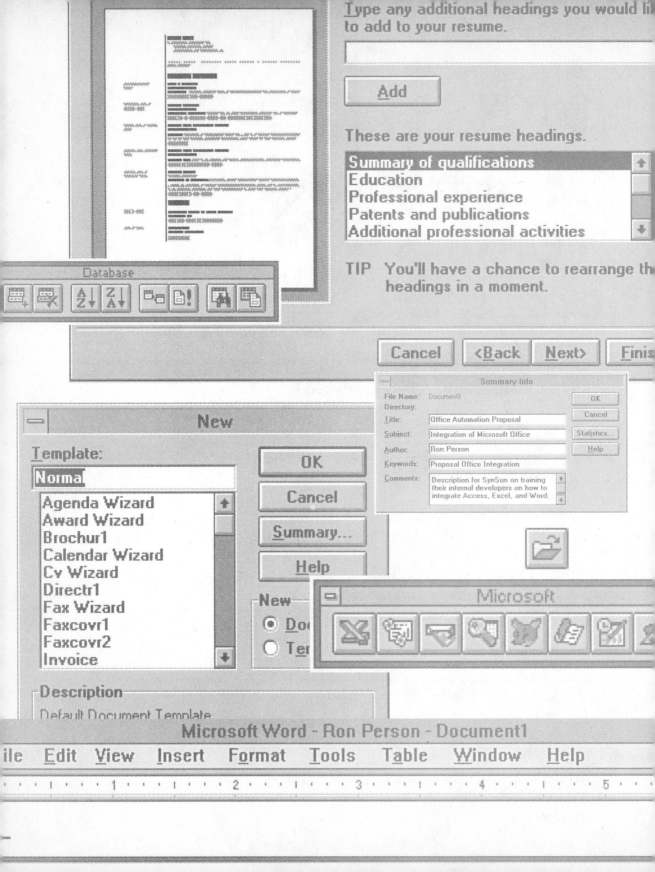

Type any additional headings you would like to add to your resume.

Add

These are your resume headings.

Summary of qualifications
Education
Professional experience
Patents and publications
Additional professional activities

TIP You'll have a chance to rearrange the headings in a moment.

Cancel   <Back   Next>   Finis

Database

Summary Info

File Name: Document8
Directory:
Title: Office Automation Proposal
Subject: Integration of Microsoft Office
Author: Ron Person
Keywords: Proposal Office Integration
Comments: Description for SynSun on training
            their internal developers on how to
            integrate Access, Excel, and Word.

OK
Cancel
Statistics...
Help

New

Template:

Normal

Agenda Wizard
Award Wizard
Brochur1
Calendar Wizard
Cv Wizard
Directr1
Fax Wizard
Faxcovr1
Faxcovr2
Invoice

OK
Cancel
Summary...
Help

New
● Do
○ Te

Microsoft

Description

Default Document Template

Microsoft Word - Ron Person - Document1

ile   Edit   View   Insert   Format   Tools   Table   Window   Help

Chapter 16

Creating and Editing Tables

Word for Windows has a very powerful tables feature that provides an excellent way of working with columns or tabular data and for simplifying many other tasks. You can use tables to show lists of data, personal rosters, financial information like that shown in fig. 16.1, scripts, and procedural steps. Tables can even include pasted illustrations that explain steps in a list. Fig. 16.1 shows an example of a table of data that was created and formatted by using tables. The commands available for working with tables simplify the job of arranging and formatting tables of information. You also can use tables to display side-by-side text and graphics. You can, for example, present sideheads next to text in a document (see fig. 16.2). In many cases, tables provide an easier and more flexible solution to problems you may have used tabs to solve in the past. In this chapter you learn how to create, edit, and format a table.

Following are some of the procedures you learn in this chapter:

■ Creating a table

■ Editing a table

■ Formatting a table

■ Sorting and numbering tables

■ Performing calculations in a table

What You Need to Know About Tables

If you have worked with a spreadsheet application, such as Microsoft Excel or Lotus 1-2-3, you may find working with tables similar to working with a spreadsheet. A *table* is simply a grid of columns and rows. The intersection of a column and a row is a rectangular box referred to as a *cell*. Each cell is independent and can be sized or formatted.

You can insert text, numbers, pictures, or formulas in a cell. If you enter text in a cell, the text wraps to the next line according to the width of the cell. If you adjust the width of the cell or column, the text adjusts to the new width.

You can select any cell in the table and enter or edit text or format the cell. A table enables you to present text in columns and align paragraphs or graphics.

Fig. 16.1
Producing tables
with a professional
look is simple
in Word for
Windows.

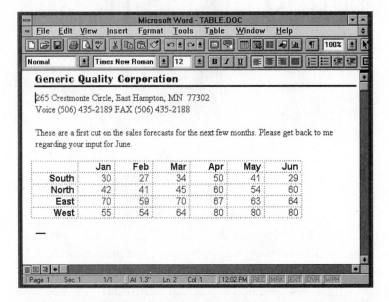

Fig. 16.2
You use tables to
create sideheads in
your documents.

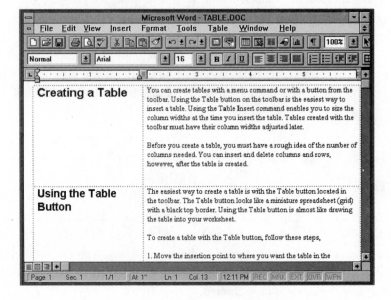

Creating Tables

You can insert a table anywhere in a document. A table can span more than one page, and you frame a table and resize and position it on the page. You can attach a caption to a table and designate headings for the table so that if the table is split within or between pages, the headings automatically are repeated at the top of the table.

What You Need to Know About Creating Tables

You can create tables using the Table Insert Table command from the pull-down menus, or you can use the Insert Table button on the toolbar. Often, using the Insert Table button is the easiest way to create a table. When you use the Insert Table button, the width of the columns is set automatically, so you may have to adjust the widths later. When you use the menu command, you can determine the width of the columns at the time you insert the table.

You also can use the Table Wizard, which is available when you choose the Insert Table command to create a table. The Table Wizard guides you step by step through the process of creating a table. After you create a table, you can use the Table Gallery command to select from a collection of predefined table layouts to simplify the task of formatting your table.

If the information you want to include in a table already appears in your document as text, you can convert the text to a table. See "Converting Text to a Table" later in the chapter for instructions on how to make these changes.

Before you create a table, it is helpful to have a rough idea of the number of columns you need. You can insert and delete columns and rows, however, after you create the table.

Creating a Table with the Table Wizard

One of the easiest ways to create a table is with the Table Wizard. The Table Wizard guides you through the process using a series of boxes that graphically present the most common choices made for preformatted tables. The Table Wizard also makes it easy to handle special situations such as repeating column headings at the top of pages when a table is longer than a single page. The Table Wizard also formats the headings and table content, and finishes by going directly into AutoFormat, which will guide you through formatting your table.

Tip

Drag tables to any location on a page by framing them as described in Chapter 23.

To create a table using the Table Wizard, follow these steps:

1. Position the insertion point where you want the top-left corner of the table.

2. Choose the Table Insert Table command, then choose the Wizard button.

3. Select the table layout from the Wizard window shown in fig. 16.3, then choose the Next button.

Fig. 16.3

In the first box of the Table Wizard, select the table layout you need.

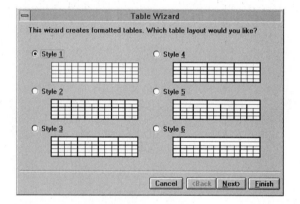

4. Select the type of column headings from the window shown in fig. 16.4, then choose the Next button.

Fig. 16.4

In the second box of the Table Wizard, select the type of column headings you want.

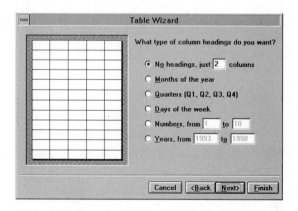

5. Select the type of row headings from the window shown in fig. 16.5, then choose the Next button.

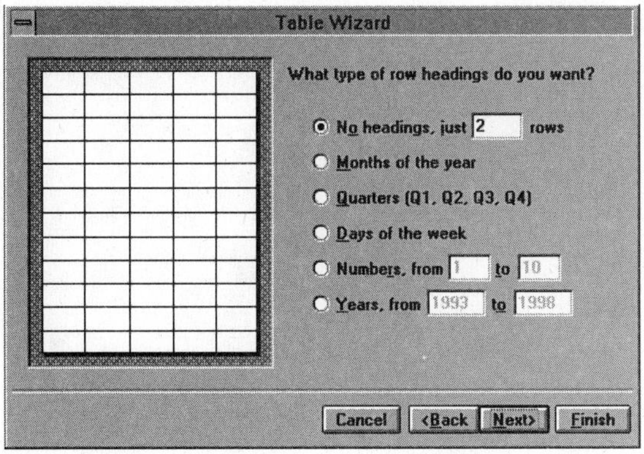

Fig. 16.5
In the third box of the Table Wizard, select the type of row headings you want.

6. Select the type of numeric or text alignment you want for the table contents as shown in fig. 16.6, then choose the Next button.

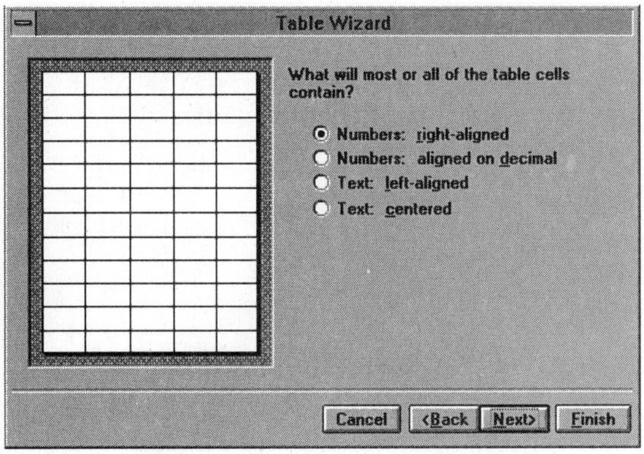

Fig. 16.6
In the fourth box of the Table Wizard, select the alignment for the table contents.

7. Select the table orientation as shown in fig. 16.7, then choose the Next button.

8. In the final Wizard window, select whether you want to see a Help window that will guide you as you create the table; then choose the Finish button.

9. Word displays the first window of the Table AutoFormat. If you do not want to use AutoFormat to format the table, choose Cancel.

Table AutoFormat presents predesigned formats for tables. It makes formatting very easy. To learn more about Table AutoFormat, see the section titled, "Formatting a Table with Table AutoFormat" later in this chapter.

Fig. 16.7

In the fifth box of the Table Wizard, select the table alignment.

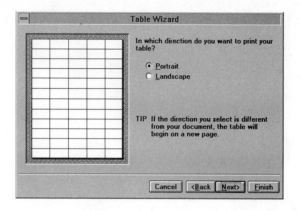

Using the Table Insert Table Command

Use the Table Insert Table command if you want to specify the width of the columns in the table at the same time as you insert the table.

To insert a table in a document, follow these steps:

1. Position the insertion point where you want the top-left corner of the table.

2. Choose the Table Insert Table command. The Insert Table dialog box appears, as shown in fig. 16.8.

Fig. 16.8

You can insert a table using the Insert Table dialog box.

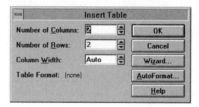

3. Select or type the number of columns you want in the Number of Columns text box.

4. If you know the number of rows you need, select or type the number of rows in the Number of Rows text box.

   If you are unsure of the numbers, don't worry. You easily can add rows and columns to the end of a table or in the middle of the table.

5. If you know how wide you want all columns, adjust the Column **W**idth box.

You easily can change column widths if you are unsure of the column width or later want to adjust the table.

6. Choose the Wizard button to be guided through the creation of a table.

7. Choose the AutoFormat button to apply predefined formats to the table when it is created.

8. Choose OK.

The table appears in your worksheet. It may be invisible, or it may show because table gridlines have been turned on (see "Displaying or Hiding Gridlines and End Marks" later in this chapter). The insertion point appears in the first cell.

Using the Insert Table Button

The easiest way to create a table is by using the Insert Table button located in the toolbar. The Table button looks like a miniature spreadsheet (a grid with a black top border. Using the Table button is almost like drawing the table into your worksheet.

To create a table using the Table button, follow these steps:

1. Move the insertion point to where you want the table in the document.

2. Click the Insert Table button and drag down and to the right.

When you click the button, a grid of rows and columns that looks like a miniature table appears. As long as you continue to hold down the mouse button, you can move the pointer within the grid to select the size of the table you want inserted. If you move the pointer beyond the right or lower borders, the grid expands. Fig. 16.9 shows the Table button expanded and a table size selected.

3. Release the mouse button when the selected grid is the size of the table you want.

If you decide you do not want to insert a table, but you have already begun the selection process with the Insert Table button, continue to hold down the mouse button and drag the pointer until it is outside the grid and then release the button. You also can drag up until the pointer is over the button and then release.

Fig. 16.9
The Table button enables you to draw the size of table you want inserted.

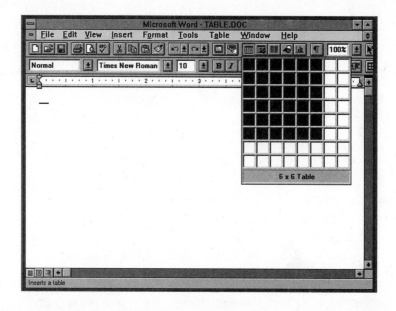

> **Note**
>
> You can store tables, like text, as an AutoText entry. If you use the same type of table repeatedly, you can save considerable time by storing the table as an AutoText entry. To store a table as a glossary, select the entire table and choose the **Edit AutoText** command. Type a name for the entry in the **Name** box and choose OK. To later insert the table glossary, type the table glossary name and press F3. For more information on creating and using AutoText, see Chapter 5, "Editing a Document."

Displaying or Hiding Gridlines and End Marks

Table gridlines can show you the outline of your cells and table, which makes working in tables easier. The end-of-cell mark indicates where the contents of a cell end, and the end-of-row mark indicates the end of the row. Fig. 16.10 shows a table in which the gridlines and end marks are turned off. Fig. 16.11 shows the same table with the gridlines and end marks turned on. You can see how they help you see the table. Gridlines do not print.

Tip
Add a custom button to any toolbar to toggle gridlines on or off. See Chapter 36 about custom buttons.

If you want gridlines on or off, choose the **Table Gridlines** command. This command toggles gridlines on or off. A check mark appears to the left of the command if gridlines are turned on. To turn end marks on or off quickly, press Shift+Ctrl+8 or click the paragraph mark in the Standard toolbar.

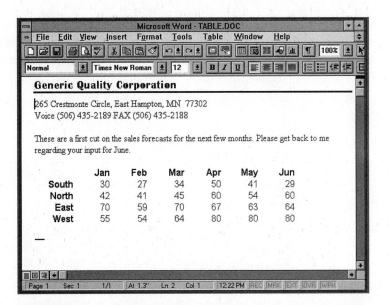

Fig. 16.10
In this table, gridlines and end marks are turned off.

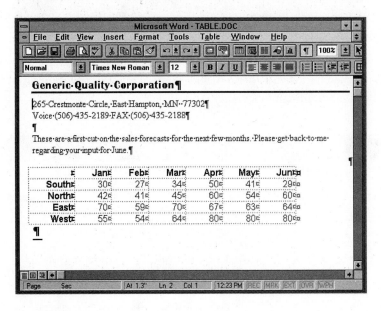

Fig. 16.11
This table is easier to see and edit because gridlines are turned on.

Typing and Moving in a Table

When you create a new table, the insertion point flashes in the first cell—the cell at the upper-left corner of the table. To insert text or numbers in the cell, just start typing.

As you enter text into a cell, you may type more characters than fit in one line. Characters simply wrap to the next line in the cell. In a Word for Windows table, the entire row of cells expands downward to accommodate the text. The same thing happens if you press Enter in a cell. The insertion point moves to the next line down, and the row becomes taller. Each cell acts like a miniature word processing page.

To move forward through the cells in the table, press the Tab key. Press Shift+Tab to move backward through the cells. When you use the Tab key to move to a cell, any text in the cell is selected. To move with the mouse, click in the cell at the point where you want the insertion point to appear.

If you reach the last cell in the table (the lower-right cell) and press Tab, you create a new row of cells at the end of the table and move the insertion point into the first cell of that row. To leave the table, you must press an arrow key or use the mouse to move the insertion point outside the table. Don't be concerned with the number of rows in a table. You add additional rows to the end of the table by pressing the Tab key when the insertion point is in the last cell of the table.

Arrow keys also help you move around in a table. Table 16.1 summarizes these keyboard movements and includes several other handy shortcuts to help you move around in a table.

Table 16.1 Shortcut Keys Used to Move in a Table

Key Combination	Function
Tab	Moves the insertion point right one cell; inserts a new row when pressed in the bottom-right cell
Shift+Tab	Moves the insertion point left one cell
Arrow key	Moves the insertion point character by character through a cell and into the next cell when the insertion point reaches the end of the current cell
Alt+Home	Moves the insertion point to the first cell in the row
Alt+End	Moves the insertion point to the last cell in the row
Alt+PgUp	Moves the insertion point to the top cell in the column
Alt+PgDn	Moves the insertion point to the bottom cell in the column

IV

Using Indents and Tabs in a Cell

Cells contain indents the same as a normal text paragraph. You can format these indents using the same techniques you use to format a paragraph. Use the ruler or choose the Format Paragraph command.

To change the indent or first-line indent within a cell, follow these steps:

1. Select the cell.

2. Choose the Format Paragraph command.

   or

   Click the right mouse button in the selected cell and choose the Paragraph command.

3. Set indents in the dialog box and then choose OK.

   or

   Drag the indent and first-line indent markers to a new location.

Pressing Tab moves you from one cell to the next in a table. Pressing Shift+Tab moves you to the previous cell. You also can set tabs within a cell. Select the cell or cells in which you want tabs, and set the tab stops in the usual way—using the ruler or the Format Tabs command. To move the insertion point to the tab stop within the cell, however, press Ctrl+Tab rather than just Tab.

Attaching Captions to Tables

You can add a caption to a table to identify it, to enable you to cross-reference the table, or to create a list of tables in your document. When you insert a caption, the table is numbered using the SEQ field code. If you insert a new table before or after an existing table, the numbering for all the tables is updated automatically. Field codes are described in more detail in Chapter 37, "Automating with Field Codes."

To attach a caption to a table, follow these steps:

1. Select the entire table by moving the insertion point in the table and choosing the Table Select Table command.

2. Choose the Insert Caption command to display the Caption dialog box or click the right mouse button in the selected table and choose the Caption command (see fig. 16.12).

Fig. 16.12

You can attach a caption to a table in the Caption dialog box.

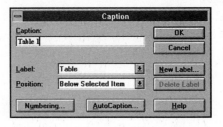

3. If it isn't already selected, select Table in the Label list.

4. Type text after the caption label in the Caption text box, if you want.

5. Select the position for the label in the Position list.

6. Choose OK.

A caption for the table then appears at the position you specified (see fig. 16.13). If the SEQ field code is displayed instead of the table number, choose the Tools Options command and select the View tab. Clear the Field Codes option and choose OK.

Fig. 16.13

A table with a caption attached.

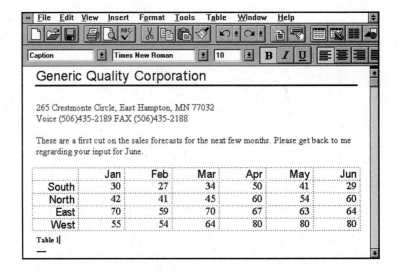

For more information on working with captions, see Chapter 31, "Adding Cross-References and Captions."

Editing Tables

After you create and fill your table, you probably have to make changes to the table. You may need to move or copy cells, or insert new cells, rows, or columns to make room for additional text or graphics. Often you need to adjust row heights and column widths. In the following sections, you learn how to carry out all these tasks.

What You Need to Know About Editing Tables

You can edit the contents within a cell using the same techniques you use to edit text or graphics in a document. You can delete characters using the Backspace and Delete keys, and move around in the text using the mouse or arrow keys. To edit the cells, rows, and columns in a table, you use different techniques, which are described in the following sections.

You can access quickly many of the commands you learn about in the following sections by using the shortcut menus. To use the shortcut menus, point to a cell or selection you have made in a table and click the right mouse button. A list of commands that you can use to edit or format the selection appears. Use the mouse to select the appropriate command.

Selecting and Editing Cells

Before you use the table editing commands, you need to select the correct cells, rows, or columns for whatever changes you are making to the table. You have two ways to select the contents of a table: by character, for which you use Word for Windows usual character-selection techniques; and by cell, for which Word for Windows offers special techniques.

When the entire cell (or cells) is selected, the entire cell appears darkened (see fig. 16.14). Word for Windows enables you to select an entire row, an entire column, or the entire table easily.

Selecting by Menu. You can select rows, columns, or the entire table by using commands from the menu.

For Related Information
- "Setting Indents," p. 306
- "Setting Tabs," p. 298
- "Understanding the Basics of Fields," p. 1073
- "Creating Tables of Figures, Other Tables," p. 917

IV

Mastering Special Features

To select cells, rows, or columns, follow these steps:

1. Move the insertion point into the cell containing the row or column you want selected. Any cell works if you need to select the table.

2. Choose Table and then choose Select Row, Select Column, or Select Table.

Fig. 16.14
A cell appears
darkened when
it is selected.

	Jan	Feb	Mar	Apr	May	Jun
South	30	27	34	50	41	29
North	42	41	45	60	54	60
East	70	59	70	67	63	64
West	55	54	64	80	80	80

Selecting by Mouse. You also can use a mouse to select the contents of a cell. Just drag across characters or double-click words in the usual way. As you can do with the keyboard, you can extend the selection beyond the cell: as soon as the selection reaches the border of a cell, you begin selecting entire cells rather than characters. In addition, you can use special selection bars with the mouse. When you move the I-beam into a selection bar, the pointer changes to an arrow. You can use the mouse to select a cell, row, or column, depending on where you click the mouse pointer. Table 16.2 summarizes the mouse selection techniques.

Table 16.2 Using the Mouse to Select in a Table	
Item to Select	**Mouse Action**
Characters	Drag across characters.
Cell	Click the cell selection area at the left inside edge of the cell.
Group of cells	Select first cell or characters; then drag to the last cell or Shift-click on last cell.
Horizontal row	Click the selection area to the left of the table; drag down for multiple rows.
Vertical column	Click the top line of the column; drag to either side for multiple columns. (The pointer appears as a solid black down arrow when positioned correctly.)
Table	Click in the selection area to the left of the top row and drag down to select all rows or Shift-click to the left of the last row.

Selecting with the Keyboard. Word for Windows provides several other keyboard techniques for selecting cells and groups of cells. These methods are listed in table 16.3.

Table 16.3 Using Shortcut Keys to Select Cells	
Key Combination	**Selects**
Tab	Next cell
Shift+Tab	Previous cell
Shift+arrow key	Character by character in the current cell and then the entire adjacent cell
F8+up or down arrow	Current cell and the cell above or below (Press Esc to end the selection.)
F8+left or right arrow	Text in the current cell (character by character) and then all of the adjacent cells (Press Esc to end the selection.)
Alt+5 (on numeric keypad)	Table

When you select with an arrow key, you first select each character in the cell. As soon as you go beyond the border of the cell, however, you begin selecting entire cells. If you change arrow directions, you select groups of adjacent cells. If you use Shift+right arrow or F8+right arrow to select three adjacent cells in a row and then you press the down-arrow key once, for example, you extend the selection to include the entire contents of the three cells below the original three.

Moving and Copying Cells

Unless you do everything perfectly the first time, you may need to reorganize data in your tables. Word for Windows gives you all the flexibility of moving and copying in a table that you have with text.

Using the Mouse to Drag and Drop Cells, Rows, and Columns. The mouse shortcuts that work with text in body copy also work on cell contents, cells, or an entire table.

To move or copy the characters in a cell or one or more cells and their cellular structure, follow these steps:

1. Select the characters, cells, rows, or columns you want to move or copy.

2. Move the mouse pointer over selected characters until it changes from an I-beam to an arrow pointed up and to the left, as shown in fig. 16.15. (The pointer still may be an arrow if you have not moved it out of the selected area.)

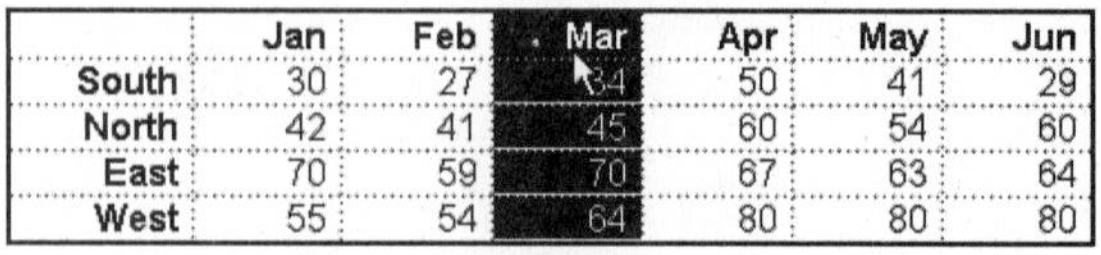

Fig. 16.15

Using the pointer to drag cells, rows, or columns.

	Jan	Feb	Mar	Apr	May	Jun
South	30	27	34	50	41	29
North	42	41	45	60	54	60
East	70	59	70	67	63	64
West	55	54	64	80	80	80

3. To move, hold down the left mouse button.

   or

   To copy, hold down Ctrl and then the left mouse button. Notice the message in the status bar.

4. Position the grayed insertion point where you want the moved or copied characters or cells to appear. Position the pointer over the top-left cell at the place where you want a range of cells to appear.

   The insertion point appears gray and displays a gray box at its bottom end.

5. Release the mouse button.

If the end-of-cell mark is included in the selection, the formatting for the cell or cells you selected is moved or copied to the destination, along with the cell contents.

Using Commands. Choosing Edit and then Cut, Copy, or Paste works much the same way in a table as with text outside a table. These commands enable you to move or copy cells within a table or copy a table to another location. You can cut and copy a single cell, multiple cells, or an entire table.

If you select only the text, number, or picture within a cell, then you copy or cut only what you have selected, just as you do in a document's body copy. But if you select the entire cell or multiple cells, you copy the cell boundaries as well.

If you select an entire cell, the Copy command copies the entire cell to the Clipboard. The Cut command moves the entire contents of the cell to the

Clipboard. The cell's boundaries remain in the table. When you paste cells from the Clipboard, the cell containing the insertion point receives the first cell on the Clipboard. The original cells in the table are replaced by the contents of the cells on the Clipboard, as shown in fig. 16.16 and fig. 16.17.

	Jan	Feb	Mar	Apr
South	30	27	34	50
North	42	41	45	60
East	70	59	70	67
West	55	54	64	80

Fig. 16.16
These selected cells are being copied.

	Jan	Feb	Mar	Apr	Apr
South	30	27	34	50	50
North	42	41	45	60	60
East	70	59	70	67	67
West	55	54	64	80	80

Fig. 16.17
The same cells pasted into a blank area.

When you paste cells, the **Paste** command becomes **Paste Cells**, and the cells are pasted as cells in a table. If you copy an entire row or column, the command becomes **Paste Row** or **Paste Column**, respectively. When you paste cells into an area not formatted as a table, they arrive as a table. When you paste a group of cells into an existing table, the table expands, if necessary, to accommodate the new cells.

You also can paste text from outside a table into a single cell in a table. Just copy or cut the text, move the insertion point inside a cell, and choose the **Edit Paste** command.

To move or copy cells, follow these steps:

1. Select the cells, rows, or columns you want to move or copy.

2. Choose the **Edit Cut** command or press Ctrl+X or click the Edit Cut button on the Standard toolbar if you want to move the cells.

   or

   Choose the **Edit Copy** command or press Ctrl+C or click the Edit Copy button if you want to copy the cells.

3. Select an area in the table that matches the shape and size of the area you selected in step 1.

   Word warns you if the shape and size of the copied cells do not match the shape and size of the cells into which you're pasting.

4. Choose the Edit Paste Cells command or press Ctrl+V or click the Edit Paste button on the Standard toolbar.

Using the Outliner. The Word for Windows outline view provides another option for reorganizing rows, columns, and cells. Switching to outline view enables you to move an entire row of selected cells by dragging the selection to the location where you want the data to appear.

To move a row of cells, follow these steps:

1. Choose the View Outline command.

    A small box, called a *body text symbol*, appears to the left of each row (see fig. 16.18).

Fig. 16.18

Drag the body text symbol for a row up or down to move the row.

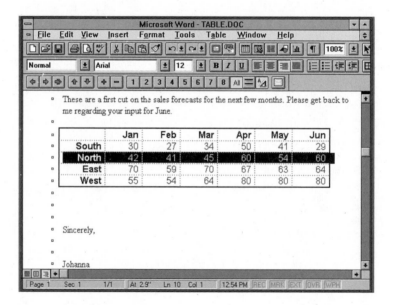

2. Select the row by clicking the body text symbol.

3. Select the up or down arrows in the outline bar or drag the body text symbol up or down to move the selected row to the desired location.

IV

Mastering Special Features

> **Note**
>
> A real shortcut for moving table rows up or down is to select the entire row and then press Shift+Alt+up or down arrow. You do not have to be in outline view for this shortcut to work, nor does the document need an outline.

Changing Column Width

When a table is first created, the columns are sized equally to fill the area between the right and left margins. You can change column or cell widths in three ways: drag the right cell border of the column in the table, drag the column marker on the ruler, or choose the Table Cell Height and Width command.

Dragging Cell Borders or Using the Ruler. To change the width of a column using the mouse, position the pointer on the right border of the column. The pointer changes to a vertical double bar when it is positioned properly. (The pointer changes even if the gridlines are turned off.) Fig. 16.19 shows the shape of the pointer when it is positioned correctly to drag a cell border. Drag this column marker to the desired column width and release the mouse button. If the entire column is selected or nothing in the column is selected, the entire column adjusts to the new width. If cells within the column are selected, only the selected cells adjust to the new width.

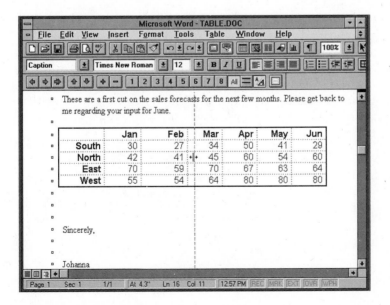

Fig. 16.19
Drag the border of a cell or selected column to change its width.

You can affect the other columns and the overall table width differently by pressing different keys as you drag the border. To see the width measurements of the columns displayed on the ruler, hold down the Alt key as you drag the border. Table 16.4 indicates the different ways you can adjust the columns.

Table 16.4 Changing Column Widths Using the Mouse	
Action	**Result**
Drag the border without holding down any keys	All columns to the right are resized in proportion to their original width.
Drag the border while holding down the Shift key	Only the width of the column to the left is changed; table width is unchanged.
Drag the border while holding down the Ctrl key	All columns to the right are adjusted equally; table width is unchanged.
Drag the border while holding down the Ctrl+Shift keys	Columns to the right are unchanged; table width is adjusted proportionally.
Double-click on border	Adjusts column-width to fit widest content.

You also can use the table markers on the ruler to change column widths. Dragging the table markers gives the same results as dragging the column borders, as discussed in the preceding paragraphs. If the ruler is not turned on, choose the View Ruler command.

Using the Column Width Command. The Table Cell Height and Width command is useful if you want to change the width of multiple columns with a single command or if you want to define the width of columns by specific amounts. The Table Cell Height and Width command also enables you to change the distance between columns. To change the width of an entire column rather than just a cell in a column, be sure to select the entire column first.

To change column width using the Column Width command, follow these steps:

1. Select the columns or cells whose width you want to change.

2. Choose the Table Cell Height and Width command and select the Column tab in the Cell Height and Width dialog box. The Column tab is displayed (see fig. 16.20).

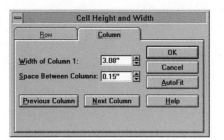

Fig. 16.20
You can set the width of any number of columns at one time in the Cell Height and Width dialog box.

3. Select or type a number in the Width of Columns text box.

4. If you want to adjust other columns, choose the Previous Column or Next Column buttons to keep the dialog box open and move to the next column. The Width of Columns label changes to tell you which row you are formatting.

5. Choose OK.

Changing Column Spacing. The Cell Height and Width dialog box enables you to control the amount of space between columns. When a table is first created, the number of columns you choose for the table are of equal size and span the distance between margins. Included in the column width is a default column spacing setting of .15 inch.

To change the spacing between columns, follow these steps:

1. Select the columns you want to adjust. Select a row if you want to adjust all columns in the table.

2. Choose the Table Cell Height and Width command and select the Column tab in the Cell Height and Width dialog box.

3. Select or type a number in the Space Between Columns text box.

   The space you set in this box is divided between the left and right margins within the cell—just as though the cell is a small page and you are entering the combined value for the left and right margins.

4. Choose OK.

The column spacing affects the cell's usable column width. If a column width is 2 inches and the column spacing is set to 0.50 inch, for example, the column width available for text and graphics is 1.5 inches.

Using the AutoFit Command. You can have Word for Windows automatically adjust the width of a column in a table to accommodate the width of the longest line of text in the column. One advantage to using AutoFit to adjust the columns in a table is that you know the columns are as wide as but no wider than they have to be to accommodate the data in the table. This feature helps you to optimize the use of space on a page.

To AutoFit column width, follow these steps:

1. Select the columns you want to AutoFit.

    If you do not select the entire column, only the selected cells are AutoFit.

2. Choose the Table Cell Height and Width command, and select the Column tab in the Cell Height and Width dialog box.

3. Choose the AutoFit button.

The column will adjust automatically. The dialog box will disappear, and you will return to the document.

Changing Row Height and Position

All rows are equal in height when you first create a table. The text and amount of paragraph spacing you add changes the height of the row. The Table Cell Height and Width command enables you to set how far a row is indented from the left margin, the height of the row, and the alignment of the row between margins. You also can change the height of rows using the vertical ruler.

Changing Row Height. You can change the height of the rows in a table using either the Table Cell Height and Width command or the vertical ruler. If you want to change several rows at the same time to the same height, using the menu command is easier.

To set row height using the Cell Height and Width command, follow these steps:

1. Select the rows whose height you want to adjust.

2. Choose the Table Cell Height and Width command and select the **R**ow tab in the Cell Height and Width dialog box. The Row tab is displayed (see fig. 16.21).

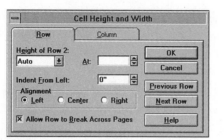

Fig. 16.21
You can control the height and indentation of rows in a table.

3. Select a **H**eight of Row option.

Option	Result
Auto	Row height automatically adjusts to the size of the text or graphic
At Least	Sets minimum row height; automatically adjusts row if text or graphic exceeds minimum
Exactly	Sets a fixed row height. Text or graphics that exceed the fixed height are cut off on-screen and at printing.

4. If you choose At Least or Exactly in step 3, type or select the row height in points in the **A**t box.

   You also can specify the height in lines (li) or inches (") by including the abbreviation after the numerical value.

5. Clear the Allow Row to **B**reak Across Pages option to keep the selected row from splitting at a page break.

   When this option is selected, if the text or graphic in a cell in the row cannot fit on the current page, the row is split and continues on the next page.

6. Choose the **P**revious Row or Next Row button if you want to format other rows. The **H**eight of Row label changes to tell you which row you are formatting.

7. Choose OK.

To set row height using the vertical ruler, follow these steps:

1. If you are not in page layout view, choose the **View Page Layout** command.

   Every row in a table has a corresponding horizontal marker in the vertical ruler (see fig. 16.22). You can adjust the height of a row by dragging its marker.

Fig. 16.22

You can use the vertical ruler on the left to set row heights.

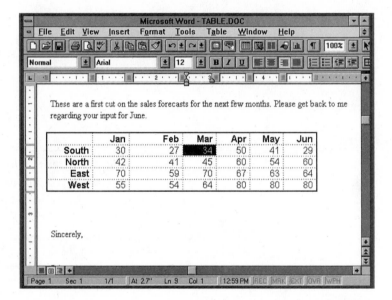

2. Drag the marker to set the height of the row you want to change.

   If you drag the marker without pressing any keys, you set the row height to at least whatever the new measurement is. The row height automatically adjusts if the text or graphics exceed this minimum setting. If you hold down the Ctrl key as you drag the marker, you set the row height to exactly the new measurement. Text or graphics that exceed the fixed height are cut off on-screen and at printing.

Changing Row Spacing. A little extra vertical spacing between rows can make your table easier to read. You can adjust the amount of space between rows using the Paragraph Spacing button on a toolbar or by choosing the Format Paragraph command.

To add space between rows, follow these steps:

1. Select the rows to which you want to add spacing.

2. Choose the Format Paragraph command and select the Indents and Spacing tab in the Paragraph dialog box.

3. Type or select a spacing in the Spacing Before or the Spacing After boxes. You can use lines (li) or point (pt) measurements by typing the number and space and then the abbreviation.

4. Choose OK.

Aligning and Indenting Rows. With Word for Windows, you can control the position of a table by changing the alignment of rows. You also can indent selected rows to align with other text in your document. Row alignment and indentation does not affect the alignment of text within the cells.

To align rows between page margins, follow these steps:

1. Select the rows you want to align.

2. Choose the Table Cell Height and Width command and select the Row tab in the Cell Height and Width dialog box. The Row tab is displayed (see fig. 16.21).

3. Select Left, Center, or Right alignment.

4. Choose OK.

The Cell Height and Width dialog box also enables you to indent selected rows. When you indent a row, the entire row shifts right by the amount you specify, just as though you were indenting a paragraph.

To indent a row, follow these steps:

1. Select the row or rows you want to indent.

2. Choose the Table Cell Height and Width command and select the Row tab in the Cell Height and Width dialog box.

3. Type or select the number of inches of indent you want in the Indent From Left box.

4. Choose OK.

Adding or Deleting Cells, Rows, or Columns

Word for Windows enables you to change the structure of a table by adding and deleting cells, rows, and columns. You can add or delete one or many cells, rows, or columns by using a single command. The Table menu changes its Insert and Delete commands, depending on what you have selected.

If a cell is selected, the Table menu displays Insert Cells and Delete Cells commands. If a column is selected, the Table menu displays the Insert Column and Delete Column commands. If a row is selected, the menu displays Insert Row and Delete Row.

Adding or Deleting Cells. You can add or delete individual cells if you don't want to add or delete entire rows or columns. The other cells in the table are shifted to accommodate the added or deleted cells.

To add cells to or delete cells from an existing table, follow these steps:

1. Select the cells you want to add or delete.

2. Choose Table and then Insert Cells or Table Delete Cells.

   The Insert Cells or Delete Cells dialog boxes appear, depending on which command you choose (see fig. 16.23 and fig. 16.24).

Fig. 16.23
The Insert Cells dialog box appears if you are inserting cells.

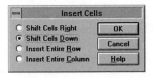

Fig. 16.24
The Delete Cells dialog box appears if you are deleting cells.

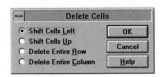

3. Choose the appropriate option button that corresponds to shifting the existing cells to the position you want. You also have the option of inserting or deleting an entire column or row.

   Choosing the Insert Cells command inserts blank cells at the location of the selected cells and shifts the selected cells either down or right.

   Choosing the Delete Cells command deletes the selected cells and shifts adjacent cells either up or left to fill the vacancy.

4. Choose OK.

If you want to delete cell contents without deleting the actual cell, select the cell contents you want to delete and press Del or Backspace.

Adding or Deleting Rows and Columns. You can insert and delete columns and rows from a table using the same commands you use to insert or delete cells. You can add columns and rows to the end of the table or insert them within the table.

If the insertion point is positioned at the last position in the last cell, press Tab to insert a new row at the end of the table.

To insert or delete rows through the middle of an existing table, follow these steps:

1. Select the row or rows where you want to insert or delete.

   When you insert a row, the selected row is shifted down and a blank row is inserted (see fig. 16.25). When you delete a row, the selected row is deleted and lower rows move up.

2. Choose Table and then Insert Rows or Delete Rows.

	Jan	Feb	Mar	Apr	May	Jun
South	30	27	34	50	41	29
North	42	41	45	60	54	60
East	70	59	70	67	63	64
West	55	54	64	80	80	80

Fig. 16.25
A table after a new row has been inserted.

If you are inserting a row or rows, you can click the Insert Table button on the Standard toolbar instead of choosing the Insert Rows command.

To insert or delete one or more columns within a table, follow these steps:

1. Select one or more columns where you want columns inserted or deleted.

   If you are inserting a column or columns, you can click the Insert Table button on the Standard toolbar instead of choosing the Insert Columns command.

2. Choose Table and then Insert Columns or Delete Columns.

   When you insert columns, the selected columns shift right to make room for the inserted blank columns. When you're deleting, selected columns are removed and columns to the right shift left to fill the gap.

If a column is inserted, the table looks like the one shown in fig. 16.26. If a column is deleted, the table looks like the one shown in fig. 16.27.

Fig. 16.26
Inserting a column
shifts existing
columns right.

	Jan	Feb	Mar	Apr		May	Jun
South	30	27	34	50		41	29
North	42	41	45	60		54	60
East	70	59	70	67		63	64
West	55	54	64	80		80	80

Fig. 16.27
Deleting a column
shifts existing
columns left to
fill the gap.

	Jan	Feb	Mar	Apr	Jun
South	30	27	34	50	29
North	42	41	45	60	60
East	70	59	70	67	64
West	55	54	64	80	80

Inserting a column as the last column requires a different procedure. To insert a column to the right of a table, follow these steps:

1. Position the insertion point at the end of a table row outside the table, which places it in front of an end-of-row mark.

   If gridlines and end marks are not displayed on-screen, refer to "Displaying or Hiding Gridlines and End Marks" earlier in this chapter.

2. Choose the Table Select Column command.

3. Choose the Table Insert Columns command or click the Insert Table button on the Standard toolbar.

To insert additional columns to the right of the table, choose the Edit Repeat command or press F4.

> ### Note
>
> If you want to insert multiple columns quickly at the right edge of the table, select from the existing table as many columns as you want to insert. (Dragging across with the right mouse button is a quick way to select these columns.) Choose the Edit Copy command. Move the insertion point to the end of the first row of the table and choose the Edit Paste command. Reselect these new columns and press Del to clear them.

Troubleshooting Editing a Table
When I try to drag and drop cells that I have selected, it doesn't work. The mouse pointer doesn't change to an arrow when I point to the selected cells.

When the drag-and-drop feature is turned off, the mouse pointer does not change to an arrow when you point to a selection, and you cannot drag the selection to a new location. To turn on drag-and-drop, choose the Tools Options command, select the Edit tab, select the **Drag and Drop Text Editing** option, and then choose OK.

When I try to insert rows or columns in a table, the Insert Rows and Insert Columns commands do not appear in the Table menu.

If the Table Insert or Delete command for rows or columns does not appear on the menu, you have selected only cells. You must select the rows or columns with which you want to work so that Word for Windows knows which Insert or Delete command to add to the menu.

For Related Information
- "Selecting Text," p. 133
- "Moving, Copying, and Linking Text or Graphics," p. 152

Merging and Splitting Cells and Creating Table Headings

Sometimes you want text or a figure to span the width of multiple cells. A heading is an example of text you may want to stretch across several columns. Word for Windows enables you to merge multiple cells in a row into a single cell. Merging cells converts their contents to paragraphs within a single cell.

Merging Cells

You can only merge cells horizontally. Selecting cells in more than one row results in the selected cells in each row being merged horizontally.

To merge multiple cells in a row into a single cell, follow these steps:

1. Select the cells you want to merge (see fig. 16.28).

2. Choose the Table Merge Cells command.

   The selected cells condense into a single cell (see fig. 16.29). You may need to reformat the contents so that the cell aligns correctly.

Creating Table Headings

To create table headings, follow these steps:

1. Select the first row and any following rows that you want to use as table headings.

2. Choose the Table Headings command.

Fig. 16.28
Select the cells you want to merge in the table.

| | Jan | Sales Forecast | | | | |
		Feb	Mar	Apr	May	Jun
South	30	27	34	50	41	29
North	42	41	45	60	54	60
East	70	59	70	67	63	64
West	55	54	64	80	80	80

Fig. 16.29
Merge cells to put text such as titles into a single, wider cell.

| | | Sales Forecast | | | | |
	Jan	Feb	Mar	Apr	May	Jun
South	30	27	34	50	41	29
North	42	41	45	60	54	60
East	70	59	70	67	63	64
West	55	54	64	80	80	80

Splitting Cells

You can return cells that have been merged to their original condition. The text in the merged cells is divided among the split cells by paragraph marks. The first paragraph is placed in the first cell, the second paragraph in the second cell, and so on. If the selected cell has not been merged, the Split Cells command is not available.

To split merged cells, follow these steps:

1. Select the cell that was merged previously.

2. Choose the Table Split Cells command.

Formatting a Table

You can format the text and cells in a table to produce attractive and professional-looking tables. You format text and paragraphs just as you do in the body text of your document. You can add borders and shading around the entire table or to selected cells to make a table more attractive and more readable. You also can draw gridlines within the table. To enhance the appearance or make important data stand out, you can use colored borders or shaded or colored backgrounds. In addition, 26 different shades and patterns are available for black-and-white laser printers—an important feature when you have to make a good impression with your document.

What You Need to Know About Formatting a Table

You can format the contents in the cells of a table using the same procedures you use to format regular text. You can change the font, font size, and font style by using the Format Font command, and you can adjust the spacing and indentation of cell contents by using the Format Paragraph command. Remember that you can access these formatting commands using the shortcut menus. Click the right button after you select the cells, columns, or rows that you want to format, and then choose the formatting command you want to use from the shortcut menu.

You use the Format Borders and Shading command to add borders, shading, and color to a table. You also can add a Borders toolbar to the screen to access the border and shading options with a mouse click. To add the Borders toolbar to your screen, click an existing toolbar with the right mouse button and choose Borders from the menu. Repeat these steps to remove the toolbar.

Formatting a Table with Table AutoFormat

Formatting a table to achieve a professional appearance could take you longer than creating and filling the table—unless you use the Table AutoFormat. Table AutoFormat, automatically applies predesigned collections of formatting to the table you select. It includes borders, shading, fonts, colors, and AutoFit column widths. If you are familiar with Excel's time saving AutoFormat, then you are already familiar with how useful this feature is.

To format a table using Table AutoFormat, follow these steps:

1. Move the insertion point inside the table.

2. Choose the Table AutoFormat command to display the Table AutoFormat dialog box shown in fig. 16.30.

3. Select from the Formats list a predefined format. Watch the Preview box to see an example of the format you select.

4. If you do not want to lose existing formats in the table, deselect the appropriate type of format in the Formats to Apply group: Borders, Shading, Font, Color, and AutoFit. The preview will change as you select or deselect formats.

5. If you want to apply only selected portions of the AutoFormat to your table, select the parts of the table you want to format from the Apply Special Formats To group: Heading Rows, First Column, Last Row, and Last Column.

6. Choose OK.

Fig. 16.30

Apply collections
of predefined
formats using the
Table AutoFormat
command.

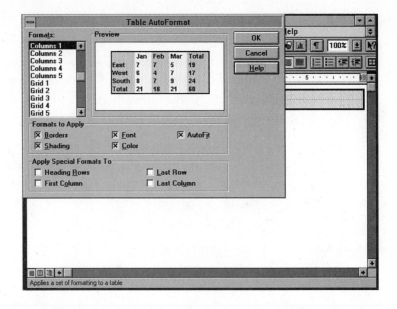

Selecting Border Formats

With Word for Windows, adding borders to a table is easy. You can add borders to individual cells, rows, and columns, or to the entire table. Fig. 16.31 shows a table formatted with multiple border styles.

Fig. 16.31

A table formatted
with multiple
border styles.

	Jan	Feb	Mar	Apr	May	Jun
South	30	27	34	50	41	29
North	42	41	45	60	54	60
East	70	59	70	67	63	64
West	55	54	64	80	80	80

To add borders to all or selected parts of your table, follow these steps:

1. Select the entire table or the cells you want to shade or border.

2. Choose the Format Borders and Shading command and select the Borders tab in the Table Borders and Shading dialog box. The Borders tab is displayed (see fig. 16.32).

3. Select the line weight and style from the Style list.

4. Select a line color from the Color list.

5. Select one of the Preset border patterns: **None**, **Box**, or **Grid**.

6. Choose OK.

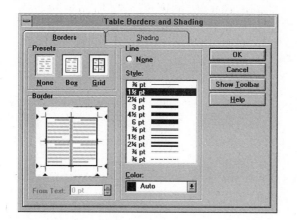

Fig. 16.32
Add borders to your table by using the Table Borders and Shading dialog box.

IV

Mastering Special Features

If you want to specify custom combinations of border types, weights, and colors, you can select which lines are affected by your Style and Color selections from the Border box.

To specify custom combinations, follow these steps:

1. Select the line type and weight from the Style options as described in the preceding steps.

2. Select the line color from the Color list.

3. Select the line or edge you want affected from the sample in the Border box. Fig. 16.33 shows the arrow-head handles that point to the lines which are affected by Style and Color selections.

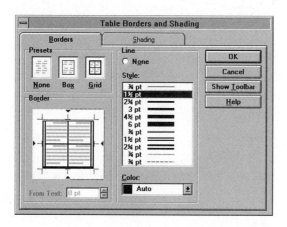

Fig. 16.33
You can select any combination of individual edges or the interior gridlines to add borders to.

Using the mouse, click the line or outside border you want changed. To change multiple lines or edges at one time, hold down the Shift key and click the lines. After you have selected lines, click a line type from the Line options.

Using the keyboard, press Alt+R to move the focus to the Border box. Press the up- or down-arrow keys to cycle through combinations of selected lines. Stop on the combination you want and press the space bar to change them to the current Style and Color selections. You can alternate among the Style, Color, and Border options until you get the right combination.

4. Watch the sample in the Border box to see the result of your choices. To remove a selected border, select the None option in the Line box. If you do not like the sample appearance, select the None Preset and return to step 1.

5. Choose OK.

Note

The preceding steps show you how to add borders to an entire table or individual cells in a table. You also can add borders to the paragraphs in a cell. To add borders to paragraphs, click the paragraph mark on the ribbon to display paragraph marks, select the paragraph mark for the paragraph to which you want to add borders, and choose the Format Borders and Shading command to add borders to the paragraph. You may have to insert a paragraph mark after the text by pressing Enter. When you apply borders to the paragraph, the extra line from this paragraph mark is removed.

Selecting Shading and Colors

You can enhance a table or selected cells with shading. Shading draws attention to a particular section of a table, or you can use it to create reserved areas on office forms.

Whatever cells you have selected are affected by the selections you make in the Table Borders and Shading dialog box. If the insertion point is located in a single cell without that cell being selected, shading is applied to the entire table.

To add shading to a table, follow these steps:

1. Choose the Format Borders and Shading command, and select the Shading tab in the Table Borders and Shading dialog box. The Shading tab appears (see fig. 16.34).

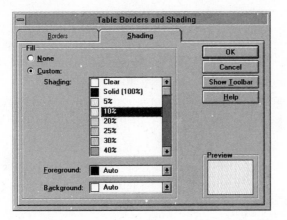

Fig. 16.34
You can add shading and color to a table by using the Shading options.

2. Select None to remove shading or Custom to apply shading.

3. If you select Custom, select the pattern or percentage of shading from the Shading list. Fig. 16.34 shows the 10% shading. Many shades are available.

4. Select a foreground color from the Foreground list. Select Auto or Black if you are printing to a black-and-white printer.

5. Select a background color from the Background list. Select Auto or White if you are printing to a black-and-white printer.

6. Check the pattern you have created in the Preview box. If it is what you want, choose OK; otherwise, return to step 3 and make other selections.

The background of selected cells are shaded when shading is applied. You can control the type of shading you want by setting the shading percentage. If you want lighter shading, choose a lower shading percentage. A higher percentage applies darker shading.

Your printer's resolution controls shading patterns. The higher the resolution—dots per inch (dpi)—the finer the shading. The resolution at which your printer prints graphics and shading is an option within the Printer Setup dialog box. To access this dialog box, choose the File Print command, choose

For Related Information
- "Formatting Characters," p. 246

- "Changing Fonts," p. 254

- "Using Paragraph Formatting Techniques," p. 289

- "Shading and Bordering Paragraphs," p. 324

IV

Mastering Special Features

the Printer button, and then choose the Options button. Experiment with the Pattern, Foreground, and Background options in the Shading dialog box to find the shading pattern that looks best.

Numbering Rows and Columns

Tip
If you frequently use the same collection of formats on a table, read about styles in Chapter 11.

You can use the Numbering button on the toolbar or the Format Bullets and Numbering command to add numbers to the cells and rows in a table. You can add numbers to just the first column in the table, or you can add numbers across rows or down columns in as many cells in the table as you want.

Adding Numbers with the Numbering Button

The quickest way to add numbering to a table is to use the Numbering button on the toolbar. When you use this method, however, you are limited to adding only Arabic-style numbers.

To add numbers to a table using the Numbering button, follow these steps:

1. Select the cells, rows, or columns that you want to number. In most cases you will want a number in the first cell of each row, so select the first column.

2. Click the Numbering button on the Formatting toolbar. The Table Numbering dialog box appears.

3. Select from one of the following options:

Option	Action
Number Each Cell Only Once	Inserts one number in each cell
Number Across Rows	Numbers across rows
Number Down Columns	Numbers down columns

4. Choose OK.

If the table is not numbered as you expected, choose the Edit Undo command and repeat the procedure with a different selection or option. To remove numbering from a table, select the cells from which you want numbrs removed; then click the Numbering button on the Formatting toolbar.

IV

Adding Numbering with the Menu

You can use the Format Bullets and Numbering command to add numbers to a table. When you use this method, you can select from a variety of numbering styles in the Bullets and Numbering dialog box.

To add numbers using the menu, follow these steps:

1. Select the cells, rows, or columns that you want to number.

2. Choose the Format Bullets and Numbering command and select the Numbered tab in the Bullets and Numbering dialog box. The Numbered tab appears (see fig. 16.35).

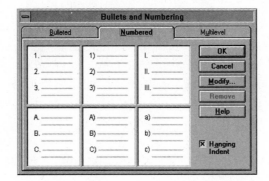

Fig. 16.35
You can select from several numbering styles in the Bullets and Numbering dialog box.

3. Select one of the numbering styles.

4. To modify the predefined style, choose the Modify button and make selections in the Modify Numbered List dialog box to change the format of the numbering and then choose OK.

5. Choose OK.

For Related Information
■ "Creating Numbered Lists," p. 557

Splitting a Table

You may have an occasion when you need to insert a paragraph or heading between rows in a table. If you start a table at the very top of a document and later decide you need to insert some text before the table, you can insert text before the table.

To insert text above the table or between rows, follow these steps:

1. Position the insertion point in the row below where you want to insert the text. Position the insertion point in the first row of the table if you want to enter text above the table.

2. Choose the Table Split Table command or press Ctrl+Shift+Enter.

   A paragraph mark formatted with the Normal style is inserted above the row.

Sorting Tables

Tables often are created to arrange data in columns and rows. You can sort the rows in a table by up to three of the columns in the table. You can sort a table that is a database of names and addresses first by the last name, for example, and then within that sort, by the first name. You can sort text, numbers, and dates in either ascending or descending order.

To sort a table, follow these steps:

1. Select the entire table to include all the rows in the sort or select only the rows you want to sort.

2. Choose the Table Sort command. The Sort dialog box appears (see fig. 16.36).

Fig. 16.36
You can sort a table by up to three columns in the Sort dialog box.

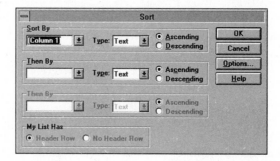

3. Select the first column you want to sort by in the **S**ort By list.

4. Select either Text, Number, or Date from the Type list.

5. Select either the Ascending or Descending option.

6. Repeat steps 3 through 5 if you want to sort by additional columns in your table. Make your selections in the Then By boxes.

7. If your table has headings that you don't want to include in the search, select the Header **R**ow option in the My List Has box.

8. To make the sort case-sensitive, choose the Options button, select the Case Sensitive option, and choose OK.

9. Choose OK.

The Edit Undo command reverses the Sorting command if you use it immediately after you sort. You may want to save your document before sorting so that you can return to it if it is sorted incorrectly.

Converting a Table to Text

You can convert the cell contents of a table to comma-separated or tab-separated text, or you can convert the contents of each cell into one or more paragraphs.

To convert a table to text, follow these steps:

1. Select the rows of the table you want to convert to text or select the entire table.

2. Choose the Table Convert Table to Text command. The Convert Table to Text dialog box appears.

3. Select a Separate Text With option from the dialog box. You can separate each cell's contents by Paragraph Marks, Tabs, or Commas.

4. Choose OK.

Converting Text to a Table

When you copy data from another application or convert a file from a word processor that did not have tables, your data may be in tabbed columns. Converting it to Word for Windows tables makes it easier to work with.

To convert text to a table, follow these steps:

1. Select the lines of text or paragraphs you want to convert to a table.

2. Choose the Table Convert Text to Table command or click the Insert Table button on the Standard toolbar. The Convert Text to Table dialog box appears (see fig. 16.37).

Fig. 16.37
Use the Convert Text to Table dialog box to separate text at the character you specify.

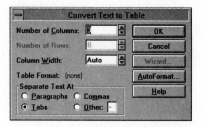

Based on the selected text, Word for Windows proposes the number of columns and rows, the width of the columns, and what separator character to use to delineate columns from the text. You can change these settings if necessary.

3. Type or select the number of columns in the Number of Columns box to specify a different number of columns.

4. Type or select the number of rows in the Number of Rows box to specify a different number of rows.

5. Type or select an exact column width in the Column Width box if you don't want to use the automatic settings.

6. Select a different separator character if the default character is incorrect.

Choose one of the following options from the dialog box:

Option	Result
Paragraphs	A paragraph separates information to be in a cell. Each paragraph becomes its own row.
Tabs	A tab character separates information in a cell. Word for Windows converts each paragraph and each line ending in a hard line break (created by pressing Shift+Enter) into a row. The number of columns is determined by the greatest number of tab characters in the paragraphs or lines.

Option	Result
Commas	A comma separates information in a cell. Word for Windows converts each paragraph and each line ending in a hard line break (created by pressing Shift+Enter) into a row. The number of columns is determined by the greatest number of commas in the paragraphs or lines.
Other	Some other character separates information in a cell. Word for Windows converts each paragraph and each line ending in a hard line break (created by pressing Shift+Enter) into a row. The number of columns is determined by the greatest number of the specified characters in the paragraphs or lines.

7. Choose OK.

Calculating Math Results in a Table

You can perform calculations in a table just as you do in a spreadsheet. In a Word for Windows table, you can add, subtract, multiply, and divide numbers, and you also can perform several other types of calculations, such as averaging and finding minimum and maximum values.

What You Need to Know About Calculating Math in a Table

To perform a calculation in a table, you must locate the insertion point in the cell where you want the result of the calculation to appear. If text or numbers are already in that cell, you should delete them. When you use the Table Formula command to sum a group of cells, Word assumes you want to sum the cells immediately above or to the left of the cell and inserts either ABOVE or LEFT in the parentheses of the SUM function in the Formula dialog box. If you want to perform other types of calculations, you must replace the SUM function with another function and specify the cells you want to use in the calculation. You specify a cell by using the cell address, which consists of the row and column designation for that cell. The first cell in the upper-left corner of a table, for example, is designated as A1, where A represents the column and 1 represents the row. You can designate a range of cells by typing the addresses for the first and last cells in the range separated by a colon.

When you perform a calculation in a cell, a field code is inserted. The field includes the function name, for example, SUM, and the cells on which the calculation is being performed. To see the field code, choose the Tools Options command and select the View tab. Select the Field Codes option and choose OK. The field code is displayed instead of the result. A shortcut for toggling between a field code and its result is to locate the insertion point within the code and press Shift+F9. If the numbers used in the calculation change, you can update the results of the calculation by selecting the cell where the results appear and pressing F9, the Field Update key.

From Here...

Tables are related to numerous other areas in Word for Windows such as calculations, desktop publishing, and forms. The following chapters give you more information about table-related topics:

- Chapter 5, "Editing a Document." AutoCorrect and AutoText are an excellent way of inserting preformatted tables that you use frequently.

- Chapter 11, "Formatting with Styles." Styles are collections of formats you can apply as a group to a table.

- Chapter 20, "Calculating Math with Formulas." Learn how to insert formulas in tables so you can do simple spreadsheet-like calculations.

- Chapter 26, "Graphing Data." Turn the numbers and labels in a table into a high-quality chart using what you learn in this chapter.

- Chapter 31, "Adding Cross-References and Captions." Cross-references enable you to correctly refer to a table, even when it is moved. Captions are titles that attach to a table to identify it.

Chapter 17

Creating Bulleted or Numbered Lists

A bulleted or numbered list is a special type of list formatted with a *hanging indent*. (A hanging indent is when the first line of a paragraph goes all the way to the left margin, but all other lines in the paragraph are indented. Chapter 10, "Formatting Lines and Paragraphs," describes hanging indents and other paragraph formatting.) Bulleted lists have a bullet at the left margin; numbered lists have a number and are numbered sequentially (see fig. 17.1). Many writers use bulleted lists to distinguish a series of important items or points from the rest of the text in a document, such as a summary of product features in a sales letter or a list of conclusions reached as a result of a research project. Numbered lists are often used for step-by-step instructions (as in this book), outlines, or other types of lists where the specific order of the information is important.

Word for Windows provides flexible, easy-to-use methods for creating bulleted or numbered lists with a variety of standardized numbering or bullet formats. You can vary the size of the hanging indent or the space between the numbers or bullets and the following text. You can also create your own custom numbering formats for numbered lists, or you can select characters from any of your installed fonts to use as a bullet in a bulleted list. Word even provides an easy way to remove bullets or numbering.

You can apply the bulleted or numbered list format either before or after you type the text for the list. You can type the text for the bulleted or numbered list and then apply the list formatting to the text; or you can place the insertion point in a blank line, apply the bulleted or numbered list format to that line, and then type the list. Either way, after you select a bulleted or numbered list format, Word for Windows sets a 1/4-inch hanging indent and adds

In this chapter, you learn how to do the following:

- Create and customize bulleted, numbered, and multilevel lists

- Create and customize numbered or bulleted headings

- Remove bulleting and numbering from lists and headings

the bullets or numbers in front of each paragraph in the selected text, or to each new paragraph you type.

Fig. 17.1

An example of the types of bulleted and numbered lists you can create.

Numbered list

Bulleted list

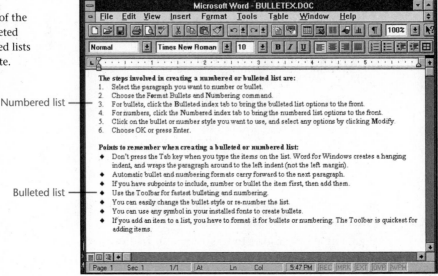

Like paragraph margin and indent formatting, the bulleted or numbered list format carries forward from paragraph to paragraph. Each time you press Enter to begin a new paragraph, Word for Windows adds a new bulleted or numbered paragraph to the list. You can add another bulleted or numbered item anywhere in a list by placing the insertion point where you want to add the new item and then pressing Enter to begin a new paragraph. Word for Windows automatically adds a bullet or number to the beginning of the new paragraph and formats the paragraph with a hanging indent to match the other paragraphs in the bulleted or numbered list. You can also use the AutoFormat feature described in Chapter 11, "Formatting with Styles," to automatically create numbered or bulleted lists.

Creating Bulleted Lists

Word for Windows offers six standard bullet shapes: round (large or small), diamond (solid or hollow), arrow, and asterisk. If you want to use a heart, pointing hand, or some other symbol as your bullet, Word enables you to select the character for the bullet from any of your installed fonts.

You can create a bulleted list in two ways: with menu commands or with a toolbar shortcut. As usual, you have many more options when you use menu commands.

Creating Bulleted Lists with Menu Commands

To create a bulleted list with menu commands, follow these steps:

1. Type the list at the left margin (without using the Tab key to indent the text) and then select it.

    or

    Place the insertion point on a blank line.

2. Choose the Format Bullets and Numbering command. The Bullets and Numbering dialog box appears (see fig. 17.2).

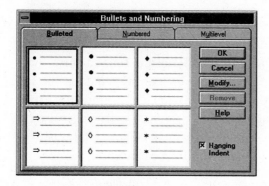

Fig. 17.2
Use the Bullets and Numbering dialog box to select the bullet and indent style options for a bulleted list.

3. Click the Bulleted tab to display the bulleted list options, if they are not already displayed.

4. Select the bulleted list format you want from the predefined choices by clicking it with the mouse or using the arrow keys. (The choices include two round bullets of different sizes, a solid diamond, a hollow arrow, a hollow diamond, and an asterisk.)

    Using the Modify button to customize a bulleted list's formatting is described in "Customizing Bulleted Lists," later in this section.

5. If you prefer a bulleted list with no hanging indent, select the Hanging Indent option in the Bullets and Numbering dialog box so that no X appears in that check box. Word for Windows sets no indent.

6. Choose OK. Word for Windows formats the current line or selected text as a bulleted list.

If you have not yet typed the bulleted list, type it now. Each time you begin a new paragraph, Word for Windows formats the paragraph as part of the bulleted list. To end the bulleted list, refer to "Ending the Bulleted List," a later part of this section.

> ### Note
>
> You can open the Bullets and Numbering dialog box by placing the pointer over the selected text and then clicking the right mouse button. A context-sensitive menu appears to the right of the insertion point; choose Bullets and Numbering to display the Bullets and Numbering dialog box.

If you want to replace an existing bulleted list with new bullets or change any of the other formatting properties of the bulleted list, select the list and then follow the instructions in "Customizing Bulleted Lists," a later part of this section. If you want to replace bullets with numbers, select the list and refer to the section "Creating Numbered Lists" later in this chapter for instructions on creating a numbered list. Word for Windows does not ask you to confirm replacing bullets with numbers. If you inadvertently change a bulleted list to a numbered list, use the Edit Undo command.

To add bulleted items anywhere in a bulleted list, position the insertion point where you want to add the new bulleted item, and press Enter to add a new paragraph to the list. Word for Windows automatically formats the new paragraph as part of the bulleted list.

Creating Bulleted Lists with the Toolbar

With the Formatting toolbar, you can easily set up a bulleted list by clicking the Bulleted List button (near the right side of the Formatting toolbar). When you create a bulleted list with the Bulleted List button, Word for Windows uses the bulleted list formatting options selected most recently in the Bullets and Numbering dialog box.

To create a bulleted list with the toolbar, follow these steps:

1. Use the View Toolbars command to display the Formatting toolbar, if it is not already displayed.

2. Type the list at the left margin and select it.

   or

   Place the text insertion point in a blank line.

3. Choose the Bulleted List button from the toolbar. Word for Windows formats the current line or selected text as a bulleted list.

If you have not yet typed the bulleted list, type it now. Each new paragraph is formatted as part of the bulleted list. Refer to the next section to end the bulleted list.

By default, Word for Windows uses a small round bullet and a 1/4-inch hanging indent to format lists with the Bulleted List button in the Formatting toolbar. If you recently selected different options in the Bullets and Numbering dialog box, however, Word uses those selections instead.

Ending the Bulleted List

If you apply bulleted list formatting to a blank line and then type the list, Word for Windows continues formatting each new paragraph you type as part of the bulleted list, until you end the bulleted list.

To end a bulleted list, follow these steps:

1. Press Enter to add a bulleted, blank line to the end of the bulleted list.

2. Move the pointer over the blank line and click the right mouse button. Word for Windows moves the insertion point to that line and displays a context-sensitive menu to the right of the insertion point.

3. Choose Stop Numbering to end the bulleted list. The bullet and hanging indent are removed from the blank line, ending the bulleted list.

Adding Subordinate Paragraphs to a Bulleted List

Sometimes the topic of a bulleted list item cannot be conveniently discussed in a single paragraph. Usually, if you require more than one paragraph to describe a single topic in a bulleted list, you want only the first paragraph for that topic to have a bullet. The remaining subordinate paragraphs for that topic do not need bullets, although they do need to have the same hanging indent as the bulleted paragraphs in the list.

Whether you are changing an existing bulleted paragraph to a subordinate paragraph or typing the bulleted list as you go along, you can change a bulleted paragraph into a subordinate paragraph by using either a context-sensitive shortcut menu or the Formatting toolbar.

Adding a Subordinate Paragraph with the Menu. To change a bulleted list item to a subordinate paragraph, follow these steps:

1. Select the bulleted list items from which you want to remove the bullets.

2. Move the pointer over the selected text and click the right mouse button. Word for Windows moves the insertion point to that line and displays a context-sensitive menu to the right of the insertion point.

3. Choose Skip Numbering. The bullet is removed from the selected paragraphs, but the hanging indent remains.

If you added a subordinate paragraph at the end of a bulleted list and you want to add another bulleted list item after the subordinate paragraph, choose the Bulleted List button from the Formatting toolbar to resume the bulleted list format.

 Adding a Subordinate Paragraph with the Toolbar. To use the toolbar to change a bulleted list item to a subordinate paragraph in the list, follow these steps:

1. Select the bulleted list items from which you want to remove the bullets.

2. Choose the Bulleted List button from the Formatting toolbar. The bullet is removed from the selected paragraphs, but the hanging indent remains.

Use the Bulleted List button to resume formatting the bulleted list.

Customizing Bulleted Lists

To customize an existing bulleted list or to make your own specifications for the formatting of a new bulleted list, use the Modify option from the Bullets and Numbering dialog box. Modify enables you to choose a character from any of your installed fonts to use as a bullet, and to specify the bullet's point size and color. You can also specify the size of the hanging indent; how much space appears between the bullet character and the text in the bulleted item; and whether the bullet is right, left, or center justified within the indent space.

You can customize a bulleted list format only by using menu commands; there is no toolbar shortcut. If your custom bulleted list format is the most recently specified format, however, the Bulleted List button will apply your custom format.

To create a custom bulleted list format, follow these steps:

1. Select the bulleted list whose format you want to customize.

2. Choose the Format Bullets and Numbering command. The Bullets and Numbering dialog box appears (refer to fig. 17.2).

3. Click the **B**ulleted tab to display the bulleted list options, if that tab is not already up front.

4. Choose the **M**odify button. The Modify Bulleted List dialog box appears (see fig. 17.3).

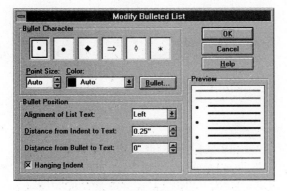

Fig. 17.3
The Modify Bulleted List dialog box lets you select custom bullet characters, colors, and point sizes for the bullet, and to choose how the bullet character is aligned in relation to the text.

5. Select the **B**ullet Character you want to use by clicking it or using the arrow keys.

Using the **B**ullet button to select a custom bullet character is described in the next part of this section, "Selecting a Custom Bullet Character."

6. Choose any of the following options:

Point Size	Type the point size you want the bullet character to be, or type **Auto** to have Word for Windows automatically select the size of the bullet.
Color	Use the list box to choose the color for the bullet. Choose Auto to have Word for Windows automatically select the color of the bullet.

(continues)

(continued)

Alignment of List Text	Use the list box to choose the alignment of the bullet within the space used for the indent. Word for Windows offers you the choice of left, right, or center justification.
Distance from Indent to Text	Type a number to set the size of the hanging indent.
Distance from Bullet to Text	Type a number to set the distance between the bullet and the text in the bulleted paragraph.
Hanging Indent Checkbox	Select this option to have each line of the numbered list indented

7. Choose OK. The Modify Bulleted List dialog box closes, and the Bullets and Numbering dialog box appears.

8. Choose OK. The Bullets and Numbering dialog box closes, and the new bullet format is applied to the bulleted list.

Caution

If you customize or reformat an existing bulleted list that contains subordinate (unbulleted) paragraphs, the subordinate paragraphs have bullets added to them.

Selecting a Custom Bullet Character

Word for Windows allows you to select any character from any of your installed fonts to use as the bullet character in a bulleted list.

To select a custom bullet character, follow these steps:

1. Choose the Bullet button in the Modify Bulleted List dialog box. Word for Windows displays the Symbol dialog box (see fig. 17.4).

Fig. 17.4

The Symbol dialog box lets you pick a bullet character from any installed font.

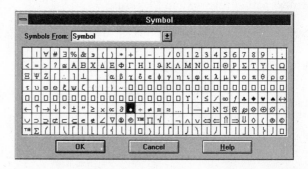

2. Select the bullet character you want from the Symbol dialog box by clicking the character or using the arrow keys. Use the Symbols From list box to select the font displayed in the Symbol dialog box.

3. Choose OK. The Symbol dialog box closes, and the bullet character you selected is shown, already selected, in the Bullet Character portion of the Modify Bulleted List dialog box.

Creating Numbered Lists

Numbered lists are much the same as bulleted lists; however, they are numbered sequentially rather than bulleted. Each paragraph you add to a numbered list is numbered so that its number is the next in sequence (after the number of the preceding paragraph). If you add a paragraph in the middle of a numbered list or rearrange the order of paragraphs in a numbered list, Word for Windows automatically renumbers all the paragraphs in the list so that they retain their sequential numbering.

Word for Windows offers six standard numbering formats and enables you to customize them. Word for Windows offers also a special type of numbered list, called a multilevel numbered list. In a multilevel numbered list, each successive indentation level in the list can be numbered. Multilevel numbered lists are described in the section "Creating Multilevel Lists" later in this chapter.

You can create a numbered list in two ways: with menu commands or with a toolbar shortcut. As usual, you have many more options when you use menu commands.

Creating Numbered Lists with Menu Commands

To create a numbered list with menu commands, follow these steps:

1. Type your list and then select it. Don't use the Tab key to indent the items on your list.

   or

   Place the text insertion point on a blank line.

2. Choose the Format Bullets and Numbering command. The Bullets and Numbering dialog box appears (refer to fig. 17.2).

3. Click the Numbered tab to display the numbered list options if they are not already displayed (see fig. 17.5).

For Related Information
■ "Formatting a Document Automatically," p. 341

Fig. 17.5

Use the Bullets and Numbering dialog box to select the numbered list format.

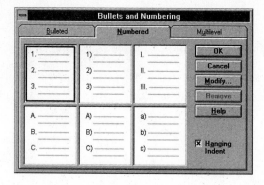

4. Select the numbering style you want from the predefined choices. Your choices include Arabic numbers, Roman numerals, and letters, with either periods or parentheses to separate the numbers from the list text.

   Using the Modify button to customize a numbered list is described in "Customizing Numbered Lists," later in this section.

5. If you prefer a numbered list with no hanging indent, select the Hanging Indent option in the Bullets and Numbering dialog box so that no X appears in that check box. Word for Windows sets no indent.

6. Choose OK. Word for Windows formats the selected text or line as a numbered list.

If you have not yet typed the numbered list, type it now. Each time you begin a new paragraph, Word for Windows formats the paragraph as part of the numbered list. To end the numbered list, refer to "Ending the Numbered List," later in this section.

Note

You can open the Bullets and Numbering dialog box by placing the pointer over the selected text and clicking the right mouse button. A context-sensitive menu appears to the right of the insertion point; choose Bullets and Numbering to display the Bullets and Numbering dialog box.

If you want to replace an existing numbered list with new numbers or change any of the other formatting properties of the numbered list, select the list and then follow the instructions in "Customizing Numbered Lists," a later part of this section. If you want to replace numbers with bullets, select the list and refer to the section "Creating Bulleted Lists" earlier in this chapter, for

IV

Mastering Special Features

instructions on creating a bulleted list. Word for Windows does not ask you to confirm replacing numbers with bullets. If you inadvertently convert a numbered list to a bulleted list, use the Edit Undo command.

To add numbered items anywhere in a numbered list, position the insertion point where you want to add the numbered item, and simply press Enter to add a new paragraph to the list. Word for Windows automatically formats the new paragraph as part of the numbered list and renumbers the paragraphs in the list so that all the numbers remain sequential.

Creating Numbered Lists with the Toolbar

A quicker way to number a list is to use the Numbered List button in the Formatting toolbar. The Numbered List button appears near the right side of the Formatting toolbar. When you create a numbered list with the Numbered List button, Word for Windows uses the numbered list formatting options selected most recently in the Bullets and Numbering dialog box.

To create a numbered list with the toolbar, follow these steps:

1. Use the View Toolbars command to display the Formatting toolbar, if it is not already displayed.

2. At the left margin, type the list and then select it.

   or

   Place the text insertion point on a blank line.

3. Choose the Numbered List button from the toolbar. Word for Windows formats the current line or selected text as a numbered list.

If you have not yet typed the numbered list, type it now; each new paragraph is formatted as part of the numbered list. To end the numbered list, refer to "Ending the Numbered list," the next part of this section.

By default, Word for Windows uses Arabic numbers and a 1/4-inch hanging indent to format lists with the Numbered List button in the Formatting toolbar. If you recently selected different options in the Bullets and Numbering dialog box, however, Word uses those selections instead.

Ending the Numbered List

As with bulleted lists, if you apply numbered list formatting to a blank line and then type the list, Word for Windows continues formatting each new paragraph you type as part of the numbered list, until you end the numbered list.

To end a numbered list, follow these steps:

1. Press Enter to add a numbered, blank line to the end of the numbered list.

2. Move the pointer over the blank line and click the right mouse button. Word for Windows moves the insertion point to that line and displays a context-sensitive menu to the right of the insertion point.

3. Choose Stop Numbering to end the numbered list. The number and hanging indent are removed from the blank line, ending the numbered list.

Adding Subordinate Paragraphs to a Numbered List

As with bulleted lists, sometimes the topic of a numbered list item requires more than one paragraph. And as with bulleted lists, you probably want only the first of several paragraphs for the same numbered list item to be numbered.

You can change a numbered paragraph into a subordinate paragraph by using either a context-sensitive shortcut menu or the Formatting toolbar.

Adding a Subordinate Paragraph with the Menu. To change a numbered list item to a subordinate paragraph by using the menu, follow these steps:

1. Select the numbered list items from which you want to remove the numbers.

2. Move the pointer over the selected text and click the right mouse button. Word for Windows moves the insertion point to that line and displays a context-sensitive menu to the right of the insertion point.

3. Choose Skip Numbering. The number is removed from the selected paragraphs, but the hanging indent remains.

If you added a subordinate paragraph at the end of a numbered list and you want to add another numbered list item after the subordinate paragraph, choose the Numbered List button from the Formatting toolbar to resume the numbered list format.

Adding a Subordinate Paragraph with the Toolbar. To use the toolbar to change a numbered list item to a subordinate paragraph in the list, follow these steps:

1. Select the numbered list items from which you want to remove the numbers.

2. Choose the Numbered List button from the Formatting toolbar. The number is removed from the selected paragraphs, but the hanging indent remains.

Customizing Numbered Lists

To customize an existing numbered list or to make your own specifications for the number format, use the Modify option from the Bullets and Numbering dialog box. Modify enables you to specify the text that comes before and after the number, to specify the numbering style, and to choose the font for the numbers. In addition, you can specify the size of the hanging indent; how much space appears between the bullet character and the text in the bulleted item; and whether the number is right, left, or center justified within the indent space.

You can customize a numbered list format by using only the menu commands; there is no toolbar shortcut to alter the format of a numbered list. If your custom numbered-list format is the most recently specified format, however, the Numbered List button will apply your custom format.

To create a custom numbered-list format, follow these steps:

1. Select the numbered list whose format you want to customize.

2. Choose the Format Bullets and Numbering command. The Bullets and Numbering dialog box appears (refer to fig. 17.2).

3. Click the Numbered tab to display the numbered list options, if they are not already displayed.

4. Choose the Modify button. The Modify Numbered List dialog box appears (see fig. 17.6).

5. Choose any combination of the following numbered list options:

Text **B**efore text box	Type the characters, if any, t1hat you want to come before each number. If you want each number enclosed in parentheses, for example, type **(** (the opening parenthesis) here.
Number list box	Select the numbering style you want. Available choices include Arabic numerals, upper- and lowercase Roman numerals, upper- and

(continues)

(continued)

	lowercase alphabet letters, and word series (1st, One, and First). You can also choose no numbers at all.
Text After text box	Type the characters, if any, that you want to come after each number. If you want each number enclosed in parentheses, for example, type) (the closing parenthesis) here.
Font button	Choose this button to use a special font or font attributes (such as bold, italic, and underline), or to set the point size for the numbers. A standard Font dialog box appears.
Start At text box	Type the starting number for your list. (If you're doing a series of lists, the starting number may be something other than 1.)
Alignment of List Text	Use this list box to select the alignment of the number within the space used for the indent. Word for Windows offers you the choice of left, right, or center justification.
Distance from Indent to Text	Type a number to set the size of the hanging indent.
Distance from Number to Text	Type a number to set the amount of space between the number and the text in the numbered paragraph.

6. Choose OK in the Modify Numbered List dialog box.

7. Choose OK in the Bullets and Numbering dialog box.

Fig. 17.6

Use the Modify Numbered List dialog box to select the starting number of the list, to select the text before and after the number, and to select the number's alignment.

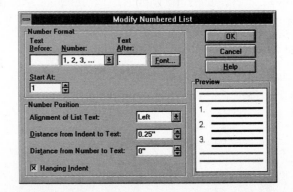

Creating Multilevel Lists

Multilevel lists are similar to numbered and bulleted lists but number or bullet each paragraph in the list according to its indentation level. Multilevel lists allow you to mix numbered and bulleted paragraphs based on indentation level.

You can create multilevel lists with up to a maximum of eight levels. You might use a multilevel list format if you want your list to have numbered items that contain indented, bulleted subparagraphs. Many types of technical or legal documents require each paragraph and indentation level to be numbered sequentially. You can also use multilevel lists to create outlines of various types.

Don't confuse multilevel lists, however, with the outline view and outlining features described in Chapter 19, "Organizing Content with an Outline," or with the heading numbering discussed later in this chapter. In the outline view and heading numbering, only paragraphs that have one of the nine heading styles are numbered. In a multilevel list, only paragraphs that have a body text style (such as Normal) can be part of the list.

You can create a multilevel list only by using the menu commands; there is no toolbar shortcut to create a multilevel list. Although you can customize the numbering formats for the various indentation levels of a multilevel list, you cannot have more than one multilevel list format in use in the same document.

To create a multilevel list, follow these steps:

1. Type and select your list. Use paragraph indenting to indent text; don't use the Tab key.

   or

   Place the text insertion point on a blank line.

2. Choose the Format Bullets and Numbering command. The Bullets and Numbering dialog box appears.

3. Click the Multilevel tab to display the multilevel list options, if the options are not already displayed (see fig. 17.7).

4. Select the multilevel numbering style you want from the predefined choices. Your choices include combinations of numbered and lettered paragraphs, technical, and legal numbering styles.

For Related Information

■ "Formatting a Document Automatically," p. 341

■ "Formatting Characters," p. 246

IV

Mastering Special Features

Using the Modify button to customize a multilevel numbered list is described in "Customizing Multilevel Lists," later in this section.

Fig. 17.7
Use the Bullets and Numbering dialog box to select the multilevel list format you want.

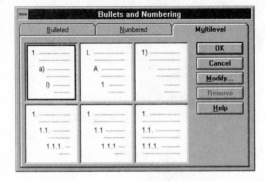

5. If you prefer a multilevel list with no hanging indent, select the Hanging Indent option in the Modify Bulleted List dialog box so that no X appears inside that check box (refer to fig. 17.3).

6. Choose OK. Word for Windows formats the selected text or line as a multilevel list.

If you have not yet typed the multilevel list, type it now. Each time you begin a new paragraph, Word for Windows formats the paragraph as part of the multilevel list and applies the appropriate numbering for that level of indentation. Use the Paragraph Indent and Unindent buttons in the toolbar (or the shortcuts Shift+Alt+right arrow and Shift+Alt+left arrow) to set the indentation level of each paragraph in the list. Word for Windows automatically adjusts the numbering to accommodate the paragraph's new level of indentation.

Ending a multilevel list is the same as ending a regular numbered list. To end a multilevel list, follow the instructions given in the preceding section for ending a numbered list. You can also add unnumbered subordinate paragraphs to a multilevel list the same way you would for a numbered list.

If you want to replace an existing multilevel list with new numbers or change any of the other formatting properties of the multilevel list, select the list and follow the instructions in "Customizing Multilevel Lists," the next part of this section. If you want to replace a multilevel list with a numbered or bulleted list, select the list and refer to the section "Creating a Bulleted List" or the section "Creating a Numbered List" earlier in this chapter for instructions on creating a bulleted or numbered list. Word for Windows does not ask you to confirm replacing a multilevel list with a bulleted or numbered list format. If you inadvertently convert a multilevel list, use the Edit Undo command.

To add a new item to the multilevel list at any indentation level, position the insertion point where you want to add the item, and press Enter to add a new paragraph to the list. Finally, use the paragraph indenting commands to indent the paragraph to the desired level. Word for Windows automatically formats the new paragraph as part of the multilevel list and renumbers the paragraphs in the list so that all the numbers remain sequential.

Customizing Multilevel Lists

Customizing a multilevel list format is similar to customizing a numbered or bulleted list. You can customize a multilevel list format by using only the menu commands.

To create a custom multilevel list format, follow these steps:

1. Select the multilevel list whose format you want to customize.

2. Choose the Format Bullets and Numbering command. The Bullets and Numbering dialog box appears (refer to fig. 17.7).

3. Click the Multilevel tab to display the multilevel list options, if they are not already displayed.

4. Choose the Modify button. The Modify Multilevel List dialog box appears (see fig. 17.8).

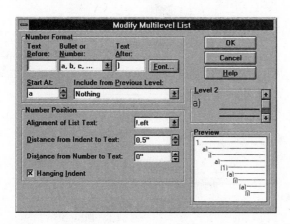

Fig. 17.8
Use the Modify Multilevel List dialog box to customize the numbering or bullet styles, alignment, and indentation levels of a multilevel list.

5. Use the Level list box to select the indentation level for which you want to adjust the formatting. You must customize each indentation level separately.

6. For each indentation level you customize, set the following options in any combination:

Text **B**efore text box	Type the characters, if any, that you want to come before each number or bullet at this indentation level.
Bullet or **N**umber list box	Select the numbering or bullet style you want. Available choices include a combination of the numbering choices available for numbered lists and the bullet choices available for bulleted lists, or no number or bullet at all.
Text **A**fter text box	Type the characters, if any, that you want to come after each number or bullet at this indentation level.
Font button	Choose this button to select any special font or font attributes (such as bold, italic, and underline), or set the point size for the numbers or bullets used at this indentation level.
Start At text box	Type the starting number for paragraphs at the selected level of indentation.
Include from **P**revious Level	Use this list box to select whether the numbering of indented paragraphs includes nothing from the previous level; or includes the number only, or the number and position from the preceding indented paragraphs. This control is not available if level 1 is selected in the Level list box.
Alignment of List Text	Select the alignment of the number or bullet within the indent space.
Distance from Indent to Text	Type a number to set the size of the hanging indent.
Distance from Number to Text	Type a number to set the amount of space between the number and the text in the numbered paragraph.
Hanging Indent	Select this option to have each bulleted list item indented.

7. Choose OK in the Modify Multilevel List dialog box.

8. Choose OK in the Bullets and Numbering dialog box.

Splitting a Numbered or Bulleted List

You may occasionally want to divide a long numbered or bulleted list into two or more smaller lists. To split a list, follow these steps:

1. Place the insertion point at the place where you want to divide the list.

2. Press Enter to create a blank line.

3. Remove the bullet or numbering from the blank line.

If you split a numbered or multilevel list, Word for Windows renumbers the list so that both lists start with the starting number (specified in the Modify Numbered List dialog box) and are numbered sequentially.

Removing Bullets or Numbering

You can remove bullets or numbering from a list by using either a menu command or the Numbered List and Bulleted List buttons in the Formatting toolbar.

To remove bulleted, numbered, or multilevel list formatting by using a menu command, follow these steps:

1. Select the list from which you want to remove bullets or numbering.

2. Choose the Format Bullets and Numbering command.

3. Choose the Remove button.

To remove list formatting by using the toolbar, do one of the following:

- To remove list formatting from a bulleted list, select the list and click the Bulleted List button in the Formatting toolbar.

- To remove list formatting from a numbered or multilevel list, select the list and click the Numbered List button in the toolbar.

Creating Numbered Headings

When you number headings, Word for Windows looks for different heading styles to determine how to number each heading paragraph. Paragraphs formatted with the heading 1 style, for example, are numbered with the first outline level (I., II., III.), paragraphs with the heading 2 style are numbered with the second level (A., B., C.), and so on. Word for Windows provides six predefined outline numbering formats for these different levels and allows you to establish your own custom numbering formats.

Only paragraphs with a heading style are numbered. You can apply heading styles by promoting or demoting the paragraphs in the outline view or by applying the appropriate heading styles. When you delete or rearrange numbered headings, Word for Windows automatically renumbers them. You can have only one heading numbering format in your document, although you can set the heading numbering so that numbering starts over at the beginning of each new document section. You can also choose to have headings appear with bullets instead of numbers.

To number headings, follow these steps:

1. Choose the Format Heading Numbering command. The Heading Numbering dialog box appears (see fig. 17.9).

Fig. 17.9
Use the Heading Numbering dialog box to choose the numbering or bulleting style for headings.

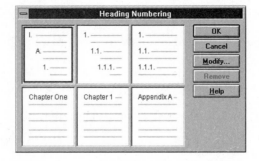

2. Select the heading numbering style you want from the predefined choices.

    Using the Modify button to customize heading numbering is described in "Customizing Numbered Headings," the next part of this section.

3. Choose OK.

The numbering format you selected is applied to all paragraphs in your document with a heading style.

IV

Mastering Special Features

Customizing Numbered Headings

To make your own specifications for the heading number format, use the Modify option from the Heading Numbering dialog box.

You can customize heading numbering by using only the menu commands; there is no toolbar shortcut.

To create a custom heading number format, follow these steps:

1. Choose the Format Heading Numbering command. The Heading Numbering dialog box appears (refer to fig. 17.9).

2. Choose the Modify button. The Modify Heading Numbering dialog box appears (see fig. 17.10).

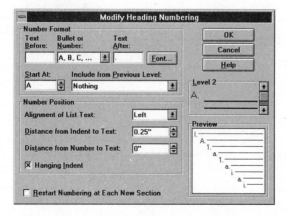

Fig 17.10
Using the options in the Modify Heading Numbering dialog box. You can vary the appearance of your heading number formats.

3. Use the Level list box to select the heading level for which you want to adjust the formatting. You must customize each heading level separately.

4. Choose or set any of the following options, in any combination:

Text **B**efore text box	Type the characters, if any, that you want to have appear before each number or bullet at this heading level.
Bullet or **N**umber list box	Select the numbering or bullet style you want. Available choices are a combination of the choices available for numbered lists and the choices available for bulleted lists, or you can choose to have no number or bullet at all.
Text **A**fter text box	Type the characters, if any, that you want to have appear after each number or bullet at this heading level.
Font button	Choose the **F**ont button to select any special font or font attributes (such as bold, italic, and underline), or set the point size for the numbers or bullets used at this heading level.
Start At text box	Type the starting number for the selected heading level.
Include from **P**revious Level	Use this list box to select whether the heading numbering includes nothing from the previous level; or includes the number only, or the number and position from the preceding heading level. This control is not available if level 1 is selected in the **L**evel list box.
Alignment of List Text	Use this list box to select the alignment of the number or bullet within the indent space.
Distance from Indent to Text	Type a number for the size of the hanging indent.
Distance from Number to Text	Type a number for the amount of space between the number or bullet and the text in the heading.
Hanging **I**ndent	Select this check box so that there is not an X in the box if you do not want a hanging indent for this heading level.
Restart Numbering	Select this check box so that there is an X in this check box if you want to have the heading numbering start over at the beginning of each new document section.

5. Choose OK to close the Modify Heading Numbering dialog box.

6. Choose OK to close the Heading Numbering dialog box.

Removing Heading Numbers

You can remove heading numbering by placing the insertion point in any heading paragraph and choosing the Remove button in the Heading Numbering dialog box.

From Here...

For information relating to numbered lists, bulleted lists, and numbered headings, review the following chapters of this book:

For Related Information

■ "Formatting Characters," p. 246

■ "Creating an Outline," p. 617

■ Chapter 11, "Formatting with Styles." Learn how to use the AutoFormat feature to create bulleted, numbered, and multilevel lists. The information on setting indents in this chapter will help you format your multilevel lists and numbered headings.

■ Chapter 2, "Getting Started in Word for Windows." Learn how to use the various controls on the toolbars.

■ Chapter 19, "Organizing Content with an Outline." Learn how to create and use headings in your document.

Chapter 18

Building Forms and Fill-In Dialog Boxes

In the past, one of the office tasks that word processors were not able to do well was fill in forms. Typewriters were always needed to fill in a form. Storage rooms and filing cabinets took up space just to keep months worth of inventory of forms that, in some cases, were so seldom used they were obsolete before ever leaving the shelf.

Word's new forms features are a big step in the direction of being able to do away with pre-printed forms. Using Word's desktop publishing features, many companies are now designing forms that they save as *templates* and print on demand. The cost savings over printing large volumes of forms can be huge.

In addition to Word's ability to produce a high-quality form on demand, Word now includes features that make it easy to fill in forms. Using the form fields in Word, you can put edit boxes, check boxes, and pull-down lists directly into your documents. The use of {fill in} and {ask} fields enable a document to pop up dialog boxes that ask for input.

In the first part of this chapter, you learn how to use the new edit box, check box, and pull-down lists within documents. These new form fields enable you to restrict the user to making only the type of entries you want them to make.

In the last part of this chapter, you see how to use a combination of field codes and simple macros to make documents that display dialog boxes asking the operator to enter data.

In this first half of the chapter, you learn to do the following:

■ How to create a template in which you can put edit boxes, check boxes, or pull-down lists

■ How to lock the template to prevent users from changing unauthorized parts of a document

■ How to specify lists of data that show-up in pull-down lists, or how to format the data that a user types in a data entry box

In the last half of the chapter, you learn to do the following tasks:

- How to use a {fill in} field to display a dialog

- How to ask for an item of data one time, yet use it throughout the document multiple times

- How to create a simple macro that controls these dialog boxes as soon as the dialog opens

Form Basics

A *form* is a special kind of protected document that includes fields where people can type information. Any document that includes form fields is a form. A *form field* is a location on-screen where you can do one of three things: enter text, toggle a check box on or off, or select from a drop-down list.

Tables provide the structure for many forms because a table's cells are an ideal framework for a form's labels and information fields. You can type labels in some cells, and insert form fields in others. Tables also make it easy to add shading and borders to forms. For example, in a table, you can place a dark border around a selected group of cells, while including no border at all around other cells. With the gridlines turned off, a table doesn't have to look like a table at all, and thus makes the ideal framework for a form.

A form can be based on any type of document. A real estate contract, for example, may include several pages of descriptive paragraphs containing form fields where you will insert information. The text in the paragraphs doesn't change—you insert information only in the form fields.

There are three types of form fields you can include in a form: text, check box, and drop-down. You can customize each of these field types in many ways. You can format a text field, for example, to accept only dates and to print dates as January 1, 1994, as 1/1/94, or in another format. Figs. 18.1, 18.2, and 18.3 show three examples of different forms

You can use forms in a variety of ways to save time, effort, and money. You can create your own commonly used business forms such as sales invoices, order sheets, personnel records, calendars, and boilerplate contracts. You can print a copy of your blank form and have it reproduced in quantity, using color if you want. Then print only the information contained in your form onto your preprinted forms—the information will be positioned correctly.

You also can automate forms that don't need to be printed at all. Distribute form templates, rather than paper forms, to people in your company. You can make forms easy-to-use by including helpful on-screen messages and automatic macros.

You can include calculations in forms. For example, add up the prices of items in a sales invoice form to show a total invoice amount. You can add form fields to other documents besides forms. When the fields are shaded, people can easily see where they should insert needed information.

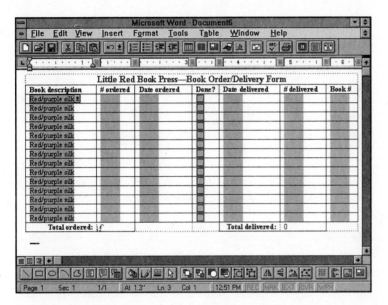

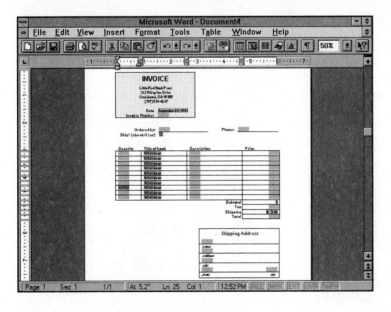

Figs. 18.1 and 18.2

Two examples of different forms.

Fig. 18.3
Another example
of a form

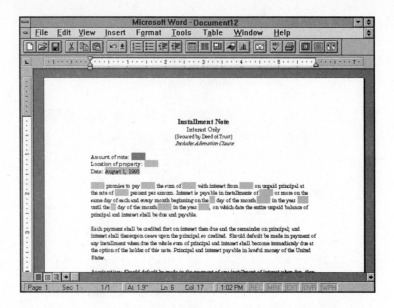

Forms are most useful when they're based on templates. This way, when someone fills in a form, they're only working on a copy, and the original stays unchanged. A form template can thus be used over and over. (You can, of course, create a form as a document instead of a template if you plan to use the form only one time.) When someone creates a new document based on your form template, they can type information only in the fields you designated when you created and protected the form. (Unless you add password protection, however, someone using the form can unprotect it and make changes to other parts of the form besides the fields. Later in this chapter, you learn how to provide maximum protection for your form templates.)

There are two important tools you can use to create forms: the Insert Form Field command, which you use to insert and customize form fields, and the Forms toolbar, which contains tools for building and customizing forms (see fig. 18.4).

Fig. 18.4
The Forms toolbar
includes tools to
help you build and
customize forms.

You can display the Forms toolbar by choosing the Insert Form Field command and choosing Show Toolbar, or by choosing the View Toolbars command and selecting Forms from the Toolbars list. Alternatively, you can click with the right mouse button on the Standard toolbar and select Forms from the drop-down list of toolbars that appears.

Building Forms

Building a simple form is a three-part process. First, you create a new template and build the *form structure*—the framework for the form—and add labels, formatting, shading and borders, and anything else that won't change when users fill in the form. Next, you insert form fields where you want to type information when you fill in the form. Finally, you protect and save the form.

To learn how to make more complex forms, refer to the upcoming section "Customizing Form Fields."

Creating and Saving the Form Structure

Another way you might create a form is by using frames. By framing a table or selected text, you can position it anywhere on the page you want (see fig. 18.5). In this way, you can separate the portion of a document that contains fields where you must insert information from other parts of the document where the text may not change.

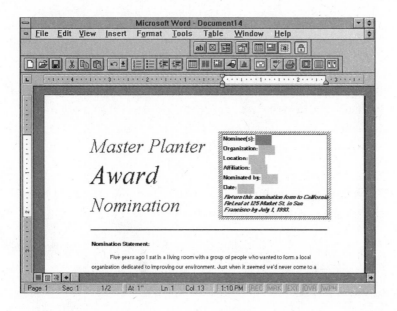

Fig. 18.5
By framing selected text that includes form fields, you can create a form like this.

Before you begin designing your form on your computer, it may be helpful to sketch it out on paper, particularly if you're using a table as the structure for your form. That way you'll know how many rows and columns you need in your table, and you'll know where to type labels and where to insert form fields. Even if you change it as you go, it's easier to start with a plan.

To create and save the form structure as a template, follow these steps:

1. Choose the File New command. The New dialog box appears.

2. Select from the Template list the template you want to use as the basis for your form. In most cases, you can use the Normal template.

3. Select Template from the New group.

4. Choose OK.

5. Establish the form structure in one of these ways:

Insert a table by choosing the Table Insert Table command, or by using the Table button on the Standard toolbar. Type labels and any other text that will not change in the form. Format the table with lines, borders, and shading.

Create a form based on paragraphs by inserting form fields where you need them as you type the text of your document. Read the next section, "Adding Form Fields," to learn how to insert form fields.

At the top of your document, insert the table or type the text that will contain form fields. Select, frame, and position this portion of your document. Then type the remainder of the form, which includes text that will not change when you fill in the form.

6. Choose the File Save As command to save the template. Type the name for your template in the Save As box, then choose OK. Leave your template open so you can add the form fields.

Tip
If you created a new form as a document, you can still save it as a template. Just save the file again with an appropriate name (using the DOT file extension) in the TEMPLATE directory.

Notice that templates are normally saved in the TEMPLATE directory under the directory containing Word.

Adding Form Fields

Once you've established the structure for your form—whether it's a table a framed block of text, or a paragraph—you can add the form fields. Form fields enable the user to enter data. There are three types of form fields: text, check box, and drop-down. You can add form fields to your template by using a menu command or by clicking buttons on the Forms toolbar.

To add form fields to your document using a menu command, follow these steps:

1. Position the insertion point where you want the form field to appear.

2. Choose the **Insert Form** Field command. The Form Field dialog box appears (see fig. 18.6).

Fig. 18.6
The Form Field
dialog box.

3. Select **Text**, **Check Box**, or **Drop-Down** from the Type group.

4. Choose OK. The form field appears in your document (see fig. 18.7).

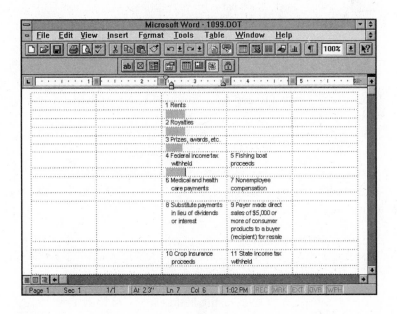

Fig. 18.7
A form field
appears in your
document.

To add form fields to your document using the Forms toolbar, follow these steps:

1. Display the Forms toolbar by choosing the **Insert Form** Field command and choosing the **Show Toolbar** button. The Forms toolbar appears (see fig. 18.8).

Alternatively, use another technique to display the Forms toolbar. (Refer to the section on "Using the Toolbars" in Chapter 2, "Getting Started in Word for Windows," for more information about displaying toolbars.)

Fig. 18.8
You can use the Forms toolbar to simplify form creation.

2. Position the insertion point where you want a form field.

3. Click one of the form field tools displayed at the left side of the Forms toolbar:

 To insert a text field, click the Text button.

 To insert a check box, click the Check Box button.

 To insert a drop-down list, click the Drop-Down button. (Note that a drop-down list is empty until you customize it by adding items to the list; see the later section, "Customizing Drop-Down Form Fields.")

A form field appears in your document.

4. Repeat Steps 2 and 3 to add more form fields to your document.

 Notice that the Forms toolbar contains a Shading Options button. If you select this tool, form fields appear as shaded rectangles on your screen. If you don't select this tool, text fields appear with no shading or border, check box fields appear with a square outline, and drop-down fields appear with a rectangular outline.

Although the preceding steps insert text boxes, check boxes, or lists, you cannot use these form fields until you protect the document or template, as described in the next section.

Refer to the later section, "Customizing Form Fields," to learn how to customize each of the form fields you add to your document. For example, you can customize a Text field so that the current date automatically appears; you can customize a drop-down field to add items to the drop-down list.

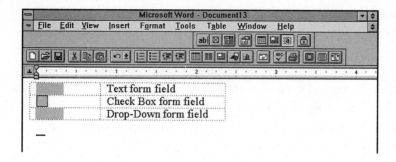

Fig. 18.9
Form fields appear shaded when you click the Shading Options button on the Forms toolbar.

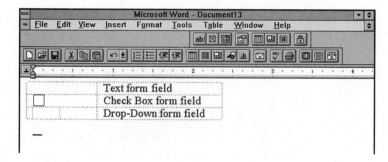

Fig. 18.10
If you don't click the Shading Options button, Text form fields don't show at all, and check box and drop-down form fields are outlined.

Protecting and Saving the Form

Until you protect a document containing form fields, you can edit any part of it, text or form fields. Once the document is protected, you can fill in a form field, but you can't edit the document.

A protected form is different from an unprotected form in several ways. For example, a protected document appears in page layout view, and you cannot edit the document—you can only insert a response into a form field. You can't select the entire document, and you can't use most commands, including formatting commands. Tables and frames are fixed, and fields with formulas display results, rather than the formula.

You can easily unprotect a document when you want to edit it—unless someone has protected it with a password. To learn how to use password protection, refer to the upcoming section, "Protecting and Unprotecting a Form with a Password."

To learn how to protect only part of a form, see the later section "Protecting Part of a Form."

Tip
If you're creating a form with a lot of form fields that are the same, save time by copying one or more existing form fields and pasting them into a new location.

Tip
Even if you don't want form fields shaded in your final on-line form, use shading while you create your form to make the fields easy to see and edit.

As long as you designated your new document as a template, then Word automatically saves it as a template (using the extension DOT) and proposes saving it in the TEMPLATE subdirectory, where it *must* remain in order for Word to find it when you create a new document. To use your form as a template, don't change these defaults. (You can, however, specify that all templates be stored in a different subdirectory by choosing the **Tools Options** command, selecting the File Locations tab, and modifying the User Templates.)

To protect and save your form, follow these steps:

1. Choose the **Tools Protect Document** command. The Protect Document dialog box appears (see fig. 18.11).

Fig. 18.11

After you protect a document, you can't edit it.

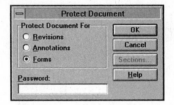

2. Select Forms, and choose OK.

3. Choose the **File Save As** command. (See fig. 8.12.) Type a name in the File **Name** box, and make sure that Document Template is selected in the Save File as Type list, and that the TEMPLATE subdirectory within the WINWORD6 directory is selected in the **Directories** list.

4. Choose OK to save the file as a template.

Fig. 18.12

Be sure to save your form as a template.

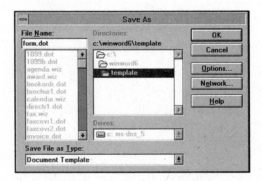

To unprotect your form, choose the Tools Unprotect Document command.

If your form is protected with a password, you must enter the password in order to unprotect your form. See the upcoming section, "Protecting and Unprotecting a Form with a Password."

To protect or unprotect your form using the Forms toolbar, click the Protect button on the Forms toolbar. When the button appears pressed, the form is protected; when the button appears raised, the form is unprotected.

Word has two ways of saving forms. You can save the complete form, including fields, labels, and the information you enter in a form. Or you can save just the information you entered into a form so that you can use this data with another program. See the section "Saving an On-Screen Form," later in this chapter, for details on the second method.

Using an On-Screen Form

The great advantage to forms is that you *can't* edit them—instead, you open a blank copy of the form (thus preserving the original), and then move from field to field, filling in information as needed.

The three types of form fields (text, check box, and drop-down) look different from each other on-screen, and you respond to each differently (see fig. 18.3).

Your form may be customized several ways. For example, you can customize a Text field to hold only dates and to format the date you enter in a certain way. Any type of field may have a help message attached so that when you enter the field or press F1, instructions for using the field appear in the status bar. In some fields, a particular response may cause some action in another part of the form; for example, a positive response to a check box field may activate another field later in the form. Be alert to what happens on-screen as you fill in your form.

To open a form, follow these steps:

1. Choose the File New command. The New dialog box appears (see fig. 18.14).

2. From the Template list, select the name of your form.

3. Choose OK. An unnamed copy of the form appears on-screen, and the first field in the form is highlighted.

Tip
Someone may have changed the names of your WINWORD6 directory and TEMPLATE subdirectory; accept these changed names if they appear as the defaults.

Tip
When you give someone an on-line form to use, be sure to give that person the template. Tell the person to copy the template into the TEMPLATE directory under the WINWORD6 directory.

For Related Information
- "Creating Tables," p. 509

- "Using Templates as a Pattern for Documents," p. 168

Fig. 18.13
Click the arrow or press Alt+down arrow to display the items in a Drop-Down list.

Clicking this arrow displays the items in a drop-down list.

Respond to a text field by typing a text or number

Select or clear a check box by pressing the space bar

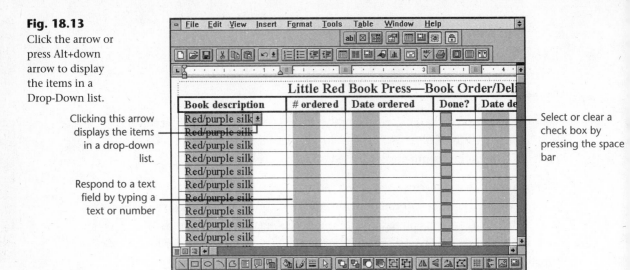

Fig. 18.14
Open a form by using the File New command.

If your form isn't based on a template, you can still use it by opening it as a regular file. Choose the File Open command, locate and select your form, and choose OK. Save it with a new name to preserve the original. For more information about opening files, see Chapter 3, "Creating and Saving Documents."

Filling in an On-Screen Form

When you open a new, protected form, the first field is selected (highlighted).

To fill in the fields in a form, follow these steps:

1. Respond to the selected field as appropriate.

   In a text field, type the requested text or number.

   Check boxes toggle on and off. Press the space bar once to place an X in an empty check box; press the space bar a second time to remove an X from the box. (Check boxes may have an X in them by default; if so, pressing the space bar once removes the X, and pressing the space bar a second time replaces the X.)

   In a drop-down field, click the arrow to display a list of selections, then click the item you want to select. Or with the keyboard, press Alt+down arrow to display the list, and press the down- or up-arrow keys to select an item from the list.

2. Press Tab or Enter to accept your entry. One of two things happens:

   If your entry is acceptable, then Word selects the next field.

   If your entry is unacceptable, Word displays an error message and returns you to the current field so that you can make a correct entry. You might get an error message, for example, when you type text in a Text field that's formatted to hold a number.

3. Continue responding to fields until you complete the form.

If you make a mistake and want to return to a previous field, hold down Shift as you press the Tab or Enter key enough times to reach the earlier field. To move to the next field without making an entry, just press Tab or Enter. You can also move between fields by pressing the up- or down-arrow keys, and you can move to the beginning or end of your form by pressing Ctrl+Home or Ctrl+End.

To edit an entry in a field you've already left, use the mouse or arrow keys to position the insertion point next to the text you want to edit and press Backspace to delete characters or type to insert characters.

If you want to insert a Tab character in a field, without moving to the next field, hold down the Ctrl key as you press Tab.

Always watch how Word interprets your response to a field. For example, if a Text field is formatted to include numbers formatted with no decimal places, and you respond by spelling out a number (four, for example), Word interprets your response as 0 (zero) because it's expecting numbers, not letters. Return to the field and type the correct response.

Tip

Except when a Drop-Down list is dropped down, you can use the up- and down-arrow keys to move between fields in a form.

Tip

Watch the status bar for messages that may appear to help you fill in each field in a form. You can also try pressing F1 to get help for a particular field when that field is selected.

If the form isn't protected, the first field isn't highlighted when you open the form, and you can't move between fields by pressing Tab or Enter. To fill in an unprotected form, use Word's normal techniques for moving the insertion point from field to field. Or better yet, protect the form by choosing the Tools Protect Document command and selecting the Forms option.

Saving an On-Screen Form

Because most on-screen forms are based on templates, they appear unnamed when you open them. You must save and name the form. (If a form is not based on a template, follow the steps outlined below to save your form with a unique name. In this way, you preserve the original for future use.)

To save a form, follow these steps:

For Related Information
■ "Using Templates as a Pattern for Documents," p. 168

■ "Typing and Moving in a Table," p. 515

1. Choose the File Save As command. The Save As dialog box appears.

2. Type a name in the File Name box, and select the directory for the form in the Directories list. You can save the form to a different drive by selecting a drive from the Drives list.

3. Choose OK.

Troubleshooting Forms

I opened a new form and the first field isn't selected.

The form isn't protected. To fill it in, protect it by choosing the Tools Protect Document command. (It may be a good idea to open the form template and protect it, so that the next time you open the form, it's protected.)

Customizing Form Fields

There are many ways you can customize form fields to make your forms more informative, more automated, and easier to use. Automatic date and time fields, for example, insert the current date or time into your form. Default entries suggest a likely response to a field. Help messages give users hints on how to fill in a particular field. Controls prevent certain types of errors. Formulas calculate results in a field. Macros run when users enter or exit a particular field. Controls prevent certain types of errors.

Formulas calculate results in a field. Macros run when users enter or exit a particular field.

You can also apply most types of formatting to form fields. For example, you can make a form field bold so that the response stands out. Or you can apply a border to a form field to add boxes in a form that isn't based on a table.

You can customize form fields while you're creating your form, by customizing fields as you insert them, or after you've created your form, by editing selected fields. To edit form fields after you've inserted them, the document must be unprotected.

To customize form fields as you insert them, follow these steps:

1. Choose the Insert Form Field command. The Form Field dialog box appears (see fig. 18.15).

2. Select the type of form field you want to insert and customize from the Type group: Text, Check Box, or Drop-Down.

3. Choose the Options button. A dialog box containing options for customizing the type of form field you've selected appears (see fig. 18.16).

Fig. 18.15
Use the Insert Form Field command to customize form fields as you insert them.

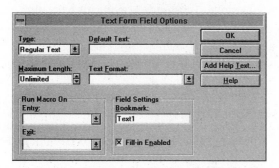

Fig. 18.16
If you select the Text form field option from the Type group, the Text Form Field Options dialog box appears when you click the Options button.

To customize an existing form field, follow these steps:

1. Unprotect your document, if it's protected, by choosing the Tools Unprotect Document command or by clicking the Protect button on the Forms toolbar.

2. Double-click the form field you want to customize, displaying the Form Field Options dialog box.

   or

   Select the form field you want to customize by clicking it, positioning the insertion point above or below it and pressing the up- or down-arrow key, or positioning the insertion point next to it and holding the Shift key as you press the right- or left-arrow key. Then do one of the following:

   Click the Options button on the Forms toolbar.

   or

   Click the form field you want to customize with the right mouse button to display the shortcut menu. Select Form Field Options.

3. Select the options you want, and choose OK.

Customizing Text Form Fields

Text fields are probably the most customizable of the three form field types. You can customize them by type (regular, number, date, or calculation, for example), by default text, by the size of the field, by the maximum number of characters in the response, or by the format of the response. As with all form field types, you can also customize Text fields by adding macros (see the later section "Adding Macros to a Form"), by adding Help text (see the section "Adding Help to a Form"), by renaming the bookmark (see "Naming and Finding Fields in a Form"), or by disabling the field for entry (see "Disabling Form Fields").

To specify the restrictions on a Text form field, follow these steps:

1. Open the Text Form Field Options dialog box (see fig. 18.17).

2. Select from these types of options (refer to the upcoming tables for details about the Type and Format options):

Tip
If you're using the same form field over and over in a form, duplicate it by placing it in AutoText (for details, see "Creating an AutoText Entry" in Chapter 5, "Editing a Document").

Tip
Specifying a field size is particularly important when you are using preprinted forms.

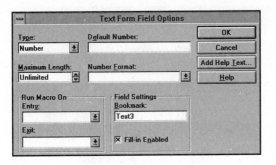

Fig. 18.17
Text form fields
have the most
customizing
options of any
form field type.

Option	Description
Type (see table 18.1)	Select from six types of text entries: Regular Text, Number, Date, Current Date, Current Time, and Calculation.
Default Text	Type in the text that you want to appear as the default entry in this field. Users can change the entry.
Maximum Length	Type or select "Unlimited" or the number of characters or numbers you want the field to accept (up to 255).
Text Format (see table 18.2)	Select from various types of text, numeric, and date formats, depending on what you've selected in the Type option.

3. Choose OK.

You will often use two or more of these options together. For example, if you select Number as the Type, then you might choose 0.00 as the Format so that a numeric response appears in two decimal places.

Table 18.1 Type Options for Text Form Field Options Dialog Box	
Select this option:	**When users should respond by typing:**
Regular Text	Text. Word formats the text according to your selection in the Text Format list.
Number	A number. Word formats the number according to your selection in the Number Format list and displays an error message if users type text.

(continues)

Table 18.1 Continued	
Date	A date. Word formats the date according to your selection in the Date Format list. Word displays an error message (A valid date is required) if users type text or a number not recognizable as a date and returns user to the current field for an appropriate response. However, nearly any response resembling a date will work.
Current Date	No user response allowed. Word enters the current date (and updates the date when the document is opened*).
Current Time	No user response allowed. Word enters the current time (and updates the time when the document is opened*).
Calculation	Enter a formula when inserting or editing this field; no user response allowed. Word applies your formula, and prints the result of the calculation in this field. For example, you can insert a simple SUM formula to add up the numbers in a column if your form is based on a table. (Word updates the result when the document is opened.*) To learn more about formulas, see Chapter 16, "Creating and Editing Tables," and Chapter 37, "Automating with Field Codes."

You can specify that Word update the date, time, or a formula when you print your form by choosing the Tools Options command, selecting the Print tab, and then selecting Update Fields   from Printing Options. Or you can use an exit macro to update the fields.

Table 18.2 Text Format Options for Text Form Field Options		
Type option	**Text Format option**	**What the entry looks like**
Regular Text	Uppercase	ALL CAPITAL LETTERS
	Lowercase	all lowercase letters
	First Capital	First letter of first word is capitalized
	Title Case	First Letter Of Each Word Is Capitalized
Number	0	123456
	0.00	123456.00
	#,##0	123,456
	#,##0.00	123,456.00
	$#,##0.00; ($#,##0.00)	$123,456.00
	0%	10%
	0.00%	10.00%

Type option	Text Format option	What the entry looks like
Date	M/d/yy	1/1/93
	dddd, MMMM dd, yyyy	Sunday, 3 January, 1993
	d MMMM, yyyy	3 January, 1993
	MMMM d, yyyy	January 3, 1993
	d-MMM-yy	3-Jan-93
	MMMM-yy	Jan-93
	MM/dd/yy h:mm AM/PM	01/03/93 2:15 PM
	MM/dd/yy h:mm:ss AM/PM	01/03/93 2:15:58 PM
	h:mm AM/PM	2:15 PM
	h:mm:ss AM/PM	2:15:58 PM
	h:mm	2:15
	h:mm:ss	2:15:58
Current Date	same as Date	same as Date
Current Time	h:mm AM/PM	3:30 PM
	h:mm:ss AM/PM	3:30:00 PM
	H:mm	15:30
	H:mm:ss	15:30:00
Calculation	same as Number	same as Number

Customizing Check Box Form Fields

You can customize check box fields, which require your user to make a simple "yes or no" response, by determining their size and by choosing whether they will be checked or unchecked by default. As with all form field types, you can also customize check box fields by adding macros (see the later section "Adding Macros to a Form"), by adding Help text (see the section "Adding Help to a Form"), by renaming the bookmark (see "Naming and Finding Fields in a Form"), or by disabling the field for entry (see "Disabling Form Fields").

To customize a check box field, follow these steps:

1. Open the Check Box Form Field Options dialog box (see fig. 18.18).

Fig. 18.18
You can make a
Check Box exactly
the size you want,
and you can
specify whether it's
checked or
unchecked by
default.

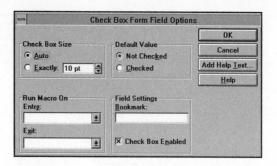

2. Determine the check box size by selecting the appropriate option:

   Select Auto to make the check box the same size as the text around it.

   Select Exactly to make the check box a specific size. Click the up or down arrow or press the up- or down-arrow key to increase or decrease the box size. Or type the size you want; for example, type **12 pt** for a 12-point box, **.25"** for a quarter-inch box, **1 pi** for a 1-pica box, or **1 cm** for a 1-centimeter box. (When you next open the dialog box, the measurement will appear in points.)

3. Determine the Default Value by selecting one of the following options:

   If you select Not Checked, the check box will be empty by default (a negative response). The user must press the space bar to check the box.

   If you select Checked, the check box will have an X in it by default (a positive response). The user must press the space bar to uncheck the box.

4. Choose OK.

Customizing Drop-Down Form Fields

A drop-down list gives users a list of up to 25 items to choose from. It helps ensure that the user's response to a field is valid because only valid responses are in the list. It also helps users fill in the form because they don't have to guess what kind of response the field requires.

You will most likely customize a drop-down form field as you insert it because there's nothing in the list until you do. You may want to add items to the list later, or remove some items, or rearrange the items, however. You can do this by editing the Drop-Down field.

To add items to the list in a Drop-Down field, follow these steps:

1. Open the Drop-Down Form Field Options dialog box (see fig. 18.19).

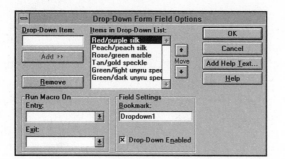

IV

Mastering Special Features

Fig. 18.19
You can add items
to a Drop-Down
list, remove items
from it, or
rearrange the
items in the list.

2. In the **Drop-Down Item** box, type the item you want to add to the list.

3. Choose the Add button.

4. Repeat Steps 2 and 3 to add more items to the list.

5. Choose OK.

To remove items from a drop-down list field, follow these steps:

1. Select the drop-down field and open the Drop-Down Form Field
   Options dialog box.

2. Select the item you want to remove from the Items in drop-down List
   list.

3. Choose the **R**emove button.

4. Repeat Steps 2 and 3 to remove more items.

5. Choose OK.

To rearrange items in a drop-down list field, follow these steps:

1. Select the drop-down field and open the Drop-Down Form Field
   Options dialog box.

2. Select the item you want to move in the Items in Drop-Down List list.

3. Move the item up by clicking the Move up arrow, or move it down by
   clicking the Move down arrow (with the keyboard, press the up or
   down arrow to select the item you want to move, press Tab to select the
   Move up or Move down arrow, and then press the space bar to move
   the selected item up or down).

4. Repeat Steps 2 and 3 to move more items.

5. Choose OK.

Formatting Form Fields

Users can't format entries in a protected form when they're filling in the form. But when you're creating a form, you can apply font and paragraph formatting to fields, as well as many other formatting options. Responses will then appear in that formatting.

You must insert a form field before you can format it. Remember, the document must be unprotected.

To format a form field, first select the form field you want to format. Then use one of the following methods to apply formatting:

- Choose the formatting command you want to use, and select the formatting options you want to apply.

- Click a formatting option on a toolbar.

- Press formatting shortcut keys.

- Click the selected field with the right mouse button to display the shortcut menu, and select Font, Paragraph, or Bullets and Numbering. Then select the formatting options you want to apply.

Disabling Form Fields

In most forms, you want users to respond to each field. But sometimes you'll want to disable a field, so users cannot respond. You may want to include a default entry in disabled fields.

To disable a form field, follow these steps:

1. Unprotect the document, if necessary.

2. Select the field you want to disable and display the Form Field Options dialog box.

3. Clear the appropriate option: Fill-in Enabled (for text fields), Check Box Enabled (for check box fields), or Drop-Down Enabled (for drop-down fields).

4. Choose OK.

Naming and Finding Fields in a Form

Each form field you insert in a document has a name: its *bookmark*. You can use this bookmark to help you find a field quickly. By default, Word numbers the fields you insert, calling them Text1, Check7, Dropdown13, and so forth. However, you can name a form field whatever you want (subject to bookmark naming rules—see Chapter 5, "Editing a Document").

To name a form field, follow these steps:

1. Unprotect the document, if necessary.

2. Select the field and display the Form Field Options dialog box.

3. In the Field Settings group, select the Bookmark text box and type the name.

4. Choose OK.

To find a named form field, follow these steps:

1. Unprotect the document.

2. Choose the Edit **B**ookmark command.

3. Type the name you want to find in the Bookmark Name box or select it from the list.

4. Choose the **G**o To button. Word displays the field, but doesn't close the dialog box. Go to another field, or choose Close to close the dialog box.

Adding Help to a Form

Adding help messages can make it much easier for users to respond correctly to a field in your form. There are two ways help messages can appear in your form when the field is selected: either in the status bar at the bottom of the screen or as a message box that appears when the user presses the F1 key. (The document must be protected in order for your help message to appear; if it isn't protected, pressing F1 displays Word help.)

You can type your own text for a help message or use an existing AutoText entry. For example, you may have an AutoText entry that reads Press F1 for Help, which you include as a status bar help message in each field for which you've included F1 help (see fig. 18.20).

To add help to a form field, follow these steps:

Fig. 18.20
Help can appear
in the status bar if
you use the Status
Bar tab.

1. Display the Form Field Options dialog box for the field to which you want to add help.

2. Choose the Add Help Text button.

3. Select the Status Bar tab to add a line of help in the status bar, or select the Help Key (F1) tab to add help that appears as a message box when the user presses F1 (see fig. 18.21).

Fig. 18.21
Help can appear
as a message box
when the user
presses F1 if you
use the Help Key
(F1) tab.

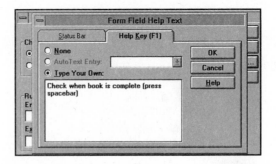

4. To add your own help message, select the Type Your Own option and type your message (up to 255 characters).

or

To use the text of an AutoText entry as help, select the AutoText Entry option, and select the AutoText entry you want to use from the list.

5. Choose OK.

6. Choose OK to close the Form Field Options dialog box and return to your document.

Tip
If you add F1 help
to a field, also
include a status
bar message read-
ing Press F1 for
help so your users
know where to
find help.

If you're including status line help messages, be aware that even if your form is protected, users can turn off the status line. Also be aware that there's no way for users to know whether F1 help is attached to a field (though a message in the status line can help, if the status line is displayed). If your form is based on a template, try including a message alerting users to the presence of F1 help in an AutoNew macro that runs when users create a new form. To learn more about macros, see Chapter 38, "Recording and Editing Macros."

Note

Help users fill in your form, or give them some instructions about what to do with the form when they're finished with it, by including a helpful message as part of an AutoNew macro that runs when users open the form. (AutoNew macros are attached to templates, and run when you create a new document based on the template. This idea works best for forms that are based on a template.)

Adding Macros to a Form

Macros can automate your forms in many ways. They can activate or deactivate fields depending on the user's response to an earlier field. They can update fields that contain calculations. They can cause Word to skip over unneeded fields.

To use a macro in a form, you must create the macro before you apply it to a particular field in the form. Macros run at one of two times: when the user enters the field or when the user leaves the field.

When you record or write macros for your form, be aware that macros use bookmarks to locate particular fields, so make sure there are no duplicate bookmark names in your form. You can find out the automatic bookmark name of any field, or give the field a new bookmark name, by selecting the field, displaying the Form Field Options dialog box, and then looking at the **B**ookmark text box (for details, see the section "Naming and Finding Fields in a Form" earlier in this chapter).

To be useful, attach your macros to the template that your form is based on. You can do this most easily as you create the macro, or you can attach a macro to your template by choosing the File **T**emplates command, then choosing the **O**rganizer button and selecting the Macros tab (for details, refer to Chapter 6, "Using Templates as Master Documents.")

To learn about creating macros, refer to Chapter 38, "Recording and Editing Macros."

Your document must be unprotected before you can apply macros to a field. And remember, before you can apply a macro to a form field, you must create the macro.

To apply a macro to a form field, follow these steps:

1. Select the field to which you want to apply a macro, and display the Form Field Options dialog box.

2. If you want the macro to run when the user enters the field, select the Entry option in the Run Macro On group and select the macro you want from the list.

   or

   If you want the macro to run when the user leaves the field, select the Exit option in the Run Macro On group and select the macro you want from the list.

3. Choose OK.

If no macros appear in either the Entry or Exit list, no macros are available for your form's template. You must either create the macro, or attach it to your template.

Protecting and Unprotecting a Form with a Password

If you don't want users to change your form, protect it with a password. In this way, anyone attempting to unprotect the form must supply the password (including you—don't forget your password).

To password-protect a document, follow these steps:

1. Choose the Tools Protect Document command. The Protect Document dialog box appears (see fig. 18.22).

Fig. 18.22
Type your password in the Password box.

2. Select the Forms option.

3. Select the Password box, and type your password. Choose OK. The Confirm Password dialog box appears (see fig. 18.23).

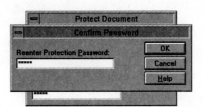

Fig. 18.23
To confirm your password, you must retype it exactly as you typed it the first time.

4. In the Reenter Protection Password box, retype your password. Spelling, spacing, and capitalization must match exactly. Choose OK. (If you don't retype the password exactly as you originally typed it, you get an error message. Choose OK and try again.)

5. Choose OK to return to your document.

To unprotect a password-protected document, follow these steps:

1. Choose the Tools Unprotect Document command, or click the Protect button on the Forms toolbar. If the document is password protected, the Unprotect Document dialog box appears (see fig. 18.24).

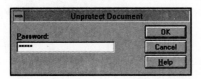

Fig. 18.24
To unprotect a password-protected document, you must enter the password exactly as you typed it originally.

2. Type the password exactly as you originally typed it in the Password box. Spelling, spacing, and capitalization must match exactly.

3. Choose OK. If you typed the password correctly, you return to your document, which is now unprotected. If you typed the password incorrectly, Word displays a message that the password is incorrect, and you must choose OK to return to your document, which remains protected.

Protecting Part of a Form

If your form is divided into sections, you can protect parts of it, while leaving other parts unprotected. You can include password protection for the protected sections.

To learn how to divide a document into sections, refer to Chapter 13, "Setting the Page Layout."

To protect or unprotect part of a form, follow these steps:

1. Choose the Tools Protect Document command. The Protect Document dialog box appears.

2. Select the Forms option.

3. Choose the Sections button to display the Section Protection dialog box (see fig. 18.25).

Fig. 18.25

You can protect part of a document if it's divided into sections.

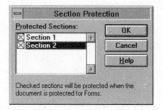

4. In the Protected Sections list, select each section you want protected so that it appears with an X in the box. Clear each section you want unprotected.

For Related Information

- "Marking Locations with Bookmarks," p. 149

- "Calculating Math Results in a Table," p.547

- "Changing Layouts Within a Document," p.432

- "A Reference List of Field Codes," p. 1099

- "Recording Macros," p. 1124

5. Choose OK to return to the Protect Document dialog box. (If you want to protect the sections with a password, do so now. For details, see the earlier section, "Protecting and Unprotecting a Form with a Password.")

6. Choose OK to return to the document.

Converting Existing Forms

The forms you want to create may already exist on paper or in another program's format. Sometimes the easiest way to convert a form is to simply retype it, but other times you may want to use existing data.

You can use a scanner to help you retype an existing form. Scan the form as a picture, and insert it into a text box. When a picture is in a text box, you can move it to the layer behind the text in your document. In the text layer, you can trace over the scanned form to create your new form. When you're finished, select and delete the scanned form. (To learn about working with pictures and text boxes, see Chapter 22, "Inserting Pictures in Your Document," and Chapter 24, "Drawing with Word's Drawing Tools.")

Though you can't import form fields from a document created by another program into a Word document, you can import text. If a form exists in another program, import the text, and then format it as you need it and add the form fields. You can change text to a table by selecting the text and choosing the Table Convert Text to Table command. To learn about importing documents into Word, see Chapter 34, "Converting Files with Word for Windows." To learn about tables, see Chapter 16, "Creating and Editing Tables."

Printing a Form

There are three ways you might want to print a form. You might want to print it exactly as it appears on-screen, including the labels, any graphics, and the data in the fields. You may want to print the data only onto preprinted forms. Or you may want to print the labels and graphics only, to create a preprinted form.

Printing the Filled-In Form

To print the entire form, including everything that appears on your screen, use Word's usual printing commands. Use this method to print forms that you've already filled in.

To print the entire form, follow these steps:

1. Fill in the form, or open a filled-in form.

2. Choose the File Print command.

3. Select the printing options you want from the Print dialog box, and choose OK.

To learn more about printing options, refer to Chapter 8, "Previewing and Printing a Document."

Printing Form Data Only

Print only data when you're using preprinted forms. Because you use the same form template to print the blank form as you use when you print only the data, the form data will line up with the fields correctly.

To print only data onto a preprinted form, follow these steps:

1. Insert the preprinted form into your printer.

2. Choose the Tools Options command.

3. Select the Print tab (see fig. 18.26).

4. Select Print Data Only for Forms from the Options for Current Document Only group, and choose OK.

5. Choose the File Print command, select printing options, and choose OK.

Fig. 18.26
Use the Tools
Options command
to print form data
only.

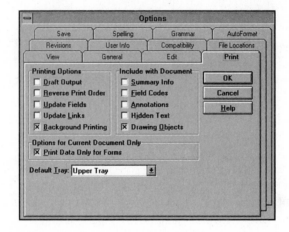

Notice that this procedure assures that each time you print this form, you will print data only. Repeat the procedure, deselecting the Print Data Only for Forms option in Step 4, if you want to print the entire form.

Printing a Blank Form

To make your own preprinted form, print the form only, without the data.

To print a blank form, follow these steps:

1. Choose the File New command, select the form you want to print from the Template list, and choose OK.

2. Without filling in the form, print it by choosing the File Print command, selecting printing options, and choosing OK.

Remember that fields in your form appear shaded if the Shading Options button is selected in the Forms toolbar. This shading will not appear when you print your forms. If you want shading to appear on a printed form, use the Format Borders and Shading command to shade selected areas of your form.

Troubleshooting Printing a Form

When I print the form data, it doesn't line up with the form fields on the preprinted form.

Be sure you're using the same form to print your data as you used to create the preprinted form.

Saving Data Only

You may want to use the data you collect in your forms with another program, such as a database. To do that, save only the data, and import the data into the other program. Word saves a copy of the data as a Text Only document (with the extension TXT), creating a comma-delimited document containing only the responses in your fields.

Many applications can read the data stored in comma-delimited files. Microsoft Excel, for example, can open and automatically separate each piece of data into a worksheet cell if the file uses the file extension CSV (comma separated values).

To save data only from your form, follow these steps:

1. Choose the Tools Options command.

2. Select the Save tab.

3. In the Save Options group, select the Save Data Only for Forms option.

4. Choose OK.

5. Choose the File Save As command to save and name your data.

For Related Information
- "Printing the Current Document," p. 227

Building Forms with Fill-In Dialog Boxes

With {fillin} fields, you can design a form letter so that you need to enter a data item (such as a name) only once—no matter how many times it appears in the letter. This is extremely useful for filling out invoices, contracts, proposals, or business forms in which the majority of the body copy remains unchanged. {fillin} fields also are useful when you need to insert personal phrases within mass mailings. Fig. 18.27 shows a document you can create to demonstrate {fillin} fields.

Fig. 18.27

Field codes can enter data or display dialog boxes that prompt users to enter data that can be used repeatedly through the document.

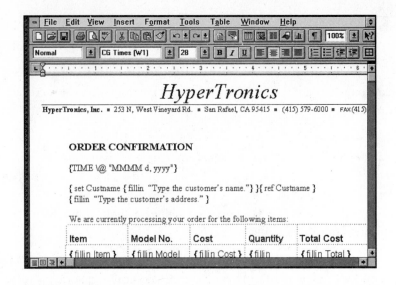

First you should create a new template for form letters.

To create a new template, follow these steps:

1. Choose the File New command. The New dialog box appears, as shown in fig. 18.28.

Fig. 18.28

Using a template on which to create a form prevents the user from accidentally changing the original.

2. Select the Template option in the New box.

   Normal already should be selected in the Template list.

3. Select a different template on which to base the letter, if you prefer. You may have created a template, for example, that includes a letterhead or company logo.

4. Choose OK.

5. Modify the template to include any body text, graphics, tables, and so on that you want in the form letter. Format the template's page layout to account for letterhead if that is used.

Keep the template open and on-screen so that you can add {fillin} fields as described in the next section.

Using {fillin} Fields

To set up your template to prompt the user to enter key information, use {fillin} fields. Fig. 18.29 shows a dialog box prompt generated by a {fillin} field. For more information on {fillin} fields, refer to Chapter 37, "Automating with Field Codes."

To insert the {fillin} field code in a document, move the insertion point to where you want the operator's input to appear. Choose the Insert Field command. Make sure [All] is selected in the categories list, then select Fill-in from the Insert Field Names list. In the Field Codes text box, move the insertion point past FILLIN, type the user prompt in quotes and choose OK.

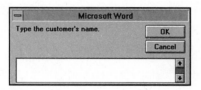

Fig. 18.29
The {fillin} field is an easy way to ask users to enter data into a dialog box. You don't need to create a macro to display the dialog box.

Alternatively, you can type the {fillin} field into the template. To do this, move the insertion point to where you want the results to appear, then press Ctrl+F9, the Insert Field key. Position the insertion point between the field characters and type the following field type and instructions:

fillin "Type the customer address."

To display the dialog box requesting the customer's name and update the {fillin} field, follow these steps:

1. Select the field character at either end of the code or text on both sides of the code to select the {fillin} field.

2. Press F9. The Fillin dialog box appears.

3. Type a customer address in the box. To start a new line in the box, Press Enter. Choose OK to complete the box and insert your entry in the document.

Tip
Enclose prompts longer than one word in quotation marks (" "). If you don't enclose a phrase in quotes, Word uses only the first word.

Tip
To update {fillin} fields throughout an entire document, select the entire document, then press F9 (Update).

The entry you typed appears in the document in the same location as the field code. Text following the inserted entry is pushed down or right, just as if you had manually typed text in the location. To switch between displaying fields and their results, press Alt+F9 or display the Options dialog box (by choosing **Tools Options**) and click the Field Codes check box in the View tab.

Reusing Field Results

If you use field codes in form letters, you can request an input from the operator one time, but have that information appear in multiple locations. To reuse an entry from one {fillin} box in other locations in a form letter, you must use three field codes:

- {set bookmark data} assigns data to a bookmark, which stores information so that it can be reused later. In the next example, the data argument for {set} is a {fillin} field so that the operator's entry is stored in the bookmark name Custname. If the data is explicit text that doesn't change, such as *Montana*, you must enclose it in quotation marks. Don't include a space in the bookmark name.

- {fillin [prompt]} displays an input box in which the operator can enter data. The brackets ([]) indicate that the prompt is optional.

- {ref bookmark} displays the contents of a bookmark at the field location. You enter this field to repeat a bookmark's contents in other locations within the document.

Fig. 18.30 shows a field code that requests the customer's name and stores it in the Custname bookmark. The {fillin} field requests the name. The {set} field sets Custname equal to the {fillin} entry. The {ref} field displays the entry stored in Custname. You can use {ref} throughout the letter following the {set} field, even though the data was entered only once.

In fig. 18.30, the {fillin} field displays a dialog box in which the user types an entry. The {set} field code then stores the entry in the bookmark Custname. (You can make up your own single words to use as bookmarks.) The data stored in Custname can be redisplayed anywhere in the document with {ref Custname}. The {ref} field code references the data stored in that bookmark. You can reuse {ref} as many times as you want in the document. Using the switches described in Chapter 37, "Automating with Field Codes," you can format the information that {ref} returns.

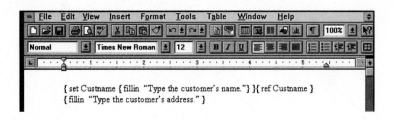

IV

Mastering Special Features

Nested fields are one field code inside of another field code. In the example, a {fillin} field is nested inside a {ref} field. The result of the {fillin} is used to supply one of the arguments required by the {ref} field. To build the *nested field* in fig. 18.30 from the inside out, follow these steps:

1. Position the insertion point before where you need to use the entry.

2. Press Ctrl+F9, the Insert Field key.

3. Between the field characters, type **fillin**, a space, then a quoted prompt to the operator, such as **"Type the customer's name."**

4. Select the field you just typed. To select field characters and field contents, select a field character at either end.

5. Press Ctrl+F9 to enclose the selection in field characters.

   This step *nests* your first field entirely inside another set of field characters. The insertion point moves directly after the first field character.

6. Directly after the first field character, type **set**, a space, then the appropriate bookmark, such as **Custname**.

   Leave a space after the bookmark, but don't leave spaces in the name.

This new nested field requests a name and stores it in the bookmark, but the entry doesn't appear on-screen. To see the field's result, you must update the field.

To update both of these new fields and see the customer's name requested and displayed, follow these steps:

1. Select the entire line or lines containing both fields.

2. Press F9 (Update Fields).

   A dialog box appears and requests the customer's name (refer to fig. 18.29).

3. Type the entry as requested.

4. Choose OK.

The {set} field stores in the bookmark the name you entered in the {fillin} field. The {ref bookmark} field displays the contents of a bookmark in the letter. You can enter a {ref bookmark} field in multiple locations in the document, wherever you need the name repeated. In fig. 18.31, the Custname bookmark is repeated at the last line on the screen. The new contents of {ref bookmark} don't appear, however, until each {ref bookmark} field is updated.

Fig. 18.31

Reuse data by repeating the {ref bookmark} combination wherever you want the data to display. The {ref} only displays the new data when it is selected and updated.

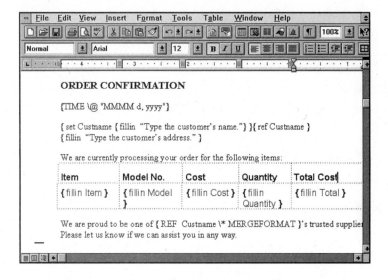

After you enter all of the field codes, choose File Save As and choose OK to save the template.

These fields display data entered in the address block; they also request and display the type, model, and cost of the items the customer ordered. The switch * mergeformat used in the {ref bookmark * mergeformat} field ensures that the formatting you applied to the field name in the document doesn't change when the field is updated. The format of field results match the format you apply to the letter *r* in *ref*.

The inclusion of the * mergeformat switch is controlled by the Preserve Formatting During Updates option in the Field dialog box. Chapter 37, "Automating with Field Codes," provides more information on switches that format and control field results.

Saving and Naming the Template

This document must be saved as a template because you opened it as one. To save your template, choose the File Save As command. Type an eight-letter name to describe your form in the File Name text box. Notice that you cannot change many of the text or list boxes. Choose OK. Word saves the template and adds the extension DOT. When you save a new template, give it a name that reflects the type of document it creates.

Updating Fields in a Form

To test the fields you entered, update them. This action will display new values, or allow you to enter new ones.

To enter data into the {fillin} fields and update the {ref} fields, follow these steps:

1. Choose File New and select a template containing {fillin} fields. Choose OK.

2. Move the insertion point to the top of the document, then press F11 to select the next field. (Press Shift+F11 to select the preceding field, or select the entire document by choosing the Edit Select All command to update all fields.)

3. Press F9 to update the selected field or, if the entire document is selected, each field in turn from the beginning to the end of the document.

4. Type the data requested and choose OK. (To preserve the previous entry, select Cancel; nothing is produced if no previous entry existed.)

If an error appears at a field's location, display the field codes in the document. Check for correct spelling and spacing. Use one space between field types, instructions, and switches.

Creating a Macro to Update Fields Automatically

Because this type of fill-in form is designed for repetitive use, you can have Word automatically prompt the user for the information as soon as the document is opened. You can do this with an automatic macro that updates all fields in the document when the document opens. With the fill-in template as the active document, follow these steps:

1. Choose the Tools Macro command. The Macro dialog box appears (see fig. 18.32).

Fig. 18.32

You can record a macro that automatically updates field codes when a document or template opens.

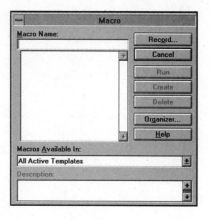

2. Type **AutoNew** in the Macro Name box.

3. In the Make Macro Available To list, select the Documents Based on [template] option, where [template] is the name of the template. The macro will be available only to this template or to documents that originate from this template. (The option of where a macro is saved is described in Chapter 38, "Recording and Editing Macros.")

4. Click the Record button.

5. Enter a description, such as **Automatically updates all fields**, in the Description box.

6. Choose OK.

The Macro Record toolbar appears on the screen and the REC indicator is highlighted in the status bar, indicating that the recorder is on. Follow these steps to record a process that updates all fields in the document:

1. Press Ctrl+5 (on numeric keypad) to select the entire document.

2. Press F9. A prompt generated by the first {fillin} field appears.

3. Choose the Cancel button for each {fillin} prompt.

4. Press Ctrl+Home to return the insertion point to the top of the document.

 5. Click the Stop Recorder button in the Macro Record toolbar.

Choose File Save All to save the macro and close the template. To test the macro, follow these steps:

1. Choose the File New command.

2. Select the template from the Use Template list.

3. Choose OK.

When you open the document, the AutoNew macro runs the update macro. Enter a response to each dialog box or choose Cancel. If the macro doesn't run correctly, record it again. If you re-record using the same name (AutoNew), Word asks whether you want to replace the previous recording. Choose Yes.

From Here...

For information relating to forms, you may want to review the following chapters of this book:

- Chapter 6, "Using Templates as Master Documents," which describes working with templates, on which most forms are based.

- Chapter 16, "Creating and Editing Tables," which describes creating and formatting a table as the framework for a form.

- Chapter 20, "Calculating Math with Formulas," which describes using formulas to perform calculations in forms.

- Chapter 27, "Desktop Publishing," which describes designing a form's layout.

- Chapter 37, "Automating with Field Codes," which includes automating fields other than form fields in a form.

- Chapter 38, "Recording and Editing Macros," which describes automating forms with macros.

Chapter 19

Organizing Content with an Outline

Many writers feel comfortable organizing their thoughts and even their schedules with outlines. If you're in that group of organized people, you are going to enjoy working with the Word for Windows outlining feature. In Word for Windows, an *outline* is a special view of your document that consists of formatted headings and body text. Nine possible outline heading levels are available: Heading 1, Heading 2, Heading 3, and so on, through Heading 9. Each heading level can have one level of body text. Assigning each heading level a different formatting style enables you and the reader to quickly discern the organization of your document.

Having an outline for your document is useful in many ways. For one thing, an outline can help you organize your thoughts as you compose a new document. At a glance, you can quickly see an overview of your document that shows only the headings. Later, an outline can help you reorganize and edit your document. By "collapsing" parts of your document so that only the headings show, you can easily move an entire section—heading, subheadings, and any associated body text. But Word for Windows has some other not-so-obvious uses for outlines: you can easily number the parts of a document, change heading-level formatting (each heading level has its own specific style), and use headings to generate tables of contents and other lists.

This chapter helps you maintain your documents and manage changes made within a workgroup. You learn how to do the following:

- Create and work with an outline

- Reorganize your document easily by using an outline

- Use outline headings to create tables of contents

Viewing an Outline

To view an outline, choose the View **O**utline command, or click the Outline View button at the left of the horizontal scroll bar (see fig. 19.1). Fig. 19.1 shows the first page of a document in the normal editing view, and fig. 19.2 shows the same document in outline view with headings displayed. Fig 19.3

shows the document in an expanded outline view, with text and subheadings displayed.

Fig. 19.1
A document in normal view that does not show outline headings.

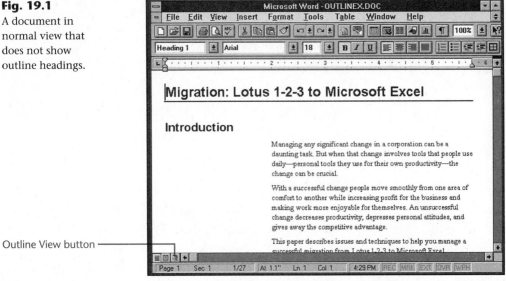

Outline View button

Fig. 19.2
Outline view that shows an overview of contents (headings only).

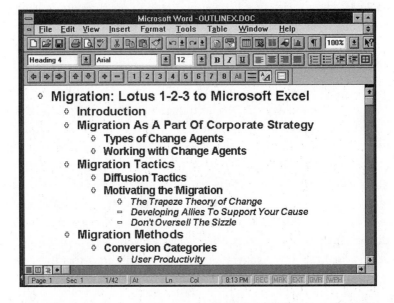

You can see that the outline view looks different from the normal editing view in several ways. First, the *Outline toolbar* has replaced the ruler. Second, the formatted headings and body text paragraphs are indented to different levels. Third, a + or – icon is displayed to the left of each heading and paragraph.

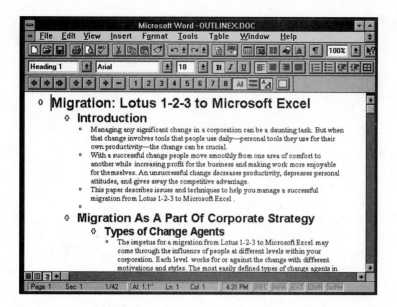

IV

Mastering Special Features

Fig. 19.3
Outline view that shows detailed contents by expanding the outline.

When you are in outline view, you have the option of viewing headings at different levels or of viewing the entire document, including all body text. You also have a choice of displaying headings at selected levels or of displaying headings and text. Seeing only the headings of a large document gives you an opportunity to see an overview of your document. You can also see where topics have been missed or misplaced.

The Outline toolbar includes buttons you can use to assign heading levels to text, promote or demote headings, and hide or display headings. Table 19.1 summarizes the functions of the buttons in the Outline toolbar.

Table 19.1 The Functions of the Buttons in the Outline Toolbar

Button	Function
◀	*Promote button.* Promotes the heading (and its body text) by one level; promotes body text to the heading level of the preceding heading.
▶	*Demote button.* Demotes the heading by one level; demotes body text to the heading level below the preceding heading.
⇒	*Body Text button.* Demotes the heading to body text.
▲	*Move Up button.* Moves the selected paragraph(s) before the first visible paragraph that precedes selected paragraph(s).

Button	Function
Table 19.1 continued	
Move Down button. Moves the selected paragraph(s) after the first visible paragraph that follows selected paragraph(s).	
Expand button. Expands the first heading level below the currently selected heading; repeated clicks expand through additional heading levels until body is expanded.	
Collapse button. Collapses body text into heading and then collapses lowest heading levels into higher heading levels.	
Buttons 1 through 8. Display all headings and text through the lowest level number you click.	
All button. Displays all text if some is collapsed; displays only headings if all text is already expanded.	
First Line button. Switches between displaying all the body text, or only the first line of each paragraph.	
Show Formatting button. Displays the outline with or without full character formatting.	
Master Doc button. Changes to master document view or back to simple outline view. If master document view is selected, the Master Document toolbar appears to the right of the Outline toolbar.	

In the sections that follow, you learn how to use these buttons to create and reorganize your outline. The Master Document toolbar is described in Chapter 32, "Assembling Large Documents."

In fig. 19.2, notice that two different types of screen icons are displayed to the left of the headings and paragraphs in the outline. A plus sign (+) means that subordinate headings (those at a lower level than the heading being examined) or paragraphs of body text are associated with the heading. A minus sign (–) indicates that no headings or paragraphs are beneath the heading.

Creating an Outline

Creating an outline does two things: organizes your work by heading, sub-heading, and body text; and applies formatting to each heading level. Styles define the formatting applied to each heading level. The first level of heading is formatted by the style Heading 1, the second level is formatted by Heading 2, and so on, through Heading 9. Body text is formatted by the Normal style. The Heading and Normal styles are predefined by Word for Windows; however, you can redefine any of those styles by using the Format Style command (see Chapter 11, "Formatting with Styles").

Word for Windows provides two ways to create an outline. The first method is to select the outline view and assign heading levels to your text by using the buttons on the Outline toolbar (while creating the document or after creating it). This chapter describes this method. The second method is to work in the normal view (or draft or page layout view) of your document and assign appropriate styles such as Heading 1 or Heading 2 to headings. To learn how to apply styles to text, see Chapter 11, "Formatting with Styles."

To create an outline in a new or existing document, follow these steps:

1. Choose the **View Outline** command.

2. Type a heading or select the text you want to convert to a heading. Select the heading by moving the insertion point anywhere within the heading's text, or by clicking to the left of the heading (but not clicking the plus or minus icon).

   If you're creating an outline from scratch (in a new file), the level 1 heading (Heading 1) is applied as you begin typing.

3. Assign the appropriate heading level by clicking in the Outline toolbar or pressing one of these shortcut keys:

	Result	Mouse Action	Shortcut Key
⇦	Promote heading one level	Click left-arrow button	Press Alt+Shift left-arrow key
⇨	Demote heading one level	Click right-arrow button	Press Alt+Shift right-arrow key
⇨	Convert heading to body text	Click double-arrow button	
⇦ ⇨	Convert body text to heading	Click right- or left-arrow button	Press Alt+Shift left- or right-arrow key

4. Press Enter to end the heading (or body text) and start a new heading (or body text) at the same level.

Note

As you work in your document in normal or page layout view, you may come to text that should be a heading in the outline. You can stay in the normal or page layout view and create this heading. One way is to format the paragraph with a heading style. Another method is to move the insertion point into the heading text and press Alt+Shift+left-arrow key. The paragraph containing the insertion point is formatted to the same heading level as the preceding outline heading in the document. Use Alt+Shift+left-arrow key or Alt+Shift+right-arrow key to adjust the heading to the level you want.

Formatting Your Outline

When you create an outline, you're actually applying styles to the headings in your document. The styles determine your document's formatting. Unless Heading 1 has been redefined in your document, for example, the style applies the Arial font in 14-point size, boldface, with extra space before and after the heading.

If you want the headings in your document to be formatted differently from the predefined heading styles, you must redefine the heading styles. If you want the level 1 headings in your outline to be formatted differently, for example, you must redefine the Heading 1 style. You can redefine styles by formatting an example or by choosing the Format Style command, choosing the Modify button, and then redefining a style. (To learn more about defining styles, see Chapter 11, "Formatting with Styles.") When you redefine a style for a heading, the format change applies to all headings formatted with that style.

Promoting and Demoting Headings

Promoting a heading means raising its level in the outline. You may promote a Heading 3 to a Heading 2, for example, to make the indent smaller. *Demoting* does just the opposite. When you promote and demote headings, Word for Windows assigns the appropriate heading style for that level.

Using the Mouse to Promote or Demote Headings —

You can use the mouse to promote or demote headings in two ways. One method uses the buttons in the Outline toolbar. Using this technique, you promote or demote only the selected heading. In the other method, you drag the heading's plus or minus icon left or right until the heading is at the level you want; with this technique, you promote or demote the heading and all subordinate text.

If you want to use the mouse to promote or demote only the selected heading(s) or text, follow these steps:

1. Choose the View Outline command (if you haven't already).

2. Select the paragraphs to promote or demote.

3. Click the Promote button (a left-arrow button) in the Outline toolbar to promote the heading.

    or

    Click the Demote button (a right-arrow button) to demote the heading.

    or

    Click the Body Text button (a double-arrow button) to convert the heading to body text.

Headings are treated independently; associated subheadings are not promoted and demoted along with the headings. Body text, however, always remains associated with its heading. This method is useful for changing only the selected heading level while leaving subordinate text or levels alone.

To promote or demote a heading and have all subordinate headings and text change at once, follow these steps:

1. Choose the View Outline command.

2. Move the mouse pointer over the plus or minus icon that appears to the left of the heading you want to promote or demote (the pointer becomes a four-headed arrow). Click and hold down the mouse button.

3. Drag the icon to the left to promote the heading and its subordinate subheadings and body text, or drag the icon to the right to demote them. (Drag to the right edge of the outline to demote a heading to body text.)

As you drag a heading to a new level, the mouse pointer becomes a two-headed arrow, and a gray vertical line appears as you drag across each of the heading levels. When the gray vertical line is aligned with the new heading level you want—that is, aligned with other headings at the level you want—release the mouse button.

Using Keyboard Shortcuts to Promote or Demote Headings

You can also use keyboard shortcuts to promote and demote individual headings (and body text). You needn't be in outline view to use this method; any view works.

To use shortcut keys to promote or demote a heading or portion of body text, follow these steps:

1. Select the heading(s) or body text to promote or demote.

2. Press Alt+Shift+left-arrow key to promote one level.

   or

   Press Alt+Shift+right-arrow key to demote one level.

   Only selected headings and text are affected; associated subheadings are not promoted or demoted along with selected headings.

No matter which method you use, when you return to the normal editing view and display the ruler, you see that the appropriate heading styles have been applied to your outline headings. (You can return to normal editing view by choosing the View Normal or View Page Layout command.)

Collapsing and Expanding an Outline

A *collapsed* outline shows only the headings down to a specific level. When an outline is *expanded* to a specific level, you see all headings down to that level, as well as body text. You can collapse an outline all the way down so that only level 1 headings show, or you can expand the outline all the way so that all headings and body text show. You can also expand the outline to show all headings and only the first line of each paragraph of body text.

Collapsing and expanding your outline can help you to write and edit. By collapsing your outline, you can see an overview of your entire document and can move around quickly in the outline. To move to a particular section, just collapse to the level of the heading to which you want to move, select the heading, and then expand the outline. You can also use shortcuts to move entire headings and all their subordinate headings and text to new locations in the outline.

To collapse or expand the entire outline, use the numeric buttons on the Outline toolbar. Click the lowest level you want to display in your outline. If you want to show levels 1, 2, and 3 but no lower levels, for example, click the 3 button.

To display all levels, including body text, click the All button. To display all heading levels but no body text, first click All to display all levels and body text (if not already displayed), and click All again to collapse the body text, leaving only the headings for all levels displayed. Clicking a number in the Outline toolbar collapses or expands your entire outline uniformly. Fig. 19.4 shows the outline presented in fig. 19.2 with only two levels of headings displayed.

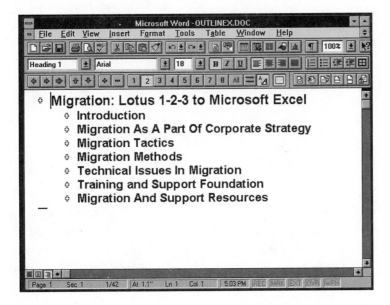

Fig. 19.4
Collapsing an outline shows only higher levels of headings.

Using the Mouse to Collapse or Expand Headings

You can use the mouse and the plus and minus buttons in the Outline toolbar, as well as the plus and minus icons in the outline, to selectively collapse or expand headings. Here are the methods you use:

■ Collapse headings and body text into the selected heading by clicking the minus button in the Outline toolbar.

- Expand contents of selected headings by clicking the plus button in the Outline toolbar.

- Expand or contract a heading's contents by double-clicking the plus icon to the left of the heading in outline view.

Using Keyboard Shortcuts to Collapse or Expand Headings

If you don't have a mouse or if you work faster on the keyboard, you can collapse and expand your outline by using shortcut keys. Table 19.2 lists the shortcut keys available. Before using a shortcut key, you must select the heading or text you want to collapse or expand.

Table 19.2 Using Shortcut Keys to Collapse and Expand Headings	
Shortcut Key	**Description**
Alt+Shift+- (hyphen)	Collapses the selected heading's lowest level and collapses all body text below the heading. Repeated presses collapse additional levels.
Alt+Shift++ (plus sign)	Expands the selected heading's next lower level. Repeated presses expand additional levels and, after all headings are expanded, body text.

Fitting More of the Outline into the Window

One of the great benefits of using an outline view of your document is the ability to get an overview of your document's organization. As you work with an outline to organize a document, you may want to view more of the outline than usually fits into the display window. Word for Windows provides two ways to fit more of an outline into the display window; you can use these methods separately or in combination.

If you expand all or some headings to display subordinate body text, you may find that parts of the outline are pushed out of the display window. To view more of the outline, you can display the first line of each body text paragraph only, instead of the entire paragraph. You can also display the outline view without the full character formatting for each heading style. Because the character formatting for many of the heading styles usually uses boldface text and fairly large point sizes, each heading takes up a lot of room on the screen. Omitting the character formatting makes the headings take up less room.

Displaying an outline without character formatting affects the display in outline view only; it does not make any permanent changes in the heading styles or their formatting. Fig. 19.5 shows the same outline as in fig. 19.2, but without the full character formatting. Notice how much more of the outline is now visible.

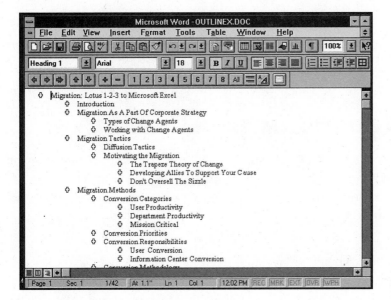

Fig. 19.5
Displaying the outline without character formatting in the headings fits more of the outline into the window.

Using the Mouse to See More of the Outline

You can use the mouse and buttons in the Outline toolbar to fit more of the outline into the display window. Use either of the following methods:

- To show only the first line of expanded body text paragraphs, click the First Line Only button in the Outline toolbar. If the body text paragraphs are already showing only the first line, clicking this button causes the entire paragraph to be displayed.

- To display the headings without full character formatting, click the Show Formatting button in the Outline toolbar. If the headings are already shown without character formatting, clicking this button causes the formatting to be displayed again.

Using Keyboard Shortcuts to See More of the Outline

If you prefer to use the keyboard, you can fit more of the outline into the display window by using shortcut keys. Table 19.3 lists the shortcut keys available.

Table 19.3 Using Shortcut Keys to See More of the Outline	
Shortcut Key	**Description**
/ (slash key on numeric keypad)	Shows or hides character formatting for headings.
Alt+Shift+L	Shows only first line of each paragraph of expanded body text. Pressing this key combination a second time displays all text.

Reorganizing an Outline

You can select outline headings in any of the normal ways, using Word for Windows selection techniques. The outline view, however, offers a shortcut for selecting that can be a real time-saver. When you select an outline heading by clicking its icon in the outline view, you select the heading and its subordinate headings and body text.

Even if you don't use an outline to organize your thoughts before you begin writing, you can use an outline later to reorganize your document quickly. After you click a heading's plus or minus icon, you can move all the subordinate headings and text as a unit. (If you select only the words in an expanded heading, you move only the heading.)

You can move selected headings (along with associated subheadings and body text) by using the mouse or keyboard. To move a selected heading upward (toward the first page) or downward (toward the last page), use any of these methods:

■ Press Alt+Shift+up- or down-arrow key.

■ Drag the heading's icon up or down.

■ Click the Move Up or Move Down button in the Outline toolbar.

By selecting multiple headings and paragraphs, you can move them as a unit. Hold Shift as you click adjacent headings and paragraphs to select them together.

Numbering an Outline

If you need numbered outlines for legal documents, bids, or proposals, you can have Word for Windows add the numbers for you.

To number your outline (from any view), use the Format Heading Numbering command. You can then select the type of numbering method. Fig. 19.6 shows some of the numbering options available. Fig. 19.7 shows an outline that uses the legal numbering style. For detailed information on numbering, see Chapter 17, "Creating Bulleted or Numbered Lists."

To quickly apply heading numbering, click with the right mouse button on any heading and select Heading Numbering from the shortcut menu that appears.

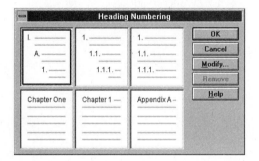

Fig. 19.6
Using the Heading Numbering option to renumber outlines.

Using Outline Headings for a Table of Contents

If you need a table of contents, Word for Windows can build one from the outline. Word for Windows constructs tables of contents by accumulating outline headings and their page numbers.

To create a table of contents from outlining, use the Insert Index and Tables command. Chapter 29, "Creating Indexes and Tables of Contents," goes into detail on how to use the Indexes and Tables dialog box shown in fig. 19.8 to create a table of contents like that shown in fig. 19.9.

To create a table of contents, follow these steps:

1. Position the insertion point where you want the table of contents to appear.

2. Choose the Insert Index and Tables command.

3. Select the Table of Contents tab.

4. Select the options you want.

5. Choose OK.

Fig. 19.7
Automatic
numbering makes
legal and proposal
documents easy to
construct.

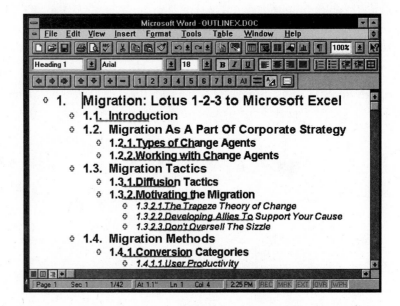

Replacing Outline Headings

Outline headings are formatted by styles—specifically, Word for Windows built-in Heading 1 through Heading 9 styles. Because you can search for and replace styles in Word for Windows, you can globally change outline headings. For details about searching and replacing, see Chapter 7, "Using Editing and Proofing Tools."

Using Custom Styles to Create an Outline

If you formatted a document with custom styles and you want to convert the document to an outline, you can replace the custom styles with outline styles.

Suppose, for example, that your document is formatted with custom heading styles called *title*, *heading*, and *subheading*. Choose the Edit Replace command. With the insertion point in the Find What text box, choose Format, select Style, and then select the style title. Then in the Replace With text box choose Format, select Style, and select the style heading 1. (Type no text in either text box.) In the Replace dialog box, choose Replace All to replace all title styles with heading 1 styles. Do the same for all other headings and subheadings in your document. Then you can view your document as an outline.

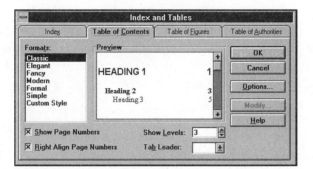

Fig. 19.8
From this dialog box, you can create a table of contents.

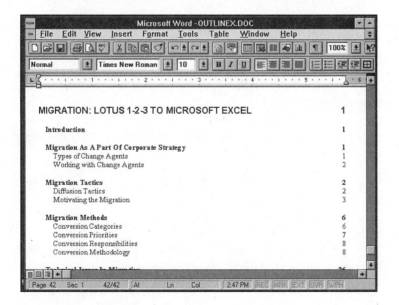

Fig. 19.9
The finished table of contents, using outline headings and document page numbers.

Globally Replacing Outline Headings

In your document, you may want to globally promote or demote heading levels. For example, you may want to change all level 3 headings to level 4 headings. To do that, replace Heading 3 styles with Heading 4 styles (see the general instructions in the previous section "Using Custom Styles to Create an Outline").

Removing Text from Within an Outline

You can remove all text from within an outline if the text is formatted with a style. You may want to remove all the text from an outline, for example, so that you can save just the headers. To remove the text, rather than replacing the style (or styles) that formats the text with another style, replace it with nothing. To remove text in an outline formatted with Word for Windows default styles, for example, replace the style Normal with nothing. For details, **see** the general instructions in the previous section "Using Custom Styles to Create an Outline."

Printing an Outline

You can print your document as seen in the outline view. To print the outline, choose the View Outline command, display the levels of headings and body text you want to print, and then choose the File Print command, or press Ctrl+P.

From Here...

For information relating to outlining, review the following major sections of this book:

- Chapter 11, "Formatting with Styles," which explains creating, applying, and changing styles.

- Chapter 29, "Creating Indexes and Tables of Contents." If your document is formatted with Word for Windows automatic styles—Heading 1 through Heading 9—you can collect these headings into a table of contents or an index.

- Chapter 32, "Assembling Large Documents." Working in outline view, you can create a master document that governs subdocuments.

Chapter 20

Calculating Math with Formulas

Have you ever wanted to perform calculations on the numbers in a Word for Windows table that you created and have the results automatically updated if the figures in the table change, much as you would in a spreadsheet? Or perhaps you would like to perform a calculation on numbers scattered throughout a document, without searching for each number and then performing the math yourself. Word for Windows simplifies these tasks with the features discussed in this chapter.

Using Word's Math Functions or a Spreadsheet?

Windows gives applications the capability to integrate results from other applications into your Word document. You can easily paste, insert, link, or embed the results from a Windows worksheet, such as a Microsoft Excel or Lotus 1-2-3 worksheet, into your Word document. Yet Word has its own basic math and table features. If you have both Word and a Windows worksheet available, you should learn the advantages and disadvantages of both.

You may want to use Word's built-in math capabilities under the following conditions:

- When problems involve simple math, such as totals or averages

- When numbers are arranged in rows and columns in a table

- When numbers are distributed throughout a document and the math result depends on those numbers

This chapter helps you maintain your documents and manage changes made within a workgroup. You learn how to do the following:

- Calculate totals or mathematical results using data from the cells in a table, much like a worksheet

- Calculate results from numbers used in the text of a document

■ When results do not need to be linked to or updated in other documents

You may want to do math in a worksheet and then paste, link, or embed the results into Word under these conditions:

■ When problems involve complex math operations unavailable in Word

■ When problems involve worksheet analysis, such as database analysis or trends forecasting

■ When numbers are arranged in different cell locations throughout a table, rather than in simple rows and columns

■ When one worksheet can be updated with that worksheet's result updating multiple linked Word documents

For Related Information

■ "Transferring Data with Copy and Paste," p. 999

■ "Linking Documents and Files," p. 1008

■ "Embedding Data," p. 1000

If you need to use a Windows worksheet to do your problem solving, you should read Chapter 33, "Using Word with Other Windows Applications." If you need to integrate a Word document with the results from a DOS worksheet, make sure that you read Chapter 34, "Converting Files with Word for Windows."

Performing Calculations

You can use two methods to calculate numbers in Word for Windows. Both methods calculate the results within a field. *Fields* are codes you place in your document to automate certain procedures. (See Chapter 37, "Automating with Field Codes," for more about field codes.)

With the first method of calculating numbers in a document, you assign bookmarks to each of the numbers you want to use in the calculation. Book-marks are a named location. You then use the bookmarks that specify the location of numbers combined with math operators and constants to write an expression to calculate the desired result.

You use the second method if you are working in a table, similar to working in a spreadsheet. With this method, you can perform the calculations within the table by referring to specific cells or ranges of cells. You can also place a calculation field that calculates a result based on the numbers in one or more tables.

Using Bookmarks to Perform Calculations in Text

To perform calculations on numbers scattered throughout a document and to allow the results of a calculation to be updated if any of the numbers change, you need to use bookmark names and fields. Performing math on numbers within a document takes two steps: you must mark the location of numbers in the text, and then enter a field code that calculates the mathematical result.

To create the bookmarks that will contain numbers used in the calculations, follow these steps:

1. Create your document and type numbers where you will be typing numbers. Save your document.

2. Choose the **Tools Options** command and select the View tab.

3. Select the Bookmarks check box, then choose OK.

4. Select a number in the document you want to use in a calculation.

5. Choose the Edit Bookmark command to display the Bookmark dialog box.

6. Type a name in the Bookmark Name edit box. Use a descriptive name that starts with a letter and has no spaces.

   Use a bookmark name that indicates the number's meaning, such as Profit, Expense, or Budget.

7. Choose the Add button. You will see the square brackets that indicate a bookmark surrounding the selected number.

8. Return to step 4 until you have assigned a bookmark to each number used in calculations.

Note

Be careful when you delete or change a number entered at a bookmark location because you may delete the bookmark. If you accidentally delete the bookmark, a math field that uses that bookmark will produce an error. To prevent yourself from deleting bookmarks, only edit the numbers in bookmarks while the screen is set so you can see bookmark end symbols. To display bookmark end symbols, choose the **Tools Options** command and select the View tab. Select the Bookmark check box, then choose OK. The ends of bookmarks will now appear as a pair of square brackets, [ ]. When you edit or delete numbers work within the brackets and do not delete them. While editing within bookmark brackets, you may find it helpful to magnify the screen with the View Zoom command.

To insert the math function or formula that calculates using the numbers you have just identified with bookmarks:

1. Position the insertion point where you want the calculation result to appear, and choose the Insert Field command. Word for Windows displays the Field dialog box (see fig. 20.1).

Fig. 20.1

Entering a calculation formula in the Field dialog box.

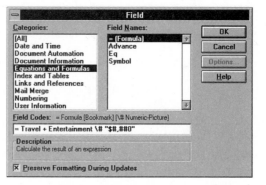

2. Select Equations and Formulas from the Categories list and select = (Formula) from the Field Names list.

3. In the Field Codes text box, type the mathematical expression for calculating the desired result, using bookmark names and mathematical operators.

   Type a formula using the bookmarks and math operators as you would expect to write a formula. For example,

   =Revenue-Cost

You can use any of the functions or mathematical operators listed under the entry for the {=} field in Chapter 37, "Automating with Field Codes."

4. Following the mathematical formula, add any formatting instructions. For more information on formatting numeric results, see the topics on general switches in Chapter 37, "Automating with Field Codes."

5. Choose OK.

The results of the field (that is, the calculation in the field) are displayed unless you have set Word for Windows to display field codes with the Tools Options command, in which case the field code and formula itself are displayed. To turn the field code display on or off, select the field (or the field's result) and press Shift+F9. To update the field, select the field and press F9.

For additional information about editing or modifying formulas entered within a field code, please see Chapter 37, "Automating with Field Codes."

Consider an example of a calculation that uses bookmarks and a formula field:

> Your budget for this quarter is $8,465 for travel and $2,500 for entertainment. This gives you $10,965.

In this example, you can apply the bookmark Travel to $8,465 and the bookmark Entertainment to $2,500. The field you use to calculate the result is

```
{=Travel+Entertainment \# "$#,##0"}
```

The advantage of using a formula field for this calculation is that you can quickly update the results whenever the numbers for the travel or entertainment budgets change. The numeric picture \# "$#,##0" is used to format the result without decimal places. Number formatting is described in Chapter 37, "Automating with Field Codes."

For Related Information
- "Marking Locations with Bookmarks," p. 149
- "Editing Fields," p. 1084
- "Formatting Field Results," p. 1085

Performing Calculations in a Table

To perform a calculation in a table, you use table references and special functions to create a field expression for calculating the desired result. *Functions* are built-in mathematical formulas that perform operations such as Sum and Average.

Specifying Table Cells in a Formula

As you enter a formula in a field in a table, you refer to individual cells or ranges of cells in the table by using column and row coordinates. The columns of a table are lettered A, B, C, and so on; the rows of a table are numbered 1, 2, 3, and so on, just as in a spreadsheet. To refer to an individual cell in a table, specify first the column letter followed by the row number. To refer to the cell in the second column of the third row of a table, for example, you use the coordinates B3.

> **Note**
>
> Unlike the cell coordinates in Excel, the cell coordinates in Word for Windows are always absolute; you do not need to use the dollar sign ($) notation used by Excel.

You can specify ranges of cells in a table by using two cell coordinates separated by a colon (:). To specify the first three cells in the row C, the third row, of a table, for example, you use the coordinates C1:C3. You can specify an entire column or row by using a range without starting or ending cells. The coordinates B:B specify all the cells in the second column of a table, and the coordinates 2:2 specify all the cells in the second row of a table. This second form of cell coordinates is useful if you expect to add or remove rows or columns from a table in which you use all the cells in your calculation. In a table with three rows, for example, if you specify a range of cells in a column with the coordinates B1:B3, and you later add another row to the table, your formula will still use only the first three cells in column B; you must manually edit the formula to include the fourth row. If, instead, you use the B:B coordinates, the fourth row is automatically included in the formula's computations.

> **Note**
>
> Formulas in tables do not automatically update themselves to reflect inserted or deleted rows or columns as they do in Microsoft Excel or Lotus 1-2-3. If you insert or delete a row or column and your formula uses specific cell references, you will have to edit the formula to adjust it to include the new cells. For example, if your formula is
>
> =B2*C5
>
> B2 and C5 will not adjust if you delete column A from the table. You must manually adjust the formula by selecting it and pressing Shift+F9 to display the field code. Edit the formula and then press F9 to recalculate it.

Entering a Formula in a Table

Many calculations that need to be done in a document are in the form of a table. Word has made it very easy to enter formulas into a table.

To enter a formula in a table, follow these steps:

1. Position the insertion point in the cell where you want the result to appear.

2. Choose the Table Formula command. Word for Windows displays the Formula dialog box (see fig. 20.2).

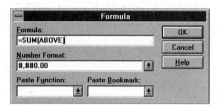

Fig. 20.2
The Formula dialog box for entering a formula in a table.

Word for Windows analyzes the table and automatically enters in the Formula text box an expression that seems most appropriate for the cell containing the insertion point. If Word for Windows cannot determine what formulas are appropriate, it leaves the Formula text box empty.

3. Type any additions to the suggested expression in the Formula text box, or delete the suggested expression and type your own, using any combination of reduction functions, cell references, bookmarks, and mathematical operators. You can use any of the functions or mathematical operators listed under the entry for the {=} field in Chapter 37, "Automating with Field Codes."

4. If you are writing your own formula, use the Paste Function list box to see a list of available functions. As you select the function from the Paste Function list box, it is pasted in the Formula text box. Table 20.1 lists the available functions and briefly describes them. For full details on these functions, refer to the entry for the {=} field in Chapter 37, "Automating with Field Codes."

   To sum a column of numbers, for example, the formula expression might look like this:

   { =SUM(D2:D10) }

IV

Mastering Special Features

SUM is the function for adding a range of numbers, and D2:D10 speci-fies the range of cells to be added—that is, the cells from row 2 to row 10 in column 4.

5. If you want your formula expression to include numbers referenced by bookmarks, you can select the bookmark names from the Paste Book-mark list box to paste them in the Formula text box.

6. To format the formula expression's results, select a format from the Number Format list box.

7. Choose OK or press Enter.

The results of the field (that is, the calculation in the field) are displayed un-less you have set Word for Windows to display field codes with the Tools Options command, in which case the field code and formula itself are dis-played. To turn the field code display on or off, select the field (or the field's result) and press Shift+F9. To update the field, select the field and press F9.

Table 20.1 Functions Available for Table Formulas

Function Name	Description
ABS	Absolute value of a number
AND	Logical AND
AVERAGE	Average of specified numbers
COUNT	Count of nonblank numbers
DEFINED	Logical value; 1 if bookmark name or merge field defined; 0 if not defined
FALSE	Logical False, always equal to 0
IF	IF expression, which returns one of two values based on a condition
INT	Integer part of a number
MAX	Largest of the specified numbers
MIN	Smallest of the specified numbers
MOD	Modulus (division remainder) of the specified numbers

Function Name	Description
NOT	Logical NOT, which inverts the logical state of another expression or function
OR	Logical OR
PRODUCT	Product of specified numbers
ROUND	Number rounded to the specified decimal places
SIGN	Sign of a number: 1 if the number is positive, –1 if the number is negative, or 0 if the number is zero
SUM	Sum of the specified numbers
TRUE	Logical True, always equal to 1

Using Table Values in a Formula outside the Table

You can also refer to a table's cells in a formula field that is not part of the table. To do this, you must first select the entire table (Table Select Table) and then give the table a bookmark name (Edit Bookmark). Now specify cells in the table by using the table's bookmark name and including the cell references inside square brackets, as in

> { =SUM(Budget[C:C]) }

or

> { =SUM(Budget[B2:B5]) }

This example shows a formula field expression that displays the sum of all the numbers in the third column of a table that was given the bookmark name Budget.

Recalculating Formulas

Formula fields, whether you enter them in a table or elsewhere in your document, do not update automatically, as do some other types of fields. To update a formula field, you must update the fields manually, using one of these methods:

- Place the insertion point in the field (or its result) and press Alt+Shift+U or F9 to update the field.

For Related Information
- "Marking Locations with Bookmarks," p. 149

- "Creating Tables," p. 509

- "Editing Tables," p. 519

- "Editing Fields," p. 1084

- "Formatting Field Results," p. 1085

- Move the pointer over the field (or its result) and click the right mouse button. Word for Windows moves the insertion point to that line and displays a context-sensitive menu to the right of the insertion point. Choose Update Field from this menu.

- To update all the fields in the document, select the entire document by using **E**dit Select **A**ll or pressing Ctrl+A. Then press Alt+Shift+U or F9 to update the fields.

You can also set Word for Windows to update all fields, including formula fields, every time you print the document.

To update fields when you print, follow these steps:

1. Choose the **T**ools **O**ptions command.

2. Select the Print tab to display the Print options.

3. Select the **U**pdate Fields check box.

For Related Information
- "Updating Fields," p. 1096

Word for Windows will update all the fields in the document each time you print the document.

Troubleshooting Calculations

Calculating results in Word can be difficult. A minor mistake in how you enter a formula will cause an error message to appear instead of a result.

The error message !Error at TRAVEL *appears. TRAVEL is a bookmark in my trip statement that contained the amount spent on TRAVEL.*

Choose **E**dit **G**o To or press the F5 key to display the Go To dialog box. Select Bookmark from the Go to **W**hat list, select Travel from the **E**nter Bookmark Name list, choose Go To, and choose Close. When the bookmark is selected, you may find that Travel includes a letter or symbol that Word cannot interpret as a number for calculation.

The error message !Undefined Bookmark, TRAVEL *appears where the formula result should be.*

The bookmark named Travel was deleted. Use the **E**dit **B**ookmark command to create a new bookmark that will hold the number.

When the number that has been named with a bookmark is changed, the bookmark is lost, so the formula can't recalculate.

Before you edit or change a number, choose the Tools Options command and select the View tab, and then select the Bookmarks check box and choose OK. This will display square brackets, [ ], around the area defined by a bookmark. When you edit a number, make sure you edit or delete only within the square brackets. If you have already deleted the bookmark, you will need to reenter a number and use that number as the location on which to re-create the bookmark.

From Here...

For information relating to entering mathematical formulas in fields, you may want to review the following chapters of this book:

- Chapter 5, "Editing a Document."

- Chapter 37, "Automating with Field Codes."

Chapter 21

Displaying Formulas and Equations

If you are a scientist or engineer, you might have wished for an easy way to enter equations and formulas in a polished document instead of having to draw them by hand. Word for Windows simplifies all these tasks with its built-in equation editor. With the Equation Editor, you can insert mathematical symbols and operators, such as integrals and fractions. You can also control the size, placement, and formatting of the different elements in an equation. The Equation Editor, which is a derivative of *MathType* 3.0™ (a dedicated equation editor published by Design Science, Inc.), is a *graphical editor*. What you see on-screen is what you get when you print your document. This makes creating equations much easier than with a character-based editor that uses codes, such as TeX™. When you have finished creating the equation, it is inserted as an object in your Word document. You can quickly open the Equation Editor with the equation displayed when you need to edit it.

In this chapter, you learn to do the following:

- Create an equation

- Format an equation

- Work with matrices

- View equations

- Edit equations

- Print equations

What You Need to Know about Displaying Formulas and Equations

Word for Windows comes with an Equation Editor that enables you to easily create publishable equations within a document. An equation created with the Equation Editor is inserted in your document as an object, just as you can insert pictures, graphs, and spreadsheet tables (see fig. 21.1). To edit the equation, you must reopen the Equation Editor; you cannot edit the equation from within Word for Windows. You can, however, position and resize an equation from within a Word for Windows document, as with any object.

Fig. 21.1
You can insert an
equation in a
document by using
the Equation
Editor.

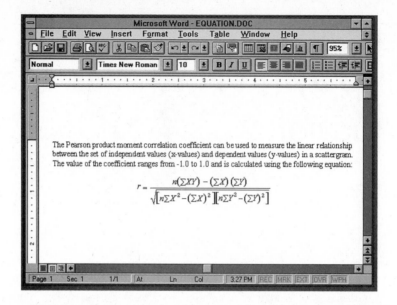

Note

If you did not choose to install the Equation Editor when you set up Word for Windows, it will not appear in the list of object types. You must run the setup program again to install the Equation Editor. You do not have to reinstall the entire program; just tell the setup program to install only the Equation Editor.

When you first open the Equation Editor, you are presented with a screen containing a single slot (see fig. 21.2). Slots demarcate the different components of an equation. If you are entering a fraction, for example, one slot is available for the numerator, and another slot is available for the denominator. You move from one slot to another by clicking a slot or by pressing the arrow and Tab keys, filling in the slots with text and symbols to create your equation.

The Equation Editor has several tools for simplifying the task of creating an equation. Just below the menu bar are buttons that access the symbol and template palettes. To access these palettes, you simply click the button for the palette you want to open. The template palettes, displayed in the second row of the toolbar, contain collections of ready-made templates that enable you to create the different components in an equation. For example, the second template from the left in the second row of buttons contains a collection of templates for entering fractions and roots (see fig. 21.3). The dotted areas within a template represent the slots into which you enter symbols and numbers. Several template palettes contain a variety of templates for creating fractions, roots, summations, matrices, integrals, and many other mathematical expressions.

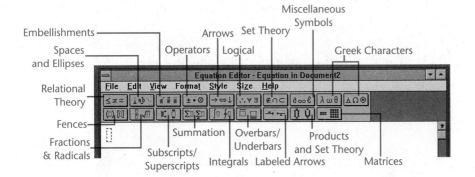

Fig. 21.2
The Equation Editor window has menus commands and palettes to help you build your equations.

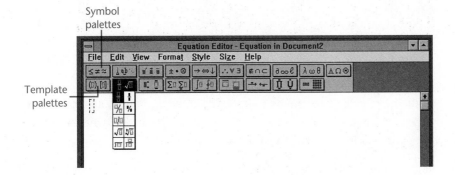

Fig. 21.3
The Equation Editor contains a template palette that has been opened.

In the first row of the toolbar are several palettes for entering symbols, including math operators, Greek symbols, arrows, and so on. The best way to become familiar with both the template and the symbol palettes is to experiment with them, one by one, inserting the template or symbol to see what it looks like.

Building an Equation

Constructing an equation consists largely of using the template and symbol palettes and the keyboard to assemble the equation piece by piece. Text and symbols are entered into slots, which are either separate from or part of a template. (An example of a slot is the one that appears on-screen when the Equation Editor is first opened.) Text or symbols are entered into the slot that contains the insertion point. You can use the mouse, or the arrow and Tab keys, to move the insertion point from one slot to another.

The templates take care of most of the tasks that deal with positioning and spacing of equation building. Other commands are available to fine-tune spacing and alignment of the components of an equation. Commands are available for controlling the font type and font size of the various elements in an equation as well.

Fig. 21.4 shows a partially completed equation in the Equation Editor. Notice the slot near the end of the equation into which characters have yet to be inserted.

Fig. 21.4

The Equation Editor with a partially completed equation.

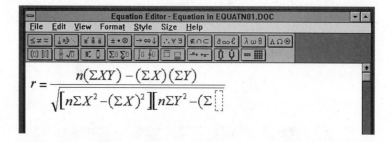

$$r = \frac{n(\Sigma XY) - (\Sigma X)(\Sigma Y)}{\sqrt{\left[n\Sigma X^2 - (\Sigma X)^2\right]\left[n\Sigma Y^2 - (\Sigma)\right]}}$$

Inserting an Equation

You use the Insert Object command to open the Equation Editor and create an equation. The equation you create is inserted in the document where the insertion point was located when you chose the Insert Object command.

To insert an equation in a document, follow these steps:

1. Position the insertion point where you want to insert the equation you will create.

2. Choose the Insert Object command and select the Create New tab.

3. Select Microsoft Equation 2.0 from the Object Type list box and choose OK.

   When you choose OK, the Equation Editor opens (refer to fig. 21.2).

4. Create the equation in the Equation Editor. (See the following sections for detailed instructions on creating an equation.)

5. Choose the File Exit and Return to Document command to close the Equation Editor and return to the document. You are asked whether you want to save the equation in the document.

   or

Choose Update (or press F3) to insert the equation in the document without closing the Equation Editor window.

If you choose to update your equation without closing the Equation Editor, you can return to the document in the same way you would switch to any other program: press Ctrl+Esc to use the Task List, or press Alt+Tab until the document window is active.

Typing in the Equation Editor

Typing in the Equation Editor is similar to typing in a Word for Windows document although there are some important differences. Whenever you type in the Equation Editor, text is entered in the slot containing the insertion point. As with a Word for Windows document, you can use the Backspace and Del keys to delete characters.

Unless you use the Text style from the Style menu, the space bar has no effect. The Equation Editor takes care of the spacing in an equation. When you type an equal sign, for example, the Equation Editor adds spacing before and after it. If you press the Enter key, a new line is started.

If you want to type regular text, choose the Text style from the Style menu or press Ctrl+Shift+E. Then you can enter text as you normally would, using the space bar to insert spaces. Choose the Math style from the Style menu or press Ctrl+Shift+= to return to the Math style. You normally work with this style when creating an equation.

Selecting Items in an Equation

You might need to select an item within an equation—to change the point size or reposition the item, for example. To select characters within a slot, use the mouse to drag across characters. If you use the keyboard to do this, press the Shift+arrow key combination as you normally would. To select an entire equation, choose the Edit Select All command or press Ctrl+A.

To select embedded items (items not contained in a slot), such as character embellishments (carets, tildes, prime signs, and so on) or integral signs, press and hold down the Ctrl key. When the mouse pointer changes to a vertical arrow, point to the embedded item and click to select it.

Entering Nested Equation Templates

Complex equations involve templates nested within templates. The result is an equation involving many templates, each nested within the slot of a larger template. An example of nested templates is the square root nested within the denominator of the equation shown in fig. 21.4.

To enter a template within an existing equation, follow these steps:

1. Place the insertion point where you want to insert the template.

2. Use the mouse to choose a template from one of the template palettes. The template is inserted immediately to the right of the insertion point.

   or

   Use one of the shortcut keys listed in table 21.1 to insert the template.

3. Type text or enter symbols in each slot in the template. The insertion point must be positioned in the slot before you begin entering text or symbols.

   To position the insertion point with the mouse, point to the slot and then click.

   or

   Use the arrow and Tab keys to position the insertion point.

Table 21.1 lists the shortcut keys for inserting templates.

Template	Description	Shortcut Key
	Table 21.1 Shortcut Keys for Inserting Templates	
(∷)	Parentheses	(or)
[∷]	Brackets*	[or]
{∷}	Braces*	{ or }
|∷|	Absolute Value	|
▯	Fraction*	F
▯/▯	Slash Fraction*	/
▦⌐	Superscript (high)*	H
▦⌐	Subscript (low)*	L
▦⌐	Joint sub-/superscript*	J
√▯	Root*	R
∜▯	Nth Root	N

Template	Description	Shortcut Key
∑⬚	Summation	S
∏⬚	Product	P
∫⬚	Integral*	I
🔲	Matrix (353)	M
⬚	Underscript (limit)	U

To use these shortcuts, press Ctrl+T and then the shortcut key. You can insert the items marked with an asterisk by pressing just the Ctrl key and the shortcut key—you do not have to press T first.

Entering Symbols

Many fields of mathematics, science, and medicine use symbols to represent concepts or physical structures. With the Equation Editor, you can insert a symbol in a slot by following these steps:

1. Position the insertion point where you want to insert the symbol.

2. Use the mouse to select the symbol you want from one of the symbol templates.

   or

   Use one of the shortcut keys listed in table 21.2 to insert the symbol.

Table 21.2 lists the shortcut keys for inserting symbols. To use these shortcuts, press Ctrl+S and then the shortcut key.

Table 21.2 Shortcut Keys for Inserting Symbols		
Symbol	**Description**	**Shortcut Key**
∞	Infinity	¦
→	Arrow	A
∂	Derivative (partial)	D
≤	Less than or equal to	<
≥	Greater than or equal to	>

(continues)

Table 21.2 Continued		
Symbol	**Description**	**Shortcut Key**
✕	Times	T
∈	Element of	E
∉	Not an element of	Shift+E
⊂	Contained in	C
⊄	Not contained in	Shift+C

Adding Embellishments

The Equation Editor has several embellishments—such as prime signs, arrows, tildes, and dots—that you can add to characters or symbols.

To add an embellishment, follow these steps:

1. Position the insertion point to the right of the character you want to embellish.

2. Choose the embellishment icon from the embellishment palette (third button from the left in the top row of buttons).

   or

For Related Information
- "Embedding Data," p. 1000

- "Sizing Frames," p. 710

- "Moving and Positioning Frames," p. 699

Use one of the shortcut keys listed in table 21.3 to add an embellishment.

Table 21.3 Shortcut Keys for Inserting Embellishments		
Icon	**Description**	**Shortcut Keys**
	Overbar	Ctrl+Shift+–
	Tilde	Ctrl+~ (Ctrl+" on some keyboards)
	Arrow (vector)	Ctrl+Alt+–
	Single prime	Ctrl+Alt+'
	Double prime	Ctrl+" (Ctrl+~ on some keyboards)
	Single dot	Ctrl+Alt+.

Formatting an Equation

Once you have created an equation, you can format it to appear exactly as you want. You can work on the spacing of the elements in the equation, adjust the positioning and alignment within the equation, and change the font and font size for any element.

Controlling Spacing

You can modify several spacing parameters by using the Format Spacing command (for example, line spacing or row and column spacing in matrices).

To modify the spacing setting used by the Equation Editor, follow these steps:

1. Choose the Format Spacing command. A dialog box appears that displays a scrolling list of dimensions (see fig. 21.5).

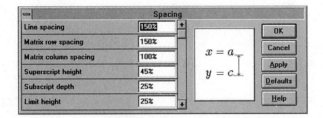

Fig. 21.5
You can control the spacing used by the Equation Editor in the Spacing dialog box.

2. Select the text box next to the dimension you want to modify. Use the scroll bar to move through the list of dimensions. The dimension you select is displayed in the diagram to the right of the dialog box.

3. Type a new measurement.

The default unit of measure is points. You can specify other units by typing the appropriate abbreviation from the following list:

Unit of Measure	Abbreviation
Inches	in
Centimeters	cm
Millimeters	mm
Points	pt
Picas	pi

4. Choose Apply or OK.

Choosing Apply applies the modified dimension to the current equation and leaves the dialog box open. This enables you to continue modifications. Choosing OK applies any modifications and closes the dialog box.

In practice, you probably should specify the spacing dimensions as a percentage of the point size given for Full size type, which is set in the Size Define dialog box. The advantage to this approach is that if you change the type size, you don't have to redefine your spacing dimensions; spacing will always be proportional to the type size.

Unless you are using the Text style, the Equation Editor takes care of the spacing between elements in an equation. You can insert spaces manually if you like, using the mouse or keyboard. You can use four spacing symbols for manually inserting spaces. These symbols are located in the second symbol palette from the left in the top row. You can also access these symbols with shortcut keys. Table 21.4 lists the spacing symbols and shortcut keys.

Table 21.4 Shortcut Keys for Inserting Spaces		
Icon	**Function**	**Shortcut Keys**
a͟b	Zero space	Shift+space bar
a͟b	One point space	Ctrl+Alt+space bar
a͟b	Thin space	Ctrl+space bar
a͟ b	Thick space (two thin spaces)	Ctrl+Shift+space bar

You can insert as many spaces together as you like. To delete a space, use the Del or Backspace key, as you would with text.

Positioning and Aligning Equations

If you are not satisfied with the automatic positioning of the elements in an equation, you can adjust the positioning of any selected item by using the Nudge commands. First select the item (see "Selecting Items in an Equation" earlier in this chapter). Then use one of the following keystrokes to move the item, one pixel at a time:

Keystrokes	Function
Ctrl+left-arrow key	Moves item left one pixel
Ctrl+right-arrow key	Moves item right one pixel
Ctrl+down-arrow key	Moves item down one pixel
Ctrl+up-arrow key	Moves item up one pixel

The Equation Editor enables you to align horizontally one or more lines of single or multiple equations, using either the Format menu or the alignment symbol. You can align lines to the left, center, or right; or you can align lines around equal signs, decimal points, or alignment symbols. To align a group of equations, simply choose one of the alignment commands from the Format menu. To align lines within an equation, position the insertion point within the lines; then choose one of the alignment commands.

To insert an alignment symbol, position the insertion point and choose from the Spaces palette (second button in the top row of buttons) the alignment symbol at the far left of the top row of symbols. The alignment symbols are used as a reference point around which one or more lines of single or multiple equations are aligned. They override the Format commands.

Selecting Fonts

Usually, when you work in the Equation Editor, you will use the Math style from the **S**tyle menu. When you use the Math style, the Equation Editor automatically recognizes standard functions and applies to them the Function style (typeface and character formatting, for example). The Variable style is applied otherwise. If the Equation Editor fails to recognize a function, you can select it and apply the Function style manually. Other styles are available, such as Text, Greek, and Matrix-Vector. Styles are simply a combination of font and character formatting assigned to characters that are selected or about to be typed. You can modify the font and character formatting (that is, make the font bold or italic by selecting these styles in the Style Define dialog box).

To define the font and character attributes for a style, follow these steps:

1. Choose the **S**tyle **D**efine command.

2. Select the style you want to define.

3. Select the font from the list of available fonts.

4. Select the Bold or Italic boxes if you want bold or italic.

5. Choose OK.

You use the Text style to type regular text. Selecting this style applies the Text style to the text you type, and enables you to use the space bar to enter spaces as normal. With the other styles, spacing is handled automatically by the Equation Editor.

Use the Other style when you want to select a font and character format that is not one of the standard styles. Selecting the Other style opens a dialog box in which you can choose a font and character format for characters that are selected or about to be entered.

Selecting Font Sizes

Along with providing several predefined font styles, the Equation Editor offers certain predefined font sizes. The Full size is the choice you normally work with when you are building equations. You also have selections for subscripts, sub-subscripts, symbols, and subsymbols. You can use the Other size option for those cases in which you want to specify a size not defined by one of these standard sizes.

To apply a font size to an equation, follow these steps:

1. Select the characters whose point size you want to modify.

If you do not select any characters, the size you choose will apply to characters you type subsequently.

2. Choose the Size menu.

3. Choose the size you want from the Size menu. If no defined size matches your needs, choose Size Other and specify a size in the Other Size dialog box.

You can modify the default settings for each of the sizes listed in the Size menu by using the Size Define command. Follow these steps:

1. Choose the Size Define command.

2. Select the box to the right of the size you want to define.

When you select a box, the element you are defining is highlighted in the diagram on the right side of the dialog box.

3. Type a new size.

4. Choose OK.

To apply a size, select one from the Size menu; then type the characters you want the size applied to. Alternatively, you can select the characters after they have been typed and then choose a size.

For Related Information
■ "Using Fonts Correctly," p. 276

Working with Matrices

The Matrix template palette includes several vectors and matrices of pre-defined sizes. You can also select one of the template symbols in the bottom row of the palette to open a Matrix dialog box. In this box, you can specify the dimensions of the matrix or vector, as well as control several other matrix characteristics.

To insert a matrix template, click the matrix template button (the last button on the right of the bottom row). Then click the palette you want. Selecting a template from the last row of icons opens the Matrix dialog box (see fig. 21.6). In the Matrix dialog box, you can specify the dimensions of the matrix and make several other selections. You can specify how the elements in rows and columns are aligned and whether the column widths and row heights are equal (rather than based on widest or highest entry). By clicking the space between the rows and columns in the dialog box, you can select one of three types of partition lines: solid, dashes, and dotted. As you click the space, you cycle through the three types of lines, then back to no line. You use the Format Spacing dialog box to control the spacing between rows and columns.

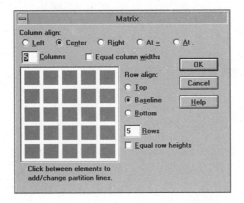

Fig. 21.6
You can specify the dimensions of the matrix in the Matrix dialog box.

You can use the Tab key to move from left to right through the matrix, one element at a time. Pressing Shift+Tab will move you right to left through the matrix. You can also use the arrow keys to move from element-to-element in a matrix.

To format an existing matrix, select the entire matrix and then choose the Format Matrix command. Make your selections from the dialog box and choose OK.

> **Note**
>
> To create a determinant, you can nest a matrix within absolute value bars. Insert the absolute value bar template first, and with the insertion point inside the absolute value bars, insert a matrix template.

Viewing Equations

You can choose from three predefined magnifications of the equation in the Equation Editor window. Alternatively, you can use the View Zoom command to set a custom magnification for viewing your equation. To change the view, open the View menu. To display the equation at the actual size you want it to appear in the document and on the printed page, select 100%. Select 200% and 400% to display the equation at twice and four times the actual size, respectively. To set a custom magnification, choose the View Zoom command and select the Custom option in the Zoom dialog box. Next enter the magnification you want in the Custom text box; then choose OK. These commands are useful when you want to adjust the spacing in an equation or closely examine small items in it.

Editing an Equation

To edit an equation, you must return to the Equation Editor. To open the Equation Editor, follow these steps:

1. Double-click the equation you want to edit, or select it. Then choose the Edit Object command.

2. Make your editing changes.

3. Choose the File Update command to update the equation without closing the Equation Editor.

or

Choose the File Exit and Return to Document command to close the Equation Editor and return to the document. You are asked whether you want to save the equation in the document.

Printing Equations

To print equations, you need to have one of these three kinds of printers: a PostScript printer; a laser printer that lets you download fonts; or a dot-matrix or DeskJet printer used with a font-scaling utility, such as TrueType or Adobe Type Manager. For more information on fonts, see Chapter 9, "Formatting Characters and Changing Fonts." The Help facility in the Equation Editor contains extensive information on using printers and fonts with the editor. To access a help screen, follow these steps:

1. Choose the Help Contents command in the Equation Editor.

2. Choose the Reference Information topic and then Printers and Fonts.

3. Select one of the topics under the Printers and Fonts category.

You can obtain a printout of the help screen by choosing the File Print Topic command.

From Here...

For more information on creating equations and formulas, review the following chapters:

- Chapter 33, "Using Word with Other Windows Applications." Learn how to exchange and link data between Word and other Windows applications.

- Chapter 20, "Calculating Math with Formulas." Learn how to carry out calculations in a Word document.

- Chapter 22, "Inserting Pictures in Your Document." Learn how to insert pictures and other graphics into your Word documents, and how to resize, crop, and format graphic objects.

For Related Information

- "Understanding Your Printer Capabilities," p. 278

- "Using Fonts Correctly," p. 276

- Chapter 23, "Framing and Moving Text and Graphics." Learn how to frame text and graphics so that you can position them on the page exactly where you want them and wrap text around them.

- Chapter 26, "Graphing Data." Learn how to create a chart from data in a document or from data imported from a worksheet.

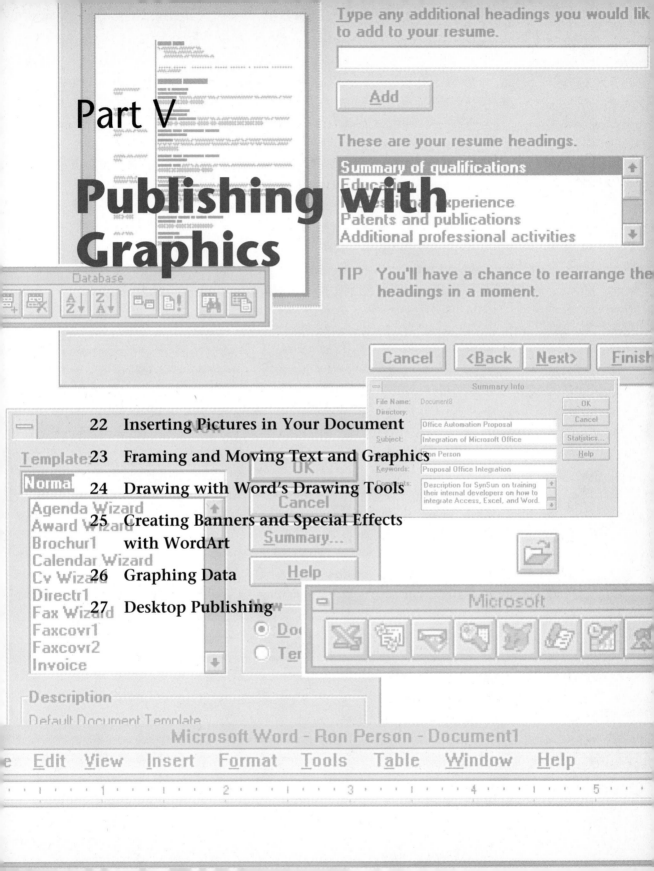

Part V

Publishing with Graphics

22   Inserting Pictures in Your Document

23   Framing and Moving Text and Graphics

24   Drawing with Word's Drawing Tools

25   Creating Banners and Special Effects
        with WordArt

26   Graphing Data

27   Desktop Publishing

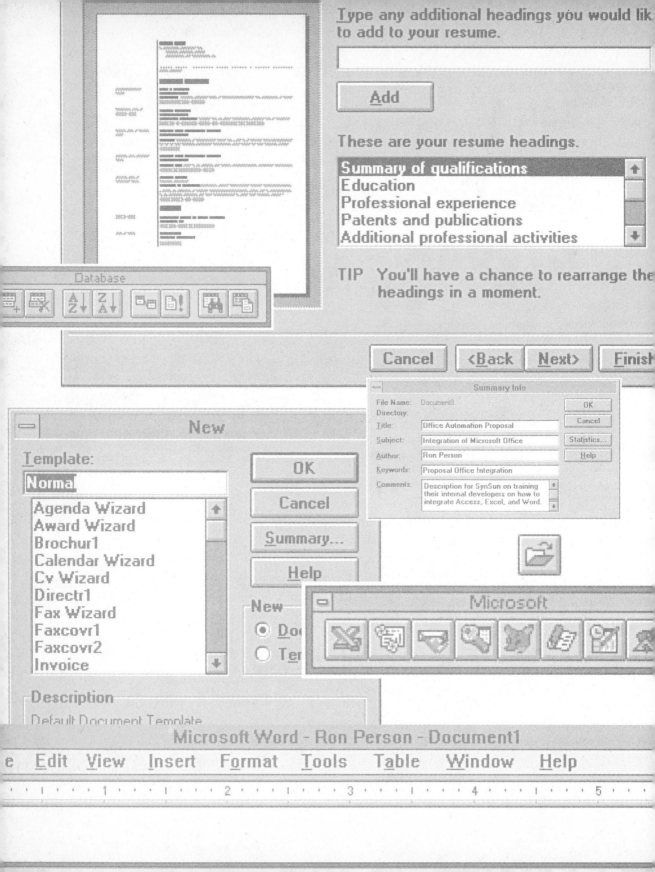

Type any additional headings you would lik
to add to your resume.

Add

These are your resume headings.

Summary of qualifications
Education
Professional experience
Patents and publications
Additional professional activities

TIP You'll have a chance to rearrange the
      headings in a moment.

Cancel   <Back   Next>   Finish

Summary Info

File Name: Document8
Directory:
Title: Office Automation Proposal
Subject: Integration of Microsoft Office
Author: Ron Person
Keywords: Proposal Office Integration
Comments: Description for SynSun on training
            their internal developers on how to
            integrate Access, Excel, and Word.

OK
Cancel
Statistics...
Help

Database

New

Template:

Normal

Agenda Wizard
Award Wizard
Brochur1
Calendar Wizard
Cv Wizard
Directr1
Fax Wizard
Faxcovr1
Faxcovr2
Invoice

OK
Cancel
Summary...
Help

New
○ Do
○ Ter

Description
Default Document Template

Microsoft

Microsoft Word - Ron Person - Document1

e Edit View Insert Format Tools Table Window Help

· · · | · · · 1 · · · | · · · · | · · · 2 · · · · | · · · | · · · 3 · · · · | · · · 4 · · · · | · · · | · · · 5 · · ·

Chapter 22

Inserting Pictures in Your Document

With Word for Windows, you can illustrate your ideas by using pictures created with a graphics program. If a picture is worth a thousand words, think how much typing you can save! Even if your picture is worth somewhat less than a thousand words, illustrating your document with graphics can make your pages more appealing—which means that readers pay more attention to your words. Fig. 22.1 shows a brochure enhanced with graphic elements.

Pictures that you insert in your Word for Windows documents come from many sources. Some come from a stand-alone graphics program, which you can use to create illustrations ranging from the simple to the sophisticated. Some—including photographs—come from scanners that digitize artwork for use in a computer. Some pictures come from clip art packages that provide ready-to-use artwork. Word for Windows includes many clip art images in the CLIPART subdirectory.

All the pictures you insert come from a source outside Word for Windows (and can be used in many programs besides Word for Windows). That makes the pictures different from the graphics objects you create with Microsoft WordArt, Microsoft Graph, or the Drawing toolbar. (You can learn about each of these built-in programs in Chapter 25, "Creating Banners and Special Effects with WordArt," Chapter 26, "Graphing Data," and Chapter 24, "Drawing with Word's Drawing Tools"). Using one of the built-in graphics programs, you can create a graphic that exists only as a part of your Word for Windows document.

In this chapter you learn how to insert many different types of graphics and work with them in your document. You learn how to do the following:

- Insert previously-created graphics into your document, and how to copy graphics into your document

- Edit, size, crop, and move graphics

- Add lines and borders to graphics

- Hide graphics so you can work faster with text

Fig. 22.1
Graphics can make
your document
more appealing to
readers.

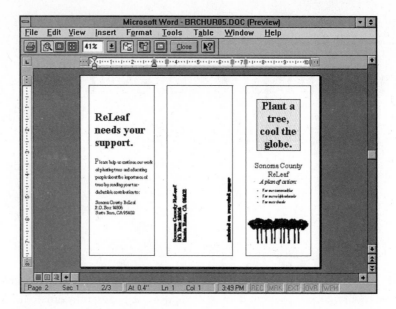

Fig. 22.1
Graphics can make
your document
more appealing to
readers.

Stand-alone graphics programs often are more powerful than the simple built-in programs that come with Word for Windows. Thus, Word for Windows gives you the flexibility to include a range of graphics in your documents—from simple drawings that you create yourself without leaving Word for Windows, to sophisticated graphics that you or someone else makes with a powerful stand-alone graphics program.

Reviewing Compatible Formats

Word for Windows is compatible with many of the most frequently used graphics programs. You can import pictures created with any of the following programs or in any of the formats listed:

Program Format	File Extension
PC Paintbrush	PCX
Tagged Image File Format	TIF (scanned images)
Windows Metafile	WMF
Encapsulated PostScript	EPS
Windows Paintbrush	BMP
Windows Bitmap	BMP

Program Format	File Extension
Computer Graphics Metafile	CGM
HP Graphic Language	HGL
DrawPerfect	WPG
Micrografx Designer	DRW
Micrografx Draw	DRW
Macintosh or Windows PICT	PCT

Your favorite graphics program might not be listed. Many programs easily export graphics (or even part of a graphic) from the native format to a commonly used format. If your program isn't listed, see whether it can save graphics in one of the formats in the preceding list, so that you can use it in Word for Windows.

Installing the Import Filters

To import pictures into a document, Word for Windows uses special "import filters." One filter is required for each type of file you want to import. If you selected the Complete Setup option when you installed Word for Windows, all the graphics import filters were put into your system. If you selected a Custom installation, you might not have installed all the filters. To see which filters are installed (and consequently which types of graphics you are able to import), read the contents of the List Files of Type list in the Insert Picture dialog box. This dialog box appears when you choose the Insert Picture command. If you need to install an additional graphics filter, refer to Appendix B, "Installing Word for Windows." It gives you information on setting up additional features after you have installed Word.

Inserting and Copying Pictures into Your Document

You can insert a picture in the text of your document, or in a frame or table. When you work with the Drawing toolbar, you can insert a picture in a text box or picture container. Inserting a picture directly in your text is the simplest way to put an illustration in your document. Other techniques, however, offer advantages. Inserting a picture in a frame enables you to wrap text around the picture. Inserting a picture in one cell of a table enables you to position the picture adjacent to text in the next cell. Inserting a picture in a text box enables you to layer the picture above or below the text.

You can use one of three ways to insert a picture in your document. First, you can insert pictures by using the Insert Picture command. This command asks you to locate the file name and then inserts the picture from disk. If you use this method, you don't even need to own the program used to create the picture. Second, you can open the program used to create the picture, and copy the picture into the Windows Clipboard. Then you can paste the picture into your Word for Windows document. Third, you can insert picture objects by using the Insert Object command to open a graphics program from within Word for Windows. You can use this command to insert a picture that you can later edit using the program that created it.

Tip

You can automatically include a caption with each picture you insert by choosing the Insert Caption command and selecting the AutoCaption option.

Inserting Pictures into Your Document

You can insert a picture in your document without ever opening the program used to create the picture. As with opening or saving a Word for Windows file, you must first locate the file before you insert a picture.

You can insert a picture with or without a link to the graphics program used to create the picture. By linking to the graphics program, you might be able to reduce the size of your document (see the next section, "Minimizing File Size through Linking.")

To insert a picture, follow these steps:

1. Position the insertion point where you want to insert the picture.

2. Choose the Insert Picture command. The Insert Picture dialog box appears (see fig. 22.2).

3. Locate your picture file. If it is not in the current drive, select from the Drives list the drive containing your file. From the Directories list, select the directory that contains your file.

4. From the File Name list, select the picture file you want to insert.

   You can restrict the File Name list to a particular file type. In the List Files of Type box, simply select the file type you want to list.

5. If you want to see the picture before you insert it, select the Preview Picture option. A miniature version of your picture appears in the

Preview box. If you want help finding your file, choose the Find File button. Then use the Find File features to locate your file. (Refer to Chapter 4, "Managing Documents and Files," for more information on the Find File features.)

6. Choose OK.

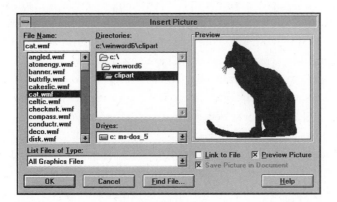

Fig. 22.2
Use the Insert Picture dialog box to locate a picture you want to insert. The Preview box shows the selected picture—a Word for Windows clip art image.

V

Publishing with Graphics

When you insert a picture in your Word for Windows document, it falls into place at the location of the insertion point. If you add or delete text preceding the picture, the picture moves with the edited text. Unless you frame and position the picture, it stays with the text. For details on framing a picture and positioning it independently of the text, refer to Chapter 23, "Framing and Moving Text and Graphics."

Note

If you cannot insert a picture because it's in a format Word doesn't recognize, open the picture in Windows Paintbrush or some other graphics program. Then save the picture in a format Word does recognize, such as BMP.

Note

If you format a paragraph to have line spacing of an exact amount—one inch, for example—and you insert in that paragraph a picture two inches high, you won't see all of it. You can reformat the paragraph containing the picture for any line spacing other than Exactly, and the paragraph will adjust to fit the picture. For more information, see Chapter 10, "Formatting Lines and Paragraphs."

Minimizing File Size Through Linking. When you insert a picture in your document, Word usually includes a representation of the picture. Each time you open your document, you see the picture. However, this method can make your Word for Windows file quite large: the file size is increased by the file size of the picture (which can be very large).

Another way to insert a picture is to link it to the program used to create the picture, but not store a copy of the picture in your Word for Windows file. In this way, each time you open your document, Word refers to the program used to create the picture so that Word can draw a representation of the picture. If the program is not available, Word displays an empty box where the picture should appear. This method has the advantage of minimizing your file size, as Word does not store a copy of the picture in your document. But the method has two disadvantages: first, it takes longer to display the picture; second, if the program used to create the picture is not available, you can't see or print it. Use this method for minimizing file size only when you work with your Word for Windows document on a computer that contains the graphics program used to create your pictures.

To minimize file size through linking, follow these steps:

1. Position the insertion point where you want the picture to appear. Then choose the Insert Picture command and select the picture you want to insert.

2. In the Picture dialog box, select the Link to File option. Then deselect, or clear, the Save Picture in Document option.

3. Choose OK.

If you move the original picture file, you must update the link. (For more information, refer to Chapter 33, "Using Word with Other Windows Applications.")

Minimizing File Size Through File Format. When you insert a picture that you created on another computer, such as a Macintosh, Word saves two versions of the picture: the version that works with Word (the "native" version) and the version that came from the Macintosh. This feature is handy if you ever need the Macintosh version again some time, but it makes your file larger. You can conserve file size by saving only the native version of the picture.

To minimize file size through file format, follow these steps:

1. Choose the Tools Options command.

2. Select the Save tab.

3. Select Save Native Picture Formats Only from the Save Options group.

4. Choose OK.

Copying Pictures into Your Document

Sometimes the easiest way to get a picture you created with a graphics program into Word for Windows is to use the Clipboard to copy the picture. You can even link the picture to the original file when you paste it into Word; in this way, you can update the picture if you later make changes to the original. To link a picture, the graphics program must support the older Dynamic Data Exchange (DDE) or the newer technology, Object Linking and Embedding (OLE). Some of the programs that support the older DDE technology are Lotus 1-2-3 for Windows, Microsoft Access 1.1, Microsoft Excel 4.0, and WordPerfect for Windows. Programs that support both DDE and the newer OLE 2.0 technology are Microsoft Excel 5.0 and CorelDRAW! 4.0.

To copy a picture into your document, follow these steps:

1. Start your graphics or charting program. Then open the file containing the picture you want to copy into your Word for Windows document.

2. Select the picture or chart.

3. Choose the Edit Copy command.

4. Switch to your Word for Windows document.

5. Position the insertion point where you want to insert the picture.

6. Choose the Edit Paste command.

   or

   Choose the Edit Paste Special command to link the picture to the original file. Select Paste Link from the Paste Special dialog box. In the As list, select the format for your picture (formats vary depending on what type of picture you copied). Select the Display as Icon option if you want to display an icon, rather than the picture, in your text. (You can double-click the icon to display and edit the picture.)

When you paste in a picture with a link, you get some choices. If you paste the picture as an object, you can edit it later. If you paste the picture as a picture, it might take up less space. To get an idea of the best way to paste in your picture, read the Result box at the bottom of the Paste Special dialog box as you select each of the different formats in the As list.

For more information about how to work with links, refer to Chapter 33, "Using Word with Other Windows Applications."

Inserting Picture Objects in Your Document

A *picture object* is a picture in your Word for Windows document that you can edit. You edit the picture by double-clicking it to display the program used to create the picture, if the program is available. All the data that creates a picture object is contained within the Word document. The picture is not linked to a file outside the document. A picture object is not linked back to an original file, instead all of the data that creates the object is stored within the Word document.

Tip
Paintbrush uses embedded objects, so updating the original file does not affect the embedded file. You must double-click the embedded object, and then manually edit it to update the Paintbrush object in the Word document.

You can insert many types of picture objects in your document. If CorelDRAW! is installed on your computer and you put in the CorelDRAW! filter when you installed Word, you can insert a CorelDRAW!, CorelCHART!, or CorelPHOTO-PAINT! object. If Microsoft Excel 5.0 is installed, you can embed an Excel chart as an object. You can insert an equation, graph, picture, or WordArt image as objects, and you can insert a Microsoft Word Picture object.

Tip
If you're copying in pictures from Microsoft applications, display the Microsoft toolbar. This will help you quickly start Microsoft applications.

You can insert new or existing picture objects. If you insert new picture objects, Word displays the graphics program you've chosen, and you must draw the picture. For example, if you choose to insert a new CorelDRAW! picture object, Word starts CorelDRAW! and presents you with a blank drawing screen. You draw the picture, and then you choose a command to return to your Word document with the picture.

If you insert existing picture objects, the existing picture appears in your document. Whether you insert new or existing picture objects, you can always double-click one of these objects to display the program used to create the picture. Then you can edit the picture. Alternatively, you can use a command to edit the picture.

To insert a new picture object, follow these steps:

1. Position the insertion point where you want to insert the picture object.

2. Choose the Insert Object command. The Object dialog box appears (see fig. 22.3).

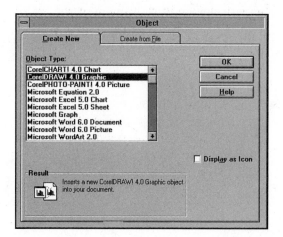

Fig. 22.3
When you insert a new picture object, Word displays the program you use to create it.

3. Select the Create New tab.

4. From the Object Type list, select the type of picture object you want to insert. Select the Display as Icon option if you want to display an icon rather than the picture.

   Icons can be used if a picture will take too much room in a document. The icon displays on-screen or when printed. You can double-click the icon to see its contents.

5. Choose OK. The program you use to create the picture starts.

6. Create the picture.

7. Return to your Word document. The way that you do this varies from one program to another. In Microsoft Excel or WordArt, simply click the Word document somewhere outside the picture. In Microsoft Word Picture, click the Close Picture button. In other programs, choose the File Exit and Return to Document command. Then answer Yes when a message box asks whether you want to update your document.

For more information on working with other applications, see Chapter 33, "Using Word with Other Windows Applications."

To insert a Microsoft Word Picture object, follow these steps:

1. Position the insertion point where you want to insert the Microsoft Word Picture object.

Tip

A quick way to insert a Microsoft Word Picture object is to display the Drawing toolbar and click the Picture Container tool.

2. Choose the Insert Object command and select the Create New tab.

3. From the Object Type list, select Microsoft Word 6.0 Picture. (Select the Display as Icon option if you want to display an icon rather than the picture.)

4. Choose OK. The Microsoft Word Picture screen appears, and the Drawing toolbar is displayed at the bottom (see fig. 22.4).

Fig. 22.4

You can insert or draw a picture in Microsoft Word Picture.

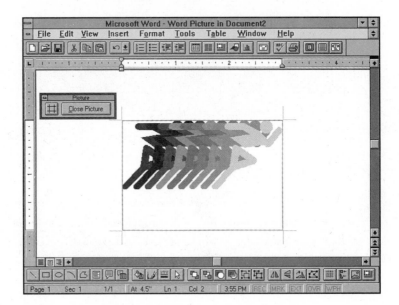

5. Insert a picture by choosing the Insert Picture or Insert Object command. Alternatively, you can draw a picture by using the tools on the Drawing toolbar, or you can type text. You can select and edit text and pictures in the Picture window (see the section "Working with Pictures" later in this chapter).

   Click the crop marks button to shrink the picture edges to fit a picture you've drawn.

6. Choose the Close Picture button.

To insert an existing picture object, follow these steps:

1. Position the insertion point where you want to insert the picture object.

2. Choose the Insert Object command. The Object dialog box appears (see fig. 22.5).

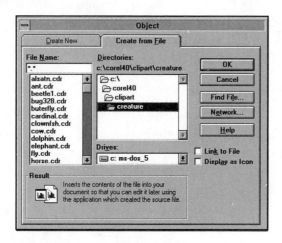

Fig. 22.5
You can insert an existing picture object and edit it later.

3. Select the Create from File tab.

4. In the File Name list box, type or select the file name of the picture you want to insert. Locate the file, if necessary, by selecting choices from the Directories and Drives lists. Or choose the Find File button to get help in locating the file.

5. Select the Link to File option if you want the picture in your Word document to update when you change the original picture.

6. Select the Display as Icon option if you want to display an icon rather than the picture.

7. Choose OK.

Read the message in the Result box at the bottom of the Object dialog box to see the results that the currently selected options have produced in your document.

Inserting Pictures in Frames and Text Boxes

By inserting a picture in a frame or framing a picture you've already inserted, you free the picture from the text. You can move a framed picture anywhere on the page by simply dragging the picture. You can also wrap text around it.

Framed pictures are very useful with desktop publishing projects. For more information on working with frames, see Chapter 23, "Framing and Moving Text and Graphics."

Inserting a picture in a text box offers some advantages. You can move a picture in a text box to the layer below the text in your document so that the picture appears to be behind the text. You can also use tools in the Drawing toolbar to quickly format a text box with fill and line colors and with styles. For more information on working with the Drawing toolbar, see Chapter 24, "Drawing with Word's Drawing Tools."

To frame a picture, follow these steps:

1. Choose the Insert Picture command and select the picture you want to insert. Choose OK to insert the picture at the insertion point in your document. Make sure that the picture remains selected.

   or

   If the picture you want framed is already inserted in your document, select the picture by clicking it.

2. To frame the selected picture, choose the Insert Frame command.

   or

   Click the Frame tool on the Word for Windows, Drawing, or Forms toolbar.

Alternatively, you can first create a frame and then insert the picture in the frame (simply reverse the preceding steps 1 and 2, drawing the frame with a crosshair). The frame reshapes itself to the shape of the picture, and the picture resizes itself to the width of the frame.

To insert a picture in a text box, follow these steps:

1. Display the Drawing toolbar by choosing the View Toolbars command. Select Drawing from the Toolbars list.

2. Click the Text Box tool in the Drawing toolbar.

3. Move the crosshair into the document and drag the crosshair to draw a text box.

4. When you see the insertion point flashing at the upper-left corner of the text box, choose the Insert Picture command. Select the picture you want to insert; then choose OK. The text box reshapes to the shape of the picture, and the picture resizes to the width of the text box.

Use the techniques described in the following section, "Working with Pictures," to resize or crop the text box to fit the picture, if necessary. Use the Fill Color, Line Color, and Line Style tools on the Drawing toolbar to change the fill and edges of the text box.

Working with Pictures

After you insert a picture in your document, you can manipulate the picture in many ways. You can scale it to a smaller or larger size, proportionally or non-proportionally. You can size the picture to the exact dimensions you want. You can crop it, cutting away portions you don't want to use. You can add a border to the picture; and you can move, copy, or paste the picture. You can frame it or insert it in a text box, freeing the picture for positioning anywhere on the page. Finally, you can wrap text around the picture.

You can work with pictures in any view. (An exception is a picture in a text box, which appears only in the page layout view or the Print Preview screen.) The page layout view shows you exactly where the picture is positioned and how text wraps around it. Working with pictures in the page layout view can be slow, however, as even the fastest computers slow down when scrolling a graphic. The normal view displays the picture at the left margin and scrolls a little more quickly than the page layout view. To save scrolling time, you can hide pictures.

Selecting Pictures

Before you change a picture, you must select it. When a picture is selected, it has square selection handles on all four corners and sides—eight in all. With a mouse, you can use the selection handles to size, crop, or scale the picture. Selected pictures appear differently if they're in a text box or framed (see fig. 22.6).

To select a picture with the mouse, follow these steps:

1. Display the picture on your screen.

2. Click the picture.

For Related Information

■ "Framing Text, Pictures, and Other Objects," p. 688

■ "Wrapping Text around a Frame," p. 708

■ "Drawing and Coloring Shapes and Lines," p. 727

■ "Including Text or Another Picture in a Drawing," p. 759

■ "Creating a WordArt Object," p. 775

■ "Embedding Data," p. 1000

■ "Linking Documents and Files," p. 1008

V

Publishing with Graphics

To select a picture with the keyboard, follow these steps:

1. Position the insertion point to one side of the picture.

2. Press Shift+left-arrow key to select a picture to the left of the insertion point. Or press Shift+right-arrow key to select a picture to the right.

Clicking an inserted picture selects it. Double-clicking a picture often has a very different effect: it brings up a graphics program in which you can edit the picture. Word for Windows OLE technology makes this action possible.

Fig. 22.6
A selected picture has eight selection handles (top). A text box containing a picture (middle) has a gray border and may have a colored fill or border. In the page layout view, a selected framed picture (bottom) has a shaded border.

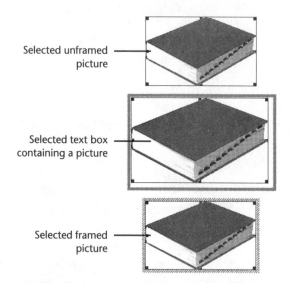

Selected unframed picture

Selected text box containing a picture

Selected framed picture

Note

You can select inserted pictures, which exist as part of your text, by dragging across them or using other text-selection techniques. The pictures appear in reverse color when you do this. When you select a picture this way, you can format it with paragraph-formatting commands but not with picture-formatting commands. You can use this technique to align a picture that exists on a line by itself. For more information on paragraph formatting, see Chapter 10, "Formatting Lines and Paragraphs."

Resizing and Cropping Pictures

After you insert a picture in your document, you can scale the picture to a smaller or larger size. You can also size it to the exact dimensions you want, or crop away parts of the picture you don't want to use. Resizing is useful when you need a picture to be a certain size in your document. Cropping helps when you want to zoom in on the most important part of the picture.

You can change the dimensions of a picture in three ways:

- Scale the picture larger or smaller by a percentage (proportionally or non-proportionally)

- Size the picture to an exact width and height

- Crop away part of the picture

You can make any of these changes with the mouse or keyboard commands.

Resizing and Cropping with the Mouse. Using the mouse to scale, size, or crop a picture is visual: it enables you to see how your changes look while you're making them. At the same time, you can monitor your picture's dimensions because a readout in the status bar tells you its exact size. (You can display the status bar by choosing the **T**ools **O**ptions command and selecting Status **B**ar on the View tab.) If you use the mouse to change a picture, and you later want to see what its dimensions are, select the picture. Then choose the **F**ormat Picture command. The entries in the Crop From, Scaling, and Size groups tell you the picture's current dimensions.

To change a picture, you select it and drag the small black selection handles that appear on the sides and corners of the picture. After you select the picture and move the mouse pointer over the selection handles, the pointer changes shape: it turns into a two-headed arrow if you're resizing the picture (left side of fig. 22.7) or a cropping tool if you're cropping the picture (right side of fig. 22.7).

Fig. 22.7
You can resize a picture by dragging its handles (left) or crop the picture by holding Shift as you drag the handles (right).

Each of the eight selection handles surrounding a selected picture has a specific purpose. The corner handles enable you to scale or crop from two sides. When you use a corner handle to resize a picture, the picture remains proportional. The side handles enable scaling and cropping from just one side.

When you use a side handle to resize, the picture's proportions change. Whenever you drag a handle, the opposite handle stays anchored to its current position.

When you resize a picture by dragging a handle toward the center of the picture, you make the picture smaller. When you crop a picture by dragging toward the center, you cut away part of the picture. When you drag the handle away to resize a picture, you make the picture larger. If you're cropping, you add a blank border after you pass the picture's original edges. Fig. 22.8 shows an original picture (left example) that has been sized smaller (top left example) and cropped (bottom right example).

Fig. 22.8

The original picture (left) becomes smaller or larger when you resize it (top right). Some of it is cut away when you crop it (bottom right).

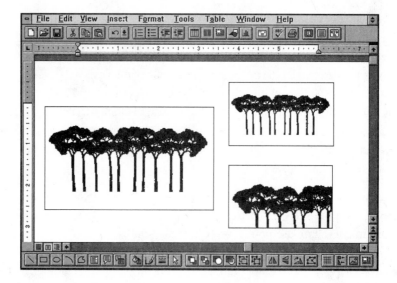

As you drag the handles to resize or crop the picture, you see a dotted-line box that represents the picture's new size and shape. When you release the mouse button, the picture snaps to fit inside the box.

To resize a picture with the mouse, follow these steps:

1. Select the picture.

2. Move the mouse pointer over a black selection handle until it turns into a two-headed arrow.

3. Drag a corner handle to scale the picture proportionally, or drag a side handle to scale a picture nonproportionally. The status bar reads Scaling and gives the picture's proportions. (Proportional changes keep the height and width proportions the same.)

4. Release the mouse button when the picture is the size you want.

To crop a picture, follow these steps:

1. Select the picture.

2. Press and hold down the Shift key.

3. Drag any black selection handle. Notice that the status bar reads Cropping and gives the picture's dimensions.

4. Release the mouse button when only the part of the picture you want to show is within the box boundary.

Resizing and Cropping with the Picture Dialog Box. You can use the Picture dialog box to scale, size, or crop a picture. The Picture dialog box includes boxes in which you must enter measurements. Each box has up and down arrows to its right; you can click the up arrow to increase the measurement, or click the down arrow to decrease it.

To scale, size, or crop a picture with the Picture dialog box, follow these steps:

1. Select the picture.

2. Choose the Format Picture command. The Picture dialog box appears (see fig. 22.9).

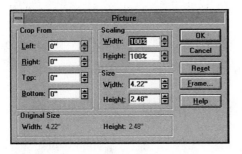

Fig. 22.9
You can crop, scale, and size a picture to specific dimensions.

3. If you want to crop the picture, use the Crop From group. Enter the crop amount in the **Left**, **Right**, **Top**, or **Bottom** box (or click the up or down arrows to increase or decrease the crop amount).

   To crop one-half inch off the bottom of the picture, for example, type .5 in the **Bottom** box. To crop one-quarter inch off the right side, type .25 in the **Right** box.

4. If you want to scale your picture by a percentage, use the Scaling group. In the **W**idth or **H**eight box (or both), enter the percentage by which you want to scale the picture.

   To scale the picture to half its original size, for example, type **50** (for 50%) in the **W**idth box, and **50** in the Height box. To double its size, type **200** (for 200%) in both boxes.

   Typing the identical scaling amount keeps the scaled picture proportional. If you type a different scale in the **W**idth and **H**eight boxes, the picture is distorted.

5. If you want to make your picture an exact size, use the Size group. Enter the dimensions for your picture in the Width and He**i**ght boxes.

   If you want your picture to be exactly three inches wide, for example, type **3** in the **W**idth box; if you want the picture to be two inches high, enter **2** in the Height box.

> **Note**
>
> If you make a mistake, or change your mind and want to return the picture to its original dimensions, they are listed in the Original Size box at the bottom of the Picture dialog box.

6. Choose OK.

The percent you enter in the Scaling boxes is always a percent of the original size, not of the previous percent; therefore, it is easy to return to the original size.

Resetting the Picture to its Original Dimensions. You can easily reset your picture to its original dimensions (even if you changed it with the mouse rather than the Picture dialog box). Follow these steps:

1. Select the picture.

2. Choose the Format Picture command.

3. Choose the Reset button.

Adding Lines and Borders

Unless a border is part of your original composition, pictures arrive in your document with no lines around their edges. You can easily add lines or a box.

Many line styles, widths, and colors are available. Pictures in text boxes are an exception to this rule—they are formatted with fill color, line color, and style selections that you make from the Drawing toolbar.

The Picture Borders dialog box contains the Shading tab, which you can use only when a picture is framed. You can add shading to a frame, but the shading does not change the picture—it applies only to the frame around the picture. It is, therefore, of minimal use when you're working with pictures. On the Borders tab is the From Text option, which you can use only when text is framed. The From Text option sets the distance between the text and the border and does not apply to pictures. Refer to Chapter 23, "Framing and Moving Text and Graphics," to learn more about frames. Refer to Chapter 10, "Formatting Lines and Paragraphs," to learn about shading.

Adding Boxes Around a Picture. A box is the same on all four sides of a picture, unless it is a shadowed box. This type of box adds a black drop shadow on both the right and bottom sides of the box.

To add a box around a picture, follow these steps:

1. Select the picture.

2. Choose the Format Borders and Shading command. The Picture Borders dialog box appears (see fig. 22.10).

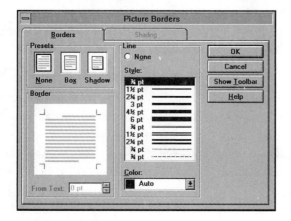

3. Select the Borders tab.

4. Select Box or Shadow from the Presets group (with a mouse, just click the appropriate icon). The Box option adds lines of the selected style and color to all four sides of the picture; the Shadow option adds a black drop shadow as well (see fig. 22.11).

Tip
You can quickly display the Picture Borders dialog box by clicking on a picture with the right mouse button to display the shortcut menu, and then selecting the Borders and Shading command.

Fig. 22.10
You can add borders and lines of many styles and colors to your pictures.

V

Publishing with Graphics

Fig. 22.11
Boxes and shadow
boxes add
definition to
pictures.

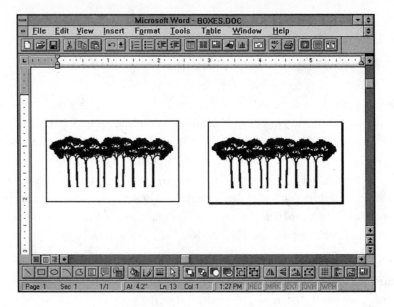

5. From the Line group, select the line Style you want for the box.

6. From the Color list, select a color for the box.

7. Choose OK.

Adding Lines Around a Picture. You can add lines to any or all sides of a selected picture. Use lines instead of a box when you want lines on only some sides of the picture. Use lines also when you want the sides of the picture to have different line styles.

The easiest way to add lines to a picture is to select your line style and color and then click the sides of the sample picture where you want lines. The lines appear in the selected line style and color on each side where you clicked. If you want lines of different styles or colors on different sides, select the sides you want to alter, and then select the style and color you want for them. Any line style or color selection you make applies to a side while it is selected.

To add lines around a picture, follow these steps:

1. Select the picture.

2. Choose the Format Borders and Shading command. Select the Borders tab.

3. Select Border. Click the side of the sample picture where you want a line to appear. The side is selected: a line appears on that side in the selected style and color (see fig. 22.12). (Click the side a second time to remove the line.) Selected sides have black, triangular selection handles at each end. Press and hold down Shift to select multiple sides (or to deselect a selected side).

Fig. 22.12
Select the sides of the picture where you want lines to appear. While the sides are selected, you can change their line style and color.

To use the keyboard, select Border and press any arrow key to cycle through various combinations of lines.

4. From the Line group, select the line Style you want for the selected lines or future lines.

5. From the Color list, select the line color you want for the selected lines or future lines.

6. Choose OK.

To remove a line or box from a picture, follow these steps:

1. Select the picture.

2. Choose the Format Borders and Shading command. Select the **Borders** tab.

3. To remove either a box or all the lines, select None from the Presets group.

   or

   To remove a line, select Border and click the line you want to remove. Alternatively, select None in the Line group.

4. Choose OK.

Tip
Select Box from the Presets group to add lines quickly on all four sides in the selected line style and color. Then select and change the lines that you want to be different.

V

Publishing with Graphics

Moving or Copying a Picture

You can use either the mouse or keyboard commands to move or copy any picture. But the way the picture behaves when you move or copy it depends on what type of container holds the picture. If it is not in a container—that is, if you simply inserted or copied the picture—it remains tightly linked to the text. Moving the picture means relocating it in the text; you even see an insertion point as you drag it to a new location. Moving or copying an inserted picture is the same as moving or copying text. If a picture is framed or in a text box, however, and you're working in the page layout view, you can drag the picture freely around on the page, regardless of where text appears.

For more information on moving pictures in text boxes, refer to Chapter 24, "Drawing with Word's Drawing Tools." If you want to learn more about working with frames, see Chapter 23, "Framing and Moving Text and Graphics."

To move a picture, follow these steps:

1. Select the picture.

2. Choose the Edit Cut command (Ctrl+X or Shift+Del). Move the insertion point to the place where you want to move the picture. Then choose Edit Paste (Ctrl+V or Shift+Ins).

   or

   Drag the picture to its new location.

To copy a picture, follow these steps:

1. Select the picture.

2. Choose the Edit Copy command (Ctrl+C or Ctrl+Ins). Move the insertion point where you want to copy the picture in your document. Then choose Edit Paste (Ctrl+V or Shift+Ins).

   or

   Press and hold down the Ctrl key while you drag the picture to its new location.

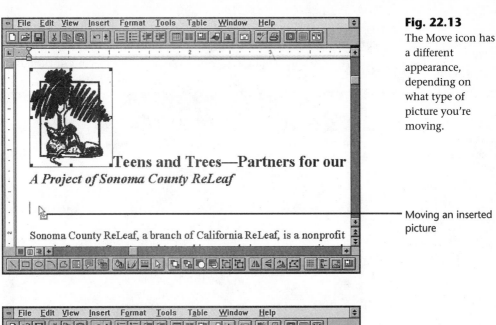

Fig. 22.13
The Move icon has a different appearance, depending on what type of picture you're moving.

Moving an inserted picture

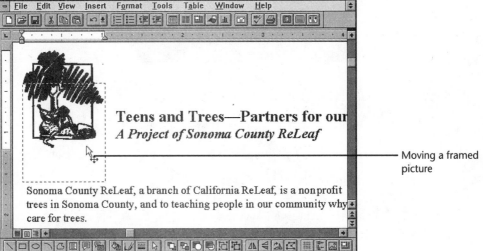

Moving a framed picture

Displaying and Hiding Pictures

Pictures use up a lot of your computer's memory. Thus, they can slow you down when you're working, especially if there are several pictures in your document. Hiding pictures is a good way to save time when you don't need to see them. You might display the pictures while you're inserting and formatting them. Then you can hide them while you work on the text in your document.

When hidden, pictures appear as placeholders—simple line borders in your document (see fig. 22.14). You can select and work with them just as though they were displayed. Hidden drawings don't appear in your document.

Fig. 22.14

Hidden pictures appear as line borders (boxes) in your document.

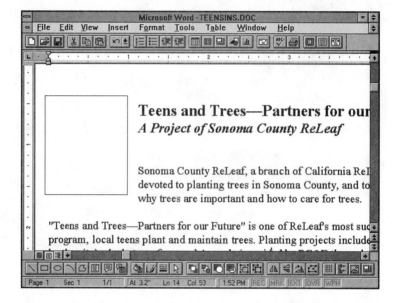

To hide pictures, follow these steps:

1. Choose the Tools Options command and select the View tab.

2. In the Show group, select the Picture Placeholders option.

3. Choose OK.

To display pictures, follow these steps:

1. Choose the Tools Options command and select the View tab.

2. In the Show group, deselect, or clear, the Picture Placeholders option.

3. Choose OK.

Separate commands exist for hiding pictures and drawings you create with the Drawing toolbar.

To hide drawings you've made with the Drawing toolbar, choose the Tools Options command and select the View tab. In the Show group, deselect, or clear, the Drawings option.

Editing and Converting Pictures

To edit a picture, you must have on your computer the program used to create the picture. If the program is not available, when you attempt to edit the picture, Word places it in a Microsoft Word Picture window.

To edit pictures, follow these steps:

1. Double-click the picture to edit.

   or

   Select the picture and choose either the Edit Picture command or the Edit Object command. (The name of the command depends on the type of picture you've selected.)

   Either the program used to create the picture or Microsoft Word Picture appears on your screen.

2. Make your changes to the picture. In Microsoft Word Picture, you can replace the picture or enhance it by using tools on the Drawing toolbar.

3. Choose the File Update command and then the File Exit command in some programs, such as CorelDRAW!; in other programs, such as Excel, simply click your document.

   or

   Choose the Close Picture button to close Microsoft Word Picture and return to your document.

Note that if you use the Edit Picture command to edit a picture with Microsoft Word Picture, Word converts the picture to an object. The next time you select the same picture for editing, the Edit Word Picture Object command appears instead.

Converting Picture Objects

You can convert a picture object from its original format to a different format. You might want to convert a picture created in CorelDRAW! to a picture that can be edited by Microsoft Word Picture. You might do this, for example, if you do not own CorelDRAW! but you want to edit the picture.

An alternative exists that preserves your picture in its original format. You simply specify that the picture be activated in a different format, but not converted.

For Related Information

- "Aligning Paragraphs," p. 295

- "Shading and Bordering Paragraphs," p. 324

- "Framing Text, Pictures, and Other Objects," p. 688

- "Moving and Positioning Frames," p. 699

- "Wrapping Text around a Frame," p. 708

- "Including Text or Another Picture in a Drawing," p. 759

V

Publishing with Graphics

For Related Information

- "Editing Embedded Objects," p. 1006

To convert an inserted picture or picture object, follow these steps:

1. Select the picture you want to convert.

2. Choose the Edit Object command. (The name of the object varies, depending on the program used to create it.)

3. From the submenu, select Convert. The Convert dialog box appears; the current format of your picture is displayed as Current Type near the top of the dialog box (see fig. 22.15).

Fig. 22.15
You can convert pictures and picture objects into another format.

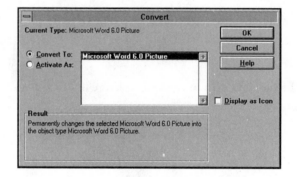

4. Select Convert To. Then select the format to which you want to convert your picture or picture object.

    Select Display as Icon if you want to display your converted picture as an icon.

5. Choose OK.

To activate a picture in a different format without converting, follow these steps:

1. Select the picture you want to activate in a different format.

2. Choose the Edit Object command.

3. From the submenu, select Convert.

4. Select Activate As. Then select the format in which you want to activate your picture or picture object.

5. Choose OK.

From Here...

For information relating to pictures, review the following chapters of this book:

- Chapter 10, "Formatting Lines and Paragraphs," shows how to format paragraphs. You can use paragraph-formatting commands to format pictures that are inserted, but not framed or in a text box. For example, you can use paragraph formatting to center an inserted picture if it is in a paragraph by itself.

- Chapter 23, "Framing and Moving Text and Graphics," shows how to frame a picture and position it where you want it on the page. Framed pictures can move independently of the text in your document.

- Chapter 24, "Drawing with Word's Drawing Tools," show how to draw with tools on the Drawing toolbar, explains how to insert pictures in text boxes and how to format the text boxes.

- Chapter 27, "Desktop Publishing," covers building newsletters, brochures, stationery, and other projects using Word.

- Chapter 33, "Using Word with Other Windows Applications," describes how to work with pictures that are linked to their source programs.

V

Publishing with Graphics

Chapter 23

Framing and Moving Text and Graphics

Word for Windows has many features that help make your pages look graphical—boxes, lines, columns, pictures, and much more. Frames, however, take your document a step beyond traditional word processing and into the world of page layout. Frames allow you to move objects freely on the page.

In Word for Windows, you can frame many types of objects, including text, tables, drawings, inserted pictures, WordArt logos, captions, charts, equations, and even blank space (in case you want to add noncomputer art to your document after you print it). You can frame objects singly or together. (For example, you can frame a picture with a caption.) You can add lines, borders, and shading to frames.

After you frame an object, you can position it anywhere you want on the page—like hanging a picture on a wall. You can drag it into position with a mouse or specify its precise position on the page with a command. Text automatically wraps around any framed text or object.

By positioning a framed object on the page, you free the object from its surrounding text. Frames are a critical tool in helping you use Word for Windows to design a pleasing, professional, and creative page layout.

Using frames, you can accomplish the following:

- Position text, pictures, tables, or any object wherever you want them on the page

- Wrap text around text, pictures, tables, or any object

In this chapter, you learn to do the following:

- Frame pictures and other graphic objects

- Insert text or graphics in a blank frame

- Change the position of frames

- Group text and other objects so that you can position them as a unit anywhere in your document and wrap text around them

- Leave a blank space—with or without a border—where you can paste in noncomputer graphics after you print your document

Fig. 23.1 shows an example of how you can use frames.

Fig. 23.1

With frames, you can position text and graphics anywhere on the page. On the left, framed text is used as a sidehead. On the right, text wraps around framed text in the top part of the newsletter, and a framed picture is positioned exactly where it's needed at the bottom.

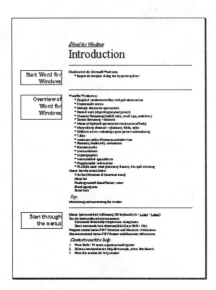
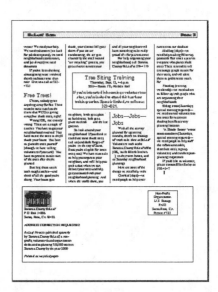

Framing Text, Pictures, and Other Objects

Framing text or an object sets it apart from the rest of your document. You can frame a paragraph or a picture so that it becomes a graphic element on the page that attracts the reader's attention. You can create a blank frame and type text inside it or insert a picture—or both. You can frame a picture and a caption together so that they exist as a unit and aren't separated when you later edit the document.

To create a frame, you can select the object—or objects—that you want to frame and choose a command or click a button. For quick framing, three of Word's toolbars—the Word for Windows, Forms, and Drawing toolbars—contain frame buttons. Several shortcut menus—the Picture, WordArt, Equation, and other object shortcut menus—contain framing commands. Alternatively, you can draw a frame and then insert text or a graphic inside it.

You can create a frame in any view. Page layout and print preview are the only views, however, that accurately show where a frame is positioned in your document and how text wraps around the frame. If you create a frame in the normal view, Word for Windows displays a dialog box to suggest that you switch to page layout view.

In this section, you learn how to create frames; in later sections in this chapter, you learn how to move, size, and border frames, as well as how to wrap text around them.

You can use the Edit Undo command to remove a frame you've just inserted.

Framing Text

You can frame any amount of text—from one character to an entire page. When you first frame selected text, the frame is the same size as the text. If you change the size of the frame, the text wraps to accommodate the frame's new dimensions. Similarly, if you add text to a frame, the frame expands downward to accommodate the new text. If you frame only part of a paragraph, the framed text becomes a separate paragraph and moves outside the paragraph that contains it.

After you frame text, it becomes an object you can move, border, and shade. Framed text is bordered by a box drawn in a narrow line, and other text on the page wraps around it.

You can frame text that's already in your document, or you can insert a blank frame and type text inside it (see the section "Inserting Text or Graphics in a Blank Frame" later in this chapter).

In page layout view, you can see your frame interact with the rest of the text on the page. You can see how frames appear in the normal view in the section "Working in Different Views" later in this chapter.

To frame text, follow these steps:

1. If you're not in page layout view, choose the View Page Layout command.

2. Select the text you want to frame.

3. Choose the Insert Frame command or click the Frame button on the Word for Windows toolbar. Selection handles and a shaded border appear around the edges of your framed text (see fig. 23.2).

V

Publishing with Graphics

Fig 23.2

Newly framed objects have selection handles on the corners and sides, and a shaded border around the edges.

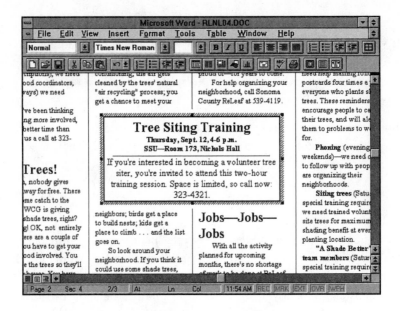

Fig 23.2

Newly framed objects have selection handles on the corners and sides, and a shaded border around the edges.

Framed objects that are selected have eight selection handles on the corners and sides. Selection handles appear as small, black squares, which you can use to size your frame. (See the section "Sizing Frames" later in this chapter.)

If you are in the normal view when you insert a frame, Word for Windows displays a dialog box suggesting that you switch to the page layout view. Choose Yes if you want to switch to page layout view.

Tip

Frame buttons are included on the Forms and Drawing toolbars, as well as on the Word for Windows toolbar.

Formatting Text Within a Frame

When you frame text, it keeps the same text and paragraph formatting it had before you added the frame. You can change the formatting in any way you want by using Word's usual selection techniques and formatting commands. You can even use styles to format text within a frame, or include framing as part of a style. Sometimes framing text in a box makes the text look different enough that you *should* change its formatting. For example, big text in a small frame may look awkward; make the frame larger. Similarly, small text in a huge frame gets lost; make the text larger.

For variety, use any text and paragraph formatting commands to change the appearance of text within a frame. Choose a different font, or add spacing between lines. Use bold or italic. Add borders or shading to framed text (see the section "Bordering and Shading Frames" later in this chapter). Align the text however you want inside the frame: no matter where the frame is positioned, the text remains aligned within the frame as you specify.

Watch out for indentations inside a frame; if you have a two-inch-wide frame, and the text inside the frame has one-inch left and right margin indents that you set before inserting the frame, you get a frame containing a vertical string of characters trying to fit within impossible specifications (see fig. 23.3). To fix it, reduce the indentations or widen the frame.

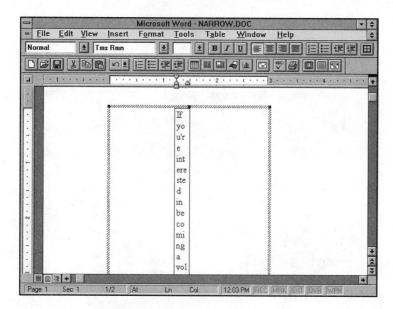

V

Publishing with Graphics

Fig. 23.3
When a frame contains text with indents that are too wide, select the text and reduce the indentations.

Framing Pictures and Other Graphic Objects

If you frame an inserted, embedded, drawn, or copied picture or other graphic in your document (such as a Microsoft WordArt object or a piece of clip art), you can easily move the graphic wherever you want it in your document. You can frame a graphic that's already in your document, or you can insert a blank frame and then insert the graphic inside it (see the section "Inserting Text or Graphics in a Blank Frame" later in this chapter). When you frame an existing graphic, the frame is the size of the graphic; when you insert a graphic into a frame, the graphic conforms to the size of the frame. A selected unframed picture looks different from a selected framed picture (see fig. 23.4).

In page layout view, you can see your frame interact with the rest of the text on the page. You can see how frames appear in the normal view in the section "Working in Different Views" later in this chapter.

To frame a picture or graphic, follow these steps:

1. Select the graphic by clicking it. You also can use the keyboard to position the insertion point next to the graphic, and then press Shift+up- or down-arrow key to move the insertion point across the graphic. A graphic selected with the mouse appears with selection handles on each corner and side. A graphic selected with the keyboard appears reversed.

2. Choose the Insert Frame command or click the Frame button on the toolbar.

Fig. 23.4
A selected graphic has square handles on the corners and sides (left); once framed, a shaded border appears around the selected graphic (right).

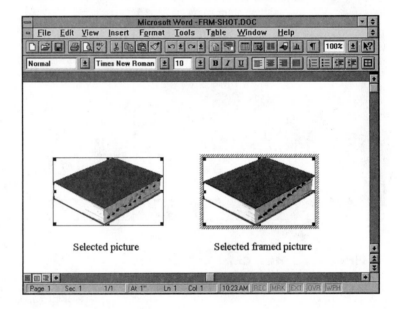

You can remove a frame from a graphic (see the upcoming section "Removing a Frame"). If you remove a frame, however, the graphic loses its position. To later reposition the graphic with the Format Frame command, first frame the graphic.

Tip
If you want to position a graphic in the layer behind your text, insert it in a text box or picture container. See Chapter 24, "Drawing with Word's Drawing Tools."

Framing Tables

A framed table can work as an illustration in a financial or business document, such as an annual report. Framing a table is like framing text: you select a row or the entire table and insert the frame. You cannot frame just a cell; if you select a cell and choose the Insert Frame command, you frame the entire row containing the selected cell. You also cannot frame a single column in a table; if you select a column and insert a frame, you frame the entire table.

To frame a row or a table, follow these steps:

1. Select the row you want to frame, or select the entire table.

To Frame	Select
A row	One cell or an entire row
A table	One column or the entire table

2. Choose the Insert Frame command or click the Frame button on the toolbar.

Framing a table makes it a movable object on the page. In a report, for example, you may want to center a table containing pertinent data to give it prominence on the page. Or you may want the flexibility to move the table around to different locations on the page—to see what looks best. You can move a framed row to a different location on the page and make it a separate table.

Inserting a Blank Frame

Sometimes you want to insert a blank frame to leave a space for a photograph or artwork to be inserted during copying or offset printing. Or, you may want to insert a blank frame and then type text in it or insert a graphic into it. When you create a blank frame, you draw it to the size you want.

To insert a blank frame, follow these steps:

1. Make sure that no text, table, or other object is selected.

2. Choose the Insert Frame command or click the Frame button on the toolbar. A crosshair appears on-screen, and a message in the status bar at the bottom of the screen reads Click and drag to insert a frame (see fig. 23.5).

3. Click and hold the left mouse button where you want to start the frame, drag to where you want the frame to end, and release the button.

Like text, a blank frame is automatically formatted with a border. Use the Format Borders and Shading command to change the frame's border (see "Bordering and Shading Frames" later in this chapter).

Fig. 23.5

When you insert a
blank frame, you
draw it to size.

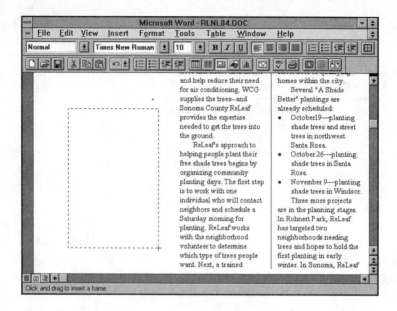

Inserting Text or Graphics in a Blank Frame

When you draw an empty frame, it appears with a flashing insertion point at the top left corner. To include text in the frame, type the text. To include a graphic in the frame, choose the Insert Picture or Insert Object command. Or copy a graphic from another application and paste it inside the frame.

Text wraps inside a frame just as it does in a Word document. When you type text in a frame, the frame stays the same width as you drew it, but gets taller as you continue typing. When you insert a graphic into a frame, the graphic becomes as wide as the frame, and the frame adjusts in height to the graphic.

You cannot draw a picture inside a frame to frame the picture. Instead, first draw the picture, and then select and frame it.

Framing Objects Together

To include multiple objects in a frame, simply select them all and choose the Insert Frame command or click the Frame button. The objects are framed as one, and you can move them as a unit on the page.

You can add text, a picture, or an object to an existing frame by positioning the insertion point inside the frame and typing the text, or by inserting the picture or object as usual. You can move the insertion point inside a frame with the keyboard by pressing the arrow keys. With the mouse, click the frame to select it, and then press the right- or down-arrow key to position the insertion point at the bottom right of the frame. Press Enter to add a new line inside the frame.

Including a Caption in a Frame

There are two ways to include a caption in a frame: create the object and caption separately and frame them together, or frame the object and then add a caption. You can use either technique with captions you type yourself or with Word's automatic captions.

To frame an object and caption together, select them both and choose the Insert Frame command or click the Frame button. To add a typed caption to a framed object, position the insertion point inside the frame and type the text (see the previous section "Framing Objects Together"). To add an automatic caption to a framed object, select the frame and choose the Insert Caption command. To learn about captions, see Chapter 31, "Adding Cross-References and Captions."

Working in Different Views

In page layout view, you can see where framed objects are positioned and how the text wraps around them (see fig. 23.6). In any view besides page layout, a framed object or text appears at the left margin with one or more small black squares at the left margin (see fig. 23.7). You usually work with frames in page layout view.

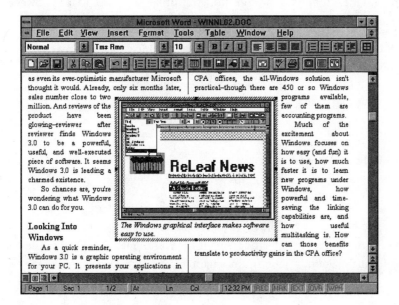

Fig. 23.6

In page layout view, a framed object appears in place in your document.

Fig. 23.7

In normal view, a framed object appears with black squares in the left margin when paragraph marks are displayed.

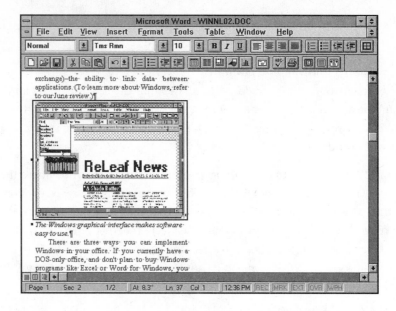

You can select a framed object in any view, and you can format it in any view with the Format Frame command (options include sizing the framed object, positioning it, and wrapping text around it). You can even insert a frame in normal view, although Word for Windows advises you to switch to page layout view. In normal and outline views, however, you see the framed object aligned to the left margin, not positioned. Unlike page layout view, however, you cannot move the object by dragging it with the mouse.

Working in normal view is faster—anything graphical takes longer to redraw on your computer screen in Word for Windows or any other program. If you're working very fast and you're on a deadline, do your layout in page layout view and switch to normal view for typing.

To switch to page layout view, choose the View Page Layout command.

Troubleshooting Frames

The following troubleshooting tips will help you solve some of the more frequently asked questions about creating frames.

When you frame multiple lines with paragraph end marks, the frame extends from margin to margin. Size the frame using techniques described in the section "Sizing Frames" later in this chapter.

I tried to put a drop cap in my frame, but couldn't.

A drop cap is already framed, and you can't create a frame within another frame. You can drag an existing frame inside another existing frame, and you can select an existing frame along with unframed text and frame the two together. However, neither of these techniques will cause text in the larger frame to wrap around the smaller frame. Use some other technique to emphasize your text, such as a raised initial cap. See Chapter 27, "Desktop Publishing," for ideas.

Selecting and Removing Frames

In most Windows programs, as in many other programs, you must select an object before you can do something to it so that the program knows where to apply your actions. In Word for Windows, before you can move, border, size, position, or wrap text around a framed object, you first must select it.

Removing a frame is not the same as removing the framed text or object—the text or object remains, whereas the frame and its positioning go away. To remove a frame you must select the frame and choose a command—pressing the delete key removes the frame and its contents.

Selecting a Framed Object

You can select a framed object using the mouse or the keyboard. Usually, the easiest way is to use the mouse. Again, make sure that you are in page layout view. Text is an exception because you can position the insertion point inside the framed text and choose the Format Frame command to select the frame (and then format it).

A selected frame appears with black selection handles on its corners and sides. In page layout view, it also appears with a shaded border. If you move the mouse pointer across the selected frame, the arrow or insertion point changes. On top of the selection handles, the insertion point turns into a two-headed arrow (used to size the frame); on top of the border surrounding the frame, it turns into a four-headed arrow (used to move the frame). See the section "Moving and Positioning Frames" later in this chapter for details.

Note that when you see a shaded border around framed text or a framed object, the frame may not be selected. The shaded border, which appears only in page layout view, simply indicates that the text or object is framed and that the insertion point is inside the frame. Only when you see square selection handles on each corner and side of a frame is the frame selected (see fig. 23.8).

For Related Information

■ "Inserting and Copying Pictures into your Document," p. 661

■ "Creating Tables," p. 509

■ "Formatting Characters," p. 246

■ "Starting Paragraphs with a Drop Cap," p. 269

■ "Controlling Your Document's Appearance On-Screen," p. 115

V

Publishing with Graphics

Fig. 23.8

A graphic or text
might be selected
even if the frame
is not (left); you
see selection
handles inside the
shaded frame
border when a
frame is selected
(right).

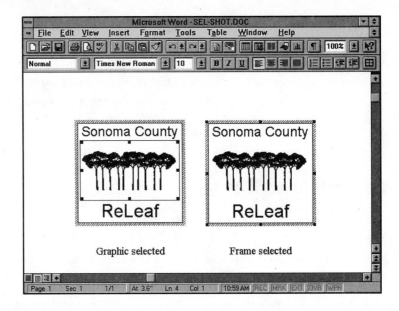

In normal view, you cannot see frames. However, you can use the Format Frame command to change a selected frame.

To select a frame with a mouse, follow these steps:

1. Choose the View Page Layout command if you are in any view besides page layout.

2. Click the framed text or object to display the shaded frame border, and then click the shaded border to select the frame.

   or

   Position the mouse pointer over the edge of the framed object until it turns into a four-cornered arrow. Then click the mouse button to select the frame.

   or

   Click the framed text or object to display the shaded frame border, and then choose the Format Frame command. Make your selections and choose OK.

To select a frame with the keyboard, follow these steps:

1. Choose the View Page Layout command if you are in any view besides page layout.

2. Position the insertion point inside the frame.

3. Choose the Format Frame command.

4. Make your frame formatting choices, then choose OK.

Removing a Frame

Removing a frame does not remove its contents. You can remove a frame from a paragraph or a table, for example, and even though the frame is gone, the paragraph or the table is still there.

Removing a frame does remove frame formatting. If text is wrapped around the framed paragraph, it doesn't wrap after you remove the frame. If the framed table was positioned in the center of the page, it moves back to where it was before you inserted the frame.

To remove a frame, follow these steps:

1. Select the framed object, or select the blank frame.

   For text, position the insertion point inside the framed text.

2. Choose the Format Frame command.

3. Choose the Remove Frame button.

A frame is a paragraph-level formatting command, and like a paragraph, the paragraph mark at the end of a frame stores the information defining the frame. If you delete the paragraph mark, you delete the frame (but not the paragraph). If you position the framed text, the text loses its position and moves back to where you inserted it. If two paragraphs are in a frame, and you delete the paragraph mark for the second paragraph, the second paragraph moves outside of the frame and the first stays in.

Moving and Positioning Frames

A frame separates an object from the text on a page so that you can move the object independently. Word for Windows by default anchors a framed object to the paragraph where you created it, not to the page. (You can easily override this default—see "Anchoring a Frame.") Every framed object also retains its connection to its roots—if you remove the frame, the object moves back to the beginning of the paragraph to which it's anchored.

V

Publishing with Graphics

Tip
If you want to remove a frame *and* the framed object, select the frame and press Delete.

You can move or position a framed object in two ways: you can select and drag it with the mouse, or you can select the object, choose the Format Frame command, and specify its precise position on the page.

Tip

Use the View button on the Word for Windows toolbar to help you position objects. The Zoom Page Width button shows the full width of a page and is helpful when you're moving a framed object.

If a framed object is linked to another program, and you move part of it (for example, the caption) away from its original position, you break the link for the part of the text you moved. Similarly, if you designate a framed object as a bookmark, and you move part of the bookmark, then you remove the part you moved from the bookmark. If you frame and move the entire bookmark, however, Word for Windows remembers the bookmark and still finds it, even in its new position.

> **Note**
>
> Text boxes and picture containers, which you can create using the Drawing toolbar, are similar to frames. You can place text or graphics inside them, add borders (and even shading), and move them freely on the page. You even can place them in the layer behind your text. However, you cannot wrap text around them. Choose the container—frame, text box, or picture container—that works best for you. To learn more about the Drawing toolbar, see Chapter 24, "Drawing with Word's Drawing Tools."

Moving a Frame with a Mouse

Using a mouse is probably the easiest way to move a framed object. It isn't as precise, however, as positioning the frame using the Frame dialog box (discussed in the next sections on positioning frames).

Tip

If you don't like where you've moved a frame, quickly choose the Edit Undo command to return it to its original position.

By default, framed objects move with their surrounding text. If you add or delete text near the framed object, causing the text to move up or down on the page (or even to the next page), the object stays with its related text. If you want a framed object linked to its position on the page, regardless of where the surrounding text moves, choose the Format Frame command, and deselect or clear the Move with Text option. (The option is deselected if no X appears in its box.)

To move a framed object with the mouse, follow these steps:

1. In page layout view, select the framed object or text you want to move.

2. Move the mouse pointer over the frame until it turns into a four-headed arrow (see fig. 23.9).

3. Hold down the left mouse button, drag the framed object to its new location, and release the mouse button. The frame appears as a dotted line as you move it.

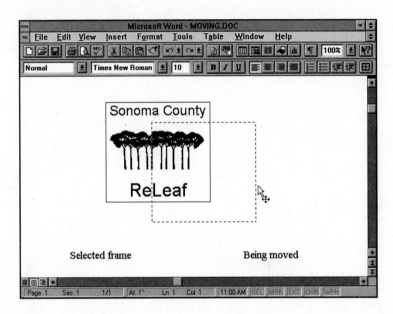

Fig. 23.9

The easiest way to move a frame is to select it (left) and then drag it to its new position (right).

You can use Word for Windows automatic scrolling feature to move a framed object from one page to another. In any view, select the object you want to move, drag it to the top of the screen (if you want to move it to the preceding page) or to the bottom of the screen (if you want to move it to the next page). By "pushing" the object into the top or bottom of your screen, you cause the text to scroll. If you continue holding the mouse button, the pages continue to scroll, and the frame continues to move. Release the mouse button when you get to the page where you want to move your framed object. If the status bar is displayed, you can see what page you're on when you release the mouse button.

Moving and Copying Frames

You can move and copy frames using Word's usual Edit Cut, Copy, and Paste commands. To move a frame, select and cut it, position the insertion point where you want to move it, and paste it. To copy a frame, select and copy it, then position the insertion point where you want to copy it, and paste. You can also copy a frame by holding down the Ctrl key while you drag the frame with a mouse.

Frames have a shortcut menu for quick moving and copying. Click the frame with the right mouse button to display the shortcut menu, then select the command you want (see fig. 23.10). The contents of the shortcut menu vary depending on where you click and what the frame contains. For example, if you click a framed picture with the left mouse button to select it, then click the frame with the right mouse button to display the shortcut menu, the shortcut menu displays commands for both editing the picture and formatting the frame.

Fig. 23.10
Click the frame with the right mouse button to display the shortcut menu.

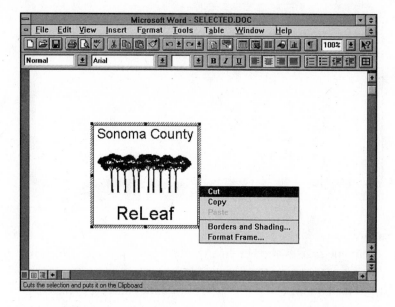

Positioning a Frame Horizontally

Positioning a frame with a command is different from dragging it with a mouse. Dragging is visual, but it's not precise. When you position a frame using a command, you specify exactly where it appears on the page.

When you position a frame horizontally, you define its exact position relative to the left, center, or right of the margin, column, or page. If you're working with facing pages, you can position the frame relative to the inside or outside of the margin, column, or page.

You can position a frame at the left margin, for example, to have the frame appear flush against the left text margin. You can position a frame at the outside edge of the page in a facing page layout to have the frame appear in the outside margin (if the frame is wider than the margin, then text wraps around it; if the margin is wider than the frame, then the frame is completely within the margin). You can position a frame at the center of the page in a two-column layout to have text in both columns wrap around the frame. Or you can position a frame to the left or right of a column, to place the frame flush with the text on either side of the column (see fig. 23.11).

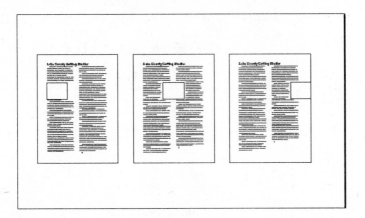

Fig. 23.11
Positioned left relative to the margin (left); positioned center relative to the margins (center); positioned right relative to the page (right).

V

Publishing with Graphics

Alternatively, you can position a frame some absolute distance relative to the margin, page, or column. For example, you may want a frame to appear one-quarter inch away from the left edge of the page, because most printers can't print to the edge of a sheet of paper. If you position a frame with an absolute distance, the distance is measured from the left edge of the margin, page, or column. To position a frame some absolute distance from the right edge, add the distance to the width of the frame and subtract it from the width of the page. For example, to position a one-inch frame one-quarter inch from the right edge of an 8 1/2-inch page, set its absolute distance at 7.25".

To position a frame horizontally, follow these steps:

1. In page layout view, select the framed object.

2. Choose the Format Frame command or choose Format Frame from the shortcut menu. The Frame dialog box appears (see fig. 23.12).

3. In the Horizontal Position box, select the horizontal position for your frame.

Fig. 23.12

Use the Frame
dialog box to
position a frame
horizontally or
vertically.

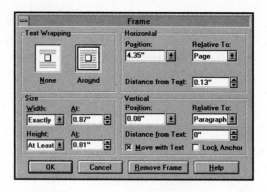

Type or Select	To Position the Frame
A measured distance	At a measured distance from the left of the margin, page, or column
Left	At the left side of the margin, page, or column
Right	At the right side of the margin, page, or column
Center	Centered between the left and right margins, page edges, or column edges
Inside	At the inside edge of the margin, page, or column
Outside	At the outside edge of the margin, page, or column

4. In the Relative To box, select the boundary you want your frame positioned relative to.

Select	To Position the Frame Relative to
Margin	The left or right margin
Page	The left or right edge of the page
Column	The left or right edge of the current column

5. In the Distance from Text box, type the amount of space you want between the frame and the text on the left and right sides of the frame, or click the up or down arrows to increase or decrease the distance.

6. Choose OK.

Positioning a Frame Vertically

Positioning a frame vertically anchors it somewhere between the top and bottom of the page. You can position the frame at the top, bottom, center, or some absolute distance relative to the margin, page, or paragraph.

You can center a frame between the top and bottom edge of the page, for example, or between the top and bottom margin. You can position the frame flush against the top or bottom margin. Or you can position the frame some absolute distance from the top margin or edge of the page. Alternatively, you can position a frame at the top, bottom, or center of the paragraph the frame is anchored to. Or you can position a frame some absolute distance from a paragraph—a negative number places the frame before the paragraph, whereas a positive number places the frame below the paragraph (see fig. 23.13).

Unless you deselect the Move with Text option, a frame moves with the paragraph it's anchored to. If the paragraph moves to the next page, so does the frame—but it remains positioned in the same relative place. If you center a frame vertically between the top and bottom margins, for example, then add so much text before the frame that the paragraph it's anchored to moves to the top of the next page, the frame also moves to the next page, but it is still centered on the page.

Tip
If a frame contains only text, or contains multiple objects, you can double-click a selected frame to quickly display the Frame dialog box. (Double-clicking on a picture allows you to edit the picture.)

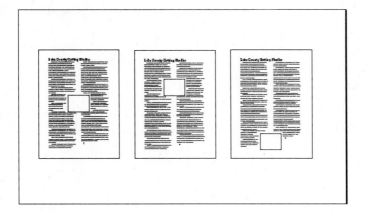

Fig. 23.13
A frame centered vertically between the margins (left); two inches relative to the top margin (center); and relative to the bottom margin (right).

To position a frame vertically on the page, follow these steps:

1. In the page layout view, select the frame.

2. Choose the Format Frame command or choose Format Frame from the shortcut menu. The Frame dialog box appears.

V

Publishing with Graphics

3. In the Vertical Position box, select or type the vertical position for your frame.

Type or Select	Positions the Frame
A distance in inches	At a measured distance from the top of the margin, page, or paragraph
Top	At the top margin, top of the page, or top edge of the paragraph
Bottom	At the bottom margin, bottom of the page, or bottom edge of the paragraph
Center	Centered between the top and bottom margins or page edges, or centered between the top and bottom of the paragraph

4. In the Relative To box, select the boundary you want the frame positioned relative to.

Select	Positions the Frame Relative to
Margin	The top or bottom margin
Page	The top or bottom edge of the page
Paragraph	The top or bottom of the current paragraph

5. In the Distance from Text box, type the amount of space you want between the frame and the text above or below the frame. Or click the up or down arrows to increase or decrease the distance.

6. If you don't want the frame to move with its surrounding text, deselect the Move with Text option so that no X appears in the option box.

With this option unselected, the frame stays anchored to its spot on the page, no matter how the text moves. If you select this option, a frame moves with its surrounding text.

7. Choose OK.

Positioning a Frame in a Margin

Because you can move or position a frame independently of the text on the page, you can move it into the margin, or partially into the margin with text wrapping around it. You frame a picture, for example, and move it to the top left of the first page of a newsletter to give the masthead a graphic effect (see fig. 23.14). Or you can use a style to format tips in a training document as italicized and positioned in the inside margins. Perhaps your document's style is to include headings in the left margin of each page. Positioning text in a margin can give it emphasis in your document; positioning a graphic in a margin can make your page more interesting. Be creative!

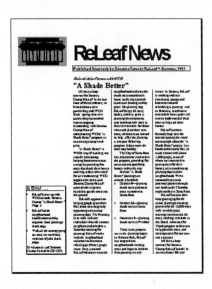

Fig. 23.14
You can frame text or graphics for positioning in margins.

One use for frames in margins is to create *sideheads*—subheadings that appear not above text, but outside of text in the margin. If you create sideheads, be sure to select the Move with Text option in the Frame dialog box so that sideheads stay with the paragraphs they're attached to.

When you position a frame in a margin, remember your printer's limitations. Most laser printers cannot print within one-quarter of an inch from the paper's edges.

Anchoring a Frame

A frame is always anchored to a paragraph. Initially, it is anchored to the paragraph where you created it. As you move a frame, the anchor moves to the nearest paragraph. A frame always appears on the same page as the paragraph it's anchored to.

You can move a frame's anchor to another paragraph without moving the frame itself. If you then lock the anchor, you can be sure the frame remains in the same position on the page, but always prints on the same page as the paragraph. For example, you may position a frame at the center of a page and anchor it to a paragraph; if the paragraph moves to the next page, the frame does too, but it still prints in the center of the page. Similarly, if a frame is too big to fit on a page with the paragraph it's anchored to, both the frame and the paragraph move to the next page.

You can display anchors in order to move them.

To display anchors, follow these steps:

1. Choose the Tools Options command and select the View tab.

2. In the Show group, select Object Anchors. Anchors appear as anchor icons in the left margin.

To move an anchor, follow these steps:

1. Display the anchors in page layout view, and select the framed, anchored object.

2. Drag the anchor icon to a new paragraph.

To lock an anchor to a paragraph, follow these steps:

1. Make sure the frame is positioned inside the paragraph where you want it.

2. Choose the Format Frame command.

3. Select the Lock Anchor option.

If you want a frame to stay on a specific page and not move with the paragraph it's anchored to, in the Frame dialog box deselect, or clear, the Move with Text and the Lock Anchor options.

Wrapping Text Around a Frame

If a frame is smaller than the page or column it's in, you may want to wrap text around it. By default, when you first insert a frame, the surrounding text wraps around the frame. If text does not wrap around a frame, then the text stops above and continues below the frame, with no text to either side of the frame.

Text wraps around a frame no matter how many columns of text are on a page (see fig. 23.15). In order for text to wrap, however, at least one inch of text must be on the left or right of the frame. You can specify how much distance there is between the frame and the text that wraps around it.

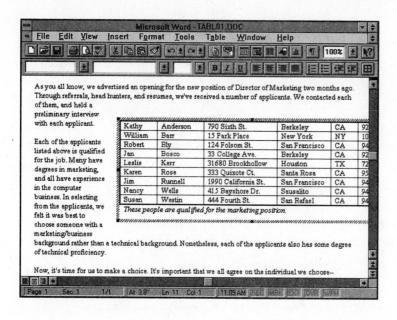

Fig. 23.15
By default, text
wraps around a
frame.

Publishing with Graphics

To wrap text around a framed object and specify the distance between the frame and text, follow these steps:

1. In page layout view, select the frame.

2. Choose the Format Frame command. The Frame dialog box appears.

3. In the Text Wrapping group (top left), select the Around option (see fig. 23.16).

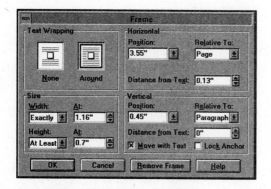

Fig. 23.16
Select Around to
have text wrap
around the frame.

4. From the Horizontal group (top right), select the Distance from Text option. Type, in decimal numbers, the distance you want between the frame and the text to its left and right; or click the up or down arrows to increase or decrease the distance.

5. From the Vertical group (bottom right) select the Distance from Text option. Type, in decimal numbers, the distance you want between the frame and the text above and below; or click the up or down arrows to increase or decrease the distance.

6. Choose OK.

The Distance from Text options usually are measured in decimal inches. If you want to use some other measurement system, however, type the distance measurements in the appropriate increments followed by the appropriate abbreviation (**pt** for points, **pi** for picas, or **cm** for centimeters). You can change your measurement system by choosing the Tools Options command and selecting the General tab. Then in the **M**easurement Units list, select inches, centimeters, points, or picas.

If later you don't want text to wrap around the frame, select the frame and choose Format Frame. Select None from the Text Wrapping group. Deleting the frame also causes text to no longer wrap around the object.

Sizing Frames

Tip

If you specify a wide Distance from Text, you may create a space around the frame that is too narrow for text. You need at least an inch of space around a frame for text to wrap around it.

When you first insert a frame around text or an object, the frame is selected. Square black selection handles appear on each corner and side of a selected frame—eight in all—and a shaded border appears around the outside of the frame (only in page layout view). The frame is the same size as the text or object.

You can size a frame using the mouse or keyboard. Using a mouse, drag one of the handles to size the frame. With the keyboard, use the Format Frame command to size a frame. You can size a frame proportionally so that it becomes larger or smaller but keeps its shape, or nonproportionally so that it stretches into a new shape.

When you size a frame that contains only a graphic, you size the graphic. When you size a frame that contains only text, the text rewraps, but the frame remains large enough to hold the text. (If you make the frame too large for the text, the frame will include blank space at the end of the text.)

If you use a mouse to size a frame that contains multiple objects, you can make the frame larger or smaller than the objects it contains (in this way you can crop the frame's contents). You also can make a frame larger or smaller than the object or objects it contains by sizing it using the Format Frame command rather than the mouse—use this technique when you want to make a frame larger than the single object it contains.

You can select a frame around a graphic object rather than the graphic itself only when the frame is larger than the graphic. The frame might be larger than the graphic if your graphic is framed together with text (such as a caption) or if you have used the Format Frame command to specify for the frame an exact measurement which is larger than the graphic.

Sizing Frames with a Mouse

Using a mouse to size a frame is quick, and it gives you visual control over the frame's appearance (as well as its position). If only text or a single object is in the frame, the frame's contents adjust to fit your frame's new size. If multiple objects are in the frame, you can size the frame so that it is smaller or larger than its contents.

When you size a framed picture with the mouse, you really are sizing the picture—the frame adjusts to fit. But sizing pictures is a little different from sizing frames: a picture remains proportional when you size it by dragging corner handles, but it changes proportions (distorting the picture) if you drag side handles. If you hold Shift while you size a picture—framed or not—you crop the picture rather than size it. To size a frame using a mouse, follow these steps:

1. In page layout view, select the frame so that the black selection handles appear on all four sides and corners, and the shaded frame border appears.

2. Move the mouse pointer over one of the selection handles so that it turns into a two-headed arrow. This arrow is the sizing arrow (see fig. 23.17).

:Leaf

Fig. 23.17
Use the two-headed sizing arrow to size the frame.

3. Click and hold the left mouse button, then drag the sizing arrow to reshape the frame. A dotted-line box shows you the frame's new shape as you drag the arrow.

If you are sizing a framed picture, drag a corner handle to keep the picture proportional. If you are sizing framed text, hold Shift as you drag a corner handle to keep the frame proportional. Do not hold Shift as you drag the corner handle on a picture unless you want to crop the picture.

4. Release the mouse button when the frame is the size you want.

Note

Be careful: if you specify an exact size for a text frame and later size the frame by using the mouse, you *can* size the frame smaller than text. The reason is that the frame is still set to an exact size in the Frame dialog box, and you now are changing the exact size. To fix this, choose Auto for the frame's **Width** or **Height** in the Frame dialog box.

Sizing Frames with the Keyboard

By using the Format Frame command to size a frame, you can specify the frame's precise dimensions.

By default, a frame's size is set to "auto" width and height. If you change the size of the object, the frame adjusts to be the same size. You can make the frame a fixed size, however. You can make the frame's width and height the exact size you want with the Exactly option, specifying the frame's exact dimensions. You also can use the At Least option to specify that the frame be at least a certain height. (This feature is most useful for text, when you want the frame to be an exact width, and you want it to be at least a certain height, but always tall enough to include all the text.)

If you make a frame an exact size rather than the auto size, the frame is likely to be a different size than its contents. If the frame is larger than its contents, you insert a blank space below the contents. If the frame is smaller than the contents, you hide, or crop, part of the contents. The text or graphic itself does not change size. (If you want to change the size of a graphic, use the mouse technique described in the preceding section to drag the selection handles, or use the Format Picture command.)

To size a frame with the keyboard command, follow these steps:

1. Select the framed text or object. The square, black selection handles and the shaded frame border appear.

2. Choose the Format Frame command. The Frame dialog box appears.

3. Select **W**idth and **H**eight options in the Size group.

Select	To Size a Frame this Way
Auto	Sizes the frame so that it is the same size as the framed object
At Least (Height only)	Makes the frame at least as tall as you specify, but always tall enough to include the entire text or graphic
Exactly	Makes the frame exactly the size you specify

4. If you select Exactly for your **W**idth, specify the exact width of your frame in the At box. Type the width, or click the up or down arrow to increase or decrease the width.

5. If you select At Least or Exactly for your **H**eight, specify the minimum or exact height of your frame in the A**t** box. Type the height, or click the up or down arrow to increase or decrease the width.

Bordering and Shading Frames

Word automatically borders text that you frame, but not graphics. However, you can easily add borders and shading to frames.

When you add borders and shading to framed text, the appearance is the same as unframed text: borders appear around the outside edge or edges of the text and between paragraphs, as you specify, and shading appears behind the text. For details about using the Borders dialog box or the Borders toolbar, see the section "Shading and Bordering Paragraphs" in Chapter 10, "Formatting Lines and Paragraphs."

Framed graphics can act a little differently. You can apply a border to both the graphic and the frame; if the frame is larger than the graphic, you see both (see fig. 23.18). To create this effect, select and border the picture and the frame separately. Within the frame, center the picture, using paragraph alignment, and include blank lines above and below the picture. Use this technique to create a double border. Shading appears in the frame, but not behind the graphic. If the frame is larger than the graphic, you see shading

Tip
You may want to size a frame larger than the object it contains, to add another object or more text inside the frame.

inside the frame, but not behind the graphic. You can add blank lines above and below the picture, size the frame so that it is wider than the graphic, and use paragraph formatting to center the graphic within the frame to create a shaded border around a graphic. For details about using the Borders dialog box or the Borders toolbar, see the section "Adding Lines and Borders" in Chapter 22, "Inserting Pictures in Your Document."

Fig. 23.18
This bordered and shaded frame is larger than the bordered picture inside it, creating a double border.

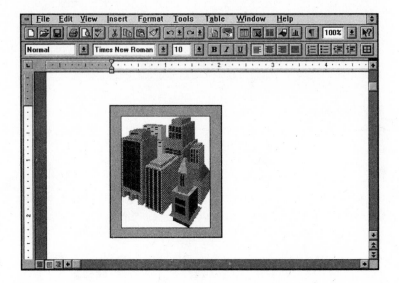

To add borders or shading to frames, follow these steps:

1. In page layout view, select the frame you want to border or shade.

2. Choose the Format Borders and Shading command. Select the Borders tab and select the borders you want around the edges of the frame. Select the Shading tab and select the shading you want within the frame.

   or

   Display the Borders toolbar and select border and shading options.

For Related Information
■ "Shading and Bordering Paragraphs," p. 324

■ "Inserting and Copying Pictures into your Document," p. 661

You can quickly border a frame using a shortcut menu. Click a selected frame with the right mouse button, then select Borders and Shading.

From Here...

For information relating directly to frames, you may want to review the following chapters of this book:

- Chapter 10, "Formatting Lines and Paragraphs," for information on customizing your documents.

- Chapter 22, "Inserting Pictures in Your Document," for information on adding graphics to your documents.

- Chapter 27, "Desktop Publishing," for information on creating professional-looking layouts.

Chapter 24

Drawing with Word's Drawing Tools

Word 6 makes it easier than ever to include drawings in your documents. A drawing can be as simple as a circle, or as complex as a painting on a canvas. With the Drawing toolbar, you can create a drawing without leaving your document—you draw right on the page.

Although the Drawing toolbar includes simple tools for drawing, filling, and coloring lines and shapes, these simple tools are powerful enough that they may be all you ever need for illustrating your pages with graphics.

What You Need to Know About Drawing

When you create a drawing by using tools from the Drawing toolbar, you work directly on a page in your document in the page layout view. The objects you create are location-independent—you can move them anywhere on the page (or even onto another page) by simply dragging them.

When you first draw objects, those objects appear on top of any text on the page. Your document, however, exists in three layers: the text layer, the layer above the text, and the layer below the text. You can move drawn objects, or the entire drawing, between these layers. Within your drawing, you can move objects in front of or behind each other.

Although you draw your lines and shapes one at a time, you can group them into a whole drawing. That way, you don't have to worry about keeping track of each individual piece of a drawing, and you can work with the drawing as a whole, moving or resizing it as a single piece. You can ungroup the pieces of your drawing whenever you want.

You will find the Drawing toolbar useful in some of the following ways:

- Illustrating concepts better explained with pictures than with words alone.

- Making newsletters, brochures, and flyers more interesting with graphics.

- Adding emphasis to important points in your document with shapes and colors.

- Highlighting portions of imported pictures with callouts.

- Nesting blocks of text within a document.

**For Related
Information**

■ "Inserting
   Pictures
   and Picture
   Objects,"
   p. 662, 666

■ "Framing and
   Moving Text
   and Graphics,"
   p. 687

■ "Desktop
   Publishing,"
   p. 827

A drawing can include other things than objects you draw with tools from the toolbar. You can insert a graphic you've created in a different program into a drawing, and you can include text in your drawing.

You can work on your document without displaying drawing objects. To hide drawing objects, choose the Tools Options command and select the View tab; then in the Show group, clear the Drawings check box. To display the drawing objects, select the Drawings check box.

**Figs. 24.1
and 24.2**

You can create simple or complex drawings using tools on the Drawing toolbar.

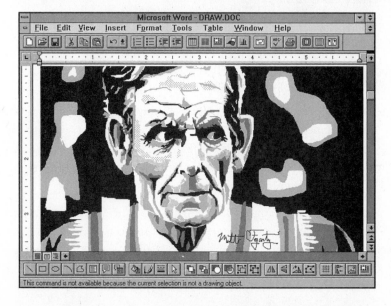

Displaying and Understanding the Drawing Toolbar

To use Word's drawing tools, you must display the Drawing toolbar. When you do, Word switches to the page layout view. Each button on the Drawing toolbar has a specific purpose: some tools draw lines or shapes; some tools allow you to add color or change the appearance of a line or shape; some tools help you position the objects you draw where you want them; some tools insert special objects on your page.

Displaying the Drawing Toolbar

The Drawing toolbar is one of seven predefined toolbars available with Word for Windows. Unlike other toolbars, it appears at the bottom of your screen.

Fig. 24.3
The Drawing toolbar gives you tools for drawing directly onto the page.

You can display the Drawing toolbar by choosing the View Toolbars command and selecting Drawing from the Toolbars list. Or, you can click the Drawing Toolbar button on the Standard toolbar. Alternatively, you can click with the right mouse button on the Standard toolbar and select Drawing from the drop-down list of toolbars that appears.

To display the Drawing toolbar, follow these steps:

1. Choose the View Toolbars command.

2. Select Drawing from the Toolbars list.

To display the Drawing toolbar using the mouse:

■ Click the gray area of any displayed toolbar with the right mouse button, and select Drawing from the drop-down list of toolbars that appears.

   or

■ Click the Drawing Toolbar button on the Standard toolbar.

Understanding the Drawing Tools

Each button on the Drawing toolbar performs a specific function. Browse through the tools and their descriptions to get an idea of what you can do with the Drawing toolbar; then refer to later sections in this chapter to learn how to use each tool.

Table 24.1 Drawing Buttons

Drawing Button	Function
Line button	Draws straight lines. Lines are vertical, horizontal, or at a 30-, 45-, or 60-degree angle if you hold Shift as you draw.
Rectangle button	Draws rectangles, or squares when you hold Shift as you draw.
Ellipse button	Draws ellipses or circles when you hold Shift as you draw.
Arc button	Draws an elliptical arc or a circular arc when you hold Shift as you draw.
Freehand/Polygon button	Draws a curving freehand, straight-line-segment polygon, or composite shape. Line segments are vertical, horizontal, or at a 30-, 45-, or 60-degree angle if you hold Shift as you draw.
Text Box button	Draws a text box into which you can type text or insert a picture created in another program.
Callout button	Inserts a callout.
Callout Formatting button	Formats a callout.
Fill Color button	Fills a selected shape with color, or sets the default fill color if no shape is selected.
Line Color button	Colors a selected line (or the line around a selected shape), or sets the default line color if no line is selected.
Line Style button	Changes the style of a selected line (width, pattern, arrowheads), or sets the default line style if no line is selected.

Drawing Button	Function
Selection button	Draws a selection box around objects in the drawing.
Bring to Front button	Brings a selected drawing object in front of other drawing objects.
Send to Back button	Sends a selected drawing object behind other drawing objects.
Top of Text Layer button	Brings selected drawing objects in front of the text layer.
Behind Text Layer button	Sends selected drawing objects behind the text layer.
Group button	Groups together selected drawing objects.
Ungroup button	Ungroups a selected group of drawing objects.
Flip Horizontal button	Flips selected drawing object(s) left to right.
Flip Vertical button	Flips selected drawing object(s) top to bottom.
Rotate button	Rotates selected drawing object(s) 90 degrees to the right.
Reshape button	Reshapes a freehand or polygon line by letting you drag points along the line.
Drawing Grid button	Establishes an invisible drawing grid.
Align button	Aligns a selected object to the page or selected objects to each other.
Picture Container button	Inserts a picture container (same as choosing the Insert Object Microsoft Word 6.0 Picture command).
Frame button	Frames selected drawing object, or inserts empty frame.

V

Publishing with Graphics

Note

As you move the pointer over a button, watch the status bar for the button description. To get a more visual display of the button name, choose the View Toolbars command, then select the Show ToolTips check box and choose OK. While ToolTips is on, a name tag appears under the pointer when you place the pointer on a toolbar button.

For Related Information
- "Customizing and Creating Toolbar," p. 1052

Note

If you insert or draw invisible objects (such as empty picture frames, or shapes with no fill or line), or if you lose objects that become layered behind other objects, use the Selection tool to draw a section box around the area where you've lost the object. All objects inside the selection box will be selected, and you can see their square selection handles, even if they're behind another object.

Choosing the Line and Color for Drawing

When you draw a line, a shape, or even a text box, it appears in some color, in some pattern, and in some line style. You can set Drawing toolbar's current color and line style used for drawing.

If you want to begin drawing shapes filled with red and with all lines drawn in green, first make sure that no drawing object is selected. Then select red as the fill color and green as the line color before you begin working. You can, of course, select a drawn object and change its color, fill, or line style at any time (see the section "Changing Lines and Shapes" for details).

If a drawing object is selected when you choose new colors, fill colors, or line patterns, your choices will change the selected object. Your choices will also be the colors and line patterns used for the next drawing.

Caution

When you go to change color or line pattern for the next drawing, make sure you do not have a drawing object selected. If a drawing object is selected, its color and line pattern will be changed.

You can choose new colors or line patterns in two ways: by using a menu command to make multiple choices at once, or by making individual choices using buttons on the Drawing toolbar.

Using a Menu Command to Change Drawing Color or Line Pattern

By using a menu command, you can choose fill color and pattern, line color and style, and size and position all at once. This method is the quickest for making several choices at the same time.

Note that when you choose the Format Drawing Object command, you display the Drawing Defaults dialog box. This dialog box is the same one you use to change selected objects. However, when a drawing object is selected, the dialog box name changes to the Drawing Object dialog box.

To make several choices at once, follow these steps:

1. Be sure that no object is selected in your drawing. A safe way to do this is to move the insertion point into text.

2. Choose the Format Drawing Object command. The Drawing Defaults dialog box appears.

3. Select the Fill, Line, or Size and Position tab to make your default selections. See the following table for details.

4. Choose OK.

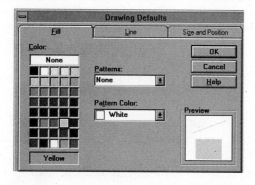

Figs. 24.4, 24.5, and 24.6
You can make all your default choices at once by using the three tabs in the Drawing Defaults dialog box.

V

Publishing with Graphics

Fig. 24.5

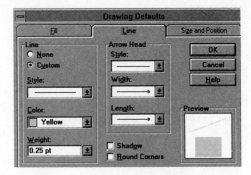

Fig. 24.6

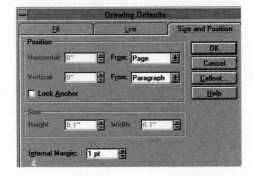

Table 24.2 explains the options you can change for your defaults in each of the three tabs.

Table 24.2 Options for the Fill, Line, and Size and Position Tabs		
Fill Tab		
Selection	**How to use it**	**Result**
Color	Click on the fill color you want. Or, with the keyboard, select the color grid by pressing Alt+C, then select your color by pressing arrow keys.	Objects you draw will contain this fill color.
Patterns	Select the percent fill or pattern you want the list.	Fill color will appear from in this fill pattern.
Pattern Color	Select the color you want your pattern to be from the list.	Fill pattern will appear in this color.

Selection	How to use it	Result
Preview	Look at the Preview box to see how your selections appear.	Shows the color and pattern of filled shapes.

Line Tab

Selection	How to use it	Result
None (Line group)	Select this option for no lines.	A line is invisible. A shape has no borders.
Custom (Line group)	Select this option to format lines.	Makes **S**tyle, **C**olor, and **W**eight options
Style (Line group)	Select from the list of dotted and dashed line style options.	Lines and the borders around shapes appear in this line style.
Color (Line group)	Select from the list of color options.	Lines and the borders around shapes appear in this color.
Weight (Line group)	Select from the list of line weight options. Line weights are measured in points; a point is 1/72 of an inch.	Lines and the borders around shapes appear in this line weight (width).
Style (Arrow Head group)	Select from the list of arrowhead style options.	Select the line with no arrowheads to remove arrowheads. Arrowheads appear at the end or ends of lines. Or, removes arrowheads.
Width (Arrow Head group)	Select from the list of arrowhead width options (these options pertain to the width of the arrowhead, not to the weight of the line). An arrowhead Style must be selected.	Arrowheads in the selected width appear at the end or ends of lines.
Length (Arrow Head group)	Select from the list of arrowhead length options (these options pertain to the length of the arrowhead, not to the length of the line). An arrowhead Style must be selected.	Arrowheads in the selected length appear at the end or ends of lines.

(continues)

Table 24.2 Continued

Selection	How to use it	Result
Shadow	Select this option for drop-shadows on your	Lines and shapes appear with a black drop shadow. lines.
Round Corners	Select this option for rounded corners on shapes.	Shapes with corners have rounded, rather than squared, corners.
Preview	Look at the Preview box to see how your selections appear.	

Size and Position Tab

Selection	How to Use it	
Horizontal (Position group)	Not available for defaults (an object must be selected).	
Vertical (Position group)	Not available for defaults (an object must be selected).	
Lock Anchor (Position group)	Select this option if you want objects to be permanently anchored to the paragraph in which you draw them.	See the later section, "Positioning Lines and Shapes" for details.
Height (Size group)	Not available for defaults (an object must be selected).	
Width (Size group)	Not available for defaults (an object must be selected).	
Internal Margin	Select from the scrolling list the internal margin—that is, the distance between the text inside a text box or callout and the edge of the text box or callout.	
Callout	If a callout is selected when you choose this button, Word displays the Format Callout dialog box.	

Setting Colors and Line Patterns Using the Drawing Toolbar

You can set color and line style using the Drawing toolbar. Be sure that no object is selected and then make the selections you want from the toolbar. For example, if you want all your lines to be drawn in red, select the color red from the color grid that appears when you click the Line Color button. Refer to the following table for an overview of the selections you can make using the Drawing toolbar; refer to the next section, "Drawing Shapes and Lines," for details about using these tools.

Button		Default Settings Available
	Fill Color button	Select the default fill color.
	Line Color button	Select the default line color.
	Line Style button	Select the default line style.

Drawing and Coloring Shapes and Lines

Drawing in Word is like working on paper: you create your image line by line and shape by shape. The objects you draw appear directly on the page where you're working, and you can move them anywhere on the page—even underneath the text. In this way, Word acts more like a true graphics program than like a traditional word processing program; in the word processing program, pictures are part of the text, rather than existing independently of the text.

Understanding the Drawing Screen

When you select a drawing button and then move the pointer onto the page, the arrow turns into a crosshair (it looks like a +). You draw an object by holding down the left mouse button as you drag the crosshair. You can drag the crosshair in any direction to draw. When you release the mouse button, the object is completed. (The freehand button works slightly differently; you must click once on the starting point or double-click anywhere to complete a freeform shape.)

When you draw any object, it appears in the selected default fill color and line style. However, you can easily change the color, style, or shape of any object you draw. The object you draw appears in the layer above the text, and it appears on top of any other objects you've drawn. In this section, you learn how to select colors and line style as you draw.

Fig. 24.7
You can build complex drawings in Word by drawing and coloring shapes.

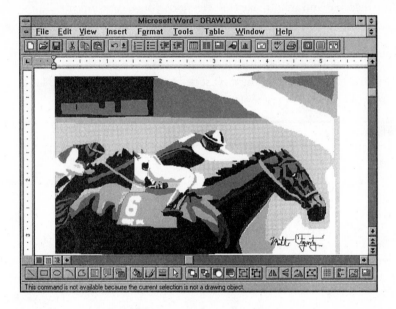

As you draw, the movement of your drawing crosshair is constrained by the drawing grid. If you have a half-inch grid, for example, lines and rectangles appear in half-inch increments. See the later section, "Using the Drawing Grid," for details.

Each object you draw is anchored to the paragraph it is closest to. You can freely move objects (see the later section, "Moving, Copying, and Positioning Lines and Shapes," for details), and when you do, the anchor moves to the paragraph nearest the object. Anchors are important, because the drawing always appears on the same page as the paragraph to which it is anchored, and because if you delete the paragraph, the drawing is deleted, too. For more details about anchoring, see the later section, "Positioning Lines and Shapes."

If you change your mind about the button you selected, press Esc to deselect it, or click a blank part of the page to type text, or click another drawing button.

Scrolling the Page

You can draw objects on any part of a page, but when you first open a document or first start a new document, you can see only the top part of the first page. To draw on other parts of the page or on other pages, use Word's scrolling techniques to display the area where you want to draw. For details about scrolling and changing pages, refer to the section "Moving in the Document" in Chapter 5, "Editing a Document."

Like most professional-quality graphics programs, Word offers a scrolling shortcut: when you drag a drawing object to move it, bumping the edge of the screen with the object causes the screen to scroll in that direction. For example, if you drag a circle downward so that it touches the bottom edge of your screen, your screen scrolls downward. In this way, you can move an object or objects further than the displayed area of your document.

Basic Procedure for Drawing

The general process for creating a drawing is to select the colors and line styles you want to use, click the drawing button you want to use to select it, and draw an object on the page.

Immediately after you draw your object, and before you do anything else, the object is selected. It appears, as shown in fig. 24.8, with square selection handles at its edges. While the object is selected, you can change it. If a shape's fill color isn't quite right, for example, while the shape is selected, you can select a different fill color to change it. You can reshape a selected object by dragging its selection handles.

Fig. 24.8
A selected object has square handles at its edges. You can change an object while it's selected.

When you click the page to draw a new object, or when you click a different drawing button in the toolbar, the object is deselected. You can simply point to a drawn object and click the left mouse button to select it again. See the later sections "Selecting Shapes, Lines, and Whole Drawings" and "Changing Lines and Shapes" to learn how to select objects and change your drawing.

After you draw a line or shape, the crosshair turns back into an I-beam for typing text, unless you double-clicked the Drawing button to select it. In that case, the crosshair remains so you can draw additional lines or shapes. The crosshair changes back to an I-beam when you click the page, or to another drawing button when you click a different drawing button on the toolbar.

To draw a line or shape, follow these steps:

1. Display the Drawing toolbar.

2. Select a fill color, line color, and line style.

3. Click the drawing button you want to use. Double-click the button if you want to draw more than one line or shape.

4. While holding down the left mouse button, drag the crosshair on your page to draw an object. Release the mouse button to complete most shapes; click once on the starting point or double-click anywhere to complete a freeform shape.

To change an object while it's still selected:

Select a different fill color, line color, or line style.

or

Drag selection handles to reshape the object (a special tool helps you reshape a freeform object; see the later section, "Changing the Shape of a Freeform Shape.")

or

Refer to later sections in this chapter to learn more ways to change a selected object.

Tip
Quickly duplicate a drawing by holding down the Ctrl key as you drag a copy to a new location.

Tip
You can press the Esc key to cancel a line or shape before it's completed.

Selecting Shapes, Lines, and Whole Drawings

When you first draw an object, it remains selected until you click the mouse button somewhere else on-screen. Selection handles appear at each corner or end. You can change a selected object in many ways: you can change its color, its line, or its size; you can move it to another layer; you can rotate or flip it; you can frame or align it.

The "select and do" principle applies to drawing objects just as it does to text: you must select an object before you can do something to it. You can easily select one object, multiple objects, or your entire drawing.

Although you can select all objects using the techniques described in this section, there is a special button for selecting freeform or polygon shapes when you want to reshape them by changing the line segments that comprise them. See the later section, "Changing the Shape of a Freeform Shape," for details about reshaping freeforms and polygons.

Fig. 24.9 shows several selected objects:

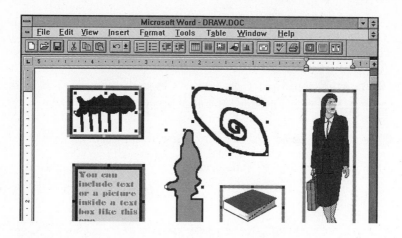

V

Publishing with Graphics

Fig. 24.9
When objects are selected, you can change them in many ways.

To select one drawing object, follow these steps:

1. With no drawing button selected, move the I-beam over the object you want to select until it turns into a selection arrow with a four-cornered arrow below it (see fig. 24.10).

Fig. 24.10
When you see the selection arrow, you can click to select the object underneath the arrow.

2. Click the mouse button on the object.

To select several objects one by one, follow these steps:

1. Click the first object to select it.

2. Hold the Shift key.

3. Click the other objects you want to select. Release the Shift key when you're finished selecting objects.

To select several objects all at once, follow these steps:

1. Click the Selection button.

2. Move the tool to the page, where it turns into a crosshair. Position the crosshair somewhere outside all the objects you want to select.

3. Click and hold the mouse button, and drag to draw a selection square around all the objects you want to select. The selection square appears as a dotted line.

4. Release the mouse button. The selection square disappears, and all the objects inside the selection square are selected.

To deselect a single object from a group of selected objects:

Hold down the Shift key and click the object you want to deselect.

To deselect all objects:

Click somewhere outside the selected objects.

Troubleshooting the Selection Process

The following troubleshooting tips will help you answer some of the more frequently asked questions about selecting.

I drew a selection box around objects, but not all of them were selected.

A selection box must completely enclose all objects you want to select. Make sure no part of any object you want to select is outside the selection box.

I clicked on an object to select it, but I couldn't select it.

If an object such as a square or circle is unfilled, you must click its edge to select it. You can't select an unfilled object by clicking in its center.

Drawing and Coloring Lines

With the Line tool, you can draw straight lines in your choice of colors, weights, and styles. Lines can end in a variety of arrowheads, if you want.

As with most tools, you can hold down the Shift key as you draw to constrain the way the tool works. Holding Shift as you draw a line ensures that the line appears vertical, horizontal, or at a 30-, 45-, or 60-degree angle. Be sure to use this feature when you want perfectly vertical or horizontal lines; if you don't, your line might print at a slight angle, even if it looks right on the screen.

The Control key is also a constraint key. Hold it to draw a line from the center outward, instead of drawing from one end to the other.

You can use a different tool, the Freehand/Polygon tool, to draw squiggly or jagged lines. In reality, a squiggly or jagged line is a polygon with no fill. You can learn more about the Freehand/Polygon tool in the later section "Drawing and Coloring Freeform Shapes and Polygons."

To draw a straight line, follow these steps:

1. Display the Drawing toolbar.

2. Click the Line Color button to display the line color palette, which is shown in fig. 24.11. Click the line color you want.

Fig. 24.11
Use the Line Color button to select a line color.

3. Click the Line Style button to display the line style palette, which is shown in fig. 24.12. Click the line style you want.

Fig. 24.12
Use the Line Style button to choose a line weight or style.

4. Click the Line button and move the mouse arrow to the page, where it turns into a crosshair for drawing. Double-click the Line button if you want to draw more than one line.

5. Click and hold down the left mouse button while you drag the crosshair in any direction to draw a line. When you release the mouse button, the line is completed. Fig. 24.13 shows how a line remains selected after it is drawn.

If you want to draw a perfectly horizontal or vertical line, or a 30-, 45-, or 90-degree line, press the Shift key before you click the mouse button to draw, and hold it until after you release the mouse button to complete your drawing.

V

Publishing with Graphics

Fig. 24.13
When you finish
drawing a line, it
remains selected,
with square
selection handles
at each end.

To draw a squiggly or jagged line, follow these steps:

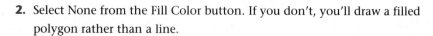

1. Display the Drawing toolbar.

2. Select None from the Fill Color button. If you don't, you'll draw a filled polygon rather than a line.

3. Select a line color from the Line Color button, and a style from the Line Style button.

4. Select the Freehand/Polygon button.

5. To draw a squiggly line, click and hold down the mouse as you draw your squiggly line. Don't release the mouse button until you're finished; if you do, you'll draw a straight line segment.

   or

   To draw a jagged line, click the left mouse button where you want the line to start, and then click where you want each corner of the line.

6. Double-click at the end of the line to complete it. Don't click the beginning point of the line; if you do, you'll connect the beginning and end points to create a shape rather than a line.

Drawing and Coloring Arrows

An arrow is a special kind of line formatted to include arrowheads at either or both ends. You can include arrowheads on straight or squiggly lines, but not on arcs or other shapes. Although you can use the Line Color and Line Style tools on the Drawing toolbar to choose line color and style for your arrow, you must use the Drawing Object dialog box to add arrowheads to lines.

To draw an arrow, follow these steps:

1. Draw a line in the color and style you want.

2. While the line is selected, display the Drawing Object dialog box. Choose the Line tab.

3. In the Arrow Head group, make selections from these three option lists:

Option	Select from these items on the list
Style	From the list, select the arrowhead style you want (open or closed, one end or the other, or both ends).
Width	Select the arrowhead width. The top arrowhead is the narrowest; the bottom the widest.
Length	Select the arrowhead length. The top arrowhead is the shortest; the bottom the longest.

4. Choose OK.

Drawing and Coloring Rectangles or Squares, and Ellipses or Circles

With the rectangle and ellipse tools, you can draw rectangles, squares, ellipses (ovals), or circles. By default, the tools draw rectangles and ellipses; if you hold the Shift key as you draw, the tools draw perfect squares and perfect circles. The shapes you draw with these tools can be empty or filled, bordered or not, in color or in blacks and grays.

Like the Shift key, the Control key is also a constraint key. Hold it to draw a rectangle, square, ellipse, or circle from the center outward.

Squares and rectangles normally have 45-degree corners. However, you can select an option that rounds the corners of selected squares and rectangles.

To draw a rectangle or square, or an ellipse or circle, follow these steps:

1. Display the Drawing toolbar.

2. Click the Fill Color button to display the fill color palette, which is shown in fig. 24.14. Click the fill color you want. This is the color that will appear inside the shape you draw; choose None if you want an empty shape.

3. Click the Line Color button to display the line color palette, which is shown in fig. 24.15. Click the line color you want. This is the color of the edge around the shape; choose None if you do not want a line around the edge.

Tip
To remove an arrowhead from an arrow, select the arrow and display the Drawing Object dialog box. From the Style option, select None.

V

Publishing with Graphics

Fig. 24.14
Use the Fill Color button to select a fill color—the color that will fill the inside of your shape.

Fig. 24.15
Use the Line Color button to select a line color.

4. Click the Line Style button to display the line style palette, which is shown in fig. 24.16. Click the line style you want. This is the style of the edge around your shape.

Fig. 24.16
Use the Line Style button to choose a line weight or style.

5. Click the Rectangle or Ellipse button and move the mouse arrow to the page, where it turns into a crosshair for drawing. To draw more than one rectangle or square, or ellipse or circle, double-click the rectangle or ellipse button.

6. Click and hold down the left mouse button while you drag the crosshair in any direction to draw a rectangle, square, ellipse, or circle. When you release the mouse button, the shape is complete.

To draw a perfect square or circle, press the Shift key before you click the mouse button to draw, and hold it until after you release the mouse button to complete your drawing. Hold the Control key as you draw to draw from the center outward.

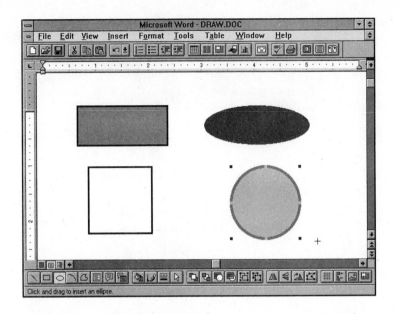

Fig. 24.17
When you finish drawing a shape, it remains selected, with square selection handles at each corner.

To draw a square or rectangle with rounded corners, follow these steps:

1. Select the square or rectangle whose corners you want rounded. Choose this option as a default if you want all corners rounded.

2. Choose the Format Drawing Object command.

3. Select the Line tab.

4. Select the Round Corners option.

5. Choose OK.

Note

To fill a shape, including wedges and freeforms or polygons, with a "screen" or "percent screen," use a fill color and pattern. Select the shape and then double-click it to display the Drawing Object dialog box. Select the Fill tab. Select a color from the Color grid, and from the Patterns list, select 5%, 10%, or one of the other percents. In effect, you create a tint of the color you selected. If the screened shape goes behind text, use a light screen—no darker than 20%.

> **Note**
>
> To help you measure or align drawing objects, use Word's temporary "guidelines." Click and hold the mouse button on the ruler at the top of the screen to display a guideline; then drag the line left or right to measure an object or check the alignment of multiple objects. The guideline disappears when you release the mouse button.

Drawing and Coloring Arcs and Wedges

An arc is one quarter of an ellipse or circle. If you don't select a fill color or pattern, an arc is simply a line drawn in the selected line color and style. Similarly, if you don't select a line color or style (but do select a fill), an arc is a wedge without an outline.

As with the other drawing tools, two constraint keys work when you draw arcs and wedges. Hold Shift as you draw if you want your shape to be one quarter of a perfect circle. Hold Control as you draw if you want to draw your shape from the center.

To draw an arc or wedge, follow these steps:

1. Display the Drawing toolbar.

2. Click the Fill Color button to display the fill color palette, which is shown in fig. 24.18. Click the fill color you want. This is the color that will appear inside the shape you draw; choose None if you want an arc with no fill—that is, if you want an arced line only.

Fig. 24.18
Use the Fill Color button to select a fill color—the color that will fill the inside of your shape.

3. Click the Line Color button to display the line color palette, which is shown in fig. 24.19. Click the line color you want. This is the color of the outside edge around the arc; choose None if you want no line around the edge—that is, if you want a filled wedge with no border.

Fig. 24.19
Use the Line Color
button to select a
line color.

4. Click the Line Style button to display the line style palette, which is shown in fig. 24.20. Click the line style you want. This is the style of the outside edge around your arc.

Fig. 24.20
Use the Line Style
button to choose a
line weight or
style.

5. Click the Arc button and move the mouse arrow to the page, where it turns into a crosshair for drawing. Double-click the arc button if you want to draw more than one arc or wedge.

6. Click and hold down the left mouse button while you drag the crosshair in any direction to draw an arc or wedge. When you release the mouse button, the shape is completed.

If you want your arc to be one quarter of a circle, press the Shift key before you click the mouse button to draw, and hold it until after you release the mouse button to complete your drawing. Hold the Control key as you draw to draw from the center outward.

Drawing and Coloring Freeform Shapes and Polygons

The freehand, or polygon, tool is very versatile. With it, you can draw a curve, a squiggle, a jagged line, a straight line, or a closed polygon. A completed freeform or polygon is composed of any combination of line segments—straight or curved—connected by nodes. For example, a stop-sign-shaped polygon is composed of eight straight sides with eight connecting corners (see fig. 24.22).

V

Publishing with Graphics

Fig. 24.21
When you finished drawing a shape, it remains selected, with square selection handles at each corner.

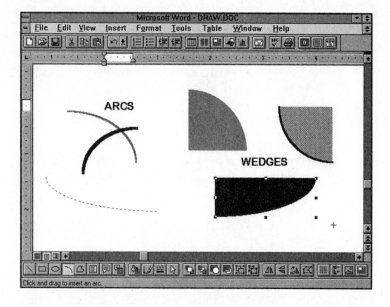

Fig. 24.22
A freeform shape or polygon is composed of line segments connected by nodes.

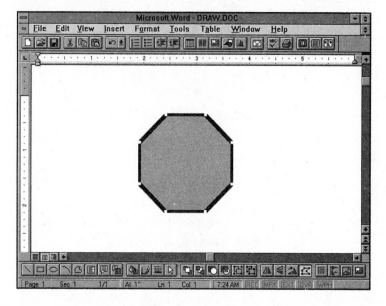

When you draw a freeform shape, lines appear in the selected line color or style; closed polygons appear with the fill you selected, and are bordered in the line color or style you selected.

Only one constraint key works with freeform shapes and polygons. Hold the Shift key as you draw to keep your straight line segments perfectly vertical, horizontal, or at a set angle.

You can reshape a freeform shape or a polygon in two ways. When the shape is selected as it is after you draw it, you can drag its corner handles, as you do any shape, to stretch it into a different size and shape. Or you can reshape it by dragging any of the nodes that connect its segments. To reshape a freeform or polygon in this way, you must use a special selection button. See the later section, "Changing the Shape of a Freeform Shape" for details about reshaping a freeform shape in this way.

To draw a freeform shape or polygon, follow these steps:

1. Display the Drawing toolbar.

2. Click the Fill Color button to display the fill color palette. Click the fill color you want. This is the color that appears inside the shape you draw; choose None if you do not want fill—that is, if you want only a line.

3. Click the Line Color button to display the line color palette. Click the line color you want. This is the color of the edge around the shape; choose None if you want no line around the edge—that is, if you want a filled shape without a border.

4. Click the Line Style button to display the line style palette. Click the line style you want. This is the style of the edge around your shape.

5. Click the Freeform button and move the mouse arrow to the page, where it turns into a crosshair for drawing. Double-click the Freeform/ Polygon button if you want to draw more than one freeform shape or polygon.

6. Draw your shape using one of these techniques:

    To draw a shape composed of straight line segments, click the left mouse button to start the shape, move the crosshair to the end of the first line segment and click again, and continue moving the crosshair and clicking to define each line segment.

    or

    To draw a curving shape, click and hold the left mouse button to start the shape; then drag the crosshair in a curving fashion to draw.

    or

    To draw a composite shape, including straight and curved line segments, click and hold the mouse button when you want to draw a curved line segment, and click once when you want to draw a straight line segment.

Fig. 24.23
When you finish drawing a shape, it remains selected, with square selection handles at each corner.

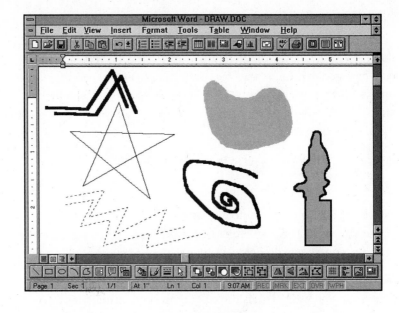

Tip
Use the Freeform button to trace complex drawings that you import from another software program. You can then modify the drawing in Word and delete the original image.

Tip
Press the Esc key to cancel the most recent line segment in a polygon shape.

7. Complete your shape in one of two ways:

   For an open shape or a line, double-click the mouse button when you finished drawing. (If you selected a fill color or pattern, Word connects the last and first points and fills the shape; select None as your fill color and pattern if you want just a line.)

   or

   For a closed shape, click once on the beginning point of your shape.

Creating Shadowed Lines and Shapes

You can instantly add a black drop-shadow to a line or shape by selecting an option. The black shadow appears below and to the right of the object you draw. As shown in fig. 24.24, drop-shadows add an interesting three-dimensional effect to lines, rectangles, and ovals (drop-shadows cannot be automatically applied to arcs or freeforms, but you can add them manually as described by a following tip).

To create a drop-shadow, follow these steps:

1. Select the line or shape you want to shadow. Alternatively, choose this option before you begin drawing if you want all lines and shapes shadowed.

2. Choose the Format Drawing Object command.

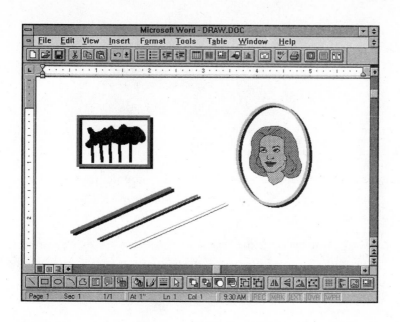

Fig. 24.24
Drop-shadows
create a three-
dimensional effect.

3. Select the Line tab.

4. Select the Shadow option.

5. Choose OK.

Using the Drawing Grid

The drawing grid constrains the movement of your crosshair as you draw.
It acts like a magnetic grid of invisible intersecting lines that attract your
crosshair and do not allow the crosshair to stray outside the grid. Use the
drawing grid to help you draw straight lines, and to get the sides of objects
you draw to appear in certain increments. For example, to draw squares with
sides measured in one-quarter inch increments, set your drawing grid at .25".

The grid also works when you move objects, by aligning those objects to the
grid. Use the grid to help you keep drawing objects lined up in relation to
each other.

By default, the grid's starting point is at the top left corner of the page. You
can change its origin, however. For example, you may want the grid to originate at the top left margin of the page rather than the top corner of the page.

To set the drawing grid, follow these steps:

1. Click the Drawing Grid button to display the Snap to Grid dialog box,
   which is shown in fig. 24.25.

Tip
To create a drop-
shadow for an arc
or freeform, dupli-
cate the shape,
offset it from the
original by a little,
layer it behind the
original, and
change it to black.

V

Publishing with Graphics

Fig. 24.25

The drawing grid helps you draw straight lines or draw shapes with sides of a particu- lar size.

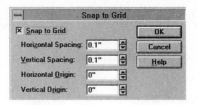

2. Select the Snap to Grid option.

3. Select Horizontal Spacing, and type the side-to-side spacing increment you want for the grid. Or use the arrows or arrow keys to increase or decrease the increment.

4. Select Vertical Spacing, and type the top-to-bottom spacing increment you want for the grid. Or use the arrows or arrow keys to increase or decrease the increment.

5. Choose OK.

To turn off the drawing grid, follow these steps:

1. Click the Drawing Grid button to display the Snap to Grid dialog box.

2. Deselect, or clear, the Snap to Grid option.

3. Choose OK.

To set the drawing grid's point of origin, follow these steps:

1. Click the Drawing Grid button to display the Snap to Grid dialog box.

2. Select the Snap to Grid option.

Tip

If the grid is off, you can turn it on temporarily by holding down the Alt key as you drag. Alternatively, if the grid is on, you can turn it off temporarily by holding Alt as you drag.

3. Select Horizontal Origin, and type the distance from the left edge of the page that you want the grid to begin. Or use the arrows or arrow keys to increase or decrease the increment.

4. Select Vertical Origin, and type the distance from the top edge of the page that you want the grid to begin. Or use the arrows or arrow keys to increase or decrease the increment.

5. Choose OK.

Troubleshooting Your Drawings

The following troubleshooting tips will help you answer some of the more frequently asked questions about drawing.

I drew a shape, but none appeared.

"None" is selected as both your fill color and line color. Select a color.

I can't draw small shapes.

The increments in the drawing grid are too large. Turn off the drawing grid or decrease its increments.

Changing Lines and Shapes

Drawing in Word is similar to drawing on paper, because in both cases you build your image bit by bit, drawing individual lines and shapes until the result looks the way you want it to. Working in Word has a big advantage over paper, however, because you can easily change your picture until you get it just right.

You can change the objects in your picture in many ways. You can change the fill and line color, the line style and weight, and the size and shape of an object. You can rotate and flip objects, and you can completely redesign freeform objects.

You can make changes to a single selected object, or to several selected objects. If you are working with several objects, you might want to consider grouping them so that they become a single object; see the upcoming section, "Grouping and Ungrouping Lines and Shapes."

What You Need to Know About Changing Objects

Changing an object can be similar to designing it in the first place. For example, you change the color of a line the same way you first choose the color of the line: by selecting a color with the Line Color button or from the Drawing Object dialog box. The difference is whether an object is selected. When no object is selected, choosing colors and line styles sets the default colors and styles; when objects are selected, choosing colors and line styles changes the selected objects.

In short, when you want to change an object, you must make sure that it is first selected.

When you change an object's characteristics, however, those characteristics remain in effect for subsequent objects that you draw. Thus changing color, line style, and other characteristics of a selected object has the same effect as changing defaults.

Basic Procedure for Changing Drawing Objects

The most important rule to remember about changing drawing objects is "select and do." In order to change an object, you must first select the object. To select an object, click it; to select several objects, hold Shift as you click the objects. For details about selecting, refer to the earlier section, "Selecting Shapes, Lines, and Whole Drawings."

There are two ways to change a selected object or a group of selected objects. You can make a selection from one of the toolbar tools; for example, you can change a circle's fill color by selecting the circle, and then selecting a different color from the Fill Color button.

The second way to change an object or object is to display the Drawing Object dialog box, which includes Fill, Line, and Size and Position tabs, each with many options. There are four ways you can display the Drawing Object dialog box. For details about how to use the Drawing Object dialog box, see the earlier sections, "Choosing Line and Color Defaults," and "Drawing and Coloring Shapes and Lines."

For details about changing objects, see the remaining subsections in this section of the chapter.

To change an object or objects, follow these steps:

1. Select the object or objects you want to change.

2. Select the change from the Drawing toolbar or from the Drawing Object dialog box.

To display the Drawing Object dialog box:

Double-click the line, square, rectangle, ellipse, circle, or arc you want to change. Do not use this technique to change a freeform or polygon.

or

Click with the right mouse button on the object you want to change. Select Format Drawing Object from the shortcut menu that appears.

or

Select the object you want to change and choose the Format Drawing Object command.

or

Click the Line Styles button and select More from the menu.

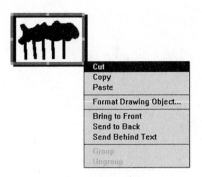

V

Publishing with Graphics

Fig. 24.26
Click with the
right mouse
button on a
selected object
to display the
shortcut menu.

Fig. 24.27
Choose More from
the Line Styles
button menu to
display the
Drawing Object
dialog box.

Changing or Removing a Shape's Fill or Pattern

A shape's fill is the color inside a shape, whether it is a rectangle, an ellipse,
an arc, or a freeform shape. It is also the color inside a text box or a callout.
You can also change the pattern, and the color of the pattern, that fills a
shape. Patterns include *screens,* or percentages of a color, as well as many
designs.

To change or remove a shape's fill or pattern, follow these steps:

1. Select the shape or shapes.

2. Do one of the following two things:

   Click the Fill Color button and select a fill color from the palette that
   appears. To remove the fill, select None.

   or

   Display the Drawing Object dialog box, select the Fill tab, and select a
   fill color from the Color palette, a fill pattern from the Patterns list, and
   the color of the pattern from the Pattern Color list. To remove the fill,
   select None from the Color palette. Choose OK when you finish.

Fig. 24.28

You can use the Drawing Object dialog box to select a fill color as well as a fill pattern.

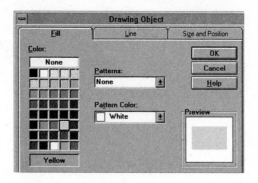

Changing Line Style and Color

Line color is like fill color: it is the color of a line, whether the line stands alone or whether it is the border around the edge of a shape. Line style is either the weight (width) of a line, or it is the appearance of the line, whether it is solid, dotted, or dashed. The weight, or width, of lines is measured in points, and a point is 1/72 of an inch. If you want a hairline-weight line, choose a 1/4-point line; for a line about the width of a pencil line, try a 1-point line. If you want a very thick line, type your own measurement in the Drawing Object dialog box you use to determine line weight; for example, a 36-point line is about 1/2 inch wide.

Line color and style apply not only to individual lines, but also to the edges around shapes.

To change the color of a line or of the line around a shape, follow these steps:

1. Select the line or shape.

2. Do one of the following two things:

 Click the Line Color button and select a line color from the palette that appears.

or

Display the Drawing Object dialog box, select the Line tab, and select a line color from the Color list in the Line group. Choose OK when you're finished.

To change the style of a line or of the line around a shape, follow these steps:

1. Select the line or shape.

2. Do one of the following two things:

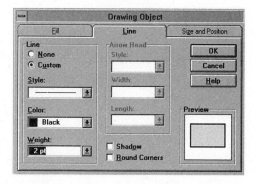

Figs. 24.29 and 24.30
You can use the Line Color palette (top) to quickly change the line color of a selected line or shape, or you can use the Drawing Object dialog box (bottom) to select line color.

V

Publishing with Graphics

Click the Line Style button and select a line style from the palette that appears.

or

Display the Drawing Object dialog box and select the Line tab. In the Line group, select a line style from the Style list and select or type a line width from the Weight list. Choose OK when you're finished.

Removing the Line Around a Shape

Often the line around the edge of a shape is a different color from the shape. If you want the object to appear as if it has no line around its edge, you can remove the line or make it the same color as the shape. The shape is slightly smaller if you remove the line.

To remove a line from around a shape or shapes, follow these steps:

1. Select the shape or shapes.

2. Do one of the following two things:

   Click the Line Color button and select None or the same color as the shape from the palette that appears.

   or

Display the Drawing Object dialog box, select the Line tab, and select None or the same color as the shape from the Line group. Choose OK.

Changing Arrows or Removing Arrowheads

Arrowheads appear at the ends of lines, and unlike other line colors and styles, don't apply to shapes. You can place arrowheads on either or both ends of a line, and you can select the width and length of the arrowheads. You can remove the arrowheads from a line. (To change the width of the line, see the earlier section, "Changing Line Style and Color"; to change the length of a line, see the later section, "Resizing a Line or Shape.")

To change an arrow or remove an arrowhead, follow these steps:

1. Select the arrow you want to change or the arrowhead you want to remove.

2. Display the Drawing Object dialog box and select the Line tab.

3. To change an arrow, select different Style, Width, and Length options in the Arrow Head group. To remove an arrowhead, select the line that shows no arrowheads (the top line in the list).

4. Choose OK.

Resizing a Line or Shape

When a shape is selected, it has square selection handles at its corners and sides. When a line is selected, it has selection handles at each end. You can resize the object, making it smaller or larger, by dragging these handles. Alternatively, you can use the Drawing Object dialog box to set precise measurements for any object.

Keep these rules in mind as you resize a shape:

- If you drag a side handle, you resize only from that side.

- If you drag a corner handle, you can resize from two directions at once.

- If you hold the Shift key as you drag a corner handle on a shape, the object retains its proportions (a square stays square, a circle stays round, and a freeform retains the same shape). Hold the Shift key as you resize a line to keep its angle.

- If you hold the Ctrl key as you resize, you resize from the center outward.

To resize a line or shape, follow these steps:

1. Select the line or shape so that its selection handles appear.

2. Click and hold the mouse button on any selection handle, and drag the handle to resize the line or shape. When you release the mouse button, the shape assumes its new size.

or

Display the Drawing Object dialog box and select the Size and Position tab. In the Size group, type or select measurements for the object's Height and Width. Choose OK.

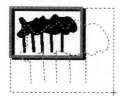

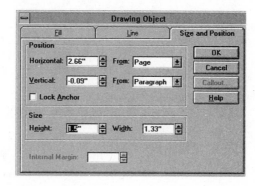

Figs. 24.31 and 24.32

You can resize an object by dragging its handles (left) or by specifying precise measurements in the Drawing Object dialog box (right).

Changing the Shape of a Freeform Shape

The Reshape button enables you to drag an existing line end point in a freeform shape to a new position.

Reshaping a freeform line is amazing the first time you see it done. After you draw a freeform shape and then click the Reshape button, you find that the shape is composed of small lines connected by movable handles called *nodes*. You can drag any of these nodes to change the shape.

As you reshape a freeform or polygon object, you can add or delete nodes. Adding a node in between two existing nodes can give you another node with which to smooth a curve. Deleting a node will make a line straighten to join the nodes on either side of the deleted node.

To reshape a freeform or polygon object, complete the following steps:

1. To display the nodes linking the individual line segments, select the freehand or polygon object, and then click the Reshape button.

2. Move the pointer to a node. When it turns into a crosshair, hold the mouse button and drag the node to a new location. Release when the node is where you want it. Repeat to move other nodes.

3. Click in the background when you finish.

Fig. 24.33 and 24.34

Use the Reshape button to re-arrange the line segments that comprise a polygon.

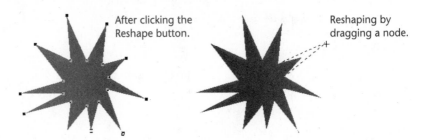

After clicking the Reshape button.

Reshaping by dragging a node.

To add or delete nodes on a freeform or polygon shape, follow these steps:

1. Display the nodes linking the individual line segments by selecting the freehand or polygon object, and then clicking the Reshape button, or by double-clicking the freeform shape.

2. To add a node, point to the line where you want the node, hold down the Ctrl key, and click the mouse button.

or

To remove a node, point to the node, hold down the Ctrl key, and click the mouse button.

Rotating Shapes and Lines

You can rotate a selected line or shape in 90-degree increments. Each time you select the rotation button, the object rotates 90 degrees to the right. You can rotate a single selected object or a group of selected objects.

You can rotate a text box or callout, but not the text or picture inside it. Use WordArt to rotate text.

To rotate an object or objects, follow these steps:

1. Select the object or objects you want to rotate.

2. Click the Rotate button.

Flipping Shapes and Lines

Flipping selected objects turns them horizontally (left to right) or vertically (top to bottom). You can flip a callout, but not the text inside it.

Fig. 24.35
Each time you click the Rotate button, the selected object rotates 90 degrees to the right.

To flip an object or objects, follow these steps:

1. Select the object or objects.

2. Click the Flip Horizontal button to flip the object or objects from right to left.

or

Click the Flip Vertical button to flip the object or objects from top to bottom.

Troubleshooting When You Change an Object

The following troubleshooting tips can help you answer some of the more frequently asked questions about changing objects.

I made a change, but my object didn't change.

Your object was not selected. Select the object you want to change, then make the change.

I tried to resize an object, but it moved instead.

You didn't drag on a selection handle. To resize an object, drag it by a selection handle, not by a side. Dragging an object by its side moves it.

Moving, Copying, Deleting, and Positioning Lines and Shapes

You can easily move an object, or a group of objects, from one part of your drawing to another, or from one part of your document to another. One way to move an object is to drag it to a new location. Another way is to cut it from one place and paste it somewhere else. When you move something a long distance, this method may be the best.

Copying objects enables you to duplicate shapes you want to use again—in the current document, or in another document or even another program.

Delete unwanted objects by selecting them and then pressing the Delete key or choosing the Edit Clear command. You can restore them if you immediately choose the Edit Undo command.

Moving Lines and Shapes

The quickest way to move an object is to drag it to a new position on the page. If you drag to the edge of the screen, the page automatically scrolls. In this way, you can move objects beyond the area of the page that is displayed.

To move longer distances, or to move objects between documents, use Word's cut and paste commands. Once an object is cut, you can paste it as many times as you want.

To move an object or objects by dragging, follow these steps:

1. Select the object or objects you want to move.

2. Position the move arrow over the object, but not on a selection handle.

3. Click and hold the mouse button, and drag the object to its new location. Release the mouse button when the object is where you want it.

   You can hold the Shift key as you drag to move an object in a straight line.

To move an object or objects long distances using cut and paste, follow these steps:

1. Select the object or objects you want to cut and paste.

2. Choose the Edit Cut command, or click the object with the right mouse button and select the Cut command from the shortcut menu, or press Ctrl+X, or click the Cut button on the Standard toolbar.

3. Position the insertion point where you want to move the object. (Just as with text, you cannot paste a drawing object into a location unless text is already there.)

4. Choose the Edit Paste command, or click the screen with the right mouse button and select the Paste command from the shortcut menu, or press Ctrl+V, or click the Paste button on the Standard toolbar.

Another way to move an object is to drag its anchor. For details about object anchors, see the later section, "Positioning Lines and Shapes."

Copying Lines and Shapes

You can use Word's copy and paste commands to duplicate shapes you want to use over—whether in the current document or another document. After an object is copied, you can paste it as many times as you want.

To copy an object or objects, follow these steps:

1. Select the object or objects you want to copy.

2. Choose the Edit Copy command, or click the object with the right mouse button and select the Copy command from the shortcut menu, or press Ctrl+C, or click the Copy button on the Standard toolbar.

3. Position the insertion point where you want to copy the object.

4. Choose the Edit Paste command, or press the right mouse button and select the Paste command from the shortcut menu, or press Ctrl+V, or click the Paste button on the Standard toolbar.

Deleting Shapes and Lines

You can easily remove a shape or group of shapes from your drawing.

To delete an object or objects, follow these steps:

1. Select the object or objects you want to delete.

2. Press the Delete key.

You can also remove an object by selecting it and then cutting it using the Edit Cut command. Use this technique if you want to later paste the object somewhere else.

Aligning Lines and Shapes to Each Other or to the Page

There are two ways you can align objects: to each other or to the page. When you align objects to each other, they line up on the side you specify: left, right, top, or bottom; or they line up at their centers. Similarly, when you

V

Publishing with Graphics

Tip

You can also copy an object by holding down the Control key as you drag the object.

Tip

If you delete an object or objects and then realize you still want them, choose the Edit Undo command before doing anything else.

align objects to the page, they line up to the left, right, top, bottom, or center of the page. To align objects to each other, you must select more than one object; however, you can align a single object to the page.

After an object is aligned, you can drag it to move it to another location on the page.

Fig. 24.36, 24.37, and 24.38

You can align objects to each other (center) or to the page (bottom).

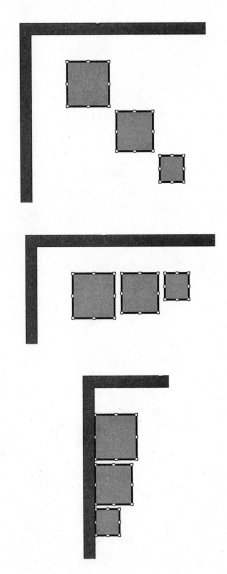

To align objects, follow these steps:

1. Select the objects you want to align to each other, or select the object or objects you want to align to the page.

2. Click the Align button.

3. From the Horizontal group, select Left, Center, or Right alignment. Select None if you don't want to align the object or objects horizontally.

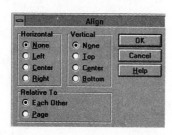

Fig. 24.39
You can align objects horizontally or vertically, relative to each other or the page.

4. From the Vertical group, select Top, Center, or Bottom alignment. Select None if you don't want to align the object or objects vertically.

5. From the Relative To group, select Each Other if you selected multiple objects and want to align them relative to each other, or select Page if you selected one or more objects and want to align them relative to the edges of the page.

6. Choose OK.

Positioning Lines and Shapes

There are two ways you can position objects that you draw. You can use the Drawing Object dialog box to specify how far the object should be positioned from the margins, edges of the page, column, or paragraph. Or you can frame an object, and use frame commands to position an object on the page (for details about framing, see the upcoming section, "Framing Objects to Move Them into the Text"). In either case, you can drag an object after it has been positioned to move it to another location.

To specify an exact position for an object or objects, follow these steps:

1. Select the object or objects.

2. Display the Drawing Object dialog box, which is shown in fig. 24.40.

3. Select the Size and Position tab.

4. Make selections in these options:

V

Publishing with Graphics

Select Horizontal and then From, and type or select the distance you want the object to be positioned from the margin, page, or column.

Select Vertical and then From, and type or select the distance you want the object to be positioned from the margin, page, or paragraph.

5. Choose OK.

Fig. 24.40

You can specify an exact position for an object, relative to the margin, page, column, or paragraph.

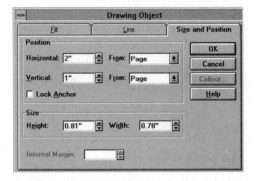

Objects are always anchored to the paragraph nearest to where you draw them. When you move an object by dragging it, the anchor moves to the paragraph nearest to the object's new location—unless you lock the anchor. In that case, the object stays with the paragraph, even if the paragraph moves. Anchors also provide another way you can move objects. If you display the anchors, which appear in the margin, you can drag an object's anchor to a new paragraph, and the object moves to that paragraph.

To lock an object's anchor, follow these steps:

1. Select the object.

2. Display the Drawing Object dialog box and select the Size and Position tab.

3. Select the Lock Anchor option.

4. Choose OK.

To display and move anchors, follow these steps:

1. Choose the Tools Options command, and select the View tab.

2. In the Show group, select the Object Anchors option.

3. Select an object to display its anchor.

4. Drag the anchor to another paragraph to move the anchor.

Object anchor

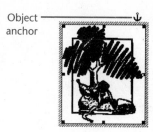

Teens and Trees—
A Project of Sonoma C

Sonoma County ReLeaf, a b
devoted to planting trees in
why trees are important and

Fig. 24.41
Objects are anchored to paragraphs; you can move objects by dragging their anchors to a new paragraph.

Including Text or Another Picture in a Drawing

You can include either text or a picture created in another application in a drawing or in your document using two tools from the Drawing toolbar—the Text Box button and the Picture Container button. In a Text Box, you can include text or a picture. In a Picture Container, you can insert a picture. A Text Box is more versatile, because you can format, move, flip, rotate, or layer it using tools on the Drawing toolbar.

There are other ways to include pictures in your document or put text in a box: for example, you can use the Insert Picture or Insert Object command to insert a picture, and you can frame text to put it in a box. But there are some advantages to using the Drawing toolbar. First, you can include a text box as part of your drawing. Second, you can move a text box to the layer behind the text. Third, you can use the other tools on the Drawing toolbar to quickly format text boxes.

Fig. 24.42 shows a drawing that includes text.

Inserting Text Boxes

A text box is a graphic box with text inside it. It is filled with the fill color you've selected and edged with the line color and style you selected. Like any drawing object, it floats freely on the page, so you can drag it to move it to a new location. You can resize or reshape it; the text inside rewraps to fit the new size or shape.

Text inside a text box is the same as regular text in Word. You can edit it, align it, format it, cut and paste it, or copy it just like any other text. Use Word's normal editing and formatting commands and shortcuts to edit and format text inside a text box. A text box does not automatically resize when you add more text; you must manually resize the text box if you insert more text than you can see (see the earlier section, "Resizing a Line or Shape").

You can also insert pictures created in other applications in text boxes.

Fig. 24.42
Text is sometimes an important part of your drawing.

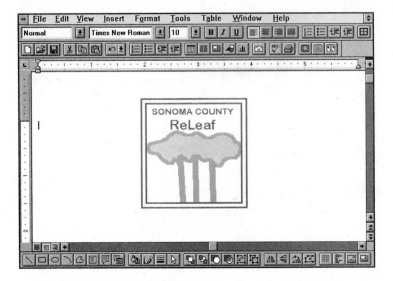

Because text boxes float freely on the page, you can position them anyplace: in a margin, in the text, or beneath the text. Because of their freedom of placement, text boxes—whether they contain text or inserted pictures—can be very useful with desktop publishing projects.

Fig. 24.43
Text boxes, like this pull-quote, can be dragged anywhere on the page—even in the margin.

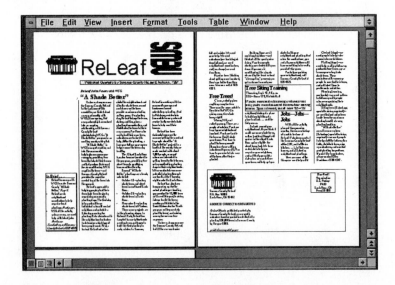

To draw a text box, complete the following steps, follow these steps:

1. Click the Text Box button. The mouse pointer becomes a crosshair.

   Hold down the Shift key if you want a square text box.

2. Move the crosshair where you want to start drawing your text box.

3. Click and hold the mouse button, and drag from one corner to the opposite corner where you want the text box.

4. Release the mouse button.

When you release the mouse button, a flashing insertion point appears in the text box, indicating that you can begin typing text. Type continuously; the text wraps when you reach the margin. If you type more text than will fit in the box, the box contents scroll so that you can see what you are typing; the full contents may not be visible. If you later decide to change the size or shape of the text box, the text inside wraps to fit the new shape.

Although you can rotate or flip a text box, you can't rotate or flip the text inside it. Use WordArt to rotate text and create many other special text effects. WordArt is described in Chapter 25.

When you see the flashing insertion point, you can use the Insert Picture command to insert a picture inside the text box.

Note

If you want text in your document to wrap around text in a box, you must use a frame rather than a text box. With no object selected, click the Frame button, then drag the crosshair to insert an empty frame. An insertion point flashes in the top left corner of the frame. Type and format your text, then move the framed text wherever you want it—text in your document will wrap around it. You can also insert a picture into a frame. Framing text or an object is described in Chapter 23.

Inserting Picture Containers

If you want to include in your drawing a drawing created in another program, such as Windows Paintbrush or CorelDRAW!, you can insert it in a picture container. After it's in the picture container, you can resize or crop it. To move it on the page, however, you must first frame it. To border it, you must use the Format Borders and Shading command or the Borders toolbar.

Use a picture container for your picture when you don't want to use the drawing tools to format it, and when you don't need to position the picture in the layer beneath the text. If you do want to use drawing tools to format the box holding the picture, or you want to layer the picture beneath the text, insert it into a Text Box rather than a Picture Container. See the previous section, "Inserting Text Boxes" for details.

To learn more about working with inserted pictures, refer to Chapter 22, "Inserting Pictures in Your Document."

If you want, you can insert an empty picture container into your document and draw your objects inside it. In this way, you don't have to group your objects into a whole drawing: they are already grouped in the picture container.

To insert a picture container, follow these steps:

1. Click the Picture Container button. The mouse pointer becomes a crosshair.

   Hold down the Shift key if you want a square picture container.

2. Move the crosshair where you want to start drawing your picture container.

3. Click and hold the mouse button, and drag from one corner to the opposite corner where you want the picture container.

4. Release the mouse button. The Picture window appears.

Fig. 24.44

You can insert or draw a picture in a picture container.

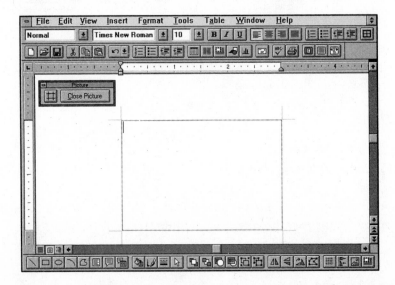

To insert a picture into a picture container, follow these steps:

1. Insert a picture container.

2. Choose the Insert Picture command.

3. Locate and select the picture you want to insert.

4. Choose OK. The picture appears in the picture container. You can add to it using the drawing tools.

5. Choose the Close Picture button.

You also can use drawing tools to draw a picture in the picture container. If you do, click the Margins button to shrink the picture container's margins to exactly fit your picture.

Troubleshooting Text Boxes and Picture Containers

The following troubleshooting tips will help you answer some of the more frequently asked questions about text boxes and picture containers.

I inserted a picture I created in CorelDRAW! in a picture container, but I can't move it around on the screen, and the line color won't change.

Use the Frame button to frame the picture container if you want to move it around on the page. Use the Format Borders and Shading command, or the Borders toolbar, to change the line around the edge of a frame. Alternatively, insert the picture in a text box rather than a picture container. Use a text box to hold your picture if you want to use drawing tools to change the line color and style or the fill color, or if you want to move the picture to the layer behind the text.

For Related Information
■ "Creating a WordArt Object," p. 775

■ "Inserting and Copying Pictures into Your Document," p. 661

■ "Framing Text, Pictures, and Other Objects," p. 688

V

Publishing with Graphics

Adding and Changing Callouts

Callouts are a very handy addition to any document in which you include illustrations that need some explanation. Callouts are a special type of text box that include a pointer which you can accurately aim at any location on the document. You can include text or an inserted picture in a callout.

Like text boxes, callouts appear in the fill and line colors that you've selected, and in the line style you've selected. If you want a callout to appear as text only, select None as your fill and line colors. You can change, move, and layer callouts like any drawing object.

A special formatting command exists for designing and pointing your callout. It allows you to very accurately specify how the callout looks and how it's attached to the text.

Fig. 24.45 shows how a callout can clarify your document.

Fig. 24.45
Callouts help explain illustrations in your document.

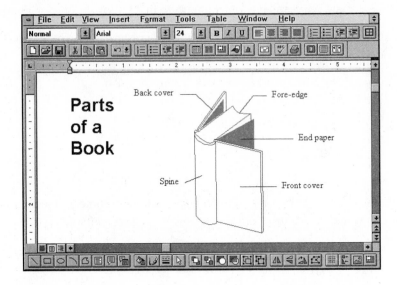

Inserting a Callout

When you insert a callout, you draw a line from where you want the callout to point to where you want the callout text in relation to what it's pointing to.

To insert a callout, follow these steps:

1. Click the Callout button.

2. Move the crosshair to the place in your document where you want the callout to point.

3. Click and hold the mouse button, and drag to where you want the callout text.

4. Release the mouse button.

5. Type the callout text.

Changing a Callout

You can apply all the same colors and line styles to a callout as you do to any object you draw. You can move a callout to a different layer—which is often handy when you're working with pictures inserted from another program.

But besides these formatting features, callouts also have a special dialog box for changing the callout's specifications. You can determine how many segments comprise the callout line, and what their angles are; you can determine how the callout line is attached to the callout text; and you can determine whether there is a border around the callout text.

To format a callout, follow these steps:

1. Select the callout you want to format.

2. Click the Format Callout button to display the Format Callout dialog box, which is shown in fig. 24.46.

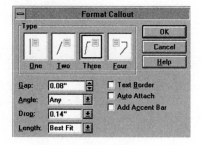

Fig. 24.46
You can determine many aspects of a callout's appearance using the Format Callout button.

3. In the Type group, select one of the four callout types shown: One, Two, Three, or Four. Types One and Two use a straight line; type Three uses a two-part line; type Four uses a three-part line.

4. Select from among these additional options (not all options are available for all callout types):

Select this option	For this effect
Gap	Type or select the distance between the callout line and the callout text.
Angle	Type or select the angle at which you want the callout line. It can be Any, or a degree.
Drop	Type or select the position where you want the callout line attached to the callout text: attached at an exact distance from the top, or attached at the Top, Center, or Bottom.

(continues)

V

Publishing with Graphics

(continued)

Select this option	For this effect
Length	Type or select the length you want the callout line: Best Fit, or measured precisely.
Text Border	Select this option if you want a border around the text (it appears in the selected line color and style).
Auto Attach	Select this option if you want the callout line at the bottom of the callout text (rather than at the top) when text is to the left of the callout line.
Add Accent Bar	Select this option to include a vertical line next to the callout text.

5. Choose OK.

The selections you make in the Format Callout dialog box apply to the current callout and the next callouts you create.

> **Note**
>
> You can display the Format Callout dialog box by displaying the Drawing Object dialog box and selecting the Size and Position tab, and then choosing the Callout button. Use this method to format many aspects of the callout at once.

For Related Information

■ "Inserting and Copying Pictures into Your Document" p. 661

■ "Wrapping Text Around a Frame," p. 708

■ "Creating Captions," p. 955

Rearranging a Drawing's Layers

Word has three layers with which you can work, giving you great flexibility in how you can use pictures. The text layer is where text appears—it's the layer you're accustomed to working with in a word processing program. Uniquely, Word has two additional layers: the drawing layer above the text and the layer behind the text. You can move any object, or your entire picture, between these layers.

When an object or picture is in the drawing layer above the text, it obscures text, as shown in fig. 24.47. Objects in the text layer force the text to wrap around the object. This is apparent when in page layout view or print preview, as shown in fig. 24.48. When you move an object behind text, you can see it through the text, as fig. 24.49 illustrates.

When you first draw an object, it appears in the drawing layer on top of the text. Within this drawing layer, objects are layered—one on top of the other, with the most recently drawn on top. You can move objects in front of or behind one another within the drawing layer.

There are four separate tools on the Drawing toolbar for rearranging layers: two for moving objects in front of and behind other objects in the drawing layer, and two for moving objects behind or in front of the text layer.

To move an object or drawing into the text layer, you must frame it. Framing an object is a good idea when you want to wrap text around a drawing or an object. An unframed drawing object remains in the layer above or below the text, but text does not wrap around it.

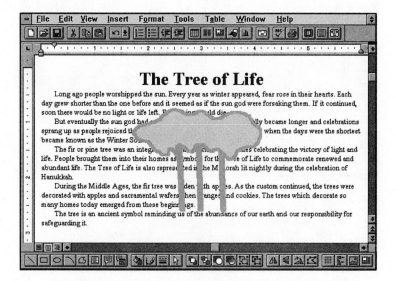

Fig. 24.47
An object in the drawing layer obscures the text below it.

What You Need to Know About Rearranging Layers

Like most procedures in Word, a simple rule applies when you're moving objects in front of or behind each other, or between the layers in the document: select and do. Select the object you want to move, and then choose the button that moves it to the layer where you want it. You can select and rearrange a single object or multiple objects.

Moving Objects in Front of or Behind Each Other

Each new object you draw appears on top of other objects in the drawing layer. You can select any object and move it to the top of all the other objects, or beneath all the other objects. If you have several objects to arrange, think about the order in which they are to appear. Select the top object and move it to the back, then select the second object and move it to the back, and so on through all the objects. When you're finished, you've moved the last object furthest back, and the objects are in the right order.

Fig. 24.48
You have to frame an object if you want text to wrap around it.

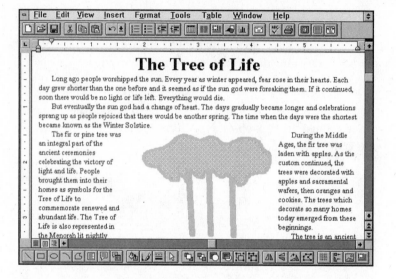

Fig. 24.49
You can see through the text to an object layered behind the text.

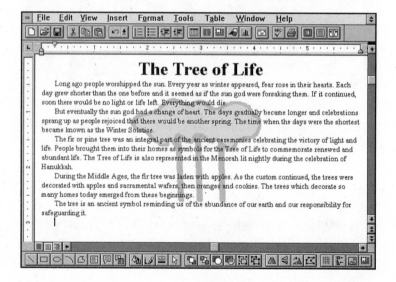

To move objects in front of or behind each other, follow these steps:

1. Select the object or objects you want to move.

2. Select one of the following two tools:

Select this button to move the object(s) to the front of all the other objects in the drawing layer

 Select this button to move the object(s) behind all the other objects in the drawing layer

Layering Objects Below or Above the Text

You can move any single object, or your entire drawing, below the text. You can then see the drawing through your text. Use this technique to create interestingly shaped backdrops for your text (rather than the simple square boxes or shading that the Format **B**orders and Shading command allows). You can even use this technique to create a watermark, by placing a drawing in your document's header so that it appears on every page.

Selecting objects that are behind the text layer is the same as selecting objects that are in the drawing layer.

Remember, when you first draw objects, they appear in the drawing layer on top of the text.

To move an object or objects behind the text layer, follow these steps:

1. Select the object or objects.

2. Select one of these two tools:

 Select this button to move the object(s) behind the text layer

 Select this button to move the object(s) in front of the text layer

Tip
If an object is hidden behind another object so that you can't see it, select the top object and move it behind the hidden object.

Framing Objects to Move Them into the Text

If you want text to wrap around an object or picture you draw, you must frame it. You can use the Insert Frame command to do this, but it's easiest to just use the Frame button on the Drawing toolbar. After a drawing object is framed, you can use the Format Fra**m**e command, discussed in Chapter 23, "Framing and Moving Text and Graphics," to assign the framed object a fixed position or size, or to remove the frame.

When you frame a drawing object, text automatically wraps around it.

You can also insert an empty frame and type text or insert a picture inside it. Use this technique when you want text in your document to wrap around text in a box (you can't frame a text box) or when you want to insert a picture that you plan to frame anyway (it saves a step over inserting and then framing a picture container).

You must use the Format Borders and Shading command, or the Borders toolbar, to add color, follow these steps to a frame.

To frame an object or objects, follow these steps:

1. Select the object or objects.

2. Click the Frame button.

To insert an empty frame, follow these steps:

1. Click the Frame button. When you move the mouse pointer onto the document, it becomes a crosshair.

2. Drag the crosshair to draw the size of the frame. An insertion point flashes in the top left corner of your frame; use it to type text or insert a picture.

To remove a frame from an object or text, follow these steps:

1. Select the frame.

2. Choose the Format Frame command. The Frame dialog box appears.

3. Choose the Remove Frame button.

Grouping and Ungrouping Lines and Shapes

Grouping objects together fuses them into a single object. When related objects are grouped, they are easier to move and size. You can ungroup objects if you later need to separate them.

The fig. 24.50 shows several objects before and after being grouped.

When you apply commands to grouped objects, they are applied as if the objects were a single object. In some cases, the command may work differently than when you apply it to individually selected objects. For example, when you rotate two separate objects, each rotates around its own center. When you rotate two objects that are grouped as one, however, they rotate around the group's center. The effect is different. Other changes you make, such as fill and line color, apply the same to individual objects as they do to grouped objects.

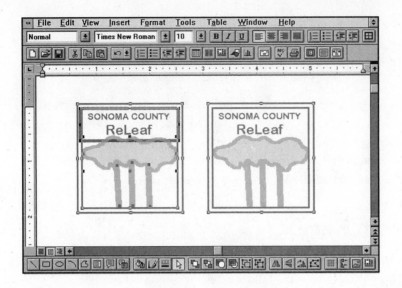

Fig. 24.50
Grouping objects
fuses them into a
single object.

Grouping Objects

It's very often useful to group objects that make up a single picture when that picture is completed. That way, you can select, size, or move the picture as a unit without accidentally separating some of its elements. When you click a group to select it, it appears with the same corner and side selection handles as any single object. You can use these handles the same as you do on an individual object.

You can group groups as well as individual objects. You might want to separate the components of a complex drawing into several smaller groups for easier handling.

To group objects, follow these steps:

1. Select the objects you want to group.

2. Click the Group button.

Ungrouping Groups

If you want to change any individual part of a group, you must first ungroup it. For example, if you want to change the color of one of the objects making up a grouped picture, but not other parts, ungroup the picture first.

To ungroup a group, follow these steps:

1. Select the group.

2. Click the Ungroup button.

Troubleshooting Grouping

I ungrouped a group, but I still can't select a certain object.

You can group groups as well as individual objects. Your group probably includes multiple groups; try ungrouping each of them. What appears to be a group may actually be a picture that has been imported from another graphics program. Pictures drawn in Microsoft Draw for Word for Windows 2 cannot be ungrouped. They are treated as a single object.

From Here...

For information relating directly to drawing with the Drawing toolbar, you might want to review the following major sections of this book:

- Chapter 23, "Framing and Moving Text and Graphics," teaches you how to frame text and inserted pictures so that you can position them where you want them.

- Chapter 25, "Creating Banners and Special Effects with WordArt," teaches you how to use WordArt to create artistic text, how to rotate text, and how to include WordArt images in your pictures.

- Chapter 27, "Desktop Publishing," teaches you a little about design and some rules of layout.

- Chapter 31, "Adding Cross-References and Captions," teaches you how you can add a caption to a picture you create.

Chapter 25

Creating Banners and Special Effects with WordArt

Words can serve as more than abstract symbols that we read for meaning. Words sometimes work as graphics that not only convey meaning, but also attract attention and create memorable images. You see examples of words used as graphics every day: pull-quotes in magazines lighten a page of text and attract attention to important points; logos turn words into symbols that you recognize without even reading; decorated words embellish the mastheads in newsletters; special text-effects add interest to advertisements.

With WordArt, you can turn ordinary words into graphics. You can pour text into a shape, flip or stretch letters, condense or expand letter spacing, rotate or angle words, or add shading, colors, borders, or shadows to text. By combining WordArt effects, you can create hundreds of interesting designs.

You can use WordArt with a mouse or your keyboard—either way, you can create great graphics.

Figs. 25.1 through 25.3 show some examples of finished WordArt objects.

What You Need to Know About WordArt

WordArt is an OLE-based add-in program that comes free with Word for Windows (OLE stands for *object linking and embedding*). Because of the OLE technology, WordArt objects you insert in your document remain linked to the

The following list contains just some of the tasks you learn how to do with WordArt:

- Apply text treatments such as fonts, styles, and sizes

- Apply special effects such as rotation, slanting, shaping, and arcing

- Apply colors, borders, and shading

- Apply typographic aids such as aligning and adjusting character spacing

WordArt program. You can edit WordArt objects easily; the image in your Word for Windows document updates to reflect the edit changes. Because WordArt is built into Word for Windows, you can't run WordArt by itself—you can run it only from within Word for Windows (and other Windows programs that support OLE). Further, you can't create a separate WordArt file—WordArt images are part of your Word for Windows file. To learn more about object linking and embedding, refer to Chapter 33, "Using Word with Other Windows Applications."

Fig. 25.1
WordArt created this newsletter banner. The two words "ReLeaf" and "News" are two separate WordArt objects framed together.

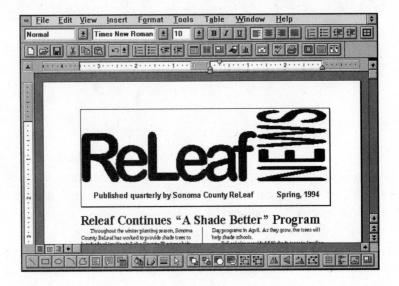

Fig. 25.2
WordArt created this logo, which can be used for stationery.

Fig. 25.3
WordArt created this simple motto for use on a flyer.

You must install WordArt before you can use it. You may have installed WordArt when you installed Word (WordArt is installed if it is listed in the Object Type list in the Object dialog box). If you didn't install WordArt with your original Word installation, you can install it now. You must use your original Word disks to install WordArt. Insert disk number one (the setup disk) and display the Program Manager. Choose the File Run command. In the Command Line box, type **A:\SETUP** (or substitute the appropriate drive letter) and choose OK or press Enter. Follow the screen instructions to install WordArt.

Creating a WordArt Object

After starting WordArt, creating a WordArt object is a two-part process: you type the text to be included in the image, and then you add whatever special effects you want. At any time before you close WordArt, you can change the text or the special effects. You never leave your document when you work with WordArt—you create your WordArt object directly on the page of your document using WordArt commands and buttons.

A WordArt object behaves in the same manner as any other picture that you insert into a Word document. You insert it at the insertion point, and the object moves with the text that surrounds it. You can size the object to make it proportionally larger or smaller, or you can crop it to hide part of the image. You can add a border around it. If you frame the object, you can release it from the position where you inserted it and move it anywhere on the page. You can wrap text around the framed object. If you insert the object in a text box (which you draw using the Text Box button on the Drawing toolbar) you can move the object to the layer behind the text. The section "Editing a WordArt Object" later in this chapter describes how you can work with a WordArt object after you have created it.

Because WordArt graphics are based on text, fonts are the raw materials you have for creating WordArt objects. Windows comes with some fonts, such as Arial and Times New Roman. Your printer may contain more fonts, and you can purchase additional fonts to install on your computer. Any font installed on your computer is available for use in WordArt.

Starting WordArt
Because WordArt is an OLE-based program that works only within other programs, it doesn't look like other programs. When you work with WordArt in

Word, WordArt does not appear in a window of its own; instead, WordArt menus and buttons replace the Word menus and buttons.

> **Note**
>
> In programs that use OLE 1.0 and don't allow their menus to be replaced, WordArt does appear in a window of its own. You see this window in the later section, "Editing a WordArt Object."

To start WordArt, follow these steps:

1. Position the insertion point where you want the WordArt object to appear in your document.

2. Choose the **Insert Object** command. The Object dialog box appears (see fig. 25.4).

Fig. 25.4
To start WordArt, select it in the Object dialog box.

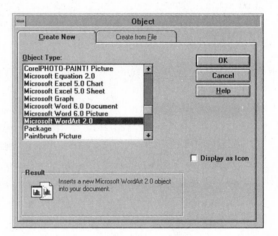

3. Select the Create New tab.

4. From the Object Type list, select Microsoft WordArt 2.0.

5. Choose OK.

When you have started WordArt, you see the screen shown in fig. 25.5. You enter and edit the text of your WordArt image in the Enter Your Text Here dialog box. As you edit your text and add special effects, you see the results of your work in the shaded box in the working area of your page (when you start WordArt, this shaded box contains the words Your Text Here).

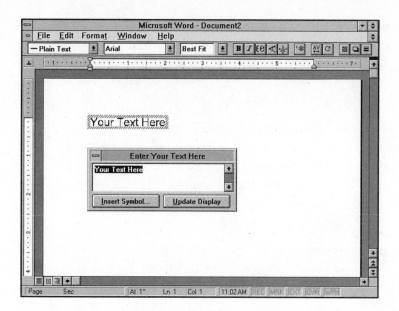

Fig. 25.5
This is how your screen looks when you first start WordArt. You can watch your image develop as you create it.

V

Publishing with Graphics

Entering and Editing the Text

When you start WordArt, the text in the Enter Your Text Here dialog box is selected. You can type as much text as you want in this dialog box. The size of the WordArt image is limited by the size of your page, however, so type no more than can fit within the width or length of your page. By default, a new WordArt object is two inches wide, and as tall as the text you type.

You can watch your WordArt image change in the shaded box as you enter text and add special effects. The shaded box marks the spot where your finished WordArt image appears in your document.

To enter and edit text to be used in the WordArt object, follow these steps:

1. Select the existing text in the Enter Your Text Here dialog box (this text is selected already if you just started WordArt) and type the text for your graphic image. The text you type replaces the selected text. Press Enter when you want to start a new line.

    or

    Edit the text by positioning the insertion point in the Enter Your Text Here dialog box and using standard Word editing techniques. If necessary, use the scroll bar to locate the text you want to edit.

2. Choose the Update Display button to see your new text in the shaded box on your page.

Choose the Insert Symbol button if you want to insert a symbol in your text. In the Insert Symbol window, select the symbol you want to use in your graphic image, and choose OK or press Enter. (For additional information on inserting symbols, see the "Changing the Font or Font Size and Inserting Symbols" section later in this chapter.)

Understanding WordArt's Commands, Lists, and Buttons

WordArt's special effects are available through commands listed in the WordArt menus and through lists and buttons on the WordArt toolbar. You can apply any of these effects at any time, and the image in the shaded box on your page changes to reflect your choices. You can combine many of the effects to create your own unique designs.

WordArt's commands are few and simple. Commands listed in the File and Window menus apply not to WordArt specifically, but to your Word document. The Edit menu has only one command, Edit WordArt Text, which selects the text in the Enter Your Text Here dialog box to enable you to edit the text (you can do the same thing by dragging across the text in the dialog box). All of the Format menu commands duplicate buttons on the WordArt toolbar; you can use either the keyboard or the mouse to create WordArt objects. The Help menu provides help specifically for WordArt.

The WordArt toolbar contains three lists and 11 buttons. The lists contain options for shaping the text or choosing a different font or size. Choosing some of the buttons displays a dialog box; these buttons are duplicated by menu commands. Other buttons apply effects that you can toggle on and off. Here's what the WordArt toolbar looks like:

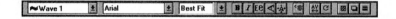

The following table describes the commands and buttons contained in WordArt (they are also described in the section "A Description of WordArt Special Text Effects," in WordArt help). WordArt's commands and buttons are described in detail in the later section, "Adding Special Effects."

Table 25.1 WordArt Commands and Buttons

Menu Command	List or Button	Description
Edit Edit WordArt Text		Selects the text in the Enter Your Text Here dialog box. You can do the same by dragging across the text.

Menu Command	List or Button	Description
Format Spacing Between Characters		Increases or decreases spacing between characters. Turns kerning on or off.
Format Border		Adds a border, in your choice of width and color, around edges of each letter.
Format Shading		Applies shading or a pattern to text, in color or in black and white.
Format Shadow		Adds a shadow to each letter, in a selection of styles and colors.
Format Stretch to Frame		Stretches text vertically and horizontally to fit the box the text is in.
Format Rotation and Effects		Rotates the text or applies different effects depending on the shape applied. You can slant straight text, or change the arc of curved text.
	Shape list	Lists all the different shapes you can pour text into.
	Font list	Lists fonts on your computer. All are available in WordArt.
	Font Size list	Lists different font sizes, measured in points (there are 72 points per inch). The Best Fit option fits the font to the size of the box.
		Applies bold formatting to text.
		Applies italics to text.
		Makes all letters the same height, regardless of case.
		Flips each letter on its side (90 degrees counter-clockwise).
		Selects alignment of text within the WordArt frame (centered text is the default).

Exiting WordArt

When your WordArt image is complete, exit WordArt by clicking the working area of your page somewhere outside the Enter Your Text Here dialog box or the WordArt image. When you exit WordArt, the Enter Your Text Here dialog box disappears, the Word menus return, and your WordArt image appears in your document.

Getting Help in WordArt

WordArt's Help program works just like Word Help, and you access both programs the same way. To access WordArt Help, WordArt must be displayed on your screen when you issue the Help command.

To get help in WordArt, follow these steps:

1. Display WordArt.

2. Choose the **Help Contents** command to see a list of topics in WordArt help; choose **Help Search** For Help On to display the Search dialog box.

For information about using Help, you can choose the **Help** How To Use Help command, or refer to the "Getting Help" section in Chapter 2, "Getting Started in Word for Windows."

Troubleshooting WordArt

For Related Information
■ "Formatting Characters and Changing Fonts," p. 243

■ "Inserting Pictures into Your Document," p. 659

■ "Including Text or Another Picture in a Drawing," p. 759

WordArt isn't listed in the Object dialog box.

WordArt isn't installed. Install it by running the Setup program on your original Word disks.

My screen looks funny when I start WordArt.

WordArt replaces Word's menus and toolbar.

How do I get out of WordArt?

Just click the page outside the WordArt image or the Enter Your Text Here dialog box.

Adding Special Effects

When you add a special effect to your WordArt image, the image changes immediately and you instantly see the result of each effect you choose. You can experiment with different effects and get quick feedback about how they look.

You can add many different types of special effects to create your WordArt image. All of the effects apply to the text rather than to the border or background of your text. You can "pour" your text into a shape, to mold the text into a form of your choice. You can change the font, the size, or the style of the text. You can flip the individual letters or rotate the whole text. You can apply borders or shading to the letters. You can combine the effects to develop a look of your own. Fig. 25.6 shows just a few of the special effects you can achieve with WordArt.

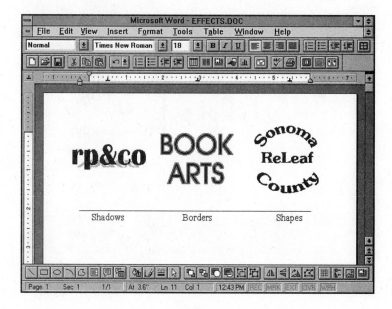

Fig. 25.6
You can create many different special effects with WordArt.

What You Need To Know about WordArt Effects

The effects you apply in WordArt apply to all the text in the Enter Your Text Here dialog box. You cannot apply an effect to just a few of the letters in the dialog box.

Choosing some of the commands or buttons displays a dialog box from which you make selections. To remove the effect, choose the same command or button and select a different option. Most of the buttons that don't display a dialog box toggle on and off; for example, if you have flipped the letters and want them straight up again, choose the Flip Letters button a second time.

The commands listed in the WordArt menus are all duplicated by buttons on the toolbar, so you can apply WordArt effects using either the keyboard or a mouse.

Shaping the Text

By applying one special WordArt effect—pouring your text into a shape—you can create an interesting sign or logo (see fig. 25.7). WordArt's toolbar includes a Shapes list that displays a grid of different shapes. When you select one of these shapes, the text in the Enter Your Text Here dialog box "pours" into that shape.

Fig. 25.7

By "shaping" text, you can create an interesting logo or sign.

Some shapes produce different results depending on how many lines of text you are shaping. The circle shape, for example, turns a single line of text into a circle, but turns multiple lines of text into a vertical half-circle. The button shape turns three lines into a button, but turns a single line into an arch. Experiment to get the result you want.

To shape text, follow these steps:

1. Start WordArt, and type text in the Enter Your Text Here dialog box.

2. Choose the Shapes list (see fig. 25.8).

3. Select the shape you want.

Changing the Font or Font Size and Inserting Symbols

You can change the *font* (the letters' style) or size of the font in your WordArt object by selecting from lists in the WordArt toolbar. You can use the same fonts in WordArt that you use in Word. You can use any font installed on your computer, whether the font came with Windows, was built into your printer, or is a font you purchased separately.

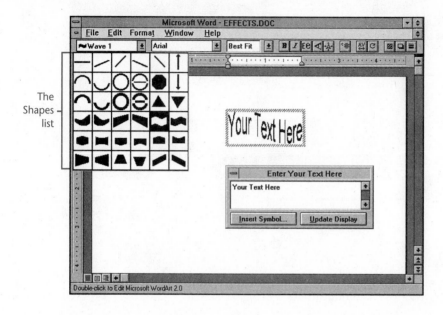

The Shapes list

The default WordArt font size is Best Fit. Using this setting fits your text into the standard two-inch WordArt frame. If you select a smaller or larger font size, the size of the WordArt frame changes to fit your text.

Because you can use only one font per WordArt image, your symbol selections are dependent on the font you are using. By inserting a symbol, you can access symbols contained in your font that are not shown on your keyboard. The Windows TrueType fonts Arial and Times New Roman, for example, include copyright symbols, fractions, and accented letters.

To change the font or font size, follow these steps:

1. Start WordArt, and type text in the Enter Your Text Here dialog box.

2. Select a font from the Font list in the WordArt toolbar (see fig. 25.9).

3. Select a font size from the Font Size list in the WordArt toolbar (see fig. 25.10). Select Best Fit if you want WordArt to choose the size that best fits the WordArt frame. If the size you want is not listed, type it in the Font Size box.

V

Publishing with Graphics

**Figs. 25.9
and 25.10**
You can select or
type a font size.

The Font list

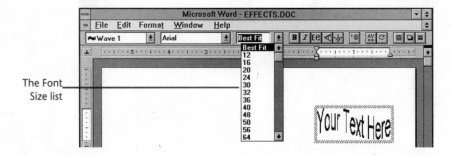

The Font
Size list

To insert a symbol, follow these steps:

1. Start WordArt, and type text in the Enter Your Text Here dialog box.

2. Position the insertion point where you want the symbol to appear.

3. Choose the Insert Symbol button. The Insert Symbol dialog box appears
(see fig. 25.11).

Fig. 25.11
The Insert Symbol
dialog box gives
you access to
symbols not
shown on your
keyboard.

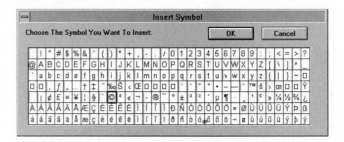

4. Select the symbol you want to insert.

5. Choose OK.

Applying Bold, Italics, or Even Caps

You can apply bold and italicized character formats in WordArt just as you
do in Word. WordArt also enables you to make all the letters in your text the

same height, regardless of case (see fig. 25.12). Each of these three effects—Bold, Italic, and Even Caps—toggle on and off through buttons on the toolbar. To apply Even Caps, for example, you click the Even Caps button; to remove this effect, you click the button a second time.

Fig. 25.12
Bold and Italics are the same in WordArt and Word, but the Even Caps effect is unique to WordArt.

To apply (or remove) Bold, Italics, or Even Caps, follow these steps:

1. Start WordArt, and type text in the Enter Your Text Here dialog box.

2. Click the Bold button, the Italics button, or the Even Caps button.

Flipping and Stretching Letters

Flipping letters creates a different effect than rotating the entire text—the Flip effect flips each individual letter (see fig. 25.13). Stretching letters stretches them to fit the WordArt frame (by default, a two-inch square frame), as shown in figure 25.14. Although you can change the size of letters in a WordArt image by changing the size of the WordArt frame (see the later section, "Editing a WordArt object"), stretching text is the only way to lengthen it vertically.

The Flip and the Stretch buttons toggle on and off on the WordArt toolbar; click the appropriate button to choose the effect, and click it again to remove the effect. To stretch text, you also can choose a menu command; like the button, the menu command toggles on and off.

V

Publishing with Graphics

Fig. 25.13
Examples of
flipped text.

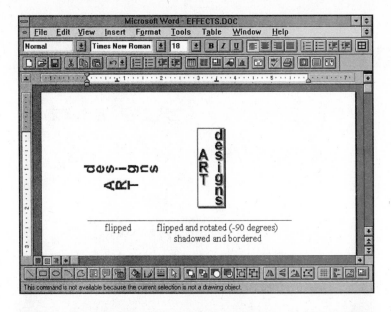

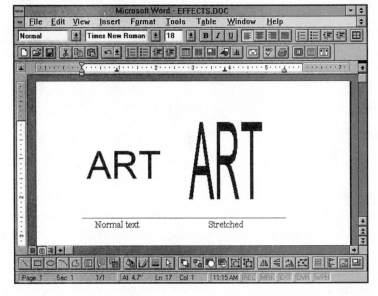

Fig. 25.14
An example of
stretched text.

To flip or stretch text, follow these steps:

1. Start WordArt, and type text in the Enter Your Text Here dialog box.

2. Click the Flip button to flip the letters, or the Stretch button to stretch
    letters. Alternatively, choose the Format Stretch To Frame command to
    stretch letters.

Rotating, Slanting, and Arcing Text

The Rotation and Effects command or button enables you to rotate your WordArt image, slant the letters, change the angle of the arc, or reduce the height of the letters. The Special Effects dialog box that you see when you choose this command or button changes depending on what shape you have selected for your image. You can rotate and slant images that you have poured into noncircular shapes. You also can rotate and change the arc or letter height for images that you have poured into circular shapes. Fig. 25.15 shows some of the effects you can achieve with the Rotation and Effects command or button.

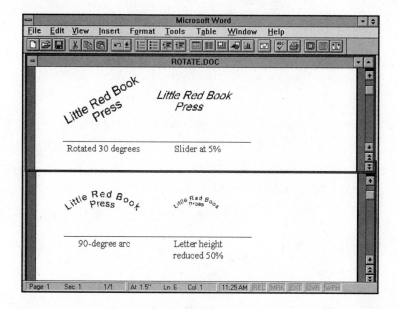

Fig. 25.15
You can change the angle, arc, or height of letters.

V

Publishing with Graphics

To rotate, slant, or arc text, follow these steps:

1. Start WordArt, and type text in the Enter Your Text Here dialog box.

2. Click the Rotation and Effects button or choose the Format Rotation and Effects command.

    The Special Effects dialog box appears (see fig. 25.16 and 25.17).

3. To rotate your WordArt image, select Rotation and select a rotation degree. For example, 90 degrees rotates the text to a vertical position, reading from bottom to top.

Figs. 25.16 and 25.17

If you have selected a circular shape, you can change rotation, arc angle, and letter height (left); if you have selected some other shape, you can change rotation or use Slider to change the slant (right).

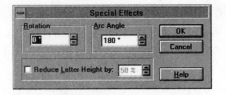

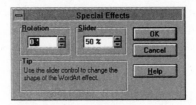

4. To slant your text, select Slider and select a percent. 100% angles the text backward; 50% is normal; 0% angles the text forward (similar to italics).

5. To change the angle of the arc, select Arc Angle and select a percent. The default, 180 degrees, is a half-circle; 90 degrees is a quarter-circle.

6. To reduce the letter height, select Reduce Letter Height By and select a percent. The default, 50%, reduces the letter height by half; 100% makes the letters very small.

7. Choose OK.

Aligning the Text

By default, text in a WordArt image is centered; however, WordArt offers other text-alignment options. You can change the text's alignment to the left or right. You also can *stretch justify* it to stretch the letters to fit the WordArt frame, *letter justify* it to space the letters out to fit the frame, or *word justify* it to space the words to fit the frame. These alignment effects are shown in fig. 25.18.

To align text, follow these steps:

1. Start WordArt, and type text in the Enter Your Text Here dialog box.

2. Click the Alignment button on the toolbar. A list of alignment options appears (see fig. 25.19).

3. Select the alignment style you want.

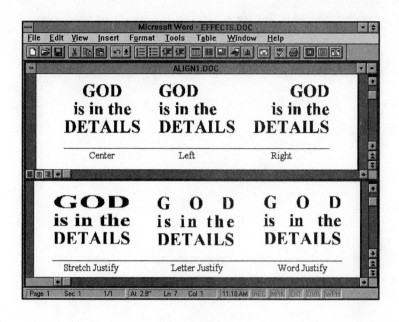

Fig. 25.18
You can align and
justify text six
ways.

Fig. 25.19
You can align your
text to the center
or a side of the
WordArt frame, or
you can justify it
to fill the frame.

V

Publishing with Graphics

Adjusting Spacing Between Characters

Graphic artists appreciate the ability to control the spacing between letters
and words in their text. *Kerning* means adjusting the spacing between character pairs, and WordArt gives you the option of turning on kerning to optimize the spacing between certain adjacent letters. In general, kerning
tightens the spacing between letter pairs such as *AV* and *Td*. If your type
is any larger than normal reading size, kerning can make your type
more readable.

Tracking adjusts the spacing between all letters. In WordArt, you can loosen
or tighten the tracking, or set it to an exact percent of normal (see fig. 25.20).

To adjust the spacing between letters and words, follow these steps:

1. Start WordArt, and type text in the Enter Your Text Here dialog box.

2. Click the Spacing Between Characters button or choose the Format
   Spacing Between Characters command.

Fig. 25.20
You can tighten or loosen tracking to adjust spacing between characters.

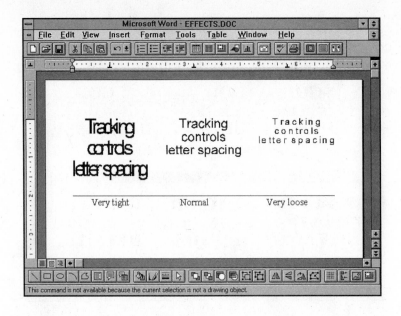

The Spacing Between Characters dialog box appears (see fig. 25.21).

Fig. 25.21
You can control the precise spacing between characters in your WordArt image.

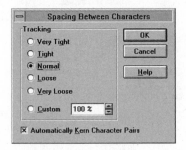

3. Select a tracking option: Very Tight (60% of normal), **Tight** (80%), Normal (100%), Loose (120%), or Very Loose (150%). Or select Custom and select a percent of normal.

4. Select the Automatically Kern Character Pairs option if you want WordArt to automatically kern characters. Deselect (clear) the option to turn off kerning.

5. Choose OK.

Adding Borders
When you apply borders in a WordArt image, you apply them to the characters, not to the frame around the edge of the image (to border the frame, exit WordArt, select the WordArt image, and choose the Format Borders and

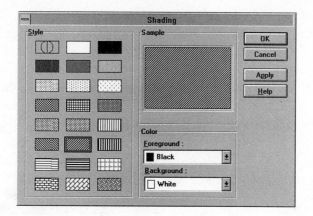

Fig. 25.25
The Sample box in
the Shading dialog
box shows you
how your
selections look.

Follow these steps to add color to text:

1. In WordArt, click the Shading button or choose the Format Shading
   command.

2. In the Style group, select the solid background option (top middle) and
   select the color you want from the Background list.

   or

   Select the solid foreground option (top right) and select the color you
   want from the Foreground list.

3. Choose Apply to see the effect of your choice on your text without
   closing the Shading dialog box, or choose OK or press Enter to close the
   dialog box.

Follow these steps to add shading to text:

1. In WordArt, click the Shading button or choose the Format Shading
   command.

2. In the Style group, select a shading option (the second and third rows
   are dotted shading patterns; the fourth row includes patterns small
   enough to work as shading).

3. Select the shading color you want from the Foreground list, and select
   White from the Background list.

4. Choose Apply to see the effect of your choice on your text without
   closing the Shading dialog box, or choose OK or press Enter to close the
   dialog box.

Adding Shadows

Like borders, shadows apply to the letters in your WordArt image, not to the edge of the WordArt frame (to add a shadowed border, exit WordArt, select the WordArt image, and choose the Format Borders and Shading command—for more information, see "Shading and Bordering Paragraphs" in Chapter 10, "Formatting Lines and Paragraphs"). You can add many different types of shadows to your letters, in a variety of colors (see fig. 25.26).

Fig. 25.26
Many different shadow styles are available in WordArt.

You can add a shadow using either the Shadow button or a command. To choose a color for a shadow, however, you must display the Shadow dialog box. You can display the Shadow dialog box either by clicking More in the Shadow palette that appears when you click the Shadow button, or by choosing the Format Shadow command. Text remains black, unless you change its color using the Shading button or command (see the earlier section "Adding Color, Shading, or a Pattern").

To add shadows to letters, follow these steps:

1. Start WordArt, and type text in the Enter Your Text Here dialog box.

2. Click the Shadow button. The Shadow palette appears (see fig. 25.27).

   or

   Choose the Format Shadow command. The Shadow dialog box appears (see fig. 25.28).

Fig. 25.27
Choose from the
shadow styles
shown.

Fig. 25.28
By choosing the
Format Shadow
command, you
can choose both
shadow style and
color.

3. From the Shadow palette, click the shadow style you want to use. Click More if you want to display the Shadow dialog box.

   or

   In the Shadow dialog box, select Choose a Shadow and select a shadow style. Then select Shadow Color and select the color you want the shadow to be.

4. You need do nothing more if you selected a shadow from the Shadow palette; if you selected from the Shadow dialog box, choose OK or press Enter.

Editing a WordArt Object

You can edit a WordArt object several ways. You can change the image itself by restarting WordArt and editing the text or choosing different special effects. In this section, you learn how to select your WordArt object and restart WordArt; earlier sections of this chapter ("Creating a WordArt object" and "Adding Special Effects") discuss how to edit text and add special effects to your WordArt object.

Many other methods of editing WordArt objects also are available to you. You can resize, crop, move, or copy a WordArt image by using the same techniques you use for any inserted picture. These techniques are covered in "Working with Pictures" in Chapter 22, "Inserting Pictures in Your Document." You can insert a WordArt object in a text box that you draw using the Drawing toolbar; see "Including Text or Another Picture in a Drawing" in Chapter 24, "Drawing with Word's Drawing Tools." By framing and positioning a WordArt object, you can move it freely on the page and wrap text

For Related Information
■ "Formatting Characters and Changing Fonts," p. 243

■ "Working with Pictures," p. 671

around it; see Chapter 23, "Framing and Moving Text and Graphics." You can add a caption; see Chapter 31, "Adding Cross-References and Captions." Later in this section, Table 25.2 provides an overview of using these techniques to edit your WordArt object.

Shortcuts for adding a border or caption or for framing your WordArt object are included in the WordArt shortcut menu. You can display that menu by clicking the WordArt object with the right mouse button.

All the techniques for editing a WordArt object share one rule: Select, then do. You must select your WordArt image before you edit it. In some cases, selecting the WordArt object is part of the process of editing; for example, you can double-click the WordArt image to select the image and start WordArt for editing. In other situations, you must select the WordArt object before you can edit it. A WordArt object selected with the mouse appears with square selection handles on all sides and corners; selected with the keyboard, it appears reversed. Figs. 25.29 and 25.30 show images selected with both techniques.

Figs. 25.29 and 25.30
With a mouse, you can select a WordArt object by clicking on it (left); with the keyboard, hold Shift while you press an arrow to cross the WordArt object (right).

You select a WordArt object in the document as follows:

■ With a mouse, click the WordArt object. The WordArt object appears with selection handles on the sides and corners.

    or

■ With a keyboard, position the insertion point to one side of the WordArt object, hold down the Shift key, and press an arrow key to cross the graphic. The WordArt object appears reversed.

When you change a WordArt image, you can use WordArt in the usual way (displaying the Enter Your Text Here dialog box and replacing the Word menus and toolbar with WordArt menus and buttons), or you can display WordArt in a dialog box. The WordArt 2.0 dialog box is shown in fig. 25.31.

To edit a WordArt object, follow these steps:

1. Select your WordArt object and start WordArt using one of the following techniques:

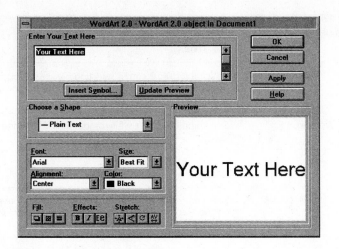

Fig. 25.31
You can open the
WordArt dialog
box to edit your
WordArt object.

■ Double-click your WordArt object.

■ Select your WordArt object and choose the Edit WordArt 2.0 Object
command. From the menu that opens, choose Edit to display
WordArt in the usual way, or Open to display the WordArt 2.0 dialog
box.

■ Click your WordArt object with the right mouse button to display
the shortcut menu. Select Edit WordArt 2.0 to edit your image in the
usual way, or select Open WordArt 2.0 to edit your image using the
WordArt dialog box.

2. Make your changes and exit WordArt. For details, see the earlier
sections in this chapter.

Table 25.2 shows an overview of different ways you can edit your WordArt
object.

Table 25.2 Techniques for Editing a WordArt Object—An Overview	
To...	**Do This...**
Move a WordArt object	Select it and drag it to a new location
Copy a WordArt object	Select it and choose any Copy command or shortcut; or, drag it while holding down the Ctrl key
Paste a WordArt object	Position the insertion point where you want the graphic, and choose any Paste command or shortcut

(continues)

V

Publishing with Graphics

Table 25.2 Continued	
To...	**Do This...**
Resize a WordArt object	Select and drag a corner selection handle for proportional resizing; drag a side handle for nonproportional resizing
Crop a WordArt object	Select and hold Shift while dragging any selection handle
Crop or resize a WordArt graphic	Select and choose the Format Picture command
Frame a WordArt object	Select and choose the Insert Frame command, or click on the graphic with the right mouse button and select Frame Picture
Position a WordArt object	Frame the graphic and choose the Format Frame command
Border a WordArt object	Select and choose the Format Borders and Shading command or click on the graphic with the right mouse button and select Borders and Shading
Add a caption to a WordArt object	Select and choose the Insert Caption command or click on the graphic with the right mouse button and select Caption

For Related Information

- Working with Pictures," p. 671

- "Framing and Moving Text and Graphics," p. 687

- "Including Text or Another Picture in a Drawing," p. 759

- "Adding Cross-References and Captions," p. 949

From Here...

For information relating to WordArt, you may want to review the following major sections of this book:

- Chapter 22, "Inserting Pictures in Your Document," and Chapter 23, "Framing and Moving Text and Graphics," teach you to work with WordArt objects after you've created them.

- Chapter 27, "Desktop Publishing," teaches you to use graphics in publications such as newsletters, flyers, and brochures.

- Chapter 33, "Using Word with Other Windows Applications," describes how to work with embedded OLE objects like those from WordArt.

Chapter 26

Graphing Data

With Microsoft Graph, you can create informative and impressive charts for your Word for Windows documents. You can turn an overwhelming table of numbers into a chart that shows important trends and changes. You can relegate the detailed numeric table to a location where it doesn't slow down communication. Fig. 26.1 shows a Word for Windows document enhanced by a chart. Microsoft Graph is not just a small charting application; it has the capability of Microsoft Excel, the most capable Windows spreadsheet, graphics, and database program.

Microsoft Graph is an *applet*. Applets are small applications designed to work with Windows programs that have Object Linking and Embedding (OLE) capability. Applets add additional features to OLE-capable applications. Microsoft Graph is a separate program that embeds charts and their data into Windows applications such as Microsoft Word for Windows.

Charts embedded into a Word for Windows document contain both the chart and the data that creates the chart. When you activate Microsoft Graph, it loads the selected chart and its data so that you can make changes. You cannot save the chart or data separately; they are embedded into your Word for Windows document.

Creating a Chart

Charts arecreated from data entered into a data sheet. With Microsoft Graph, you can create a new chart in Word for Windows in a number of ways. The text and numbers in the data sheet can be:

- Selected from a table in the Word for Windows document
- Typed into Microsoft Graph

In this chapter, you learn to do the following:

- Create charts
- Format data sheets

V

Publishing with Graphics

Tip
Many of the tips found in the charting chapters of Que's book *Using Excel 5 for Windows,* Special Edition, also work in Microsoft Graph.

- Copied in from any Windows document

- Imported from a Microsoft Excel, Lotus 1-2-3, or text file

- Read in from an existing Microsoft Excel chart

 To start Microsoft Graph using the mouse, click the I-beam where you want the chart to appear in your document, and then click the Graph button in the toolbar.

Fig. 26.1
A Word for Windows document enhanced by a chart.

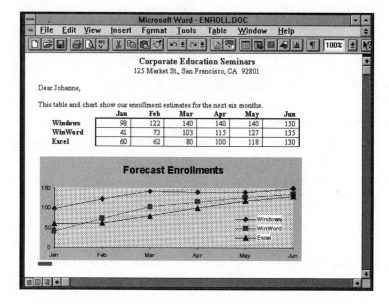

To start Microsoft Graph using the keyboard, position the insertion point where you want the chart to appear in your document and choose the Insert Object command. Select the Microsoft Graph object from the list in the Object Type dialog box and then choose OK.

Microsoft Graph opens in an application window on top of your Word for Windows application. Microsoft Graph opens with default data in the data sheet and chart (see fig. 26.2). The chart reflects the data in the sample data sheet. (If you select data in a Word for Windows table before starting Microsoft Graph, the opening chart uses that data.) If you change the data in the data sheet, you change the chart. When you close the Microsoft Graph application, you can embed the chart and its related data into your document.

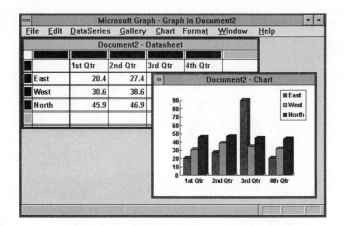

Fig. 26.2

A sample data sheet and chart.

You can change the data in the Microsoft Graph data sheet in many ways. You also can choose different types of charts from the Gallery menu. The Chart menu enables you to add or remove chart items, such as legends, arrows, and titles. You can change the appearance or position of selected chart items or data in the sheet by using the commands in the Format menu.

Understanding the Data Sheet Layout

Microsoft Graph plots data points from the data sheet as *markers* in the chart. Markers appear as lines, bars, columns, data points in X-Y charts, or slices in a pie chart. With the Microsoft Graph default settings, a row of data points appears in a chart as a *series* of markers; a series of values appears in the chart connected by a line, or as bars or columns of the same color. In fig. 26.3, for example, the row labeled East corresponds to one line in the 3-D line chart.

In this default orientation, known as Series in Rows, the text in the first row of the data sheet becomes the *category names* that appear below the *category (X) axis* (the horizontal axis). The text in the left column becomes the *series names*, which Microsoft Graph uses as labels for the legend. (The *legend* is the box that labels the different colors or patterns used by each series of markers.) If you change orientation and want to return to the default orientation, choose the DataSeries Series In Rows command.

If your data uses the reverse orientation on the data sheet so that each data series goes down a column, you must choose the DataSeries Series In Columns command. When you use that command, Microsoft Graph takes the category names (x-axis labels) from the left column of the data sheet and the series names (legend labels) from the top row (see fig. 26.4).

V

Publishing with Graphics

Fig. 26.3
By default, each row of data translates to a series of data points in the chart.

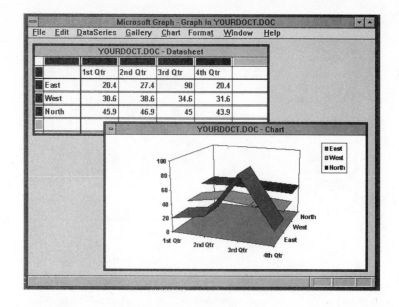

Fig. 26.4
A data series with a column orientation.

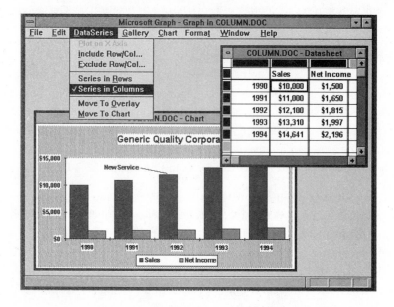

When you create a Microsoft Graph chart, be sure that you have text for each series name (legend labels), text for each category label (x-axis), and a number for each data point.

Typing Data for a New Chart

To manually create a chart, type over the numbers and text that appear in the default data sheet. When you change the default data sheet, you update the chart.

If you change numbers or text in the data sheet after you open it, you make corresponding changes in the chart. The program includes the chart rows or columns of data you add to the data sheet. Later sections in this chapter describe methods for editing data and for including or excluding rows or columns from the chart.

Creating Charts from a Table

In a Word for Windows document, you quickly can convert data in a table into a chart. Fig. 26.5 shows a table and its subsequent chart in a document.

To create a chart from a table in a Word for Windows document, follow these steps:

1. In the table, enter the data and text in the layout you want to use in a Microsoft Graph data sheet.

   Use the Table menu or the table button on the Standard toolbar to insert and format a table.

2. Select the table.

3. Click the Graph button in the toolbar or choose the Insert Object command. Select Microsoft Graph from the Object Type list, and then choose OK.

   Microsoft Graph starts. After a moment, Microsoft Graph loads the table's data into the data sheet. The chart updates.

4. Format, modify, and size the chart and data sheet. If your data series are in columns, you need to choose the DataSeries Series In Columns command.

5. Choose the File Exit And Return To Document command.

6. To update the chart in the document, choose Yes at the prompt.

Microsoft Graph closes. In your document, the chart (preceded by a blank line) appears below your table.

V

Publishing with Graphics

Fig. 26.5

A table and its
subsequent chart
in a document.

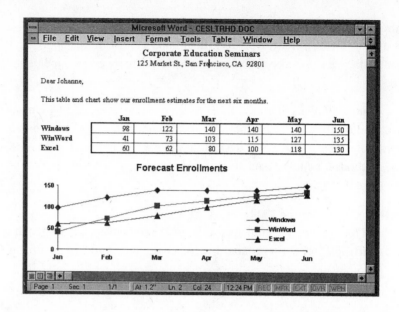

Copying Data from Word for Windows or Other Applications

You can copy data from applications and paste it into the data sheet to create
a chart. You can create a chart, for example, from a series of text and numbers aligned on tabs in Word for Windows, or you can copy a range of cells
from a Microsoft Excel worksheet. ("Importing Excel Charts," later in this
chapter, describes how to import a range from Microsoft Excel or use a
Microsoft Excel chart as a basis for a Microsoft Graph chart.)

You must use tabs to separate data and text in a word processing document
if you want to copy the information into separate data sheet cells. Fig. 26.6
shows the same Word for Windows document as in fig. 26.5, but the data
and labels are separated by right-align tabs. You must arrange data and text
as you want them to appear in the Microsoft Graph data sheet.

To copy data from a document or Microsoft Excel worksheet and create a
chart, follow these steps:

1. Select the tabbed data or range of Microsoft Excel cells.

2. Choose the Edit Copy command.

3. Position the insertion point where you want the chart, and then click
the Graph button or choose the Insert Object command. Select
Microsoft Graph from the list, and then choose OK.

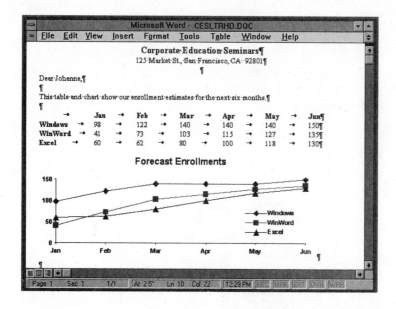

Fig. 26.6
Data and labels
separated by tabs.

4. Activate the data sheet and erase all existing data by choosing the Edit Select All command or by pressing Ctrl+A. Then choose the Edit Clear command or press the Del key. When the Clear dialog box appears, choose OK.

5. Ensure that the top-left cell in the data sheet is selected, and then choose the Edit Paste command.

   The data is pasted into the data sheet, and the chart updates.

6. Format, modify, or size the chart and data sheet as necessary.

7. Choose the File Exit And Return To Document command.

8. Choose Yes when asked whether you want to update the chart in the document.

   The chart is inserted at the insertion point.

Importing Worksheet or Text Data

You may want to use data you have in an ASCII text file, or in a Microsoft Excel or Lotus 1-2-3 worksheet for a chart. You can save time by importing this data directly into the Microsoft Graph data sheet.

To import data into the data sheet, follow these steps:

1. Erase all unwanted data from the data sheet, and then select the cell where you want to position the top left corner of the imported data. If you are importing an entire chart's worth of data, select the top left cell of the data sheet.

2. Choose the File Import Data command. The Import Data dialog box appears (see fig. 26.7). Find and select the file from which you want to import data.

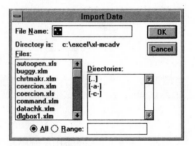

Fig. 26.7
The Import Data dialog box.

3. Specify the amount of data you want imported. To import all data, choose the All button. To import a range of data, enter the range or range name in the Range box. Use a range format such as A12:D36.

4. Choose OK.

To import data from a worksheet, you must have the worksheet converter files loaded. If they are not loaded, run the Word for Windows Setup program (the icon for this program is in the Word for Windows program window). Select the options to install the converters you choose without reinstalling all of Word for Windows. You must use your original Word for Windows installation disks to load the converters. For additional information on installing or reinstalling Word for Windows see Appendix B, "Installing Word for Windows."

Importing a Microsoft Excel Chart

With Microsoft Excel, you can create mathematical models that generate charts, and you can link the charts to Word for Windows documents. If you change the Excel worksheet that contains your mathematical model, you change the chart. These changes are reflected in the Word for Windows document. (This concept is described in Chapter 33, "Using Word with Other Windows Applications.")

Importing a Microsoft Excel chart into Microsoft Graph to embed the chart into the Word for Windows document has other advantages. Because embedded charts keep the data with the chart, another person can update the chart without using Microsoft Excel or the original Microsoft Excel worksheet. Links are not broken if the source worksheet or chart in Microsoft Excel is renamed or moved to a different directory.

To import a Microsoft Excel chart and the chart's related data, follow these steps:

1. Position the insertion point where you want the chart; start Microsoft Graph by clicking the Chart button in the toolbar, or by choosing the **Insert Object** command.

2. Choose the File Open Microsoft Excel Chart command. To overwrite existing data in the data sheet, choose OK when prompted.

   The Open Microsoft Excel Chart dialog box appears (see fig. 26.8).

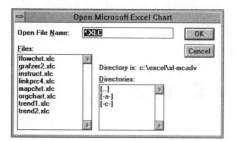

Fig. 26.8
The Open Microsoft Excel Chart dialog box.

3. Select the drive, directory, and file name of the Microsoft Excel chart, and then choose OK. Microsoft Excel charts use the file extension XLC.

   The chart opens in Microsoft Graph and the associated data appears in the data sheet. Data series that were in rows in Microsoft Excel are in columns in the Microsoft Graph data sheet, but the chart is correct.

Editing Existing Charts

Updating existing Microsoft Graph charts in a Word for Windows document is easy. With a mouse, double-click the chart. With the keyboard, select the chart by moving the insertion point next to the chart, and then pressing Shift+left or right arrow to move across the chart. After the chart is selected, choose the Edit Microsoft Graph Object command.

Microsoft Graph opens and loads the data and chart. You then can use any of the procedures described in this chapter to modify your chart or data.

Entering Data for Overlay Charts

Overlay charts overlay one two-dimensional chart type with another. Overlay charts can display clearly the relationships between different types of data or data with widely different scales.

Overlay charts consist of a *main* chart (the underlying chart foundation that uses the Y-axis on the left) and an overlay chart (the overlay that covers the main chart and uses a second Y-axis on the right). You can create an overlay chart by choosing the Gallery Combination command. You also can create an overlay chart from existing charts by selecting a data series (line, bar, or column) and choosing the DataSeries Move To Overlay command. This procedure moves the selected series out of the main chart and into the overlay chart.

The Gallery Combination command divides the data series into halves. The first half creates the main chart, and the second half creates the overlay chart. When the total number of series is odd, the main chart receives the large number of series.

For Related Information

■ "Moving and Positioning Frames," p. 699

■ "Creating Tables," p. 509

■ "Embedding Data," p. 1000

Editing the Data Sheet

Working in the data sheet is similar to working in a Word for Windows table or a Microsoft Excel worksheet. Because the data sheet cannot be printed, however, it does not have a wide range of font formatting options. Another difference is that you can edit cellular data directly in a cell or within an editing box.

Selecting Data

Moving and selecting cells in the data sheet uses many of the same techniques used in Microsoft Excel. If you are using a mouse, you can use the scroll bars to scroll to any location on the data sheet. You can select parts of the data sheet using the following methods:

■ To select a cell, click it.

■ To select multiple cells, drag the mouse across them.

■ To select a row or column, click its header.

- To select multiple rows or columns, drag across the headers.

- To select all of the cells in the data sheet, click in the blank rectangle at the top left corner where row and column headings intersect.

If you are using the keyboard, use the keys shown in the following tables to move the insertion point or select cells and their contents:

To move	Press
A cell	Arrow key in the direction to move
To first cell in row	Home
To last cell in row	End
To top left data cell	Ctrl+Home
To lower right data cell	Ctrl+End
A screen up/down	Page Up/Down
A screen right/left	Ctrl+Page Up/Down

To select	Press
A cell	Arrow key in the direction to move
A range (rectangle) of cells	Shift+arrow key or F8 (enters Extend mode). Arrow key, and then F8 (exits Extend mode)
A row	Shift+space bar
A column	Ctrl+space bar
The datasheet	Shift+Ctrl+space bar or Ctrl+A or Edit Select **All**
Undo selection	Shift+backspace or move

Tip

Selecting the entire worksheet and pressing Del erases the entire worksheet.

V

Publishing with Graphics

Replacing or Editing Existing Data

The easiest way to replace the contents of a cell is to select the cell by moving to it or by clicking it, and then typing directly over the cell's contents. When you press Enter or select a different cell, the change takes effect.

To edit the contents of a cell, select the cell by moving to it or by clicking it. Press F2, the Edit key, or double-click the cell. A simple edit box appears and shows the contents of the cell. You can edit the cell's contents as you would edit the contents of any edit box. After you finish editing, choose OK.

Inserting or Deleting Rows and Columns

Microsoft Graph expands the chart to include data or text you add in rows or columns outside the originally charted data. If you add rows or columns of data and leave blank rows or columns, Microsoft Graph does not include the blank rows or columns as part of the chart.

To insert or delete rows or columns in the data sheet, select the rows or columns where you want to insert or delete, and then choose the Edit Insert Row/Col or the Edit Delete Row/Col command. The shortcut keys for inserting and deleting are Ctrl++ (plus) and Ctrl+– (minus), respectively. If you do not select an entire row or column, a dialog box appears and asks you to select whether you want to affect the rows or columns that pass through the selected cells.

The Microsoft Graph data sheet cannot have more than 256 columns or 4,000 rows. If you need a larger data sheet, create the chart in Microsoft Excel or an advanced charting application and link or paste it into Word for Windows.

Copying or Moving Data

Copy or move data in the data sheet using normal Windows techniques. Select the cells you want to copy or move, and then choose the Edit Copy or Edit Cut command. (The shortcut keys for these commands are Ctrl+C and Ctrl+X, respectively.) Select the cell at the top left corner of the area where you want to paste the data and choose the Edit Paste command or press Ctrl+V. The pasted data replaces the data it covers. To undo the paste operation, choose the Edit Undo command before choosing another command.

Including and Excluding Data from a Chart

When you add data or text to the data sheet, Microsoft Graph immediately redraws the chart, even if the data is not adjacent to other data in the table. This redrawing is inconvenient if you want to add a row or column of data to the table but not include the data in the chart.

You can see which rows and columns of data are included in the chart because their row or column headings are bold. Excluded rows or columns are grayed.

To include or exclude a row or column with the mouse, double-click the row or column heading. The double-click toggles the row or column between being included and being excluded.

To include or exclude a row or column with the keyboard, select the entire row or column and then choose the DataSeries Include Row/Col or the DataSeries Exclude Row/Col command.

Changing Data by Moving a Graph Marker

Microsoft Graph enables you to move column, bar, lines, or X-Y markers on 2-D charts. As you move the data point, the corresponding data changes in the data sheeta convenient feature for smoothing a curve so that it matches real-life experience or for "fudging" numbers so that they fit the results you want.

To change values on the datasheet by moving markers on the chart, follow these steps:

1. Open the worksheet and chart. Activate the chart. The chart must be a two-dimensional column, bar, or line chart.

2. Hold down the Ctrl key and click the column, bar, or line marker you want to change. A black handle appears on the marker.

3. Drag the black handle to the new height. When you drag the black handle, a tick mark on the vertical axis moves, showing you the value of the new location.

4. Release the mouse when the marker is at the location you want.

The corresponding data in the data sheet changes.

Changing the Chart Type

When Microsoft Graph first opens, the chart appears as a three-dimensional column chart. Many different chart types are available. You select the chart type appropriate for the data you want to graph.

Try to choose the appropriate chart type before you begin customizing. To change the chart type after you customize, follow the procedure described in the later section, "Customizing an Existing Chart Type."

Selecting the Original Chart Type

When you build charts, you can use any of the 81 predefined chart formats. The easiest way to create charts is to select the predefined chart closest to the type you want. You then can customize the predefined chart until it fits your needs.

For Related Information
■ "Selecting Text," p.133

■ "Moving, Copying, and Linking Text or Graphics," p.152

To use a predefined chart, follow these steps:

1. Select the Gallery command.

2. From the menu, choose one of these charts:

Area	Combination
Bar	3-D Area
Column	3-D Bar
Line	3-D Column
Pie	3-D Line
X-Y (Scatter)	3-D Pie

After you make your choice, the Chart Gallery dialog box appears. This dialog box shows the predefined formats available for the chart type you have chosen. Fig. 26.9 shows the gallery available for 3-D column charts.

Fig. 26.9
The gallery of predefined formats for 3-D Column charts.

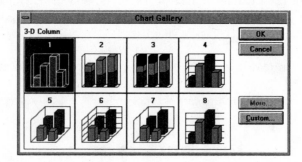

3. To select a chart format, click its square or type its number.

4. If you do not see the format you want and the More button is available, choose the More button to see additional formats of this chart type.

5. If you want a variation from the chart formats shown, choose the Custom button.

The Format Chart dialog box appears (see fig. 26.10). Select options to modify the chart format. The options in this dialog box are different for each chart type.

6. Choose OK.

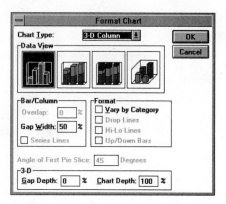

Fig. 26.10
The Format Chart
dialog box.

You can access the customizing options available through the Custom button
in step 5 at any time by choosing the Format Chart or Format Overlay command.

The following table describes the two-dimensional chart types available
through the Gallery menu.

Tip
To select from the
Gallery the chart
type you want,
double-click the
box containing the
type. This action
selects the type
and chooses OK.

Chart	Description
2-D Line Chart	Compares trends over even time or measurement intervals plotted on the category (X) axis. (If your category data points are at uneven intervals, use an X-Y scatter chart.)
2-D Area Chart	Compares the continuous change in volume of a data series.
2-D Bar Chart	Compares distinct (non-continuous) items over time. Horizontal bars show positive or negative variation from a center point. Frequently used for time management.
2-D Column Chart	Compares separate (non-continuous) items as they vary over time.
2-D Pie Chart	Compares the size of each of the pieces making up a whole unit. Use this type of chart when the parts total 100 percent for the first series of data. Only the first data series in a worksheet selection is plotted.
X-Y (Scattergram) Chart	Compares trends over *uneven* time or measurement intervals plotted on the category (X) axis.
Combination Chart	Lays one chart over another. These charts are useful for comparing data of different types or data requiring different axis scales.

V

Publishing with Graphics

The following table describes the three-dimensional chart types available through the Gallery menu.

Chart	Description
3-D Area Chart	3-D area charts for the same types of data as those used in 2-D area charts.
3-D Bar Chart	3-D bar charts for the same type of data as those used in 2-D bar charts.
3-D Column Chart	3-D column charts for the same types of data as those used in 2-D column charts. You can create 3-D column charts with the columns adjacent to each other or layered into the third dimension.
3-D Line Chart	3-D line charts for the same types of data as those used in 2-D line charts. 3-D line charts also are known as *ribbon charts*.
3-D Pie Chart	Shows labels or calculates percentages for wedges. Only the first data series from a selection is charted as a pie. Wedges can be dragged out from the pie.

Customizing an Existing Chart Type

You can save yourself work by deciding on the type of chart you want before you customize it. Use the Gallery command to try different types of charts, and then customize the one you decide to use. If you use the Gallery command to change the chart type after you customize a chart, you may lose some of your custom selections.

To change or customize a chart type without losing custom formatting, choose the Format Chart or Format Overlay command and then select from the available options. The Format Overlay command is only available when the chart is a combination chart.

Using the Format Chart command changes the basic type or customizes the main or background chart. Format Overlay changes or customizes the overlay chart. Figs. 26.11 and 26.12 show the Format Chart and Format Overlay dialog boxes that enable you to customize the main or overlay charts. Both dialog boxes offer the same options.

Options in the Format Chart and Format Overlay dialog boxes are available only when appropriate for the type of chart that is active. The options in these dialog boxes include the following:

Option	Description
Chart Type	Changes the basic chart type to one of the types shown in the Gallery menu and retains custom formats.
Data View	Changes the type of marker or axis presentation within a specific chart type.
Bar/Column Overlap	Overlaps bars or columns by a percentage if you enter a positive number. 50 is full overlap. A negative number separates individual bars or columns.
Bar/Column Gap Width	Specifies the space between groups of bars or columns. Measured as a percentage of one bar or column width.
Format Vary by Category	Specifies a different color or pattern by category for each marker in all pie charts or any chart with one data series.
Format Drop Lines	Drops a vertical line from a marker to the category (X) axis. Used on line or area charts.
Format Hi-Lo Lines	Draws a line between the highest and lowest lines at a specific category. Used on 2-D line charts.
Format Up/Down Lines	Draws a rectangle from the opening price to closing price on open-high-low-close types of line charts used to track stock prices.
Angle of First Pie Slice	Specifies the starting angle in degrees for the first wedge in a pie chart. Vertical is zero degrees.
3-D Gap Depth	Specifies the spacing in depth between markers as a percentage of a marker. 50 sets the space of the depth between markers to 50% of a marker width.
3-D Chart Depth	Specifies how deep a 3-D chart is relative to its width. Enter a number (between 20 and 2000) as a percentage of the chart width. The 50 makes the depth 50% of the width.

V

Publishing with Graphics

If you did not choose a combination chart as your first chart type, you can change your chart to include an overlay. To add data series to an overlay or to create an overlay, select the data series in the data sheet or select the markers in the chart. Choose the DataSeries Move to Overlay command.

When you add a data series as an overlay to an existing chart, the data series will be marked on the left by a large white dot. To change the format of an overlay, use the Format Overlay command as described earlier in this section.

Fig. 26.11
The Format Chart
dialog box.

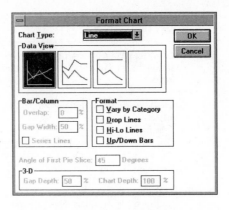

Fig. 26.12
The Format
Overlay dialog
box.

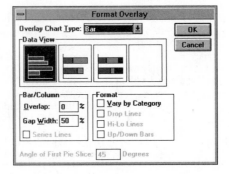

To remove a data series from the overlay, select the data series or the markers, and then choose the DataSeries Move To **Main** command. To completely remove an overlay, move all of the data series in the overlay back to the main chart.

Formatting the Data Sheet

The proper formatting of your data sheet is important for reasons other than ensuring the ease and accuracy of data entry. The format of dates and numbers in the data sheet controls the format of dates and numbers in the chart.

Adjusting Column Widths in the Data Sheet

When numbers are entered in unformatted cells, they appear in General format. If the column is not wide enough to display the full number, the number's format changes to scientific format. 6,000,000, for example, changes to 6E+6. When a number is too large to fit in a cell, the cell fills with # signs.

Microsoft Graph uses the same numeric and date formatting methods as Microsoft Excel—methods also shared by many of the numeric and date formatting switches used with Word for Windows field codes. Microsoft Graph has all of Microsoft Excel's custom numeric and date formatting capability.

To adjust column width with the mouse, move the pointer over the line separating the column headings until the pointer changes to a two-headed arrow. Drag the column separator line to the column width you want and release the mouse button.

To adjust column width by keyboard, select cells in the columns you want to adjust, then choose the Format Column Width command. The Column Width dialog box appears. In the Column Width edit box, type a number representing the width of the column, and then choose OK.

You can return column widths to their standard setting by choosing the Standard Width check box in the Column Width dialog box.

Formatting Numbers and Dates

Microsoft Graph has many predefined numeric and date formats. You can choose from these formats to format the data sheet and chart or to create your own custom formats.

The format of the first data cell in a series defines the numeric or date format for that series in the chart. You can even enter a date such as 12-24-92 as a label for a category axis. You can then format the cell with a different date format (such as *d-mmm*, and the date appears as 12-Dec).

To format data cells, follow these steps:

1. Select the data cell or range you want to format. You can select entire rows or columns at one time.

2. Choose the Format Column WidthFormat Number command.

   The Number dialog box displays a list of different numeric and date formats.

3. Select from the list the numeric or date format you want to apply to the selected data cells.

4. Choose OK.

V

Publishing with Graphics

The items in the list may appear strange until you understand the symbols used to represent different numeric and date formats. The following table explains these symbols:

Character	Purpose
#	Position holder for numbers that use comma placeholders. It *will not* represent blank values, such as the trailing zeros to the right of the decimal.
0	Position holder for leading or trailing zeros
$	Displays a dollar sign. Values are rounded up because of no trailing zeros.
( ) parentheses	Enclose negative numbers
m	Represents months (m = 6, mm = 06, mmm = Jun, mmmm = June)
d	Represents days (d = 6, dd = 06, ddd = Tue, ddd = Tuesday)
y	Represents years (yy = 93, yyyy = 1993)
h	Represents hours
m following h	Represents minutes
AM/PM	Indicates 12-hour clock. No AM/PM indicates 24-hour clock.

The following table gives examples of the different formats:

Format	Entry	Result
#,###	9999.00	9,999
#,###.00	9999.5	9,999.50
$#,###	9000.65	$9,001
0.00 ;(0.00)	5.6	$5.60
0.00 ;(0.00)	-9.834	($9.83)
mmm	12	Dec
dd	6	06
yy	1991	91
hh:mm AM/PM	6:12	06:12 AM

Microsoft Graph also enables you to format numbers differently, depending upon whether they are positive or negative numbers. The format pattern that defines these two formats has two parts—one for positive and one for negative. You use a semicolon to separate positive and negative format patterns. For example,

$#,##0.00 ;($#,##0.00)

produces a different appearance for positive and negative numbers, as shown in the following example:

The number	Appears as
89875.4	$89,875.40
–567.23	($567.23)

In the format example, you see that a space separates the end of the positive number and the semicolon. You can use this space when you are formatting negative numbers in parentheses. This space appears after the positive number in the column to balance the trailing parenthesis on a negative number and helps positive and negative numbers align when a column has right alignment.

Custom Formatting of Numbers and Dates

If the format you need is not in the Number Format list, you can create your own custom formats by typing them into the Format text box. Use the same characters as those used in the predefined formats. After you create a custom format, it appears at the bottom of the Number Format list so that you can reuse it. *Using Excel for Windows,* Special Edition, published by Que, covers creating custom formats extensively.

For Related Information
- "Formatting Characters," p. 246
- "Formatting Field Results," p. 1085

Adding Items to a Chart

You can add many items to your Microsoft Graph charts that make the charts more informative and easier to read.

Some of the items you add are movable and some are fixed. Items fixed in position appear with white handles at their corners when selected. You cannot move or resize fixed items. You can move or resize items that display black handles when selected.

Adding Titles and Data Values

You can use the Chart menu to add or delete most items from a chart. To add a title or data point to a fixed location on a chart, for example, follow these steps:

1. Choose the Chart Titles command.

The Chart Titles dialog box appears (see fig. 26.13).

Fig. 26.13

The Chart Titles
dialog box.

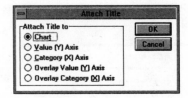

2. Select one of the option buttons.

3. Choose OK.

Depending upon your option choice in step 2, a default title of Title, X, Y, or Z appears at the appropriate location in the chart.

4. While that default title is selected, type the title text you want to use. Press Enter to move to a second line. Edit using normal editing keys.

5. To finish the text, Press Esc or click outside the text.

To remove fixed text, select the text and then press the Del key or choose the Edit Clear command.

To attach numbers or labels that move with the data point in a bar, column, or line chart, follow these steps:

1. Choose the Chart Data Labels command.

2. Select the Show Value or Show Label option. If you are working with a pie chart, the Show Percent option is available.

3. Choose OK.

To delete data point values or labels, select them and press Del, or choose the Chart Data Labels command and select the None option.

Adding Floating Text

You can use *floating text* to add comment boxes or to create boxes for embellishing or covering parts of a chart.

To add floating text, make sure that no other text is selected and then type. You don't have to choose a command; just type. Your text appears in a floating box surrounded by black handles. To complete the box, click outside it or press Esc.

When you first type a title or if you select it by clicking it, black *handles* (squares) surround the text. The black handles on selected text indicate that you can resize and move the enclosing box by dragging it to a new location or by dragging a handle to resize the box. You can format floating text boxes to include colors and patterns.

To select text with the keyboard so that it can be formatted, press the arrow keys until the text you want formatted is enclosed by black or white handles. Floating text cannot be moved by keyboard.

To edit the text in a floating text box, click the text to select it, and then click where you want the insertion point. If you are using a keyboard, you must retype the text. To delete a floating text box, select the text and then press the Del key, or use Edit Clear.

Adding Legends, Arrows, and Gridlines

To add a legend, choose the Chart Add Legend command. The legend that appears is enclosed with black handles. To move a legend, select it and then choose the Format Legend command, or drag the legend to a new location and release it.

To change the labels in the legend, change the series labels in the data sheet. You cannot resize a legend.

To add arrows to your charts, make sure an arrow is not selected, and then choose the ChartAdd Arrow command. If an arrow is selected, the Chart Delete Arrow command replaces the Chart Add Arrow command. Notice that arrows have black handles at either end so that you can resize them. To move an arrow, drag with the pointer on the arrow's shaft. You can format arrows to appear with different heads and thicknesses, or as a line.

To add gridlines to a chart, choose the Chart Gridlines command. The Gridlines dialog box that appears has many check boxes for vertical and horizontal gridlines. To delete gridlines, choose the Chart Gridlines command again and clear the check boxes for the gridlines you don't want.

Formatting the Chart and Chart Items

After you select a predefined chart format and add chart items, you can customize your chart. You can change the colors, patterns, and borders of chart items; the type and color of the fonts; the position and size of some chart items; and you can add lines, arrows, titles, legends, and floating text. By selecting an axis and then a format command, you can change the scale and the appearance of tick marks and labels. You also can rotate 3-D charts and create picture charts, in which pictures take the place of columns, bars, or lines.

Customize charts by selecting an item in the chart, and then choosing a format command, as in the following steps:

1. Select the chart item you want to customize by clicking it or by pressing an arrow key until the chart item is selected.

2. Choose the Format menu and a formatting command to format the item. A dialog box appears that provides choices for the type of formatting you want to apply or change.

3. Select the changes you want to make from the dialog box.

4. Choose OK.

As a shortcut, you can double-click any chart item—such as an arrow, bar, or chart background—to produce that item's Pattern dialog box. You then can change the item's pattern, border, color, or line weight, or choose one of the buttons in the dialog box to display another dialog box such as Font, Scale, or Text.

Sizing Your Chart
Your charts look best in Word for Windows if you resize the chart in Microsoft Graph. Resizing the chart in Word for Windows changes the size, but does not correct text placement, readjust the scale, and so on. By sizing the chart in Microsoft Graph before you update it in Word for Windows, you use Microsoft Graph's capability to reposition and resize elements in the chart.

Change the size of the chart as you would change the size of any window. You can drag its borders or corners with the mouse. You can choose the Size command from the Document Control Menu, press Alt+- (hyphen), and then press the arrow keys to resize the window. Make the chart's window the size you want the chart to be when you paste it into the Word for Windows document.

Although you can change the magnification of the graph, doing so does not change the size of the chart when pasted into the document. A magnified view can be useful when you are formatting or positioning text or arrows. To magnify or shrink your view of the chart, select the **Window** menu and choose a percentage to magnify or shrink.

Changing Patterns and Colors

To add patterns or colors to an item, choose the Format **Pattern** command, and then select the colors, patterns, shading, and line widths you want for the item. With a mouse, double-click an item to display the item's Pattern dialog box.

To return to the default colors, patterns, and borders, select the chart items you want to change, choose the Format Patterns command, and then select the Automatic option.

Note

Microsoft Graph supplies only 16 colors, but you can blend them to create your own colors. To create your own color palette, choose the Format Color Palette command. When the Palette dialog box appears, select the color you want to replace, and then choose the Edit button. When the custom palette appears, type in new color numbers or click in the palette, and then choose OK. The custom color replaces the color you previously selected. To return to the original color settings, choose the Default button.

Formatting Fonts and Text

Every data sheet is formatted with a single font, size, and style. You can use a different font, size, or style, however, for each text item in the chart.

To change an item's font, size, or style, select the item, and then choose the Format Font command. Select a font, size, or style. With a mouse, double-click the item, and then choose the Font button to tunnel through to the

Font dialog box. The Font dialog box looks like other Font dialog boxes in Word for Windows, but it enables you to select different types of character backgrounds.

To rotate or align text—such as the text on an axis—select the text or axis, and then choose the Format Text command. Select the text orientation from the options and choose OK.

Formatting Axes

Microsoft Graph automatically scales and labels the axes, but you can select any axis and change its scale. You also can change how frequently labels or tick marks appear on an axis, or the orientation and font of text.

Microsoft Graph scales charts to even amounts. To rescale your charts, select the axis (vertical or horizontal) and then choose the Format Scale command. (A shortcut is to double-click an axis. When the Pattern dialog box appears, choose the Scale button.) A different dialog box appears, depending on which axis you select.

If you select the Category (X) Axis, you can change tick marks types and spacing or labels spacing along the horizontal axis. If you select the Value (Y) Axis, you can change the beginning and ending values of the vertical axis, and the amount of increments and type of tick marks on that axis. Fig. 26.14 shows the Format Axis Scale dialog box that appears when you select the Value (Y) Axis.

Fig. 26.14

Format Axis Scale dialog box for the Value (Y) Axis.

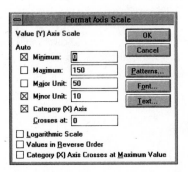

To thin out the number of tick marks or overlapping labels along the category (X) axis, select the axis, and then choose the Format Scale command. The Format Axis Scale dialog box for the Category (X) Axis appears (see fig. 26.15). Select the text boxes for either or both the Number Of Categories (or Series) Between Tick Labels and Number Of Categories (or Series) Between Tick Marks options. If you enter five in a box, for example, every fifth tick mark and label is displayed. Choose OK.

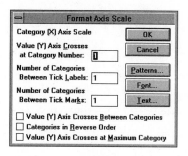

Fig. 26.15
The Format Axis Scale dialog box for the Category (X) axis.

To change how tick marks appear on an axis scale, double-click the axis or select the axis, and then choose the Format Pattern command. In the Axis Patterns dialog box that appears, you will be able to change the type of axis line, as well as the positioning of tick marks on the axis.

Rotating 3-D Charts

You can rotate the angle of your 3-D chart to display the chart's best view. To rotate a 3-D chart, follow these steps:

1. Choose the Format 3-D View command. The Format 3-D View dialog box appears (see fig. 26.16).

2. Select the Elevation, Perspective, or Rotation buttons by clicking them or typing values into them. Changing their values affects the wire frame sample chart.

3. When the wire frame sample is oriented so that you can see the chart as you want, choose OK.

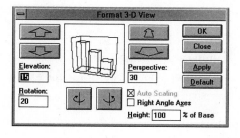

Fig. 26.16
The Format 3-D View dialog box.

For Related Information
- "Formatting Characters," p. 246

- "Moving and Positioning Frames," p. 699

- "Sizing Frames," p. 710

The Apply button enables you to apply the new orientation to the chart and keep the dialog box open—a helpful feature when you want to experiment. Choose the **Default** button to return to the original orientation.

Exiting or Updating Graphs

You can keep Microsoft Graph open and update the chart in Word for Windows, or close Microsoft Graph and update the chart. Updating the chart embeds the chart and its data in the Word for Windows document. You cannot save the chart and data separately—they must be saved as embedded objects within the Word for Windows document.

You need not close Microsoft Graph to see your chart or its changes in the Word for Windows document. To keep Microsoft Graph open and update the new or existing chart in the document, choose the File Update command.

When you exit Microsoft Graph, you are given a chance to update the new or existing chart in Word for Windows. To exit Microsoft Graph, choose the File Exit and Return to document command. If you made changes since the last update, you are prompted to update the chart in the document. Choose Yes to update the chart.

From Here...

If you are familiar with charting in Microsoft Excel, use what you learned in Microsoft Excel to learn about Microsoft Graph. For more detailed information on Microsoft Graph, refer to the book *Using Excel for Windows*, Special Edition, published by Que Corporation. Many of the descriptions, tips, and tricks used in this best-selling book apply to Microsoft Graph.

- Chapter 22, "Inserting Pictures in Your Document." Learn how to use charts or graphs you have created in more complex graphics applications.

- Chapter 23, "Framing and Moving Text and Graphics." With the information you learn in this chapter, you can frame a graph and move it anywhere on the page.

- Chapter 37, "Automating with Field Codes." Graphs are actually controlled by field codes that are normally hidden. Chapter 37 enables you to reveal and edit these codes.

Chapter 27

Desktop Publishing

In the years since word processing programs and desktop publishing programs have both come to be widely used, the two have grown more and more alike. Word processing programs have gained graphics capabilities. Desktop publishing programs have gained text editing capabilities. But until now, no one program really served both needs—the need to work powerfully with text and the need to incorporate graphics and illustrations easily.

Word for Windows successfully bridges the narrowing gap between word processors and desktop publishers. It has the very powerful text handling capabilities that serious publishers need, but at the same time it has surprisingly sophisticated graphics capabilities as well. And like all desktop publishing programs, what Word for Windows cannot do graphically, it can import from other specialized programs.

Word for Windows desktop publishing capabilities include the following:

- The ability to produce typeset-quality text using any font available on your printer or computer, in scalable sizes ranging from unreadable to bigger than the page

- The ability to lay out text in columns and to vary the number and style of columns throughout your document

- The ability to incorporate lines, boxes, and shading

- The ability to draw pictures directly on the page and to layer them in front of or behind the text

- The ability to manipulate text into a graphic form

- The ability to insert into your publication illustrations created in other graphics programs

In this chapter, you learn to do the following:

- Understand the basic elements of design

- Use templates and other tools to work more efficiently

- Design with text

- Create envelopes, letterhead, and brochures.

V

Publishing with Graphics

■ The ability to drag text and other objects freely on the page, with text wrapping around them

■ The ability to use templates to save time when you produce periodicals, and styles to ensure consistent formatting throughout a publication. Use Word for Windows to create publications including newsletters, catalogs, brochures, stationery, business cards, manuals, price lists, advertisements—anything that needs to make a visual impact on readers.

Fig. 27.1
This newsletter was created using Word for Windows desktop publishing features.

Fig. 27.1 shows an example of desktop publishing using Word for Windows.

As you venture into the world of desktop publishing, keep in mind that desktop publishing is not a single skill—rather, it is the successful and creative use of many different skills. Throughout this chapter, you see examples of how you can use Word for Windows as a desktop publishing program, and you read about the skills you need to do similar projects yourself. You also see references to earlier chapters in this book where you can learn more about the skills you need. But to become a successful desktop publisher, first become familiar with Word's basic features and capabilities. Learning these features makes your publishing job easier.

Designing Your Publication

When you approach the task of designing a publication, you're confronted with a question that is at the same time both simple and overwhelming: How will it look? If graphic design isn't your trade, the task can seem daunting. But if you break this big job into bite-size pieces, it becomes much more manageable.

A good way to start to answer the question of how your publication will look is to look around you. If you're designing a newsletter or brochure, look at other newsletters or brochures. If you're designing an ad, browse through a magazine or newspaper similar to the one where your ad may appear. Look at desktop publishing magazines and books that teach about design. Notice what works and doesn't work. Notice what you like and don't like. Make some notes.

After you do some research into what other designers are doing, you see that desktop publishing isn't so hard—that design is simply arranging text and graphics on a page in an effective way. With Word for Windows, you have the tools to do it yourself.

Planning Your Publication

Planning is the first step in producing a successful publication. Start the planning process by analyzing your task. If you understand specifically what you have to work with, designing your publication is easier. Your design takes form as you clarify your intent. Don't try to design the ideal newsletter; instead, design *your* newsletter.

If you follow a logical sequence of steps that lead you from concept, through visual brainstorming, to implementing the design, you can design an effective publication. Try following these six steps in planning your publication:

1. *Research the task.* Find out as much as you can about the publication you plan to design. Make sure you understand its content, its purpose, its audience, its central message, and its tone. If you're working with a client (or boss), ask specific questions about what he or she envisions. Use this information to develop, refine, and analyze your ideas and to choose the final design.

V

Publishing with Graphics

2. *Develop preliminary ideas.* On a couple of blank sheets of paper, draw small boxes (an inch square or so) in the shape of your publication. Visually brainstorm ideas for a design. Work fast on these thumbnail sketches, and don't censor yourself. Do lots of them. Don't show them to your client.

3. *Refine the design.* Go through your thumbnails and pick three that work the best. Draw each of them in more detail in full size. Take time with these drawings and think about all the details—text size, graphics, color. In this chapter, read the sections "Using the Building Blocks of Design" and "Understanding the Elements of Effective Design" for ideas about designing your publication.

4. *Analyze the potential designs.* Carefully analyze each of your three detailed designs. Do they meet the needs you've outlined for this publication? Can you implement them in Word for Windows? Do you have the tools (printers, scanners, and so on) and resources (writers, illustrators, and so on) you need to produce them?

5. *Make the decision.* From among your three designs, choose the one that best meets all the criteria you've outlined for this publication.

6. *Implement the design.* Now comes the fun part: working with Word for Windows to produce your publication.

Using the Building Blocks of Design

When you design a publication, you're working with a specific medium. In the same way that a sculptor works with clay or a painter with paint and canvas, you work with text, graphics, and illustrations on paper. Your goal is to integrate the building blocks of design into a pleasing publication.

As you work on your design, keep three goals in mind:

■ Design with variety, but be consistent in applying your design variations.

■ Strive for a unified tone by choosing design elements that complement one another.

■ Remember that the goal of any publication is to communicate—design your publication to serve that goal.

The Page. When you think about your publication's design, think about the whole page. It is the skeleton of your design, and it contains every other piece of your design: the text, the graphics, the illustrations, and even the paper.

At its simplest level, a designed page is divided into two elements: positive space and negative space. The positive space is occupied by anything you put on the page—text, graphics, and illustrations. The negative space surrounds the positive space.

The text, lines, boxes, graphics, and illustrations you place on a page form a design of their own when you see them against the surrounding negative space. Strive to make this design work. One way to see whether it works is to cut pieces in the shape of your positive images from black paper and arrange them on a white background. How can you best arrange the pieces? Another way to see whether your design works is to squint at the page until everything turns into a blur. In this way you simplify complex images into their basic shapes. Does the arrangement work, or can you move things around to make it work better?

One of the most basic rules for designing a page is this: keep the positive images together as much as you can so that you break up the negative space as little as possible.

An excellent tool for designing a page is the grid system (see fig. 27.2). To create a design grid, divide your page into equal-sized rectangles using vertical and horizontal lines. Then place all the objects on a page within that grid so that everything is the size of some whole number of rectangles. If your grid has six vertical columns, for example, you may have two columns of text on the page (each as wide as three grid columns) or three columns of text (each as wide as two grid columns), but not four or five columns of text. If you include photos or other illustrations, they are as wide as any whole number of columns, but not one and one-half or three and one-half columns wide. If your grid has three horizontal rows, you may place photos in the top third, the middle third, or the bottom third of the page, but not halfway between the top and middle thirds. This example might be a good grid for a newsletter you fold into thirds to fit in a business-size envelope.

By using the grid and remembering to keep objects together on the page, you can create a harmonious design.

Fig. 27.2
You can design
your publication
using a grid
system. All the
pieces of your
publication should
fit within the grid.

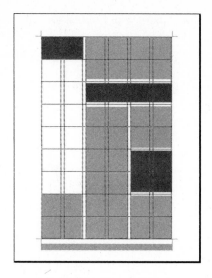

Text. Text is the first object you put on a page. Even if it is the only object on the page, you can make your publication interesting by varying the uses of text and designing an effective layout.

There are two basic types of fonts you can use in a publication: serif and sans serif. *Serif* fonts have characters of uneven thickness with small strokes, or serifs, at the tips of each letter. *Sans serif* fonts have characters of uniform thickness, and no serifs. Serif fonts are considered easier to read for body copy; sans serif fonts are preferred for display type above 14 points or so. Windows includes a serif font, Times New Roman, and a sans serif font, Arial (see fig. 27.3). Your printer may have additional fonts, and you can purchase others.

Fig. 27.3
Serif fonts like the
popular Times are
considered easier
to read for body
copy. Sans Serif
fonts like Arial
work well for signs
and display type.

Serifs—Serif (Times)

Sans serif (Arial)

Text performs several functions on the page. It is the body copy, the headings and subheadings, and the titles. Sometimes text is even a graphic when you use it as a drop-cap at the beginning of a paragraph, a pull-quote in a newsletter, or a logo in an advertisement.

Body copy lends color to your publication. If body copy is dense and closely spaced, it looks dark. If body copy is open and widely spaced, it looks much lighter. Readability aside, decide how you want your publication to look. You can adjust your treatment of the body copy through your choice of font, size, and line spacing to achieve the look you want.

One of the most important rules of working with body copy is to keep it consistent. Don't arbitrarily vary the font, size, or line spacing.

Lines, Boxes, and Shading. Lines, boxes, and shading are the graphics built into Word for Windows and desktop publishing programs that you can use to enhance your document's readability and add interest.

You can use lines in many ways: above headings or subheadings, between articles, in headers and footers, or around pull-quotes. Boxes perform a similar function. Use them to enclose lists, to set apart explanatory text, or to highlight tables of contents. Use shading to emphasize important text or to separate sidebars from their main stories.

As you do with text, use lines, boxes, and shading consistently. If you place 2-point lines over some subheadings, place them above all subheadings. If you shade important sidebars, don't shade unimportant information as well. Such graphic devices help readers identify elements on the page.

Use graphics, but don't overuse them. Don't let them overpower your text. If body copy is light, make your graphics light, too. Work within your design grid.

When you include graphics in your publication, make sure they serve a purpose. Don't just include them to have lines on the page. Remember, the goal of a publication is to communicate. Just like text, graphics can help you accomplish that goal.

Illustrations. Illustrations in a publication explain and entertain. They can take many forms: photos, line drawings, clip art, and computer graphics. They can come into your publication from another program or from a scanner. Sometimes you just leave a blank space for noncomputer illustrations in a publication that you plan to print and then take to a commercial printer for duplication.

Like lines and boxes, illustrations should be meaningful in your publication. If you don't really have a use for them, don't use them: do something graphical with the text instead. Illustrations should also be appropriate. Don't use frivolous clip art in a serious journal.

Make sure the illustration's quality is adequate to the job—if you want to use photos, be sure you have the equipment to scan and print them at the resolution you need.

Give illustrations the weight they deserve in your publication. Run an important picture big, and a less important one small. If you have two illustrations, run one big and another small for variety. Focus on your illustrations, cropping away parts you don't need.

Paper. The color and texture of the paper on which you choose to print your publication form the negative space in your design. Even though paper is the last step in the production of your publication, it should be present in your design from the beginning.

Paper is critical in setting the tone of your publication. A cool, smooth, gray paper sets a formal tone, whereas textured and colored paper sets a less formal tone. So many types of paper are available that you easily can find one to match the feeling you want to achieve.

Be aware that any paper that is not white provides less contrast with your text. If the paper is dark, you may need to compensate for lost contrast by using larger or bolder text.

Consider your printer's limitations when you select a paper style. If you plan to mail your publication, paper weight might be a consideration—don't risk increasing postage costs because you've chosen a heavy paper.

Understanding the Elements of Effective Design

Some designers claim that designs should be "SAFE"—Simple, Appropriate, Functional, and Economical.

In your design, strive to achieve the goals of unity, focal point, balance, scale, consistency and contrast, direction, and simplicity.

Unity. Gestalt theory proposes that the whole is greater than the sum of the parts. In design, this theory means the elements of your page work together to form a whole that is stronger than the individual pieces.

You can achieve unity five ways. *Proximity* means that you arrange objects on the page near each other, creating perceptual groups (which helps you keep positive space together on the page as well). *Similarity* means that you use design elements that are similar to each other. *Repetition* means that you repeat elements in a design (it doesn't necessarily mean you repeat them identically). *Continuation* means that you find ways to move the reader's eye from one area of the design to another, in the direction you want the eye to move. *Closure* means that you let the reader's eye complete a shape or thought by leaving out a little bit.

Focal Point. Good design has a focal point. Focal points are especially helpful in complex designs, and they help guide the reader's eye into your publication.

You can create a focal point in many ways:

- *Contrast one form or shape.* Include a circle among squares.

- *Change direction.* Include a diagonal among horizontal lines.

- *Change color.* Place a spot of red on a white background.

- *Change placement.* Ungroup one item and move it away.

- *Change scale.* Make one item smaller or larger than the rest.

- *Simulate depth.* Overlap objects, make something transparent, or place something larger farther down on the page than something smaller.

- *Create a feeling of motion.* Make something blurry or repeat it. Whatever interrupts the eye from a pattern creates a focal point.

Include a focal point, but keep the other rules of design in mind too, and don't let your focal point overwhelm your design.

Balance. Balance is the universal aim of composition. It occurs in design when two forces of equal weight pull in opposite directions (see fig. 27.4). There are two kinds of balance: symmetrical and asymmetrical.

Fig. 27.4
An example of asymmetrical balance: the size of the "YES" balances the dark color of the "NO."

Whereas symmetrical balance is more formal, asymmetrical balance is more visually interesting and exciting. You can achieve it using many techniques:

- *Shape.* Use a simple, large shape to balance a more complex small shape.

- *Texture.* Use a small amount of texture to balance a larger smooth area.

- *Color.* A small spot of bright color balances a large area of neutral color.

- *Value.* A small area of dark balances a large area of light.

- *Size and number.* Two small objects can balance one large object.

- *Direction.* A face looking inward balances a page.

- *Structure.* Sans serif type can balance serif type.

Scale. Organize elements on the page so that they are in proportion to one another. Although you can create interest by varying size, and you can create a focal point by changing scale, maintain a sense of proportion throughout your document.

Don't place a huge headline in a small space at the top of a newsletter, for example; it looks crowded. On the other hand, don't place a tiny headline in a big space. Don't use a thick rule over small type; the rule overwhelms the type. But don't use a hairline rule with big, bold type; the rule gets lost. Be particularly aware of the proportions of positive and negative space in your design.

Consistency and Contrast. Consistency is important in any design. It makes the reader's job easier because she knows what to expect and where to find what she's looking for in your publication. Consistent use of type, graphics, and illustrations signals meaning and is important to communication. Design all your body copy to be the same size, for example, and don't vary line spacing arbitrarily. Do the same with other text elements in your publication.

Place elements on the page in a consistent manner and remember in a facing page layout to design the full two-page spread, because readers see two pages when they open your publication.

Strive also for consistent tone in your publication. If you're preparing a business report with conservative type and graphics, don't print it on party-pink paper. On the other hand, if you are preparing a wild party invitation, get a little crazy with fonts and graphics. But as always, keep the other rules of good design in mind as you do so.

At the same time you strive to keep related elements in your publication consistent, you also should aim for contrast between elements. Subheadings should not be too close in size and style to body copy, for example; if they are, readers can't determine quickly which is which. Contrast makes the page more interesting. Without contrast, the page assumes an all-over unbroken gray tone that doesn't attract the eye anywhere.

Consistency and contrast may seem to be contradictory elements, but they aren't. Be consistent at the detail level, but apply contrast in your design.

Direction. Readers read from the top left of a page to the bottom right. In general, your publication should do the same. Direction can be obvious, or it can be very subtle. In a newsletter, for example, placing the nameplate at the top of the first page and the first article just below it is obvious—you can assume that readers start at the top and read to the bottom. Creating direction in an ad may be a little less obvious; nonetheless, you can design successfully if the most important element of the ad is at the top and the remainder is below it.

Simplicity. Word for Windows has so many text and graphic capabilities that it may be tempting to use them all in your publication. Don't do it. Every part of your design serves a purpose: to further communication. Let communication be your guide and don't let your design get in the way of it. You even must use tools of emphasis with restraint; otherwise, they create a noisy design in which no single element is heard above the rest.

Strive for simple elegance.

Using Word for Windows Desktop Publishing Capabilities

By now, you should have a pretty good idea of what your publication should look like. Now it's time to use Word for Windows to put it together. In this section, you learn which features of Word for Windows you can use in your desktop publications and where in this book to find out more about each feature. You also find tips about designing effectively with Word for Windows desktop publishing features.

V

Publishing with Graphics

Tools to Help You Work

Word for Windows includes many tools you can use as you're designing and developing a publication. You use them to help you work faster and more efficiently. The following sections describe these tools in more detail.

Working in Different Views

Normally, while you're working on a publication, you work in the Page Layout view so that you can see all the page elements (lines, columns, positioned graphics, and so on) and how they will print.

In Page Layout view, use the page size drop-down list on the Standard toolbar (see fig. 27.5) or choose the View Zoom command to set the page width as you want it. The Page Width option is a good working size because you see the whole width of the page, but at a readable size (on most screens). Whole Page shows you the entire page from top to bottom—switch to this view frequently to see how your page is shaping up as a whole. If your publication includes facing pages, select Two Pages so that you can see how your pages look side by side; after all, that's what the reader sees when he opens your publication. All page layout views are completely editable.

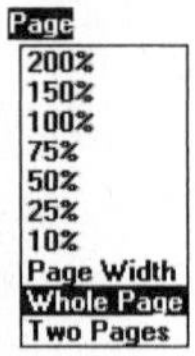

Fig. 27.5
Switch frequently
between close-up
and zoom-out
views to see how
your publication is
shaping up.

To select the Page Layout view, choose the View **P**age Layout command. To hide everything on the screen except your page, choose the View F**u**ll Screen command. Press Esc or click the Full Screen icon to return to the normal page.

Changing the Viewing Options

Most people like to work with the page as it will appear when printed. When you're editing text, however, you might want to display nonprinting characters such as paragraph marks and section breaks. And when you've inserted pictures, you might want to hide them so that you can work faster. When you're working on a page layout with columns, you might want to display text boundaries so that you can see the edges of each column. To maximize the size of your working screen, you can turn off the status bar, scroll bars, and vertical ruler. Choose the Tools Options command and select the View tab to make any of these selections.

Using the Toolbars

Word for Windows provides 11 different toolbars you can use to help you work more quickly. Each toolbar contains tools, or buttons, that you can click for quickly executing a command. Choose the View Toolbars command or click the right mouse button in a toolbar to show a list of the toolbars you can display.

Using Templates

If you use the same layout over and over, create a template to save formatting and any text and graphics that you use each time. Newsletters are good candidates for templates: you can include the nameplate, headers and footers, styles for formatting, columns, mailers, postal indicia, mastheads, and anything else you use each issue. Templates save you the time of re-creating the issue from scratch each time. See the section, "Maintaining Consistent Formatting," later in this chapter.

You use a template each time you choose the File New command. To use a custom template, select it from the Template list in the New dialog box.

Using Wizards

Word for Windows includes Wizards that create instant awards, calendars, fax cover sheets, memos, newsletters, and more. Wizards include all the formatting and graphics needed in a publication—you just supply the text. Use them when you need a quick design. To use a Wizard, choose the File New command and select a template that ends with the word Wizard. Wizards are described in Chapter 6, "Creating or Changing Templates."

Using Styles

When you use repetitive formatting, format with styles. A *style* is a set of remembered formatting characteristics, such as font and size and text alignment. Word for Windows includes many built-in styles, but you can create your own. Styles are easy to apply, and when you format with styles, you can make global formatting changes instantly by simply changing the style. The quickest way to apply an existing style is to choose it from the drop-down list of styles on the Formatting toolbar.

Spelling and Grammar Checkers

Professionals don't let their work go out the door with mistakes. Use Word for Windows spelling checker always and use the grammar checker when

V

Publishing with Graphics

you're unsure about wording. Don't let the spelling checker substitute for careful proofreading, however; it doesn't catch misused words (such as to, too, and two, or there, their, and they're). *Caveat:* We all make mistakes sometimes, and making mistakes isn't the end of the world.

To check spelling, choose the Tools Spelling command or press F7. To check grammar, choose the Tools Grammar command.

For Related Information

- "Controlling Your Document's Appearance On-Screen," p. 115

- "Checking your Spelling," p. 200

- "Checking your Grammar," p. 207

- "Using Templates as a Pattern for Documents," p. 168

- "Using Wizards to Guide You in Creating Documents," p. 174

- "Using the Toolbars," p. 42

Laying Out the Page

Your publication's page layout includes the size of its pages, page orientation, and margins. These global choices are among the first you make as you start to assemble your publication.

Paper Size

You can design your publication to use a standard paper size, such as letter or legal. Or you can select a custom paper size. To select paper size, choose the File Page Setup command, then select the Paper Size tab and make your selections.

- Select a standard size paper for newsletters, flyers, stationery, reports, catalogs, and brochures. Be aware of what sizes of paper your printer can accommodate.

- Choose a custom paper size to create invitations, business cards, envelopes, and other items that are smaller than usual. Most laser printers include a manual paper feed for printing custom paper sizes.

Paper Orientation

Word for Windows can print your publication vertically on the page, called *portrait* orientation, or horizontally, called *landscape* orientation. Paper orientation applies to any page size. To select paper orientation, choose the File Page Setup command, select the Paper Size tab, and select either Portrait or Landscape.

- Use portrait orientation for most publications, such as newsletters and catalogs.

- Use landscape orientation to create two-fold (three-panel) brochures, signs, and horizontally oriented advertisements.

Margins

Margins are the distance between text and the edges of the page. You can set top, bottom, left, and right margins for any size page. To set margins, choose the File Page Setup command, select the Margins tab, and set your margins.

In any type of publication, margins may be your most important tool in creating unified white space on the page—whenever possible, be generous with your margins. Don't crowd the page.

Also, don't vary margins arbitrarily from page to page in your document.

Facing Pages for Newsletters, Catalogs, Magazines, and Books

You see facing pages when you open a magazine or book: the left and right pages face each other. To create facing pages, select mirror margins. Instead of left and right margins, you set inside and outside margins. Very often the inside margin is wider than the outside margin—both for design and to accommodate binding. To select facing pages, choose the File Page Setup command, select the Margins tab, and select the Mirror Margins option.

- Use facing pages to create a newsletter, magazine, catalog, book, or any other type of publication that you plan to print on both sides of a sheet of paper and for which you want wider inside margins.

- When you're using mirror margins, position page numbers on the outside edges of each page.

Binding Gutters for Extra Margin Width

Whether or not you're using facing pages, you can add extra space to the gutter for binding. If you add extra space on facing pages, you add it to inside edges; on regular pages, you add space to the left edge. Gutters don't change your margins but rather are added to margins. Gutters make the printing area of your page narrower, however. To add gutters, choose the File Page Setup command, select the Margins tab, and select the gutter width you want using the Gutter option.

- Use gutters in any document in which you need extra margin space for binding. Examples include price lists, training manuals, and reports.

- Consider adding extra gutter width any time you design with facing pages.

Changing the Page Layout Within a Document

You can vary page layout options such as margins, headers and footers, number of columns, page numbers, and even page size and orientation within a single document. Any time you want to make these changes, you must insert a section break. A new section can start on the same page, the next column, the next page, or the next odd- or even-numbered page. To insert a section break, choose the Insert Break command and select an option from the Section Breaks group.

- Use a section break in a newsletter to separate a one-column nameplate from the three-column text of the newsletter.

- Use a section break to separate an envelope and letterhead, each with unique margins, in a single document.

- Use section breaks to start each new chapter in a book; therefore, each chapter can start on a right-facing page.

- Use section breaks to separate a report into sections so that each section can have unique headers and footers, or unique page numbering.

Including Headers and Footers

Headers and footers appear in the top and bottom margins of each page in your document. They can include any font in any size, as well as illustrations, lines and boxes, automatic page numbers, the date or time, and even chapter numbers. You can format headers and footers using any of Word for Windows formatting commands. To add headers and footers, choose the View Header and Footer command.

- Use headers and footers in any type of multipage publication, including newsletters, books, reports, catalogs, price lists, and much more.

- Use headers and footers to repeat text or graphics consistently on every page.

- Headers and footers can be different from section to section, or on the first page of a document. On a newsletter, for example, you usually want the first-page headers and footers to be different from those on remaining pages.

Positioning Text and Graphics in the Margins

Usually text is confined to the space between margins on your page—with the exception of headers and footers. But sometimes you want text and graphics to appear in the left or right margin of your page. You can use text in the margin if you frame the text or graphic and then position it in the margin. If you position a framed object so that it is only partially inside a margin, text on the page wraps around it. To frame text or an object, select it and choose the Insert Frame command. To position a framed object, drag it with the mouse or select it and choose the Format Frame command.

For Related Information
■ "Setting Margins," p. 402

■ "Creating Headers and Footers," p. 414

■ "Changing Layouts Within a Document," p. 432

- Position pull-quotes, sidebars, and illustrations in the margin of a newsletter.

- Create an ad, flyer, or res'um'e with an illustration or big headline that extends across both the margin and text, with text wrapping around it.

Designing with Text

Text is the primary building block of most publications—because most publications are meant to be read. Although decisions about text may seem simple, they are important to your design.

Consistency is the first rule in working with text on the page: make your titles, headings, subheadings, pull-quotes, captions—any text you use regularly in your publication—consistent from use to use.

Selecting the Font

Windows comes equipped with two TrueType fonts that you use often in your desktop publishing projects: Times New Roman, a serif font; and Arial, a sans serif font. Your printer may include additional fonts, and you may purchase still others. Any fonts you've installed in Windows are available in Word for Windows, but even if you have only Times and Arial, you have enough variety for desktop publishing. To change fonts, position the insertion point where you want a new font to begin, or select existing text, and then choose the Format Font command. Or select a different font from the fonts list on the Formatting toolbar.

- If your publication includes paragraphs of text to read, a serif font like Times is best—the serifs carry the eye from letter to letter and make reading easier. If you have a big, bold headline to be seen from a distance, a sans serif font like Arial is a better choice.

- Mix fonts but use only two or three (at most) per publication. Set body copy in Times, for example, and headlines in Arial.

■ Use unusual or decorative fonts only when you have an unusual purpose. Use them sparingly.

■ Make readability your primary consideration when you select a font.

Selecting the Font Size

With TrueType, you can make letters as tiny or as big as you want—from 1 to 1,638 points (non-TrueType printer fonts may be limited in size). Use 72-point type to create a one-inch letter. To change font size, position the insertion point where you want a new font size to begin, or select existing text, and then choose the Format Font command. Or select a different font from the font size list on the Formatting toolbar.

■ Text for reading should be between 9 and 11 points for most fonts (although readability varies considerably among fonts, so print a sample before you decide). Text for subheadings and headlines should be from 14 points and up.

■ If your publication includes titles, headings, and subheadings, size them consistently throughout your publication (an easy way to size headings is to use styles—see "Maintaining Consistent Formatting" later in this chapter). Be sure you have enough difference in the size of body text, subheadings, headings, and titles so that the reader can tell which is which at a glance.

Choosing Text Styles and Color

You can apply bold, italic, bold italic, and other styles to most fonts (you may not be able to choose these styles for some specialty fonts). You also can apply color to text—you see it in color on-screen, but you need a color printer to print color. To change font color, position the insertion point where you want a new color to begin, or select existing text, and then choose the Format Font command.

■ Use text styles sparingly and meaningfully. Save bold for headlines and subheadings in a publication or for big headlines in flyers and ads. Reserve italics for titles and occasional emphasis. Use all caps rarely; small caps is a better design choice (all caps are hard to read and were used for emphasis or contrast when people used typewriters, not computers capable of producing typeset-quality output).

■ Color is useful in publications that are never printed but rather are used on-screen or in a presentation that you project in front of an audience.

In an ad or flyer or to create a banner or newsletter nameplate, try dark or light gray. Make the text big to compensate for the loss of contrast when text is lighter than black.

Using Typesetting Characters

Special typesetting characters take the place of a typewriter's straight quotation marks and double dashes, and they're easy to insert in Word for Windows. Instead of a double dash, use an em dash (like a wide hyphen). Instead of straight quotation marks, use opening and closing quotation marks. To insert typesetting characters, choose the Insert Symbol command and select the Special Characters tab.

- An em dash is the width of your point size—if your text is 10 points, an em dash is 10 points wide. Use it to indicate a pause. An en dash is half the width of your point size; use it between numbers or times (for example, "from 9–12 p.m.").

- Always use "typesetting" quotation marks in a publication, rather than straight quotation marks. Typesetting quotation marks curve inward toward the text (see fig. 27.6). Use an opening quotation mark at the beginning of a quote and a closing quotation mark at the end; both single and double quotation marks are available.

> "Eat your peas," she said.
> regular quote marks
>
> "Eat your peas," she said.
> typesetting quotes

Fig. 27.6
Always use typesetting quotation marks in a publication.

- Word for Windows includes other special characters, such as trademark and registration symbols, that you should use when appropriate.

Controlling the Letter Spacing

Word for Windows automatically controls the spacing between letters, and usually Word's setting is fine. You optionally can expand or condense spacing (called *tracking* when you use it on all your text), and you can turn on *kerning*, which adjusts the spacing between letter pairs. Usually, kerning reduces the space between adjacent letters like *AV* or *Yo* that are too far apart with normal spacing. In Word for Windows, you can turn on automatic kerning, or you can kern letter pairs individually. To change letter spacing, select the text, and then choose the Format Font command. Select the Character Spacing tab.

- Turn on automatic kerning for type larger than body copy size—usually over 10 points.

- Kern headlines as needed. To kern individual letter pairs, position the insertion point between the two letters and condense the spacing as needed.

- For large headlines, select the entire headline and condense the spacing slightly, until it looks tight but not crowded.

- Sometimes you can condense, or track, text slightly to make it fit on a line when space is tight.

- Use expanded type only for special effects.

Using Titles, Headings, and Subheadings

Appropriate titles, headings, and subheadings help guide readers through text. When you see a title, you know an article is about to begin. When you see a subheading, you know a new concept is starting. These "meaning markers" are invaluable to readers.

- Format titles, headings, and subheadings consistently. In your newsletter, for example, make the titles of all feature articles 24 points bold; make less important titles 18 points bold; and make subheadings 12 points bold.

- For titles, headings, and subheadings, choose a font that contrasts with the body copy font. A sans serif font is a good choice.

- Use styles to maintain consistent formatting.

Determining Alignment and Justification

Text can be left-aligned, centered, right-aligned, or justified (aligned to both margins). To align text, select the text or position the insertion point inside the paragraph you want to align and choose the Format Paragraph command. Select the Indents and Spacing tab and make a selection from the Alignment list. Or, select the Left Align, Center, Right Align, or Justify button on the Formatting toolbar.

- Always use left-aligned text for body copy. It is easiest to read because the reader's eye knows exactly where to go to start a new line.

- Use centered text sparingly—for invitations, logos, and, occasionally, headlines.

- Use right-aligned text only when you have a specific reason to do so, such as in tables, or in a header or footer on a right-facing page.

- When you use justified text (even on both sides), Word for Windows must increase the spacing between words. Be sure to use hyphenation with justified text to avoid gaping spaces between words.

Adjusting Line and Paragraph Spacing

In Word for Windows, you can add extra space before and after paragraphs, and you can adjust the spacing between the lines in a paragraph. In typographical terms, the spacing between lines is called *leading* (pronounced "ledding"). You can adjust line spacing, or leading, by lines ("1.5 lines" or "double") or by some specified amount ("At Least" or "Exactly"). If you specify an amount, you measure it by points, the same way font size is measured. Normal leading for 10-point type, for example, is 12 points; to increase leading, you increase line spacing to a larger point size. To adjust line and paragraph spacing, choose the Format Paragraph command and select the Indents and Spacing tab. Make selections from the Spacing group.

- Add spacing before subheadings to help them stand out from the rest of your text.

- Add spacing after paragraphs instead of pressing Enter twice each time you finish a paragraph. Often half a line of extra spacing looks better than a whole line. If you need to change the spacing later, you can select all the paragraphs and make the change quickly.

- Use styles to apply line spacing consistently in your document.

- Increase line spacing (leading) when lines in your paragraph are longer than about 40 characters. Long, tightly spaced lines are hard to read because the reader's eye gets lost as it travels back to the left margin.

- Increase line spacing for graphical effect in pull-quotes, invitations, flyers, and other occasions when you're using type decoratively.

Keeping Text Together

Word for Windows breaks text at the bottom of a page regardless of whether the page ends at the beginning of a paragraph or between the lines of a two-line subheading. You can prevent unwanted breaks, however. To keep text together, select the text and choose the Format Paragraph command. Select the Text Flow tab.

- Select the **Widow/Orphan Control** option to prevent single lines at the beginning of paragraphs from appearing at the bottom of a page, or single lines at the end of a paragraph from appearing at the top of a page. Widows and orphans are bad form in any publication.

- Select the Keep Lines Together option when you don't want a paragraph to break between two pages.

- Select the Keep with Next option when you want a subheading to stay with the paragraph that follows it.

Maintaining Consistent Formatting

Styles are one of word processing's greatest inventions (one that is shared by most desktop publishing programs). A *style* is simply a set of remembered formatting commands that you can apply instantly and change globally. Styles are invaluable to desktop publishers because they save time, enforce consistent formatting, and allow for experimentation. Styles are often included in templates. You can create or apply a style by choosing the Format Style command.

- Use styles to format body copy, subheadings, headings, titles, pull-quotes, tables, lists—just about everything. You save time creating your publication because you have to invent your formatting only once. And your publication benefits from a consistent appearance.

- Use styles to experiment with design. If you format your whole publication with styles, you can change formatting throughout your publication just by changing the style. If you don't like the change, try something else.

- Use Word for Windows built-in heading styles, Heading 1 through Heading 9, to format anything you may later want to collect into tables, lists, or cross-references. You can change the style—you just have to keep the name.

Indenting Paragraphs

Don't press Tab to indent the first line of every paragraph. Instead, create an automatic indent. It saves time because each new paragraph you create is indented automatically. You can create indents by using the ruler or the Paragraph dialog box. To indent paragraphs, select the paragraph and choose the Format Paragraph command. Select the Indents and Spacing tab and make selections from the Indentation group. Or select the paragraph and drag the indentation markers on the horizontal ruler.

- Don't make paragraph indents too deep—half an inch is too deep for most paragraphs. Try a quarter inch.

- Use hanging indents to create lists.

Creating Lists

Word for Windows includes two tools to help you make lists quickly and attractively: the Bulleted List button and the Numbered List button. Both are on the Word for Windows toolbar.

- Always use a hanging indent to create an itemized list (this chapter contains bulleted lists with hanging indents). You can get a hanging indent by clicking the Bulleted or Numbered List button, by using the Bullets and Numbering dialog box, by using the ruler, or by using the Paragraph dialog box.

- Customize lists by using dingbats rather than bullets. Choose the Insert Symbols command to insert a special character.

Using Text as Graphics

Text becomes a graphic when you use it as a logo, as a newsletter nameplate, as a drop cap (see fig. 27.7), or any time you make it decorative rather than expository. You can change text to a graphic in many ways in Word for Windows: by using WordArt, by creating a drop cap, by enclosing it in a border or shading it, or even just by making it big and setting it apart from the rest of your text. To create a drop cap, select the first letter of a paragraph and choose the Format Drop Cap command.

- Use text as a graphic when you don't have any other illustrations for your publication. Drop caps, pull-quotes, and boxed text all can relieve a long expanse of unbroken text and add interest to the page.

■ Use WordArt to create logos, signs, and banners. Also use it for simpler purposes—such as rotating or stretching text, or adding a simple drop-shadow.

■ Frame text when you want to move it freely on the page, with other text wrapping around it.

■ Use the Drawing toolbar to group text with objects. Use these creations to illustrate your publication or to attract attention in an ad.

Fig. 27.7
Text can be effective as a graphic.

For Related Information
■ "Changing Fonts," p. 254

■ "Setting Indents," p. 306

■ "Adjusting Line and Paragraph Spacing", p. 318

■ "Applying, Copying, and Removing Styles," p. 355

■ "Creating Styles," p. 359

■ "Creating Bulleted Lists," p. 350

■ "Creating Numbered Lists," p. 557

> Summer is upon us and provides a welcome change at Redwood Empire Ballet. The discipline of dance class, rehearsals, and performances takes a break. Instead our students enjoy a wider selection of dance disciplines in a less formal atmosphere, all simply for the joy of learning something new.
>
> Of course the Board of Directors and REB staff are already busy planning for the

Working with Columns

Many published documents are formatted with columns. Columns are usually easier to read than full-width text—studies show that the optimal line length for reading is about one and one-half to two alphabets. And columns make a page look more graphical than uninterrupted text because they create blocks of text surrounded by white. Because text and white space are two of the primary building blocks in desktop publishing, columns often are an early design decision.

You can create two types of columns in Word for Windows: snaking (or newspaper-style columns) and side-by-side columns. You create snaking columns by using a formatting command, and you create side-by-side columns by using a table.

Creating Snaking, Newspaper-Style Columns

You commonly see snaking columns in newsletters, magazines, brochures, and newspapers—wherever text is continuous from one column to the next. Columns can be any width you want—and they can be the same width or different widths. You can control the space between columns, and you can add lines between columns. To create columns, position the insertion point inside the section you want formatted as columns and choose the Format Columns command. Or select the number of columns you want using the Columns button on the Standard toolbar.

- The width of a column is the length of a line. For best readability, lines of text should be one and one-half to two alphabets wide.

- If columns are wide (thus lines are long), add extra spacing between the lines.

- The narrower the column, the less space you need between columns. But be sure to include enough space so that the columns remain visually separate.

- Word for Windows includes an option for creating columns of different widths. Use this option for an asymmetrical appearance, but use it consistently in your publication. In a layout with facing pages, mirror uneven columns on left- and right-facing pages.

- Include lines between columns to add a graphic effect to pages and to separate columns. Don't let the lines "outweigh" the text—their weight should be in proportion to the text. Smaller text and narrower columns need a lighter weight line than larger text or wider columns.

- If text is justified, the edges of columns form a visual line, and you probably don't need lines between these columns—unless you want to create a multiline effect.

- Columns are an excellent basis for creating an underlying grid structure around which you can design your document.

- To override columns, frame text and position it so that it crosses columns. Text in the columns wraps around a frame.

- If you position illustrations or framed text on a page of columns, size it to equal one or more column widths. If you have a three-column layout, make pictures one column or two. If you have a six-column grid, however, in which you use three columns of text, pictures can be in multiples of half a column.

Controlling Column Length

You usually determine column length by page length, but you can control the length of columns in two ways: by balancing columns at the end of a publication and by forcing text to start at the top of the next column.

- Balance columns when you don't have enough text to fill the page—your half page of text should be in columns of equal length. Balance columns by inserting a section break at the end of the text. Use this technique on the last page of a newsletter, for example.

- Force a new column to start by inserting a column break or by inserting a continuous section break and formatting it as a new column. Use this technique for creating brochures or any other design that requires columns to be a specific length.

Varying the Number of Columns in a Publication

In Word for Windows, you can create snaking columns in your whole document, or in *sections*. In many publications, you see a first section with only a single column—the title—followed by another section with multiple columns—the text. Insert a section break wherever you want to format different parts of the document with different numbers or styles of columns (see fig. 27.8). To insert a section break, position the insertion point where you want the break and choose the Insert **Break** command. Select an option from the Section Breaks group.

- Use a section break after a title when you want a one-column title followed by multicolumn text.

- Insert a section break wherever you want to start new column formatting.

- Insert two continuous section breaks when you want two sections with different numbers or styles of columns separated by a blank line. If you want a horizontal line to separate two sections with different numbers of columns, insert three continuous section breaks, with the middle section formatted as a single column including one paragraph with a single-line border.

Lake County Getting Shadier

Throughout this planting season, Sonoma County ReLeaf has worked with The Utility Company to provide shade trees to hundreds of families in Lake County. The trees help cool homes in an area very much in need of heat relief. Families profit not only by enjoying a cooler environment, but also by saving money on their utility bills, which can be substantially reduced as leafy trees shade their homes and lessen their need for air conditioning.

Three plantings this spring finished up the season in Lake County. The Utility Company gave 100 trees to schools in the Konocti School District for their Earth Day programs in April. As they grow, the trees will help shade schools.

The Utility Company also provided 540 shade trees to families in Hidden Valley, a community outside of Middletown.

Finally, a planting in June at senior centers and homes helped celebrate the opening of The Utility Company's new service center in Clearlake. The Utility Company provides shade trees as part of their "A Shade Better" program, directed locally by Sonoma County ReLeaf.

Throughout this planting season, Sonoma County ReLeaf has worked with The Utility Company to provide shade trees to hundreds of families in Lake County. The trees help cool homes in an area very much in need of heat relief. Families profit not only by enjoying a cooler environment, but also by saving money on their utility bills, which can be substantially reduced as leafy trees shade their homes and lessen their need for air conditioning.

Three plantings this spring finished up the utility bills, which can be substantially reduced as leafy trees shade their homes and lessen their need for air conditioning.

Three plantings this spring finished up the season in Lake County. The Utility Company gave 100 trees to schools in the Konocti School District for their Earth Day programs in April. As they grow, the trees will help shade schools.

The Utility Company also provided 540 shade trees to families in Hidden Valley, a community outside of Middletown. The planting took place at the end of April.

Finally, a planting in June at senior centers and homes helped celebrate the opening of The Utility Company's new service center in Clearlake.

The Utility Company provides shade trees as part of their "A Shade Better" program, directed

Fig. 27.8
Section breaks make it possible for you to format a publication with varying numbers and styles of columns.

V

Publishing with Graphics

Creating Side-by-Side Columns

With short paragraphs of text that you want to appear side by side, a table may be a better formatting choice than columns. You can format a table so that borders appear or do not appear. To create a table, choose the Table Insert Table command, or use the Table button on the Standard toolbar.

- Use a table to create side-by-side columns of numbers or data.

- Use tables when you need to do extensive formatting with borders or shading, and need great flexibility about where the borders and shading appear, as in a form.

- Use a table to format text inside a frame into columns.

- Don't overuse lines—especially heavy lines—in tables.

Creating Sideheads

Headings and subheadings usually appear above text, but your design may place them to the side of paragraphs instead. You can use frames to create sideheads. To create a sidehead, select the sidehead text and frame it using the Insert Frame command. Then position the sidehead in the margin by selecting it and choosing the Format Frame command.

For Related Information

- "Creating Columns," p. 383

- "Changing Columns," p. 393

- "Creating Tables," p. 509

- "Formatting a Table," p. 536

- "Positioning a Frame in a Margin," p. 706

- Set wide margins and position framed subheadings in the margins to create sideheads. Using this technique you can create the illusion of a two-column layout, with only the subheads in one column.

- Use sideheads when you want to create a simple design with a light look—sideheads contribute to a light look by using wide margins.

- Use styles to format and position sideheads so that they have a consistent appearance.

Incorporating Illustrations

Illustrations are an important building block in most publications. They can take many forms: photographs that you scan or for which you leave a blank space, pictures that you insert from other programs, clip art, drawings that you create in Word for Windows using the Drawing toolbar, and even text that is transformed into an illustration.

Including Photographs

You can include photographs in your publication in two ways. You can scan photographs and insert them as pictures, or you can leave a blank space where you manually paste a photo after you print your publication. To insert a scanned photo, choose the Insert Picture command. To create a blank frame, make sure nothing is selected and choose the Insert Frame command. Then drag the crosshair to create the blank frame.

- Unless you have a high-resolution scanner and printer, photos print at poor resolution. Include scanned photographs in your publication when you don't need high-quality output or when you have the equipment to produce high-quality output.

- If you don't have the equipment but need high-quality output, use a service bureau to scan your photos and print your pages. Use your own equipment for proofing before you get a final high-quality print.

- If you are going to reproduce your publication in quantity using a commercial offset printer, leave a blank space for photos and have a typesetting shop or your printer make half-tones. Paste the half-tones onto your printed originals before you take them to the commercial printer for duplication. You can create a blank space by inserting an empty frame.

Creating Illustrations in Other Programs

You can use graphics programs to create illustrations that you include in a Word for Windows publication. The program can be as simple as Windows Paintbrush or as sophisticated as Aldus Freehand or CorelDRAW!—as long as the program is compatible with Word for Windows or can create a file in a format compatible with Word for Windows. To include an illustration in your document, choose the Insert Picture or Insert Object command.

- When you need illustrations beyond the scope of what Word for Windows can produce, create them in programs other than Word for Windows and insert them into your Word for Windows document.

- If you aren't an illustrator yourself, hire one to prepare drawings for your publication. Art students may be more affordable than professionals if your budget is limited.

- Find out which graphics formats are compatible with Word for Windows by choosing the Insert Picture command and reading the file types in the List Files of Type list. Install filters for other formats by running the Word for Windows setup program.

Adding Captions

Some experts say that people look first at pictures and second at captions in your publication. Word for Windows makes including captions easy, and it even numbers them for you automatically. To add a caption, choose the Insert Caption command.

- Include captions for your illustrations.

- Frame captions together with illustrations if you want to move them freely on the page as a unit.

Sizing and Cropping Illustrations

In Word for Windows you can size an inserted illustration proportionally or nonproportionally. You can crop, or cut away the edges of, an illustration. You can crop a selected illustration by holding Shift while you drag a selection handle.

- Illustrations should be in proportion to the text—and to each other—in your publication. Don't let illustrations overpower text. Make an important illustration larger than a less important illustration.

- Size illustrations to fit within your layout grid—if you have a four-column grid, illustrations may be one, two, three, or even four columns wide but not half a column or one and one-half columns wide.

- Crop illustrations to focus on what's important about them—you don't have to use the whole photo if it's not relevant.

Knowing Where to Position Illustrations

Using your layout grid helps you position illustrations on the page. To learn about using a grid, read the earlier section, "Using the Building Blocks of Design," and see figure 27.2.

- Position illustrations on your grid. Often you can position them by aligning them to a column or margin.

- Place important illustrations above the fold in newsletters and magazines (usually above the horizontal center of the page).

- Position illustrations as close as possible to the text they illustrate.

Drawing in Word for Windows

You can use the Word for Windows Drawing toolbar to create surprisingly sophisticated illustrations right in your publication. You can create drawings in your document by displaying the Drawing toolbar (choose the View Toolbars command and select the Drawing toolbar) and using any of its drawing tools. For details, see Chapter 24, "Drawing with Word's Drawing Tools."

- If you're artistic, use buttons on the Drawing toolbar to create simple or sophisticated illustrations for your publication.

- Use Word for Windows drawing tools to create lines and boxes that are unattached to the page. You can use the Rectangle button, for example, to draw a border around the edge of a page.

- Use the Alignment button to center a border on the page. To duplicate a border on all pages, create and copy it on the first page, and paste it on the remaining pages, centering it vertically and horizontally relative to each page.

- Share drawings you create in Word for Windows with other Word documents, or even with other programs in Windows, by copying and pasting them.

Repeating Graphics on Every Page

Include graphics that you want to repeat on every page in headers or footers. The graphics do not have to be confined to the space within the top and bottom margins. To create headers or footers, choose the View Header and Footer command. With the insertion point inside the header or footer pane, choose the Insert Picture command to insert an existing picture, or use drawing tools to create a drawing. Alternatively, choose the Insert Object command to create a WordArt logo or other graphic.

- ■ Use headers and footers to create rules that appear at the top and bottom of every page in a publication. Rules can appear by themselves or in conjunction with text.

- ■ Create a watermark by placing a large graphic in a header, setting it to overlap the margin, and moving it into the layer behind the text layer. A watermark should be a light enough color that you can read text through it.

Creating Transparent Graphics

Any drawing that you create with Word for Windows drawing tools you can layer behind text. This way you can read text through the drawing. Display the Drawing toolbar and draw objects to create transparent graphics.

- ■ If you want to read text through a drawing, create the drawing using buttons on the Drawing toolbar and send it to the layer behind the text.

- ■ Use transparent graphics to create eye-catching illustrations for ads and flyers. Use them under big, bold text.

Creating Logos with WordArt

WordArt enables you to manipulate text in ways that turn text into a graphic. You can pour text into a shape, rotate it, flip it, stretch it, border it, shadow it, and much more. To create a WordArt logo, choose the Insert Object command and select the Create New tab. Select Microsoft WordArt 2.0 from the Object Type list. For details about using WordArt, see Chapter 25, "Creating Banners and Special Effects."

- ■ Use WordArt to create logos for business identity materials—letterhead, business cards, envelopes, brochures, and anything else you need.

■ Use WordArt to rotate text; for example, rotate a newsletter's nameplate so that it's vertical, and position it on the left side of the front page of the newsletter.

■ Use WordArt in combination with drawing tools to create advertising graphics.

Using Ready-Made Computer Art

Many companies sell computer *clip art*—pictures on a disk that you can insert into your publication. You can buy specialized collections of clip art related to topics such as business, sports, seasons, and other topics. Look in the back of desktop publishing magazines for ads selling clip art and call the companies you're interested in for samples. Word for Windows includes a good collection of clip art images in the Clipart folder. To insert an illustration from Word for Windows clip art collection, choose the Insert Picture command and select a file from the Clipart subdirectory located within the WINWORD directory.

For Related Information
■ "Inserting and Copying Pictures into your Document," p. 661

■ "Drawing and Coloring Lines," p. 732

■ "Creating a WordArt Object Graphic," p. 775

■ "Inserting a Blank Frame," p. 693

■ Use clip art with restraint. Many designers don't use it at all because it looks too "canned."

■ Use clip art as the basis for creating your own illustrations. Size it, crop it, color it, or use it together with other art to create something unique.

Leaving a Blank Space for Pictures

Not all art is in your computer. If you want to add an illustration after you print your publication, leave a blank space for it by creating an empty frame. To create an empty frame, choose the Insert Frame command when you have nothing selected. Drag the crosshair to draw the frame.

■ Leave a blank space in your publication for noncomputer illustrations. This technique works well when you are going to reproduce your publication in quantity by photocopying or offset printing.

■ You can border an empty frame if you want to include a line around the picture you insert by hand.

Wrapping Text Around Graphics (and Other Text)

The capability to wrap text around graphics and other text is one of the primary features that makes Word for Windows a desktop publishing program.

In Word for Windows, you can frame any graphic or block of text and wrap the text of your publication around it. You also can border, shade, or color a frame.

Framing and Moving Text and Objects

When you frame text or an object, you can move it anywhere on the page. You can move it by dragging it with the mouse, or you can position it relative to some anchor on the page, such as a margin or column. By default, text wraps around a frame (if at least one inch is available for text). To frame an object, select it and choose the Insert Frame command. To position a frame, select it and choose the Format Frame command and make selections from the Horizontal and Vertical groups.

- Even though you can move frames anywhere, design within your grid. Don't position frames between columns so that you have narrow or uneven strips of text on either side of the frame. When *Newsweek* positions text this way, they are working within a multiple-column grid.

- For precision, use the Frame dialog box to position frames relative to some anchor on your grid, like a column edge or margin.

- In a template, create frames for repetitive blocks of text such as a teaser box ("What's Inside") on the front page of a newsletter. Then just change the contents each issue.

- Use a frame when you want to position something in a margin. If the framed object overlaps body copy, text wraps around it. Use this technique to create sideheads, for example.

- You can use a frame when you want a story in a newsletter to override columns (see fig. 27.9). If you want a two-column-wide story in a three-column layout, for example, create a frame the width of two columns and position it relative to the left or right margin.

Framing and Grouping Items Together

When you want to group items so that they behave as a single item, frame them together. You either can select existing items—such as a picture and its caption—and then add a frame, or you can create a frame and insert objects or type text inside it. Items that are framed together move as a unit on the page, and text wraps around them.

If you're working with buttons on the Drawing toolbar, use the Group button to group items such as drawings and their callouts. You can move drawings you create and group using the Drawing toolbar anywhere on the page, but you must frame them if you want text to wrap around them.

Fig. 27.9

When you want text to override columns, frame it.

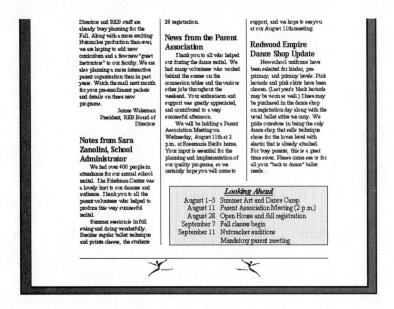

If you want to frame an inserted picture together with callouts (which you create using the Drawing toolbar), insert the picture in a text box, create the callouts, and then group the picture and callouts. Although you cannot frame the individual items together, you can frame the group.

To frame objects together, select them and choose the Insert Frame command. To group drawing objects, select them and click the Group button on the Drawing toolbar.

- Frame illustrations and their captions together so that they stay together.

- Frame pictures and callouts together so that they move easily as a unit.

- In a newsletter, frame together the items needed to create a mailer on the back page. Then position the frame at the bottom margin. A table provides a good skeleton for organizing the items in a mailer and can be framed.

For Related Information

- "Framing Text, Pictures, and Other Objects," p. 688

- "Moving and Positioning Frames," p. 699

- "Wrapping Text Around a Frame," p. 708

- "Framing and Moving Text Objects and Graphics," p. 687

Using Lines, Boxes, and Shading

Lines, boxes, and shading can add graphic interest to a publication, even if you don't have any illustrations to use. In Word for Windows, lines, boxes, and shading apply to selected paragraphs and frames. You can add lines and boxes around inserted pictures or WordArt images, but you cannot shade an inserted picture or WordArt image.

Putting Information in a Box

You can select a paragraph or group of paragraphs and add a box around them. The box is as wide as the margins or column; if you want it narrower, indent the paragraph. To box text, select it and choose the Format Borders and Shading command. Select the Borders tab and select Box, or create your own box using the Border group.

- Add a box around important text in a newsletter. It can be as little as a pull-quote or as much as several paragraphs of information.

- Don't crowd text with a box. Include enough space between the box and the text inside it and surrounding it.

- Don't let the box outweigh the text. If text is small, use a lightweight (thin) line. Use heavy lines only when they don't overpower the text.

Creating an Empty Box for Illustrations Added After Printing

You can create an empty box by inserting a frame when no text or object is selected. You can use the Frame dialog box to specify an exact size for the frame, and you can include a border if you want. After you've created the box, you can move it anywhere on the page, and text wraps around it. To create an empty box, make sure nothing is selected and choose the Insert Frame command. Drag the crosshair to draw a box.

- If you plan to include noncomputer illustrations in your publication, include an empty box where you can paste your illustration after you print your publication. Use this technique when you print only one original and then have your publication duplicated at a copy shop or commercial printer.

- If your illustration is the wrong size for your publication, you can have a commercial printer scale it to the right size (some typesetting and art stores also scale illustrations). To determine the percent to scale your illustration, divide the width you have for the illustration in your publication by the width of the current illustration. The result is the percent by which you should have the illustration scaled. If a photo is 4" wide, for example, but you have only a 2" space for it, divide 2 by 4 to get 50 percent. You then can multiply the height of the existing photo by the percent to get the height to make your empty box. Using the same example, if the photo is 3" tall, multiply 3" by .5 (which is 50 percent) to get 1-1/2". Now you know to have the photo reduced to 50 percent and to create a 1-1/2" by 2" box for it in your publication. (If you find yourself calculating percentages often, graphic arts stores sell proportion wheels that do the calculation for you.)

Lines Above and Below Paragraphs

Lines, or rules, above paragraphs can serve as text separators—complementing, or sometimes even replacing, subheadings, or dividing stories in a newsletter. To place lines above and below text, select the text and choose the Format Borders and Shading command. Select the Borders tab and create lines by clicking at the top and bottom of the sample box in the Border group. Select a line style from the Style list.

- Use lines above and below paragraphs the same way you use text—consistently. If you include a 2-point line above some subheadings, include one above all. If you place lines above and below some pull-quotes, use them with all pull-quotes.

- Keep lines in proportion to the text surrounding them and in proportion to your overall design. Don't use big, bold lines in a publication with a light appearance; don't use skinny little lines with a big, heavy headline in an ad.

Including Lines Between Columns

In the Columns dialog box, you can select an option to add lines between columns. The lines extend from the top of the section to the bottom of the longest column in the section. Use this option, rather than the drawing tools or the Borders and Shading dialog box, to include lines between columns. To add lines between columns, position the insertion point in the text that is formatted as columns, choose the Format Columns command, and select the Line Between option.

- Don't crowd the page. Make sure the space between columns is wide enough to comfortably accommodate the lines.

- If text is justified, its edges create a visual line. You may not need lines between the columns as well.

Shading and Coloring Paragraphs

With the Borders and Shading dialog box, you can add shading or a color behind paragraphs. You can blend foreground and background colors to create just about any hue imaginable. To shade or color text, select it and choose the Format Borders and Shading command. Select the Shading tab and select an option from the Shading list.

For Related Information

■ "Enclosing Paragraphs in Boxes and Lines," p. 325

■ "Shading Paragraphs," p. 332

■ Shading and coloring are good techniques for adding emphasis to important paragraphs or for setting sidebars apart from the rest of the text. Shading adds color to a page and can give it a graphical appearance without illustrations.

■ Be sure text is readable through the shading. For most text, 20 percent is as dark as you should shade a paragraph. Before finalizing this choice, however, print a few samples to see how shading looks and how it works with the text size you plan to use.

■ You can create "reverse" type by formatting text as white and adding a black or dark background. Don't reverse small type or large quantities of text. Reversed text is best in a sans serif font and usually looks best in bold style.

■ You can create horizontal gray or patterned bars by formatting a blank line in your text with shading.

■ Don't even think about placing a pattern behind text.

Printing Your Publication

Printing means two things to a publisher: printing an original from your own printer and printing quantities of your publication, usually done by a copy shop or commercial offset printer. For a few publications, all printing is accomplished on a laser printer.

Many desktop publishers have laser printers for typeset-quality output at 300 dots per inch, or even more. Some people have lower resolution printers, and some have higher resolution or color printers. But no matter what type of printer you have, you still can create attractive publications. If your own printer cannot do the job, service bureaus can do it for you. Call any local commercial printer or typesetting shop for names of shops that can print your original.

V

Publishing with Graphics

Most publications go outside your office for duplication in quantity. This approach has many advantages—saving time, saving wear and tear on your laser printer, printing in a larger format than your own printer can accommodate, printing in color, and binding your publication.

Understanding Your Own Printer's Capabilities

Because most publications end up on paper, a printer is an important tool for desktop publishers. Get to know yours: What is its printing resolution? What fonts does it contain? How do shaded areas look when printed? How fast or slow is it? Do large publications stall it? Does heavy paper jam it? Do you have easy access to your printer? Before you even begin your design, consider your printer's capabilities. If they don't meet your needs, try to find outside resources for printing your final publication and use your own printer for drafts.

Printing an Original for Outside Duplication

If you're printing limited quantities of a publication, you don't need to add color, you don't need a larger size than your printer can accommodate, and you don't need high-quality photographs, you might be able to use your printer to print final copies of your publication. Many publishers use their laser printers to print a single original of their publication and then take the original to a copy shop or commercial offset printer for duplication.

If you print only an original, invest in a ream of good-quality, smooth, bright white paper that is heavier than the bond weight paper you use day to day. Print your original on this good-quality paper. It holds up well and provides a good surface for pasting on any illustrations you must add before you take your publication to the printer.

Find out from your commercial printer how to present your artwork—if your print job is a newsletter, you may need to create printing spreads of facing pages, paste on noncomputer illustrations, and add a tissue overlay on which you mark areas to be printed in color. Do any final paste-up before you take your original to the printer.

Getting Your Printing Job Typeset

Any printer available in Windows is available to Word for Windows; that also includes typesetting equipment. If your publication is very high-quality—a magazine to be printed on glossy paper or an ad to go in a national magazine—you may want your text printed at higher resolution than is available on most laser printers. Many typesetting service bureaus can print Word for

Windows documents at resolutions beginning at 1200 dots per inch (compared to 300 dpi for most laser printers). The price is generally per-page.

If you want typeset output, call typesetters in your area to find out whether they can take a disk containing a Word for Windows document or how you can save your document so that they can print it. Be sure you understand how they need the file—what format, what disk size—before you take your file to them. You may be able to install the printer your typesetter is using and print to a file to create a file for the typesetter. To print to a file, choose the File Print command and select the Print to File option.

Typesetters generally offer two options: printing a positive or a negative image. Sometimes you can save money or time with a negative rather than a positive because commercial offset printers must convert to a negative before going to press anyway. Work closely with commercial printers to find out what they need before you have your publication typeset.

Desktop Publishing Examples

In this section you'll find examples of desktop publishing projects, along with descriptions of how they were created. Don't try to re-create them exactly as they are: rather, use them as examples of what you can do. Be creative!

Creating a Page Full of Business Cards

You can create a page full of your own business cards and print them on card-weight paper on a laser printer (see fig. 27.10). Many business supply companies sell card-weight laser printer paper perforated for business cards. If you include crop marks in the margins, you can cut the page easily into individual cards.

Set up a page with .75" left and right margins and .5" top and bottom margins. This way you can divide the page into ten standard 3-1/2" by 2" business cards. Divide the page into two columns, with no spacing between. Then display text boundaries.

In the top left corner, create a business card, using text, graphics, lines, shading, and whatever else you want. Keep in mind that the cards should be 2" tall, and you should allow some white space on all four sides of the card. Select all the text and graphics on the card and insert a frame around them. Format the frame so that it is exactly 2" tall (its width is already accurate

For Related Information
- "Previewing Pages Before Printing," p. 222

- "Printing the Current Document," p. 227

V

Publishing with Graphics

because it is the same width as the column). Align the frame to the top and left margins.

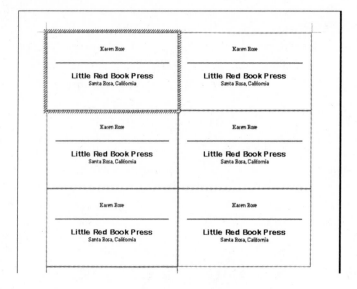

Fig. 27.10

You can create a page full of business cards using margins, columns, and frames of an exact size.

Tip

The next time you want to create business cards, use this same document because you've already positioned all the frames exactly where they should be. Change the top left card; then copy the text from card to card without changing the frames. Save the file with a new name. If you plan to create several business cards, create a template.

Now copy the frame to the top right of the page by dragging it while holding down the Control key. While the frame is selected, align it to the top and right margins.

Create the remaining cards by copying them and aligning them into fixed positions on the page. Cards on the left side of the page should all be aligned to the left margin; the cards on the right, to the right margin. The second row of cards should be 2" from the top margin; the third row, 4" from the top margin; the fourth row, 6" from the top margin; and the fifth row, 8" from the top margin.

Use the Drawing toolbar to draw crop marks for cutting at the corners and between rows and columns.

Creating a Folded Brochure

Notice the integration of text, graphics, and illustrations in the brochure shown in fig. 27.11. Notice the contrast in type sizes and styles, and yet the consistency in type style from panel to panel. All the bulleted lists use hanging indents with consistent formatting. Notice also how WordArt was used to rotate text for the return address panel.

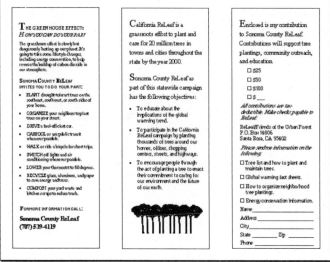

To create a two-fold brochure (with three panels), set up a page in landscape orientation with equal left and right margins. Then divide the page into three equal columns. The spacing between the columns should be double the left or right margins because you fold the brochure between the columns to create the brochure's panels. If the left and right margins are one-half inch, for example, the spacing between columns should be one inch. A two-fold brochure printed on letter-size paper fits perfectly into a business envelope. You can create a three-fold brochure (with four panels) on legal-size paper; it also fits in a business envelope.

Use column breaks at the bottom of each column to force text to start at the top of the next column. Or if you want to include different page-level formatting for columns, insert a section break and then format the new section start as "New Column." Use this approach, for example, if you want to vary the vertical alignment between columns. To start the second page (back side of your brochure), insert a new page section break.

If you want a box around each panel, draw the first one using the Box button on the Drawing toolbar, using rulers to guide you, and then copy and paste the box for the other panels (this way they're the same size on each panel). Send the boxes to the layer behind text.

Working on a brochure is easier if you select Text Boundaries on the View tab in the Options Dialog box. That way you see nonprinting boundaries for each column.

Creating an Ad

In the ad shown in fig. 27.12, notice the use of graphics, including lines, a shaded box of text, and an illustration. The size of the headline contrasts with other text, creating a focal point, and the picture is balanced by the shaded box of text diagonally across from it. Notice also that one font is used consistently in the headline and subheading text, whereas a contrasting font is used for the times table.

Fig. 27.12
This ad is based on a table, but you also can use columns to achieve the same effect.

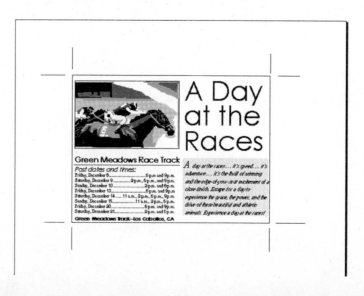

To create the ad shown in fig. 27.12, based on a table, set up a page in land-scape orientation. Select margins that leave the working page the size you want your ad.

Create a two-column, two-row table the size of the page. In the top left cell, insert a picture or draw one using Word's Drawing toolbar (this one, remark-ably, was drawn using the Drawing toolbar). Add a box around the picture.

In the bottom left cell, type the race schedule. Use right-aligned tabs with dot leaders for the table of times. Use a sans serif font for headings and a serif font for the times table.

At the top right, create a big headline (the text is not bold—only big). Use the same font as you used for headings in the bottom left cell. Adjust the letter spacing so that all lines are the same length and reduce the line spac-ing—often a good idea for multiline headlines.

At the bottom right, type the text of the ad using the same font as in the times table. Increase line spacing and italicize the text. Select the text—not the cell—and add a 10 percent shaded background to the paragraph.

Format the table with a border around the outside and use the Line button on the Drawing toolbar to create crop marks (display text boundaries to see where to put the crop marks).

Creating a Simple Newsletter

The simple two-column newsletter shown in fig. 27.13 is easy to produce, yet its design is effective. In the newsletter, text wraps around an illustration that is positioned in the center of the page, and a drop cap at the beginning of the text helps draw in the reader's eye.

To create this newsletter, set up a portrait-oriented page. On the first two lines, create the nameplate and issue line. Type the headline and by-line for the text. Format all the text; then select and border the nameplate and issue line.

Beneath the by-line, insert a continuous section break. Format this second section for two columns with a line between them. Type the text of the news-letter, including a drop-cap for the first letter. For the text, use 10-point Times New Roman; for the subheadings, use 12-point bold with one extra line of spacing before. Use styles to format body copy and subheadings.

Fig. 27.13
This simple two-
column newsletter
is easy to create.

Insert your picture, border it, and add a caption. Frame the picture and caption together and then center them between the margins, at about 3" from the top of the page (adjust this position for the best-looking text wrap).

Add a footer formatted with a line at its top. Include an automatic page number. Also include a header if your newsletter is longer than one page, but omit it for the first page. If you include a header, balance it with the footer by including a similar horizontal line (because all the necessary information is in the footer, a line may be all you need in the header).

Creating Letterhead and an Envelope

In the "business system" shown in fig. 27.14, notice the subtle use of graphics and the consistency between the envelope and letterhead. This project is designed to be a template.

Create a new two-page template with a next page section break between the pages. Use the Page Setup dialog box to size the first page at 9.5" by 4.125", landscape orientation. Select standard letter size for the second page.

Because the graphics are contained in headers and footers (so that they don't interfere with typing the text of the letter), set the margins for typing the text of the envelope and letter. On the envelope, the top margin is about 2.5", for example, whereas the left margin is about 4". For the letterhead, the top margin is about 2".

Create separate headers and footers for each page of this document and specify that they appear .25" from the edge of the page. On the envelope, create the WordArt logo in the top left of the header and use left-aligned tabs to line up the return address information (the top line is diamond-shaped bullets). Reverse the process in the letterhead: use right-aligned tabs and create the logo at the right edge of the header. For both pages, use only diamond-shaped bullets in the footer.

On both the envelope and the letterhead, include dummy text formatted as you want it. On the letterhead, include a date field as the first line.

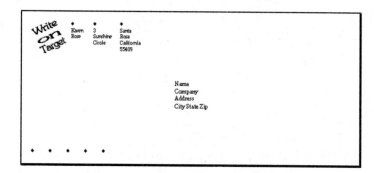

Fig. 27.14
This letterhead and envelope are in the same document.

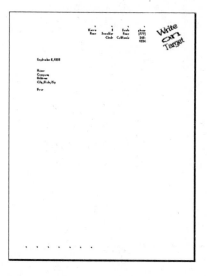

Creating a Four-Column Newsletter

The four-column, two-page newsletter shown in fig. 27.15 includes inserted illustrations, WordArt graphics in the nameplate, framed boxes of text, and a back-page mailer based on a table. Its design is based on a four-column grid.

If you use your newsletter periodically, create as much of it as does not change and save that part as a template. To do so, create a new template file.

Fig. 27.15

This four-column newsletter includes inserted illustrations, WordArt graphics, and framed text.

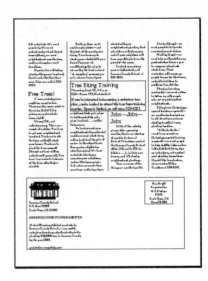

The first line of the newsletter contains a logo and nameplate; the logo is the width of the first column, and the nameplate is the width of the remaining three columns. When you first insert the logo and create the nameplate, make a guess at column widths; after you create the columns, refine the size of the logo and the width of the nameplate so that they fit within the grid.

At the top left margin, insert the logo (the logo in fig. 27.15 was created in a graphics program). Size it to be the width of one column. Then set a left-aligned tab to line up with the second column, press Tab, and type the news-letter name. Create the rotated "news" as a WordArt object and position it flush with the right margin.

To create the subtitle below the nameplate, set the left indent flush with the tab you used for the nameplate. Then type the text, center it, and add the box and shading. Because the left margin is indented, the subtitle is centered over the three right-most columns, and the box is the width of three right-most columns rather than the full width of the page.

Start a new line and type placeholders for the title of the first article.

Now you change from a one-column format to a four-column format. Press Enter to start a new line and remove the left indent. Insert a continuous sec-tion break. Then format the new section for four columns with a line between.

In the first column, create the "teaser" box, using placeholder text. Frame it and position it at the bottom of the column, aligned to the left edge of the column. If the line between columns to the right of the box disappears, make the frame narrower.

At the end of the first column, insert a column break. In the second column, type a paragraph of placeholder text for the newsletter story. Press Enter and insert a continuous section break. Change the column format to one and insert a two-column table. In the left column of the table, include the return address; in the right column, create the postal indicia. Use paragraph indents to center the postal indicia where you want it, and select just its text and add a box. Then select the whole table and add a box around it. Frame the table and position it at the bottom of the page. It appears on page 1 in your template, overlapping the teaser box; as you add text to the issue, it moves to the bottom of the next page. If you add too much text, it moves to a third page. Delete some text if the text moves to a third page.

Now you have included as much of your newsletter as does not change. Save it as a template. When you're ready to create your first issue, open the tem-plate and replace the date and teaser placeholder text. Then select the placeholder for the first paragraph of text and begin typing the text of your newsletter. Or use Word for Windows Insert File command to insert the text of your article from a file previously created. To create the boxed text on the back page, type the text, box and frame it, and position it in the middle of the page relative to the margins horizontally and wherever it looks best vertically.

Save the issue with a unique file name.

From Here...

You may want to review the follow chapters:

- Chapter 22, "Inserting pictures in your Document," for more information on placing graphics.

- Chapter 24, "Drawing with Word's Drawing Tools," for more information on designing unique documents.

V

Publishing with Graphics

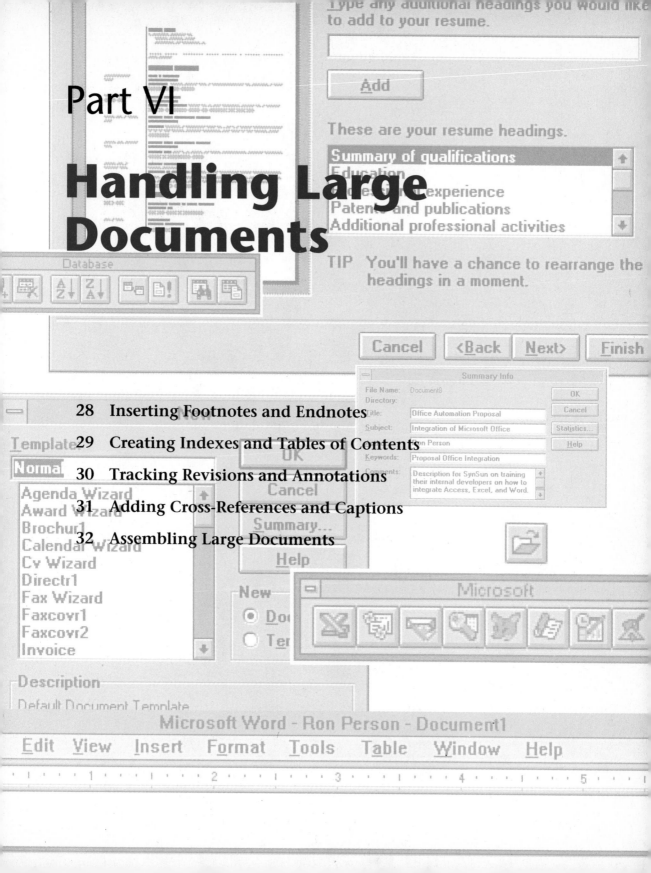

Part VI

Handling Large Documents

28   Inserting Footnotes and Endnotes

29   Creating Indexes and Tables of Contents

30   Tracking Revisions and Annotations

31   Adding Cross-References and Captions

32   Assembling Large Documents

Type any additional headings you would li
to add to your resume.

Add

These are your resume headings.

Summary of qualifications
Education
Professional experience
Patents and publications
Additional professional activities

TIP You'll have a chance to rearrange th
headings in a moment.

Database

Cancel   <Back   Next>   Finis

Summary Info

File Name: Document8
Directory:
Title: Office Automation Proposal
Subject: Integration of Microsoft Office
Author: Ron Person
Keywords: Proposal Office Integration
Comments: Description for SynSun on training
              their internal developers on how to
              integrate Access, Excel, and Word.

OK
Cancel
Statistics...
Help

New

Template:

Normal

Agenda Wizard
Award Wizard
Brochur1
Calendar Wizard
Cv Wizard
Directr1
Fax Wizard
Faxcovr1
Faxcovr2
Invoice

OK
Cancel
Summary...
Help

New
⦿ Do
○ Ter

Microsoft

Description

Default Document Template

Microsoft Word - Ron Person - Document1

le   Edit   View   Insert   Format   Tools   Table   Window   Help

· · · I · · · 1 · · · I · · · 2 · · · I · · · 3 · · · I · · · 4 · · · I · · · 5 · · ·

Inserting Footnotes and Endnotes

Footnotes and endnotes have long been a staple of academic treatises—supplying additional information about a topic in the text or providing a reference. Footnotes and endnotes save you from having to clutter the text of your document with every piece of information you have. Instead, you can include parenthetical or reference information as a footnote or endnote listing. Because each note is referenced in the text, finding this extra information when you need it is easy. Fig. 28.1 shows examples of footnotes being placed in a document.

What You Need to Know About Inserting Footnotes and Endnotes

Inserting, editing, and formatting footnotes and endnotes is easy in Word. Basically, a footnote consists of two parts: a footnote reference in the text (usually a superscripted number after the text) and the footnote at the bottom of the page, separated from the body text by a separator line. An endnote is similar, except that the entry for an endnote appears at the end of the section or document, set apart from the text by a separator.

The process of creating footnotes and endnotes involves two basic steps. First, you insert the note reference to mark the location in the document where a footnote or endnote is referred to. The note reference usually is a number. After Word inserts the note reference, you type the note entry (customizing the separator if you prefer). The note entry is the text information that appears in the footnote or endnote. Several options are available for specifying

In this chapter, you learn the following:

- The difference between footnotes and endnotes

- How to insert a footnote or endnote

- How to manage footnotes or endnotes with the ability to find, delete, copy, or move them

- How to convert a footnote to an endnote, and an endnote to a footnote

- How to apply custom formats, numbering, and positioning to footnotes or endnotes

VI

Handling Large Documents

where footnotes and endnotes appear, the type of separator line that is used, and the style of numbering used for the reference numbers.

Fig. 28.1

You can add footnotes to a document to provide additional information or to indicate references.

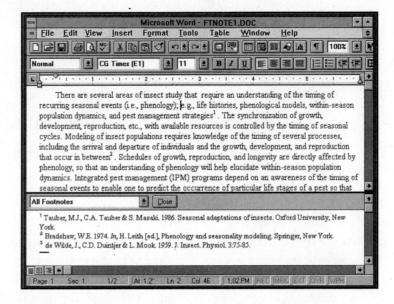

Inserting Footnotes and Endnotes

When you insert a footnote or endnote, Word for Windows inserts a reference mark in the text at the current insertion point. This is usually a sequential number that identifies the note you are adding. You are then given the opportunity to type the text that the reference mark refers to.

If you are in the normal view, a pane opens at the bottom of the window. In that pane, you can type either a footnote or an endnote, depending on the type of note you selected. If you are in page layout view, Word moves the insertion point to the bottom of the page for footnotes, or to the end of the document for endnotes. Entering footnotes and endnotes becomes as visual and as easy as if you were manually writing in a notebook. But Word automatically adjusts the page lengths as footnotes fill up the page. And endnotes at the end of the document are continually pushed to the last page as your document gets longer.

> **Note**
>
> Footnotes usually make a document more difficult to read because they clutter the bottom of each page. However, many academic institutions require footnotes in their papers, probably because it makes grading easier for teaching assistants. (They don't have to work as hard if they can see that you crammed your paper full of someone else's thinking.) Endnotes are more frequently used in scholarly publications because they do not interfere with reading, but they do make the research accessible for those who need more information. Before you choose between footnotes and endnotes, check with the institution for whom you are writing.

To create a footnote or endnote, follow these steps:

1. Position the insertion point after the text where you want to insert a reference mark.

   Word inserts the reference mark at the insertion point, unless you have selected text, in which case it positions the mark before the selection.

2. Choose the Insert Footnote command. The Footnote and Endnote dialog box appears (see fig. 28.2).

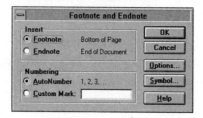

Fig. 28.2
In the Footnote and Endnote dialog box, you choose the type of note and how it should be numbered.

3. Select either the Footnote or the Endnote option.

4. Accept the default AutoNumber to have Word number your footnotes. For custom reference marks, see "Changing the Appearance of Reference Marks" later in this chapter.

5. Choose OK. Word displays the note pane (normal view) or the bottom margin (page layout view) so that you can type your footnote.

6. Type the text of your footnote or endnote.

VI

Handling Large Documents

If you're in the normal view of your document, you type in a special note pane, which appears when you choose OK in Step 5. At this point, the screen is divided into two parts: the text of your document on top, showing the note reference; and the note pane below, showing the note entry (see fig. 28.3).

Fig. 28.3

The note pane is at the bottom of the screen.

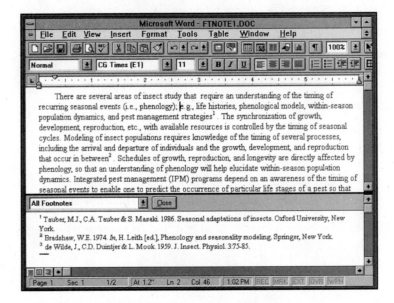

If you're in the page layout view of your document, you don't see the note pane. Instead, you type the note directly on the page (see fig. 28.4). If you are entering a footnote, you type at the bottom of the page. If you are entering an endnote, you type at the end of the document.

7. If you are in normal view, leave the note pane visible and press F6 or click in the document to move back to the document window. You can also click in the document to move the insertion point. Or close the note pane by choosing the Close button or the View Footnote command (which is turned on when you insert a footnote).

or

If you are in page layout view, you can use Shift+F5 (the Go Back key) to return to where you inserted the reference. You can use the mouse to click at any location in the document.

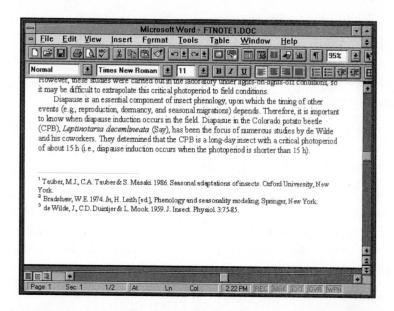

Fig. 28.4
You type footnotes
directly on the
bottom of the page
when in page
layout view.

Note

You can insert multiple references to the same footnote or endnote. For example, you can refer to the same footnote text several times in a document without having to repeat the footnote text. To do this, you use the Insert Cross-Reference command and the NOTEREF field.

To insert an additional reference to a note that has already been inserted in your document, position the insertion point where you want to insert the reference mark. Choose the Insert Cross-Reference command. Select either Footnote or Endnote from the Reference Type list box; then select either Footnote Number or Endnote Number from the Insert Reference To list box. Finally, select the footnote or endnote you want to refer to in the For Which Footnote or For Which Endnote list box. Choose the Insert button and then the Close button. Next select the reference mark you just inserted and select either Footnote Reference or Endnote Reference from the Style drop-down list on the Formatting toolbar to apply the correct formatting to the reference mark.

You can insert a cross-reference to another note within the text for a note, using the procedure just described. For more information on working with cross-references, see Chapter 31, "Adding Cross-References and Captions."

Changing the Appearance of Reference Marks

In the preceding procedure, it is assumed that footnotes and endnotes use the default numbering scheme. You set default numbering by selecting the

AutoNumber option when creating a footnote or endnote. Footnotes are automatically numbered using Arabic numerals (1, 2, 3, and so on), and endnotes are numbered using Roman numerals (i, ii, iii, and so on). With this option selected, footnotes are renumbered when additional footnotes are added, deleted, moved, or copied.

You can create footnotes or endnotes with a custom reference mark. To use a custom reference mark when you create the note, select the Custom Mark option from the Footnote and Endnote dialog box.

In the Custom Mark text box, you can type up to 10 characters, such as asterisks or daggers; or you can choose the Symbol button and select a symbol from the Symbol dialog box. Custom marks are not automatically updated, but custom reference marks don't interfere with any automatically numbered footnote references already in your document.

To change an existing reference mark, select the mark, choose the Insert Footnote command, and type a new mark in the Custom Mark text box. Choose OK. Word displays the footnote pane (normal view—choose Close to close it) or the bottom margin (page layout view—press Shift+F5 to return to your document).

Editing and Viewing Footnotes and Endnotes

Tip
Insert a footnote with Alt+Ctrl+F. Insert an endnote with Alt+Ctrl+E.

Research papers, theses, and technical documents are rarely completed in a single pass. They usually require multiple rewrites and, after review, usually require additional footnotes or endnotes. To make changes, you will need to know how to view and edit existing footnotes and endnotes.

Viewing Footnotes and Endnotes

If you choose to leave the note pane open, it will scroll along with the document to display the notes that correspond to the note references displayed in the text.

Word offers some handy shortcuts for viewing existing notes. If you have a mouse and are in normal view, you can open the note pane by double-clicking any note reference in your document, and you can close the pane and move back to the note reference by double-clicking any note entry in the pane. You also can open the note pane by holding down the Shift key while you drag the split bar down. (The split bar is the black bar above the up arrow in the right scroll bar.) Close the pane by dragging the split bar back up or by double-clicking the split bar.

Once you have opened the note pane, you can switch between viewing footnotes and endnotes by selecting either All Endnotes or All Footnotes from the drop-down list at the top of the pane.

You can also use the View Footnotes command to view footnotes and endnotes. When you are in normal view, choosing this command will open the note pane. When you are in page layout view, a dialog box appears if your document has both footnotes and endnotes, giving you a choice to view either the footnotes or endnotes area.

Formatting and Editing Footnotes and Endnotes

Footnote and endnote text can be formatted and edited just like any other text. You can use the ribbon, ruler, toolbar, and menu commands for formatting notes. The default point size is 10 points for the note text and 8 points for the reference mark.

You can easily change the formatting of all your footnotes by redefining the Footnote and Endnote Reference and Footnote and Endnote Text styles. Choose the Format Style command and select the style you want to change from the Styles list. Choose the Modify command button and then choose the appropriate command from the Format submenu. Make the desired formatting changes in the dialog box that is displayed and choose OK. Repeat these steps for any other formatting changes you want to make, choose OK, and then choose Close. Finally, choose the Close button. See Chapter 11, "Formatting with Styles," for more information on working with styles.

Finding Footnotes

If you are in page layout view, you can double-click the number to the left of a footnote or endnote reference to return to where you inserted the reference. You can return to the note associated with a reference by double-clicking the reference mark. This method allows you to quickly move back and forth between the document and the note while in page layout view. You can edit notes in page layout view just like any other text; simply scroll to the note and make the desired changes.

Tip
Use shortcut menus displayed with the right mouse button to quickly format in the note pane.

For Related Information
- "Formatting with Styles," p. 337
- "Cross-Referencing Text and Figures," p. 964
- "Creating Indexes and Tables of Contents," p. 893

VI

Handling Large Documents

You can use the Edit Go To command to locate notes. Choose the Edit Go To command or press F5 to display the Go To dialog box. Select either Footnote or Endnote in the Go to What list box, enter the number of the note you want to find in the text box, and choose the Go To button. To find the next or previous note, leave the text box blank and choose either the Next or Previous button. Choose Close to close the Go To dialog box.

For Related Information
■ "Using Find and Replace," p. 187

You can also use the Edit Find command to locate notes. Choose the Edit Find command, position the insertion point in the Find What text box and choose the Special button. Select either Endnote Mark or Footnote Mark from the list and choose the Find Next button repeatedly until you find the note you are looking for.

Deleting, Copying, and Moving a Footnote or Endnote

To delete, copy, or move a footnote or endnote, you work with the reference mark and not the actual note text. If you delete, copy, or move the actual note text, the reference mark is left in place where it was originally inserted. When you delete, copy, or move a reference mark, Word automatically renumbers all numbered notes.

To delete a footnote or endnote, you must select the reference mark for the footnote and press Del or Backspace. Deleting the note's text leaves the reference mark in the text.

If you want to remove all the footnotes or endnotes in a document, choose the Edit Replace command and choose the Special button. Select Endnote Mark or Footnote Mark from the list, clear any contents in the Replace With text box, and choose Replace All.

> **Caution**
>
> Be careful deleting text that contains footnotes or endnotes. If you select and delete text that contains a footnote marker, you also delete the footnote or endnote.

To copy or move a note with the Edit Copy/Edit Cut commands, follow these steps:

1. Select the reference mark for the note you want to move.

2. If you want to copy the note, choose the Edit Copy command. You can also choose the Copy button in the Standard toolbar.

   or

   If you want to move the note, choose the Edit Cut command. You can also choose the Cut button in the Standard toolbar.

3. Position the insertion point at the new position where you want the note reference.

4. Choose the Edit Paste command. Or you can choose the Edit Paste button in the Standard toolbar.

To copy or move a note with the mouse, follow these steps:

1. Select the reference mark for the note you want to move.

2. To move the note, drag the selected note reference to the new location and release the mouse button.

   or

   To copy the note reference, hold down the Ctrl key and drag and drop the note reference to the location you want to copy it to.

For Related Information
■ "Moving, Copying, or Linking Text or Graphics," p. 152

Converting Footnotes and Endnotes

So you've worked and slaved to get an article written for the *Arabian Rain Forest Review*, and it's finally done. After waiting for three weeks, you get a letter stating that if you resubmit the article by tomorrow, it will be published. But you used footnotes, and they want you to redo your article with endnotes. Because you typed it with Word, you don't have a problem; you can convert existing footnotes to endnotes, or endnotes to footnotes. You can convert all the notes in a document or individual notes.

To convert all notes, follow these steps:

1. Choose the Insert Footnote command.

2. Choose the Options button to display the Note Options dialog box; then choose the Convert button.

3. Select one of the options in the Convert Notes dialog box (see fig. 28.5).

Fig. 28.5
Use the Convert
Notes dialog box
to convert
footnotes to
endnotes, or
endnotes to
footnotes.

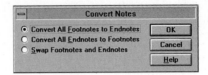

4. Choose OK to close the Convert Notes dialog box, choose OK to close the Note Options dialog box, and then choose the Close button to close the Footnote and Endnote dialog box.

To convert individual notes, follow these steps:

1. Choose the View Normal command if you are not already in normal view.

2. Choose the View Footnotes command.

3. Select All Footnotes or All Endnotes in the view box at the top of the note pane.

4. Select the note you want to convert in the note pane.

5. Click the right mouse button to display the shortcut menu.

6. Choose either the Convert to Footnote or Convert to Endnote command.

Customizing Note Settings

You can override the default note settings to suit your particular needs in several ways. You can customize the separator—the line that separates notes from the document text and from each other if they continue across more than one page. You also can add a continuation notice specifying that a note continues on the next page.

By default, footnotes appear on the bottom of the page in which their reference marks appear. If you want, you can specify that footnotes are printed directly beneath the document text if the text on a page does not extend to the bottom. Endnotes normally appear at the end of the document. You can specify that they appear at the end of each section in a document.

Finally, you can change the numbering scheme for notes. You can change the starting number for notes or choose to have note numbering restart on each page or at the beginning of each section, rather than having the notes numbered sequentially from the beginning of the document. You can also change the number format used for footnotes and endnotes.

Customizing Note Separators

Footnotes and endnotes are separated from the text in a document by a *separator*. When a footnote continues from one page to the next, Word inserts a *continuation separator* line between the document text and the continued footnote.

To customize separators, follow these steps:

1. Choose the View Normal command if you are not already in normal view.

2. Choose the View Footnotes command.

3. Select either All Footnotes or All Endnotes from the view list at the top of the pane.

4. To edit the separator line, select Footnote Separator or Endnote Separator from the view list.

    The default is a two-inch line. You can keep the line, delete it, or add characters before or after the line. You can change the characters that are used as the separator or use graphics characters if you want.

5. To edit the continuation separator line, select Footnote Continuation Separator or Endnote Continuation Separator from the view list.

    The Continuation Separator is the separator between the document text and the remainder of a note that continues across more than one page. Word proposes a margin-to-margin line. You can edit this line the same way as the separator line.

6. Choose the Close button or press Alt+Shift+C to close the note pane.

To reset the default settings for the note separators, follow Steps 1 through 4 in the preceding procedure, choose the **Reset** button and choose **Close**.

A *continuation notice* is text that explains that footnotes or endnotes continue on the next page. You can add a continuation notice in the note pane.

VI

Handling Large Documents

To add a continuation notice, follow these steps:

1. Choose the View Normal command if you are not already in normal view.

2. Choose the View Footnotes command.

3. Select either All Footnotes or All Endnotes from the view list at the top of the pane.

4. Select either Footnote Continuation Notice or Endnote Continuation Notice from the view list.

5. Type the text you want to use for the continuation notice.

6. Choose the Close button or press Alt+Shift+C to close the note pane.

To view the text, switch to page layout view. You can only edit the continuation text in the note pane. To reset the default settings for the continuation notice, follow Steps 1 through 4 in the preceding procedure, choose the Reset button, and then choose Close.

Placing Footnotes

You can specify where the footnotes or endnotes you create are to appear in your document. Traditionally, footnotes appear at the bottom of the page. Word for Windows places them at the bottom margin, below the footnote separator. You can change the placement so that footnotes appear immediately below the text in a document.

Endnotes normally appear at the end of a document. You can choose to have endnotes appear at the end of each section in a document, provided that the document is divided into sections.

To change the position of footnotes, follow these steps:

1. Choose the Insert Footnote command.

2. Choose the Options button. The Note Options dialog box appears (see fig. 28.6).

3. Select either the All Footnotes or All Endnotes tab.

4. Select one of the following options from the Place At drop-down list:

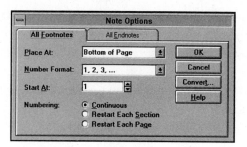

Fig. 28.6
Select the position of notes in the Note Options dialog box.

Option	Function
Bottom of Page	Places footnotes at the bottom margin of the page on which the footnote references appear (the default setting).
Beneath Text	Prints footnotes after the last line of text. This style is handy when the text is much shorter than a page.
End of Section	Prints the endnotes at the end of the section.
End of Document	Prints endnotes at the end of the document.

5. Choose OK and then choose the Close button.

Fig. 28.4, shown earlier in this chapter, shows a document with the footnotes placed at the bottom of the page, just below the document text. Fig. 28.7 shows the same document with the endnotes collected at the end of the document.

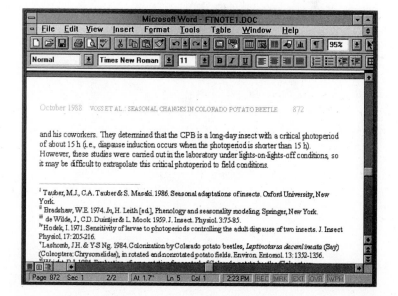

Fig. 28.7
A document in page layout view that shows endnotes collected at the end of the document.

VI

Handling Large Documents

If you specify endnotes to appear at the end of each section, you can choose to print the endnotes at the end of the current section (the choice Word for Windows proposes), or you can save them for a later section. Place the insertion point in the section in which you want to suppress the endnotes. Choose the File Page Setup command and select the Layout tab. Select Suppress Endnotes to save endnotes for the next section, or clear Suppress Footnotes to include the endnotes with the current section.

Customizing Numbering

You can change how you number your footnotes. To customize the numbering of footnotes, follow these steps:

1. Choose the Insert Footnote command.

2. Choose the Options button. The Note Options dialog box appears (refer to fig. 28.6).

3. Select either the All Footnotes or All Endnotes tab.

4. To change the starting number, type a new number in the Start At text box, or scroll the up and down arrows to select a new number.

5. Select one of the following Numbering options:

Option	Result
Continuous	Numbering is continuous from beginning to end of document.
Restart Each Section	Numbering is restarted in each section of the document.
Restart Each Page	Numbering is restarted on each page of the document (available only for footnotes).

6. Choose OK and then choose Close.

From Here...

Review the following chapters to learn more about features and techniques that may be related to work requiring footnotes and endnotes:

- Chapter 29, "Creating Indexes and Tables of Contents." Most scholarly works require an index and a table of contents or a table of figures. This chapter shows you how to do these.

- Chapter 31, "Adding Cross-References and Captions." Documents that require notes usually require cross-references from one location in text to another location, figure, or table.

- Chapter 32, "Assembling Large Documents." If your work becomes longer than approximately 50 pages, you may find better performance by separating your document into smaller subdocuments.

VI

Handling Large Documents

Chapter 29

Creating Indexes and Tables of Contents

In this chapter, you learn how to build references for a document so that it is easy for people to use. Imagine trying to locate a specific topic in a long reference book with no table of contents, trying to get information from a long technical document without a good index, or trying to remember where you saw a useful chart or table in a book with no list of figures. Word for Windows is equipped with powerful tools for creating these reference aids.

Creating Indexes

An index, such as the one found at the end of this book, lists topics covered in a book or document and provides the page numbers where you can find the topics. Without an index, your readers will have difficulty locating information in a long document or one that is filled with references.

In Word for Windows, creating an index involves two steps. First, you must identify in the document each entry you want indexed. Second, you must collect these entries into an index.

Word for Windows has the ability to create simple indexes, such as the following:

```
Printing, 5, 12, 25
Publishing, 37, 54, 68
```

Word for Windows also can create indexes that use subentries so that specific topics are easier to locate:

In this chapter, you learn how to do the following:

- Create, format, and edit index entries, and then compile and format an index.

- Use a concordance file to automatically create index entries.

- Create and format a table of contents based on heading or other styles, and to create table of contents entries based on any text.

- Create tables of figures or other tables based on figure caption or other styles, or based on any text.

```
Printing
        Envelopes, 37, 39
        Merge, 43-45
```

If you need more in-depth or complex indexing, Word for Windows is capable of creating indexes that include different characters as separators, unique formatting, and multiple levels of subentries, as in the following example:

```
Printing
        Envelopes: 37, 39-42
        Mail Merge
                Data document: 54-62
                Main document: 50-55, 67, 72
        Conversion, See WordPerfect conversion
```

Creating Index Entries

Identifying an entry, such as a word, to be included in your index can be as simple as selecting the word and choosing a command. As an alternative, you can position the insertion point where you want the entry referenced, choose a command, and type the word to index. This second method gives you the flexibility to decide how the topic will appear in the index.

> **Note**
>
> When creating index entries, you should select the entire word or phrase to be indexed. Remember that you can select entire words by double-clicking the word or by moving to the beginning of the word and pressing Shift+Ctrl+right arrow.

To create an index entry in your document, follow these steps:

1. Select the word or words to index or position the insertion point where you want the entry.

2. Choose the Insert Index and Tables command. Word for Windows displays the Index and Tables dialog box.

3. Click the Index tab to display the indexing options, if they are not already displayed (see fig. 29.1).

4. Choose the Mark Entry button. Word for Windows displays the Mark Index Entry dialog box.

   The Mark Index Entry dialog box includes the selected word or words (see fig. 29.2). If no word or words are selected, type the index entry.

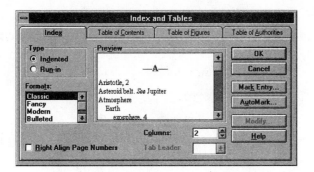

Fig. 29.1
Use the Index and
Tables dialog box
to create index
entries and
compile indexes.

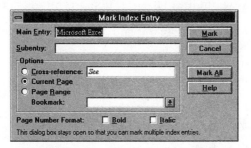

Fig. 29.2
Creating an index
entry in the Mark
Index Entry dialog
box.

Note

If the selected text contains a colon (:), Word for Windows prefaces the colon with a
backslash (\). If you type text that contains a colon, you must preface the colon with
a backslash yourself. As you learn in "Creating Multiple-Level Index Entries" later in
this chapter, the colon has a special meaning in an index entry. The backslash character tells Word for Windows to ignore the colon's special meaning and instead to
include it in the index entry text.

5. In the Main Entry text box, make no change if the index entry looks
   the way you want it; or type and edit the index entry as you want it to
   appear in the index.

6. Select among the index entry Options.

   Select the Cross-reference option to create a cross-reference index entry.
   Cross-reference index entries are described later, in the section "Creating Cross-Reference Index Entries."

   Select Current Page to have the index entry refer to the current page
   only.

Tip
You can also open
the Mark Index
Entry dialog box
by pressing
Alt+Shift+X.

Select Page Range and type or select the name of a bookmark from the drop-down list if you want the index entry to refer to the range of pages spanned by the bookmark (see Chapter 5, "Editing a Document," for more information on using bookmarks, and the later section of this chapter, "Including a Range of Pages").

7. Select among the Page Number Format options.

Select Bold to print the index page numbers for this entry in boldface text.

Select Italic to print the index page numbers for this entry in italic text.

8. Choose Mark to mark only this entry for inclusion in the index.

or

Choose Mark All to have Word for Windows search the entire document and mark all index entries that match the text in the Main Entry text box for inclusion in the index.

The Mark Index Entry dialog box remains open after marking the index entry whether you choose Mark or Mark All. To create additional index entries, scroll your document and select additional text, or move the insertion point to where you want the next index entry and type the entry directly into the Main Entry text box, repeating Steps 5 through 8.

9. Choose Close to close the Mark Index Entry dialog box.

Repeat these steps for every index entry in your document.

Note

You can add to the index entry character formatting that will affect how the entry appears in the compiled index by selecting text in the Main Entry or Subentry text boxes and using the character formatting shortcut keys. If you want the main index entry to be in bold, for example, select all of the text in the Main Entry text box and press Ctrl+B to apply bold character formatting. When the index is compiled, this entry appears in bold. (The character formatting shortcut keys are listed in Chapter 9, "Formatting Characters and Changing Fonts.")

Including a Range of Pages

As you create an index, you probably will want to reference a range of pages for an index entry, as in the following example:

```
Desktop Publishing, 51-75
```

To do this, you first must select the range of pages and assign a bookmark to the selection (see Chapter 5, "Editing a Document," for more information on using bookmarks). Then, when you insert the index entry, you use the bookmark name in the Bookmark text box (part of the Page **R**ange option) to indicate the range of pages for the entry.

You want to use a range name to mark the span of pages rather than an actual number of pages because editing, insertions, and deletions may move the topic so that it spans different page numbers than those typed. By using a bookmark, Word for Windows calculates the new location of the bookmark so that the index will be up to date.

To reference a range of pages, first create the bookmark by following these steps:

1. Select the pages you want to reference in the index entry.

2. Choose **E**dit **B**ookmark.

3. Type a name of up to 20 characters in the **B**ookmark Name text box.

4. Choose OK.

Now create the index entry and use the bookmark to describe the page range involved in the reference by following these steps:

1. Position the insertion point where you want to insert the index entry.

2. Choose the Insert Index and Tables command.

3. Click the Index tab to display the Index options, if necessary.

4. Choose the Ma**r**k Entry button.

5. In the Main Entry text box, make no change if the index entry looks the way you want it, or type an index entry.

6. Select Page **R**ange, and type the bookmark name in the text box, or select it from the drop-down list.

7. Select other options as necessary.

8. Choose Mark to create the index entry. The Mark Index Entry dialog box remains open.

9. Choose Close to close the Mark Index Entry dialog box.

> **Note**
>
> You can also select text and set bookmarks after you open the Mark Index Entry dialog box. Open the Mark Index Entry dialog box, and then use the usual procedure to set a bookmark; the Mark Index Entry dialog box stays open.

Customizing Index Entries

When you choose the Mark Entry option of the Insert Index and Tables command, enter descriptive text, and choose OK, you actually are entering a hidden {XE} field code into the document at a point directly after the insertion point or the selected text. These field codes are a powerful feature that can help you automate Word for Windows and customize the results of some commands, like the Insert Index and Tables command.

To see the hidden text of the field codes inserted by the Mark Entry option of the Insert Index and Tables command, choose the Tools Options command, and then select the View tab. Select Hidden Text from the Non-Printing Characters group and choose OK. The hidden text in the index field is now displayed at all times. Deselect this check box when you want to hide the {XE} field text.

Tip
You can also display hidden text in {XE} fields by clicking the Show/Hide button on the Standard toolbar.

Some example field codes for index entries are as follows:

Field Code	Result in Index
{XE "Printing"}	Printing, 56
{XE "Printing Envelopes" \r "PagesEnv"}	Printing Envelopes, 72-80
{XE "Printing Envelopes" \b \i}	Printing Envelopes, 56

You can modify and edit these codes to give them more capabilities or formatting than is built into the Insert Index and Tables Mark Entry command. The section "Formatting an Index" later in this chapter covers formatting in detail.

Index entries appear in the compiled index capitalized exactly as they are in the {XE} index entry fields. If your document contains index entries for the words *computer* and *Computer*, Word for Windows creates a separate entry in the finished index for each word. If you want only one entry for both words, you must edit the text in the {XE} field to have the same capitalization.

Assembling a Simple Index

After you create an entry for each index entry or subentry you want collected into an index, you can compile the index. Follow these steps to create your index:

1. Position the insertion point where you want the index.

   If you are creating an index for a master document, use the View Master Document command to switch to master document view, and make sure that the insertion point is not in a subdocument.

2. Turn off the display of hidden text and field codes so that the document will be repaginated properly as the index is created.

3. Choose the Insert Index and Tables command.

4. Click the Index tab to display the index options, if they are not already displayed (see fig. 29.3).

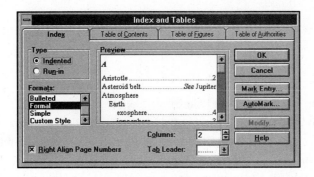

Fig. 29.3
Compiling an index with the Index and Tables dialog box.

VI

Handling Large Documents

5. Choose from two types of indexes: indented or run-in. Select Indented to indent subentries under major entries in the index as in the following example:

```
Printing
     Envelopes, 56
```

Select Run-in to include subentries on the same line as their major entries, with words wrapping to the next line if necessary, as in the following example:

```
Printing: Envelopes, 56
```

6. Select among seven Formats for the index; a sample of the format you select is shown in the Preview box.

   If you select Custom Style, the Modify button is enabled. Choose Modify to adjust the style of the text used in the index. Word for Windows displays a standard Style dialog box, except that style editing is limited to the Index Heading and Index styles 1 through 9. Refer to Chapter 11, "Formatting with Styles," for more information on editing styles.

7. Set the number of columns in the index in the Columns text box.

8. Use the Right Align Page Numbers check box to turn the right alignment of page numbers on or off.

   If Right Align Page Numbers is selected, then the Tab Leader list box is enabled.

9. Select the leader style (none, dots, dashes, or a solid line) in the Tab Leader list box.

10. Choose OK. Word for Windows repaginates the document and compiles the index. Figure 29.4 shows a sample index.

When you use the Insert Index and Tables command to compile an index, you are actually inserting a hidden field code, {INDEX}. Chapter 37, "Automating with Field Codes," describes field codes in detail; the following example shows the field code for the index shown in figure 29.4. To view the index field code, place the insertion point in the index and press Shift+F9. Press Shift+F9 while the insertion point is in the field to again view the index's text.

```
{INDEX \h "A" \c "2" }
```

If you choose Custom Style for your index, no index heading to separate the index entries (such as separating the A's from the B's) is included in the index. If you want to include a heading in an index with a custom style, you must manually add the \h code to the {INDEX} field code. In the index field code example shown above, the "A" after the \h indicates that the index heading should contain the letter of the alphabet for the index entries below that heading. To edit the index field code, place the insertion point in the index and press Shift+F9 to display the field code, and then edit the text in the field code as you would any other text. To display the index with the new heading, follow the instructions later in this section on updating indexes.

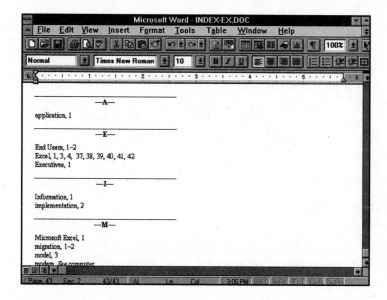

Fig. 29.4
A sample index.

Formatting an Index

You can change the appearance of an index by formatting the index and by formatting individual index entries.

Formatting an Index Using Styles. The easiest and fastest way to change the character and paragraph formatting of an index is by using styles. Word for Windows supplies automatic styles for index entries: Index heading, Index 1, and so on through Index 9. Index heading is the style Word for Windows uses to format the letters at the beginning of each section of your index. In fig. 29.4, the index heading style has been changed to add a border over the index heading paragraph so that a line is drawn between sections in the index. To redefine a style, choose the Format Style command. For more information on using styles, see Chapter 11, "Formatting with Styles."

> **Note**
>
> You can access several formatting options for indexes by using switches in the INDEX field. For example, you can specify which characters are used to separate index headings using the \h switch, or you can change the characters used to separate the index text from the page numbers (the default is a comma plus a space) with the \e switch. To add these switches, place the insertion point over the index and press Shift+F9 to display the INDEX field (or use the **T**ools **O**ptions command; select the View tab, and select the **F**ield Codes check box). Next, type in the desired switches. See Chapter 37, "Automating with Field Codes," for more information on the switches you can use with the INDEX field.

Formatting an Index Directly. You also can format the index directly, using the Format commands, the ribbon, and the ruler. If you update your index, however, you will lose all direct formatting changes. For this reason, you should redefine the styles for your index to make formatting changes, or only apply formatting directly to an index which you have fixed as text by unlinking the {INDEX} field.

Formatting Index Entries. You can also apply character formatting to individual index entries by directly formatting the text in the {XE} index entry field. Any character formatting you apply to text in the index entry field is applied to that index entry as Word for Windows compiles the index. The character formatting in the index entry field is applied to the text for that entry in addition to any formatting dictated by the index style. Character formatting applied directly to text in the {XE} field is unaffected if you update or replace the index.

You can apply character formatting to individual index entries in two ways. You can format the text in the Mark Index Entry dialog box as you create the index entry, or you can edit the index entry field itself. To format the text as you create the index entry, select text in either the Main Entry or **S**ubentry text boxes, and use the character formatting shortcut keys. To make an entry appear in italics, for example, select the text in the Main Entry text box, and press Ctrl+I. (The character formatting shortcut keys are listed in Chapter 9, "Formatting Characters and Changing Fonts.")

To edit the {XE} index field itself, click the Show/Hide button on the Standard toolbar so that hidden text and printing codes are displayed, or use the **T**ools **O**ptions **V**iew command to display Hidden text. Select all or part of the text in the {XE} field and use the ribbon or Format Font command to apply character formatting as you would with any other text.

Note

If you used the Insert Page Numbers command to have Word for Windows display chapter numbers with page numbers (for example, 4-27), then the chapter numbers are also shown with the page numbers in your index.

Updating or Replacing an Index

If you later add index entries to your document and want to update your index, move the insertion point within the {INDEX} field code (or the text that results from the code) and then press F9 (the Update Field key). Word for Windows updates the index, adding any new index entries and updating the page numbers for all index entries. Any formatting changes that you made to the index by redefining index styles or formatting individual index entries is kept; any formatting that you performed directly on the index text is lost.

Occasionally, you may want to completely replace an index, especially if you have made extensive changes in a document, or if you want to completely change the appearance of the index. To replace an index, place the insertion point within the {INDEX} field code (or the text that results from the code) and then use the Insert Index and Tables command as you would for compiling a new index. After you choose OK to begin compiling the index, Word for Windows asks whether you want to replace the existing index. Respond Yes to replace the selected index; Word for Windows compiles a new index, replacing the existing index. If you respond No, then Word for Windows still compiles a new index, but adds another {INDEX} field to the document.

Caution

If you use the Insert Index and Tables command to replace an index or to compile more than one index, Word for Windows resets all of the index styles (Index heading and Index 1 through 9) to have the characteristics of the index format you choose in the Index and Tables dialog box. If you want to keep any changes you have made to the index styles, use the F9 (Update Fields) key to update an index instead of replacing it.

Deleting an Index

To delete an index, select the index and press Del. You can select the entire index quickly by clicking the mouse button in the left margin over the section break at either end of the index. To select and delete an entire index quickly using the keyboard, place the insertion point to the left of the first entry, press F8, press the down-arrow key once, and press Del. Another alternative is to use the Tools Options command to display field codes, select the {INDEX} code, and press Del.

Fixing an Index as Text

An index is actually created with a hidden field code, {INDEX}. As long as the field code is there, you can quickly update the index by selecting the code and pressing F9.

In some cases, you may want to change the field code to its text result so that the index cannot be changed or updated. You may want to fix the field code so that you can reformat the index and formatting is not lost if someone selects the document and presses F9 to update other fields, or so that you can save the document to another word processing format while preserving the index.

To fix the index field code so that it changes to text, select the index or field code so that the entire index is selected. This is most easily done by dragging across one end of the index, which causes the entire index to be selected. Then press Shift+Ctrl+F9, the Unlink Field key combination.

Creating Multiple-Level Index Entries

If you have ever looked up a topic in an index and found the topic listed with a dozen or so page numbers, you know the value of a multiple-level index. When you expect to have several occurrences of a topic, you can help your reader by using categories and subcategories to divide the topic into more specific references. In Word for Windows, these entries are called *multiple-level index entries*, and they're easy to create.

The following is an example of the difference between a regular and a multiple-level index:

Index type	Result
Regular	Computers, 1, 6, 17, 25, 33-37, 54

Multiple-level	Computers
	    hard disk drives, 6
	    modems, 17
	    software, 1, 25
	    processor types, 33-37, 54

To create a multiple-level index entry, follow these steps:

1. Position the insertion point where you want the index entry, or select the text you want indexed.

2. Choose the Insert Index and Tables command.

3. Click the Index tab to display the index options, if necessary (refer to fig. 29.3).

4. Choose Mark Entry. Word for Windows displays the Mark Index Entry dialog box (refer to fig. 29.2).

5. In the Main Entry text box, type the name of the main category, or edit the selected text until the main category item is as desired.

6. Type the name of the subcategory in the Subentry text box.

   If you want to create sub-subentries, separate each subentry level in the Subentry text box with a colon (:).

7. Select other options as needed and choose Mark.

   The Mark Index Entry dialog box remains open so you can scroll through your document and create additional index entries. Repeat Steps 5 through 7 for each index entry with a subentry.

8. Choose Close when you are finished creating index entries.

Follow this procedure for each index entry and subentry. To create the following multiple-level index entry, for example, you would type **Computers** in the Main Entry text box, and **Hard disk drives** in the Subentry text box (Step 6):

```
Computers
      Hard disk drives, 54, 65
```

You also can create sub-subentries, as in the following example:

```
Computers
      Hard disk drives
            Maintenance, 54
            Performance, 65
      Processors, 102
```

All of the above sub-subentries were made with **Computers** in the Main Entry text box, and the following text in the Subentry text box:

```
Hard disk drives:Maintenance
Hard disk drives:Performance
Processors
```

Notice how each subentry level is separated from the previous level by a colon (:). You can have up to 9 levels of subentries. The index entry fields for these entries would look like this:

```
{XE "Computers:Hard disk drives:Maintenance" }
{XE "Computers:Hard disk drives:Performance" }
{XE "Computers:Processors" }
```

Creating Cross-Reference Index Entries

You can use the Insert Index and Tables command to create cross-reference indexes. A *cross-reference* index gives the reader information such as "Modem, see Computers."

To create a cross-reference index entry, follow these steps:

1. Select the word or words to index or position the insertion point where you want the entry.

2. Choose the Insert Index and Tables command. Word for Windows displays the Index and Tables dialog box.

3. Click the Index tab to display the indexing options, if necessary.

4. Choose the Mark Entry button. Word for Windows displays the Mark Index Entry dialog box.

   The Mark Index Entry dialog box includes the selected word or words (refer to fig. 29.2). If no word or words are selected, type the index entry.

5. In the Main Entry and Subentry text boxes, make no change if the index entry and subentry look the way you want; or type and edit the index entry and subentry as you want them to appear in the index.

6. Select Cross-reference, and type the cross-reference topic in the Cross-reference text box.

7. Select among other options as needed and choose Mark to mark only this entry or Mark All to mark all words in the document matching the Main Entry.

The Mark Index Entry dialog box remains open so you can scroll through your document and create additional index entries. Repeat Steps 5 through 7 for each index entry.

8. Choose Close when you are finished creating index entries.

Repeat these steps for each index entry. As with all other index entries, Word for Windows inserts an {XE} field code each time you mark an index entry. If you view the cross-reference index field, you will notice that it includes a special switch—\t—to create the cross-reference entry. The text in front of the \t switch is the index entry, and the text after the \t switch is the cross-reference text. The following line shows a cross-reference index field:

```
{XE "Graphics" \t "See Desktop Publishing" }
```

The above index entry field produces the following entry in the compiled index:

```
Graphics. See Desktop Publishing
```

Automatically Creating Index Entries

If you have a large number of index entries to create, or you want to regularize the capitalization of your index entries, you can have Word for Windows create index entries for you. To automatically create index entries, you must first make a *concordance file* containing the words or phrases you want to index and their corresponding entries and subentries. After you create the concordance file, you can use the AutoMark option of the Insert Index and Tables command to mark the index entries. You can add index entries to your document automatically or manually, in any combination.

Creating a Concordance File. The concordance file is a Word for Windows document file containing a single, two-column table, and no text outside the table. The first column of the table contains the words and phrases that you want to index, and the second column of the table contains the entry and subentry that should appear in the index for the indexed word or phrase.

To create a concordance file, follow these steps:

1. Use the File New command to create a new document file.

2. Choose the Table Insert Table command. Word for Windows inserts a two-column table into the document.

3. In the first column of the table, type the word or words you want to index.

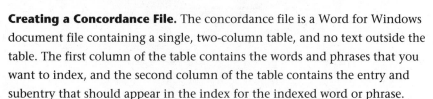

4. In the second column of the table, type the text that you want to appear in the index for each entry.

   To create an index subentry, separate each subentry level with a colon, as described earlier in this chapter for multi-level indexes. You cannot use a concordance file to create cross-reference index entries.

5. Perform Steps 3 and 4 for each word or phrase you want to index, adding additional rows to the table, as necessary. See Chapter 16, "Creating and Editing Tables," for more information on tables.

6. Save and close the concordance file.

Creating Index Entries from a Concordance File. To create index entries from the concordance file, follow these steps:

1. Turn off the display of hidden text, if necessary. Use the Show/Hide button on the Standard toolbar or the Tools Options command.

2. Choose the Insert Index and Tables command.

3. Click the Index tab to display the index options, if necessary.

4. Choose the AutoMark button. Word for Windows displays the Open Index AutoMark File dialog box (see fig. 29.5), which operates like the standard File Open dialog box.

Fig. 29.5
Selecting the concordance file to automatically create index entries.

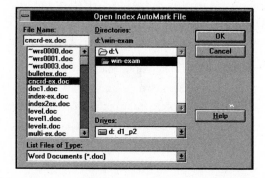

5. Select the disk drive and directory, as necessary, and then select the concordance file that you want to use.

   If the concordance file you want is not listed, use the List Files of Type list box to change the files displayed in the File Name list, or try another disk or directory.

6. Choose OK.

Word for Windows searches through your document, and inserts an index entry at every location where a word or phrase matches a word or phrase in the first column of the table in the concordance file.

After inserting the index entries, create the index as described earlier in this chapter. If you later make changes in the concordance file, just use the Insert Index and Tables AutoMark command again. Word for Windows adds any new index entries and updates any existing index entries to reflect changes in the concordance file.

Creating Tables of Contents

A table lists selected items included in your document, along with their page numbers. Building a table of contents at the beginning of a document is probably the most common use of this feature. You also can create tables of figures, photos, tables, or other items. Figure 29.6 shows one of the types of tables of contents you can create.

You have two ways to create a table of contents: by using heading styles or by using special table of contents entry fields. The easiest way to create a table of contents is to collect heading styles. (Styles are discussed in Chapter 11, "Formatting with Styles.")

Creating a Table of Contents Using Outline Headings

If you know you want a table of contents, you may want to format your document headings using the built-in heading styles, heading 1, heading 2, and so on. When you compile a table of contents, Word for Windows recognizes these heading styles and uses the text with those styles to create the table of contents. Word for Windows provides nine heading levels, heading 1 through heading 9. You choose which heading levels to use when creating a table of contents.

The heading styles used to create tables of contents or lists are the same heading styles used automatically when you create an outline. If you prefer to work with Word for Windows' outliner, you may want to outline your document before or as you write, and then use the outline headings to create your table of contents. Chapter 19, "Organizing Content with an Outline," describes how to create and use outlines.

For Related Information
- "Marking Locations with Bookmarks," p. 149
- "Formatting with Keyboard Shortcuts," p. 250
- "Creating Styles," p. 359
- "Creating a Table," p.509
- "Adding or Deleting Cells, Rows, or Columns," p. 531
- "Editing Fields," p. 1084
- "A Reference List of Field Codes," p. 1099

VI

Handling Large Documents

Fig. 29.6

Word for Windows can create tables of contents in many formats and for different items.

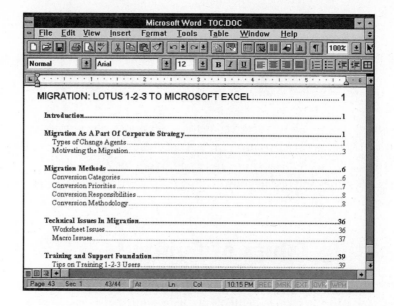

MIGRATION: LOTUS 1-2-3 TO MICROSOFT EXCEL.................................1

Introduction..1

Migration As A Part Of Corporate Strategy.......................................1
Types of Change Agents...1
Motivating the Migration..3

Migration Methods...6
Conversion Categories...6
Conversion Priorities...7
Conversion Responsibilities...8
Conversion Methodology..8

Technical Issues In Migration...36
Worksheet Issues..36
Macro Issues...37

Training and Support Foundation...39
Tips on Training 1-2-3 Users...39

Before you can create a table of contents, you must apply heading styles to each of your headings you want to list in a table of contents. (To create a table of figures or other table, refer to the later section in this chapter.) To apply heading styles, move the insertion point into the text and then use one of the following methods, which are listed from the easiest to most complex:

■ Select the desired heading style from the style list box in the ribbon.

■ Press Ctrl+Shift+left arrow or Ctrl+Shift+right arrow to change a paragraph into a heading style and move it to a higher or lower style.

■ Choose the Format Style command and select the desired heading style from the Styles list and choose OK.

You can apply heading styles as you type in the headings, using either the mouse or keyboard methods.

To create a table of contents from headings formatted with heading styles, follow these steps:

1. Position the insertion point where you want the table of contents to appear in your document.

   If you are creating a table of contents for a master document, use the View Master Document command to switch to master document view, and make sure that the insertion point is not in a subdocument.

2. Turn off the display of hidden text and field codes so that the document will be repaginated properly as the table of contents is created.

3. Choose the Insert Index and Tables command.

4. Click the Table of Contents tab to display the table of contents options, if necessary (see fig. 29.7).

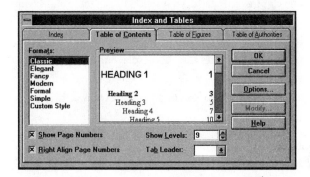

Fig. 29.7
Creating a table of contents with the Index and Tables dialog box.

5. Select among seven Formats for the table of contents; a sample of the format you select is shown in the Preview box.

   If you select Custom Style, the Modify button is enabled. Choose Modify to adjust the style of the text used in the table of contents. Word for Windows displays a standard Style dialog box, except that style editing is limited to TOC styles 1 through 9. The TOC styles are used for each of the heading styles; TOC1 for heading 1, and so on. Refer to Chapter 11, "Formatting with Styles," for more information on editing styles.

6. Select Show Page Numbers to turn the display of page numbers on or off.

7. Set the number of heading levels to show in the table of contents in the Show Levels text box.

8. Use the Right Align Page Numbers check box to turn the right alignment of page numbers on or off.

   If Right Align Page Numbers is selected, then the Tab Leader list box is enabled.

9. Select the leader style (none, dots, dashes, or a solid line) in the Tab Leader list box.

VI

Handling Large Documents

10. Choose OK. Word for Windows repaginates the document and compiles the table of contents.

Figure 29.6, shown earlier, shows a table of contents built from heading styles.

When you use the Insert Index and Tables command to create a table of contents, you are inserting a hidden field code, {TOC}. Field codes are described in detail in Chapter 37, "Automating with Field Codes"; the following example shows the field code for the table of contents shown in figure 29.6. To view the table of contents field code, place the insertion point in the table of contents and press Shift+F9. Press Shift+F9 while the insertion point is in the field to again view the table of contents text.

```
{TOC \o "1-9" }
```

In the above table of contents field, the \o switch tells Word for Windows to create the table of contents from outline headings; the numbers in quotation marks after the switch indicate the range of heading levels to include in the table of contents.

Note

Create a table of contents early in your work, then you can use it to navigate through your document. If you put the table of contents at the end of the document, you can press Ctrl+End to go to the end, check the table of contents to identify the page number you want, and then use the Edit Go To command (or press F5) to go quickly to that page.

Creating a Table of Contents Using Any Style

You may want to create a table of contents or some other table for a document that does not use heading styles, or you may want to include references to items that have a style other than one of the heading styles. You can create a table of contents based on any styles used in the document.

To create a table of contents that includes entries based on styles in addition to (or instead of) the built-in heading styles, follow these steps:

1. Turn off the display of hidden text and field codes so that the document will be repaginated properly as the table of contents is created.

2. Position the insertion point where you want the table of contents to appear in your document.

If you are creating a table of contents for a master document, use the View Master Document command to switch to master document view, and make sure that the insertion point is not in a subdocument.

3. Choose the Insert Index and Tables command.

4. Click the Table of Contents tab to display the table of contents options, if necessary (refer to fig. 29.7).

5. Choose Options. Word for Windows displays the Table of Contents Options dialog box (see fig. 29.8).

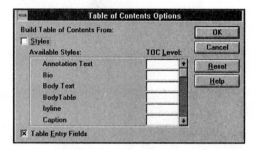

Fig. 29.8
The Table of Contents Options dialog box enables you to choose what items are included in the table of contents.

6. To create a table of contents that contains *only* entries compiled from certain styles, select the Styles check box so that there is an X in the box, and select Table Entry Fields so that there is not an X in the box.

or

To create a table of contents that contains *both* entries compiled from heading or other styles and from table entry fields, select Styles and Table Entry Fields so that there is an X in both check boxes.

Creating a table of contents based on table entries is described in the next section of this chapter.

7. For every style in the Available Styles list that you want included in the table of contents, type the table of contents level for that style in the corresponding TOC Level text box. You may use levels 1 through 9.

If you don't want a style included in the table of contents, make sure that its TOC Level text box is empty.

8. Choose OK to accept the options you set. Word for Windows closes the Table of Contents Options dialog box.

9. Set any other options in the Index and Tables dialog box, as necessary.

10. Choose OK to compile the table of contents. Word for Windows closes the Index and Tables dialog box and creates the table of contents.

Creating a Table of Contents Using Any Text

Some documents don't lend themselves to heading styles, or you may want to include references to items that don't have heading or other styles. In those cases, you can insert a table of contents field code, along with a descriptive entry, at the beginning of each appropriate section in your document (or wherever you want the listing to be referenced in the table of contents). Word for Windows then can collect these fields and descriptions into a table of contents.

A *field* is a hidden code enclosed in special characters that look like braces ({}). They are used to automate features of Word for Windows. Field codes were used earlier in this chapter for indexes. For more information on fields, see Chapter 37, "Automating with Field Codes."

Marking Table of Contents Entries. To insert table of contents fields into your document, follow these steps:

1. Position the insertion point where you want the table of contents entry.

2. Choose the Insert Field command.

3. Select Index and Tables in the Categories list.

4. Select TC in the Field Names list.

5. Position the insertion point in the Field Codes box, leaving one space after the TC entry.

6. Type an opening quotation mark ("), type the text of the table of contents entry, and type a closing quotation mark.

   To create the first entry in the table of contents shown in figure 29.6, for example, type the following in the Field Codes box (the \l switch is explained in Step 7):

   TC "MIGRATION: LOTUS 1-2-3 TO MICROSOFT EXCEL" \l 1

7. Type a space, a backslash, and the letter **l** (as shown above); next, type the number for the level at which you want this entry to appear in the finished table of contents. You may specify levels 1 through 9.

8. Choose Options to add additional switches to the TC entry; otherwise skip to Step 11. Refer to the {TC} section of Chapter 37, "Automating with Field Codes," for information on the available switches.

9. Select the desired switch in the Switches list, and then choose Add to add the switch to the TC field, and type any additional text needed for the switch in the Field Codes text box.

10. Choose OK to close the Field Options dialog box.

11. Choose OK to insert the table of contents entry and close the Field dialog box.

Repeat these steps for each table of contents entry you want. The field codes you insert will not be visible in your document unless you have turned on the Hidden Text option in the View tab of the Tools Options command.

> ### Note
>
> You can bypass the Insert Field command by using the Insert Field key combination, Ctrl+F9. Position the insertion point where you want the table of contents entry, press Ctrl+F9 (a pair of field characters will appear), and type **TC** *"text" switches*, where *text* is the text you want to appear in the table of contents and *switches* is the \l switch and level number, followed by any of the optional field code switches you want to use.

Editing Table of Contents Entries. You can edit a table of contents entry as you would any other text in your document. Any character formatting that you apply to the text in the table of contents entry will also appear in the finished table of contents. To display the table of contents entry text, use the Show/Hide button on the Standard toolbar to display the hidden text, or use the Tools Options View options to turn on the display of Hidden Text.

Creating the Table of Contents. To collect {TC} field codes into a table of contents, follow these steps:

1. Turn off the display of hidden text and field codes so that the document will be repaginated properly as the table of contents is created.

2. Position the insertion point where you want the table of contents to appear in your document.

3. Choose the Insert Index and Tables command.

VI

Handling Large Documents

4. Click the Table of Contents tab to display the table of contents options, if they are not already displayed (refer to fig. 29.7).

5. Choose Options. Word for Windows displays the Table of Contents Options dialog box (refer to fig. 29.8).

6. To create a table of contents that contains *only* entries compiled from table entry fields, select the Styles check box so that there is no X in the box, and select Table Entry Fields so that there is an X in the box.

   or

   To create a table of contents that contains *both* entries compiled from heading or other styles and from table entry fields, select Styles and Table Entry Fields so that there is an X in both check boxes.

   Creating tables of contents based on styles is described in the preceding section of this chapter.

7. Choose OK to accept the options you set. Word for Windows closes the Table of Contents Options dialog box.

8. Set any other options in the Index and Tables dialog box, as necessary.

9. Choose OK to compile the table of contents. Word for Windows closes the Index and Tables dialog box and creates the table of contents.

Troubleshooting Tables of Contents

The following troubleshooting tips will help you solve some of the more frequent difficulties with tables of contents.

Table of contents entries created from any text don't appear in the compiled table of contents.

Table of contents entries you created from any text (by creating a {TC} field) are included in the compiled table of contents only if you select the Table Entry Fields check box in the Table of Contents Options dialog box, or if the \f switch is in the {TOC} field. To correct this problem, do one of the following:

■ Follow the instructions in the section "Replacing a Table of Contents or Other Table" later in this chapter to replace the table of contents. Make sure that you choose the Options button and then select the Table Entry Fields check box in the Table of Contents Options dialog box.

■ Manually edit the {TOC} field, adding the \f switch to the field, then update the table of contents as described in the section "Updating a Table of Contents or Other Table" later in this chapter.

The page numbers for entries in the table of contents are incorrect.

If you make extensive changes to a document, the pagination of your document may change, so that the page numbers in a table of contents no longer match the actual page numbers of the heading or table of contents entry. If you compile a table of contents while hidden text is displayed, your document may not paginate correctly. To correct the page numbers in your table of contents, update the table of contents as described in the section "Updating a Table of Contents or Other Table" later in this chapter.

For Related Information
■ "Creating Styles," p. 359

■ "Editing Fields," p. 1084

■ "A Reference List of Field Codes," p. 1099

Creating a Table of Figures or Other Tables

You can create tables of other things besides contents, such as figures, photos, charts, equations, tables, or any other items. These tables usually appear in a document after the table of contents.

You can create tables of figures or other special-purpose tables of contents in two ways. First, you can compile the special purpose tables based on the style of the text, or you can manually insert table of contents entries into the document.

Creating Tables of Figures and Other Tables Using Styles

The easiest way to assemble tables of figures or other special-purpose tables is to use the Figure Caption, Equation, and other styles built into Word for Windows. If you use the Insert Caption command to create all of your figure captions, for example, you can easily build a table of figures. Refer to Chapter 31, "Adding Cross-References and Captions," for more information on creating captions.

To create a table of figures, equations, or tables based on one of Word for Windows' caption styles, follow these steps:

1. Position the insertion point where you want the table of figures to appear in your document.

If you are creating a table of figures for a master document, use the View Master Document command to switch to master document view, and make sure that the insertion point is not in a subdocument.

2. Turn off the display of hidden text and field codes so that the document will be repaginated properly as the table of figures is created.

3. Choose the Insert Index and Tables command.

4. Click the Table of Figures tab to display the table of figures options, if necessary (see fig. 29.9).

Fig. 29.9

Creating a table of figures with the Index and Tables dialog box.

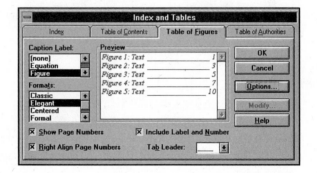

5. Select the appropriate caption in the Caption Label list.

6. Select among the Formats for the table; a sample of the format you select is shown in the Preview box.

If you select Custom Style, the Modify button is enabled. Choose Modify to adjust the style of the text used in the table of figures. Word for Windows displays a standard Style dialog box. Refer to Chapter 11, "Formatting with Styles," for more information on editing styles.

7. Select Show Page Numbers to turn the display of page numbers on or off.

8. Use the Right Align Page Numbers check box to turn the right alignment of page numbers on or off.

If Right Align Page Numbers is selected, then the Tab Leader list box is enabled.

9. Select the leader style (none, dots, dashes, or a solid line) in the Tab Leader list box.

10. Choose Options if you want to change the style on which the table of figures is based (otherwise, skip to Step 12). Word for Windows displays the Table of Figures Options dialog box (see fig. 29.10).

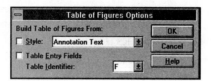

Fig. 29.10
The Table of Figures Options dialog box enables you to choose how the table of figures is built.

11. To create a table of figures that contains *only* entries compiled from a selected style, select the **Style** check box so that there is an X in the box, and then select the style in the list box. Also, select Table Entry Fields so that there is not an X in the box.

or

To create a table of figures that contains *both* entries compiled from the selected style and from table entry fields, select **Styles** and **Table Entry Fields** so that there is an X in both check boxes. Next, select the text style in the Style list box, and select the table identifier in the Table Identifier list box.

Creating a table of figures based on table entries and table identifiers is described in the next section of this chapter.

12. Choose OK. Word for Windows repaginates the document and compiles the table of figures.

When you use the Insert Index and Tables command to create a table of figures, you are actually inserting the same {TOC} hidden field code used to create a table of contents. A table of figures is really just a special variety of table of contents. The following example shows the field code for a table of figures:

```
{TOC \c "Figure" }
```

In the above table of contents field, the \c switch tells Word for Windows to create the table by using the text in paragraphs marked with {SEQ} fields, and the text in quotation marks after the switch indicates which items to group together in the same table. {SEQ} fields are the hidden codes inserted by the Insert Caption command. If you use the Insert Caption command to insert a figure caption, for example, the following code is inserted into the document:

```
{SEQ Figure \* ARABIC }
```

Refer to Chapter 37, "Automating with Field Codes," for more information on fields, and Chapter 31, "Adding Cross References," for more information on inserting captions.

Creating Tables of Figures and Other Tables Using Any Text

Another way to collect special tables is to use field codes instead of (or in addition to) styles. These field codes do three things:

- They mark the spot in the text you want to reference by page number.

- They include the text you want to appear in the table.

- They include an identifier that defines into which table they should be accumulated.

You can type these field codes directly into a document or use the Insert Field command to insert them. The field codes you insert look similar to the following:

```
{TC "Automated publishing" \f p}
```

In the command, *TC* is the field code, *"Automated publishing"* is the text that appears in the table, and the \f switch indicates that the table will be built from fields. The *p* is an identifier that associates this entry with other entries with the same identifier. This entry will be accumulated in a table with other field codes that have the *p* identifier.

The letters you use are up to you. The code for tables, for example, could be simply *t*. Some examples of how you may group items in different tables are listed in the following table:

Item	Field code identifier
Charts	c
Figures	f
Lists	l
Pictures	p
Tables	t

Marking List Entries. To insert field codes that mark what will be included in tables, follow these steps:

1. Position the insertion point on the page where you want the table to reference.

2. Choose the Insert Field command.

3. Select Index and Tables in the Categories list.

4. Select TC in the Field Names list.

5. Position the insertion point in the Field Codes box, leaving one space after the TC entry.

6. Type an opening quotation mark ("), type the text of the table entry, and type a closing quotation mark (").

7. Press the space bar once, and type \f, (the *f* indicates that the table is being built from fields).

8. Press the space bar to insert a space, and then type a single-character list identifier, such as **g**, for graphs. Use the same single-letter character for all items to be accumulated in the same table.

9. Use the Options button to add additional switches to the TC entry. (Refer to the {TC} section of Chapter 37, "Automating with Field Codes," for information on the available switches.)

10. Choose OK to insert the table entry and close the Field dialog box.

Repeat these steps for each entry you want. The field codes you insert do not appear in your document unless you turn on the Hidden Text option in the View tab of the Tools Options command. Your TC field code should look similar to the following:

```
{TC "Graph Showing Learning Retention" \f g}
```

Another, and often quicker, way to enter the field code is to position the insertion point, press Ctrl+F9 to insert the field code braces, {}, and then type the code and text inside the braces.

Creating the Table. To create a table that accumulates all the items belonging to a single identifier, such as *f* for figures or *g* for graphs, follow these steps:

1. Turn off the display of hidden text and field codes so that the document repaginates using only the text that will print.

2. Position the insertion point where you want the table to appear.

3. Choose the Insert Index and Tables command.

4. Click the Table of Figures tab to display the table of figures options, if the options are not already displayed (refer to fig. 29.7).

5. Choose Options. Word for Windows displays the Table of Figures Options dialog box (refer to fig. 29.10).

6. To create a table that contains *only* entries compiled from table entry fields, select the Styles check box so that there is no X in the box, and select Table Entry Fields so that there is an X in the box.

   or

   To create a table that contains *both* entries compiled from a selected style and from table entry fields, select Styles and Table Entry Fields so that there is an X in both check boxes, and select the style in the **Styles** list box.

   Creating tables based on styles is described in the preceding section of this chapter.

7. Select the table identifier in the Table Identifier list box, for example, *G* for graphs.

8. Choose OK to accept the options you set. Word for Windows closes the Table of Figures Options dialog box.

9. Set any other options in the Index and Tables dialog box, as necessary.

10. Choose OK to compile the table. Word for Windows closes the Index and Tables dialog box and creates the table.

For Related Information
■ "Creating Captions," p. 955

■ "Editing Fields," p. 1084

■ "A Reference List of Field Codes," p. 1099

If you display the resulting field code, it should appear similar to the following:

```
{TOC \fG \c}
```

The above {TOC} field produces a table from any TC fields that contain the *g* identifier. By using different list identifiers, you can include multiple tables for different entries in a document (for example, charts, graphs, lists, and so on).

Creating a Table of Authorities

If you work with legal documents, you are familiar with tables of authorities. A *table of authorities* lists where citations occur in a legal brief; the citations can be references to cases, statutes, treatises, constitutional provisions, and so on.

To create a table of authorities, you first create the citation entries in your document and then compile the table of authorities.

Creating Citation Entries

To create citation entries in your document, follow these steps:

1. Select the citation text or position the insertion point where you want the entry.

2. Choose the Insert Index and Tables command. Word for Windows displays the Index and Tables dialog box.

3. Click the Table of Authorities tab to display the table of authorities options, if necessary (see fig. 29.11).

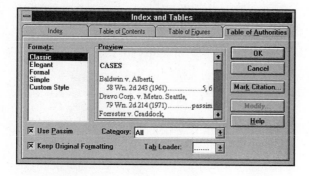

Fig. 29.11
The Index and Tables dialog box, showing the Table of Authorities options.

4. Choose the Mark Citation button. Word for Windows displays the Mark Citation dialog box.

   The Mark Citation dialog box includes the selected citation (see fig. 29.12) in both the Selected Text box and the Short Citation text box. If no citation is selected, type the citation entry.

5. In the Selected Text box, edit the text so that the long form of the citation entry looks the way you want it to appear in the table of authorities.

Tip
You can also open the Mark Citation dialog box by pressing Alt+Shift+I.

VI

Handling Large Documents

You can use any of the character formatting shortcut keys (such as Ctrl+B) to apply formatting to the text in the Selected Text box, and press Enter to add line breaks to the text.

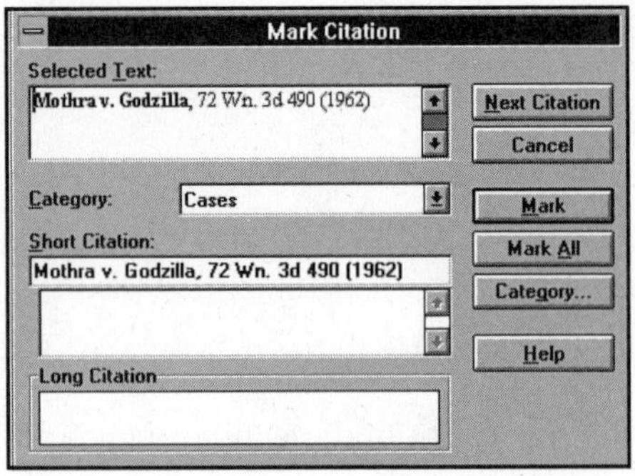

Fig. 29.12

Creating a citation entry in the Mark Citation dialog box.

6. Select the citation category in the Category list box.

7. Edit the text in the Short Citation text box so that it matches the short citation form that you use in your document. Word for Windows searches for and marks short citations in your document by matching the text in the Short Citation text box, so be sure that capitalization, punctuation, and abbreviations are the same.

8. Choose **Mark** to mark only this entry for inclusion in the table of authorities.

   or

   Choose Mark All to have Word for Windows mark the current citation and then search the entire document and mark all long and short citations that match your entries in the Mark Citation dialog box.

   The Mark Citation dialog box remains open after marking the citation, whether you choose Mark or Mark All.

9. To create additional citation entries, scroll your document and select additional text, repeating Steps 5 through 8, above.

   or

   Choose Next Citation to have Word for Windows search your document for common abbreviations used in legal citations (*in re*, *v.*, *Ibid.*, or *Sess.*), and then repeat Steps 5 through 8, above.

10. Choose Close to close the Mark Citation dialog box.

Repeat these steps for every citation entry in your document.

Editing Citation Entries

After you create a citation entry, you cannot edit it through the Insert Index and Tables command. Instead, you must edit the text in the hidden field code that is inserted in the document directly after the selected text whenever you create a citation entry in the Mark Citation dialog box.

To see the hidden text of the field codes inserted by the Mark Citation option, choose the Tools Options command, and then select the View tab. Select Hidden Text from the Non-Printing Characters group and choose OK. The hidden text in the index field is now displayed at all times. Unselect this check box when you want to hide the {TA} field text.

Edit and format the hidden text in the citation entry field the same way you would any other text in your document.

Assembling a Table of Authorities

After you create an entry for each citation you want collected into the table of authorities, you can compile the table. Follow these steps to create your table of authorities:

1. Position the insertion point where you want the table.

    If you are creating a table of authorities for a master document, use the View Master Document command to switch to master document view, and make sure that the insertion point is not in a subdocument.

2. Turn off the display of hidden text and field codes so that the document will be repaginated properly as the table of authorities is created.

3. Choose the Insert Index and Tables command.

4. Click the Table of Authorities tab to display the index options, if necessary.

5. Select among four Formats for the table of authorities; a sample of the format you select is shown in the Preview box.

    If you select Custom Style, the Modify button is enabled. Choose Modify to adjust the style of the text used in the index. Word for Windows displays a standard Style dialog box. (Refer to Chapter 11, "Formatting with Styles," for more information on editing styles.)

Tip

You can also display hidden text in {TA} fields by clicking the Show/Hide button on the Standard toolbar.

VI

Handling Large Documents

6. Select the **Passim** check box (so there is an X in it) to substitute the term *passim* whenever a citation has five or more different page numbers.

7. Select the Keep Original Formatting check box to have the citation appear in the table of authorities with the same formatting it has in the document text.

8. Select the tab leader style (none, dots, dashes, or a solid line) you want to use for the page numbers in the **Tab** Leader list box.

9. In the Category list box, select the category for this table of authorities. The All selection includes all of the other categories in a single table.

10. Choose OK. Word for Windows repaginates the document and compiles the table of authorities.

When you use the Insert Index and Tables command to compile a table of authorities, you are inserting the {TOA} hidden field code. To view the index field code, place the insertion point in the index and press Shift+F9. The following example shows a typical field code for a table of authorities.

```
{TOA \H \C "1" \P}
```

Customizing Citation Categories

You can change Word for Windows' predefined citation categories, or add your own categories.

To customize the citation categories, follow these steps:

1. Choose the Insert Index and Tables command. Word for Windows displays the Index and Tables dialog box.

2. Click the Table of Authorities tab to display the table of authorities options, if necessary.

3. Choose the Mark Citation button. Word for Windows displays the Mark Citation dialog box.

4. Choose the Category button. Word for Windows displays the Edit Category dialog box (see fig. 29.13).

5. In the Category list, select the category you want to change. Word for Windows permits up to 16 different categories, and only predefines the first 7. The remaining categories in the Category list are simply numbered 8 through 16.

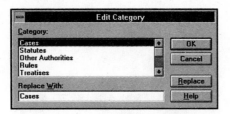

Fig. 29.13
Creating custom-
ized citation
categories in the
Edit Category
dialog box.

6. Type the new category name in the Replace With text box.

7. Choose the Replace button to change the category name.

8. Repeat Steps 5 through 7 for each category you want to customize.

9. Choose OK to close the Edit Category dialog box.

**For Related
Information**
■ "Formatting
with Keyboard
Shortcuts,"
p. 250

Updating, Replacing, or Deleting Tables of Contents and Other Tables

You can easily update, replace, or delete any table of contents, table of figures, table of authorities or other tables you create with the Insert Index and
Tables command.

Updating a Table of Contents or Other Table

As you add or delete text from a document, you will also add or delete various table entries. If you add new headings to a document, additional figures,
or other items, you will need to update the various tables in your document.

To update any table of contents or other table, follow these steps:

1. Place the insertion point in the table's field code (or the text resulting
   from it).

2. Turn off the display of hidden text, so that the document will paginate
   correctly as the table is updated.

3. Press F9, the Update Fields key. Word for Windows displays a dialog
   box similar to the one shown in figure 29.14 (the exact title of the dialog box depends on the type of table you are updating).

4. Select Update Page Numbers Only if you have only added or deleted
   text from the document, without adding or deleting table or citation
   entries.

   or

Select Update Entire Table if you have added or deleted table or citation entries in the document.

5. Choose OK.

Fig. 29.14
Word for Windows
asks you how
extensive the table
update should be.

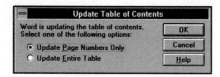

If you choose to update a table, any formatting you applied to the table by editing the styles used by the table will be unchanged. If you formatted the table directly, then updating page numbers leaves that formatting in place, but updating the entire table causes the formatting to be replaced by the style formatting.

Tables that have been unlinked so that their text is fixed can not be updated; instead, you must recreate the table if you want an updated version.

Replacing a Table of Contents or Other Table

Occasionally, you may want to completely replace a table of contents or other table, especially if you have made extensive changes in a document, or if you want to completely change the appearance of the table. To replace a table of contents or other table, place the insertion point within the table's field code (or the text that results from the code) and then use the Insert Index and Tables command as you would for compiling a new table of contents, table of figures, or table of authorities. After you choose OK to begin assembling the table, Word for Windows asks whether you want to replace the existing table. Respond Yes to replace the selected table; Word for Windows compiles a new table, replacing the selected one. If you respond No, then Word for Windows still compiles a new table, but adds another table field ({TOC} or {TOA} field) to the document.

Deleting a Table of Contents or Other Table

To delete any table of contents, table of figures, or table of authorities, just select the table and press Del, or use the Tools Options command to turn on the view of field codes, and then delete the table field.

Limiting Tables of Contents and Other Tables

If you need to create a table of contents or other table for part of a document, you need to modify the field codes with switches. To modify the field codes, use the Tools Options command, select the View tab, and then select Field Codes so that you can see the {TOC} or {TOA} field codes. Type the switches inside the field code braces as shown in the following table. After modifying the field code, you must update the entire table as described in the preceding section of this chapter. For more information on modifying field codes, refer to Chapter 37, "Automating with Field Codes."

Switch	Argument	Use
\b	bookmarkname	{TOC \o \b NewIdeas} The table of contents that is built is only for the area named NewIdeas. The \o indicates that the table of contents is built from heading styles.
\o	"1-4"	{TOC \o "1-4"} The table of contents is built from a limited selection of heading styles, Heading 1 through Heading 4.

For more information on page numbering or limiting the scope of a table of contents, refer to Chapter 32, "Assembling Large Documents."

For Related Information
■ "Editing Fields," p. 1084

■ "A Reference List of Field Codes," p. 1099

Formatting Tables of Contents and Other Tables

If you format a table of contents, table of figures, or other table using the format commands or the ribbon and ruler, that formatting will be lost if you update the entire table (updating page numbers only will not affect formatting). You can use two methods to format tables of contents, tables of figures, or other tables so that formatting is not lost when tables are updated. With the first method, you apply formatting to the table by editing the styles used by the table. The second method uses switches that are inserted within the TOC or TOA field to add or preserve formatting. The following two sections explain these methods in detail.

VI

Handling Large Documents

Formatting with Styles

Levels within a table of contents each have a specific style—TOC1, TOC2, and so on. By redefining these styles, you can change the format of the table of contents, and that new format will still be used when you update the table of contents. For a table of figures or authorities, you change the formatting of the Table of Figures and Table of Authorities styles.

This method of changing styles is useful if you want to format one level of the table of contents differently from other levels. You may, for example, want the first level of the table, TOC1, to be in bold 12-point Times Roman without tab leaders (dots or dashes before the page number) and all other levels to use the Normal font with tab leaders.

Word for Windows' original TOC (Table of Contents) styles are based on the Normal style, with added indents, so your table of contents will look similar to the rest of your document. To redefine the TOC, Table of Figures, or Table of Authorities styles, choose the Format Style command and use the **Styles** list to select the style you want to redefine (such as TOC1 for the first level of table of contents entries). Next, choose the **Modify** button to open the Modify Style dialog box, which gives you options for redefining styles.

Choose the Format button and select the font, border, and other formatting options for the style you want to change. After making the formatting changes to the style, choose OK; Word for Windows applies the changes in style to all text in your document that uses that style. When the original Style dialog box reappears, continue to redefine styles, or choose the Close button.

Formatting with Field Code Switches

The second method of formatting a table of contents or figures so that formatting is preserved when you update the table employs switches you include with the TOC field code. You can use many switches to format the entire table of contents or figures. Chapter 37, "Automating with Field Codes," discusses these switches in more detail.

To make changes, first display the field codes by choosing the Tools Options command, selecting the View tab, and then selecting the Field Codes check box (so that it has an X in it). Add your switch(es) inside the field code braces to tell Word for Windows how you want the table formatted after it updates. For example, if the TOC field code appears as

```
{TOC \fG \* charformat}
```

the entire table of graphs uses the formatting applied to the first letter of TOC. In this case, the bold and italic on *T* apply to the entire table. The \ * *charformat* switch applies the formatting of the first character in the field code to the entire result.

Some useful switches are in the following table:

Switch	Argument	Use
*	charformat	{TOC \o * charformat} Apply formatting of first character in field code to entire result of field. For example, change the fonts of the entire table of contents.
*	mergeformat	{TOC \o * mergeformat} Retain formatting in field results that you applied manually. Formatting of updated results applies on a word-for-word basis. For example, change the tab leader throughout the table of contents.
*	upper	{TOC \f t * upper} Change all characters in the table of contents to uppercase.
*	lower	{TOC \f g * lower} Change all characters in the table of contents to lowercase.
*	firstcap	{TOC \o * firstcap} Change all words in the table of contents to use a capital for the first letter.
*	roman or * ROMAN	{TOC \o * roman} Change numbers in the table of contents to Roman numbers. *roman* produces iv; *ROMAN* produces IV.

After making changes in the TOC field, you must select the field and press F9 (Update) to see the results of the changes.

From Here...

The topics in this chapter—indexes, tables of contents, tables of figures, and tables of authorities—go beyond the normal business letter, but are an integral part of many professional documents. Documents that require these features usually also require headers, footers, footnotes or endnotes, and the other features used in professional typing. To learn more about these and

For Related Information

■ "Editing Fields," p. 1084

■ "A Reference List of Field Codes," p. 1099

VI

Handling Large Documents

other features, and to learn more about the flexibility available in Word for Windows when you modify the field codes that some commands insert in the document, review the following major sections of this book:

- Chapter 5, "Editing a Document," describes how to mark page ranges by using bookmarks.

- Chapter 11, "Formatting with Styles," describes how to define, edit, and use styles such as the index, heading, and figure caption styles used to produce indexes, tables of contents, and tables of figures.

- Chapter 16, "Creating and Editing Tables," describes how to create a table and how to add rows to tables, skills which are necessary if you choose to create a concordance file to automatically create index entries.

- Chapter 31, "Adding Cross-References and Captions," describes how to insert and edit figure captions in your document. Figure captions are used to create tables of figures.

- Chapter 32, "Assembling Large Documents," describes how to create and view master documents, and how to include tables of contents and other tables in large documents.

- Chapter 37, "Automating with Field Codes," describes how to view and edit fields, and contains a list of all of the available field codes and their various options, including all of the field codes used to created indexes, tables of contents, and other tables.

Chapter 30

Tracking Revisions and Annotations

Because you don't work in a vacuum, Word for Windows is ready to work with other people, too—right on your computer screen. Using revision marks and annotations can eliminate errors and time spent transferring changes from paper to computer. Soon after you start using these features, you may wonder how you ever did without them.

Whether you work in a group or alone, revision marks keep track of changes made to a document. Each piece of added or deleted text is marked with the date, time, and reviewer's name. In effect, revision marks create an automatic history of the review process. Even if an edited document did not have revision marks turned on, you can create them by comparing the document to the original.

Word for Windows lets you use annotations just as you would jot notes in the margin, without worrying about these comments accidentally appearing in a final draft. Annotations enable you and other reviewers to include comments and questions in a special window, marked by the reviewer's initials and attached to the text being commented on.

What You Need to Know About Revisions and Annotations

Annotations do not alter the visible contents of a document but are linked to selections in the document, like invisible footnotes. Annotations are equally useful for reviewers' comments or for notes and questions to yourself. Revision marks, however, are useful for keeping a record of specific changes when

This chapter helps you maintain your documents and manage changes made within a workgroup. You learn how to do the following:

- Mark revisions and edits so that they are easy to see and can be accepted or rejected

- Compare two documents for changes

- Annotate a document with remarks or notes that do not print with the main document

VI

Handling Large Documents

you let someone else edit your document or when you want to review your own changes. Revision marks do not track changes to formatting, such as tab settings or point sizes.

Using the Revision Marks Feature

Revising a document is often a job shared by several people. For example, several people might work together to produce an annual report, or a book might be reviewed by more than one editor. If a revised document has no marks, it can be hard to find everything that was changed or who did it. Revision marks show where the document has been changed and by whom, allowing the originator to accept or reject any of the changes.

Adding revision marks is simple. Before someone makes revisions, turn on revision marking. Revisions to the document are then marked automatically as the reviewer makes changes (see fig. 30.1).

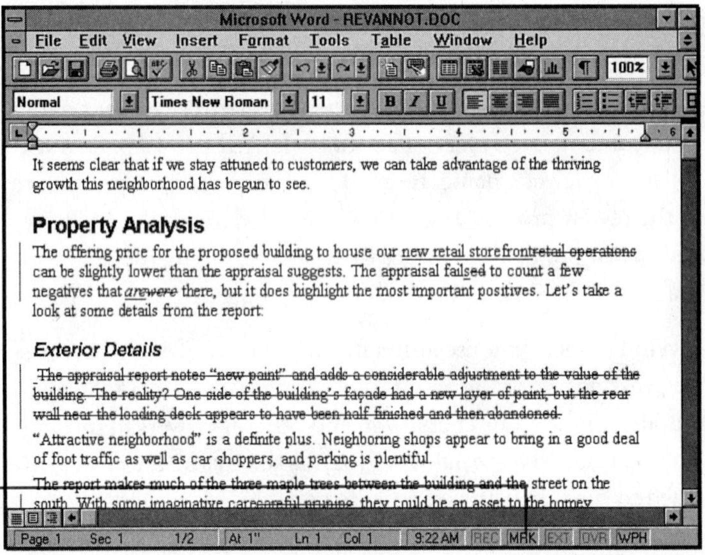

Fig. 30.1
With revision marking turned on, you can see exactly what additions and deletions a reviewer has made.

MRK indicator ──────

When you view revision marks, you get a general idea of how much is changed in your document, as well as the details of specific words and letters that were edited. You can also hide revision marks to see exactly what the document would look like if you accepted the changes.

Marking Revisions

When revision marking is turned on, revision bars appear in the margin next to any lines where text has been inserted or deleted. Revision marks indicate the actual text that has changed—inserted text is underlined, and deleted text has strikethrough formatting. The section "Customizing Revision Marks" later in this chapter tells how you can change these marks.

Before you turn on revision marking, you should save a copy of the original document. This can help later if you need to merge revisions from several reviewers or compare a reviewed file to create revision marks.

To mark revisions in the active document, follow these steps:

1. Choose the Tools Revisions command. The Revisions dialog box appears (see fig. 30.2). You turn on revision marking in the Revisions dialog box.

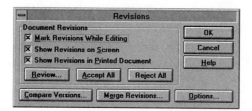

2. Select the Mark Revisions While Editing check box.

3. If you do not want to be distracted by revision marks while reviewing a document, deselect the Show Revisions on Screen check box.

4. Choose OK.

Tip
Double-clicking the MRK indicator in the status bar, shown in fig. 30.1, is a shortcut to display the Revisions dialog box.

To turn off revision marking, choose the Tools Revisions command and deselect the Mark Revisions While Editing check box.

While revision marking is turned on, any text inserted in the document or deleted from it is marked. If you move a selection of text, two sets of marks appear: deleted text where you moved it from, and inserted text where you moved it to. If you delete text marked as inserted, the text simply disappears. Only original text, when deleted, appears with revision marks for deleted text.

Note

You can turn on revision marking for all documents at once, if they are based on the NORMAL.DOT template. Open the NORMAL.DOT template, choose the **Tools** Revisions command, select the **Mark** Revisions While Editing check box, and save the template. You can also deselect the Show Revisions on **Screen** and Show Revisions in Printed Document check boxes to hide revision marks until you actually review the revisions.

Showing Revisions

When a document comes back from your reviewers or you return to a document after editing it yourself, you can look over the changes. If revision marks are not visible in the document, choose the Tools Revisions command and select the Show Revisions on **Screen** check box.

The document now appears with revision bars in the margin, marking where text has been inserted or deleted. If multiple reviewers made revisions, each reviewer's changes appear in a different color. If you want to continue tracking revisions but without seeing revision marks, choose the Tools Revisions command and deselect the Show Revisions on **Screen** check box.

By default, Word prints documents with revision marks showing. To print a document without revision marks, choose the Tools Revisions command and deselect Show Revisions in **Printed** Document.

Note

If you customize your user information, you can keep track of your own editing sessions separately. For each session you want to distinguish, choose the **Tools Options** command, select the User Info tab, and change the **Name** text box. For example, start with First Draft, then use Style Review for another editing session, and then use Final Draft. Each set of revisions appears in its own color, and the Review Revisions dialog box shows those names. Be sure to restore your original name later, because other Word for Windows features use this information.

Accepting or Rejecting All Revisions

Word for Windows makes using or discarding revisions easy. To incorporate all the revisions marked in the document, choose the Tools Revisions command and Accept All. When prompted to accept the revisions, answer Yes and choose Close. All the deleted text disappears, the inserted text is incorporated into the document, and revision bars are removed.

Rejecting all revisions means restoring your document to its contents before it was reviewed. To reject all revisions, choose the Tools Revisions command and Reject All. When prompted to reject all revisions, answer Yes and choose Close. Inserted text disappears, deleted text is restored, and revision bars are removed.

You cannot undo these commands. As a safety measure, save your file with a new name before you accept or reject all revisions. You then have a copy of original and revised drafts for later reference or comparison. Remember that any formatting changes made by reviewers remain, whether you accept or reject revisions.

Accepting or Rejecting Individual Revisions

You'll probably want to use some but not all of the revisions made to your document. You can look through the document, jumping directly from revision to revision, and choose whether to accept or reject each change.

To accept or reject individual revisions, follow these steps:

1. Choose the Tools Revisions command.

2. Choose the Review button. The Review Revisions dialog box appears (see fig. 30.3).

   In the Review Revisions dialog box, you can review all revision marks, and see which reviewer made a revision and when.

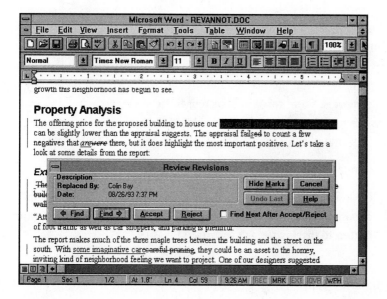

Fig. 30.3
The Review Revisions dialog box.

3. Choose one of the Find buttons to find either the next or the previous revision in the document and to show which reviewer made the change and when.

4. Choose the Accept button to keep the change, or choose the Reject button to discard it. If the Find Next After Accept/Reject check box is selected, Word immediately finds and selects the next revision.

5. If you change your mind, choose the Undo Last button to restore the most recent revision that you accepted or rejected.

6. Choose one of the Find buttons to locate the next revision.

While the Review Revisions dialog box is on-screen, you can click anywhere in the document to edit the text, or you can select another revision to display information about it. To see what the revision would look like if accepted, choose Hide Marks. Then choose Show Marks to display the revision marks again.

> **Note**
>
> A quick way to locate only revisions marked as inserted text is to choose the Edit Find command, select the Find What text box, and press Ctrl+N. To search for anything except inserted text (including deleted text and unchanged text), select the Find What text box and press Ctrl+N twice.

Customizing Revision Marks

Usually, revision bars in the margins are red, the revision mark for inserted text is an underline, deleted text has a line through it, and changes made by up to eight reviewers are marked in different colors. (If you have more than eight reviewers, Word for Windows reuses the earlier colors.) You can customize each of these marks to your liking. For example, you can mark deleted text as a subdued color, such as light gray, and inserted text as green.

To customize revision marks, follow these steps:

1. Choose the Tools Options command and select the Revisions tab, or choose the Tools Revisions command, and then choose the Options button to display the tab shown in fig. 30.4.

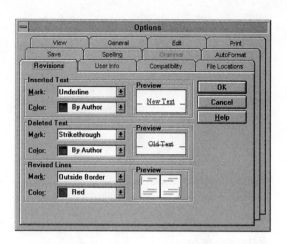

Fig. 30.4
As you customize revision marks in the Revisions tab of the Options dialog box, you can preview the appearance of changed text in a document.

2. Select styles from the Mark list boxes under Inserted Text, Deleted Text, and Revised Lines.

3. If you do not need color to distinguish reviewers, select a color from the Color list boxes under Inserted Text and Deleted Text.

4. Choose OK.

If you select By Author under Color in the Inserted Text and Deleted Text sections, each reviewer's changes appear in a different color for up to eight reviewers. The Revised Lines options specify the appearance of the revision bars in the margins of your document.

Protecting Documents for Revisions

Protecting a document for revisions ensures that revisions are being tracked. If a reviewer turns off revision marking in your document, you could have a good deal of extra work finding where revisions are and who made them. For increased security, you can add a password so that only you can unprotect the document.

When a document is protected for revisions, Word for Windows tracks all revisions and does not allow revision marks to be removed by accepting or rejecting them. Reviewers can add annotations as well as revise the document directly. For more information, see the section "Using Annotations" later in this chapter.

To protect a document for revisions, follow these steps:

1. Choose the **Tools Protect Document** command. The Protect Document dialog box appears (see fig. 30.5).

Fig. 30.5

The Protect
Document dialog
box.

2. Select the **Revisions** option.

3. If you want to keep other users from unprotecting the document, type a password in the Password text box.

4. Choose OK. If you entered a password, Word for Windows prompts you to reenter the password for confirmation.

To unprotect a document, choose the **Tools Unprotect** command. While the document is protected for revisions, any revisions made to the document will be tracked until it is unprotected, and you cannot choose to accept or reject any revisions. If you defined a password, you must enter it before the document can be unprotected. If you are using the routing feature of Word for Windows, you can protect the document when you add a routing slip. See Chapter 8, "Previewing and Printing a Document," for more information on routing documents.

Merging Revisions and Annotations

Several different reviewers may have worked on separate copies of a document instead of routing the same copy. If so, filtering through all the revision marks and annotations in multiple files can be tedious. To make the work easier, you can combine all the changes into the original document and see them together. You need the original document and any revised documents from it.

To merge revisions and annotations, follow these steps:

1. Open one of the revised documents.

2. Choose the **Tools Revisions** command.

3. Choose the **Merge Revisions** button. The Merge Revisions dialog box appears.

4. Select the original, unrevised document and choose OK.

5. Repeat these steps for each revised version of the document that you want to merge into the original.

Word for Windows merges the revision marks and annotations into the original document, where you can see and evaluate them in one place.

Troubleshooting Revisions

Why don't I have any revision marks in my document?

You can see revision marks only if revision marking was turned on while the document was being edited. Choose the Tools Revisions command, choose the Review button, and then choose the Find button. If no revision marks are found, you can add them by comparing your document with the original version of the file. See the section "Comparing Documents" later in this chapter.

Why do I see a revision bar in the margin but no revision marks?

There may be revision marks inside hidden text, field codes, or annotations. To see these, choose the Tools Options command, select the View tab, and then select the Field Codes and Hidden Text check boxes.

How can I see the reviewer name and time information in the Review Revisions dialog box?

Information about each revision appears only after you find the revision. Choose one of the Find buttons to search for revisions.

Why can't I turn off the option for tracking revisions?

If the document is protected for revisions, the Mark Revisions While Editing check box is grayed. To turn off this option, choose the Tools Unprotect command, asking the document's author for the password if necessary.

Comparing Documents

You can pinpoint revisions by comparing the current document to an earlier version. When you compare two documents, Word applies revision marks to your current document wherever it differs from the earlier version. The two documents you're comparing must have different names or locations on the disk.

For Related Information
■ "Sending Documents to Others in Your Workgroup" p. 238

To compare two versions of a document, follow these steps:

1. Open the document in which you want to see revisions.

2. Choose the Tools Revisions command. The Revisions dialog box appears. You can choose options from the Document Revisions section of the dialog box to determine how the revisions appear.

3. Choose the Compare Versions button. The Compare Versions dialog box appears.

4. From the Original File Name list, select a file to which you want to compare the current file.

5. Choose OK. Word for Windows compares the two documents and, based on the options you selected on the Revisions tab, marks any revisions that appear in the current document.

You can select or reject any of the revisions by using the following options in the Revisions dialog box:

For Related Information
■ "Using the Revision Marks Feature," p. 934

Choose This	To Do This
Review	Display each revision mark so that you can accept, reject, or ignore it. The Review Revisions dialog box provides these options.
Accept All	Leave the selection unchanged and remove the revision marks.
Reject All	Reverse all changes and remove revision marks.

Using Annotations

Revisions are useful for tracking editing changes in a document, whereas annotations are best for attaching comments to a document. Because annotations are linked to specific parts of a document, they are just like notes scribbled in the white space—except that annotations are more convenient.

You may have had the experience of printing a final copy of a document and then noticing a note to yourself that you forgot to delete. The annotation feature takes care of that problem by keeping comments separate from the rest of your text; they aren't printed unless you specifically decide to print

them. Annotations are the ideal place to store questions and notes to yourself
or to an author whose work you're reviewing.

Inserting Annotations

When you insert an annotation, Word marks the location in the document
and opens the Annotations pane. Here you can type your comments and
even format them.

To insert an annotation, follow these steps:

1. Select the word or passage you want to comment on, or position the
    insertion point in the text.

2. Choose the Insert Annotation command or press Alt+Ctrl+A to insert
    an annotation mark and open the Annotations pane (see fig. 30.6).

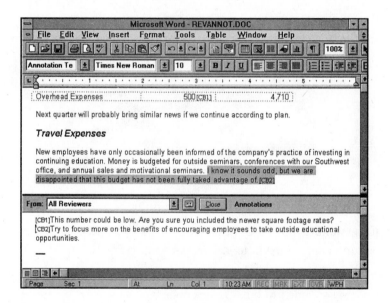

Fig. 30.6
The Annotations
pane showing the
reviewer's initials
and the text of the
annotation.

3. Type your annotation in the Annotations pane. You can use font and
    paragraph formatting just as you normally would.

The annotation mark, like a hidden-text footnote, contains the reviewer's
initials and a number—for example, [CB1]. Annotations are numbered in
sequence. In the Annotations pane, a corresponding mark precedes the annotation text.

To close the Annotations pane, choose the Close button or double-click any annotation mark in the pane.

Finding and Viewing Annotations

 There are several ways to display annotation marks in a document. When the Annotations pane is open, annotation marks always appear. Because annotation marks are formatted as hidden text, they appear also when hidden text is showing (when you choose View Hidden Text in the Tools Options dialog box). Finally, you can show annotation marks by clicking the Paragraph Marks button on the Standard toolbar.

To find a specific annotation mark, follow these steps:

1. Choose the View Annotations command. The Annotations pane appears.

2. Choose the Edit Go To command to display the Go To dialog box. In the Go To dialog box, you can go to a particular reviewer's next annotation or type the number of an annotation (see fig. 30.7).

Fig. 30.7
The Go To dialog box.

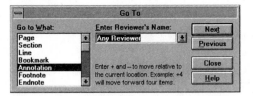

3. Select Annotation from the Go to What list box.

4. If you want to find a specific reviewer's annotation, type or select the person's name in the Enter Reviewer's Name box.

5. If you want to find a specific annotation, type a number in the Enter Reviewer's Name text box. For example, type 3 for the third annotation or +2 for the second annotation after the current selection.

6. Choose the Next or Previous button. The Next button changes to Go To if you type a number rather than select a reviewer's name.

> **Note**
>
> If you don't need to specify the reviewer, you can find annotations quickly by choosing the Edit Find command and then selecting Annotation Mark from the Special pull-down list. The Annotations pane appears automatically when an annotation is found. (This pane does not appear when you use the Go To command.)

When you select an annotation in the Annotations pane, Word for Windows highlights the corresponding document text. This is why it's most useful to select the text in question when you insert annotations. You can adjust the size of the Annotations pane by dragging the split box—the thick, black line between the vertical scroll bars of the document and Annotations panes.

Including or Deleting Annotations

An annotation often consists of comments or questions about the selected text. If the annotation contains suggested text, however, you can easily move the text into your document. Simply select the text in the Annotations pane and drag it into your document. Similarly, you can copy the text by holding down the Ctrl key while dragging. (If you cannot drag the text, choose the Tools Options command, select the Edit tab, and then choose the Drag-and-Drop Text Editing check box.)

To delete an annotation, select the annotation mark in your document and press the Del or Backspace key. The annotation mark must be selected: trying to backspace or delete when the cursor is next to the annotation mark does not delete it.

Note

You can easily remove all annotations at once. Choose the Edit Replace command, type ^a in the Find What text box, leave the Replace With text box empty, and choose the Replace All button.

If several reviewers added annotations to separate copies of an original document, you can merge all the annotations into the original document for convenient evaluation. To merge annotations, see the section "Merging Revisions and Annotations" earlier in this chapter.

Protecting Documents for Annotations Only

At times, you might want reviewers to comment on your document but not to change it directly. You can allow annotations but no revisions by protecting your document for annotations.

To protect a document for annotations, follow these steps:

1. Choose the Tools Protect Document command and select the Annotations option.

VI

Handling Large Documents

2. If you want to keep others from unprotecting the document, type a password in the Password text box.

3. Choose OK. If you entered a password, Word prompts you to reenter the password for confirmation.

No changes except annotations can be made to the document until it is unprotected, and menu commands that could make changes are unavailable. When anyone tries to edit the document, a beep warns that the document is protected.

To unprotect a document, choose the Tools Unprotect command. If you defined a password, you must enter it before the document can be unprotected.

Printing Annotations

To get a printed copy of an annotated document, you can either print just the annotations or print them at the end of the document.

To print annotations only, follow these steps:

1. Choose the File Print command.

2. Select Annotations from the Print What drop-down list box.

3. Choose OK.

Word prints the contents of the Annotations pane, adding the page number where each annotation mark occurs in the document.

To print a document with annotations, follow these steps:

1. Choose the Options button in the Print dialog box.

2. Select the Annotations check box, which automatically selects the Hidden Text check box, and choose OK.

3. Select Document from the Print What list box.

4. Choose OK.

Because annotation marks in a document are formatted as hidden text, all hidden text is printed. The annotations are printed at the end of the document, along with the page number of the accompanying annotation mark.

Troubleshooting Annotations

When I try to delete an annotation comment, why doesn't the annotation mark go away?

To delete an annotation, select the annotation mark in the document text and press Backspace or Del. You must select an annotation mark first, before pressing Backspace or Del, because it is a special nontext character, like a field.

I don't remember deleting an annotation, but now it's gone. Why?

If you delete the text surrounding an annotation mark in the middle of a document, the mark is deleted, even if the mark is not visible.

How do I change the initials in an annotation mark?

The initials are taken from the User Info tab of the Options dialog box. If you change your initials there, future annotations will contain the new initials.

From Here...

For information relating directly to revising documents, you may want to review the following major sections of this book:

- Chapter 19, "Organizing Content with an Outline." The outlining features help you organize and work with your documents.

- Chapter 28, "Inserting Footnotes and Endnotes." Footnotes and endnotes are advanced features that help you with your professional and academic documents.

- Chapter 29, "Creating Indexes and Tables of Contents." Often, you will need to add a table of contents and an index to a professional document. This chapter provides the information you need to create these items in Word.

For Related Information

- "Finding Files," p. 95

- "Finding and Replacing Special Characters," p. 198

- "Controlling Printing Options," p. 232

VI

Handling Large Documents

Chapter 31

Adding Cross-References and Captions

Cross-references and captions greatly simplify the job of creating complex or illustrated documents. *Cross-references* refer to text or objects in some other part of your document, or in another document. *Captions* label and number illustrations in your document. You can update cross-references and captions automatically, so that when you insert them you can be sure they will remain accurate.

Cross-references and captions simplify your job when you create a document, and they also make your reader's job easier. Cross-references give readers quick access to related information in other parts of your document; captions provide consistent and accurate labeling for the illustrations that augment text.

Figs. 31.1 and 31.2 show examples of a cross-reference and a caption.

What You Need to Know About Cross-References and Captions

Because cross-references and captions are *fields*, Word can update them automatically whenever you print the document. (Fields are hidden text that perform special functions, such as linking parts of a document together. Chapter 37 describes fields in detail.) Alternatively, you can update them yourself by selecting them and pressing F9. If you have included page

In this chapter, you learn ways to use cross-references and captions:

■ How to cross-reference headings, bookmarks, and page numbers in the current document or in related documents

■ How to label pictures, tables, and other illustrations

■ How to add captions automatically when you insert objects

VI

Handling Large Documents

numbers in cross-references throughout your document, for example, and you subsequently add text (so that page numbers change), the cross-references update to show the new page numbers. Or if you include automatically numbered captions for figures and then add more figures, Word renumbers existing figures.

Fig. 31.1

Both the section title and the page number are cross-references. If either changes, the text on this page reflects that change.

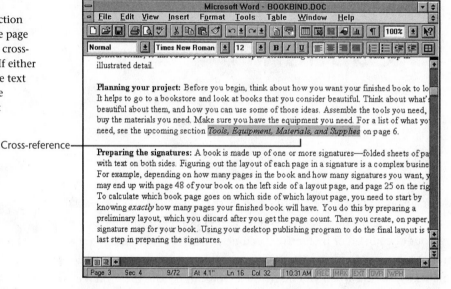

Fig. 31.2

Word numbers captions automatically; callouts describe parts of the figure.

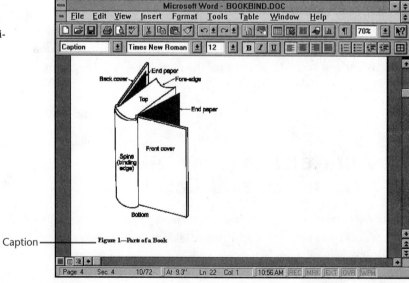

In a cross-reference, the entire text (except any text you type yourself) is a field result. In a caption, however, only the chapter and caption number are fields. For example, in a caption reading *Figure 1*, the word *Figure* is not a field result, but the number *1* is.

As a rule, you see the results of fields in your document; they look like text (see fig. 31.3). If you choose the Tools **O**ptions command, however, and on the View tab, select Field Codes in the Show group, you see a code inside brackets—the field code—instead of text (see fig. 31.4). Deselect this option to see the result of your field, rather than the code.

For Related Information
■ "Understanding the Basics of Fields," p. 1073

Creating Cross-References

A cross-reference refers the reader to information in another part of your document (or another document that is part of the same master document). You have the option of including page numbers in cross-references. If the content or location of the information changes, you can update the cross-reference to reflect those changes.

You can cross-reference several types of information, including headings formatted with Word's built-in heading styles (Heading 1 through Heading 9), page numbers, footnotes and endnotes, captions, and bookmarks. When you apply a cross-reference in your document, Word finds the referenced information and inserts that information at the cross-reference. If you cross-reference a heading, for example, Word inserts the text of that heading at the location of the cross-reference. If you cross-reference a page number, Word inserts the correct page number.

Cross-references generally contain two types of text: text that you type, and the cross-reference information that Word inserts. You may type, for example, the words **For more information see page** and then insert a cross-reference to a page number.

You can include multiple references within a single cross-reference in your document. For example, you may want your cross-reference to read: "For more information see ... on page ... ," with Word filling in both a heading title and a page number.

VI

Handling Large Documents

Fig. 31.3

The cross-reference field code result in text that can be formatted or edited.

Field result

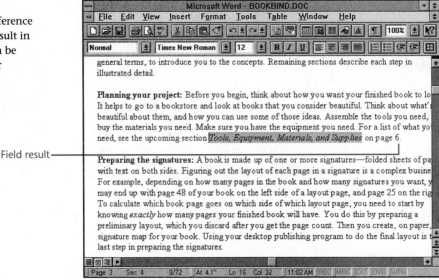

Fig. 31.4

You can use the Tools Options command, the View tab, and the Field Codes option to display field codes.

Field codes

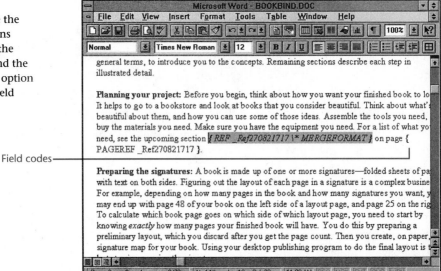

Adding Cross-References

Because cross-references contain two kinds of text—the text you type and the cross-reference itself—creating a cross-reference is a two-part process. You type the introductory text and then insert the cross-reference. In many cases, you insert two cross-references—one for a title and one for a page number.

Word leaves the Cross-reference dialog box open so that you can insert as many cross-references as you need.

When you use the Cross-reference dialog box, you make three choices for each cross-reference you insert. This process involves narrowing down your options. First you select the general category of your cross-reference; for example, you select Heading because your cross-reference is based on one of Word's built-in heading styles (Heading 1 through Heading 9). You next select what part of that heading you want to reference: the heading text, the page number where that heading appears, or the heading number (if you have included heading numbering). Finally, you select the specific heading you want to reference—the Cross-reference dialog box lists all the headings. Each reference type (Heading, Bookmark, Footnote, and so on) has different specific options.

Caution

Before you can insert a cross-reference, you must have marked the item you want to reference. You can use a heading style, bookmark, footnote, endnote, or caption to mark a location. If you have not marked locations in one of these ways, the lists in the Cross-reference dialog box will not display items for you to cross-reference.

To add a cross-reference, follow these steps:

1. Type the introductory text preceding the cross-reference. For example, you might type "See the following page. " Leave the insertion point where you want the cross-reference to appear.

2. Choose the Insert Cross-reference command. The Cross-reference dialog box appears (see fig. 31.5).

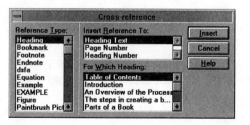

Fig. 31.5
The Cross-reference dialog box stays open while you complete your cross-reference.

3. In the Reference Type list, select the type of item you want to reference.

VI

Handling Large Documents

For example, you might select Heading if you want to cross-reference to a title or subtitle formatted with a heading style.

4. In the Insert Reference To list, select the information about the item that you want to reference.

The list varies, according to which reference type you have selected. For example, if you had selected Heading as the Reference Type, you could reference the heading's text title, the page number of the heading, or the heading number.

5. In the For Which list box, select the specific item you want to reference.

Word lists all the items of the selected type that it finds in your document. If you had selected Heading as the Reference type, you would see a list of all headings in the document.

6. Choose Insert to insert the cross-reference.

7. If you want to add additional text in your document before closing the Cross-reference dialog box, click in your document and type the text. Then you can repeat Steps 3 through 6 to insert an additional cross-reference. Choose Close when you're finished. (Close appears after you insert a cross-reference.)

Cross-Referencing Another Document

Tip
You can include a cross-reference in a header or footer. You may want to include a cross-reference, for example, which displays the title of a chapter inside a header.

To include a cross-reference to another document, both documents must be part of a master document. Master documents are used to create a large document from many smaller subdocuments. To insert a cross-reference, choose the View Master Document command, and in the master document view, insert cross-references in the usual way (see the earlier section, "Adding Cross-References"). When you are in the master document view, the Cross-reference dialog box lists all the headings, bookmarks, and so on that are contained in the documents linked to this master document.

Updating Cross-References

You can update cross-references and captions by simply selecting them and pressing the F9 key. To update all the cross-references in your document, select the entire document and press F9. Cross-references update automatically when you print your document.

Formatting Cross-References

In your document, a cross-reference looks like text (even though it is a field result), and you can edit it just like text. When the insertion point is inside a cross-reference field, the entire cross-reference is highlighted. The field is selected, but the text is not. Within the highlighted field, however, you can select text and edit it using any of Word's usual editing techniques. When you cross-reference a heading, for example, you may want it to appear in italics. After you insert the cross-reference, select the text in the usual way and apply italics using a command or shortcut. For more information about selecting fields, see the section "Editing and Deleting Cross-References and Captions" later in this chapter.

Creating Captions

Captions help readers reference the illustrations you include in your document. In Word, a caption includes a label, a number, and (optionally) a chapter number. A caption may read, for example, *Figure 7* or *Table II-ii*. You can type additional text after the label and number.

When you create a caption, you can select from a list of preexisting labels such as *Figure* or *Table*, or you can create your own labels. You can select from a list of predefined numbering styles, such as *1 2 3*, *A B C*, or *I II III*. You can place a caption above or below your illustration.

You can include captions in your document in one of two ways. You can instruct Word to include a caption each time you insert a particular type of object; for example, you may want a caption for each picture you insert. Or you can select an object and create a caption for it manually.

Captions update automatically when you insert additional captions in your document. The first caption you insert, for example, may read *Figure 1* and the second *Figure 2*. If you insert a new caption between Figure 1 and Figure 2, the new caption is numbered *Figure 2* and the previous Figure 2 becomes *Figure 3*.

Word formats captions with the Caption style. The style that follows Caption is Normal, therefore when you press Enter after inserting a caption, Word automatically sets the next paragraph's style to Normal. You can change the formatting of the Caption style by using the Format Style command, or by defining a new Caption style by example. For details, see Chapter 11, "Formatting with Styles."

For Related Information

- "Marking Locations with Bookmarks," p. 149

- "Creating Numbered Headings," p. 567

- "Creating Captions," p. 955

- "Understanding the Basics of Fields," p. 1073

VI

Handling Large Documents

Captions work well with cross-references. You can create a cross-reference to any type of caption. If the caption number or label changes, you can update the cross-reference to reflect that change. (For information about updating, see the earlier section, "Creating Cross-References.")

Inserting Captions Manually

You can insert captions manually for figures, tables, objects, and even text. Use this technique when the illustrations are already inserted in your document, or when you include various types of illustrations (pictures and tables, for example), and you want them to have a consistent labeling and numbering scheme.

A caption always includes a label and number, but you can also add text to further explain your illustrations. For example, you may want a caption to read *Table 1Summary of Annual Sales*. For each type of label you include, Word creates a separate numbering sequence. If you have already inserted Figure 1 and Figure 2, for example, and then insert a caption with the label *Table*, the caption reads *Table 1* rather than *Table 3*.

To insert a caption manually, follow these steps:

1. Select the object for which you want a caption.

2. Choose the Insert Caption command. The Caption dialog box appears (see fig. 31.6).

Fig. 31.6
Captions
include labels and
numbers, and you
can add additional
text as well. In this
example, "Figure"
is the label and "1"
is the number.

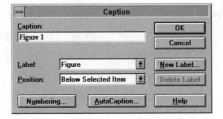

3. With the insertion point after the proposed label and number in the Caption text box, type any additional text you want in your caption.

4. You can select a different label from the Label list box. Word numbers each type of label separately.

5. You can select a different location for your caption—above or below the selected item—from the Position list box. Fig. 31.7 shows a caption placed below an illustration.

Fig. 31.7
Word inserts the caption above or below the selected item.

6. Choose OK or press Enter.

When you return to your document after inserting a caption, the insertion point flashes at the end of the caption. The caption is formatted with the Caption style. Press Enter to start a new paragraph formatted with the Normal style.

> **Note**
>
> Because captions are formatted with a style, be sure to put them on a line by themselves; otherwise, Word formats with the Caption style the entire paragraph where you insert the caption.

Inserting Captions Automatically

If you plan to insert many illustrations of a certain type in your document, you can specify that Word include a caption for each. If you intend to illustrate your document with many pictures, for example, you can have Word include a caption for each picture. You determine what label Word uses in the captions.

You can include automatic captions for as many different types of objects as you want. The captions either can share a label (and thus share a numbering scheme), or captions for each type of object can have a unique label and a

VI

Handling Large Documents

separate sequence of numbers. If you want to add explanatory text after an automatic caption, position the insertion point at the end of the caption and type the text.

Insert automatic captions before you begin inserting your illustrations. If you insert automatic captions after you have inserted some of your illustrations, select the existing illustrations and add their captions manually (see the earlier section, "Inserting Captions Manually," for information on this procedure). If the manually and automatically inserted captions use the same label, Word updates the caption numbers to keep them sequential.

To include automatic captions, follow these steps:

1. Choose the Insert Caption command.

2. Choose the AutoCaption button. The AutoCaption dialog box appears (see fig. 31.8).

Fig. 31.8
You can use automatic captions for many types of objects.

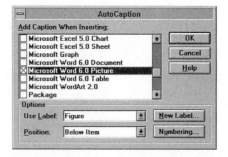

3. In the Add Caption When Inserting list, select the type of object for which you want Word to add automatic captions. Select several types of objects if you want them all to have the same label and numbering scheme.

4. Select Options for the type of object you selected. From Use Label, select the type of label for the object; from Position, select Above Item or Below Item.

   To create a unique label, choose New Label (for details, see the upcoming section "Creating New Caption Labels"). To change the numbering style or include chapter numbers, choose Numbering (see the "Changing Caption Numbering" later in this section).

5. Repeat steps 3 and 4 to add automatic captions for additional types of objects. By first selecting the object (step 3) and then selecting options (step 4), you can create a separate label and numbering scheme for each type of object for which you insert automatic captions.

6. Choose OK.

Creating New Caption Labels

You can create a new caption label at any of three times when working in your document: when you insert the caption manually, when you insert automatic captions, or after you have inserted your captions.

When you create a new label, Word adds it to the list of existing labels; the new label is available the next time you create a caption.

To create a new label for a manual caption, follow these steps:

1. Select the object for which you want a caption and choose the Insert Caption command.

> **Note**
>
> You can't drag across an existing label in the Caption box to select it; to change a label, you must choose the Insert Caption command, and then select a caption from the Label list or create a new one by choosing New Label.

2. Choose New Label. The New Label dialog box appears (see fig. 31.9).

Fig. 31.9
Create your own label by typing it in the Label box.

3. In the Label text box, type the text of the label you want. Choose OK or press Enter to close the New Label dialog box.

4. Choose OK to close the Caption dialog box.

Your new label appears in the Caption list box of the Caption dialog box, as shown in fig. 31.10.

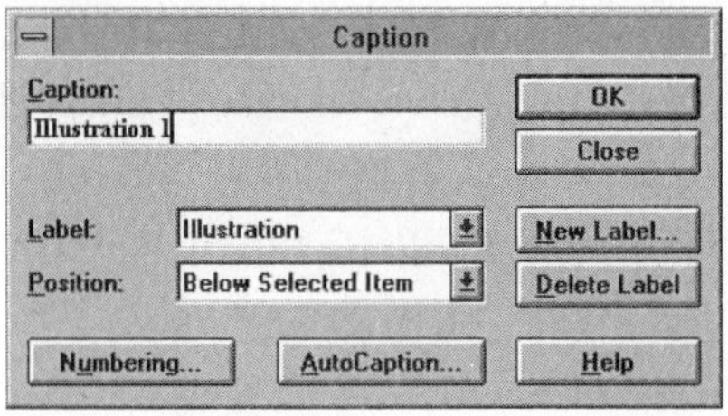

Fig. 31.10

Your new label
appears in the
Caption box.

To create new labels for automatic captions, follow these steps:

1. Select the Insert Caption command.

2. Choose AutoCaption to produce the AutoCaption dialog box (refer to fig. 31.8).

3. From the Add Caption When Inserting list box, select the object type for which you want automatic captions.

4. Choose New Label.

5. In the Label box, type the text of the label. Choose OK or press Enter to exit the New Label dialog box.

6. Choose OK or press Enter.

Changing Caption Labels

You can change the labels for captions you already have inserted in your document. When you change the label for an existing caption, all captions with that label-type change. If you change *Figure* to *Table,* for example, all the captions labeled as *Figure* change to *Table.*

To change labels for existing captions, follow these steps:

1. Select a caption with the label type you want to change. If you want to change all captions with the label *Figure* to the label *Table,* for example, select one *Figure* caption.

2. Choose the Insert Caption command.

3. Select a different label from the Label list, or choose New Label and create a new label.

4. Choose OK or press Enter.

Deleting a Caption Label

When you create new caption labels, they are added to the list of existing labels. You can delete these new labels from the list, but you can't delete Word's built-in labels (like Figure and Table). To delete the label, choose the Insert Caption command, select the label from the Label list, choose Delete Label, and then choose Close or press Enter.

If you delete the label from an existing caption, the caption number remains, and the numbering scheme for that label type is unchanged. To learn about editing captions, see the section "Editing and Deleting Cross-References and Captions" later in this chapter.

Changing Caption Numbering

You can change the caption numbering style for manual or automatic captions when you insert the captions. Alternatively, you can change the numbering style for existing captions in your document. When you change the caption numbering style, the change affects all captions with the same label type as the caption you changed.

To change caption numbering when you insert captions, follow these steps:

1. For manual captions, select the object for which you want to insert a caption and choose the Insert Caption command. In the Caption dialog box, choose Numbering.

   or

   For automatic captions, choose the Insert Caption command. In the Caption dialog box, choose AutoCaption. Select the type of object for which you want automatic captions, then choose Numbering.

   The Caption Numbering dialog box appears (see fig. 31.11).

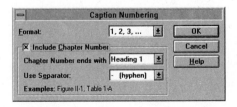

Fig. 31.11
You can change the format of the caption number, and you can include chapter numbers in your captions.

2. To change the style of the numbers, select an option from the Format list. For example, select 1, 2, 3; or a, b, c; or A, B, C; or i, ii, iii; or I, II, III.

3. Choose OK to return to the previous dialog box.

4. Choose OK or press Enter to return to your document.

To change caption numbering style for existing captions, follow these steps:

1. Select a caption of the label-type whose numbering style you want to change. For example, if you want to change all the "Figure 1-*x*" captions to "Figure A-*z*" captions, select a single "Figure 1" caption.

2. Choose the Insert Caption command.

3. In the Caption dialog box, choose Numbering.

4. Select a different numbering style from the Format list.

5. Choose OK to return to the Caption dialog box.

6. Choose Close to return to your document. All captions using the same label-type reflect your new numbering style.

You also can change numbering by selecting a captioned object, rather than a caption. If you use this technique, close the Caption dialog box by choosing Close in Step 4 rather than OK. If you choose OK, you add an extra caption.

Including Chapter Numbers in a Caption

In a caption, you can include the current chapter number, if you format your chapters with one of Word's built-in heading styles (Heading 1 through Heading 9), and if you have selected a heading numbering style. A caption with a chapter number may read, for example, "Figure 1A" or "Table II:ii."

This technique works well with a document containing several chapters. In a document containing only one chapter, all the chapter numbers are the same—Chapter 1, "What's New in Word for Windows."

To include chapter numbers in your captions, follow these steps:

1. Format all chapter titles and subheadings with built-in heading styles: Heading 1 through Heading 9. Be sure to format the title of each chapter as Heading 1.

2. Choose the Format Heading and Numbering command. In the Heading Numbering dialog box, select a heading numbering style. Choose OK.

3. For manual captions, select the object for which you want to insert a caption and choose the Insert Caption command. In the Caption dialog box, choose Numbering.

   or

   For automatic captions, choose the Insert Caption command. In the Caption dialog box, choose AutoCaption. Select the type of object for which you want automatic captions, then choose Numbering.

4. In the Caption Numbering dialog box, select the Include Chapter Number option.

5. In the Chapter Number ends with list box, select the lowest level of heading you want to include in your caption number. If you want only the chapter number, for example, select Heading 1 to get a caption such as *Figure 1-3*. If you want to include the chapter and first subheading number, however, select Heading 2 for a caption such as *Figure 1.2-3*.

6. In the Use Separator list, select the punctuation you want to separate the chapter number and the caption number. Options include a hyphen, a period, a colon, or an em-dash (a wide hyphen).

7. Choose OK to return to the previous dialog box.

8. Choose OK or press Enter to return to your document.

Formatting Captions

The Caption format style is the Normal style, with the addition of bold and a line space before and after the paragraph. You can reformat all your captions automatically by making changes to the Caption style. Alternatively, you can select the caption and apply manual formatting. Because most captions are a single line (and therefore, a single paragraph), you can apply paragraph formatting commands such as indentations and alignment, as well as text formatting commands such as italics or another font.

Editing Captions

You can edit captions in several ways. You can change their labels or numbering styles, as described in the previous sections, "Changing Caption Labels" and "Changing Caption Numbering." You can format captions, as described in the previous section, "Formatting Captions." You can update captions, as described in the upcoming section "Updating Captions."

VI

Handling Large Documents

You also can edit captions' text. Editing a caption's text does not affect other captions of the same type. You can add text to the end of a caption called *Figure 1,* for example, and no other *Figure* captions are affected. You also can edit the field portion of a caption; that edit also does not affect other captions of the same type. To learn how to edit the field, see the section "Editing and Deleting Cross-References and Captions" later in this chapter.

Updating Captions

When you insert new captions using a label you previously have used in your document, Word includes the correct sequential caption number. Word renumbers existing captions when you insert a new caption between existing captions.

For Related Information
- "Creating Numbered Headings," p. 567

- "Inserting and Copying Pictures into your Document," p. 661

- "Working with Pictures," p. 671

- "Framing and Moving Text and Graphics," p. 681

When you delete or move something a caption references, however, you must update it by selecting it and pressing F9. To update all the captions in your document at once, select the entire document and press F9.

Framing a Caption with Its Object

When you move an object for which you have inserted a caption, the caption does not move with the object. If you want the object and caption to move together, frame them as a single object. When an object and caption are framed together, you can use the mouse to drag them anywhere in your document. To learn more about frames, see Chapter 23, "Framing and Moving Text and Graphics."

To frame an object and its caption, follow these steps:

1. Select the object and its caption.

2. Choose the Insert Frame command.

   or

   Click the Frame button on the Word for Windows or Drawing toolbar.

Alternatively, you can frame the object and *then* insert its caption—the caption is included automatically inside the frame.

Editing and Deleting Cross-References and Captions

Cross-references and captions are fields; by default, you see in your document the result of the fields. You may see, for example, a cross-reference such as

Editing Cross-References or a caption such as *Figure 3*. If you display fields, however, rather than field results, you see field codes, such as `{REF _Ref270669594\* MERGEFORMAT }` or `{ SEQ Figure \* ARABIC }`. Word uses fields so that it can update cross-references and captions if the information changes.

You can edit either the field result or the field code. Editing the field result is the same as editing text, however, the next time the field code is updated, the editing will be lost unless you unlock the results as described in Chapter 37. You can also edit the field code when it is displayed. You may want to edit the field code as a quick way of changing a reference or as a means of inserting a special formatting. Editing field codes and adding formatting switches is described in Chapter 37. Many cross-references and captions also include normal text preceding or following the field. Edit this text using Word's usual text-editing techniques; for details, see Chapter 5, "Editing a Document."

The key to editing a cross-reference or caption is in selecting and displaying the field code that creates the cross-reference or caption. To make selecting a field code easier, you can set viewing options to shade data from fields codes.

To shade any data from field codes, follow these steps:

1. Choose the **Tools O**ptions command and select the View tab.

2. Select one of the following items from the Field Shading list:

Never	Field codes and results are never shaded.
Always	Field codes and results are always shaded.
When Selected	Field codes and results are shaded only when they are selected or the insertion point is in the field code.

3. Choose OK.

You can switch the entire document beween field codes and results by pressing Alt+F9.

To edit or format a field result, move the insertion point within the field result. If the Field Shading option is on, the field results turn light gray (see fig. 31.12). Select the text you want to edit or format. Fig. 31.13 shows selected text within a field result.

VI

Handling Large Documents

To delete a field code and its result, select across one field code marker or across the entire field result. The entire field result will turn darker (see fig. 31.14). Press the Delete key. It is easier to select and delete field codes if you display the field codes rather than field results.

Fig. 31.12

A field result displays with light shading when the insertion point is inside and Field Shading is turned on.

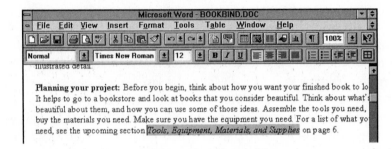

Fig. 31.13

This field result shows darker selected text that can be edited or formatted.

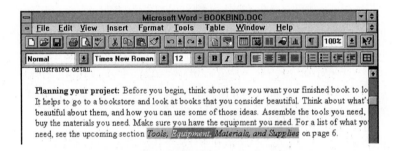

Fig. 31.14

Selecting the entire field result displays the entire result with dark shading. The field code can be deleted at this point.

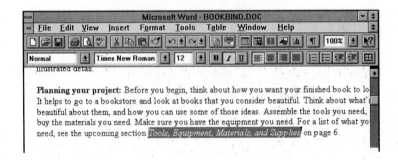

To update the field, select it and press F9. To update a field, you either can highlight it by positioning the insertion point inside it, or you can select it by dragging across it.

From Here...

For information relating to cross-references and captions, review the following chapters:

- Chapter 5, "Editing a Document." Refer to the section "Marking Locations with Bookmarks" to learn how to create bookmarks, which you can use in cross-references.

- Chapter 11, "Formatting with Styles." Learn how to use Word's built-in heading styles in cross-references and for chapter numbers in captions.

- Chapter 27, "Desktop Publishing." See examples of captions in desktop publishing projects.

- Chapter 28, "Inserting Footnotes and Endnotes." Learn how to create footnotes and endnotes, which you can use in cross-references.

- Chapter 37, "Automating with Field Codes." Learn the basics about field codes; both cross-references and captions are field codes.

Tip
To select quickly the next field following the insertion point, press F11. To select the field prior to the insertion point, press Shift+F11.

VI

Handling Large Documents

Chapter 32

Assembling Large Documents

You can work with any size document in Word for Windows, but several considerations dictate the most efficient approach to working with large documents. Large documents, as well as documents with many graphics, fields, bookmarks, and formatting, consume more memory and disk space. They can be slow to load, save, and work in, depending on how much memory you have and the speed of your computer.

Although you can break a document up into smaller documents and work with and print these smaller files individually, there are many advantages to combining these smaller *subdocuments* into a *master document*, and using Word for Windows powerful master document feature to organize and work with the large document. When you work in the *master document view* of a large document (see fig. 32.1), it is like working with an outline, so it is much easier to move around the document and to organize the document using the same techniques you use to organize an outline (see Chapter 19, "Organizing Content with an Outline"). There are also several tools in the master view that you can use to manage the subdocuments in a master document.

When you switch to normal view for the master document, it's just like working on a single document, so you can use the standard procedures for adding page numbers, tables of contents, indexes, and cross-references, avoiding the complications of trying to accomplish these tasks using individual files. You can print the master document just as you would any file, so you don't have to open and print each individual file. When necessary, you can still work with the individual subdocuments. For example, when you want each subdocument to have its own header and footer, you work with the documents individually. Also, different people can work on the individual

In this chapter, you learn to do the following:

- Work with a master document

- Work with subdocuments

- Insert tables of contents, indexes, and cross references.

subdocuments in a master document. Then you can open the master document to pull together all the subdocuments and make editing changes that affect the whole document—for example, adding a table of contents and an index—and print the entire document all at once.

Fig. 32.1

You can use the master document view to manage a large document.

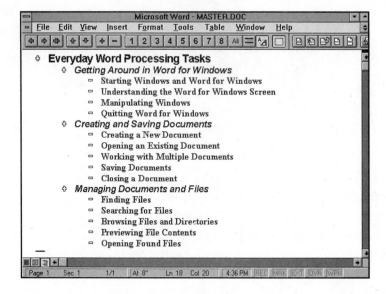

Most of this chapter focuses on using master documents to work with large documents, because this is the most efficient and flexible way to manage large documents. However, you also learn how to break a large document into individual files and treat these files separately. You learn how to create tables of contents and indexes that span the information contained in these individual files.

Another technique covered is using the Insert File command to insert a document into the master document. The inserted source documents become part of a master document, as if they were created there. This is useful for creating contracts or proposals by inserting paragraphs saved on disk. The inserted material is not linked back to the source. Two disadvantages to this method exist. If a source document changes, you must manually change the master. Also, the master document can become as large and as slow as if you had typed a large document.

Documents of 20 or fewer pages give the best performance in Word for Windows. If your documents are significantly larger than 20 pages, you can segment the documents into multiple files and rejoin them using the techniques described in this chapter.

What You Need to Know About Assembling a Large Document

Assembling a large document consists of dividing the document into smaller *subdocuments* and then combining the subdocuments into a *master document*. You can work with two views in the master document. The *master document view* (refer to fig. 32.1) is similar to the outline view, and allows you to organize your document using the same techniques you use to organize an outline with the buttons on the Outlining toolbar. Using the buttons on the Master Document toolbar, you can move and delete entire subdocuments, insert new subdocuments, combine subdocuments, and demote a subdocument so that it becomes part of the master document text. If you need to work with one of the subdocuments, you can quickly open it from the master document.

To view the entire document to edit and format it, you can switch to normal view. In normal view, you can work with the document just as if it were a single document. You can add a table of contents, index, and cross-references just as in any other document. You need to be in normal view when you want to print the document. You can print in the master document view if you want to obtain an outline of your document.

Creating a Master Document

There are three ways to create a master document. You can create a master document from scratch by entering an outline for your document, using one of the heading levels to indicate the beginning of each subdocument. You then create the subdocuments from the headings, using one of the buttons on the Master Document toolbar. You can also create a master document from an existing document or combine several documents into a master document. The three ways of creating a master document are discussed in the following sections.

Whatever method you use to create your master document, you must work in the master document view and use the built-in heading styles (Heading 1-Heading 9) for the headings in your outline. You can use the promote and demote buttons on the Outlining toolbar to create your headings; Word for Windows automatically uses the heading styles. You can also apply the heading styles using the Style box on the Formatting toolbar.

VI

Handling Large Documents

Creating a New Master Document

You create a new master document in a blank document using the master document view. To create a new master document, follow these steps:

1. Open a new document.

2. Choose the View Master Document command.

   When you switch to the master document view, the Outlining and Master Document toolbars are displayed at the top of the screen (see fig. 32.2). These buttons are used to promote and demote outline headings and work with subdocuments. Table 32.1 summarizes the functions of the individual buttons on the Outlining and Master Document toolbars.

Fig. 32.2
The Outlining and Master Document toolbars.

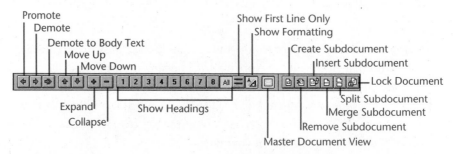

Table 32.1 Functions of the Outline and Master Document Toolbars	
Button	**Function**
⬅	Promotes the heading (and its body text) by one level; promotes body text to the heading level of the preceding heading.
➡	Demotes the heading by one level; demotes body text to the heading level below the preceding heading.
⬆	Moves the selected paragraph(s) before the first visible paragraph that precedes the selected paragraph(s).
⬇	Moves the selected paragraph(s) after the first visible paragraph that follows the selected paragraph(s).
⇛	Demotes a heading to body text.
✛	Expands the first heading level below the currently selected heading; repeated clicks expand through additional heading levels until body is expanded.

Button	Function
▬	Collapses body text into heading, then lowest level headings into higher level headings.
1 2 3 4 5 6 7 8	Display all headings and text through the lowest level number you click.
All	Displays all text if some is collapsed; displays only headings if all text is expanded.
▤	Toggles between showing all the body text in an outline and only the first line of text.
ᴬ𝐴	Toggles between showing normal character formatting in outline view and normal view.
▣	Toggles between showing outline and master document view.
▤	Creates subdocuments from selected outline items.
▥	Removes the selected subdocument, leaving the text in the master document.
▦	Inserts the file selected in the Insert Subdocument dialog box into the master document.
▤	Merges selected subdocuments into one subdocument.
▤	Splits the selected portion of a subdocument into another subdocument.
▦	Locks and unlocks the file for the selected subdocument.

3. Type an outline for the master document.

   You can use the buttons on the toolbar to promote and demote headings as you enter your outline. Decide on a heading level that designates the beginning of a subdocument. For example, you might use Heading Level 2 to indicate the beginning of each subdocument.

4. Select the headings you want to create your subdocuments from.

   You can select as many headings as you want, but you must be sure that the first heading in the selection is the same level as the one you are using to indicate the beginning of subdocuments, as shown in fig. 32.3.

Fig. 32.3
The first heading level in your selection should be the level you want to convert to subdocuments.

5. Click the Create Subdocument button on the Master Document toolbar.

   Word for Windows divides the master document into subdocuments, one subdocument for each heading level that you designated as the subdocument heading. Each subdocument is enclosed in a box and a subdocument icon appears in the upper-left corner of the box, as shown in fig. 32.4.

6. Save the master document.

Fig. 32.4
Word for Windows creates a subdocument for each subdocument heading level.

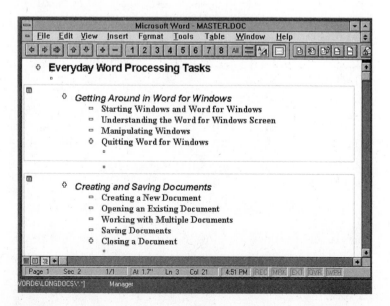

When you save the master document, Word for Windows automatically saves each of the subdocuments as a file. Word for Windows assigns a file name to each subdocument, using the first characters in the heading for the subdocument. For example, the file names for the subdocuments created from the outline shown in fig. 32.3 are GETTING.DOC, CREATING.DOC, and MANAGING.DOC. Word for Windows uses numbers or other characters in the file name if the file names based on the headings conflict with other files.

Caution

If you decide to rename a subdocument or save it in a different location on your hard disk, be sure to do it while you are in the master document; then save the master document again. First you must open the subdocument from within the master document. To do this, double-click the subdocument icon in the upper-left corner of the box enclosing the subdocument. Then use the **F**ile Save **As** command to save the subdocument with a new name or in a new location. This keeps the links between the master document and the subdocuments from being broken.

Creating a Master Document from an Existing Document

If you already created a document, you can convert it to a master document. To do so, use the Outlining toolbar in the master document view to set up headings in the document, and then create subdocuments from these headings, as described in the previous section.

To create a master document from an existing document, follow these steps:

1. Open the document you want to convert to a master document.

2. Choose the View Master Document commmand.

3. Use the buttons on the Outlining toolbar to assign heading levels to your document and to rearrange the headings, if necessary.

   For more information about working with outlines, see Chapter 19, "Organizing Content with an Outline." As discussed previously, you must use the built-in heading styles for the headings.

4. Complete Steps 4 through 6 as outlined in "Creating a New Master Document" earlier in this chapter.

Creating a Master Document by Combining Documents

Another method for creating a master document is to insert existing Word for Windows documents into a master document. You can either start a master document from scratch, inserting documents to build the master document, or you can insert Word for Windows documents into an existing master document.

To insert an existing document into a master document, follow these steps:

1. Open a new document or an existing master document.

2. Choose the View Master Document command.

3. Move the insertion point where you want to insert the document.

 4. Click the Insert Subdocument button on the Master Document toolbar.

5. In the File Name text box, type the name of the file you want to open, or select the file you want to open from the File Name list in the Insert Subdocument dialog box.

   The file is inserted into the master document with its original file name. Word for Windows uses the formatting from the master's documents template if it is different from the subdocument's template. The original formatting is preserved in the subdocument file if you open it separately.

Troubleshooting

I selected the headings that I wanted to convert to subdocuments and clicked the Create Subdocument button, but my subdocuments did not divide up as I intended.

The key to creating subdocuments from the headings in a master document is to make sure that when you select the headings that you want to create subdocuments from, you select all of the headings you want to convert to subdocuments and that the first heading in the selection is assigned the heading level you want to use to begin all subdocuments. For example, if the first heading in the selection is assigned heading level 2, all sections beginning with heading level 2 will be converted to subdocuments.

For Related Information
■ "Creating an Outline," p. 617

Working with the Master Document

When you have set up your master document, you can use the master document and normal views to work with the document. In master document view, you can view the overall structure of the document, and reorganize the sections in the document. For example, it is very easy to reorder the subdocuments that make up the master document by using the mouse and the buttons on the Outlining toolbar. You can also open the individual subdocuments in the master document view. You should work in the master document view when you need to make changes that affect the overall document.

In normal view, you can work with the document just as if it were a single document. You can format the document, add page numbers, tables of contents and other tables, indexes, and cross-references. When you switch to normal view, each subdocument that makes up the master document is a *section* (see Chapter 13, "Setting the Page Layout"). You can apply section formatting to these sections. For example, you can set up different headers and footers in the individual sections.

Formatting the Master Document

Formatting a master document is no different than formatting a single document. You can create templates, styles, and AutoText for the master document and format all or any part of the master document. If a subdocument is based on a different template than the master document, the master document's template styles override the subdocument styles. If you open a subdocument file outside of the master document, the original template styles will still be in effect.

To insert headers and footers that are the same for the entire master document, set them up in the master document. If you want different headers and footers for the individual subdocuments, set them up in each subdocument. You can also modify the page numbers, margins, and other section-level formatting within subdocuments, and insert new section breaks within a subdocument. When you insert an existing file into a master document, any section formatting in that document is maintained. This helps if you already set up headers and footers in the individual documents you combine to create a master document and you want to maintain those headers and footers in the master document.

Another benefit of working in the master document is that you can move text and graphics among subdocuments without opening the individual subdocuments. You can even use the drag-and-drop technique for moving text and graphics from one subdocument to another. You need to be in the normal view of the master document to move text and graphics. See Chapter 5, "Editing a Document," for more information on moving text and graphics.

Tip
To ensure consistency when you or a team are writing large documents, read Chapter 6, "Using Templates as Master Documents," and Chapter 11, "Formatting with Styles."

VI

Handling Large Documents

Printing a Master Document

Printing a master document is as simple as printing a single document. The ability to print an entire long document at once is one of the advantages that a master document has over working with individual files. To print the entire document, you must be in normal view. You then use the File Print command to print the document (see Chapter 8, "Previewing and Printing a Document").

To print an outline of your document, switch to master document view. You can then collapse or expand the outline to include exactly the heading levels you want to include in your outline and print the outline.

Sharing a Master Document

One advantage of using a master document to manage a long document is that several users can work together on the subdocuments in the master document at the same time. Word for Windows has a locking feature that allows any user to open a master document, but have read-write access to only those subdocuments that that user created. You will have read-only access to subdocuments created by other users. Word for Windows uses the Author field in the summary information for a subdocument to determine who the author of a subdocument is.

Word for Windows does allow you to unlock any locked document. For this reason, if you want to provide absolute protection for a document against changes, use the techniques described in Chapter 3, "Creating and Saving Documents," to apply password protection to the document. Also, you will not be able to work on a subdocument if another user on the network already opened that document. See Chapter 3 for more information on opening documents on a network.

To lock or unlock a subdocument, follow these steps:

1. Select the subdocument you want to lock or unlock.

2. Click the Lock Document button on the Master Document toolbar.

   A padlock icon displays just below the subdocument icon when a subdocument is locked (see fig. 32.5).

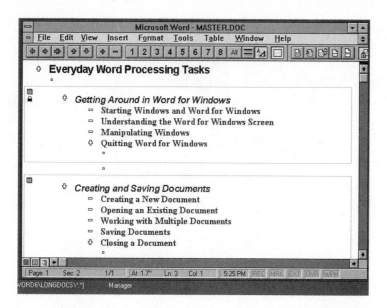

Fig. 32.5
The padlock icon
in a subdocument
indicates that the
subdocument is
locked against
changes.

Troubleshooting

I am able to open a subdocument outside of the master document and then edit and save it, but whenever I open the same subdocument from within the master document, I am unable to edit and save it.

The reason for this is that the subdocument has been locked in the master document. If you look just below the subdocument icon for the subdocument you are trying to work with, you will see a padlock symbol, which indicates that the subdocument is locked. When you open a locked subdocument, it is opened as a read-only document, and cannot be edited and saved with the same name. To unlock the subdocument, locate the insertion point anywhere in the subdocument and click the Unlock Subdocument button, the last button on the Master Document toolbar.

Working with Subdocuments within the Master Document

You can work with subdocuments while you are in the master document view of a master document. You can open a subdocument from within a master document if you need to edit the subdocument. You can also rearrange the order of subdocuments, and merge, split, or remove subdocuments.

For Related Information

- " Opening an Existing Document," p. 72

- "Saving a Document," p. 80

- "Using Styles versus Direct Formatting," p. 337

- "Using Templates as a Pattern for Documents," p. 168

VI

Handling Large Documents

Opening Subdocuments from Within a Master Document

You can quickly open a subdocument when you are in the master view of a document. This is handy if you need to edit the subdocument. To open a subdocument, open the master document, switch to master document view, and double-click the subdocument icon for the subdocument you want to open. If you make any editing changes in the subdocument, be sure to save it. When you do, the changes are saved in both the subdocument and the master document.

Rearranging Subdocuments in a Master Document

When you work in a master document, it is easy to rearrange the order of the subdocuments in the master document by using the same methods you use to move the contents of an outline. You can move headings within a subdocument or move entire subdocuments.

To move a subdocument within a master document, follow these steps:

1. Click the subdocument icon to select the entire subdocument.

2. Drag the subdocument to the new location.

   A gray line appears on-screen as you drag the selection. Drag the gray line to the point where you want to move the selection and release the mouse button.

   or

   Hold down the Alt+Shift keys and use the up- and down arrow keys to relocate the subdocument.

You can also move individual headings within a subdocument by using the same techniques. For more information about working with outlines, see Chapter 19, "Organizing Content with an Outline."

Splitting, Merging, and Deleting Subdocuments

If a subdocument becomes larger than you would like, you can split it into subdocuments. Or you can merge smaller subdocuments into one large subdocument.

To split a subdocument, follow these steps:

1. Open the master document and switch to the master document view.

2. Position the insertion point where you want to split the document.

3. Click the Split Subdocument button on the Master Document toolbar.

4. Save the master document so that Word for Windows will save and name the new subdocument.

To merge two or more subdocuments, follow these steps:

1. Open the subdocument and switch to the master document view.

2. If necessary, move the subdocuments you want to merge next to each other.

3. Select the entire contents of the subdocuments you want to merge.

4. Click the Merge Subdocument button on the Master Document toolbar.

5. Save the master document to save a new file for the merged subdocuments.

   Word for Windows uses the file name of the first subdocument.

To remove a subdocument from a master document, follow these steps:

For Related Information
■ "Promoting and Demoting Headings," p. 618

1. Open the subdocument and switch to the master document view.

2. Click the subdocument icon to select the subdocument you want to remove.

3. Press Delete to remove the subdocument and its contents from the master document.

   When you delete a subdocument, the subdocument file is still stored on the hard drive.

   or

   Click the Remove Subdocument button on the Master Document toolbar to remove the subdocument and retain the text in the master document.

Caution

To delete a subdocument from a master document, do so while in the master document view. If you simply delete the file from your hard disk, when you try to open the master document you will get an error message informing you that the subdocument is missing.

VI

Handling Large Documents

Inserting Tables of Contents, Indexes, and Cross-References

When you work with a master document, one of the main advantages is that you can use the same techniques you use in a single document to create tables of contents and other tables, indexes, and cross-references. To insert a table of contents or index into a master document, open the master document and switch to normal view. Then use the normal methods for inserting the table of contents or index (see Chapter 29, "Creating Indexes and Tables of Contents"). You also must be working in the normal view of the master document to insert cross-references that make references across documents. For more information on inserting cross-references, see Chapter 31, "Adding Cross-References and Captions." When you update tables of contents, indexes, or cross-references, be sure to do so from within the master document to avoid error messages.

Troubleshooting

When I work on subdocument containing cross-references, I get many error messages. The same is true of the subdocument that contains my table of contents and index.

To work on cross-references and tables of contents and indexes, you must be in the master document. This is because cross references, tables of contents, and indexes make references across documents. To replace the error messages in your subdocuments, open the master document, select the text containing the error messages, or position the insertion point anywhere in a table of contents or index, and press F9. The fields used to return this information will be updated.

Working with Individual Files

Another technique for assembling large documents is to print the smaller documents separately. For large documents that would overload memory if they were inserted or linked into one large master document, this technique is preferable.

When you use this technique, you must set the starting numbers for pages, paragraphs, footnotes, and so on for each individual file to maintain sequential numbering across the larger document. You must also use RD (Referenced Document) field codes for creating tables of contents and indexes. The table of contents and index are created in a separate document, and an RD field code is inserted for each of the individual files that make up the document. You cannot use cross-references across files when you work with individual files.

Setting Starting Numbers

To set the starting numbers for the individual files, you start with the first file in the series. You repaginate the file, and then note the number of the last page and of any other sequentially numbered items, such as paragraphs, lines, footnotes, and items numbered using the SEQ fields (tables or figures, for example). Next, you open the second file in the series and use the appropriate commands to set the starting numbers for each sequentially numbered item in that document. Follow this procedure for each of the individual files. To save time and to minimize the possibility that you have to repeat the process of setting starting numbers, carry out this procedure after all editing changes have been made.

To set the starting page numbers, follow these steps:

1. Choose the Insert Page Numbers command.

2. Choose the Format option.

3. Type or select the appropriate page number in the Start At text box (one higher than the number of the last page in the preceding file).

4. Choose OK and then choose Close.

To set the starting footnote numbers, follow these steps:

1. Choose the Insert Footnote command.

2. Choose the Options button.

3. Type or select the appropriate number in the Start At text box (one higher than the number of the last footnote in the preceding file).

4. Choose OK and then choose Close.

To set the starting line numbers, follow these steps:

1. Choose the File Page Setup command.

2. Select the Layout Tab.

3. Choose the Line Numbers option.

VI

Handling Large Documents

4. Choose the Add Line Numbering option.

5. Type or select the appropriate line number in the Start At text box (one higher than the number of the last line in the preceding file).

6. Choose the Continuous option in the Restart Field.

7. Choose OK twice.

To set the starting number for paragraphs, follow these steps:

1. Select the group of paragraphs you want to renumber.

2. Choose the Format Bullets and Numbering command.

3. Select the Numbered tab and choose the Modify option.

4. Type the appropriate number in the Start At text box (one higher than the number of the last numbered paragraph in the preceding file).

5. Choose OK.

To set the starting numbers of items numbered using the SEQ field, follow these steps:

1. Choose the Tools Options command and select the View tab.

2. Select the Field Codes option and choose OK.

3. Find the first SEQ field and type \r followed by the appropriate number (one higher than the last number in that sequence of items).

4. Repeat Step 2 for each sequence in the document.

Note

See Chapter 37, "Automating with Field Codes," for information on using the {SEQ} field code to create a sequentially numbered series of items. Also, you can learn how to insert chapter numbers using the {SEQ} code in "Inserting Chapter Numbers," later in this chapter.

Creating Chapter Numbers

When you print the individual documents separately (not linking in a master document), you must insert the chapter number. To do so, you add the chapter number to the header or footer, next to the page number code. The entry in the header or footer for Chapter 2, for example, might look like this:

```
2-{page}
```

If the order of the chapters changes, you must edit the chapter numbers that appear in the header or footer to maintain the proper sequencing.

Printing Individual Files

After you set the starting numbers for each of the files, you can print them individually. To print several documents with one command, use the File Find File command. When you choose this command, Word for Windows finds all the files in the path specified in the Search dialog box. You can edit this path if necessary (see Chapter 4, "Managing Documents and Files"). After you have a list of the correct files, follow these steps to print the files:

1. Press and hold down the Ctrl key and click the name of each file you want to print.

   or

   Press Shift+F8 and use the arrow keys to move to the file you want to print. Press the space bar to select the file. Repeat this step for each file you want to print.

2. Choose the Commands button and then choose **Print**.

3. Choose OK to print the files.

Creating a Table of Contents

When you print the smaller documents separately, you must insert RD fields to create indexes and tables of contents. The RD fields are inserted into a document separate from the individual documents. Insert one RD (Reference Document) field for each separate file that makes up the larger document. You then use the Insert Index and Tables command to create the index and table of contents from the document containing the RD fields. This document then contains only the index and table of contents, not the text of the documents. You can print the table of contents and index separately and combine it with the larger document.

To create a separate index or table of contents, follow these steps:

1. Open a new file to contain the RD fields.

2. Press Ctrl+F9, the Insert Field key.

For Related Information
- "Numbering Lines," p. 315
- "Inserting Page Numbers," p. 424
- "Printing Found Files," p. 111
- "Understanding the Basics of Fields," p. 1073

VI

Handling Large Documents

3. Type **rd** followed by a space and the name and path of the first file that makes up the document. If the files are all in the current directory, you do not need to include the path (**rd chapt1.doc**, for example). Use the full path name if the files are located in different directories. Use a double backslash where a single backslash normally is used in a path name.

4. Use the arrow keys to move outside the field and press Enter to start a new paragraph.

5. Repeat Steps 2 through 4 for each of the files that makes up the document.

6. Position the insertion point where you want to locate the table of contents and choose the Insert Index and Tables command to create a table of contents.

7. Press Ctrl+Enter, the page break key, to separate the table of contents and index.

8. Position the insertion point where you want to locate the index, and choose the Insert Index and Tables command to create an index.

9. Choose the Insert Page Numbers command to set the appropriate page numbers for the table of contents and index.

See Chapter 29, "Creating Indexes and Tables of Contents," for more information on creating a table of contents.

To set separate starting page numbers for the table of contents and the index, you must insert a section break between them. Choose the Insert **B**reak command, select the Next Page option, and choose OK.

Fig. 32.6 illustrates the field code view of a document set up to print the table of contents and index for a book.

Inserting Chapter Numbers

In documents assembled in a master document, you can use the SEQ field to print chapter numbers with the page numbers.

First you must put a SEQ field at the beginning of each chapter, as in the following steps:

1. Open the first subdocument in the master document.

2. Move the insertion point to the beginning of the subdocument.

3. Press Ctrl+F9 to insert a pair of field characters, {}.

4. Type **SEQ** *identifier* **\h** in the brackets.

   Identifier is a name you assign to the sequence (here, a chapter). The **h** code hides the result of the field so that it is not displayed in the document. The identifier may be a name such as WordBook. Use this identifier for all chapters in the same master document or book.

5. Repeat this process at the beginning of each subsequent chapter.

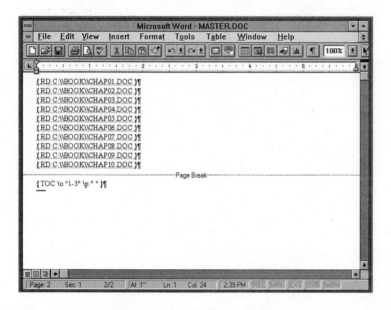

Fig. 32.6
The RD field codes that create a table of contents.

Now use this SEQ field to create a chapter/page number combination in each subdocument. For the first source document included in your master document, follow these steps:

1. Choose the View Header and Footer command.

2. Select header or footer from the list box.

3. Position the insertion point where you want the chapter and page numbers to appear in the header or footer.

4. Press Ctrl+F9, and type **SEQ** *identifier*.

5. Use the arrow key to move the insertion point outside the field bracket, and type a dash or the character you want to separate the chapter number from the page number.

6. Click the page button to insert a page field code.

The entry in the header or footer will look similar to the following:

```
{seq WordBook}-{page}
```

7. Choose the Close button.

8. Save the file.

You must set the starting page number for the second and subsequent files in the series of files included in the master document. When you use a master document to assemble a large document, you usually do not have to set the starting page numbers because Word for Windows automatically assembles the final document into one file and numbers the pages sequentially. When the page numbering includes the chapter number, however, the page numbers have to restart at 1 for each chapter. See "Setting Starting Numbers," earlier in the chapter, for instructions on how to set the starting page number.

To set the page numbering in each subsequent chapter, follow these steps:

For Related Information

■ "Inserting Page Numbers," p. 424

■ "Understanding the Basics of Fields," p. 1073

1. Choose the Insert Page Numbers command.

2. Choose the Format button.

3. Type or select 1 in the Start At text box.

4. Choose OK twice.

In the individual files, the SEQ field that outputs the chapter number always results in the number 1. When you assemble the master document, however, and the SEQ fields are updated, a sequence of chapter numbers results.

From Here...

The following chapters help you learn more about the most important concepts of assembling large documents:

- Chapter 19, "Organizing Content with an Outline." Learn how to organize and manage large documents using Word's excellent outlining feature.

- Chapter 29, "Creating Indexes and Tables of Contents." Learn how to add indexes and tables of contents to your documents to make it easier for your readers to use them.

- Chapter 37, "Automating with Field Codes." Learn how to automate many tasks in Word for Windows by using fields.

VI

Handling Large Documents

Part VII

Word & Other Applications

33   Using Word with Other Windows Applications

34   Converting Files with Word for Windows

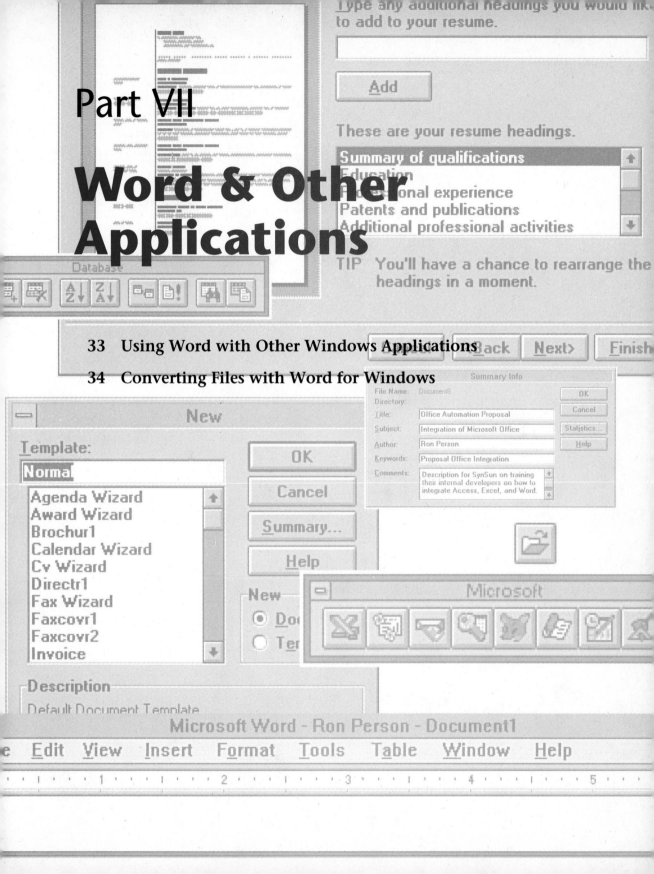

Type any additional headings you would lik
to add to your resume.

Add

These are your resume headings.

Summary of qualifications
Education
Professional experience
Patents and publications
Additional professional activities

TIP You'll have a chance to rearrange the
headings in a moment.

Database

Cancel   <Back   Next>   Finish

Summary Info

File Name:	Document8	OK
Directory:		Cancel
Title:	Office Automation Proposal	Statistics...
Subject:	Integration of Microsoft Office	Help
Author:	Ron Person	
Keywords:	Proposal Office Integration	
Comments:	Description for SynSun on training their internal developers on how to integrate Access, Excel, and Word.	

New

Template:

Normal

Agenda Wizard
Award Wizard
Brochur1
Calendar Wizard
Cv Wizard
Directr1
Fax Wizard
Faxcovr1
Faxcovr2
Invoice

OK
Cancel
Summary...
Help

New
◉ Do
○ Te

Microsoft

Description

Default Document Template

Microsoft Word - Ron Person - Document1

e Edit View Insert Format Tools Table Window Help

Chapter 33

Using Word with Other Windows Applications

One of the unique advantages of Windows applications is their capability to exchange and link information easily with other Windows applications. With Word for Windows, you also can import or link to files from many DOS applications, such as Lotus 1-2-3 worksheets and graphs, AutoCAD drawings, or dBASE database files. Through the use of Microsoft Query, you even can insert or link your Word documents to data found in a SQL server or mainframe. Fig. 33.1 shows a letter with links to a Microsoft Excel worksheet and chart.

If you are used to working with a single application, the value of linking, embedding, or pasting data might not be immediately apparent to you. After you begin to link, embed, or paste data, however, you will see how tasks involving multiple applications come together to produce a single integrated document. You can use Word for Windows with other applications, for example, to do the following:

■ Create mail-merge data documents from a mailing list file kept in dBASE or Microsoft Excel, or from a network or mainframe file.

■ Create sales projections, financial analyses, inventory reports, and investment analyses with worksheets and charts in Microsoft Excel or Lotus 1-2-3 for Windows, and link or embed these charts and tables into Word for Windows documents.

■ Keep client reminder letters and call-backs up to date by linking contact-management software such as Act or PackRat to Word for Windows documents.

In this chapter, you learn the following:

■ The advantages, and disadvantages of pasting, linking, or embedding data from other applications

■ The available data formats

■ How to embed then convert all or part of data from an OLE 1.0 or OLE 2.0 application into a Word document

■ How to link all or part of a file into a document so that changes in the source file appear in the Word document

- Produce proposals and contracts that include designs from the major drafting programs.

- Produce advertising or marketing materials that include artwork created in different Windows or DOS drawing and design applications.

Starting Applications from the Microsoft Toolbar

You can quickly start other Microsoft applications installed on your computer by clicking the appropriate button in the Microsoft toolbar. If the application for the button you click is already running, the application will activate. To display the Microsoft toolbar, choose the View Toolbars command, select Microsoft from the Toolbars list, and choose OK.

The buttons on the Microsoft toolbar are listed in table 33.1.

Table 33.1 The Microsoft Toolbar Buttons	
Button	**Start or Activate Application**
	Microsoft Excel
	Microsoft PowerPoint
	Microsoft Mail
	Microsoft Access
	Microsoft FoxPro
	Microsoft Project
	Microsoft Schedule+
	Microsoft Publisher

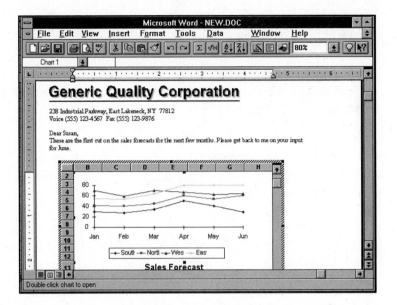

Fig. 33.1
Word documents
can have data
linked or embed-
ded from other
Windows applica-
tions like this table
and chart from
Microsoft Excel.

Choosing to Paste, Link, or Embed Data

Note

This chapter includes references to source and destination documents. The *source* is the file on disk or document in an open application that supplies data. The *destination* is the document that receives the data.

You can look at the various methods of exchanging data in a number of different ways: you can evaluate whether the source of the data is a file or is in an active application; you can evaluate whether you are exchanging text or graphic data; or you can evaluate which of the different procedures can be used.

Word for Windows provides the following primary methods for exchanging data:

- *Embedded data.* The source data is encapsulated and inserted within the Word for Windows document. The data is contained within the Word document as an integral unit.

Advantage: The data, such as a Microsoft Excel worksheet or chart, is stored within the Word for Windows document. You do not need to be concerned with broken links, renaming files, or sending linked files with the document, because it is all self-contained. Editing is done by simply double-clicking the embedded data, which then starts the source application and loads the data.

Disadvantage: Do not use this when you want to be able to change one source file and have many destination documents change. Each file containing embedded data must be updated individually. The original source and the embedded data are not linked. Word files containing embedded data can be very large.

- *Linking Data.* The source data is located in a source file on disk or in a Windows application.

  Advantage: The user can update the linked data when opening the Word document or while the document is open. Links may be live so that a change in one document is immediately reflected in another document. Changes to the source document are available to all linked documents, so updating multiple destination documents is easy.

  Disadvantage: The source data is updated by starting the source application and manually opening the source file and editing it. When you ship a Word document with links to other files, the other files and applications must be available.

- *Pasting Data.* The source data is converted to text or a graphic and inserted into Word.

  Advantage: The source data takes up less storage than embedded data. There is no link—the information appears as a *snapshot*. The source application does not have to be available.

  Disadvantage: The source data cannot be edited or updated; it must be re-created.

- *Inserting or importing from a file.* The source data remains in a file on disk separate from the Word document. Updating the Word document is done manually, or can be automated through a macro. The source application does not need to be available to the user's computer, but a converter file to convert the source file must be installed in Word.

Advantage: You do not need the source application because Word for Windows converts the file or graphic while inserting it. Changes to the source document may affect multiple destination documents.

Disadvantage: Changes to the data will be lost when you update the inserted file.

The following commands are used for exchanging data:

- *File Open and conversion.* Use this command if the data is in a disk file, and you transfer large amounts of non-graphic data infrequently. Use this method to load large dBASE files, text files, or worksheets as a new Word for Windows document. See Chapter 34, "Converting Files with Word for Windows," about converting files.

- *Insert File.* Use this command if the data is in a disk file and you need only portions of the file, or you want to insert the file within an existing Word for Windows document. Data can be brought in unlinked or linked to the disk file (source). Updates from the source on disk can be controlled automatically or manually.

- *Insert Picture.* Use this command for a graphic in a disk file. You can bring in graphics unlinked or linked to the source file. Updates from the source on disk can be controlled automatically or manually. This is described in Chapter 22, "Inserting Pictures in Your Document."

- *Insert Object.* Use this command to embed an object from another Windows application. Objects package all the data that you select and place it within the Word document. You do not need to be concerned with links to external files. Data in objects can be edited.

- *Insert Database.* Use this command to paste or link database information, like that used for mailing lists or product information, into your Word document. The database information can be from many different personal computer, mainframe, or network databases. This topic is described in Chapter 14, "Managing Mail Merge Data."

- *Edit Paste.* Use this command to paste data into a Word document that has been copied from a running Windows application.

- *Edit Paste Special without linking.* Data can be pasted in numerous different formats including as a picture, unformatted text, formatted text, or an embedded object. Data must be re-pasted to be updated.

■ *Edit Paste Special with linking.* Data can be pasted in numerous different formats including as a picture, unformatted text, formatted text, or an embedded object. Data is linked to the source. When the source changes, the data can be updated.

Note

Before Word for Windows exchanges data with files or applications that use a data format other than Word for Windows or text, you must install the appropriate file converter. Before you can open dBASE files or insert ranges from a Microsoft Excel worksheet, for example, you must install the dBASE and Microsoft Excel converter files. If you did not install the converter files when you installed Word for Windows, you can rerun Word for Windows installation program or run the Word for Windows Setup program item icon and install them without completely reinstalling Word for Windows. You will need your original installation disks. Appendix B describes the installation process.

What You Need to Know about Data Formats

When you link data or embed an object, you have a choice of the form in which the data is stored. The data from the source can appear in the Word for Windows document in different forms such as tabbed text, a formatted table, a picture, or a bit map, depending on the source application. Microsoft Excel data, for example, can appear in a number of forms. If you copy a range of Microsoft Excel cells and then use the Edit Paste Special command to paste them into a Word for Windows document, you see the following alternatives in the Data Type dialog box:

■ *Object.* The data is an embedded object with all data stored in the object inside the Word document. No link is maintained with the source document.

■ *Formatted Text (RTF).* Text transfers with formats. Worksheets appear formatted as tables. You can edit or reformat data.

■ *Unformatted Text.* Text is unformatted. Worksheets appear as unformatted text with cells separated by tabs. You can edit or reformat data.

- *Picture*. Pictures, text, database, or worksheet ranges appear as a picture. You can format them as pictures, but you cannot edit text in Word for Windows. Unlinking changes them to drawing objects.

- *Bit map*. Pictures, text, or worksheet ranges appear as a bit-mapped picture. You can format them as pictures, but you cannot edit text in Word for Windows. Resolution is poor.

Exchanging Data Through Files

One of the easiest ways to bring large amounts of textual or numeric data into Word for Windows from another Windows or DOS application is to use the **File Open** command. This command is useful for opening dBASE files containing mailing list data or opening and formatting text files downloaded from a mainframe.

Chapter 3, "Creating and Saving Documents," describes how to change the List Files of Type pull-down list to the All Files (*.*) option. This option lists all files so that you can see and open non-Word for Windows files. If you installed the appropriate file converter, Word for Windows will open and convert the file simultaneously. Converting files is described in detail in Chapter 34, "Converting Files with Word for Windows."

Transferring Data with Copy and Paste

The simplest way to transfer small amounts of data or graphics from one application to another is to copy and paste in the same way that you move text or graphics within a document.

To copy from one Windows application to a Word for Windows document, follow these steps:

1. Select the text, cells, or graphic in the source document.

2. Choose the Edit Copy command.

3. Press Alt+Tab until the title for Word for Windows appears on-screen. Release the Alt key to activate Word for Windows.

4. Position the insertion point where you want the data to appear in the document.

5. Choose the Edit Paste command.

Text is pasted into the document as formatted text; Microsoft Excel worksheet cells or ranges paste in as a table; graphics paste in as a bit-mapped picture. None of them are linked to their source document, but if you double-click a pasted picture, the appropriate drawing program on your computer will activate and load the picture.

Embedding Data

When you need to include information from a Windows application in your Word document, and you want a copy of the information to go with the Word document, then you should use an embedded object. Embedded objects take the data from the source application and embed it into the Word document. If the recipient of the Word document wants to edit the embedded data, they can use their copy of the source application to make changes.

If you have worked with the WordArt or Microsoft Graph applets, you are familiar with embedded objects and how they work. Although these programs are applets (small applications), other major applications with Object Linking and Embedding (OLE) capabilities can embed their data into Word for Windows documents.

Consider the following advantages to embedding objects:

■ File management and tracking of source documents is not a problem—the source data goes with the Word document.

■ Linked data is not destroyed when a source document cannot be found during an update.

■ Updating an embedded object is done in the source application. If the source application is OLE 1.0 compliant, then the source application starts and loads the data. If the source application is OLE 2.0 compliant, you can edit the data without leaving the Word document.

There are also the following disadvantages to embedding objects:

- The recipient must have the source application to edit the embedded object. However, the embedded object can be converted if the appropriate conversion filter has been installed.

- The Word for Windows document becomes large, containing the Word for Windows document as well as all the embedded data.

Creating an Embedded Object

You can embed data in two ways. Both methods produce the same results. You can create completely new data and then embed it, all in the same action, or you can insert an existing file as an object. Once the data is embedded it is referred to as an object.

Applications that can embed data work in two different ways. Applications using OLE 1.0 run and activate the source application you selected and display a blank document in which you can create your embedded object. Applications that use OLE 2.0 leave Word active on the screen. Word's menus and toolbars change to reflect the application you selected. But you are still looking at the full Word document.

Fig. 33.2 shows how Windows Paintbrush appears when you insert a Paintbrush object. Paintbrush uses OLE 1.0. Notice that Word is behind while Paintbrush is active and waiting for the object to be created. The Paintbrush application's title bar says `Paintbrush Picture in Document1`.

Fig. 33.3 shows how WordArt appears when you insert a WordArt object. Because WordArt uses OLE 2.0, it enables you to work within the Word document. While a WordArt object is active in the Word document, Word's menus and toolbars change to those of WordArt.

Embedded objects display as field codes when you display field codes. To see field codes, select the document, and then press Shift+F9. The following shows some of the embedded objects you may see:

```
{ EMBED MSWordArt.2 \s }
{ EMBED MSEquation.2 }
{ EMBED Word.Document.6 }
{ EMBED Package }
```

Fig. 33.2
Some Windows applications activate the source application in a window when you edit an embedded an object.

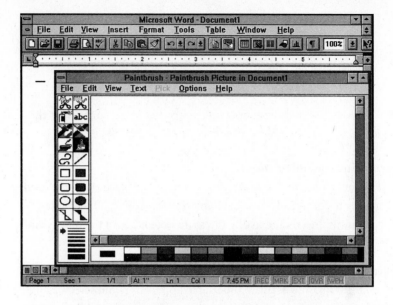

Fig. 33.3
Some Windows applications enable you to create or edit an object while you remain in the Word document.

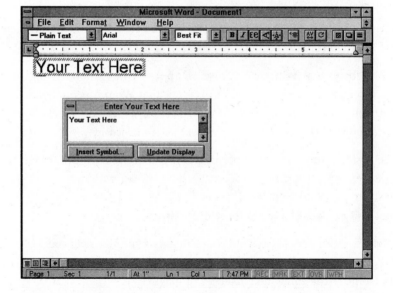

Creating a New Object. To create a new object and embed it, follow these steps:

1. Position the insertion point in the destination document where you want to insert the object.

2. Choose the Insert Object command.

3. Select the Create New tab. The tab lists the types of objects you can embed (see fig. 33.4).

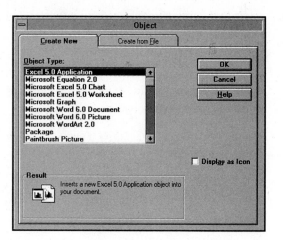

Fig. 33.4
From the Create New tab of the Object dialog box, select the type of data you want to embed into your Word document. The Result box describes the type of object.

4. From the Object Type list, select the type of object you want to insert.

5. Select the Display as Icon check box if you want the embedded object to appear as an icon in the Word document. In most cases, you will not select this check box.

6. Choose OK.

Create the data you want contained in the object. If a blank worksheet opens, for example, create the worksheet. If a blank drawing window appears, draw the object.

Embedding New Objects. To embed the new object once you have created it, use one of the following methods:

■ If you are working in an OLE 2.0 application—one where Word's menus have changed—click outside the object or use the method described in the application's manual or Help file to update the object and close the application.

■ If you are working in an OLE 1.0 application, one where the application appears in a separate window, do one of the following:

Choose the File Close and Return to Document command if you are editing a Word document embedded in a Word document.

or

Choose the File Exit command and respond with Yes if you want the destination document updated.

or

Choose the File Update command to update the embedded object but keep the application and object open.

An object appears in the Object Type List only if the application you use to create the object is registered with Windows and is capable of producing OLE objects.

Select the Display as Icon check box if you believe that the embedded data will take up too much room in the document, or if the data is backup information that needs to be displayed only when requested. Data that appears as an icon displays as an application-specific icon on-screen and when printed. When on-screen, the user can double-click the icon to read the actual data or see the graphic. Although the icon takes up less space on-screen, it still consumes the same amount of memory as a normally embedded object.

Embedding an Existing File or Object. To embed a file that already exists, follow these steps:

1. Position the insertion point in the destination document where you want to insert the object.

2. Choose the Insert Object command.

3. Select the Create from File tab. The tab displays directories and file lists, as shown in fig. 33.5.

4. Change to the directory containing the file you want to insert. If you need to connect to the network, choose the Network button. If you need to find the file, choose the Find File button.

5. Type or select the file name in the File Name list box.

6. Select the Display as Icon check box if you want the embedded file to appear as an icon on-screen and in print. Icons take up less screen

space, but the same memory. You can read the contents of an icon by double-clicking it.

7. Choose OK.

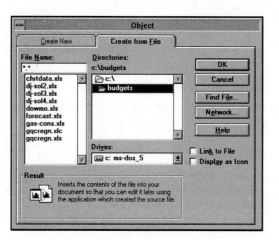

Fig. 33.5
From the Create from File tab of the Object dialog box, select the file you want to embed. The Result box describes the type of object.

The data you embed appears as a single object in the document. If you select the object, you will see it enclosed by black handles. You can edit that object at any time by double-clicking the object.

Embedding Part of a File. The preceding two methods required that you embed an entire file. The following method describes how to embed a portion of a file—for example, a range from an Excel worksheet. This example requires only as much memory as the range requires, so the Word document will be smaller.

To create an embedded object that is part of a file, follow these steps:

1. Position the insertion point in the destination document in which you want to insert the object.

2. Activate the application containing the data and select the portion of the data you want to embed. If you are using a Windows spreadsheet like Excel, you select the cells you want to embed. If you are using a Windows database, such as Access, you select the data you want to embed.

3. Choose the Edit Copy command or its equivalent in the application.

4. Switch to Word by pressing Alt+Tab or clicking the Word window.

5. Choose the Edit Paste Special command.

6. Select the object listed at the top of the As list in the Paste Special dialog box.

7. Choose OK.

The embedded data appears as a single object in your document. When it is not selected, it appears like a normal text or graphic. When the object is selected, you will see the object surrounded by black handles. Double-click the object to edit it, using its source application.

Editing Embedded Objects

Embedded objects are easy to edit. With the mouse, simply double-click the embedded object. With the keyboard, select the object by moving the insertion point to one side of the object and pressing Shift+arrow key across the object. Once the object is selected, choose the Edit Object command at the bottom of the Edit menu. From the submenu, choose the Edit command. If the object's application is not open, it opens; if it is open, the application activates. The object then loads so that you can make changes.

To exit the object after you edit or format it, use the same procedures used to exit when you created the object:

- If Word's menus changed when you edited the object, click in the Word document to return to Word and embed the object.

- If the object's application opened in a separate window, do one of the following:

  Choose the File Close and Return to Document command if you are editing a Word document embedded in a Word document.

  or

  Choose the File Exit command and then choose the Return command to close the application and update the embedded object.

  or

  Choose the File Update command to update the embedded object but keep the object's application and object open.

Converting Embedded Objects

One problem you may face when exchanging files with others in your workgroup is receiving an embedded object you cannot open or edit. Suppose, for example, that you receive a Word document that contains an embedded Excel worksheet, but you do not have Excel. You can still work with this file, read the Excel worksheet, and even edit the worksheet.

Note

If you want to read or edit the embedded object, you do not have to have the object's application, but you must have installed the converter required to convert that application's files. These converters can be installed at any time by selecting the Word Setup program in the Program Manager. You need your Word installation diskettes.

To convert an embedded object into a different format, follow these steps:

1. Select the embedded object by clicking it or by moving the insertion point to one side, and then pressing Shift+arrow key. Black handles appear around the object when it is selected.

2. Choose the Edit Object command from the bottom of the Edit menu.

3. Choose Convert from the submenu. The Convert dialog box appears.

4. Select the Convert To option if you want to permanently convert the object to another format. Select the Activate As option if you want to temporarily convert the object so that you can read or edit it. The object is stored back into the document in its original format.

5. Select the type of conversion you want from the Object Type list box.

6. Choose OK.

If you must return the Word document to its original creator, but you need to read or edit the object for which you do not have an application, use the Activate As option in the Convert dialog box. This converts the object only while you are reading or editing it. Once the object is closed, it is converted back to its original format and stored back in the document. Using the Activate As option enables the original document creator to reopen the object using the original application that created it.

Troubleshooting Embedded Objects

A newly installed program is supposed to be capable of embedding objects, yet the application does not appear in the Object Type list after I choose Insert Object.

Make sure that the OLE-compatible application is registered in the OLE registration database. (Normally this is done automatically during installation.) If you move or rename an application, the registration may not be correct anymore. If an OLE application does not appear in the Object Type list of the Object dialog box, switch to the File Manager and open the Windows directory. Start the Registration Info Editor by double-clicking the file named REGEDIT.EXE; or by keyboard, select that file and press Enter.

In the Registration Info Editor, choose the File Merge Registration File command. In the Merge Registration File dialog box, change to the directory containing the application you want to register. In that directory you should find files with the file extension REG. Select a file, and then choose OK. Repeat this process for each REG file in the application's directory. If this does not enable you to use embedded objects from the application, call the support telephone line for that application.

Double-clicking an embedded object opens a different application than I expected.

Double-clicking an embedded object normally opens the file that created that object. If that application is not open, but an application that can read that file is available, the substitute application that is available will open.

If an unlinked picture or bitmap (BMP) file is in Word and you double-click it, Word's native drawing tools appear for you to edit the pasted object.

A file contains an object for which the original application is not available. The object needs to be edited.

If the proper conversion files were installed in Word, you will be able to convert the object from its current format into the format of an available application. You have a choice of leaving the object in its new converted format or only converting temporarily. To learn more about converting objects, refer to "Converting Embedded Objects" earlier in this chapter.

Linking Documents and Files

Linking data between applications enables one document to show the changes that occur in another document. This capability can be very useful in many business situations. For example, you may have an engineering proposal that is constructed from a standard Word template. But the drawings within the template are linked to graphics files and the cost estimates and schedules are linked to worksheet files. When you open the proposal in Word, or at any time, you can update the linked data so that the graphics, cost estimates, and schedules are always current.

There are two ways to link files. You can link the entire file using the Insert File command, or you can link data between Windows applications with the Edit Paste Special command. Linking creates a communication channel between two open Windows applications. Data can be sent through this channel when information in the source changes, or when you manually request an update.

Linking Documents to Entire Files

If you need to include in your Word for Windows document a graphic or portions of a file or worksheet, you should become familiar with the methods for inserting files and importing graphics. Linking to files on disk has these advantages:

- The data resides in a disk file.

- All or part of a word processing, worksheet, or database file can be inserted and linked.

- Only a source file on disk is required. The source application need not be open or even on the system.

- The operator controls when the file or graphic data updates. This feature enables you to "freeze" the data in the destination document until you want an update.

- Files and graphics from DOS applications can be linked into Word for Windows documents.

Linking to files has the following disadvantages:

- Renaming or moving a source file can disturb the link. You then must edit the link so that the Word for Windows document can find it.

- Links cannot exist across a network unless you are using enhancements to Windows.

- Editing an inserted picture can break its link and change the graphic into an embedded object.

To link into your document a file or a portion of a file that is on disk and for which you have an installed converter, follow these steps:

1. Position the insertion point in the destination document at the place where you want the source data to appear.

2. Choose the Insert File command. The File dialog box opens (see fig. 33.6).

Fig. 33.6

Link a file or portion of a file into your document using the Insert File command.

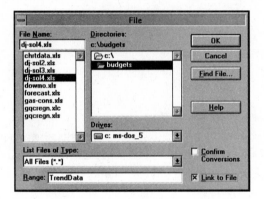

3. Change to the directory containing the source file. In the File Name box, type or select the name of the file you want to insert. If you do not see the file, change the List File of Type to All Files (*.*).

4. To insert a portion of the file, type the name (for Microsoft Excel files), the bookmark (for Word for Windows files), or range name (for 1-2-3 files) in the Range text box.

5. To link rather than insert the source document into the target document, select the Link to File check box.

6. If you want to see a dialog box that will confirm the file type before Word converts it, choose the Confirm Conversions check box.

7. Choose OK.

8. If you choose to confirm the conversion, the Convert File dialog box appears so that you can confirm the type of file conversion. Select the file type and choose OK. (You must have the appropriate converter installed to convert other word processing, worksheet, or database files.)

If you are inserting a worksheet file and did not enter a range name, a dialog box appears from which you can select to insert the Entire Worksheet or select from the list of named ranges in the worksheet. When you later update the inserted worksheet, by selecting it and pressing F9, you again will have an opportunity to select the range to be updated.

Inserting a file without linking enters data as though it were typed. Worksheets are entered as Word for Windows tables.

If you select the Link to File check box, a link is created to the source document, using a LINK field code such as the following:

```
{LINK ExcelWorksheet C:\\FINANCIAL\\FORECAST.XLS Result
➡\* mergeformat \r \a}
```

In this example, the Result range within the Microsoft Excel worksheet was copied and pasted into the Word for Windows document as Formatted Text (RTF), as indicated by the argument \r. (The [ccc] indicates you should type this as one long line.)The following arguments specify the form for linked data:

\r	Formatted Text (RTF)
\t	Unformatted Text
\p	Picture
\b	Bit map

> **Note**
>
> Before you can use the Insert File command to insert data into a document, the source document must have been saved to disk.

Linking Documents to Part of a File

The Edit Paste Special command is useful primarily when you want to link two Windows applications and use features in a source application to update data or graphics in your Word for Windows document. You might use the command if you have a financial worksheet and charts in Microsoft Excel, for example, and the results and charts are part of an integrated Word for Windows report. You need to be able to work in Microsoft Excel and use its functions and its links to mainframe data. When the worksheets and charts change, however, the changes should pass immediately to the integrated report in Word for Windows, where you can print them.

The advantages to using links created by Paste Special are these:

- You can link a single source document to many destination documents. Changes in the single source are available to all the destination documents.

- The data resides in the source application's document. You can use the source application and all of its features to update the source document.

- The data or graphic is not embedded in the Word for Windows document—only the result is shown—so the document is much smaller than a document with embedded data.

- You can bring in all or part of a word processing, worksheet, or database file.

- Updates can be done automatically whenever the source data changes or manually when you request them.

Note some disadvantages to using links created by Paste Special:

- Renaming or moving a source file can disturb the link. You must edit the link so that the Word for Windows document can find the source file.

- The source application and file must be on disk and available to Word for Windows if you want to edit the data or graphic.

- Not all Windows applications can link data.

- Automatic updates can slow down computer response time.

- Windows requires enhancement software to create links across networks.

Creating Links with Copy and Paste Special. Creating a link between Word for Windows and a Windows application is as easy as copying and pasting. When you give the paste command, you create a link that updates automatically.

VII

Word & Other Applications

> **Note**
>
> If you copied data from a source application, but the **E**dit Paste **S**pecial command
> does not enable you to link, that source application may not be able to create linked
> data.

To copy a range or a portion of a document and link it into the Word document, follow these steps:

1. Position the insertion point in the Word document where you want the linked data or graphic to appear.

2. Activate the source application and document, and make sure the source is saved with the file name it will keep.

3. Select the portion of the source document you want to link.

4. Choose the Edit Copy command.

5. Activate the Word document.

6. Choose the Edit Paste **S**pecial command.

7. Select the Paste Link option.

8. From the As list, select the type of data format you want in the document.

9. Choose OK.

Troubleshooting Linked Files

When the link is updated an error message appears that says Error! Not a valid Filename.

This error is caused when the link cannot find the source file that is supposed to contain the source data. This could be caused by the source file being deleted, renamed, or moved to another directory. First, choose the Edit Undo command to restore the last linked data instead of displaying the error message. Do not save the document to the original file name until you fix the problem.

You can use any of the following methods to resolve the problem of a lost link:

■ Reconnect the link if you know where the original data file has moved or its new name. This is usually the best and easiest solution if the original file can still be found. Reconnecting a link is described in "Reconnecting Links When Names or Path Names Change" later in this chapter.

■ Delete the linked data producing the error and re-create it with a new source. This is the best solution if the original file is lost and you need a link to a source file in another application.

■ Lock a link so that the image of the last data is maintained and the field code that creates the link is kept for possible future use. This enables you to use the last image or text from the source data, while preserving the link field code in case the source document is later found or recreated. Locking a link is described in "Locking Links to Prevent an Update" later in this chapter.

■ Freeze the text or image from the last link so that the text or data is like a normal unlinked graphic or text in the document. When you *freeze* linked data, you are undoing the link to the source document, but maintaining the text or graphic image in your Word document. The field code that maintained the link is deleted. To freeze linked data as it appears currently in the document, see "Converting Linked Data to Fixed Data" later in this chapter.

Managing Links

For Related Information
■ "Creating a Master Document," p. 971

■ "Converting Files from Word Processors, Spreadsheets, or Databases," p. 1021

Keeping track of the many links into a large or complex document can be a difficult task. You can use the Edit Links command to make the job easier. When you choose the Edit Links command, the Links dialog box, shown in fig. 33.7, opens and displays a list of all the links, their type, and how they update. From the buttons and check box, you can update linked data, open linked files, lock links to prevent changes, cancel the link, change a link between automatic and manual, or change the file names or directories where the linked data is stored.

Passing Linked Documents to Other Computer Users. If you want to change the linked data in your document, you must have the source document the link is connected to as well as the application that created the data.

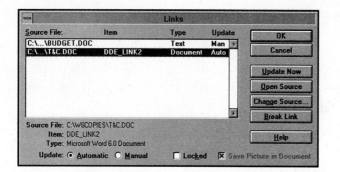

Fig. 33.7
The Links dialog box enables you to update, unlink, or protect links. If the source file moves or is renamed, you can relink to the source using the Links dialog box.

When you give a document containing links to other users, make sure that you give them the source documents. They will need the source application if they want to make edits in the original data.

Reducing the Size of a Linked File. The linked data that appears in your word document is actually a representation of the real data that exists in a source document. But this image still requires memory. If your document displays a link to a large graphics file, the representation of the graphics file alone can be very large.

You can reduce the size of a file containing links by not storing the graphic representation; instead, you store only the field codes that describe the links. When the document opens, these field codes reestablish the link to the source document and regenerate an image in your Word document.

The advantages to storing only the link is that your Word document file size can be significantly reduced if your document contains links to large graphics. The disadvantage to storing only the links is that documents with large files take longer to load as the images are re-created, and links that cannot be re-created will appear as rectangular placeholders on-screen.

To store a document as a reduced size file, follow these steps:

1. Choose the Edit Links command.

2. Select the link you want stored as a link field without the graphic image.

3. Deselect the Save Picture in Document check box.

4. Choose OK.

Opening the Source Document. In your Word for Windows document, you can edit linked data such as text or numbers just as though you typed them in the document. But as soon as you update the link, your changes disappear. To change linked data so that it remains, you need to edit the source document. The source application and source document must be open when you edit the link.

To open a source document that may be closed, follow these steps:

1. If you want to open a file specific to one link, select the linked data.

2. Choose the Edit Links command to display the Links dialog box shown in fig. 33.8.

3. From the Source File list, select the link you want to open. If you selected linked data in Step 1, that link is already selected.

4. Choose the Open Source button. The source application opens.

5. Make your updates, edits, or formatting changes to the source document.

6. If you have made all the changes you want, save and then close the source document.

If the link is automatic, the Word for Windows document updates immediately. If the link is manual, you must update the linked data to see the change. Update linked data by selecting it and pressing F9.

Caution

When you rename or move a source file, make sure that the destination document is open; save the destination document after renaming or moving the source file. This step is recommended because the {LINK} field in the destination document stores the file and path name of the source file. You can see these names by selecting linked data and pressing Shift+F9. If you rename or move the source file while the destination document is closed, the {LINK} field will not be able to update itself to the new file or path name. If a link is accidentally lost, you can reconnect the link by using the technique described in "Reconnecting Links When Names or Path Names Change" later in this chapter.

> **Note**
>
> To preserve manually applied formatting during an update to linked data, use the * mergeformat and * charformat field switches described in Chapter 37, "Automating with Field Codes." To preserve wide titles in a table, do not merge cells to give a title extra width in a cell. Instead, change individual cell widths to allow space for a wide title.

Converting Linked Data to Fixed Data. To convert linked information to text or a graphic, select the linked information and then press Shift+Ctrl+F9 to unlink. The information changes into text, a picture, or a bit map—as if you had pasted it and not paste-linked it. You can also select the link, choose the Edit Links command, choose the Break Link button, and then confirm with Yes.

Updating Links. To update individual links in a document so that the destination file receives new information, select the linked text or graphic, and then press F9. To update links selectively without scrolling through the document, choose the Edit Links command. When the Links dialog box appears, select the links you want to update (use Ctrl+click to select multiple links), and then choose the Update Now button.

When you want to update all the links in an entire document, select the entire document by pressing Ctrl and clicking in the left boundary, or press Ctrl+5 (numeric pad). Then press the F9 key or choose the Edit Links command and choose the Update Now button.

Changing Links between Automatic and Manual. Using the Edit Paste Special command creates an automatic link; pasted data normally updates immediately when the source information changes. This automatic updating process can slow your computer's operation if changes are frequent. If you do not need to see immediate changes, however, you can change an automatic link to a manual link.

To change between manually or automatically updated links, follow these steps:

1. Select the linked data or graphic.

2. Choose the Edit Links command.

3. From the Update options at the bottom of the dialog box:

■ Choose Manual to update a link by manually selecting it and pressing F9.

■ Choose Automatic to automatically update a link when the source data changes.

4. Choose OK.

To update a manual link, select the linked information and press F9. To prevent a link from updating, lock the link, as described later in "Locking Links to Prevent an Update."

Reconnecting Links When Names or Path Names Change. If a source's location, file name, or range name changes, you need to update the field code that creates the link to reflect the new directory and file name. To update a linking field, choose the Edit Links command, select the link you need to edit, and then choose the Change Source button to display the Change Source dialog box (see fig. 33.8). From this dialog box, you can select or type a new file name, path name, or item. (The item is a range name in a worksheet or bookmark in a Word document.)

Fig. 33.8
You can reconnect source files to the destination even if the source file has been moved or renamed.

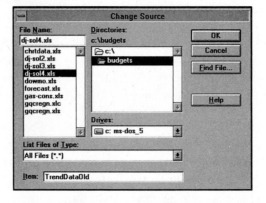

If you are familiar with the operation and editing of field codes as described in Chapter 37, "Automating with Field Codes," you can display the field code for the link and edit the file name, path name, and item name directly. Remember that two backslashes are needed to separate subdirectories in a path name within a field code.

Locking Links to Prevent an Update. You may want to prevent accidental updating of a link by locking the field. When the field is locked, its data will not change. The linking field code is preserved, however, so that at a later time you can unlock the field and update the linked data.

To lock a field, follow these steps:

1. Select the field you want to lock.

2. Choose the Edit Links command (or press Ctrl+F11), select the Locked check box, and choose OK.

To unlock a locked field, follow these steps:

1. Select the field you want to lock.

2. Choose the Edit Links command (or press Shift+Ctrl+F11), deselect the Locked check box, and choose OK.

For Related Information

■ "Automating with Field Codes," p. 1071

From Here...

Integrating data from many different sources is one of the ways Word can really help you. For more information related to using or formatting information from different sources you may want to examine the following chapters:

■ Chapter 14, "Managing Mail Merge Data." Learn how to retrieve databases and paste or link them to your Word document. These capabilities are useful for bringing in mail list information, product data, sales histories, and so on.

■ Chapter 32, "Assembling Large Documents." Bring many smaller documents together into one large document of manual or book size so that the entire document can be cross-referenced, indexed, or have a table of contents built.

■ Chapter 34, "Converting Files with Word for Windows." Use data from other applications that do not provide linking or embedding or in cases where you want to import an entire file.

■ Chapter 37, "Automating with Field Codes." Field codes are used to create and maintain linked or embedded data. Manually editing these links provides formatting capabilities that can't be achieved through dialog boxes.

Converting Files with Word for Windows

In this chapter, you learn how to make the transition to Word for Windows smoothly and how to use Word for Windows with other word processing, spreadsheet, and database programs that still may be a part of your operations.

If you are experienced with a word processor, you may meet frustration in the first days of transition from your old word processing program to Word for Windows. Whenever people move from a known system to a similar but different system, they encounter learning interference. The old similar ideas and muscle memory get in the way of the new ideas and new muscle coordination. Within a few weeks of using Word for Windows, however, you will be handling more work with better quality and greater ease.

Converting Files from Word Processors, Spreadsheets, or Databases

Word for Windows is made for offices using a mix of word processors and spreadsheets from different software manufacturers. Because Word for Windows reads and writes the files of many major word processors, working in an office that has more than one word processor is not a problem for standard business writing. You also can insert all or portions of major spreadsheet and database files.

Examining the File Types that Word for Windows Converts

Converting a file means changing the way information in the file is formatted from a format used by one application to a format used by another

This chapter explains how to convert files to and from other word processor formats. In this chapter, you learn the following:

- How to open document files created by another word processor and save them in Word for Windows format

- How to save Word for Windows files in a file format that is used by another word processor

- How to improve the way that Word for Windows handles file conversions to and from other file formats

application. Word for Windows is able to convert a variety of word processor, spreadsheet, and database file formats. Word for Windows can either convert files from another format to its own format or convert its own files to other formats.

You convert a file to Word for Windows format by opening the file. When you open a file created by another word processor, spreadsheet, or database program, Word for Windows uses a *converter* to read the file from the disk drive. The converter reads (retrieves) the file from the disk, stores it in your computer's memory, and changes it to a form that Word for Windows can use, without changing the original contents of the file you opened. Specific instructions to convert files to Word for Windows format are given in the next part of this section.

You convert a file from Word for Windows format to another word processor format by saving the file. Word for Windows also uses converters to enable you to save files in formats that can be used by other word processors. In-struction to save files in a format other than Word for Windows format are in the next section of this chapter, "Saving Word for Windows Documents to Another Format."

Word for Windows is supplied with a variety of converters. Many of the word processor converters enable you to either open or save files in a particular format. The spreadsheet and database converters, however, only allow you to *open* a file in that format—not save it. You can always save a document in Word for Windows format, however, including spreadsheets and databases.

Word for Windows can open files in the following word processor, spread-sheet, and database formats:

Program	Description
Microsoft Excel	XLS; Versions 2, 3, 4, and 5*
dBASE	DBF; II, III, III+, IV
DisplayWrite and DisplayWriter	Versions 4, 4.2, 5, and 5.2*
Microsoft Windows Write	WRI
Microsoft Word for DOS	DOC and styles; Version 3.0 through 6.0
Microsoft MultiMate	Versions 3.3, 3.6, Advantage, Advantage II, and 4.0

Program	Description
Multiplan	SLK; Versions 3.x and 4.2*
Rich Text Format	RTF (stores formatting and graphics as ANSI characters)
Text Only (ASCII)	With or without line breaks
Text Only (PC-8)	With or without line breaks
Text with Layout	Column and tabs are preserved
Microsoft Publisher for Windows	Version 1.x
Microsoft Word for Windows	DOC; Versions 1.0, 1.1, 1.1a, and 2.0
Microsoft Word for the Macintosh	Versions 4.x and 5.x
Microsoft Works for DOS	WKS and WK1 files; Versions 1.0, 2.0, and 3.0
Microsoft Works for Windows	WKS and WK1 files; Version 2.0
Lotus 1-2-3	WKS Versions 1A and WK1 2.x and 3.x*
WordPerfect for DOS	Versions 4.1, 4.2, 5.0, and 5.1
WordPerfect for Windows	Version 5.x
WordStar	Versions 3.3, 3.4, 3.45, 4.0, 5.0, 5.5, 6.0, and 7.0

*Word for Windows cannot save to this file format, although it can open it.

Installing Converters

During the Word for Windows installation process (described in Appendix B), you have the opportunity to select the types of converters you want to install on your hard disk. From your selections, Word for Windows copies the appropriate converters into the directory you specify for Word for Windows. The installation process also makes changes to the WIN.INI file, which contains start-up characteristics for Windows applications.

You can add converters after Word for Windows has been installed by running the Word Setup program.

You will need the original installation floppy disks. You will be given the opportunity to install selected converters rather than reinstalling all of Word for Windows.

When the file converters are installed, you can open or save to different word processing formats using the Word for Windows File Open and File Save As commands. Word for Windows converts the files as you open or save them.

When spreadsheet or database converters are installed, you can insert all or a portion of a spreadsheet or database by using the Insert File command. You do not have to convert data in a database or spreadsheet file that you are using for a mail merge. Word for Windows converts the data as it performs the merge.

Converting a File into Word for Windows Format

To open a file created by another word processor, follow these steps:

1. Choose the File Open command or click the Open button on the Standard toolbar. Word for Windows displays the Open dialog box (see fig. 34.1).

Fig. 34.1

To convert a file, open it with the standard file Open dialog box.

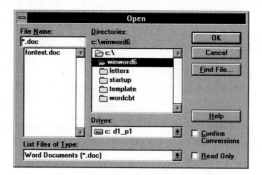

2. Type or select a file name in the File Name box Use the Drives, Directories, or List Files Of Type boxes to find the document when necessary.

3. Choose OK.

   Word for Windows analyzes the file's contents, and attempts to convert the file automatically. If Word for Windows cannot determine the file's format, it displays the Convert File dialog box shown in fig. 34.2. Word for Windows also displays the Convert File dialog box if it cannot find the converter necessary to convert the file.

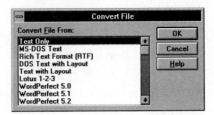

Fig. 34.2
Select the source
format for a file
conversion.

4. If the Convert File dialog box appears, select the program the file came
   from, and then choose OK.

The next time you save this document, Word for Windows will ask you if
you want to overwrite (replace) the file with the Word for Windows 6 format.
Choose Yes to replace the file. If you choose No, Word for Windows displays
a Save As dialog box. If you have much editing to do, continue to save the
document in Word for Windows format. When you are ready to send the
document to a user who does not have Word for Windows, use the procedure
in the next section of this chapter, "Saving Word for Windows Documents to
Another Format," to save the document to another word processing format.

Inserting all or a portion of a spreadsheet or database file is described in
Chapter 15, "Mastering Envelopes, Mail Merge, and Form Letters."

If the document file you convert contains graphics, Word for Windows will
automatically convert the graphics. Refer to Chapter 22, "Inserting Pictures
in Your Document," for more information about importing and converting
graphics.

If you want to confirm all file conversions, select the Confirm Conversions
check box in the Open dialog box (so that there is an X in it). Refer to fig.
34.1.

If you have several files that you want to convert at the same time, use the
BatchConversion macro in the CONVERT.DOT template supplied with Word
for Windows. This template is located in the Word for Windows program
directory. Refer to Chapter 38, "Recording and Editing Macros," for information on using macros.

Tip
When Word asks
whether you want
to overwrite the
original file, an-
swer No. Your
original file then
remains un-
changed as a
backup.

Troubleshooting Converting a File into Word for Windows

The original document contained pictures that are missing in the converted file.

Word for Windows will automatically attempt to convert any pictures in a file that you open. If Word for Windows cannot locate either the graphics file that contains the picture or a convertor for the graphics file, the picture is not included in the converted document. Refer to Chapter 22, "Inserting Pictures in Your Document," for information on converting graphics files and for information on the graphics file converters.

The fonts in the converted document aren't the same as the fonts in the original document.

The original document might contain fonts that you do not have installed on your system. When this happens, Word for Windows substitutes an available font for the missing font, making the best match it can. You can alter the font substitutions that Word for Windows makes by following the instructions in the section "Controlling Font Conversion in Documents," later in this chapter.

Saving Word for Windows Documents to Another Format

For Related Information

■ "Merging Mailing Lists and Documents," p. 470

■ "Inserting Pictures in Your Document," p. 659

■ "Editing and Converting Pictures," p. 683

■ "Running a Macro," p. 1132

Word for Windows can save files to the same word processing formats it converts. This feature is useful if you work in a company that uses different types of word processors. Word for Windows documents cannot be saved to spreadsheet or database formats.

Word for Windows uses the same converters described earlier to convert Word for Windows documents into other word processing formats. If you do not see the format you need in the Save File As Type box, rerun the Word for Windows installation program and install the converter you need.

To save a Word for Windows document to a non-Word for Windows format, follow these steps:

1. Choose the File Save As command.

2. Type the document name in the File Name text box. Use a different file name than the original file so that you do not write over the original file.

3. Select a file format from the Save File As Type pull-down box.

4. Choose OK.

Seeing Which Converters You Have Installed

When you install converters, the conversion files with the file extension CNV are copied into the same directory in which Word for Windows is installed. The installation program also modifies the WIN.INI file. The WIN.INI file is a text file that stores configuration information for Windows and some Windows applications.

You can see which converters are installed for Word for Windows by opening the WIN.INI file and examining the segment of that file that starts with the title [MSWord Text Converters]. WIN.INI can be found in the Windows directory. When you open the Windows directory, Word will convert the file from text.

Microsoft does not recommend modifying the [MSWord Text Converters] segment of WIN.INI. Instead, use the Word for Windows setup program to modify WIN.INI automatically. If you must make changes to the WIN.INI, make a backup copy you can use in case your modifications do not work. When you save WIN.INI with your modifications, choose the File Save **As** command and select Text Only (*.TXT) from the Save File as **Type** pull-down list. WIN.INI must be saved as a text file.

Caution

Be certain that you save the WIN.INI file as a Text Only file, otherwise Windows will not operate correctly.

Information in the [MSWord Text Converters] segment uses the following syntax:

```
Converter_class_name=application_name, filename, filename_extension
```

By looking in WIN.INI, you can see the types of converters you have installed and where they are located. The following list shows a sample [MSWord Text Converters] segment:

```
[MSWord Text Converters]
DOS Text with Layout=DOS Text with Layout, C:\WINWORD\TXTWLYT.CNV, asc
Text with Layout=Text with Layout, C:\WINWORD\TXTWLYT.CNV, ans
WrdPrfctDOS50=WordPerfect 5.0, C:\WINWORD\WPFT5.CNV, doc
WrdPrfctDOS=WordPerfect 5.1, C:\WINWORD\WPFT5.CNV, doc
WordPerfect 4.2=WordPerfect 4.2, C:\WINWORD\WPFT4.CNV, doc
WordPerfect 4.1=WordPerfect 4.1, C:\WINWORD\WPFT4.CNV, doc
MSWordWin=Word for Windows 1, C:\WINWORD\WORDWIN1.CNV, doc
MSWordDos=Word for DOS, C:\WINWORD\WORDDOS.CNV, doc
MSWordMac4=Word for Macintosh 4.0, C:\WINWORD\WORDMAC.CNV, mcw
MSWordMac=Word for Macintosh 5.0, C:\WINWORD\WORDMAC.CNV, mcw
RFTDCA=RFT-DCA, C:\WINWORD\RFTDCA.CNV, rft
MSBiff=Excel Worksheet, C:\WINWORD\XLBIFF.CNV, xls
ATdBase=Ashton-Tate dBASE, C:\WINWORD\DBASE.CNV, dbf
Lotus123=Lotus 1-2-3, C:\WINWORD\LOTUS123.CNV, wk1 wk3
WordStar 5.5=WordStar 5.5, C:\WINWORD\WORDSTAR.CNV, doc
WordStar 5.0=WordStar 5.0, C:\WINWORD\WORDSTAR.CNV, doc
WordStar 4.0=WordStar 4.0, C:\WINWORD\WORDSTAR.CNV, doc
WordStar 3.45=WordStar 3.45, C:\WINWORD\WORDSTAR.CNV, doc
WordStar 3.3=WordStar 3.3, C:\WINWORD\WORDSTAR.CNV, doc
Windows Write=Windows Write, C:\WINWORD\WRITWIN.CNV, wri
```

Modifying Conversion Options

You can control how some of Word's converters operate—how features convert or whether a feature converts. Some of the modifiable converters are as follows:

Microsoft Word for the Macintosh

Microsoft Word for DOS

Microsoft Works

RFT-DCA

Text with Layout

Some of the ways in which these converters can be modified are whether mail-merge fields are converted, whether INCLUDE fields are converted, and whether you want a document to convert as close to the same print layout or with the greatest use of compatible features in Word for Windows.

To modify the different options available for each of the modifiable converters, use the Tools Macro command to run the EditConversionOptions macro in the CONVERT.DOT template supplied with Word for Windows. Refer to Chapter 38,

"Recording and Editing Macros," for information on running macros. Changes you make to the conversion options are stored in MSTXTCNV.INI in the \WINDOWS directory.

Improving Conversion Compatibility

Not all word processors have the same features, and not every word processor handles the same features in the same way. For this reason, files that you convert to Word for Windows from other word processing programs may display on the screen or print differently. WordPerfect, for example, wraps blank spaces at the end of a line to the next line, while Word for Windows 6 allows the blank spaces to extend beyond the right margin. As another example, Word for the Macintosh displays borders in tables differently than Word for Windows.

You can alter Word for Windows behavior to more closely match the behavior of another word processor to improve the compatibility of documents that you convert to or from Word for Windows. When you save a document, Word saves the compatibility options with the document. If you change the compatibility options, remember that you are only changing the behavior of that document; if you later convert the document back to its original format, or to another word processor format, the document will behave as any other document would in those word processors.

To change the compatibility options for a document, follow these steps:

1. Open and convert the document, if necessary.

2. Choose the Tools Options command.

3. Click the Compatibility tab to display the compatibility options, if they are not already displayed (see fig. 34.3).

4. To set the recommended compatibility options for the document's original format, select the original word processor format in the Recommended Options For list box.

5. Select or unselect the various compatibility options in the Options list.

6. To set the options for the current document only, choose OK.

   or

To set the options as the default for all future conversions from the file format in the Recommended Options box, choose **Default**. Word for Windows prompts you to confirm the change to the default compatibility options.

Fig. 34.3
Select the
Compatibility tab
for a converted
document in the
Options dialog
box.

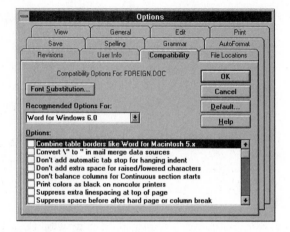

Controlling Font Conversion in Documents

If you convert a document that contains fonts not installed on your computer, Word for Windows will substitute available fonts for the unavailable fonts. Word does not actually replace the unavailable fonts in the document with the substituted fonts, it just uses the substitute font for display and printing purposes. This way, if you convert the file back to its original word processor format, the original fonts are still in the document and the document will still display and print correctly in the original word processor. This feature is especially important if you are working in an office with a mixed network (PC and Macintosh computers) or in an office that uses several different word processors.

Font Conversions for Documents Converted to Word for Windows
Although Word for Windows tries to make the best match from available fonts for an unavailable font, it may not always select the font that you agree is the best substitute. Word for Windows provides an easy method to handle this issue: you can tell Word for Windows which fonts to substitute for the unavailable fonts.

To change the font substitutions for a document, follow these steps:

1. Open and convert the document, if necessary.

2. Choose the Tools Options command.

3. Click the Compatibility tab to display the compatibility options, if they are not already displayed.

4. Choose the Font Substitution button. Word for Windows displays the Font Substitution dialog box (see fig. 34.4).

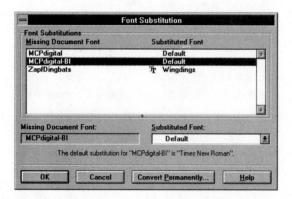

Fig. 34.4
Change the font substitutions for a converted document in the Font Substitution dialog box.

5. Select the unavailable font in the Missing Document Font list.

6. Select the font that you want to substitute in the Substituted Font list box. In fig. 34.4, the Wingdings font has been substituted for the ZapfDingbats font.

7. Choose OK.

    or

    Choose Convert Permanently if you want Word for Windows to actually replace the missing fonts with substituted fonts. Word asks you to confirm your choice to permanently replace the substituted fonts.

Word for Windows saves the font substitutions with the document. The font substitutions are also stored in a file named FONTSUB.INI in the Word for Windows program directory. The next time you convert a file from the same word processor format, Word for Windows uses the new font substitutions in the FONTSUB.INI file.

Font Conversions for Documents Converted from Word for Windows to Another Format

Unless you specify otherwise, Word for Windows uses the same fonts in a document that you save to another word processor format as are in the original Word document (see the section "Saving Word for Windows Documents to Another Format," earlier in this chapter for information on saving a document in another format). If you know that the file you convert will not be used on a computer with the same fonts you have, you can control the font substitutions that Word for Windows makes when you convert a file from Word format to another word processor format.

Word for Windows uses *font-mapping files* that tell Word for Windows which font, size, and style to use for each change in fonts in the converted file.

Sample font conversion files are stored in the Word for Windows directory with the TXT file extension. These files contain a description of how to use the file and a sample mapping. For these files to be used during conversion, they must be in the Word for Windows directory and renamed or copied with the file extension DAT. Make sure that you save the modified and renamed file in text format.

Some of these mapping files map fonts according to each font change in the original font. For example, the first font may be Helv 12 point, the second font may be Times Roman 14 point, and so on. For font mappings that work this way, you may need a different DAT file for different word processing documents.

The font-mapping file names are a three-letter abbreviation for the format being converted, an underscore, and then three-letter abbreviation of the format being converted to. The intermediary format for these conversions is Rich Text Format (RTF). Some of the TXT files containing font-mapping information are as follows:

Format	From Word
RFT-DCA	RTF_DCA.TXT
Microsoft Word 5, Macintosh	RTF_MW5.TXT
Word for DOS	RTF-PCW.TXT
WordPerfect 5.0/5.1	WP5_RTF.TXT

To modify the font-mapping information, open the appropriate mapping file in Word for Windows and follow the instructions in the file. When you have finished making the changes, use the File Save As command to save the mapping file with a DAT extension. For more information, choose the Help Search for Help on command, type **readme**, and then press Enter twice.

From Here...

As explained in this chapter, you can use the macros in CONVERT.DOT to convert several files at once or to edit the conversion options for some file formats, and that you can convert documents that contain graphics. For more information on these and other topics, you may want to review the following major sections of this book:

- Chapter 15, "Mastering Envelopes, Mail Merge, and Form Letters," for information on using spreadsheet and database files as data sources for mail merges so that you do not have to convert the files.

- Chapter 22, "Inserting Pictures in Your Document," for instructions on installing and using picture converters for use when converting documents that contain graphics.

- Chapter 38, "Recording and Editing Macros," for a description of how to use template macros, such as the macros supplied in the CONVERT.DOT template.

Type any additional headings you would like to add to your resume.

[ ]

Add

These are your resume headings.

Summary of qualifications
Education
Professional experience
Patents and publications
Additional professional activities

TIP You'll have a chance to rearrange the headings in a moment.

Cancel **<Back** **Next>** **Finis**

Summary Info

File Name: Document8
Directory:
Title: Office Automation Proposal
Subject: Integration of Microsoft Office
Author: Ron Person
Keywords: Proposal Office Integration
Comments: Description for SynSun on training their internal developers on how to integrate Access, Excel, and Word.

OK
Cancel
Statistics...
Help

New

Template:

Normal

Agenda Wizard
Award Wizard
Brochur1
Calendar Wizard
Cv Wizard
Directr1
Fax Wizard
Faxcovr1
Faxcovr2
Invoice

OK
Cancel
Summary...
Help

New
● Do
○ Te

Microsoft

Description
Default Document Template

Microsoft Word - Ron Person - Document1

le Edit View Insert Format Tools Table Window Help

· · · 1 · · · 1 · · · 1 · · · 2 · · · 1 · · · 3 · · · 1 · · · 4 · · · 1 · · · 5 · ·

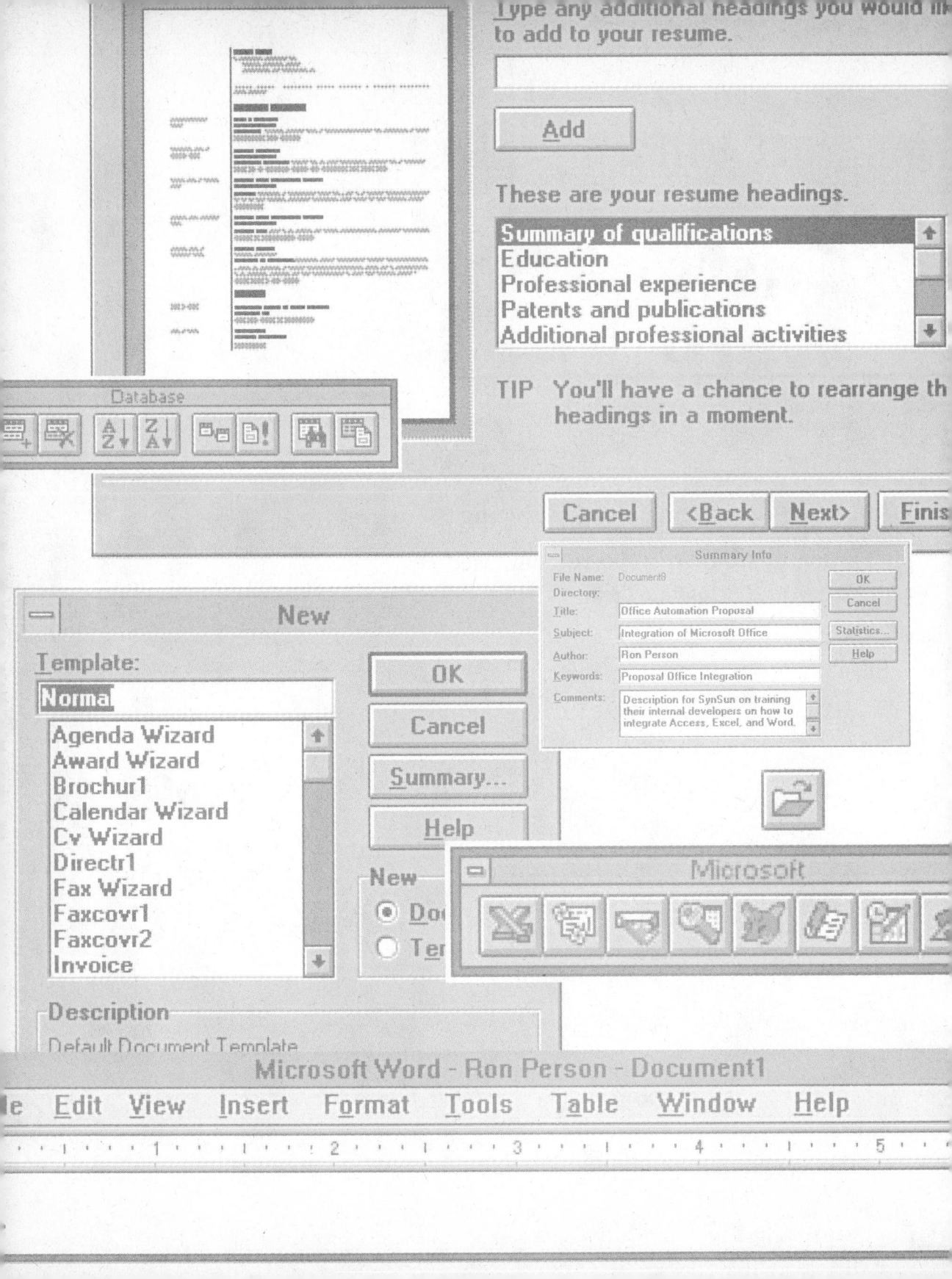

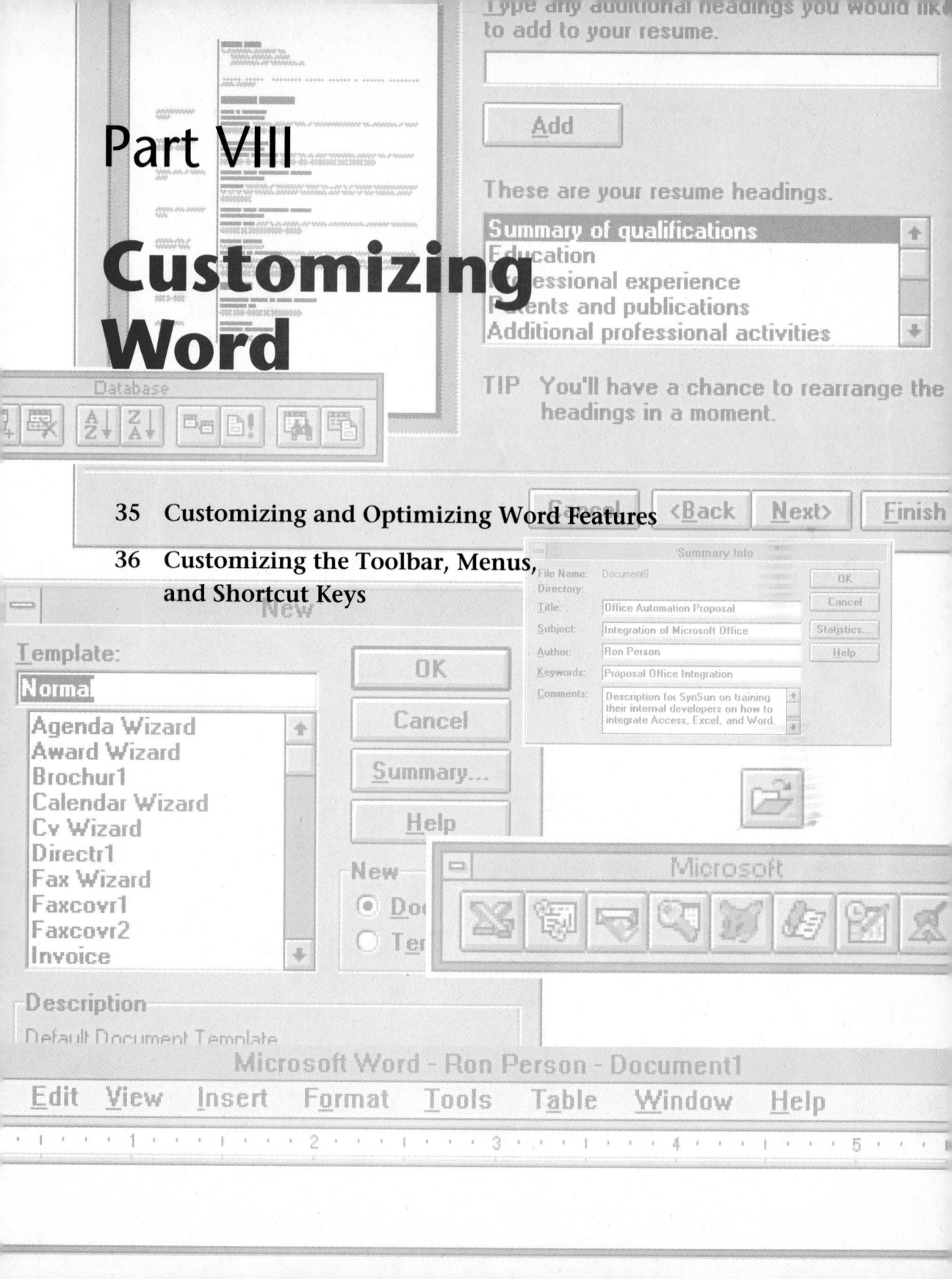

Part VIII

Customizing Word

35 Customizing and Optimizing Word Features

36 Customizing the Toolbar, Menus, and Shortcut Keys

Chapter 35

Customizing and Optimizing Word Features

As you use Word for Windows, you might want to customize it to fit the way you work or to make trade-offs between increased performance and features. Other chapters have shown you how to customize Word features such as menus, toolbars, and shortcut keys. But there are many other ways in which you can customize Word. This chapter contains suggestions and options to help you fine-tune Word and customize it for your way of working.

In this chapter, you learn about the following topics:

- Improving the performance of Word for Windows

- Optimizing memory usage

- Starting Word or documents automatically

- Customizing the workspace and display

- Personalizing the mouse

> **Note**
>
> For the instructions in this chapter, it is assumed that Word for Windows 6 has been installed in the C:\WINWORD directory. If you have installed Word in a different directory, please substitute your Word directory's name in the following examples.

Customizing Commonly Used Features

Other chapters of this book discuss techniques for customizing many Word for Windows features. The following list indicates some commonly customized features and the chapters in which they are discussed:

If You Want to Customize	Refer to
Dictionary	Chapter 7, "Using Editing and Proofing Tools"
Document on startup	Chapter 6, "Using Templates as Master Documents"
Documents that are frequently used	Chapter 6, "Using Templates as Master Documents"
Font on startup (default font)	Chapter 9, "Formatting Characters and Changing Fonts"
Imported file handling	Chapter 34, "Converting Files with Word for Windows"
Menus or commands	Chapter 36, "Customizing the Toolbars, Menus, and Shortcut Keys"
Page settings on startup	Chapter 13, "Setting the Page Layout"; Chapter 6, "Using Templates as Master Documents"
Paragraph settings on startup	Chapter 10, "Formatting Lines and Paragraphs"; Chapter 6, "Using Templates as Master Documents"
Procedures or commands	Chapter 38, "Recording and Editing Macros"; Chapter 39, "Building More Advanced Macros"
Screen display	Chapter 2, "Getting Started in Word for Windows"
Shortcut keys	Chapter 36, "Customizing the Toolbars, Menus, and Shortcut Keys"
Toolbars	Chapter 36, "Customizing the Toolbars, Menus, and Shortcut Keys"

Improving the Performance of Word for Windows

Depending on the work that you do and the capability of your computer, Word for Windows may not perform as fast as DOS-based word processors. Factors such as slower 80386 computers, large graphics files, and long tables can make Word perform more slowly. You can make a number of trade-offs, however, to improve the speed of Word for Windows.

Modifying Word for Windows Settings

You can improve Word's performance by choosing certain options within Word for Windows. Significant performance improvements can also be made by increasing the memory available to Windows or by increasing the effective speed of your computer's hard disk.

To improve Word's performance from within Word for Windows, follow these steps:

1. Choose the Tools Options command. The Options dialog box appears (see fig. 35.1).

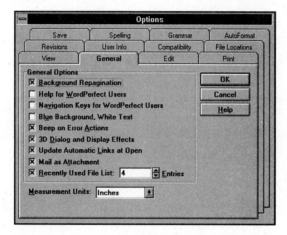

Fig. 35.1

You can use the Options dialog box to customize many Word for Windows options.

VIII

Customizing Word

2. Select the tab listed in the first column of the following table; then select or deselect the option or check box to make the performance trade-offs you want:

Tab	Option or Check Box	To Improve Performance
View	Draft Font	Select for faster performance; the document does not print as it appears on-screen.
View	Picture Placeholders	Select for faster performance; pictures display as empty rectangles on-screen.
Print	Draft Output	Select to print faster on dot-matrix printers; the document does not use the fonts shown on-screen. Some character formatting may be lost.
Print	Background Printing	Deselect to work faster on-screen; you cannot print while you work.

(continues)

(continued)

Tab	Option or Check Box	To Improve Performance
Save	Allow Fast Saves	Select to save more quickly by saving only the changes made to documents; files become larger and cannot be converted by other programs when saved with fast save.
Save	Always Create Backup Copy	Deselect to save more quickly; no duplicate copy (file extension BAK) is made during saves.
Save	Automatic Save	Deselect to avoid being interrupted by timed saves to disk; no periodic saves are made unless you remember to make them yourself.
General	Background Repagination	Deselect for better performance; page break markers and automatic page numbering aren't correct until you repaginate.
General	Update Automatic Links at Open	Deselect to open files faster; linked data is not correct unless the individual link (or the entire document) is updated.

3. Choose OK.

You also can gain a few percentage points of performance by limiting the type or number of fonts you use. Use one or both of the following methods to improve performance by way of font selection:

■ Do not use several different fonts within a single document. This guideline is in keeping with a general rule of desktop publishing which suggests that no more than three fonts should be used in a document.

■ Use TrueType fonts sparingly. TrueType fonts slow computer and printer performance slightly. Instead, use the built-in fonts provided by the currently selected printer.

Printer fonts appear in the Font list of the Font dialog box (choose Format Font) with a miniature printer to the left of their name.

To make sure you do not use TrueType fonts, follow these steps:

1. Start the Control Panel found in the Main group of the Program Manager.

2. Start the Fonts application and choose the TrueType button.

3. In the TrueType dialog box, deselect the Enable True Type Fonts check box.

4. Restart Windows so the change takes effect.

Your document becomes printer specific when you use printer fonts, so you might want to use styles when formatting it. Doing so makes it easier to change fonts throughout the document if you have to change printers.

Managing System Memory

Having more memory available can make Word run faster and enable you to work more efficiently in larger or more complex documents. You can get a significant improvement in performance by increasing your computer's memory to 4M or higher if you run one application at a time, or 8M or higher if you run multiple applications at the same time.

You also can improve performance (although the gains are not as significant) by making the proper selections of Word features and using wise file and application management practices. The following tips can also help you improve performance:

■ Exit all applications that are not being used while you are working in Word for Windows. Other applications also require memory.

■ Close unneeded documents in Word or data files in other open Windows applications. Each document and application requires a portion of Windows' limited system resources memory.

■ Increase the size of the disk cache space to increase the performance of scrolling, searching and replacing, using the Go To command, and opening and saving files. To increase the size of Word's cache, use the Notepad accessory to open the WIN.INI text file from the \WINDOWS directory. In the [Microsoft Word 6.0] section, add or edit a line such as

    CacheSize=256

Recommended settings are 256K or 512K. Make changes in 64K increments. Increasing the cache size reduces the memory available to other applications while Word is running. You must restart Word after changing the WIN.INI file for the change to take effect.

■ Increase the size of bitmap memory to increase the speed with which Word displays and scrolls pictures. Use this technique only if your computer has a large amount of memory and you need to see pictures displayed instead of using Picture Placeholders. To increase the size of memory reserved for Word's bitmap pictures, use the Notepad accessory to open the WIN.INI text file from the \WINDOWS directory. In the [Microsoft Word 6.0] section, add or edit a line such as

BitMapMemory=1024

The default setting is 256K. Increasing the cache size reduces the memory available to other applications while Word is running. You must restart Word after changing the WIN.INI file for the change to take effect.

- Open the AUTOEXEC.BAT file using the Notepad and check which drive is specified in the Set Temp= line. Set Temp= should specify a drive containing at least 2M of available space. Use the File Manager to be sure that this drive contains enough available space. Defragmenting the Temp drive can also improve performance.

- Use a disk defragmenting utility to consolidate your hard disk so that information can be read and written more quickly. Disk fragmentation occurs normally as you save and delete files. As time passes, files are saved in pieces scattered over the disk in order to make the best use of available space. Unfortunately, this process slows down read and write operations. Defragmenting reorganizes information on the disk so that each file is stored in a single contiguous location.

- Make sure your AUTOEXEC.BAT file includes a line that runs the SmartDrive. SmartDrive is a program that comes with Windows which uses your computer's RAM to increase the apparent speed of your hard disk. The line that starts SmartDrive might look like the following:

C:\WINDOWS\SMARTDRV.EXE

This line should be one of the first lines in the AUTOEXEC.BAT file.

- Do not create large documents exceeding 30 to 50 pages in length. Instead, create smaller documents and link them together using the techniques described in Chapter 32, "Assembling Large Documents."

Starting Word or Documents on Startup

If you use Word for Windows as your primary Windows application, you might want it to run or load as an icon each time you start Windows. This section explains how to do that, as well as how to create icons in the Program Manager that will start Word and immediately load a specified document.

Loading or Running Word When Windows Starts

You can load Word as an icon or run Word immediately when Windows starts. All you need to do is make a simple change to the WIN.INI text file located in the \WINDOWS directory. But before proceeding, use the File Manager to determine the disk drive and directory that contain WINWORD.EXE, the Word program file.

To modify your WIN.INI so that it loads or runs Word on startup, follow these steps:

1. Open the Notepad application from the Accessories group in the Program Manager.

2. Choose the File Open command and select All Files (*.*) from the List Files of Type list.

3. Open the WIN.INI file from the \WINDOWS directory.

4. Move to the [windows] group within the text file.

5. Type or edit the LOAD or RUN line as follows (use LOAD to load Word as an icon; use RUN to run Word):

        LOAD=C:\WINWORD\WINWORD.EXE

    or

        RUN=C:\WINWORD\WINWORD.EXE

6. Choose the File Save command to save the altered WIN.INI text file.

7. Choose the File Exit command.

The next time you restart Windows, Word loads or runs according to your instructions. If it does not, check the path name and spelling.

For Related Information
- "Controlling Printing Options," p. 232
- "Linking Documents and Files," p. 1008

VIII

Customizing Word

You also can make Word start when Windows starts by copying a Word icon into the Startup group of the Program Manager. To do so, arrange the Program Manager so that you can see a group containing a Word icon and the Startup group. Click the Word icon and hold the Ctrl key down as you drag the Word icon over to the Startup group; then release the mouse button. Using Ctrl+drag to move the Word icon creates a copy of the icon in Startup, leaving the original icon at its original location. The next time you start Windows, Word runs automatically.

Loading Documents When Windows Starts

To run Word and load a specific document when Windows starts, arrange the Program Manager and the File Manager side by side on-screen so that you can see items in both applications. Be sure that the Startup group window is visible in the Program Manager and that the Word document file you want to start is visible in the File Manager window. Click the Word file and hold down the Ctrl key as you drag the file from the File Manager over to the Startup group window. Release the file icon over the Startup group window to drop it into that group. Using Ctrl+drag to move the Word icon creates a copy of the icon in Startup, leaving the original icon at its original location. The next time you start Windows, Word runs and automatically loads that document.

Loading a Document When Word Starts from an Icon

You can set up multiple Word icons, designing each icon so that it loads a different Word document. First, you need to know how to create multiple Word icons. In the Program Manager, you can copy any icon by holding down the Ctrl key and dragging the icon to another group window.

After you have created one or more Word icons, you need to modify them so that Word loads a document when it starts.

To modify one of the Word icons, follow these steps:

1. Select the icon to be modified and choose the File Properties command. The Program Item Properties dialog box appears.

2. Select the Command Line edit box and press the End key. This step moves the insertion point to the end of the line that starts Word. This line should look like the following:

    C:\WINWORD\WINWORD.EXE

3. Edit this line to include the path name and file name of the Word document you want to load, such as

C:\WINWORD\WINWORD.EXE C:\BUDGET\JUNE.DOC

4. While the dialog box is on-screen, you can edit the Description line to describe the type of file the icon loads (instead of just leaving the default "Microsoft Word").

5. Choose OK to enter your changes.

The next time you start Word from this icon, the document you specified opens automatically.

Starting Word with Special Settings

You can modify Word's icon in the Program Manager to start Word by using special characteristics.

To modify the properties of Word's icon, follow these steps:

1. Activate the Program Manager and select a Word icon.

2. Choose the File Properties command.

3. Edit the command line to include one of the following switches after WINWORD.EXE/N:

/n	Open WinWord without a new document.
filename	Open WinWord with the specified file name.
/m*macroname*	Open WinWord and run the macro found in a file opened at the same time. Make s ure you do not leave a space between the /m switch and the macro name.
/a	Open WinWord without templates or add-ins.
/mHelpQuickPreview	Open WinWord and run the Quick Preview Demo.

Make sure there is a space between WINWORD.EXE and the switch.

4. Choose OK.

An example of a command line that would open Word without opening templates or add-ins is

C:\WINWORD\WINWORD /a

You can string these switches together. For example, to open a document file named LETTER.DOC and then run the UpdateName macro stored in that document's template, use a command line like the following:

C:\WINWORD\WINWORD LETTER.DOC /mUpdateName

The next time you start Word, it will run with the special characteristic you have added.

Making Menus, Toolbars, and Shortcut Keys Globally Available

For Related Information
■ "Creating a New Template," p. 179

If you find that a template has menus, toolbars, and shortcut keys that you use frequently, you can make them available without using the Organizer to transfer them to the NORMAL.DOT template. (The Organizer is a feature described in Chapter 6, "Using Templates as Master Documents.") Instead, copy the template file (DOT extension) containing these features into the \WINWORD??\STARTUP directory. The template files are usually located in the \WINWORD\TEMPLATE directory.

Make sure you copy a template into the STARTUP directory. If you move a template out of the TEMPLATE directory, it will not appear in the New dialog box when you choose the File New command.

Customizing the Workspace and Display

For Related Information
■ "Transferring Template Contents Using the Organizer," p. 182

■ "Customizing the Toolbar, Menus, Shortcut Keys," p. 1051

If you work at your computer a lot, even small things like customizing screen colors or arranging screen elements can help you reduce stress.

To change the display or your Word for Windows workspace, follow these steps:

1. Choose the Tools Options command. The Options dialog box appears (refer to fig. 35.1).

2. Select the tab listed in the first column of this table. Then select or deselect the associated option or check box depending on your display preferences:

Tab	Option or Check Box	To Change
General	Recently Used File List	The number of files shown under the File menu listed as having been recently opened.
General	Measurement Units	The units used on the ruler (choice of inches, centimeters, points, or picas).
General	Beep on Error Actions	The status (on/off) of the audible beep that sounds for each error.
General	Blue Background, White Text	To a white-on-blue screen, reducing the eye strain caused by reading a black-on-white screen.
View	Status Bar	The appearance of the status bar at the bottom of the screen.
View	Horizontal or Vertical Scroll Bar	The appearance of the horizontal or vertical scroll bars. Remove them if you use only the keyboard.
File Locations	File Types	The location of files used by Word. Select the file type and choose the Modify button. You can change the locations for Documents, Clipart Pictures, User Templates, Workgroup Templates, User Options, AutoSave Files, Dictionaries, Tutorial, and Startup.

3. Choose OK.

Customizing Mouse Settings

You can customize the mouse to operate more slowly; you can also switch the button actions between left and right sides.

To customize the mouse, follow these steps:

1. Start the Control Panel found in the Main group of the Program Manager.

2. Start the Mouse program.

VIII

Customizing Word

3. Change any of the following options:

Mouse Tracking Speed	The speed of the on-screen pointer moves with respect to your movement of the hand-held mouse. Use the slow setting while learning.
Double Click Speed	The speed with which you must double-click for a double-click to be accepted. Use the slow setting while learning.
Swap Left/Right Buttons	Swaps the active mouse button to the opposite side. Use for operating the mouse from the opposite hand.
Mouse Trails	Produces a shadowed trail of mouse pointers that makes the pointer easier to see on LCD panel displays (used in laptop computers). This option is available in Windows 3.1 only.

4. Choose OK.

5. To close the Control Panel, double-click its program Control menu or press Alt+F4.

Many of the newer mice have additional customizing options available (such as changing the size of the pointer or reversing the color of the pointer). These options, if available, also appear in the Mouse dialog box described above.

Customizing Word for the Hearing or Movement Impaired

Windows applications can be made more accessible for users with unique needs, whether those needs are for hearing, vision, or movement.

The hard of hearing can contact Microsoft Sales and Service on a text telephone at 800-892-5234. Technical support is available on a text telephone at 206-635-4948.

Microsoft distributes free a software package called Access Pack for Microsoft Windows that makes the keyboard easier to operate for the movement or hearing impaired. The Access Pack is available free as the file ACCESS.EXE. It can be downloaded from CompuServe, GEnie, or the free Microsoft Download Service. Contact Microsoft Download Service by modem at 206-936-6735. Use these communication settings:

Baud rate	1200, 2400, or 9600
Parity	N
Data bits	8
Stop bits	1

You also can order a copy of the Access Pack by calling 206-637-7098.

From Here...

Tips and features on how to customize Word are discussed throughout this book. Many of these settings can be altered through dialog boxes that you use frequently. For information about customizing a specific feature, check the chapter that describes that feature. You may want to review the following chapters that cover important aspects of customization:

- Chapter 6, "Using Templates as Master Documents." Learn how to create and use templates that act as patterns for other documents. Templates can contain custom toolbars, menus, styles, and AutoText.

- Chapter 9, "Formatting Characters and Changing Fonts." Learn how to customize the default font used in the startup document.

- Chapter 36, "Customizing the Toolbar, Menus, and Shortcut Keys." Learn how to create toolbars, menus, and shortcut keys that execute procedures you need for your specific tasks.

- Chapter 37, "Automating with Field Codes." Learn how to create documents that update automatically or prompt the operator for input.

- Chapter 38, "Recording and Editing Macros." Learn how to record simple tasks as macros that you can play back when needed.

- Chapter 39, "Building More Advanced Macros." Learn how to modify simple recorded macros to make them more useful.

VIII

Customizing Word

Chapter 36

Customizing the Toolbar, Menus, and Shortcut Keys

Part of the power of Word for Windows comes from its flexibility; you can change its shape to fit your work habits. You can create menus, toolbars, shortcut keys and buttons that allow you to do things your way. You can add Word commands that don't normally appear on the menu or toolbar. You can even assign macros that you create to commands, tools, buttons, or shortcut keys.

> ### Note
>
> Custom key assignments, menus, and toolbars combined with Word for Windows easy-to-create macros enable you to build a word processor tailored to the work you do. This capability also holds a danger: you have the potential to modify the global menus and keyboard assignments so much that Word for Windows becomes difficult for other operators to use. For this reason, you probably should assign your menus, toolbar buttons, and key assignments to templates rather than assigning them globally.

Understanding Where and When Customizing Occurs

You have the ability to *assign* one of Word's built-in commands or one of your macros to a menu command, toolbar button, or shortcut key. However,

In this chapter, you learn about the following topics:

- How and where customized features are stored

- How to add, remove, and rearrange tool-bar buttons

- How to assign Word's built-in commands or your macros to a tool

- How to transfer toolbars to other templates

- How to add or remove menus or commands

- How to create custom shortcut keys or custom toolbars

unless you know a few rules about assigning commands and macros, you may cause conflicts. When conflicts occur, a different command or macro than the one you expected will run. When you assign a macro to a command, button, or shortcut key, it can be a *global* assignment or specific to a template.

Global assignments—assignments that apply to *all* documents—are stored in the NORMAL.DOT template. Such global assignments may conflict with the custom menus, toolbars, or shortcut keys you create in a template. Suppose, for example, you assign Ctrl+C to a Calculate macro in your Invoice template. Ctrl+C is a global assignment for the Edit Cut command and is stored in NORMAL.DOT. If a document based on your Invoice template is open, which assignment takes precedence? To avoid confusion, Word for Windows follows a strict hierarchy: template assignments always take precedence over the global assignments stored in NORMAL.DOT.

When you create custom menus, toolbars, or shortcut keys, always remember to open a document that uses the template you want to change. Then, in the Customize dialog box, select either All Documents (NORMAL.DOT) or the specific template that should contain the new menu, toolbar, or shortcut key.

Customizing and Creating Toolbars

Word for Windows enables you to customize toolbars and create your own toolbars and tools. Specifically, you can do the following:

- Change any of the supplied toolbars

- Design and edit your own toolbars

- Draw your own tool faces

- Assign macros to custom tools

> **Note**
>
> You must have a mouse to modify toolbars or create custom tools.

Adding Tools

Word offers hundreds of tools, each with its own built-in commands, that you can add to any toolbar. Adding a tool is as easy as dragging the tool from a dialog box and dropping it at the desired location on the toolbar. The following example shows how you can add a tool to a toolbar.

To add a new tool to the toolbar, follow these steps:

1. Be certain that the toolbar you want to change is displayed. If you want the tool to appear only when documents that use a specific template are open, open a document that uses that template.

2. Use the right mouse button to click the toolbar, and then choose Customize from the shortcut menu.

3. When the Customize dialog box appears (see fig. 36.1), make sure the Toolbars tab is selected.

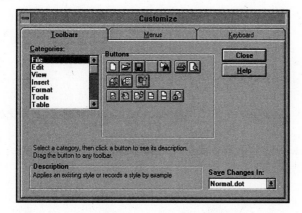

VIII

Customizing Word

Fig. 36.1
Add a tool by dragging it from the Customize dialog box and dropping it on a toolbar.

4. Select a tool category from the Categories list; your selection determines the items that appear in the Buttons group (either tools or lists of commands that do not have associated tool faces).

5. If you want this toolbar change to apply only to documents that use a specific template, select that template from the Save Changes In list. (Remember that a document using that template must be open.) If you want the change to apply to all toolbars in all documents, select the NORMAL.DOT template.

6. Select the tool you want by clicking it. A description of its action or command appears in the Description box.

7. Drag the tool from the dialog box and drop it onto the toolbar in the location where you want it to appear.

8. Repeat Steps 6 and 7 as necessary to add more tools, and then choose Close to close the Customize dialog box.

Some of the tools that appear in the Buttons group do not have tool faces. If you drag one of these tools to a toolbar or document, the Custom Button dialog box appears. This dialog box enables you to select a custom tool face or to draw a new tool face. For further instructions, see the "Drawing a New Tool Face" later in this chapter.

At this point, the standard toolbar may appear a bit crowded, especially if you are working with a standard VGA screen. Some tools might have vanished off the right end of the screen. You can eliminate this crowding by removing tools, changing the spacing between tools and changing the width of a pull-down list (see the next section of this chapter for details). If you have many tools you want to add, you might want to create your own custom toolbar (a process described later in this chapter).

To move or copy tools from one toolbar to another, open the Customize dialog box while both the toolbar containing the tool you want to copy or move and the toolbar on which you want to place the tool are displayed onscreen. To move the tool, drag it from one toolbar to another. To copy the tool, hold down the Ctrl key while you drag the tool's button from one toolbar to another.

Reorganizing Tools

If a toolbar gets crowded, you need to remove tools, slide tools left or right (so you can fit more tools on the bar), or reorganize the tools.

To return a predefined toolbar to its originally installed condition, follow these steps:

1. Open a document that contains the toolbar you want to reset.

2. Choose the View Toolbars command.

3. Select the toolbar(s) you want to reset from the Toolbars list, and then press the Reset button.

4. In the dialog box that appears, select the template in which you want the selected toolbar(s) reset. If you want the reset to apply to all documents, select All Documents (NORMAL.DOT).

5. Choose Yes when you close the document and are asked if you want to save changes to the template.

To change the width of a pull-down list (like the one that represents the Style tool), follow these steps:

1. Click the right mouse button while the pointer is positioned on the toolbar, and then choose Customize from the shortcut menu. The Customize dialog box appears at the Toolbars tab.

2. While the Customize dialog box is on-screen, click a pull-down tool, such as the Style, Font or Font Size tool, on the toolbar.

3. Move the mouse pointer to the right side of the tool. When the double arrow appears, click and drag the arrow left or right to resize the list box (see fig. 36.2).

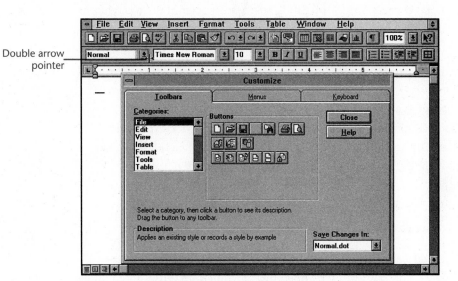

Double arrow pointer

Fig. 36.2
When the Customize dialog box is open, you can click a list tool and drag it to a new width.

VIII

Customizing Word

4. Choose Close from the Customize dialog box.

If you want to remove a tool from the toolbar, complete the following steps:

1. Click the right mouse button when the pointer is positioned on the toolbar, and then choose Customize from the shortcut menu. The Customize dialog box appears with the Toolbars tab selected.

2. While the Customize dialog box is on-screen, drag the tool off the toolbar into the document area.

3. Release the mouse button.

Tip
You can visually
group tools on the
toolbar by drag-
ging together tools
in the group and
leaving spaces to
mark the left and
right ends of the
group.

You can move groups of tools left or right to put spacing between groups. To slide a group away from another group, click the tool at the end where you want to make space. Drag the tool one-half a tool width away from the location for the space; drop the tool in the location where it would be if the space existed.

To reorganize a toolbar and move tools into new locations, follow these steps:

1. Click the right mouse button when the pointer is positioned on the toolbar, and then choose Customize from the shortcut menu. The Customize dialog box appears with the Toolbars tab selected.

2. While the Customize dialog box is on-screen, drag a tool to a new location between two existing tools (place the center of the tool you're moving between the tools that appear on either side of the desired location).

3. Release the mouse button.

Creating Your Own Toolbar

If you need to add many new tools, you might want to create your own toolbar. This technique is especially useful for creating a toolbar designed to work with documents that use a specific template. For example, you may want to create a custom toolbar to work with your Invoice template. Its tools and their arrangment may be designed specifically for invoicing.

To create your own toolbar, follow these steps:

1. If you want this toolbar to appear with documents using a specific template, you must begin by opening a document that uses that template.

2. Click the right mouse button when the pointer is positioned on the toolbar and then choose Toolbars from the shortcut menu (or choose the View Toolbars command). The Toolbars dialog box appears (see fig. 36.3).

Fig. 36.3
Create a new
toolbar by
choosing the New
button and typing
the new toolbars
title.

3. Choose the New button.

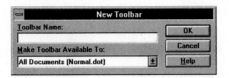

Fig. 36.4

Type your custom toolbar's name and select the template in which it should be stored.

4. Type the title for the toolbar in the Toolbar Name edit box. The name can be any length and can contain spaces.

5. From the Make Toolbar Available To list, choose the template (and the set of documents using that template) with which the toolbar should appear. Select All Documents (NORMAL.DOT) if you want the toolbar to be available at all times.

6. Choose OK.

The Customize dialog box appears with the Toolbars tab selected. Your new toolbar appears at the top left of the screen; initially it is only large enough for one tool.

7. Drag the tools you want from the Customize dialog box to the new toolbar.

8. Choose Close after you finish. The new toolbar contains the tools you copied onto it.

Tip

Do not type toolbar names that are too long. Extremely long names can make the shortcut menu for the toolbar so wide that normal names do not display.

VIII

Customizing Word

You also can create a toolbar quickly by displaying the Customize dialog box and dragging one of the tools onto your document. The toolbar that appears is called Toolbar1, Toolbar2, or the next sequentially numbered toolbar name. You cannot rename this type of toolbar.

In either case, the name of your new toolbar now appears at the bottom of the Toolbars list. You can treat it like any other toolbar.

To delete a custom toolbar, click the right mouse button while the pointer is positioned on the toolbar, and then choose Toolbars from the shortcut menu or choose the View Toolbars command. Choose your custom toolbar from the Toolbars list and then choose the Delete button. Respond with Yes to confirm you want to delete it.

To delete a custom toolbar, choose the View Toolbars command; or click the right mouse button while the pointer is positioned on the toolbar, and then choose Toolbars from the shortcut menu.

Putting a Command or Macro on a Toolbar

You provide yourself with fast access to frequently used Word commands by placing standard tools on the toolbar. But Word for Windows also enables you to accomplish some other useful goals by putting tools of your own making on the toolbar. With custom tools you can do the following:

- Run Word commands that are not on menus or tools

- Run your macros

- Change fonts

- Insert AutoText

- Apply styles

You even get to select or draw a tool face for your custom tools!

You can save time later by looking through the global list of Word for Windows commands now. Take the time to scan through the commands listed in the All Commands category on the Toolbars tab of the Customize dialog box. Many of these commands are very useful. Most of them perform a function for which you normally would have to choose a command and make a selection from a dialog box. Creating tools for them can save you time.

To assign a command or macro to a button on the toolbar, follow these steps:

1. Display the toolbar to which you want to add the tool.

2. Click the right mouse button while the pointer is positioned on the toolbar, and then choose Customize from the shortcut menu or choose the View Toolbars command. When the Toolbars dialog box appears, choose the Customize button.

3. Select either All Commands, Macros, Fonts, AutoText, or Styles from the Categories list.

4. Drag one of the commands, macros, AutoText names, or styles from the central list onto your toolbar. The Custom Button dialog box appears (see fig. 36.5). Your custom buttons can contain a text label, an icon, or a tool face that you draw.

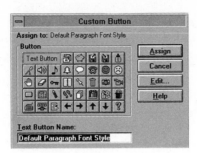

Fig. 36.5

Assign custom buttons by using the Custom Button dialog box.

5. Choose one of the predrawn buttons, type a text label, or draw your own tool face as described in "Choosing Custom Tool Faces," the next part of this section.

6. Choose the Assign button and then choose Close in the Customize dialog box.

Choosing Custom Tool Faces

When you add your own tools or a tool that does not have a face, you have the opportunity to create the tool face.

To create custom buttons for your toolbar, follow these steps:

1. Drag and drop the faceless tool or feature from the Customize dialog box to the toolbar. The Custom Button dialog box appears.

2. Choose one of the following options:

   Text Button. Type the label in the Text Button Name box that you want to appear within the button.

   Icons. Click a face if you want to use that face on the tool.

3. Choose Assign if you want to use the text label or the tool face as it is. If you want to draw your own tool face, see "Drawing Your Own Tool Face" later in this section.

4. Choose Close when the Customize dialog box reappears.

Tools that have your macro assigned to them do not display a description in the status bar.

For Related Information

- "Recording Macros," p. 1124

- "Creating Styles," p. 359

- "Inserting Frequently Used Material," p. 142

VIII

Customizing Word

Tip

You can create a *storage toolbar* to hold tools that you need infrequently, but don't want to reselect or redraw when needed.

If you have tools that you need occasionally and you don't want to reselect or redraw them every time you need them, create a toolbar used for storage. Drag copies of tools you think you might need again onto this toolbar. If you need one of these tools later, just display the storage toolbar you created. Then open the Customize dialog box and drag a copy of the needed tool to an active toolbar. To drag a copy, press the Ctrl key while dragging.

Drawing Your Own Tool Faces

To draw a custom tool face, follow these steps:

1. Perform the steps given earlier in "Choosing Custom Tool Faces," but do not choose the Assign button in Step 3.

2. If you want to modify a tool face that appears in the Button group, select that tool face. If you want to start drawing with a clear background, select the Text Button icon.

3. Choose the Edit button to display the Button Editor dialog box. If you selected a tool face to edit, it appears in the Picture box. See fig. 36.6.

Fig. 36.6

Draw custom tool faces by clicking a color and then dragging in the Picture box. Use the Move buttons to reposition your drawing on the tool.

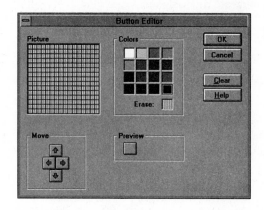

4. Use the Button Editor to draw a tool face in the Picture box.

   Click a color and then click or drag in the Picture box to paint. Click the Erase color and then drag over the Picture to erase cells. Watch the Preview box to see what the tool looks like at its actual size. Click the Move buttons to reposition your drawing within the tool face.

5. Choose OK to accept the drawing, and paste it onto the tool.

Transferring Toolbars with the Organizer

At times, you will want to transfer a toolbar from one template to another. You or a coworker might create a template that has a toolbar you can use in another template. It's easy to transfer toolbars between open templates.

To transfer toolbars between two open templates, follow these steps:

1. Open a template containing the toolbar you want to copy. Also open the template that you want to receive a copy of the toolbar.

2. Unprotect the templates if they are protected. You cannot transfer from or to a protected template.

3. Activate the template the toolbar will come from.

4. Choose the Tools Macro command. The Macro Dialog box appears.

5. Choose the Organizer button in the Macro dialog box; select the Toolbars tab. See fig. 36.7.

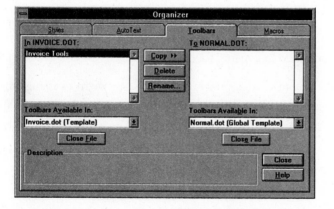

Fig. 36.7
Select a toolbar from any open template, and copy it to any other open template.

6. From the Toolbars Available In list, select the template containing the toolbar.

7. In the right side of the Organizer, select from the Toolbars Available To list the template you want to receive a copy of the toolbar.

8. In the left side of the Organizer, select from the In *TemplateName* list the toolbar you want copied.

9. Choose the Copy button.

   The toolbar is copied from the template on the left side to the template on the right side.

10. If you want to copy additional toolbars, return to Step 4. If you are finished, choose the Close button. When you return to the documents and close them, you are prompted to save the templates and the changes to their toolbars.

Customizing the Menu

Word offers far more commands than could ever be put on the menu at a single time. But you can put any of Word's hundreds of commands on an existing or custom menu. In fact, you can also add to the menu any macro, style, font, or AutoText that you want to be readily available. You can add these features to the menus associated with a specific template or to the global menus associated with the NORMAL.DOT template.

Adding Commands to Menus

You can add a command to any predefined menu or custom menu that you build. To make your menus easier to use, you can also add separator lines between groups of commands, and you can place a new command anywhere on the menu.

To add a command to a menu, follow these steps:

1. Before you customize a menu, open any document to change the global menu or open the specific template to change the menu associated with that template.

2. Choose the Tools Customize command and then select the Menus tab in the Customize dialog box. See fig. 36.8.

Fig. 36.8
You can add to Word's menus any of hundreds of commands or your own macros, styles, and AutoText.

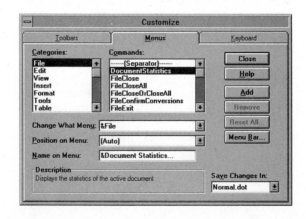

3. Select from the Save Changes In pull-down list the template you want the custom menu attached to (select NORMAL.DOT for the global menu).

4. Select from the Categories list the type of feature you want to add.

5. Select from the box at the top center the specific item you want to add. Depending on the choice you made in Step 4, this item could be a command, style name, macro name, AutoText, or font name.

   If you want to add a separator line between groups of related commands on a menu, select the choice

   ```
   -----------(Separator)------------
   ```

6. Select from the Change What Menu list the menu to which you want to add the command. Notice that you can even add commands to shortcut menus.

7. Select from the Position on Menu list the location for the new command. Here are your choices:

   Auto. Word attempts to group new commands

   At Top. New command placed at top of menu

   At Bottom. New command placed at bottom of menu

   Existing Command. Replaces existing command with new command

8. Type the name of your command in the Name on Menu box.

   Type an ampersand (&) before the letter you want underlined as the *hot key*. Pick a letter that hasn't been used before in that menu. Word makes a recommendation for the command's name, but you do not have to accept it. You can edit the recommended name.

9. Choose Add.

10. Return to Step 3 to add more commands or choose Close.

Caution

It's very easy to choose the Close button instead of the Add button, because in most dialog boxes, you choose OK or Close after you finish. If your new command doesn't appear on the menu, try the procedure again, making sure that you choose the Add button before closing the dialog box.

The macro description, displayed in the Description box at the bottom of the dialog box, appears in the status bar at the bottom of the screen when the newly added command is selected on the menu.

Removing or Resetting Commands

To remove a predefined or custom command from a menu, follow these steps:

1. Open a document with a menu containing the command you want to remove.

2. Choose the Tools Customize command and then select the Menus tab.

3. Select from the Save Changes In list the template for this document (select NORMAL.DOT if the menu is available to all documents).

4. Select the menu containing the command you want to remove from the Change What Menu list.

5. Select from the Position On Menu list the command you want to remove. Commands appear on the list in the same order in which they appear on the menu.

6. Choose the Remove button.

7. Continue to work in the Menus tab if necessary, or choose Close if you are finished.

Tip
Quickly remove menu commands by pressing Alt+Ctrl+ – (minus sign) and clicking the menu command.

To remove built-in or custom commands from menus, press Alt+Ctrl+ – (minus sign). The pointer changes to a large bold minus sign. Click the menu and then choose the command you want to remove. (It is not considered polite to remove all commands from another user's computer unless they are a power user.)

Notice that when you remove a command, the other commands on the menu move up. Press the Esc key if you decide not to remove a command and want to return the pointer to normal.

To restore menus to the original configuration provided by Word for Windows, follow these steps:

1. Open a document containing the menu you want to restore.

2. Choose the Tools Customize command and then select the Menus tab.

3. Select from the Save Changes In list the template that contains the menu.

4. Choose the Reset All button.

5. Respond Yes when asked to confirm that you want to reset the menu in that template.

Adding or Removing Menus

When you create templates designed for a specific type of work, you may want to remove menus that are not needed. In some cases, fewer menus means fewer training and support problems. You can remove entire menus and add your own menus that contain custom commands.

To add a custom menu, follow these steps:

1. Open a document that uses the template that is to contain the added menu.

2. Choose the Tools Customize command and then select the Menus tab.

3. Select from the Save Changes In list, in the lower right corner, the template to contain the new menu.

4. Select the Menu Bar button.

5. Type the name of the new menu in the Name on Menu Bar edit box. Place an & (ampersand) before the activating letter or *hot key*.

6. Select from the Position on Menu Bar list box the menu you want to appear to the left of your menu. See fig. 36.9.

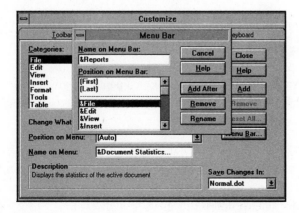

Fig. 36.9
From the Menu Bar dialog box, you can remove entire menus or add new menus for your custom commands.

7. Choose the Add After button.

8. Return to Step 4 to add more menus, or choose Close to return to the Customize dialog box.

9. Continue to add commands to the new menu from the Customize dialog box, or choose Close to return to the document.

Note

You may accidentally (or purposefully) delete the Tools menu or the Tools Customize command. You are then faced with that sinking-in-the-pit-of-the-stomach feeling because you seem to have no way to reset the menu (it looks like you can't get to the Customize dialog box). But there is a way! Use the View Toolbars command or click the right mouse button on a toolbar; then choose Customize. When the Customize dialog box appears, select the Menus tab and restore the menu or command you deleted.

To remove a menu, follow the above procedure to select the template and display the Menu Bar dialog box. Select the menu from the Position on Menu Bar list box and then choose the Remove button.

Restore menus to their original display by selecting the template containing the menu from the Save Changes In list and then choosing the Reset All button. Respond Yes to confirm that you want to reset the menus.

Assigning Commands and Macros to Shortcut Keys

Shortcut keys enable you to perform routine operations quickly without moving from the keyboard to the mouse. You should consider assigning shortcut keys to frequently used menu options.

Many of Word for Windows' commands and options are assigned to shortcut keys in the global template, NORMAL.DOT. Pressing Ctrl+B, for example, applies boldface to selected text. These key combinations are global; they work with all documents unless they have been deleted.

If you did not assign a key combination to a macro when it was created, you can assign it using the following procedure.

To assign key combinations to Word's predefined commands, your own macros, styles, fonts, or AutoText, follow these steps:

1. Open a document that uses the template that you want to contain this shortcut keystroke.

2. Choose the Tools Customize command and select the Keyboard tab. See fig. 36.10.

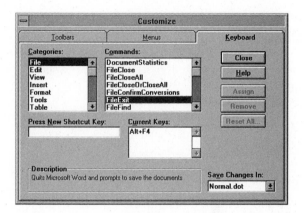

Fig. 36.10
Assign shortcut keys to almost any of Word's features to increase your work efficiency.

3. Select from the Save Changes In list the template you want to contain the shortcut.

4. Select from the Categories list the type of feature.

5. Select a specific feature from the list at the top center of the dialog box.

   Check the Current Keys list to see if the command you have selected has an existing shortcut key. It may already have one assigned.

6. Select the Press New Shortcut Key box, and then press the shortcut key combination you want. To enter a combination, you must press a letter while holding down an individual key or combination of the Ctrl, Alt, and Shift keys (Ctrl+Alt+Q, for example). Remove a key combination from the edit box by pressing the backspace key.

Tip
You can create double-keystroke combinations, such as Alt+B,F, by pressing Alt+B, releasing them both, and then pressing F.

Caution

If the keystroke combination you press in Step 6 has already been assigned, you see the command it has been assigned to under the title Currently Assigned To: on the left side of the dialog box. (This message only appears while you are assigning a keystroke.) Combinations that have not been assigned display [unassigned].

VIII

Customizing Word

7. Choose the Assign button.

8. Continue to make more shortcut key assignments or choose Close.

To return to the default keyboard assignments, display the Customize dialog box and select the Keyboard tab. Select the template containing the shortcut keys you want removed; then choose the Reset All button. Word for Windows restores the original shortcut keys for that template.

From Here...

For information relating directly to toolbars, menus, and shortcut keys, review the following chapters:

- Chapter 5, "Editing a Document." Learn how to use the AutoText feature to insert frequently used material.

- Chapter 11, "Formatting with Styles." Learn how to apply a combination of formats that have been assigned a name.

- Chapter 38, "Recording and Editing Macros." Learn how to record and edit simple macros.

- Chapter 39, "Building More Advanced Macros." Learn how to modify and troubleshoot macros.

Part IX

Automating Your Work

37 **Automating with Field Codes**

38 **Recording and Editing Macros**

39 **Building More Advanced Macros**

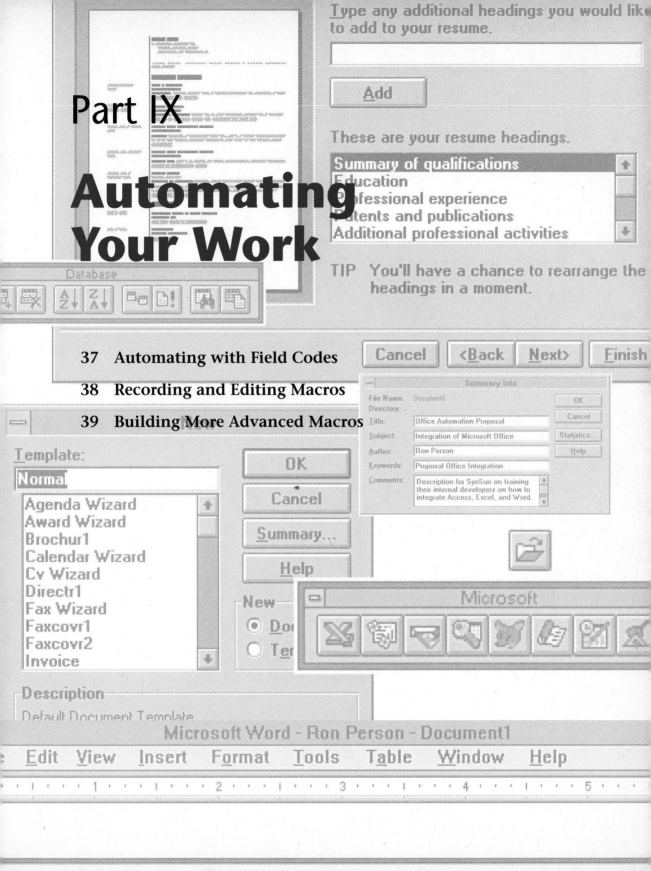

Type any additional headings you would like to add to your resume.

[ ]

Add

These are your resume headings.

Summary of qualifications
Education
Professional experience
Patents and publications
Additional professional activities

TIP   You'll have a chance to rearrange the headings in a moment.

Cancel   <Back   Next>   Finis

Database

Summary Info

File Name: Document8
Directory:
Title: Office Automation Proposal
Subject: Integration of Microsoft Office
Author: Ron Person
Keywords: Proposal Office Integration
Comments: Description for SynSun on training
              their internal developers on how to
              integrate Access, Excel, and Word.

OK
Cancel
Statistics...
Help

New

Template:

Normal

Agenda Wizard
Award Wizard
Brochur1
Calendar Wizard
Cv Wizard
Directr1
Fax Wizard
Faxcovr1
Faxcovr2
Invoice

OK

Cancel

Summary...

Help

New
○ Do
○ Ter

Microsoft

Description

Default Document Template

Microsoft Word - Ron Person - Document1

le   Edit   View   Insert   Format   Tools   Table   Window   Help

· · · I · · · 1 · · · I · · · 2 · · · I · · · 3 · · · I · · · 4 · · · I · · · 5 · · ·

Chapter 37

Automating with Field Codes

Fields are a necessary, but often invisible, part of such features as a table of contents, an index, or a table of authorities. Fields also perform such simple tasks as inserting the date or displaying a data-entry box. They also display the text edit box, check box, and drop-down list used in forms. The value you gain from using fields comes from the repetitive work they can automate for you.

Fields are hidden codes you type into a document or insert by using commands from the Insert menu. You normally see the results of fields, such as dates, page numbers, text linked to other documents, or mail-merge data. You also can see the field code for an individual field or for all fields in a document.

If you have used worksheet functions in Microsoft Excel or Lotus 1-2-3, you are familiar with the concept of fields. Fields are similar to functions. Most worksheet functions are mathematically and financially oriented; Word for Windows fields are oriented toward words, document processing, and mail-merge functions.

Fig. 37.1 and fig. 37.2 show two views of the same document. Fig. 37.1 shows the field codes in the document. Fig. 37.2 shows a document after the fields it contains have been updated. As you can see, the field codes create an auto-mated document that you can use repeatedly.

In this chapter,
you learn to do
the following:

■ Build tables
  of contents

■ Edit fields

■ Lock and un-
  lock fields

Tip
Microsoft Word
fields are similar
to functions in
a spreadsheet
program.

IX

Automating Your Work

Fig. 37.1
Display field
codes in the
document by
pressing Alt+F9
for the whole
document or
Shift+F9 for the
selected area.

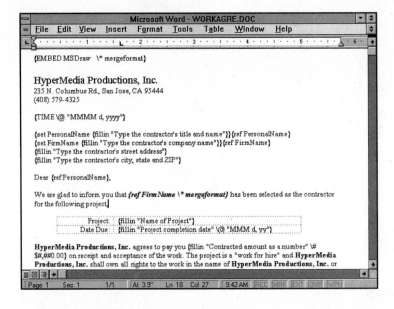

Fig. 37.2
When the field
results are
displayed, the
document looks
as though it was
typed.

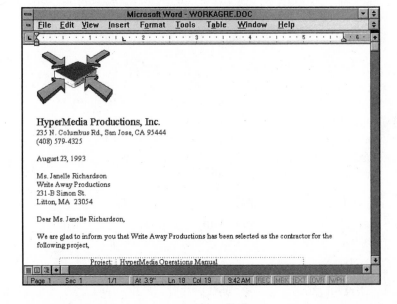

In Word for Windows, most fields update to produce a new result only when you print, print merge, or select and then update the field. You can update fields individually or throughout the entire document.

Many of the other features described in this book use fields, although you may not have been aware of them. In Chapter 13, "Setting the Page Layout," for example, the dates and page numbers in headers and footers are created with fields; in Chapter 29, "Creating Indexes and Tables of Contents," the indexes and tables of contents are created with fields. Fields are used in Chapter 32, "Assembling Large Documents," Chapter 34, and "Converting Files with Word for Windows," to assemble large documents, create mail-merge letters, and integrate the output from different Windows applications.

More than 60 different types of fields codes are available. With these field codes, you can do the following:

- Build tables of contents, tables of authorities, and indexes

- Build mailing lists, labels, and form letters

- Prompt operators for information used repeatedly in a document

- Insert dates, times, or document summary information

- Link Word for Windows documents or data in other Windows applications with the current Word for Windows document

- Update cross-referenced page numbers automatically

- Calculate math results

- Enable operators to jump between related words or contents

- Start macros

This chapter gives you an introduction to fields, covering how to view, insert, update, edit, and format the fields. Near the end of this chapter is a list of field codes and examples.

IX

Understanding the Basics of Fields

In this section you learn about the types of fields, their components, how to print fields, and how they appear in your documents.

Examining the Types of Fields
Fields can change your documents in a number of ways. Three types of Word for Windows fields are available: result fields, action fields, and marker fields.

Tip
For a full listing of field codes and descriptions choose the Help Contents command, select Reference Information, and then select Field Types and Switches.

Automating Your Work

Result fields produce a result in your document by inserting information. This information may be from the computer or document, such as the {author} and {date} fields. Other fields, such as {fillin}, display a dialog box that requests information from the operator and then inserts the information into the document.

Action fields do something to the document but don't insert visible text. The action is performed either when you update the field, as in the {ask} field, or when you click the field, as in the {gotobutton} and {macrobutton} fields. The {ask} field, for example, displays a dialog box and prompts you to enter information. But instead of displaying the information, Word for Windows stores it in a bookmark you designate.

Marker fields produce neither results nor actions. A marker field simply marks a location in the document so that you can find the location when you build such things as indexes and tables of contents. The index entry {xe} and table of contents entry {tc} fields are marker fields.

Understanding the Parts of Fields

Fields contain three parts: field characters, field type, and field instructions. A field that displays the current date in a format like Sep 12, 94, may look like the following:

```
{date \@ "MMM d, yy"}
```

where the braces ({ and }) are field characters, date is the field type, and \@ "MMM d, yy" is the field instruction.

Field characters define the beginning and end of a field. Although they look like braces, { and }, you cannot type the field characters. You create them by choosing a menu command that creates a field.

The second part of a field, the *field type*, defines the type of action the field performs. The field type follows the first field character, {, and must be a field type (see "A Reference List of Field Codes" later in this chapter), an equal sign (=), or a bookmark name.

The third part of a field, the *field instructions*, defines the type of action performed. You can customize the action of some fields by giving different instructions.

Arguments are numbers or text used to control a field's action or results. If an argument contains more than one word, the argument usually must be enclosed in quotation marks (" "). (Exceptions are described in each field's description.) You can use the {ask} field, for example, to prompt the operator for text to be assigned to the bookmark `First_Name` as follows:

```
{ask First_Name "Enter the first name."}
```

If a field result, such as a Fillin dialog box, shows only the first word of the text you typed, you have probably forgotten to enclose the rest of the argument in quotation marks. Word for Windows uses the first word of the argument but doesn't see the rest unless it is in quotation marks.

Tip
Enclose text
arguments in
quotation marks.

Bookmarks in fields are the same as bookmarks you assign to text. They name a location or selection of text. Fields use bookmarks to take action on the text or object in the document having that bookmark name. Fields also can store information in a bookmark or use the page number or sequence value of a bookmark's location.

Identifiers distinguish between different parts of the same document. You may use the letter `F` as an identifier of figures, for example, and the letter `P` as an identifier of pictures.

Text includes words or graphics used by the field. If you are entering a text argument with more than one word, you need to enclose all the text argument in quotation marks.

Switches toggle field results on or off. Type switches with a backslash (\) followed by the switch letter. Switches can be specific to a field or can be general and used by different fields. A field can contain as many as 10 field-specific switches and 10 general switches. Field-specific switches are described in "A Reference List of Field Codes" later in this chapter.

Field Code Shortcut Keys

Table 37.1 lists shortcut keys that can make your work with fields quicker and easier. These shortcut keys and their equivalent commands are described in the appropriate sections throughout this chapter.

IX

Automating Your Work

Table 37.1 Field Shortcut Keys

Key Combination	Function
F9	Update fields in the selection
Shift+F9	Toggle the selected field codes between the code and result
Ctrl+F9	Insert field characters, { }, to manual type field
Ctrl+Shift+F9	Unlink—Permanently replace a field with its last result
Alt+Shift+F9	Equivalent to double-clicking on selected {gotobutton} and {macrobutton} fields
F11	Go to next field
Shift+F11	Go to previous field
Ctrl+F11	Lock field to prevent updates; field remains
Ctrl+Shift+F11	Unlock field to allow updates
Alt+Shift+D	Insert {date} field
Alt+Shift+P	Insert {page} field
Alt+Shift+T	Insert {time} field

Viewing and Printing Field Codes

Fields appear two different ways: as a field code and as the field result. Field results display as though they were typed. You normally don't see the field codes when you work in your document, but if they return text, you see their results after the fields have been updated. If the fields have not been updated, you see the fields' previous results.

Some fields produce no visible result. Instead, they produce an action that affects other field codes. The fields that do not produce results include {ask}, {data}, {nextif}, {next}, {print}, {rd}, {set}, {skipif}, {ta}, {tc}, and {xe}. (See "A Reference List of Field Codes" later in this chapter for more information.)

Displaying Field Codes

You may need to see field codes on-screen so that you can review them, delete them, or edit them. You can display the field codes throughout the entire document or for an individual field.

To display field codes on-screen throughout the entire document, follow these steps:

1. Choose the Tools Options command.

2. Select the View tab.

3. Select the Field Codes check box.

Or if you are using the keyboard, press Alt+F9.

To display an individual field code, follow these steps:

1. Move the insertion point within the field code or its result.

2. Press Shift+F9.

   or

   Click the right mouse button and choose Toggle Field Display from the Shortcut menu.

These commands switch the display between showing field codes or the result. Your document probably will change its word wrap when you reveal or hide field codes. This change is due to the differences in length between the field codes and their results.

Note

A fast way to switch all the fields in a selected area between displaying field codes or their results is to select the area containing the field or move the insertion point inside the field and then press Shift+F9. This key combination toggles between displaying results and field codes in the selected range.

A few field codes do not display. The {xe} (index entry), {tc} (table of contents entry), and {rd} (referenced document) field codes are formatted automatically as hidden text. To see these codes when you display field codes, you must choose the Tools Options command, then select the View tab, then select the Hidden Text check box and choose OK.

Most fields do not update automatically to show you the most current result. You must update fields manually or by using a macro. When you load a document that contains fields, each field shows its previous result. This feature enables you to load a document, such as a contract or form letter, and update only the items you want changed.

Displaying Field Results as Shaded

The result of fields—whether they are text, dates, or numbers—appear on-screen just as though they were entered normally. If you are working in forms or documents where you want to see which items are fields, you can shade the result of fields at certain times so that they stand out.

To shade field results, follow these steps:

1. Choose the Tools Options command.

2. Select the View tab.

3. Select from the Field Shading drop-down list the time when you want field results shaded: Never, Always, or When Selected.

4. Choose OK.

Printing Field Codes

You probably should keep a printed copy of your documents and macros. These copies help you if you ever lose the file or if someone else takes over your operation.

To print a copy of the document so that you can see the field codes, follow these steps:

1. Choose the File Print command.

2. Choose the Options button from the Print dialog box.

3. Select the Print tab and select the Field Codes check box under the Include with Document group.

4. Choose OK to return to the Print dialog box, and then print your document.

Remember to unselect the Field Codes check box when you want to return to printing just the document.

Inserting Field Codes

You can enter fields in a number of ways. Several commands enter field codes at the insertion point's position. Some of the commands that insert field codes include the following:

Edit Paste Special Paste, Paste Link

Insert Page Numbers

Insert Annotations

Insert Date and Time

Insert Field

Insert Symbol

Insert Form Field

Insert Footnote

Insert Caption

Insert Cross-reference

Insert Index and Tables

Insert File

Insert Picture

Insert Object

You also can insert field codes into a document by using the Insert Field command and then choosing the appropriate field codes from the Field dialog box. Or you can type field codes directly into a document by pressing Ctrl+F9 to insert the field characters, { }, and then typing between the field characters.

IX

Automating Your Work

Inserting Field Codes

To insert field codes with the **Insert Field** command, follow these steps:

1. Position the insertion point in the document at the location where you want the field result.

2. Choose the **Insert Field** command.

   Fig. 37.3 shows the Field dialog box, from which you can select field types and instructions.

Fig. 37.3

The Field dialog box inserts fields and enables you to select appropriate switches to change format or actions.

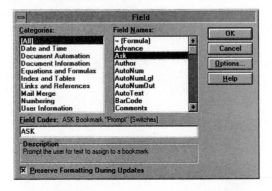

3. Select the type of field you want from the Categories list or select All.

4. Select a field type from the Field Names list.

5. Select a switch to modify the field by choosing the Options button, when it is not gray. Select switches or bookmarks as described in the following text; then choose OK in the Option dialog box.

6. Choose OK.

When you choose OK, some fields update immediately. When you insert the {fillin} field, for example, Word for Windows displays the Fillin dialog box that prompts you for an entry.

Inserting Field Code Switches or Bookmarks

Some field codes have mandatory or optional switches. Some codes also require a bookmark, a named location in the document. You can find out what a field code needs and what is mandatory in two ways: look for a short prompt in the Field dialog box or select Help for a full explanation.

In the Field dialog box, shown in fig. 37.3, look to the right of the Field Codes label in the lower third of the dialog box to see a short prompt that shows what you can put in the field code that is selected in the list.

If you need further explanation of the switches and bookmarks for a field code, select the field in the Field Names list and then press F1. Doing so displays the Help window with a full explanation for the selected field.

To insert switches or bookmarks into a field code, follow these steps:

1. Follow the steps in the previous procedure and select a field from the Field Names list.

2. Choose the Options button. The Field Options dialog box appears (see fig. 37.4).

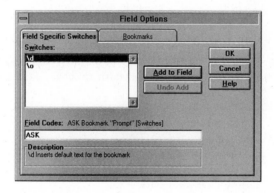

Fig. 37.4
After you choose Options, you can read a description of the switches available and choose the one you want from a list.

3. Select the Field Specific Switches tab.

4. Select a switch from the Switches list and check the switch Description at the bottom of the dialog box. Choose Add to Field if you want to add the switch. Continue to add more switches if needed.

5. If the field code requires a bookmark, select the Bookmarks tab.

6. Select a bookmark from the Name list and choose the Add to Field button.

7. Choose OK from the Field Options dialog box.

8. Choose OK from the Field dialog box.

IX

Automating Your Work

The field code you have built is then inserted into your document at the location of the insertion point.

Inserting Field Codes Manually

After you are familiar with the field code syntax, you can manually enter the field codes quickly. Because you are not prompted and do not have lists of correct switches, making mistakes is easier.

To enter a field code manually, follow these steps:

1. Position the insertion point in the document at the location where you want the field action or result.

2. Press Ctrl+F9.

   Even if fields are not displayed currently, Word for Windows shows the field characters you have just inserted. The insertion point appears between two field characters, { }.

3. Enter the field name followed by a space; then type the field instructions. If the field references a path name, be sure to type two backslashes instead of a single backslash to separate directories.

4. Update the field code by pressing F9.

An incorrect syntax in the field code causes a beep when you press F9 to see the results. Select the field and press Shift+F9 to see the field code and switches.

Another method of manually entering fields is to position the insertion point where you want the field, type the field type and instructions, select them, and then press Ctrl+F9. Word for Windows encloses the selection in field characters, { and }. This method works well when you need to nest fields inside other fields (see "Creating Complex Fields by Nesting" later in this chapter).

> **Note**
>
> Remember that although the field characters appear to be braces, they are not. Fields do not work if you type brace characters. You can create a matching set of field characters only by pressing Ctrl+F9 or using a command to insert the field characters and field code.

Moving Between Fields

You can find fields in two ways: use a shortcut key to find the next field or use the Edit Find command to find a specific field type.

To move to and select the next field after the insertion point, press F11 (Next Field). If you do not have an F11 key, press Alt+F1. To move to and select the preceding field before the insertion point, press Shift+F11 (Previous Field) or Alt+Shift+F1.

Note

The F11 and Shift+F11 shortcuts do not find the {xe} (index entry), {tc} (table of contents entry), or {rd} (referenced document) fields. You can find these fields by first displaying hidden text using the **Tools Options** command, selecting the View tab, and then selecting the Hidden Text check box. After the codes are visible, you can use the **Edit Find** command.

To find a specific field code, follow these steps:

1. Choose the Tools Options command.

2. Select the View tab.

3. Select the Field Codes check box to display field codes. For some field codes, you may have to select the Hidden Text check box in this same tab also. Then select the OK button.

4. Choose the Edit Find command from the menu bar.

5. In the Find What text box, type the field type you want to find, such as **fillin**. Do not type the field characters.

6. Choose the Find Next button.

7. Choose Cancel or press Esc in the Find dialog box if you want to edit the field.

8. Press Shift+F4 to find the next field of the same type.

   The insertion point moves to the next field of the type you requested.

Editing Fields

You can edit field codes or their results manually. This approach is useful for correcting the results of a field or for changing the information or switches inside a field code after it has been created. By editing simple fields, you can change them into larger, nested fields containing multiple parts, which you then can use to accomplish complex tasks.

To edit a field code, follow these steps:

1. Choose the Tools Options command.

2. Select the View tab.

3. Select the Field Codes check box or select the text enclosing the field and press Shift+F9 to display the fields.

4. Move the insertion point inside the field.

5. Edit the field as you edit text. Make sure that you preserve the correct syntax of the parts within the field. You cannot edit the field characters, { }.

To see the results of your editing, select the field and press F9 (Update Field).

You can change the results of a field by editing the results on-screen as if you were editing normal text. If you edit the results, however, you do not want the field code to update when it prints. To make sure the field code does not update, choose the File Print command, select the Print tab, and make sure the Update Fields check box is not selected.

Note

Some fields, such as {include}, {dde}, and {ddeauto}, use DOS path names (directory names). When you type path names in fields, you must use double backslashes (\\) wherever the path name normally has a single backslash (\). Keep this fact in mind if you have to change the directory path name used in a field. Always use a backslash before any quotation mark (") within a quoted string. For example, the field

```
{fillin "Who wrote \"Brahm's Lullaby\""}
```

places quotation marks around the phrase "Brahm's Lullaby" when it appears in the prompt of a Fillin dialog box.

Creating Complex Fields by Nesting

When you nest fields, you put one or more fields inside another field. This technique enables you to use the result of one field to change the actions of another. You can nest the {fillin} field inside the {set} field, for example, so that the typed entry in the {fillin} field can be stored by the {set} field in a bookmark. The text in the bookmark then can be redisplayed at other locations with the {ref} field:

```
{set Name {fillin "Type the name"}}
```

This method is used in the letter shown in fig. 37.1 and fig. 37.2.

To nest a field inside another field, follow these steps:

1. Display the field codes, if they are not already displayed, by choosing the Tools Options command, selecting the View tab, and selecting the Field Codes check box.

2. Insert the first field into the document using your normal method.

3. Position the insertion point inside the existing field at the point where you want the nested field.

4. Insert the nested field by following the Insert Field procedure for this code, or by pressing Ctrl+F9 and typing the field type and its instructions between the field code characters, { }.

5. Return to Step 3 and insert additional field codes if necessary.

6. Select the field and press F9 (Update Field) to check the results.

Deleting Fields

Delete a field by selecting it and pressing Del. A quick way to select and delete fields is to press F11 (Next Field) until the appropriate field is selected and then press Del. If you manually select fields by dragging across them, you need to drag across only the character field, { }, at one end to select the entire field code.

Formatting Field Results

You can format the results from field codes in two ways. You can format the results of a field code as you do any other text or graphics, or you can insert formatting switches within a field code. If you use formatting switches within

IX

Automating Your Work

a field code, they take priority over manual formatting when the field code updates.

Formatting the result of a field code is the same as formatting any item in a document. You select what you want to format and then choose a command. The next time the field code updates, however, it may lose the formatting you have applied. This situation can happen if the formatting you apply is different from the formatting contained in the switch within the field code.

Switches enable you to format the results of a field. When the field updates, the formatting specified by the switch applies itself again to the field code result. You can insert switches within a field code by selecting the switch from the Field Options dialog box as described in "Inserting Field Code Switches or Bookmarks" earlier in this chapter. You also can add or change a switch by editing an existing field code.

You can format field results in three ways:

- * mergeformat. Format the field results with multiple formats by inserting this switch in the field and then choosing the Format Font or the Format Paragraph commands.

- * charformat. Format the field results with a single character format by inserting this switch in the field and then formatting the first character of the field type.

- *General switches*. These switches enable you to format such things as date, time, and numeric formats. Enter a general switch within the field code, after the field type.

The * mergeformat and * charformat switches are described in the following sections. The general switches are listed in table 37.2. The following sections also describe the switch types, numeric pictures, and date-time pictures used in the switches and explain how to use them in your fields.

Table 37.2 General Switches for Formatting Fields		
Switch	**Syntax**	**Effect**
*	{field-type * switchtype}	Formats the text result with case conversion, number conversion, or character formatting

Switch	Syntax	Effect
\#	{field-type \# numericpicture}	Formats the numeric result to match a "picture" showing the pattern of numeric format
\@	{field-type \@ date-timepicture}	Formats the date or time result to match a "picture" showing the pattern of date-time format
\!	{field-type \!}	Locks a field's results

The following fields' results cannot be formatted with general switches:

{autonum}	{rd}
{import}	{eq}
{autonumlgl}	{tc}
{macrobutton}	{gotobutton}
{autonumout}	{xe}

Formatting Numbers, Dates, and Text Case

In the following sections, the {fillin} field is used to illustrate how each * switch works. The {fillin} field displays a dialog box in which you can type sample text or numbers, which enables you to type an entry and see the switch affect what you type.

To duplicate the examples, press Ctrl+F9, type **fillin**, type a space, then type the switch type and switch. To update the field and see the results, select the field and press F9. Remember that you can switch quickly between viewing the field codes and their results by pressing Shift+F9.

Preserving Manual Formats

The * charformat and * mergeformat switches are two of the most valuable switches. They enable you to retain formats you have applied to a field result. Without the use of these switches, your manual formatting of a field's result is removed when the field updates.

Tip

Always use a single space to separate the field instructions, such as formatting switches, from the field type, such as fillin.

IX

Automating Your Work

Switch Type	Effect
* charformat	Formats the field result the same as the format of the first character of the field type, the character after {. This format takes precedence over other formatting. Formatting the f in the {fillin} field as boldface, for example, produces a boldface field result.
* mergeformat	Preserves your manual formatting of a field's result. Character and paragraph formatting you apply to a field result are preserved after the field updates. The updated field results are reformatted on a word-by-word basis using the original formatting as a template. If the updated results have more words than the originally formatted result, the extra words use the format of the first character after the opening field character, {. If the previous field result was not formatted, mergeformat acts like charformat.

In the following example, format the first letter in the field name fillin with the character format you want to apply to the entire result:

```
{fillin "Type a sample result" \* charformat}
```

Formatting remains even after updating the field.

In the following example, format the results of the field with character or paragraph formatting:

```
{fillin "Type a sample result" \* mergeformat}
```

After the field updates, the * mergeformat field reapplies the formats you applied previously. Your formats are reapplied according to word-by-word locations. If the updated field contains words in a different order, the formatting may not coincide with the updated position of words.

Note

When you first format a field that uses the * mergeformat switch, make sure that the field result has the maximum number of words you expect as a result for this field. mergeformat reapplies formatting on a word-by-word basis, ensuring that all subsequent field results with fewer words are formatted as you expect.

Converting Uppercase and Lowercase Text. The following switches change the capitalization of the field's results.

Switch	Result
* upper	Converts characters in the field results to all uppercase
* lower	Converts characters in the field results to all lowercase
* firstcap	Converts the first letter of the first word in the field result to a capital; converts other letters to lowercase
* caps	Converts the first letter of each word in the field result to a capital; converts other letters to lowercase

Example:

```
{fillin "Type a sample result" \* upper}
```

Formatting Numeric. Types The following switches change how a numeric result displays:

Switch	Result
* Arabic	Uses Arabic cardinal numbers such as 1, 2, 3, and so on. If the field-type is {page}, the switch overrides the page-number formatting set by the Edit Header/Footer dialog box.
* ordinal	Converts a numeric field result to an ordinal Arabic number. When used with the {page} field, it produces page numbers such as 18th.
* roman	Converts a numeric field result to Roman numerals, such as XV for xviii. Type the switch as * **Roman** for uppercase Roman numerals or * **roman** for lowercase Roman numerals.
*alphabetic	Converts a numeric field result into its alphabetical equivalent. The number 5 results in the letter *e*, for example. Type the switch as * **Alphabetic** for uppercase letters or * **alphabetic** for lowercase letters.

Example:

```
{fillin "Type a number" \* ordinal}
```

Formatting Numbers as Text. The following switches convert numeric results into a text equivalent. This process is useful for calculated numeric results that appear in documents—a check or invoice amount. Use the capitalization switches described in "Converting Uppercase and Lowercase Text" to change the capitalization of a number as text.

Switch	Result
* cardtext	Converts a numeric field result into text with the first letter in uppercase. The number 35 results in Thirty Five, for example.
* ordtext	Converts a numeric field result to ordinal text. The number 35 results in Thirty Fifth, for example.
* hex	Converts a numeric field result into a hexadecimal number.
* dollartext	Converts a numeric field result into a text amount and fractional dollar. For example, 53.67 becomes Fifty three and 67/100.

Example:

```
{fillin "Type a number" \* cardtext \* upper}
```

Formatting with Custom Numeric Formats

You can format numeric field results so that they appear in the numeric format you want. You can, for example, define your own custom formats that round results to the desired precision, display only significant numbers, include text, or have different formats for positive, negative, and zero results.

To format numeric results, you create a numeric picture. The switch for a numeric picture is \#. A numeric picture is a pattern that follows the switch and is composed of symbols that define placeholders, commas, and signs.

To format numeric fields with character formatting, such as boldface and italic, format the numeric picture. Formatting the negative portion of a numeric picture in italic, for example, produces italic formatting of negative results.

The examples use a fillin data-entry box that enables you to type into a data-entry box any number or text. To duplicate one of the examples, use the Insert Field command to display the Field dialog box. Select the Fillin field and then type the \# switch and the numeric picture following fillin in the Field Codes edit box. Leave a single space between the field name, the switch, and the numeric picture. The result should look similar to the following:

```
{fillin \# $#,##0.00}
```

To update the field so that a dialog box asks for your entry, select the field and press F9. To toggle the display between showing field results and field codes, press Shift+F9.

You can use the following characters to generate numeric pictures:

```
0  #  x  .  ,  á  +
```

You also can specify formatting variations for positive, negative, and zero results and can include text, sequence names, and other symbols and characters in a numeric picture. The following sections describe how to use these characters in numeric pictures.

Positive, Negative, and Zero Formatting Variations. You can specify three different numeric pictures that Word for Windows can use, depending on the sign of the field's result. The three numeric pictures must be separated by semicolons (;). If the field result is positive, Word for Windows uses the numeric picture to the left of the first semicolon. If the result is negative, Word for Windows uses the numeric picture between the two semicolons. And if the result is 0, Word for Windows uses the numeric picture to the right of the second semicolon. The numeric picture does not have to be in quotation marks if it contains only numeric formatting. If the numeric picture contains text or space characters, you must enclose the entire numeric picture in quotation marks. For example, the numeric pictures in this field

```
{fillin \# #,##0.00;(#,##0.00);0}
```

produce 4,350.78 when the field result is 4350.776; 4,350.78 when the result is –4350.776; and 0 when the result is 0.

> **Note**
>
> The right parenthesis,), accompanying a negative number can cause positive and negative numbers to misalign. If this problem occurs, align the numbers by using a decimal tab or insert a space in the positive format to the right of the last zero.

The 0 Placeholder. Put a 0 in a numeric picture wherever you want a 0 to display when a number is missing. The field {fillin \# 0.00}, for example, produces the following results:

Tip
Use the general format (*) switches described in this chapter to change a number such as 35 into Thirty Five or Thirty Fifth. You even can change numbers such as 35.60 into Thirty Five and 60/100.

Tip
If you are familiar with how to create custom numeric and date formats in Microsoft Excel, you know how to create custom formats in Word for Windows.

IX

Automating Your Work

Number	Result
.646	0.65
250.4	250.40

Most currency formats use two 0s (zeros) to the right of the decimal.

The # Placeholder. The # character is a digit placeholder used when you do not want leading or trailing 0s (zeros) in results. The field {fillin \# #.00}, for example, produces the following results:

Number	Result
0.6	.60
250.4	250.40

The x Placeholder. The x character is a digit placeholder that truncates, or cuts off, numbers that extend beyond the x position. For example,

```
{fillin \# #.#x}
```

produces .24 when the numeric result is .236.

The Decimal Point. Use the decimal point along with other numeric picture characters to specify the decimal location in a string of digits. Change the character used as the decimal separator by selecting a country from the International program in the Windows Control Panel.

The Thousands Separator. Use the thousands separator (usually a comma) along with the # or 0 numeric picture characters to specify the location of the thousands separator in a result. Change the character used as the thousands separator by selecting a country from the International program in the Windows Control Panel.

The Minus Sign (–). Used in a numeric picture, this character displays a minus sign (–) if the result is negative and a blank space if the number is positive or 0.

The Plus Sign (+). Used in a numeric picture, this character displays a plus sign (+) if the result is positive, a minus sign (–) if the result is negative, and a space if the result is 0.

Text. Use text formatting within a numeric picture to include measurements or messages along with the numeric result. Enclose text and the numeric picture in quotation marks (" "). The text displays in the field result in the same location as it appears in the numeric picture. For example, the numeric picture

```
{fillin \# "Amount owed is $#,##0.00"}
```

produces "Amount owed is $4,500.80" when the user types 4500.8 into the Fillin dialog box.

If the text string contains a character that Word for Windows might interpret as an operator or as field information, enclose that character in apostrophes (' '). In the following example, the dashes on either side of the zero, - 0 -, normally do not display for the 0 result. But by enclosing the entire numeric picture in double quotation marks and the numeric picture for - 0 - in apostrophes, you can tell Word for Windows to display - 0 - for zero results:

```
{fillin \# "0.0;(0.0);'- 0 -'"}
```

If you use text in a numeric picture that includes positive, negative, and zero format variations, enclose the entire pattern in quotation marks, as in

```
{fillin \# "0.0;(0.0);Enter a non-zero number"}
```

If the text itself contains quotation marks, precede the text's quotation marks with a backslash (\), as follows:

```
{fillin "Who wrote \"Brahm's Lullaby\"?"}
```

Other Characters. You can use symbols and characters in the numeric picture, and they appear in the result. This feature is useful when you need to format a numeric result to include dollar signs, percent symbols, and international currency. A simple example is the use of the dollar sign, as in

```
{fillin \# $#,##0;($#,##0)}
```

or the percent sign, as in

```
{fillin \# #0%}
```

To enter ANSI characters such as the cent, pound, Yen, and section symbols, turn on the numeric keypad (press Num Lock until the Num Lock light is on) and hold down the Alt key as you type the appropriate four-number ANSI code. (These codes are listed in Appendix C, "Windows Character Tables.") The character appears when you release the Alt key. Do not leave a space between the character entered and the numeric picture.

IX

Automating Your Work

Formatting Date-Time Results

You can format date and time field results so that they appear in standard or custom formats. To format date-time results, you create a date-time picture. The switch for a date-time picture is \@. A date-time picture is a pattern composed of characters that define date and time formats such as month, day, and hour. Word for Windows uses the pattern as a sample format. For example, the field and pattern

```
{date \@ "MMMM d, yyyy"}
```

displays the computer's current date in the format December 24, 1992.

To format date-time pictures with character formatting such as boldface and italic, format the first letter of each portion of the date-time picture. In the preceding example, you can format the first M in boldface and italic to make the entire month boldface and italic but leave the day and year as they were.

You can use the following characters to generate date-time pictures:

```
M  d  D  y  Y  h  H  m  am  pm  AM  PM
```

You also can include text, sequence names, and other characters and symbols in a date-time picture. The following sections describe how to use these characters in date-time pictures.

The Month Placeholder. Uppercase M is the month placeholder (lowercase m designates minutes). The four formats are as follows:

M	1 through 12
MM	01 through 12
MMM	Jan through Dec
MMMM	January through December

The Day Placeholder. Uppercase or lowercase d is the day placeholder. The four formats are as follows:

d or D	1 through 31
dd or DD	01 through 31
ddd or DDD	Mon through Sun
dddd or DDDD	Monday through Sunday

The Year Placeholder. Uppercase or lowercase y is the year placeholder. The two formats are as follows:

yy or YY	00 through 99
yyyy or YYYY	1900 through 2040

The Hour Placeholder. Uppercase or lowercase h is the hour placeholder. Lowercase designates the U.S. 12-hour clock. Uppercase designates the international 24-hour clock. The four formats are as follows:

h	1 through 12
hh	01 through 12
H	1 through 24
HH	01 through 24

The Minute Placeholder. Lowercase m is the minute placeholder (uppercase M designates months.) The two formats are as follows:

m	0 through 59
mm	00 through 59

Morning and Afternoon Indicators. You use uppercase or lowercase AM and PM with h or hh 12-hour clock formats to designate morning or afternoon. You can select characters other than AM/am and PM/pm by using the Control Panel to change settings in the International icon. The four formats are as follows:

\@ h AM/PM	8AM and 6PM
\@ h am/pm	8am and 6pm
\@ h A/P	8A and 6P
\@ h a/p	8a and 6p

Text Characters. Use text formatting in date-time pictures to include measurements or messages with the results. Enclose text and the date-time picture in quotation marks (" "). If the text includes characters that Word for Windows can interpret as field information characters, such as a minus (–) or zero (0), enclose those characters in apostrophes (' '). The text displays in the field result in the same location it appears in the date-time picture. For example, the field and date-time picture

```
{date \@ "Job complete at HH:mm"}
```

displays a result such as Job complete at 12:45.

Other Characters. You can use the colon (:), hyphen (-), and comma (,) in the date-time picture. These characters display in the result in the same position in which they are used in the date-time picture. The date-time picture \@ "HH:mm" displays 23:15, for example, and the date-time picture \@ "MMM d, yy" displays Jun 15, 92.

Updating, Unlinking, or Locking Fields

As you learned earlier in the chapter, many field codes update automatically. You can update some codes manually, however. In some cases, you don't want field codes to update; for example, you may have a letter that begins with an automatic date field. You do not want the date on a completed letter to change the next time you open the letter.

Another instance where you want to control updating is when you have data from an application such as Microsoft Excel linked into your Word document. You probably do not want the link refreshed each time you update the document—you may not know at that time whether the data in the source Excel worksheet is correct. Using the methods described in the following sections, you can update the document without updating the Excel data and then return at a later time to update just the Excel data.

Updating Fields

Updating a field produces a new result or action from the field—perhaps a change in text, numbers, or graphics. Some fields may not produce a visible change but instead affect the results in other fields.

Different fields update at different times. Fields such as {date} update when the document opens or when updated by command. Fields such as {next} take affect only during print merge. Fields such as {fillin} update when you select the field and press the F9 (Update) key. Other fields may update during printing, print merge, or repagination.

To update a field manually, select the field and press F9 (Update Field). You can select the field by selecting the text around it, using one of the selection methods described in previous chapters, or by pressing F11 (Next Field) or Shift+F11 (Previous Field) to move to and select the field. If field codes are visible, you can select a specific field by dragging across one of the field characters. You also can select a visible field code by moving the insertion point inside the field and pressing F8 (Extend Selection) until the field is selected.

If Word for Windows beeps when you attempt to update a field, the field is locked, there is a syntax error in the field code, or that field code does not update—the fields that generate equations on-screen, for example.

If you want to update only part of a document, select only the portions of the document you want to update and press F9. To update fields in a table, select the portion of the table you want to update using any table selection method and then press F9.

To update an entire document, select the entire document either by pressing Ctrl and clicking in the selection bar (the blank area to the left of the document), by choosing the Edit Select All command, or by pressing Ctrl+5 (on the numeric keypad). Press F9 to update fields.

The following list shows fields unaffected by F9 (Update Field). Fields with an asterisk update automatically.

Field	Use
*{autonum}	Automatic numbers with Arabic (1, 2, 3 and so on) format
*{autonumlgl}	Automatic numbers with legal (1.1.1 and so on) format
*{autonumout}	Automatic numbers with outline format
{eq}	Math formulas
{gotobutton}	On-screen buttons that jump to a location when double-clicked
{macrobutton}	On-screen buttons that run a macro when double-clicked
{print}	Send information to the printer

Undoing or Stopping Updates

You can undo field updates if you choose the Edit Undo Update Fields command (or press Alt+Backspace or Ctrl+Z) immediately after updating one or more fields. This capability gives you a chance to make changes throughout a

IX

Automating Your Work

document, see how they affect the document, and then remove the changes if necessary.

Tip
The status bar displays the percentage of updates completed.

If you are updating a document and want to stop the updates, press Esc. This method is handy if you have selected the entire document and realize that you do not want to update all fields.

Locking Fields to Prevent Updates

When you want to prevent a field from changing, you can lock it. Locking fields is useful if you want to archive a file that will not change, to prevent accidental changes, or to prevent updating a link to a file that no longer exists. Word for Windows does not update a locked field. If you attempt to update a locked field, you hear a beep and see a warning in the status bar that an attempt was made to update a locked field.

To prevent a particular field from being updated while those around it are updated, lock the field. Select the field and then press Ctrl+F11 (Lock Field). To unlock the field, press Shift+Ctrl+F11 (Unlock Field). (If you do not have an F11 key, use Alt+Ctrl+F1 and Alt+Shift+Ctrl+F1, respectively.)

Locking a field is different from unlinking a field with Shift+Ctrl+F9. Unlinked fields replace the field code with the results. You are unable to return to a usable field code.

Unlinking Fields

You may want to unlink fields and convert them to their fixed results. Unlinking and then converting fields freezes the result at its current value, removes the field code, and ensures that the result does not change if updated. You may want to unlink field codes that link pictures, charts, and text into your document before you pass the document to someone else. If you do not want to pass all the linked documents as well as your Word document, you should unlink the linked field codes before you give another user the document.

To unlink a field, select the field code and press Ctrl+Shift+F9 (Unlink Field).

Getting Help on Field Codes

Word for Windows has over 60 field codes that enable you to automate many of the features in documents you work in repetitively. Although most field codes are not difficult to use, much information is required about switches, bookmarks, and so on. You can use three ways to get help about field codes:

the Help menu system, Help about specific fields in the Field dialog box, and Help while you are editing a field in the document.

To get general or specific help about field codes, open the Help menu system. Choose the **Help** Contents command and then select Using Word. Next, from the Automating Your Work section, select Inserting Information with Fields. If you need help about a specific field code, choose the **Help** Contents command and then select Reference Information, then select Field Types and Switches. Now select Field Types and you will see a listing of fields in alphabetical order. Select the one you need information about.

To see a description and examples of a field code before you insert them in a document, follow these steps:

1. Choose the Insert Field command.

2. Select the field from the Field Names list.

3. Press F1, the Help key.

4. Read the Help information. You can move to other help topics while the Help window is open.

5. Press Alt+F4 to close the Help application.

To see a description and example of a field code while you are in the document, follow these steps:

1. Press Alt+F9 to display field codes in the document.

2. Select the field code or move the insertion point inside the field code.

3. Press F1, the Help Key.

4. Read the Help information.

5. Press Alt+F4 to close the Help application.

The Help window that appears contains the syntax, descriptions, and examples of how you can use the field code.

A Reference List of Field Codes

Exploring all the power and possibilities available with field codes is beyond the scope of this book. The following list shows some of the more frequently used field codes and their functions:

Function	Field Code
Date, Time, Summary Info	`date, time, author, createdate`
Index	`xe, index`
Forms	`formtext, formcheckbox, formdropdown`
Linking, embedding, and importing	`embed, import, include, link, dde, ddeauto`
Mathematical calculations	`eq`
Mail merge	`data, mergerec, mergefield, next, nextif, ref`
Numbering	`autonum, autonumlgl, autonumout`
Page numbering	`page, numpages`
Prompting	`ask, fillin`
Reference figures, objects, or locations	`pageref, ref, seq, xe`
Symbol	`symbol`
Table of Contents	`tc, toc`

In the following list of field codes, the syntax of each field code shows whether the code contains field instructions, such as bookmarks, prompts, or switches. Remember that a *bookmark* is a name assigned to a selection or insertion point location. A bookmark also can be a name used to store information for future use by a field code. A *prompt* is a text message that appears on-screen when the field code updates. The prompt must be enclosed in quotation marks (" "). A *switch* alters the behavior or format of a field code in some manner. A field may use multiple switches. Included in some field code descriptions is an explanation of the specific switches used in that field code.

In the following sections, the syntax shows the order in which you must enter information between field characters. Italicized words are information used by the field type. Optional information is enclosed in square brackets.

{ask}
Syntax:

```
{ask bookmark "prompt" [switches]}
```

Displays a dialog box asking the user to enter text. Word for Windows assigns that text to the bookmark, which then can be used throughout the document to repeat the typed text. The following field code, for example, displays a dialog box asking the operator to enter the first name. Word for Windows stores the typed information in the bookmark named `Firstname` so that it can be used by other fields in the document:

```
{ask Firstname "Enter the first name"}
```

If you type **Mary** in response to the dialog box, you can repeat `Mary` throughout the document by using the field code `{ref Firstname}`.

Switch	Result
\o	Requests a response to the dialog box only at the beginning of the first document during a print merge.
\d	Defines default text for the dialog box. If no default exists, the last entry is repeated. Use \d" " if you want nothing as the default.

Updates during printing merge. You cannot use `{ask}` fields in footnotes, headers, footers, annotations, or macros.

If you want a dialog box for data entry, which you can update by pressing the F9 key, see the `{fillin}` field code.

{author}
Syntax:

```
{author ["new_name"]}
```

Inserts or replaces the author's name as it appears in the document's Summary Info box.

The new name can be up to 255 characters long.

Updates when you press F9 or when you print.

{autonum}
Syntax:

```
{autonum}
```

Results in an Arabic number (1, 2, 3, and so on) when inserted at the beginning of a paragraph or outline level. Numbers display in the document in sequence and update as other `{autonum}` paragraphs are inserted or deleted. Use the Format Bullets and Numbering command to insert these fields more easily.

IX

Automating Your Work

{autonumlgl}

Syntax:

{autonumlgl}

Displays a number using legal numbering (1.2.1) format when inserted at the beginning of a paragraph or outline heading. See also {autonum}.

{autonumout}

Syntax:

{autonumout}

Displays a number using outline number (I, A, 1, a, and so on) format when inserted at the beginning of a paragraph or outline heading. See also {autonum}.

{autotext}

Syntax:

{*autotext AutoTextEntry*}

The AutoTextEntry is the name in the Edit AutoText command under which text or an object is stored. Updating this field results in the latest definition stored in AutoText.

{bookmark}

Syntax:

{*bookmark*}

Bookmarks are names that refer to text or graphics. They appear not as {bookmark}, but showing the actual bookmark name in braces, such as {Premise}. Different field codes use bookmarks in different ways. Some fields return or display contents of the bookmark. Some fields return or display the page number where the bookmark's contents are located. You load data into a bookmark by using the Insert Cross-reference command or by displaying an input box for operator entry using {ask} or {fillin} field control.

Bookmarks may be up to 40 characters in length and cannot include spaces. Use only letters numbers and underscore characters (_). If you need to separate words, use an underline instead of a space.

If the bookmark FirmName contains the text Generic Quality Corporation, for example, the text appears in the document at every location of the field {ref FirmName}.

Updates when you press F9, when you choose File Print Merge, or when you choose File Print the first time (when in a header or footer). See also {ref bookmark}.

{comments}

Syntax:

```
{comments /"new_comments"/}
```

Inserts or replaces comments from the document's Summary Info box a ppearing in the document.

Updates when you press F9 or when you print or print merge.

{createdate}

Syntax:

```
{createdate}
```

Inserts the date the document was created as shown in the Summary Info box. Formats according to the system's default format.

Updates when you press F9, when you choose File Print Merge, or when you choose File Print the first time (when in a header or footer).

{database}

Syntax:

```
{database /switches/}
```

Used to insert data from an external database.

{date}

Syntax:

```
{date ["date_format_picture"]}
```

Results in the current date or time when the field was updated.

Updates when you select this field and press F9 or print. Format with the date-time picture-switches listed in the section "Formatting Date-Time Results" earlier in this chapter.

{edittime}

Syntax:

```
{edittime}
```

Results in the number of minutes the document has been edited since its creation, as shown in the Summary Info box.

Updates when you press F9 or when you when you merge a mail document.

{embed}

Syntax:

```
{embed object}
```

Results in embedding an object into a Word for Windows document. For example,

```
{embed ExcelChart \s  \* mergeformat}
```

embeds a Microsoft Excel chart into the document. For more information, see Chapter 33, "Using Word with Other Windows Applications."

{=}

Syntax:

```
{= formula}
```

Displays the result of a mathematical calculation, such as

```
{ = Sales - Cost}
```

Expressions can use bookmarks to define the locations of numbers or can use row and column locations in document tables. See Chapter 5, "Editing a Document," to learn how to create bookmarks. Calculations on bookmarks can use common arithmetic operators, such as + (plus) and * (multiply). Calculations on row and column contents in a table use functions such as Average, Count, Sum, and Product. Calculations are described in Chapter 20, "Calculating Math Formulas."

Updates when you press F9 or print merged documents. If the expression is in the header or footer, it is updated once when you print.

Following are examples of expression fields:

Field Code	Result
{= Sales - Cost}	Subtracts the value in Cost from the value in Sales.
{= if (Sales > 450,Sales*.1,Sales*.05)}	Tests whether the value in Sales is greater than 450; if it is, the result is the Sales value multiplied by .1; if not, the result is the sales value multiplied by .05.
{= if (Sales > 450,Sales*.1,Sales*.05)*2}	Multiplies the result of the if statement by two.

Note

If you need to create a large mathematical expression, build it in pieces within the field characters. As you complete each integral unit (one that can calculate by itself), select the entire field and press F9 to see whether the result is correct. Select the completed expression and press Ctrl+F9 to enclose that expression in another set of field characters. This method enables you to find errors in construction as you go rather instead of trying to find problems in a large completed expression.

You can lose a bookmark used in calculations by carelessly deleting a character. If you delete a value as well as the spaces that enclosed the value, you may have deleted the bookmark. In this case the formula no longer works because the bookmark no longer exists. You can re-create the bookmark to restore the formula. If you are in doubt as to whether a bookmark still exists, press F5 twice and select the bookmark. See whether the correct value is selected in the document. If the bookmark is a name with data stored in it rather than a document location, you may not be able to go to the bookmark.

Use the following math operators with bookmarks only:

Operation	Operator
Plus	+
Minus	-
Multiply	*
Divide	/
Exponentiate	^
Less than	<
Less than or equal to	<=
Greater than	>
Greater than or equal to	>=
Parenthetical	( )
Absolute value	Abs
Integer	Int
Sign	Sign
Test for error	Define

IX

Automating Your Work

(continues)

(continued)

Operation	Operator
Modulus (remainder)	Mod
Round	Round
And	And
Or	Or
Not	Not

When you refer to a cell in a table, use the A1 format, where rows are numbered starting with 1 and going down. Columns have letters beginning with A at the leftmost. If the expression is in the same table as the cells, only the A1 reference in brackets, [], is needed.

You should use the functions and operators in the following table for any math calculations within a table. Chapter 20, "Calculating Math with Formulas," covers math in tables. Functions can result to 1 for TRUE or 0 for FALSE.

Function	Name/Examples	Type/Result
Abs	Absolute value `{= Abs -4}`	Operator Results in 4
And	Logical And `{= And (Sales>500,Cost<300}`	Operator Returns 1 if both arguments are true; 0 if either argument is false (maximum of two arguments).
Average	Averages arguments `{= Average (Budget[R1C1:R1C2])}`	Reduction function Averages the content of cells in row 1, column 1 and row 1, column 2 from the table named Budget.
Count	Counts arguments `{= Count (Budget[C1])}`	Reduction function Counts the number of numeric items in the cells of column 1 in the table Budget. Empty cells and text count as zero.

Function	Name/Examples	Type/Result
`Defined`	Checks for errors `{Defined (Sales)}`	Operator Results in 1 if Sales bookmark exists and expression evaluates without error; otherwise, results in 0.
`Int`	Results in integer `{= Int (Sales)}`	Operator Deletes decimal fraction of an argument. To round numbers, use the Round operator.
`Max`	Returns largest argument `{= Max (Budget[R1C1:R2C2])}`	Reduction function Returns the maximum value in the table named Budget within the range R1C1 to R2C2.
`Min`	Returns smallest argument `{= Min (Budget[R1C1:R2C2])}`	Reduction function Returns the maximum value in the table named Budget within the range R1C1 to R2C2.
`Mod`	Returns remainder `{= Mod (500,23.6)}`	Operator Returns the modulus. In the example, it is the remainder of 500 divided by 23.6.
`Not`	Reverses logical value `{= Not (Test)}`	Operator Returns 1 if the Test is 0 or if condition in Test is false; returns 0 if the Test is not zero or if condition in Test is true.
`Or`	Logical Or `{=Or (Sales$mt500,Cost$lt300)}`	Operator Returns 1 if either condition is true; returns 0 if either condition is false.
`{= Product (Budget[R1C1:R2C1],2)}`		Returns the product of values in the range R1C1 to R2C1 of the table Budget and the number 2.
`Round`	Rounds value to specified digits `{= Round (SalesTotal,2)}`	Operator Returns the value of SalesTotal rounded to two decimal places.

IX

Automating Your Work

(continues)

(continued)

Function	Name/Example	Type/Result
Sign	Tests for sign of arguments	Operator
	{= Sign (Profit)}	Returns 1 if Profit is positive, 0 if Profit is zero, or –1 if Profit is negative.
Sum	Totals arguments	Reduction function
	{= Sum(Budget[R1C1:R2C1])}	Returns the sum of values in the range R1C1 to R2C1 of the table Budget.

{filename}

Syntax:

```
{filename}
```

Results in the file name as shown in the Summary Info box.

Updates when you press F9, when you choose mail merge documents, or if in the header or footer, when you choose the File Print command.

{fillin}

Syntax:

```
{fillin [" "prompt"] switch}
```

Produces a dialog box, like the one shown in fig. 37.5, that displays a generic box used for data entry. You can type a response in the dialog box. The result appears at the field location or can be used by other fields in which {fillin} is nested. Enclose the prompt and default text in quotation marks. {fillin} is also demonstrated in Chapter 15, "Mastering Envelopes, Mail Merge, and Form Letters," in descriptions about automating mail merge.

Updates when you press F9 or when you mail merge. Updates once in header or footer when you choose the File Print command.

Switch	Result
\d	Default text follows the switch. The default text appears in the text edit of the dialog box and is used if no entry is made. Enclose the default text in quotation marks. Use \d " " if you do not want any text to appear in the dialog box.

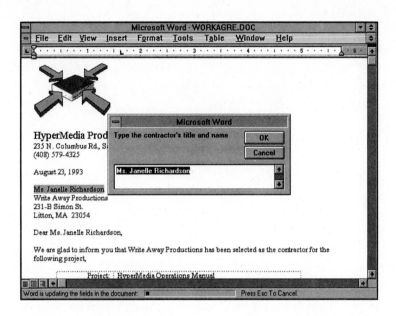

Fig. 37.5
Fillin fields display
a data entry dialog
box that displays a
message prompt-
ing the user to
type a correct
entry.

For example, you can add the following:

```
{FILLIN "Type your company." \d "MegaCorp" \* mergeformat}
```

{gotobutton}

Syntax:

```
{gotobutton destination button_text}
```

Produces a button in the document at the field's location. Double-clicking this button (or selecting the field by pressing F11 and pressing Alt+Shift+F9) moves the insertion point to the *destination*. Use any destination you would when you're using F5 (Go To). *destination* can be any location acceptable to the Edit Go To command.

Create a button to surround the *button_text* by putting the field into a single-celled table or into a paragraph and then formatting it to have a border. The *button_text* appears within the button. Do not enclose *button_text* in quotation marks.

{if}

Syntax:

```
{if expr1 oper expr2 if_true_text if_false_text}
```

Use this field when you want Word for Windows to change a field action or result depending on some value or text in the document. The {if} field uses the operator *oper* to compare the value of *expr1* to *exper2*.

expr1 and *expr2* can be bookmarks of selected text, bookmarks assigned to store text, or R1C1 cell addresses from a table. *oper* is a mathematical operator separated from the *expr1* and *expr2* arguments by spaces. Allowed operators include the following:

=	equal
>	greater than
>=	greater than or equal to
<	less than
<=	less than or equal to
<>	not equal to

if_true_text is a result that produces text when the *expr1 oper expr2* statement is true. *if_false_text* is the result when the statement is false. If they are text, enclose them in quotation marks. Consider the following example:

```
{if daysdue >= 30 "As a reminder, your account is more than thirty
days overdue." "Thank you for your business."}
```

If the `daysdue` bookmark contains 12 when the field is updated, the field results in `Thank you for your business.` If the `daysdue` bookmark contains 45 when the field is updated, the field results in `As a reminder, your account is more than thirty days overdue.`

Updates when you press F9 or when you mail merge. If in a header or footer, updates when you choose the File Print command. See also `{nextif}` and `{skipif}`.

{includepicture}
Syntax:

```
{includepicture filename [\c converter]}
```

Inserts the contents of the *filename*. Use `\c` *converter* to specify a converter file if the included file must be translated before being imported. You insert the `{includepicture}` by using the Insert Picture command.

Switch	Result
\c	Specifies the converter file to be used for files Word for Windows does not convert automatically. The appropriate converter file must have been installed in Word.

{includetext}

Syntax:

```
{includetext filename [bookmark] [\c converter]}
```

Inserts the contents of the *filename* at the location *bookmark*. Use `\c con-verter` to specify a converter file if the included file must be translated before being imported. The `{includetext}` is described in Chapter 32, "Assembling Large Documents."

Switch	Result
\c	Specifies the converter file to be used for files Word for Windows does not convert automatically. The appropriate converter file must have been installed in Word.

{index}

Syntax:

```
{index [switches]}
```

Accumulates all the text and page numbers from the `{xe}` (index entry) fields or from outline headings and then builds an index. Insert this field by choosing the Insert Index And Tables command. See also `{xe}`.

You use *switches* to specify the range of the indexes or the separator characters:

Switch	Result
\b	Specifies the amount of text indexed
\c	Creates multicolumn indexes
\d	Specifies the separator character between a sequence number and a page number
\e	Specifies the separator character between the index entry and page number
\f	Creates indexes using xe fields of a specified type
\g	Specifies the page range separator
\h	Specifies heading letter formats used to separate alphabetical groups
\l	Specifies the page number separator
\p	Specifies the alphabetical range of the index
\r	Puts sublevel indexes on the same level
\s	Includes the sequence number with page number

{info}

Syntax:

```
{[info] type ["new_value"]}
```

Results in information from the Summary Info dialog box according to the *type* you use. Available types include the following:

```
author          numpages

comments        numwords

createdate      printdate

edittime        revnum

filename        savedate

keywords        subject

lastsavedby     template

numchars        title
```

Updates when you press F9 or when you print merge. If in the header or footer, when you choose the File Print command.

{keywords}

Syntax:

```
{keywords ["new_key_words"]}
```

Inserts or replaces the key words from the Summary Info box.

Updates when you press F9 or when you print merge. If in the header or footer, when you choose the File Print command.

{lastsavedby}

Syntax:

```
{lastsavedby}
```

Inserts the name of the last person to save the document, as shown in the Summary Info box.

Updates when you press F9, or when you print merge. If in the header or footer, when you choose the File Print command.

{link}

Syntax:

```
{link class_name file_name [place_reference] [switches]}
```

Links the contents of a file into the Word for Windows document. The link is created using the Edit Paste Special command with the Paste Link option. This field updates when you press F9.

If the linked file cannot be updated, the results remain unchanged.

Switch	Result
\a	Updates link when source data change
\b	Inserts a Windows bit map
\d	Does not store graphic data with file (smaller file size)
\p	Inserts linked data as a picture
\r	Inserts linked data as an RTF file (with converted formatting)
\t	Inserts linked data as text

{macrobutton}

Syntax:

```
{macrobutton macroname instruction_text}
```

Displays the *instruction_text* on-screen. The macro specified by *macroname* runs when you double-click the on-screen *instruction_text* or select it and press Alt+Shift+F9. Create a button to surround the text by putting the field into a single-celled table or into a paragraph and then formatting it to have a border. The *instruction_text* must fit on one line. Do not enclose *instruction_text* in quotation marks.

{mergefield}

Syntax:

```
{mergefield merge_name}
```

Inserted using the Tools Mail Merge command. Defines the field, column, of data used at this location from the source file.

Do not edit this field code.

{mergerec}

Syntax:

```
{mergerec}
```

Inserts the number of the current print merge record.

{mergeseq}

Syntax:

```
{mergeseq}
```

Inserts the number of the current print merge sequence.

{next}

Syntax:

```
{next}
```

No result appears, but the field instructs Word for Windows to use the next record in the data file. {next} is used in mailing label templates, for example, to increment the mailing list from one record (label) to the next. {next} is inserted in labels created from the MAILLABL template.

{nextif}

Syntax:

```
{nextif expr1 oper expr2}
```

No result appears. {nextif} acts like a combination of the {if} and {next} fields. You can use {nextif} to specify a condition that data file records must satisfy before you use them for mail merge or form letters.

{numchars}

Syntax:

```
{numchars}
```

Inserts the number of characters in the document as shown in the Summary Info box.

Updates when you press F9 or when you print merge. If in a header or footer, updates when you choose the File Print command.

{numpages}

Syntax:

```
{numpages}
```

Inserts the number of pages contained in the document when it was last printed or updated. The number comes from the Summary Info box. See also {page}.

Updates when you press F9 or when you print merge. If in a header or footer, updates when you choose the File Print command.

{numwords}
Syntax:

```
{numwords}
```

Inserts the number of words in the document as shown in the Summary Info box.

Updates when you press F9 or when you print merge. If in a header or footer, updates when you choose the File Print command.

{page}
Syntax:

```
{page [page_format_picture] [switch]}
```

Inserts the page number for the page where the field code is located. Use numeric picture or format switches to format the number.

Updates when you press F9 or when you print merge. If in a header or footer, updates when you choose the File Print command.

{pageref}
Syntax:

```
{pageref bookmark |* format switch}
```

Results in the page number on which bookmark is located. This field produces a cross-reference page number that updates itself.

Updates when you select it and press F9, or when you choose the File Print command.

{print}
Syntax:

```
{print ""printer_instructions"}
```

Sends the printer_instructions text string directly to the printer without translation. You use this field to send printer control codes to a printer or to send PostScript programs to a PostScript printer.

IX

Automating Your Work

{printdate}

Syntax:

```
{printdate [|@ Date_time-picture] [switch]}
```

Inserts the date on which the document was last printed, as shown in the Summary Info box. The default date format comes from the Control Panel. For other date formats, use a date-time picture, as described in the section "Formatting Date-Time Results" earlier in this chapter.

{quote}

Syntax:

```
{quote ""literal_text""}
```

Inserts the *literal_text* in the document. Update by selecting the field code and pressing F9 or by printing with print merge.

{rd}

Syntax:

```
{rd filename}
```

No result appears. {rd} helps you create a table of contents or index for large documents that cross multiple files. See Chapter 32, "Assembling Large Documents," for more information.

{ref}

Syntax:

```
{[ref] bookmark [switches]}
```

Results in the contents of the *bookmark*, which specifies a selection of text. The formatting of the bookmark displays as in the original. You can use a bookmark within field characters, such as {datedue}, and produce the same result as {ref datedue}. You must use the {ref bookmark} form, however, to avoid using bookmark names that conflict with field types. If a bookmark's name conflicts with that of a field type—{ask}, for example—use {ref ask} whenever you want to refer to the bookmark.

Updates when you press F9 or when you print merge. If in the header or footer, updates when you choose the File Print command.

{revnum}

Syntax:

```
{revnum}
```

Inserts the number of times the document has been revised, as shown in the Summary Info box. This number changes when the document is saved.

Updates when you select the field and press F9, or when you print merge. If in the header or footer, updates when you choose the File Print command.

{savedate}

Syntax:

```
{savedate}
```

Inserts the date the document was last saved, as shown in the Summary Info box. To change formats, use a date-time-picture, as described in "Formatting Date-Time Results" earlier in this chapter.

Updates when you select the field and press F9, or when you print merge. If in the header or footer, updates when you choose the File Print command.

{section}

Syntax:

```
{section}
```

Inserts the current section's number.

Updates when you select the field and press F9, or when you print merge. If in the header or footer, updates when you choose the File Print command.

{seq}

Syntax:

```
{seq seq_id [bookmark] [switches]}
```

Inserts a number to create a numbered sequence of items. Use this field for numbering figures, illustrations, tables, and so on. *seq_id* specifies the name of the sequence, such as Figure. *bookmark* specifies a cross-reference to the sequence number of a bookmarked item. If you insert the following field wherever you need a figure number,

```
{ref chap}.{seq figure_num}
```

the field produces an automatically numbered sequence of chapter number, period, and figure number—5.12. You must define the bookmark chap at the beginning of the document, and it must contain the number of the chapter. figure_num tracks only a specific sequence of items.

IX

Automating Your Work

Updates the entire sequence when you select the entire document and press F9. Unlink (fix as values) the figure numbers by selecting them and pressing Shift+Ctrl+F9.

Switch	Result
\c	Inserts the sequence number of the nearest preceding item in a numbered sequence.
\n	Inserts the next sequence number. If no switch is used, Word for Windows defaults to \n.
\r	Resets the sequence number as specified. The following field restarts the sequence numbering to 1 when it reaches 10, for example: {seq figurenum \r 10}.

{set}

Syntax:

```
{set bookmark ""text""}
```

No result appears. Use this field to store text (data) in a bookmark. You then can use the bookmark in multiple locations to repeat that text. See also {ref}.

{set} is not allowed in annotations, footnotes, headers, or footers.

Updates when you select the field and press F9, or when you print merge.

{skipif}

Syntax:

```
{skipif expr1 oper expr2}
```

No result displays. You use this command in print merge to skip merges to meet specified conditions.

Updates when you print merge.

{styleref}

Syntax:

```
{styleref "style_id" [switch]}
```

Displays the text of the nearest paragraph containing the specified style, *style_id*. This field is useful for accumulating headings and topics that contain a specific style; for example, to create a dictionary-like heading.

{subject}

Syntax:

```
{subject ["new_subject"]}
```

Inserts or replaces the subject found in the Summary Info box.

Updates when you select the field and press F9, or when you print merge.

{symbol}

Syntax:

```
{symbol character [switches]}
```

Inserts a symbol character. Inserted by using the Insert Symbol command.

Switch	Result
\f	Font set used, {symbol 169 \f "courier new bold"}
\s	Font size used, {symbol 169 \f Helv \s 12}

{tc}

Syntax:

```
{tc ""text"" [switch] [table_id]}
```

No result shows. {tc} marks the page and associates a text entry for later use when building a table of contents. See also {toc}.

text is the text that should appear in the table of contents.

table_id is a single letter used to identify a distinct table. This letter should follow the \f switch, with one space between the switch and the *table_id* letter.

Switch	Result
\f	Defines this {tc} as belonging to the table indicated by the *table_id*. This switch enables you to accumulate tables of contents for different topics.
\l	Specifies the level number for the table entry. The default is 1.

IX

Automating Your Work

{template}

Syntax:

{template *[switches]*}

Inserts the name of the document's template as shown in the Summary Info dialog box.

Updates when you select the field and press F9, or when you print merge. If in the header or footer, updates when you choose the **File Print** command.

{time}

Syntax:

{time *[time_format_picture]*}

Results in the time or date when the field was updated. Reformat by using a *time_format_picture*, as described in "Formatting Date-Time Results" earlier in this chapter.

Updates when you select the field and press F9, or when you choose the **File Print** command.

{title}

Syntax:

{title *["new_title"]*}

Inserts or replaces the document title as shown in the Summary Info box.

Updates when you select the field and press F9, or when you print merge. If in the header or footer, updates when you choose the **File Print** command.

{toc}

Syntax:

{toc *[switches]*}

Shows a table of contents built by accumulating the text and page numbers of {tc} fields throughout the document. Constructing a table of contents based on {tc} fields is described in Chapter 29, "Creating Indexes and Tables of Contents."

Switch	Result
\a	Builds a table of figures with no labels or numbers.
\b	Builds a table of contents for the area of the document defined by the bookmark, as in {toc \b firstpart}.

Switch	Result
\c	Use SEQ as a table identifier.
\d	Defines a sequence separator number.
\f	Builds a table of contents from {tc} fields with specific tableids.
	The following field builds a table of contents from only those fields with the tableid graphs: {toc \f graphs}.
\l	Controls the entry levels used in the table of contents.
\o	Builds a table of contents from the outline headings. The following field builds a table of contents from the outline using heading levels 1, 2, and 3: {toc \o 1-3}
\p	Defines the separator between a table entry and its page number.
\s	Uses a sequence type to identify the sequence used in the table of contents.

{xe}

Syntax:

```
{xe "index_text" [switch]}
```

No result appears. Specifies the text and associated page number used to generate an index. You generate the index by choosing the Insert Index and Tables command. See Chapter 29, "Creating Indexes and Tables of Contents," for examples.

Switch	Result
\b	Toggles the page numbers for boldface.
\f	Specifies the type. Indexes can be built on this specific type of XE.
\i	Toggles the page numbers for italic.
\r	Specifies a range of pages to be indexed.
\t	Specifies the use of text in place of page numbers.

IX

Automating Your Work

From Here...

For information about how you use field codes to do specific tasks or how some commands insert field codes in documents, refer to the following chapters:

- Chapter 13, "Setting the Page Layout," page numbering and use of field codes.

- Chapter 15, "Mastering Envelopes, Mail Merge, and Form Letters," inserting merge codes to control what data fields are used in merge documents.

- Chapter 17, "Creating Bulleted or Numbered Lists," using field codes that insert bullets, symbols, and sequential numbers.

- Chapter 18, "Building Forms and Fill-In Dialog Boxes," inserting field codes that produce text boxes, check boxes, and pull-down lists.

- Chapter 20, "Calculating Math with Formulas," using field codes to work on numbers in tables or bookmarks.

- Chapter 22, "Inserting Pictures in Your Document," using field codes that link pictures to a file.

- Chapter 28, "Inserting Footnotes and Endnotes," using field codes that control footnotes and endnotes and their style.

- Chapter 29, "Creating Indexes and Tables of Contents," using field codes that compile indexes and tables of content.

- Chapter 30, "Tracking Revisions and Annotations," using field codes that display or hide annotations.

- Chapter 31, "Adding Cross-References and Captions," using field codes that enable you to link and update cross-references between bookmarks or section titles.

- Chapter 32, "Assembling Large Documents," using field codes that control the order, page numbering, indexes, and tables of contents when you construct a document from many files.

- Chapter 33, "Using Word with Other Windows Applications," using field codes that specify how linked data between documents will be controlled.

Chapter 38

Recording and Editing Macros

Word for Windows macros enable you to automate frequent procedures and command choices with minimal effort. The easiest way to create a macro is to record your keystrokes and commands with the macro recorder. You also can modify recorded macros or write them directly—once you know WordBASIC, the programming language included with Word for Windows. You can test and modify your macros using the Word for Windows macro editor.

You can assign your macros or Word for Windows built-in commands to buttons in your documents, buttons on toolbars, custom menu commands, or new shortcut keys. You can turn Word for Windows into a word processor specially designed to handle the work you face or the industry you are in.

In some word processors, all automation must be done with macros. Word for Windows is more powerful and flexible. Word for Windows also gives you styles, AutoFormats, Style Gallery, field codes, and AutoText entries to make your work easier. Many of the tasks performed by macros in other word processors can be done more efficiently with these features:

Feature	Function
Styles	Manually applies a collection of formats. Redefining the collection of formats in a style changes the appearance of the style throughout the document
AutoFormats	Automatically applies styles to documents that have a consistent layout
Style Gallery	Displays a list of named document types. Selecting from the list shows you what your document will look like using this predefined layout and style

This chapter is an introduction to using the macro language, WordBASIC, that comes with Word. In this chapter, you learn how to do the following:

- Record macros

- Save macros for use with any document or for use with a specific document

- Run macros that are global or specific to a template

- Edit macros that you have recorded

IX

Automating Your Work

(continues)

(continued)

Feature	Function
Field codes	Automates entries such as the current date or filling a form
AutoText	Repeats frequently used text, tables, or pictures

If you need to accomplish a mix of these features or automate an entire task involving multiple features, then use macros.

This chapter introduces you to the fundamentals of macros. To learn how to make your recorded macros work better, read Chapter 39, "Building More Advanced Macros."

Recording Macros

Macros can be recordings of keystrokes and commands or sophisticated programs you build. Even simple recorded macros can signficantly improve your work efficiency. Some of the simple tasks and procedures you can easily automate with a macro include the following:

- Opening, selecting, and updating a document filled with field codes

- Adding custom zoom or edit buttons to the toolbar

- Creating a shortcut key to toggle table gridlines on or off

- Opening and arranging collections of files that are used together

- Removing styles or heading levels

- Opening a document and immediately moving to the last location edited

- Opening a document and immediately switching to outline view

- Storing different display and work settings so you can switch between them easily

- Copying selected data from the active sheet to the end of a second document

- Requesting data from the user, checking it, and entering it in a bookmark (a hidden location placeholder)

■ Reformatting the active document to meet prerecorded layout and print settings

Deciding How Your Macro Will Work

Before you create a macro, you need to decide whether it affects a specific portion of the document, the currently selected portion, or the entire document. If the macro always affects a specific part of a document, insert bookmarks in the document that name the specific text or graphic so that the macro can find these parts easily. If you want a macro to work on whatever is selected when you run it, then make your selection before you begin recording the macro.

You also must decide whether you want to make a *global macro* (a macro that can be used with any document) or a *template macro* (a macro that can be used only with documents based on that template).

Specifying Where Macros Are Stored

Macros are stored in three different ways—as commands, global macros, or template macros. *Commands* are built-in macros stored within the Word for Windows program, WINWORD.EXE. Many of these built-in macros are menu commands, such as File New or Bold. Many of these commands do not exist on the menu, but are useful when added to a shortcut key or toolbar button, or used within one of your macros. Macros that you record or write are stored as a *global* or *template* macro. Global macros are stored in the NORMAL.DOT template and are available to all documents and templates. Template macros are stored in a specific template and are available to only those documents based on that template.

You can ensure that a macro is available in all documents by declaring it as a global macro. If you store too many macros as global macros, however, you clutter your NORMAL.DOT file with macros used for a specific purpose or for a specific document. You should save macros designed for a specific purpose with the appropriate template. Save macros as a global macro only when they need to be shared by many documents.

Tip
Storing a macro as a global macro ensures that it is available in all documents.

When you record your macro you will be given the opportunity of selecting whether the macro will be a global macro, stored in NORMAL.DOT and available to all documents, or whether it will be stored in a specific template and available only to documents based on that template. Should you change your mind later about where you want the macro stored, you can use the Organizer, described in Chapter 39, "Building More Advanced Macros," to copy the macro from one template to another.

IX

Automating Your Work

Preparing to Record a Macro

Before you record a macro, there are a few things you may want to do in preparation. This preparation is something that becomes automatic after you have recorded a few macros, but if you are new to the process, running through the following checklist can prevent you from having to re-create the macro many times. You should consider the following items in the order they are described:

1. Practice the procedure you want to record and know the order in which you want to choose commands or select items.

2. Decide whether you want the macro to be global, so any document can use it, or to be template specific, so only documents based on that template can use it.

3. Decide on a macro name that is descriptive, but does not include spaces or unusual characters. It must begin with a letter.

4. Decide how you want to run your macro. They can be run from the Tools Macro command, a button on the document, a toolbar button, a custom menu command, a shortcut key. Macros also can be run automatically when you open or close a document, or start or exit Word.

5. Open a document of the type in which you want to use the macro. If you want the macro available to all documents, then the document should be based on NORMAL.DOT. If you want to use the macro only with documents from a specific template, then open a document based on that template. You can see which template a document is based on by choosing the File Templates command.

Tip
Before you start recording your macro, make sure the appropriate template is open.

The template you want your macro stored in must be open before you start recording. This does not mean you have to open the DOT file that contains a template. Opening a document based on a template automatically opens the template and hides it.

Prepare the document so it is in the same condition in which you would begin the manual work that you now want to automate.

Decide whether you want to select the text or object and then run the macro, or if you want the macro to make the text and object selections. The first case enables you to use the macro on items you select manually. In the second case, the macro will always try to find the same text or object.

Decide how you want to move or make selections during the recording. Some of the most frequent ways of recording moves and selections are

- Naming a location with the Edit **B**ookmark command before the recording starts. During the recording you can then select or return to that named location with Edit Go To.

- Moving to a relative or specific position in the document using the Edit G**o** To command and any move code described in Chapter 5, "Editing a Document." You can use locations such as P12L2, page 12 line 2.

- Moving to the last edited location, Shift+F5.

- Moving to the beginning of the document, Ctrl+Home.

- Moving to the end of the document, Ctrl+End.

- Selecting the entire document with Edit Select All or Ctrl+A.

- Not selecting anything, so the macro affects whatever is selected when you run it.

What Gets Recorded

Before you record a macro you need to understand what is recorded while the recorder is on. This will help keep you from recording unwanted changes, help you when you need to delete actions from a recorded macro, and will help you set up Word prior to starting the macro recorder.

Dialog boxes are only recorded if you choose OK. The settings for all options in the dialog box are recorded. If you don't want some of the options to change when the macro runs, then you must edit the macro and remove the dialog options you don't want changed. (This is easy if you read this chapter and the following one.) Dialog boxes that contain tabs, such as Tools **O**ptions, only record the contents of a tab when you choose OK in that tab. For example, if you want to record Save, View, and Edit options, then you must choose the Tools Options command for each set of options, select the options, then choose OK. You must do this once for each set of options.

Some items, such as the Ruler, toggle between on and off. The macro recorder records a single statement, `ViewRuler`. If the Ruler is already on, then `ViewRuler` turns the Ruler off. If the Ruler is off, then `ViewRuler` turns the Ruler on. That means that running a recorded macro could actually turn off the Ruler when you wanted it to stay on.

Some macro statements, such as ViewNormal, only record when you change to it. If you are in page layout view and switch to normal view, the ViewNormal statement is recorded. But, if you are already in normal view and you select the View Normal command, nothing is recorded.

Recording a Macro

Mouse actions are limited while the recorder is on. You can choose commands, but you cannot move or select within the document. If you are unfamiliar with using the keyboard to select or move, see the list of keyboard methods in the previous section and read the descriptions on using the keyboard and the Edit Go To command in Chapter 5, "Editing a Document."

To record a macro, follow these steps:

1. If you plan to use the macro with a template, open a document based on that template. If you plan to make the macro global, open any document.

2. Choose the Tools Macro command, then choose the Record button. Alternatively, you can double-click the REC indicator in the Status bar or click the Record button on the Macro toolbar. The Record Macro dialog box appears (see fig. 38.1).

   This starts the macro recorder. The REC indicator in the Status bar appears bold when recording is on and the Macro Stop and Pause tools appear on-screen.

3. Type the macro's name in the Record Macro Name text box.

   Enter a descriptive name. Macro names must begin with a letter and can be up to 36 characters long. Do not use spaces. A combination of uppercase and lowercase letters is best (PrintEnvelope, for example).

Fig. 38.1

Type macro names that begin with a letter and are up to 36 characters in length.

4. If you want to assign the macro to a tool on a toolbar, a command on a menu, or a shortcut key combination, then choose one of the buttons in the Assign Macro To group. (Assigning macros is described in Chapter 36, "Customizing the Toolbar, Menus, and Shortcut Keys.") If you do not assign the macro, you can run it from the Tools Macro command. If you want, you can assign or reassign macros after the macro has been created.

5. Select the template in which to store your macro from the Make Macro Available To pull-down list. This list only shows templates for documents that are open.

6. Enter a description in the Description text box to help you remember what the macro does. This description displays in the Macro dialog box and in the Status bar.

7. Choose OK.

The REC indicator in the Status bar changes to bold and the Macro Recording toolbar displays at the top left of the document window. The recorder is on and recording all your commands and keyboard actions.

If you want to pause the macro momentarily so you can check commands or the document, click the Macro Pause tool in the Macro Recording toolbar. Click the tool a second time to restart macro recording.

Complete the process you want to record. If you make a mistake, choose the Edit Undo command as you would normally. If you are in a dialog box, choosing Cancel prevents the dialog box from being recorded. Text that has just been typed and is backspaced out is not recorded.

To stop the recording, choose the Tools Macro command, then choose the Stop Recorder button to turn off the macro recorder. Choose Close to close the Macro dialog box. If you are using the mouse, you can click the Macro Stop button on the Macro Recording toolbar. The REC indicator in the status bar turns gray when the recording stops.

Recording a Sample Macro

The following procedure illustrates how easily you can record a macro. Follow these steps to record a macro that sets up Word for Windows screens and options for the way you might want to work. This type of macro is convenient when many people use the same computer, but each person prefers different custom settings. Running the macro enables you to quickly restore toolbar, view, and other settings.

Tip

The macro recorder does not record commands used inside applets like the Equation Editor or Microsoft Graph.

IX

Automating Your Work

Before starting the recorder, set up Word for Windows so the commands and options you choose will be recorded. The previous section, titled "What Gets Recorded," describes some rules about preparing to record.

To make sure this macro records your toolbar selections, makes the transition to normal view, and turns the Ruler on, prepare Word for Windows. Hide all toolbars with the View Toolbars command. Turn off the Ruler with the **View Ruler** command. Choose the View Page Layout command so the transition back to normal view will be recorded.

To turn on the recorder and name your macro, follow these steps:

1. Open a document. Since this will be a global macro attached to NORMAL.DOT, any document will do.

2. Choose the Tools Macro command, then choose the Record button or double-click the REC indicator in the status bar to display the Record Macro dialog box.

3. Type **MyWorkspace** in the Record Macro Name text box.

4. Skip the Assign Macro To group. You can use the methods in Chapter 36, "Customizing the Toolbar, Menus, and Shortcut Keys," to assign the macro at a later time.

5. Select the All Documents (NORMAL.DOT) item from the Make Macro Available To list.

6. Enter **Changes Word to my workspace settings** in the Description text box as shown in fig. 38.2.

Fig. 38.2

The Record Macro dialog box enables you to name the macro, store it in a template, and assign it to a toolbar, menu, or keystroke.

7. Choose OK.

The macro recorder is now on. The Macro Recording toolbar will appear on-screen. Follow the next steps to record the MyWorkspace macro:

1. Choose the View Normal command to return the screen to normal view.

2. Choose the View Ruler command to display the ruler that you had previously turned off.

3. Choose the View Toolbars command and select the Standard, Formatting, and Drawing check boxes. Deselect the Macro Record check box, which is on because you are recording a macro. (This will hide it so you will not be able to use it to pause or stop the macro.) Choose OK.

4. Choose the View Zoom command, enter **85%** in the Percent edit box. Choose OK.

5. Choose the Tools Options command, then select the Edit tab. Select the Typing Replaces Selection and Drag-and-Drop Text Editing check box. Choose OK to record your selections for this tab.

6. Choose the Tools Options command, then select the Save tab. Select the Allow Fast Saves check box and deselect the Automatic Save Every __ Minutes check box. Choose OK to record your selections for this tab.

7. Double-click the REC indicator. Alternatively, choose the Tools Macro command, then choose the Stop Recording button, and finally choose Close.

To save the macro, choose the File Save All command. If you attempt to close a document attached to a template and that template contains an unsaved macro, you will be asked whether you want to save changes to the template.

Your macro is now stored in the NORMAL.DOT template, so it will be available no matter which document is active. Keep the MyWorkspace macro you just recorded; you will use it when you learn how to edit a macro.

Troubleshooting Recording a Macro

After restarting Word, the macro is no longer available.

This problem may be caused by two different things. You may have forgotten to save the macro, or you may have stored the macro in a template that is not available when you restart Word. To make sure you save a macro after recording it, choose the File Save All command. When you are asked whether you want to save changes to the template, respond with a yes. The second problem occurs if you save the macro to a specific template rather than saving it to the NORMAL.DOT template. Macros that are stored in a specific DOT file are only available when a document based on that template (DOT file) is open.

While recording a macro, the wrong command is chosen.

For Related Information
■ "Creating a New Template," p. 179
■ "Marking Locations with Bookmarks," p. 149

If you are in a dialog box while the recorder is on, choose the Cancel button or press Esc to close the dialog box. None of your selections in the dialog box will be recorded. If you have already completed a command or closed a dialog box, then choose the Edit Undo command and the last command will be removed from the macro. If too many commands have been choosen to use the Edit Undo command, then use the editing techniques at the end of this chapter and the next chapter to remove the incorrect macro statement from the recording. Remember which command you want removed. The macro statement you want to remove will have a similar name.

Running a Macro

After you record a macro, you should test it. Save your document so that if the macro doesn't do what you wanted, you can recover your document and edit it.

The following list describes the ways you can run a macro:

■ Select the macro from the Macro dialog box, then choose the **Run** button.

■ Create an Auto macro that runs when you open or close a document, or start or exit Word for Windows.

■ Click a {MACROBUTTON} field code in a document. {MACROBUTTON} field codes display a button in a document that runs a macro. See Chapter 37 to learn about inserting field codes.

■ Click a standard or custom tool in a toolbar.

■ Choose a custom command from a menu.

■ Press a shortcut key combination.

■ Run the macro under the control of another macro.

■ Run the macro under the control of a Dynamic Data Exchange command.

The Auto macros are described in the following chapter. Creating custom tools, buttons, commands, and shortcut keys is described in Chapter 36, "Customizing the Toolbar, Menus, and Shortcut Keys."

You can run a global macro at any time because NORMAL.DOT is always available. If you want to run a macro that is stored in a specific template, then you must have an open document that is based on that template.

To run a macro, follow these steps:

1. Activate a document on which the macro is designed to work. If the macro is designed to work with items preselected, select those items.

2. Choose the Tools Macro command to display the Macro dialog box. See fig. 38.3.

Fig. 38.3
A shortcut for running the macro is to double-click its name in the Macro dialog box.

3. Select from the Macros Available In pull-down list the location of the macro—All Active Templates, NORMAL.DOT (global), or Word's built-in commands.

4. Select or type the macro or command name in the Macro Name list box.

5. Choose the Run button.

If you assigned your macro to a shortcut key, menu command, or tool, you also can run a macro by following Step 1 in the preceding steps, then pressing the macro shortcut key, choosing the command, or clicking the tool.

IX

Automating Your Work

Troubleshooting Macros

The macro does not appear in the Macro Name list of the Macro dialog box.

For Related Information

■ "Using Templates as a Pattern for Documents," p. 168

■ "Transferring Template Contents Using the Organizer," p. 182

■ "Putting a Command or Macro on a Toolbar," p. 1058

■ "Adding Commands to Menus," p. 1062

■ "Assigning Commands and Macros to Shortcut Keys," p. 1066

Make sure a document based on the template that contains your macro is open. Or open a new blank document based on that template. Choose the name of this document or template from the Macros Available In pull-down list of the Macro dialog box. If you want the macro to be available at all times, then use the Organizer to transfer a copy of the macro out of its current template into the NORMAL.DOT template.

Editing a Macro

The steps recorded by your macro are stored on a macro document as WordBASIC statements. You can see this document and edit these statements much like a normal document. By editing a macro, you can remove commands recorded by mistake, modify recorded commands, or make your macros more efficient.

You can view or edit your recorded macro, MyWorkspace, by following these steps:

1. Choose the Tools Macro command.

2. Select from the Macros Available In group where the macro is stored. (The MyWorkspace macro just recorded was stored in NORMAL.DOT and is global.)

3. Select or type the name in the **Macro Name** text box or list.

4. Choose Edit.

Fig. 38.4 shows the newly recorded macro, MyWorkspace, in the macro editing window.

When you open a macro for viewing or editing, Word for Windows displays a macro editing bar at the top of the screen. The buttons on the bar are helpful when you troubleshoot macros.

The title bar shows the name and context of the macro being displayed—Global: MyWorkspace. The macro begins with the words Sub MAIN and ends with End Sub. All macros within WordBASIC are considered *subroutines* (subprograms) that run under Word for Windows.

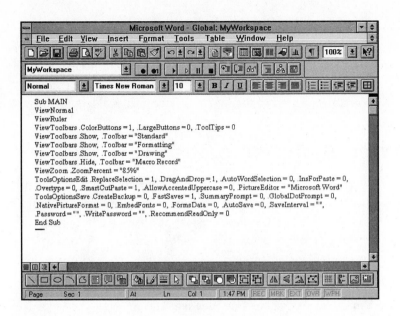

Fig. 38.4
Editing a macro uses the same editing techniques as a normal document. Macro statements match the command and options you chose during the recording.

In your recording, you started by choosing the View Normal command. Notice that the first statement is ViewNormal. Each statment that follows describes a command you chose.

Each item that follows ToolsOptionsEdit and ToolsOptionsSave corresponds to a selection in a list, edit box, option button, or check box. Notice that the items following these commands name an item in the dialog box. A 0 value indicates a check box is not selected; a 1 indicates that it is selected. You can get help and a greater explanation on any of these WordBASIC statements by clicking within the statement and pressing F1.

When you are in the macro editor, use standard Word for Windows editing procedures and menu commands to edit, type, or delete macro statements and functions. You can tab to indent lines. Tabs are in fixed locations and you cannot format the characters in the macro code.

The capability to edit macros is useful even if you only record macros and never program in WordBASIC. With simple edits you can correct typographical errors, delete commands, copy macros or parts of macros from one document or template to another, and reorganize a macro by cutting and pasting.

While a macro is open, the macro edit bar remains on-screen. You can switch between macro windows and other document windows like you would change between any Word for Windows documents; choose the document from the **W**indow menu, click an exposed portion, or press Ctrl+F6.

IX

Automating Your Work

For Related Information

- "Selecting Text," p. 133

- "Understanding and Modifying Recordings," p. 1139

To close your macro editing window, activate the macro's window. Then choose the document control menu icon by pressing Alt+- (hyphen). Choose the Close command. This closes the window and keeps the macro in memory. (It does not save the macro to disk.) If you choose the File Close command instead, you close the macro window and the document containing the macro.

Saving a Macro

Your new macro is stored in memory but is not automatically saved to disk. You can lose your macro if you forget to save it. Template macros must be saved before you close the template to which they are attached; global macros must be saved before you exit Word for Windows. Just as you save preliminary versions of documents every fifteen minutes or so, occasionally save versions of your macros to protect against accidental deletion.

For Related Information

- "Using Templates as a Pattern for Documents," p. 168

- "Transferring Template Contents Using the Organizer," p. 182

To save a macro to disk, choose the File Save All command. The Save All command goes through your open templates and documents, including any macros you opened to view or edit, and determines whether they have been newly created or changed. Word for Windows prompts you to specify whether to save the changes and newly created macros. If you close a document that has unsaved macros in its template, then you are given a chance to save the macros to the document. If you attempt to exit Word and there are global macros that have not been saved to the NORMAL.DOT template, then you will be asked if you want to save those macros.

Using Word for Windows Sample Macros

Word for Windows has sample macros associated with the templates saved in the WINWORD\TEMPLATE directory during installation. You can copy these macros from the sample templates to your own documents or templates using the Organizer as described in the next chapter.

Word comes with a collection of macros located on the template MACRO60.DOT. If you want to use, edit, or review these macros, use the File New command to open a document based on this template. Use the procedures described in this chapter to read a macro's description or edit the macro. Use the Organizer described in Chapter 39 to transfer one of the macros in MACRO60.DOT to another template.

From Here...

For information relating directly to recording macros, you may want to review the following major sections of this book:

- Chapter 6, "Using Templates as Master Documents." Templates act as a pattern for a new document. They store custom features such as macros that you define.

- Chapter 39, "Building More Advanced Macros," describes how to modify and troubleshoot recorded macros.

IX

Automating Your Work

Chapter 39

Building More Advanced Macros

After you learn how to record macros that perform small tasks, you should learn how to modify your recorded macros so they handle special situations, prompt the user for data entries, or operate automatically when you open or close documents. And none of these changes require learning how to program.

If you do want to learn how to program, you may want to learn more about WordBASIC. WordBASIC is the language in which macros are recorded. It is a version of the world's most-used programming language, BASIC. If you go beyond what this chapter teaches, you can learn how to write your own custom dialog boxes, control other Windows applications, and much more. But for now, this is the place to learn how to make your recorded macros even better.

Understanding and Modifying Recordings

When the macro recorder is on, every time you choose a command, tool, or shortcut key, Word stores a WordBASIC statement in a macro document. That WordBASIC statement is the equivalent of choosing the command. In most cases, you can read the statement and tell immediately which command is being referenced. Some of them are obvious, such as Bold, PasteFormat, or InsertTableOfContents.

One of the most familiar features of the Word for Windows program is its reliance on the dialog box to store information from the user. A dialog box is composed of one or more dialog elements: scrolling lists, check boxes, text boxes, option buttons, and so on. When you make a selection in a dialog

In this chapter, you learn how to do the following:

- Modify recorded macros

- Display an input dialog box and enter the typed information anywhere in your document

- Understand what is recorded from dialog box selections

- Run macros automatically

- Manage macros

- Debug macros using buttons on the Macro toolbar

- Learn more about the functions and statements in WordBASIC

IX

Automating Your Work

box, Word for Windows stores the selections as a WordBASIC statement in a macro that resides in a template. If you are familiar with how this dialog information is stored, you can modify it or delete unnecessary parts.

Understanding Dialog Recordings

Each time your record information from a dialog box in Word for Windows, all the information in the dialog box is stored in the macro document. The dialog box information is stored in the following format:

```
CommandName.Argument1 = Value, .Argument2 = Value,...
```

In this convention, CommandName is the menu and command that, when chosen, displays the dialog box. These are known as WordBASIC *statements*. A statement runs a Word for Windows command. Each argument, such as .Argument1, corresponds to an element within the dialog box—for example, the name of a check box. The value for each argument describes the condition of that argument—1 or 0 if a check box is selected or cleared, for example, or text enclosed in quotes for the contents of an edit box. For example, the Font tab of the dialog box from the Format Font command is recorded as follows:

```
FormatFont .Points = "11", .Underline = 1, .Color = 0,
➡.Strikethrough = 0, .Superscript = 0, .Subscript = 0, .Hidden = 0,
➡.SmallCaps = 0, .AllCaps = 0, .Spacing = "0 pt",
➡.Position = "0 pt", .Kerning = 0, .KerningMin = "", .Tab = "0",
➡.Font = "Times New Roman", .Bold = 1, .Italic = 0
```

The statement FormatFont describes the dialog box. Each element of the dialog box follows this. For example, .Points = "11" means that the point size was set to 11. Notice the .Font. You can read which font was selected. Check boxes are recorded as 1 for selected and 0 for deselected. Notice that the .Bold check box is selected, but the .Italic check box was not.

The recorded macro is a straightforward guide to the user's selections within the dialog box. Each option in the dialog box is represented by an item in the recorded macro.

Dialog item names are preceded with a period, text values are enclosed in quotation marks, and selected or cleared values for Bold, AllCaps, and so on, are identified by a 0 for clear and a 1 for selected. When an item (.Color, for example) requires the user to choose from among several values in a list, the number of the selected value is stored in the argument. (As in many instances when dealing with computer languages, you should start counting at 0, not 1). Auto is the first choice in the .Color list box, so the .Color item's value is 0.

Using What You Want from a Recording

There are two very simple edits you can make to your recorded macros that can improve them. (Editing is described in Chapter 38, "Recording and Editing Macros.") Using the previous WordBASIC code as an example, you can edit the line to change the action of the statement. If the code was originally

```
FormatFont .Points = "11", .Underline = 1, .Color = 0,
➡.Strikethrough = 0, .Superscript = 0, .Subscript = 0, .Hidden = 0,
➡.SmallCaps = 0, .AllCaps = 0, .Spacing = "0 pt",
➡.Position = "0 pt", .Kerning = 0, .KerningMin = "", .Tab = "0",
➡.Font = "Times New Roman", .Bold = 1, .Italic = 0
```

you can change the size of the font to 14 by changing the argument `.Points` to `.Points = "14"`. Or you can make the font different by editing the font argument to be `.Font = "Arial"`.

Check boxes that are selected in a dialog box, such as `.Bold = 1`, can be deselected by changing their corresponding argument to a 0, such as `.Bold = 0`. The value for an item selected from a list becomes the number of that item in the list. (Remember counting starts at 0.) For example, instead of the color being Automatic, which is the first (or 0) item, you could edit the `.Color` argument to use the fourth color so the argument would appear as `.Color = 3`.

An important concept is that a statement only changes the listed arguments following the statement. For example, if you use the previous `FormatFont` statement on selected text, all the recorded characteristics of the text will be changed. Even if you only wanted the bold to be recorded, you actually record all the items in the dialog box. When you run this recording on text with the Bookman font, the `.Font` statement changes the font to Times New Roman—even though you only wanted bold.

The solution is to record the entire dialog box, then delete the arguments you do not want. For example, if you want your recording to only change the bold characteristic, you should edit the statement to look like

```
FormatFont .Bold = 1
```

Modifying the MyWorkspace Macro

Some recorded macros will not run the way you want unless you first do some editing to them. Other macros can be made more efficient. The following code is the MyWorkspace macro recorded in Chapter 38:

IX

Automating Your Work

```
Sub MAIN
ViewNormal
ViewRuler
ViewToolbars .ColorButtons = 1, .LargeButtons = 0, .ToolTips = 0
ViewToolbars .Show, .Toolbar = "Standard"
ViewToolbars .Show, .Toolbar = "Formatting"
ViewToolbars .Show, .Toolbar = "Drawing"
ViewToolbars .Hide, .Toolbar = "Macro Record"
ViewZoom .ZoomPercent = "85%"
ToolsOptionsEdit .ReplaceSelection = 1, .DragAndDrop = 1,
➥.AutoWordSelection = 0, .InsForPaste = 0, .Overtype = 0,
➥.SmartCutPaste = 1, .AllowAccentedUppercase = 0,
➥.PictureEditor = "Microsoft Word"
ToolsOptionsSave .CreateBackup = 0, .FastSaves = 1,
➥.SummaryPrompt = 0, .GlobalDotPrompt = 0, .NativePictureFormat = 0,
➥.EmbedFonts = 0, .FormsData = 0, .AutoSave = 0, .SaveInterval = "",
➥.Password = "", .WritePassword = "", .RecommendReadOnly = 0
End Sub
```

Note

The ➥ character indicates that the lines should be entered as one line. Don't include it with the lines when you type them.

You could improve this code by deleting the following two lines so that color buttons and large buttons are not changed and so that the macro toolbar is not hidden when you run the macro:

```
ViewToolbars .ColorButtons = 1, .LargeButtons = 0, .ToolTips = 0

ViewToolbars .Hide, .Toolbar = "Macro Record"
```

Another improvement is to make the macro so it only changes the dialog box items you wanted, not everything. The statements `ToolsOptionsEdit` and `ToolsOptionsSave` recorded all the settings in the dialog box. But you only wanted to change a few options. In the Edit tab you wanted to change the Typing Replaces Selection and Drag-and-Drop Text Editing options. In the Save tab, you wanted to change the Allow Fast Saves check box and deselect Automatic Save Every __ Minutes. Since you don't want these other items in the dialog box to be affected, remove their corresponding arguments. The edited code should look like the following code:

```
Sub MAIN
ViewNormal
ViewRuler
ViewToolbars .Show, .Toolbar = "Standard"
ViewToolbars .Show, .Toolbar = "Formatting"
ViewToolbars .Show, .Toolbar = "Drawing"
ViewZoom .ZoomPercent = "85%"
```

```
ToolsOptionsEdit .ReplaceSelection = 1, .DragAndDrop = 1
ToolsOptionsSave .FastSaves = 1, .AutoSave = 0
End Sub
```

Using Input Boxes to Enter Data

One of the things you will probably want to add to your recorded macro is the ability to request an entry from the user. WordBASIC has a very simple statement, InputBox$, that displays a pre-built dialog box for data entry. In the following examples, you will learn how to display the Input dialog box, prompt the user for an entry, then take their entry and insert it at the appropriate location in the document. You will also learn how to request a numeric entry, do a math operation on it, and insert the result in the document.

Preparing to Create a Data Entry Macro

The easiest way to create a data entry macro is to create a template that contains bookmarks at the locations where data will be inserted. When the user does a File New and opens a new document based on the template, all the appropriate text and graphics will be there, as well as the bookmarks that indicate where the macro should insert entries. If you want to duplicate the following code, you should create a document, then use the Edit Bookmark command to put two bookmarks in. The first bookmark is named TextLocation and marks where a name will be inserted. The second bookmark is NumberLocation and marks where a number will be inserted. Save this document as a template.

Close the template you have just created and use the File New command to open a new document based on that template. Turn on the macro recorder and name the new macro InputData.

To create a base recording you can modify, follow these steps while the macro recorder is on:

1. Press Ctrl+Home to move the insertion point to the beginning of the document.

2. Choose the Edit Go To command, select Bookmark from the Go to What list, then select TextLocation from the Enter Bookmark Name list, and choose OK. The insertion point should move to the TextLocation position.

3. Type a name.

4. Choose the **Edit Go To** command, select Bookmark from the Go to What list, then select NumberLocation from the Enter Bookmark Name list, and choose OK. The insertion point should move to the NumberLocation position.

5. Type a number.

6. Choose the **Tools Macro** command and choose the Stop Recording command, then choose Close.

Your recording has given you a basic macro that you can now modify. You can edit your macro by choosing the Tools Macro command, selecting the InputData macro from the Macro Name list, and then choosing the Edit button. Your macro code should look similar to the following code:

```
Sub MAIN
StartOfDocument
EditGoTo .Destination = "TextLocation"
Insert "Name"
EditGoTo .Destination = "NumberLocation"
Insert "10"
End Sub
```

Displaying the INPUT Dialog Box

In the following procedures you will learn how to modify your recorded macro to produce the macro shown in the upper window of fig. 39.1. This macro asks the user to type a name into an Input box and then inserts the name at the bookmark, TextLocation. The macro then asks the user to type a number into an Input box. The number comes from the Input box as text so it must be converted back to a number (Val), it is then multiplied by 1.2, converted back to text (Str$), and the number is finally inserted at the bookmark NumberLocation.

This macro uses an Input box to ask the user for an entry. Fig. 39.2 shows the first input box displayed by the macro in fig. 39.1. The `InputBox$` statement uses the following layout

```
InputBox$(Prompt$[,Title$][,Default$])
```

where `Prompt$` is text in quotes that tells the operator what to enter. `Title$` is optional and is also text in quotes that is used as a title for the Input dialog box. `Default$` is the optional text in quotes that will appear in the edit box when the dialog box displays. Choosing OK without making an entry results in the default. If the user clicks Cancel, an error occurs that can be trapped for with an `On Error` statement.

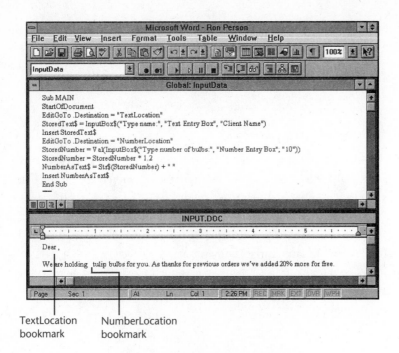

Fig. 39.1
The macro in the upper window displays dialog boxes that prompt for data. The macro then inserts the data at the correct locations in the letter in the lower window.

TextLocation
bookmark

NumberLocation
bookmark

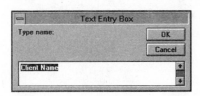

Fig. 39.2
Use the `InputBox$` statement to add a dialog box to your recorded macro.

The first part of the code asks for and inserts a name:

```
StartOfDocument
EditGoTo .Destination = "TextLocation"
StoredText$ = InputBox$("Type name:", "Text Entry Box",
➥"Client Name")
Insert StoredText$
```

The StartOfDocument statement moves the insertion point to the beginning of the document. The EditGoTo was the recorded move to the bookmark named TextLocation. The text that the user types into the Input box will be stored in the text variable StoredText$. A variable is a name that can hold information for later use. The $ at the end of the variable means that it will only hold text values. What the user typed is then inserted at the current insertion point by the Insert statement.

IX

Automating Your Work

The second part of this example asks for a number. The number is then multiplied by 1.2 and inserted in the document:

```
EditGoTo .Destination = "NumberLocation"
StoredNumber = Val(InputBox$("Type number of bulbs:",
➥"Number Entry Box", "10"))
StoredNumber = StoredNumber * 1.2
NumberAsText$ = Str$(StoredNumber) + " "
Insert NumberAsText$
```

Working with a number takes a little more work because `InputBox$` returns a number as text, which will not work with math. To convert this number as text into a true number, the `InputBox$` statement is put inside a `Val` statement. This produces a true number that is stored in the variable `StoredNumber`. The amount in `StoredNumber` is multiplied by 1.2 and then stored back into the same variable `StoredNumber`. `StoredNumber` then gets converted back into text and has a blank space added to the end. The resulting number as text is now stored in `NumberAsText$`, which gets inserted by the `Insert` statement.

Notice that WordBASIC automatically created a numeric variable from the word StoredNumber as soon as it was used. Text variables are created by ending the variable name with $. (WordBASIC does have the ability to dimension variables at the beginning of each module.)

The finished macro looks like this:

```
Sub MAIN
StartOfDocument
EditGoTo .Destination = "TextLocation"
StoredText$ = InputBox$("Type name:", "Text Entry Box",
➥"Client Name")
Insert StoredText$
EditGoTo .Destination = "NumberLocation"
StoredNumber = Val(InputBox$("Type number of bulbs:",
➥"Number Entry Box", "10"))
StoredNumber = StoredNumber * 1.2
NumberAsText$ = Str$(StoredNumber) + " "
Insert NumberAsText$
End Sub
```

Creating Automatic Macros

You may want some macros to run automatically at certain times. To run a macro automatically you only need to give them a special name. Table 39.1 describes Word for Windows five automatic macros.

Table 39.1 Running Macros Automatically	
Macro name	**Function**
AutoExec	Global macro that runs when you start Word for Windows. For example, the macro could change to a selected directory, prompt the user for preferences, or prompt for a document or template to start up in.
AutoExit	Global macro that runs when you exit Word for Windows. For example, closes applications that Word for Windows macros opened, or automatically opens another application.
AutoNew	Global or template macro that runs when you create a new document based on the template containing AutoNew. For example, displays an instruction message to help new users or update arguments in a new document.
AutoOpen	Global or template macro that runs when you open an existing document. For example, updates arguments in an existing document, or automatically inserts text from a specified file.
AutoClose	Global or template macro that runs when you close a document. For example, saves a changed document to a predetermined file name.

To prevent an automatic macro from running, hold down the Shift key when you perform the action that starts the macro. To prevent AutoOpen from running when you open a document, for example, hold down the Shift key while you choose the OK button from the File **O**pen command.

> **Tip**
> You can prevent an automatic macro from running by holding down the Shift key when you perform the action that starts the macro.

As Table 39.1 indicates, automatic macros are especially useful for performing operations that set up a document when it opens. A handy use of the AutoNew macro, for example, is to update all fields in a document when you open a template for that document. This is especially useful for templates containing date and time fields and {fillin} field codes. The macro to update an entire document might appear as follows:

```
Sub MAIN
   EditSelectAll
   UpdateFields
   StartOfDocument
End Sub
```

This macro is useful when saved as an AutoNew macro with a template used for forms and containing field codes such as {fillin}. When a new document opens from a template having this macro, each field code is updated. For example, all the {fillin} input boxes are displayed in turn.

Managing Macros

After a while, you may have accumulated macros you really don't need. Others may be poorly named (Can you remember what Macro7 does?) or better suited to another template. You should keep your macros up to date and well organized. This section discusses how to manage your macros.

Deleting Macros

To delete a macro, follow these steps:

1. If the macro is a template macro, open the template or a document attached to it. If the macro is a global macro, open any document.

2. Choose the Tools Macro command.

3. Select the macro or command type—All Active Templates or NORMAL.DOT—from the Macros Available In group, then select the macro from the Macro Name list.

4. Choose the Delete button. You will be asked if you want to delete the macro. Choose Yes to delete it.

5. Choose Close.

You cannot delete a macro that is in an open edit window. If you delete a macro currently assigned to the menu or toolbar, Word for Windows unassigns the macro when it is deleted. All of your changes are stored in memory until you save them to disk (see "Saving Macros" earlier in this chapter).

Renaming Macros

When you want to rename a macro, you must open the template in which that macro is stored. If the template is protected, you must unprotect it before renaming will work.

To rename a macro, follow these steps:

1. If the macro is stored in a specific template, open the template. If the macro is a global macro, open any document. (Opening any document also opens the NORMAL.DOT template, but NORMAL.DOT stays hidden.)

2. If the template is protected, choose the Tools Unprotect command.

3. Choose the Tools Macro command.

4. Choose the Organizer button to display the Organizer dialog box.

5. Select from one of the Macros Available In lists the template containing the macro name you want to rename.

6. Choose the Rename button.

    The Rename dialog box appears as shown in fig. 39.3.

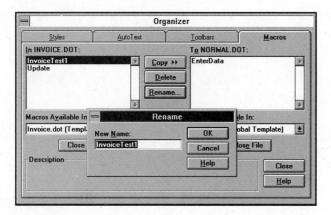

Fig. 39.3
Select the macro you want to rename, then choose the Rename button to type in a new name.

7. Type the new name in the New Name text box.

8. Choose OK.

9. Choose Close if you have no more changes.

Copying Macros Between Templates

At times you will want to transfer a macro from one template to another. You or a co-worker may create a template that has a macro you can use in another template. Or you may want to transfer one of the sample macros included with Word into one of your templates. It's easy to transfer macros between any templates that are open. It's just as though you are copying your macro into the other template.

To transfer macros between two open templates, follow these steps:

1. Open the template containing the macro you want to copy. Also open the template that you want to receive a copy of the macro. If the macro is a global macro, then you can open any document based on NORMAL.DOT

2. If the template is protected, choose the Tools Unprotect command.

IX

Automating Your Work

3. Choose the **T**ools Macro command.

4. Choose the Organizer button from the Macro dialog box. Select the **M**acros tab of the Organizer dialog box to display the dialog box as shown in fig. 39.4.

Fig. 39.4
Select a macro from any open template and copy it to any other open template.

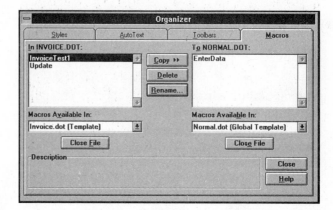

5. In the left side of the Organizer, select from the Macros A**v**ailable In list the template containing the macro.

6. In the right side of the Organizer, select from the Macros A**v**ailable In list the template you want to receive a copy of the macro.

7. In the left side of the Organizer, select from the In *TemplateName* list the macro you want copied. (TemplateName can be the name of any template which currently has a document open.)

8. Choose the Copy button.

   The macro will be copied from the template on the left side to the template on the right side.

9. If you want to copy additional macros, return to Step 4. If you are finished, choose the Close button. When you return to the documents make sure you save the macros.

Getting Help on Macros

Word for Windows contains extensive help for macros. You can choose the **H**elp Content command to see the index of major help topics. To get an overview and detail on specific procedures, select the underlined topic Programming with Microsoft Word by clicking it or by pressing the Tab key until it is selected, and then press Enter.

You also can get information about a specific macro statement or function. For example, you may have recorded a macro and need to know which argument values are appropriate to turn a dialog option on or off. To find out about a specific macro statement, function, or argument, use the **Tools Macro** command to select a macro, then change to the edit window. Move the insertion point into the macro statement or argument you need information about, then press F1 (Help). Fig. 39.5 shows the help screen for the Bold macro statement and function. The numeric values that can be used or returned by Bold are shown.

For Related Information
■ "Using Word for Windows Sample Macros", p. 1136

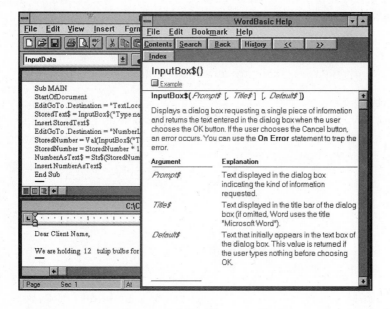

Fig. 39.5
Help for the currently selected WordBASIC statement displays when you press F1. To display InputBox$ help as shown here, the insertion point was moved into InputBox$ and F1 was pressed.

An excellent way to learn more about WordBASIC is to record macros, then use the F1 key as described here to learn more about the statements and functions involved in your recording. You can also examine or modify the sample macros that come with Word. These sample macros are described in Chapter 38 in the section "Using Word for Windows Sample Macros."

Tip
You can learn learn more about WordBASIC by recording macros, then using the F1 key as described here to learn about the statements and functions involved in your recording.

IX

Automating Your Work

Debugging Macros

Even the best programmers usually have a few errors (or bugs) in their programs at first. Long, complex macro recordings or manually entered WordBASIC programs are more prone to errors than short recordings, but any macro can contain an error that prevents it from working properly. Fortunately, Word for Windows contains special troubleshooting tools to help you find problems and correct them.

When you choose the Tools Macro Edit command and select a macro to edit, Word for Windows automatically switches to a troubleshooting or "debugging" mode. The macro edit bar appears at the top of the screen to aid you in testing and troubleshooting your macros. The buttons on this bar enable you to control the operation of your macro and pinpoint problems. For example, you can run the macro one statement at a time. As the macro runs, you can watch its effect on a target document and isolate problems as they occur. This process is much easier than running a macro and seeing it zip through its operations, only to stop abruptly and display a macro error message.

To debug your macro, you need to run it from within a target document. The easiest way is to put a target document in one window and the macro in another, then use one of the step buttons to watch how each macro statement affects the document.

To make troubleshooting easier, set up the macro and document in two windows. Make sure that you open your macro window using the Tools Macro Edit command, then follow these steps:

1. Choose the Window Arrange All command to see the document in which you want to work and the macro editing window.

2. Reposition the windows so that you can work in the document, but watch the code in the macro window.

3. Activate the document window in which you want to run the macro.

Each button in the edit icon bar can help you see the macro's effect on the document. To operate these buttons by keyboard, press Alt+Shift+the underlined letter shown in Table 39.2. The macro toolbar that appears when a macro document is open, as shown in fig. 39.6.

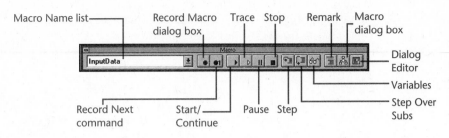

Macro Name list

Record Macro dialog box

Trace Stop

Remark Macro dialog box

InputData

Dialog Editor

Variables

Step Over Subs

Record Next command

Start/ Continue

Pause Step

Fig. 39.6

Use the Macro toolbar to help you troubleshoot your macros. Operate the toolbar with the mouse or the shortcut keys in Table 39.2.

Table 39.2 describes the buttons in the edit bar.

Table 39.2 Using the Edit Bar

Button	Function
Macro Name List	Lists the names of open macros. Select from the list the macro you want to troubleshoot.
Record Dialog	Displays the Record Macro dialog box so you can record or stop a recording.
Record Next	Records the next command you choose. WordBASIC command is inserted at the current insertion point in the macro.
Start/Continue	Runs the active macro or continues the macro after a pause. If the macro has paused for a step or trace, the Start button appears as Continue.
Trace	Runs the macro from start to finish, highlighting each statement as it executes.
Pause	Pauses the macro.
Stop	Stops the macro.
Step	Runs the macro one line at a time, highlighting the statement being executed, then pausing until the Step button is pressed again. By *stepping* through the macro, you can see how it is operating and where problems occur.
Step SUB	Runs the macro on the target document one subroutine at a time, pausing on the first line of the subsequent subroutine until the Step SUB button is pressed again.
Vars	Displays a dialog box that shows the current values of the variables used in the macro and provides a way to reset the variable assignments during macro execution.
REM	Adds or removes a REM from the front of a line. REM remarks a line so it stays in code but does not run.
Macro Dialog	Display the Macro dialog box so you can run, edit, delete, or transfer a macro.
Dialog Editor	Opens the dialog editor used to create custom dialog boxes.

IX

Automating Your Work

If an error or alert box displays, press F1 for help with that macro statement or function.

From Here...

For more information about programming with WordBASIC use either the on-line Help system or purchase the WordBASIC manual from Microsoft.

Word's on-line Help system has extensive help, reference information, and examples. To get to the table of contents for WordBASIC on-line help, choose the **Help Contents** command. When the table of contents appears, select `Programming with Microsoft Word`. You will see the table of contents for WordBASIC help. You can get help about a specific statement or function by moving the insertion point into that statement or function and pressing the F1 key.

To purchase a copy of *Using WordBASIC*, Microsoft's manual on WordBASIC, contact Microsoft Sales and Service at 1-800-426-9400.

Part X
Reference

Appendix A Service and Support

Appendix B Installing Word for Windows

Appendix C Windows Character Tables

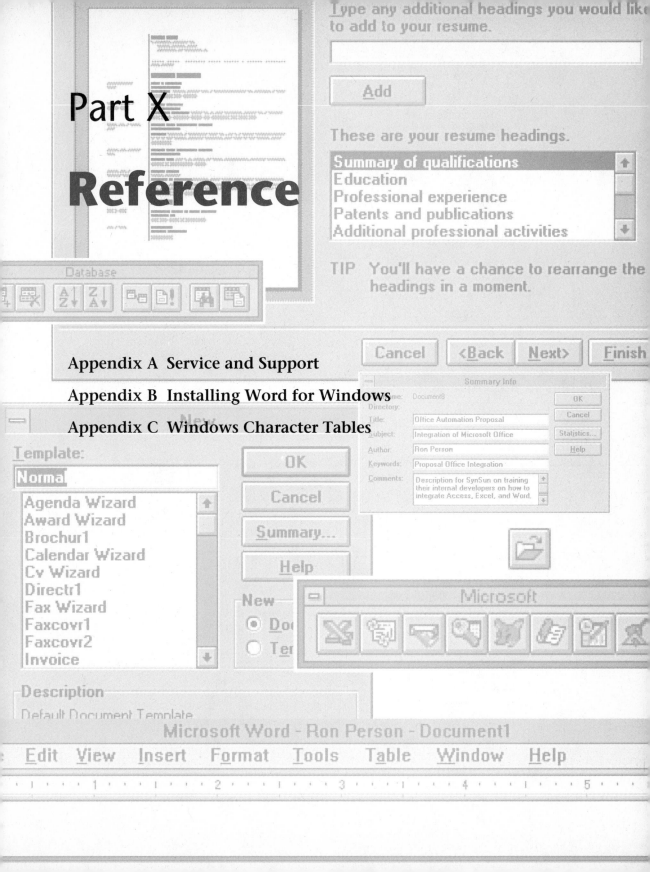

Type any additional headings you would li[k]
to add to your resume.

[   ]

[**Add**]

These are your resume headings.

Summary of qualifications	↑
Education	
Professional experience	
Patents and publications	
Additional professional activities	↓

TIP You'll have a chance to rearrange th[e]
headings in a moment.

[Cancel] [<Back] [Next>] [Finis]

Database

New

Template:

Normal

Agenda Wizard	↑
Award Wizard	
Brochur1	
Calendar Wizard	
Cv Wizard	
Directr1	
Fax Wizard	
Faxcovr1	
Faxcovr2	
Invoice	↓

[**OK**]

[**Cancel**]

[**Summary...**]

[**Help**]

New
● Do[c]
○ Te[m]

Description
Default Document Template

Summary Info

File Name:	Document8	[OK]
Directory:		[Cancel]
Title:	Office Automation Proposal	[Statistics...]
Subject:	Integration of Microsoft Office	[Help]
Author:	Ron Person	
Keywords:	Proposal Office Integration	
Comments:	Description for SynSun on training their internal developers on how to integrate Access, Excel, and Word.	

Microsoft

Microsoft Word - Ron Person - Document1

[E]dit   [V]iew   [I]nsert   [F]ormat   [T]ools   [T]able   [W]indow   [H]elp

· · · 1 · · · | · · · 2 · · · | · · · 3 · · · | · · · 4 · · · | · · · 5 · ·

Support Services

Resources, Consulting, and Support

Microsoft Corporation

Microsoft Corporation
One Microsoft Way
Redmond, WA 98052-6399
206-882-8080
206-462-9673, Word for Windows support line
206-635-7070, Excel support line
206-637-7098, Windows support line
800-426-9400, Microsoft product-support line
6AM-6PM, M-F, Pacific time

Microsoft maintains a telephone support line for technical questions concerning Windows, Excel, and Word for Windows.

CompuServe

CompuServe
5000 Arlington Centre Boulevard
P.O. Box 20212
Columbus, OH 43220
1-800-848-8199

CompuServe is a computer service available to your computer through a telephone connection. CompuServe gives you access to databases, sample files, and question-and-answer forums concerning hundreds of topics and industries. CompuServe contains an Excel forum, a troubleshooting service, and libraries of worksheets and macros.

The Excel and Microsoft Windows services are provided by Microsoft Corporation. To access the many Windows forums and libraries, type GO MSOFT at any menu prompt. To directly access the applications forums and libraries, type GO MSAPP at any menu prompt. For information on how to use CompuServe, contact CompuServe directly.

Que Corporation

Que Corporation
201 W. 103rd Street
Indianapolis , IN 46290
317-581-3500

Que Corporation is the world-wide leader in computer book publishing. Other books available about Windows applications by Ron Person or Karen Rose include *Using Excel 5 for Windows*, *Using Windows 3.1*, Special Edition; and *Windows 3.1 QuickStart*. Call Que for a free catalog. Corporate and volume discounts are available.

Ron Person & Co.

Ron Person & Co.
P.O. Box 5647
Santa Rosa, CA 95402
415-989-7508   Voice
707-539-1525   Voice
707-538-1485   FAX

Ron Person & Co., based in San Francisco, is one of the original twelve Microsoft Consulting Partners, Microsoft's highest rating for consultants who support their major customers. Ron Person is both a Microsoft Excel and Word for Windows Consulting Partner. The firm also is a Microsoft Registered Developer for Excel and Word for Windows. In addition to writing three best-selling books on Windows applications, *Using Excel*, *Using Word for Windows*, and *Using Windows 3.1*, they are recognized leaders in training corporate developers and support personnel in Microsoft Visual Basic for Applications and macro languages.

Appendix B

Installing Word for Windows

In this appendix, you learn what hardware components are required to run Word for Windows and how to install the program with different features and settings.

Hardware Requirements

To provide acceptable performance in the Windows environment, your computer system must satisfy the following minimum hardware requirements:

- Personal Computers running Windows 3.1 or later and using 80386, 80486SX, 80486, or Pentium processors.

- 4M or more of memory. Performance increases dramatically with at least 8M of memory.

- Graphics cards compatible with Windows 3.1 or later. High resolution monitors can take advantage of the large buttons on the toolbars.

- Hard disk or file server.

- At least one floppy disk drive.

- An operating system that runs Windows 3.1 or higher.

In addition, Word for Windows supports the following:

- The wide range of printers and plotters supported by Windows, including Hewlett-Packard LaserJet-compatible and PostScript-compatible laser printers.

- A mouse or other pointing device.

- Networks supporting Windows 3.1 or higher.

Installing Word for Windows

Before you install Word for Windows, you must have Windows 3.1 or higher installed. Windows is a separate software package from Microsoft that enables you to run Word for Windows, Microsoft Excel, and other Windows applications.

Before you begin the Word for Windows installation, check your hard disk and decide where you want to install Word. The default directory used during installation is C:\WINWORD. During installation, you are given a chance to change this directory. If you have an existing version of Word for Windows on the disk, the installation program gives you the option of overwriting it, but you can insure that old files are deleted by first copying out of C:\WINWORD any documents or templates you want to save and then deleting all of the old Word for Windows. Once the old files are deleted, install Word for Windows 6.

Starting the Installation Process

During the installation process you can use the mouse to make selections. If you use the keyboard you can press Tab to select options or buttons. After selecting a check box or button with the Tab key, press the space bar to complete the selection. Pressing Enter is the same as OK. Pressing Esc is the same as Cancel.

To begin installing Word for Windows, follow these steps:

1. Make a backup copy of your original floppy disks. It is also a good idea to make a backup copy of WIN.INI and REG.DAT located in the \WINDOWS directory as well as AUTOEXEC.BAT and CONFIG.SYS located in the root directory, C:\. Should the installation fail you can copy these files back to their original location to restore your computer's startup settings to their original condition.

2. Protect your original floppy disks from accidental change. On 5 1/4-inch disks, put a write-protect tab over the square cut notch on the edge. On 3 1/2-inch disks, slide the write-protect notch to the open position.

3. Start Windows.

4. Choose the File Run command from the Program Manager or File Manager.

5. When the Run dialog box appears, insert Disk 1 in the floppy disk drive, type **a:setup** or **b:setup**, depending upon the disk drive you use, and press Enter. You may get a message to close any running applications before continuing. Use Alt+Tab to switch to other applications and close them.

6. If this is the first time you have installed Word for Windows, a dialog box appears and prompts you for your name and company. Use the Tab key to move between edit boxes and press the Backspace key to remove errors. Click the Continue button or press Enter to continue.

   If these floppy disks have been used previously, a message will show the name of the initial installer.

7. When you continue a Setup dialog box will ask for the path where you want Word for Windows installed. The default path is C:\WINWORD. If you want to change where Word is installed, for example if drive C does not have enough space, choose the Change Directory button and specify a new drive and directory. See fig. B.1. Then choose OK.

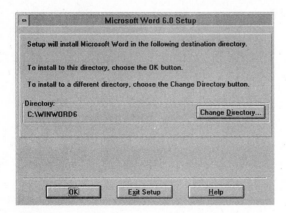

Fig. B.1
You can keep the default installation directory of C:\WINWORD or install in any drive or directory.

If Setup finds a different version of Word for Windows in the directory you specify, you are given the option of overwriting it. To keep the existing version of Word for Windows and put the new version in a different directory, choose the Change Directory button. Specify a new path.

Choosing the Features to Install

The Setup dialog box gives you an opportunity to choose how much of Word for Windows you want installed. Click the box describing the type of installation you want. Using the keyboard, press the arrow keys to select a box, and then press Enter. You can choose one of three levels of installation, as shown in fig. B.2.

Fig. B.2
You can elect to install three different levels of Word features.

Tip
If you later decide to add Word for Windows features that you did not install initially, you can rerun the Word for Windows setup and install the features you want using Complete/Custom.

Tip
If you are unsure which type of installation to choose, choose Custom Installation and read the rest of this appendix before completing the installation. Through the use of Custom you can select or deselect files and see how much disk space is required and how much is available.

The following table describes the installation levels:

Selection	Description
Typical	Installs Word for Windows as it is most commonly used. Gives you an opportunity to accept or reject automatically adding the Word for Windows path to the AUTOEXEC.BAT file.
Complete/Custom	Installs only those portions of Word for Windows features that you select. It enables you to see all the possible features, add-ins, sample files and filters that can be installed. You can also use this option to add features you have not installed previously. This option also enables you to see how much disk space is required for different features.
Laptop (minimum)	Installs only the basic Word for Windows files.

If you decide on the Complete/Custom installation, the Complete/Custom dialog box appears. You can select all or part of different features. Each feature requires additional storage on your hard disk. See fig. B.3. The lower-left corner of the dialog box shows you how much storage you have available and how much storage is required for the options you have selected.

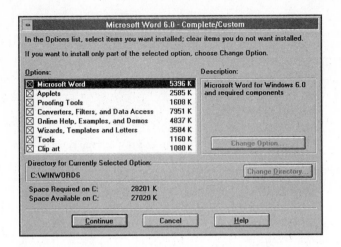

Fig. B.3
In the Custom install, you can select the features you want installed and see the amount of disk space required.

With the mouse, remove files and features you do not want by clicking a check box to remove the X.

With the keyboard, press Alt+O to select the Options list, if the list is not already selected. Use the up- or down-arrow key to move between features. Press the spacebar to select or clear a check box.

The different features you can install are as follows:

Feature	Description
Microsoft Word	Fundamental word processing. You can deselect this option if you want to install additional features without installing Word. You will be warned that you are not installing Word.
Applets	Miniature applications that run with Word for Windows. Applets include the Button Editor, Equation Editor, Microsoft Graph, and WordArt.
Proofing Tools	Word processing enhancements, such as spell checker, thesaurus, and grammar checker.
Converters, Filters, and DataAccess ODBC.	Filters that enable Word for Windows to convert other documents, spreadsheets, database, snd graphics files. Data access features enable you connect Word to external databases using
Online Help, Examples and Demos	On-line learning aids to help you learn features in Word for Windows. Sample files and computer based training demonstrations are also available.

(continues)

(continued)

Feature	Description
Wizards, Templates, and Letters	Templates and Wizards help you build standard forms, mailing labels, and so on.
Tools	Macros tools such as the Dialog Editor and Setup program.
Clip Art	Drawings and pictures you can insert into documents.

As you select or deselect features and files, watch the amount of disk storage required and available at the lower-left corner of the dialog box.

If you want to select a subset of features, select the feature under the Options list, then choose the Change Option button. Choose OK to return to the main Options list.

Fig. B.4
Select the Change Option button to select a subset of features like these subsets of Help.

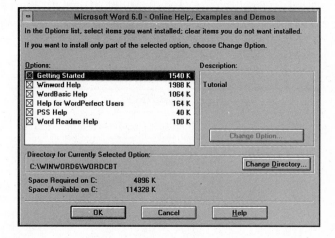

Choose the Continue button from the main Options list when you finish selecting the features to install.

> **Note**
>
> If you have Microsoft Excel or a previous version of Word for Windows already installed, you should make sure that you include the conversion filters for Microsoft Excel and Word for Windows 2 or 1.X. If you previously used WordPerfect or work with people who still use WordPerfect, you should install the conversion filters for WordPerfect 5.0, 5.1, DrawPerfect Import, and DrawPerfect Export.

Finishing the Installation

The last item you need to specify for the installation process is the group window in which you want the Word for Windows 6 icons to appear. In the Choose Program Manager Group dialog box, select the group window you want, then choose OK.

The final step of the installation is to insert and remove the numbered floppy disks as the setup program requests them. For each disk, press Enter or choose OK when you have the next disk inserted in the floppy drive.

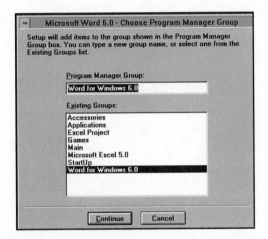

Fig. B.5
Choose an existing or new group window in the Program Manager for the Excel icons.

Word for Windows will prompt you as to whether you want to manually change your AUTOEXEC.BAT file or if it should automatically update the file. If you choose to manually update the AUTOEXEC.BAT file, you should modify the path to include the directory containing WINWORD.EXE. A path that includes Word for Windows might look like the following:

PATH C:\EXCEL;C:\WINDOWS;C:\WINWORD;C:\VB;C:\DOS;C:\

If setup did not change your AUTOEXEC.BAT you also will need to add a line that runs the Share utility. This utility is normally in the DOS directory, so the line you will add might appear as follows:

C:\DOS\SHARE.EXE

You can use the Windows Notepad accessory to open and modify the AUTOEXEC.BAT file. Save the file back to the root directory. Notepad automatically saves the file in text format. You will need to shut down windows and restart your computer before the new AUTOEXEC.BAT takes effect. The installation program will prompt you to restart Windows.

When Word for Windows is installed, make sure that you store your original and backup floppy disks in safe, but separate locations.

Character Sets

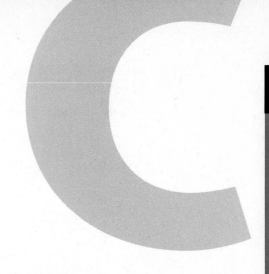

Each of the characters, numbers, and symbols that you see on the screen or in a document is assigned a numeric code as part of a character set. Some of the codes are part of the standard ASCII and ANSI character sets; others are extensions to the basic character sets. This appendix lists the codes in some common fonts for the character sets used in Windows-based applications and on the Macintosh.

Most of the time, it's easiest to insert symbols with the Symbol command on the Insert menu. If you prefer using the keyboard to the mouse, you can insert symbols by typing their codes or by pressing shortcut keys.

However, if you are editing a WordBasic statement or a Word field, or specifying a symbol in the Find or Replace dialog box, you can't use the Symbol dialog box to insert the symbol. You must specify a symbol by typing its code or key combination.

For online instructions, double-click the Help button on the Standard toolbar. Then type **symbols**.

To insert symbols by typing the character code, follow these steps:

1. Position the insertion point where you want to insert a symbol.

2. Make sure the NUMLOCK key is on.

3. In Word for Windows, hold down ALT, then, using the numeric keypad, type **0** (zero) followed by the appropriate code. For example, to insert an uppercase Ç character, type **0199** on the numeric keypad while holding down ALT.

Windows Character Set

Code	Times New Roman	Symbol	Code	Times New Roman	Symbol
0			26		
1			27		
2			28		
3			29		
4			30	Nonbreaking hyphen	Nonbreaking hyphen
5					
6			31	Optional hyphen	Optional hyphen
7					
8			32	Space	Space
9	Tab	Tab	33	!	!
10	Carriage Return	Carriage Return	34	"	∀
			35	#	#
11	Line break	Line break	36	$	∃
12	Hard page break	Hard page break	37	%	%
			38	&	&
13	Paragraph mark	Paragraph mark	39	'	϶
			40	(	(
14	Column break	Column break	41	)	)
15			42	*	*
16			43	+	+
17			44	,	,
18			45	-	−
19			46	.	.
20			47	/	/
21			48	0	0
22			49	1	1
23			50	2	2
24			51	3	3
25			52	4	4
			53	5	5

Code	Times New Roman	Symbol	Code	Times New Roman	Symbol
54	6	6	84	T	Τ
55	7	7	85	U	Υ
56	8	8	86	V	ς
57	9	9	87	W	Ω
58	:	:	88	X	Ξ
59	;	;	89	Y	Ψ
60	<	<	90	Z	Ζ
61	=	=	91	[	[
62	>	>	92	\	∴
63	?	?	93	]	]
64	@	≅	94	^	⊥
65	A	Α	95	_	_
66	B	Β	96	`	
67	C	Χ	97	a	α
68	D	Δ	98	b	β
69	E	Ε	99	c	χ
70	F	Φ	100	d	δ
71	G	Γ	101	e	ε
72	H	Η	102	f	φ
73	I	Ι	103	g	γ
74	J	ϑ	104	h	η
75	K	Κ	105	i	ι
76	L	Λ	106	j	φ
77	M	Μ	107	k	κ
78	N	Ν	108	l	λ
79	O	Ο	109	m	μ
80	P	Π	110	n	ν
81	Q	Θ	111	o	ο
82	R	Ρ	112	p	π
83	S	Σ	113	q	θ

(continues)

Windows Character Set Continued

Code	Times New Roman	Symbol	Code	Times New Roman	Symbol
114	r	ρ	144		
115	s	σ	145	'	
116	t	τ	146	'	
117	u	υ	147	"	
118	v	ϖ	148	"	
119	w	ω	149	•	
120	x	ξ	150	–	
121	y	ψ	151	—	
122	z	ζ	152	˜	
123	{	{	153	™	
124					154	š	
125	}	}	155	›	
126	~	~	156	œ	
127			157		
128			158		
129			159	Ÿ	
130	‚		160	Nonbreaking Space	Nonbreaking Space
131	ƒ				
132	„		161	¡	ϒ
133	…		162	¢	′
134	†		163	£	≤
135	‡		164	¤	⁄
136	ˆ		165	¥	∞
137	‰		166	¦	ƒ
138	Š		167	§	♣
139	‹		168	¨	♦
140	Œ		169	©	♥
141			170	ª	♠
142			171	«	↔
143			172	¬	←

Code	Times New Roman	Symbol	Code	Times New Roman	Symbol
173	-	↑	203	Ë	⊄
174	®	→	204	Ì	⊂
175	-	↓	205	Í	⊆
176	°	°	206	Î	∈
177	±	±	207	Ï	∉
178	²	"	208	Ð	∠
179	³	≥	209	Ñ	∇
180	´	×	210	Ò	®
181	µ	∝	211	Ó	©
182	¶	∂	212	Ô	™
183	·	•	213	Õ	∏
184	¸	÷	214	Ö	√
185	¹	≠	215	×	·
186	°	≡	216	Ø	¬
187	»	≈	217	Ù	∧
188	¼	…	218	Ú	∨
189	½	|	219	Û	⇔
190	¾	—	220	Ü	⇐
191	¿	↵	221	Ý	⇑
192	À	ℵ	222	Þ	⇒
193	Á	ℑ	223	ß	⇓
194	Â	ℜ	224	à	◊
195	Ã	℘	225	á	⟨
196	Ä	⊗	226	â	®
197	Å	⊕	227	ã	©
198	Æ	∅	228	ä	™
199	Ç	∩	229	å	Σ
200	È	∪	230	æ	⎛
201	É	⊃	231	ç	⎜
202	Ê	⊇	232	è	⎝

Code	Times New Roman	Symbol
233	é	⌈
234	ê	|
235	ë	⌊
236	ì	⌠
237	í	⟨
238	î	⎩
239	ï	|
240	ð	
241	ñ	⟩
242	ò	∫
243	ó	⌠
244	ô	|
245	õ	⌡
246	ö	⎞
247	÷	|
248	ø	⎠
249	ù	⌉
250	ú	|
251	û	⌋
252	ü	⎫
253	ý	⎬
254	þ	⎭
255	ÿ	

Index

Symbols

Placeholder in numeric formatting, 1092
(…) ellipsis following commands, 40
* (asterisk) wild card, 72, 98
: (colon) specifying cell ranges, 634
? (question mark) wild card, 72, 98
~ (tilde) character, 100
¶ button (Standard toolbar), 126
0 Placeholder in numeric formatting, 1091
3-D charts, 825-826
   bar charts, 812-814
   column charts, 812-814
   line charts, 812-814
   pie charts, 812-814

A

ABS function, 636
accepting revisions in documents, 936-938
Access Pack program (Microsoft), 1048
action fields, 1074

activating, 37
Active window, 32, 34
Add Fonts dialog box, 283
Add-ins, 173-174
   loading, 173-174
   removing, 174
   WordArt, 773-775
   see also programs
adding
   commands to menus, 1062-1064
   menus, 1065-1066
adjusting formulas, 634
ads (publications), 868-869
advanced macros, 1139-1154
Advanced Search command (Search dialog box), 96
Advanced Search dialog box, 97
   Network button, 103
   Summary tab, 99
   Timestamp tab, 101
Agenda Wizard, 175
aliases for styles, 366-367
alignment
   lines/objects, 755-757
   paragraphs, 295-298
      Formatting toolbar, 297
      keyboard shortcuts, 297-298

   menu commands, 296-297
   troubleshooting, 298-300
   publications, 846-847
   vertical, 436-437
   WordArt method, 788-789
Alt key combinations, 39
alternating styles, 375
anchoring
   frames, 707-710
   objects, 758
AND function, 636
Annotation command (Insert menu), 943
annotations, 89, 933-947
   deleting, 945
   displaying, 944-945
   inserting, 943-945
   merging, 940-941
   printing in documents, 946
   protecting, 945-946
   removing all, 945
   troubleshooting, 947
   unprotecting, 946
Annotations command (View menu), 944
Annotations pane, 943

ANSI
  character sets, 1167
  characters, formatting in
    fields, 1093
appending
  cells (tables), 532
  headers/footers, 414-417
  line numbers
    (documents), 315-317
  spelling dictionary, 203
  summary information,
    108-109
Application Control menu,
  32
Application icon, 32
Application window, 32
applying styles, 340-341
  AutoFormat command,
    343-345
      maximizing, 348-349
      options, 347-348
  character styles, 356-358
  paragraph styles, 356
  reviewing formatting
    changes, 345-347
  standard styles, 351-354
  Style Gallery command
    (Format menu), 349-350
arcs, 738-739
area charts, 812-814
arguments
  fields, 1075
  linked data, 1011
Arrange All command
  (Window menu), 79, 159,
  1152
arranging windows, 79
arrow-shaped pointer
  (mouse), 36
arrows
  charts, 821-822
  drawing, 734-735
  removing, 750
ASCII
  character sets, 1167

text files, importing into
  Microsoft Graph,
  805-806
ASD files, 85
assigning passwords
  (documents), 89-90
Attach Template dialog box,
  181
attaching
  macros to forms, 597-598
  templates to documents,
    180-181
AutoCaption dialog box,
  958, 960
AutoClose macro, 1147
AutoCorrect command
  (Tools menu), 147
AutoCorrect dialog box, 148
AutoCorrect feature, 18
  creating entries, 146-148
  deleting entries, 148-149
  options, 148
AutoExec macro, 1147
AUTOEXEC.BAT file, 2, 31,
  1160
AutoExit macro, 1147
AutoFit Command (tables),
  528
AutoFormat button
  (Standard toolbar), 344
AutoFormat command
  Format menu, 338,
    343-345
      maximizing, 348-349
      options, 347-348
  Table menu, 537
AutoFormat dialog box, 343,
  345
AutoFormat feature, 18
AutoFormat tab (Options
  dialog box), 347
AutoMark, 907
automatic captions, 957-959
automatic index entries,
  907-909
automatic macros,
  1146-1147

automatically backing up
  documents, 86-87
AutoNew macro, 1147
AutoOpen macro, 1147
AutoSave files, 85-86
AutoText
  creating entries, 143-144
  deleting entries, 145
  inserting, 142-146
  printing entries, 146
  Spike, 145-146
AutoText button (Standard
  toolbar), 143
Autotext command (Edit
  menu), 143-144
AutoText dialog box, 145
AVERAGE function, 636
Award Wizard, 175

B

Back button (Help window),
  53
background printing, 234
background repagination,
  161
backing up documents
  automatically, 86-87
  sequential backups, 82
BAK files, 86
balance (publication
  design), 835-836
balancing columns, 398
base styles, 371-373
BatchConversion macro
  (CONVERT.DOT template),
  1025
bit maps
  data exchanges, 999
  font creation, 282
  memory, 1041
blank frames, 693-694
Bookmark command (Edit
  menu), 149, 151, 595, 897,
  1127, 1143
Bookmark dialog box, 149,
  151, 631

bookmarks, 149-152, 1075
  creating, 149-150
  deleting, 151-152
  field codes, 1080-1082
  form fields, 595
  going to, 130
  manipulating
    bookmarked text,
    150-151
  math operations,
    631-633, 1105
  naming, 150
  selecting, 151
Border dialog box, 791
borders, 324
  changing styles, 331-332
  frames, 713-714
  paragraphs, 324-335
    enclosing, 329
    shading, 334
  tables, 538-540
  WordArt images, 790-791
Borders and Shading
  command (Format menu),
  325, 328, 538, 541,
  677-678
Borders button (Formatting
  toolbar), 326, 335
Borders dialog box, 294
Borders tab
  Paragraph Borders and
    Shading dialog box, 326
  Picture Borders dialog
    box, 677
  Table Borders and
    Shading dialog box, 538
Borders toolbar, 43, 326
box borders (pictures),
  677-678
boxes
  changing styles, 331-332
  creating, 325-331
boxing text, 861
Break command (Insert
  menu), 162, 386, 398, 432,
  439, 842, 986

Break dialog box, 386-387,
  398, 432, 439
breaking
  pages, 439-440
  paragraphs, 437-439
Brochur1 template, 169
building
  equations, 643-648
  forms, 577-583, 603-611
    {fillin} fields, 605-606
    reusing field results,
    606-608
    saving/naming
    templates, 609
    updating fields,
    609-611
built-in heading styles
  (master documents), 971
built-in macros, 1125
Bulleted List button
  Formatting toolbar, 552
  Standard toolbar, 849
bulleted lists, 550-557
  customizing, 554-557
  ending, 553
  Formatting toolbar,
    552-553
  menu commands,
    551-552
  subordinate paragraphs,
    553-554
  removing bullets, 567
Bulleted tab (Bullets and
  Numbering dialog box),
  551
Bullets and Numbering
  command (Format menu),
  543, 551, 984
Bullets and Numbering
  dialog box, 309, 551, 557,
  563, 565
  Bulleted tab, 551
  Multilevel tab, 563
  Multilevel tabs, 565
  Numbered tab, 557

business cards, 865-866
Button Editor dialog box,
  1060

C

calculations, 630-631
  bookmark method,
    631-633
  tables, 633-637
  troubleshooting, 638-639
Calendar Wizard, 175
callouts, 27, 763-766
  changing, 764-766
  inserting, 764
cancelling links, 158
cancelling print jobs, 227
capitalization, 200,
  1088-1089
Caption command (Insert
  menu), 855, 919, 956
Caption dialog box, 517,
  956
Caption Numbering dialog
  box, 961
Caption style, 955
captions, 949-966
  automatic insertion,
    957-959
  chapter numbers inserted
    in, 962-963
  deleting/editing, 964-966
  editing, 963-964
  formatting, 963
  frames, 695
  framing, 964
  in publications, 855
  inserting manually,
    956-957
  labels, 959-961
  numbering, 961-962
  tables, 517-519
  updating, 964
cartridge fonts, 277

case conversion, 268-269
category (X) axis, 801
category names, charts, 801
Cell Height and Width
  command (Table menu),
  527
Cell Height and Width
  dialog box, 527, 529
cells (tables), 507
  appending/deleting, 532
  column width, 525-528
  copying/moving, 521-525
  editing, 519-521
  indents/tabs, 517
  merging, 535
  splitting, 536
Change Case command
  (Format menu), 268
Change Case dialog box,
  268
Change Source dialog box,
  1018
chapter numbers, 984-988
  captions, 962-963
character formatting in
  indexes, 902
Character Spacing tab (Font
  dialog box), 249, 267
character styles, 337
characters
  applying styles, 356-358
  character styles versus
    paragraph styles, 355
  character sets, 1167
  custom bullets, 556-557
  em dashes, 845
  formatting, 243-254
    command method,
      247-250
    copying formats,
      259-260
    default formatting,
      259
    Formatting toolbar,
      251-254
    keyboard shortcuts,
      250-251

selecting, 246
special options,
  260-269
troubleshooting, 254
viewing characters,
  244-246
removing styles, 359
tracking, 789
WordArt formatting,
  784-785
Chart commands
  (Microsoft Graph)
  Add Arrow, 821
  Add Legend, 821
  Data Labels, 820
  Gridlines, 821
  Titles, 820
charts, 799-801
  adding items, 819-822
  columns, 816-817
  data, 803-805
  data sheets, 801-802
  editing, 807-808
  formatting
    axes, 824
    fonts and text,
      823-824
    numbers/dates,
      817-819
    patterns/colors, 823
  from tables, 803
  inserting/deleting rows/
    columns, 810
  Microsoft Excel, 806-807
  sizing, 822-823
  types, 811-816
  updating, 826
Check Box Form Field
  Options dialog box, 591
  customizing, 591-592
Check Box form fields, 574
check boxes (dialog boxes),
  47-49
Check Errors button (Mail
  Merge toolbar), 480
Checking and Reporting
  Errors dialog box, 480

circles, 735-738
citations (Table of
  Authorities)
  customizing, 926-927
  editing, 925
  entries, 923
Clear command (Edit
  menu), 40
clearing tabs, 302-336
clicking mouse, 38
clip art, 858
Clipboard, 152-153, 158
Close and Return to
  Document command (File
  menu), 1004
Close command (File
  menu), 60, 79, 90
closing
  dialog boxes, 52
  document windows,
    60-61
  documents, 79, 90-91
  files, 60-61
  Help window, 55-56
  windows, 160
closure (publication design),
  835
codes
  fields, 1075-1076
  in fields, 1071-1073
  special characters,
    198-199
collapsing outlines, 620-622
collating print jobs, 228
colors
  arcs/wedges, 738-739
  arrows, 734-735
  changing
    command method,
      723-726
    Drawing toolbar, 727
  character formatting, 264
  charts, 823
  freehand drawings,
    739-742
  lines, 732-734, 748-749

selecting, 722-723
tables, 540-542
WordArt images, 792-793
column breaks, 397-398
column charts, 812-814
Column tab (Cell Height and Width dialog box), 527
Column Width dialog box, 817
columns, 383-400
  balancing, 398
  changing, 393-399
  charts, 816-817
    inserting/deleting, 810
  creating, 383-393
  editing text, 391
  formatting, 19
  landscape-oriented pages, 384
  length/width, 384-385, 852
  new, 397-398
  newspaper-style, 851-852
  number of columns, 394-395
  parallel, 383
  publications, 850-854
  removing, 397
  sections, 385-387, 852
  side-by-side, 853
  sideheads, 853-854
  snaking, 383
  tables
    inserting/deleting, 533
    numbering, 542-543
  viewing, 392-393
  width/spacing, 395-397
    equal, 387-388
    tables, 525-528
    unequal, 389-391
Columns button (Standard toolbar), 387, 394, 851
Columns command (Format menu), 386-387, 851
Columns commands (Microsoft Graph)

DataSeries Move to Main, 816
DataSeries Move to Overlay, 808, 815
DataSeries Series, 801, 803
Columns dialog box, 388, 393-394
combination charts, 812-814
combined documents, creating master documents from, 976
command buttons (dialog boxes), 47, 52
command macros, 1125
commands, 34
  (...) ellipsis following, 40
  adding to menus, 1062-1064
  assigning to shortcut keys, 1066-1068
  Control menu
    Maximize, 58, 79
    Minimize, 58
    Restore, 58
  creating styles, 362-364
  deselecting, 40
  dialog boxes, 47-52
  Edit menu
    Autotext, 143, 144
    Bookmark, 149, 151, 595, 897, 1127, 1143
    Clear, 40
    Copy, 154, 523, 884, 999, 1013
    Cut, 153, 523, 884
    Data Source, 457
    Find, 187, 884, 1083
    Go To, 129, 638, 1127-1128, 1143
    Links, 158, 1014-1019
    Main Document, 476
    Object, 654, 683, 1006
    Paste, 153, 524, 665, 885, 997, 1000

Paste Special, 157, 665, 997, 1011-1014
Picture, 683
Repeat, 259, 294
Replace, 142, 187, 190, 369, 884
Select All, 638, 1127
Undo, 139, 142, 1013
Undo Formatting, 410
Undo Replace, 192
Undo Spelling, 203
Undo Update Fields, 1097
Word Picture Object, 683
WordArt 2.0 Object, 797
WordArt Text, 778
File menu
  Close, 60, 79, 90
  Close and Return to Document, 1004
  Exit, 31, 1004
  Find File, 74, 84, 93, 96, 98, 235, 985
  Import Data, 806
  Merge Registration File, 1008
  New, 69, 70, 578
  Open, 71, 73, 75, 997, 999, 1024
  Page Setup, 315, 317, 404, 412, 429, 840, 983
  Print, 111, 146, 601, 215, 946, 1078, 1084
  Print Preview, 161, 224
  Printer Setup, 469
  Properties, 1044
  Save, 64, 73, 85
  Save All, 85, 304, 1136
  Save As, 64, 73, 81, 82, 1026
  Send, 238
  Summary Info, 83, 171

Templates, 172, 182, 371, 1126
Update, 1004
Win Fax, 237
Format menu
AutoFormat, 338, 343-349
Borders and Shading, 325, 328, 538, 541, 677-678
Bullets and Numbering, 543, 551, 984
Change Case, 268
Columns, 386-387, 851
Drawing Object, 723
Drop Cap, 271, 849
Font, 250, 259, 1086
Frame, 698
Heading and Numbering, 568-569, 625, 962
Matrix, 654
Options, 1084
Paragraph, 162, 289, 296, 319, 438, 1086
Picture, 673
Spacing, 649
Style, 352, 356, 362, 617, 883, 955
Style Gallery, 338, 341, 349-350
Tabs, 300, 517
formatting characters, 247-250
grayed commands, 42
Help menu
Contents, 52, 780, 1099
Search, 53
Insert menu
Annotation, 943
Break, 162, 386, 398, 432, 439, 842, 986
Caption, 855, 919, 956

Cross-reference, 953
Database, 451, 997
Date and Time, 428
Field, 479, 632, 1079-1080, 1090
File, 970, 997, 1010
Footnote, 879-882, 885, 888, 890, 983
Form Field, 576, 579, 587
Frame, 670, 689, 692, 964
Index and Tables, 625, 894, 985
Object, 644, 662, 667, 776, 800, 803, 804, 997, 1003
Page Numbers, 424, 983, 988
Picture, 662, 664, 763, 997
Symbol, 273, 1167
Install menu, 661
Style, 617
Microsoft Graph
Chart Add Arrow, 821
Chart Add Legend, 821
Chart Data Labels, 820
Chart Gridlines, 821
Chart Titles, 820
Columns, DataSeries Move to Main, 816
Columns, DataSeries Move to Overlay, 808, 815
Columns, DataSeries Series, 801-803
Edit Clear, 820
Edit Delete Row/Col, 810
Edit Insert Row/Col, 810
File Exit, 826
File Update, 826
Format 3-D View, 825-826

Format Chart, 813-814
Format Color Palette, 823
Format Column Width, 817
Format Overlay, 813-814
Format Pattern, 823, 825
Format Scale, 824-825
Gallery Combination, 808
Rows, DataSeries Series, 801
placing on toolbars, 1058-1059
removing from menus, 1064-1065
selecting, 40-42
drag and drop commands, 42
grayed commands, 42
keyboard method, 41
shortcut menus, 40-41
Style menu, 651
Table menu
AutoFormat, 537
Cell Height and Width, 527
Convert Table to Text, 545
Convert Text to Table, 546, 601
Delete Cells, 532
Delete Columns, 533
Delete Rows, 533
Formula, 547, 635
Headings, 535
Insert Cells, 532
Insert Columns, 533
Insert Rows, 533
Insert Table, 509, 512-513
Merge Cells, 535
Select Column, 534
Select Table, 517, 637
Sort, 462, 544

Split Cells, 536
Split Table, 544
toolbars, 42-46
  displaying/hiding,
    44-45
  Help, 44
  moving/sizing, 45-46
Tools menu
  AutoCorrect, 147
  Customize, 1062,
    1064, 1067
  Envelopes and Labels,
    466, 497
  Grammar, 208, 840
  Hyphenation, 140
  Language, 213
  Macro, 609, 1028,
    1061, 1126,
    1133-1134, 1148
  Macro Edit, 1152
  Mail Merge, 455,
    458-459, 461, 472
  Options, 42, 51, 56,
    67, 74, 84, 124, 1029,
    1039, 1077
  Protect Document,
    582, 598-600, 940
  Record Macro, 1128
  Revisions, 935, 938
  Spelling, 147, 201, 840
  Thesaurus, 212
  Unprotect, 940,
    1148-1149
  Unprotect Document,
    583, 599
  Word Count, 214
View menu
  Annotations, 944
  Field Codes, 158
  Footnote, 880
  Footnotes, 883,
    886-888
  Full Screen, 17, 120
  Header and Footer,
    416, 842, 987
  Master Document,
    899, 954, 972, 975

  Normal, 120, 223, 244,
    886-888, 1131, 1135
  Outline, 124, 524, 613,
    617
  Page Layout, 121, 161,
    223, 689, 1130
  Ruler, 293, 303,
    1130-1131
  Toolbars, 20, 44, 297,
    326, 355, 719, 994,
    1054, 1056, 1058,
    1130-1131
  Zoom, 121-124, 223,
    393, 1131
Window menu
  Arrange All, 79, 159,
    1152
  New Window, 159
  Remove Split, 160
  Split, 160
WordArt program,
  778-779
see also keyboard
  shortcuts
Compare Versions dialog
  box, 942
comparing document
  revisions, 941-942
compiling
  indexes, 899-901
  table of authorities,
    925-926
complex fields, 1085
components of fields,
  1074-1075
components of macro
  recording, 1127-1128
CompuServe, 1159
concordance files
  automatic index entries,
    907-909
  creating, 907
condensed lines, 320
conditional field inclusion
  (mail merges), 498-499
CONFIG.SYS file, 2, 1160

Confirm Password dialog
  box, 599
Connect Network dialog
  box, 103
Contents button (Help
  window), 53
Contents command (Help
  menu), 40, 52, 780, 1099
continuation (publication
  design), 835
continuation notices for
  endnotes/footnotes, 887
continuation separator lines,
  887
contrast (publication
  design), 836
Control menu commands
  Maximize, 58, 79
  Minimize, 58
  Restore, 58
controlling mail merges,
  485-486
Convert dialog box, 684,
  1007
Convert File dialog box, 75,
  1010, 1024
Convert Notes dialog box,
  886
Convert Table to Text
  command (Table menu),
  545
Convert Table to Text dialog
  box, 545
Convert Text to Table
  command (Table menu),
  546, 601
Convert Text to Table dialog
  box, 546-547
CONVERT.DOT template
  (BatchConversion macro),
  1025
converting
  embedded objects into
    different formats, 1007
  endnotes/footnotes,
    885-886

files, 999, 1021-1033
forms, 600-601
non-Word files, 475
pictures, 683-684
tables to text, 545
text to tables, 545-547
Copy button (Standard
  toolbar), 154
Copy command (Edit
  menu), 154, 523, 884, 999,
  1013
Copy dialog box, 112
copying
  and linking documents,
    1013
  cells (tables), 521-525
  character formats,
    259-260
  data into other formats,
    999-1000
  files, 111-112, 804-805
  footnotes/endnotes,
    884-885
  frames, 701-702
  lines/objects, 755
  macros to other
    templates, 1149-1150
  mouse method, 155-157
  pictures, 665-666, 680
  styles, 358
  template options,
    177-178
  text/graphics, 154-155
  tools to other toolbars,
    1054
COUNT function, 636
counting words
  (documents), 214
Create Data Source dialog
  box, 456, 476
Create Header Source dialog
  box, 500
Create Labels dialog box,
  495
Create New tab (Object
  dialog box), 644, 667, 776

cropping
  illustrations in
    publications, 855-856
  pictures, 672-676
    mouse method,
      673-675
    Picture dialog box,
      675-676
cross format saves
  (documents), 88
cross hair pointer (mouse),
  36
cross-application data
  sources, 459-460
cross-document cut/paste
  operations, 160
Cross-reference command
  (Insert menu), 953
Cross-reference dialog box,
  953
cross-references, 24, 949-966
  deleting/editing, 964-966
  formatting, 955
  indexes, 906-907
  master documents, 982
  other documents in
    master documents, 954
  troubleshooting, 982
  updating, 954
Ctrl+B keys (Bold attribute),
  1066
Custom (Grammar Rules
  group), 210
custom bullet characters,
  556-557
Custom Button dialog box,
  1058, 1059
custom dictionaries (spell
  checking), 205-206
custom labels, 497-498
custom menus, 1065
custom number formats in
  fields, 1090-1093
custom paper size, 413
custom styles, 626-627
custom tabs, 302

custom templates, 68-70,
  179-180
  based on existing
    documents, 180
  based on existing
    templates, 179
custom tool faces, 1054,
  1059-1060
custom toolbars, deleting,
  1057
Customize command (Tools
  menu), 1062, 1064, 1067
Customize dialog box, 373,
  1052, 1055, 1062, 1068
Customize Grammar
  Settings dialog box, 210
Customize Keyboard dialog
  box, 274
customizing, 1037-1049
  bulleted lists, 554-557
  citations in tables of
    authorities, 926-927
  display, 1046-1047
  document revision
    marks, 938-939
  form fields, 586-600
    Check Box type,
      591-592
    Drop-Down type,
      592-594
    Text type, 588-591
  global assignments,
    1051-1052
  hearing-impaired needs,
    1048-1049
  index entries, 898-899
  menus, 1062-1066
  mouse performance,
    1047-1048
  multilevel lists, 565-566
  numbered headings,
    569-571
  numbered lists, 561-562
  pull-down lists, 1055
  Symbol dialog box,
    274-275

template assignments, 1051-1052
toolbars, 22, 1052-1062
Word for Windows, 1037-1038
workspace, 1046-1047
Cut button (Standard toolbar), 153
Cut command (Edit menu), 153, 523, 884
cutting cross-document operations, 160
Cv Wizard, 175

D

data entry macros, 1143-1144
Data Form, 22, 460-464
    records, finding/editing, 460-462
    scrolling, 464
Data Form button (Database toolbar), 461
Data Form dialog box, 461
data formats (file exchanges), 998-999
data management (mail merges), 448-449
data sheets, Microsoft Graph, 808
    copying/moving data, 810
    editing data, 809, 811
    formatting, 816-819
    replacing data, 809
    selecting data, 808-809
Data Source commands (Edit menu), 457
data sources (mail merges), 453-460, 471
    changing, 483
    creating, 454-458, 476-477, 483
    cross-application data sources, 459-460
    existing, 458-459

field changes, 462-463
managing, 460-464
record changes, 463
sorting, 462
specifying, 474-476
Data Type dialog box, 998
Database command (Insert menu), 451, 997
Database dialog box, 451, 453
Database toolbar, 43, 449-450
    Data Form button, 461
    Delete Record button, 463
    Insert Record button, 463
    Manage Fields button, 462
databases
    compatibility, 21, 451
    converting files from, 1021
    inserting into files, 450-453
datasources (merges), 500-502
Date and Time command (Insert menu), 428
Date and Time dialog box, 428
date/time
    field results, formatting, 1094-1096
    formatting in charts, 817-819
    headers/footers, 416
    options, 428
Day Placeholder, date/time formatting, 1094
debugging macros, 1152-1154
Decimal Point, numeric formatting, 1092
default settings
    characters, 259
    directories, 66-67
    indents, 313-315

margins, 403, 405
Page Setup dialog box, 413-414
templates, changing, 178-179
Define command (Style menu), 651
DEFINED function, 636
defragmenting utilities, 1042
Delete Cells command (Table menu), 532
Delete Cells dialog box, 532
Delete Columns command (Table menu), 533
Delete key, 40
Delete Record button (Database toolbar), 463
Delete Rows command (Table menu), 533
deleting
    annotations in documents, 945
    AutoText entries, 145
    bookmarks, 151-152
    caption labels, 961
    cells (tables), 532
    columns (tables), 533
    cross-references, 964-966
    custom toolbars, 1057
    field codes and results, 965
    fields, 1085
    files, 112-113
    footnotes/endnotes, 884-885
    headers/footers position, 423-424
    indexes, 903-904
    lines/objects, 755
    macros, 1148
    manual page breaks, 162
    rows (tables), 533
    soft fonts, 282-284
    styles, 366
    subdocuments, 981
    symbols, 274

tables of contents, 928-929
tables of figures, 928-929
text, 138-139, 369
demoting headings, 618-620
deselecting
    check boxes to change macros, 1141
    commands, 40
    drawing objects, 731-732
    text, 134
designing publications, 829-837
    balance, 835-836
    contrast, 836
    direction, 837
    focal point, 835
    graphics, 833
    illustrations, 833
    page design, 831
    paper selection, 834
    planning, 829-830
    scale, 836-837
    text, 832-833
    unity, 834-835
desktop publishing, 827-873
destination (linking text), 157
destination documents, 995, 1016
dialog boxes, 47-52
    and macro recording, 1140
    check boxes, 48-49
    closing, 52
    command buttons, 52
    Custom Button, 1058-1059
    Help button, 54-55
    list boxes, 51-52
    option buttons, 48-49
    tabbed dialog boxes, 16
    tabs, 48
    text boxes, 49-51
dingbats (characters), 272
direction (publication design), 837

directories, 64-66
    changing, 65-66
    default, 66-67
Directories list box, 65
disabling form fields, 594
discarding revisions in documents, 936-938
disk cache, 1041
disk drives, 65-66
display, customizing, 1046-1047
displaying
    annotations in documents, 944-945
    Drawing toolbar, 719
    equations/formulas, 641-643
    nonprinting characters, 200
    paragraph marks, 286-289
    pictures, 681-682
    ruler, 303
    shortcut menus, 41
    status bar, 77
    styles, 378-379
    tab characters, 299
    Task List, 57
    toolbars, 44-45
DOC files, 64
Document Control menu, 32
Document Statistics dialog box, 83
Document View icons, 223
Document window, 32
documents
    backing up, 86-87
    base styles, 371-373
    closing, 79, 90-91
    closing document windows, 60-61
    converting to master documents, 975
    copying and linking, 1013

counting words, 214
creating, 63-67
creating master documents, 976
cross format saves, 88
cross-document cut/paste operations, 160
designing templates from, 180
desktop publishing, 827-873
destination, 995
    renaming after source document, 1016
embedding data, 995
embedding objects, 1000-1008
linking, 996, 1008-1019
loading at startup, 1044-1045
multiple open windows, 159-160
naming, 81-82
navigating, 127-133
    bookmarks, 130
    going to pages, 129-130
    keyboard methods, 129
    mouse methods, 127-129
    moving insertion point, 131-133
new, 67-71
    NORMAL.DOT template, 69
    Template Wizards, 70-71
    templates, 70
    troubleshooting, 71
opening, 72-76
    existing Word for Windows documents, 72-74
    from File Manager, 75
    non-Word for Windows files, 74-75

recently-used files, 74
    troubleshooting, 76
passwords, 89-90
renaming, 82
repaginating, 440
revisions, 933-939
saving, 80-90
    automatic backups,
        86-87
    automatically, 85-86
    cross formatted saves,
        88
    Fast Save option, 87
    new names, 82
    protected files, 88-90
    reduced files, 1015
    replacing original,
        84-85
    summary information,
        83-84
    troubleshooting, 90
saving to other formats,
    1026-1027
scrolling
    keyboard methods,
        129
    mouse methods,
        127-129
soft page breaks, 161
source, 995, 1016
troubleshooting, 78
viewing, 103-109
    Find File dialog box,
        103-104
    multiple pages, 226
    multiple sections,
        159-160
    previewing
        documents, 105-107
    sorting file lists,
        104-105
    summary information,
        107-108
Wizard templates,
    174-175
zooming, 121-124

DOT files, 167
dot leaders, *see* tab leaders
double words (spelling
    checks), 200, 203
double-clicking mouse, 38
draft copies (documents),
    232-233
drag and drop commands,
    42
dragging objects, 754
dragging mouse, 38
drawing, 717-772
    arcs/wedges, 738-739
    arrows, 734-735
    changing objects,
        745-746
    color selection, 722-727
    custom tool faces, 1060
    deselecting objects,
        731-732
    drawing grid, 743-744
    Drawing screen, 727-728
    freehand shapes,
        739-742, 751-752
    line patterns, 722-727
    lines, 732-734
    objects, 730-732
    rearranging layers,
        766-770
        above/below text, 769
        beneath other objects,
            767-769
        framing objects,
            769-770
    scrolling pages, 728-729
    selecting objects, 731-732
    shadowed shapes,
        742-743
    shapes, 735-738
    troubleshooting, 744-745
Drawing Defaults dialog
    box, 723
    Fill tab, 724
    Line tab, 725-726
    Size and Position tab, 726
Drawing Object command
    (Format menu), 723

Drawing Object dialog box,
    723, 734, 746-747, 757
    Fill tab, 747
    Line tab, 734, 748
    Size and Position tab, 757
Drawing toolbar, 43, 661,
    683, 717, 767
    buttons, 719-722
    displaying, 719
drawing tools, 717-718
drawings
    in publications, 856
    including text/pictures,
        759
    picture containers,
        761-763
    text boxes, 759-761
Drictr1 template, 170
Drop Cap command
    (Format menu), 271, 849
Drop Cap dialog box, 271
drop caps, 26, 269-272
Drop-Down Form fields,
    574, 593
duplicating paragraph
    formats, 294

E

Edit Bar, 1153
Edit Category dialog box,
    926
Edit commands (Microsoft
    Graph)
    Clear, 820
    Delete Row/Col, 810
    Insert Row/Col, 810
Edit menu commands
    Autotext, 143-144
    Bookmark, 149, 151, 595,
        897, 1127, 1143
    Clear, 40
    Copy, 154, 523, 884,
        999, 1013
    Cut, 153, 523, 884
    Data Source, 457

Find, 187, 884, 1083
Go To, 129, 638,
   1127-1128, 1143
Links, 158, 1014-1019
Main Document, 476
Object, 654, 683, 1006
Paste, 153, 524, 665, 885,
   997, 1000
Paste Special, 157, 665,
   997, 1011-1014, 1013
Picture, 683
Repeat, 259, 294
Replace, 142, 187, 190,
   369, 884
Select All, 638, 1127
Undo, 139, 142, 1013
Undo Formatting, 410
Undo Replace, 192
Undo Spelling, 203
Undo Update Fields, 1097
Word Picture Object, 683
WordArt 2.0 Object, 797
WordArt Text, 778
editing
   captions, 963-964,
      964-966
   citations, 925
   cross-references, 964-966
   data sheets, 808-811
   embedded objects, 1006
   equations, 654-655
   field codes, 1084
   field results, 965
   full screen view, 120-121
   footnotes/endnotes, 883
   headers/footers position,
      422-423
   index fields, 902
   linked text, 158
   macros, 1134-1136
   main documents (mail
      merges), 478-483
   Microsoft Graph charts,
      807-808
   multiple documents,
      78-80

normal view, 120
outline view, 124
page layout view, 121
pictures, 683
Print Preview mode, 225
records, 460-462
screen view, 116-126
single documents, 76-78
summary information,
   108-109
tables, 519-535
tables of contents, 915
templates, 71, 175-179
   changing default
      settings, 178-179
   copying features to
      normal template,
      177-178
   default formats, 177
text in columns, 391
text boxes (dialog boxes),
   49-51
undoing edit selections,
   142
WordArt objects, 795-798
WordArt text, 777-778
ellipses, 40, 735-738
em dashes, 272, 845
embedded objects
   converting into different
      formats, 1007
   creating, 1001-1006
   editing, 1006
   troubleshooting, 1008
embedding
   data, 995
   files, 1004
   objects, 1003
   objects in documents,
      1000-1008
   portions of files, 1005
embellishments, 648
empty frames, 858
enabling TrueType fonts,
   280-281
end marks (tables), 514

End of document marker,
   35
ending
   bulleted lists, 553
   multilevel lists, 564
   numbered lists, 559-560
endnotes, 877-881
   converting to footnotes,
      885-886
   editing, 883-885
   finding, 883-884
   formatting, 883
   inserting, 878-881
   numbering, 890
   placing, 888-890
   reference marks, 881-882
   separators, 887-888
   viewing, 882-883
Enter key, 39, 77
Enter Your Text Here dialog
   box, 777, 785
Envelope Address dialog
   box, 492
Envelope Options dialog
   box, 469, 492
envelopes, 24, 466-470,
   870-871
   graphics, 470
   mail merges, 491-493
   POSTNET codes, 469-470
Envelopes and Labels
   command (Tools menu),
   466, 497
Envelopes and Labels dialog
   box, 466, 469, 497
   Labels tab, 494
equally-spaced columns,
   387-388
Equation Editor, 641-645
equations
   building, 643-648
   displaying, 641-643
   editing, 654-655
   embellishments, 648
   fonts
      selecting, 651-652
      sizes, 652-653

inserting, 644-645
inserting symbols,
  647-648
nested equations,
  645-647
positioning, 650-651
printing, 655
selecting equation items,
  645
spacing, 649-650
symbols, 647-648
viewing, 654
Excel, *see* Microsoft Excel
Exit command (File menu),
  31, 1004
exiting
  Word for Windows,
    30-31
  WordArt, 780
expanding outline view,
  622-624
  keyboard shortcuts, 624
  mouse method, 623
expression fields, 1104
Extend Selection mode
  (text), 134, 137
extensions (files), 64
externally created
  illustrations, 855

F

faces on tools, 1059-1060
facing pages, 406-407, 841
FALSE function, 636
Fast Saves option
  (documents), 87
Fax addressing dialog box,
  238
Fax Wizard, 175
Faxcovr1 template, 170
Faxcovr2 template, 170
faxes, 237-238
field characters, 1074
field codes, 1071-1122

bookmarks, 1080-1082
creating tables of figures,
  920-922
deleting, 965
displaying, 1077-1078
editing, 1084
embedded objects, 1001
formatting results,
  1085-1087
help, 1098-1099
indexes, 898-899
inserting, 1079-1082
limiting in tables of
  contents, 929
locating, 1083
printing, 1076-1079
reference list and
  explanations of
  function, 1100-1121
shading data from, 965
switches, 930-931,
  1080-1082
tables of contents,
  914-916
viewing, 1076-1079
Field Codes command (View
  menu), 158
Field command (Insert
  menu), 479, 632,
  1079-1080, 1090
Field dialog box, 632, 1079
field instructions, 1074
Field Options dialog box,
  915, 1081
field results, 1078
  deleting, 965
  editing/formatting, 965
field types, 1074
fields, 471, 1073-1076
  capitalization, 1088
  codes, *see* field codes
  complex, 1085
  components, 1074-1075
  databases, 449
  data sources (mail
    merges), 462-463
  deleting, 1085

documents, 949
formatting, 1089-1096
locking, 1019, 1098
mail merges, 454
manual formatting,
  1087-1088
math operations, 632
moving between, 1083
nested, 607, 1085
RD (Reference
  Document), 985
shading, 1078
switches for formatting,
  1086-1087
undoing updates,
  1097-1098
unlinking, 1098
updating, 1096-1097
see also form fields
Figure captions, 917-920,
  955
File command (Insert
  menu), 970, 997, 1010
file converters, 1022,
  1027-1028
  data exchanges, 998
  improving compatibility,
    1029-1030
  installing, 1023-1024
  modifying, 1028-1029
  WIN.INI file inclusion,
    1028
File dialog box, 1010
File Exit command
  (Microsoft Graph), 826
File Locations tab (Options
  dailog box), 67, 85, 172
File Manager (Windows), 75
File menu commands
  Close, 60, 79, 90
  Close and Return to
    Document, 1004
  Exit, 31, 1004
  Find File, 74, 84, 93, 96,
    98, 235, 985
  Import Data, 806

Merge Registration File, 1008
New, 69-70, 578
Open, 71, 73, 75, 997, 999, 1024
Page Setup, 315, 317, 404, 412, 429, 840, 983
Print, 111, 146, 215, 946, 1078, 1084
Print command, 601
Print Preview, 161, 224
Printer Setup, 469
Properties, 1044
Save, 64, 73, 85
Save All, 85, 304, 1136
Save As, 64, 73, 81, 82, 1026
Send, 238
Summary Info, 83, 171
Templates, 172, 182, 371, 1126
Update, 1004
Win Fax, 237
File Page Setup dialog box, 306
File Update command (Microsoft Graph), 826
files
    ASD, 85
    AUTOEXEC.BAT, 31, 1160
    BAK, 86
    closing, 60-61
    concordance
        automatic index entries, 907-909
        creating, 907
    CONFIG.SYS, 2, 1160
    converting, 475, 999, 1021-1026
    copying, 111-112, 804-805
    deleting, 112-113
    directories, 64-66
    DOC, 64
    DOT, 167
    embedding, 1004

embedding portions thereof, 1005
Find File command, 93
finding, 22, 74, 95-103
    by date, 101
    by summary information/file text, 98-100
    different drives/ directories, 96-97
    including networks in searches, 103
    saving search criteria, 102
    specific file types, 97-98
    troubleshooting, 103
font-mapping, 1032
FONTSUB.INI, 1031
importing data into documents, 996
inserting data into documents, 996
inserting databases, 450-453
large documents
    footnote numbers, 983
    printing, 985
linking, 1008-1019
listing, 72, 74
managing, 94-95, 109-113
    copying, 111-112
    deleting, 112-113
    file selection, 110
    opening files, 110-111
    printing, 111
multiple backups, 84
naming, 64
opening, 110-111, 1022
previewing, 105-107
printing, 111
printing documents to files, 236-237
REG.DAT, 2, 1160
selecting, 110

starting numbers of large documents, 983-984
summary information, 108-109
TXT, 1032
viewing information, 103-109
    Find File dialog box, 103-104
    previewing documents, 105-107
    sorting file lists, 104-105
    summary information, 107-108
WIN.INI, 2, 282, 1160
    checking for file converters, 1027
    running Word at startup, 1043
Word for Windows opening formats, 1022-1023
    see also documents
files conversion, 1025-1026
Fill tab (Drawing Defaults dialog box), 724, 747
Fill-In dialog boxes, 603-611, 1084
FILLIN fields, 501
{fillin} fields, 605-606
filling on-screen forms, 584-586
Filter Records tab (Query Options dialog box), 488
Final Draft, 936
find and replace operations, 187-200
    formatting, 193-197
    special character, 198-200
    styles, 197
    text
        finding, 187-190
        Replace All button (Replace dialog box), 192
        replacing, 190-193

Find command (Edit menu), 187, 884, 1083

Find dialog box, 187-189, 1083

Find File button (Open dialog box), 95

Find File command (File menu), 74, 84, 93, 96, 98, 235, 985

Find File dialog box, 93, 96, 103

Find Font dialog box, 194

Find in Field dialog box, 461

Find Language dialog box, 194

Find Paragraph dialog box, 194

Find Style dialog box, 195

finding
  files, 22, 74, 95-103
    by date, 101
    by summary information/file text, 98-100
    different drives/directories, 96-97
    including networks in searches, 103
    saving search criteria, 102
    specific file types, 97-98
    troubleshooting, 103
  footnotes/endnotes, 883-884
  records, 460-462
  sections (documents), 435-437

First Draft, 936

Flesch-Kincaid index, 211

flipping lines/objects, 753

flipping/stretching letters (WordArt), 785-786

floating text in charts, 821

focal points (publication design), 835

folded brochures, 866-868

font cartridges, 221-222

Font command (Format menu), 250, 259, 1086

Font dialog box, 247-250
  Character Spacing tab, 249, 267
  Font tab, 248-249

font mapping in TXT files, 1032

Font tab (Font dialog box), 248-249

font-mapping files, 1032

fonts, 255, 276-284
  cartridge fonts, 277
  changing, 254-258
  charts, 823-824
  converting in documents, 1030-1033
  Equation Editor, 651-653
  find and replace operations, 194
  Formatting toolbar, 257-258
  limiting to improve performance, 1040
  listing, 51
  points, 257
  printer capabilities, 278
  printer/screen fonts, 245-246
  publications, 843-844
  resident fonts, 276
  scalable fonts, 277
  screen fonts, 257
  screen soft fonts, 278
  size, 257-261
  soft fonts, 277, 282-284
  substitution in documents, 1031
  system fonts, 277
  TrueType, 245, 279-281, 1040
  type management programs, 278
  typefaces, 276
  Windows 3.0, 279

WordArt operations, 782-784

FONTSUB.INI file, 1031

footers, *see* headers/footers

Footnote and Endnote dialog box, 879-882

Footnote command
  Insert menu, 879-882, 885, 888, 890, 983
  View menu, 880

footnotes, 877-881
  converting to endnotes, 885-886
  editing, 883-885
  finding, 883-884
  formatting, 883
  inserting, 878-881
  numbering, 890, 983
  placing, 888-890
  reference marks, 881-882
  separators, 887-888
  viewing, 882-883

Footnotes command (View menu), 883, 886-887, 888

For Casual Writing (Grammar Rules group), 210

Form Field command (Insert menu), 576, 579, 587

Form Field dialog box, 579, 587

Form Field Options dialog box, 595-598

form fields, 574-576
  appending to forms, 578-580
  bookmarks, 595
  customizing, 586-600
    Check Box type, 591-592
    Drop-Down type, 592-594
    Text type, 588-591
  disabling, 594
  formatting, 594
  help messages, 595-597

form input data, 234
Form toolbar, 580
Format 3-D View command,
  825-826
Format Callout dialog box,
  765-766
Format commands
  (Microsoft Graph)
    Chart, 813-814
    Color Palette, 823
    Column Width, 817
    Overlay, 813-814
    Pattern, 823, 825
    Scale, 824-825
Format Chart dialog box,
  814
Format menu commands
    AutoFormat, 338,
      343-349
    Borders and Shading,
      325, 328, 538, 541,
      677-678
    Bullets and Numbering,
      543, 551, 984
    Change Case, 268
    Columns, 386-387, 851
    Drawing Object, 723
    Drop Cap, 271, 849
    Font, 250, 259, 1086
    Frame, 698
    Heading and Numbering,
      568-569, 625, 962
    Matrix, 654
    Options, 1084
    Paragraph, 162, 289, 296,
      319, 438, 1086
    Picture, 673
    Spacing, 649
    Style, 352, 356, 362, 883,
      955
    Style Gallery, 338, 341,
      349-350
    Tabs, 300, 517
Format Overlay dialog box,
  814

Format Painter button
  (Standard toolbar), 18, 294,
  358
Format Spacing dialog box,
  653
formats for indexes, 900
formatted text, data
  exchanges, 998
formatting
    callouts, 764-766
    captions, 963
    characters, 243-244,
      246-254
      command method,
        247-250
      copying formats,
        259-260
      default formatting,
        259
      flipping/stretching,
        785
      Formatting toolbar,
        251-254
      keyboard shortcuts,
        250-251
      rotating/slanting,
        785-788
      special options,
        260-269
      troubleshooting, 254
      WordArt, 784-785
    characters in indexes, 902
    charts, 822-826
    columns, 19
    cross-references, 955
    data sheets, 816-819
    date/time field results,
      1094-1096
    dates/numbers, 1087
    equations, 649-650
    field results, 965
    fields with switches,
      1086-1087
    find and replace
      operations, 193-197
    footnotes/endnotes, 883
    form fields, 594

headers/footers position,
  422
indexes, 901-903
line numbers, 430-431
manual, 379-381
master documents, 977
methods, 339-341, 379
negative numbers with
  right parenthesis,),
  1091
numbers, 1089-1090
outlines, 618
page numbers, 426-427
paragraphs
    duplicating formats,
      294
    Formatting toolbar,
      292-293
    menu commands, 291
    options, 285-286,
      289-295
    ruler, 293
    shortcut keys, 291-292
    troubleshooting, 295
removing all options, 196
sections (documents),
  435
Style Gallery, 19
styles, 337-381
tables, 536-542
    AutoFormat
      command, 537
    borders, 538-540
    shading/colors,
      540-542
tables of contents,
  929-931
text in frames, 690-691
text case, 1087
versus styles, 337-339
see also styles
formatting field code results,
  1085-1087
Formatting toolbar, 43, 289
    applying standard styles,
      352

Borders button, 326, 335
Bulleted List button, 552
characters, 251-254
font changes, 256-258
indents, 312
Numbered List button, 559
numbered lists, 559
paragraphs
    aligning, 297
    formatting, 292-293
Style box, 339
styles, selecting, 253-254
forms, 573-611
    attaching macros, 597-598
    based on templates, 576
    building, 577-583
    converting, 600-601
    customizing form fields, 586-600
    Fill-In dialog boxes, 603-611
        {fillin} fields, 605-606
        reusing field results, 606-608
        saving/naming templates, 608-609
        updating fields, 609-611
    form fields, 578-580
    on-screen forms, 583-586
        filling, 584-586
        saving, 586
        troubleshooting, 586
    passwords, 583
    printing, 601-603
        blank forms, 602
        data, 602
        full form, 601-602
        troubleshooting, 602-603
    protecting, 598
    protecting/saving, 581-583
    saving as templates, 578

section protection, 599-600
structure, 577-578
unprotecting, 583, 599
forms feature, 23
Forms toolbar, 43, 579, 599
Formula command (Table menu), 547, 635
Formula dialog box, 635
formulas, 629-639
    adjusting, 634
    displaying, 641-643
    out of table formulas, 637
    recalculating, 637-639
    tables, 635-637
four-column newsletters, 871-873
Frame button (Standard toolbar), 689
Frame command
    Format menu, 698
    Insert menu, 689-670, 692, 964
Frame dialog box, 703, 705
frames, 687-715
    anchoring, 707-710
    blank frames, 693-694
    bordering, 713-714
    captions, 695, 964
    copying, 701-702
    empty, 858
    graphics, 155, 691-692
    inserting pictures, 669-670
    moving, 700-702
    multiple objects, 694-695
    positioning, 702-707
    removing, 699
    selecting, 697-699
    shading, 713-714
    sizing, 710-713
    tables, 692-693
    text, 689-691
    text/objects in publications, 859-860
    troubleshooting, 696-697
    viewing, 695-696

freehand drawings, 739-742, 751-752
Full Screen command (View menu), 17, 120
Full Screen toolbar, 121
Full Screen view, 17, 116, 120-121
functions (math calculations), 1106-1108
functions of field codes, 1073

G

Gallery Combination (Microsoft Graph), 808
General tab (Options dialog box), 74, 161
gestalt theory (publications), 834
global assignment of customization, 1051-1052
global macros, 1125
Go To command (Edit menu), 129, 638, 1127-1128, 1143
Go To dialog box, 130-131, 638, 884, 944
grammar checking documents, 207-211
Grammar command (Tools menu), 208, 840
Grammar dialog box, 207-209
Grammar tab (Options dialog box), 207-211
graph markers, 811
Graph, see Microsoft Graph
graphics
    appending to AutoText, 143
    copying, 154-157
    envelopes, 470
    frames, 691-692
    see also frames

framing, 155
moving, 153-154
programs, 660-661
publication design, 833
text as graphics, 849-850
see also pictures
graphics boxes, 861-862
grayed commands, 42
gridlines
    charts, 821-822
    tables, 514
grouping objects, 771
guidelines for macros,
    1126-1127
gutters, 406-408, 841

H

handles (floating text), 821
hanging indents, 306,
    308-309, 549
hard hyphens, *see*
    nonbreaking hyphens
hard page breaks, *see*
    manual page breaks
hardware requirements, 1-2,
    1159-1160
Header and Footer
    command (View menu),
    416, 842, 987
Header and Footer dialog
    box, 418
Header and Footer toolbar,
    490
Header Options dialog box,
    500
header records, 471
headers/footers, 414-424
    appending, 414-417
    date/time insertion, 416
    deleting, 423-424
    editing, 422-423
    first page, 419-420
    formatting/positioning,
        422
    in document sections,
        417-421

margin position, 421-422
master documents, 977
odd/even pages, 420-421
overlapping, 416
publications, 842, 857
relinking, 418
removing, 420
standardizing, 419
Heading Numbering
    command (Format menu),
    568-569, 625, 962
Heading Numbering dialog
    box, 568-569, 962
headings
    demoting, 618-620
    in publications, 846
    outlines, 628
    promoting, 618-620
    styles, 351, 909
    subordinate headings,
        619-620
    tables, 535
Headings command (Table
    menu), 535
hearing-impaired needs,
    1048-1049
Help, 52-56
    closing Help window,
        55-56
    dialog box help, 54-55
    field codes, 1098-1099
    for macros, 1150-1151
    form fields, 595-597
    jumping topics, 54
    keyboard shortcut (F1),
        52
    Mail Merge Helper, 448
    searching topics, 53-54
    shortcut menus, 16
    Tip of the Day feature,
        15-16
    WordArt program, 780
Help button (Standard
    toolbar), 379
Help for WordPerfect Users
    dialog box, 56

Help menu commands
    Contents, 40, 52, 780,
        1099
    Search, 53
hidden text, 261-264
hiding
    pictures, 681-682
    toolbars, 44-45
History button (Help
    window), 53
horizontally positioning
    frames, 702-704
hot words (Help), 54
Hour Placeholder, date/time
    formatting, 1095
hyphenation, 139-142
Hyphenation command
    (Tools menu), 140
Hyphenation dialog box,
    141

I

I-beam shaped pointer, 36
icons
    padlock, 978
    Split window icons, 35
    subdocument, 978
    Word, 1044-1046
IF function, 636
illustrations
    graphics boxes, 861-862
    publications, 854-858
        captions, 855
        clip art, 858
        design, 833
        empty frames, 858
        externally created, 855
        headers/footers, 857
        logos with WordArt,
            857-858
        photographs, 854
        positioning, 856
        sizing/cropping,
            855-856
        transparent graphics,
            857

Import Data command (File menu), 806
Import Data dialog box, 806
import filters, 661
importing data from files to documents, 996
importing into Microsoft Graph
  ASCII text files, 805-806
  Microsoft Excel charts, 806-807
Inactive window, 34
indents, 306-315
  default settings, 313-315
  Formatting toolbar, 312
  hanging indents, 306, 308-309
  in table cells, 517
  keyboard shortcuts, 313
  nested indents, 306
  outdenting, 307
  paragraphs, 312, 849
  rows (tables), 531
  ruler, 310
  setting, 307-308
Indents and Spacing tab (Paragraph dialog box), 296, 308, 531, 849
Index and Tables command (Insert menu), 625, 894, 985
Index and Tables dialog box, 894, 906, 914
Index Style dialog box, 900
index tab (Options dialog box), 139
indexes, 893-909, 985
  automatic entries, 907-909
  compiling, 899-901
  creating entries, 894-896
  cross-reference, 906-907
  customizing entries, 898-899
  deleting, 903-904
  editing fields, 902
  field codes, 898-899

  fixing as text, 904
  formats, 900
  formatting, 901-903
  master documents, 982
  multiple-level, 904-906
  page ranges, 897-898
  replacing, 903
  styles (entries), 901
  troubleshooting, 982
  updating, 903
Indexes and Tables dialog box, 625
Indicators, 33
Input dialog boxes in macros, 1143-1146
Insert Cells command (Table menu), 532
Insert Cells dialog box, 532
Insert Columns command (Table menu), 533
Insert key, 77
Insert menu commands
  Annotation, 943
  Break, 162, 386, 398, 432, 439, 842, 986
  Caption, 855, 919, 956
  Cross-reference, 953
  Database, 451, 997
  Date and Time, 428
  Field, 479, 632, 1079-1080, 1090
  File, 970, 997, 1010
  Footnote, 879-882, 885, 888, 890, 983
  Form Field, 576, 579, 587
  Frame, 670, 689, 692, 964
  Index and Tables, 625, 894, 985
  Object, 644, 662, 667, 776, 800, 803-804, 997, 1003
  Page Numbers, 424, 983, 988
  Picture, 662, 664, 763, 997
  Symbol, 273, 1167

Insert Merge Field button (Mail Merge toolbar), 478
insert mode, 77
Insert Picture dialog box, 662
Insert Record button (Database toolbar), 463
Insert Rows command (Table menu), 533
Insert Table button (Standard toolbar), 513-514
Insert Table command (Table menu), 509, 512-513
inserting
  annotations in documents, 943-945
  AutoText, 142-146
  blank frames, 693-694
  bookmarks in field codes, 1081-1082
  callouts, 764
  columns (tables), 533
  data from files to documents, 996
  databases into files, 450-453
  equations, 644-645
  field codes manually, 1082
  footnotes/endnotes, 878-881
  manual page breaks, 162
  math formulas/functions, 632
  page breaks, 439-440
  page numbers, 424-425
  picture containers in drawings, 761-763
  pictures in documents, 662-665
  rows (tables), 533
  special characters, 272-276

switches in field codes, 1081-1082

symbols in equations, 647-648

text boxes in drawings, 759-761

insertion point, 33, 35, 76, 131-133

Install menu commands, 661

installing

file converters, 1023-1024

import filters, 661

printers, 217-219

soft fonts, 282-284

Word for Windows, 1-8, 1159-1166

WordArt, 775

INT function, 636

interacting with WIndows applications, 993-1019

intra-workgroup printing, 238-239

Invalid Merge Field dialog box, 482

Invoice template, 170

J–K

joining text in publications, 848

jumping Help topics, 54

justification in publications, 846-847

kerning, 267-268, 789-790, 845-846

keyboard

Alt key combinations, 39

creating lines, 328

navigating documents, 129

selecting

commands, 41

text, 135-138

sizing frames, 712-713

terminology, 38-40

keyboard shortcuts

bold text (Ctrl+B), 196

Bookmark (Ctrl+Shift+F5), 149

case conversion (text), 269

collapsing outlines, 622

Copy (Ctrl+C), 154

Cut (Ctrl+X), 153

Exit (Alt+F4), 31

expanding outline view, 624

Find (Ctrl+F), 187

Font (Ctrl+D), 256

font selection (Ctrl+Shift+F), 196

formatting characters, 250-251

formatting text, 345

Go To command (F5), 130

Help (F1), 52

hiding text, 262

indents, 313

manual page breaks, 162

Maximize command (Ctrl+F10), 79

New command (Ctrl+N), 69

Normal command (Alt+Ctrl+N), 119

Open command (Ctrl+O), 73

Outline command (Alt+Ctrl+O), 119

Page Layout command (Alt+Ctrl+P), 119

paragraph alignment, 297-298

Paste (Ctrl+V), 153

Print (Ctrl+Shift+F12), 227

promoting/demoting keyboards, 620

redefining styles (Ctrl+Shift+S), 367

removing manual styles (Ctrl+Q), 381

Repeat (F4), 294

Replace (Ctrl+H), 190

Save command (F12), 81

Save command (Shift+F12), 85

Select (Ctrl+5), 638

Spelling (F7), 201

Spike (Ctrl+F3), 145

Thesaurus (Shift+F7), 212

Undo (Ctrl+Z), 139, 142

Unspike (Shift+Ctrl+F3), 145

Update Fields (F9), 607

see also commands

L

Label Options dialog box, 494-496

labels, 24

captions, 959-960

custom, 497-498

mail merges, 494-498

Labels tab (Envelopes and Labels dialog box), 494

landscape-oriented pages, 384

Language command (Tools menu), 213

Language dialog box, 213

language formatting, 194

language options (documents), 213

large documents, 969, 985

Layout tab (Page Setup dialog box), 315, 317, 429

leaders, *see* tab leaders

leading, 320

left mouse button controls, 35

Legal Wizard, 175

legends, charts, 801, 821-822

Letter Wizard, 175

Letter1 template, 170
Letter2 template, 170
Letter3 template, 170
letterheads, 870-871
    mail merges, 490
line borders (pictures),
    678-679
line breaks, 323
line charts, 812-814
line numbers, 315-317,
    429-431
    appending, 315-317
    formatting, 430-431
    removing/supressing,
        317, 431
Line Numbers dialog box,
    315, 430
line patterns
    changing, 723-727
    selecting, 722-723
Line tab
    Drawing Defaults dialog
        box, 725-726
    Drawing Object dialog
        box, 734, 748
linefeeds, 466
lines
    aligning, 755-757
    changing styles, 331-332
    copying, 755
    creating, 325-331, 328
    deleting, 755
    drawing, 732-734
    flipping, 753
    leading, 320
    moving, 754-755
    positioning, 757-759
    publications, 847, 862
    removing, 749-750
    resizing, 750-751
    rotating, 752
    spacing, 318-323
    style/color, 748-749
Link/Unlink button (Header
    and Footer dialog box),
    418

linking
    converting to text/
        graphics, 1017
    data in documents, 996
    documents, 1008-1019
    documents to parts of
        files, 1011-1014
    files, 1008-1019
    manual, 1017
    pictures to documents,
        664
    sharing documents with
        other users, 1014
    text, 157-158
    troubleshooting,
        1013-1014
    updating linked
        documents, 1017
Links command (Edit
    menu), 158, 1014-1019
Links dialog box, 158, 1014
list boxes (dialog boxes), 47,
    51-52
list entries, marking in
    tables of figures, 921
listing
    files, 72, 74
    fonts, 51
lists, 549-571
    bulleted lists, 550-557
        customizing, 554-557
        ending, 553
        Formatting toolbar,
            552-553
        menu commands,
            551-552
        subordinate
            paragraphs, 553-554
    multilevel
        creating, 563-565
        customizing, 565-566
        ending, 564
    numbered, 557-562
        customizing, 561-562
        ending, 559-560

        Formatting toolbar,
            559
        menu commands,
            557-559
        subordinate
            paragraphs, 560-561
    numbered headings
        creating, 567-569
        customizing, 569-571
        removing, 571
    publications, 849
    removing bullets/
        numbers, 567
    splitting, 567
loading
    add-ins, 173-174
    documents at startup,
        1044-1045
locating field codes, 1083
locking
    fields, 1019, 1098
    subdocuments, 978
logos (WordArt), 857-858

M

Macro command (Tools
    menu), 609, 1028, 1061,
    1126,
    1133-1134, 1148
Macro dialog box, 609,
    1061, 1129, 1132, 1150
macro edit bar, 1135
Macro Edit command (Tools
    menu), 1152
Macro Pause tool, 1129
Macro Record toolbar, 610
macro recorder, 1127-1128
Macro Recording toolbar,
    1129-1131
Macro toolbar, 1128
MACRO60.DOT template,
    1136
macros, 1123-1154
    activating, 1132-1134
    advanced, 1139

assigning to shortcut
keys, 1066-1068
attaching to forms,
597-598
AutoClose, 1147
AutoExec, 1147
AutoExit, 1147
automatic, 1146-1147
AutoNew, 1147
AutoOpen, 1147
BatchConversion, 1025
built-in, 1125
changing
by deselecting check
boxes, 1141
by editing WordBASIC
statements, 1141
command, 1125
components, 1127-1128
copying to other
templates, 1149-1150
data entry, 1143-1144
debugging, 1152-1154
deleting, 1148
editing, 1134-1136
entering data with input
boxes, 1143
global, 1125
guidelines for recording,
1126-1127
Help, 1150-1151
Input dialog boxes,
1144-1146
managing, 1148-1150
modifying recordings,
1139-1141
MyWorkspace, 1141-1143
placing on toolbars,
1058-1059
planning operation, 1125
recording, 1124-1132
recording dialog box
information, 1140
renaming, 1148-1149
sample, 1136
recording, 1129-1131

saving, 1131, 1136
template, 1125
troubleshooting, 1134
updating fields (forms),
609-611
Mail Merge command (Tools
menu), 455, 458-459, 461,
472
Mail Merge Helper, 448,
454-455, 471, 485
data sources, 455-458
envelopes, 491-493
starting, 472
Mail Merge Helper dialog
box, 455, 460, 472, 491
Mail Merge toolbar, 484-485
Check Errors button, 480
Insert Merge Field button,
478
View Merged Data
button, 479
mail merges, 24, 447-464,
470-502
conditional field
inclusion, 498-499
controlling, 485-486
custom labels, 497-498
data management,
448-449
data sources, 453-460
creating, 454-458,
476-477
creating documents,
483
cross-application data
sources, 459-460
existing, 458-459
field changes, 462-463
managing, 460-464
record changes, 463
sorting, 462
specifying, 474-476
envelopes, 491-493
errors, 479-482
fields, 454
labels, 494-498

letterheads, 490
main documents,
473-474
editing, 478-483
multiple data sources,
500-501
optimizing, 498-502
performing, 483-484
rule-building, 489-490
selecting records, 486-490
suppressing lines in
labels, 500
user input, 501-502
Mail Sign In dialog box, 238
Main Document (Edit
menu), 476
main documents, 471
data sources, 483
editing, 478-483
specifying, 473-474
Manage Fields button
(Database toolbar), 462
Manage Fields dialog box,
462
managing data sources (mail
merges), 460-464
managing files, 94-95,
109-113
copying, 111-112
deleting, 112-113
file selection, 110
opening files, 110-111
printing, 111
see also files
manipulating bookmarked
text, 150-151
manipulating windows,
57-61
manual caption insertion,
956-957
manual formats in fields,
1087-1088
manual formatting, 379-381
manual links, 1017-1018
manual page breaks,
161-162

manual styles, 381

Manual1 template, 170

Manuscr1 template, 170

Manuscr3 template, 170

margins, 306, 402-411

  changing, 410-411

  default measurement, 405

  document sections, 405-406

  headers/footers position, 421-422

  measured margins, 403-408

  page layout, 841

  positioning frames, 706-707

  publications, 842-843

  resetting, 410

  setting visually, 408-411

Margins tab (Page Setup dialog box), 404

Mark Citation dialog box, 923

Mark Index Entry dialog box, 894, 898, 905

marker fields, 1074

markers in charts, 801

marking

  list entries in tables of figures, 921

  revisions in documents, 935-936

Master Document command (View menu), 899, 954, 972, 975

Master Document toolbar, 971-972

master document view, 116, 972-975

master documents, 969, 976-979

  chapter numbers, 986-988

  converting documents to, 975

  creating, 971-976

  creating from combined documents, 976

  inserting documents into, 976

  troubleshooting, 976, 979

math calculations (tables), 547-548

math functions, 629-639

  bookmarks, 631-633

  calculations, 630-631

  table calculations, 633-637

  troubleshooting, 638-639

  versus spreadsheets, 629-630

math operators (bookmarks), 1105

Matrix command (Format menu), 654

Matrix dialog box, 653

Matrix template palette, 653-654

MAX function, 636

Maximize command (Control menu), 58, 79

Maximize icon, 33

maximizing windows, 58, 79

measured margins, 403-408

Memo Wizard, 175

Memo1 template, 170

Memo2 template, 170

Memo3 template, 170

memory

  bitmap, 1041

  Clipboard, 152-153

  managing to improve performance, 1041-1042

  printers, 221-222

  RAM, 63

Menu bar, 33-34

Menu Bar dialog box, 1066

menus, 34

  adding, 1065-1066

  customizing, 1062-1066

  removing, 1065-1066

Merge Cells command (Table menu), 535

Merge dialog box, 485-486, 487

Merge Registration File command (File menu), 1008

Merge Registration File dialog box, 1008

Merge Revisions dialog box, 940

merges

  cells (tables), 535

  annotations in documents, 940-941

  revisions in documents, 940-941

  subdocuments, 981

  see also Mail Merges

Microsoft Corporation, 1159

Microsoft Excel

  charts, importing, 806-807

  worksheets, 804-805

Microsoft Graph

  charts, 799-801

    adding items, 819-822

    data, 803

    data from Word for Windows or other programs, 804-805

    data sheets, 801-802

    editing, 807-808

    editing overlays, 808

    formatting, 822-826

    from tables, 803

    inserting/deleting rows or columns, 810

    types, 811-816

    updating, 826

  commands

    Chart Add Arrow, 821

    Chart Add Legend, 821

    Chart Data Labels, 820

    Chart Gridlines, 821

Chart Titles, 820
Columns, DataSeries Move to Main, 816
Columns, DataSeries Move to Overlay, 808, 815
Columns, DataSeries Series, 801, 803
Edit Clear, 820
Edit Delete Row/Col, 810
Edit Insert Row/Col, 810
File Exit, 826
File Update, 826
Format 3-D View, 825-826
Format Chart, 813-814
Format Color Palette, 823
Format Column Width, 817
Format Overlay, 813-814
Format Pattern, 823, 825
Format Scale, 824-825
Gallery Combination, 808
Rows, DataSeries Series, 801
data sheets, 808
copying/moving data, 810
editing, 811
editing data, 809, 811
formatting, 816-819
replacing data, 809
selecting data, 808-809
importing
ASCII text files, 805-806
Microsoft Excel charts, 806-807
Microsoft Query, 475

Microsoft Toolbar, 43
starting programs, 994
Microsoft Word Picture objects, 668
MIN function, 636
Minimize command (Control menu), 58
Minimize icon, 33
minimizing
picture size
file format method, 664-672
linking, 664
windows, 58
Minute Placeholder, date/time formatting, 1095
mirror margins, 417
Mirror Margins option (Page Setup dialog box), 407
MOD function, 636
Modify Heading Numbering dialog box, 569
Modify Location dialog box, 85
Modify Multilevel List dialog box, 565-569
Modify Numbered List dialog box, 561-562
Modify Style dialog box, 366, 368, 372, 374-375
modifying
file converters, 1028-1029
macro recordings, 1139-1141
MyWorkspace macro, 1141-1143
screen display, 124-126
Word icon, 1045-1046
see also editing
Month Placeholder, date/time formatting, 1094
mouse, 35-37, 39
clicking, 38
collapsing outlines, 621-622
creating lines, 328

customizing
performance, 1047-1048
deselecting text, 134
dragging, 38
expanding outline view, 623
move/copy operations, 155-157
navigating documents, 127-129
pointer shapes, 36-37
promoting/demoting headings, 619-620
resizing/cropping pictures, 673-675
selecting table items, 520
selecting text, 133-135
sizing frames, 711-712
splitting windows, 160
terminology, 37-38
Mouse pointer, 32, 35
Mouse program, 35
moving
between fields, 1083
cells (tables), 521-525
footnotes/endnotes, 884-885
frames, 700-702
Full Screen toolbar, 121
insertion point, 131-133
lines/objects, 754-755
pictures, 680
subdocuments in master documents, 980
text/graphics, 153-154
text/objects in publications, 859-860
toolbars, 45-46
tools to other toolbars, 1054
windows, 59
multilevel lists
creating, 563-565
customizing, 565-566
ending, 564

Multilevel tab (Bullets and Numbering dialog box), 563, 565
multiple documents
  editing, 78-80
  saving, 85
  see also documents
multiple open windows, 159-160
multiple references within cross-references, 951
multiple users of master documents, 978
multiple-level indexes, 904-906
MyWorkspace macro, 1141-1143

N

naming
  bookmarks, 150
  documents, 81-82
  files, 64
  styles, 359-360
navigating
  documents, 127-133
    bookmarks, 130
    going to pages, 129-130
    keyboard methods, 129
    mouse methods, 127-129
    moving insertion point, 131-133
  tables, 515-516
negative numbers, 1091
nested equations, 645-647
nested fields, 607, 1085
nested indents, 306
Network button (Advanced Search dialog box), 103
networks in file searches, 103

New command (File menu), 69-70, 578
New dialog box, 69-70, 83, 167, 578
New Document button (Standard toolbar), 69
new documents, 67-71
  NORMAL.DOT template, 69
  Template Wizards, 70-71
  templates, 70
  troubleshooting, 71
New Label dialog box, 959
New Style dialog box, 363-364
New Template option, 179
New Window command (Window menu), 159
newsletters, 829-830, 869-870
  four-column, 871-873
  see also publications
Newsletter Wizard, 175
newspaper columns, 383, 851-852
  see also snaking columns
nodes (freehand drawings), 751
nonbreaking hyphens, 140
nonprinting characters, 200
Normal command (View menu), 120, 244, 223, 886-888, 1131, 1135
Normal style, 339
  changing, 369-370
Normal template, 169
  copying features to other templates, 177-178
  default formats, 177
normal view, 116, 120
Normal View tab (Options dilalog box), 256
NORMAL.DOT template, 68-69, 304, 1066
NOT function, 637

Note Options dialog box, 885, 890
Number dialog box, 817
numbered headings
  creating, 567-569
  customizing, 569-571
  removing, 571
Numbered List button
  Formatting toolbar, 559
  Standard toolbar, 849
numbered lists, 557-562
  customizing, 561-562
  ending, 559-560
  Formatting toolbar, 559
  menu commands, 557-559
  subordinate paragraphs, 560-561
Numbered tab (Bullets and Numbering dialog box), 557
numbering
  captions, 961-962
  footnotes, 890
  lines, 429-431
  lists, 567
  outlines, 625
  pages, 424-427
  table rows/columns, 542-543
Numbering button (Standard toolbar), 542
numbering lines (documents), 315-317
numbers
  chapters, 984-985
  formatting
    as text, 1089-1090
    custom, 1090-1093
    in charts, 817-819
    in fields, 1089
    with 0 Placeholder, 1091
numeric pictures, 1091

O

Object command
Edit menu, 654, 683, 1006
Insert menu, 644, 662, 667, 776, 800, 803-804, 997, 1003
Object dialog box, 644, 667, 776
objects
aligning, 755-757
anchoring, 758
callouts, 27
changing drawing objects, 745-747
copying, 755
creating, 1002-1003
cut and paste operations, 754-755
data exchanges, 998
deleting, 755
drawing, 729-732
embedded, 1000-1008
converting into different formats, 1007
creating, 1001-1006
editing, 1006
flipping, 753
framing multiple objects, 694-695
grouping, 771
moving, 754-755
picture objects
documents, 666-669
frames/text boxes, 669-670
positioning, 757-759
rotating, 752
troubleshooting, 753, 772
ungrouping, 771-772
WordArt, 775-780, 795-798

OLE (Object Linking and Embedding), 773, 799, 1000
on-screen forms, 583-586
filling, 584-586
saving, 586
troubleshooting, 586
Open button (Standard toolbar), 73
Open command (File menu), 71, 73, 75, 997, 999, 1024
Open Data Source dialog box, 452, 458, 475, 494
Open dialog box, 65, 73, 95, 1024
Open Index AutoMark File dialog box, 908
opening
documents, 72-76
existing Word for Windows documents, 72-74
non-Word for Windows files, 74-75
recently-used files, 74
troubleshooting, 76
files, 110-111
to convert formats, 1022
Word for Windows formats, 1022-1023
source documents, 1016
subdocuments, 980
Wizards, 17
operators (math calculations), 1106-1108
optimizing mail merges, 498-502
optimizing Word for Windows, 1037-1049
option buttons (dialog boxes), 47-49
Option command (Tools menu), 51
optional hyphens, 140-142

Options command
Format menu, 1084
Tools menu, 42, 56, 67, 74, 84, 124, 1029, 1039, 1077
Options dialog box, 230, 1039
AutoFormat tab, 347
File Locations tab, 67, 85, 172
General tab, 74, 161
Grammar, 209
Grammar tab, 207, 211
index tab, 139
Normal View tab, 256
Print tab, 231, 263, 602
Save tab, 84-86, 603
Spelling tab, 204, 206
View tab, 77, 124, 286
OR function, 637
ordering subdocuments in master documents, 980
Organizer, 182-183
Organizer dialog box, 376, 1149-1150
orientation (paper), 840
outdenting, 307
Outline command (View menu), 124, 524, 613, 617
Outline toolbar, 615-616
outline view, 116, 124
Outliner, 524
outlines, 613-628
collapsing, 620-622
creating, 617-618
documents, printing, 978
expanding, 622-624
fonts, 277
formatting, 618
headings, 909-912
numbering, 625
printing, 628
removing text, 628
reorganizing, 624-625
replacing headings, 626-628

styles, 626-627
tables of contents,
    625-626
viewing, 613-616
Outlining toolbar, 971-972
overlapping headers/footers,
    416
overlay charts, 808
overriding, 379-381
overtype mode, 77-78, 139

P

padlock icon, 978
page breaks, 439-440
page design (publications),
    831
page layout, 401-443,
    840-843
    changing, 842
    facing pages, 841
    gutters, 841
    margins, 402-411, 841
        measured margins,
            403-408
        setting visually,
            408-411
    orientation, 840
    paper size, 840
    sections, 432-434
        finding, 435-437
        formatting, 435
        removing, 434
        types, 435
Page Layout command
    (View menu), 121, 161,
    223, 689, 1130
Page Layout view, 116
    editing documents, 121
    previewing print jobs,
        222-226
Page Number Format dialog
    box, 426
page numbers, 424-427
Page Numbers command
    (Insert menu), 424, 983,
    988

Page Numbers dialog box,
    424
page ranges in indexes,
    897-898
Page Setup button (Header
    and Footer toolbar), 490
Page Setup command (File
    menu), 315, 317, 404, 412,
    429, 840, 983
Page Setup dialog box, 222,
    315, 403-404, 406, 412,
    429
    default settings, 413-414
    Layout tab, 315, 317, 429
    Margins tab, 404
    Paper Size tab, 412
    Paper Source tab, 441
pages, 161-162
    background repagination,
        161
    going to, 129-130
    manual page breaks,
        161-162
paper
    publication design, 834
    selecting paper source
        (printers), 441-443
    size/orientation, 411-413,
        840
Paper Size tab (Page Setup
    dialog box), 412
Paper Source tab (Page Setup
    dialog box), 441
Paragraph Borders and
    Shading dialog box, 325,
    328
    Borders tab, 326
    Shading tab, 326,
        332-333
Paragraph command
    (Format menu), 162, 289,
    296, 319, 438, 1086
Paragraph dialog box, 291,
    296, 438, 848
    indentation options,
        307-308

Indents and Spacing tab,
    296, 308, 531, 849
Text Flow tab, 291, 431,
    438, 848
paragraph styles, 337
paragraphs, 285-336
    aligning, 295-298
        Formatting toolbar,
            297
        keyboard shortcuts,
            297-298
        menu commands,
            296-297
        troubleshooting,
            298-300
    applying styles, 356
    bordering, 325-335
    breaking, 437-439
    displaying paragraph
        marks, 286-289
    drop caps, 269-272
    find and replace
        operations, 194
    formatting
        duplicating formats,
            294
        Formatting toolbar,
            292-293
        menu commands, 291
        options, 285-286,
            289-295
        ruler, 293
        shortcut keys, 291-292
        troubleshooting, 295
    indenting, 312
    paragraph styles versus
        character styles, 355
    publications
        indenting, 849
        shading/coloring, 863
        spacing, 847
    shading, 332-335
    spacing, 318-323
        adjusting, 318-319
    starting numbers, 984

parallel columns, 383
passim, tables of authorities, 926
passwords, 89, 90, 583, 598-599
Paste button (Standard toolbar), 153
Paste command (Edit menu), 153, 524, 665, 885, 997, 1000
Paste Special command (Edit menu), 157, 665, 997, 1011-1014
Paste Special dialog box, 157, 1006
pasting
   cross-document operations, 160
   data into other formats, 999-1000
   data in documents, 996
patterns
   charts, 823
   shading, 332
photographs in publications, 854
Picture Borders dialog box, 677
Picture command
   Edit menu, 683
   Format menu, 673
   Insert menu, 662, 664, 763, 997
   Install menu, 661
picture containers, 763
Picture dialog box, 664, 675-676
pictures, 659-685
   box borders, 677-678
   converting, 683-684
   copying, 665-666, 680
   cropping, 672-676
   displaying/hiding, 681-682
   editing, 683
   frames/text boxes, 669-670

import filters, 661
   including in drawings, 759, 761-763
   line borders, 678-679
   moving, 680
   resetting, 676
   resizing, 672-676
      mouse method, 673-675
      Picture dialog box, 675-676
   selecting, 671-672
   see also graphics
pictures and data exchanges, 999
pie charts, 812-814
planning operation of macros, 1125
pointer shapes (mouse), 36-37
points (fonts), 257
positioning
   equations, 650-651
   frames, 702-707
   headers/footers, 422
   illustrations in publications, 856
   lines/objects, 757-759
POSTNET codes, 469
predefined templates, 169-172
Present1 template, 170
Presrel1 template, 170
Presrel2 template, 170
Presrel3 template, 170
Preview Icon Bar, 224-225
previewing
   documents, 105-107
   print jobs, 222-226
Print command (File menu), 111, 146, 215, 221, 601, 946, 1078, 1084
Print dialog box, 111, 216, 601, 1078
Print Preview command (File menu), 161, 224
Print Preview mode, 225

Print Setup dialog box, 216, 219, 221
Print Setup Options dialog box, 220
Print tab (Options dialog box), 231, 263, 602
Print to File dialog box, 236
printer fonts, 245-246
printer orientation, 277
Printer Setup command (File menu), 469
printers
   font capabilities, 278
   installing, 217-219
   memory and font cartridges, 221-222
   selecting, 215-217
   selecting paper source, 441-443
   special setups, 219-220
Printers dialog box, 222
printing, 215-239
   annotated documents, 946
   AutoText entries, 146
   background printing, 234
   cancelling print jobs, 227
   current document, 227-232
      hidden attributes, 230-232
      multiple copies, 227-228
      specified ranges, 228-230
   documents, 442
      as files, 236-237
      intra-wrokgroup printing, 238-239
      to fax machines, 237-238
   draft copies, 232-233
   envelopes, 466-470
      graphics, 470
      POSTNET codes, 469-470

equations, 655
field codes, 1078-1079
files, 111
files of large documents, 985
form input data, 234
forms, 601-603
    blank form, 602
    data, 602
    full form, 601-602
    troubleshooting, 602-603
hidden text, 263
linefeeds, 466
master documents, 978
outlines, 628
outlines of documents, 978
previewing print jobs, 222-226
publications, 863-865
    originals for duplication, 864
    printer capacity, 864
    typesetting, 864-865
reversing print order, 233
selecting paper source, 234-235
small documents as large contiguous documents, 982-986
unopened documents, 235-236
Update Links option, 233
updating fields, 233
PRODUCT function, 637
product support, 1159-1160
Program Item Properties dialog box, 1044
programs
    Access Pack, 1048
    graphics, 660-661
    Microsoft Graph, 799-826
    Mouse program, 35
    SmartDrive, 1042
    starting with Microsoft toolbar, 994

type management programs (fonts), 278
Word Setup, 1023
WordArt, 773-775
promoting headings, 618-620
Properties command (File menu), 1044
Protect button (Forms toolbar), 599
Protect Document command (Tools menu), 582, 586, 598-600, 940
Protect Document dialog box, 582, 598-600, 940
protected files, 88-90
protecting
    documents
        for annotations, 945-946
        for revisions, 939-940
    forms, 581-583, 598
proximity (publication design), 834
publications, 865
    ads, 868-869
    alignment/justification, 846-847
    balance, 835-836
    boxing text, 861
    business cards, 865-866
    columns, 850-854
        length, 852
        newspaper-style, 851-852
        sections, 852
        side-by-side, 853
        sideheads, 853-854
    contrast, 836
    designing, 829-837
    direction, 837
    drawing, 856
    focal point, 835
    folded brochures, 866-868

fonts, 843-844
framing/moving objects, 859-860
gestalt theory, 834
graphics, 833
graphics boxes, 861-862
grouping, 859-860
headers/footers, 842
illustrations, 833, 854-858
    captions, 855
    clip art, 858
    empty frames, 858
    externally created, 855
    headers/footers, 857
    logos with WordArt, 857-858
    photographs, 854
    positioning, 856
    sizing/cropping, 855-856
    transparent graphics, 857
letterheads/envelopes, 870-871
lines
    above/below paragraphs, 862
    between columns, 862
lists, 849
margin items, 842-843
newsletters, 869-873
page design, 831
page layout, 840-843
    changing, 842
    facing pages, 841
    gutters, 841
    margins, 841
    orientation, 840
    paper size, 840
paper selection, 834
paragraphs
    indenting, 849
    shading/coloring, 863
planning, 829-830
printing, 863-865

originals for
   duplication, 864
   printer capacity, 864
   typesetting, 864-865
scale, 836, 837
spacing, 847
spelling/grammar checks,
   839-840
styles, 839, 848
templates, 839
text, 832-833
   as graphics, 849-850
   joining, 848
   kerning/tracking,
      845-846
   styles/color, 844-845
   typesetting characters,
      845
titles/headings, 846
toolbars, 839
unity, 834-835
view options, 838-839
Wizards, 839
see also documents
pull-down lists, 1055
Purchord template, 170

Q–R

Query Options dialog box,
   488

RAM (random access
   memory), 63
RD (Reference Document)
   fields, 985
Read Only option (Open
   dialog box), 73
Read-Only Recommended
   option (documents), 88, 90
readability statistics, 211
Reapply Style dialog box,
   367
rearranging drawing layers,
   766-770
   above/below text, 769

beneath other objects,
   767-769
   framing objects, 769-770
recalculating formulas,
   637-639
reconnecting links, 1018
Record Macro command
   (Tools menu), 1128
Record Macro dialog box,
   1128, 1130
recording
   macros, 1124-1132
   sample macros,
      1129-1131
records, 471
   Data Form operations,
      460-462
   data sources (mail
      merges), 463
   databases, 448
   mail merges, 486-490
rectangles, 735-738
redefining stylesm 367-369
   normal style, 369-370
   standard styles, 354-355
Redo button (Standard
   toolbar), 142
references
   footnotes/endnotes,
      881-882
   in cross-references, 953
reformatting tab stops, 301
REG.DAT file, 2,1160
relinking headers/footers,
   418
Remove Split command
   (Window menu), 160
removing
   add-ins, 174
   arrows, 750
   bullets/lists, 567
   character styles, 359
   columns, 397
   commands from menus,
      1064-1065
   drop caps, 272

frames, 699
headers/footers, 420
line numbers, 317, 431
lines, 749-750
manual styles, 381
menus, 1065-1066
numbered headings, 571
optional hyphens, 142
outline text, 628
page numbers, 425-426
picture borders, 679
sections (documents),
   434
shading (paragraphs), 335
shortcut menus, 41
tabs, 304-336
tools from toolbars,
   1054-1056
TrueType fonts from use,
   1040
underlined text, 266
window splits, 160
see also deleting
Rename dialog box, 1149
renaming
   documents, 82
   macros, 1148-1149
   styles, 366-367
   subdocuments, 975
reorganizing
   outlines, 624-625
   tools on toolbars,
      1054-1056
repaginating documents,
   440
Repeat command (Edit
   menu), 259, 294
repeating character
   formatting, 260
repetition (publication
   design), 834
Replace All button (Replace
   dialog box), 192
Replace command (Edit
   menu), 142, 187, 190, 369,
   884

Replace dialog box, 190-191
replacing
  headings (outlines), 628
  indexes, 903
  outline headings,
    626-628
  tables of contents, 928
  tables of figures, 928
  text, 139
  see also find and replace
    operations
Report1 template, 170
Report2 template, 170
Report3 template, 170
resetting
  margins, 410
  pictures, 676
resident fonts, 276
resizing
  lines, 750-751
  pictures, 672-676
Restore command (Control
  menu), 58
Restore icon, 33
restoring menus to original
  state, 1064-1065
restoring window size, 58
result fields, 1074
Resume Wizard, 175
Resume1 template, 170
Resume2 template, 170
Resume4 template, 170
reusing field results (forms),
  606-608
reversing print order, 233
Review AutoFormat Changes
  dialog box, 345-346
Review Revisions dialog box,
  936-937
reviewing formatting
  changes, 345-347
revision bars in text, 935
revision marks, 345-346, 934
  all documents, 936
  customizing, 938-939

revisions
  as inserted text, 938
  comparing document,
    941-942
  documents, 933-947
  marking in documents,
    935-936
  merging in documents,
    940-941
  protecting documents,
    939-940
  showing in documents,
    936
  troubleshooting, 941
  unprotecting documents,
    940
Revisions command (Tools
  menu), 935, 938
Revisions dialog box, 935
right mouse button controls,
  35
right parenthesis,) in
  negative number
  formatting, 1091
right-clicking mouse, 38
Ron Person & Co., 1160
rotating lines/objects, 752
ROUND function, 637
Row tab (Cell Height and
  Width dialog box), 529
rows
  charts, 810
  tables
    height/position,
      528-531
    inserting/deleting, 533
    numbering, 542-543
    spacing, 530
Rows, DataSeries Series
  command (Microsoft
  Graph), 801
RTF files in data exchanges,
  998
Rule groups (grammar
  checking documents),
  209-211

Ruler, 35
  formatting paragraphs,
    293
  indents, 310
  margins, 410-411
Ruler command (View
  menu), 293, 303,
  1130-1131
running macros, 1132-1134

S

sans serif fonts, 254, 832
Save All command (File
  menu), 85, 304, 1136
Save As command (File
  menu), 64, 73, 81-82, 1026
Save As dialog box, 61, 66,
  81, 305
Save button (Standard
  toolbar), 81, 85
Save command (File menu),
  64, 73, 85
Save Data Source dialog box,
  457, 477
Save tab (Options dialog
  box), 84-86, 603
saving
  documents, 80-90
    as reduced files, 1015
    automatic backups,
      86-87
    automatically, 85-86
    cross formatted saves,
      88
    Fast Save option, 87
    new names, 82
    protected files, 88-90
    replacing original,
      84-85
    summary information,
      83-84
    to other formats,
      1026-1027
    troubleshooting, 90

form structures, 577-578
macros, 1131, 1136
multiple documents, 85
on-screen forms, 586
search criteria (files), 102
scalable fonts, 277
scale (publication design), 836-837
screen display, 115-126, 245-246
screen
    elements, 31-35
    fonts, 245-246, 257, 283
    magnification, 122
    soft fonts, 278
    view, selecting, 116-120
Scroll bar, 33
scrolling Data Forms, 464
scrolling documents, 127-129
scrolling pages, 728-729
Search button (Help window), 53
Search command (Help menu), 53
Search dialog box, 95, 98, 985
    Advanced Search command, 96
    Help topics, 53
searching Help topics, 53-54
Section Protection dialog box, 600
sections, 385-387, 432-434
    finding, 435-437
    formatting, 435
    headers/footers placement, 417-421
    margins, 405-406
    master documents, 977
    page numbers, 427
    protecting in forms, 5 99-600
    removing, 434
    types, 435

Select All command (Edit menu), 638, 1127
Select Column command (Table menu), 534
Select Table command (Table menu), 517, 637
selecting, 37
    bookmarks, 151
    colors (drawing), 722-723
    commands, 40-42
        drag and drop commands, 42
        grayed commands, 42
        keyboard method, 41
        shortcut menus, 40-41
    drawing objects, 731-732
    equation items, 645
    files, 110
    frames, 697-699
    line patterns, 722-723
    paper source, 441-443
    paper source (printers), 234-235
    pictures, 671-672
    printers, 215-217
    records (mail merges), 486-490
    Rule groups (grammar checking documents), 209-211
    screen view, 116-120
    tables, 136
    text, 49, 133-138
    views, 403
Send command (File menu), 238
separators for footnotes/ endnotes, 887-888
SEQ field, 986-987
sequential backups (documents), 82
series names, charts, 801
serif fonts, 254, 832
setting
    default directories, 66-67
    gutters, 408

measured margins, 404-405
tabs, 300-336
Setup dialog box, 4, 1162
shading
    fields, 1078
    frames, 713-714
    paragraphs, 324-335
    removing, 335
    tables, 540-542
    WordArt images, 792-793
shading data from field codes, 965
Shading dialog box, 792-793
Shading Options button (Forms toolbar), 580
Shading tab (Paragraph Borders and Shading dialog box), 326, 332-333
Shading tab
    Picture Borders dialog box, 677
    Table Borders and Shading dialog box, 541
Shadow dialog box, 794
shadowed shapes, 742-743
shadows (WordArt images), 794-795
shaping text, 782
sharing styles, 375-377
shortcut keys
    assigning commands, 1066-1068
    assigning macros, 1066-1068
    cell selection (tables), 521
    fields, 1075-1076
    inserting embellishments, 648
    inserting symbols, 647-648
    inserting templates, 646-647
    moving/copying text, 154-155

paragraph formatting, 291-292
spacing in equations, 650
styles, 373-374
table navigation, 516
shortcut menus, 16
displaying, 41
removing, 41
selecting commands, 40-41
Show/Hide ¶ button (Standard toolbar), 289
Show/Hide Hidden Character button (Standard toolbar), 458
showing revisions in documents, 936
side-by-side columns, 853
sideheads, 853-854
SIGN function, 637
similarity (publication design), 834
Size and Position tab (Drawing Defaults dialog box), 726
Size and Position tab (Drawing Object dialog box), 757
Size Define dialog box, 650
sizing
frames, 710-713
keyboard method, 712-713
mouse method, 711-712
illustrations in publications, 855-856
toolbars, 45-46
windows, 58, 59
SmartDrive program, 1042
snaking columns, 383
see also columns; newspaper columns
Snap to Grid dialog box, 743
soft fonts, 277
installing, 283

installing/deleting, 282-284
soft page breaks, 161
soft returns, 323
Sort command (Table menu), 462, 544
Sort dialog box, 544
sorting
data sources (mail merges), 462
file lists, 104-105
tables, 544-545
source (linking text), 157
source documents, 995, 1016
spacing
columns, 395-397
line breaks, 323
lines/paragraphs, 318-323
publications, 847
rows (tables), 530
Spacing Between Characters dialog box, 790
Spacing command (Format menu), 649
special characters
codes, 198-199
find and replace operations, 198-200
formats, 260
case conversion, 268-269
color, 264
hidden text, 261-264
kerning, 267-268
superscripts/subscripts, 264-265
underlining, 265-267
inserting, 272-276
keyboard insertion, 275-276
Symbol dial box, 273-275
special effects (WordArt), 780-795
aligning text, 788
borders, 790-792

character formatting, 784-785
color/shading, 792-793
flipping/stretching letters, 785-786
fonts/symbols, 782-784
kerning, 789-790
rotating/slanting text, 787-788
shadows, 794-795
shaping text, 782
Special Effects dialog box, 787
special print setups, 219-220
specialty fonts, 254
spell checking documents, 200-207
appending dictionary, 203
AutoCorrect feature, 146-149
custom dictionaries, 205-206
double words, 203
options, 204-205
troubleshooting, 207
Spelling button (Standard toolbar), 201
Spelling command (Tools menu), 147, 201, 840
Spelling dialog box, 200-201, 204
Spelling tab (Options dialog box), 204, 206
Spike (AutoText), 145-146
Split Cells command (Table menu), 536
Split command (Window menu), 160
Split Table command (Table menu), 544
Split window icons, 35
splitting
cells (tables), 536
lists, 567
subdocuments, 980-981
tables, 543-544

spreadsheets
   converting files from,
      1021
   versus Word math
      functions, 629-630
squares, 735-738
standard styles, 351-355
Standard toolbar, 43
   ¶ button, 126
   AutoFormat button, 344
   AutoText button, 143
   Bulleted List button, 849
   Columns button, 387,
      394, 851
   Copy button, 154
   copying character
      formatting, 260
   Cut button, 153
   Format Painter button,
      18, 294, 358
   Frame button, 689
   Help button, 379
   Insert Table button, 513
   New Document button,
      69
   Numbered List button,
      849
   Numbering button, 542
   Open button, 73
   Paste button, 153
   Redo button, 142
   Save button, 81, 85
   Show/Hide ¶ button, 289
   Show/Hide Hidden
      Character button, 458
   Spelling button, 201
   Undo button, 142
   Zoom buttons, 119
standardizing headers/
   footers, 419
starting
   Mail Merge Helper, 472
   Microsoft Graph, 800
   programs with Microsoft
      toolbar, 994
   Word for Windows,
      29-31, 1043-1046

Word installation
   program, 2-3,
   1160-1161
   WordArt, 775-776
starting numbers
   files of large documents,
      983-984
   large document files, 983
   page numbers, 988
   paragraphs, 984
statements (WordBASIC),
   1140
Status Bar, 33, 77
Status Bar tab (Form Field
   Options dialog box), 596
Strictly (Grammar Rules
   group), 209
style areas, 378-379
Style box (Formatting
   toolbar), 339
Style command (Format
   menu), 352, 356, 362, 617,
   883, 955
Style dialog box, 352, 356,
   363
Style Gallery, 19
Style Gallery command
   (Format menu), 338, 341,
   349-350
Style Gallery dialog box, 350
Style menu commands, 651
styles, 337-381
   aliases, 366-367
   alternating, 375
   applying, 340-341
      AutoFormat command
         (Format menu),
         343-345
      AutoFormat options,
         347-348
      character styles,
         356-358
      maximizing
         AutoFormat
         command, 348-349
      paragraph styles, 356

reviewing formatting
      changes, 345-347
   Style Gallery
      command (Format
      menu), 349-350
base styles, 371-373
based on existing styles,
   364-365
changing, 365-373
copying, 358
creating, 359-365
   based on existing
      styles, 364-365
   by example, 360-362
   names, 359-360
   with menu
      commands, 362-364
deleting, 366
displaying, 378-379
find and replace
   operations, 195, 197
formatting methods,
   339-341
formatting tables of
   contents, 930
Formatting toolbar,
   253-254
index entries, 901
lines, 748-749
naming, 359-360
normal style, 369-370
overriding, 379-381
publications, 839, 848
redefining, 367-369
removing, 359
renaming, 366-367
sharing, 375-377
shortcut keys, 373-374
standard styles, 351-355
tables of figures, 917-920
updating, 370-371
versus formatting,
   337-339
see also formatting
Styles dialog box, 378
subdocuments, 969

icon, 978
locking, 978
master documents, 971, 979-981
multiple users in master document, 978
renaming, 975
troubleshooting, 979
unlocking, 978
subentries (indexes), 893
subordinate headings, 619-620
subordinate paragraphs
bulleted lists, 553-554
numbered lists, 560-561
subroutines (macros), 1134
subscripts, 264-265
SUM function, 637
Summary Info command (File menu), 83
Summary Info command command (File menu), 171
Summary Info dialog box, 81, 83-84, 171
summary information, 83
appending, 108-109
editing, 108-109
finding files with, 100
Summary tab (Advanced Search dialog box), 99
superscripts, 264-265
suppressing
line numbers, 317, 431
lines in labels (mail merges), 500
switches
field codes, 930-931, 1080-1082
field results, 1075, 1086
fields, 1086-1087
indexes, 902
switching
applications, 57
documents, 57-58
full-screen document windows, 79

Symbol command (Insert menu), 273, 1167
Symbol dialog box, 273-275, 556
symbols
deleting, 274
inserting in equations, 647-648
WordArt operations, 782-784
see also special characters
system fonts, 277
system memory, 1041-1042

T

tab leaders, 300
tab styles, 303
tabbed dialog boxes, 16
Table AutoFormat dialog box, 537
Table Borders and Shading dialog box, 538, 541
Table menu commands
AutoFormat, 537
Cell Height and Width, 527
Convert Table to Text, 545
Convert Text to Table, 546, 601
Delete Cells, 532
Delete Columns, 533
Delete Rows, 533
Formula, 547, 635
Headings, 535
Insert Cells, 532
Insert Columns, 533
Insert Rows, 533
Insert Table, 509, 512-513
Merge Cells, 535
Select Table, 517, 637
Sort, 462, 544
Split Cells, 536
Split Table, 544

Table Numbering dialog box, 542
table of contents, 985-986
from outline headings, 625-626
master documents, 982
troubleshooting, 982
Table of Contents Options dialog box, 913, 916
Table of Figures Options dialog box, 919, 922
Table Wizard, 175, 509-511
tables, 507-548
appending/deleting elements, 531-534
AutoFit Command, 528
calculations, 633-637
captions, 517-519, 955
cells
copying/moving, 521-525
merging, 535
splitting, 536
charts, 803
column width, 525-528
converting text to tables, 545-547
converting to text, 545
creating, 509-519
Insert Table button (Standard toolbar), 513-514
Insert Table command, 512-513
Table Wizard, 509-511
editing, 519-535
formatting, 536-542
AutoFormat command, 537
borders, 538-540
shading/colors, 540-542
formulas, 635-637
frames, 692-693
gridlines/end marks, 514
headings, 535

indents/tabs, 517
math calculations,
   547-548
navigating, 515-516
numbering rows/
   columns, 542-543
out of table formulas, 637
rows, 528-531
selecting, 136
sorting, 544-545
splitting, 543-544
troubleshooting, 534-535
versus tabs, 300
tables of authorities,
   923-927
tables of contents, 909-917
   creating, 915-916
   deleting, 928-929
   editing, 915
   field codes, 914-916
   formatting, 929-931
   limiting field codes, 929
   outline headings,
      909-912
   replacing, 928
   troubleshooting, 916-917
   updating, 927-928
   varied styles, 912-914
tables of figures, 917-922
   creating, 921-922
   creating with field codes,
      920-922
   deleting, 928-929
   replacing, 928
   updating, 927-928
tabs, 298-305
   clearing, 302-336
   custom, 302
   defaults, 304-305
   displaying tab characters,
      299
   in table cells, 517
   removing, 304-336
   ruler, 302-304
   setting, 300-336
   Tabs dialog box, 300-302

troubleshooting, 305
   versus tables, 300
   see also individual tab
      listings
Tabs command (Format
   menu), 300, 517
Tabs dialog box, 300
Task List, 57
Template Wizards, 68, 70-71
   troubleshooting, 71
templates, 68-70, 165-168
   as document patterns,
      168-172
   assignments, 1051-1052
   attaching to documents,
      180-181
   changing default settings,
      178-179
   CONVERT.DOT, 1025
   copying features to
      normal template,
      177-178
   copying macros to,
      1149-1150
   custom, 179-180
   default formats, 177
   editing, 71, 175-179
   forms, 576
   global, 1066
   including features
      globally, 1046
   insertion shortcut keys,
      646-647
   MACRO60.DOT, 1136
   macros, 1125
   predefined, 169-172
   publications, 839
   saving forms as
      templates, 578
   transferring contents,
      182-183
   transferring toolbars
      between, 1061-1062
   troubleshooting, 172
   Wizards, 174-175

Templates and Add-ins
   dialog box, 173, 371
Templates command (File
   menu), 172, 182, 371,
   1126
text, 1075
   aligning, 436-437, 788
   appending to AutoText,
      143
   case conversion, 268-269
   color characters, 264
   converting to/from
      tables, 545-547
   copying, 154-157
   deleting, 138-139, 369
   editing in columns, 391
   em dashes, 272, 845
   Extend Selection mode,
      134, 137
   floating, 821
   formatting numbers as,
      1089-1090
   frames, 689-691
      see also frames
   hidden text, 261-264
   including in drawings,
      759-761
   linking, 157-158
   moving, 153-154
   paragraph styles versus
      character styles, 355
   publication design,
      832-833
   removing from outlines,
      628
   replacing, 139
   revision bars, 935
   rotating/slanting
      (WordArt), 787-788
   selecting, 49, 133-138
      keyboard method,
         135-138
      mouse method,
         133-135
   shaping, 782
   spiking, 145-146

superscripts/subscripts, 264-265
tracking, 789
troubleshooting, 138
umlauts, 272
underlining, 265-267
vertical position, 265
word-wrap feature, 77
WordArt, 777-778
see also documents
text boxes (dialog boxes), 47
inserting pictures, 669-670
troubleshooting, 763
editing, 49-51
text files (ASCII), 805-806
Text Flow tab (Paragraph dialog box), 291, 431, 438, 848
Text Form Field Options dialog box, 588-590
Text form fields, 574, 588-591
text-editing actions, 50
Thesaurus, 212-213
Thesaurus command (Tools menu), 212
Thesaurus dialog box, 212
Thesis1 template, 170
Thousands Separator in numeric formatting, 1092
tildes, 272
time in headers/footers, 416
Timestamp tab (Advanced Search dialog box), 101
Tip of the Day feature, 15-16
Title bar, 33
titles in publications, 846
TOC Style dialog box, 911
tool faces, 1054
Toolbar, 20, 33, 35, 42-46
Borders toolbar, 326
creating, 1056-1057
customizing, 22, 1052-1062
Database toolbar, 449-450

displaying/hiding, 44-45
Drawing toolbar, 661, 717
Formatting tolbar
indents, 312
paragraphs, 292-293, 297
Forms toolbar, 579
Help, 44
Macro Record toolbar, 610
Macro Recording, 1129, 1131
Master Document, 971
moving/sizing, 45-46
Outline toolbar, 615-616, 971
placing commands upon, 1058-1059
placing macros on, 1058-1059
publications, 839
transferring between templates, 1061-1062
WordArt, 778
Toolbars command (View menu), 20, 44, 297, 326, 355, 719, 994, 1054, 1056, 1058, 1130-1131
Toolbars dialog box, 46, 1056, 1058
tools
adding faces to, 1059-1060
adding to toolbars, 1052-1054
copying to other toolbars, 1054
custom faces, drawing, 1060
Macro Pause, 1129
moving to other toolbars, 1054
removing from toolbars, 1054-1056
reorganizing on toolbars, 1054-1056

Tools menu commands
AutoCorrect, 147
Customize, 1062, 1064, 1067
Envelopes and Labels, 466, 497
Grammar, 208, 840
Hyphenation, 140
Language, 213
Macro, 609, 1028, 1061, 1126, 1133-1134, 1148
Macro Edit, 1152
Mail Merge, 455, 458-459, 461, 472
Option, 51
Options, 42, 56, 67, 74, 84, 124, 1029, 1039, 1077
Protect Document, 582, 598-600, 940
Record Macro, 1128
Revisions, 935, 938
Spelling, 147, 201, 840
Thesaurus, 212
Unprotect, 940, 1148-1149
Unprotect Document, 583, 599
Word Count, 214
tracking, 789, 845-846
transferring
macros between templates, 1149-1150
template contents, 182-183
toolbars between templates, 1061-1062
transparent graphics, 857
troubleshooting
annotations, 947
Clipboard, 158
cross-references, 982
documents
editing, 78
opening, 76
saving, 90

1210 troubleshooting

drawing, 744-745
embedded objects, 1008
files conversion,
  1025-1026
finding files, 103
formatting characters,
  254
frames, 696-697
grouping objects, 772
indexes, 982
linked files, 1013-1014
macro recording,
  1131-1134
master documents, 976,
  979
math calculations,
  638-639
object selection, 732
objects, 753
on-screen forms, 586
paragraphs, 295, 298-300
picture containers, 763
printing forms, 603
revisions, 941
spell checking, 207
subdocuments, 979
tables, 534-535
tables of contents,
  916-917, 982
tabs, 305
templates, 172
text, 138
text boxes, 763
WordArt, 780
TRUE function, 637
TrueType dialog box, 281
TrueType fonts, 245,
  279-281, 1040
TXT files, 1032
type management programs
  (fonts), 278
typesetting
  characters, 845
  publications, 864-865
typing, 39

U

umlauts, 272
underlining text, 265-267
Undo button (Standard
  toolbar), 142
Undo command (Edit
  menu), 139, 142, 1013
Undo Formatting command
  (Edit menu), 410
Undo Replace command
  (Edit menu), 192
Undo Spelling command
  (Edit menu), 203
Undo Update Fields
  command (Edit menu),
  1097
undoing edit selections, 142
undoing field updates,
  1097-1098
undoing spelling changes,
  203
unequally-spaced columns,
  389-391
unformatted text in data
  exchanges, 998
ungrouping objects, 771-772
unlinking, 1017
  fields, 1098
unlocking
  subdocuments, 978
unopened documents,
  235-236
Unprotect command (Tools
  menu), 940, 1148-1149
Unprotect Document
  command (Tools menu),
  583, 599
Unprotect Document dialog
  box, 599
unprotecting
  documents
    for annotations, 946
    for revisions, 940
  forms, 583, 599

unspiking text, 145
Update command (File
  menu), 1004
Update Links option
  (printing), 233
updating
  all document fields, 1097
  captions, 964
  cross-references, 954
  fields, 233, 1096-1097
  indexes, 903
  links, 1017
  manual links, 1018
  styles, 370-371
  tables of contents and
    figures, 927-928
  undoing in fields,
    1097-1098

V

vertical ruler, 530
vertically aligning text,
  436-437
vertically positioning
  frames, 705-706
View dialog box, 378
View menu commands
  Annotations, 944
  Field Codes, 158
  Footnote, 880
  Footnotes, 883, 886-888
  Full Screen, 17, 120
  Header and Footer, 416,
    842, 987
  Master Document, 899,
    954, 972, 975
  Normal, 120, 223, 244,
    886-888, 1131, 1135
  Outline, 124, 524, 613,
    617
  Page Layout, 121, 161,
    223, 689, 1130
  Ruler, 293, 303,
    1130-1131

Toolbars, 20, 44, 297, 326, 355, 719, 994, 1054, 1056, 1058, 1130-1131
Zoom, 121-124, 223, 393, 1131
View Merged Data button (Mail Merge toolbar), 479
View Options (Options dialog box), 125, 126
View tab (Options dialog box), 77, 124, 286
viewing
columns, 392-393
documents, 103-109
Find File dialog box, 103-104
multiple sections, 159-160
previewing documents, 105-107
sorting file lists, 104-105
summary information, 107-108
equations, 654
footnotes/endnotes, 882-883
formatted characters, 244-246
frames, 695-696
index field codes, 900
multiple pages, 226
optional hyphens, 140
outlines, 613-616
publications, 838-839
views, 403
visually setting margins, 408-411

W

wedges, 738-739
Weektime template, 170
width (columns), 395-397

wild-card characters, 72, 98
Win Fax command (File menu), 237
WIN.INI file, 282, 1160
checking for file converters, 1027
file converters, 1028
running Word at startup, 1043
Window menu commands
Arrange All, 79, 159, 1152
New Window, 159
Remove Split, 160
Split, 160
Windows
terminology, 37-40
version 3.0, 279
windows, 57-61
arranging, 79
closing, 160
closing document windows, 60-61
maximizing, 79
moving, 59
multiple open windows, 159-160
sizing, 58-59
splitting, 160
switching
applications, 57
documents, 57-58
Wizard dialog box, 70
Wizards, 17, 174-175
opening, 17
publications, 839
Table Wizard, 509-511
Word Count command (Tools menu), 214
Word Count dialog box, 214
Word for Windows
compatibility, 28
exiting, 30
file opening formats, 1022-1023

hardware requirements, 1-2, 1159-1160
improving performance, 1038-1042
installing, 1-8, 1159-1166
interacting with WIndows applications, 993-1019
new features, 15-28
product support, 1159-1160
screen elements, 31-35
starting, 29-31
Word for Windows 2.0 toolbar, 44
Word icon, 1044-1046
Word Picture Object command (Edit menu), 683
word processors, converting files from, 1021-1026
Word Setup program, 1023
word-wrap feature, 77
WordArt, 773-798
commands/options, 778-779
creating objects, 775-780
editing objects, 795-798
exiting, 780
help, 780
installing, 775
logos, 857-858
special effects, 780-795
aligning text, 788-789
borders, 790-792
character formatting, 784-785
color/shading, 792-793
flipping/stretching letters, 785-786
fonts/symbols, 782-784
kerning, 789-790
rotating/slanting text, 787-788

shadows, 794-795
shaping text, 782
starting, 775-776
text operations, 777-778
troubleshooting, 780
WordArt 2.0 dialog box, 797
WordArt 2.0 Object command (Edit menu), 797
WordArt Text command (Edit menu), 778
WordArt toolbar, 778
WordBASIC programming language, 1139
WordBASIC statements, 1140-1141
worksheets
linking to documents, 1011
Microsoft Excel, 804-805
workspace, 1046-1047

X-Y-Z

x Placeholder in numeric formatting, 1092
X-Y (Scatter) charts, 812-814
Year Placeholder, date/time formatting, 1095
Zoom buttons (Standard toolbar), 119
Zoom command (View menu), 121-124, 223, 393, 1131
Zoom dialog box, 122
zooming documents, 121-124

Shortcut Keys

A (+) sign in these tables indicates that you should hold down the first key while pressing the second key, as in Alt+A. A comma (,) indicates that you should release the first key before pressing the second key, as in Alt,A. If your keyboard has only 10 function keys, use Alt+F1 for the F11 key and Alt+F2 for the F12 key.

Function Keys

Key	Function	Key	Function
F1	Help	Ctrl+F7	Move document window
Shift+F1	Help pointer (Context-sensitive help)	Ctrl+Shift+F7	Update linked information to the source
F2	Move selection to insertion point on Enter	F8	Extend selection/extend mode
Shift+F2	Copy selection to insertion point on Enter	Shift+F8	Shrink selection
		Ctrl+F8	Size document window
Ctrl+F2	Print preview	Ctrl+Shift+F8	Select column with arrow
F3	Insert glossary entry	F9	Update field
Shift+F3	Alternate between three letter cases	Shift+F9	Toggle selected field display
		Ctrl+F9	Insert field characters {}
Ctrl+F3	Cut to spike	Ctrl+Shift+F9	Unlink field
Ctrl+Shift+F3	Insert from spike	Alt+F9	Toggle document field display
F4	Repeat previous command		
Shift+F4	Repeat Find or Go To	Alt+Shift+F9	Activate field
Ctrl+F4	Close active document window	F10	Activate menu
Alt+F4	Close Word	Shift+F10	Activate shortcut menu
F5	Go To	Ctrl+F10	Maximize document window
Shift+F5	Go back to previous positions	Alt+F10	Maximize Word window
Ctrl+F5	Restore document window	F11	Next field
Ctrl+Shift+F5	Insert bookmark	Shift+F11	Previous field
Alt+F5	Restore Word window	Ctrl+F11	Lock field
F6	Next pane	Ctrl+Shift+F11	Unlock field
Shift+F6	Previous pane	F12	Save as
Ctrl+F6	Next document window	Shift+F12	Save
Ctrl+Shift+F6	Previous document window	Ctrl+F12	Open
F7	Spelling	Ctrl+Shift+F12	Print
Shift+F7	Thesaurus		

Outlining Keys

Key	Function	Key	Function
Alt+Shift+ left arrow	Promote heading	Alt+Shift++	Expand outline
Alt+Shift+ right arrow	Demote heading	Alt+Shift+ _	Collapse outline
		Alt+Shift+1 through 9 (cannot use keypad)	Show through indicated numeric level
Alt+Shift+up arrow	Move paragraph/ heading up	Alt+Shift+A	Show all levels
Alt+Shift+down arrow	Move paragraph/ heading down		

New File	File Open	File Save	Print	Full Page Print View	Spell Check	Edit Cut	Edit Copy	Edit Paste	Copy Format	Undo	Redo

...ction Keys Used with Fields

	Function	Key	Function
Shift+F7	Update linked information in data source	Shift+F11	Go to previous field
	Update selected field	Ctrl+F11	Lock field
Ctrl+U	Update link	Ctrl+Shift+F11	Unlock field
..F9	Toggle selected field between codes and result	Alt+Shift+D	Insert DATE field
..9	Toggle document between code and result	Alt+Shift+P	Insert PAGE field
		Alt+Shift+T	Insert TIME field
.F9	Insert field characters {}	Alt+Ctrl+A	Insert Annotation
.Shift+F9	Unlink field	Alt+Ctrl+F	Footnote
.hift+F9	Produce result in field	Alt+Ctrl+E	Endnote
	Go to next field	Alt+Shift+I	Mark index entry
		Alt+Shift+O	Mark citation entry

...ting

	Function	Key	Function
.A	Select all of document	Ctrl+Shift+Enter	Column break
.Backspace	Delete left word	Ctrl+hyphen	Optional hyphen
.Del	Delete right word	Ctrl+Shift+hyphen	Nonbreaking hyphen
.Shift+C	Copy format	Alt+up arrow	Move to previous frame
.Shift+V	Paste format	Alt+down arrow	Move to next frame
.-Enter	Line Break	Ctrl+up arrow	Move to left column
.Enter	Page break	Ctrl+down arrow	Move to right column

...agraph Formatting

	Function
.E	Center
	Justify
	Left align
.M	Indent
.hift+M	Decrease indent from left
.R	Right align
.T	Create hanging indent
.Shift+T	Decrease hanging indent
.) (zero)	Add/Close space before paragraph
	Single space lines
.2	Double space lines
.5	One-and-one-half space lines

Style Formatting

Key	Function
Ctrl+Shift+S	Apply Style/Open Style Dialog
Ctrl+Q	Remove direct formatting
Ctrl+K	AutoFormat
Ctrl+Shift+N	Apply Normal style
Alt+Ctrl+1	Apply Heading 1 style
Alt+Ctrl+2	Apply Heading 2 style
Alt+Ctrl+3	Apply Heading 3 style
Ctrl+Shift+L	Apply List style

...aracter Formatting Keys

.hift+A	All Caps	Ctrl+U	Continuous underline	Ctrl+[	Decrease by 1 point
	Bold			Ctrl+Shift+]	Increase kerning
.hift+D	Double-underline	Ctrl+Shift+W	Word underline	Ctrl+Shift+[	Decrease kerning
.hift+F	Font	Ctrl+Shift+Z	Remove formatting	Ctrl+space bar	Reapply current style
.hift+H	Hidden	Ctrl+=	Subscript	Ctrl+Shift+*	Display non-printing characters
	Italic	Ctrl++	Superscript		
.hift+K	Small caps	Ctrl+Shift+>	Increase font size	Ctrl+space bar	Removes non-style formatting
.hift+P	Point size	Ctrl+Shift+<	Decrease font size		
.hift+Q	Create symbol	Ctrl+]	Increase by 1 point		

Auto-Format	Auto-Text	Insert Table	Insert Excel Object	Format Columns	Insert Drawing	Insert Chart	Show/Hide Characters	Zoom View		Help